AUSTRALIAN DICTIONARY

OF BIOGRAPHY

General Editors
BEDE NAIRN
GEOFFREY SERLE

AUSTRALIAN
DICTIONARY
OF BIOGRAPHY

VOLUME 10 : 1891-1939

Lat-Ner

General Editors
BEDE NAIRN
GEOFFREY SERLE

Deputy General Editor
CHRISTOPHER CUNNEEN

Section Editors
G. C. BOLTON
K. J. CABLE
R. J. O'NEILL
J. R. POYNTER
HEATHER RADI

MELBOURNE UNIVERSITY PRESS

First published 1986

Typeset by Abb-typesetting Pty Ltd, Collingwood, Victoria
Printed in Australia by Griffin Press Limited
Netley, South Australia, for
Melbourne University Press, Carlton, Victoria 3053
U.S.A. and Canada: International Specialized Book Services, Inc.,
P.O. Box 1632, Beaverton, OR 97075
United Kingdom, Ireland and Europe: Europa Publications Limited
18 Bedford Square, London WC1B 3JN

National Library of Australia Cataloguing-in-Publication entry

Australian dictionary of biography. Volume 10.
   1891–1939, Lat–Ner.
   ISBN 0 522 84327 1.
   ISBN 0 522 84236 4 (set).

   1. Australia—Biography—Dictionaries. 2. Australia
   —History—1891–1901. 3. Australia—History—1901–
   1945. I. Nairn, Bede, 1917–   . II. Serle, Geoffrey, 1922–
920'.094

PREFACE

This volume of the *Australian Dictionary of Biography*, containing 659 entries by 445 authors, is the fourth of six for the 1891-1939 section. The two volumes of the 1788-1850 section and the four of the 1851-1890 section have already been published. The late Douglas Pike was general editor for volumes 1 to 5, Bede Nairn for volume 6, and Nairn and Geoffrey Serle for volumes 7 to 10. Nairn retired as joint general editor on 31 January 1984. The chronological division was designed to simplify production, for more than 7000 entries will be included in volumes 1-12. (Volumes 1-2, for 1788-1850, had 1116 entries; volumes 3-6, for 1851-1890, 2053; and 4000 are planned for volumes 7-12). The placing of each individual's name in the appropriate section has been determined by when he/she did his/her most important work (*floruit*). A general index volume will be published after the three sections are completed.

The selection of names for inclusion required prolonged consultation. After quotas were estimated, working parties in each State and the armed services working party prepared provisional lists, which were widely circulated and carefully amended. Many of the names were obviously significant and worthy of inclusion as leaders in politics, business, the armed services, the professions, the arts, the labour movement, etc. Many others have been included as representatives of ethnic and social minorities and of a wide range of occupations, or as innovators, notorieties or eccentrics. Many had to be omitted through pressure of space or lack of material, and thereby joined the great mass whose members richly deserve a more honoured place; however, many thousands of these names, and information about them, are accumulating in the biographical register at the *Dictionary* headquarters in the Australian National University.

Most authors were nominated by working parties. The burden of writing has been shared almost equally by the staff of universities and other tertiary institutions and by a wide variety of other specialists.

The *Australian Dictionary of Biography* is a project based on consultation and co-operation. The Australian National University has borne the cost of the headquarters staff, of much research and of some special contingencies, while other Australian universities have supported the project in various ways. Its policies were originally determined by a national committee, composed mainly of representatives from the departments of history in each Australian university. At Canberra the editorial board has kept in touch with all these representatives, and with the working parties, librarians, archivists and other local experts, as well as overseas correspondents and research assistants in each Australian capital. With such varied support the *Australian Dictionary of Biography* can truly be called a national project.

ACKNOWLEDGMENTS

Special thanks are due to Professor K. S. Inglis and Dr A. Barnard for their guidance as chairman and acting chairman of the editorial board and to Professor G. M. Neutze, director of the Research School of Social Sciences, Australian National University, and Mr P. Grimshaw, business manager of the research school. Those who helped in planning the shape of the work have been mentioned in earlier volumes.

Within Australia the *Dictionary* is greatly indebted to many librarians and archivists in Canberra and in each State; to the secretaries of many historical and genealogical societies; to the Australian War Memorial, Australian National Gallery and Department of Veterans' Affairs, in Canberra; to the registrars of probates in the various States, and of Supreme and Family Courts, whose generous co-operation has solved many problems; and to the Department of Defence for authenticating many details. Warm thanks for the free gift of their time and talents are due to all contributors and to all members of the editorial board and the working parties. For particular advice the *Dictionary* owes much to the late Brigadier M. Austin, and to B. Gandevia, G. McKeown, Bernard Smith, Daniel Thomas and C. W. Wrigley and the staff of the Petherick Room, National Library.

Essential assistance with birth, death and marriage certificates has been provided by the generous co-operation of registrars in New South Wales, Queensland, South Australia, Tasmania, Western Australia, the Northern Territory and the Australian Capital Territory, and by the government statist, Victoria; by the reference librarian, Alexander Turnbull Library, Wellington, New Zealand; by the General Register Office, Edinburgh, Scotland; by Bureaux of Vital Statistics in State Health departments in Arkansas, California, Colorado, Hawaii, Indiana, Iowa, Louisiana, Massachusetts, New Hampshire, New York, Washington, D.C., South Carolina and Wisconsin, in the United States of America; by the registrar-general in Fiji; by the Superior Court, Montreal, and the registrar-general, Ontario, in Canada; the principal civil status officer, Port Louis, in Mauritius; the registrar, Supreme Court, Barbados; by the mayors of Cannes and La Boussac, in France; by the civil status officers, Velaine, Belgium, and Genoa and Siena, Italy; and by the Royal Danish Embassy and the Embassy of the Federal Republic of Germany.

For assistance overseas, thanks are due to Sean Murphy, Dublin, Ireland; to Information Systems Consultants Inc., Bethesda, Maryland, in the United States of America; to the archives and/or libraries of the universities of Birmingham, Cambridge, Leeds, London, Manchester and Oxford and of the Imperial College of Science and Technology, London, in England, of the universities of Edinburgh, Glasgow, and St Andrews in Scotland, and of Trinity College, University of Dublin, in Ireland, of the University of Liège in Belgium, and of California, also Harvard and Stanford universities in the United States of America.

Thanks are also due to the Linnean Society of London, the Public Record Office, the Royal Academy of Music, the Royal College of Music, all in London, to the Ministry of Defence, Middlesex, in England; to the Royal College of Surgeons of Edinburgh, Scotland; the Dictionary of Canadian Biography; and other individuals and institutions who have co-operated with the *Dictionary*.

The special services to the *Dictionary* over many years of Nan Phillips merits particular notice of her death in 1984. So do the deaths in 1984-85 of 'Bunny' Austin, Denis Murphy and John Reynolds, friends and advisers, as well as contributors.

Andrew Brudenall, a young member of the *Dictionary* administrative staff of outstanding promise, died in a tragic accident in 1985. The *Dictionary* deeply regrets these deaths and those of such notable contributors as Harry Adlam, R. W. Baker, Diane Barwick, Macfarlane Burnet, Eleanor Dark, D. K. Darling, Denison Deasey, A. B. Doyle, Alban Doyle, E. Beatrix Durie, Harley W. Forster, A. J. Gray, D. A. Herbert, V. Hodgman, Roy H. Holden, Frederick Howard, F. C. Hutley, R. B. Joyce, R. M. Jukes, Michael C. I. Levy, T. B. McCall, J. M. Main, S. Merrifield, R. S. Neale, Ralph Pervan, R. T. M. Pescott, A. A. Phillips, E. R. Pretyman, D. Bruce Ross, E. J. Semmens, Merab Harris Tauman, W. V. Teniswood, K. A. Townley, Sydney Walker, Mervyn J. Wasson, Judah Waten, George F. Wieck and Keith Willey.

Grateful acknowledgment is due to the director and staff of Melbourne University Press; to the editorial and research staff in Canberra: Frank Brown, Martha Campbell, Suzanne Edgar, Gillian Fulloon, James Gibbney (now retired), Emma Grahame, Helga Griffin, Paula Harris, Diane Langmore, Merrilyn Lincoln, Patti Sharp, Ann Smith and Margaret Steven: to Michal Bosworth, Hilary Carey, Ruth Frappell and Susan Hogan in Sydney, Betty Crouchley in Brisbane, Joyce Gibberd in Adelaide, Wendy Birman in Perth, Margaret Glover and Gillian Winter in Hobart, Mimi Colligan in Melbourne and Léonie Glen and Sally O'Neill in London: and to the administrative staff: Marion Consandine, Annie Gan, Edna Kauffman, Alison Manners, Ivy Meere, David Turner and Margaret Tyrie.

COMMITTEES

AUTHORS

ABBOTT, Dennis:
Littler, F. M.
ABBOTT, Jacqueline:
MacKinnon, E.
ADAMS, David:
Moore, Sir N.
ADAMS, J. D.:
Lind, Sir A. E.; McGregor, M.
AGARS, Mervyn:
Leahy, T. J.
ALEXANDER, Fred:
Murdoch, Sir W.
ALEXANDER, H.:
Macdonald, L.
ALLEN, Judith:
Leigh; Miles, B.; Montefiore.
ALLEN, Margaret:
Martin, C.
ALLINGHAM, A.:
Love, J. S.
ANDERSON, Hugh:
Macdonald, D.; Neilson.
ANDREWS, B. G.:
*Locke; Macartney, C.; Macleod, W.; Mahony,
F.; Morton, F.*
ANDREWS, E. M.:
Mann, E.
APPLEYARD, R. T.:
Marmion.
ARNOLD, John:
Minogue.
ARNOT, Jean F.:
MacPherson, M.
ASHBOLT, Allan:
McMahon, G.
ASTBURY, Leigh:
Longstaff, Sir J. C.
ATCHISON, John:
*Livingston-Learmonth; Longworth, W. &
T.; McRae, C.; Mathews, H.; Meares; Miller,
R.; Moore, S.*

BACKHOUSE, Sue:
Lovett.
BAIN, Mary Albertus:
Male.
BAINTON, Helen:
Monk.
BAKER, R. W.*:
McDougall, D.
BANKS, Maxwell R.:
Loftus-Hills.
BARBER, Ross:
Lesina.
BARTROP, Paul R.:
McNamara, D. J.
BATE, Weston:
Littlejohn, W. S.

BATTYE, O. K.:
Nanson, J.
BENNETT, Arthur L.:
Murphy, E.
BENNETT, Scott:
*Lee, Sir W. H.; Lewis, Sir N. E.; McCall;
Miles, E; Millen, J.*
BERESFORD, Quentin:
McGee.
BERNDT, Catherine:
Mondalmi.
BERTRAND, Ina:
Lovely.
BERZINS, Baiba:
Leeson; Ley.
BETTISON, Margaret:
Luffman, L.
BIRMAN, Wendy:
*Lawley; Lee Steere; Liebe; McCallum, A.;
McClintock; Monger.*
BIRRELL, J.:
Mollison.
BISKUP, P.:
Mouton.
BLACK, Alan W.:
Lowrie.
BLACK, David:
Lynch, P.
BLACKBURN, C. R. B.:
Mills, A. E.
BLAINEY, Geoffrey:
Lewis, E.
BLAKE, L. J.:
Leason.
BLYTH, Judy:
Mather, J.
BOLTON, G. C.:
Mitchell, Sir J.; Moran, C.; Morgans.
BONDS, Alan:
Lynn.
BONNIN, Nancy:
Mackness.
BOURKE, Helen:
Mayo, G.
BRADY, Wendy:
McNess.
BRAZIER, Jan:
Lawrence, C.
BRIGNELL, Lyn:
Matthews, S.
BROWN, Elaine:
Mackay, G.
BROWN, Greg:
Moulds.
BROWNE, Geoff:
*Leckie, J. W.; Linton, Sir R.; Livingston, T.;
McCutcheon.*
* deceased

BROWNE, Margaret:
Martin, W.
BUCK, A. R.:
Lee, C. A.
BURGIS, Peter:
McEachern; Moncrieff, G.
BURGMANN, Verity:
McNamara, M.; McNamara, W.; Matthias.
BURNESS, Peter:
Loynes; McIntosh, H.; Mackay, J.; Maguire.
BUTCHER, R. Dunbavin:
Le Souef.
BUTLER, Roger:
Moffitt.
BYRNE, Geraldine:
Miller, H.

CABLE, K. J.:
McCabe; MacCallum, Sir M.; McKellar, J.; Matthews, C.; Micklem.
CAHILL, A. E.:
Moran, P.
CAIN, Frank:
MacKay, W.; Moore, N.
CAMERON, Catherine:
Lefroy.
CAMPBELL, Jean:
Minns.
CAMPBELL, Keith O.:
McMaster, Sir F. D.
CAMPBELL, Ruth:
Madden, Sir J.
CARMENT, David:
Mackay, D.; Nelson, H.
CARNELL, I. G.:
Mulvany.
CASTLES, Alex C.:
Murray, Sir G.
CHAMBERLAIN, W. M.:
McCash; McLeish.
CHAMBERS, Don:
Mackrell.
CHAPMAN, Barbara:
Nerli.
CHAPMAN, Peter:
Mills, C.
CHAPMAN, R. J. K.:
Meagher, R. J.
CHERRY, T. M.*:
Michell, J.
CLOSE, Cecily:
Lothian.
COBB, Joan:
Nangle.
COLLIGAN, Mimi:
Lemmone; Moore, E.
CONDON, Brian:
Muirden.
CONNELL, W. H.:
McCarthy, L.
CONROY, Denise K.:
Macgregor, L.
CONSANDINE, Marion:
McMillan, R.

COOK, Peter:
McNamara, D. L.
COOPER, James G.:
Lyons, T.
COPE, Graeme:
Laycock.
COPE, Malcolm:
McCawley.
CORRIS, Peter:
Melvin.
COSTAR, B. J.:
Moore, A. E.
COULTHARD-CLARK, C. D.:
Legge; Macnaghten; Milne, E.; Murray, P.
COURTNEY, R. C. H.:
Lihou; Murphy, B.
COWPER, Norman:
McCrae.
CROCKER, W. R.:
Naylor, H.
CROFT, Julian:
Lower.
CROSS, J. J.:
McLaren, S. B.
CROUCHLEY, Betty:
Marconi; Mayne; Milne, J.; Murphy, P.
CUNNEEN, Chris:
Lyne, Sir W.; McIntosh, H. D.; McKivat; Mansour; Messenger; Miles, W.

DARLING, B. B.:
Nash.
DARRAGH, Thomas A.:
Mahony, D.
DAVIDSON, Jim:
Melba.
DAVIS, R. P.:
McPhee; Mercer.
DE GARIS, B. K.:
Leake.
DE SERVILLE, P. H.:
Manifold, Sir W.; Manifold, W., J. & E.; Neil.
DEWDNEY, J. C. H.:
Lynch, A.
DICKER, Matthew:
Moore, J. C.; Munro, E.
DILGER, David:
Lillico.
DINGSDAG, Don:
Nelson, C.
DOUGAN, Alan*:
Marden.
DOW, Gwyneth:
Montgomery, C.
DUCKER, Sophie C.:
Lucas, A. H.
DUNSTAN, David:
Liston; Luxton; McEacharn; Morell.

* deceased

EDGAR, Suzanne:
  Lindsay, D.; Lucas, Sir E.; McPherson, J.;
  Melrose, Sir J.; Miethke; Murdoch, M.;
  Muskett.
EDGELOE, V. A.:
  Mitchell, Sir W.
EDWARDS, Eric J.:
  McMillan, Sir R.
ELLIS, A. S.:
  Montgomery, S.
EMILSEN, Susan E.:
  Macintyre.
ENGEL, Frank:
  McLaren, C.
EVANS, Lloyd:
  McWilliam.
EWER, Peter:
  Mair.

FAHEY, Charles:
  Lazarus; McClelland, H.
FAIRFAX, Denis:
  Moyes.
FARRELL, Frank:
  Lysaght, A.; Macdonell, D.; Magrath.
FENDLEY, G. C.:
  Nanson, E.
FENTON-SMITH, J.:
  Lister.
FINLAY, E. M.:
  McWhae; Miller, Sir E.; Mitchell, I. & J.
FINLAY, H. A.:
  McWhae; Neighbour.
FINN, Rosslyn:
  Massie.
FIRTH, J. F.:
  Lithgow.
FISHER, Anthony:
  Maughan; Mitchell, E.
FITZSIMONS, T.:
  Munro, A.
FLETCHER, Jim:
  McCormick, P.
FLOWER, Cedric:
  Moore, J. D.
FOLEY, Meredith:
  Littlejohn, E. L. P.; Muscio, F.
FORBES, John R.:
  Lawton, T.
FORBES, M. Z.:
  Levien, R. H.
FORSTER, Frank M. C.:
  Meyer.
FRASER, Alan:
  McCloughry; Murphy, A.
FREDMAN, L. E.:
  Levy.
FRENCH, M.:
  Leahy, J.
FRIEND, Warren:
  MacDougall, J.
FRY, Eric:
  Miller, M.

FRY, Gavin:
  Lawlor.
FULLOON, Gillian:
  McPhillamy; Marks, P.; Mathias; Muscio, F.

GARDEN, Donald S.:
  Lawson, Sir H.
GARDINER, Lyndsay:
  Morres.
GARRISSON, A. D.:
  McNamara, F.
GARTON, S.:
  Neitenstein.
GELLIE, G. H.:
  McCracken.
GIBBERD, Joyce:
  Minchin.
GIBBNEY, H. J.:
  Lynas; Mahon; Matheson.
GIBBS, Desmond:
  Lawton, J. T.
GILL, J. C. H.:
  Longman, A. H.; Lukin; McGill; Macleod,
  T.; Morgan, G.
GILL, K. E.:
  Macgroarty.
GILLISON, Joan:
  McMillan, S.
GLOVER, Margaret:
  Lithgow.
GOLLAN, Robin:
  Miller, Sir D.
GOOT, Murray:
  Lumsdaine; McDonald, A.
GOSSE, Fayette:
  Latimer; Matters.
GRAINGER, G. C.:
  McGregor, G.
GRANT, Donald:
  Lovekin.
GRAY, Anne:
  Linton, J. & J.; Longstaff, W. F.; McCubbin, L.
GREEN, Dorothy:
  Muskett.
GREEN, O. S.:
  Leslie.
GREGG, D. R.:
  Lewis, A. N.
GREGORY, C. J.:
  Mackay, J. H.
GREGORY, Helen:
  Marchant.
GREGORY, J. S.:
  Morrison, G.
GRIFFIN, Helga M.:
  Lawrence, M.
GRIFFIN, James:
  Leahy, M. J.; Mannix; Mummery.
GROENEWEGEN, P. D.:
  Mills, R.
GUNSON, Niel:
  Murdoch, P.
GUYATT, Joy:
  Moroney; Mullan.

REED, T. T.:
Marryat.
REEVES, Andrew:
McVicars.
REYNOLDS, John*:
Miller, E. M.
RICHARDS, Eric:
Lyons, H.; McCann, Sir C.; Mitchell, T.;
Muecke.
RICKARD, John:
McLean, A.
ROBERTS, Alan:
Lees, S. E.
ROBERTSON, J. R.:
McNeill.
ROBINSON, D. J.:
McDowall, V.
ROE, J. I.:
Nelson, W.
ROE, Michael:
Macartney, Sir W.; Miller, E. M.
ROLFE, Amanda M.:
McColl; McKenzie, H.
ROUTH, S. J.:
McDougall, C.
RUSSELL, K. F.:
Maudsley.
RUTLAND, Suzanne D.:
Marks, P. J.
RUTLEDGE, Martha:
Lee, I. L.; Lee, J. R.; Leist; Leverrier; Lyon;
McCrae; Mackaness; Marks, T.; Marlowe;
Meeks; Millen, E.; Moore, C.; Morton, F.;
Mutch; Neild.

SAUNDERS, Malcolm:
Moore, E.
SCHEDVIN, C. B.:
McPherson, Sir C.
SCOTT, Bruce:
McAulay.
SEKULESS, Peter:
March.
SELLECK, R. J. W.:
Long, C. R.
SENYARD, J. E.:
Lockwood, J.
SERLE, Geoffrey:
Lynch, A. A.; McCay, Sir J.; McClelland, D.;
MacDonald, J.; MacFarland; Mackey;
Mackinnon, D.; Mackinnon, Sir L.;
Maloney; Monash; Murdoch, Sir K.;
Murray, J., grazier.
SERLE, Œnone:
Martyn, N.
SHANAHAN, Mary:
MacRory.
SIMMONS, H. L. N.:
Mansour.
SIMPSON, Caroline:
Macarthur Onslow, R.
SIMPSON, Pat:
Loton.

SISSONS, D. C. S.:
Muramats; Murdoch, J.
SMITH, Ann G.:
Laurie; Laver, C. & F.; Lemmon; Lewis, E.;
Lewis, F.; Lewis, W. H. H.; McComas;
McLaren, S. G.; Macnamara, Dame A.;
Murray, R.
SMITH, Bernard:
Lindsay, P. C.; Meldrum.
SPAULL, Andrew:
McBride; McRae, J.
SPEARRITT, G. D.:
May, S.
SPEARRITT, Peter:
Mair; Martin, L.; Molesworth, V.
STANNAGE, Tom:
Molloy.
STAUNTON, Anthony:
Lowerson.
STEPHENS, Geoffrey:
Montgomery, Sir H.
STEVEN, Margaret:
Lucas, W.
STIMSON, A. J.:
Moncrieff, A.
STIRLING, Alfred*:
McDougall, F.
STRACHAN, Pat:
Mott.
STREMSKI, R.:
Lee, W. H.; McHale.
SULLIVAN, Rodney:
Lennon.
SUNTER, Anne Beggs:
Murphy, G. R.
SUTTON, R.:
Lynch, T.; McGlinn; Marks, D.
SWEETING, A. J.:
Lind, E. F.; Mackenzie, W. K.
SWIFTE, L. B.:
Murphy, G. F.

TAMPKE, J.:
Muller.
TAYLOR, Cheryl:
McLaren, J.
TEALE, Ruth:
Long, G. M.
THOMAS, David:
McCubbin, F.
THOMIS, Malcolm I.:
Melbourne; Michie.
THORNTON, Robert:
Mitchell, S.
THWAITES, Jack:
Lord, C. E.
TINDALE, Norman B.:
Milerum.
TODD, R. K.:
Morant.
TREVENA, Bill:
Mennell.

* deceased

xvii

AUTHORS

A NOTE ON SOME PROCEDURES

Among our authors and readers and, indeed, on the editorial board, there is strong disagreement on whether certain facts should normally be included—such as cause of death, burial or cremation details, and value of estate. In this volume our practices have been as follows:

Cause of death: normally included, except in the case of the very old.

Burial/cremation: included when details available.

Value of estate: normally included for certain categories such as businessmen, and when the amount is unusually high or low. In recent years, when the practice developed of early distribution of assets in order to avoid estate and probate duties, the sum is not always meaningful; moreover it is not always possible to ascertain the full facts. Hence we have resorted to discretionary use.

Some other procedures require explanation:

Measurements: as the least unsatisfactory solution we have used imperial system measurements (as historically appropriate), followed by the metric equivalent in brackets. Round metric figures are used when the number is clearly approximate, e.g., 500 miles (800 km).

Money: we have retained £ for pounds for references prior to 14 February 1966 (when the conversion rate was A£1 = A$2).

Religion: stated whenever information is available, but often there is no good evidence of actual practice, e.g., the information is confined to marriage and funeral rites.

[q.v.]: the particular volume is given for those included in volumes 1-9 but not for those in this and future volumes. Note that the cross-reference [q.v.] now accompanies the names of all who have separate articles in the *Dictionary*. In volumes 1-6 it was not shown for royal visitors, governors, lieut-governors and those Colonial Office officials who were included.

Small capitals: used for relations and others when they are of substantial importance but not included in their own right; these are also marked q.v.

Five-year rule: a few men and women, whose *floruit* was pre-1940 but who lived to an advanced age, have been excluded on the ground that they died too recently for proper historical consideration. No one is included who died less than five years before date of publication, except some sportsmen whose years of fame were long ago.

CORRIGENDA

Every effort is made to check every detail in every article, but inevitably a work of the size and complexity of the *Dictionary* includes some errors.

Corrigenda have been published with each volume and a list is included with volume 10 showing corrections made since the publication of volume 9 (1983).

Only corrections are shown; additional information is not included; nor is any re-interpretation attempted. The only exception to this procedure is when new details become available about parents or births, deaths and marriages.

Documented corrections are welcomed. Additional information, with sources, is also invited and will be placed in the appropriate files for future use.

A copy of cumulative corrigenda up to volume 7 and the lists published with volumes 8 and 9 are available from the publishers at cost of postage.

REFERENCES

The following and other obvious works of reference have been widely used but not normally acknowledged:

Australian encyclopaedia, 1-2 (Syd, 1925), 1-10 (1958), 1-12 (1983).

Biographical register for various Australian parliaments: (A. W. Martin & P. Wardle *and* H. Radi, P. Spearritt & E. Hinton *and* C. N. Connolly—New South Wales; G. C. Bolton & A. Mozley—Western Australia; K. Thomson & G. Serle *and* G. Browne—Victoria; D. B. Waterson *and* D. B. Waterson & J. Arnold—Queensland; H. Coxon, J. Playford & R. Reid— South Australia; S. & B. Bennett—Tasmania; and J. Rydon—(Commonwealth)

D. Blair, *Cyclopaedia of Australasia* (Melb, 1881)

B. Burke, *A genealogical and heraldic history of the colonial gentry,* 1-2 (Lond, 1891, 1895)

O'M. Creagh and E. M. Humphris (eds), *The V.C. and D.S.O.: a complete record . . .* 1-3 (Lond, 1934)

Dictionary of national biography (Lond, 1885-1981)

H. M. Green, *A history of Australian literature,* 1-2 (Syd, 1961, 2nd edn 1971), revised by D. Green (Syd, 1984-85)

C. A. Hughes and B. D. Graham, *A handbook of Australian government and politics 1890-1964* (Canb, 1968); *Voting for the Australian House of Representatives 1901-1964,* with corrigenda (Canb, 1975), for *Queensland Legislative Assembly 1890-1964* (Canb, 1974), for *New South Wales . . .* (1975), *Victoria . . .* (1975), and *South Australian, Western Australian and Tasmanian Lower Houses . . .* (1976)

F. Johns, *Johns's notable Australians* (Melb, 1906), *Fred Johns's annual* (Lond, 1914); *An Australian biographical dictionary* (Melb, 1934)

A. McCulloch, *Encyclopedia of Australian art* (Lond, 1968), 1-2 (Melb, 1984)

E. M. Miller, *Australian literature . . . to 1935* (Melb, 1940), extended to 1950 by F. T. Macartney (Syd, 1956)

W. Moore, *The story of Australian art,* 1-2 (Syd, 1934), (Syd, 1980)

P. C. Mowle, *A genealogical history of pioneer families in Australia* (Syd, 1939; 5th edn Adel, 1978)

P. Serle, *Dictionary of Australian biography,* 1-2 (Syd, 1949)

Who's who (Lond), and *Who's who in Australia* (Syd, Melb), present and past editions.

ABBREVIATIONS USED IN BIBLIOGRAPHIES

AAA	Amateur Athletic Association	Fr	Father (priest)
AAO	Australian Archives		
ABC	Australian Broadcasting Commission/Corporation	G, Geog	Geographical
		Govt	Government
ACT	Australian Capital Territory		
Adel	Adelaide	HA	House of Assembly
Agr	Agriculture, Agricultural	Hist	History, Historical
AIF	Australian Imperial Force	Hob	Hobart
ALP	Australian Labor Party	HSSA	Historical Society of South Australia
ANU	Australian National University, Canberra		
ANU Archives	ANU Archives of Business and Labour	Inst	Institute, Institution
		introd	introduction, introduced by
ANZAAS	Australian and New Zealand Association for the Advancement of Science	ISN	Illustrated Sydney News
A'sian	Australasian	J	Journal
Assn	Association	JCU	James Cook University of North Queensland, Townsville
Aust	Australia, Australian		
AWM	Australian War Memorial, Canberra	LA	Legislative Assembly
		LaTL	La Trobe Library, Melbourne
		Launc	Launceston
Basser Lib	Adolph Basser Library, Australian Academy of Science, Canberra	LC	Legislative Council
		Lib	Library
		Lond	London
Battye Lib	J. S. Battye Library of West Australian History, Perth	Mag	Magazine
Bd	Board	Melb	Melbourne
BHP	Broken Hill Proprietary Co. Ltd	MDHC	Melbourne Diocesan Historical Commission (Catholic), Fitzroy
bibliog	bibliography	MJA	Medical Journal of Australia
biog	biography, biographical	ML	Mitchell Library, Sydney
Brisb	Brisbane	MS	manuscript
		mthly	monthly
c	circa	nd	date of publication unknown
CAE	College of Advanced Education	NG	New Guinea
Canb	Canberra	NL	National Library of Australia, Canberra
cat	catalogue		
CO	Colonial Office, London	no	number
C of E	Church of England	np	place of publication unknown
Col Sec	Colonial Secretary	NSW	New South Wales
Com	Commission	NSWA	The Archives Authority of New South Wales, Sydney
comp	compiler		
CSIRO	Commonwealth Scientific and Industrial Research Organization	NT	Northern Territory
		NZ	New Zealand
cttee	committee	Oxley Lib	John Oxley Library, Brisbane
Cwlth	Commonwealth		
		p	page, pages
Dept	Department	pc	photocopy
DNB	Dictionary of National Biography	PD	Parliamentary Debates
		PIM	Pacific Islands Monthly
		PP	Parliamentary Papers
ed	editor	PRGSSA	Proceedings of the Royal Geographical Society of Australasia (South Australian Branch)
edn	edition		
Edinb	Edinburgh		
Eng	England	priv print	privately printed

ABBREVIATIONS

PRO	Public Record Office	SLNSW	State Library of New South Wales
Procs	*Proceedings*		
pt	part, parts	SLSA	State Library of South Australia
PTHRA	*Papers and Proceedings of the Tasmanian Historical Research Association*	SLT	State Library of Tasmania
		SLV	State Library of Victoria
pub	publication, publication number	*SMH*	*Sydney Morning Herald*
		Soc	Society
Q	*Quarterly*	supp	supplement
QA	Queensland State Archives, Brisbane	Syd	Sydney
Qld	Queensland	TA	Tasmanian State Archives, Hobart
RAHS	Royal Australian Historical Society (Sydney)	Tas	Tasmania, Tasmanian
		T&CJ	*Australian Town and Country Journal*
RG	Registrar General's Office		
RGS	Royal Geographical Society	*Trans*	*Transactions*
RHSQ	Royal Historical Society of Queensland (Brisbane)	UK	United Kingdom
RHSV	Royal Historical Society of Victoria (Melbourne)	UNSW	University of New South Wales
RMIT	Royal Melbourne Institute of Technology	UNE	University of New England, Armidale
Roy	Royal	Univ	University
RWAHS	Royal Western Australian Historical Society (Perth)	UPNG	University of Papua New Guinea
1st S	First Session	*V&P*	*Votes and Proceedings*
2nd S	Second Session	*VHM(J)*	*Victorian Historical Magazine (Journal)*
2nd s	second series		
SA	South Australia	v, vol	volume
SAA	South Australian Archives, Adelaide	Vic	Victoria
Sel	Select	WA	Western Australia

Lat

LATHAM, Sir CHARLES GEORGE (1882-1968), farmer and politician, was born on 26 January 1882 at Hythe, Kent, England, son of Thomas Latham, coastguard, and his wife Isabella, née Isum. Orphaned in childhood, he arrived in New South Wales with his siblings in 1890. On 24 June 1903 at Hay he married Marie Louisa von Allwörden.

After working at various rural jobs Latham moved to Western Australia in 1910, attracted by advertisements promising land to prospective farmers. He took up newly opened country at East Kumminin (from 1917 Narembeen) on the eastern wheat-belt, obtaining a homestead block and 1000 acres (405 ha) of conditional purchase land through the Industries Assistance Board with a maximum advance from the Agricultural Bank. He asserted in 1921 that 'a man who has made a good pioneer is a better man than he who has been more or less spoon fed'. A successful pioneer, he cleared salmon gum, gimlet and morrell by chopping and burning and battled the dry climate by carting water, learning by trial and error to avoid the salt.

The 'roos' which ate his first crops were shot and he erected fences against the advancing front of rabbits; he carted supplies 50 miles (80 km) from the railhead at Doodlakine and later carried wheat to the new railhead at Bruce Rock.

Superphosphate increased his very poor initial wheat yields and he survived the 1914 drought; he shared machinery and worked together with his neighbours. By 1921, when he entered parliament, Latham was a successful wheat-farmer with 2000 acres (809 ha) of land.

On 15 March 1916 Latham had enlisted in the Australian Imperial Force as a private in the 20th Battalion and embarked for active service in October. In December he became an acting corporal with the 4th Training Battalion. Promoted corporal in January 1917 he reached France with the 16th Battalion in October, and was wounded in action in March 1918. In September-October that year he was attached to the United States Army. Promoted sergeant in April 1919, he returned to Australia in July and was discharged next month.

Latham was a leader in the new rural community. He became a member of the Bruce Rock Road Board when the district was gazetted in 1913 and, in 1924, first chairman of the Narembeen Road Board. He was also foundation president of the local Farmers and Settlers' Association and in 1921 secured Country Party endorsement for the safe Legislative Assembly electorate of York. He won the election and held the seat until his resignation in 1942.

The parliamentary Country Party in the early 1920s was divided over party autonomy and identity in coalition. Following the 1923 split on this issue, Latham joined most of his colleagues in forming the Majority or Ministerial Country Party, in defiance of the party organization.

With his fellows he joined the new United Party in 1924 and did not rejoin the official Country Party until four years later. In 1930 he became its parliamentary leader. From the beginning he expressed farmers' interests and ideology, arguing for orderly marketing, closer settlement, improved rural services and the opening up of more agricultural land, including light land. Land 'lying idle' must, he said, be harnessed to 'the development of the State'.

In 1930 Latham led the Country Party into coalition with the Nationalists on strong terms. In 1930-33 he was deputy premier and minister for lands, immigration and health in the Mitchell [q.v.] ministry. During the Depression he fought for the reduction of farmers' debts but opposed the radicalism of the newly formed Wheat Growers' Union. Unsympathetic towards the protests of the unemployed, he wanted to turn fire-hoses on demonstrators.

From 1933, with the Country Party the larger of the non-Labor parties in the assembly, Latham was leader of the Opposition. In 1942 he resigned to fill a Senate vacancy but was defeated in the 1943 election.

He became deputy director of the Commonwealth Loans and National Savings Organization in Western Australia and in 1946 returned to State parliament as member for East (later Central) Province in the Legislative Council. He held the seat until he retired in 1960.

Latham had another spell in a coalition ministry in 1952-53 as minister for agriculture in the McLarty-Watts government and ended his parliamentary career as president of the Legislative Council (1958-60). He had been appointed K.C.M.G. in 1948.

Latham was an effective, dedicated party leader, politically astute, strong willed and persuasive. In his later career, as a respected dignitary and 'father figure', he organized the financing and purchase of West Perth premises for party headquarters, named Latham House. Predeceased by his wife, he died on 26 August 1968, survived by two sons, and was

1

cremated. His estate was sworn for probate at $69 632.

West Australian, 16 Mar 1921, 27 Aug 1968; *Northern Advertiser*, 5 Sept 1968; Reminiscences of Sir Charles Latham, July 1962 (PR 3234, OH921 tr Battye Lib).   LENORE LAYMAN

LATHAM, SIR JOHN GREIG (1877-1964), politician, diplomat and chief justice, was born on 26 August 1877 at Ascot Vale, Melbourne, eldest of five children of Victorian-born Thomas Latham and his Scottish wife Janet, née Scott. The father was a tinsmith who, shortly before John's birth, had become founder and secretary of the Victorian Society for the Protection of Animals, a post he held for thirty-one years. The family moved to Ivanhoe shortly after, where Thomas became a justice of the peace and town councillor. Both he and his wife were devout Methodists who encouraged their four sons and daughter to make their way by industry and high moral purpose. 'In the home', their father recalled, 'we did not allow conversation to degenerate into mere small-talk'. John Latham abandoned the religion while at university but retained the elevated tone for the rest of his life.

From George Street State School, Fitzroy, Latham won a scholarship to Scotch College and thence progressed to the University of Melbourne (B.A., 1896). While teaching at the Hamilton Academy in 1897-98 he began to master his nervousness and temper his earnest intensity with a formidable reserve. A boyhood stammer was alleviated through elocution lessons and avoided by use of synonyms. In 1899 he returned to the university to study law, supporting himself as a resident tutor in logic and philosophy at Ormond [q.v.5] College. After winning the Supreme Court prize, he was admitted to the Victorian Bar in December 1904 and entered Selborne Chambers. Progress was slow (in his first six months as a barrister he earned just one guinea) and for some years most of his work was in petty sessions and the County Court. On 19 December 1907, with Methodist forms, he married Eleanor Mary (Ella) Tobin, herself an arts graduate, to whom he had been engaged for over four years.

Latham's success was achieved by uncommon ability and extraordinary industry. His forensic style, based on careful preparation and strictly logical presentation, was more effective with judges than juries. He embarked on his career some years after his more fortunate contemporaries and had none of their advantages of connexion and independent means. He supplemented his income by teaching and journalism, lecturing at the university in logic and, later, in contracts and personal property, and contributed reports to the *Argus* at a penny a line. He joined with (Sir) Walter Murdoch [q.v.] and others in forming a quarterly magazine, and even co-edited an *Australasian Students' Song Book* (1911). In 1908 he succeeded his friend Edward Shann [q.v.] as Australian correspondent of the London *Standard*, a vehicle for Imperial sentiment. This last post was combined with service on the political committee of the Deakinite Liberal Party, secretaryship of the Imperial Federation League's Victorian branch and, later, membership of the Victorian group of the Round Table. As early as 1909 he was invited to become a parliamentary candidate. With (Sir) Frederic Eggleston [q.v.8], he was a foundation member of the 'Boobooks', a fellowship of young professional men formed in 1902 to dine and digress at monthly meetings. His membership overlapped with a group of fly-fishing enthusiasts, including the surgeon (Sir) Thomas Dunhill [q.v.8] and physician (Sir) Richard Stawell [q.v.], who repaired to the Snowy Mountains over the Christmas holidays along with a similar group of Sydney men, (Sir) Thomas Bavin [q.v.7] and Colonel J. W. Macarthur-Onslow [q.v.] among them. (The annual gathering coalesced in the 1920s as the Waterfall Fly Fishing Club, when J. T. Lang [q.v.9] publicized its existence as a sinister cabal of politicians, judges and businessmen.)

There were other personal, less advantageous enthusiasms. In 1907 he helped to form an Education Act Defence League to resist the teaching of Scripture in government schools. In 1909 he was an organizer of a Rationalist Society in Melbourne and in 1910 of a tour of Australia by a prominent British free thinker Joseph McCabe. Latham was also a keen lacrosse player, captain of Victoria, and in 1908 represented Australia against a visiting Canadian team. Yet that year he acknowledged that he was 'working day and night' at his profession. How, then, are we to understand his compulsive accumulation of offices and responsibilities? Certainly he had a strong sense of public duty; but was there something more, a need that never left him to gain recognition by achievement? While outsiders saw a tall, aloof, impassive man, seemingly impatient of all human frailty, his circle of male friends knew a different, more companionable Jack Latham. In their company he could unbend and find reassurance. One of them, the observant Walter Murdoch, urged Latham: 'Don't be too intolerant of those who, perhaps because they are not so capable of clear and sustained thinking as you are, are less exultant than you in the powers of human thought and more helplessly conscious of its limitations'.

At the outbreak of World War I Latham was

earning £2000 a year at the Bar. About 1916 he moved from Northcote and bought a house at Malvern. At the request of Bavin, secretary of the New South Wales branch of the Universal Service League, he became secretary of the Victorian branch when it was formed in 1915 and he and his wife campaigned vigorously for the introduction of conscription. In 1917, following allegations of sabotage in the naval dockyards, he was appointed head of Naval Intelligence with the honorary rank of lieutenant-commander (on his recommendation Bavin was put in charge in Sydney). In this office he formed habits of mind that persisted throughout his public life: an apprehension of the grave menace of Bolshevism and a conviction that sedition should be prosecuted with the full weight of the law.

In 1918 he contemplated seeking National Party endorsement for the Federal seat of Flinders. The seat was won by S. M. (Viscount) Bruce [q.v.7]. Latham went instead to London as adviser to the minister for the navy, Sir Joseph Cook [q.v.8], in the party of prime minister W. M. Hughes [q.v.9]. Latham contributed to the work of the Imperial War Conference and Imperial War Cabinet but, unable to persuade Cook to allow him a real measure of responsibility, he won the right to submit his memoranda directly to the prime minister. Though recognizing Hughes's achievement in representing Australian interests, Latham was critical of his excesses and affronted by his manner. He conceived an antipathy to Hughes that remained throughout his political career. At the Versailles Peace Conference Latham served on the committee that determined the Czechoslovakian borders and probably formulated the definition of 'C class' mandates that permitted Australia to secure control over German New Guinea. For his services abroad stretching over fifteen months, he received £300 and in 1920 was appointed C.M.G.

On returning to the Bar in 1919 Latham made swift progress. Assisted by the appointment to the High Court of Australia of (Sir) Hayden Starke [q.v.], who had been the senior advocate at the Melbourne Bar, Latham developed his practice in size and scope, with an emphasis on taxation, commercial and arbitration matters but taking in some important constitutional cases. He reported to his English friend Lionel Curtis at the end of 1920 that he had 'been in at least one court, and usually more than one, on every day since the beginning of the year'. In 1922 he took silk. He joined the Melbourne Club, and belonged also to the Australian and Naval and Military clubs.

At the end of 1921 Latham had been invited to become a judge of the Supreme Court of Victoria. He declined, explaining that he was 'very keenly interested in matters in which a judge cannot properly allow himself to be interested'. Essentially, he was concerned with the conduct of national affairs. Business and conservative interests became increasingly impatient in the post-war years with the National government's economic interventionism and inexpedient interference in industrial relations. Latham shared his clients' disapproval of such policies and retained his hostility towards the prime minister for what he now regarded as an unprincipled debauchery of public life. Campaigning on the slogan 'Hughes Must Go', he stood in 1922 as an Independent Liberal Union candidate for the Federal seat of Kooyong and defeated the Nationalist member, Sir Robert Best [q.v.7]. Following that election, Latham attended meetings of the Country Party, advised its leader (Sir) Earle Page [q.v.] and drafted its memoranda during the negotiations that forced Hughes's resignation from office in 1923.

In parliament Latham first sat on the back-benches, studying briefs and giving occasional speeches which were described as 'like lumps of ice tinkling into a tumbler'. He addressed the House as he would the bench, his manner prim and his voice high-pitched. One journalist christened him 'the disembodied brain' while another called him 'the last proud scion of a long line of pokers'. But the relentless flow of argument commanded attention and he learned to vary his rhythm and leaven his speeches with a dry wit.

In 1925 he joined the National Party and was appointed attorney-general from 18 December, replacing the easygoing (Sir) Littleton Groom [q.v.9] whose amendments to the Immigration Act had failed to sustain deportation proceedings against the leaders of the seamen's strike, Tom Walsh [q.v. Pankhurst] and Jacob Johnson. Latham's solution was to amend the Crimes Act with a provision declaring revolutionary and seditious associations to be unlawful and making it an offence to belong to such an association. Reforms of industrial relations proved more difficult in an increasingly difficult economic climate. Like many conservatives, Latham leaned sometimes to the abolition of a mechanism which neither contained costs nor brought industrial peace, sometimes to the strengthening of that mechanism so that its determinations could be enforced. In the 1926 referendum Latham sought to augment the power of the Commonwealth to close loopholes created by the overlapping jurisdiction of the Commonwealth Court of Conciliation and Arbitration and State tribunals. But he was almost relieved when the defeat of the referendum proposal freed him from the responsibility of preparing a comprehensive national code.

In 1927 he suggested to cabinet that while

it was well-nigh impossible to proscribe strikes, the lock-out provisions of the Arbitration Act were all too effective, with the result that 'employers fight with their hands tied'. His recommendation that all strike and lock-out penalties be removed from the legislation was rejected. He therefore prepared the Arbitration Act of 1928 which strengthened the penalty provisions, introduced secret ballots into union proceedings, and forced the court to take economic effects into consideration when making awards.

Minister of industry from 10 December 1928, as well as attorney-general, he harried the maritime, transport and timber-workers' unions by discriminating application of the provisions of the Arbitration and Crimes Acts. Yet in 1929 he conceded that the government had failed to impose industrial peace and joined with Bruce in requesting that the States hand over their powers of industrial registration. When that initiative failed, he helped to formulate the proposal to abandon the field of industrial regulation (except for the maritime industry) to the States, the issue on which the government was defeated in the House in September and the principal reason for its defeat at the polls next month.

Latham's reputation for bias towards employers in administration of the law was not wholly justified, at least not in the conspiratorial terms in which it was usually propounded. It is true that he did not prosecute businessmen with the vigour applied to unionists: Mr Justice Starke made scathing criticism of the settlement made in 1928 with the notorious tax evaders, the Solomon brothers. It is true, also, that he maintained links with some of the principal enterprises whose interests were affected directly by his decisions as attorney-general: throughout the 1920s he held general retainers from a wide range of shipping, mining and other clients. Yet there is no evidence to impugn his integrity. He opposed what was regarded as the government's flagrant act of favouritism in withdrawing prosecution of the mine owner John Brown [q.v.7] for locking out his workers. His one-sidedness arose not from any illicit relationship with business clients (for he had declared openly that 'there was much to be said in favour of the attorney-general being a practising member of the bar') but from his inability to understand union militancy except as the result of seditious agitation.

Bruce having lost his seat in the 1929 election, Latham assumed the leadership of the Nationalists and for the next eighteen months he was leader of the Opposition. He was not averse to vigorous criticism of the Labor administration and its members and he orchestrated an attack on E. G. Theodore [q.v.], following the conservative Queensland government's exhumation of the Mungana

affair, to force the treasurer's suspension from the ministry in 1930; but he restrained his diehards and sought to project the image of a responsible, constructive Opposition. There were critics of such restraint in a period of mounting discord, and as the desire grew to reconstruct the National party on a more popular basis, so Latham's limitations became more apparent. He accepted pressure to make way for the former Labor minister J. A. Lyons [q.v.] and the formation of the United Australia Party was announced in May 1931. Latham's friends warmly commended his unselfishness. Labor was defeated at the general election of 19 December. Latham was closely involved in the unsuccessful negotiations for a coalition of the U.A.P. and the Country Party, and he served in the U.A.P. ministry from 6 January 1932 as attorney-general and minister for external affairs and for industry.

Latham had maintained his interest in international affairs. In 1926 he led the Australian delegation to the League of Nations General Assembly in Geneva and, with Bruce, attended the Imperial Conference in London. He had always been a supporter of Imperial links and opposed the move towards their legal definition, views developed in the Macrossan [q.v.5] lectures he delivered in 1928, published as *Australia and the British Commonwealth of Nations* (1929). But the earlier basis of Australia's Imperial relationship, summarized in Bruce's slogan 'Men, Money and Markets', could hardly be maintained in the circumstances of the Depression. Immigrants were no longer needed at a time when more than a quarter of the workforce was unemployed, loans had to be repaid and markets were all too few. By implementing the Ottawa Agreement of 1932 to extend the principle of preferential trade within the British Commonwealth, the government hoped to find a basis of recovery whereby the protectionist demands of its urban manufacturing supporters could be satisfied without estranging the Country Party. Rural interests were placated further with special assistance schemes. In 1932 Latham also attended the disarmament conference at Geneva and the reparations conference at Lausanne. In 1934 he toured South-East Asia, the first such initiative by a minister for external affairs.

As attorney-general he intervened for the Commonwealth in the Privy Council appeal in Trethowan's [q.v.] case. He introduced the Financial Agreement Enforcement Act in 1931: Lang's response, instructing State civil servants not to comply with Commonwealth orders, triggered his dismissal by the governor. Still preoccupied with the menace of sedition, Latham enacted a new Crimes Act in 1932, banned the transmission of communist papers through the post, and even launched an investigation of the Australian Pensioners' League, but some of his more draconian initiatives were quashed by the High Court.

As deputy prime minister, senior conservative in the Lyons ministry and close counsellor of the prime minister, Latham was a central figure in Federal politics. In 1933 he was appointed privy councillor. Yet throughout these years, and even during his previous period in office, there were persistent rumours that he would abandon politics. Sometimes the likelihood of his retirement was attributed to a preference for the law, sometimes to an inability to endure the financial sacrifice created by his dependence on ministerial salary. Of the loss in income caused by his political responsibilities there can be no doubt: when he first became attorney-general his practice was said to be worth £6000 a year; and even though he continued to accept briefs, the strain told on his health. The preference for legal practice is more dubious. He cared greatly to be in the centre of public affairs, and in his later years it was his experiences as a minister and not as chief justice that he was wont to recall with relish; perhaps he found the forthright style of Bruce more congenial than the drift and compromise of the Lyons administration.

It was evident by 1933, however, that he had set his sights on the post of chief justice of the High Court and that the only remaining obstacle was the reluctance of Sir Frank Gavan Duffy [q.v.] to vacate that post. It was predicted that Duffy's son would be appointed to the Supreme Court of Victoria, Duffy himself would retire, Latham would take his place, and the ambitious young Victorian attorney-general, Robert Menzies, would replace Latham in Kooyong and succeed him as attorney-general in Canberra. All these things came to pass. Latham retired from politics in 1934 and was appointed G.C.M.G. He was made chief justice on 11 October 1935.

His early years on the bench were made difficult by the play of fierce animosities among his colleagues, and it was no small achievement that he kept them in a working relationship with each other—Starke and Evatt were an especially combustible combination. Later the chief justice obtained more joint judgments. As a judge he was vulnerable to the temptation to interrupt counsel too often and at too great length. His most significant contributions were in constitutional law where he insisted on a strictly legal approach. When Commonwealth legislation was challenged, he asked not whether the legislation went further than was reasonably necessary, for he considered that no business of the court, but simply whether it was legislation 'with respect to' the powers enumerated in the Constitution. He took a decidedly generous view of the Commonwealth's defence powers and on some important cases, notably the Communist Party case of 1951, failed to carry his colleagues with him. But in general his judgments, which he reached with impeccable precision of reasoning, left the law much as he found it. He retired from the High Court in 1952.

Legislation was passed in 1940 to enable Latham to become Australia's first minister to Japan while still chief justice. He had a long-standing interest in Japan and was better informed about it than almost any of his contemporaries, but he did not reach Tokyo until the close of 1940 after Japan had concluded a pact of mutual assistance with the Axis powers, and his mission was accordingly constricted. He 'spoke with firmness and frankness' to successive Japanese foreign ministers on the 'hope for friendly relations and the resolution to resist attempts at Japanese domination'. In September 1941 he left Japan for consultations in Singapore, but fell ill and was back in Melbourne when the Pacific War began.

Latham had been chancellor of the University of Melbourne (1939-41). He was foundation president of the Australian Congress for Cultural Freedom, president of the Australian-American Association (1951-64), a local founder and president of the League of Nations Union, president of the Free Library Movement of Victoria (1937-48), the Australian Elizabethan Theatre Trust (1954-61) and the Victorian Amateur Athletic Association (1943-56). He was a director of Humes Ltd and of several other companies.

Even as an old man, Latham took enormous pride in his achievements and was always willing to talk about them. Those achievements were substantial. From humble origins he had attained the most senior post in his chosen profession and he had come very close to winning the highest political office. He was industrious, loyal and of unquestioned integrity. In the end, perhaps, he lacked the thrust required to succeed in politics and the creative spark that separates the distinguished jurist from the competent one. The intellectual certainty that Walter Murdoch had described in 1912 narrowed his imagination and stunted his sympathy with human frailty. But he gave fully of his energies to the many causes he served.

His retirement years were spent in Melbourne with his wife, who predeceased him by four months. Ella Latham, C.B.E., had been president of the Royal Children's Hospital, Melbourne, in 1933-54. She had supported her husband in his political career and accepted the lengthy separations imposed first by his overseas missions, then by the shift of Federal parliament to Canberra, and later by the perambulations of the High

Court. She and their three children were important to Latham, and the deep distress caused by the wartime death of their elder son was eased by the more continuous companionship they afforded each other in their later years. To the end he remained an indefatigable correspondent. Latham died on 25 July 1964 at Richmond and, despite his rationalist principles, was cremated after a memorial service at Wesley Church conducted by Rev. Sir Irving Benson. His estate was valued for probate at £74 365. His daughter Winifred Mary had died in 1953. He was survived by his third child Lieut-Colonel Peter Greig Latham. A portrait by William Dargie is in the High Court, Canberra.

Latham's younger brother Leslie Scott (1879-1950) was a leading Melbourne physician. Another brother Alan Thomas (1883-1974) was secretary (1918-41) of the Victorian Society for Protection of Animals and honorary secretary (1939-67) and fellow of the Royal Historical Society of Victoria.

Latham's elder son RICHARD THOMAS EDWIN (1909-43) was educated at Scotch College and the University of Melbourne (B.A., 1930), was president of the Students' Representative Council in 1929 and Victorian Rhodes scholar for 1931. He graduated from the University of Oxford (B.A., 1934) with first-class honours in jurisprudence and was elected a fellow of All Souls. The father's pride in his son's achievement was tempered by disappointment that he taught and practised in London. During the Spanish Civil War he drove a lorry for a relief society. He joined the Foreign Office on the outbreak of World War II and worked as a clerk in the refugee section where he was an outspoken critic of the British treatment of internees. Accepted by the Royal Air Force in 1941, he trained in Canada and was commissioned as an observer. His aeroplane failed to return from a flight over the Norwegian coast on 15 April 1943. While sharing his father's aptitude and industry, he possessed greater warmth, and friends such as (Sir) Keith Hancock, to whose *Survey of British Commonwealth affairs* he contributed a chapter on law and the Commonwealth, believed he showed outstanding promise.

Z. Cowen, *Sir John Latham and other papers* (Melb, 1965); C. Edwards, *Bruce of Melbourne* (Lond, 1965); J. R. Williams, *John Latham and the conservative recovery from defeat* (Syd, 1969); W. J. Hudson, *Billy Hughes in Paris* (Melb, 1978); F. Cain, *The origins of political surveillance in Australia* (Syd, 1983); P. G. Edwards, *Prime ministers and diplomats* (Melb, 1983); *Meanjin Q*, 21 (1962), no 1, p 78; *Aust Bar Gazette*, 1 (1964), no 4, p 3; *Aust Law J*, 38 (1964), p 188; *VHJ*, 35 (1964), p 95; *Table Talk*, 2 Aug 1928; *Bulletin*, 8 Aug 1964; D. J. E. Potts, A study of three Nationalists in the Bruce-Page government of 1923-1929 (M.A. thesis, Univ Melb, 1972); Latham papers (NL); Cabinet papers (AAO).   STUART MACINTYRE

LATIMER, WILLIAM FLEMING (1858-1935), draper and politician, and HUGH (1896-1954), accountant and politician, were father and son. William was born on 28 November 1858 at Lisblake near Enniskillen, Fermanagh, Ireland, son of William Lattimer, farmer, and his wife Sarah, née Fleming. Educated at the Erasmus Smith School at nearby Florence-Court, he was apprenticed at 15 to a softgoods firm at Blacklion, Meath. After serving his articles he spent two years in Glasgow, Scotland, and from 1880 managed a large softgoods warehouse at Mount Mellick.

Deciding to migrate, Latimer reached Sydney on 17 March 1883 and soon started work for W. Perry & Co. At Burwood on 23 September 1884 he married Charlotte Creighton, also from Fermanagh. That year he established a softgoods shop at 126 Queen Street, Woollahra, installing a manager. Two years later he took over its management and moved there to live. Business flourished and about 1896 he visited Ireland.

On his return Latimer was elected in 1897 to the Woollahra Municipal Council. He remained an alderman until he retired in December 1932, serving as mayor in 1900-10 and 1918-20 and on the executive of the Municipal Association of New South Wales in 1902-03. Standing as an unattached free trader, he was defeated for the Legislative Assembly seat of Woollahra in 1898, but won as a Liberal in 1901. He represented the electorate until he resigned on 16 February 1920 on being nominated to the Legislative Council; he did not stand for election to the reconstituted council in 1933. He served on the Parliamentary Standing Committee on Public Works in 1907-10 and attended to his parliamentary and municipal duties assiduously. Genial and reliable, he was described by J. T. Lang [q.v.9] as an 'ornament' in local government circles, who 'raised no antagonism and was friendly to all'.

By 1914 Latimer had sold his Queen Street shop and moved to Ashfield, but in 1923 was living at Roslyn Street, Bellevue Hill. He set up a family company, W. F. Latimer Ltd, and from 1930 was a director of Biber Furs Ltd. Intensely interested in all local affairs, he was a deacon of the Woollahra Congregational Church and was furious when Sunday tennis (which he described as 'this Godlessness') was allowed. With a neat beard and, when younger, a splendid waxed moustache, he had a merry laugh and cheery smile. Latimer died at his Bellevue Hill home on 21 July 1935 and was buried with Congregational forms in

South Head cemetery. His wife, two sons and daughter survived him, and with his sister inherited his estate valued for probate at £14 301.

His second son Hugh was born on 5 October 1896 at Queen Street, and named after his sixteenth-century ancestor Bishop Hugh Latimer. Educated at Woollahra Superior Public and Fort Street Boys' High schools, he was working as a clerk when he married Jean McClelland at the Congregational Church, Burwood, on 8 November 1919. He became an accountant with David Jones [q.v.2] Ltd, and later set up as a consulting chartered accountant. He lived at Bellevue Hill.

Latimer was elected to the Woollahra council in 1923 and, like his father, was an alderman for thirty-one years. He was mayor in 1932-35 and 1949-51 and a vice-president of the Local Government Association of New South Wales in 1947-49. He relentlessly opposed the government's plan to merge Woollahra with the Sydney Municipal Council in 1949 and urged the transfer of the Rose Bay flying boat base. He promoted kindergartens, baby health centres, Redleaf Pool and open-air concerts in Cooper's Park. A quiet and private man, he 'lived and breathed Woollahra'. In 1933 he had been elected to the reconstituted Legislative Council and remained a member until his death; he became Opposition whip in 1946. He was an elder of St Stephen's Presbyterian Church, treasurer of Eastern Suburbs Hospital and a life governor of Prince Henry Hospital.

A diabetic, Hugh Latimer died of coronary vascular disease in the Woollahra council chambers on 10 May 1954 and was cremated with Presbyterian forms. Survived by his wife and son, he left them an estate valued for probate at £17 641. His son William Fleming (d. 1969) was elected to his place on the Woollahra council and served for fifteen years before being run over by a vehicle driven by a council employee, making a total of seventy-two years continuous service on the council by three generations of Latimers.

Cyclopedia of N.S.W. (Syd, 1907); J. Jervis and V. Kelly, *History of Woollahra* (Syd, 1960); *PD* (NSW), 1935-36, p 35, 1954-55, p 6; *SMH*, 6 Dec 1919, 5 Feb 1920, 29 Aug, 11 Oct, 27 Nov 1922, 19 Dec 1934, 22, 23 July 1935, 13 May 1936, 13 Dec 1939, 14, 28 Mar 1950, 29 July 1951, 14, 16, 18 Mar 1953, 11 May 1954, 29 June 1957, 27 Sept 1969; *Fighting Line*, 27 Oct 1920; family information from Mr Hugh Latimer, Woollahra, Syd.

FAYETTE GOSSE

LAURIE, HENRY (1837-1922), journalist and philosopher, was born on 22 September 1837 at Comely Bank, Edinburgh, son of William Francis Hunter Laurie, writer to the signet, and his wife Christina, née Bayne. After attending the Edinburgh Academy, he studied literature and mental and moral philosophy at the University of Edinburgh in 1856-60. A gifted student, strongly influenced by A. Campbell Fraser, he won essay and poetry prizes and the Staten gold medal in moral philosophy. Laurie did not graduate: a breakdown in health induced, instead, his migration to Canada and, in September 1864, to Victoria. He settled at Warrnambool where, in January 1866, having failed to become a school inspector, he was appointed town clerk.

At Warrnambool Laurie pursued his literary interests as a member of the Shakespearian and Western Caledonian societies and as a contributor to Richard Osburne's [q.v.5] *Warrnambool Examiner.* In October 1867 he relinquished his clerical position for a five-year lease of the *Examiner* in partnership with William Fairfax, an experienced printer and journalist. The partners, in collaboration with George Robertson [q.v.6], published Laurie's penetrating pamphlet, *Conservatism and democracy*, in 1868 and in 1872 they established the bi-weekly (later more frequent) *Warrnambool Standard.* From 1877 Laurie was sole proprietor of the paper which competed so successfully with the *Examiner* as to absorb it in 1880. J. F. Archibald [q.v.3] who, as an apprentice, followed Laurie from the *Examiner* to the *Standard*, greatly admired the stylish editing (and the courageous support of free selection) of his 'scholarly' if 'somewhat moody' employer; he acknowledged that Laurie taught him to cut.

In August 1881 the lecturer in logic at the University of Melbourne, Frederick Joy Pirani, died after a fall from his horse. Laurie, with excellent credentials from Edinburgh and author of a timely article in the November issue of the *Victorian Review* supporting the establishment of a chair of philosophy, was, in December, appointed in Pirani's place. He sold the *Standard* and next year commenced duty as lecturer in mental and moral philosophy as well as in logic. In May 1886, on assuming the new Melbourne chair, he became the first professor of mental and moral philosophy in Australia; that year he received an honorary LL.D. from St Andrew's University. On 11 January 1871 in Melbourne, with Presbyterian forms, Laurie had married Frances, daughter of William Spalding, a Scottish professor of rhetoric and logic. With his wife and three sons he was among the first to occupy the professorial houses built on the Melbourne campus in 1887.

Devoted to the search for truth, Laurie was much praised as a teacher. He delivered his lectures from full notes with 'convincing earnestness'; his aim was not to present a systematic formulation of his own philosophical position which, stemming from the Scottish common-sense school, was based on his belief in the veracity of consciousness, but to elucidate the theories of others and to encourage fair-minded yet searching criticism. His students, among whom were E. Morris Miller, (Sir) Walter Murdoch and (Sir) John Latham [qq.v.], were taught, in plain terms, to think for themselves. Latham judged Laurie 'the best of the Profs'. In 1893 he was first president of the mental science and education section of the Australasian Association for the Advancement of Science and in his address urged the establishment of psychological laboratories. In 1911-14 he served on the special committee appointed by the 1911 Australasian Medical Congress to ascertain the extent of mental deficiency in Australia.

Laurie's *Scottish philosophy in its national development* (Glasgow, 1902) was his main published work. Other important writings are *Some thoughts on immortality* (Melbourne, 1901), originally the last of a series of lectures on Kantian ethics, and an investigation of the ideas of J. S. Mill, 'Methods of inductive inquiry', published in *Mind* (1893).

Laurie's interests continued to range beyond philosophy. For several years in the 1890s he wrote the leading article in the *Australasian* and in 1901 several of his poems were published in *Pro patria et regina* (edited by William Knight). He delivered university extension lectures on Robert Browning and contributed a paper at the 1912 Browning centenary celebrations in London. In 1921 he published *Plato in English literature*, an address to the Classical Association of Victoria.

In spite of his success Laurie, 'a tall, spare man with square red beard and heavy red eyebrows', was excessively shy. He was too inhibited to attend the dining club he formed with a friend and few outside his intimate circle knew what a fine conversationalist he was. He remained a devout Christian.

After his retirement in 1911 Laurie lived at The Righi, South Yarra. Predeceased by his wife, he died at home on 14 May 1922 and was buried in Boroondara cemetery. A portrait by Tom Roberts [q.v.] is held by the University of Melbourne.

R. Osburne, *The history of Warrnambool* (Prahran, Melb, 1887); E. Scott, *A history of the University of Melbourne* (Melb, 1936); J. La Nauze, *Walter Murdoch* (Melb, 1977); S. Lawson, *The Archibald paradox* (Melb, 1983); S. A. Grave, *History of philosophy in Australia* (Brisb, 1984); *Alma Mater* (Univ Melb), May 1897; *A'sian J of Psychology and Philosophy*, Mar 1923, Mar 1930; *Warrnambool Standard*, centenary issue, 2 Oct 1972.

ANN G. SMITH

LAVATER, LOUIS ISIDORE (1867-1953), composer, musician and writer, was born on 2 March 1867 at St Kilda, Melbourne, eldest child of George Theodore Adams Lavater, civil servant, and his English-born wife Emily Challinor, née Swindells. His Swiss-born father had migrated to Victoria after the 1851 gold rush. He was educated at St Kilda Grammar School, Wesley College and the University of Melbourne where in 1884 he began to study medicine, later abandoning it for music, a subject dearer to his heart although he did not complete his degree.

From March 1885 to January 1887 Lavater worked for the London Chartered Bank of Australia and in 1888 was secretary to the orchestral committee of the Melbourne Centennial Exhibition. In 1892 he moved to Colac where he taught music and opened a school, offering a wide range of subjects.

With the enthusiasm that was to accompany most of his ventures he conducted the Methodist choir and produced operas and oratorios for the Colac Lyric Club as well as writing and conducting for local and Melbourne fêtes, benefits and entertainments. Where musical gaps existed he proceeded to fill them, forming an orchestra, Liedertafel, and ladies' choir. He also organized a circulating library of sheet music, played for the cricket team and was its secretary, and published light verse and humorous paragraphs in local papers.

On 4 February 1912 Lavater married Catherine Annie Churchland at Wesley Church, Melbourne. Two years later they left Colac for Melbourne where Catherine died on 12 July 1914. On 22 November 1916 Lavater married Beatrice Kathleen Stephens, a nurse from New Zealand. This marriage ended unhappily in divorce in June 1936.

Lavater was a versatile and prolific composer, but his music only ever earned him a precarious living, which the £1 a week pension eventually granted him by the Commonwealth Literary Fund alleviated slightly. Much of his work remained in manuscript but he did publish orchestral, choral and chamber music, sonatas, pieces for the piano, violin and cello, motets and part-songs and *Nina*, a ballet suite which was performed in London and Australia. He was author of *The licentiate pianist's handbook* (1928, 1945) and received the gold medal from the London College of Music. He was much in demand as an adjudicator at local and interstate musical competitions.

Although music was always the major component in his life, he was the author of four collections of poetry: *Blue days and grey days* (1915), *A lover's ephemeris* (1917), *This green mortality* (1922) and 'Changing harmonies' which remained unpublished. In 1926 he edited an anthology, *The sonnet in Australasia*, which had a favourable critical reception, and he also translated Swedish poems. His interest in Swedish literature and music earned him the honour of associate of the Royal Swedish Academy of Music. Lavater's own poetry at its best was intelligent, lyrical and often sensuous. He published short stories, although not nearly as many as he would have liked; in some of these, especially the earlier ones, the prose is polished and humorous and demonstrates a predilection for the mysterious and macabre.

Lavater lectured to clubs and societies on diverse topics. He edited *Verse* magazine, wrote book reviews, and was sometime music critic for the *Sun-News Pictorial*, the *New Graphic* and *Listener In*. He belonged to a variety of clubs and societies, including the Buonarotti Club, Dickens Fellowship, Fellowship of Australian Writers, Melbourne Literary Club, Australian Literature Society, Australian Artists' Association, Bread and Cheese Club, Arts and Crafts Society of Victoria and P.E.N. International. He was sometime Melbourne secretary of the British Music Society, president of the Association of Music Teachers of Victoria, and librarian, examiner and president of the Musical Society of Victoria. In 1935 his determination was the main impetus behind the foundation of the Guild of Australian Composers, whose aim was to encourage and make Australian works more widely known both at home and overseas.

This dream of Lavater's was still unrealized when he died suddenly at St Kilda on 22 May 1953. But his influence lived on in the younger writers and musicians whose talent he encouraged. The impression remains of a picturesque, unpretentious, kindly and generous man with a keen sense of humour, and a passionate desire to further the development of music and literature that was distinctively Australian.

S. Nemet, *History of the Musical Society of Victoria 1861-1981* (Melb, nd); W. A. Orchard, *Music in Australia* (Melb, 1952); *Meanjin Q*, 10, no 4, 1951, p 364, 12, no 3, 1953, p 319, 322, 358; *A'sian*, 9 Sept 1939; Lavater papers (SLV).

VALERIE KENT

LAVER, CHARLES WILLIAM (1863-1937), medical practitioner, and FRANK JONAS (1869-1919), cricketer, were the third and fifth of the seven surviving sons of Jonas Laver, farmer from Somerset, England, and his wife Mary Ann, née Fry, a connexion of Elizabeth Fry the prison reformer. Jonas arrived in Melbourne on the *Maitland* in 1846, married there in 1854 and settled with his wife at Chinamans Creek, near Castle-maine, where Charles was born on 26 June 1863. Frank was born on 7 December 1869 at Castlemaine. Charles and Frank, with their brothers William [q.v.], Alfred, Arthur, Ralph and Rudolph, made up an unusually talented family.

Charles worked as a drover and took up land in North-West Western Australia in the 1880s, forming friendships with (Sir) John and Alexander Forrest [qq.v.8], before attending the University of Melbourne in 1887-91. He continued his medical studies overseas, graduating L.C.R.P. and L.R.C.S. (Edinburgh), L.M. (Edinburgh and Glasgow) and L.F.P.S. (Glasgow) in 1894. Returning to Melbourne, he quickly forsook his Collins Street practice for a prospector's life in Western Australia; but after his marriage to Edith Beatrice Attewell in London on 2 June 1904 he practised in various Western Australian country towns, winning renown for unselfish devotion to goldfields patients and, as 'Mr the Doctor', to the Aborigines.

Laver's great faith in Western Australia led to his reputation as the 'super-optimist'. He had several interests on the Golden Mile, Kalgoorlie, and in the flotation of the British Flag, Craigiemore and Barneycoat mines at Laverton, the town named after him. He had some success at mining but his sheep-farming experiments at Yundamindra station were under financed and collapsed.

An Anglican, Laver died at Kalgoorlie on 14 May 1937 and was buried there, survived by his wife, two daughters and four sons, one of whom, Jack, also had a distinguished medical career.

Frank was educated at Castlemaine Grammar School and in 1887-95 worked as a clerk in the government Law Department before joining his brother Ralph's Collingwood fruit-preserving business. 'A gangling, heavy-legged six-footer' (the height and leanness a family trait), he joined the East Melbourne Cricket Club about 1887. In the 1892-93 season, during which he made a record 352 not out for his club, he was selected for Victoria and made 104 against South Australia; in later years he often captained Victoria. He played for Australia against the visiting Englishmen in 1901-02 and toured England in 1899, 1903-04, 1905 and 1909. A. G. Moyes describes him as 'a splendid medium-fast off-spinner and rough and ready batsman'. His Test triumphs included 7 wickets for 61 at Nottingham in 1905 and 8 for 31 at Manchester in 1909. In 15 Tests against England, Laver took 37 wickets at an average of 25.97. In Sheffield Shield matches he made 2760 runs and took 108 wickets.

Laver was popular with team members as player-manager in England in 1905 and 1909. In 1911-12 he was again players' candidate for manager and when the Australian Board of

Control for International Cricket Matches insisted on the appointment of G. S. Crouch, six players led by Clem Hill [q.v.9] declined to tour. In 1905 Laver wrote *An Australian cricketer on tour*. He was also a prominent baseballer, captaining the Australian team which visited the United States of America in 1897.

Frank married Katie Myrtle Adele Major on 15 September 1914. He died at East Melbourne on 24 September 1919 after visiting his Northern Territory property with his brother Alfred. Survived by his wife, son and daughter, he was buried in Brighton cemetery.

ALFRED EDMUND (1858-1927) was born on 16 November 1858. As a youth a prominent Castlemaine footballer and cricketer, he established himself as a vigneron at Woodbrook, marrying Margaret Ellen Williamson (d. 1904) at Castlemaine on 22 March 1882. In 1891 he became superintendent and secretary of the Castlemaine Benevolent Asylum and in 1896-1924 directed the Melbourne Benevolent Asylum. He died at Marrickville, Sydney, on 15 August 1927, survived by his wife Flora, née Dash, whom he had married on 2 April 1911, and by three children of his first marriage.

RALPH HERBERT (1874-1962), youngest of the brothers, was born on 14 July 1874. He and Rudolph (b. 1872) were educated in Germany where Rudolph remained to become a highly successful electrical engineer. Ralph returned to Melbourne and with Otto Jung's help established Laver Bros in 1893 in Collingwood as a greengrocery and then a preserving factory. The firm developed a large trade throughout Australia and with England and China. After Frank's death Ralph was joined by Arthur (1860-1927), a successful grazier. Ralph retired to Warrandyte about 1935. He died at Canterbury on 24 September 1962.

J. Smith (ed), *Cyclopedia of Victoria*, 3 (Melb, 1905); A. G. Moyes, *Australian cricket* (Syd, 1959); H. H. Wilson, *Westward gold* (Adel, 1973); A. L. Bennett, *The glittering years* (Perth, 1981); J. Pollard, *Australian cricket* (Syd, 1982); *MJA*, 29 June 1935; *Argus*, 25, 29 Sept 1919, 19 May, 16 Aug 1927; *A'sian*, 27 Sept 1919; *SMH*, 20 Aug 1927; *Daily News* (Perth), and *Kalgoorlie Miner*, 15 May 1937; G. W. Laver, The consummation of a youthful dream (MS, Univ Melb Archives); Monash papers (NL); family information. ANN G. SMITH

LAVER, WILLIAM ADOLPHUS (1866-1940), violinist and professor of music, was born on 20 August 1866 at Castlemaine, Victoria, fourth of seven surviving sons of Jonas Laver, farmer, and his wife Mary Ann, née

Fry. William (Willie to intimates) probably attended the local Castlemaine school. It is not known from whom he received his early violin tuition. In 1881 the famous German violinist August Wilhelmj heard Laver play and, impressed with the boy's potential, offered to have him trained in Germany. Jonas had died in 1880; his widow refused Wilhelmj's offer, but in 1882, she undertook the journey with William and three other sons Arthur, Rudolph and Ralph [q.v.]. They were accompanied by an old family friend Otto Jung who had become guardian of the under-age boys when their father died and who continued to care for them after their mother's death at Frankfurt-am-Main in 1885 or 1886.

At the Hoch Conservatory of Music at Frankfurt William's teachers were Professor Bernhard Scholz, Hugo Heermann, Bernhard Cossmann, James Kwast and Ivan Knorr. Laver was admitted to the intimate circle surrounding Brahms, and Frederic Lamond, considered the greatest Beethoven pianist of the day, became his closest friend. In 1882 Laver was the student chosen by the school to attend the first performance of Wagner's *Parsifal* at Bayreuth; later he became an authority on Wagner.

In 1887 Clara Schumann offered Laver a conducting post at Nottingham, England. He refused on hearing that Francis Ormond [q.v.5] was to establish a chair of music at University of Melbourne. Though not yet 22 and with his studies unfinished, he applied for the position, travelling to London to lobby the selection committee, and mounting a vigorous campaign in Australia through his brothers and their contacts. He arrived in Melbourne on 13 May 1889 with detailed plans for a conservatorium on the Frankfurt model. Neither the attempt to realize these plans nor his application for the chair was successful. He was declared below the age limit for the professorship and lost the appointment in 1890 to G. W. L. Marshall-Hall [q.v.].

Laver established himself in Melbourne as a private teacher and on 7 March 1894 at Brighton, with Presbyterian forms, he married one of his pupils, Agnes Grant MacIntyre Robertson. Common interests had drawn him into friendship with Marshall-Hall, despite his own rather withdrawn temperament and Marshall-Hall's flamboyance, and in 1894 he offered his plans and private practice as a basis for a university school of music. The proposal was accepted and on 28 February 1895, when Laver was acting professor during Marshall-Hall's study leave, the university's Conservatorium of Music was opened in the Queen's Coffee Palace, Rathdowne Street, Carlton; within a few years it was rehoused in Albert Street, East Melbourne, and in 1910 in a new building in the university grounds. Two of Laver's students from the 1890s, Adelaide Burkitt and William Murdoch [q.v.], won international fame, while Percy Grainger's [q.v.9] attendance at the Hoch Conservatory may have stemmed from Laver's advice.

In 1900 when Marshall-Hall's dismissal resulted in the establishment of a rival conservatorium Laver, now in opposition to his old friend, resumed the acting professorship of the university conservatorium and then, unsuccessful in a second bid for the chair, became vice-director under F. S. Peterson [q.v.]. In this capacity he visited and reported upon European music centres in 1903. After Peterson's death in 1914 Laver's supporters fought a long and acrimonious battle for his succession as professor; but, instead, Marshall-Hall was reinstated. Laver finally became third Ormond professor of music after Marshall-Hall's death next year.

Laver toured Australia and New Zealand as a violinist in 1905 and frequently conducted, notably for the 1913 Wagner Centenary at the Melbourne Auditorium. He was a distinguished editor, mainly of Bach and Beethoven, and composer of a small number of orchestral and vocal works. He represented the university on the advisory committee of the Teachers' Registration Board of the Education Department and was chairman of the University of Melbourne Examination Board (Music). He also examined at interstate universities and for the (Sir William) Clarke [q.v.3]-South Province scholarship founded at the Royal College of Music, to which he was elected an honorary member in 1936.

Late in 1925 Laver retired from the Ormond chair to his retreat, Eothen at Kinglake, where he lobbied tirelessly for the preservation of bushland. In 1938 as acting professor during (Sir) Bernard Heinze's sabbatical leave, he opened the Grainger Museum at the university. He died at Kinglake on 2 July 1940, survived by his wife, three sons and a daughter, and was buried in Brighton cemetery. A portrait by W. B. McInnes [q.v.] is held by the university.

E. Scott, *A history of the University of Melbourne* (Melb, 1936); I. Moresby, *Australia makes music* (Melb, 1948); G. Blainey, *A centenary history of the University of Melbourne* (Melb, 1957); J. Bird, *Percy Grainger* (Melb, 1977); T. Radic, *G. W. L. Marshall-Hall*, music monograph 5, Univ WA (Perth, 1982); Melba Memorial Conservatorium, *Con Amore*, 10 (1943), 12 (1946); *Punch* (Melb), 9 Nov 1916; *Argus*, 3 July 1940; G. W. Laver, The consummation of a youthful dream, (MS, Archives), and J. Barrett, Professor Marshall-Hall (lecture, 21 Mar 1935, Grainger Museum), and Univ Melb Conservatorium prospectus, 1898, and Council of Univ Melb, Minute-book, 1888-89 (Central Registry), Univ Melb; family information.

MAUREEN THÉRÈSE RADIC

LAW, SYDNEY JAMES (1856-1939), politician, was born on 23 November 1856 at Redfern, Sydney, son of John Law, cabinetmaker, and his wife Sarah Anne, née Pollard, both Londoners. As a young man, he learned shorthand, but first prospered hawking drapery 'on the time payment system'. In 1881 he opened a drapery store at Balmain. He soon acquired other property in the area and was a provisional director of the New Balmain Steam Ferry Co. formed in 1892. He had married Mary McLean on 4 July 1883 at St Barnabas' Anglican Church.

In 1889 Law was vice-president then president of the local branch of the Free Trade and Liberal Association of New South Wales, but when the Balmain Labor Electoral League was formed in 1891 he joined it. He unsuccessfully sought pre-selection for the 1891 election but by late that year had become president of the local league. In 1894 he was elected to the Legislative Assembly for Balmain South, which he represented until 1904. About 1894 he joined the Balmain Labourers' Union. The involvement in the Labor Party of a small businessman like Law provoked internal critics but, at the local level at least, he provided organizing and publicizing skills and a certain respectability.

Law was no high-flier. In parliament he concerned himself largely with local issues. He also supported female franchise and shared Labor's opposition to the Federal constitution, but after its adoption he was defeated for the Federal seat of Dalley. Increasingly resentful of caucus discipline, Law, by voting in November 1902 with the Opposition on the estimates for the Attorney-General's Department, found an opportunity to demonstrate his dissatisfaction with the action of the attorney-general B. R. Wise [q.v.] in freeing Moss Friedman, who had been found guilty by a jury of receiving. Rebuked by J. T. McGowen [q.v.] for failing to support the government, Law resigned his seat and party membership. His resignation caused a flurry of interest in the press: standing as Independent Labor, he won the lively by-election.

While Law did not plan his defection, he was attracted by the development of a revitalized free-trade, now liberal, movement which was catching up free traders, sectarian Protestants, temperance, women's and business groups into a powerful party. He was a member of the Evangelical wing of the Church of England, a temperance supporter, an Orangeman and in 1901 an original member of Rev. William Dill Macky's [q.v.8] Australian Protestant Defence Association. For many sectarian Protestants, Labor seemed a tool of the Catholic Church and Law, with a strongly self-righteous streak, was an awkward colleague. In 1904 as a Liberal Reform candidate he won

Rozelle. He tried to maintain a base among sectarian Protestants and working men but was defeated in 1907. A strong element of sectarianism marked his last three campaigns.

Late in 1907 Law began business as an auctioneer and estate agent. He was moderately successful and in the 1920s moved his residence to more fashionable Drummoyne. He died there on 7 October 1939 and was buried in the Anglican section of Waverley cemetery. His wife, son and daughter survived him.

B. Nairn, *Civilising capitalism* (Canb, 1973); I. Wyner, *With banners unfurled* (Syd, 1983); *SMH*, 25 July, 19, 29 Nov 1902; *Balmain Observer*, 27 July, 28 Sept, 21 Dec 1907; *Daily Telegraph* (Syd), 4 July 1894; L. G. Lynch, A community study—Balmain 1860-1894 (Ph.D. thesis, Univ Syd, 1982).

MARK LYONS

LAWLEY, SIR ARTHUR, 6th BARON WENLOCK (1860-1932), governor, was born on 12 November 1860 in London, fourth son of Beilby Richard Lawley, 2nd Baron Wenlock, and his wife, Lady Elizabeth, née Grosvenor. Educated at Eton and Trinity College, Cambridge (he did not graduate), he was captain in the 10th (The Prince of Wales's Own Royal) Regiment before becoming the duke of Westminster's private secretary in 1892. He had married Annie Allen Cunard on 12 October 1885. In 1896-99 he was deputy, then administrator in Matabeleland; he was decorated for his advice to the northern district columns early in the South African War. In 1901 Lawley was appointed K.C.M.G. and commissioned as governor of Western Australia.

He travelled to Australia with the duke and duchess of York on board the *Ophir* and, after arriving at Albany and presenting his credentials in Perth, sailed on 3 May to Melbourne where he represented Western Australia at the opening of the Federal parliament. In Perth on 21 May he received Premier Throssell's [q.v.] resignation, the first of a series of political crises to occur during his stewardship: between May 1901 and July 1902 Lawley asked seven times for an administration to be formed. Three contenders, F. Illingworth [q.v.9], F. H. Piesse [q.v.] and (Sir) Walter Kingsmill [q.v.9] failed; G. Leake and A. E. Morgans [qq.v.] succeeded, but soon collapsed. Refusing dissolutions to both Leake and Morgans, Lawley argued that because of Federal and State elections early in 1901, the legislature was still fresh from the constituency. When Leake, who had gathered support for a second term, died in June 1902, the governor summoned (Sir) Walter James [q.v.9] from the cross-bench.

Lawley led the State's social life with aplomb. He toured the south-west with the governor-general Lord Hopetoun [q.v.9] in December 1901. He was tactful and unperturbed by ructions that year in the Perth City Council. Lady Lawley identified herself with community welfare; a children's cottage by the sea at Cottesloe bears her name. She reputedly approved F. S. Drake-Brockman's [q.v.8] suggestion that Mount Lawley be named for her husband only on condition that no licensed hotels be built within that suburb.

Lawley left Western Australia in 1902 to become lieut-governor of the Transvaal; in 1906-11 he was governor of Madras. Part of his brief in both cases was to initiate electoral reform. Characteristically firm yet fair, Lawley was a diplomatic and able administrator, with a strong sense of duty. Affable and engaging, with a dashing appearance, he was an excellent sportsman, but the accidental death of his only son blighted his enthusiasm for hunting. He was appointed G.C.I.E. in 1906 and G.C.S.I. in 1911.

In London Lawley entered commercial life in the City as director of several companies; some, like Dalgety [q.v.4] & Co. Ltd with whom he remained till 1930, had Australian connexions. In World War I he was a commissioner for the British Red Cross Society at Boulogne, France. In 1927 he visited the Fairbridge [q.v.8] Farm School at Pinjarra, Western Australia, and he remained president of the Child Emigration Society (later Fairbridge Society) until his death.

In June 1931 he succeeded his brother Algernon as 6th and last Baron Wenlock. Survived by his wife and two daughters, he died on 14 June 1932 at Freiberg, Germany, and was buried at Escrick, Yorkshire, England.

PD (WA), 1901-02, p 21; Dept of Education (WA), *Education Circular*, May 1902; *Education Supplement*, May 1927; *West Australian*, 2 Jan 1906, 20 Dec 1912; *The Times*, 15, 16, 20, 22 June 1932; Col Sec, GD 1901-02 (Battye Lib).

WENDY BIRMAN

LAWLOR, ADRIAN (1889-1969), painter, writer and critic, was born on 30 August 1889 in London, son of Andrew Lawlor, butler and later farmer, and his wife Margaret, née McIntosh. Christened Andrew, he changed his name to Adrian when a youth. He was educated at a private school in Surrey and in 1910, after the death of his mother, migrated to Australia with one of his two younger sisters. On 9 May 1916 at a civil ceremony in Melbourne he married Eva Nodrum, twenty years his senior and a member of the family leather business of Charles Nodrum & Co. for which Lawlor was to work for many years as clerk and leather sorter. Enlisting in the Australian Imperial Force six months after his marriage, Lawlor served on the Western Front as a private in the 21st Battalion. On his return in 1919 he moved with his wife to Broom Warren, a cottage at Warrandyte where they spent the next thirty years.

In 1921 Lawlor began writing literary articles, poetry and stories which were published in a variety of journals including the *Bulletin, Vision* and *New Triad*. Having achieved some minor success as a writer, he took up painting in 1929 and after brief periods of study at the National Gallery School and with A. D. Colquhoun [q.v.8] embarked on a vigorous and prolific decade as an artist. Under the guidance of Arnold Shore [q.v.], George Bell and William Frater [qq.v.7,8] he moved rapidly into prominence among Melbourne modernist artists. In 1930-40 he held eight one-man exhibitions and showed over 500 works.

Lawlor and Bell strongly resisted the proposal to form an Australian Academy of Art in 1937 and next year set up the opposing Contemporary Art Society with Lawlor as secretary. His book, *Arquebus* (1937), and pamphlet, *Eliminations* (1939), dealt brilliantly with the controversy. He was a guide lecturer at the 1939 *Herald* Exhibition of French and British Contemporary Art and spoke on art at public meetings. After a relatively unsuccessful exhibition in 1940, following the destruction of his house and nearly all his paintings in the 1939 bushfires, he gave up painting and concentrated on criticism for the Melbourne *Sun* and *Art in Australia*; he continued with his regular Australian Broadcasting Commission session 'Art Front' (after 1945 'Art Review') in which he championed the cause of progressive art and culture.

Lawlor's semi-autobiographical novel, *Horned capon*, was privately published in 1950. His wife died in 1953 and on 6 March 1954 he married a librarian, Margaret Sweatman. The marriage soon ended in divorce and in 1955-65 Lawlor lived as a semi-recluse at St Kilda, supported by a war service pension. In 1966 he assembled his remaining paintings and held a retrospective exhibition at the Argus Galleries, Melbourne.

Childless, Lawlor died at Heidelberg on 6 September 1969 and was cremated. His paintings are represented in the State galleries of Victoria, South Australia and Western Australia and in the Australian National Gallery where there is also a portrait of Lawlor by Albert Tucker. A major exhibition of his work was held at Heide Park and Art Gallery, Melbourne, in 1983.

Bernard Smith, *Australian painting 1788-1970* (Melb, 1971); G. Fry, *Adrian Lawlor, a portrait* (Melb, 1983); Lawlor papers (LaTL); Contemporary Art Soc, records (SLV).   GAVIN FRY

LAWRENCE, CHARLES EDWARD (1885-1968), entertainer and broadcaster, was born on 28 March 1885 at Hotham, Melbourne, elder child of Victorian-born parents Charles Joseph Lawrence, clerk, and his wife Nellie, née Quick. As a boy soprano Lawrence sang in his church choir and at eisteddfods. On leaving school he 'pushed a pen and used a billing machine' before opting to use his musical talents. In 1909 the strong-arm wrestler George Hackenschmidt engaged him as a support act in New Zealand. Next year he went to Perth. In 1910-11 in Melbourne Lawrence turned to beach entertainments at St Kilda, playing with Edward Branscombe's Jesters at the Arcadia and next season with J. & N. Tait's [qq.v.] Follies. In Melbourne on 15 April 1912 he married Eva May Spence before touring Australasia and South Africa in 1912-13 as support to English entertainer Margaret Cooper.

In the summer of 1913-14 Lawrence joined Rob and Will Thomas's English Pierrots at St Kilda beach where he was known for his 'pianologues'. The company followed a rhythm of summers at St Kilda and winters in New Zealand or Western Australia. After Rob Thomas died in 1920 the leading performers (including Lawrence) bought the company, but next season they did not continue.

Lawrence toured the vaudeville circuits and in 1926 began working as a radio entertainer on 2FC in Sydney; he made the transition smoothly. He entertained at the piano with the patter song his mainstay, appeared in such revues as Laurence Halbert's 'Radio Revellers' and '2FC Follies', and acted as compère of many hospital and concert parties. Through the Depression years people flocked to the free community-singing that Lawrence began conducting in mid-1930 at Ashfield, and later at Sydney Town Hall and suburban and country centres. In 1931 he appeared on the cover of *Wireless Weekly* with his 'community smile', a short chubby man with slightly receding hair and twinkling eyes behind round rims.

His popularity on radio led to his engagement in November 1931 as commentator for the pioneer newsreel *Cinesound Review*. With his gags, puns and gentle humour Lawrence provided the entertainment quality which director Ken Hall required. In April 1932 Lawrence moved to 2UW, combining his usual items with sporting sessions. For the 1934 cricket Tests 2UW linked with 3DB in Melbourne; Lawrence was one of a team of comedians in both cities used to fill adjournments in play. A follower of horses, he helped to inaugurate 2UW's racing session and with Eric Welch [q.v.] of 3DB relayed Melbourne races.

During World War II Lawrence, whose voice lacked the serious timbre needed for war items, continued to do the 'at home' and novelty items for *Cinesound*. He ceased narrating in the early 1950s but, ever the old trouper, continued for some time to compère on the Sydney *Show Boat*. Predeceased by his wife, he died childless on 12 November 1968 in Sydney Hospital and was cremated.

A genial and professional showman, Lawrence based his humour, never overtly vulgar, on gags, corn and gentle wit, derivative mainly from the English stage. His distinctive voice, which gave pre-war *Cinesound* newsreels their character, is his legacy.

St Kilda by the Sea Annual, 1915-16; *Wireless Weekly*, 1 Feb, 22 Nov 1929, 22 Aug 1930, 24 Apr 1931, 5 July 1935; *Film Weekly*, 5 Nov 1931; *People* (Syd), 26 Jan 1955; *Punch* (Melb), 2 Oct 1913; *Table Talk*, 24 Feb 1921; *SMH*, 27 Sept 1930, 13 Nov 1969.

JAN BRAZIER

LAWRENCE, GORDON ORD (1896-1960), dentist, was born on 11 November 1896 at Geraldton, Western Australia, tenth child of William Chipper Lawrence, police inspector, and his wife Jane Charlotte, née Howell. He was educated in Western Australia and was apprenticed for eighteen months to the leading Perth dentist James Alexander Wright before enlisting in August 1916 in the Australian Imperial Force as a private in the Dental Corps. Remaining in Australia, next April he was promoted staff sergeant; however, he was discharged from the A.I.F. in June, having re-enlisted for home service. He entered the dental school of the University of Melbourne in 1919 (B.D.Sc., 1922). Lawrence registered with the Dental Board of South Australia in 1925 and was a dental house surgeon at the (Royal) Adelaide Hospital for three years. From 1927 he also practised at suburban Largs Bay and, from 1937, at Semaphore. At the University of Adelaide he was an instructor in prosthetic dentistry from 1936 and thereafter divided his interests between his practice and university teaching; from 1930 he was also an honorary dental surgeon at the Adelaide Hospital. On 9 February 1929 at Unley Lawrence had married Alice Eileen Dobson, secretary; they had no children.

He was a tall, dark, impressive man, gentle and with an inquiring and inventive mind. A perfectionist, he contributed substantially to dental research and education in South Australia; his insistence upon the highest standards of clinical dentistry is remembered by his students and colleagues. His original work (1938-40) included the Lawrence matrix, an ingenious instrument for the improved restoration and contour of compound cavities, which received world acclaim. At a time when there were few Australian studies of dental materials, and when wartime shortages and quality variation in raw materials were a problem, Lawrence did basic work on impression pastes and reversible agar gels. He was awarded a doctorate of dental science by the University of Adelaide in 1945 for a thesis on these matters and other studies, including the hot oil sterilization of dental handpieces. Lawrence loved working with his hands; his hobby was the making of fine gold jewellery.

Lawrence died suddenly of myocardial infarction at Memorial Hospital, North Adelaide, on 6 August 1960 and was cremated. He was survived by his wife (d. 1967) who was inconsolable; in her will she endowed the G. O. Lawrence scholarship for postgraduate studies in conservative dentistry.

Advertiser (Adel), 9 Aug 1960.

GEOFFREY W. PAGE

LAWRENCE, MARJORIE FLORENCE (1907-1979), dramatic soprano, was born on 17 February 1907 at Dean's Marsh, near Winchelsea, Victoria, fifth of six children of William Lawrence, butcher and fiddler, and his wife Elizabeth, née Smith, church organist, who died when Marjorie was 2. Reared by her paternal grandmother until she too died, Marjorie was educated at local schools; from the age of 10 she was a regular soloist. Her musical tastes were refined by the local Anglican parson and gramophone records of Nellie Melba [q.v.] and Clara Butt. At 18, despite her father's opposition, she left for Melbourne with her brother Cyril in search of work, paying Ivor Boustead to train her voice—she never had to unlearn anything he taught. Forced home by impecuniousness, she failed to gain a place in the Ballarat South Street competitions, but at Geelong in 1928 won the *Sun* Aria contest.

John Brownlee [q.v.7] advised Marjorie to study in Paris. Experiencing financial hardship, she boarded with a French family to acquire the language and manners, and learned her craft from Cécile Gilly who extended the upper range of her voice. In January 1932 Lawrence made her début as Elisabeth in *Tannhäuser* at Monte Carlo; it was acclaimed by critics as comparable with those of Chaliapin and Caruso. Elbowed out of a contract in Paris by a jealous soprano, she sang a season at Lille; then, steering clear of intrigues, she sang Ortrud for the Paris Opera from 25 February 1933 followed by a number of dramatic leads over four seasons. Now the company's leading dramatic soprano, she privately entertained celebrities like Honegger and James Joyce.

Her triumph in New York (18 December 1935) introduced six seasons with the Metropolitan Opera at home and on tour (with her brother Cyril her manager), mostly in Wagnerian leads. Her physical grace enchanted audiences. She herself danced Salome's erotic dance, and as Brünnhilde she scored another first by riding a horse on stage into the immolation flames of *Götterdämmerung*.

Marjorie Lawrence visited Australia in 1939, 1944, 1951, 1966 and 1976; she kept a promise in 1939 to perform first at Winchelsea, which honoured her with an escort of one hundred horsemen. More popular in Melbourne than in Sydney, she quarrelled briefly with the Australian Broadcasting Commission over its cringe to foreign performers. Her repertoire now ran to some twenty-five major roles in four languages. Neville Cardus wrote of the 'unselfconscious pathos' and 'intimate poetry' in her performances, of the 'superb range' of her powerful voice, 'rich in vocal splendour' throughout. Her timbre had a certain exciting wildness, first noted and accepted by Gilly. A disciplined and versatile musician, Lawrence prescribed an 'iron constitution, calm and an ordered life' to aspiring singers. Despite her huge collection of Parisian gowns and hats (her passion—one had a brim of a half-map of Australia), she disdained the temperamental hauteur of prima donnas and met people with informal warmth.

A sudden attack of poliomyelitis in 1941 left her almost completely paralysed in both legs. Married on 29 March 1941 at City Hall, New York, to Thomas King, osteopath and Christian Scientist, she used the Sister Kenny [q.v.9] treatment to provide a slow, laborious method to use her legs partially. Other helpful factors, she said, were her husband's support, her faith in God and her Australian upbringing. Her first public reappearance in 1942 was followed by her New York Venus in a chair (when Sir Thomas Beecham called her 'the greatest living dramatic soprano'), her reclining Isolde at Montreal, and Amneris at Cincinnati carried off stage on a palanquin. By 1947 she sang Elektra upright on a wheeling platform designed by her husband. A film in 1955, which she criticized as untrue to her life, was based on her humorous, candid autobiography, *Interrupted melody* (New York, 1949). She was not engaged to sing the lead herself.

Lawrence made extensive tours to entertain troops in Australia (1944), occupied Europe (1945, 1948) and Vietnam (1966), sang at Buckingham Palace and the White House, and continued to perform until 1952, after which she taught at Tulane, Southern Illinois, and Arkansas universities. In summer she ran opera workshops and sponsored children's opera at her home Harmony Range, Hot Springs, Arkansas. Grateful students established the Marjorie Lawrence Lincoln Endowment Fund for handicapped people attending performances of 'the Met' at the Lincoln Center, New York.

Marjorie Lawrence died of heart failure on 13 January 1979 at St Vincent's Hospital, Little Rock, Arkansas, and was buried in Greenwood cemetery. For her work in France she had received the cross of the Légion d'honneur (1946); she was also appointed C.B.E. in 1976.

B. and F. Mackenzie, *Singers of Australia* (Melb, 1967); *People*, 14 Feb 1951; *Opera Australia*, Mar 1979; *Sun-News Pictorial*, 16 Apr 1928, 17 June 1939; *Age*, 19 Oct 1928, 14 June 1941, 12 June 1976 (green guide), 15 Jan 1979; *Herald* (Melb), 2 July 1937, 17 June 1939, 16 Jan 1979; *SMH*, 17 June, 31 July, 1, 2, 3 Aug 1939, 15 Sept 1944, 1 Aug 1954, 20 May 1977; *Australian*, 16 June 1976; *Courier Mail* (Brisb), 18 Jan 1979; NL biog files.   HELGA M. GRIFFIN

LAWSON, ABERCROMBIE ANSTRUTHER (1870-1927), botanist, was born on 13 September 1870 at Hamilton, Ontario, Canada, fourth son of William Lawson, sailor and shipyard worker, and his wife Janet (Jessie) Kerr, née Coupar. The family from Fifeshire, Scotland, had migrated to Hamilton in 1866 and in 1881 moved to Toronto, where Lawson was educated at the Harbord Street Collegiate Institute. When his father's health failed, his mother wrote novels and worked as a journalist to educate the ten children. After a year at the University of Toronto, Lawson claimed to have studied medicine and botany at the University of Glasgow, Scotland, in 1895-96. He graduated at the University of California, Berkeley (B.S., 1897; M.S., 1898). After a year as assistant in botany he spent 1901 at the University of Chicago with Professors Coulter and Chamberlain in the new Hull laboratories and was awarded a Ph. D. (1901). Lawson returned to California and spent five years teaching at Stanford University under Professor D. H. Campbell. In 1907 he was appointed lecturer in botany at the University of Glasgow and in 1910 was awarded D.Sc. for papers on the special morphology of the Coniferales.

In 1913 Lawson became foundation professor of botany at the University of Sydney. The university had obtained the services of a man well versed in and strongly committed to the theory of evolution which was then revolutionizing comparative morphology, a major branch of botanical studies. His research interests, based on collections and observations made on major expeditions, contrasted with the more descriptive and less theoretical concerns of economic botany and traditional taxonomy which had dominated botanical research in Australia.

From the first day Lawson stressed laboratory work and pressed for a new building to house his department. Insisting on adequate laboratory facilities, he rejected attempts to locate the department in the arts building and soon occupied a large part of the Macleay [q.v. 5] Museum. World War I delayed his plans but a new building, largely to his design and built on to the museum, was opened in 1925. Lawson also emphasized the importance of field excursions as a teaching technique, a long-hallowed tradition of Scottish universities. About 1925 he formally introduced the study of ecology into the teaching programme.

An entertaining lecturer and assiduous in his attention to students, Lawson retained a close interest in teaching methods. While at Glasgow he had visited the principal European botanical institutions to study teaching methods and research techniques, and in 1923 visited several Canadian universities. His enthusiasm had its reward. Not long after his arrival in Sydney botany had become a major field of study within the university's science programme and by the early 1920s its first honours students had graduated.

By the 1920s Lawson had built up a very productive research team including John McLuckie and Patrick Brough, his former students from Glasgow. His main research interest was in the origin and evolution of gymnosperms, non-flowering seed-bearing plants such as conifers and cycads. He firmly championed the study of native plants and joined the campaign which resulted in the Wildflowers and Native Plants Protection Act, 1927. His work on the origin and evolution of Australian flora was published posthumously by McLuckie.

Lawson's popular extension lectures on Australian flora were illustrated by lantern slides, made from photographs taken on many excursions, which he had coloured by hand using a difficult and exacting technique perfected by himself. A collection of 1000 slides was given to the university on his death. This artistic flair pervaded his private life, and he had a fine collection of antique furniture and English, French and Chinese porcelain, paintings (one by Turner) and etchings. Lawson's character baffled his acquaintances. Intensely proud of his Scottish descent, he was reserved yet given to whimsy. He affected a certain naivety which friends claimed belied his true nature. He never married. According to an obituarist 'he treated women with a detached courtesy as of a celibate priest. For the friendship of men he had that genius which the old Greeks have idealised'. Handsome and clean-shaven, he had classically moulded features and wavy hair. He resided at the Australian Club and later at Potts Point.

He was a fellow of the Linnean societies of London and New South Wales, and of the Royal Society of Edinburgh (winning its Makdougall-Brisbane prize for 1916-18) and a member of the Royal Society of New South Wales. In 1926 the University of Adelaide conferred upon him an *ad eundem* D.Sc. Before his election as a fellow of the Royal Society, London, could be confirmed, Lawson died on 26 March 1927 in St Luke's Hospital, following an operation for a diseased gall bladder; he was buried in the Presbyterian section of South Head cemetery. His brother Andrew was professor of geology in 1899-1928 at the University of California. Another brother, James Kerr-Lawson, was a noted portrait painter. His portrait of A. A. Lawson hangs in the botany department, University of Sydney.

Francis E. Vaughan, *Andrew C. Lawson* (Glendal, California, 1970); *Dictionary of American biography*, supp 5, 1951-55 (NY, 1977); *Nature* (Lond), 119, 21 May 1927; *Hermes* (Syd), 33 (1927), no 1; *Univ Syd Science J*, 11, 1927; *SMH*, 3 June 1919, 4 Dec 1924, 28 Mar, 2 Apr 1927; miscellaneous records, Botany Dept, Univ Syd; Botany School papers (Univ Syd Archives).   C. J. PETTIGREW

LAWSON, SIR HARRY SUTHERLAND WIGHTMAN (1875-1952), politician and lawyer, was born on 5 March 1875 at Dunolly, Victoria, only surviving son of John Wightman Lawson, Presbyterian minister from Scotland, and his twenty-two-years younger, native-born wife Penelope Bell, née Hawkins. In 1884 John retired to Forest Hall, a fine old home on the outskirts of Castlemaine. Harry was educated at Castlemaine Grammar School and briefly at Scotch College, Melbourne, hastening home after the death of his father in 1892 to become an articled clerk to F. K. Best, Castlemaine barrister and solicitor. After his mother's death in 1898 he continued to live at Forest Hall with his three sisters until his marriage with Presbyterian forms at East Malvern on 8 October 1901 to Olive Adele Horwood, daughter of a former Castlemaine iron foundry proprietor.

As a young man Lawson was extensively involved in local affairs. Tall and amiable, he was a teetotaller, prominent in the Presbyterian Church as a founder of the Young Men's Fellowship, and a champion cricketer and footballer. His popularity led to his election to the Castlemaine Borough Council in 1899 and a few weeks later pushed him into politics. In November he was asked to stand as a Turner [q.v.] Liberal candidate at a ministerial by-election to oppose (Sir) James McCay [q.v.] who had been selected in the new McLean [q.v.] ministry. McCay had been Lawson's headmaster at Castlemaine Grammar. Lawson, aged only 24, won the seat and held it until 1904, defeating McCay again in 1900; in

1904-27 he represented Castlemaine and Maldon and in 1927-28 Castlemaine and Kyneton.

During his first decade in parliament Lawson was not a lively member. He spoke infrequently, though a 'discriminating supporter' of the various Liberal governments. In 1907 Melbourne *Punch* described him as 'unimportant' and 'innocuous' and lamented Castlemaine's loss of a good footballer in return for a poor politician. However, Lawson attended carefully to his local duties, travelling around his electorate on his bicycle which, at least once, carried him the seventy miles (113 km) to a Melbourne sitting. He continued as a Castlemaine councillor until 1915 and was mayor in 1905-06. Some of Lawson's energy was also devoted to his law studies; in 1908 he was admitted as a barrister and solicitor and joined F. S. Newell in a partnership at Castlemaine with branches at Maldon and Newstead.

From about 1910 Lawson became more active in parliament and rose in stature among the Liberals. He was convivial, temperate and a good, if unimaginative, speaker. In 1913-15 he served as president of the Board of Land and Works and as commissioner of crown lands and survey in the Watt [q.v] and then the Peacock [q.v.] governments. In November 1915 he was promoted to the portfolios of attorney-general, solicitor-general and public instruction. Education was one of his particular interests and he sought to promote secondary, especially technical, education. He also resisted the extreme anti-German sentiment which tried to force the closure of Lutheran schools in western Victoria. Frank Tate [q.v.], director of education, liked Lawson and had far more support from him than from most other ministers of education.

When (Sir) John Bowser's [q.v.7] 'Economy' faction of the National (formerly Liberal) Party overthrew Peacock in the November 1917 elections, Lawson followed Peacock out of office. In March 1918 Bowser was forced to resign and the Nationalists turned to Lawson as a compromise party leader and premier. Lawson won the support of the 'Economy' faction by including seven of its members in the ministry which was sworn in on 21 March; he retained for himself the portfolios of attorney-general (until 7 July 1919) and labour (until 21 October 1919 when he took control of lands) and served also, from 20 January until 21 September 1920, as solicitor-general. He successfully met a challenge by Bowser in June 1919 over the question of cabinet composition, securing Bowser's resignation from the ministry and his own confirmation as leader.

Further difficulties arose when the election of October 1920 left the Nationalists two short of a majority in the assembly. Lawson, appointing himself minister of agriculture and, from 21 February 1921, of water supply, was now dependent on the support of the Country Party, led by John Allan [q.v.7]. In July the withdrawal of this support over Lawson's determination to abolish the wheat pool caused the government to fall. The consequent election, however, did not alter the balance of power and Lawson continued to govern, winning renewed Country Party backing by the introduction of a wheat pool which, ostensibly voluntary, was in practice compulsory.

Early in 1923 Lawson visited Britain to negotiate loan and migration agreements. He spent a month on the Continent, where Mussolini impressed him as 'the man whom Providence wanted to lead Italy', and before returning to Australia toured North America, arriving home in July to face a restless Country Party and some dissident Nationalists—the 'Metropolitan Liberals' who complained of dilatoriness and ineptitude within the cabinet. He was saved from defeat on 30 August only by the support of the Labor Party, and in September he agreed to the formation of a composite National-Country Party ministry, with Allan as his deputy. The coalition, however, never had the full support of the Victorian Farmers' Union and when the V.F.U. at its annual conference in March 1924 refused to agree to an electoral alliance Lawson had his Country Party ministers dismissed and formed a new, purely Nationalist cabinet, taking for himself the treasurership as well as the premiership.

Within a month another National-Country Party coalition with a change of leader was mooted. Lawson, weary of the turmoil and doubting his ability to survive, took the opportunity offered by the death of Sir John Mackey [q.v.] to resign and stand for the vacant Speakership. His election appeared a foregone conclusion but his Labor and Country Party enemies united to appoint his 'old and jealous rival' Bowser, forcing Lawson to retreat ignominiously to the back-bench.

Among the achievements of Lawson's premiership were his fostering of the State Electricity Commission and the development of the Yallourn brown-coal deposit; his encouragement of land settlement schemes; and the formation of the Melbourne and Metropolitan Tramways Board, the Forests Commission and the Charities Board. W. Calder [q.v.7], chairman of the Country Roads Board, and W. Cattanach [q.v.7], chairman of the State Rivers and Water Supply Commission, became firm friends. Lawson's government also perpetuated the six o'clock closing of hotels and combated the police strike of 1923. Whereas during the 1903 railway strike Lawson had been one of the minority of parliamentarians to advocate negotiation rather than suppression by legislation ('Mercy first and last should brightest shine', he urged, quoting Milton), as premier in 1923 he was adamant that there could be no forgiveness 'for desertion of the post of duty' and introduced Draconian legislation. He was also able to call on his erstwhile headmaster, hustings and legal opponent, but by now his firm friend McCay to work with Sir John Monash [q.v.] in arranging the Special Constabulary Force.

Lawson was always praised as honest, courteous, good tempered and conscientious. But friends such as (Sir) Frederic Eggleston [q.v.8] were forced to acknowledge his lack of originality or interest in political principle. Astute outsiders could be bluntly critical: 'His honesty is beyond question', wrote one journalist, 'but so is his opportunism'. In 1924 Lawson emphasized: 'It is of great importance to remember that Parliament's chief duty is to govern'. Earlier he had quoted Pope:

For forms of Government let fools contest,
What e'er is best administered is best.

Handicapped as they were throughout 1918-23 by the lack both of a strong group cohesion and a parliamentary majority, the Nationalists had in Lawson a usefully pragmatic leader who was able to hang on to power and achieve legislation of a utilitarian kind.

After moving to the back-bench Lawson again became quiet. He nurtured his business interests and his legal practice which from about 1930 as Lawson & Co. included a Melbourne branch. In 1926 he was elected president of the National Federation and next year became the party's election director. Rumour in December 1927 that he intended to contest a Legislative Council seat proved false, but in October 1928 he resigned from the assembly to stand successfully for the Senate. In January 1933 he was appointed K.C.M.G. and from October that year served as honorary minister in the Lyons [q.v.] government, representing the Treasury and the Department of Commerce in the Senate. In 1934 he was also minister for external territories and for a few months acting postmaster-general. He did not stand for re-election later that year.

In retirement Lawson worked in his law firm and served on the boards of several companies including the Colonial Mutual Life Assurance Society, Perpetual Executors & Trustees Co., Mount Lyell Mining & Railway Co. and Robert Harper [q.v.9] & Co. Ltd. He resigned from the board of the *Argus* during World War II when that paper was critical of (Sir) Robert Menzies. From 1939 he lived in Melbourne. He was appointed to the Capital Issues Advisory Board in 1941, was a trustee of the Melbourne Cricket Ground and of the Shrine of Remembrance and belonged to the Australian Club.

Lawson's son and biographer R. S. Lawson, while proud of his father's achievements, wrote of him as over-protective towards his children, 'dutiful, thrifty . . . demanding' and sometimes 'pretty grumpy', an egotist who became with success 'a little pompous and platitudinous'. Lawson's youngest son, a member of the Royal Australian Air Force, was killed in 1941; his wife died in 1949. Lawson died at East Melbourne on 12 June 1952, survived by three sons and four daughters. He was cremated after a state funeral at Toorak Presbyterian Church, leaving an estate valued for probate at £33 083. A portrait by John Longstaff [q.v.] is held by Castlemaine Art Gallery; outside the gallery stands a bronze bust by Paul Montford [q.v.], unveiled in 1930.

B. D. Graham, *The formation of the Australian Country Parties* (Canb, 1966); C. Edwards, *Brown power* (Melb, 1969); J. Iremonger et al (eds), *Strikes* (Syd, 1973); R. S. Lawson, *Sir Harry Lawson, premier and senator* (Melb, 1976); G. Cresciani, *Fascism, anti-fascism and Italians in Australia, 1922-1945* (Canb, 1980); G. Serle, *John Monash* (Melb, 1982); *Melb Graduate*, June 1953; *Punch* (Melb), 19 Dec 1907, 26 July 1917; *Herald* (Melb), 25 July 1921, 25 Jan 1922, 7 Sept 1923, 15 Dec 1924, 25 Oct 1930; *Table Talk*, 17 Feb 1927; *Today*, 1 Mar 1934; *Argus*, 13 June 1952; *Castlemaine Mail*, 14 June 1952; W. Osmond, F. W. Eggleston (1875-1954) (Ph.D. thesis, Univ Syd, 1980); F. W. Eggleston, Confidential notes (Menzies Lib, ANU); Eggleston papers (NL).

DONALD S. GARDEN

LAWSON, HENRY (1867-1922), short-story writer and balladist, was born on 17 June 1867 at Grenfell, New South Wales, eldest of four surviving children of Niels Hertzberg (Peter) Larsen, Norwegian-born miner, and his wife Louisa [q.v.], née Albury. Larsen went to sea at 21 and, after many voyages, arrived in Melbourne in 1855 where he jumped ship and joined the gold rush. He and Louisa were married in 1866 and Henry (the surname changed when the parents registered the birth) was born about a year later, by which time the marriage was already showing some signs of stress. The family moved often as Peter followed the gold but, in August 1873 with the birth of their third child imminent, they finally settled back at Pipeclay where they had started from. Peter took up a selection which Louisa managed; she also ran a post office in his name while she worked as a building contractor around Mudgee.

Existence for the Lawsons, however, remained precarious. The selection even at its best was only marginally productive. With Peter often absent, Louisa was lonely and vulnerable: responsibility began to fall on Henry's young and rather frail shoulders and intensified in him a tendency to reclusiveness and introversion and a personal conviction that he was somehow different from others in a way that cut him off from them. There were happy times: Louisa was imaginative and a brilliant raconteuse and Peter was an accomplished musician. But failing communication between husband and wife, Peter's increasingly frequent absences and the exacerbating effect of continual hardship seemed to outweigh such lighter moments. The young Lawson was often alone, often worried about the problems of the selection, and much disturbed by the apparent estrangement of his parents, a situation about which he was more knowledgeable than the younger children and which caused him keener suffering. Outside the family, he was one of those children who seem inevitably to become the butt for juvenile ridicule and cruelty. He had little opportunity for boyhood friendship and little talent for it when rare opportunities arose. He several times expressed to his father a reluctance to grow older even as worry, fears and oppression were denying him most of the joys of childhood.

Lawson was 8 before Louisa's vigorous agitation led to a school being established in the district, and he was 9 before he actually entered the slab-and-bark Eurunderee Public School as a pupil in the care of the new teacher John Tierney. In the same year, 1876, after a night of sickness and earache, he awoke one morning slightly deaf. For the next five years he suffered hearing deficiency. When he was 14 the condition deteriorated radically and he was left with a major and incurable hearing loss. For Lawson, already psychologically isolated, the deeper silence of partial deafness was a crushing blow.

When his much-interrupted schooling (three years all told) ended in 1880, Lawson worked with his father on local contract building jobs and then further afield in the Blue Mountains. In 1883, however, he joined his mother in Sydney at her request. Louisa had abandoned the selection and was living at Phillip Street with Henry's sister Gertrude and his brother Peter. He became apprenticed to Hudson Bros Ltd as a coachpainter and undertook night-class study towards matriculation. Yet, as the story ('Arvie Aspinall's Alarm Clock') which he based on that time of his life suggests, he was no happier in Sydney than he had been on the selection. His daily routine exhausted him, his workmates persecuted him and he failed the examinations. Over the next few years he tried or applied for various jobs with little success. Oppressed anew by his deafness, he went to Melbourne in 1887 in order to be treated at the Victorian Eye and Ear Hospital. The visit,

happy in other ways, produced no cure for his affliction and thereafter Lawson seems to have resigned himself to living in the muffled and frustrating world of the deaf.

Meanwhile he had begun to write. Contact with his mother's radical friends imbued in him a fiery and ardent republicanism out of which grew his first published poem, 'A Song of the Republic' (*Bulletin*, 1 October 1887). He followed this with 'The Wreck of the Derry Castle' and 'Golden Gully', the latter growing partly out of memories of the diggings of his boyhood. At the same time he had his introduction to journalism, writing pieces for the *Republican*, a truculent little paper run by Louisa and William Keep (its precarious and eccentric existence is celebrated in the poem 'The Cambaroora Star'). By 1890 Lawson had achieved some reputation as a writer of verse, poems such as 'Faces in the Street', 'Andy's Gone With Cattle' and 'The Watch on the Kerb' being some of the more notable of that period.

Early in 1891 Lawson was offered, as he put it, 'the first, the last and the only chance I got in journalism'. The offer came from Gresley Lukin [q.v.5] of the Brisbane *Boomerang* and was eagerly accepted. Lawson became a prolific contributor of prose and rhymes to the *Boomerang* and also to William Lane's [q.v.9] *Worker*. But his luck had not changed: by September the *Boomerang* was in trouble and Lawson's services were dispensed with. Once again he found himself in Sydney dividing his time between odd jobs, writing and occasional carousing with friends, chief among whom at this time was E. J. Brady [q.v.7].

Whether it was a matter of luck or temperament, Lawson seemed unable to attain equilibrium or direction in his writing or his lifestyle. His promising early poems had been followed by a rush of versifying on a wide range of topics, contemporary and reminiscent; and his first published story, 'His Father's Mate' (*Bulletin*, December 1888), though uneven and sentimental, had given glimpses of his extraordinary ability as a writer of short stories. By 1892 a number of sketches together with the magnificent 'The Drover's Wife' had fully borne out the initial promise. Yet Lawson seemed in a rut: failing to concentrate his energies and gifts much beyond what was required for subsistence, spending more and more time in favourite bars around Sydney. Recognizing something of Lawson's inner faltering, J. F. Archibald [q.v.3] suggested he take a trip inland at the *Bulletin*'s expense. With £5 and a rail ticket to Bourke, he set out in September 1892 on what was to be one of the most important journeys of his life.

Much of what Lawson saw in the drought-blasted west of New South Wales during succeeding months appalled him. 'You can have no idea of the horrors of the country out here', he wrote to his aunt, 'men tramp and beg and live like dogs'. Nevertheless, the experience at Bourke itself and in surrounding districts through which he carried his swag absolutely overwhelmed him. By the time he returned to civilization, he was armed with memories and experiences—some of them comic but many shattering—that would furnish his writing for years. 'The Bush Undertaker', 'The Union Buries its Dead' and some of the finest of the Mitchell sketches were among the work he produced soon after his return. *Short stories in prose and verse*, the selection of his work produced by Louisa on the *Dawn* press in 1894, brought together some of these stories albeit in unprepossessing form and flawed by misprints. But *While the billy boils* (1896) was Lawson's first major short-story collection. It remains one of the great classics of Australian literature.

Though the creative pressure of his outback experience showed almost immediately in his writing, Lawson's life in other respects settled back into the depressingly familiar hole-and-corner existence. After six months he went to New Zealand where he worked eventually as a telegraph linesman, turning his back on journalism and alcohol. He returned to Sydney on 29 July 1894 to take a position on the newly formed *Daily Worker* only to see it wound up three days later. He consoled himself with drink and Bohemian exploits with a circle of friends that now included J. Le Gay Brereton [q.v.7]. The release in December of *Short stories in prose and verse*, did little to lift his spirits or his income.

Within a year, however, Lawson seemed poised to achieve both the recognition and the stability he had been seeking. In 1895 he contracted to publish two books with Angus [q.v.7] & Robertson [q.v.]; and he met Bertha Marie Louise Bredt (1876-1957), daughter of Bertha McNamara [q.v.]. After a brief and, on Lawson's part, characteristically intense and impulsive courtship, they were married on 15 April 1896. That year Angus and Robertson brought out the two books, *In the days when the world was wide and other verses* and *While the billy boils*, as arranged; both were well received.

Following an abortive trip to Western Australia in search of gold, the Lawsons returned to Sydney where Henry, now a writer and public figure of some note, embarked on a colourful round of escapades in which large amounts of alcohol and the company of his Dawn and Dusk Club friends, including Fred Broomfield, Victor Daley [qq.v.7,8] and Bertram Stevens [q.v.], were central ingredients. The Lawsons' move to Mangamaunu in the South Island of New Zealand was arranged by Bertha with the express intention of removing him from this kind of life. They left on 31 March 1897, but the venture was not a success, creatively or otherwise. Lawson's initial enthusiasm for the Maoris whom he taught at the lonely, primitive settlement soon waned. As well, there is evidence in some of his verse of that time ('Written Afterwards', 'The Jolly Dead March') that he was realizing, for perhaps the first time since their romantically rushed courtship and marriage and subsequent boisterous, crowded life in Western Australia and Sydney, both the responsibilities and the ties of his situation. Lawson's growing restiveness was deepened by promising letters from English publishers. Bertha's pregnancy strengthened his resolve and they left Mangamaunu in November 1897, returning to Sydney in March after Bertha's confinement. Lawson spent the enforced wait in Wellington writing a play ('Pinter's Son Jim') commissioned by Bland Holt [q.v.4]; it turned out to be too unwieldy to stage.

Lawson went back to old friends and old ways in Sydney. He had returned with one overriding aim: to get to London, where he felt certain there would be more opportunity for him to live by his pen. He expressed a mounting sense of frustration and bitterness by drinking heavily—he entered a home for inebriates in November 1898—and by writing a personal statement to the *Bulletin*. This appeared in the January 1899 issue under the title 'Pursuing Literature in Australia'. Abstemious and industrious throughout the ensuing year, Lawson worked on books contracted earlier with Angus & Robertson—*On the track* and *Over the sliprails* (stories) and *Verses popular and humorous*. But he would probably not have realized his goal of 'seeking London' had it not been for the generous help of David Scott Mitchell, the governor Earl Beauchamp [qq.v.5,7] and George Robertson. He set off on 20 April 1900 for England. With him went his wife, his son Joseph and his daughter of just over two months, Bertha.

Lawson himself in later years provided fuel for the idea that his English interlude, so eagerly anticipated, was in fact a catastrophe: 'Days in London like a nightmare'; 'That wild run to London/That wrecked and ruined me'. But he had some successes in London, the opportunity was certainly there for him to establish himself upon the literary scene and he may have been in some ways simply unlucky. On arrival he retained the services of J. B. Pinker, one of the best literary agents in England, and was soon receiving enthusiastic encouragement from critic and publisher's reader Edward Garnett and William Blackwood, editor of *Blackwood's Edinburgh Magazine*. The four Joe Wilson stories—generally regarded by critics as the peak of his achievement—were written in London, and

Blackwood published two new Lawson collections in two years: *Joe Wilson and his mates* (1901) and *Children of the bush* (1902). But the strain of family life in unfamiliar surrounds and an unkind climate, his wife's serious illness (she spent three months from May 1901 in Bethlem Royal Hospital as a mental patient) and the consequent return to the soul-destroying task of writing under pressure to pay the bills, all sapped Lawson's early resilience and affected his health, the quality of his work and the nature of his literary aspirations and plans. By April 1902 he was arranging for Bertha to return home with the children. He followed soon after and they were all back in Sydney before the end of July.

From that time Lawson's personal and creative life entered upon a ghastly decline. A reconciliation with Bertha soon after their return was short lived. In December 1902 he attempted suicide. In April next year Bertha sought and obtained a decree for judicial separation. He wrote a great deal despite his often squalid circumstances but his work alternated between desperate revivals of old themes and inspirations and equally desperate and unsuccessful attempts to break new ground. Maudlin sentimentality and melodrama, often incipient even in some earlier work, invaded both his prose and poetry. Among later books were *The skyline riders and other verses* (1910); *My army, o my army! and other songs* (1915); and *Triangles of life and other stories* (1913). He was frequently gaoled for failure to pay maintenance for his children and, after 1907, was several times in a mental hospital. Though cared for by the loyal Mrs Byers, he became a frail, haunted and pathetic figure well known on the streets of Sydney; in his writing, images of ghostliness proliferated and increasingly a sense of insubstantiality blurred action and characters. Loyal friends arranged spells at Mallacoota, Victoria, (with Brady) in 1910 and at Leeton in 1916. But his state of mind, physical condition and alcoholism continued to worsen. The Commonwealth Literary Fund granted him £1 a week pension from May 1920. He died of cerebral haemorrhage at Abbotsford on 2 September 1922.

Lawson was something of a legendary figure in his lifetime. Not surprisingly, as dignitaries and others gathered for his state funeral on 4 September, that legend was already beginning to flourish in various exotic ways. The result was that some of his achievements were inflated—he became known, for example, as a great poet—and others obscured. Lawson's reputation must rest on his stories and on a relatively small group of them: *While the billy boils*, the Joe Wilson quartet of linked, longer stories and certain others lying outside these (among them, 'The Loaded Dog', 'Telling Mrs Baker' and 'The Geological Spieler'). In these he shows himself not only a master of short fiction but also a writer of peculiarly modern tendency. The prose is spare, cut to the bone, the plot is either slight or non-existent. Skilfully modulated reticence makes even the barest and shortest sketches seem excitingly full of possibility, alive with options and potential insights. A stunning example is 'On the Edge of a Plain' but almost any Mitchell sketch from *While the billy boils* exemplifies these qualities. Though not a symbolist writer, Lawson had the capacity to endow accurately observed documentary detail with a significance beyond its physical reality: the drover's wife burning the snake; the black goanna dying 'in violent convulsions on the ground' ('The Bush Undertaker'); the 'hard dry Darling River clods' clattering on to the coffin of the unknown drover ('The Union Buries its Dead') are seemingly artless yet powerful Lawsonian moments which, in context, transform simple surface realism into intimations about the mysteries, the desperations and the tragedies of ordinary and anonymous lives.

Lawson failed fully to assimilate one of the most vital inspirations of his writing life—his experience in the western outback. It was the source of most of his best work, but he returned to it again and again, coming close to Hemingway-like self-parody as he sought to gain creative renewal from a seam already thoroughly mined. Only the Joe Wilson series allowed him temporary freedom from this enslavement, because these four connected stories are about the rare joys, awkward intimacies and frequent sorrows of a marriage that is slowly, imperceptibly, deteriorating. As a subject it clearly owed much to those lonely months at Mangamaunu and it did not rejuvenate Lawson's art because he could not pursue the theme without coming into unacceptably close engagement with the realities of his own marriage. In any case, Lawson's withholding, austere prose was ill suited to analytic probing, which is why *Joe Wilson*, fine piece of work though it is, seems constantly on the point of disintegration.

The decline of his creative ability, as it were before his very eyes, in the years from about 1902 onwards (though the malaise is traceable earlier than that in, for example, *On the track* and *Over the sliprails*) was one of the great tragedies of Lawson's troubled life. Too much evidence exists to show with what deep and continued seriousness he aspired to be a memorable writer for his artistic decline to be regarded in any less important light. To this disaster were added personal crosses—deafness, a marital failure that deeply grieved him—which even a stronger temperament would have found hard to withstand. That he managed to dredge out of disadvantage, adversity and often appalling hardship so many magnificent stories is testimony to a toughness and determination that he is perhaps not often enough given credit for.

His statue by George Lambert [q.v.9] is in the Domain, Sydney; his portrait by Longstaff [q.v.] is in the Art Gallery of New South Wales and another by Norman Carter [q.v.7] is at Parliament House, Canberra.

B. L. Lawson and J. Le G. Brereton (eds), *Henry Lawson by his mates* (Syd, 1931); D. Prout, *Henry Lawson, the grey dreamer* (Adel, 1963); W. H. Pearson, *Henry Lawson among Maoris* (Canb and Wellington, 1968); A. A. Phillips, *Henry Lawson* (New York, 1970); B. Matthews, *The receding wave* (Melb, 1972); C. Roderick (ed, and for bibliog), *Henry Lawson criticism, 1894-1971* (Syd, 1972) and *The real Henry Lawson* (Adel, 1982); S. Murray-Smith, *Henry Lawson* (Melb, 1975); M. Clark, *In search of Henry Lawson* (Melb, 1978); B. Kiernan, *The essential Henry Lawson* (Melb, 1982); *Quadrant*, July 1979, Aug 1983. BRIAN MATTHEWS

LAWSON, JAMES (1884-1965), stock and station agent and soldier, was born on 16 February 1884 at Halifax, Yorkshire, England, son of James Lawson, police officer, and his wife Elizabeth, née Dickinson. Educated at Heath Grammar School, Halifax, he became a clerk at the Todmorden branch of the Manchester and Liverpool Bank. He came to Australia in 1905. Fair-haired, of powerful build and commanding presence, he had the traditional Yorkshireman's directness of manner and character and a dry sense of humour—qualities liked by his neighbours in the Wimmera district of Victoria. By 1912 he was a hotelkeeper at Rupanyup, and that year on 6 March he married Effie Maude Franklin at St Peter's Church, Melbourne.

In England Lawson had served in the Duke of Lancaster's Own Imperial Yeomanry and in 1912 he was commissioned second lieutenant in the 19th Australian Light Horse Regiment, Victorian Mounted Rifles. On 20 August 1914 he joined the Australian Imperial Force in the same rank and embarked for Egypt with the 4th Light Horse Regiment. They served dismounted at Anzac from 20 May 1915 until the evacuation; Lawson had been promoted lieutenant in February and in January 1916 in Egypt he became commander of 'C' Squadron. In 1916-18 his regiment served with the Egyptian Expeditionary Force under General Sir Edmund Allenby in Sinai and Palestine. Lawson was promoted major in May 1917 and from then commanded 'A' Squadron.

On 31 October 1917 Allenby, planning his main advance through the heavily fortified Gaza area, made a diversionary thrust at Beersheba. British infantry on the south-west formed the guard, while Australian cavalry charged the Turks from the south-east. Lawson's squadron and a squadron of the 12th Australian L.H.R. led the attack, storming the enemy trenches with wild and spectacular success; the official historian, (Sir) Henry Gullett [q.v.9], noted that the 'enemy had been beaten rather by the sheer recklessness of the charge than by the very limited fighting powers of this handful of Australians'. Lawson's leadership and personal valour in this key operation won him the Distinguished Service Order. After the fall of Gaza his regiment joined Allenby's advance into Syria, linked up with a force under Lawrence of Arabia and took part in the capture of Damascus in September 1918. Lawson was mentioned in dispatches twice in 1917-18.

He returned home in January 1919 and his A.I.F. appointment ended in April. He became a stock and station agent at Rupanyup, reverting to part-time soldiering with the Australian Military Forces as a major in the 19th L.H.R.; he was promoted lieut-colonel and commander of the regiment in 1927. In 1931-33 he commanded the 5th Cavalry Brigade as a temporary colonel and in 1929 received the Volunteer Officers' Decoration. During World War II, with the acting rank of brigadier, he held administrative command of a training brigade based at Geelong. He was placed on the retired list, A.M.F., as an honorary colonel in November 1943.

Never a man to pull his rank, Lawson was active in civic affairs, was master of his Masonic Lodge in 1922-23, sat for many years on the Wimmera League Football Tribunal and supported the local Anglican Church and volunteer fire brigade. In 1952 he retired to Melbourne where he was a member of the Naval and Military Club. Survived by his wife, son and daughter, Lawson died on 29 September 1965 at his daughter's home at Brighton and was cremated. He is depicted in George Lambert's [q.v.9] painting of the battle of Beersheba at the Australian War Memorial, Canberra.

H. S. Gullett and C. Barrett, *Australia in Palestine* (Syd, 1919); H. S. Gullett, *The A.I.F. in Sinai and Palestine* (Syd, 1923); T. E. Lawrence, *Revolt in the desert* (Lond, 1927); *London Gazette*, 6 July 1917, 15 Jan, 14 June 1918; *Herald* (Melb), 29 Sept 1965; local and family information; records (AWM). J. P. HALDANE-STEVENSON

LAWSON, JAMES ROBERT (1860-1926), auctioneer, was born on 10 October 1860 at Pyrmont, Sydney, second of nine children of James Lawson, publican from Scotland, and his Yorkshire-born wife Emma, née Glen. About 1864 his father set up a furniture warehouse and later also as a cabinetmaker. James was apprenticed to his father and had an early training in quality furnishings. Describing himself as an importer, he married Maria Rossiter at St Paul's Anglican Church, Canterbury, on 20 January 1885. They visited London where Lawson 'studied all aspects of the auctioneering business and also fine art, antiques'.

On his return he set up as a cabinetmaker and in 1886 established Jones, Lawson Bros & Co., auctioneers, with premises at 39 Castlereagh Street. It was the first of many short-lived partnerships, some of which ended acrimoniously. In 1887 he auctioned the contents of four Irish country houses, a collection which W. Hardy Wilson [q.v.] noted in 1922 was 'by far the most important sale of pictures and antiques that had been held in Australia'. In partnership with Francis Broughton by 1889, Lawson petitioned to be declared bankrupt on 3 March 1891 because of his partner's insolvency. He moved to smaller rooms but fire destroyed 'all assets, books and private papers' of his new firm, Lawson Bros & Co., and an office clerk was later convicted of embezzling £600. Lawson owed £2098. He worked as an auctioneer for Harris & Ackman and was discharged from bankruptcy on 8 February 1893.

In partnership with John Charles Smith by 1896, Lawson auctioned some 5000 books, including two volumes of autographed letters, for Sir Henry Parkes [q.v.5], in March. After Smith's death in 1899 he set up Lawson, Caro & Co. Ltd, trading at 128-130 Pitt Street, until the partnership was voluntarily dissolved on 17 March 1904. On 31 March, with William Augustus Little, he formed James R. Lawson & Little, Pitt Street, which lasted until 1914. Lawson then traded on his own until he took his sons into partnership in 1921.

Almost all notable collections sold by auction in Sydney passed through Lawson's rooms. They included the dispersal of the effects of the late Miss Wentworth of Vaucluse House in February 1900. In August 1916 he was at the late John Norton's [q.v.] house, St Helena, to sell its contents—rooms filled with massive furniture, costly pictures and Napoleonic relics. For the sale of Captain G. W. Eedy's treasures in 1921, he and J. R. Tyrrell [q.v.] arranged a throne draped with velvet to display each item, while Lawson 'waxed lyrical on the rostrum', a new practice that soon became common. As well as the fine arts, the firm had a large share of the ordinary second-hand trade and often sold surplus effects for the government.

Lawson, always dressed for the occasion, auctioned with style and kept tight control of the crowd. He was delightfully portrayed by Norman Lindsay [q.v.] as a koala wearing top hat and frock coat. According to his son, Lawson 'had an outstanding personality, a brilliant brain and also a great love of the good things of life. His business integrity was of the highest'. He moved house many times, living at Canterbury in 1904-19, Clifton Gardens in 1920-25 and Turramurra where he died of cerebro-vascular disease on 5 November 1926; he was cremated with Presbyterian forms. His wife, two sons and four daughters survived him and inherited his estate valued for probate at £32 243. The firm was carried on at 236 Castlereagh Street by his son Maxwell until 1969.

J. R. Tyrrell, *Old books, old friends, old Sydney* (Syd, 1952); T. Ingram, *A question of polish* (Syd, 1979); *SMH*, 5 Sept 1896, 6 Nov 1926; *Daily Telegraph* (Syd), 6 Nov 1926; M. J. Lawson, Notes, *and* M. B. Reymond, Lawson's (MSS, held by James R. Lawson & Co.); Bankruptcy file no 3391, *and* NSW Companies Office, Company packets, no 1839 (NSWA); ML printed cat (under J.R. Lawson); information from B. H. Badgery, Sydney.

MAX KELLY

LAWSON, LOUISA (1848-1920), newspaper proprietor, was born on 17 February 1848 on Edwin Rouse's station, Guntawang, near Mudgee, New South Wales, second of twelve children of Henry Albury, stationhand, and his wife Harriet, née Winn, needlewoman. Baptized an Anglican, Louisa was educated at Mudgee National School where J. W. Allpass proposed making her a pupilteacher. Instead, she was kept home to help to care for her younger siblings and she resented the drudgery. On 7 July 1866 at the Wesleyan parsonage, Mudgee, Louisa married Norwegian-born Niels Hertzberg Larsen who called himself Peter. A handyman and gold digger, he was fluent in several European languages and teetotal. They joined the Weddin Mountain gold rush and later selected forty acres (16 ha) at Eurunderee. By the time of Henry's [q.v.] birth in 1867, they had anglicized the spelling of Larsen.

Between 1867 and 1877 Louisa bore five children. Peter was often away, either at the goldfields or contract building with his father-in-law; Louisa took in sewing, sold dairy produce and fattened cattle. She was an expert four-in-hand driver. The women in her family believe that she was the original for the hardworking, resourceful, kindly and long-suffering bushwomen who feature in her son's stories. The Lawsons joined a Mudgee spiritualist group. Louisa had had a strict Methodist upbringing and though she ceased to attend church she remained deeply religious. When she and the children moved to Sydney in 1883, she found friends through the Progressive Spiritualist Lyceum at Leigh House. She kept up a pretence of being separated from her husband by misfortune, but the marriage had ended.

Peter sent money irregularly to help to

support the children and Louisa considered taking legal action. Instead she did sewing and washing and took in boarders. In 1887 she bought the ailing *Republican* (1887-88). Her father though illiterate was a great story-teller. She shared that talent and her poetry, inspired by the death of her infant daughter, had been published in the *Mudgee Independent*. She and Henry edited and wrote most of the *Republican*'s copy using 'Archie Lawson' for editorial purposes. In 1888 she started *Dawn*, announcing that it would publicize women's wrongs, fight their battles and sue for their suffrage. It offered household advice, fashion, poetry, a short story and extensive reporting of women's activities both locally and overseas. Louisa added a political editorial on the importance to women of the divorce extension bill. *Dawn* was an immediate commercial success. On 31 December 1888 Peter died, leaving £1103 to Louisa. She enlarged her printing plant and accepted job printing. In 1889 Mrs Lawson was employing ten women, including female printers.

The New South Wales Typographical Association, which refused membership to women, tried to force Mrs Lawson to dismiss her printers. It appealed to advertisers to boycott *Dawn* and harassed the women at their work. Louisa countered with a proclamation of her support for trade unionism. In a different context she advocated the protection of a union for married women and crèches for the benefit of the overworked mothers of large families and those forced to take paid employment. Her practical philanthropy included the Sydney Ragged Schools for which she organized the collection of old clothes and the seeds, bulbs and a prize for a floral competition.

In May 1889 Louisa launched the campaign for female suffrage and announced the formation of the Dawn Club. Who ordained that men only should make the laws which both women and men must obey, she asked, but her case rested on more than abstract justice. Woman's vote was needed to change evil laws and to protect women and their children. At the Dawn Club women met regularly to discuss 'every question of life, work and reform' and to gain experience in public speaking; she persuaded the Sydney Mechanics' School of Arts' debating clubs to admit her and encouraged other women to join. In 1893 she became the first woman elected to its board of management. Through *Dawn* she created the public knowledge of women's affairs which helped to move opinion towards enfranchising women. She revealed the instances where the law failed to protect them or where by other means they were prevented from making a reasonable living. She blamed prostitution on men and evil laws and urged parents to equip

daughters to earn their living and not keep them at home as unpaid domestic labour. In editorials she presented feminist arguments for opening the legal profession to women, appointing them as prison warders, factory inspectors and magistrates, and giving hospital appointments to female doctors. She added advice on health and the care of children, stressing diet, rest and exercise, and in her fashion page and paper pattern service encouraged women to dress sensibly but attractively. *Dawn* had an extensive country readership and intercolonial and overseas subscribers. It was in regular communication with English and American feminists.

When Mrs Dora Montefiore [q.v.] formed the Womanhood Suffrage League of New South Wales in 1891, Louisa was invited to join and was elected to its council. She allowed it to use *Dawn*'s office for meetings and printed its literature free of charge. She frequently spoke at league meetings and although she had enormous energy she was reported in need of a rest by the end of the year. About this time her relationship with Henry became strained although his first volume of verse was published on the *Dawn* press in 1894. She was a savage critic of drunkenness.

Again busy in the campaign in 1892, Louisa was a member of the league's delegation to the premier in October. Her outburst that women needed the vote 'to redeem the world from bad laws passed by wicked men' was unfavourably reported in the press. She was again exhausted and took a well-earned holiday. The failure of the Australian Joint Stock Bank caused her some financial difficulty but *Dawn* survived. She was drawn into the dispute in the league over allowing speeches on subjects other than the suffrage at its meetings. When her friend Lady Windeyer [q.v.] was outvoted and resigned as president, Louisa in December 1893 withdrew from its council. Although she gave as her reason her recent move to Tempe, she had wept on hearing of the president's resignation. She remained a financial member of the league and continued to do its printing and supply publicity in *Dawn*.

In 1895 and 1897 Mrs Lawson took out a miner's right, presumably to demonstrate an inconsistency in the electoral law. At the celebratory meeting after women were enfranchised in New South Wales in 1902, she was publicly acclaimed as the originator of the suffrage campaign. She had become involved in protracted legal proceedings in an attempt to protect a patent which she had taken out on a mailbag fastener and for which she was meagrely compensated. She was thrown from a tram and suffered a fractured knee and injured her spine in 1900, taking over a year to recover, but in 1902 she was again active politically. On the council of the Women's Progressive Association she resumed her campaign to secure appointment of women to public office.

Following her accident she lost some of the vitality and inventiveness which had helped to make *Dawn* a success. Her friend Mrs E. J. Todd, who had been one of her journalists, remembered her as 'so full of original ideas that she always seemed to have plenty to spare for others'. Novelties disappeared from *Dawn* and there were fewer lively short-paragraph news items. Advertising fell away and in 1905 *Dawn* closed.

Afterwards Louisa lived in lonely and increasingly impoverished circumstances. She secured a publisher for two volumes of verse and sold a few poems and a number of short stories. She enjoyed her garden in which she had planted natives. Her 'Dolley Dear' poems capture the humour and warmth of the old woman's love for children. Louisa died in the Hospital for the Insane, Gladesville, on 12 August 1920. She had been living alone before being admitted in 1918, her memory failing but still strong willed. She was buried with Methodist forms in the Anglican section of Rookwood cemetery. Her estate, valued for probate at £629, was left to her son Peter who was father of nine of her beloved grandchildren.

A block of Housing Commission flats at North Bondi was named after her in 1952. In most surviving photographs, she is stern faced. Big-boned, as befitted a country-woman, she is to be remembered for her reply to the editor of the *Bulletin*'s 'Red Page': 'And why shouldn't a woman be tall and strong?'.

B. Kiernan, *The essential Henry Lawson* (Melb, 1982); E. Fry (ed), *Rebels and radicals* (Syd, 1983); *Woman's Budget*, 28 Aug 1920; *Aust Literary Studies*, 9 (1980), no 3, 10 (1982), no 4; *Daily Telegraph* (Syd), 17 Oct 1892; *Nation*, 25 Oct 1958, 14 Dec 1962; Louisa Lawson papers, scrapbook, poems *and* B. Lawson, Memoir of Henry Lawson, *and* G. O'Connor, Louisa Lawson and her life work, *and* Rose Scott papers (ML).   HEATHER RADI

LAWSON, WILLIAM (1876-1957), author, was born on 2 September 1876 at Low Fell, Gateshead, Durham, England, second son of Nicholas Lawson, chemical agent, and his wife Emma Jane, née Ridley. In 1880 the Lawsons migrated to New Zealand. His father joined the New Zealand Insurance Co. and in 1884 was transferred to Brisbane. Here Will completed his education at Brisbane Grammar School. After his family returned to New Zealand in 1892, he worked briefly as a clerk in the Wellington office of the Union Steamship Co. of New Zealand; then, at his father's insistence, he transferred to the local branch of the Australian Mutual Provident Society, where he remained for the next eighteen years.

Inspired by Henry Lawson's [q.v.] poetry, Lawson began to write ballads on sea and railway subjects; 'Stokin' was published in the Sydney *Bulletin* on 7 July 1900, signed 'Quilp N'. His first collection of verse, *The red west road*, appeared in Wellington in 1903. On 22 August 1905 at Johnsonville Lawson married Vera Willis; they had no children.

In 1912 Lawson moved to Sydney to work on the *Evening News*. He continued to publish in the *Bulletin* and the *Lone Hand*, and met many of their writers and artists. During World War I, medically unfit for active service, he returned to New Zealand to write for various newspapers. After the war he worked as a publicity officer and compiled tourist guides. One of his clients was *Smith's Weekly* and in 1923 he joined its staff in Sydney. Over the following decade Lawson alternated between Sydney and New Zealand, working as a journalist, publicist and travel agent. He also toured extensively in the United States of America and East Asia.

Will Lawson's first novel, *The laughing buccaneer* (Sydney, 1935), was, he claimed, written in six weeks because he was 'broke'. Like many of his sixteen published novels, it is a historical romance, set at the time of 'Bully' Hayes [q.v.4]. The best of these, *When Cobb and Co. was king* (Sydney, 1936), has plenty of excitement and romance and less of Lawson's typical clichéd plotting and writing. After becoming a freelance author, he aimed to write at least two books a year, publishing five in 1945. Lawson produced seven volumes of verse, four non-fictional works and numerous uncollected poems, short stories and articles; he also 'specialized in railroad stories'.

In 1938 Lawson was granted a Commonwealth literary pension of £26 a year; by 1952 it had been increased to £208. He was an active member and sometime State secretary of the Fellowship of Australian Writers, which in May 1952 held a special meeting in his honour. Hazel-eyed, he had 'a craggy face, a strong beak of a nose, large ears and thick untidy hair'. For much of his life he was a heavy drinker and 'awkward in his cups'. In 1942 his wife left him and returned to New Zealand. His good angel, as he wrote in his unpublished autobiography, was Henry Lawson's widow Bertha, who 'saved me from the grog'. Together they wrote *My Henry Lawson* (Sydney, 1943). Lawson lived with her at Northbridge until her death in 1957. He died a few months later, on 13 October, in the home of the Little Sisters of the Poor, Randwick, and was buried in the Catholic section of Botany cemetery.

Mid-Pacific Mag, July 1917, p 64; *Christchurch Sun*, 11 Nov 1931; *People* (Syd), 28 Dec 1955; *Nth Aust Mthly*, 4 (Feb 1958), p 55; *Southerly*, 19 (1958), p 29; *NZ Free Lance*, 2 Sept 1905; *SMH*, 19 May 1938, 14 Oct 1957; *Bulletin*, 23 Nov 1949, 13 May 1953; W. Lawson *and* F. Johnson *and* C. Roderick papers (ML) *and* A. G. Stephens papers (NL).
                                        ELIZABETH WEBBY

LAWTON, JOHN THOMAS (1878-1944), Presbyterian clergyman, educationist and social reformer, was born on 13 March 1878 near Digby, Victoria, eldest of eight children of James Lawton, carrier and later farmer, and his wife Susan, née Whyte, both Victorian born. Educated at Grassdale State School and privately, Lawton excelled scholastically and at 20 became a pupil-teacher. In 1903 he entered Ormond [q.v.5] College, University of Melbourne (B.A., 1907; M.A., 1909) as a theological student and became the college's champion athlete. After a period as travelling secretary to the Australian Student Christian Movement, on 26 May 1910 at Hawksburn Presbyterian Church he married Bertha Maria Davies, daughter of a wealthy hardware merchant. That year Lawton was ordained and inducted into the new parish of Sunshine. In 1913 he became Presbyterian foreign missions secretary in New South Wales and in 1915-19 was minister at South Yarra, Melbourne, where he founded the School of the Pathfinder, a Montessorian day-school conducted by Margaret Lyttle (1875-1944).

A pacifist, Lawton joined the Australian Imperial Force as chaplain in October 1918. Arriving in London in April 1919, he attended a London University summer school in 1919 where Homer Lane spoke on the psychology of education. Back in Melbourne in December, Lawton lectured on psychology and sociology for the Workers' Educational Association. He resigned his ministry and in 1921 established St Andrew's College at Kew; Margaret Lyttle was directress of the junior school.

St Andrew's trained a generation of students, mostly girls, into ideals of truth, individual freedom and self-government. Believing in the perfectibility of human nature, Lawton envisaged a new social order which would challenge commercialism and exploitation. He attacked advertising, the cinema and the financial world, and promoted the pacifism of Kagawa, Schweitzer and Gandhi. He allowed his student council wide powers, encouraged participation in decision-making and banned classroom competition. The senior girls responded with speech-night pageants based on H. G. Wells and Van Loon, plays in Esperanto and participation in student Christian organizations. To the popular misconception of St Andrew's as 'the school where they do what they like', Lawton's riposte was 'the school where they like what they do'. Indeed, the curriculum was varied and comprehensive and Lawton attracted talented staff.

The Depression and Margaret Lyttle's departure to establish Preshil, Kew, forced the school's closure in 1933. Lawton returned to the ministry. From Hartwell he wrote on social and fiscal issues, broadcast over the radio and worked for the Christian Social Order Movement, the Kagawa Co-operative Fellowship and, less actively, the Workers' Co-operative Movement and the Movement Against War and Fascism. Sometimes called 'the red parson', he took a Christian Socialist stance and shunned the Communist Party of Australia in order to keep his ministry.

Tall and eloquent, Lawton was a sincere, strong-willed, at times dogmatic, man whose social conscience often cost him his peace of mind. He died of cerebro-vascular disease on 24 December 1944 at East Melbourne. Survived by his wife, four sons and one daughter, he was buried in Box Hill cemetery.

Other men laboured: fifty years with the Student Christian Movement (Melb, 1946); C. A. White, *The challenge of the years* (Syd, 1951); *Centenary history of South Yarra Presbyterian Church, 1854-1954* (np, nd); *Middle Way*, June-Dec 1940; *Hartwell Presbyterian Messenger*, vol 3, no 7 (Jan 1945); Presbyterian Church of Vic, *Procs of the General Assembly*, 7 May 1945; *Aust J of Education*, 14, Mar 1970; *Truth* (Melb), 4, 11 May, 28 Sept 1935; R. C. Petersen, Experimental schools and educational experiments in Australia, 1906-48 (Ph.D. thesis, Univ Syd, 1968); D. R. Gibbs, John Thomas Lawton (1878-1944) (M.Ed. thesis, Univ Melb, 1978); family papers (held by Rev. R. Lawton, Korumburra, Vic).
                                        DESMOND GIBBS

LAWTON, THOMAS (1899-1978), footballer, was born on 16 January 1899 at Congumbogan, Queensland, seventh child of James Thomas Lawton, sawmill manager, and his wife Ruth Herbert, née Hall. Lawton was educated at Brisbane Grammar School, which he represented in Rugby, cricket, swimming and rowing. He enlisted on 12 January 1918 in the Australian Imperial Force, serving briefly in France as a gunner. In 1919 he entered the faculty of science at the University of Queensland, and represented the State at Rugby against New South Wales in an unsuccessful effort to revive the amateur code in the north after a wartime hiatus.

While at the University of Sydney studying medicine in 1920, Lawton was elected

Queensland Rhodes scholar. He entered New College, Oxford (B.A., rural economy, 1924), and represented the university at Rugby, swimming and athletics.

The Rugby Union suspended Lawton as a suspected professional in 1923 on a charge of having played Rugby League in Queensland, but he was exonerated when it was shown that there was no Rugby Union available at the time. In 1924 he was a reserve for England against Ireland. He was widely popular at Oxford but according to London sports commentators was not always treated on his merits when university Rugby teams and club officers were selected. While in England he seems to have enjoyed an excellent living standard, kept souvenirs of fine clubs and hotels in England and Europe and compiled a remarkable collection of labels of exotic beverages.

In 1925 Tommy Lawton played in New Zealand as vice-captain of a New South Wales team. In 1927, as a member of the Sydney Western Suburbs club, he was selected in A. C. Wallace's [q.v.] renowned 'Waratahs' for an eight-month tour of Britain, France and Canada and was outstanding in the five-eight position. Lawton settled in Brisbane, probably in 1929, and greatly assisted the revival of the Queensland Rugby Union organization. He was captain of the Australian team which defeated the New Zealand 'All Blacks' in all three Test matches that year—a feat still unsurpassed. In 1930 he led Australia to victory in the first Test against the British Isles. His last appearance was in a drawn series against New Zealand in 1932. A writer in the Sydney crowd of 28 000 pronounced him 'still the master at 33'. Photographs of Lawton in his playing days portray a handsome, somewhat patrician figure, full-lipped, with high cheekbones.

Lawton had worked for a time with Gibbs, Bright & Co. in Melbourne. On 24 March 1933 at Mosman, Sydney, he married a divorcee, Maud Howe Leeze Archibald, née Rich. They soon retired to a small farm at Mount Nebo near Brisbane where Lawton lived frugally until a few years before his death on 28 June 1978 at Greenslopes Repatriation Hospital. His wife predeceased him and he was survived by two sons and a daughter.

Lawton was one of the finest inside-backs produced by Australian Rugby Union. For a five-eight he was exceptionally tall, being six feet (183 cm) and over twelve stone (76 kg) in a period when international players were markedly slighter than their modern counterparts. His great ability to lead and to 'steady' a team lay in his straight running, his very sure handling and fine tactical kicking. He was also a noted goalkicker. A grandson, also named Thomas Lawton, represented Australia at Rugby from 1983.

W. H. Bickley (ed), *Maroon* (Brisb, 1982); *Isis* (Oxford), Dec 1921, Feb 1925; *Sporting Life* (Lond), 7 Feb 1924, 15 Jan 1928; *Oxford University Gazette*, 23 Dec 1924; *Referee*, 9 Jan 1923, 23 July 1930, 26 Oct 1932; *SMH*, 6 July 1929, 9 May 1932, 3 July 1978; T. Lawton papers (held by Mrs G. W. Lawton, Mt Gravatt, Brisb).   JOHN R. FORBES

LAY, PERCY (1892-1955), soldier and farmer, was born on 8 February 1892 at Ballan, Victoria, son of Edward Lay, farmer, and his wife Annie, née Slack, both Victorian born. Before enlistment in the Australian Imperial Force on 19 August 1914 he worked as a sheep and cattle dealer for W. J. Andrews of Ballarat. He was posted to the 8th Battalion and embarked for Egypt on 19 October. The 8th landed at Gallipoli on 25 April 1915 and from then until the evacuation Lay continually volunteered for dangerous patrols. He was promoted lance corporal in June, corporal in February 1916 and sergeant next August. On the Western Front particularly, in 1916-17, he showed the remarkable coolness, courage and determination which made him a legend in his own battalion and in the A.I.F.

Lay won his first decoration during fighting near Pozières on 18 August 1916. When the 7th and 8th Battalions attacked, he and three others managed to get into the enemy trenches but were assaulted with bombs. When Lay's bombs were exhausted and he realized that the second attacking wave would not reach the trench he left it, carrying one of his men who was wounded; despite heavy fire he successfully brought him in. When his company was relieved in the front trench he remained behind and assisted the relieving company commander. His own company commander recommended him for the Victoria Cross but on 20 January 1917 he was awarded a Croix de Guerre avec Palme.

For his courageous actions during the 2nd battle of Bullecourt on 8-9 May 1917 Lay was awarded the Military Medal. When his unit was exposed to constant artillery barrage and repeated counter-attacks Lay, wounded during the first few hours, declined to go to the rear until the battalion was relieved. During the attack he was of 'invaluable assistance' and at one stage left a newly captured post to bring in six prisoners, 'belting the hide off them with his tin hat'.

At Polygon Wood near Ypres on 20 September 1917 Lay won the Distinguished Conduct Medal. When his platoon commander was wounded he took charge and led the platoon through a barrage to the assembly position, into the attack, and on to the final objective. The success of the attack was very much due to his inspiration. Nine days later, in the field, he was commissioned second lieutenant. At Broodseinde, east of Ypres, on

4 October he was awarded the Military Cross. After all the other company officers had become casualties he took command during a critical period of the attack. During the final fight for the ridge his unit was opposed by a field-gun firing at point-blank range. Ordering his company to take cover he and two other men worked to the right flank of the gun position. They then attacked with bomb and bayonet, killing the entire crew and capturing the gun. General Sir William Birdwood [q.v.7] sent him a personal letter of congratulations.

Before the 3rd battle of Ypres concluded Lay was to again show his courage. During the Canadian attack at Passchendaele he reconnoitred the German forward positions on the Keiberg. C. E. W. Bean [q.v.7] described Lay's reconnaissance as 'magnificent scouting'. He was detached in 1918 for special duty with Dunsterforce in Persia and in February was promoted lieutenant, A.I.F. On 9 March 1919 he embarked for Australia and was demobilized in June, soon afterwards establishing a small farm at Alphington, Melbourne.

During World War II Lay served in garrison, works and training units in Victoria, reaching the rank of major. He then remained at Alphington until illness forced him to enter Heidelberg Repatriation Hospital. He died there, unmarried, on 28 August 1955 of a cerebral tumour and was cremated. His estate was sworn for probate at £19 459.

An archetypal digger, 'Perce' Lay was greatly admired by his mates. Many felt that he was the bravest man in the A.I.F. and he was often compared to Albert Jacka [q.v.9] and others. His medals and a portrait by W. B. McInnes [q.v.] are held by the Australian War Memorial.

C. E. W. Bean, *The A.I.F. in France*, 1917-18 (Syd, 1933, 1937); W. D. Joynt, *Breaking the road for the rest* (Melb, 1979); J. L. Turner (ed), *The war diaries of Captain Percy Lay, 1914-19* (priv print, Ballarat, 1981); *London Gazette*, 1 May, 17 July, 16, 23 Nov 1917; *Reveille* (Syd), July 1933; *Age, Argus* and *Courier Mail* (Brisb), 29 Aug 1955; *Bulletin* (Syd), 7 Sept 1955; P. Lay file, War Records Section (AWM).   J. G. WILLIAMS

LAYBOURNE-SMITH, LOUIS; see SMITH, LOUIS LAYBOURNE

LAYCOCK, FREDERICK (1839-1909) and BURDETT (1861-1941), wool traders and blanket and textile manufacturers, were father and son. Frederick was born on 13 April 1839 at Harden Beck near Bradford,

Yorkshire, England, second son of Joshua Laycock, wool and waste dealer, and his wife Elizabeth, née Birt. Following his elder brother Burdett to Australia in 1857, he spent some time on the Bendigo goldfield but returned to England none the richer in 1859. Subsequently a potato and fruit wholesaler and woollen waste trader at Bradford, he married Mary Jowett there at the Zion Chapel, with Baptist forms, on 22 January 1861; after her death in 1865 he married, on 1 January 1866, a widow Elizabeth Ambler, née Wigglesworth (d. 1881). In 1878, with debts of several hundred pounds, he again decided to try his luck in Victoria where his nephew Edmund Jowett [q.v.9] was doing well.

Arriving in Melbourne in February 1879 he formed a six months partnership with William Hudson, a Brunswick rag merchant; then with his son Burdett he partnered F. & F. Pearson in a waste and flockmaking venture until its stormy dissolution in March 1884. Continuing the business in association with Burdett and Samuel Nettleton, his second wife's relation by marriage, Laycock used the proceeds of an insurance settlement on his burned-out Yarraville factory to build the South Melbourne works which were to become the cornerstone of a commercial and manufacturing empire.

The firm of Laycock, Son & Nettleton, initially seriously undercapitalized, grew by ploughback, family loans and the reluctant support of banks until, by gradually diversifying its interests into bedding, wool-scouring and the importing of kapok, timber and upholsterers' supplies, it employed in Melbourne alone 81 people in 1890 and represented a capital investment of some £30 000. There was already a branch in Sydney. In 1893 the company began selling wool on its own account in Bradford. Under the control of Frederick's younger brother Alfred and, after 1907, Walter Andrews, a Nettleton relative, this side of the business quickly expanded to include tops-making for the American and European markets and, through wholly owned subsidiaries formed during the early 1930s, spinning and combing. In 1896 the firm became one of the first Australian companies to begin wool-carbonizing. In 1897 the company entered the Queensland market in partnership with Alfred J. Littledike, a Brisbane bedding manufacturer, and, after a characteristically thorough investigation of the blanket industry, added the Laconia woollen mill to its original works in 1904. Selling directly to retailers, the mill became the principal source of the Laycocks' Australian success. A New Zealand wool-buying agency followed in 1906.

Frederick Laycock died of cerebral haemorrhage at his home, Belmont, Glen Iris, on 3 April 1909, leaving an estate valued for probate in Victoria and New South Wales at £55 858. Buried in the Baptist section of Boroondara cemetery, he was survived by his third wife Lavinia Georgina, née Witford, whom he had married in Melbourne on 9 November 1882, and by their five daughters and Burdett, the son of his first wife.

Burdett was born on 25 October 1861 at Heaton near Bradford. Educated at Allerton, Wilsden and Cottingley, he began work as a 10-year-old half-timer at Thomas Baines's Cottingley mill and spent several years learning the woollen trade with his grandfather in Bradford.

After his father's death and an awkward parting of the ways with Samuel Nettleton in 1910, Burdett reorganized the firm as Laycock, Son & Co. and admitted his sons Frederick Cornelius and Edwin Burdett to full partnership in 1915. Active in the Victorian Chamber of Manufactures in 1911-36, he was also a member of the Central Wool Committee during World War I and sometime chairman of the Australian Woollen Manufacturers' Association. Profiting from government contracts during the war, the company re-entered the Sydney market and established a short-lived buying operation in South Africa during the 1920s. In 1933 it purchased Mt Fyans, a 15 300-acre (6190 ha) pastoral property near Darlington in the Western District.

Burdett Laycock died after several years of failing health at his home, Frognall, Camberwell, on 26 December 1941 and was buried in Box Hill cemetery, leaving an estate sworn for probate at £37 543. He had married Mary Ann Cornelius in St Paul's Church, Melbourne, on 25 October 1883; she survived him with their sons and two daughters.

Demanding, quick-tempered and indomitable, both father and son lived for their business and family. Neither was active in community affairs. Frederick summed up the Laycock philosophy: 'A man without ambition is not much use in a competitive world'.

N. J. Holt, *The house of Laycock, 1879-1959* (Melb, priv print, 1959); *Age*, 5 Apr 1909; *Argus*, 5, 7 Apr 1909; T. G. Parsons, Some aspects of the development of manufacturing in Melbourne 1870 to 1890 (Ph.D. thesis, Monash Univ, 1970); Laycock, Son & Co. Pty Ltd papers (ANU Archives).
GRAEME COPE

LAYH, HERBERT THOMAS CHRISTOPH (1885-1964), bank clerk and soldier, was born on 3 April 1885 at Hamilton, Victoria, son of German-born Carl Layh, accountant, and his English wife Jane Emma, née Remfry. Nothing is known of his early education; he probably attended local schools at Hamilton.

On 13 September 1900 Layh became a clerk with the Hamilton Savings Bank, later taken over by the State Savings Bank of Victoria, and was transferred to Melbourne in 1906; in 1908 he completed the senior examinations of the Bankers' Institute. He resigned from the bank on 25 June 1912 while employed as a clerk at its head office in Melbourne and in July joined the Melbourne branch of the newly founded Commonwealth Bank of Australia. On 30 December 1909, at St Michael's Anglican Church, Carlton, he had married Beatrice Olive Akeroyd; they had a daughter and a son.

Layh had taken an active interest in military training in the citizen forces. On 12 October 1908 he was commissioned second lieutenant in the 5th Australian Infantry Regiment, Melbourne, and in July 1913 became militia adjutant of the 60th (Prince's Hill) Infantry. On 14 August 1914 he was appointed to the Australian Imperial Force as a lieutenant and allotted to H. E. ('Pompey') Elliott's [q.v.8] 7th Battalion which sailed from Melbourne in October. In Egypt, on 3 April 1915, he was promoted captain. He landed at Gallipoli with his battalion on the first day of the campaign and was shot in the hip and leg as his boat grounded at Anzac beach. Returning to duty on 1 July, he was posted on 26 August to command 'A' Company and from then until 9 September was also second-in-command of the 7th Battalion.

Layh's battalion remained at Anzac until the evacuation and in January 1916 underwent reorganization and training in Egypt. On 28 January his temporary rank of major became substantive. Layh was transferred on 24 February, with other officers and men, to form the nucleus of the new 59th Battalion of the 15th Infantry Brigade. This battalion reached France in June and took part on 19 July in the ill-fated battle of Fromelles. During part of the battle Layh took temporary command, an appointment confirmed on 27 July with promotion to lieut-colonel. On 9 May 1917 he was wounded by a gas-shell during operations at Favreuil and was evacuated. Transferred to the 57th Battalion on 3 April 1918, he commanded it in the 2nd battle of Villers-Bretonneux, then on 1 May was transferred to command the 60th Battalion, also in the 15th Brigade. He commanded that brigade temporarily from 9 to 20 July 1918 then returned to lead the 60th Battalion in operations at Lihons from 8 to 12 August.

After these operations Layh's active service ended and on 13 October 1918 he embarked for Australia. His service in the A.I.F. had been outstanding and can be measured by his promotions, honours and awards. He was awarded the Distinguished Service Order in December 1916 and a Bar to it in

1918, and in 1919 he was appointed C.M.G. He was also mentioned in dispatches three times. On 18 December 1924 he was awarded the Volunteer Officers' Decoration.

Layh resumed duty on 28 January 1919 with the Commonwealth Bank of Australia, Melbourne Branch; he resigned from the bank's service on 30 June 1924. His wife died in June 1934 and on 7 April 1937 he married a widow, Olive Blanche Turner, née Hood, at the Office of the Victorian Government Statist, Melbourne; on his marriage certificate he described himself as a clerk. His second wife predeceased him and when he died after being struck by a car on 10 April 1964, he was living at Box Hill. He was cremated with Anglican rites. The children of his first marriage survived him.

C. E. W. Bean, *The story of Anzac* (Syd, 1921, 1924), and *The A.I.F. in France*, 1916-18 (Syd, 1929, 1933, 1937, 1942); A. Dean & E. W. Gutteridge, *The Seventh Battalion, A.I.F.* (Melb, 1933); *London Gazette*, 29 Dec 1916, 2 Jan, 25 Dec 1917, 16 Sept, 31 Dec 1918, 1 Jan 1919; War diaries, 57th and 59th Battalions, AIF (AWM); Archives, State Bank of Victoria (Melb).   WARREN PERRY

LAZARUS, DANIEL BARNET (1866-1932), mining director and politician, was born on 20 October 1866 at New Chum, Bendigo, fifth child of Polish-born Barnet Lazarus, gold-mine owner, and his London-born wife Dina, née Abraham. He was educated at Bendigo High School and toured Europe with his brother Samuel in 1883. His father had arrived in Bendigo in 1852 and in partnership with George Gibbs became a pioneer of quartz-mining. Their claim on the Saxby reef was reported to have produced £136 000 net profit between 1864 and Barnet's death in 1880; he left £80 000 to his three sons. After a visit to Europe Daniel managed the family properties and with a syndicate of speculators floated the Prince of Wales and Frederick the Great mines. He believed that Bendigo's mines, especially its neglected western reefs, needed British investors. A proud Bendigonian, he joined the committees of the hospital, benevolent asylum and art gallery and enthusiastically supported establishment of vineyards and orchards. After his second visit to Europe in 1889 Lazarus was elected to the Sandhurst (Bendigo) City Council in 1890. At 26 he was the youngest mayor in Victoria when elected in 1893 and the first locally born mayor of Bendigo.

Lazarus was returned to the Legislative Assembly at a by-election in October 1893, and survived as a Liberal at the general election in September 1894. He lost his seat in October 1897 but held it again in 1900-02. He was a member of the royal commission on state forests in 1897. In 1896 Lazarus supported legislative attempts to reform the iniquitous tribute system of employment in mines and in 1900 campaigned for improved ventilation in Bendigo's deep quartz-mines. Although an investor himself, he supported Bendigo's engine drivers in their attempt to win a wage increase from the mine-magnate George Lansell [q.v.5] in December 1899. This support for local liberal issues led the Bendigo *Independent* to describe Lazarus, in 1897, as an attentive and vigorous member who was listened to by both sides. However, on issues such as votes for women, 'one man one vote' and reform of the Legislative Council, he was anything but liberal. By October 1900 the *Independent* had branded Lazarus as a conservative in the mould of Murray Smith [q.v.6] and suggested that his 'political prayer book and shorter and longer catechism' was the *Argus*. On 27 September 1905 Lazarus married a divorcee Mary Watson, née de Fraza, in Melbourne at the Office of the Government Statist.

The stocky Lazarus was a sportsman and keen follower of horse racing. A member of the Victoria Racing Club and the Victorian Amateur Turf Club, with his brother Dr Samuel Lazarus he owned several horses. He died childless on 9 March 1932 of a cerebral haemorrhage in Melbourne and was buried in the Jewish section of White Hills cemetery, Bendigo; his many relatives were requested to eschew mourning clothes. His wife survived him. His estate, sworn for probate at £24 513, was partly left to Jewish charities.

W. B. Kimberly, *Bendigo and its vicinity* (Ballarat, 1895); *Bendigo Independent*, 3 Aug 1880, 8 Oct 1897, 26, 27 Oct 1900; *Table Talk*, 27 Oct 1893; *Age* and *Argus*, 10 Mar 1932; *Bendigo Advertiser*, 10, 12 Mar 1932.   CHARLES FAHEY

LAZZARINI, CARLO CAMILLO (1880-1952), tailor and politician, was born on 24 April 1880 at Wombat, New South Wales, son of Piedro Lazzarini, labourer, of Italy, and his wife Hannah, née Stubbs, of Sydney. Educated at the Young convent and public school, he was apprenticed to a tailor. He joined the Young Labor League, campaigned for J. C. Watson [q.v.] in 1898 and 1901, and became secretary of the league.

Moving to Sydney, Charlie Lazzarini was active in the Labor Party and in the tailors' union, and was secretary and president of the Federated Clothing Trades' Union in 1912-17 and its delegate on the Labor Council of New South Wales. He joined the party opposition to W. A. Holman [q.v.9] and, a strong anti-conscriptionist in World War I, was a member of the Industrial Vigilance Committee in 1916-19 which took over the party machine and expelled Holman, W. M. Hughes [q.v.9] and many others in 1916. He took part in Catholic social activities and became a district secretary of the Hibernian Australasian Catholic Benefit Society. In 1915 he was at the formation meeting of the Irish National Association of New South Wales, called by A. T. Dryer [q.v.8].

Lazzarini was an influential member of the successful moderates in the kaleidoscopic factionalism in the Labor Party and was on the executive in 1916-17. In 1917 he was vice-president of the No Imperial Federation League. That year he defeated ex-Laborite T. S. Crawford [q.v.8] for the seat of Marrickville in the Legislative Assembly. On 26 April 1919 at St Brigid's Church, Marrickville, he married Myra Hurley. Next year he was a director of the *Freeman's Journal*.

A member for Western Suburbs in 1920-27 and party whip in 1920-21, Lazzarini was minister for state industrial enterprises in James Dooley's [q.v.8] ministries in 1921-22. He continued as a prominent member, with P. F. Loughlin and P. J. Minahan [qq.v.], of the Catholic-reformist Labor group in 1922-25. He backed majority parliamentary opinion against union extremists led by J. S. Garden [q.v.8] and, to 1923, the executive, which was dominated by the Australian Workers' Union headed by J. Bailey [q.v.7]. In 1925 Lazzarini became chief secretary in J. T. Lang's [q.v.9] first cabinet, and confronted problems associated with the increasing number of motor cars, bus competition with government trams and allegations of corruption in the police force. He was acting secretary for mines in 1927.

With other Labor parliamentarians he clashed with Lang over the new 'red rules' foreshadowed at a special conference in November 1926. After they had been adopted by the Easter 1927 party conference and Lang confirmed as leader independent of caucus and cabinet, the premier reconstructed his ministry in May, omitting Lazzarini. But he remained in the party and won Marrickville in October.

Lazzarini maintained his rage against Lang and by 1936 was one of the few caucus members openly opposed to 'one-man control'. In August, with R. J. Heffron, E. M. Horsington, and M. A. Davidson [q.v.8], he was expelled from the party, but was readmitted next year. He remained a strong critic of Lang, and in 1938 joined Heffron in the Industrial Labor Party and was part of the pressure that led to a unity conference in August next year, at which the Lang forces were defeated. He was an assistant minister in (Sir) William McKell's ministry in 1941-44, and was still in parliament when he died of coronary vascular disease on 26 November 1952. Buried in Rookwood cemetery, he was survived by his wife and a son. Hubert Peter Lazzarini (1886-1952), a Labor member of the Federal parliament in 1919-31 and 1934-52, was his brother.

SMH, 26 Mar 1917, 10 Oct 1921, 11 Dec 1923, 11, 30 July 1925, 24 Aug 1936, 17 May 1941, 27 Nov 1952; 3 *Fighting Line*, 22 Apr 1920; *Freeman's J* (Syd), 13 Oct 1921, 18 June 1925.

BEDE NAIRN

LEA, ARTHUR MILLS (1868-1932), entomologist, was born on 10 August 1868 at Surry Hills, Sydney, second son of Thomas Lea, a currier from Bristol, England, and his Sydney-born wife Cornelia, née Dumbrell. Leaving public school at 15 he joined a firm of chartered accountants. He had become interested in insects while a child and continued to study them in his own time. In 1891 he became assistant entomologist in the New South Wales Department of Agriculture and in 1895 he was appointed government entomologist in Western Australia. On 13 May 1896 he married Nellie Blackmore. When their son died soon after birth, the local Anglican pastor's refusal to bury the unbaptized infant left Arthur Lea embittered with the Church for the rest of his life.

At the first opportunity the Leas left Western Australia. In 1899 he was appointed government entomologist in Tasmania where he soon succeeded (his predecessor, having been dismissed under pressure from farmer groups because he failed) in controlling the codling moth, a fruit pest. Lea elucidated the life history of this moth, as well as that of another serious pest, the underground grass grub, with the help of local farmers and orchardists. His capacity to imbue others with his enthusiasm and to enlist their help was characteristic of Lea's entire career. His handbook on pests of orchards and farms and some eighty papers on pest insects and their control established his world-wide reputation in economic entomology.

Lea's first and most enduring passion was the study of beetles. By 1911, when he applied by invitation for the position of entomologist at the South Australian Museum, he could cite published descriptions of 1853 new species. Appointed on an annual salary of £300 he at last was able to indulge his love of beetles during both his working and leisure hours. He embarked on a series of collecting trips which took him to many different parts of Australia and offshore islands. The material thus acquired, added to that obtained earlier in his career and through his encouragement of other collectors, enabled Lea to bequeath to the South Australian Museum what is still the most representative and diverse collection of beetles in Australia.

In 1919, as a member of the South Australian Weevil Commission, Lea developed a method of protecting wheat accumulated during the war from insect pests: it saved some £1 500 000. He was consulting entomologist (1911-32) to the South Australian Department of Agriculture and lecturer in forest entomology (1912-24) at the University of Adelaide. In 1924 a twelve-month appointment with the government of Fiji to study ways of controlling the coconut moth, which was attacking copra crops, took him to Queensland, Java, Malaya and Borneo in search of a parasite. Lea wanted to take the live parasite (a fly) that he found eventually in Malaya, to Fiji by aeroplane but his wife, who had accompanied him, opposed this dangerous mode of transport, and the insects died on board ship. The same species of fly later was introduced to Fiji with great success, but Lea did not get the credit due.

On his return to Adelaide in 1925 he plunged with renewed energy into his revisionary work on beetles, particularly on the huge family of weevils which had commanded most of his attention, but his eyesight began to fail and he came to rely more and more on his assistant, Norman B. Tindale, to make drawings and check details. He published over 280 formal papers, as well as numerous articles in newspapers and magazines, and described 5432 new species of beetles. His private hobby was philately.

Lea was a large man with luxuriant hair and moustache. Frank, genial and generous he was described by those who knew him well as a delightful fellow in camp, whimsical and self-sacrificing. Known to have been hypertensive for many years, Lea died suddenly on 29 February 1932 in Adelaide and was buried in West Terrace cemetery. His wife and three daughters survived him.

H. M. Hale, 'Obituary and bibliography of Arthur Mills Lea', Sth Aust Museum, *Records*, 4 (1932), p 411; *Aust Museum Mag*, 4 (1932), p 342; *Vic Naturalist*, 49 (1932), p 15; *Advertiser*, 1 Mar 1932, 14 Jan 1933; *Herald* (Adel), 1 Mar 1932; *SMH*, 2, 5 Apr 1932; family papers held by Mr C. L. Gellie, Panorama, Adel, and Mr D. A. A. Shepherd, Clarendon, SA; personal notes by Miss A. M. Lea, Myrtle Bank, Adel, and Dr N. B. Tindale, Palo Alto, California; personal information from Mr P. B. McQuillan, New Town, Tas, and Miss A. M. Lea.

E. G. MATTHEWS

LEACH, JOHN ALBERT (1870-1929), teacher and naturalist, was born on 19 March 1870 at Ballarat West, Victoria, son of William Leach, English-born coachsmith, and his wife Bedelia, née Honan, from Ireland. After matriculation from Creswick Grammar School, where he was dux, Leach worked as an unpaid student teacher at Dana Street State School, Ballarat, before gaining his trained teacher's certificate at the Melbourne Training College in 1890. He began a lifetime of professional employment with the Education Department of Victoria by teaching briefly at Mount Prospect and Footscray State schools and serving as head-teacher at Goyura (Rosebery) in the Mallee.

In 1892, before his marriage to Emily Hannah Lamert Gillman on 19 October at Christchurch, Ballarat, he received a longer-lasting appointment to Bengworden (Bairnsdale). He studied science at the Bairnsdale School of Mines, deepened his interest in natural history and pursued his hobbies of debating, cricket, tennis and horse-riding. He first became involved in adult education when in 1898 he was transferred to Moormung (Rosehill) State School where he conducted evening classes in physics. He went on to lecture to the Workers' Education Association and was for twenty-five years a member of the University Extension Board, acting as secretary for seven years.

In 1901 Leach returned to Melbourne to study part time for his B.Sc. He graduated in 1904 with exhibitions in biology and geology and next year won a scholarship in biology. His great enthusiasm was the study of Nature; he gained his M.Sc. in 1906 and his D.Sc. in 1912 with a two-part thesis on the myology of *Strepera* and a revision of the lampreys of Victoria.

From 1904 Leach, as the Education Department's visiting teacher of nature study, was an inspiration to other teachers. His subject was soon accepted into the school curriculum and in February 1905 he became teacher of nature study and geography at the Melbourne Continuation (High) School and, in March, lecturer in nature study and botany at the Training College. He was appointed organizing inspector of nature study in 1907 and in 1911 and 1912 published a complete scheme for the teaching of the subject in the *Education Gazette and Teachers' Aid*. Leach led many field excursions and, although these were planned for small groups, attendance swelled and the trips soon became regular features of school life. In October 1909 Leach also helped to found the Gould [q.v.4] League of Bird Lovers; its membership of 25 000 in its first year was a tribute to his organizing ability. He was made a senior inspector of schools in 1920, rising to assistant chief inspector in 1924.

Leach contributed monthly articles to the *Education Gazette* on natural history subjects from 1905 until 1919. With others he produced a series of six geography textbooks for elementary schools and a more advanced book for teachers. In 1908, assisted by H. W.

Wilson, he published 'Nature-study: a descriptive list of the birds native to Victoria, Australia' as a supplement to the December issue of the *Education Gazette*. This was the forerunner of *An Australian bird book* (Melbourne, 1911) which ran to nine editions. His other major publication was *Australian nature studies* (Melbourne, 1922). He had two books in preparation when he died, one a collection of his weekly radio talks on natural history which he had broadcast over 3LO from the mid-1920s.

Leach was a member of the Field Naturalists' Club of Victoria and the Royal Australasian Ornithologists' Union. He was president of the R.A.O.U. in 1922-24 and a painstaking editor of the *Emu* in 1914-24. He was also convener of their checklist committee, a demanding position as nomenclature decisions for the revised edition of the *Official checklist of the birds of Australia* (1926) called for wise and temperate adjudication. Leach was also a colonial member of the British Ornithologists' Union and a corresponding fellow of the American Ornithologists' Union.

Of medium height and solidly built, Leach was endowed with a sober temperament but was nevertheless capable of enjoying a joke, frequently at his own expense. He died of pericarditis and pleurisy on 3 October 1929 at Richmond and was cremated with Presbyterian forms; he was survived by his wife, son and one of his two daughters. In 1930 members of his nature-study classes formed the Leach Memorial Club which met monthly for many years, participating in botanical, historical and geological excursions.

H. M. Whittell, *The literature of Australian birds* (Perth, 1954); Education Dept (Vic), *Vision and realisation*, L. J. Blake ed (Melb, 1973); *Emu*, 29 Jan 1930, p 230; C. Barrett, 'The doctor', in J. A. Leach, *An Australian bird book*, 8th ed (Melb, 1945); *The Gap*, 1965, p 34; Education Dept (Vic), *Education Mag*, 28, 1971, p 423; *Age* and *Argus*, 4 Oct 1929.   TESS KLOOT

LEADBEATER, CHARLES WEBSTER (1854-1934), theosophist and Liberal Catholic 'bishop', was born on 16 February 1854 at Stockport, Cheshire, England, son of Charles Leadbeater, book-keeper, and his wife Emma, née Morgan. With little theological training, Leadbeater was made deacon by the bishop of Winchester in December 1879 and priested by him next year. In 1882 he joined the ultra-Anglo-Catholic 'Confraternity of the Blessed Sacrament', and next year joined the Theosophical Society. He soon resigned his curacy at Bramshott, Hertfordshire, spending the years 1884-89 at the society's headquarters at Adyar, India, and in

Ceylon. Returning to England, he became closely associated with Annie Besant and wrote the first of his enormous output of books on theosophy and related subjects.

In the early 1900s Leadbeater became the most prominent of the society's lecturers, undertaking several tours of Europe, the United States of America and Australia. Although allegations of sexual irregularities with young boys led to a brief disgrace, and his reinstatement caused a split in the society in America, by 1909 he had become second only to Mrs Besant in the theosophist hierarchy. About this time he discovered an Indian boy, Krishnamurti, who, he claimed, would in time become the latest manifestation in the flesh of the 'World Teacher', the Lord Maitreya.

In 1914 Leadbeater moved to Australia and met 'Bishop' James Ingall Wedgwood, who on 22 July 1916 raised him to the 'episcopate' of the Old Catholic Church. In consultation with their 'spirit masters', they developed a whole new elaborate ritual and theosophical symbolism for what became in 1918 the Liberal Catholic Church. In 1922 Leadbeater succeeded Wedgwood as 'presiding bishop'. Leadbeater presided over a religious community at The Manor, a rambling mansion overlooking Taylor's Bay in the Sydney suburb of Mosman. In 1923-24, as patron of the Order of the Star in the East, he was a prime mover in the building of a huge amphitheatre on the northernmost end of Edwards Beach in preparation for the coming of the 'World Teacher'. The presence of Leadbeater and G. S. Arundale [q.v.7] made Sydney a major theosophist centre in the 1920s.

In 1918 Leadbeater had been the subject of police inquiries when dissident theosophists in California brought to the notice of the New South Wales attorney-general the earlier allegations of sexual perversion and the fact that he now had charge of a number of children of Australian theosophists. These inquiries, and a further series which followed local complaints in 1922, were inconclusive. There were no prosecutions, but press reports of the second affair caused a public scandal.

Leadbeater left Australia in 1929 for Adyar to take over the leadership of the Theosophical Society from Mrs Besant whose health was failing. He was back in Sydney for several months in 1930 and from February to May 1932, when he consecrated a successor as 'regionary bishop' for Australia. He was again returning in 1934 when he became ill and died in Perth on 1 March. He was cremated in Sydney, his ashes being distributed among various theosophical centres.

The pseudo-mysticism, elaborate ritual and doctrinal latitudinarianism of his 'Liberal Catholic Church' had a certain appeal in the climate of the 1920s. Although it declined rapidly after his death, vestiges survive in Sydney, Brisbane, Melbourne and Perth half a century later. Leadbeater himself was a large man, impressive in his Roman purple cassock, with a carefully clipped beard and piercing, almost hypnotic dark eyes. Inclined to be pompous, yet occasionally displaying 'a rather loud sense of humour', he may have been, as Gandhi said, a humbug, but his activities, even the least savoury of them, were probably the product of massive self-delusion: he seems to have lived out his life in the shadowy borderlands between antinomianism and clinical megalomania.

P. F. Anson, *Bishops at large* (Lond, 1964); J. Roe (ed), *Twentieth century Sydney* (Syd, 1980); G. J. Tillett, *The elder Brother* (Lond, 1982); *SMH*, 21 June 1921, 2 Mar 1932; AG and Justice special bundle, 5/7771.2 (NSWA).   W. G. McMINN

LEAHY, JOHN (1854-1909), politician, was born on 15 July 1854 at Schull, Cork, Ireland, eldest son of Patrick Leahy, farmer, and his wife Mary, née Coghlan. Educated at local schools, in 1875 he migrated to Queensland where he was said to have worked as a rural labourer, then acted as postmaster at Windorah before settling at Thargomindah in 1883. There on 11 February 1886 he married Annie Colbert.

Employed by the Bulloo Divisional Board, of which he was a member in 1889-93, he also held a partnership in a cordial manufactory, became part-owner of the *Thargomindah Herald* established by his younger brother Patrick James in 1884, and was proprietor of the Royal Hotel in 1886-89. Secretary of the school of arts in 1886, he was president of the hospital in 1895, the year he and his brother were prominent in making Thargomindah the first town in Queensland with a reticulated artesian water supply. In 1886 John represented Bulloo in a delegation to parliament over crown lands. He has been accredited with originating the system of land classification introduced in 1901.

Succeeding his friend John Donaldson [q.v.4] as member for Bulloo in 1893, he entered parliament as an Independent and promptly led the opposition to Sir Thomas McIlwraith's [q.v.5] railway border tax. In 1899 he engineered a back-bench revolt against Premier (Sir) James Dickson [q.v.8] in favour of (Sir) Robert Philp [q.v.]. He was rewarded by appointment as secretary for railways and public works from 1 February 1901 to 17 September 1903 and was vilified by Labor for his retrenchment policies in the great drought.

On 23 July 1907 Leahy (Opposition), George Jackson (Ministerialist) and W. J. Maughan (Labor) were nominated for the

Speakership. After an inconclusive ballot the Kidstonites threw their weight behind Leahy in return for Jackson's election as chairman of committees. At first bitterly resented by Labor, Speaker Leahy soon gained the respect of all sides for his measured handling of procedures, especially during the constitutional crisis over electoral reform in November 1907.

Leahy was widely read with a preference for didactic poetry. He attempted by repartee and satire to cast himself as a trenchant parliamentary critic, but he was an ineffective debater and his contributions, mainly on western lands, finances and local government, were delivered in a torrent of words, with tangled diction and in a rich brogue. In essence, he was a strong party numbers man, a follower rather than a leader, uncompromising and opinionated with little personal appeal until redeemed by the Speakership.

Popularly known as 'Bulloo', Leahy died suddenly of haematemesis at New Farm, Brisbane, on 20 January 1909 following a bout of influenza and was buried in the Roman Catholic section of Toowong cemetery after a state funeral. His wife, son and four daughters survived him.

Leahy had held directorships in the Queensland Meat Export Agency Co. and the Australian Estates & Mortgage Co., executive positions in the Queensland Woolbrokers' Association, the Queensland Irish Association, the National Agricultural and Industrial Association of Queensland and the Brisbane Chamber of Commerce. On his death his partners James Forsyth [q.v.8] and Philp bought Leahy's interest in Thylungra station.

His brother Patrick James (1860-1927) developed grazing, mercantile and newspaper interests, was member for Warrego for nearly six years from 1902, for three months from November 1907 was secretary for public works and mines in the Philp ministry, and was a member of the Legislative Council in 1912-22. Another brother, Daniel Vincent, was a barrister in Brisbane.

Alcazar Press, *Queensland, 1900* (Brisb, nd); C. A. Bernays, *Queensland politics during sixty (1859-1919) years* (Brisb, nd, 1919?); A. L. Petrie, *Reminiscences* (Brisb, 1926); D. J. Murphy and R. B. Joyce (eds), *Queensland political portraits 1859-1952* (Brisb, 1978); *Centenary Bulloo shire-Thargomindah 1880-1980* (Thargomindah, 1980); Commercial Publishing Co. of Syd, Ltd, *Annual Review of Qld*, Dec 1902, p 286; *Pastoralists' Review*, 15 Feb 1909; *Brisbane Courier*, 2 Nov 1895, 18 Mar, 24 July 1907, 21, 22, 23 Jan 1909; *Catholic Press*, 7 Oct 1907.   M. FRENCH

LEAHY, MICHAEL JAMES (1901-1979), explorer, was born on 26 February 1901 at

Toowoomba, Queensland, fourth of nine children of Irish migrants Daniel Leahy, railway guard, and his wife Ellen, née Stone. He was educated at Christian Brothers' College, Toowoomba. He eventually became leader of the most enterprising expatriate 'clan' on the New Guinea frontier, where from the 1930s a million people were brought under Australian control. He can be said to have closed the European freebooting saga begun by Cortes in the sixteenth century.

After a 'rough and ready' childhood, Mick became a railway clerk but abandoned the job as a dead end. A non-smoker and near-teetotaller, tall, well-built, brown-eyed, ruminative, eloquent, commanding, restless and indefatigable, he abandoned freelance timber-cutting in 1926, leaving his 'T-model Ford on the side of the road' on hearing of the Edie Creek gold strike. Misgauging the rugged, humid terrain, lacking equipment, suffering from near-fatal malaria, he retreated to contract construction and labour management and, joined by his brothers Patrick (1899-1963), James (1909-81) and Daniel (b. 1912), learned the skills of prospecting and survival.

In 1930 Mick and Michael Dwyer were staked to prospect the Ramu tributaries. Tracing the Dunantina they glimpsed the Goroka valley, then unexpectedly were led south to the junction with the unknown Wahgi where bloated corpses intimated dense populations westwards although the interior of New Guinea was thought to be 'simply a continuation of precipitous mountains and miasmic jungles'. With only sixteen carriers and few guns, they encountered Highlands groups who perceived them as ancestors and tried to rub off their white skins, crossed the cordillera and descended by canoe to Port Romilly on the Gulf of Papua to learn they had traversed the mainland and discovered the Purari headwaters.

In November 1930 Leahy and Dwyer were the first Europeans into the Gafuku (Asaro) valley. Mick accepted a stake from New Guinea Goldfields Ltd in 1931 and, after aerial reconnaissance, a decisive factor in Highlands exploration and then almost unique to New Guinea, led an expedition into the Watut valley. On a second trip to the Watut, Mick was caught unprepared for a Kukukuku pre-dawn attack, was battered and partly deafened by a 'pineapple-stone' club and his brother Paddy was seriously wounded. No longer crediting the dictum that 'nothing more lethal than a walking stick was needed to patrol or prospect', Mick henceforth went well-convoyed, demarcated his camps with fishline and sentinels, practised forbearance but shot to kill. According to his adulatory retainers '*Masta Mick*' never missed; between them some hundred warriors were shot. Women, children and non-belligerents were sacrosanct; protecting his carrier line and teaching the heinousness of killing white men were paramount. His attitude on preventive measures hardened ('I'd like to murder the murdering bastards') as he became increasingly disgusted by Highlanders' indiscriminate savagery, though he admired their virility and ceremonious skills. Uncharacteristically solicitous for that time, he lost only one 'boy' through illness during ten expeditions.

Spurred perhaps more by fame than fortune, Leahy took correspondence lessons in photography and journalism and carefully kept a diary. His meticulously organized expeditions in 1933 brought himself, Danny and Charles Marshall of N.G.G.L. to a Pisgah view of the populous Wahgi valley from Mount Erimbari on 15 February. In April with J. L. Taylor, representing an administration urged by the League of Nations to fill in cartographical blanks, the Leahys crossed Chimbu territory to Mount Hagen, tracked the Baiyer River towards the Sepik and, via the lower Jimi, returned to climb Mount Hagen and explore south to the Wahgi-Nebilyer divide. Although Mick providently wrote to his friend, Father William Ross, at Alexishafen, to bring his mission quickly to 'the real New Guinea', he could not take communion because of the nubile girls who were offered transactionally and who gave themselves so unabashedly to verify, as one acknowledged cheerfully fifty years later, his appetising humanity. Mick deprecated the passing of perceived primeval sexual freedoms and detested mission-civilized (especially Lutheran) 'pimps'. To Taylor, Mick said: 'Jim, good country, good climate, good kanakas, too good to find gold in'.

Further expeditions in 1934 began with a punitive sortie against the killers of prospector Bernard McGrath at Finintigu, followed by probes north, south and west of Mount Hagen, the climbing of Papua's highest peak, Mount Giluwe (14 340 feet, 4300 m), the penetration of the Enga to twenty miles (32 km) past Wabag and confirmation that the Wahgi joined the Purari. The Highlands were now open: aerodromes were enthusiastically stamped out by myriad bare feet and villagers sent to the coast to bring back amazing tales of white men's cargo. Mick's photographs and films remain a unique record of the saga of 'first contact' in an award-winning film of the same name (1983).

When Sir Hubert Murray [q.v.] submitted that the Papuan patrol officer Jack Hides [q.v.9] had discovered Mounts Giluwe and Ialibu and the Purari source, an acrimonious public controversy erupted. Mick went to London with his brother Jim in 1935 and forced a hearing with the Royal Geographical Society, after branding its members as 'phonies'. In 1936 he received its Murchison grant and his reports were published in its journal. The Anti-Slavery and Aborigines Protection Society then protested about the killings to the League of Nations. An administration enquiry duly conducted by Jim Taylor exonerated Mick but Italian diplomats noted his reprisals in justifying action in Abyssinia. Further recognition came in Britain and the United States of America where with ghost-writer Maurice Crain he published *The land that time forgot* (1937). In 1959 he was made an honorary member of the U.S. Explorers' Club and in 1971, with moonwalker Neil Armstrong, received its Explorers' medal. They had explored respectively the last terrestrial and the first extra-terrestrial 'unknowns'.

The Leahys found appreciable pay-dirt only at Kuta (Western Highlands). On 5 March 1940 Leahy married at St John's Church, Darlinghurst, Sydney, a 19-year-old North Queenslander Jeannette Gwendolin Best; she was an alumna of Sydney Church of England Girls' Grammar School. Jim Taylor was best man; Margaret Dovey (later Whitlam) was bridesmaid. They had five children who went into professions and business but Mick could not acknowledge three mixed-race sons at Mount Hagen who came under Danny's patronage and thrived. When the Australian New Guinea Administrative Unit offered Mick only a sergeant's rank, he organized an assignment to the U.S. chief engineer as a Royal Australian Air Force flight lieutenant. He glided into remote Telefomin to build an airstrip and was awarded the U.S. Medal of Freedom with bronze palm in 1948.

Post-war Australia offered him in 1952 a mere M.B.E. which he temporarily declined when refused a £25 000 war service loan. He felt he had earned generous Highlands agricultural leases, and saw vendetta in being overlooked but, after years of delay, acquired mixed farming properties at Zenag on the Wau-Lae road. He locked horns with kiaps and villagers over policies, rights and tenure, was left off the Morobe District Advisory Council until protests were lodged, and was a hapless litigant against the administration. Yet he prospered after Papua New Guinea's independence although he had fulminated in the press against E. G. Whitlam's campaign for it, envisaging aid from 'hardworking, frugal and generous Australians' being despoiled by cargo cultists. In 1968 he could decline to have a black university student in his house because it would upset his servants and, though well-read, hoped George Wallace would win the American presidency. Survived by his wife, he died on 7 March 1979 and was buried at Zenag with Catholic rites. Ewunga, his trusty 'shoot-boy', after whom he had named his most promising gold-bearing creek, hoped to join him soon. Two natural sons came unrecognized to his funeral in a Mercedes-Benz and wept. Leahy belonged to the Imperial Service Club, Sydney, and the Returned Servicemen's League, Lae. His portrait hangs in the Pioneers' Club, Mount Hagen.

His brothers also settled in New Guinea as farmers. James pioneered the coffee industry and was a principal in the Highlands oligopoly, Collins & Leahy.

C. Simpson, *Plumes and arrows* (Syd, 1962); Second Waigani Seminar, *The history of Melanesia* (Canb and Port Moresby, 1968); J. P. Sinclair, *The outside man* (Melb, 1969); C. Ashton, 'The Leahy family', J. Griffin (ed), *Papua New Guinea portraits* (Canb, 1978); R. Connolly and R. Anderson, *First contact* film (Syd, 1983), and research material for film (held by them, Syd); *Pacific Islands Mthly*, Aug, Dec 1935, Mar 1940; *Geog J*, 87 (1936), no 3, p 229; *Cwlth Law Reports*, 1960-61, p 6; *PNG Law Reports*, Supreme Court, 1971-72, p 442; *J of Papua New Guinea Soc*, 3 (1969), no 1, p 32, 6 (1972), no 2, p 85; *Post-Courier*, 15 July 1970; *Bulletin*, 2 Mar, 24 Apr, 22 May, 26 June, 10 July, 7 Aug 1979, 5 July, 9, 16 Aug 1983; *Times* (Papua New Guinea), 29 May 1981; I. Willis, An epic journey (M.A. sub-thesis, UPNG, 1969); personal information.
                                        JAMES GRIFFIN

LEAHY, THOMAS JOSEPH (1888-1964), Australian Rules footballer, was born on 13 January 1888 at Goodwood, Adelaide, son of George Joseph Leahy, carpenter and West Adelaide football supporter, and his wife Annie, née McKenzie. Tom was educated at Christian Brothers' College, Wakefield Street, where he captained the football team. Like his brothers, he was also a handball player and at 19 represented his State in Sydney. As a lad he had played football for Albert Park and in 1905 he played his first games for the West Adelaide team, of which his brother George was secretary. Two other brothers, Bernie and Vin, also played and largely because of the Leahys the struggling club became a power and won the premierships in 1908 and 1909, confirming its quality by winning the Australian club championship in 1908.

Late in 1909 a rift in the club caused the Leahys to transfer to North Adelaide, with Bernie as captain. Already established as a top ruckman in interstate matches following the 1908 carnival, Tom Leahy was an automatic selection for the 1911 and 1914 carnivals. He won the Magarey medal for South Australia's best and fairest player in 1913 and captained Norths in 1915, the last season before World War I halted competition until 1919. A warehouseman, on 29 November 1917 he married Agnes Shannon, shop assistant; they had one daughter.

Leahy became captain-coach of North Adelaide in 1919, when it was runner-up to Sturt for the premiership; he guided it to the flag next year and was named 'best afield' in the grand final. He made his fourth appearance in a carnival in 1921. That year he was defeated by one vote in the election of the club committee and retired as a player.

The 6 ft. 4 ins. (193 cm), raw-boned Leahy had an iron constitution and massive hands; he was famous for holding the ball in one hand when preparing to kick. Also acknowledged as the greatest ruckman in the game, he was a consistent matchwinner in 200 home and interstate matches. A key figure in three premiership teams, he had been selected in every South Australian team from 1906 until 1921. He was suspended once, after being charged with striking a Norwood player in 1914. Leahy wrote to the press alleging unjust treatment and protested his innocence for the rest of his life. He claimed that in 1935 he accepted a position on the tribunal which heard charges against reported players, so that he could protect them from unwarranted suspensions.

After retiring he coached Norwood (to two premierships and a second) and other league teams. He was belatedly appointed a life member of the South Australian National Football League in 1945 and in 1944-64 was the resident officer at Football House, Hindmarsh Square. In 1946 he helped to form the Past Players and Officials Association; he also lectured and wrote about the evolution of the game. Though retiring, Leahy was courteous, obliging and always ready to help a young player. Scrupulously fair, he ignored attempted bribes.

He died in Royal Adelaide Hospital on 7 May 1964 and after a requiem Mass in St Francis Xavier's Cathedral was buried in Centennial Park cemetery.

Sth Aust Football Budget, 19 Apr 1980; *Advertiser* (Adel), 27 Sept 1924, 11 June 1958, 13 Apr 1959, 8 May 1964; information from Mr G. Joseph, Adel.   MERVYN AGARS

LEAK, JOHN (1892?-1972), soldier, teamster and garage proprietor, was born probably in 1892 at Portsmouth, Hampshire, England, son of James Leak, miner. He migrated to Australia before World War I, becoming a teamster at Rockhampton, Queensland.

Leak enlisted as a private in the Australian Imperial Force on 28 January 1915 and embarked with the 5th Reinforcements for the 9th Battalion on the transport *Kyarra*, joining his unit on 22 June at Gallipoli. Early in 1916 the battalion was posted to the Western Front and disembarked at Marseilles bound

for northern France to engage in the Somme offensive in July. The village of Pozières on the Amiens-Bapaume highway on a ridge overlooking the Somme was a vital objective of the allies and was taken after four days of savage fighting. The 1st Australian Division, flanked by British divisions, and with the 9th Battalion spearheading its attack, moved towards Pozières on 22 July. Next day Leak was one of a party ordered to capture a German strong-point which was holding up the battalion's advance. His party became pinned down in an old German trench by heavy machine-gun fire. Their grenades were outranged by the Germans' superior 'egg' bombs. Leak dashed from cover and, under heavy fire, ran towards the enemy post, hurling three grenades to great effect. On reaching the enemy trench he leapt in and bayoneted the three remaining Germans.

Later in this engagement his party was driven back. Leak was the last to withdraw at each stage, hurling bombs to cover his companions' retreat. By the time reinforcements arrived his courage and energy had done much to weaken the enemy's defence and the post was taken again. For 'conspicuous bravery' he was awarded the Victoria Cross. He was wounded on 21 August 1916 at Mouquet Farm and rejoined the 9th Battalion on 15 October 1917. On 7 March 1918 he was severely gassed at Hollebeke, Belgium, and was unable to resume duty until 26 June. Late in life, he suffered from bronchitis and emphysema. He married Beatrice May Chapman on 30 December 1918 in the Parish Church of St John Baptist, Cardiff, Wales.

On 9 February 1919 Leak embarked for Australia and was discharged from the A.I.F. in Queensland on 31 May. After two years in Queensland he moved to New South Wales for two and a half years. Further moves took him to South Australia and then to Esperance in Western Australia where he became a mechanic and garage proprietor. He was married again on 19 January 1927 to Ada Victoria Bood-Smith. On retirement he settled at Crafers, South Australia. Survived by four sons and three daughters, he died at Redwood Park on 20 October 1972 and was buried in Stirling cemetery.

C. E. W. Bean, *The A.I.F. in France*, 1916 (Syd, 1929); L. Wigmore (ed), *They dared mightily* (Canb, 1963); *London Gazette*, 9 Sept 1916; *Reveille* (Syd), June 1931, Jan 1932, Aug 1935; records (AWM).
          HELEN MAYS

LEAKE, GEORGE (1856-1902), lawyer and premier, was born on 3 December 1856 in Perth, eldest son of George Walpole Leake [q.v.5] and his wife Rose Ellen, née Gliddon. George attended Bishop Hale's [q.v.4] School and the Collegiate School of St Peter, Adelaide, before being articled in his father's legal firm. In 1880 he was admitted to the Bar and partnership in the firm but in 1882 became acting crown solicitor and next year was confirmed in the post, which he retained until 1894.

In 1890 Leake was elected to the Legislative Assembly for Roebourne but resigned after three weeks when he was excluded from the Forrest ministry although (Sir) John Forrest [q.v.8] had approached him about the attorney-generalship months before, and later considered offering him the colonial secretaryship. Without a ministerial salary, Leake could not afford to give up the crown solicitorship, so he deferred his political ambitions. In 1894, however, he won Albany by one vote.

His return to parliament coincided with the formation of the first organized Opposition, crystallized by controversy over state aid to education; he became an active member. When his leader George Randell [q.v.6] failed to press the education issue hard enough for his satisfaction, Leake moved in effect a motion of no confidence in the government's education policy. The motion was withdrawn in return for an undertaking that the government would legislate to abolish state aid. Leake had declared that he was fully prepared to turn Forrest out and form a government if he could attract enough support. This was not a realistic aspiration then, but his confrontationist style added a new dimension to Western Australian politics and was too much for Randell who crossed the floor, leaving leadership of the Opposition to the 38-year-old newcomer. The political temperature subsequently dropped and although Leake spent much of the 1896 session in England his colleagues did not replace him as leader.

Momentous changes were occurring in the colony with the gold rushes. Forrest's strategy was to use gold-induced prosperity to develop the agricultural and pastoral industries and so ensure long-term economic growth even after the gold ran out. This made sense, but was a source of grievance to the large goldfields population and discontent simmered over such issues as the high freight rates charged by the railways and the tariffs levied on imported food. Leake's free-trade inclinations made him a natural critic of the food duties and, as the goldfields won political representation, his following grew in size and vigour. After the 1897 election, at which Leake himself was unopposed, there were 14 members with oppositionist sympathies in a House of 44. By the end of the decade Forrest's majority had been reduced to six or eight and the government was suffering occasional defeats as well as making frequent concessions to its more liberal opponents.

The writing was on the wall well before Federation gave Forrest the opportunity to move to a new sphere.

Leake was a delegate to the Australasian Federal Convention of 1897-98; his few speeches were mainly in defence of the need for a strong Senate as a bulwark of State rights. His real contribution, however, was made within the colony as a spokesman for the Federal cause and president of the local Federal League. This reawakened conflict with Forrest who, though himself sympathetic to Federation, was inhibited by the negative attitude of many of his followers and the conservatism of the Legislative Council. Thus Western Australia did not hold referenda on the Commonwealth bill in 1898 or 1899. The issue was not in principle a 'party' matter, but Leake and his Opposition allies, with massive support on the goldfields and considerable support in Perth, tended to be ranged against the government and the agricultural and pastoral interests. Forrest's bid to make the bill more acceptable to his sympathizers, by gaining concessions for Western Australia, was seen by Leake and the Federalists as a device for delaying a referendum; and they sabotaged it by asking prominent Federalists in the other colonies to refuse to negotiate with Forrest.

Leake probably misjudged Forrest's motives. Certainly the progress of the movement would have been smoother had the two men worked in concert, as they eventually did in 1900 when Forrest finally persuaded the council to let the bill go to the people without special concessions. The result was a resounding affirmative vote, on the goldfields and in most of the colony—a triumph for Leake and his legal and political associate (Sir) Walter James [q.v.9].

Forrest's departure from State politics ushered in a period of confusion. Following the election of 1901, Forrest's successor George Throssell [q.v.] could not form a ministry; the governor sent for Frederick Illingworth [q.v.9], who had taken over the leadership of the Opposition in August 1900 when Leake had resigned his seat to make a business trip to England. Illingworth also failed to form a ministry, partly because of the non-co-operation of Leake, now member for West Perth. A 'party' meeting agreed that Leake should take office with Illingworth as treasurer; the governor concurred.

Leake was vulnerable, for even with the support of the 8 Labor members, who were generally aligned with the government, he could only muster 22 votes in a house of 50. He nevertheless retained office for five months before being defeated on a no confidence motion by F. H. Piesse [q.v.], prominent in the rural wing of the old Forrest group. Governor Sir Arthur Lawley [q.v.]

refused to allow Leake a dissolution but invited Piesse and, when he failed, A. E. Morgans [q.v.] to form a cabinet. Leake and his Labor allies caused a sensation by energetically contesting the ministerial by-elections to such effect that three ministers were defeated. When he too was refused a dissolution, Morgans had to resign after only a month in office.

The political crisis ended when Leake formed a new administration in December 1901. He broadened the basis of his cabinet by including a rural representative, which began a process of realignment which, by 1905, saw the virtual coalescence of the groups which Forrest and Leake had led in the 1890s and a two-party system emerging on Labor versus non-Labor lines. Leake did not live to see this: he collapsed and died on 24 June 1902 at the age of 45.

Though his two administrations had totalled only about twelve months, Leake had, with the aid of James, enacted some important legislation. The Trade Unions Act confirmed the legality of unions of employees and employers alike; the Workers' Compensation Act extended the principle of compensation beyond cases of employer negligence; and the Industrial Conciliation and Arbitration Act, carefully worked up in conjunction with union and Labor representatives, replaced the ineffective measure of 1900 and provided a workable arbitration system.

George Leake was a Western Australian version of the turn-of-the-century, Australian-born, liberal lawyer-politician of which Sir Edmund Barton [q.v.7] and Alfred Deakin [q.v.8] are the most celebrated examples. Leake concentrated on public service but was renowned as a courtroom advocate; in 1898 he was appointed Q.C. As a politician he was a combative debater although sometimes impatient of detail. He was the only contemporary prepared to confront Forrest on his own terms and by so doing, and in his comings and goings from office in 1901, he did much to ensure the rapid transformation of Western Australian politics from a pre-party to a two-party system.

Leake was affable, popular and witty. He invested in mining, but not very successfully. A keen cricketer in his youth, he was later a committee-member of the Western Australian Turf Club. He was an Anglican. On 15 September 1881 he had married Louisa Emily, daughter of the former Chief Justice Sir Archibald Burt [q.v.3], his father's old antagonist, and sister of Septimus Burt [q.v.7], a major political adversary in the 1890s. Leake was survived by his wife, a daughter and four sons, one of whom, Francis Walpole, followed his father into the firm of Leake, James & Darbishire (in 1919 amalgamated with Stone & Burt to become Stone,

James & Co.), and in 1939 became the third generation of Leakes to take silk. George Leake was buried in East Perth cemetery. His appointment as C.M.G. was gazetted posthumously.

J. S. Battye (ed), *Cyclopedia of Western Australia*, 1 (Adel, 1912); F. K. Crowley, *Forrest: 1847-1918*, 1 (Brisb, 1971); B. K. de Garis in P. Loveday et al (eds), *The emergence of the Australian party system* (Syd, 1977), and in C. T. Stannage (ed), *A new history of Western Australia* (Perth, 1981); G. S. Reid and M. R. Oliver, *The premiers of Western Australia 1890-1982* (Perth, 1982); E. Russell, *A history of the law in Western Australia and its development from 1829 to 1979* (Perth, 1980); *Inquirer*, 21 Jan 1874; *Morning Herald* (Perth) and *West Australian*, 25 June 1902; J. S. Bastin, The West Australian Federation movement (M.A. thesis, Univ Melb, 1952); L. Hunt, A political biography of Walter Hartwell James 1894-1904 (M.A. thesis, Univ WA, 1974); J. S. Kalajzich, The life of George Leake (MS, Battye Lib); Leake papers (Battye Lib); Deakin papers (NL).   B. K. DE GARIS

LEANE, EDWIN THOMAS (1867-1928), ALLAN WILLIAM (1872-1917) and SIR RAYMOND LIONEL (1878-1962), soldiers, were sons of Thomas John Leane, shoemaker, and his wife Alice Ann, née Short, daughter of an Adelaide shoemaker. They and two brothers all served in World War I. Nine of their sons served in either World War I or World War II.

Thomas John (1842-1900) migrated to South Australia from Cornwall, England, in 1857 with his parents, three brothers and three sisters. He followed his father in the shoemaking trade. As he grew older he was strongly attracted to Nonconformist religious teachings, became a temperance adherent and was accepted as a Wesleyan lay preacher. He married Alice Short in 1865 and they settled in a house in Rose Street, Prospect, which remained the family home for the rest of their lives.

Edwin Thomas, eldest of eight surviving children, was born on 25 August 1867 at Prospect and was educated at North Adelaide Public School and Whinham College before becoming a book-keeper and later an insurance manager. He joined the South Australian Garrison Artillery (militia) about 1888 as a gunner and transferred to the 3rd South Australian Infantry Regiment in 1890, reaching the rank of captain. On 15 June 1891, at St Paul's Church, Adelaide, he married Katie Mary Walker Machin; they had eight children. Edwin volunteered for service in the South African War in 1900-01 as a subaltern with the 4th South Australian Contingent of Imperial Bushmen and was mentioned in dispatches. After the war he settled in Sydney, becoming resident secretary of the Colonial

Mutual Life Assurance Society Ltd. He was described as 'a big man, both physically and mentally'.

On 14 September 1914 Leane joined the Australian Imperial Force as a captain in the 12th Battalion. Because of illness in Egypt, and possibly his age, he was transferred to the Australian Army Ordnance Corps; his administrative ability was finally to carry him to the top levels of the A.I.F. Ordnance Service. Promoted major in April 1915 he served at Gallipoli as deputy assistant director of ordnance services, 2nd Division, from late July until the evacuation, and held the same appointment in Egypt in January-March 1916 and until July in France and Belgium. In August he was promoted lieut-colonel and transferred to A.I.F. Headquarters, London. After leave to Australia in February-July 1917 he was posted to France and in November became the head of the ordnance services, 1st Anzac Corps. From February 1918 this responsibility was widened to include the whole A.I.F. in France. He was promoted colonel in November and became a deputy director in the A.I.F. Repatriation and Demobilization Department, London, before returning to Australia in September 1919; his A.I.F. appointment ended in November.

He had been mentioned in dispatches five times, appointed C.B.E. and awarded the Belgian Croix de Guerre. Three of his sons, Allan Edwin (died of wounds 1917), Geoffrey Paul and Reuben Ernest, served with the 48th Battalion, and a fourth son Maxwell with the Royal Australian Navy. Edwin Leane was appointed administrator of Norfolk Island in 1924; although he was officially commended for his administration, the Australian government terminated his office in 1926 because of his personality clashes with prominent Norfolk Islanders. Survived by his wife and six of their children, he died of cancer at Camberwell, Melbourne, on 27 August 1928 and was buried in Box Hill cemetery.

Thomas Leane's second son Ernest Albert (b. 1869) enlisted at the age of 45 and served with the 27th Battalion as a warrant officer. His two sons, one of whom, Arnold, was killed in action in 1916, also served in the battalion.

Allan William was born on 11 May 1872 at Mount Gambier. When 18 he joined the militia and was commissioned as an infantry officer in 1893. He later moved to Perth where he worked as an indentor and estate agent and in 1908 joined the 11th Australian Infantry Regiment as a lieutenant; he was promoted captain in 1912. Leane enlisted in the A.I.F. as a major in the 28th Battalion on 28 April 1915 and reached Gallipoli in September. He was second-in-command of his battalion from January 1916 and commanded it in France from 29 July as a temporary lieut-

colonel, providing inspiring leadership during the battle of Pozières. He was promoted lieut-colonel on 29 November but died of shrapnel wounds received at Delville Wood on 4 January 1917 and was buried at Dernancourt. He was married with one son.

Raymond Lionel was born on 12 July 1878 at Prospect. Educated at North Adelaide Public School until 12, he began work in a retail and wholesale business. After his firm sent him to Albany, Western Australia, he became interested in militia soldiering and was commissioned in the 11th (Perth Rifles) Infantry Regiment in 1905. On 14 June 1902, at Christ Church, Claremont, Perth, he married Edith Louise Laybourne, sister of Louis Laybourne Smith [q.v.]. For six years they lived at Claremont where Raymond was elected to the local council. At the time of his marriage he was employed as a commercial traveller. In 1908 he bought a retail business at Kalgoorlie and became a successful merchant. He also resumed militia training with the Goldfields Infantry Regiment and was a captain by 1910.

On 25 August 1914 Raymond Leane enlisted in the 11th Battalion, A.I.F., as a captain and company commander. His battalion went ashore with the covering force during the landing at Gallipoli on 25 April 1915 and Leane's 'C' Company moved into the Plugge's Plateau sector. On 4 May he led an attempt to capture Gaba Tepe fort, a Turkish position close to the beach which enfiladed the Australian trenches. C. E. W. Bean [q.v.7] considered him the ideal choice for this hazardous enterprise. After landing at dawn Leane's small force was pinned close to the beach by heavy fire so that no advance could be attempted. Having been given full discretion to depart from his orders as he thought fit, he organized a withdrawal and successfully brought off his men and their wounded with the aid of the Royal Navy. For this he was awarded the Military Cross. He was slightly wounded on 28 June in an assault on Pine Ridge and again on 31 July when he led a successful attack against Turkish defences and held the position thereafter against heavy counter-attacks. This position became known as 'Leane's trench'. Promoted temporary major on 5 August, he commanded the 11th Battalion from 11 September and was promoted temporary lieut-colonel on 8 October. He remained at Gallipoli until evacuation on 16 November. He was twice mentioned in dispatches for service at Anzac. While there he had been nicknamed 'Bull'; his 'tall square-shouldered frame, immense jaw, tightly compressed lips, and keen, steady, humorous eyes made him the very figure of a soldier'.

In Egypt, on 26 February 1916, Leane was confirmed as major and appointed commander of the 48th Battalion; promoted lieut-colonel on 12 March, he took his unit to France in June. After a week at Fleurbaix the battalion moved into the Pozières sector and on 7 August repulsed a heavy German counter-attack. The 48th served at Mouquet Farm and Gueudecourt in 1916 and at Bullecourt, Messines, Wytschaete and Passchendaele in 1917. At Bullecourt Leane's younger brother and second-in-command Major Benjamin Bennett Leane (1889-1917) was killed on 10 April and his nephew Captain Allan Edwin Leane died of wounds on 2 May.

Severely wounded at Passchendaele on 12 October, Raymond Leane did not resume duty until late January 1918. He commanded the 48th at Albert in March-April, was appointed temporary colonel commanding the 12th Brigade on 19 April and was confirmed in rank and promoted temporary brigadier general on 1 June. Under his leadership the 48th Battalion was prominent in halting the German advance on Amiens on 5 April and he commanded the 12th Brigade at Villers-Brettoneux in April-May, in the attack on Proyart on 8 August and in the battles of the Hindenburg outpost line in September. His A.I.F. appointment ended on 3 January 1920. He had been mentioned in dispatches eight times and his decorations included, as well as the Military Cross, the Distinguished Service Order and Bar and the French Croix de Guerre; he was appointed C.M.G. in 1918 and C.B. in 1919. His brother Ben, three nephews and several other relatives had served under him in the 48th Battalion which led to its being known throughout the A.I.F. as 'the Joan of Arc Battalion' (Made of all-Leanes).

As a commander Raymond Leane won the affection of his men by his constant concern for their well-being; he gained their respect by his strength of character, firm discipline and high sense of duty. In action he was cool and alert, directing and encouraging, heedless of danger.

After demobilization he was appointed police commissioner by the South Australian government in May 1920, gave distinguished service until 1944 and was knighted on retirement. Leane had taken over a restive force which had been poorly led and whose morale was low. He soon displayed a capacity to remedy reasonable grievances, through both departmental conferences and the police union. His men remained in awe of him, but most came to see him as just and sensitive. He introduced a school for recruits and a system of promotion which stressed merit more than seniority; his major contributions were in police education and conditions of service. In 1928 with strong government backing he crushed the Port Adelaide wharf strike, enrolling some 3000 special constables; and during the Depression ruthlessly curbed demonstrations by the unemployed which he

judged to be communist inspired. His son Geoffrey was deputy commissioner of police in 1959-72.

Raymond Leane had commanded the 3rd Infantry Brigade, Australian Military Forces, in 1921-26 as a lieut-colonel, was transferred to the unattached list in 1926 and placed on the retired list in 1938. In World War II he commanded a group in the Volunteer Defence Corps. After his retirement he lived quietly at Plympton, Adelaide, until his death on 25 June 1962. Survived by his wife, five sons and a daughter, he was buried in Centennial Park cemetery.

Bean described Sir Raymond Leane as 'the head of the most famous family of soldiers in Australian history'. The family was known during the war and for long afterwards as 'the Fighting Leanes of Prospect'. Raymond's wife Edith typified the devotion, courage and skill of the Leane womenfolk. His portrait by George Bell [q.v.7] is in the Australian War Memorial. The Leane brothers and their sons provide a remarkable example of family enlistment—every male member of military age offered himself for active service and was accepted.

W. Devine, *The story of a battalion* (Melb, 1919); C. E. W. Bean, *The story of Anzac* (Syd, 1921, 1924), and *The A.I.F. in France*, 1916-18 (Syd, 1929, 1933, 1937, 1942); *Reveille* (Syd), Mar, Oct 1930, June, July 1932, July, Sept 1933, Dec 1934; *Advertiser* (Adel), 14 May 1920, 24 June 1921, 30 Apr 1926, 28 June 1962; *Observer* (Adel), 7 June 1924, 21 Aug, 18 Sept 1926; *News* (Adel), 29 Apr 1926; *Mail* (Fremantle), 21 July 1932; E. T. and R. L. Leane files (war records section), and B. B. Leane papers (AWM); information from Mr G. M. Leane, Plympton, Adel, Mr R. F. Leane, Rostrevor, Adel, Mrs P. Benton, Warradale, Adel, Mrs E. T. McEllister, Erindale, Adel, Mr R. L. Johnson, Medindie, Adel.   RONALD HOPKINS

LEARMONTH, F. V. C. L.; *see* LIVINGSTONE-LEARMONTH

LEASON, PERCY ALEXANDER (1889-1959), artist, was born on 23 February 1889 at Kaniva, Victoria, second of six children of James Leason, farmer, and his wife Mary Campbell, née Crothers. Both parents were Australian born. As a boy he practised drawing in a cubby-house studio and with a mate from Kaniva State School, Desmond Harris, printed and illustrated a threepenny weekly sheet. He weathered an art school at Nhill—'The town's name represents what I learnt'—and in 1906 was apprenticed to Sands [q.v.6] & McDougall in Melbourne as a lithographic artist.

At work Leason became friendly with fellow apprentice Dick McCann. The pair collaborated on a number of posters ('I allus has one at eleven', commissioned by the Carlton Brewery, became famous), bolstered meagre incomes by the sale of surreptitiously executed drawings and attended evening classes at the National Gallery of Victoria. Leason was a splendidly talented draughtsman. McCann said of him: 'He could draw anything at all in perspective or at any angle'.

His apprenticeship served, Leason joined the Lithographic Artists' Union and tried to earn a living with 'odds and ends of illustrations', renting a studio with William Frater [q.v.8], McCann and others. He experimented briefly with spiritualism. Several years of Bohemian existence ended with his marriage to his cousin Isabella Cargill Chapman at Terang, with Presbyterian forms, on 15 April 1916, by which time he had achieved some success as a book-illustrator.

Next year Leason moved to Sydney as chief designer for (Sydney Ure) Smith [q.v.] & Julius; he illustrated Harley Matthews's [q.v.] *Saints and soldiers* and, for Angus [q.v.7] & Robertson [q.v.], *Selected poems of Henry Lawson* [q.v.] before succeeding David Low [q.v.] as political cartoonist for the *Bulletin* in May 1919. Leason's special talent was for depicting the acquaintances of his Wimmera childhood and his full-page 'After the Show' published on 2 March 1922 was the first of many bucolic comedies. He continued to contribute to the *Bulletin* after 1924 when he returned to Melbourne as cartoonist for *Punch* at £1750 a year. His famous 'Wiregrass' cartoons, based on a Kaniva-like hamlet, were begun in *Table Talk* (which had incorporated *Punch*) in January 1926. He lived at Eltham.

Leason achieved moderate recognition as a painter with 'On the Beach', 'Morning' and 'Morning Glow', purchased by the National Art Gallery of New South Wales; his first Melbourne exhibition in 1927 enhanced his reputation. But contentment eluded him. Shy, but fierce in controversy, he was disturbed by the modernist movement; he became a firm disciple of the realist Max Meldrum [q.v.] and joined the Twenty Melbourne Painters group. His antipathy to 'decadent' art was lifelong.

Leason's anthropological interests also got him into hot water. In 1928 after making copies of rock paintings in caves near Glenisla for the National Museum of Victoria he contended that some figures described by the ethnologist John Mathew [q.v.] in 1897 were nothing but natural stains in the rock. Further studies of the Cave of the Serpent at Mount Langi Ghiran and of rock paintings in the Mootwingee range, New South Wales, led him to another tenet, still maintained after a visit to Europe in 1957, that cave-art animals were painted from dead subjects. The first of several publications outlining his ideas, 'A new view of Western European cave art', appeared in the *Journal of the Prehistoric Society of Great Britain* in 1939. Inspired by Frederick Wood Jones [q.v.9], Leason also collected biographical notes on Victorian full-blood Aborigines and in 1934 painted twenty-eight portraits, ascribing his work to 'a deep affection for the Australian scene and much concern for the vanishing aborigines'.

In 1937 Leason visited the United States of America and next year settled permanently in New York. After working as an illustrator, mainly for *Collier's Magazine*, he established an art colony on Staten Island. He exhibited widely and opened an art school where he taught a modified form of Meldrumism and formulated a 'diagrammatic pyramid' to explain his theories on the history of art. In 1945 he won the Audubon Artists' Hollander Prize and in the 1950s was elected a fellow of the London Royal Society of Arts and of the Staten Island Institute of Arts and Sciences; he had been president of the institute in 1945-51. The self-portrait displayed at his last one-man exhibition at the Chase Gallery, New York, in November 1958 showed a man of stocky build with a bald, well-shaped head, wide mouth and the dancing eyes of the humorist.

Leason died of heart disease on 11 September 1959 at Staten Island, survived by his wife, four daughters and two sons. His early works are represented in Australian State galleries and at Castlemaine, Victoria, but most of his paintings are held privately in the U.S.A.

L. J. Blake, 'Percy Leason', *VHM*, 39 (1968), p 158; *Herald* (Melb), 19 Sept 1925, 9 June 1934; *People* (Syd), 3 Jan 1951; *Sun-News Pictorial*, 16 June 1967; Leason papers (LaTL).   L. J. BLAKE

LECKIE, ALEXANDER JOSEPH (1881-1966), musician, was born on 31 August 1881 at Newtown, Geelong, Victoria, son of Alexander Veitch Leckie, Scottish-born salesman, and his Geelong-born wife Mary Louisa, née Wright. After state school education in Geelong he found a post with the Geelong Town Council while continuing organ studies with R. J. Shanks in Melbourne. In 1904 he resigned as assistant town clerk, and as organist of All Saints Church, Newtown, and went to London to study organ, singing and piano at the Royal College of Music (A.R.C.M., 1906; F.R.C.O., 1907). He was an excellent student although his piano teacher assessed him as 'an earnest and intelligent pupil, but too sceptical and independent. This hinders his progress'. He returned in 1907 to become organist at St John's, Camberwell, Melbourne.

In 1908-17 Leckie succeeded G. A. D'Arcy-Irvine [q.v.8] as organist and choirmaster at St George's Anglican Cathedral in Perth. There, on 14 October 1909, he married Hilda Tate. He bought D'Arcy-Irvine's extensive piano-teaching practice and was soon presenting organ and piano recitals with local groups and artists. In 1910 he became foundation president of the Western Australian Music Teachers' Association; he conducted the Metropolitan Liedertafel (later Gleemen) in 1912-32 and in 1913-23 conducted the Metropolitan Orchestral Society which he had founded. In 1918 he extended his choral activities with the formation of the Perth Ladies Choir, which he re-formed in 1932 as the Oriana Ladies Choir and directed until 1946. The honorary representative of the Royal College of Music in Perth, Leckie had in 1913 gained his Mus. Bac. from the University of Adelaide.

He had a long association with the University of Western Australia as president of the University Music Society, examiner for the Australian Music Examinations Board and as founder and conductor of the University Choral Society (1931-45). He also gave university extension lectures in the 1930s and in the newly formed department of music in 1954.

Perceiving the musical potential of radio early in its development, Leckie was musical director of 6WF in the late 1920s. He later gave talks for the Australian Broadcasting Commission in programmes such as the Argonauts' Club and Catherine King's Women's Session in addition to performing in chamber music groups such as the Amati Trio.

Leckie's major contribution to music in Western Australia lay in his performances; his encouragement of amateurs and local musicmaking, both instrumental and choral; and in his dedication to raising programming and teaching standards. He translated a number of Hugo Wolf's songs and wrote several musical perception texts for the A.M.E.B. syllabus. He gave his pupils a firm foundation for development in singing and keyboard. His quiet sense of humour, neat turn of phrase and open mind helped him to foster the development of music in the State. In 1963 he was appointed M.B.E.

Predeceased by his wife, Leckie died in Perth on 17 September 1966 and was cremated. Two daughters and a son survived him.

Who's who in broadcasting in Western Australia (Perth, 1933); A. H. Kornweibel, *Apollo and the pioneers* (Perth, 1973); *Canon*, 11, no 3 (Oct 1957), p 75; family papers held by Mrs B. Walton, Dalkeith, Perth.   BRIAN POPE

LECKIE, JOHN WILLIAM (1872-1947), manufacturer and politician, was born on 14 October 1872 at Alexandra, Victoria, son of James Leckie, Scottish-born butcher, and his wife Mary, née Reilly, from County Cork, Ireland. Educated at Scotch College, Melbourne, in 1885-90, he captained the football team and was twice champion athlete; in 1917-18 he was president of the Old Scotch Collegians' Club. From 17 Jack Leckie played football for Fitzroy as a rugged half-back and in 1895 was a member of their first premiership side. He studied medicine for two years at the University of Melbourne, but quarrelled with his father; after being 'cut off without a shilling' he went to Western Australia where he dug for gold at Kalgoorlie and continued his football career with Fremantle. After his father's death in 1897 Leckie returned to Alexandra to run the family farm and store. On 7 April 1898 at St Matthew's Anglican Church, Prahran, Melbourne, he married May Beatrix Johnston (d. 1910). He moved to Melbourne in 1912 and co-founded the firm of Leckie & Gray, lithographic printers and canister manufacturers.

Leckie was a member of the Alexandra Shire Council in 1900-11 and president in 1904-05. In 1906, as an Anti-Socialist Protectionist, he unsuccessfully contested the Federal seat of Mernda against Robert Harper [q.v.9]. He became known as a hard-working and very effective Liberal Party organizer but was unable to secure Liberal endorsement for a Federal seat. Instead, in December 1913, having been encouraged to stand by W. A. Watt [q.v.], he won a by-election for the Legislative Assembly seat of Benambra. Leckie's early political views reflected his rural background: 'every pound spent in developing the country was worth two to the state, every pound spent on city improvements was worth only one'. In 1916 he joined (Sir) John Bowser's [q.v.7] Economy Party. He married Hattie Martha Knight at Hawthorn with Anglican rites on 4 April 1917.

World War I drew Leckie into Federal politics. Rejected for military service on medical grounds, he became chairman of the State Recruiting Committee in 1917 and that year won Indi as a 'Win the War' Nationalist. His strong support for the war effort co-existed with his pronounced independent streak; he disagreed with Sir William Irvine [q.v.9] over the value of the second conscription campaign, perceiving a detrimental effect on recruitment, and criticized Prime Minister Hughes's [q.v.9] failure to fulfil his pledge to quit after the defeat of the 1917 referendum.

In December 1919 Leckie lost Indi to a Victorian Farmers' Union candidate and after failing to win the State seat of Upper Goulburn in 1921 he devoted himself to the cause of manufacturing. An executive member of the Industries Protection League and of the Chamber of Manufactures, he served as treasurer of the latter body. He was also a member of the Victorian Apprenticeship Commission. In 1934 he campaigned as a United Australia Party member and a representative of secondary industry to win a Senate seat.

During his first Senate term Leckie was occasionally sharply critical of his own governing party. In October 1940 he became minister assisting the ministers for trade and customs and labour and national service in the government of (Sir) Robert Menzies, whom his eldest daughter Pattie Maie had married in 1920. He was the first minister for aircraft production in June-October 1941 and minister assisting the minister for munitions between June and August. A loyal supporter of Menzies, Leckie became deputy opposition leader in the Senate on Menzies' return to party leadership in 1943. He was defeated in the September 1946 elections, but remained a senator until June 1947.

Leckie was a hard-hitting, honest and practical politician whose speeches were often laced with humour. His principal recreation was bushwalking. He died of cancer at his Hawthorn home on 25 September 1947, only three months after leaving parliament, and was cremated after a state funeral. He was survived by his wife and their son and by three daughters of his first marriage. His son Roland John, a member of the Legislative Assembly in 1950-52, became Victorian crown prosecutor and a judge of the County Court.

HATTIE MARTHA LECKIE (1886-1965) was born on 3 January 1886 at St Kilda, Melbourne, second daughter of Archibald Knight, merchant, and his wife Laura, née Mundy. Educated at a private school, she worked as a journalist, known professionally as Hattie Knight, in Sydney and Melbourne. In 1922 she joined the newly launched Melbourne *Sun-News Pictorial* as special feature writer and art critic. She later broadcast for the Australian Broadcasting Commission on various topics, including women's issues and current affairs, and founded the A.B.C. Women's Association. In 1931 a collection of her clearly written essays, described by Nettie Palmer as 'a plea for individualism in the arts and in society', was published as *Candour and cant*. She died at Cheltenham on 21 June 1965.

All About Books, 15 June 1931; *Scotch Collegian*, Nov 1947; *PD*(Cwlth), 1917-18, p 3070; *Argus*, 24 Dec 1913, 30, 31 Oct 1917, 4 Aug 1934, 26 Sept 1947; *Punch* (Melb), 5 Feb 1914; information from Judge Leckie, Melb.   GEOFF BROWNE

LE COUTEUR, PHILIP RIDGEWAY (1885-1958), educationist, was born on 26 June 1885 at Kyneton, Victoria, only son of Methodist parents George Thomas Le Couteur, pharmaceutical chemist, and his wife Fanny Byron, née Maling, both Victorian born. Educated at Middle Park State School and Warrnambool Academy, he served an apprenticeship in a pharmacy before entering the University of Melbourne in 1903 to study arts. In 1904 he won a Queen's College residential scholarship and, graduating B.A. in 1906 with the Hastie scholarship in logic and philosophy, became a tutor there. A triple blue in cricket, football and lawn tennis, he was also active in student entertainments.

After beginning a medical degree in 1907 Le Couteur won the Victorian Rhodes scholarship for 1908 and, taking out a Melbourne M.A., proceeded to University College, Oxford, where he completed the final classical school with third-class honours. He won an Oxford cricket blue and in 1911 a place in *Wisden* for making 160 runs and taking 11 wickets for 69 against Cambridge. He played regularly for Gentlemen versus Players, wrote for the *Windsor Magazine* on the psychology of cricket, and took a great interest in the development of 'that little bowling deceit', the googly. He was also a member of the Oxford String Quartette.

Le Couteur studied experimental psychology at the University of Bonn, Germany, under Professor O. Külpe and K. Bühler until early 1913 when he was appointed lecturer in mental and moral philosophy in the newly established University of Western Australia. He began duties in March after marrying Emma Holdsworth, the musically gifted daughter of E. H. Sugden [q.v.], master of Queen's, on 8 February at the Methodist Chapel, Bedale, Yorkshire. Le Couteur worked hard to establish his department which was the first in Australia to include a psychological and pedagogical laboratory. During World War I he captained a rifle club; consideration for his young family and for his father after the deaths of his mother and sister forced a reluctant decision against enlistment.

In 1918 Le Couteur succeeded Otto Krome [q.v.9] as headmaster of Methodist Ladies' College, Melbourne. The position proved difficult, as control of the school was shared with the foundation president W. H. Fitchett [q.v.8], a living legend and a bulwark against reform. For ten years Le Couteur served on various university committees and school councils and captained the Hawthorn-East Melbourne Cricket Club. Unsuccessful in applications for the headmastership of Sydney Grammar School in 1921 and the mastership of Queen's in 1927, he became head of Bishop Hale's [q.v.4] School, Perth, in 1929.

In 1931 he was appointed headmaster of Newington College, Sydney, succeeding C. J. Prescott [q.v.].

Le Couteur's term at Newington covered the difficult Depression and war years, yet saw a remarkable increase in pupils and the opening of a preparatory school, Wyvern House, in 1938. With his wife Le Couteur developed the school's musical life, encouraging the belief that 'it is manly to be cultured and refined'. On retirement in 1948 he took a counselling position with Communication Engineering Ltd and maintained an interest in the Fairbridge [q.v.8] Farm School movement.

A man for whom family ties and friendships were important, 'Pip' believed that 'education includes all those influences which enable us to get the most out of life'. He combined an ardent Platonism with Spartan simplicity. He was 'the traditional pipe-smoking, scholarly headmaster type . . . with a rare sense of humour . . . a dreamer . . . whose dream stuff could be (and often was) translated into reality'. He died at Gunnedah, New South Wales, on 30 June 1958 and was buried in Rookwood Methodist cemetery. His wife, two daughters and three sons survived him.

D. S. Macmillan, *Newington College 1863-1963* (Syd, 1963); F. Alexander, *Campus at Crawley* (Melb, 1963); R. M. Heath, *A short history of the Le Couteur and Sugden families* (Gunnedah, NSW, 1979); A. G. T. Zainu'ddin, *They dreamt of a school* (Melb, 1982); *Aust Q*, Dec 1945; *SMH*, 5 Sept 1931, 10 Dec 1948; *Bulletin*, 16 July 1958; M. D. Hancock, Headmasters of Hale School 1890-1959 (typescript Battye Lib); file 0422/255 (Univ WA Archives); Monash papers (NL).

A. G. THOMSON ZAINU'DDIN

LEE, ALFRED (1858-1923), businessman and book collector, was born on 8 June 1858 near Dublin, eldest surviving son of Frederick Norman Lee, army officer, and his wife Elizabeth, née Finlay. His father, who had served in the Crimean War with the 19th Regiment, received a land grant in New Zealand and in 1867 took his wife and three children there. Alfred attended Christchurch and Auckland Grammar schools and in 1874 was sent to Sydney with £10.

Soon after his arrival he was employed as a commercial traveller by Enoch Taylor & Co., boot and shoe importers; he became manager for Australia in 1884 and was senior partner in 1888-1923. He travelled widely on the firm's behalf. At St Clement's Anglican Church, Yass, he married MINNIE DODDS (1860-1938) on 10 March 1879. They lived first at The Willows, Yass, then at North Sydney. Early in 1886 they bought Glen Roona, Old South Head Road (later Penkivil Street), Bondi, where they lived out their lives.

In his early thirties Lee began collecting Australiana, influenced by his friend Frank Bladen, editor of *Historical Records of New South Wales*. His collection attracted the attention of another close friend David Scott Mitchell [q.v.5], especially when his London agents beat Mitchell to some prize such as the handwritten journal of Sir Joseph Banks [q.v.1], acquired by Lee in 1888. Mrs Lee and Mitchell's confidante Rose Scott [q.v.] were also friends. Mitchell urged Lee to give his library of over 10 000 volumes to the nation at the same time as Mitchell himself. Lee, married with five children, felt unable to do this but agreed in December 1906 to sell his collection to Mitchell, who gladly paid him £5700—cost price plus 2½ per cent (according to Lee's descendants). He handed over 'every volume, pamphlet, leaflet, print, portrait, drawing and medallion bearing on Australasia that I was possessed of'. Unlike Mitchell, the Lees had made their collection available to such scholars as Professor E. E. Morris [q.v.5] of Melbourne and Professor Hocken from New Zealand, and missed such visitors.

In 1901 Lee, with Bladen and Mitchell, had been a founder and in 1901-04 a vice-president of the (Royal) Australian Historical Society; Mrs Lee was its first female member. He was also a member of the Royal Society of New South Wales from 1906. As a young man he had played Rugby football for the Waratah Club in 1877 and from 1883 was a trustee of the Sydney Cricket Ground; he was an 'ardent' cyclist and later a horticulturist.

Widely read, Minnie Lee was a member of the Society of Women Writers of New South Wales. During (and after) World War I she was a hard-working member of the executive of the Australian Red Cross Society and was honorary director of the Lady Mayoress's Red Cross Sewing Guild which had some 2000 workers. She was also active in Sydney in the Citizens' Association and the National Council of Women. A warm and gracious hostess in her own home and as honorary secretary of the Victoria League's hospitality committee, she welcomed overseas visitors, who appreciated her kindness.

Lee died at Bondi on 2 August 1923 and was buried in the Anglican section of Waverley cemetery. His estate was valued for probate at over £61 000. He was survived by his wife, son and three of his four daughters.

SMH, 21 June 1919, 27 Apr 1929, 29, 30 Sept 1938; *Daily Telegraph* (Syd), 11 Aug 1923; N. S. G. Butler, A collection of Australian historical books amidst other achievements (MS, ML).

K. A. JOHNSON

LEE, BETSY (BESSIE) (1860-1950), temperance evangelist, was born on 10 June 1860 at Daylesford, Victoria, daughter of Henry Vickery, butcher and miner, and his wife Emma Susan, née Dungey. Her mother died of consumption in 1868 and her father was unable to keep his five children together. Bessie was sent to Melbourne relations who mistreated her during their bouts of drunkenness. In 1869 she went to Enoch's Point and the care of another uncle and his wife of stern principles and no sympathy for the young.

The lonely child had little formal schooling, but she read voraciously, began to write verse and also experienced religious conversion before her teens. A miner, Robert Lee, introduced her at 17 to his younger brother Harrison (Harry), whom she married on 14 March 1880 at St Peter's Church of England, Melbourne. The Lees lived mainly in a depressed area of Richmond. For most of his life Harrison Lee was a shift worker with the railways, which left the young and childless Bessie with time on her hands and a propensity to dwell on her constant ill health.

The marriage was not a success. Lee did not approve of his wife's ecstatic social conscience. She began Sunday school classes and sick visiting. She toured slums, refuges and gaols with Dr John Singleton [q.v.6]. She went to hear the evangelist, Mrs Hampson, about 1883 and soon afterwards launched on her own career of public speaking. In 1884 the American temperance lecturers, Booth and Glover of the Blue Ribbon Gospel Temperance Army, won her into the active prohibition camp. She helped to pioneer the Woman's Christian Temperance Union in Victoria in 1887 but fell into disfavour because of her uncomfortable belief in the sinfulness of all sexual intercourse that had no procreative intention. Leaving the executive of the W.C.T.U. she accepted the sponsorship of the powerful Victorian Alliance for the Suppression of the Liquor Traffic in 1890-96, and fought district local option battles over whether numbers of hotels should be reduced, maintained or increased. Besides incessant travelling, speech-making and pledge-taking, she wrote copiously for daily newspapers and the temperance press. She acknowledged heavenly direction as a speaker and was admired for her fluency and sincerity; she reacted well under pressure and attracted a following, mainly of women, who slaved for her. With no income of her own, she was dependent on the generosity of temperance supporters.

1896 saw the first of her countless trips abroad, principally to Britain, New Zealand and the United States of America. Harrison Lee died on 17 January 1908. When this news reached Andrew Cowie, a well-to-do farmer of Winton, New Zealand, he wrote offering marriage. A widower with a large grown-up family, Cowie had been attracted by Mrs Lee's effective campaigning. He agreed to her terms and, after a brief resistance, Bessie gave in and they were married at Winton on 17 November 1908. Auckland became Mrs Lee Cowie's headquarters between globe-trotting expeditions. Andrew Cowie died on 10 December 1928 aged 82, and Bessie entered the final phase of her career. In New Zealand, where she was a foundation member of the United Labour Party, she had resumed office in the W.C.T.U. and was appointed a world missionary. She spent some years in Hawaii before settling at Pasadena, California. In 1947 her last campaign brought her national headlines in America. She died at Pasadena on 18 April 1950. Her written works include *Marriage and heredity* (Melbourne, 1893), *One of Australia's daughters: an autobiography* (London, 1906) and *One of God's lamplighters: incidents in my life work* (London, 1909).

J. Cocker and J. M. Murray (eds), *Temperance and prohibition in New Zealand* (Lond, 1930); *Alliance Record*, 1 Feb 1902; *Pasadena Star News*, 19, 20 Apr 1950; *New Zealand Herald*, 24 Apr 1950; A. M. Mitchell, Temperance and the liquor question in later nineteenth century Victoria (M.A. thesis, Univ Melb, 1966).   ANN M. MITCHELL

LEE, CHARLES ALFRED (1842-1926), storekeeper and politician, was born on 13 November 1842 at Parramatta, New South Wales, sixth surviving son of Benjamin Lee and his wife Lucy Ann, née Poulton; his elder brother was Benjamin [q.v.5]. Educated at West Maitland Grammar School, Charles entered a Maitland store, rising to the position of partner in his early twenties. On 18 July 1865 at Penrith he married Clara Jane Tindale.

A successful merchant, Lee moved to Tenterfield in 1869 for its bracing climate and purchased the Maryland Store. He served as an alderman on the first Tenterfield Municipal Council in 1872-76 and was mayor in 1875-76. Appointed a justice of the peace in 1875, Lee held many local offices such as president of the Tenterfield Prince Albert Memorial Hospital board and of the School of Arts, and coroner in 1873-76. As chairman of the Tenterfield Railway League in the 1880s, he corresponded with Sir Henry Parkes [q.v.5] and, retiring from his business, succeeded Parkes to the Legislative Assembly seat of Tenterfield in 1884.

A staunch and consistent free trader, Lee was sympathetic to the rural interest and the small selector, and joined the Farmers and Settlers' Association. He captured public attention on 7 December 1893 when he carried an adjournment motion which censured the attorney-general (Sir) Edmund Barton [q.v.7] and the minister of justice Richard O'Connor [q.v.] for accepting private legal briefs to act against the State Railway Department. They immediately resigned and parliament was prorogued. Lee was minister of justice from 27 August 1898 to 3 July 1899, when he became secretary for public works until Reid's [q.v.] free-trade ministry fell on 13 September. Seen as 'remarkably humanitarian', Lee introduced prison libraries, lights in prison cells and nightdresses for female prisoners. He sat on the royal commission on city railway extension in 1897 and the Parliamentary Standing Committee on Public Works in 1889-92 and 1894-99.

In April 1901 Lee was elected as a compromise leader of the newly formed Liberal Party of New South Wales after the controversial withdrawal of the favoured candidate (Sir) Joseph Carruthers [q.v.7]. Lee inherited a divided party, unprepared for the elections ten weeks later. Respected by those around him, he was, however, hampered by his 'quiet, unostentatious manner' as leader of the Opposition and the Liberals were defeated soundly on 3 July. A 'staunch and reliable party man' but 'no fighter' in Opposition, Lee held the party together for the return of Carruthers, then resigned as leader because of ill health on 17 September 1902.

From 30 August 1904 to 20 October 1910 Lee was secretary for public works in the Liberal-Reform governments of Carruthers and (Sir) Charles Wade [q.v.]. With a tremendous capacity for work and a heartfelt commitment to rural development, he instigated and presided over an extensive public works programme. In January 1905 he chaired the Water Conservation and Irrigation Conference which initiated the Murrumbidgee Irrigation Scheme, involving the building of Burrinjuck dam and the creation of the town of Leeton, to which he gave his name. The many public works with which he was associated included the Cataract dam for the Sydney water supply, negotiation of the sale of W. Sandford's [q.v.] iron and steel works at Lithgow to Charles Hoskins [q.v.9], and the expansion of the State rail network.

Lee would brook no dissension in his department, as was revealed by his removal of Thomas Keele (by having him appointed to the Sydney Harbour Trust) as chairman of the Metropolitan Board of Water Supply and Sewerage in March 1908 for public criticism of government policy; Lee was intractable throughout the heated controversy that followed. He was a consistent opponent of female enfranchisement because, he argued, women as a class were not taxpayers; it was, ironically, held to be the female vote that saved him from electoral defeat in 1907 and

1910. During his later years in parliament he remained a champion of the small man on the land and a stern critic of centralism. When he stood down in February 1920 he had represented his constituents for thirty-six years.

Suffering from chronic nephritis, Lee lived in quiet retirement at Claremont, Tenterfield, till his death on 16 August 1926. He was buried with Anglican rites in the Tenterfield cemetery. Three daughters and two sons survived him; two of his sons were killed in World War I. His estate was valued for probate at £14 042. The *Daily Telegraph* had acknowledged as early as 1894 that Lee's 'parliamentary career has been marked by a sterling integrity to principle'. He was not to betray that integrity for the rest of his political life: few politicians could have claimed so much.

J. C. Wharton (ed), *The jubilee history of Parramatta* (Parramatta, 1911); W. F. Morrison, *The Aldine centennial history of New South Wales* (Syd, 1890); *T&CJ*, 4 June 1887, 7 Aug 1907; *SMH*, 31 Jan 1891, 17 Apr, 22 June, 2 July 1901, 17, 18 Sept 1902, 18 Aug 1926; *Daily Telegraph* (Syd), 5 July 1894; *Tenterfield Star*, 19 Aug 1926; *Aust Worker*, 25 Aug 1926; *Bulletin* (Syd), 26 Aug 1926; J. H. Carruthers autobiography (typescript, ML and NL); Parkes correspondence (ML).   A. R. BUCK

LEE, GEORGE LEONARD (1860-1939), soldier, was born on 25 June 1860 at West Maitland, New South Wales, son of John Lee, draper and later merchant, and his wife, Mary Ann née Eckford. Educated at Sauchu House School, West Maitland, and Armidale Grammar School, he worked for a while in the family business, John Lee & Sons, West Maitland. He was a well-known horseman and sportsman, keen on polo.

On 4 October 1889 Lee was commissioned in the local troop of the New South Wales Lancers and during the maritime strike of 1890 acted as adjutant of the partially paid cavalry and mounted rifles who were enrolled as special police in Sydney. Next year he was sent to England for training and by October 1892 had qualified in an equitation course at the Cavalry School, Canterbury, at an Army Service Corps school and at the School of Musketry, Hythe; he also trained for several months with the 20th Hussars at Aldershot. After returning home he joined the New South Wales Permanent Military Forces in December 1892 as a captain and from then until June 1902 was adjutant of the New South Wales Lancers. The New South Wales Mounted Brigade's book of confidential reports contains laudatory references to him. During that time he was also acting staff officer, Mounted Brigade, for over two years, and commandant of the Cavalry School. On 2 January 1896 he married Emma Onus

Town at St Ann's Anglican Church, Home-bush, Sydney; they had no children.

On the outbreak of the South African War in October 1899 the New South Wales Lancers mobilized a draft to go from Sydney to reinforce their squadron which was proceeding to the war from England after training there. Lee, now a major, was in charge of the draft which joined the squadron in South Africa on 6 December. Lee then took command of the Lancer contingent from Captain C. F. Cox [q.v.8]. His unit, part of Lieut-General French's force, was employed in operations around Colesberg, the relief of Kimberley, and actions at Paardeberg, Poplar Grove, Driefontein, Zand River, Johannesburg, Pretoria, Diamond Hill and in the Transvaal east of Pretoria to 26 October 1900 when the squadron's year of service ended. For his work in South Africa Lee was mentioned in dispatches and awarded the Distinguished Service Order.

Resuming duty with the Australian Military Forces, Lee was assistant adjutant general and chief staff officer in Victoria in 1902-07. Appointed to the Administrative and Instructional Staff in 1904, he became a lieut-colonel in 1909, having held brevet rank since 1902. He served in New South Wales from June 1907, and was commandant in Tasmania in 1911-12 and in Queensland in 1912-17. After that he was temporarily in command in New South Wales, with the honorary rank of major general from July 1918 until he was transferred to the retired list on 13 May 1920 as honorary lieut-general. He was aide-de-camp to the governor-general in 1915-20, and in 1917 was appointed C.M.G.

Warm tributes to Lee's personality and ability include praise of his fine horsemanship, geniality and ripe judgement; there was 'no hypocrisy in his make up' and he would not tolerate it in anyone under him. In retirement he worked two oyster leases at Port Stephens, New South Wales. He was a member of the Union Club, Sydney. Survived by his wife, he died on 13 April 1939 at Burwood and was cremated with Anglican rites.

Aust Defence Dept, *Official records of the Australian military contingents to the war in South Africa*, P. L. Murray ed (Melb, 1911); *London Gazette*, 23 Jan 1917; *Navy, Army, Air and Munitions J*, 13 April 1939; Diary of Major G. L. Lee, Oct 1899-Feb 1900, *and* Letter-book of NSW Mounted Brigade 1894-96 held by P. V. Vernon, Lindfield, Syd; file of newspaper cuttings on G. L. Lee held by Army Museum, Victoria Barracks, Paddington, Syd; personal information from Mr R. B. Lee, Newport Beach, Syd.   P. V. VERNON

LEE, IDA LOUISA (1865-1943), historical geographer, was born on 11 February 1865 at Kelso, near Bathurst, New South Wales,

third of eight children of George Lee [q.v.5], grazier, and his wife Emily Louisa, née Kite, both born at Kelso; she was a granddaughter of William Lee [q.v.2]. With her five sisters, she grew up at Leeholme, Kelso, and rode to school; she became a keen horsewoman.

On a visit to England, Ida Lee married Charles John Bruce Marriott (1861-1936) on 14 October 1891 at the parish church, Felixstowe, Suffolk. Marriott had captained Cambridge, Blackheath and England at Rugby football. In 1892-1903 he taught and was a housemaster at Highgate School, Hampstead, where Ida's only child was born in October 1892. She took part in school life and in 1897 published a slender volume, *The bush fire and other verses*. Marriott was secretary of the Rugby Football Union in 1907-24; they divided their time between London and Suffolk, where he was a small landowner. Her sister Edith married J. J. W. Power [q.v.] and lived in the Channel Islands.

Mrs Marriott spent her spare time delving in British libraries, notably at the Admiralty, and discovered log-books, journals and lost charts. In 1906 *The coming of the British to Australia, 1788 to 1829* appeared under her maiden name. Articles in the *Tasmanian Mail*, *Empire Review* and *Geographical Journal* followed. She next turned her attention to the forgotten navigator (Sir) John Hayes [q.v.1], and from 'letters, family records, official notices and newspapers of the period' compiled *Commodore Sir John Hayes, his voyage and life* (1912). In October 1913 she was elected a fellow of the Royal Geographical Society of London and in 1918 the second honorary fellow of the Royal Australian Historical Society.

Her husband and son both served with the British Expeditionary Force in France in World War I. Ida continued her researches and published *The logbooks of the 'Lady Nelson'* (1915), and *Captain Bligh's second voyage to the South Sea* (1920). In *Early explorers in Australia* (1925), despite some errors in transcribing Allan Cunningham's [q.v.1] journal, she displayed considerable knowledge of 'systematic botany and botanical taxonomy' and updated Cunningham's nomenclature. Her last book, *The voyage of the Caroline*, appeared in 1927, but she continued to correspond with museums and libraries. In an article in *Geographical Journal* (April 1934), she argued that the British first sighted Australia in 1682 when the *Trial* was wrecked on the Tryal rocks off the West Australian coast: she had found the original letter from the ship's captain in the India Office.

As a young woman, Ida Marriott had been photographed wearing a feather-boa and frivolous hat; she had an elegant figure, widely spaced eyes, regular features and a warm smile. In her late sixties, when she lived at the

Dower House, Sizewell, she was described as 'a charming lady . . . usually dressed in black in a rather Victorian style, but with great dignity and "presence" '. Survived by her son, she died at Norwich on 3 October 1943.

Although A. W. Jose [q.v.9] in 1906 chided her for errors in *The coming of the British* and later scholars have indicated that she occasionally failed to make it clear when she made omissions, contemporary reviewers warmly welcomed her books: C. H. Bertie [q.v.7] wrote that 'Mrs. Marriott's books are distinguished for the amount of original research work she has put into them'. Ida Lee's scholarly output was unusual for a woman of her time and background.

The Home, 1 Mar 1932, p 37, 55; *Argus*, 28 Feb 1913, 10 July 1915; *SMH*, 12 Sept 1925; *A'sian*, 9 Apr 1921, 25 July 1925; *The Times*, 28 Dec 1936; Ida Marriott papers (ML); information from W. G. McMinn, Univ Newcastle, NSW; family information.   MARTHA RUTLEDGE

LEE, JOHN HENRY ALEXANDER (1853-1927), sailor, surveyor and military engineer, was born on 13 May 1853 in Calcutta, India, son of David Henry Lee, merchant and tea-planter, and his wife Clara, née Moubray. He was a grandson of the celebrated polymath Dr John Lee, principal of the University of Edinburgh. He left school in Britain at 14 to train for the merchant service. After three years in H.M.S. *Worcester*, at the end of which he gained a first class extra certificate, he joined the firm of Devitt & Moore whose fleet plied between Britain and the Australian colonies. He served seven years with this line, passing the examination for ship's mate.

In 1877 Lee gave up the sea, settled in New South Wales, and found work as a surveyor in country districts. In 1879 he joined the Surveyor-General's Department as a draughts-man in the Sydney office. On 15 September 1880, at St Paul's Church, Melbourne, he married Anna Maria Anderson, a 23-year-old Scotswoman who had only recently arrived in the colony after having been shipwrecked; they had two daughters.

In 1883 Lee was commissioned as a lieutenant to command the newly raised New South Wales Naval Artillery Volunteers. Five years later he was given the task of choosing men for the army's proposed submarine mining unit, and was himself appointed to command it, as a captain. In 1891 he was sent to England for training with the Royal Engineers. He returned with satisfactory certificates from the electrical and the submarine mining courses as well as from that on the Brennan [q.v.3] torpedo which was widely used in coastal defence. In January 1894 he

was promoted major, his command being No.3 (Submarine Mining) Company of the New South Wales Engineers.

On the outbreak of war in South Africa in 1899 Lee applied to join a contingent from Australia but could not be spared from submarine mining duties. In January 1902 he was allowed to join the 1st Battalion, Australian Commonwealth Horse, as second-in-command. The regiment reached South Africa too late to take part in the major campaigns, but was used in May to clear scattered Boer units. There was little fighting. For a period Lee acted as brigade major to the column commander. Early in June he was promoted lieutcolonel to command the 1st Battalion, but hostilities were at an end and the unit was disbanded. He reverted to major and returned to his former unit in Sydney, by this time a company of the Australian Engineers.

In April 1903 Lee was promoted lieutcolonel and assumed command of the Corps of Australian Engineers in New South Wales. His command included two field companies, a submarine mining company and an electric company. He served on the defence committee of the 2nd Military District, and in 1906 was member of a committee to consider all Australian coastal defences. That year he was seconded in his corps and appointed to command the 4th Military District, with headquarters in Adelaide. His term was twice extended until October 1911 when he was placed on the retired list with an honorary colonelcy.

Lee was appointed inspector of rifle ranges for the Commonwealth. When war broke out in August 1914 he was made transport officer in Sydney, handling the embarkation of units of the Australian Imperial Force. He filled this appointment until the end of July 1918. Lee died at the home of one of his daughters, in Auckland, New Zealand, on 18 December 1927. He was buried in Weikumete cemetery with Anglican rites. His record shows that he was competent and versatile. It was his misfortune that he had so few chances of active service.

H. T. Burgess (ed), *Cyclopedia of South Australia*, 1 (Adel, 1907); Aust Defence Dept, *Official records of the Australian military contingents to the war in South Africa*, P. L. Murray ed (Melb, 1911); R. McNicoll, *The Royal Australian Engineers, 1835 to 1902* (Canb, 1977); Roy Com into the military service of New South Wales, Report, *PP* (NSW), 1892-93, 7, p 881; *Argus*, 21 Dec 1927.   RONALD McNICOLL

LEE, JOHN ROBERT (1885-1957), engineer and politician, was born on 19 October 1885 at Hedleyhope, Lanchester, Durham, England, son of James Lee, coalminer, and his wife Jessie, née Watson. Educated at Lead-gate, Jack trained as a plumber and worked for the Weardale and Consett Water Co., Dur-ham. In 1910-11 he studied for the Methodist ministry at Cliff College, Sheffield, and prob-ably migrated to New South Wales late in 1912. He served as a probationary Methodist minister at Yanco and Gilgandra from 1913 to 1914 when he abandoned his vocation and took up wheat-farming.

A member of the Gilgandra Rifle Club, Lee enlisted in the Australian Imperial Force at Gilgandra on 9 October 1915 and was prom-inently associated with the 'Coo-ee', 'Walla-bies' and 'North Coaster' recruiting marches. After training at the Royal Military College, Duntroon, he was commissioned on 25 July 1916. He embarked on 31 October and served with the 21st Battalion in France. Promoted lieutenant on 17 May 1917 he was injured on 14 November and returned to Aus-tralia in May next year. He worked in a re-cruiting depot until demobilized in Septem-ber, but remained on the reserve of offi-cers.

Lee set up as a waterworks and sanitary engineer in Sydney and on 28 February 1920 at St Andrew's Cathedral married Gladys Irene Dickinson; they were childless. Defeated as a Nationalist for the Federal seat of Hunter in 1919, he was elected next year to the Legislative Assembly for Botany which he represented until 1927 when he won Drum-moyne. He was lively as Nationalist whip in 1922-27 and served as chairman of the select committee on the administration of the Hous-ing Board in 1923-24.

From October 1927 to November 1930 Lee was minister of justice in (Sir) Thomas Bavin's [q.v.7] government. He investigated the perennial problem of those gaoled for fail-ure to pay maintenance and devised a scheme to employ them at the basic wage, building roads. However in February 1929 the plan caused a storm of protest from the Kuring-gai Chase Trust and the unions—Jack Bailey [q.v.7], president of the Australian Workers' Union, described it as 'a return to the convict system'. Lee doggedly continued with his scheme. He was also criticized for the early release of prisoners.

Defeated at the general election in Novem-ber 1930, Lee regained Drummoyne in 1932 and held the seat until 1941. He was a State council-member of the National and United Australia parties in 1931-33 and 1934-37. Disgruntled at his exclusion from (Sir) Ber-tram Stevens's [q.v.] ministries, he joined other malcontents in the U.A.P. in constantly needling the government, and vigorously attacked (Sir) Michael Bruxner's [q.v.7] metropolitan transport policy and the un-popular Gaming and Betting Act amendment bill. On 27 July 1939 Lee crossed the floor and

voted for a Labor censure motion which Stevens narrowly survived. On 3 August Stevens was defeated when Lee and nine others voted for E. Spooner's [q.v.] motion recommending a new financial policy.

Later that year Lee chaired the select com-mittee on the conduct and administration of trotting in New South Wales. Called up in July 1940, he assisted with recruiting and in 1941-43 served as a staff captain with the Citizen Military Forces.

Handsome, with regular features and wide-set eyes, Lee was a member of the Commer-cial Travellers' Club, and enjoyed golf, bowls and gardening. He was an alderman on Drum-moyne Municipal Council in 1934-37 and mayor in 1936, a director of John Thompson & Co. Pty Ltd and Ferrier & Dickinson Ltd, and a member of the New South Wales Prot-estant Federation. In retirement he was 'a frequent visitor to the House, particularly during the luncheon adjournment'. Late in life he moved to Gordon. He died at Pymble on 2 November 1957 and was cremated with Anglican rites. His wife survived him.

D. Aitkin, *The colonel* (Canb, 1969); *PD* (NSW), 5 Nov 1957, p 1513; Methodist Church of Aus-tralia, *Minutes*, 1913, 1914; *SMH*, 7 Mar 1922, 27 May 1925, 27 Mar, 19 Oct, 22 Nov 1928, 15 Jan, 18 Feb 1929, 20, 21, 27 Feb, 17, 30 Mar, 7 May, 8 July 1930, 13 June 1932, 26 Aug 1938, 30 Mar, 28 July, 4 Aug 1939, 4 Apr, 2 July 1940, 7 July, 13 Aug 1943; *Mudgee Guardian*, 6 Sept 1934.

MARTHA RUTLEDGE

LEE, MARY (1821-1909), suffragist, was born on 14 February 1821 in Monaghan, Ire-land, daughter of John Walsh. In 1844 she married George(?) Lee, organist and vicar-choral of Armagh Cathedral; they had four sons and three daughters. In 1879 Mary, widowed, sailed with her daughter Evelyn for Adelaide to nurse her sick son John Benjamin; after his death next year they remained, Mary becoming devoted to 'dear Adelaide' which she could not in any case afford to leave.

For the rest of her life Mary Lee, 'once the slip of an old red-hot Tory stem', worked single mindedly for political and social reform. Her qualities of leadership, conviction and perseverance matched the social and political climate of late nineteenth-century South Aus-tralia. Initially interested in Jewish coloniza-tion, she later became ladies' secretary of Rev. J. C. Kirby's [q.v.5] Social Purity Society working for legal changes in women's sexual and social status. Through the society's inten-sive lobbying and its stimulus of public and parliamentary debate, substantial alterations, including raising the age of consent to six-teen, were incorporated in the Criminal Law Consolidation Amendment Act (1885). Kirby gave Lee the principal credit for this. She and other Purity Society members, recognizing that women's suffrage was essential to their further improved status, inaugurated the South Australian Women's Suffrage League in July 1888. Through her work in the league, initially as co-secretary and soon as secretary, Mary Lee played a major part in South Australian political history. She saw the suffrage as her 'crowning task' and, under (Sir) Edward Stirling's [q.v.6] presidency, steered the campaign skilfully, combining her experience of political processes with her knowledge of women's social disabilities and of the value of publicity to awaken public interest and understanding.

Unafraid of controversy, determined and sometimes abrasive, she publicized her commitment in the *Register*. 'If I die before it is achieved, like Mary Tudor and Calais, "Women's enfranchisement" shall be found engraved upon my heart'. She regarded manhood suffrage as 'only half a victory' and female suffrage as 'the pivot on which turns the whole question of the moral, social and industrial status of women'. The league's objects from July 1888 remained simply enfranchisement on equal terms with men, without claiming access to parliamentary seats. From 1891 Lee worked harmoniously with the league's second president, Lady Colton; Stirling and Catherine Helen Spence [q.v.6] became vice-presidents.

In frequent speeches, newspaper articles and letters, Mary Lee illustrated her case by using historical, literary and biblical allusions; this did not prevent the 'abuse' and 'obloquy' of opponents, most of whom argued on traditional grounds against women voting. Short, plump and erect, she went energetically about the city, suburbs and country, speaking eloquently at league meetings and socials, at Democratic clubs and, despite her dislike of total abstinence, at Woman's Christian Temperance Union meetings. She planned the league's wider strategies and also collected shilling subscriptions and organized petitions and deputations. A practical Christian, she had adopted the social reformist ideas of the Primitive Methodist minister Hugh Gilmore [q.v.4].

Acting on her concern at working women's conditions, and simultaneously promoting the suffrage cause, she proposed the formation of women's trades unions at a public meeting on sweating in December 1889. After the Working Women's Trades Union was founded next year she was secretary for two years; her visits to clothing factories and workshops, to persuade employers to adopt the union's log of prices, met with some success. As the union's vice-president in 1893 she was delegate to the Trades and Labor Council where she worked on a sub-committee examining sweating in the clothing trades with Augusta Zadow [q.v.] and on the Distressed Women's and Children's Committee, which distributed relief clothes and food to women suffering in the economic depression. She was also a member of the ladies' committee of the Female Refuge.

A supporter of the single tax, Mary Lee responded fluently, proclaiming women's suffrage, to a toast to the ladies at a farewell to Henry George [q.v.4] in 1890. She corresponded with New Zealanders and with women in other colonies, notably Lady Windeyer in Sydney, whom she advised on organizing the Womanhood Suffrage League of New South Wales on South Australian league principles, and Rose Scott [q.v.].

In parliament Stirling's successful 1885 resolution for female suffrage was followed, from 1886, by seven suffrage bills, five having a property qualification; six failed to gain the required statutory majority. Lee joined league deputations to premiers Playford [q.v.], Holder [q.v.9] and Downer [q.v.8] and from 1889 worked untiringly on numerous parliamentary petitions. With United Labor Party backing from 1891, the issue was approaching realization. Premier Kingston's [q.v.9] minister for education presented a female suffrage bill in 1893; an attached referendum condition caused its failure and her patience snapped. *Quiz* deplored her hot temper when she called the Labor Party 'a lot of nincompoops'. Kingston acknowledged public demand and political pressure for female suffrage; his government presented an unencumbered bill in July next year. Mary Lee had organized a colony-wide petition which yielded 11 600 signatures; the document—400 feet (122 m) long—was presented to the House of Assembly in August. Women 'deluged' members with telegrams and thronged the galleries; over fifty members spoke, flippantly or seriously. The Constitution Amendment Act was passed on 18 December 1894, making South Australian women the first in Australia to gain the parliamentary vote, and on the same terms as men. Additionally, it gave them the right to postal votes and to stand for parliament; these were unique provisions anywhere.

Mary Lee, exhausted but jubilant, received congratulatory letters from Kingston and Chief Secretary (Sir) J. H. Gordon [q.v.9]. In 1895 two trade unions nominated her to stand for parliament; she declined, preferring to work 'on the side of right . . . unfettered by pledge or obligation to any party whatever'. On her 75th birthday in 1896, at the Adelaide Town Hall Kingston handed her a purse of fifty sovereigns, publicly donated through the Mary Lee Testimonial Fund, with a 'handsomely bound and artistically engrossed' address which acknowledged that the achievement of women's suffrage 'is mainly due to your persistent advocacy and unwearied exertions'. At public meetings before the March 1896 elections Lee advised women on their voting duties.

That year the government appointed her the first female official visitor to the lunatic asylums and she performed this task with courage and compassion for twelve years. In 1898 she backed the medical superintendent on the contentious issue of Paris Nesbit's [q.v.] release from Parkside Lunatic Asylum, maintaining that special provision should be made for such brilliant and disturbed patients. She visited the Destitute Asylum regularly as a friend to the inmates.

As her financial resources dwindled, Lee asked (Sir) Josiah Symon [q.v.] to arrange the sale of her library. In 1902 Kirby initiated an appeal for her relief in the *Express and Telegraph* and the *Australian Woman's Sphere*, but with poor response. Kirby observed that many had benefited from her work, but her advanced views and outspokenness had not made her widely loved. Although her daughter Evelyn worked in the Telegraph Department, Mary's last years were blighted by poverty; she complained bitterly to Rose Scott that her public work had all been at her own expense. She died in her North Adelaide home on 18 September 1909 and was buried in the Wesleyan cemetery, Walkerville, with her son Ben. Her daughter and a son in England survived her. Her work remained unrecorded until 1980, her only memorial her tombstone, a small white marble scroll, engraved 'Late Hon. Sec. Women's Suffrage League of S.A.'.

H. Jones, *Nothing seemed impossible* (Brisb, 1985);United Trades and Labor Council of SA, *Minutes*, 5 May 1891, 17 Mar, 5 May, 7 July 1893; *Govt Gazette* (SA), 20 Feb 1896; *Quiz and the Lantern*, 24 Nov 1893, 20 Feb 1896; *Aust Woman's Sphere*, 10 May 1902; *Register*, 21, 27 July 1888, 30 June 1896, 20 Sept 1909; *Observer* (Adel), 22 Mar 1890, 6 June 1891, 21 May 1892, 14 Sept 1895, 26 Feb, 14 Dec 1898, 25 Sept 1909; *Express and Telegraph*, 7 Apr 1902; H. Jones, Women's education in South Australia (Ph.D. thesis, Univ Adel, 1980); United Trades and Labor Council of SA, Minutes, 5 May 1891, 17 Mar, 5 May, 7 July 1893 (SAA); Adel Lunatic Asylums, copy of minutes from visitors' book, 1897-1907 (SAA); R. Scott correspondence, and Lady Windeyer papers (ML); J. Symon letters (NL).   HELEN JONES

LEE, SIR WALTER HENRY, (1874-1963), wheelwright, farmer and premier, was born on 27 April 1874 at Longford, Tasmania, son of Robert Lee, wheelwright, and his wife Margaret, née Flood. He was educated at Longford State School to primary level and went into his father's business at Longford.

On 17 August 1898 he married Margaret Matilda Barnes at Longford. After 1900 with his brother James he ran the firm of Lee Bros which was well known in northern Tasmania for its wagons and farm implements. Lee sat in the House of Assembly for the rural division of Wilmot from April 1909 to November 1946, first as an Anti-Socialist, then as a Liberal, and later as a Nationalist. His obvious skills in political and parliamentary affairs soon brought rewards, and he was successively whip and in 1915 leader of the Opposition.

During the 1916 election Lee and the Liberals attacked the Labor government's 'reckless' spending of public money and promised a more 'businesslike' administration. Lee made no promises concerning public works, for he claimed that money for such matters was needed for the Empire's cause, but liberalization of land laws was promised 'in order to stop the flow of our young men into the overcrowded cities'. Despite failing to exceed Labor's total vote, the Liberals won half the seats and Lee became premier and minister for education (15 April 1916-12 August 1922), chief secretary until 31 March 1922 and treasurer from 1 April 1922. The first Lee government was a talented group containing two former premiers (Sir Neil Lewis and W. B. Propsting [qq.v.]), and one future premier (J. B. Hayes [q.v.9]). Its first term was relatively plain sailing for a conservative wartime government. In the 1919 election Lee led the recently formed National party to victory over the Labor Party by 14 per cent of the vote, though winning only 16 of 30 seats. He was knighted in 1920 and appointed K.C.M.G. in 1922.

The weak condition of the Tasmanian economy became evident soon after the war. Manufacturing was at a low ebb, wartime inflation had been severe, and there was a large deficit. The Lee government promoted hydro-electric power generation and new industries, though Lee was criticized for undercharging for electricity used by these industries such as the woollen mills at Launceston. The government also established a popular soldier settlement scheme. However, the economic problems were intractable and at the June 1922 election the government's precarious position was emphasized by a larger deficit, an inefficient public service and a premier criticized for his increasingly autocratic style of government. In addition the new Country Party led by E. F. B. Blyth attacked Lee personally in an exceedingly bitter campaign. The result was a split anti-Labor vote with the Country Party holding the balance of power. When parliament resumed the Labor party unsuccessfully moved a vote of no confidence, but Lee resigned and advised the governor to send for

Blyth. Blyth arranged a meeting of both parties and J. B. Hayes became premier of Tasmania's first coalition government. Lee remained as treasurer and minister for education. His term as premier had been a record.

After a year in office unable to resolve the economic situation, Hayes resigned in August 1923 in favour of Lee who secured an adjournment of parliament and became premier, treasurer and minister for railways. In October he stunned Tasmanians by announcing a drastic financial programme. It included public service retrenchment, abolition of the agent-general's office, a reduction in the number of members of parliament, introduction of fees for high school students and the abolition of dental clinics and medical inspections for schoolchildren. Many taxes were to be increased. Though Lee survived a Labor no confidence motion, he was defeated on a move to consider the proposals in committee. His government had survived for ten weeks. Lee asked for a dissolution but J. A. Lyons [q.v.] was called upon to form a Labor government. Lee resigned as party leader and Lyons won the 1925 election.

In 1928 when the Nationalists, led by (Sir) John McPhee [q.v.], were returned to office Lee served as deputy premier and minister for lands and works, and in turn minister for agriculture and closer and soldier settlement. During 1933 Lee acted increasingly for McPhee whose health had begun to fail. It was a government marked by severe economic orthodoxy and caution. Public works were slashed, borrowing curtailed and salaries reduced. McPhee resigned and Lee became premier and treasurer on 15 March 1934 for the third time, only to lose office to Labor in the June election after a campaign in which Lee's personality and competence became an issue. Lee continued to play an active role in parliament until he failed to win the endorsement of the new Liberal Party for the 1946 election when he lost his seat, having stood as an Independent Liberal.

Lee was a short, dapper man, forthright and vigorous in his views, thorough in administration with a sound knowledge of public finance. He was a master of parliamentary tactics, excelling in debate, particularly in his ability to ridicule opponents. A perpetual opponent of Labor, he was yet sufficiently liberal in his views for it to be claimed that he had been offered the post of agent-general in London by the Ogilvie Labor government of 1934.

Lee had taken up land at Quamby Bend about 1923 where he and two sons established Barunah, the dairy-farm where he lived until his death. A devout Methodist and lay preacher, Lee died on 1 June 1963 at Westbury and was buried in Longford cemetery.

Predeceased by his wife, he was survived by three sons and three daughters.

Examiner (Launceston) and *Mercury*, 3 June 1963.   SCOTT BENNETT

LEE, WALTER HENRY (DICK) (1889-1968), footballer, was born on 19 March 1889 at Collingwood, Melbourne, son of Walter Henry (Wal) Lee, labourer, and his wife Isabella, née Turnbull, both Collingwood born. Wal Lee played Australian Rules football for Britannia (precursor of the Collingwood Football Club) in 1882-88 and was the club's trainer in 1889-91. After helping to found the Collingwood Football Club in 1892 he served as head-trainer until 1942; his exceptional service was rewarded by appointment as a life governor of the (Royal) Melbourne Hospital in 1920.

In order to distinguish him from his well-known father, the younger Lee was called Dick or Richard—most people never realized that Richard was not his true name. After completing his primary schooling at Gold Street State School he became a boot-clicker with a local boot manufacturer, Pitman & Son, and followed his father into football.

Between 1906 and 1922, during what was then a Victorian Football League record seventeen consecutive seasons, Lee played 230 V.F.L. games for Collingwood and kicked 713 goals. He headed the V.F.L. goal-kicking ladder eight times (1907-10, 1914, 1916-17, 1919) and tied for the lead twice (1915, 1921)—a record which has not been challenged. Lee was players' representative for nine years (1909-12, 1915-19), vice-captain twice (1910-11) and captain twice (1920-21). He played in three premiership teams (1910, 1917, 1919) and after retirement as a player served Collingwood for an additional sixteen years as vice-president (1923-34, 1950-53). Injuries seriously hindered his playing career.

Lee twice (1910, 1915) won the greatest distinction bestowed on footballers in his day, Champion Player of the Colony. He could star in defence or on the ball as well as at full-forward and he was one of the truly great high marks, arguably the equal of Roy Cazaly [q.v.7]. Lee's marking has been described as 'freakish' and photographs of him taking the ball high over other players have been reproduced countless times. He was also a great kick, extremely adept with drop-kick or punt but especially proficient in the place-kick. According to Harry Collier (captain of Collingwood 1935-39) Lee could place-kick a goal from the boundary line without seeing daylight between the goalposts—even at a rival ground with kids throwing oranges trying to knock the ball over!

Lee was 6 feet (183 cm) tall with a muscular physique and wavy black hair. After a lengthy courtship he married Zella Dixon on 2 March 1927 with Baptist forms at Fitzroy; they had no children. Outside football, Lee worked as a carrier until his death on 11 September 1968 at his Northcote home. Survived by his wife, he was buried in Coburg cemetery.

P. Taylor, *Collingwood Football Club 1892-1948* (Melb, nd, 1950?); G. Atkinson, *Everything you've ever wanted to know about Australian Rules football* (Melb, 1982); S. Rodgers (comp), *Toohey's guide to every game ever played* (Melb, 1983); Collingwood Football Club, *Annual Reports*, 1892, 1906-34, 1942, 1950-53, and *Newsletter*, Feb 1965, Oct 1968; *Age*, 12 Sept 1968.   R. STREMSKI

LEE, YET SOO WAY; *see* WAY LEE

LEEHY, MARY AGNES (1873-1960), Sister of St Joseph, was born on 10 April 1873 at Bundarra, New South Wales, eldest of six children of Irish parents Thomas Leehy, miner and drover, and his wife Julia, née Kavanagh. She moved with her family to Merriwa where she attended the Catholic school. During her father's long absences droving, her mother raised the children with a respect for authority, regard for frugality and an ability to manage their resources, allied to staunch Catholic faith and practice.

In May 1890 Mary joined the black-habited Sisters of St Joseph at Lochinvar; she was professed on 13 February 1893, taking the religious name Mary Aquin. Until 1911 she taught in small country convent schools in the diocese of Maitland. She returned to Lochinvar in 1911 as sister assistant and was involved with the boarding-school there. She supervised the addition to the Lochinvar buildings of school, refectory and dormitory accommodation. In 1917-23 Mother Aquin was sister guardian and in 1923-29 superior of the newly founded convent and school at Taree. She remained at Lochinvar for the rest of her life as sister guardian in 1929-35, assistant in 1935-41 and in 1941-55 mother-general.

Despite straitened finances during World War I and the Depression, Mother Aquin was able to have built a chapel, large enough to accommodate sisters, invalids and novices as well as 200 boarders, in a dignified and traditional architectural style. On her return from Taree she saw to the addition of a novitiate wing and more sleeping accommodation in the busy and growing complex. Early in her third term of office she applied to have the Lochinvar Sisters of St Joseph given official Pontifical status and from 1943 became known as mother-general. She supervised the building of a music block, dormitory and school extensions, including a library. When Mother Aquin stepped down in 1955 the number of sisters had increased from 32 in 1890 to some 260 in the congregation's 35 houses. Throughout her terms of office she had made regular visitations to all the sisters in the diocese. She acted as an advisory councillor until she died on 19 May 1960 in St Joseph's Convent, Lochinvar, and was buried in the Catholic cemetery.

A legend in her time, Mother Aquin was a matriarchal leader of the Sisters of St Joseph in the Maitland diocese, known by schoolchildren and parents, businessmen and clergy as a capable, even dynamic, planner and builder. She had a commanding presence as well as a reputation for quick, perceptive decisiveness, fairness and a maternal concern for her sisters. Her letters to her mother reveal close and affectionate family bonds; they give a dimension of warmth to her image of an energetic leader who was a model of her own teachings about prayer, hard work and a drive for excellence in every sphere.

Family letters and written memoirs (Archives of St Joseph's Convent, Lochinvar, NSW); personal information.   MARGARET M. PRESS

LEEPER, ALEXANDER (1848-1934), educationist and publicist, founder of the collegiate system in the University of Melbourne, was born on 3 June 1848 in Dublin, son of Alexander Leeper, D.D., Anglican curate, later chaplain to the lord lieutenant of Ireland, and his wife Catherine, daughter of William Henry Porter, president of the Royal College of Surgeons in Ireland. A brilliant boy, Leeper won prizes and exhibitions at Kingstown School, Trinity College, Dublin (B.A., 1871; LL.D. (hon.), 1884), and St John's College, Oxford. After a youthful flirtation with moderate Irish nationalism, he settled into 'four passionate loyalties': 'the Church, the Classics, the Act of Union, the British Empire'.

Leeper first visited Australia in 1871, tutoring the sons of (Sir) George Wigram Allen [q.v.3] in Sydney and falling in love with their sister Adeline Marian, then 16. In 1872 he applied unsuccessfully for the Melbourne chair of classics. In 1874, driven by incipient tuberculosis and drawn by love for Adeline, he returned from Oxford to Sydney before accepting an appointment at Melbourne Church of England Grammar School, where in a few months in 1875 he founded the school library and helped to create *The Melburnian* and *Liber Melburniensis.* Leeper and Adeline were briefly engaged in 1875 but could not overcome her father's objections until 1879 when they married on 30 December at Glebe, Sydney. They had two daughters and two sons.

In 1876 Leeper had been appointed principal of Trinity College, founded by the Church of England in 1872 to be the first college affiliated with the University of Melbourne. He took over 'farming' the infant institution and its five students from G. W. Torrance [q.v.6], determined to develop a new Australian form of collegiate life. 'A pertinacious, anxious, busy, bustling person, full of immense enthusiasm for a hundred things at once', Leeper and his vice-principal (Sir) Winthrop Hackett [q.v.9] gained university affiliation in 1876, began tutorials in 1877, opened a new building in honour of bishops Perry and Moorhouse [qq.v.5] and established a theological school in 1878. Leeper so rapidly established an academic role for Trinity that after his reappointment in 1881 as first warden his predecessor was almost forgotten.

Though Trinity's tutorial programme was broad in subject-matter, Leeper's passion for classical studies was evident in his own teaching and writing. He published, with H. A. Strong [q.v.6], *A guide to classical reading intended for the use of Australian students* (1880) and a translation of *Thirteen satires of Juvenal* (1882). In 1881 he produced the first Latin play mounted in Victoria. His college was also a school for citizenship, where strict rules of conduct (including compulsory chapel) were tempered by the close relationships possible between resident tutors and students. But Trinity's financial base remained precarious, and the continuance of the collegiate system was only ensured with the opening of Ormond [q.v.5] College under (Sir) John MacFarland [q.v.] in 1881 and of Queen's College under E. H. Sugden [q.v.] in 1888. The three colleges and their formidable, if rarely consonant, heads came to dominate the university academically and in large degree politically, with Leeper's service on the University council (1880-87 and 1900-23) outdistanced only by MacFarland's. To his chagrin, Leeper never succeeded in matching Ormond's endowments, though he won a new building and other benefactions from Sir William Clarke and his brother Joseph [qq.v.3], and in 1890, from Janet, Lady Clarke [q.v.3], a new home for Leeper's most daring innovation, collegiate university residence for women.

In 1883 Trinity had become the first college in Australia to admit non-resident women to college lectures. A trip abroad in 1884 convinced Leeper that women should be allowed accommodation in the same colleges as men. Despite Bishop Moorhouse's [q.v.5] fears that squatters would withdraw their sons if 'penniless' girls were admitted, Leeper was permitted in 1886 to set up, in Parkville, a hostel for women (dubbed, inevitably, Hostiles). He opposed, however, the siting of Lady Clarke's new building in the college grounds, and insisted that while Trinity women might attend tutorials and communion services, social contact between the sexes must be severely restricted.

Ambiguities in the new policy led to serious conflict with the Council of Trinity College Hostel (later Janet Clarke Hall) which wanted constitutional separation from Trinity and the right to enrol non-residents from other colleges; Leeper and the Trinity council insisted that the hostel was an integral part of Trinity and its principal merely a deputy of the warden. After heated public dispute the principal and the council resigned in 1892, and Leeper 'farmed' the hostel to a married Trinity tutor until 1901.

While Leeper was preoccupied with the hostel his informal and none-too-consistent mode of discipline in Trinity broke down. In 1890 discontents dismissed by the council as trivial flared into crisis. The warden's effigy was burned, and in September two expelled ringleaders (one (Sir) Stanley Argyle [q.v.7]) left college in a spectacular procession of twenty-four hansom cabs carrying thirty-four sympathizers, leaving only twelve depressed survivors in residence. Amid much clamour a committee of the Church assembly conducted a public investigation, concluding that 'sundry irregularities, rash promises and serious errors of judgement had been proved against the Warden', and severely criticizing Leeper's financial management. The Trinity council greatly resented the committee's strictures and after further public dispute the bishop and the diocesan council buried the matter in 1897 by simply 'removing from the books all reference to the Trinity College Enquiry of 1890'.

Leeper's second twenty years as warden were more peaceful, and many students recorded respect and even affection for the tall, gaunt 'Bones', impulsive and authoritarian though he remained. Causes outside the college roused his energies, as in the campaign against the reappointment of G. W. L. Marshall-Hall [q.v.] as Ormond professor of music in 1900. Incompatibility of opinion and temperament appeared when Marshall-Hall provided the music for Leeper's production of *Alcestis* in 1898; Leeper did not want his musically promising daughter to study under a man of questionable reputation. He nevertheless abstained from the first agitation, emerging to 'make a stand for righteousness' only in 1900 when he organized a petition against reappointment. A Norman Lindsay [q.v.] cartoon depicted him as the murderer of Justice. Marshall-Hall was to resume the chair briefly in 1915, Leeper's opposition then proving as ineffectual as it was vehement.

Leeper's bitterest prejudices were political. He had little interest in Australian politics, his outlook remaining Imperial and his accent Irish. Australian nationalism, even in forms as trivial as the kangaroo stamp, repelled him. His commitment against Home Rule became ever more strident, Asquith's bill of 1912 provoking him to lead the local Ulster and Loyal Irish Association to defend the integrity of the Empire, 'the main bulwark of civil and religious liberty in the world'.

The outbreak of war in 1914 raised these passions to a pitch of xenophobia. In the university council he campaigned for the dismissal of two German members of staff and prevented their reappointment after 1915. As a member of the Council of Public Education he moved in 1916 for the deregistration of Lutheran schools. In 1915 and regularly thereafter he urged the university council to campaign vigorously for recruiting, and in 1916 persuaded synod to support conscription. Leeper claimed that the referendum 'No' vote represented merely the views of 'the shirkers, the pro-Germans, the Sinn Feiners, the Mannixites, the I.W.W. traitors, the pacifists, and the cranks' against the 'imperious moral obligation to defend the Empire'. In 1917 he railed against student shirkers; in 1918 his hatreds concentrated on the St Patrick's Day procession during which Dr Mannix [q.v.] appeared to pay respect to the Sinn Fein and refuse it to the king. With Herbert Brookes [q.v.7], Leeper organized the Citizens' Loyalist Committee and chaired a large meeting of 'Loyalist Melbourne'.

In other matters Leeper was usually more moderate, if seldom mild. From 1899 and 1900 he was a council-member of Melbourne Grammar and of Melbourne Church of England Girls' Grammar School, which he had persuaded the Church to establish by acquiring the existing Merton Hall. The Classical Association of Victoria, formed in 1913, was an abiding involvement, while his selective interest in modern literature found him producing a Browning play, organizing the Shakespeare Society, and admiring the novels of George Eliot, if little more modern. Active in Church affairs, in Trinity's theological school and as a lay canon of St Paul's Cathedral and a member of synod, he habitually defended the rights of the laity against the presumptions of bishops and, remarkably, favoured the ordination of women, though even he could scarcely envisage a woman bishop. His intervention to prevent a High Church appointment to the archbishopric in 1918 caused resentment, and he was isolated in Church affairs for a time. He felt even more bitterly the aftermath of his retirement from Trinity in March

1918, when his successor (Sir) John Behan [q.v.7] foiled his intention to remain on the college council; only once thereafter did he set foot in the college he had ruled for forty-two years. He was also disappointed by his defeat in the university council elections of 1923.

Leeper's principal interest in retirement was the Public Library, Museums and National Gallery, of which he was a trustee in 1887-1928, becoming president in 1920. He had assembled a notable library for Trinity, which was named in his honour on his retirement. 'A firm believer in the immense educational influence of the Public Library', he fought to raise the status of librarians. He defended the conglomerate of library, gallery and museums in Swanston Street against separatists, and although his primary interest was in the library he took his duties as the trustees' nominee on the Felton [q.v.4] Bequests' Committee (1920-28) very seriously. While occasionally pernickety in library and gallery matters, he was an influential advocate of the importance of such institutions to any enlightened society.

Leeper died at his home in Kensington Road, South Yarra, on 6 August 1934, and his ashes were buried at South Head cemetery, Sydney, beside his first wife Adeline (d. 1893). Notable portraits by Rupert Bunny [q.v.7] hang in Trinity and Janet Clarke Hall, and the National Gallery of Victoria has another by John Longstaff [q.v.]. A portrait by B. C. Edwell and a drawing by John Shirlow [q.v.] are held by the family.

On 17 February 1897 Leeper had married Mary Elizabeth Moule. The second marriage produced two daughters and one son Geoffrey Winthrop, first professor of agricultural chemistry in the University of Melbourne. The two sons of the first marriage made their careers in the British Foreign Office.

ALEXANDER WIGRAM ALLEN LEEPER (1887-1935) was born on 4 January 1887 and educated at Melbourne Grammar School, University of Melbourne and Balliol College, Oxford. He entered the Foreign Office in 1918 after publishing *The justice of Rumania's cause* (London, 1917). In 1924 as first secretary he was seconded to advise S. M. (Lord) Bruce [q.v.7] on reorganization of the Department of External Affairs. The Leeper report is an important document in the history of Australian foreign policy, arguing for closer effective co-ordination with British policy by creating the position of liaison officer in London, which R. G. (Lord) Casey was the first to occupy. First secretary in Vienna in 1924-28, and a counsellor in the Foreign Office in 1933, Leeper was appointed C.B.E. in 1920 and C.M.G. in 1935. His unfinished *History of medieval Austria* was published in 1941.

Sir Reginald (Rex) Wildig Allen Leeper, C.B.E., C.M.G., K.C.M.G., G.B.E. (1888-1968) had a distinguished career as a British diplomat and as the 'architect' of the British Council.

E. Scott, *A history of the University of Melbourne* (Melb, 1936); W. K. Hancock, *Country and calling* (Lond, 1954); G. Blainey, *A centenary history of the University of Melbourne* (Melb, 1957); E. D. Lindsay, *The Felton Bequest, an historical record 1904-1959* (Melb, 1963); R. Rivett, *Australian citizen; Herbert Brookes 1867-1963* (Melb, 1965); G. McInnes, *The road to Gundagai* (Lond, 1965); L. B. Cox, *The National Gallery of Victoria, 1861 to 1968* (Melb, 1970); J. A. Grant (ed), *Perspective of a century* (Melb, 1972); T. Radic, *G.W.L. Marshall-Hall* (Perth, 1982); *Age*, 7 Apr 1934, 2 Jan 1935; *Argus*, 7, 8 Aug 1934, 2 Jan 1935; *Herald* (Melb), 3 Feb 1968; Queen's College Archives (Melb); Trinity College Archives (Melb); Univ Melb Archives.

J. R. POYNTER

LEES, HARRINGTON CLARE (1870-1929), Anglican archbishop, was born on 17 March 1870 at Ashton-under-Lyne, Lancashire, England, eldest son of William Lees, cotton salesman, and his wife Emma, née Clare. He was head boy at the Methodist Leys School and a scholar of St John's College, Cambridge, graduating in 1892 with a second class in theology and a prize in New Testament Greek. Preaching and interpretation of the Bible were to be lifelong interests. He received the degree of M.A. in 1896 and D.D. in 1921. A keen sportsman, he developed 'athlete's heart' while at Cambridge.

Lees became a deacon in 1893 and a priest next year. On 9 December 1895 at St Andrew's, Southport, Lancashire, he married Winifred May Cranswick. After serving curacies at Reading, Berkshire, and Childwall, Lancashire, and a chaplaincy at Turin, Italy, he was vicar of three evangelical parishes: St John's, Kenilworth, Warwickshire (1900-07), Christ Church, Beckenham, Kent (1907-19) and Swansea, Glamorganshire (1919-20) where, according to the archbishop of Wales, 'He got possession of the town in a wonderful way'. He was always popular. Honorary chaplain to military depots in England during World War I, he was mentioned in 1919 by the British Red Cross Society for services.

Having refused the offer of the bishopric of Bendigo, Victoria, in 1919, Lees next year accepted appointment as archbishop of Melbourne. He was consecrated in St Paul's Cathedral, London, on 1 November and enthroned in St Paul's Cathedral, Melbourne, on 15 February 1921. In appearance he differed markedly from his predecessor. Lowther Clarke [q.v.8] was of big build, Lees was like a sprightly wicket-keeper. Of middle height,

head set well back on wide shoulders, with dark eyes and aquiline nose, he was described by Melbourne *Punch* in 1925 as showing 'a wondrous juvenility that defies his years'. Earlier, he had sported a fine moustache.

Lees is remembered as archbishop in three ways. First he was an attractive, Christian man with a most real pastoral sense. Uniformly affable, he was a welcome visitor at vicarages and took a lively interest in all diocesan activities. At the Bishopscourt ordination retreats conversation was permitted at meals so that the bishop and candidates might become better acquainted. Lees was no party man and did all he could to keep antagonisms, such as those aroused by the establishment of Ridley College, in check. He was on good terms with the leaders of the other Christian denominations and was a foundation member of the Old Melburnians' Masonic Lodge. In 1922-24 he was president of the Melbourne College of Divinity. He was, however, no ascetic; on one occasion he included in his round of diocesan engagements 'Social duties of Cup Week', and unlike Archbishop Clarke who travelled by public transport, carrying his suitcase, Lees had the full-time use of a car and chauffeur.

Second, Lees was a great speaker. When he preached at Evensong in the cathedral it was necessary to be there at least fifteen minutes early to be sure of a seat. He took infinite pains in the preparation of his sermons and delivered them with 'fire and persuasion', making the structure clear at the start and developing his theme with many varied illustrations. From 1925 he broadcast sermons over the radio; he was described at his death as 'an ideal broadcaster'.

Third, Lees was an extremely effective administrator. He presided with distinction over the Melbourne Church Congress in 1925 and initiated the successful appeal for the building of the spires of St Paul's. He proved a competent chairman at synod; although he spoke little, he was always *en rapport* with members and had the knack of quickly distinguishing essential from non-essential matters. His chief administrative changes concerned the enlargement of the Mission of St James and St John and the Church of England kindergarten system.

Between 1905 and 1919 Lees wrote at least fifteen theological works including *The King's way* (1910) and *The practice of the love of Christ* (1915). He was the author of numerous articles and pamphlets and contributed to J. Hastings's *Dictionary of Christ and the Gospels*.

Overwork contributed to Lees's early death from coronary vascular disease on 10 January 1929 at Bishopscourt, East Melbourne. He was the first archbishop of Melbourne to die in office and many thousands attended his funeral service at St Paul's Cathedral before his cremation. Winifred Lees had died in 1927 and he was survived by his second wife Joanna Mary, née Linnell, of Beckenham, Kent, whom he had married at Westminster on 19 April 1928. He had no children. A fine portrait by John Longstaff [q.v.] is in the Melbourne Chapter House.

T. B. McCall, *The life and letters of John Stephen Hart* (Syd, 1963); *C of E Messenger* (Vic), and *Age*, 11 Jan 1929; *Punch* (Melb), 26 Feb 1925; *Argus*, 11, 14 Jan 1929.   J. D. McKIE

LEES, SAMUEL EDWARD (1843-1916), printer and politician, was born on 8 July 1843 in Sydney, second of seven children of Samuel Lees, painter and glazier, and his wife Caroline, née Whitehead. Samuel attended the William Street National School and then was apprenticed to a printer. By 1866 he was partner in the printing firm of Lees & Ross, Castlereagh Street, and within two years had his own business, the Metropolitan Printing Office. He advertised as 'printer, publisher, machine-ruler, book-binder and rubber stamp maker'. In 1908 he took C. P. Mortlock into partnership; the firm of Samuel E. Lees Ltd continued after his death. On 30 September 1871 he had married Sarah Amy Davies at the York Street Wesleyan Church.

A Freemason, Lees held important positions in the Loyal Orange Institution of New South Wales in the 1870s and was foreman of the grand committee of the Grand Lodge in 1876. He was president of the Protestant Alliance Friendly Society of Australasia in the 1880s, and a director of the Protestant Hall Co. Ltd and of several land and building companies.

By 1871 Lees was also involved in the Protestant Political Association of New South Wales formed in the wake of the attempted assassination of the duke of Edinburgh [q.v.4] to promote the election of Protestants to parliament and municipal councils. In 1879-1909 he represented Macquarie Ward on the Sydney Municipal Council, serving on every committee, and represented the council on the Metropolitan Fire Brigades Board from 1886. In the midst of financial stringency he was elected mayor in 1895 and initiated substantial economies in council's budget. He declined requests to stand again in 1896 in order to make a world tour. In 1904 he was lord mayor; his administration was noted for 'prudence, economy and sound judgement'.

Twice defeated for East Sydney in the 1880s, Lees was elected to the Legislative Assembly for the Nepean in 1887. Although a prominent free trader, he was defeated in 1895, but was nominated to the Legislative Council. He resigned in 1898 and regained

the Nepean but was defeated in 1901. He contributed only briefly to debates, often on municipal matters. His judgements were moderate, and he showed sympathy to the emergent Labor Party. He was interested in the overall progress and development of the colony, especially the pastoral and agricultural industries. In 1907-16 he was a vice-president of the Royal Agricultural Society of New South Wales.

Raised in the Wesleyan Methodist church, Lees was a prominent layman. After teaching and working in the York Street Church and Sunday school, for nearly forty years he was a member and office-bearer in the William Street Church. He was honorary treasurer of the Wesleyan Methodist Missionary Society. Lees was interested in charity and moral reform. In 1879 he was provisional secretary of the Sydney Coffee Palace which had a temperance purpose. He was a director of Sydney Hospital in 1882-1916 (vice-president· in 1915) and from 1895 foundation chairman of the Nepean Cottage Hospital at Penrith.

Lees died on 14 June 1916 at his Potts Point home, and was buried in Waverley cemetery. He was survived by his wife, son and four daughters. His estate was sworn for probate at £9973.

With a walrus moustache and hair parted in the middle, Lees had a dignified bearing. He was a worthy citizen, prepared to sit for years on committees whether they gave him prestige or not. Though he occasionally rose to high positions he did not have a dominating personality. What prominence he achieved in public life was due more to sturdiness and perseverance than to any brilliance. A posthumous oil portrait by Bruce Sharp hangs in the Sydney Town Hall.

Cyclopedia of N.S.W. (Syd, 1907); *Protestant Standard*, 27 May 1871; *T&CJ*, 5 Mar 1887, 14 Sept 1895, 16 Dec 1903; *Daily Telegraph* (Syd), 9 July 1894; *SMH*, 10 Dec 1903, 15 June 1916; *Methodist*, 24 June 1916; M. Lyons, Aspects of Sectarianism in New South Wales circa 1865-1880 (Ph.D. thesis, ANU, 1972); Procs of cttee and council meetings, 1895, 1904 (Syd Municipal (City) Council); information from Janet Howse, archivist, Syd Municipal Council.   ALAN ROBERTS

LEESON, IDA EMILY (1885-1964), librarian, was born on 11 February 1885 at Leichhardt, Sydney, daughter of Thomas Leeson, carpenter from Canada, and his native-born wife Mary Ann, née Emberson. Ida's schooling began at Leichhardt Public School and, after the award of a bursary, she attended Sydney Girls' High School in 1898-1902. She won a scholarship to the University of Sydney and graduated B.A. in 1906 with second-class honours in history, then worked briefly as a teacher in private schools at Bowral and Potts Point.

Teaching, however, did not attract her and on 27 August 1906 she was appointed library assistant at the Public Library of New South Wales. As a result of David Scott Mitchell's [q.v.5] bequest, the library had acquired his invaluable collection of Australian and Pacific material. Ida Leeson was transferred to the Mitchell Library in 1909 and was one of the pioneers who sorted the collection. In July 1916 she was promoted senior cataloguer, Mitchell Library, and, in June 1919, to one of the Public Library's senior positions, principal accessions officer.

Although responsible for developing the book resources of the library as a whole, Ida Leeson maintained her interest in Australian and Pacific materials. During a visit to Britain in 1927, she reported on manuscripts relating to the area in the Public Record Office and other British repositories. She scored a coup by discovering, in the P.R.O., the original of the allegedly missing third volume of Matthew Flinders' [q.v.1] 1801-08 log.

In December 1932 Ida Leeson was appointed second Mitchell librarian. The trustees had no qualms about her qualifications for the job but, reluctant to appoint a woman to a position in which she would be the obvious successor as principal librarian, they reorganized the library's senior management, reducing the status and salary of the Mitchell librarian. The move was criticized, in vain, by feminists such as Jessie Street.

Under Ida Leeson's direction the Mitchell Library, in the 1930s, consolidated its position as the pre-eminent repository of Australian and Pacific documents. Numerous important historical and contemporary collections were acquired; the library's role as the New South Wales State archival agency was considerably expanded; the manuscripts in the collection were organized and described. The 1930s were also a time of celebration: important exhibitions were mounted for the 1936 centenary of Mitchell's birth and for the 1938 150th anniversary celebrations. For the former, Ida Leeson produced *The Mitchell Library, Sydney: historical and descriptive notes*, a definitive guide.

The outbreak of war in 1939 prevented Ida Leeson being sent overseas to film records relating to the South Pacific in British and European repositories. The library's most valuable items were transferred to the country for safe-keeping; staff resources were limited and stretched; the library had to cut its opening hours; there were complaints about the curtailing of services. After the establishment of General MacArthur's headquarters in Melbourne in 1942, the dearth of intelligence information about the Pacific led to frequent requests to the library for assistance from sections of the Allied Intelligence Bureau.

In April 1944 Lieut-Colonel A. A. Conlon secured Ida Leeson's secondment to the position of research officer in the Directorate of Research (and Civil Affairs), as a captain, then major, in the Australian Military Forces. She was a key member of Conlon's 'think-tank' which included such people as (Sir) John Kerr and J. K. Murray. Later, Ida Leeson referred to Conlon as a 'life-changer'. She did not return to the Mitchell although she did not officially resign until April 1946. Towards the end of the war she became archivist-librarian for the School of Civil Affairs (from 1946 Australian School of Pacific Administration). In mid-1949 she went to Noumea to establish the library for the South Pacific Commission. She returned in April 1950 but continued to work for the commission's social development section in Sydney until 1956, compiling *A bibliography of bibliographies of the South Pacific* (1954).

After 1956 Ida Leeson continued to research for universities and private bodies and was generous with advice and assistance on a large variety of matters. She died on 22 January 1964 at Castlecrag and was cremated with Anglican rites.

Ida Leeson was awarded King George V's silver jubilee medal in 1935. She survives indelibly in the numerous published acknowledgments to her assistance, in her many published and unpublished works (only some of which bear her name), and in the collections whose destinies she guided.

J. J. M. Thompson (comp), *Alfred Conlon, 1908-1961* (Syd, 1963); J. Kerr, *Matters for judgement* (Melb, 1978); Public Lib of NSW, *Annual Report*, 1932-46; *Aust Lib J*, June 1964, p 98; Leeson papers (ML).

BAIBA BERZINS

LEE STEERE, SIR ERNEST AUGUSTUS (1866-1957), pastoralist and businessman, was born on 19 March 1866 near Beverley, Western Australia, son of Augustus Frederick Lee Steere, grazier, and his wife Ellen Elizabeth, née Roe; (Sir) James Lee Steere [q.v.] was an uncle. The family had taken the name of Lee Steere in 1675 as a condition of the marriage between Fiducia Lee and John Steere at Plastoe, Surrey. Ernest was educated at Newcastle State School and the High School, Perth, and began work at 14.

He joined his cousins John and Sam Phillips, first as a stockman, at Culham near Toodyay, and next as overseer in 1886-90 at the Grange on the Irwin River. Carrying his swag on an aged racehorse, Star of the East, in 1888 he went to assess the Murchison country and was impressed. He returned north two years later as joint owner with his uncle J. B. Roe of Belele station, a 250 000-acre (100 000 ha) sheep and cattle run. Thwarted by drought, Lee Steere was tempted by, but resisted the lure of gold. Instead he invested in mail transport between Nannine and Peak Hill; in a local butchery and the Nannine general store; and, eventually, in a merchandise and forwarding agency, successively located at Cue, Nannine, Meekatharra and Geraldton. Versatility and hard work characterized his endeavours. Never closely involved with his sidelines, he conceded that they helped to tide over fluctuations in the pastoral industry. On 16 December 1909, at St Mary's Church of England, West Perth, Lee Steere married Bridget Yelverton, daughter of C. Y. O'Connor [q.v.]; they had three daughters and three sons, two of whom died in action in World War II.

As sole owner, Lee Steere expanded the Belele Pastoral Co. to 900 000 acres (364 000 ha). Because of the absence of permanent water holes, no Aborigines lived there; however Lee Steere spoke Yamagee and soon employed many, by whom he was well liked. They knew he never carried firearms. He gradually acquired other pastoral holdings: Annean Station (transferred to his wife); Yandil near Wiluna; Chilimony merino stud and The Bowes in the Victoria district; Yanda at Mingenew; Hawthornden and Maismore at Toodyay; Elliott Creek on the Upper Gascoyne; and, with A. J. Monger [q.v.], Woongundy estate. In 1946 he gave Yanda to the State government for its War Service Land Settlement Scheme. He was a committee-member of the Fairbridge [q.v.8] Farm School at Pinjarra.

A foundation member and president in 1920-34 of the Pastoralists' Association of Western Australia, Lee Steere was also chairman of directors of Elder Smith [qq.v.4,6] & Co. Ltd (W.A.); chairman of the Australian Mutual Provident Society (W.A.) and the West Australian Trustee Executor & Agency Co. Ltd; a director of Western Australian Airways; and president of the Weld Club. He helped to float the Western Australian Worsted and Woollen Mills at Albany, the Western Australian Meat Export Co. and the Fremantle Freezing Works. Lacking political aspirations, he had conservative views but respected Labor Premier Phillip Collier [q.v.8]. He opposed additional Federal constitutional powers in the 1944 referendum and constantly supported fusion of the National and Country parties. Unostentatiously generous in the public cause, he was also considerate to less fortunate friends and relatives. Having refused the honour twice, Lee Steere was knighted in 1948.

He enjoyed watching polo, but the turf was his favourite recreation. His champions, such as Eurythmic (Perth 1919, Caulfield 1920) and Maple (Caulfield 1928), won several Australian cup and classic races. Never a heavy punter, he told his trainers that 'when these colours go on, it is like nailing a flag to a mast'; horses carrying the Lee Steere 'all red' won repute for honest and consistent performance. Under his chairmanship (1919-40), the Western Australian Turf Club was re-organized, its fixtures opened to a wider public and the totalizator invented by his wife's brother-in-law Sir George Julius [q.v.9] installed.

Lee Steere died at his home on 22 December 1957. His estate was sworn for probate at £87 574. He had been esteemed for his enterprise and fair dealing and was remembered as tolerant and understanding. Lady Lee Steere was appointed O.B.E. in 1960 for her work with the Western Australian Girl Guide Association and the Young Women's Christian Association. Their second son Ernest was lord mayor of Perth in 1972-78.

M. J. L. Uren, *Pioneer pastoralist* (Perth, 1951); *Pastoral Review*, 20 Jan 1958; *West Australian*, 3 Apr 1941, 15 Jan 1946, 1, 3, 10 Jan 1948, 26 Sept 1950, 23 Dec 1957, 1 Jan 1960, 25 July 1979; *Sunday Times* (Perth), 1 July 1957; *Weekend Mag* (Perth), 28 Jan 1967, 22 Nov 1979; Lee Steere papers (Battye Lib); papers held by Mrs E. Lefroy, Peppermint Grove, Perth, Mrs M. Dawkins, Armadale, WA, and Sir E. Lee Steere, Cottesloe, Perth.   WENDY BIRMAN

LEE STEERE, SIR JAMES; *see* STEERE

LEETE, BENJAMIN HENRY; *see* RICKARDS, HARRY

LE FANU, HENRY FREWEN (1870-1946), archbishop, was born on 1 April 1870 in Dublin, sixth of ten children of William Richard Le Fanu, civil engineer, and his wife Henrietta Victorine, daughter of Sir Matthew Barrington, 2nd baronet. The aristocratic Le Fanu family had migrated from Normandy, France, as Huguenot refugees in the late seventeenth century; in Ireland they shone in church, state and the arts. Armorial bearings assigned by the French king in 1595 were confirmed in 1929. Henry attended Haileybury School and Keble College, Oxford, where he took a second-class honours degree in modern history (B.A., 1893; M.A., 1901); he excelled at Rugby and boxing. After training at Wells Theological College, he was ordained in 1895. He was curate at Poplar,

East London, until 1899, resident chaplain to the bishop of Rochester in 1899-1901, and chaplain to Guy's Hospital, London, in 1901-04.

On 25 October 1904 Le Fanu married Mary (Margery) Annette Ingle Dredge, a vicar's daughter. Having been appointed archdeacon, he reached Brisbane on 5 January 1905, a fortnight after Archbishop Donaldson [q.v.8]. For five years Le Fanu was also sub-dean of the pro-cathedral and on 21 September 1915 was consecrated coadjutor-bishop. A forceful right-hand man, he managed diocesan business skilfully, and as warden of the Society of the Sacred Advent guided the sisterhood's educational and hospital work.

In 1929 Le Fanu became second archbishop of Perth, succeeding C. O. L. Riley [q.v.]; he was enthroned in St George's Cathedral on 19 December. Advantage had been taken of the six months interregnum to appoint an experienced local clergyman as dean of Perth in which post Riley himself had acted since 1925. Holding that the cathedral statute and other legislation passed by synod in August 1929 were *ultra vires*, Le Fanu soon sought, unsuccessfully, to amend the diocesan constitution. Later, when relations with the parishes became strained over their financial obligations, he defended the Church's episcopal structure by reminding parishes that the diocese was the prime unit of the Church's organization. For nearly seventeen years he wisely shepherded a cohesive diocese and worked harmoniously with lieutenants such as the likewise Irish-born R. H. Moore, who was dean throughout, with parish clergy, lay officers and other denominations.

Le Fanu further displayed his financial and administrative acumen during the long years of Depression, drought and war. He recognized that, as financial support from England declined, his diocese must become self sufficient. Concerned for the distressed wheatbelt parishes, he devised a scheme which relieved them of growing debts; however, several parishes had to be amalgamated. Fifty-one buildings were added to the diocese's equipment in his first ten years; fourteen churches were consecrated during his episcopate and eleven buildings licensed for public worship. They included a university college, a private girls' secondary school, and a missions to seamen institute, all of which opened in 1931. His largest venture was the Mount Hospital, Perth, acquired in 1934 and extended in 1939.

Le Fanu improved both the architectural standards of churches and the quality of clergy. Though he had no local theological college, he recruited sufficient clergy and saw the proportion of graduates rise during his episcopate; 23 of the 29 men ordained in the 1930s were born or educated within the State and the diocese supported many of them during training in Adelaide. Le Fanu recruited others when in England for the Lambeth conference of 1930 and the coronation in 1937. While the later war years brought improved finances, including contributions to missions, they depleted the staff; over a quarter of the clergy served as full-time padrés, and half the country parishes were vacant at war's end. When the armed forces requisitioned several Church schools and the girls' orphanage, alternative accommodation had to be found for the evacuees in the country.

Though he had been acting for twenty months, by virtue of seniority, it caused surprise when the bishops elected Le Fanu primate of Australia in March 1935. His abilities and Australian experience were considered more valuable than retaining the primacy's traditional attachment to Sydney. The vote was also a censure of the exceptionally 'low church' mother diocese for its long obstruction of efforts to establish a constitution for an Anglican Church in Australia which would be legally independent of England. Le Fanu valued the honour and was amused that Western Australians were 'extremely pleased' about it despite their campaign for secession from the Federation. He received a Lambeth doctorate of divinity in 1936 and was made a sub-prelate of the Order of St John of Jerusalem.

As primate Le Fanu grasped big issues, and was forthright and liberal in his actions and pronouncements. Publicly he was purely a vocal churchman, holding that the Church should be a leavening influence in the community rather than a pressure group in politics. Though he probably never considered himself a socialist, he favoured social change and propounded radical views on many social and economic questions. By 1941 he relinquished his duties as chaplain-general of the Australian forces to bishops nearer defence headquarters in Melbourne. While firmly supporting the war effort, he deplored the persecution of communists and applauded the allies' growing accord with Soviet Russia. He was an early participant in planning for post-war reconstruction.

The primate also worked assiduously for Church unity, though hampered by distance. His chairmanship of two of the normally quinquennial general synods in 1937 and 1945 won unstinted praise; shunning retirement, he hoped to lead the Australian contingent to the postponed Lambeth conference of 1948. In his seventies, heart trouble scarcely diminished his vigour and his busy schedules; he died in harness, suddenly, on 9 September 1946 and was cremated.

Having been a widower since 1926, on 26

July 1941 Le Fanu had married Winifred Maud Whiteley (d. 1979), who had helped to raise his family. He was survived by her and by the three sons and three daughters of his first marriage. His portraits, by Leon Hogan, hang in St George's College and in the Le Fanu wing of Wollaston College in Perth.

Big in frame and strong in character, Le Fanu was also humble, sensitive and rather shy. He could be incisive with ready wit, but was always quick to apologize for hurt. Even when he provoked controversy, he caused little rancour. His virtues far outweighed any shortcomings. Deeply spiritual and intensely human, he was an ideal Church leader in difficult times.

T. P. Le Fanu, *Memoir of the Le Fanu family* (Lond, priv print, 1924); C. L. M. Hawtrey, *The availing struggle* (Perth, 1949); F. Alexander (ed), *Four bishops and their see* (Perth, 1957); C of E, Diocese of Brisb, *Church Chronicle*, 1 Oct 1929, p 241; *WA Church News* (Perth), 1929-46; C of E, *Diocese of Perth Year Book*, 1939, 1946; *Brisb Cathedral Notes*, 5 Oct 1946, p 7; *West Australian*, 10, 12 Sept 1946; *The Times*, 28 Sept 1946.

J. H. M. HONNIBALL

LEFROY, SIR HENRY BRUCE (1853-1930), pastoralist and politician, was born on 24 March 1853 at Cambray, St George's Terrace, Perth, elder son of Anthony O'Grady Lefroy [q.v.5] and his wife Mary, née Bruce. He was educated in England at an Exmouth preparatory school, Elstree, and at Rugby, where he excelled at sport. When he returned to Western Australia in 1873 he managed his father's property Walebing at Victoria Plains, making it one of the best pastoral properties of the colony. At 21 he became a justice of the peace with virtually the duties of resident magistrate. Having built a fine house at Walebing, Lefroy married, on 15 April 1880 in St George's Cathedral, Perth, Rose Agnes Wittenoom, granddaughter of the colony's first Anglican chaplain, John Burdett Wittenoom [q.v.2]; they had three sons and a daughter.

Lefroy was chairman of the Victoria Plains Road Board for thirty years (and from 1909 of the Moora Road Board) and was elected for Moore to the Legislative Assembly in 1892. He accepted Sir John Forrest's [q.v.8] policies of development. He was a delegate to the Federal Council of Australasia in Hobart in 1895 and 1897, became minister for education in 1897-98 (when he moved to Perth), and minister for mines in 1898-1901.

The problem for Lefroy and his constituents was that since 1886 land in the region had been controlled by the Midland Railway Co. of Western Australia Ltd. Although the line was completed in 1894 it was not until 1907 that any sale of land began and clearing and fencing could proceed.

In 1901-04 Lefroy was agent-general for Western Australia in London, a position he held unassumingly and with distinction; he was appointed C.M.G. in 1903. Rose Lefroy had died in 1902 and on 23 November 1904 in London Lefroy married Madeline Emily Stewart Walford; they returned to Walebing that year and raised a family of a daughter and two sons. Lefroy formed an Aboriginal cricket team, which he recruited from the New Norcia Mission.

In 1911 Lefroy, a Liberal, again became member for Moore and, later, deputy leader of the Opposition. He was minister for lands and agriculture in Frank Wilson's [q.v.] second ministry from 27 July 1916. Following the Labor split over conscription in 1917, John Scaddan [q.v.] and some of his colleagues transferred their support to the government, but Wilson's leadership proved unacceptable; Lefroy, the last, gentlemanly survivor of the Forrest ministries, was thought to command the necessary prestige. From 28 June, as premier and minister for lands, he led a National Party coalition government of the Liberal, Country and National Labor parties, but was troubled by factionalism. Despite his 'considerable personal magnetism', Lefroy was unable to discipline the ill-assorted group: at one stage the establishment of a royal commission was announced without his knowledge. Members of the ministry remained too tied to their party of origin and Lefroy encountered difficulties over financial policy. In August 1918 (Sir) James Mitchell [q.v.], a back-bencher, launched a virtual censure motion on the government's alleged dilatory attitude to soldier settlement and the opening-up of unsettled areas in the south-west. Next month Lefroy himself introduced and secured the passing of a Discharged Soldiers' Settlement Act.

He also became treasurer in April 1919, but another crisis immediately erupted. It was revealed in the press that Lefroy had used his casting vote in cabinet to survive a leadership challenge. In embarrassment he resigned his portfolios on 17 April and was replaced by (Sir) Hal Colebatch [q.v.8] whom Mitchell supported. Lefroy was appointed K.C.M.G. that year.

He was defeated at the elections in 1921 and spent his last years at Walebing, helped by his young sons John and Robert. 'The Squire of Walebing' and his family were noted for their hospitality to hundreds of guests. He died there on 19 March 1930 and was buried in the Anglican section of Karrakatta cemetery. His wife and their daughter and sons, and three sons of his first marriage, survived him. Sir Anthony Langlois Bruce Lefroy (1881-1958) and Sir Edward Henry Bruce Lefroy (1887-1966) were prominent as pastoralists and in many other aspects of Western Australian life.

W. B. Kimberly (comp), *History of West Australia* (Melb, 1897); J. S. Battye (ed), *Cyclopedia of Western Australia*, 1 (Adel, 1912); R. E. Cranfield, *From Ireland to W.A.* (Perth, 1960); C. Cameron, *F.F.B. Wittenoom, pastoral pioneer and explorer* (Perth, 1979); C. T. Stannage (ed), *A new history of Western Australia* (Perth, 1981); G. S. Reid and M. R. Oliver, *The premiers of Western Australia 1890-1982* (Perth, 1982); *Western Mail* (Perth), 4 Apr 1919, 27 Mar 1930; *West Australian*, 11 Apr 1919.   CATHERINE CAMERON

LEGGE, JAMES GORDON (1863-1947), army officer, was born on 15 August 1863 at Hackney, London, eldest of eight sons and a daughter of James Henry Legge, banker, and his wife Ada Jane, née Way. He was educated at Cranleigh School, Surrey, and, after the family's arrival in Sydney in December 1878, at Sydney Grammar School and the University of Sydney from 1881 (B.A., 1884; M.A., 1887; LL.B., 1890). He was admitted to the Bar in New South Wales on 6 March 1891.

From May 1886 Legge taught at Sydney Boys' High School until September 1890 when he resigned to practise law. During the Russian scare of 1885 he had been commissioned as a lieutenant in the 3rd New South Wales Infantry Regiment but resigned next year. In October 1887 he was appointed second lieutenant in the 1st New South Wales Infantry Regiment, being promoted lieutenant in June 1892. An inaugural member of the United Service Institution in 1889, he was elected to its council in 1892, 1896 and 1903.

After three years in chambers Gordon Legge joined the permanent staff of the New South Wales Military Forces with the rank of captain, an appointment which was questioned in the Legislative Assembly. He completed *A selection of Supreme Court cases in New South Wales from 1825 to 1862* (Sydney, 1896) before taking up the appointment on 1 October 1894 and embarking on four months training with the British Army in India. On returning he became adjutant of the 2nd Infantry Regiment and applied himself to critically examining Australian defence arrangements. On 14 October 1896 he married Annie Frances Ferguson at St Andrew's Presbyterian Church, Sydney.

On the outbreak of the South African War Legge was appointed to command an infantry company which left Sydney in November 1899. On arrival he discovered that British authorities had allotted his corps to the 'Australian Regiment', comprised of contingents from several colonies and under Victorian command. His attempts to extract the New South Wales troops helped to bring about disbandment of the regiment after four months. In April 1900 Legge's company, by now a horsed squadron, was incorporated in the 1st New South Wales Mounted Rifles; until November he was adjutant of the regiment which was in action at Diamond Hill and Eland's River. He was an intelligence officer in Colonel De Lisle's force in Cape Colony in 1901-02.

Returning to Sydney via England in October 1902, Legge took up duty as staff officer to the 3rd and 4th Infantry Regiments centred on Richmond and Newcastle, and was granted brevet rank of major. He was simultaneously appointed chief instructor of district schools on infantry training and topography and retained this responsibility until 1907. In September 1903 he became secretary to a committee charged with drafting Commonwealth military regulations and was occasionally employed at Army Headquarters in Melbourne until February 1904. When the 1903 Defence Act was proclaimed in March 1904 he published a handbook on Australian military law, the Act and its regulations. That year he also published a booklet outlining rules for framing operation orders in the field.

On 1 September 1904 Legge was appointed deputy assistant adjutant general at district headquarters in Sydney with substantive rank of major; from December 1905 until May 1906 he acted as assistant adjutant general and chief staff officer. In October 1905 he had also become associated with moves to establish a department of military science at the University of Sydney; a lectureship was offered to him in November 1906 but next June he was assigned for duty at Army Headquarters. For three months he worked with the chief of intelligence, Colonel (Sir) W. T. Bridges [q.v.7], and from September directly under the minister for defence. His duties involved working on a scheme to create a national guard of 80 000 men based on universal service, which he had publicly advocated from 1899. His proposals regarding organization and training of the forces were taken up in parliament by Prime Minister Deakin [q.v.8] on 13 December, although Legge's senior officers did not completely accept them.

In June 1908 he was appointed military secretary on the Military Board with temporary rank of lieut-colonel and he became quartermaster general and third military member on the board in January 1909. He continued preparations for universal training, provided for under the 1909 Defence Act, and frequently lectured on the scheme. The political importance of his work guaranteed him prominence among his fellow staff officers. The future official war historian C. E. W. Bean [q.v.7] remarked: 'Rumour had it that he was the coming man'. He was promoted substantively to lieut-colonel on 17 December 1909 and when Field Marshal Lord Kitchener arrived that month to advise the government on a system of defence for Australia Legge was closely involved in assisting him. Because Kitchener adopted Legge's work for the 1909 Act as the basis for his own recommendations it was later claimed by Bean that what came to be popularly known as Kitchener's scheme could have been more appropriately called Legge's scheme.

In March 1910 Legge was appointed director of operations in addition to his post as quartermaster general, the intention being to bring his work on drafting universal training regulations under the chief of the general staff. Dissatisfaction with the requirement to explain and justify his proposals to the inspector general, Kitchener's staff officer Colonel (Sir) G. M. Kirkpatrick, precipitated an attempt by Legge to resign as director of operations in November. He also felt personally aggrieved, claiming that 'my grade and pay are not commensurate with the duties I am called on to perform ... I have not received the consideration promised by the late Minister'. The minister for defence, (Sir) George Pearce [q.v.], directed Legge to withdraw his resignation, but he retired as director of operations on 17 June 1911, continuing to be quartermaster general.

Legge was nominated to be Australia's representative on the Imperial General Staff in January 1912; in practice he was to be little more than a junior observer at the War Office. He sailed from Melbourne on 12 June and two days later was appointed C.M.G. He published an account of Australia's universal training system in the *Army Review* in January 1913. On 1 May 1914 he was promoted colonel and appointed chief of the general staff with effect from August. He was returning home when war was declared and arrived in Melbourne after preparations had begun under Bridges for the dispatch of a force for active service in Europe. He immediately assumed responsibility for raising a smaller contingent, the Australian Naval and Military Expeditionary Force, and a second Australian Imperial Force contingent and reinforcements.

In May 1915, Bridges, the commander of the A.I.F., was fatally wounded in action with the 1st Australian Division. Legge was appointed to succeed him on 20 May and sailed from Melbourne that day. Protests by senior A.I.F. officers led to representations to Kitchener against his selection by Generals Hamilton and Birdwood [q.v.7], the former writing that though Legge was 'a man of bril-

liant mentality' and 'probably the *cleverest* soldier in Australia' he was regarded as a 'political and self-seeker ... with a knack of quarrelling and writing'. Arriving in Cairo in mid-June Legge immediately gave offence to the general commanding in Egypt by reporting to Melbourne, without reference to his British senior, that the place was 'a totally unsuitable centre for the training of Australian troops', though as commander of the A.I.F. Legge was quite entitled to give independent advice to his government. On reaching Gallipoli he was promoted major general on 22 June and assumed command of the 1st Division. He remained with the division little more than a month before returning to Egypt to form the 2nd Division, surrendering to Birdwood the administrative command of the A.I.F.

In late August Legge embarked on the *Southland* to follow the bulk of his formation to Gallipoli. The vessel was torpedoed south of Lemnos on 2 September, but he arrived at Anzac four days later and his division was allocated responsibility for the front line from Russell's Top to Lone Pine. Next month, however, he was evacuated because of illness and did not rejoin the division until it was back in Egypt. His periods in command of the two divisions had, militarily, been relatively quiet.

In France Legge's division went into the trenches at Fleurbaix in April 1916, becoming the first Australians responsible for a sector on the Western Front. During the 1st battle of the Somme, 2nd Division was assigned the task of capturing Pozières Heights, but Legge's attack on 28-29 July failed with 3500 casualties. The British commander-in-chief attributed this defeat to inadequate preparation and omissions caused by Legge's over-confidence. A second attempt was arranged for 30 July, but delays caused deferral, for which Field Marshal Sir Douglas Haig blamed 'the ignorance of the 2nd Australian Division'—Legge 'was not much good'. Legge pointed out the serious enemy interference to which his division's preparations had been subjected, which Bean noted included 'such bombardments as never before or afterwards were faced by the A.I.F. except in the height of action'. When finally delivered on 4-5 August, 2nd Division's attack, after heavy fighting, was overwhelmingly successful. The division was again engaged at Mouquet Farm later that month before being moved to Ypres in September; it returned to the Somme for two minor but difficult attacks at Flers in November. Legge was appointed C.B. at the New Year and mentioned in dispatches in January. At the end of January, however, he was evacuated to England, ostensibly for health reasons although he protested to his corps commander, Birdwood, that he had never 'been sick for one day in France from arrival'. Having informed Birdwood that if he was not to be again given an operational command he would prefer to return to duty in Australia, Legge reached Melbourne in mid-April 1917; his A.I.F. apppointment ended on 29 April.

On 30 April he was appointed inspector general, Australian Military Forces, and investigated conditions at training camps and schools of instruction. He resumed the appointment of C.G.S. on 1 October. He immediately became involved in the second conscription referendum, and was called upon to give evidence in the unsuccessful prosecution of Queensland premier T. J. Ryan [q.v.] in December for anti-conscription statements. In March 1918 Legge was placed at the disposal of Sir Samuel Griffith [q.v.9] in his capacity as royal commissioner enquiring into reinforcing the A.I.F. In a reversal of his pre-war position Legge revealed himself in 1918 to be a strong advocate of air power for the Australian forces and was appointed to a committee which put forward a plan in January 1919. Next year he was appointed to a committee to consider a scheme for Australia's post-war citizen forces.

Substantively promoted major general on 2 January 1920, Legge relinquished the post of C.G.S. to become commandant of the Royal Military College, Duntroon, on 1 June. He found the college in a crisis because of the scarcity of applicants for a military career and severe reductions in funds. A decision in 1922 to alter the commandant's direct accountability to the minister for defence and make him answerable through the Military Board was strongly opposed by Legge but without success. On 28 June the minister announced that Legge was among officers to be retrenched for reasons of economy. He was placed on the unattached list on 1 August and transferred to the retired list with honorary rank of lieut-general in January 1924; he was awarded the Légion d'honneur in February. His enforced return to civil life before reaching the prescribed retiring age deprived Legge of a military pension. He accordingly turned to pig-farming at Weetangera near Canberra.

Legge died at Oakleigh, Melbourne, on 18 September 1947, predeceased by his wife sixteen days earlier, and was buried in Cheltenham cemetery. He was survived by two sons, the elder of whom, Stanley Ferguson Legge, became a major general. His eldest son George Ferguson Legge was killed in action in France as a private.

Legge was a commander about whom opinions widely differed. Bean stated that 'defects in judgement and experience prevented Legge, despite his high ability, from being a good leader in battle', while Major General

Sir John Gellibrand [q.v.8] considered that 'his strongly held and strongly-expressed views failed to make him *persona grata* with higher authorities'. Major General Sir Brudenell White [q.v.] stated that: 'beyond doubt he was an outstanding character . . . Perhaps he has never been given his full due. A very human and good trainer of troops, he made an able divisional commander and successfully handled the 2nd Division through some difficult periods. But organisation and administration were his forte'. His portrait by Harry Bromilow Harrison hangs on loan from the Australian War Memorial at Duntroon.

Aust Defence Dept, *Official records of the Australian military contingents to the war in South Africa*, P. L. Murray ed (Melb, 1911); C. E. W. Bean, *The story of Anzac*, 1, 2 (Syd, 1921, 1924), and *The A.I.F. in France*, 1916-18 (Syd, 1929, 1933, 1937, 1942), and *Two men I knew* (Syd, 1957); D. N. Gillison, *Royal Australian Air Force, 1939-42* (Canb, 1962); C. D. Coulthard-Clark, *A heritage of spirit* (Melb, 1979), and for bibliog; L. M. Field, *The forgotten war* (Melb, 1979); United Service Inst (NSW), *J*, 1897-99, 1903-05; *London Gazette*, 29 Dec 1916, 4 Jan, 9 Mar 1917; ANZAAS, *Report of meeting*, 23, Jan 1937; *Reveille* (Syd), June 1938; W. Perry, 'Lieutenant-General James Gordon Legge', *VHJ*, 48 (Aug 1977), no 3; *Sydney Mail*, 17 Feb 1900; *Punch* (Melb), 17 June 1909, 26 Jan 1911, 28 Aug 1913, 17 June 1915; *Argus*, 3 Aug 1922, 16 Feb 1924, 19, 20 Sept 1947; *Canb Times*, 4, 19 Sept 1947; *SMH*, 4, 19, 20, 26 Sept 1947; *Canb News*, 2 Apr 1971; file 419/10/7 (AWM); CRS A2653 item 1914, A2657/T1, B197 item 1804/1/7 (AAO).   C. D. COULTHARD-CLARK

LEGGO, HENRY MADREN (1869-1938), merchant and manufacturer, and **ARTHUR VICTOR** (1875-1942), metallurgist and merchant, were born on 28 February 1869 and 19 December 1875 at Eaglehawk, Victoria, the ninth and eleventh children of William Leggo (d. 1879), goldminer, and his wife Elizabeth Jane, née Rowe, both of Cornwall, England.

Henry was educated at Eaglehawk State School and at Slade's private school. In 1882 he became a clerk with Frederick Rickards, Bendigo grocery distributor. Henry was admitted to partnership in 1891 and in the mid-1890s purchased Rickards's interest. Trading as H. M. Leggo & Co., with premises among the largest in Bendigo, he manufactured grocers' sundries and bought a coffee, tea and spice business. Large purchases of flour and vegetables for the making of pickles and sauces stimulated the regional market through Leggo's resident buyers. The output of the salt lakes in Victoria's northern districts was absorbed in the production of cooking and rock salt. On 5 March 1890 he had married Edith Susan, daughter of Thomas Edwards, a Cornish proprietor of pyrites works at Bendigo and Ballarat.

By the early 1900s the company was one of Victoria's foremost wholesale and manufacturing concerns. Leggo closed his coffee business to concentrate on the manufacture of a range of products including condiments, preserves and canned foods. He developed an export trade, formed a limited company in 1918, mainly a family concern, and progressively transferred processing operations to Abbotsford in Melbourne. Living in Bendigo, Leggo had substantial investments in and was a director of several gold-mining companies. He was involved in local organizations as a keen bowler, clubman, football enthusiast, Freemason and trustee of the Forest Street Methodist Church.

Henry died on 1 September 1938 during a business trip to Melbourne and was buried in Bendigo cemetery. His wife predeceased him by three months and he was survived by a son and four daughters.

Arthur Victor was educated at King's College, Melbourne, and the Ballarat School of Mines. In 1892 he was appointed an assayer with Thomas Edwards's Ballarat metallurgical works. He became manager in 1896 and subsequently acquired an interest. In 1906 Leggo left the firm after a bitter legal battle instituted by Edwards over profit-sharing and disputed partnership. As A. Victor Leggo & Co. he operated a plant at Spotswood, Melbourne, for three years before establishing a metal-refining works at Bendigo in 1909, and the Victor Leggo Chemical Co. in 1913 at Yarraville as well as an organization to market his products. The head office was in Melbourne with branches in Sydney and Brisbane.

Leggo invented and patented the 'Leggo' ore roasting furnace, and during World War I pioneered the manufacture of previously imported chemicals and raw materials essential to the munitions industry. In the 1920s he claimed to be the largest producer of arsenic in the Southern Hemisphere. His company supplied chemicals for the leather, wool and rubber industries, and seed wheatpickles, sheep dip, rabbit poison, pest sprays and weed-killers to primary producers. He also had an agency for cosmetics and toiletries. Leggo was a director of Bendigo mining companies. A founder, sometime treasurer and a vice-president (1919-33) of the Australian Industries Protection League, he was a member of clubs in Ballarat, Bendigo and Melbourne, and an associate and member respectively of the London and Australasian Institutes of Mining and Metallurgy.

On 23 February 1916 Leggo had married Ruby Gertrude Crawford at Bendigo. He died suddenly of coronary vascular disease on 21 September 1942 at his home in St Kilda Road, Melbourne, and was cremated. His wife and two daughters survived him.

W. B. Kimberly, *Bendigo and its vicinity* (Ballarat, 1895); *Bendigo and district in 1902* (Melb, 1902); J. Smith (ed), *Cyclopedia of Victoria*, 2 (Melb, 1904); *Ballarat Courier*, 13 Aug 1904; *Age*, 23 Mar 1906, 23 Sept 1942; *Argus*, 23 Mar 1906, 2 Sept 1938, 24 Sept 1942; *Bendigo Advertiser*, 20 Jan 1913, 2 Sept 1938, 23 Sept 1942; information from Mr J. O'Toole, Plumrose (Aust) Ltd, Melb.

JOHN LACK

LE HUNTE, SIR GEORGE RUTHVEN (1852-1925), governor, was born on 20 August 1852 at Artramont, Wexford, Ireland, son of George Le Hunte, high sheriff, and his wife Mary, daughter of Edward Pennefather, lord chief justice of Ireland. He was educated at Eton and Trinity College, Cambridge (B.A., 1873; M.A., 1880), and called to the Bar of the Inner Temple, London, in 1881. On 14 February 1884 he married Caroline Rachel Clowes at the parish church, Eardisland, Herefordshire. Appointed private secretary to Sir Arthur Gordon in 1875, he served in Fiji in 1875-87, becoming judicial commissioner for the Western Pacific High Commission in 1883. He was transferred to the West Indies where he served as president of Dominica (1887-94), and colonial secretary of Barbados (1894-97) and Mauritius (1897). He was appointed C.M.G. in 1898.

On 22 March 1899 he assumed the administration of British New Guinea as lieutenant-governor in succession to Sir William MacGregor [q.v.5]. The two were as different 'as chalk from cheese', wrote one of their field officers. In contrast with his short, stocky and crusty predecessor, Le Hunte was 6 ft. 2 ins. (188 cm), with distinguished features, a walrus moustache and a genial nature. Contemporaries remarked upon his 'charm of manner' and his 'constant kindness of heart'. He nevertheless announced his intention of maintaining and furthering MacGregor's policies and accordingly promoted the extension of government control, supported the 'civilising influence' of missions and encouraged, though with as limited success as his predecessor, controlled European settlement. A medical department was established and a government station founded at Cape Nelson. Further policy initiatives were inhibited by lack of funds. His rule coincided with a troubled phase in the colony's history. Delay until November 1901 in the assumption of Commonwealth responsibility (in place of the joint control by Britain and Queensland) led to uncertainty about funding and in August 1900 he declared the colony to be 'within measurable distance' of the end of its resources. Over half his period in office was spent elswhere, much of it in lobbying Australian premiers.

The killing and eating of the two missionaries James Chalmers [q.v.3] and Oliver Tomkins and their Papuan companions at Goari-bari Island on 8 April 1901 further over-shadowed his time in New Guinea. Rejecting the London Missionary Society's represen-tative's plea against reprisals, Le Hunte, tak-ing 'full responsibility' for the decision, three weeks later led a punitive expedition which killed some twenty-four Goaribari, burned their skull-laden ceremonial houses and smashed their war-canoes. His report 'deplored' the necessity of taking life but added, 'the natives brought it on themselves and I believe conscientiously that they deserved it'. Unlike that led by his successor Christopher Stansfeld Robinson in 1904, it was a disciplined, orderly expedition whose 'moderation' and 'humanity' were praised by the L.M.S. Although a time-honoured strata-gem of colonial rule, the punitive expedition provoked criticism in Britain and Australia, which was largely allayed by his second, con-ciliatory expedition in March 1902.

Returning to New Guinea in May 1903 after a years leave in England, Le Hunte was appointed K.C.M.G. and governor of South Australia (July 1903-December 1908). He carried out his vice-regal duties with energy and enthusiasm, winning respect for his administrative ability, common sense and unassuming kindliness. His intelligent inter-est in the welfare of Aborigines was recog-nized, while his affection for youth earned him the title, 'the children's governor'. He contin-ued to give Alfred Deakin [q.v.8] and Atlee Hunt [q.v.9] candid and frequent advice on the administration of Papua. Reflecting in 1906 on thirty-one years of colonial service, he wrote, 'every day of it has been a happy one'. In December 1908 Le Hunte accepted the post of governor of Trinidad and Tobago, declining reluctantly to extend his 'run in an Australian paddock'. Despite personal frugal-ity his position involved financial burden and he advised Deakin: 'Unless a Governor here has considerably more private means than I . . . he will find the struggle very hard'.

Appointed G.C.M.G. in 1912, he retired in 1915 to Crowborough, Sussex. In December 1917 he was appointed to the London Appeals Tribunal. Predeceased by his son, and sur-vived by his wife and daughter, he died of cancer on 29 January 1925 at Crowborough and was buried with Anglican rites.

G. Murray, *A man's life* (Lond, 1934); H. T. Bur-gess (ed), *Cyclopedia of South Australia*, 1 (Adel, 1907); Alcazar Press, *Queensland, 1900* (Brisb, nd); *British New Guinea Annual Report*, 1898-1903; *Public Service Review* (SA), June 1903; *SA Literary Societies' J*, 10 Jan 1909; *Syd Mail*, 4 Mar 1899; *The Times*, 30 Jan, 4 Feb 1925; Report, 5 Aug 1905, Walter Malcolmson papers (ML); Atlee Hunt *and* Alfred Deakin papers (NL); S. J. Way letters (SAA); A1 03/3487 (AAO, Canb).

DIANE LANGMORE

LEIDIG, GEORG FRIEDRICH (1870-1925), Lutheran clergyman, was born on 16 December 1870 at Marktsteft, Bavaria, Ger-many, eldest son of Johann Michael Leidig, woodworker, and his wife Maria Philippina, née Enzenberger, who died when Friedrich was 12. Leidig was unhappy working in a bakery and, helped by an uncle, completed studies at the Neuendettelsau Mission Semi-nary, Bavaria (1887-91). He arrived in South Australia in 1891, was ordained at Light Pass by Rev. G. J. Rechner [q.v.6] and proceeded to Bethesda Mission on Lake Killalpanninna, Cooper Creek. In 1892 Leidig went to Point Pass, near Eudunda, to serve a scattered rural parish, ultimately comprising eight churches.

Three years later he realized his vision of a boarding institution as a centre to instruct his confirmees, train teachers for Lutheran day schools and to offer higher education. Imman-uel Preparatory School (later Evangelical Lutheran College) opened at Point Pass on 27 February, with Leidig as its head. Its facilities were extended in 1900 and 1914, and it edu-cated some students to matriculation. Lei-dig's increasing duties precluded the develop-ment of his own pedagogical skills. A big, tall man, he was a strict disciplinarian whose vehemence could make him appear brusque and impatient in class; but in their troubles his students found him understanding and fatherly. He had married Maria Margaretha Regina Eckardt of Gunzenhausen, Bavaria, at Yorketown on 3 August 1892. She was the loved 'mother' of all students, as well as their own three sons, two of whom studied in Ger-many. Although Leidig resisted moves to re-locate the school at Tanunda in 1910, it eventually moved to North Adelaide (1923) and Walkerville (1942); Immanuel College is now a co-educational boarding-school at Novar Gardens.

In 1899 Leidig had become associate editor of the weekly periodical of the Evangelical Lutheran Immanuel Synod in South Australia, the *Kirchen und Missions-Zeitung*. Sole edi-tor from 1907, he resigned through pressure of duties in 1911.

After Rev. J. C. Auricht's [q.v.3] death Leidig was elected in 1907 as president of the Immanuel Synod. He visited Germany, to arouse interest in the college, and Western Australia. Leidig guided his Church through difficult times, encouraging members to maintain activities for the welfare of Abori-gines (Cooper Creek until 1915; Hermanns-burg, Central Australia), diaspora work in Western Australia and Tasmania, and the col-lege. The impossibility of conducting Church's normal annual conventions during and after World War I caused the responsibil-ity for far-reaching decisions to fall on him, including finance. His family savings provided substantial interim assistance. Leidig was deeply affected by the war; but although the college was listed for closure, following State legislation of 30 June 1917, it remained open.

The onset in late 1917 of a baffling nervous breakdown forced him to relinquish more and more work and to retire from Point Pass early, in 1921. Five Lutheran Church bodies, ranging from Queensland to South Australia, amalgamated on 8 March 1921, as the culmination of developments which he had largely initiated in 1910 and had fostered since. But he could only be a passive onlooker, not a guiding light of the new United Evangelical Lutheran Church in Australia. Leidig and his wife retired to Tanunda where, when he was 'totally helpless and bodily and mentally quite infirm', they received financial support from old scholars. He died from cerebral haemorrhage at Tanunda on 11 August 1925, and was buried in the Langmeil church cemetery.

T. Hebart, *The United Evangelical Lutheran Church in Australia (U.E.L.C.A.)*, J. J. Stolz translator and ed (Adel, 1938); G. A. Keller (comp), *Immanuel College jubilee souvenir 1895-1970* (priv print, Adel, 1945); *Lutheran Herald*, 31 Aug 1925; G. F. Leidig file (Lutheran Church Archives, Nth Adel).   H. F. W. PROEVE

LEIGH, KATHLEEN MARY JOSEPHINE (1881-1964), crime entrepreneur, was born on 10 March 1881 at Dubbo, New South Wales, eighth child of native-born parents Timothy Beahan, bootmaker, and his wife Charlotte, née Smith. Reputedly she was neglected and at 12 was incarcerated in Parramatta Industrial School for Girls. In Sydney from 18 she soon 'got into trouble'. On 2 May 1902 Kate married James Lee (Leigh), whom police described as an illegal bookmaker and petty criminal. He was imprisoned in 1905 for assaulting and robbing their Glebe landlord with his wife's assistance. Moreover, a perjury conviction and five years imprisonment were the outcome of her attempt to 'clear' her spouse by alleging that he only attacked the landlord when he found him in bed with Kate, who was negotiating their arrears of rent. Upon release from gaol, their separation continued.

Her relationship with Samuel 'Jewey' Freeman, brought her wider contacts with the criminal underworld. He and Ernest 'Shiner' Ryan were convicted for the armed robbery of the payroll for the Eveleigh railway workshop on 18 June 1914—reputedly the first armed robbers to use a getaway car in the history of Australian crime. Leigh tried to give Freeman an alibi but was again sen-

tenced to five years imprisonment for perjury early in 1915. Although police recorded only thirteen minor convictions (mostly prostitution-related, despite her later denials that she ever worked as a prostitute), they noted that she often provided bail and alibis for gangsters and racketeers.

In 1919-55 Leigh's main enterprise was the lucrative 'sly-grog' trade, induced by six o'clock closing. In Sydney on 26 September 1922 she married Edward Joseph Barry (d. 1948), dealer. From her Surry Hills home she became an organized crime entrepreneur, supplying at extortionate prices the fullest available range of illicit goods and services, including after-hours drinking venues, sly-grog, prostitution, illegal betting, gambling and, from the mid-1920s, cocaine. Acquiring the title 'Queen of the Underworld', Leigh obtained loyalty and protection from a male network of gangsters, but often had to protect them and was adept with a rifle. Rival gangs eroded her profits from the cocaine trade by standing over and slashing decoys (often working prostitutes) with razors. In March 1930 she shot and killed 'Snowy' Prendergast when he and other gangsters broke into her home. She was not indicted for the killing, or for shooting Joseph McNamara on 19 December 1931.

Perhaps feeling the pinch of competition, her rival Tilly Devine [q.v.8] publicly denounced Leigh as a 'white slaver' and 'dope-pusher', who enjoyed immunity from prosecution by means of unnamed Labor contacts in municipal politics. In 1930 Kate Leigh was charged with possessing cocaine and with consorting; sentenced to two years imprisonment, she was allowed to pay a £250 fine in lieu of serving the second year. During the Depression she also processed stolen goods for resale: in 1933 she and two men were convicted of receiving hosiery; however a young policeman secured suspension of her sentence on condition she returned to her family at Dubbo for two years.

Despite frequent police raids and numerous minor convictions, Leigh's sly-grog trade continued throughout the 1930s and 1940s. Her wealth was legendary. At times described as corpulent, 'flowsy' and leathery-skinned she was noted for her court-room appearances in silver fox furs and large-brimmed hats, her fingers cluttered with diamond rings. In January 1950 she flew to Western Australia and married 'Shiner' Ryan (d. 1957) on 18 January at Fremantle. They lived together in Sydney for six months, Kate continuing business as usual. After disputes about domicile he returned to Fremantle. In 1954 she was declared bankrupt for failing to pay some £6191 in arrears of taxes. Continuing to live at Surry Hills, she died on 4 February 1964 and was buried in Botany cemetery with Catholic rites. Her daughter survived her.

Much of the press, ignoring her connexion with organized crime, treated her as the kindly provider of a social service in a repressive era, against whom no real 'wrong-doing' was convincingly proved, and pointed to her wartime patriotism and generosity to the unemployed.

V. G. Kelly, *Rugged angel* (Syd, 1961); A. McCoy, *Drug traffic* (Syd, 1980); NSW Clerk of the Peace, Depositions, *R. v Kate Leigh*, Central Criminal Court, 20 Nov 1905 (9/7085), 29 Mar 1915 (9/7195), *and* NSW Court Reporting Branch, Transcript, *R. v Kathleen Barry* and two others, Syd Quarter Sessions, 15 Apr 1933 (6/1175), *and* NSW Col Sec, Special Bundle, Police Offences (Drugs) Act (3/2376 2, NSWA).   JUDITH ALLEN

LEIGHTON, ARTHUR EDGAR (1873-1961), chemical engineer and administrator, was born on 17 June 1873 at Christchurch, Surrey, England, son of James Leighton, linen draper and later a farmer, and his wife Martha, née Hamer. He was educated at Westminster Wesleyan Training College and the Birkbeck Literary and Scientific Institution (later, Birkbeck College, University of London). In the consulting firm of William Macnab he grappled with chemical problems, including work for Fletcher Moulton of the celebrated cordite patent case (1892-95). After experience at the royal gunpowder factory at Waltham Abbey in cordite production, in 1903 he was appointed to the government of India's department of military supply at the newly constructed explosives factory at Aravunkadu (southern India); he became assistant manager. While on leave in England in 1907 he met C. Napier Hake, chief inspector of explosives for Victoria, who recommended him as designer and manager of the cordite factory to be established by the Commonwealth government at Maribyrnong, Melbourne. He was appointed in January 1909 and full production was achieved by June 1912. On 2 April 1914, at St Mark's Anglican Church, Darling Point, Sydney, he married Norma Stogdale of Melbourne.

On an information-collecting mission to England via India, Leighton was requisitioned by the British government and appointed technical adviser on the manufacture of explosives to the Ministry of Munitions (1915-18). He initiated a scheme for attracting Australian chemists to work in the munitions programme; over 100 responded and from this flowed similar schemes for technicians and tradesmen. In July 1916 Leighton was appointed general manager of an arsenal planned for Australia. From his office in Australia House, London, he enlisted scientists

and engineers with expert knowledge of fighting equipment. In 1919 (Sir) Winston Churchill praised Leighton's work on the erection of explosives factories, his contribution to the running of the huge Gretna Works and the recruitment of Australian chemists. That year having returned to Australia, Leighton was appointed chairman of the board of management of the Commonwealth government factories and instituted the Defence Research Laboratories. In 1921-38 he was controller-general of munitions supply. He took a leading part in the preliminaries which led to the establishment of aeronautical research in the mid-1920s. During the 1930s he retained his staff by adapting his factories to the production of such domestic items as lipstick containers.

Leighton retired in November 1937 but returned as controller-general in May 1938-June 1939 and in 1940-46 as consultant on explosives. He was responsible for radical changes in the manufacture of cordite and the use of 'gun paper' made from pinus radiata as a replacement for cotton. An alternative source of glycerine was established using sugar as raw material. Absolute standards of measurement were introduced at Maribyrnong before the National Standards Laboratory was established. In association with private industry Leighton directed the construction of twenty-three annexes to produce chemicals not manufactured in Australia. An ambition to produce an Australian gun, conceived in 1919, was achieved in 1937 with the anti-aircraft three-pounder. In 1941 Essington Lewis [q.v.] attributed the successful local production of the first pitch-measuring machine to Leighton's establishment of the Meteorological Laboratory.

He finally retired in April 1950 aged 76. Applauding his ability, single-mindedness and courage, R. G. (Lord) Casey wrote: 'the history of explosives and allied chemical production in this country is the history of your personal efforts . . . you are the father of munitions production'.

Leighton had become a fellow of the Institute of Chemistry of Great Britain and Ireland in 1907 and served on its council. In 1921 he was president of the Victorian branch of the fledgling Australian Chemical Institute, playing a key role in the tortuous negotiations leading to the granting of a royal charter. In 1953 he was general president and he wrote a history of the institute.

Of medium stature, pleasant, modest and cheerful, Leighton was possessed of an equanimity hardly ever ruffled save when niceties of book-keeping threatened the progress of urgent projects. An abrasive exchange between him and (Sir) David Rivett [q.v.] and others in February 1930 over the proper ambit of forest products research by the Council for Scientific and Industrial Research led to a permanent coolness between the two men. Widely read, Leighton was never at a loss for a quotation or anecdote to illustrate his point. In his youth he was an enthusiastic cricketer and his later recreation was golf. He was a member of the Melbourne and Naval and Military clubs. He twice declined Imperial honours at the end of World War I, but was appointed C.M.G. in 1937.

Survived by his wife, son and daughter, Leighton died on 6 November 1961 in Melbourne and was cremated. Though he was brought up a Methodist, the rigour of religious observances had diminished his zeal. The Leighton medal, endowed by his daughter, is the premier award of the Royal Australian Chemical Institute.

D. P. Mellor, *The role of science and industry* (Canb, 1958); British Ministry of Munitions, *Newsletter*, 26 Mar 1943; Dept of Supply (Cwlth), *Newsletter*, 12 Apr 1950; Aust Chemical Inst, *Procs*, 1954; family papers including autobiographical notes (held by Miss A. Leighton, Glen Iris, Melb).   L. W. WEICKHARDT

LEIST, FREDERICK WILLIAM (1873-1945), artist, was born on 21 August 1873 at Surry Hills, Sydney, eighth surviving and fifteenth child of Edward Frederick Leist, builder, and his wife Harriet Eliza, née Norris, both Londoners. Fred was educated at Crown Street Public School and, while training as a furniture designer in the workshops of David Jones [q.v.2] Ltd, studied art at Sydney Technical College before becoming a student of the Art Society of New South Wales; under Julian Ashton's [q.v.7] tuition he learned *plein air* techniques. On 29 January 1898 he married Ada Sarah Roberts with Methodist forms.

As a black-and-white artist Leist drew for the *Bulletin* in the 1890s and became staff artist on the *Sydney Mail*; he was also local representative for the London *Graphic* from 1900. According to William Moore [q.v.] he 'was the first to portray the Australian girl as a definite type'. Leist was an original councilmember of the Society of Artists, Sydney, in 1895 and, after their merger, of the Royal Art Society of New South Wales. However in 1907 he was one of the twelve who re-established the Society of Artists.

Next year Leist, with his wife and daughter, went to London. He joined the staff of the *Graphic* and illustrated for magazines and publishing companies, but he found that the *Graphic* 'worked the tail off me'—he wanted time to paint. From 1910 to 1925 he exhibited regularly at the Royal Academy of Arts. His first successful picture, 'The Mirror', a portrait of his daughter, was hung on the line at the Royal Academy in 1911 and

next year at the Salon de la Société des Artistes Français. At the 1914 Royal Academy exhibition his painting of two Spanish guitar players, 'The Rivals', was acclaimed. The *Review* critic wrote: 'it is a composition in light and a pattern of colour, given power and meaning by restraint'. Noted for his studies of handsome women, Leist was elected to the Royal Society of British Artists and to the Chelsea Arts Club in 1913 and next year to the Royal Institute of Oil Painters; later he also exhibited with the Royal Society of Portrait Painters.

During World War I Leist worked for the War Office designing recruiting posters. Then in September 1917 he was appointed an official war artist with the Australian Imperial Force and attached to 5th Division headquarters as an honorary lieutenant. From September to December and from June to August 1918, 'dodging shells and mustard gas', he produced about 150 small sketches, drawings and water-colours, and a portrait of Lieut-General Sir Talbot Hobbs [q.v.9]. He later fulfilled commissions to paint four large battle scenes including 'Battle of Polygon Wood' and 'Capture of Mont St Quentin'. The striking colours of these battle scenes are in strong contrast to the delicacy and muted tones of his water-colours such as 'The Lacemaker'.

In London Leist consolidated his reputation: he was represented in the 1918 exhibition of Australian war artists at the Grafton Galleries and showed regularly at the Royal Academy and with sundry societies. In 1922 the National Art Gallery of New South Wales paid £400 for his 'Shadows' and 'Between the Lights'. He painted a miniature picture for the Queen's Dolls' House and his decorations 'did much to make the Chelsea Arts Club's ball one of the events of the year'. In May 1924 he designed the costumes and painted a vast back-cloth depicting the Rocky Mountains, fir trees and wigwams for Samuel Coleridge-Taylor's oratorio, *Song of Hiawatha*, at the Albert Hall. That year he was elected to the council of the Royal Institute of Oil Painters. He painted two huge murals for the Australian pavilion at the British Empire Exhibition at Wembley in 1924-25, and designed and supervised the construction of a large action model, with real water, of Sydney Harbour and its foreshores. An American millionaire D. P. Davis visited Wembley and offered Leist a lucrative contract. In 1925-26 he produced similar models and murals at St Augustine and Tampa, Florida. He travelled through Texas, New Mexico and Arizona and was deeply impressed by Taos Indians.

Leist joined his wife in Sydney in December 1926 and lived at Mosman. He held one-man shows of his American paintings with a few Australian landscapes at the Macquarie

Galleries, Sydney, and the Fine Art Society Gallery, Melbourne, in 1927, and at the Blaxland Gallery, Sydney, and the Sedon Gallery, Melbourne, in 1934, this time including such early paintings as 'The Mirror' and 'The Rivals'. In 1929-38 he taught painting at East Sydney Technical College. He also painted portraits—those of Sir Littleton Groom [q.v.9], Sir Earle Page and P. J. Lynch [qq.v.] are in Parliament House, Canberra. In 1934 he published an article, 'Mural Decoration', in *Art in Australia*. He joined the Australian Water-Colour Institute and the XV Group of Independent Artists, and in 1937 was a foundation member of the Australian Academy of Art, but soon resigned.

'Tall and lean, with the deep facial lines that come of much laughter and much experience', Leist had loved travel and adventure and wrote humorously about his encounters with bootleggers. Survived by his wife and daughter, he died in St Vincent's Hospital of cerebral thrombosis on 18 February 1945 and was cremated with Presbyterian forms. One of the most versatile Australian artists, Fred Leist was essentially a decorative painter and 'a colourist of no mean order, interested above all in problems of reflected light'.

A. Gray, *Masterpieces of the Australian War Memorial* (Adel, 1982); *Art and Architecture*, 5, Jan 1908; *Review* (Lond), June 1914; *Triad* (Syd), Apr 1927; *Society* (Syd), 1 Sept 1927; *SMH*, 25 June 1918, 14, 15 Jan 1927, 25 Apr 1934, 8 Apr 1938, 19 Feb 1945; *Sydney Mail*, 22 Nov 1922, 8, 22 June 1927; *Age*, 31 Aug, 1 Sept 1927; *A'sian*, 10 Sept 1927.   MARTHA RUTLEDGE

LEITCH, SIR WALTER (1867-1945), businessman, was born on 6 November 1867 at Edgerston, Roxburghshire, Scotland, son of George Leitch, farm servant, and his wife Isabella, née Wilson. He was educated at nearby Morebattle before moving to London to enter the Civil Service in 1884. Shortly after, he joined the London-based Quaker firm of Joseph Baker & Sons, manufacturers and exporters of baking and confectionery machinery, with whom he was to be associated for the rest of his working life. Leitch came to Australia in 1889 to exhibit the firm's wares and remained in Melbourne as the Australian manager of a prospering business from 1890. In 1905-08 he was also general manager of the Welsbach Light Co. of Australasia Ltd, a British company that imported gas-light fittings, but he returned full time to the service of Joseph Baker and in 1913 was rewarded with a place on the London board.

Leitch was thrust into government service soon after his return from the United Kingdom in 1914 because of his firm's large-scale involvement in war production, at first in the manufacture of field kitchens and later in munitions engineering. In June 1915 he was appointed to the Federal Munitions Committee and next year to the Directorate of Munitions whose task was to restrict the import of metals and machinery into Australia and augment Empire supplies by arranging the export of Australian steel. In 1917 he became director of the newly established Commonwealth Bureau of Commerce and Industry whose ambitious but poorly designed brief was to provide post-war assistance to Australian industries; he resigned from this ineffective body within the year. In the course of his official duties Leitch had come into contact with nearly all the leading politicians, civil servants and businessmen, and his appointment as C.B.E. in 1918 confirmed his new status in Melbourne society. He was described by Melbourne *Punch* that year as having 'a look of good health', 'a big frame . . . quick, decisive manner, and . . . a keen sense of humour'.

Business affairs took Leitch away from Australia in 1919-22 when Joseph Baker & Sons merged with its main rival, Perkins Engineering, and extended its operations in the United States of America, Leitch swapping his seat on the main board for a place on the board of the American subsidiary. On his return to Australia he accepted the delicate position of importers' representative on the recently established Tariff Board, remaining a member until heavy business commitments, which necessitated interstate and overseas travel and which included his directorship of Swallow [q.v.6] & Ariel from 1924, forced his retirement in 1929.

That year Leitch was appointed Victorian agent-general in London, the first non-political occupant of the post. Always hard-working, he successfully used his commercial skills and contacts to find new markets for Victorian produce; his three-year term of office was extended for twelve months before his return to Melbourne, with a newly conferred knighthood, in June 1933. In Melbourne he joined the board of G. J. Coles & Co. in 1936 and continued to mix private business with public office by serving as a commissioner of the State Savings Bank in 1935-39 and as president of the Victorian Baby Health Centres Association in 1933-34 and of Melbourne's (Royal) Dental Hospital from March 1938. A Presbyterian, he was a leading figure in the Scots community.

Sir Walter died on 7 July 1945 at Toorak and was cremated. Childless, he was survived by his wife EMILY BERTHA (1873-1957), née Main, whom he had married on 23 March 1898 at Scots Church, Melbourne. After making provision for his wife, Leitch left his estate, valued for probate at £11 435, for charitable and educational purposes, including the establishment of scholarships at Morebattle School.

Lady Leitch, daughter of John Main, secretary of the Victorian Education Department in 1889-91 and later a barrister, was one of the early women graduates of the University of Melbourne's medical school. She practised at Malvern before her marriage and was an original member of the honorary medical staff of the Queen Victoria Hospital. In 1914-18 she worked at the Anzac buffet and was later associated with the formation of the district nursing service. In 1934-50 she was a member of the board of management of the (Royal) Women's Hospital (vice-president, 1940). She died at South Yarra on 10 March 1957, leaving £9216 to the Victorian Women Graduates Association which established the Lady Leitch scholarship for women graduates.

E. Scott, *Australia during the war* (Syd, 1936); A. Muir, *The history of Baker Perkins* (Cambridge, 1968); Education Dept (Vic), *Vision and realisation*, L. J. Blake ed (Melb, 1973); *Industrial Aust and Mining Standard*, 18 Apr 1929, p 271; *Argus*, 14 June 1917, 11 Mar 1922, 15 Jan 1929, 3 June 1933, 9 July 1945; *Age*, 8 Aug 1917, 12 Nov 1957; *Punch* (Melb), 9 May 1918; *Herald* (Melb), 24 June 1933; *Sun-News Pictorial*, 28 Aug 1934; *SMH*, 19 Oct 1936.   D. T. MERRETT

LEMMON, JOHN (1875-1955), union organizer and politician, was born on 15 July 1875 in the Melbourne Trades Hall caretaker's cottage at Carlton, eighth of ten children and third son of caretaker Samuel Lambert Lemmon, a wood-turner from London, and his Irish-born wife Matilda, née Thompson. Jack was nourished on unionism. A framed document in the cottage testified to his father's part in the eight-hour movement, while Matilda who died in 1938 aged 96 'mothered' the Trades Hall for fifty years, at first as her husband's caretaking partner and from 1902 as his successor.

After education at the Trades Hall 'Tinpot' School and Rathdowne Street State School, Lemmon became a carpenter's apprentice and joined the Timber Workers' Union at 15. For five years he made sash frames, learning that it paid the boss to keep him at this one task and that the apprenticeship system needed reform—a conclusion reinforced when he forsook carpentry for tailoring. Working as a cutter, he studied at the Working Men's College and some time after 1901 set up his own business as 'Our Boys' Tailor at Footscray.

When the Cutters and Trimmers' Union was reorganized in 1899 Lemmon was vice-president; he later became secretary and in 1905 was president of the Victorian Clothing Operatives' Union. He was a delegate to the Trades Hall Council in 1900-07 and from March 1900, as secretary of the Trades Hall Organizing Committee, worked alongside S. Barker, J. W. Billson [qq.v.7] and H. E. Beard. He was prominent in the 1900 anti-sweating campaign. Lemmon combined practical talents with a studious bent. When his fellow organizers were presented with marble clocks or gold watch chains in 1901, he received fifty books on political economy and history. It was said that after losing bids as a Labor candidate for the Legislative Assembly seat of Footscray in 1901 and 1902 and a try for the Senate in 1903 he was helped to a Williamstown victory in 1904 by perusal of the speeches of Pitt and Walpole.

Lemmon closed his business when he entered parliament and, after marrying Edith Ruddock on 25 April 1905 at the Dromana Methodist Church, settled at Williamstown. By assiduous attention to his political duties, aided by a wife devoted to charitable works, he held the seat continuously until May 1954, a Victorian and British Commonwealth record term. Tall and handsome, in 1904 'the baby of the House', he was still in 1913 'the beauty man of the Labor Party', though he was untidy and later acquired a stoop. His essential earnestness was, according to Melbourne *Punch*, enlivened by bright, sometimes fanatical, eyes and a Continental haircut.

Secretary of the State Parliamentary Labor Party in 1913-38, Lemmon had little aspiration for party leadership or interest in political theory but served four times as minister of public instruction and of labour: under Elmslie [q.v.8] in December 1913, Prendergast [q.v.] in July-November 1924 and Hogan [q.v.9] in May 1927-November 1928 and from December 1929 until May 1932, losing the labour portfolio which, during the Depression had been only nominally his, in March. In April that year he supported T. Tunnecliffe's [q.v.] rejection of the Premiers' Plan, thereby aligning himself against Hogan.

Education was Lemmon's forte. He was president of the Working Men's College in 1910 and Trades Hall representative there until 1924, and sat on the University of Melbourne council in 1932-39. But he never threw off the traditional Labor bias towards technical schools. Fees were retained in high schools after his government abolished them in technical schools in 1927 and in 1930 Lemmon blocked the plans of the director of education M. P. Hansen [q.v.9] to establish multipurpose secondary schools; for months the two men, who also clashed over departmental appointments, were not on speaking terms. The project dearest to Lemmon was the passage in 1927 of the apprenticeship bill which, after years of effort, set up an apprenticeship authority.

Lemmon served on the Murray waters royal commission of 1910-11 and on the select committee and royal commission into the marketing and transportation of grain in 1911 and 1912-13. His long parliamentary service made him an authority on standing orders but although he liked to air his knowledge of May's *Parliamentary privileges* he refused the Speakership in December 1952, feeling he was 'past it'. He was a member of the Australian Natives' Association (president in 1910-11), honorary secretary of the Victorian Association of Friendly Societies and a trustee of the Melbourne Cricket Ground.

Lemmon died of cancer on 28 October 1955 at Hawthorn and was cremated after a state funeral. He left an estate valued for probate at £16 518. His wife, two daughters and a son, Nelson, who had a successful career in Federal politics, survived him.

R. J. W. Selleck, *Frank Tate* (Melb, 1982); *Aust J of Education*, 14, no 2 (1970), p 168; *V&P* (LA Vic), 1911, 2 (14); *PD* (LA Vic), 1927, p 1067, 1955-56, p 1321; *Tocsin*, 16 Mar, 21 Dec 1899, 7 Mar 1901; *Punch* (Melb), 18 Dec 1913, 4 Sept 1924; *Labor Call*, 4 Sept 1924; *Table Talk*, 20 Oct 1927; *Herald* (Melb), 5 Sept 1927, 15 July, 26 Aug 1938, 7 June 1954, 29, 31 Oct 1955; *Age*, 29 Oct 1955; *Argus*, 24 Feb, 30 Apr 1932; ANU Archives (E 138/7).   ANN G. SMITH

LEMMONE, JOHN (1861-1949), flautist and composer, was born on 22 June 1861 at Ballarat, Victoria, son of John Lemon, originally Lamoni, a goldminer from Greece, and his English wife Mary, née Baker. Raised in a musical family, he progressed from a tin whistle to the fife, and played in his school's and in the Golden City drum and fife bands. At 12 he bought his first flute with gold he had panned himself.

In 1874 the family moved to Melbourne where John continued to study the flute and became principal flute with Lyster's [q.v.5] Royal Italian Opera Company. He learned some harmony and theory, but claimed to have been largely self taught. On a visit from Adelaide where he played with the Theatre Royal Orchestra, he made his solo début at a Melbourne benefit for the musician Herr Elsasser in May 1884 at the same time as Nellie Melba [q.v.], then Mrs Armstrong. Acquiring the requisite foreign chic by changing his name to Lemmone, he toured Australia and Asia with soprano Amy Sherwin [q.v.6] in 1887-89. On 11 December 1889 he married Isabella Jeffrey Lindsay Stewart at Darlinghurst, Sydney. Tours of Australia, New Zealand and Asia followed with singers Janet Patey, Signor Foli and Charles Santley and violinist Pablo Sarasate.

In London in 1894 Lemmone renewed his acquaintance with Melba whose influential introductions furthered his career. He played obbligati at Melba's fashionable soirées where he met celebrated artists and notabilities of the day. He appeared at the Albert Hall and toured with soprano Adelina Patti. His English successes led to a South African tour with Amy Sherwin in 1896.

On his return to Australia in 1897 Lemmone took up concert management, arranging tours by pianist Mark Hambourg and singer Marie Narelle. When Melba toured Australia in 1902 Lemmone was her personal and business manager and associate artist. Though he managed the visit of the Polish pianist Paderewski in 1904, Melba took precedence over his other interests. In 1910 he travelled overseas selecting singers for her 1911 J. C. Williamson [q.v.6] opera season, after which he toured with her to New Zealand, North America and Europe. During World War I he arranged Melba's fund-raising concerts in Australia and England. In 1919 when he suffered a nervous illness in Sydney, Melba organized a benefit for him which raised over £2000.

The calm and friendly Lemmone was a good foil for the volatile *prima donna*. Melba valued him as a friend; the *Bulletin* described him in 1918 as her 'devoted chum'. Their association did however somewhat obscure Lemmone's talent as flautist and composer of many impressionistic pieces for flute. When he retired in 1927 his musical abilities were undiminished. Even in 1938 his 'vitality and infectious air of personal enjoyment' emerged when he performed on radio for the Australian Broadcasting Commission.

Lemmone enjoyed an enduring relationship with Sydney soprano and singing teacher Mabel Isobel Irene Batchelor, and was a director of her family's furniture business. They married on 28 September 1943 at Paddington after Isabella's death. He died on 16 August 1949 at Darlinghurst and was cremated. His wife and a son from his first marriage survived him.

B. and F. Mackenzie, *Singers of Australia* (Melb, 1967); N. Melba, *Melodies and memories*, J. Cargher introd and notes (Melb, 1980); *Tatler* (Melb), 14 Aug 1897; *Argus*, 19 May 1884, 29 Aug 1938; *Punch* (Melb), 6 Jan 1898; *Sydney Mail*, 30 Sept 1908; *Bulletin*, 21 Feb 1918; *SMH*, 17 Jan 1919, 16 Aug 1949; *Herald* (Melb), 24 July 1924; *Smith's Weekly* (Syd), 28 July 1927; Theatre programme collection (LaTL); information from Mr R. W. and Miss W. M. Lemmon, Gilderoy, Vic, and Mr R. Mitchell, Newtown, Syd; Lemmone papers (Performing Arts Museum, Melb). MIMI COLLIGAN

LENEHAN, HENRY ALFRED (1843-1908), astronomer, was born on 28 August

1843 in Sydney, eldest son of Andrew Lene-han (1815-1886), cabinetmaker, and his Irish wife Susannah, née Templeton. Born in Sligo, Ireland, Andrew probably reached Sydney on 31 August 1835 in the *Jane Goudie*. Later described by Governor FitzRoy [q.v.1] as 'an ingenious and reputable cabinetmaker', he used both local and imported timber to make furniture, examples of which are prized. He was elected to the Sydney Municipal Council in 1850 and was a fellow of St John's College, University of Sydney.

Henry was educated by the Benedictines at St Mary's College, Lyndhurst, and worked in his father's business until he joined the Australian Joint Stock Bank as a clerk in 1865. Sent to Ipswich, Queensland, he was transferred to Rockhampton, then became a drafts-man in the Railway Department. Returning to Sydney he was appointed assistant to the government astronomer, H. C. Russell [q.v.6], on 9 August 1870. Next year, on 4 November at Hunters Hill, he married Louisa Ann Temple-ton, née Cullen, and widow of his cousin; she died childless in 1875. At Villa Maria, Hunters Hill, he married Bertha Rose Phillips on 9 September 1876; they lived at North Sydney.

For thirty-seven years Lenehan worked under the forthright and uncompromising Russell and was responsible for cataloguing accurate star positions, using the transit instrument. His work was increased when Sydney Observatory agreed to share in a plan to make a photographic catalogue of the stars over the whole sky. During Russell's absences he was acting government astronomer in 1875, 1887, 1901 and from November 1903 until he was appointed government astronomer on 1 January 1907.

Lenehan reorganized the transit work and many thousands of observations were made. In 1903-04 he co-operated with Otto Klotz of the Dominion Observatory, Ottawa, in making observations of trans-Pacific longitudes and closed the circuits of longitudes around the world. Measurements of the force of gravity were made at Sydney Observatory and of magnetic elements at the branch observatory at Red Hill, near Pennant Hills, in 1904 by Oskar Hecker of the Zentralbureau der Internationalen Erdmessung, Berlin, and in 1906 by Alberto Alessio from the Italian cruiser *Calabria*. Lenehan erected at Red Hill a small building for magnetic work no longer possible in Sydney because of the electric trams. He had constant trouble with the meteorologist H. A. Hunt [q.v.9]: on 21 November 1905 he recorded in his diary that 'Mr Hunt is doing his best to press his own importance upon his subordinates and the public generally—in fact trying to usurp management'. In 1908 Lenehan organized the observatory's participation in an expedition to Flint Island to observe a total solar eclipse, observations of Daniel's comet and preparations to observe Halley's comet.

A keen sailing man, Lenehan was an early member of Royal Prince Alfred Yacht Club. Elected a fellow of the Royal Astronomical Society, London, in 1894, he was a council-member of the Royal Society of New South Wales for many years (president, 1905-06) and 'always to the fore when any work was to be done'. He had suffered a cerebral haemorrhage in 1892 and spent six months leave in Britain and Europe. He died suddenly at Normanhurst on 2 May 1908 and was buried in the Catholic section of Gore Hill cemetery. His wife and their three sons and three daughters survived him; he was held in great affection by his family.

Cyclopedia of N.S.W. (Syd, 1907); C. Craig et al, *Early colonial furniture in New South Wales and Van Diemen's Land* (Melb, 1972); Roy Astronomical Soc, *Monthly Notices*, 69 (1909), p 248; Roy Soc NSW, *J*, 42 (1909), p 33; *Descent*, 6 (1972), no 1; *SMH*, 3 May 1908.
                                                                        HARLEY WOOD

LENEHAN, ROBERT WILLIAM (1865-1922), lawyer and soldier, was born on 16 August 1865 at Petersham, Sydney, eldest son of Irish-born Christopher Henry Lenehan, grocer, and his wife Marie Louise, née Gannon. Educated at St Ignatius' College, Riverview, he was admitted as a solicitor in 1891 and except for time spent on war service practised law in New South Wales until his death. On 30 January 1889, at St Ignatius' College chapel, he married Harriett Emma Mary Hodge.

Commissioned in 1890 in the 1st Infantry Regiment (Volunteers), New South Wales Military Forces, Lenehan transferred to the Field Artillery in 1894, becoming a major in 1898. 'A burly man, heavily moustached . . . and with a splendid seat on a horse, he was a commanding figure'. Volunteering for service in the South African War, he was appointed a squadron commander (captain) in the New South Wales Mounted Rifles and embarked from Sydney on 17 January 1900. After active service in the Orange Free State and the Transvaal, which earned him the Queen's Medal with six clasps, he was promoted major and appointed in February 1901 to command the Bushveldt Carbineers (B.V.C.). This special corps, raised from local volunteers from the Pietersburg district, operated in the wild country of northern Transvaal. As local volunteers were fewer than expected, Lenehan was allowed to enlist time-expired Australians and other servicemen.

After some initial successes the B.V.C.

became the subject of an international incident later that year over the alleged shooting of a German missionary and Boer prisoners. After a long court of inquiry Major Lenehan and four of his officers were court-martialled. Lieutenants H. H. Morant [q.v.] and P. J. Handcock [q.v.9] were sentenced to death and executed by firing squad. Lenehan was charged with two offences: failing to report the shooting of a Dutch member of the B.V.C. (alleged to have been a traitor) and the shooting of two men and a boy. Found not guilty of the second charge but guilty of the first he was reprimanded, the lightest possible sentence. He was subsequently deprived of his command (which was disbanded) and his employment was terminated. Sent under escort to Cape Town, in February 1903, he was imprisoned there until deported to Australia by the first available berth.

On his return Lenehan was not permitted to rejoin his unit and was denied a war gratuity by the British War Office. Major General Sir Edward Hutton [q.v.9], general officer commanding the Commonwealth Military Forces, urged Lenehan to resign but he refused and sought an inquiry to clear his name. Hutton repeatedly tried to have him placed on the retired list but government and public disquiet in Australia increased as some facts surrounding the B.V.C. affair became known. Finally, replying to a Commonwealth government request, the War Office admitted that there was nothing against Lenehan other than evidence presented at the court-martial. In parliament on 27 July 1904 Prime Minister Watson [q.v.] was very critical of the treatment Lenehan had received. He was restored from the reserve of officers to the active military list, backdated in seniority to 1 July 1903 and placed in command of an artillery field battery. Awarded the Volunteer Officers' Decoration, he was promoted in January 1913 to lieut-colonel commanding the 4th Field Artillery Brigade. He was employed on home service duties in World War I, principally in training reinforcements for the Australian Imperial Force.

In 1917 Lenehan was cited as co-respondent in a much-publicized Sydney divorce case involving Emile Guiot and his wife Ruth, and in October (Sir) George Pearce [q.v.], the minister for defence, removed him from an appointment he held at Menangle Camp. He was placed on the retired list on 20 August 1918. Survived by his wife and six of their seven children, Lenehan died in Sydney on 20 May 1922 of cirrhosis of the liver.

G. Witton, *Scapegoats of the Empire* (Melb, 1907); Aust Defence Dept, *Official records of Australian military contingents to the war in South Africa*, P. L. Murray ed (Melb, 1911); R. L. Wallace, *The Australians at the Boer War* (Canb, 1976); K. Denton, *Closed file* (Syd, 1983); F. M. Cutlack, *Breaker Morant* (Syd, 1962); *PD* (Cwlth), 1904, p 3576; *Sabretache*, Dec 1975; *SMH*, 8 Jan 1916, 27 June, 26 Oct 1917, 22 May 1922; *Herald* (Melb), 25 Oct 1917; records (AWM).

E. J. H. HOWARD

LENNON, WILLIAM (1849-1938), merchant and politician, was born on 8 December 1849 in Dublin, son of William Lennon, draper, and his wife Ann, née Martin. He arrived in 1855 with his family in Melbourne where he received sufficient schooling to be employed in 1870 as a clerk with the Victorian Mines Department. In 1874 Lennon joined the Bank of Australasia. Posted to Creswick, he made friends with pioneer trade unionists David Temple and W. G. Spence [q.v.6] and on 29 November 1877 at St Patrick's Cathedral, Ballarat, married Irish-born Mary Cecilia Ryan.

In 1881 he opened the bank's Townsville branch and subsequently supervised its North Queensland expansion. Promoted to a Sydney sub-inspectorship in 1885 he resigned next year to manage the Townsville office of Burns [q.v.7] Philp [q.v.] & Co. Ltd. Clashes, particularly with Burns over administrative procedures and salary levels, led in 1896 to resignation and the establishment of his own mercantile and auctioneering business in Townsville. A 'bouncing' community figure, Lennon was a director of the Bank of North Queensland and the Townsville Gas Co., and a member of the Divisional Board of Thuringowa, the Townsville Harbour Board, Grammar School Board of Trustees, School of Arts, and Chamber of Commerce.

In 1899 he unsuccessfully stood as an Independent against his old employer Philp for the seat of Townsville. After 1900 he joined the Labor Party; having stood unsuccessfully in 1904, he was elected to the Legislative Assembly for Herbert in 1907 and deputy leader of the Parliamentary Labor Party in October 1909. Lennon acted as leader for some eighteen months before the 1912 general strike but subsequent election campaigns enabled the formidable T. J. Ryan [q.v.] to eclipse him as the obvious successor to Bowman [q.v.7], who was ailing. On Labor's accession to power in 1915 Lennon was allocated the senior ministry of agriculture and stock in recognition of his administrative ability and knowledge of the troubled sugar industry. In 1916, although one of his two sons fighting at the front won the Military Cross, he was attacked by Empire loyalists because he campaigned against conscription and supported Home Rule for Ireland.

In September 1919 he became Speaker of the assembly until an interregnum at Government House gave the Labor government an opportunity to move against the obstructive Legislative Council. In January 1920 Lennon resigned his seat to accept appointment, on a salary of £1000 a year, to the previously unremunerated office of lieutenant-governor. In a series of manoeuvres, lampooned by some as at best comic opera, he appointed himself to a seat in, and subsequently the presidency of, the Legislative Council. The conservative press was particularly galled at Lennon's alleged misuse of the vice-regal prerogative, resurrecting from the conscription debate his denunciation of British imperialism and his 1910 description of the office of State governor as 'effete'. Following a cabinet recommendation, Lennon augmented Labor's 'suicide squad' in the council with a further fifteen new appointees prepared to vote out of existence a House their party deemed undemocratic and anachronistic. In March 1922 Queensland became the only Australian State to abolish its Upper House. Lennon had achieved 'the most important single constitutional reform in Queensland history'. He continued as lieutenant-governor until May 1929 when he returned to private life after the Moore [q.v.] government cancelled his salary.

Lennon's impact on Queensland would have been greater if he had not been overshadowed by the political giants Ryan and Theodore [q.v.]. His lack of trade union experience and support was balanced by the valuable commercial and banking expertise he brought to the Labor cabinet. His most notable ministerial achievement was his contribution to the stabilizing of the sugar industry which after 1915 developed into one of the world's most successful examples of state regulation of agricultural output, pricing and marketing; it had been achieved in partnership with industry representatives and without detriment to the principle of private ownership. Queensland agriculture was transformed as other producers, notably grain-growers and dairymen, successfully demanded similar reforms. Lennon's approach to agriculture was influenced by his commitment to the co-operative movement and his prior association with co-operative commercial ventures in Brisbane. He emphasized the interdependence of producers and consumers and sought 'to dispense with, as far as possible, the services of the middle man'.

As member for Herbert Lennon embodied the values and attitudes of a Queensland regionalist. He was resentful of metropolitan privilege and argued against establishment of a university in Brisbane until all country children had access to free primary education. While minister he decentralized the Department of Agriculture and Stock and was vigilant lest the welfare of white sugarworkers was undermined by the use of cheap coloured labour.

William Lennon was a middle-class reformer whose political ambition and Irish sympathies were most easily accommodated in the Labor Party. A contemporary wrote that his 'passionate opposition to social injustice is extraordinarily strong for one who has not graduated in the school of adversity'.

After leaving public life Lennon remained active in the South Brisbane Bowling Club and the Queensland Irish Association. Survived by his wife, two sons and three daughters, he died in Brisbane on 5 May 1938 and was buried as a Catholic in Toowong cemetery. His family, in accordance with his wishes, declined the offer of a state funeral.

The Labour government of Queensland (Brisb, 1915); C. Lack (ed), *Three decades of Queensland political history, 1929-1960* (Brisb, 1962); D. J. Murphy, *T.J. Ryan* (Brisb, 1975); D. J. Murphy and R. B. Joyce (eds), *Queensland political portraits 1859-1952* (Brisb, 1978); D. J. Murphy et al (eds), *Labor in power ... Queensland 1915-1957* (Brisb, 1979); K. Buckley and K. Klugman, *The history of Burns Philp* (Syd, 1981); *PD* (Qld), 1909, p 133, 1915, p 414, 1916-17, p 752, 1917, p 1000; *Truth* (Brisb), 18 Feb 1917; *Brisbane Courier*, 7, 9 Jan 1920; *Courier Mail*, 7 May 1938; *Worker* (Brisb), 10 May 1938.   RODNEY SULLIVAN

LE RENNETEL, PIERRE FRANCOIS (1851-1904), Marist Father, was born on 30 April 1851 in the parish of La Boussac, Brittany, France, son of Pierre Le Rennetel, farmer, and his wife Perrine Victoire, née Aubin. Brought up at St Malo, he was educated at the minor seminary at St Méen. His studies for the priesthood at the Marist seminary at Lyon were interrupted when he joined the French corps of Papal Zouaves raised by Charette during the later stages of the Franco-Prussian War. In 1872 he entered the Marist scholasticate at Belley and on 2 October 1873 was professed at Ste Foy-lès-Lyon, continuing his studies there. He studied theology at Belley in 1875-76 and at St Mary's College, Dundalk, Ireland, where he was ordained priest on 24 August 1877 and taught for two years.

Le Rennetel had applied for a Pacific islands appointment, but was sent instead to Sydney where he arrived in November 1879. After a short time at St Michael's, Cumberland Street, he was transferred to St Patrick's, Church Hill. In 1883, while Dr Gillett was overseas, he acted as rector of St John's College, University of Sydney. He refused permanent appointment, but remained a fellow, and was appointed in November 1883 parish priest of St Patrick's, where he remained until his death. He was regarded highly by Cardinal Moran [q.v.] who made him a diocesan consulter and considered him for the diocesan seminary he was planning. In 1886 Le Rennetel had to go to some lengths to counter Moran's nomination of him as a bishop.

Efficient at managing finances, Le Rennetel built a convent for the Sisters of Mercy, assisted the Marist Brothers with their monastery, pushed through the construction of Federation Hall and built a presbytery for the priests. 'His sound common sense, wide knowledge of the world, high culture, and marked ability in the pulpit' helped to make St Patrick's an extraordinary centre of devotion and the Marists gave a valuable French element to a predominantly Irish-Australian Church. He supported Home Rule, and genuinely loved the Irish, who affectionately referred to him as 'Father O'Rennetel'.

During the 1890s depression Le Rennetel, with Fathers Ginisty and Piquet [q.v.], unstintingly worked for the unemployed and destitute, many of whom lived at The Rocks. He claimed not only to know all his poor parishioners but also most of the Chinese in the area. He actively and practically encouraged young men's associations and liked to boast of his young men.

In 1898 Le Rennetel went to Europe for a break: extraordinary tributes and affectionate farewells testify to his popularity. Similar tributes marked his return in February 1899 and silver jubilee as a priest in 1902. Dark with an aquiline nose and flowing beard, Le Rennetel was a witty, sought-after speaker, also highly regarded within the French community. He gave retreats and missions in all New South Wales dioceses and also preached in Queensland, Tasmania and New Zealand. He suffered from disseminated sclerosis and died of cerebral haemorrhage on 25 July 1904 at St Patrick's presbytery. After a funeral attended by an estimated 40 000 people he was buried in Waverley cemetery.

Freeman's J (Syd), 21 May 1898, 11 Feb 1899, 30 Aug 1902; *Catholic Press*, 9 Aug 1902, 28 July, 4 Aug 1904; Le Rennetel personal file (Archives of the Marist Fathers, Rome).   JOHN HOSIE

LESINA, VINCENT BERNARD (JOSEPH) (1869-1955), journalist and politician, was born on 1 November 1869 at Araluen, New South Wales, son of Alexander Lesina, Italian-Swiss goldminer, and his Irish-born wife Margaret, née McGrath. Educated at the Catholic orphanage, Parramatta, St Joseph's, Newtown, and St Benedict's, Sydney, Lesina accompanied his mother to Auckland, New Zealand, where he worked in various jobs.

In 1887, after they had returned to Sydney, he was apprenticed to a signwriter. A public speaker by 19, Lesina studied privately, joined the Henry George [q.v.4] movement and helped John Farrell [q.v.4] to produce the *Lithgow Enterprise and Land Nationaliser*. While working as a house-painter in Melbourne he became first secretary of the Victorian Homestead League. On 27 March 1895 he married Phoebe Eleanor Cullen in Sydney with Gospel Temperance Church forms; they had three sons.

Before moving to Queensland in 1896 Lesina reputedly wrote for the *Worker, Gosford Times, Orange Leader, Gloucester Gazette*, Sydney *Weekly News, Democrat, Australian Standard, Evening News* and *Australian Town and Country Journal*. In 1896-1900 he edited the Charters Towers *Eagle*. He easily won Clermont for Labor at the 1899 election and retained it until 1912, having been re-elected in 1902, 1904 and 1909 and returned unopposed in 1907 and 1908.

Described by Bernays as a 'nervy, restless dark little man of passing good looks', Joe Lesina was an eloquent, if verbose, speaker possessed of considerable wit, biting sarcasm and devastating invective, together with a capacity for detailed research and factual inventiveness. He advocated White Australia and even 'white Empire'.

Lesina never rose to any position of power or influence in the Labor Party. His only notable contribution to social reform was the adoption, at the sixth Labor-in-Politics Convention in 1910, of the abolition of capital punishment (enacted in 1922). Initially he had the support of the trade unions, the central political executive, the *Worker* (in which he was a regular columnist) and such influential Labor figures as Matt Reid [q.v.], but most of his intra-party support had gone by the time of the 1906 'split' with Kidston [q.v.9].

During the 1904-06 period, although twice censured by his party, Lesina refused to 'surrender' Labor Party policy and socialist principles, even for desired electoral reform. He was strongly critical of his parliamentary colleagues, particularly for their failure to oppose government measures contrary to Labor policy. But J. B. Dalton's view that Lesina's political career 'was one of shameless duplicity and mercenary self-interest' seems unjustified. More convincing is D. P. Crook's assessment of him as the self-appointed 'watch-dog of Labor principles . . . [who] characteristically reflected the sensitivity of militant Labor for the preservation of the Labor platform in toto'. Ultimately his flamboyant individualism and his idealistic yet politically naive behaviour brought about his political demise.

In 1909 Lesina's public dispute with Dave Bowman [q.v.7] over Labor's policy on the liquor trade and certain other aspects of nationalization led to his expulsion from the party. Born 'an utterly irreconcilable free-lance', he was uncontrollable by party discipline.

Lesina wrote for John Norton's [q.v.] Brisbane *Truth* after 1904. On his retirement from parliament he moved to Sydney and was a member of the Australian Journalists' Association in 1916-36. Little is known of his later life. In 1917 he was with the Dubbo *Daily Liberal* and during 1924-26 and 1928-29 he seems again to have worked for Sydney *Truth*. He was editor of a daily newspaper at Katoomba in 1930-31. During the 1930 New South Wales elections he was on the publicity staff of the A.J.A. Lesina died at Parramatta on 14 July 1955 and was buried in the Catholic section of Rookwood cemetery.

C. A. Bernays, *Queensland politics during sixty (1859-1919) years* (Brisb, nd, 1919?); J. Larcombe, *Notes on the political history of the labour movement in Queensland* (Brisb, 1934); D. J. Murphy et al (eds), *Prelude to power* (Brisb, 1970); *Brisbane Courier*, 10 May 1907; S. A. Rayner, The evolution of the Queensland Labour Party to 1907 (M.A. thesis, Univ Qld, 1947); J. B. Dalton, The Queensland labour movement, 1899-1915 (B.A. Hons thesis, Univ Qld, 1962); T. O'Sullivan, Reminiscences of the Queensland parliament, 1903-15 (nd, Oxley Lib, Brisb).   ROSS BARBER

LESLIE, WILLIAM DURHAM (1857-1933), businessman, was born on 21 November 1857 at Wattle Mill, Sale, Victoria, third child of Scottish parents James Leslie, black-smith and engineer, and his wife Margaret, née Durham. His father had migrated to Victoria on the advice of P. H. McArdle, Scottish-born Gippsland businessman, and was later McArdle's partner. Leaving Sale Common School at 15, William worked on the *Gippsland Times* as a proof-reader and later became a counter-hand for James Cromie, then Gippsland's largest softgoods merchant. On 31 March 1882 at Sale he married Cromie's Irish niece Mary Margaret Hanna; of their eight children, three sons and two daughters survived infancy.

In 1888 Leslie commenced business for himself as general draper in Foster Street, Sale. He assumed control of the Cromie business in 1895 and added to it saddlery, foot-wear, grocery, kitchen hardware and confectionery departments and tea-rooms, making W. D. Leslie & Co. (Pty Ltd from 1922) Gippsland's largest emporium. A parking area for wagons and buggies took in the former site of James Leslie's smithy and engineering shop; a furniture business, bought in 1901, was relocated opposite the large complex. Leslie was the first Gippsland businessman to organize his store into departments, each operating under a manager, with sales transactions being sped on overhead wires to the centrally located cashier. He opened stores at Warragul and Traralgon, and, later selling these, added a branch store at Maffra.

Leslie lived at Mulcarie, Lansdowne Street, but also had a Melbourne home at Malvern. A member of the Commercial Travellers' Association and council-member of the Victorian Master Drapers' Association, he was also on the boards of the Gippsland Steam Navigation Co. and the Sale Butter Factory. He was president of the Sale Early Pioneers' Association and belonged to the ratepayers' association and the cemetery trust. Leslie followed his father on to the Sale Borough Council in 1896 and was mayor three times (1897, 1898 and 1903) in his eighteen years service. In 1910, as a Deakin [q.v.8] supporter, he challenged G. H. Wise [q.v.] for the Federal seat of Gippsland but was forced by illness to withdraw.

Leslie was a member of the Sale Presbyterian board of management, as well as church organist and choirmaster, and initiated the Presbyterian purchase in 1923 of William Pearson's [q.v.5] Kilmany Park for conversion into a farm home for boys. Fearless in upholding his principles, he supported the Victorian Protestant Federation in sectarian debate on appointments to the Victorian Public Service.

A skilled bowler, Leslie was in the Australian team which toured the United Kingdom in 1922. The breeding of a pedigree dairy herd and thoroughbred racehorses were other interests. Ayrshires bred on his property, Raith, won major awards at district and State shows. Leslie was a councillor of the Royal Agricultural Society of Victoria and judged at New Zealand, Melbourne and Sydney shows. In Sydney in 1933 he was knocked down by a motor cycle; the effects contributed to his death at Malvern on 2 December. He was buried in Sale cemetery and, survived by his wife and children, left an estate valued for probate at £43 152.

O. S. Green, *Sale: the early years—and later* (Sale, 1979); C. Daley, *The story of Gippsland* (Melb, 1960); *Herald* (Melb), 14 May 1930, 31 Mar 1932; *Gippsland Times*, 4 Dec 1933; information from and papers held by Mr J. W. Leslie, Sale, Vic.   O. S. GREEN

LE SOUEF, WILLIAM HENRY DUDLEY (1856-1923), **ERNEST ALBERT** (1869-1937) and **ALBERT SHERBOURNE** (1877-1951), zoo directors and scientists, were the eldest, second and fourth sons of the ten children of Albert Alexander Cochrane Le Souef [q.v.5] and his wife Caroline, née Cotton. Dudley was born on 28 September 1856 at Brighton near Melbourne, and registered as Dudley Emanuel Wales. He was educated at Crediton Grammar School, Devonshire, England. In 1874, aged 18, he was appointed assistant-secretary to the Zoological and Acclimatization Society of Victoria which had established the Melbourne Zoological Gardens. He made collecting trips overseas in 1880-88 visiting India, the United States of America, Singapore, Sumatra, England, Europe, Japan and New Guinea.

When his father, the director of the Melbourne zoo, went to Europe in 1890, Dudley took charge. He was appointed assistant-director, and in May 1902 director when his father died. On a tour of zoos that year Dudley was impressed by Karl Hagenbeck's innovative arrangements for the Berlin Zoo where high walls and moats, hidden from view by simulated rocks and logs, constrained the animals without bars. Dudley began to replace the buildings developed by his father with rock-like structures of concrete over a sheet-iron or wire base. His designs were based on photographs of large rocks in the Mount Buffalo area, taken on trips made with his friend E. J. Dunn [q.v.8], director of the Victorian Geological Survey.

Dudley was a nature photographer and presented lantern lectures in many parts of the world, as well as Australia; he was a fluent and inexhaustible speaker with a fund of anecdotes. He campaigned for the introduction of zebu-cross cattle into northern Australia. Birds were his main hobby and he was known internationally as an ornithologist. A prolific writer, he was the author of *Wildlife in Australia* (Christchurch, 1907), and with A. H. S. Lucas [q.v.] co-author of *Animals of Australia* (Melbourne, 1909) and *Birds of Australia* (Melbourne, 1911), as well as numerous papers in scientific journals and articles on natural history in newspapers and magazines. He was a foundation member, twice president, and honorary secretary of the Royal Australasian Ornithologists' Union, and in Victoria a member of the Field Naturalists' Club, the Royal Geographical Society, the Royal Society, and the National Parks Association. He was reputed to have ridden the first pneumatic-tyred bicycle in Melbourne. In 1919 when returning with the weekly wages, Dudley Le Souef was attacked viciously by a former employee. His health deteriorated and he suffered a stroke in 1922. He died, in office, on 6 September 1923 at Royal Park and was buried in Melbourne general cemetery. On 27 September 1888 in London he had married Edith Evelyn Wadeson who survived him with six children.

Ernest Le Soeuf was born on 13 September 1869 at Elwood, Melbourne, and was educated at Carlton College, the Melbourne Veterinary College and the University of Melbourne (B.V.Sc., 1911). In 1888 he was accountant to the Zoological and Acclimatization Society of Victoria. He was sent to England in 1891 for stock for the zoo and kept costs so low that he was presented with a gold watch in appreciation. In 1895 he qualified as a veterinary surgeon, working at night while studying, and was appointed honorary veterinary surgeon to the society. In 1897, on the recommendation of his father who had been invited to select a site, he was appointed director of the Perth Zoological Gardens. His father advised his council that 'I could not spare Ernie were it not that my next son Sherbourne, is not in his 21st year and could fill Ernie's position at a lower salary'. Financial support in Perth was to be so inadequate that Ernest had to be his own architect, landscape gardener and road constructor. Thoroughly trained in hatching and distributing fish for acclimatization purposes, Ernest, in addition to his responsibilities at the zoo, had to travel long distances by train, horse or bicycle to hatcheries. He was a familiar sight riding his bicycle furiously downhill to catch the Perth ferry. In 1898 he bought animals in the eastern colonies for the opening of the zoo on 17 October 1898.

An expert marksman, Ernest was a foundation member of the Cannington Mounted Rifles in 1899. In 1901 he was commissioned lieutenant in the Australian Army Veterinary Corps and in 1912 was appointed principal veterinary officer (5th Military District) with the rank of major. In 1915 he was president of the military horse buying board and in March 1916 joined the Australian Imperial Force for duty with a remount unit. Attached to the Second Light Horse Brigade headquarters in Egypt, he was wounded in August and repatriated in 1917. He left the Australian Military Forces in 1930 with the rank of colonel.

In 1919-32 Ernest Le Souef lectured part time in agriculture at the University of Western Australia and in 1923 contributed to the containment of an outbreak of rinderpest. In 1926 he was appointed lecturer (part-time) in charge of the department of veterinary science and founded a museum in the zoo used by students for practical anatomy and physiology. He also ran free veterinary classes for farmers at the zoo. In 1932 the zoo, still plagued by financial problems, was transferred on Le Souef's recommendation to the State Gardens Board. He then joined the Agricultural Bank as veterinary adviser for the Margaret River district. He retired to Perth in 1935. Kindly, friendly and courteous, he was highly regarded by his staff. He died on 27 November 1937 on a visit to Margaret River and was buried there with Anglican rites. On 20 April 1899 he had married Ellen Grace, daughter of Rev. F. A. Hagenauer [q.v.4], at Ramahyuck, Victoria. She survived him with two sons and two daughters.

Albert Sherbourne Le Souef was born on 30 January 1877 at Royal Park, Melbourne. He was educated at Carlton College and the Melbourne Veterinary College and succeeded Ernest in 1897 as secretary of the Zoological and Acclimatization Society. On his father's death he was appointed assistant director of the Melbourne zoo and in April 1903 secretary of the Zoological Society in Sydney. The cramped gardens at Moore Park, dirty and noisy, were clearly inadequate and in 1907 Sherbourne and Dr R. H. Todd were sent to Europe where, as Dudley had been, they were impressed by Hagenbeck's system. Determined to develop Sydney zoo on completely modern lines, Sherbourne opposed the government's purchase of Wentworth Park and battled tenaciously for a more suitable site. The Mosman council, disliking the society's proposal to move the zoo to the Mosman side of the harbour, was finally persuaded when it was agreed to face the enclosure south and have high concrete walls on the suburban side 'to effectively muffle the lions' roar'. Sherbourne inspected the Melbourne zoo and Dudley suggested the name Taronga, meaning 'sea view'. As first director, Sherbourne supervised the planning and development of the grounds of the Taronga Park Zoo, where all walls and fences were camouflaged. Building was not sufficiently advanced to transfer the animals from Moore Park until 1916.

Sherbourne, as his brothers did, lectured frequently. He also travelled widely, collecting animals and establishing contacts. He was a prolific contributor to journals and co-author with H. J. Burrell [q.v.7] of *The wild animals of Australasia* (London, 1926). He was active in supporting the establishment of fauna and flora reserves and in 1934 predicted that future zoos would be like Whipsnade in England—one of the earliest 'broad acre' zoos. He retired in 1940. He was a member of the Royal Society of New South Wales, a councillor of the (Royal) Zoological Society of New South Wales for almost fifty years and a corresponding member of the Zoological Society, London. He died on 31 March 1951 at Mosman and was cremated. On 22 April 1908 in Sydney he had married Mary Emily Louise Greaves, who survived him.

The youngest brother Lance was accountant and librarian at the Perth Zoo for a number of years and took charge in Melbourne during Dudley's overseas travels.

J. Seekamp, 'Past history and present trends', *Melb Zoo Newsletter*, 1967; *Emu* (Melb), 23 Jan 1924; *VHM*, 36 (1965), no 1, p 8, 37 (1966), no 4, p 221; Roy Soc WA, *J*, 6 (1965), p 75; papers and cuttings (Taronga Zoo, Syd).

A. DUNBAVIN BUTCHER

LEVERRIER, FRANCIS HEWITT (1863-1940), barrister, was born on 8 February 1863 at Waverley, Sydney, second son of Guillaume André Charles Leverrier (1826-1895), merchant, and his English wife Mary Anne Skaife, née Hewitt. Born at Saint-Servan, Brittany, France, his father came to Victoria during the gold rush, married in France in 1858 and brought his bride to Sydney where he established Leverrier, Curcier & Co., importers of French wines and spirits and luxury items. In 1863 he took his family back to Saint-Servan.

Frank was educated there by the French Christian Brothers until the family returned to Sydney in 1877. By now fluent in French and German, he briefly attended Fort Street Model School and, from 1878, Sydney Grammar School. In November 1880 he passed the senior public examination in a record seventeen subjects and gained the John West [q.v.2] medal and a scholarship at the University of Sydney. He shared a love of science and great mathematical ability with his great-uncle, the noted astronomer Urbain Le Verrier.

At the university Leverrier resided in St John's College (until asked to leave in August 1882 because of his inability to submit to college discipline—eight years later he was elected a fellow). He won the Levey, Deas Thomson [q.v.2], R. C. Want and Renwick [q.v.6] scholarships and in 1884 graduated B.A. with first-class honours, the gold medal in natural science and the Belmore [q.v.3] gold medal for agricultural chemistry. Next year he graduated B.Sc. with first-class honours and the gold medal. In December 1885 he was admitted as a student-at-law and on 21 September 1888 to the Bar. At St Charles' Catholic Church, Waverley, on 4 February 1892 he married Edith Campbell (d. 1928), daughter of a shipbroker.

While Challis [q.v.3] lecturer in 1890-1907 on the law of wrongs, civil and criminal, (from 1897 on law of status, civil obligations and crimes) at the university, Leverrier built up a large practice, mainly in Equity, from Denman Chambers. He was soon unrivalled as a patent lawyer and, holding retainers from companies all over Australia and overseas, received very high fees. According to A. B. Piddington [q.v.] he was 'one of the most brilliant of cross-examiners'. To him cross-examining was 'a scientific task . . . not a scolding-match or a sorry business of breaking a witness's nerve'. He took silk on 8 March 1911 and served on the Council of the Bar of New South Wales in 1915-25. He developed an extensive practice before the High Court of

Australia and appeared in important constitutional cases; he led for the Commonwealth in the Engineers' case of 1920.

Elected to the university senate in 1907 as a scientist and reformer, Leverrier served continuously until November 1939. Under the old constitution he was vice-chancellor in 1914-17 and 1921-23, and chairman of the finance committee. At a senate meeting in June 1925 he unavailingly defended his friend Christopher Brennan [q.v.7].

Possessing 'great mechanical inventiveness and manual dexterity', Leverrier built a dynamo to generate electricity for his Waverley home and to power his well-equipped workshop, transmitter and chemical laboratory. He was a skilled cabinetmaker and for a case involving the Welsbach patent he made a wooden model that could be taken to pieces to illustrate the working of a gas mantle. His interest in science was lifelong. A friend of Professors David [q.v.8], Threlfall and J. A. Pollock [qq.v.], he experimented in wireless telegraphy and X-rays. He was a member of the Royal Society of New South Wales from 1909 and next year was first president of the Wireless Institute of New South Wales. He was chairman of the State committee of the Commonwealth Advisory Council of Science and Industry in 1916-18 and of the provisional State advisory board of the Commonwealth Institute of Science and Industry in 1920-23, and a member of the State committee of the Council for Scientific and Industrial Research in 1926-40.

As a result of a brief from W. A. Freeman [q.v.8], in 1911 Leverrier was an original shareholder in, and later a director of, Austral Malay Tin Ltd, and profited greatly. During World War I he was a vice-president of the Universal Service League. Having refused appointment as a Supreme Court judge, he retired from practice in 1926 and from 1930 was a director of the Mutual Life & Citizens Assurance Co. Ltd. In 1937 he was awarded King George VI's coronation medal.

With a narrow, intelligent face and clipped moustache, Leverrier was modest and unassuming and shunned publicity. He played the violin and taught his sister Yvonne harmony. Warm and gentle, he was beloved by his family and had 'the gift of friendship'; he was a connoisseur of wine and a member of the Australian Club. He died at his home at Wentworth Road, Vaucluse, on 11 June 1940, the day France fell, and was cremated after an Anglican service. He was survived by a son and two daughters, of whom Andrée married (Sir) Leslie Herron, later chief justice of New South Wales. His estate was valued for probate at over £56 000. His family gave a metal-embossed Napoleonic table to the National Art Gallery of New South Wales in his memory.

Sir George Rich [q.v.] claimed Leverrier as 'my oldest friend . . . a man of outstanding ability'; while *Smith's Weekly* asserted that 'he knew so much it wasn't fair'.

Cyclopedia of N.S.W. (Syd, 1907); A. B. Piddington, *Worshipful masters* (Syd, 1929); A. Clark, *Christopher Brennan* (Melb, 1980); *NSW Law Reports*, 19 (1898), p 214; *Cwlth Law Reports*, 20 (1920), p 128; *Science and Industry*, 1920, p 190; Univ Syd Union, *Union Recorder*, 22 Sept 1960, p 190; *SMH*, 13, 18 June 1940; *Smith's Weekly* (Syd), 30 Oct 1926; *Catholic Press*, 29 Jan 1903, 25 Apr 1907; family information from, and letters and newspaper cuttings held by, Mrs A. Sheahan, Castlecrag, and Mrs S. Crawford, Turramurra, Syd.

MARTHA RUTLEDGE

LEVEY, JAMES ALFRED (1846-1944), public servant and philanthropist, was born on 30 December 1846 at Camberwell, Surrey, England, youngest of four sons of George Levey, printer, and his wife Anne, née Richards. The brothers, after completing their education in London, settled in Victoria between 1851 and 1863. Soon after his arrival in Melbourne, aged 16, James joined the Crown Lands Department as field clerk and draftsman; the surveyor-general C. W. Ligar [q.v.5] was his brother G. C. Levey's [q.v.5] father-in-law.

As the land Acts brought the department an ever increasing volume and complexity of work, Levey gained considerable administrative experience. He became secretary to the Land Warrant Board and to the board of examiners for the Survey Department (1870), and private secretary to J. J. Casey [q.v.3] during an inquiry into fraud on the part of a colleague (1874); he was a crucial witness before the Victorian Crown Lands Commission in 1878. That year he was a victim of the 'Black Wednesday' dismissals, though reinstated within ten weeks.

In 1887 Levey moved to the Chief Secretary's Department. As chief inspector of factories (1887-93) he condemned the regulations for factory sanitation as 'circumlocutionary' and urged amendments to the 1885 Factories and Shops Act to extend and rationalize the regulation of labour. In a report to parliament on the 'sweating system' in the clothing trade (1890) he recommended legal control of outwork to curb exploitation, especially of women; he noted also, at the 1890 Australasian Conference on Charity, the 'very large percentage' of outworkers living on charity. Yet he later claimed that regulation was scarcely feasible unless it were possible 'to alter human nature and make us all more charitable'.

In 1893 Levey was promoted to head the Police Department as chief clerk, an office never popular with the uniformed police.

Within three years, at 49, he retired on health grounds with a reluctantly granted life pension at half salary.

Levey's marriage on 21 August 1882 at St Peter's Church, Melbourne, to Sarah Elizabeth, daughter of Richard Grice [q.v.4], had allied him with a wealthy and influential family. In 1886 he joined the Melbourne Club and in 1888 was a foundation member of the Charity Organisation Society. Throughout his long retirement his public life centred on the administration of philanthropic bodies. President of the C.O.S. in 1902-23 and an executive member until 1944, he also served on the committee of management of the Austin Hospital for Incurables (later Chronic Diseases) in 1898-1932 and on the (Royal) Melbourne Hospital committee in 1907-44 (president, 1931-35). In 1904 he succeeded E. E. Morris [q.v.5] on the Felton [q.v.4] Bequests Committee which allocated money to charities and for the purchase of art works for the National Gallery of Victoria. During his forty years on the committee and chairmanship in 1931-44, both the Melbourne Hospital and the C.O.S. benefited substantially from the bequest. Though disclaiming any authority on art, Levey offered cautious opinions; he supported the purchase of Corot's 'The Bent Tree' in 1907 ('lovely famous') but disparaged Whistler's lithographs and Blake's drawings ('most quaint').

With his wife and two daughters Levey lived in a large house at South Yarra. They entertained extensively and made three protracted trips to Europe before World War I. After his wife's death in 1923 Levey moved into the Melbourne Club. A well-known figure in the city, immaculate in spats, gloves and bowler hat, in his nineties he would outpace the young up Collins Street hill. He regularly attended St Paul's Cathedral and enjoyed bridge and the theatre. A grandson has described him as 'the smartest old man I can remember'. He was nearly 98 when he died at East Melbourne on 11 December 1944; he was cremated. His surviving daughter was the main beneficiary of his estate, valued for probate at £16 912.

Charity Organisation Soc, Melb, *Proceedings of the 1st Australasian conference on charity* (Melb, 1890); L. B. Cox, *The National Gallery of Victoria, 1861 to 1968* (Melb, 1970); *Hospital Mag*, Jan 1945; *Table Talk*, 5 Sept 1912; *Argus*, 12 Dec 1944; Roy Melb Hospital Archives; Citizens Welfare Service, Melb, Archives; Grice papers (Univ Melb Archives).   LAURIE O'BRIEN

LEVIEN, CECIL JOHN (1874-1932), district officer and mining promoter, was born on 4 January 1874 at Bellarine, Victoria, second son of Jonas Felix Levien [q.v.5], and his wife and cousin Clara, née Levien, both Australian born. The family was Jewish, but Levien was raised as an Anglican. He was educated at Melbourne Church of England Grammar School, and later worked with little success on the Western Australian goldfields and as a farmer in New South Wales.

Enlisting in the Australian Imperial Force in March 1917, Levien trained at the Royal Military College, Duntroon, and served as a lieutenant in the military administration in New Guinea in 1919-21. Saddled with debts from his farming venture, he quickly recognized that New Guinea might offer prospects for a better life. His access to German official records indicated that payable alluvial gold might exist in the Watut River area, inland of the Huon Gulf. Noting that several Australian prospectors, particularly Arthur Darling and William ('Shark-eye') Park, had been active in German territory, he decided to wait for a significant strike before making his move. Meanwhile, he transferred to the post-war civil administration where his energy, maturity, and organizing ability were highly regarded by his superiors. 'Tall, broad-shouldered and tough', he proved a capable district officer.

In 1919 Levien opened a new government station at Buka. In 1921 he contrived to have himself posted as district officer to Morobe, where southern tributaries of the Markham River had once again become a focus for prospecting. He carefully plotted all reports of gold, and was the officer-in-charge in 1922 when Park struck rich alluvium in Koranga Creek, which flows into the upper Bulolo River. His powers under the Mining Ordinance of 1922 gave him a unique opportunity to monitor the promise of the field. In 1923 he began quietly financing Park and his partner, J. Nettleton; he also acquired alluvial leases in his wife's name. Recognizing after some months that he was involved in a conflict of interests, he resigned from government service and on 31 December took out the first miner's right issued in the Mandated Territory.

In 1923-24 Levien noted that limited drilling of the Bulolo flats, below Koranga Creek, produced encouraging results and he took out leases. He appreciated that large-scale dredging would be needed for profitable recovery. By April 1925 he had formulated an integrated plan for industrial development incorporating hydro-power to operate drills and dredges; a timber industry to defray the cost of a road or railway to the coast via the Markham; and aircraft to import personnel, building materials, and essential machinery. Levien cabled an old friend C. V. T. Wells, a Melbourne accountant, to float a development company; but interest in Australia proved inadequate.

Providentially, early in 1926 W. Royal and R. Glasson struck phenomenal alluvial gold in a higher tributary of the Bulolo, Edie Creek. The resulting publicity enabled Levien and Wells to register Guinea Gold No Liability in Adelaide in May 1926. Commissioned to undertake systematic testing of the flats to ensure that no exaggerated claims would be made, G.G.N.L.'s engineer, James Hebbard, presented an enthusiastic report. At the same time Levien was prominent in agitation which led in 1928 to the promulgation of a revised Mining Ordinance clearing the way for extensive dredging leases.

Under Levien's guidance G.G.N.L. established a field organization at Bulolo, funded deeper testing of further leases, and inaugurated an air service from the coast. Levien recognized the potential of air transport, and in December 1927 induced his fellow G.G.N.L. directors to float Guinea Airways Limited, New Guinea's pioneer aviation company, of which he became a director and major shareholder. Believing that essential development at Bulolo was well in hand, he then retired as G.G.N.L.'s field manager to continue prospecting for the company and crossed the Ramu-Markham divide in November 1929. The G.G.N.L. directors, realizing that the Bulolo leases were so extensive that international capital would be needed for appropriate development, offered options on its leases to Placer Development Ltd of Vancouver. In February 1930 an operating company, Bulolo Gold Dredging Ltd, was floated in which G.G.N.L. had shares.

This company, through the unprecedented use of G-31 air freighters to import everything needed for large-scale dredging, began to realize Levien's vision. The first of eight 2000-ton dredges started work in March 1932; but Levien did not live to see it. He died suddenly of pneumococcal septicaemia on 20 January 1932, while on a visit to Melbourne. His ashes were scattered over the Bulolo goldfields. His wife Margaret May, née Maxwell, whom he had married on 7 February 1911 in a civil ceremony in Melbourne, survived him; they had no children.

I. L. Idriess, *Gold-dust and ashes* (Syd, 1933); L. Rhys, *High lights and flights in New Guinea* (Lond, 1942); A. Healy, *Bulolo* (Canb, 1967); *SMH*, 22 Jan 1932, 14 Apr 1956; *Argus*, 21, 22 Jan 1932; C. V. T. Wells papers (NL).　　　　　A. M. HEALY

LEVIEN, ROBERT HENRY (1845-1938), solicitor and politician, was born on 17 October 1845 at Singleton, New South Wales, younger son of Alfred Levien, Jewish storekeeper, and his wife Myalla Rebecca, née MacDermod. He was baptised Henry Robert at All Saints Anglican Church, Singleton, and

was always known as Harry. The family moved to West Maitland and Levien was educated at Maitland High School. In 1866 he was articled to a Maitland solicitor, A. J. Robey. He was admitted as a solicitor on 27 September 1873 and practised at Tenterfield in 1874-75 before returning to Maitland. In 1876-79 he was an alderman on the West Maitland Municipal Council. At Ardessir (Patricks Plains) he married Harriet Emma Cousins on 22 October 1879 and moved to Tamworth.

Defeated by one vote for the Legislative Assembly seat of Wollombi in 1877, Levien topped the poll for Tamworth in 1880 and moved his legal practice to Sydney, where he was successful in police courts. He represented Tamworth until 1894 and in 1904-13, and Quirindi in 1894-1904. Although a determined Protectionist, Levien was a doggedly independent 'representative, not the delegate of my constituents'. He seldom spoke in debates and was often absent from the House. His supporters admired his bright, original personality, bluff and hearty manner and his generous if volatile temperament.

Levien served on many select committees and in 1883 chaired the committee that dismissed charges against Captain R. R. Armstrong [q.v.3]. In the mid-1880s he unsuccessfully introduced bills dealing with creditors and to facilitate Supreme Court procedures. Hasty in speech, he was forced to apologize for insulting a member in 1886 and in December next year was removed by the sergeant-at-arms for disorderly conduct. Far more serious, in 1889 the Supreme Court ordered that he be struck off the roll of solicitors for one year for allowing an unqualified clerk to practise under his name. He resigned his seat but was promptly re-elected unopposed. He served on the Parliamentary Standing Committee on Public Works in 1894-95 and 1898-1901.

In 1897 Levien successfully carried as a private member an amendment to the Australasian Federation Enabling Act to raise to 80 000 the affirmative referendum vote to be required for Federation. Next year he attracted unfavourable publicity by accusing two members, W. J. Ferguson and R. Sleath [q.v.], of murder and conspiracy during the Broken Hill strike in 1892. A royal commission found Levien's charges absolutely unproved. He apologized to the House and explained that he had acted unjustly in the heat of temper. Attending diligently to the wants of his electorate, Levien strongly advocated the resumption and subdivision of the Peel River Land and Mineral Co.'s vast estate; the Wade [q.v.] government eventually resumed 100 000 acres (40 470 ha).

Surviving 'all seasons and all changes, all campaigns and all parties', Levien could not adapt to twentieth century political parties. In 1913 he refused to apply for Liberal endorsement and his old-time campaigning methods failed badly. Heartbroken by his defeat, he tried in vain five times to re-enter parliament.

Levien was twice grand primo of the Royal Antediluvian Order of Buffaloes. He also bred and raced horses. In 1912 he chaired the royal commission into the totalisator and signed the minority report recommending its legalization. He retired from legal practice in 1933 and died on 12 July 1938; he was buried in the Anglican section of Northern Suburbs cemetery. His wife and daughter survived him, but his two sons were wounded at Gallipoli and predeceased him.

R. Milliss, *City on the Peel* (Syd, 1980); G. N. Hawker, *The parliament of New South Wales, 1856-1965* (Syd, 1971); *PD* (NSW), 1883-84, p 1116, 1889, p 1799, 1898, p 229; *NSW Law Reports*, 10 (1890), p 43; *Express* (Syd), 20 Aug 1885; *Tamworth News*, 24 June, 30 Aug 1904, 20 Oct 1909; *Tamworth Daily Observer*, 25 Oct, 11, 29 Nov, 6, 8 Dec 1913, 4, 7 July 1914; *SMH*, 14 July 1938; newspaper cuttings, vol 6, p 12 (ML).

M. Z. FORBES

LEVY, Sir DANIEL (1872-1937), lawyer and politican, was born on 30 November 1872 in London, son of Joseph Levy, tailor, and his wife Esther, née Cohen. Arriving in Sydney with his parents in 1880, he was educated at Crown Street Public School and on a scholarship at Sydney Grammar School, where he was captain in 1889 and won the senior Knox [q.v.5] prize (1889) and Morehead scholarship (1890). At the University of Sydney he graduated B.A. with first-class honours in Latin and Greek and the university medal for classics in 1893, and LL.B. with second-class honours in 1895. Admitted to the Bar on 23 August, he was associate to Mr Justice H. E. Cohen [q.v.3] in 1895-97, and several times acted as crown prosecutor. On 10 February 1902 he was admitted as a solicitor and was readmitted to the Bar on 12 November 1923.

Active in Jewish affairs as a young man, Levy edited the *Australasian Hebrew* in 1896 and was secretary of the New South Wales Board of Jewish Education in 1898-1903 and president of the New South Wales Jewish Association in 1902-03. Thereafter he continued to attend the Great Synagogue regularly.

Defeated in 1898, Levy was elected to the Legislative Assembly for Sydney-Fitzroy in 1901. As a Liberal and later Nationalist, he represented Darlinghurst (a Jewish centre) in 1904-20, Sydney in 1920-27, Paddington in 1927-30 and Woollahra in 1930-37. In Opposition from 1910, he was a talented and energetic debater. His speeches were likened to 'the spikes on the prickly pear—full of that spinosity that penetrates anything'. However he early showed signs of a pedantic manner that irritated even his own colleagues.

After serving as chairman of committees from 1917, Levy was elected Speaker on 19 August 1919 on the resignation of J. J. Cohen [q.v.8]. He was to serve fourteen years as Speaker: 1919-20, 1920-21, 1921-25, 1927-30 and 1932-37. When Labor took office in April 1920 in an evenly balanced House, with the Opposition divided into Nationalists and Progressives, Levy accepted the Speakership despite the deep disapproval of Sir George Fuller [q.v.8] and other Nationalists. He was castigated in a long and bitter speech by J. C. L. Fitzpatrick [q.v.8] who accused him of being 'a rat', 'a traitor' and 'Sir Judas Iscariot', and quoted Levy's own vociferous criticisms of Henry Willis [q.v.] for accepting the Speakership in similar circumstances in 1911. When Fuller indicated he had a likely majority Levy announced his resignation as Speaker on 8 December 1921 and James Dooley's [q.v.8] government was defeated five days later. On 20 December Fuller formed an unstable coalition ministry, but when a Nationalist, William Bagnall, offered himself as Speaker, Levy objected; Fuller perforce had Levy renominated and, having been refused a dissolution, resigned after seven hours in office. Levy remaining as Speaker was the only way to ensure a workable parliament.

In 1922 and 1934 Levy supervised changes to the standing orders to simplify the passage of bills, virtually preventing their delay by procedural means and limiting debate to the second reading and committee stages. However, he maintained that 'the very essence of Parliament is discussion and debate'. The 'most articulate Speaker' of his time, Levy frequently proclaimed the importance and dignity of his office and in 1929 suggested that its independence would be strengthened if his seat was uncontested as in the House of Commons. He asserted that so 'long as I occupy the Chair I shall continue to be impartial'. Sometimes his detachment was too much for his own party. In 1930 a Nationalist delegation and the premier (Sir) Thomas Bavin [q.v.7] requested him to be firmer with the Opposition. On the other hand, Levy and J. T. Lang [q.v.9] had a deep respect for each other. Throughout his parliamentary career Levy provoked hostility: he was taunted with his academic achievements and sometimes referred to as 'the little Disraeli'. The only time he achieved ministerial office was for a month in 1932 when he served in (Sir) Bertram Stevens's [q.v.] emergency cabinet after Lang's dismissal.

Outside his parliamentary duties and

extensive practice, Levy was public spirited. He was a trustee of the Public Library of New South Wales in 1906-37 (chairman, 1927-37), the Australian Museum, Sydney, and Sydney Grammar School, a fellow of the Senate of the University of Sydney in 1913-37, a director of Sydney Hospital in 1928-37, government representative on the board of the Benevolent Society of New South Wales, member of the East Sydney School Board, sometime secretary of the Shakespeare Society of New South Wales and a council-member of the Millions Club of New South Wales. He was knighted in 1929.

Unmarried, Levy died of cerebro-vascular disease at his home at Darling Point on 20 May 1937 and, after a state funeral, was buried in the Jewish section of Rookwood cemetery. His estate of about £60 000 was left almost entirely to his unmarried sisters. Described during the 1904 election campaign as 'one of the brightest and ablest of young Australians', Levy never quite lived up to his promise: as a scholar he published nothing of note, as a barrister he never took silk, as a speaker his skill in debate was never heard. However, in the words of Dooley, when Levy had occupied the chair, he had 'always done so in an impartial manner' and had upheld the highest traditions of his office. His portrait by Jerrold Nathan is in Parliament House, Sydney.

G. N. Hawker, *The parliament of New South Wales, 1856-1965* (Syd, 1971); *PD* (LA NSW), 1920, p 9, 1921, p 2585, 2617; *SMH*, 6 Aug 1904, 28 Apr 1920, 9 Dec 1921, 10 July 1929, 21, 22 May 1937; *Fighting Line*, 19 Aug 1913, 26 Aug 1919; unpublished paper by K. Davis and cuttings (Great Synagogue, Syd); personal information.

L. E. FREDMAN

LEWIS, ARNDELL NEIL (1897-1943), lawyer, geologist and politician, was born on 23 November 1897 at Symmons Plains, Perth, Tasmania, elder son of (Sir) Neil Elliott Lewis [q.v.] and his wife Lina Henrietta, née Youl. He was educated at Leslie House School, Hobart, where he was influenced by William Hall Clemes who became a lifelong friend. At school Lewis was a cadet-lieutenant before joining the Australian Imperial Force. He was commissioned second lieutenant in the field artillery in September 1916 and joined the 1st Field Artillery Brigade in October 1917. He served in France in 1917-19, winning the Military Cross on 27 September 1918 during the capture of the Hindenburg line.

After the war he graduated from the University of Tasmania (LL.B., 1922; LL.M., 1925; LL.D., 1930). Admitted as a solicitor to the Supreme Court on 21 July 1922, he joined the family firm of Lewis, Hudspeth, Perkins & Dear in 1924, and was acting professor of law at the university in 1925 and 1930. On 7 December 1927 he married Amy Stewart Hungerford at St David's Cathedral, Hobart. His *Text book of Australian bankruptcy law* (Hobart, 1928) reached its seventh edition in 1978; *Australian military law* (1936) was based on his doctoral thesis.

Lewis had always had an intense interest in natural history and in geology in particular. He joined the Tasmanian Field Naturalists' Club while still at school and was elected to its committee in 1913. He wrote extensively on the geology of Tasmania, contributing eighteen papers to the Royal Society of Tasmania in 1921-39. He was lecturer in geology at the university in 1927-31. Lewis made wide-ranging, substantial and enduring contributions to the geology of Tasmania, following the tradition of Robert Mackenzie Johnston [q.v.9] who had taken him on geological expeditions as a boy. His earliest contribution to the Royal Society dealt with glaciology and he maintained this interest. His conclusion, largely from the study of land-forms, that there had been three glaciations in Tasmania during the Pleistocene has been confirmed by modern studies, and his contributions to the stratigraphy of Tasmania, particularly of the Palaeozoic, formed a sound basis for future work. His detailed account of *The geology of the Hobart district* (Hobart, 1946), completed in 1939 on the day war was declared, was published posthumously by the Royal Society through the memorial fund set up after his death and edited by Dr D. E. Thomas, Tasmanian government geologist. Though it has been supplemented by more recent work it has not been replaced. Lewis thought deeply about the wider aspects of geology and when he was presented with the Royal Society of Tasmania medal in 1935 he spoke on 'our pulsating world, the influence of earth movements on human development'.

Following an unsuccessful attempt in 1931, Lewis was elected to the House of Assembly in 1932 as a National party member for Denison. He lost his seat in 1934 and despite the handicaps of reticence and modesty regained it in 1937. In May 1941 he resigned to give priority to his military duties. It was a family tradition to serve in the artillery as his father and grandfather had done, and after the war Lewis had remained with the 6th Australian Field Artillery Brigade, commanding it as lieut-colonel in 1933-38. Ill health prevented his service beyond Tasmania in World War II but he was district manpower officer for Tasmania in 1939-40 and joined the Hobart Covering Force in May 1941. In 1942-43 he commanded the 6th Garrison Battalion.

Lewis was a trustee of the Tasmanian Museum, Art Gallery and Botanical Gardens in 1925-40 and a member of the National Park Board. He had joined the Royal Society of Tasmania in 1919 and served on its council in 1925-40. He was also a prominent member of the Anglican synod. Generous in thought and action, he retained a boyish outlook. He died childless on 27 December 1943 at Hobart of hypertensive heart failure and was buried in Cornelian Bay cemetery. His wife survived him. A portrait by Florence Rodway [q.v.] is held by the family.

His brother Hubert Charles, B.A., LL.B., (1899-1979) was president of the Hobart Chamber of Commerce in 1951-53 and president of the Tasmanian Law Society in 1953-56.

Cyclopedia of Tasmania (Hob, 1931); Roy Soc Tas, *Procs*, 1943, (1944), p 248; *Mercury*, 28 Dec 1943.   D. R. GREGG

LEWIS, DAVID (DAFYDD) EDWARD (1866-1941), businessman and philanthropist, was born on 7 March 1866 at Llanrhystyd near Aberystwyth, Cardiganshire, Wales, son of David Lewis, farmer, and his wife Catherine, née Mason. His mother died at his birth and his father in 1875, and he was brought up by his maternal grandparents. His grandfather Rev. Edward Mason was an Anglican clergyman. David attended a village school which he left at 12. His formal education, though fairly brief, was of a good standard and gave him a love of learning and literature.

After leaving school, Lewis worked for a grocer. He was then apprenticed to a draper at Neath and afterwards worked for William Lewis, seemingly no relation, of Pontnewyndd, who encouraged him to attend evening classes and had much influence on him. In the mid-1880s David worked in London with Jeremiah Rother's wholesale drapery. He became greatly interested in Shavian socialism, even speaking at Hyde Park Corner.

Lewis migrated in 1890 with a small capital and found employment with the drapers Craig Williamson Pty Ltd, Melbourne, and then with Miller's of Geelong. On 9 February 1899 he married an Irish-born milliner, Marion Frances Smyth (d. 1921), at St Mary's Catholic Church, East St Kilda. After one unsuccessful business venture, in partnership with J. A. Love in 1902 he opened a drapery shop in Brunswick Street, Fitzroy, that was so successful that within a short time they opened another in Chapel Street, Prahran. When Love retired in 1910 Lewis became sole proprietor. In 1930, when he was listed as the largest single holder of Commonwealth bonds, he purchased property in Bourke Street for a city headquarters. Lewis travelled extensively in his later years, partly for business purposes, and on 8 December 1928 he had married Mary Jane Jones Evans in London. In 1936 he bought a country estate, Carabobala, near Culcairn, in New South Wales, which his energy and enterprise converted into a showplace.

Prudent and careful in financial matters, he was quietly and discreetly generous to deserving causes, particularly in the Prahran municipality. Through the influence of his first wife he became interested in the work of the Presentation Sisters for the education of girls and was a financial supporter of their convent at Windsor. In 1928 he donated £2000 to the engineering school of the University of Melbourne for laboratory extensions. Always keenly interested in youth movements, and possibly influenced by his friendship with Martin Hansen [q.v.9], Lewis was very aware of the plight of boys who were, as he had been, deprived of education through lack of money. His will established the Dafydd Lewis Trust, with a £700 000 endowment, to provide scholarships for full-time degree courses (other than in theology, arts, music or education) at the University of Melbourne for boys from Victorian state schools whose parents could not afford a university education for them. Provision was also made for students to receive assistance for postgraduate study. Lewis's generosity was widely greeted as a big step towards democratic education.

His interests were travel, politics and his extensive and valuable library. He always delighted in speaking his native language. Although formally a Methodist, he might, perhaps, be better described as an agnostic; occasional attendances at the Welsh Church in his later life were as much for the opportunity of hearing spoken Welsh, for music, and for social contact, as for anything else. A kindly man, he never forgot those who had helped him to establish himself in his new country of which he was very proud.

Lewis died at his Prahran home on 17 August 1941 and was cremated. His wife and two sons of his first marriage survived him.

Argus, 19 Aug, 23, 24 Sept 1941; *Dafydd Lewis Trust scholarship* pamphlet (Univ Melb); information from Mr J. L. Lewis, Prahran, Melb.
                                                    T. A. HAZELL

LEWIS, EDWARD POWELL (1862-1930), engineer and businessman, was born on 24 July 1862 at Heidelberg, Victoria, third son and sixth child of William Richard Lewis, publican, and his wife Martha Ann, née Price, both from Wales. His father died before Lewis was 5 and his mother ran the Old England

Hotel at Heidelberg single handed until her remarriage in 1872.

Lewis attended the Model School, Melbourne, and at 17 became an apprentice with the engineering firm of Wright & Edwards (later Atlas Iron Works). He was a quiet, reserved lad, but soon showed his aptitude for engineering work and his willingness to accept responsibility. At the end of his apprenticeship he became leading hand and in 1887 chief draftsman. On 6 February 1889 at Holy Trinity Church, Williamstown, he married Amy Isobel Dobbin and that year was appointed manager of Wright & Edwards's new works at Braybrook which handled large rolling-stock contracts for the Victorian Railways. Here he was respected both for his high standards of workmanship and his ability to 'take off his coat' and operate the machines himself. When the 1890s depression forced the firm into voluntary liquidation he defeated six hundred other applicants to become works manager at Thompson [q.v.] & Co., Castlemaine.

In 1899, financed by his friend W. B. Gray, chairman of directors of the South German Reef Gold Mining Co. at Maldon, Lewis took a bold step for a man with a young family, going into partnership with George Kelly. Operating from Melbourne premises in Little Bourke Street opposite the old works of Wright & Edwards, which they eventually purchased, the partners established a reputation for the excellence of their products. The firm's development was aided by the demand from the Western Australian deep-lead goldfields for steam-driven winders, condensing plants and pumps. Kelly & Lewis constructed plant for A. de Bavay's [q.v.8] process of zinc recovery by flotation and in 1910 began producing internal combustion engines. Wartime production included the manufacture of three aircraft engines for the Australian Flying Corps.

In 1913 the firm became a proprietary company with a capital of £50 000; after Kelly died in 1919 Lewis was sole managing director. Many men spent their whole working lives at Kelly & Lewis, with sons following fathers. Edward Lewis's habit was to visit each department at least once a day and his 'system of mental arithmetic and shirt cuff memoranda' enabled him to give instant summaries of the work in hand. Construction of a large foundry at Springvale was begun in 1921 and contracts after this time included extensions to the Yallourn power house and sluice gates for the Hume weir.

Lewis was president of the Victorian Chamber of Manufactures in 1925-27 and a director of the Chamber of Manufactures Insurance Ltd from 1924. He was a life governor of the (Royal) Melbourne Hospital from 1914. His recreations were motoring and gardening; he had a cottage at Warrandyte. An Anglican, a Freemason and Rotarian, he had National Party affiliations. He died on 10 January 1930 at his Armadale home and was buried in Springvale cemetery. Sir William McPherson and Burdett Laycock [qq.v.] were pallbearers. His estate, valued for probate at £37 205 was left to his wife and daughter and his two sons, both of whom became directors of Kelly & Lewis.

Kelly & Lewis Ltd, *Fifty years of engineering 1899-1949* (Melb, 1949); *Argus*, 18 Feb 1919, 10, 13 Jan 1930; Kelly & Lewis Pty Ltd papers (Univ Melb Archives); information from Mr L. M. Davies, New Gisborne, Vic.   C. G. T. WEICKHARDT

LEWIS, ESSINGTON (1881-1961), industrialist and wartime director of munitions, was born on 13 January 1881 at Burra Burra, South Australia, third son of John Lewis [q.v.] and his wife Martha Anne, née Brook. Essington adored his mother, whose death when he was 13 was a deep blow, but his qualities stemmed more from his father. John Lewis had the characteristics of a seasoned bushman: stamina, courage, power of observation and skill in handling horses; in his list of values the first was hard work. He was aggressive, with an overwhelming desire for order and predictability. He insisted on punctuality and obedience, urged loyalty to one's mates and was suspicious of too much talk. In the 1870s he had taken up grazing land in the Northern Territory around Port Essington, and in a patriotic spirit he named his son Essington.

Lewis attended the government school at Burra Burra. He showed no special scholastic aptitude, preferring holidays which revolved around animals and guns, and becoming an outstanding horseman while still a boy. In October 1894 he entered the Collegiate School of St Peter, Adelaide, where he excelled at sport; he was captain of the Australian Rules football team, one of the best tennis players, the champion gymnast and a fine athlete and cricketer. He continued for years to play games with intense determination, representing Norwood and South Australia at football. The *Chronicle* in 1907 adjudged him 'one of the finest footballers in the Commonwealth'.

In keeping with his father's emphasis on self-reliance, Lewis's formal education was interspersed with work in the outback; he spent 1896 and 1899 at his father's cattle-station at Dalhousie Springs. He did not go on the land; his idea of becoming a solicitor was foiled by his father ('You haven't got the brain and I'm damned if I'll give you the money'); and in the end he decided to become a mining engineer, enrolling at the South Australian School of Mines and Industries in 1901. His compulsory stint as a labourer at Mount Lyell, Tasmania, in 1903 did little to endear his chosen profession to him, but he returned to Adelaide to complete his diploma and, in 1904, he signed on with the Broken Hill Proprietary Co. Ltd at Broken Hill, New South Wales. There he made steady, if unspectacular, progress.

From the mine he moved to the treatment plant as a shift boss and late in 1905 he was transferred to the smelters at Port Pirie, South Australia. By the end of 1909 he was shift superintendent of the roasters and sintering plant and had charge of the stables and the company's wharf. The new responsibilities allowed him to show his versatility and his mastery of detail.

Lewis was 5 ft. 10 ins. (178 cm) tall, broad shouldered and handsome. Fair-haired, he was dubbed 'Snowy' by the sporting press; to his friends he was 'Essie'. In spite of an already formidable independence he was generally regarded with affection and referred to as 'big-hearted'. He often played polo at the farm of fellow worker H. C. Warren where he met Warren's niece Gladys Rosalind, daughter of wealthy mining investor and grazier James Cowan and cousin of (Sir) John Cowan [q.v.8]. They were married at St John's Church, Burnside, on 12 April 1910 and set up home at Port Pirie. Lewis demanded methodical housekeeping from his wife; at work his obsession with order and efficiency led to his appointment in 1913 as assistant manager of the smelters.

From 1913 all the excitement in the company's offices centred on plans to develop a steel industry at Newcastle, New South Wales. Lewis's responsibility again increased when he was given the task of expanding the output of ironstone at the South Australian quarry at Iron Knob; he also organized a search for limestone deposits and supervised the opening of a limestone quarry at Melrose, Tasmania. The independence conferred by the move from Port Pirie to a base at Whyalla suited Lewis's domestic arrangements; he was now able to take up residence in Adelaide where his wife had lived since contracting tuberculosis after the birth of their first child in 1911. When the Port Pirie smelters were sold to Broken Hill Associated Smelters an attempt was made by the purchasers to recruit Lewis as works manager, but he chose to remain with B.H.P.; the managing director G. D. Delprat [q.v.8] had been immensely impressed by Lewis's unusual organizing ability and had probably hinted at exciting prospects.

After the steelworks opened in March 1915 Lewis increasingly visited Newcastle. Within a year he was spending half his time there on steel and munitions business. He had initially known nothing of steel-making and had copied into one of the small black note-books, which he invariably carried, simple textbook accounts of the process. His note-books, which bulged his suitcoat and which occupied his attention during his long inter-state train trips, were an essential part of his working method. One such master notebook contained a welter of detail under hundreds of categories, penned in an extremely fine hand. It was regularly updated by the deletion of outdated pages and the insertion of loose leaves. A mass of information was ever ready in Lewis's pocket, but he did not often need to consult his books; percentages, tonnages and prices were imprinted on his memory.

Lewis's three brothers served overseas in World War I, but his own decision to enlist in 1916 was blocked by Delprat's approaches to the Federal Munitions Committee and the Department of Defence, and so he remained, perhaps uneasily, a civilian. In the war years he worked more and more as Delprat's unofficial assistant at the company's head office in Melbourne. He had moved his family to Malvern in 1915. In March 1919 he stood in for Delprat for eight months and on 23 November was appointed assistant general manager at £2500 per year.

In 1920 Lewis and Harold Darling [q.v.8], youngest of the B.H.P. directors, made a world tour, visiting scores of steel plants and iron mines in the United States of America. Delprat and his steelworks manager David Baker had been attracted to the new Duplex process of converting pig-iron into steel but Lewis's observations convinced him that the method was unsuitable for Australian conditions and his opinion carried enough weight with the board for his cable to halt the plans. He made a similar attempt to quash the installation of Semet-Solvay coke ovens; he was unsuccessful though later events were to prove his deductions correct. On the same day that Lewis submitted his report of the tour, 18 February 1921, Delprat agreed to step down, and Lewis was appointed general manager at a salary of £4000. He was the first Australian to hold the office since the resignation of S. R. Wilson in 1886.

When Lewis arrived at power the Australian steel industry was tottering and B.H.P. could not compete with imported steel. In June 1922 the fires at Newcastle were drawn and nearly 5000 men dismissed. Lewis used the chance to analyse the efficiency of plant, men and managerial methods. The rod mill and bloom mill were improved, open-hearth furnaces rebuilt and a new metal foundry erected. The changes, which extended to the safety code and the system of transport at the plant, were effective. But they might not have been accepted by the board had it not been for the strong support Darling gave Lewis. Darling, who had succeeded Bowes Kelly [q.v.9] as chairman in October, was friendly with Lewis, and in Melbourne he saw him almost daily. Suave, companionable and tolerant, he was the polished foil for Lewis's bluntness; because of their differences the two men formed a powerful partnership. The steelworks reopened in 1923 on a surer footing and in 1926 Lewis, with the new title of managing director, became the first B.H.P. executive officer to take a seat on the board.

Lewis's method of management reflected his idiosyncrasies. His letters were stiffly formal and he avoided the telephone. What he insisted upon was talking to people and seeing the plants himself. Every year in the 1920s he made regular trips to Newcastle, Whyalla and Iron Knob; his visits were planned to the last detail and he adhered to his timetable, making a fetish of punctuality—his own and that of others. His constant touring of workshops, quarries, steel mills and coal-mines gave him an astonishing grip on the business and contributed largely to his success. Always observant, he was able to note the smallest alterations which had occurred between visits. He insisted on tidiness and cleanliness, would run a finger along the handrail of a cat-walk to test it for grime, and he seems to have pioneered the Australian use of shadow boards for tools, even installing them for pots and pans in mess kitchens.

It was noticeable that Lewis had more in common with a grimy labourer than a clean-shirted clerk. He knew the names of hundreds of working men. He asked one man about his greyhounds, another about his fishing, and had a standing joke with someone else, making no distinction between a loyal company man and a communist. 'What's the magnifying glass for?', he asked an old hand, pointing to a new silhouette on a shadow board. 'That's so I can see me pay', came the retort. Men who laboured for a living personified Lewis's cult of action and he could appreciate from an old workman the banter which he would not tolerate from a manager or engineer.

Lewis made an overseas tour about every five years and encouraged his senior men to travel. Rather than recruit skilled men from British or American steelworks, he preferred to select Australians and send them overseas periodically. His candidates for promotion tended to be men in his own image—forceful production engineers—but he became increasingly aware of the value of basic training and in 1927 began what was probably the most stringent staff-training scheme yet attempted for an Australian company. He

insisted that all junior technical officers who lacked the relevant diploma should study in their spare time. He did not, however, show the same zeal for research and was partly to blame for the company's slowness to equip a large laboratory.

Unlike Delprat, Lewis encouraged B.H.P. to develop its own steel-based industries, the profits from which proved vital in the 1920s. B.H.P. By Products Pty Ltd was set up in 1923 to sell crushed slag and tar to road-makers; Ryland Bros (Australia), which made nails and wire products at Newcastle, was purchased in 1925; and the company bought shares in and eventually took control of the Melbourne-based Titan Manufacturing Co., the Commonwealth Steel Co. at Newcastle and Lysaght Bros & Co. at Parramatta. In persuading the company to acquire steel-consuming factories Lewis was able to restrict the expansion of the rival steelmakers G. & C. Hoskins [q.v.9]. A merger with the Hoskins' Australian Iron & Steel Ltd in October 1935, with Darling as chairman and Lewis manager of the new subsidiary company, established Lewis indisputably as Australia's leading industrialist. He was much sought after by public committees. In 1929 he replaced Delprat on the council of the Australasian Institute of Mining and Metallurgy and joined the executive of the Victorian Chamber of Manufactures. He was South Australian delegate to the Lawn Tennis Association of Australia in 1931. Later he became a member of the University of Melbourne's appointments board and in March 1938 he was appointed chairman of the Commonwealth Advisory Panel on Industrial Organization.

Lewis was not happy with the power of governments in wage-fixing and industrial disputes and he was also critical of high government borrowing. J. T. Lang [q.v.9] was his *bête noire*, for he considered Lang's economic policies were not merely unsound but immoral. To Lewis the Depression displayed the complete failure of democracy. To individuals whom he believed deserving he was unobtrusively generous at this time, but generally he accepted the Depression as a 'fiery furnace' which would purify the false values fostered since World War I: 'this period of adversity, although very unwelcome and unpleasant, is necessary to put us on a proper economic basis'. Events at B.H.P. seemed to justify his attitude, as the steelworks revealed their efficiency. In 1933-34 Newcastle produced a record tonnage of steel ingots and during his overseas tour of 1934 Lewis realized that his steelworks was now far ahead of most of its European rivals.

On his way to Europe and U.S.A., Lewis visited Japan and was disturbed to learn of the swift expansion of the Japanese steel and other strategic industries. He mentioned his uneasiness about Australian defence to (Sir) John Latham [q.v.], then in Japan on a goodwill mission, and on 16 May wrote to Darling: 'Japan may be described as a big gun-powder magazine and the people as fanatics and any day the two might connect and there will be an explosion'. Within a day or two of leaving Japan he drew up a plan for his fellow directors to consider, urging the creation of big stockpiles of raw materials and the manufacture of munitions. He believed that B.H.P. could build ships at Walsh Island at Newcastle and could co-operate with other companies to build aircraft. In line with Lewis's formula B.H.P. in January 1935 formed a syndicate with Broken Hill Associated Smelters to build aircraft. Next year, having been joined by General Motors-Holden's [q.v.9] Ltd and three other companies, they were registered as the Commonwealth Aircraft Corporation, and set out to build Wirraways at Fishermens Bend, Melbourne. By this time B.H.P. at Newcastle was manufacturing shell cases for 18-pounder guns and anti-aircraft guns, building a shipyard at Whyalla, and organizing the Australian manufacture of special steel necessary to make machine tools.

During World War II Lewis wielded enormous power. He was already business consultant to the Department of Defence when (Sir) Robert Menzies in May 1940 offered him the position of director of munitions. The unlimited authority Lewis promptly assumed made him in fact an 'industrial dictator'. As permanent head of the new Department of Munitions he controlled the production of all ordnance, explosives, ammunition, small arms, aircraft and vehicles and all machinery and tools used in producing such munitions. He was given a seat on the Defence Committee and had the same access to War Cabinet as the chiefs of staff. Unlike them he was exempt from the rules that regulated officers of the Crown, in particular the Public Service Act (1922). Lewis was empowered to acquire compulsorily any materials or building which he needed; he could issue contracts with private firms without calling tenders; he could spend up to £250 000 on any project without approval and he could delegate and revoke responsibilities at will.

Lewis inherited an already efficient munitions concern and he adopted the organizational procedure devised by (Sir) John Jensen. He recruited private industrial leaders as a board of directors to work in partnership with senior civil servants and appointed N. K. S. Brodribb as his deputy. The others on the board were (Sir) Harold Clapp, Sir Colin Fraser [qq.v.8], (Sir) Edward Nixon, W. J. Smith [qq.v.], T. Donaldson, (Sir) Laurence Hartnett, Colonel F. Thorpe and J. B. Chifley, the last as director of labour. The directors conferred around a massive circular table;

and Lewis listened carefully to the speakers, summed up the arguments and then announced his decision. His skill in winnowing the essential from the inessential was such that his judgements were not often queried.

A nation with a common purpose, displaying Lewis's own virtues of hard work and discipline, appealed to him; perhaps he was more at ease with his environment than he had ever been. He worked harder than ever, ignoring warnings that he might jeopardize his health, and even overcoming his hatred of publicity to speak on the national radio network in June 1940 and to the leading newspaper editors in July. He was not without his critics, and in August 1941—shortly before the fall of the Menzies government—H. V. Evatt and J. A. Beasley were particularly outspoken. Although he had vacated his seat on the board of B.H.P. in 1938, Lewis was still paid by the company, remaining a large shareholder and chief general manager. His personal assistants were B.H.P. men paid by B.H.P. These arrangements in fact reflected Lewis's desire to give rather than take during the nation's crisis (and B.H.P.'s profits fell rather than rose) but the situation lent itself to the cry that he who pays the piper calls the tune.

After Menzies's resignation Lewis had to deal with a Labor ministry. But there was no curtailment of his authority. Rather, Prime Minister Curtin increased Lewis's power by appointing him director-general of the additional Department of Aircraft Production. In this capacity Lewis hastened the output of Beauforts to replace the outmoded Wirraways, and after the Japanese bombing of Darwin on 2 February 1942 he organized the production of the new Boomerangs.

The range of munitions produced by Lewis was astonishing in its variety and versatility. His factories made grenades, land-mines, ammunition of all types, .303 rifles, machine- and sub-machine guns, including the Owen gun, and several types of heavy guns. Sophisticated optical aids were produced. Post-war critics condemned the ambitious manufacture of, as it turned out, unused tanks and torpedoes, but Lewis, without the benefit of hindsight, planned for all contingencies. Much of Australia's industrial expansion after the war was based on wartime techniques which he introduced.

Lewis had not sought honours but many came to him. In 1940 he received the bronze medal of the Australasian Institute of Mining and Metallurgy; in 1942 he was made an honorary member of the American Institute of Mining and Metallurgical Engineers; he was awarded the Kernot [q.v.5] medal by the University of Melbourne in 1943 and the Bessemer gold medal by the Iron and Steel Institute, London, next year. He refused recommendation for a knighthood, but Curtin, lavish in his praise and diverging from party policy, initiated Lewis's appointment in 1943 as Companion of Honour.

By mid-1944 Lewis's main war tasks were over and in August he left for a gruelling overseas tour. He returned in March 1945 and resigned his government appointments on 28 May. He was once again the simple steelmaster, but his attitudes to politicians and government had been modified. The deep respect he had acquired for several of the Labor leaders and his belief that an independent nation ought to be able to defend itself and could only do so with a strong central government tempered his response to future economic regulation.

Expansion and efficiency continued to be his goals for B.H.P. He led in mechanizing the coal-mining industry; he opened new ironstone quarries at the back of Whyalla and a second source of iron ore at Yampi Sound, Western Australia; from 1948 he began developing a tinplate industry at Port Kembla. After Darling's death in January 1950 he rejoined the board and became chairman, stepping down to deputy chairman in July 1952. His influence permeated important projects outside B.H.P., including General Motors-Holden's first all-Australian cars in 1948, the long-range weapons project at Salisbury and Woomera, South Australia, in 1946. He served as chairman of the Industrial Design Council of Australia and of the Australian Administrative Staff College at Mount Eliza, Victoria. An honorary fellow of the Australian Academy of Science, he chaired the fifth Empire Mining and Metallurgical Congress which met in Australia and New Zealand in 1953. He was on the council of Clyde School.

The characteristics and values which made Lewis a success in business strained his social life. He was, essentially, lonely and austere. While his brothers had successful careers— James Brook (1877-1966) as a distinguished Adelaide ophthalmologist, Gilbert as an officer in the Indian Army, and Lancelot (1885-1938) as South Australian manager of Goldsbrough, Mort [qq.v.4,5] & Co. Ltd—it was Essington who was regarded as head of the family after his father's death in 1923. He practised a stern paternalism, expecting the same formality from his grandchildren as he had demanded from his children. Wealthy from the age of 45, he scorned to use his money simply to breed more wealth, having a strong suspicion of the flabbiness it often fostered; he gave away large sums but went to great lengths to redress petty dishonesties. Formal social occasions irked him. He belonged to many exclusive clubs: the Melbourne, Australian and West Brighton in Melbourne; the Union in Sydney; the Newcastle, Broken Hill and Adelaide clubs; the Weld in Perth; the Ranelagh in London; and more than a dozen fashionable sporting clubs. But he was never a devoted clubman. He had no interest in dress; he continued to wear his clothes after they had gone out of fashion and was as renowned for his aversion to white tie and tails as for the workman's grey sweatrag he brought to social gatherings. Prudish, he disliked swearing and sexual jokes; he disapproved of women smoking, drinking beer or whisky, using nail polish and wearing shorts or slacks.

The rare holidays which Lewis allowed himself he spent among men rather than with his family; in 1924 he made a motoring-tour of the Northern Territory with Darling, Walter Duncan [q.v.8] and Robert Meares and he went again to Central Australia in 1929. His love for the isolated cattle-country never waned and in the 1950s he was a winter visitor to Liveringa Station in the Kimberleys, Western Australia. He was an enthusiastic tree-planter; in 1934 he had imported the Athel pine from California as suitable for the harsh Whyalla climate and the tree became plentiful in many outback towns and on countless sheep and cattle stations.

In old age Lewis mellowed somewhat, spending more time at Landscape, the 3500-acre (1420 ha) property he had bought at Tallarook, Victoria, twenty years earlier. He was more considerate and gentle towards his wife before her death in 1954; she had made her own life in social work and had been appointed O.B.E. in 1950. In August 1959 Lewis granted his only personal interview to a journalist, Graham Perkin of the *Age*, and on his eightieth birthday newspapers throughout the country had long articles on him.

He had once remarked that he would like to die on horseback at Landscape and thus it was, on 2 October 1961. He had always shunned photographers, but now his photograph was on the front page of every daily newspaper. The Adelaide *Advertiser* reported his death as if he were royalty and at Burra where he *was* royalty the flags flew at half-mast. St John's Church, Toorak, Melbourne, was packed for his funeral; he was cremated. His estate, valued for probate at £98 483, was mainly left to his three daughters and two sons. None of his children sought a public life but a nephew Thomas Lancelot Lewis was premier of New South Wales in 1975-76.

Among Lewis's papers was found the simple text which had ruled his life: I AM WORK. By following this precept he had made B.H.P. one of the most efficient steel companies in the world, and his influence was felt in every industry and occupation. His work in munitions was a prerequisite for many of the complex manufacturing ventures developed in Australia in the 1940s and 1950s. There can be little doubt that but for his premonition of war in the 1930s and his rare talents and dedication as an organizer during the war, Australia would have played a lesser part in fighting the Japanese in the Pacific.

G. Blainey, *The steel master* (Melb, 1971) and for bibliog.

GEOFFREY BLAINEY
ANN G. SMITH

LEWIS, FRED (1882-1956), public servant, conservationist and naturalist, was born on 4 July 1882 at Fitzroy, Melbourne, son of David Alfred Lewis, paint and colour salesman, and his wife Eliza Emma, née Whitcher. Educated at South Yarra State School, he joined the Victorian Public Service in May 1900 as a clerk in the Office of the Public Service Board, moving in 1905 to the ports and harbours branch of the Department of Public Works.

Officially, Lewis's duties from 1906 concerned immigration returns and stores requisitions, but he was probably well acquainted with his branch's administration of the Fisheries and Game Act for in 1910 he headed the clerks appointed to the newly instituted fisheries and game branch of the Department of Agriculture. When fisheries and game became a separate office in 1913 he was appointed supervising clerk under the chief inspector J. M. Semmens. Lewis became chief inspector and head of the department on 13 October 1924 after long stints as acting chief inspector, particularly during and after World War I when Semmens was on military service, and, from 1920, a member of the Commonwealth Repatriation Commission.

Lewis, who retired in 1947, had a strong influence on departmental policy. Although he was largely self taught, his scientific approach earned him the respect of naturalists, conservators, sportsmen and professional fishermen alike; he insisted on a thorough investigation of the biological implications before adding or removing an animal's name from the list of protected species and took pains to publicly justify decisions unwelcome to sportsmen. The re-establishment of the koala, almost extinct in Victoria by 1910, on a reserve at Quail Island remains his most widely recognized achievement. He also saved the mutton-bird rookeries at Cape Woolamai in the 1920s by planting marron grass to control the sand drifts and in 1928-29 demonstrated that seals did not pose a threat to the fishing industry.

Field work took Lewis to all parts of the State. Fearless in discharging his inspectorial duties, he increased contemporary knowledge of the natural history of many indigenous fauna. As well as submitting official reports he wrote for the press and published articles in the *Victorian Naturalist, Emu, Wild Life* and *National Geographic Magazine*; he contributed the chapter on fauna to A. Pratt's [q.v.] *Centenary history of Victoria* (1934). Lewis had a particularly soft spot for the koala but was said to be 'passionately fond' of all Australian animals. After retirement he joined the Victorian Field Naturalists' Club; he was vice-president from 1949, honorary secretary in 1951-55 and the club's delegate to the Victorian National Parks Association. He was also a member of the committee of management of the Sperm Whale Head (Lakes) National Park. Described by his obituarist as courteous, friendly and 'perennially young', he enjoyed tennis and gardening and was a talented nature photographer.

Lewis died of cancer on 7 August 1956 at Malvern, survived by his wife Ada Lucie Edith, née Smith, whom he had married on 20 October 1909 at the Church of Christ Chapel, South Yarra, and by a son and two daughters; he was buried in New Cheltenham cemetery.

PP (LA Vic), 1929, 1st S (23), p 1155; *Vic Naturalist*, 73 (1956-57); *Sun-News Pictorial*, 6 Dec 1937; *Herald* (Melb), 5 May 1938.

ANN G. SMITH

LEWIS, GEORGE (1844-1925), electoral officer and philanthropist, was born probably on 24 May 1844 in Sydney and named Moses, youngest of four sons of Isaac Moses, Jewish merchant, and his wife Hannah, née Aarons. His father died in 1846 and his mother in 1857 when the boy became the ward of Mrs Eliza Taggart of Woolloomooloo and was brought up as a Congregationalist. He had adopted the name George Lewis when he was appointed a supernumerary draughtsman in the New South Wales Surveyor-General's Office on 1 October 1862. On 5 November 1863 he married Jessie Webster at the Congregational Church, Strawberry Hills. In 1877 he was promoted to first-class draughtsman in charge of the reserves branch, controlling forty million acres (16m ha) of crown lands.

When the Department of Lands was reorganized in 1887 Lewis was retired with a pension equivalent to six months pay, but was almost immediately appointed the first district government officer in the newly created local government office, Colonial Secretary's Department. He was responsible, as chief electoral officer, for the electoral system which came into force in New South Wales under the Parliamentary Electorates and Elections Act (1893) which redistributed boundaries and ended plural voting. In June he was one of three members of the Electoral

District Commission appointed to enquire into municipal boundaries in New South Wales and to draft the local government bill, presented in November 1894 but withdrawn and later incorporated in the Local Government (Shires) Extension Act (1905). In December 1894 Lewis was appointed a member of the Districts Government Commission responsible for the subdivision of the Colony into shires and boroughs. In December 1895 he relinquished the post of chief electoral officer. On 15 March 1901 he was appointed the first Commonwealth chief electoral officer and in June chaired a conference in Melbourne of State representatives whose report laid the foundation of the Federal electoral scheme defined in the Commonwealth Electoral Act (1902). Lewis retired in May 1905.

A devout Congregationalist, Lewis was a quiet and generous worker in its philanthropic organizations. He was a force behind the opening of the Mission Church, Sussex Street, Sydney, in 1883, and served as a lay pastor there for many years, working also for the Pitt Street Congregational Church of which he was pastor in the late 1890s. Throughout the 1880s and 1890s he provided free Sunday breakfasts for men in the city. With Sir James Fairfax [q.v.8] he was a founder in 1882 and first chairman of the Sydney Newsboys' Brigade (later, Boys' Brigade). He was also prominent in establishing and administering the Queen Victoria Maternity Home for unmarried mothers at Annandale, donating £1500 for the purchase of the property.

Lewis died on 31 May 1925 in Sydney and was buried in the Congregational section of South Head cemetery. His wife, two sons and two daughters survived him. His estate, valued for probate at £10 880, was divided between family, friends and various charities and institutions, including the Presbyterian Church for the benefit of the Queen Victoria Maternity Home. The tact and judgement that had distinguished Lewis in the public service made him an effective social worker who 'devoted the best years of his life in the cause of the poor and unfortunate'.

PP (Cwlth), 1901-02, 2, p 203; *T&CJ*, 2 Sept 1893; *SMH*, 2, 3 June, 9 Sept 1925; Queen Vic Maternity Home, Annual Report 1899, *and* First annual report of the Syd Newsboys' Brigade, 1883-84 (ML).   JANET HOWSE

LEWIS, JOHN (1844-1923), pastoralist and politician, was born on 12 February 1844 at Brighton, South Australia, second of thirteen children of James Lewis, labourer, and his wife Eliza Margaret Hutton, née Bristow. James had arrived at Glenelg on the *Rapid* in

1838, and Eliza on the *Cygnet* in 1836. In 1844 James accompanied Charles Sturt [q.v.2] into the interior. John Lewis spent six years at small local schools and enjoyed observing the ways of the Aborigines in their seaside camps. At 12 he started work on his father's Richmond farm but, following a parental beating that he considered undeserved, he ran away at 14. Working on outback properties, he developed into an expert roughrider, bushman and an authority on sheep, cattle and horses. He rode to hounds, played polo and won the hurdle race at the first Adelaide Cup meeting.

In 1872, with his brother James and others, Lewis went overland to the Northern Territory. *En route*, the government commissioned him as a courier between the constructing parties on the north and south ends of the overland telegraph line. At Palmerston (Darwin) he equipped and ran the Telegraph Prospecting and Goldmining Co. Next year he formed the Coburg Cattle Co. near Port Essington and conducted pastoral, exploration, gold-mining and trading operations. In 1876 he returned to South Australia intending to go overseas. Instead, on 18 September he married Martha Anne Brook and settled at Burra Burra where he joined William Lister and James Shakes in a stock and station agency. Lewis conducted huge stock sales, once disposing of 47 000 sheep and 1200 cattle. In 1888 the firm became Bagot, Shakes & Lewis Ltd, one of the colony's biggest pastoral firms, with branches in many towns. In 1906 they amalgamated with Luxmoore, Dowling & Jeffrey and, later, with Goldsbrough, Mort [qq.v.4,5], & Co. Ltd. In addition to Newcastle Waters in the Northern Territory, Lewis acquired properties in South Australia, Queensland and New South Wales, some in partnership with (Sir) Sidney Kidman [q.v.9]. At Burra he served for three years on the local corporation and was prominent in community organizations.

Lewis's wife died in 1894; in 1906 he moved to Adelaide where his company took up King William Street premises and he bought an imposing home, Benacre, at Glen Osmond. On 5 July 1907 he married a widow, Florence Margaret Toll, née Mortlock. In 1898-1923 he represented the Northeast (later Northern) District in the Legislative Council. He was sometimes brusque, always brief, and forthright in his political stance. He championed the pastoral interest and, as a member of the Advisory Council of Aborigines and the Aborigines' Friends' Association, he maintained his interest in their welfare. 'Work, not talk' was 'the Honourable John's' philosophy. He had a forceful personality and remained physically robust and energetic.

Lewis was president of the Horticultural

and Floricultural Society for three years from 1899 and was a member of the Flora and Fauna Board. As president in 1913-20 of the South Australian branch of the Royal Geographical Society of Australasia, he and Thomas Gill [q.v.9] organized the publication of records of the explorers Eyre [q.v.1], Strzelecki [q.v.2] and Sturt. In 1922 Lewis published his autobiography, *Fought and won*: 'I always liked winning when I was right up against it', he was quoted in the foreword as saying. In 1923 he was appointed C.M.G.

Lewis died at Benacre on 25 August 1923; his ashes were interred at Burra cemetery. His wife and two daughters and four sons, including Essington [q.v.], survived him. John Lewis's estate was valued for probate at almost £90 000.

J. J. Pascoe (ed), *History of Adelaide and vicinity* (Adel, 1901); H. T. Burgess (ed), *Cyclopedia of South Australia*, 1 (Adel, 1907); R. Cockburn, *Pastoral Pioneers of South Australia*, 2 (Adel, 1927); G. Blainey, *The steel master* (Melb, 1971); *Register* (Adel), 1 Dec 1921, 27 Aug 1923; *Burra Record*, 29 Aug 1923; *Chronicle* (Adel), 1 Sept 1923; C. Sturt, Journal of expeditions into Central Australia (MS, SAA); PRG 247 (SAA).   R. H. B. KEARNS

LEWIS, SIR NEIL ELLIOTT (1858-1935), lawyer and premier, was born on 27 October 1858 in Hobart Town, son of Neil Lewis, merchant, and his wife Anne Maria, née Cox. He was a grandson of Richard Lewis [q.v.2] and nephew of David Lewis, colonial treasurer in 1878-79. He was educated at the High School, Hobart, winning a gold medal in 1875 and a Tasmanian scholarship which earned him a place at the University of Oxford, where he graduated from Balliol College (B.A., 1878; M.A., B.C.L., 1885). He rowed for his college.

In 1882 Lewis entered the Inner Temple and was called to the English Bar in June 1883. On his return to Hobart he was admitted to the Tasmanian Bar in December 1885 and began private practice. He formed a partnership in 1888 with his English friend Tetley Gant [q.v.8] that was expanded to Lewis, Gant & Hudspeth and, in 1918, to Lewis, Hudspeth, Perkins & Dear. Lewis took a particular interest in constitutional cases. He served as vice-president of the Articled Clerks' Association and as president of the Southern Law Society. He was still in daily attendance at his law office at his death. On 15 January 1896 at Perth, Tasmania, Lewis married Lina Henrietta, daughter of Sir James Youl [q.v.6].

He early displayed an interest in politics (he reportedly campaigned for the Conservative Party while at Oxford) and in July 1886 was elected to the Legislative Assembly for Richmond which he retained until April 1903. From March 1887 he sat in opposition to the Fysh [q.v.8] government until he became attorney-general in the Dobson [q.v.8] ministry of 1892-94.

Lewis was leader of the Opposition until November 1897 when he resigned over the Great Western Railway controversy. He had been a member of the Federal Council of Australasia and was a quiet member of the Tasmanian delegation to the 1897-98 Australasian Federal Convention. He was overshadowed by his flamboyant senior Sir Edward Braddon [q.v.7]; Deakin [q.v.8] described Lewis as 'a thoughtful and gentlemanly young lawyer'. He was thrilled to take part in the successful campaigns for the acceptance of the Constitution bill in 1898 and 1899. A fitting reward for this convinced Federalist was his appointment as minister without portfolio in the Barton [q.v.7] ministry of 1901, but Lewis, then premier, sought no Commonwealth seat and relinquished the position in April. He was appointed C.M.G. in 1901 and K.C.M.G. in 1902.

When the Braddon ministry had fallen in 1899, the leader of the Opposition B. S. Bird recommended the governor to commission his colleague Lewis. On 12 October he thus became the youngest premier to that time, with Bird as his treasurer; Lewis was also attorney-general. Although his government survived until April 1903, its history was far from illustrious. The economic times were shaky for Tasmania. As opponents of Federation had predicted, the loss of customs duties to the new Commonwealth, under the Constitution's financial arrangements, was a severe handicap. The cost of the Tasmanian contingent to the South African War was an added burden. The first Lewis government was persistently besieged, and was eventually accused by the *Mercury* of having 'failed to grasp the financial situation'. In the 1903 election all three ministers in the House of Assembly lost their seats. Sir Elliott Lewis had chosen to leave Richmond to contest Central Hobart, the only time a Tasmanian premier has suffered personal defeat in a general election. In 1906 he again lost to (Sir) Herbert Nicholls [q.v.], despite offers of other seats.

The introduction of the Hare-Clark [q.v.3] voting system in 1909 made election easier for a man with a widespread following and Lewis won Denison as an Anti-Socialist. When the Labor Party won twelve of the thirty seats Premier (Sir) John Evans [q.v.8] exhorted its opponents at a specially called meeting to combine against the Labor threat. He indicated his preparedness to step aside if need be and was taken at his word. Lewis was elected leader with a pledge of twelve months support. As premier for the second time and treasurer, Lewis called for party support and organization and encouraged the formation of the Tasmanian Liberal League during 1909.

Despite the loyalty pledge, a faction of the Liberals led by N. K. Ewing [q.v.8] began to criticize Lewis for lack of leadership, and in October 1909 Ewing successfully moved a vote of no confidence, carried with Labor support. The governor called on John Earle [q.v.8] to form the first Labor government. It was obvious that this government would fall when parliament resumed: during the one week of its existence Lewis canvassed firmer support and succeeded in forcing Ewing to disown any ambitions he had for office. Lewis duly succeeded Earle and remained in power until 1912 when, despite having led his party to victory in the election, he resigned the leadership to A. E. Solomon [q.v.] after further internal criticism from the Liberals. Lewis did not join the Solomon ministry, but in the W. H. Lee [q.v.] Liberal and Nationalist government from April 1916 he was treasurer until March 1922, minister for mines until June 1922 and chief secretary briefly in April-June 1922. He then retired from parliament. He was a member of the committee which investigated Tasmanian disabilities under Federation (1925). He had been a member of royal commissions into charitable institutions (1888) and public debts sinking funds (1915). In 1933-35 he was lieutenant-governor of Tasmania.

Lewis inherited the Werndee estate, at Lenah Valley on the outskirts of Hobart, as well as a keen interest in rural affairs. Bulky in his later years, with walrus moustache and bushy eyebrows, he 'always gave the impression that he was a country gentleman who had somehow or another become immersed in legal and political life'. He was a man of many parts—an active volunteer officer in the Southern Tasmanian Artillery, a member of the Anglican synod, a Freemason and president of the Tasmanian Amateur Athletic Association. He was vice-chancellor of the University of Tasmania in 1903-09, chancellor in 1924-33 and served on council for many years. Both as lawyer and politician Lewis was active in encouraging economic enterprises of various kinds. He was a director of the Hobart Gas Co. and of mining and insurance companies. A keen walker, he was fit enough to climb Mount Field East when over 70 and advocated exploration of the neglected south-west. His clubs were the Tasmanian and the Naval and Military.

On Sunday 22 September 1935 Lewis attended church as usual. Later in the day he walked his dog, returned home, complained of tiredness, and died in the late afternoon. His family preferred a private burial to a state funeral but on the way to Cornelian Bay cemetery the cortège stopped at St David's Cathedral for a service. His wife and sons Arndell Neil [q.v.] and Hubert Charles survived him.

Sir Elliott Lewis was not a fluent speaker, being hindered by a lifelong nervous manner, but he believed firmly in a patriarchal obligation to serve. A Labor opponent described him as 'the ideal of a cultured Christian gentleman, and political differences could not in any way affect the sweetness of his disposition'. In 1894 J. B. Walker named him as 'one of the very, very few, prominent politicians in whom public spirit is at all marked', while the *Mercury* noted that his life was 'singularly free from enmity'. Lewis possessed great administrative flair, and once when he left office proudly showed reporters an empty desk. The backroom work of the administrator perhaps suited him better than the full glare of political life.

P. B. Walker (ed), *Prelude to Federation (1884-1898)* (Hob, 1976); F. C. Green (ed), *A century of responsible government 1856-1956* (Hob, 1956); *Mercury*, 27 Feb 1903, 23, 25 Sept 1935; *Examiner*, 23 Sept 1935.   SCOTT BENNETT

LEWIS, ROBERT (1878-1947), jockey, was born on 30 November 1878 at Clunes, Victoria, ninth child and fourth son of Thomas Lewis, Welsh miner, and his London-born wife Martha Ann, née Miller. His mother was reputed to be a great horsewoman and Bobby took to a horse early, though forbidden by his father to ride with a saddle. An elder brother, a horse-breaker, taught him how to handle horses and in later life Bobby was a keen student of breeding and an acknowledged judge of horseflesh. His education in this equine atmosphere suffered in other respects, however, so that, leaving school at 10, he never achieved proficiency in reading and writing.

Lewis won his first race on the Clunes course in 1892 and his first metropolitan in Melbourne in 1895. In 1899 he went to England with his trainer J. E. Brewer but, homesick, quickly returned to resume a forty-year association with the master-trainer Jim Scobie [q.v.]. With Eric Connolly [q.v.8] and Scobie, Lewis made up that 'Triumvirate' of the turf which for over a generation dominated the Victorian racing world. Lewis was soon acclaimed by many connoisseurs as the finest jockey they had ever seen. Always physically fit he seemed to have immense power in his meagre frame. According to Scobie he never 'knocked a mount about' but rode with heels, hands and head. A brilliant judge of pace in a race, he enjoyed a good view of proceedings as he rode long and was himself clearly seen above the other jockeys.

On race days Lewis always took a Turkish bath but he rarely had to waste for a ride. One exception was in 1927 when, almost 49, he determined to meet 7 st. 6 lbs. (47 kg) to ride Ernest Clarke's Trivalve in the Melbourne Cup. Clarke had never won a Cup in thirty years as a breeder and Lewis wanted to carry the pink and pale blue jacket to victory. He succeeded. Two years later in his thirty-second Cup he rode Phar Lap to a third placing, a controversial ride as the great horse suffered a check near the start and pulled hard in the early stages. In all Lewis rode four Cup winners in thirty-three starts (The Victory, 1902; Patrobas, 1915; Artilleryman, 1919; Trivalve, 1927) and gained five minor placings. Although never successful in a Sydney Cup he won a series of major events including eight Victoria Derbys, eight Victoria Racing Club St Legers and five Fisher Plates.

Abstemious but jovial, loyal and utterly dedicated to his profession, ever ready to share his knowledge with younger riders, Lewis was only once suspended, at Randwick in 1925, when the general impression was that no fault lay with him. He handed in his licence in 1938 after forty-six years in the saddle to become a grazier with properties at Glenroy and Ferntree Gully.

Lewis died at Glenroy on 31 March 1947 survived by his wife Mary Irene, née Rowntree, whom he had married at Christ Church, Hamilton, on 15 June 1920, and by two daughters.

J. Scobie, *My life on the Australian turf* (Melb, 1929); E. Bland (ed), *Flat racing since 1900* (Lond, 1950); J. Pollard, *The pictorial history of Australian horse racing* (Syd, 1981); B. Ahearn, *A century of winners* (Brisb, 1982); M. Cavanough and D. Meurig, *The Melbourne Cup* (Melb, 1983); *Argus*, 2 Nov 1927, 1 Apr 1947; *Sun-News Pictorial*, 26 Dec 1931; *Sporting Globe*, 2 Dec 1931; *Herald* (Melb), 30 Nov 1932, 24, 27 Oct, 1, 10, 11, 15, 20, 23, 28, 29 Nov, 25 Dec 1933, 30 Nov 1936, 8 July 1938, 2 June 1947, 2 Nov 1982; *SMH*, 3 Nov 1933, 1 Apr 1947; *Star* (Melb), 26 Dec 1933; *Age*, 1 Apr 1947.
                                                    JOHN MOLONY

LEWIS, WILLIAM HOWARD HORATIO (1868-1939), motor manufacturer and dealer, was born on 11 March 1868 at Willenhall, near Wolverhampton, Staffordshire, England, third of seven children of Jonah Lewis, sheet-iron worker, and his wife Mercy, née Rudge. Educated at Birmingham High School, he arrived in Melbourne with his family in 1879, served an apprenticeship in the furniture trade and was trained as a racing cyclist by his father who, until he purchased a Gippsland farm in 1890, was caretaker of the Warehousemen's Cricket Ground. After winning the one-mile championship of Australasia

in Melbourne in December 1890, Lewis was elected treasurer of the Victorian Racing Cyclists' Association. His prowess, however, could not accommodate the change from the 'ordinary' or high-wheel machine to the 'safety' bicycle and he retired from the track (with a broken collar-bone) in December 1892.

From about 1890 Lewis ran a city bicycle manufacturing, importing and repair business, at first with Ernest Beauchamp, then as Melbourne Cycle Stores and from 1895 with C. B. Kellow [q.v.9]. In 1897, however, after his marriage to Maud Emily Paton on 1 July 1896 at the Independent Church, Prahran, he forsook cycles for Harley Tarrant's [q.v.] motor syndicate in Post Office Place; his partnership with Kellow was officially dissolved in March 1898 and the Tarrant Engineering Co. was formed next year.

Between 1901, when Tarrant and Lewis were the first in Australia to manufacture a workable petrol-driven car, and 1906, when they made the last Tarrant, they produced ten or twelve such cars, their quality proven by fine performances in the 1905 and 1906 Dunlop reliability trials. But they could not compete with cheaper imports, and for the bulk of its business the company relied on the assembling and distribution of overseas models. The agencies for Benz and De Dion acquired in 1899-1900 were the first of more than fifty held over the next forty years, including the profitable Ford agency in 1908-15; while the purchase of Alexander Smith's South Melbourne carriage works in 1903 and its metamorphosis as the Melbourne Motor Body Works presaged expansion into Exhibition, then Russell and Lonsdale streets.

Tarrant's became a proprietary company in 1907. Lewis was managing director and from 1920, when the firm styled itself Auto Cars Ltd, chairman of directors. At his death, which signalled the closure of the distributing part of the business, he was a director of the holding company Allied Motor Interests Ltd and its subsidiary Ruskin Motors Ltd, and of Yellow Cabs of Australia Ltd and Yellow Express Carriers Ltd. Earlier directorships had included De Luxe Motor Service, Sydney, Royal Blue Taxi Co., Melbourne, and Olympia Motors Pty Ltd.

Lewis served as captain in the Australian Volunteer Automobile Corps in 1911-14. He was founder and first president of the Motor Traders' Association of Victoria (later Chamber of Automotive Industries) and first president of the Federal Council of Australian Motor Traders. Politically conservative, he enjoyed golf, shooting and fishing and had a fund of good stories about the early days of motoring. He was a founding member in 1903 of the (Royal) Automobile Club of Victoria and belonged to the Commonwealth and Victoria Golf clubs.

Lewis died at his Toorak home on 4 October 1939. His wife had died in 1919 and on 1 June 1921, with Presbyterian forms, he married Dorothea Surrey (Jean), McEwan to whom he left an estate of about £18 000. A daughter from his first marriage and a son and daughter from his second also survived him. His funeral was conducted by a minister of the Church of Christ, Scientist.

K. Winser, *Story of Australian motoring* (n.p., n.d.); J. Smith (ed), *Cyclopedia of Victoria*, 2 (Melb, 1904); H. H. Paynting (ed), *The James Flood book of early motoring* (Melb, 1968); J. Goode, *Smoke, smell and clatter* (Melb, 1969); P. Stubbs, *The Australian motor industry* (Melb, 1972); *Aust Cycling Annual*, 1897; *Aust Cyclist*, 24 Mar 1898; *Business Archives and History*, 1 (1956), no 6, 3 (1963), no 2; *Australasian*, 3 Mar, 20 Dec 1890, 29 Aug 1891, 7 Jan 1893; *Argus*, 5 Oct 1939.

ANN G. SMITH

LEY, THOMAS JOHN (1880-1947), politician and murderer, was born on 28 October 1880 at Bath, Somerset, England, son of Henry Ley, butler, and his wife Elizabeth, née Bryant. His father died in 1882 and in 1886 his mother migrated to Sydney with her four children and her mother. From an early age Ley had to earn money as a paper-boy and messenger. He attended Crown Street Public School but his formal education ended at 10 when his mother withdrew him to assist her in running a grocery store that she had bought. Later he worked on a dairy-farm near Windsor.

Ley, however, had ambitions for the law. While at Windsor he studiously learned shorthand and, at 14, secured appointment as a junior clerk-stenographer in a Pitt Street solicitor's office. In 1901 he transferred to Norton [q.v.5], Smith & Co., was articled to F. Osborne in 1906 and was admitted as a solicitor on 13 March 1914. On 16 June 1898 Ley had married Emily Lewise (Louisa) Stone Vernon, daughter of a well-off Somerset doctor. The Leys lived with the widowed Mrs Vernon at Glebe until 1906, during which time they had three sons.

In 1896 Ley had joined the Sydney Mechanics' School of Arts where he began to develop his considerable debating skill. The inner city offered few opportunities for an aspiring young politician so in 1907 he moved to the developing suburb of Hurstville. Within five months he was elected to the local council. He served on council committees dealing with parks and gardens, rates and levies, building and health by-laws and street maintenance. He was involved in the local ratepayers' association and the Parents' and Citizens' executive and was active in Protestant organizations such as the Presbyterian Debating Society. Through his advocacy of prohibition and his involvement in the temperance movement, he acquired the nickname 'Lemonade Ley'.

After losing several elections for mayor, he decided not to seek re-election in 1911 and instead turned his attention to State politics. An ardent conscriptionist, he was elected in March 1917 to the Legislative Assembly for Hurstville for the National Party, led by W. A. Holman [q.v.9] after Labor split over conscription. Ley, however, was no friend of Holman. Within the Nationalists he was the leading advocate of proportional representation which, despite Holman's opposition, the government enacted in 1919. Moreover, he was one of the first Nationalists to join the Progressive Party (later the Country Party) and in 1920 was returned as a Progressive for St George.

Although detested by many in his own party, Ley was a 'fluent speaker, with a most unctuous manner', and deluded many with his community work and pious utterances. He was minister of public instruction and of labour and industry in Sir George Fuller's [q.v.8] 'seven-hour' ministry of December 1921. After this débâcle the urban Progressives were accepted back into the Nationalist fold. In 1922 Ley was returned as a Nationalist and was appointed minister of justice in Fuller's coalition ministry of 1922-25.

Ley's ministry was disastrous; virulently sectarian, he had already inflamed existing antagonisms by backing Sister Ligouri [q.v.Partridge] and now exacerbated the situation by promoting the marriage amendment (ne temere) bill. His prevarication about a prohibition plebiscite and double-crossing of Rev. R. B. S. Hammond [q.v.9] damaged his standing with the temperance lobby. There was a community outcry at his refusal to commute the death sentence on Edward Williams, an impoverished music teacher who had murdered his three daughters.

Re-elected in 1925 but now in Opposition, Ley resigned in September, allegedly at the invitation of Prime Minister S. M. (Viscount) Bruce [q.v.7], to stand for the Federal seat of Barton. The ensuing campaign and its aftermath irreparably damaged his reputation. His Labor opponent Frederick McDonald alleged that Ley had tried to bribe him to withdraw from the contest. Ley countered the accusation and won the seat. McDonald sought to have the election declared void in the Court of Disputed Returns but on 15 April 1926, on his way to meet Premier J. T. Lang [q.v.9], he mysteriously disappeared.

Ley had hoped for appointment to the Federal ministry but the prize eluded him. Instead, suspicion about him mounted. In late 1925 he had severed his connexion with Norton, Smith and established the legal firm of

Ley, Andrews & Co. He engaged in business ventures such as S.O.S. Prickly Pear Poisons Ltd and Australasian Oil Fields Ltd, about which allegations of irregularity were rife by 1927. However, that year he visited Switzerland as delegate to the League of Nations General Assembly at Geneva. The critics had included his legal partner Harry Andrews and Hyman Goldstein, politician. On 3 September 1928 Goldstein was found dead at the foot of the cliffs at Coogee.

Ignominiously defeated in the 1928 Federal elections, Ley soon left for England. He was accompanied by his mistress, Maggie Brook, whose husband had also died in mysterious circumstances, with whom he had conducted a discreet alliance since 1922. In England Ley continued his involvement in shady business ventures: he promoted an unrealized £1 million sweepstake for the 1931 Derby, engaged in dubious real estate dealings, and was a wartime black marketeer.

In March 1947 Ley was convicted and sentenced to death for arranging the death of John McBain Mudie, a barman whom he deludedly believed to be Maggie Brook's lover. Three days before the ex-minister of justice was to hang for the 'Chalkpit Murder', his sentence was commuted and he was committed to Broadmoor Criminal Lunatic Asylum, Berkshire, where he died of meningeal haemorrhage on 24 July 1947. He left his estate, valued for probate at £744 in New South Wales, to his wife and sons.

J. T. Lang, *I remember* (Syd, 1956); C. Wilson and P. Pitman, *Encyclopaedia of murder* (Lond, 1961); D. Aitkin, *The colonel* (Canb, 1969); D. Morgan, *The minister for murder* (Melb, 1979); *People* (Syd), 12 Mar 1952; Ley papers (NL).

BAIBA BERZINS

LIEBE, FRIEDERICH WILHELM GUSTAV (1862-1950), building contractor and farmer, was born on 18 January 1862 at Wittenberg, Prussia, son of Edward Liebe. After leaving school at 15 he completed a builder's apprenticeship in Germany before, in 1879, going to Vienna where he studied building at a technical school. He worked on the construction of the Budapest Opera House and, in Bulgaria, in partnership with his brother-in-law Joseph Klein, on the parliament house; they also built a military barracks, colleges, a bridge and other structures. They migrated to Adelaide in 1885. Their work attracted attention from Melbourne architects and Liebe moved to Carlton where his contracts included the Newmarket markets and Carlton houses.

Liebe went to Perth in 1892 and dissolved the partnership four years later; he was naturalized in 1900 and set up in Murray Street as a builder. He worked with leading architects, notably Porter & Thomas, J. H. Grainger [q.v.9 G. P. Grainger] and W. G. Wolf. Accustomed to construction in the grand style, he erected some of Perth's most imposing buildings, including Queen's Hall (1899), His Majesty's Theatre (1904), the art gallery (1908), several banks, and stations for the Midland Railway Co. of Western Australia Ltd. He specialized in hotel construction, the finest example of his work being the Peninsula Hotel (1906) at Maylands, classified by the National Trust in 1974. Its outstanding features included wooden architraves over the wide doors; a tulip motif in the wood, glass and plaster; pressed jarrah ceilings; a massive square dome; external lacework and Victorian decoration. The hotel was originally the headquarters of the German Club, to which Liebe belonged. An astute businessman, he had acquired prime land at Carlton and in Milligan Street, Perth, where he built substantial apartments.

In 1908 Liebe secured 6000 acres (2430 ha) at Wubin. He always denied that he suffered from expressions of anti-German sentiment but, because of the decline in building work on the outbreak of World War I, he relinquished his Perth contracting business in 1914 to concentrate on wheat-production. At one stage he employed 140 men to clear and establish his property. In the 1929-30 season his crop yielded 100 000 bags of wheat, an Australian, possibly world, individual record. Because of a depressed market, he claimed to have lost £52 900. Undaunted, he sold his city properties, extended his overdraft and turned his attention to sheep. In 1945, from a flock of 23 000, his woolclip exceeded 450 bales.

At his Waddi Forest property Liebe, noted for his strength of character, created a fraternal community based on mutual respect between employer and employees. His excellent building techniques were reflected in the quality of the seven staff camps and the farmsheds; Liebe himself lived in style at number 1 camp. Committed early to mechanization, by 1930 he owned twenty tractors, twelve trucks and much other agricultural machinery; in one year he paid £11 000 for fuel.

Stocky, with curly hair, an expansive forehead, bulbous nose and broad shoulders, he was extraordinarily strong: he thought nothing of humping a crate of galvanized iron or fighting off a raging bull. He was a genial boss, esteemed for his perspicacity. He resented high taxation, insisting that it retarded progress, employment and production. He died in Perth on 4 March 1950 and was buried in the Congregational section of

Karrakatta cemetery. Although not uninterested in women, he had never married. His estate was sworn for probate at £194 768.

J. S. Battye (ed), *Cyclopedia of Western Australia*, 1 (Adel, 1912); *Western Mail, Countryman's Mag*, 1 (9 Mar 1950), no 30, p 21; *West Australian*, 6, 18 Mar 1950; CSO 1395/1900, PR 1121/1 (Battye Lib); information from Mrs J. Lakeman, Armadale, WA.   WENDY BIRMAN

LIGHTFOOT, GERALD (1877-1966), public servant, was born on 3 May 1877 at Walker, near Newcastle-upon-Tyne, Northumberland, England, son of Thomas Bell Lightfoot, mechanical engineer, and his wife Emilie Ainslie, née Coxon. He was educated at Blackheath Proprietary School, London, and Pembroke College, University of Cambridge (B.A., 1898; M.A., 1912), where he was a foundation scholar and gained first-class honours in the mechanical science tripos. He then served in engineering firms at Colchester and Clydebank with experience in industrial research into refrigeration and asbestos sheeting. After a world voyage which included Australia and New Zealand he returned to London, studied commercial law and was called to the Bar of the Middle Temple in 1902.

In 1906 Lightfoot migrated to Australia and in 1907 joined the Commonwealth Bureau of Census and Statistics as a draftsman and computer under (Sir) George Knibbs [q.v.9]. There he contributed to the *Commonwealth Year Book* and organized the labour and industrial branch of the bureau. On 11 January 1908 he married Helen Walshe at the Church of the Sacred Heart, Carlton, Melbourne. In 1914-16 he lectured in economics and industrial law at the University of Melbourne for the extension board and the Workers' Educational Association.

In January 1916 Prime Minister Hughes [q.v.9] set up an Advisory Council of Science and Industry and took Lightfoot overseas the same month. His report, published as a Commonwealth parliamentary paper, included detailed studies of American and English scientific research institutions. In August he was appointed secretary to the executive committee of the advisory council. After the death in September 1919 of F. M. Gellatly [q.v.8], director of the proposed Institute of Science and Industry, Lightfoot was responsible for the general administration until legislation was passed in 1920 putting the institute on a regular footing under Knibbs as director from early 1921. Lightfoot played an ameliorative part in tensions between members of the advisory council and the govern-ment and became chief executive officer of the new institute.

In 1925 he was a member of the conference which led to establishment in 1926 of the Council for Scientific and Industrial Research of which he was secretary in 1926-44. He had hoped for appointment as chief executive officer, but worked loyally and effectively with (Sir) David Rivett [q.v.]. Lightfoot's thorough review of the work of the Institute of Science and Industry was perhaps the most basic document in C.S.I.R. planning in its early years, and the system of record-keeping which he instituted was impeccable. He made comprehensive missions to North America, Britain and Europe in 1929 and 1937 for the council. When he retired he was retained as a consultant until 1947.

In order to strengthen C.S.I.R. information services Lightfoot established a scientific bibliographical reference service and began publication of abstracts. In 1919-20 he had fostered publication of *Science and Industry* and in 1927-30 was foundation editor of the *Journal of the Council for Scientific and Industrial Research*. He contributed a diverse range of papers to both publications, frequently relating to areas of research he wished to see promoted. His 1938 report on overseas information centres led to further expansion of C.S.I.R.'s information services which proved to be very useful during World War II.

He was an energetic member of the Commonwealth Prickly Pear Board from 1920. In 1921 he presented a paper to the congress of the Australasian Association for the Advancement of Science surveying liquid fuel resources. A keen interest in engineering standardization led him to press for the establishment of the Standards Association of Australia (1922) on whose council he served. He promoted the formation of the National Association of Testing Authorities and was its first chairman (1947). He was a fellow of the Royal Statistical Society from 1915.

Lightfoot was widely respected within C.S.I.R. for the style and order he brought to its organization. Though he was known not to suffer fools gladly he was in his early days commended as 'a most likeable fellow, with a merry eye', who knew 'how to order a good dinner'. He died on 1 June 1966 in Melbourne, survived by three daughters and a son, and was buried in St Kilda cemetery with Catholic rites. 'His knowledge, administrative competence and dedication' had been of enormous benefit to C.S.I.R.

G. Currie and J. Graham, *The origins of CSIRO* (Melb, 1966); *PP* (Cwlth), 1929, 2 (17), 1937, 5 (89), 1937-40, 4 (99), 1944-45, 2 (9); *Government Gazette* (Cwlth), 22 Feb 1908, p 553, 16 Jan 1909, p 23, 11 Dec 1919, p 2393, 30 Dec 1920, p 2359;

CSIR, *J*, 17 (Aug 1944), no 3, p 207; *Science and Industry*, 1 (May 1919), no 1; *SMH*, 13, 15 Jan 1921, 6 Aug, 15 Sept 1937, 5 Jan 1938, 3 June 1966; *Punch* (Melb), 17 Mar 1921; information from Prof. B. Schedvin, Univ. Melb.

D. I. McDONALD

LIGUORI, SISTER MARY; *see* PARTRIDGE BRIGID MARY

LIHOU, JAMES VICTOR (1895-1918), bushman and soldier, was born on 6 February 1895 at Dubbo, New South Wales, eldest of seven children of Stephen Henry Lihou, cook and station-hand, from Guernsey, Channel Islands, and his Irish-born wife Eliza, née Kennedy. Educated at Wongarbon Public School, he was a popular and keen student. He left school at 15 to help support the family by trapping and selling rabbits. Before World War I he worked mainly as a roustabout on sheep-stations and in the wheat-harvesting season helped on local properties.

On 15 January 1916 Lihou enlisted in the Australian Imperial Force, embarking for France with the 18th Reinforcements for the 13th Battalion on 3 May and joining it on 4 October. He was wounded at Stormy Trench, north-east of Gueudecourt, on 5 February 1917 and rejoined his unit on 20 March but was wounded again at the 1st battle of Bullecourt. Lihou was promoted lance corporal on 1 October and corporal on 26 March 1918. He took part in the attack on Hébuterne at the beginning of April when the battalion assaulted enemy trenches twelve times and succeeded in capturing its objective, as well as the field beyond. For his part in this action Lihou was awarded the Military Medal; he was promoted sergeant on 27 August.

At Vaire Wood, east of Corbie, on 4 July 1918 Lihou won the Distinguished Conduct Medal. He was in charge of a Lewis-gun section in the leading wave of an attack and throughout the advance fired his gun from the hip with great effect. When an enemy post threatened to hold up the line he 'engaged it so effectually' that a bombing section was enabled to approach it from a flank, killing all the occupants.

During the 13th Battalion's attack of 18 September near Le Verguier, Sergeant Lihou and his party of seven got ahead of their company but kept moving forward; a machine-gun opened fire on them from behind. Lihou immediately rushed the machine-gun post and threw a bomb, killing three of the crew and taking the survivors prisoner. When his party reached the first objective they met with opposition from several machine-guns

and Lihou again charged ahead to bomb and capture one crew, thus enabling his section to get into the enemy trench. He then led his men along it and saw a post that was holding up another battalion. He climbed out of the trench on his own and charged the post of twenty Germans but before he could reach it was fatally wounded. He died on his way back to a dressing-station and was posthumously awarded a Bar to his D.C.M. The battalion history states that 'his cheerful, careless gallantry was such that he was regarded as a certainty for a V.C. had he been spared'. Sergeant Lihou has no known grave and is commemorated at the Villers-Bretonneux Memorial, France.

T. A. White, *The fighting Thirteenth*, (Syd, 1924); War diaries of the 13th Battalion, AIF, 1916-18, and other records (AWM); information from Mr P. Lihou, Punchbowl, Syd.

R. C. H. COURTNEY

LILLEY, CHARLES MITFORD (1890-1955), medical practitioner, was born on 28 January 1890 at Kelvin Grove, Brisbane, son of Edwyn Mitford Lilley, barrister, and his wife Kate, née Goggs, both Queensland born. His grandfather was Sir Charles Lilley [q.v.5] and Kathleen Mitford Lilley [q.v.] was a sister. Charles was educated at Brisbane Grammar School where he played in the Rugby fifteen and in 1908 was champion rifle-shot of the school's accomplished Empire Cup shooting team. He graduated from the University of Sydney (M.B., Ch.M.) in March 1914 as a student of St Andrew's College.

Lilley at first worked as resident medical officer at the Brisbane Hospital where he was briefly acting medical superintendent in 1917. Next year, after enlisting as captain with the Australian Imperial Force, he became a fellow of the Royal College of Surgeons (Ireland). He served in France from July to October with the 2nd Field Ambulance and for another year with various units.

After demobilization he was appointed to the surgical staff of the Brisbane Hospital in 1920 and remained a general consultant for thirty-four years. But Charles Lilley was first of all a general practitioner, living and practising at Bardon. He had great ability in general medicine and his skills embraced the full range of medical practice of the era. His superb surgical skill eventually became so apparent that he forsook general practice and became a consultant general surgeon in Wickham Terrace. He was without doubt in the very forefront of Australian surgeons, especially in the surgery of the head and neck. His technique was meticulous and matched by humble dedication to his craft. Dr J. V. Duhig [q.v.8] remarked that he was 'rated higher as a thyroid surgeon than anybody else in Australia in his time, while many old timers think him the best surgeon Queensland has ever had'.

Monetary reward was the least of Lilley's interests: he billed his impecunious patients with token charges and was honorary surgeon for Anglican orders of nuns. He never sought the limelight and hated sham and humbug. Unfortunately he had limited powers of communication: he was a poor public speaker, he avoided conferences, even after his election in 1931 to the Royal Australasian College of Surgeons, and he did not contribute to surgical literature because of lack of confidence in his powers of expression. The medical profession suffered because of these shortcomings, for he had unrivalled surgical experience and had much to teach. He taught by example and never shirked his Hippocratic responsibilities. He was utterly devoted to his patients and the hour of day or night mattered little if his skills were required. He was a great man and a most humble man.

Lilley's general reading was wide. Especially fond of Pepys, he spoke with authority on the British Navy in the later seventeenth century. Boating and fishing were his leisure activities. Briefly president of the Brisbane Grammar Old Boys' Asociation, he was a member of the Queensland Club from 1944.

Unmarried, Lilley died at Windsor of bronchopneumonia, arteriosclerosis and coronary disease on 16 April 1955 and was cremated with Anglican rites. His medical friends established the Charles Mitford Lilley Memorial Fund within the faculty of medicine, University of Queensland, to encourage surgical studies.

S. Stephenson, *Annals of the Brisbane Grammar School* (Brisb, 1923);T. M. Hawkins, *The Queensland great public schools* (Brisb, 1965); R. Goodman, *Secondary education in Queensland, 1860-1960* (Canb, 1968);*MJA*, 13 Aug 1955; personal information.   C. A. C. LEGGETT

LILLEY, KATHLEEN MITFORD (1888-1975), headmistress, was born on 11 December 1888 at Kelvin Grove, Brisbane, second of five children of Edwyn Mitford Lilley, barrister, and his wife Kate, née Goggs. A granddaughter of Sir Charles Lilley [q.v.5], she extended the family's association with Brisbane Girls' Grammar School to over a century.

Kathleen was educated there herself. Winning the Fairfax [q.v.4] medal for senior French in 1907, she attended the University of Sydney from 1908 and, on graduating in 1911 with third-class honours in French, joined the staff of Ipswich Girls' Grammar

School to teach English, French and gymnastics. In 1919-20, on leave from Ipswich, she undertook further studies of English at Sydney University and gained her M.A. in 1922. At the end of 1923 she became head of St Faith's Anglican College at Yeppoon on the central Queensland coast and in 1925 headmistress of Brisbane Girls' Grammar School.

As headmistress, Miss Lilley ran both the day school and the boarding school, where she lived for many years. The school itself occupied nearly all of her life—she even tended the gardens when time permitted. She continued to teach English and French (with a reputed preference for brighter students) and is remembered with affection and some trepidation by her students, who nicknamed her 'Blos'. She was rather a formidable figure: a large, handsome woman, well dressed, with presence and authority, 'an air of rectitude' and a reputation for a quick temper. She is remembered as shy; although she was close to and proud of her family (her brother Charles [q.v.] became a well-known surgeon), she led a rather isolated personal life. Professionally seen as a disciplinarian, she was justly proud of the school's consistently high results in English, and took a continued interest in physical education and sport. She was a president of the Secondary Schools' Sports Association and a member too of the Crèche and Kindergarten Association of Queensland. She was also sometime president of the female Brisbane literary club, the Scribblers'. A hint of her educational philosophy is found in one of the rare public comments she permitted herself, pressing in her last annual report for an extra year of secondary education: 'Such an extension would enable secondary school work to be done with such thoroughness and pleasure as to foster the love of learning, rather than the love of percentages, and would surely lead to the acquisition to some degree of that wisdom which is the ultimate aim of the cultivation of the mind'.

1925 to 1952 were years of the school's gradual and gentle development in her care. Miss Lilley maintained a relationship of mutual respect with the school's board of trustees throughout. Retiring in 1952 to her home at Herston, she died at Herstonville Convalescent Home on 12 July 1975 and was cremated with Church of England rites. The Kathleen M. Lilley library was built at Brisbane Girls' Grammar School in 1958 as a memorial to her.

C. A. Bernays, *Queensland politics during sixty (1859-1919) years* (Brisb, nd, 1919?); R. Goodman, *Secondary education in Queensland, 1860-1960* (Canb, 1968); Qld Women's Historical Assn, *Historical Happenings*, Aug 1975, no 122; *Brisb Girls' Grammar School Mag* (Annual Reports), 1925-52, and *Centenary Mag*, 1975; *Queenslander*, 16 July 1931; *Courier Mail*, 15 July 1975.

PATRICIA NOAD

LILLICO, SIR ALEXANDER (1872-1966), farmer and politician, was born on 26 December 1872 at Lillico's Siding on the north-west coast of Tasmania, son of Hugh Lillico, farmer, and his wife Mary Elliot, née Robson. He was educated at Don State School and left to work on his father's property. Lillico worked for two years as a miner and tributer at Zeehan and saved enough money for a deposit on 320 acres (130 ha) called Grey Peel at West Pine. On 10 June 1896, at the Wesleyan Church at Norfolk Creek (Forth), he married Frances Emma Vertigan, daughter of a farmer. They lived at Grey Peel from 1896 until 1909 when Lillico sold out, intending to farm in Victoria. Persuaded by his father to settle at Lillico's, he bought Cheviot Dale and developed it into 'one of the best farms on the north-west coast' before moving to Devonport in 1926.

Lillico was a member of the Penguin (1906-09) and Devonport (1914-20) municipal councils. A gentle and devoted family man, he was friendly and approachable with a keen sense of humour. He was a Presbyterian elder at West Pine and later for almost forty years an elder of Don Presbyterian Church.

In May 1924 Lillico, who at first had resisted nomination by local farmers, won the Legislative Council seat of Mersey. In May 1954 he retired, undefeated, having promoted the interests of his district with intense loyalty. As a member of the Parliamentary Standing Committee for Public Works examining the Hobart Bridge bill (1941), he insisted that the project be put on a proper financial basis before the bill was passed. He especially liked to be associated with the Farmers' Debt Adjustment Act (1935, amended 1936) which helped many farmers to stay on the land. Lillico is reputed to have led the majority of the council who in 1943 refused to agree to temporary transfer of State constitutional powers to the Commonwealth. As a result of the resistance by several State parliaments, the Federal Labor government was forced to hold a referendum which was defeated. He was widely respected for his sound judgement on political and social questions and always fought hard for what he thought was right. His son Alexander Elliot, later a Federal senator, was elected to the Legislative Council in 1943, creating a then unique situation in Tasmanian parliamentary history with father and son in the same House. Lillico was knighted in 1962 in recognition of 'a lifetime of distinguished public service'.

He died on 14 December 1966 at Latrobe and was buried from St Columba's Presbyterian Church, Devonport, in the old Don cemetery. His wife had died in 1961 but he was survived by their three sons. In his obituary notice the *Mercury* described Lillico as 'the unchallenged, unofficial leader of opinion in the Legislative Council' who set 'a standard of integrity of purpose which would long be remembered with gratitude'.

W. A. Townsley, *The government of Tasmania* (Brisb, 1976); *Mercury* and *Advocate* (Burnie), 16 Dec 1966.   DAVID DILGER

LIND, SIR ALBERT ELI (1878-1964), politician, was born on 21 February 1878 at East Charlton, Victoria, second son of Oliver Nicholas Lind, farmer from Björnholm, Denmark, and his Welsh wife Mary Ann, née Clay. Drought drove the family from Charlton to East Gippsland in 1882 where they settled at The Poplars, Clifton Park. Albert attended Lucknow and Bairnsdale State schools and found work in the hop and maize fields. At 12 he was apprenticed to local builders, the McKnockiter Bros, and was later in business himself as a signwriter, carpenter, painter and decorator. He was a keen sportsman, winning many local cycling races and rowing trophies around the State; he also participated in coursing.

On 31 August 1904 at Bairnsdale Lind married Flora Catherine Arthur with Presbyterian forms; they had four sons and five daughters. That year he selected 640 acres (260 ha) at Mount Taylor with his brother Ernie and worked hard to develop it into a fine dairying property. Eventually Hazel Dell covered about 3500 acres (1400 ha) which Lind held in partnership with his sons.

Lind was a councillor for the East Riding of Bairnsdale Shire in 1914-25 (president, 1917-18) and was known as a forceful advocate of greater government responsibility for rural road-works. In October 1920, as a Victorian Farmers' Union candidate, he won the Legislative Assembly seat of Gippsland East and quickly made his presence felt in debates. He constantly championed his electorate, advocating road and rail extension, the development of a port at Lakes Entrance, and the opening up of forest reserves to sawmillers, as well as forest conservation and reafforestation. In 1926 two national parks east of Orbost were named the Albert and the Lind national parks after him. In 1922 he became a member of the select committee for electricity supply and later of the Railways Standing Committee and the Parliamentary Printing Committee. He was also chairman of the Unemployment and Relief Council.

In 1935 when (Sir) Albert Dunstan [q.v.8] became premier Lind was appointed minister of forests and president of the Board of Lands and Works, holding these posts through a record term until October 1945 (with a brief interlude during the Cain ministry of September 1943). He was commissioner of crown lands and survey for a similar period, relinquishing that place temporarily from January 1942 until September 1943 for the portfolio of public instruction. He was deputy leader of the Victorian United Country Party in 1937-45 and deputy premier from October 1937 to September 1943, acting as premier on several occasions. He was chairman of committees in 1947-50.

In the McDonald governments of 27 June 1950 to 28 October 1952 and 31 October to 17 December 1952 Lind again resumed his posts in lands and forests and was also minister for soldier settlement. He was knighted in 1951.

As minister of forests Lind developed pine plantations in neglected country, particularly in Gippsland; he promoted forestry camps for the unemployed and to provide training in forestry skills for boys. Under his urging Australian Paper Manufacturers Ltd established their Maryvale mills near Morwell and after the bushfires of 1939 operated other sawmills in the Erica district to cut out damaged timber for scantling and pulpwood. In this period Lind encouraged the setting up of bushfire brigades and the building of forestry roads.

As part of his responsibility for lands he helped relieve many soldier settlers by transferring their liabilities to the general revenue account. He also assisted General Motors-Holden's Ltd to purchase land at Fishermens Bend, Melbourne, where in 1948 they were to produce the first entirely Australian-built motor car. In later years, with his long experience of parliamentary service, Lind was a member of the Legislative Assembly Standing Orders Committee (1950-61), the House Committee (1955-59) and the Public Accounts Committee (1956-61). He retired from parliament in June 1961 after having served longer than any other sitting member.

Sir Albert died on 26 June 1964, survived by his wife and eight children. Greatly honoured throughout East Gippsland, he was accorded a state funeral at Bairnsdale where he was buried. He is remembered as a tall man, straight and wiry, white-haired in later life, and as very approachable. He was aptly described by the Country Party leader George Moss as 'a bushman who never got lost'.

PD (Vic), 1961, p 3097, 1964, p 21; *Bairnsdale Advertiser*, 29 June 1964; *Age*, 25 July 1950, 27 June 1964.   J. D. ADAMS

LIND, EDMUND FRANK (1888-1944), medical practitioner and soldier, was born on 23 December 1888 at South Yarra, Melbourne, son of Edmund Frank Lind, an English-born bank-manager, and his Victorian wife Emily Margaret, née Harris. Frank was educated at Camberwell Grammar School and the University of Melbourne (M.B., Ch.B., 1914), and commenced practice at Williamstown.

He enlisted in the Australian Imperial Force on 20 August 1914 as a captain (he had joined the Melbourne University Rifles in 1910) and was posted as regimental medical officer to the 5th Battalion. At Mena Camp, Egypt, in March 1915 Lind's outspoken criticisms of training conditions led to improvements. He embarked for Gallipoli on 4 April but on 17 April, while his ship was at Mudros, was injured when he fell into the hold, fracturing his skull. He rejoined his unit on Gallipoli on 28 May.

The 5th Battalion was prominent in operations against the Turks at Lone Pine during August. In September it was withdrawn to Lemnos, on 24 October returned to the Peninsula, and on 11 December left finally for Egypt. On 2 April 1916 Lind transferred to the 8th Field Ambulance at Ferry Post with the Egyptian Expeditionary Force. Promoted temporary major on 8 June he sailed for France, joining the 5th Pioneer Battalion as R.M.O. on 12 July and serving during the costly battle of Fromelles. On 13 October he joined the 9th Field Ambulance training in England and on 14 November was promoted major.

The 9th Field Ambulance embarked for France on 23 November, accompanying the 3rd Division to the Armentières sector. Lind took part in the the battle of Messines in June 1917, organizing and controlling a collecting station for walking wounded. On 22 August he was appointed deputy assistant director of medical services, II Anzac Corps, and served during the Broodseinde and Passchendaele battles. On 11 January 1918 he was appointed D.A.D.M.S., 4th Division, and was again conspicuous in organizing the clearance of wounded during the battle of Hamel in July. Promoted temporary lieut-colonel in command of the 2nd Field Ambulance on 1 September, he efficiently organized casualties during the assault on the Hindenburg Outpost Line. On 10 October, while on leave, he was detached for transport duty to Australia, and his A.I.F. appointment ended in March 1919. He had been twice mentioned in dispatches and awarded the Distinguished Service Order.

Lind married Beulah Rotterdale McMinn on 23 June 1920 at St Paul's Cathedral, Melbourne. After re-establishing himself in medical practice at Brighton he rejoined the Mel-

bourne University Rifles, commanding the
unit in 1921-26. In 1926-29 he was a staff
officer on 4th Division Headquarters, Australian Military Forces, then was appointed to
command successively the 29th and the
29th/22nd Battalions, and from 1934 the 4th
Infantry Brigade; he was promoted colonel in
1936 and brigadier in 1938. In 1937 he was
chosen—a signal honour—to lead the Australian Military Contingent to the coronation
of King George VI.

In July 1940 Lind was appointed to command 23rd Brigade, 8th Division, 2nd A.I.F.
The brigade was deployed in the Northern
Territory, and Lind had the unhappy experience of seeing his three battalions dispersed,
one in March-April 1941 to Rabaul, the
2/21st and 2/40th on the outbreak of war with
Japan to Ambon and Dutch Timor. As Lind
pointed out, these two under-strength battalions, inadequately armed and lacking air
and naval support, faced hopeless tasks. In
civilian attire, he had visited Ambon and
Timor in May. His representations caused
him to lose favour with the chief of the General Staff, and probably cost him command of
Sparrow Force in Timor for which he
appeared the logical choice.

The brigade was reinforced by two raw militia battalions and Lind was allotted the
impossible task of defending some 28 miles
(45 km) of coastline. The first Japanese air
raid on Darwin in February 1942 caused
widespread concern at the prospect of invasion. Veteran A.I.F. troops, newly returned
from the Middle East, were rapidly deployed
in the Northern Territory. Lind, a victim of
large-scale replacement of officers, was
removed from command. He flew south on 24
March and on 28 July he was placed on the
retired list. In July 1940 he had been
appointed C.B.E.

Lind became chairman of the Services and
Citizens Party from its formation in 1943 and
in August that year unsuccessfully contested
Henty at the Federal elections. He collapsed
at his South Yarra home on 2 May 1944 and
died of acute cardiac failure; he was buried in
Box Hill cemetery. His wife, two daughters
and a son survived him. Keen-eyed, never
given to wasting words and direct in manner
and speech, Lind was none the less popular
and successful in both military and medical
circles.

A. W. Keown, *Forward with the Fifth* (Melb,
1921); A. G. Butler (ed), *Official history of the Australian Army Medical Services . . . 1914-19* (Melb,
1930, Canb, 1940, 1943); C. E. W. Bean, *The A.I.F.
in France*, 1918 (Syd, 1942); *Table Talk*, 18 Feb
1937; *Reveille* (Syd), June 1944; *Herald* (Melb), 3
May 1944; *Argus, Age,* and *Sun-News Pictorial*
(Melb), 4 May 1944.   A. J. SWEETING

LINDRUM,   FREDERICK   WILLIAM
(1888-1958) and WALTER ALBERT (1898-
1960), billiard prodigies, were the only sons
of Frederick William Lindrum, billiardist, and
his wife Harriet, née Atkins. Fred was born on
6 February 1888 at South Melbourne and
Walter on 29 August 1898 at Kalgoorlie,
Western Australia. The boys received only
brief formal education, Fred at Kalgoorlie,
Walter in New South Wales at St Francis
Boys' and the Albion Street Superior Public
schools, Paddington.

Their paternal grandfather, Frederick
William (Fred I) (d. 1880), had arrived in Adelaide from Plymouth Devon, England, as a
child in 1838, later established a vineyard at
Norwood and was a hotelkeeper in Adelaide
and at Victor Harbor. In 1862 he was a bil-
liard-saloon proprietor; and on 17 September
1865 in Adelaide, the day his son (Fred II) was
born, he defeated the visiting 'world champion' John Roberts senior (presumably in a
handicap match).

Fred II played billiards from childhood. In
1886 he moved to Melbourne and next year
won the native-born Australian championship. But by 1892 (in a pattern to be repeated
by later Lindrums) he had sunk from the top
competitive ratings and within a few years
moved to Western Australia where he opened
a billiard-room at Kalgoorlie and conducted a
bookmaking business. He spent peripatetic
years at Donnybrook, Perth, Kalgoorlie and
Broad Arrow before moving to Sydney in
1909 and finally, in 1912, to Melbourne.
There, at 317 Flinders Lane, he ran the Lindrum billiard-hall until his death on 11 April
1943. According to Walter, from 1909 to
1912 his father was the greatest billiard
player in the world but 'only . . . my brother
Fred and myself knew it. He passed over public matches to coach the two of us'.

The elder son (Fred III) was obviously his
father's first choice. Left-handed, he was
trained for convenience as a right-handed
player. (Ironically, his brother, having injured
his right hand, learned a left-handed game). In
Perth, where he helped his father to manage a
billiard-room, Fred won tournaments in 1904
and 1905 and next year became Western Australian champion. He went on to win the Australian title in Sydney in 1908. The year 1911
saw the peak of his career when in a successful defence against the English professional
Tom Reece he made breaks of 830, 840 and
1239—the last an Australian record. The
most elegant of players, a great showman,
Fred took to the drink and after a disastrous
English tour in 1911-12 never again looked a
world-class competitor. While technically
retaining the Australian championship (until
1934) he was soon eclipsed by Walter.

Fred died on 22 October 1958 at South
Yarra. On 28 July 1913 he had married

Augusta Hewett (d. 1932) at Fitzroy. He was survived by his son from this marriage and by his second wife Dorothy Anne Jane, formerly Dyer, née Graham, whom he had married on 7 April 1948.

Walter was probably driven to excel by his need to match or surpass his brother in his father's eyes: significantly, his assumption of a billiardist's career followed hot on the heels of Fred's failure. World War I, however, obscured his rise, and though after it he racked up major successes against English visitors it was not until the 1929-30 season that he went to England and immediately won recognition as the best billiard player ever seen.

On this first tour Lindrum carried almost all before him, and made sixty-seven of what his nephew Horace was to call with perhaps understandable pique his 'highly scientific but somewhat mechanical thousands at billiards'. Lindrum himself effectively encouraged this view with a modest insistence that billiard champions are not born but made, an insistence reinforced by endless, perhaps exaggerated, reminiscences of dedicated practice from early childhood. It is generally said, too, that Lindrum owed his pre-eminence to 'nursery cannons' (close cannons barely moving the balls): but Lindrum's closest rivals also, necessarily, mastered this art and, though Lindrum's largest competitive break of 4137 on 19-20 January 1932 consisted of nearly two-thirds of such cannons, it was probably a more virtuoso insistence on that play by the New Zealander Clark McConachy which led, as McConachy wished, to a change in the rules in September. Tom Newman wrote in 1929: 'It is the greatest injustice you can do to Walter Lindrum to write him down as a "scoring machine". Nothing could be more unlike him. He is showing you everything the game beautiful can show'.

Praise like Newman's—and it was chorused—must have been sweet to Lindrum's ears; but conflicting trade interests, always a major determinant in professional billiards, kept him that first season from playing for the 'world championship'. Coming back for the next season, he won an international tourney, a round-robin in which he gave 7000 start to the others and which ended in a play-off between Newman and Lindrum. This was perhaps the peak of Lindrum's career—but the tournament had been so successful that the annual world championship was abandoned.

Lindrum was also to miss the championship in his third northern season which he spent mostly on a North American exhibition tour. He finally won the cup, from Joe Davis, in May 1933 in his fourth international season and, to the consternation of the Billiard Association and Control Council (the English governing body), insisted on defending it in Australia. In 1934 in Melbourne he retained it against Davis and McConachy and in 1938 against McConachy, without the sanction of the B.A.C.C. In 1950, by which time, even in its strongholds, English billiards had given way to snooker, he refused McConachy's challenge and returned the cup to England.

It was not really the rule changes that ended Lindrum's record-breaking progress. He in fact made four breaks of over 3000—the highest 3752—against Fred in 1940-41 under the revised baulk-line rule. But he seems to have found competition an unwelcome strain, and having achieved the pinnacle in English billiards was content to stop, leaving pre-eminence in snooker to Davis. Nothing came of attempts to arrange matches under hybrid rules with the American champion Willie Hoppe. In later life, Lindrum deployed his skill to raise money for charities. He was appointed M.B.E. in 1951, and C.B.E. in 1958.

Lindrum married Rose Coates on her death-bed on 23 August 1929 in Sydney. His second marriage, to Alicia Hoskin on 9 April 1933 in London, ended in divorce in 1955. Childless, Lindrum died intestate of coronary vascular disease at Surfers Paradise, Queensland, on 30 July 1960; he was buried in Melbourne general cemetery after a funeral service at St Paul's Cathedral. His third wife Beryl Elaine, formerly Russell, née Carr, whom he married on 21 July 1956, survived him.

Lindrum was the author of several books on billiards. He was featured on the 1981 Australian 60-cent postage stamp and a technical school scholarship was founded in his memory in 1963. The cuttings, letters and telegrams on display at the Lindrum Billiard Centre in Melbourne reveal the astonishing range—probably owing something to his Freemasonry—of his acquaintances.

Fred and Walter's sister Violet was also a skilled player. Her son Horace Norman William Morrell (1912-1974) changed his name to Lindrum and became world snooker champion.

A. Ricketts, *Walter Lindrum* (Canb, 1982); *People* (Syd), 27 Sept 1950.　　　EVAN JONES

LINDSAY, DAVID (1856-1922), explorer, was born on 20 June 1856 at Goolwa, South Australia, son of John Scott Lindsay, master mariner of Dundee, and his wife Catherine, née Reid. He was educated locally and under Rev. John Hotham at Port Elliot before at 15 going to work in a chemist's shop, next with an Adelaide mining agent. In 1873 he was apprenticed as a surveyor with the government. Five years later he was appointed junior surveyor and clerk in the land office of the Department of the Northern Territory at Palmerston (Darwin). On 10 March 1881 at North Adelaide he married Annie Theresa Stuart Lindsay; the families were not related.

Next year Lindsay resigned and began business in Palmerston as a surveyor, draftsman, and land, stock and station agent. In 1883 the South Australian government commissioned him to explore the central and eastern part of Arnheim's (Arnhem) Land; his party survived fierce attacks by Aborigines, one group numbering 300. Next year he took seven men and twelve camels from Hergott Springs to the Gulf of Carpentaria, tracing the Finke River to its mouth and seeking information about Ludwig Leichhardt [q.v.2]. Lindsay surveyed the country between the overland telegraph line and the Queensland border, explored the MacDonnell Ranges, made a brief foray into the Simpson Desert, and spent six months in the country between Lake Nash and Powell's Creek.

He reported on the gold-bearing potential of mines near Port Darwin in 1886-87 for an English syndicate; he then made a notable five-week ride of 1400 miles (2250 km) across the continent to the southern coast, with only one Aboriginal companion. On his return Lindsay was made a fellow of the Royal Geographical Society, London. He spent 1888 examining the MacDonnell Ranges for precious stones and minerals and found a deposit of payable mica. From 1889 Lindsay was a broker on the Adelaide Stock Exchange.

In 1891 the local branch of the Royal Geographical Society of Australasia undertook to explore the last blank spaces on the map of south-western Australia. Lindsay was appointed to lead the venture, known as the Elder Scientific Exploring Expedition, after its backer Sir Thomas Elder [q.v.4]. The expedition, begun in May and involving forty-two camels—Lindsay was an expert camel trainer and rider—set off from Warrina and was intended to take eighteen months. When crossing what was later the Coolgardie goldfield, Lindsay telegraphed back that the country was 'possibly auriferous'. Despite severe drought he was sure they could proceed towards the Kimberleys, but in the Murchison district of Western Australia he dismissed his naturalist and the medical officer for insubordination, precipitating the resignations of two other officers. The society forbade Lindsay to replace the four and wired him to return home. In Adelaide the rebels' charges against him were heard. Lindsay was exonerated, and Elder expressed his continued confidence, announcing that he would compensate him for the loss of office;

but the abandonment of the expedition was 'a terrible disappointment' to Lindsay. In 1892 he was president of the South Australian branch of the geographical society.

News soon arrived of the discovery of gold at Coolgardie. In 1893 Lindsay overlanded camels there, sold them profitably, and resumed operating as a mining surveyor and broker: he made over £20 000 in share dealing. In 1895 in London his acclaim as an explorer helped him to publicize Western Australia's golden potential: he floated several mining companies and became colonial manager of Scottish Westralia Ltd. Next year he was again in London arranging finance for his firm, Electric Power Supply Co., to provide electricity to the goldfields. In 1897 Lindsay returned to Adelaide where he and his wife were socially prominent.

Later he moved to Sydney and by 1909 was extolling the Northern Territory's potential; but he feared that 'the yellow hordes of Asia' might enter and he believed that Aborigines should live apart from whites. In 1913 he was a member of a Federal royal commission on Northern Territory ports and railways that travelled extensively in the region. Next year Lindsay gained Federal government support to establish a meat-freezing works and cattle-station on the Macarthur River in the Northern Territory, but the war fatally delayed it.

He did some surveying for the Commonwealth and became interested in cotton-growing. While investigating that possibility he became ill and died in Darwin of valvular disease of the heart on 17 December 1922. His wife, a daughter and two of their four sons survived him.

When young, Lindsay had possessed the energy and heroic stature of an explorer: tall, bronzed and richly bearded, his chest and shoulders were broad. He was a competent but autocratic leader, who became bombastic with success.

W. B. Kimberly (comp), *History of Western Australia* (Melb, 1897); *PP* (SA), 1883-84 (239); *PRGSSA*, Nov 1889; *Aust and NZ Weekly*, 4 Apr, 9 May 1895, 27 Aug 1896; *Technical J*, 1 (Jan 1923), no 3; *Scottish A'sian*, 21 Apr 1923; *Sth Australiana*, 18, no 2, Sept 1979; *Observer* (Adel), 25 Apr 1891; *Australasian*, 24 Oct 1891, 10 Nov 1894; *Morning Herald* (Perth), 20 Jan 1896; *SMH*, 7 Apr, 2 May 1922; *New York Times*, 19 Dec 1922; David Lindsay papers (ML); CRS A3 item NT16/1657, NT14/2482 (AAO); gen cat A799, A69 (SAA).   SUZANNE EDGAR

LINDSAY, PERCIVAL CHARLES (1870-1952), SIR LIONEL ARTHUR (1874-1961), NORMAN ALFRED WILLIAMS (1879-1969), RUBY (1885-1919) and SIR ERNEST DARYL (1889-1976), artists and writers, were born at Creswick, Victoria, five of the ten children of Robert Charles William Alexander Lindsay (1843-1915), surgeon from Londonderry, Ireland, and his wife Jane Elizabeth (1848-1932), daughter of Rev. Thomas Williams [q.v.6], Wesleyan missionary. The Lindsay family, originally from Ayrshire, Scotland, had settled in Tyrone in the late seventeenth century and prospered in the linen trade. Robert, after graduating in medicine at the University of Glasgow, sailed as medical officer in the *Red Rose* and reached Melbourne on 16 June 1864. He began to practise at Creswick and on 18 May 1869 at Ballarat married Jane. The boys were educated at the local state school and at Creswick Grammar School, where Percy, Lionel and Norman in turn edited the *Boomerang*, its unofficial magazine. Their early interest in art was encouraged by their maternal grandfather who took them on regular visits to the Ballarat Fine Arts Public Gallery where Norman's imagination was fired by Solomon J. Solomon's 'Ajax and Cassandra'.

The eldest son Percival, born on 17 September 1870, early showed an interest in art, receiving encouragement from S. A. Edmonds, a local bank manager and amateur painter with whom he occasionally sketched on week-ends, and at the weekly painting class in Ballarat of Frederic S. Sheldon. Lindsay was already a competent landscape painter by the time he joined the outdoor painting class conducted by Walter Withers [q.v.] at Creswick in January 1893, as his 'Creswick 1892' (Ballarat Art Gallery), somewhat influenced by David Davies [q.v.8], indicates.

In 1895 Percy's brother Lionel encouraged him to settle in Melbourne and take classes in drawing at the National Gallery School but after a few months he went home. In 1897 he returned to Melbourne and began to draw for the illustrated press, continuing to paint, particularly around Heidelberg. On 23 March 1907 at Collingwood he married Jessie Hammond, daughter of a Creswick storekeeper. For some years he worked in the Sun Art studios in Bourke Street with Cyril Dillon.

At Lionel's suggestion he moved to Sydney in 1917 when he took over from Lionel as the principal illustrator for the New South Wales Bookstall Co., working on thirty-three of their books between 1919 and 1926, including stories by 'Steele Rudd' [q.v.8 A. H. Davis] and Vance Palmer [q.v.]. A charming Bohemian who enjoyed the company of convivial friends, Percy was the least ambitious of the Lindsays and the most competent painter in the family. His best works are in the Ballarat gallery. An exhibition of his etchings was held in the Macquarie Galleries, Sydney, in March 1929. Predeceased by his wife and survived by their son, Percy Lindsay died at North Sydney on 21 September 1952 and was cremated. His artist friends at the funeral gave three cheers for the departed.

Lionel, the third son, was born on 17 October 1874. He taught himself to draw by copying illustrations from *Punch* and other periodicals taken in the home, becoming at an early age a great admirer of the drawings of Charles Keene. An avid reader from childhood, Lionel developed an interest in astronomy from the works of Charles Dick and, on the recommendation of his maternal grandfather, joined the acting government astronomer Pietro Baracchi [q.v.7] in Melbourne, as a pupil-assistant. After a few months Baracchi advised him that art not science was his true *métier*. He returned to Creswick and took lessons in water-colour painting from Miller Marshall, an English artist.

Shortly afterwards Lionel became staff artist on the *Hawklet*. Its front page was devoted to drawings covering the crimes, accidents, suicides and social highlights of the preceding week. For copy Lionel frequented Melbourne's theatres and ringsides, the morgue and the racing track. He joined the National Gallery School and shared a studio with George Coates [q.v.8].

Norman, the fourth son, was born on 22 February 1879. Until he was about 6 his mother insisted on him remaining indoors because strenuous physical activity, as a result of a blood disorder, brought on a blistering rash. Thus confined, he taught himself to draw by copying illustrations from periodicals and by drawing about the home from life. In April 1896 Lionel began working for the *Free Lance*, modelled on the Sydney *Bulletin*. After some maternal opposition Norman joined him in Melbourne to ghost drawings for him on the *Hawklet*. Lionel was paid £2 a week by the *Free Lance* and thirty-five shillings a week by the *Hawklet* of which he gave Norman ten shillings for his work.

When the *Free Lance* failed in October the two brothers experienced a difficult time until Lionel joined the *Clarion*, a newspaper established by Randolph Bedford [q.v.7], who became his lifelong friend. With Bedford he visited the Western Australian goldfields in search of copy and advertisements; Norman became cartoonist for the *Hawklet* in his own right. He attended the life class at the National Gallery and, haunting the gallery, was particularly impressed by its Dürer engravings. He led a Bohemian life in rented rooms with his brother and his brothers' friends, frequenting theatres, music-halls, prize-fights and the courts in search of copy. They joined the students' club known as the Prehistoric Order of Cannibals, founded in 1893, whose members included Will Dyson, Miles Evergood [qq.v.8], Max Meldrum, Hugh McCrae, Ernest Moffitt [qq.v.] and

Harry Weston. Daryl, his younger brother, recalled Norman about this time as 'a thin hawk-faced boy with a mobile mouth, darting blue eyes and sensitive hands'.

On Lionel's return to Melbourne he drew for the *Tocsin*, a radical weekly that attracted articles from Victor Daley [q.v.8] and Bernard O'Dowd [q.v.], edited by Jack Castieau, a public servant. However Lionel fell out with Castieau, who did not pay for the drawings and criticized his paintings of pirates—piracy becoming something of a craze for both Lionel and Norman.

Two friends, Castieau and Moffitt, exercised a strong influence on Norman at this time. For Castieau he executed unpaid drawings for the *Tocsin* and drew its first cover design which it carried for twelve months from 19 October 1897; it depicted a worker wearing a *bonnet rouge* and hammering a tocsin bell. Norman himself affected a red bow-tie. Moffitt's influence was more profound. During the summer of 1897-98 Lionel, Norman and Moffitt spent some months living in a gardener's cottage in the grounds of Charterisville, near Heidelberg, where other young artists also foregathered. In the neglected garden Norman drew assiduously from Nature and Moffitt introduced him to the Greek pastoral poets and the works of Frederick Sandys, the Pre-Raphaelite illustrator, and urged him to go his own independent way in art. Norman began making sets of pen-and-ink illustrations to classics that appealed to him, beginning with *The idylls of Theocritus*, in line only, then turned to line and wash for *The Decameron* drawings, placing the figures in settings inspired by the Charterisville garden.

Both Lionel and Norman were reading widely, Rabelais and Dickens being favourites. But Gautier and George Moore were 'their spiritual guides' until Lionel read Thomas Common's translation of Nietzsche's *The Antichrist* and *Contra Wagner* after publication in 1896. Nietzsche became the leading influence in Norman's philosophy of art and life, reinforcing his rejection of Christianity and the Puritan values of his mother who he believed had constrained his childhood freedom unduly. Lionel was an ardent admirer of G. W. L. Marshall-Hall [q.v.] and with Castieau published a burlesque on Marshall-Hall's persecution by the University of Melbourne. Lionel assisted Desbrowe Annear [q.v.7] to paint the Greek temple required for Hall's production of Gluck's *Alceste* (1898).

He also worked for the *Weekly Times, Clarion* and the *Arena*. But times were hard and Lionel went to Sydney in search of work, completing a few drawings for the *Daily Telegraph* before moving to Brisbane where he worked briefly for a sign-painter and drew houses for *Pugh's Almanac*. In January 1899 Norman, with the help of Ray Parkinson, a journalist friend, and financial aid from J. S. C. Elkington [q.v.8], established the *Rambler*, a weekly based on the English comic magazine, *Pickme-up*, and devoted to theatre gossip, light verse and illustrated jokes. Lionel, after a difficult spell in Brisbane, joined them and wrote drama criticism, but the *Rambler* failed after a few issues. The untimely death of Moffitt in 1899 shocked the brothers profoundly. Norman's Arcadian symbolism and decorative use of the nude at that time is well illustrated in his fine woodcuts for *A consideration of the art of Ernest Moffitt* (1899); Lionel wrote the text with the assistance of Marshall-Hall.

After Moffitt's death the brothers' lives began to diverge. Returning to Brisbane, Lionel worked for the *Review*, a threepenny weekly that soon failed. Back in Melbourne he wrote book reviews and occasional verses for the *Outpost*, another short-lived weekly. His closest friend was Herman Kuhr, a French-horn player with whom he rented a cottage at East Melbourne. Enthralled by Marshall-Hall's production of Bizet's *Carmen*, and a boyhood reading of *Don Quixote*, he decided to learn Spanish and visit Spain. By early 1902 he had saved enough to leave. Adept at picking up a foreign language, Lindsay quickly made friends wherever he went, but kept a Smith and Wesson revolver in his pocket. From Marseilles he shipped as a deck passenger in a Spanish coastal steamer. On reaching Seville he stayed with the family of Rafael Paez, the cork-cutter of Melbourne who had taught him Spanish. This direct entry into local peasant life made it possible for him to share a studio with a local house-decorator and make drawings for a projected illustrated edition of Prosper Mérimée's *Carmen*—drawings both of the figure and of Moorish architecture, for which he developed a great affection.

Lionel Lindsay went on to Britain but found no publisher interested in his *Carmen* project. In London he met Phil May [q.v.5] and John Longstaff [q.v.] and began to collect Keene drawings. Then Bedford arrived and invited him to Italy. At Florence, Lionel became engaged to Will Dyson's sister Jane Ann (Jean) who was travelling with the Bedford family.

Out of pocket, Lindsay borrowed £75 from Bedford and returned to Sydney early in 1903, where A. B. Paterson [q.v.] offered him a job as a cartoonist for £4 per week with the right to contribute illustrations to the *Bulletin*. At Woollahra on 20 November he married Jean Dyson and began to make drawings and etchings of old buildings in The Rocks area, much of which was being demolished for fear of another outbreak of the plague. After these etchings were shown in the 1907 exhibition of the Society of Artists, Sydney, a new vogue for etching began. Between 1905 and 1919 Lionel illustrated twenty-six books published by the New South Wales Bookstall Co. and was active as a contributor and reader for the *Lone Hand*; he was president of the Australian Painter-Etchers' Society for three years after its foundation in 1921.

In 1926 Lindsay again visited Europe, travelling extensively in Sicily and Italy before visiting Paris and London, where Colnaghi of Bond Street offered him an exhibition. Requiring more works he returned to the Continent, painting and drawing first at Walcheren and Weesp in Holland then in Spain, working in Burgos, Segovia, Avila, Guadalupe and Madrid. In the summer heat he became ill with enteritis and, though they visited Arles, Nîmes and les Baux in France, Lindsay did not recover fully until the family took a flat in Monte Carlo. Here he worked on his copperplates, making his prints from an aluminium travelling press. In April 1927 he was able to hold an exhibition at Colnaghi's of sixty-seven etchings, dry-points and wood-engravings. They included landscapes and cityscapes, churches and other buildings of Australia, Spain and Italy. The exhibition was a great success. 'Lindsay has won', Harold Wright wrote later, 'a well-deserved place among the foremost graphic artists of our time'. He joined the Chelsea Arts Club. Invited to propose the toast to etching at the Royal Academy of Arts' dinner of 1927, he took the opportunity to attack the 'malady' of modern art as a conspiracy led by Jewish art-dealers, and gained great applause. After the dinner Sir Edward Lutyens, the architect, kissing him on both cheeks, exclaimed: 'At last an honest man!'

Lindsay was back in Sydney in October but made further overseas visits, returning in October 1930 and November 1934. He continued to exhibit regularly with the Macquarie Galleries, Sydney, and the Sedon Gallery, Melbourne, and served as a trustee of the National Art Gallery of New South Wales in 1918-29 and 1934-49. He was knighted in 1941.

Lionel Lindsay's talents were both diverse and influential. As an illustrator of books by Henry Lawson [q.v.] and 'Steele Rudd' he captured the ethos of the 'Australian legend' better perhaps than any other artist. His sympathetic rendering of the fabric of old Sydney buildings places his work at a point of origin of the conservation movement in Australia. As an art critic, both in newspapers and art magazines, he was highly influential; with J. S. MacDonald [q.v.] he established the reputation of the Heidelberg School. In books such as *A Consideration of the art of Ernest Moffitt* and *Conrad Martens, the man and his art* (1920) he pioneered the publication of art

monographs in Australia. His etching and his magnificent wood-engravings of birds and other animals, inspired by Thomas Bewick, have not been surpassed in Australia. In all his work there is a much firmer grip upon reality than there is in Norman's more imaginative flights. He assembled an important collection of prints which included works by Dürer, Rembrandt, Whistler and Meryon and an unrivalled collection of Keene drawings. Rose Lindsay described him as the most handsome man she had ever met and (Sir) Robert Menzies, a long-standing friend, referred to him as 'a master of divine and disordered conversation', a comment that might have been used to describe his engaging autobiography, *Comedy of life*, published posthumously in 1967.

Master of a good prose style, Lindsay wrote lucidly and generously about the art he admired. But his taste did not extend beyond Post-Impressionism, and he became in his later years a virulent opponent of modernism, expressing his sense of outrage in *Addled art* (1942). He did however support the award of the Archibald [q.v.3] prize to William Dobell in 1944.

Resident at Wahroonga, Lionel Lindsay died at Hornsby on 22 May 1961 and was cremated. Predeceased by his wife, he was survived by his son and daughter. His estate was valued for probate at £75 140. He left his Keene drawings to the National Gallery of Victoria and a representative collection of his work to the Toowoomba Art Gallery, Queensland, which was renamed after him. A portrait (1959) by William Dargie is in the Australian National Gallery, Canberra, and another (1941) by Nora Heysen is in the Art Gallery of New South Wales.

On 23 May 1900 in Melbourne Norman married Kathleen Agatha Parkinson, Ray's sister, and their son Jack was born on 20 October. A few weeks later Elkington, on a visit to Sydney, showed some of Norman's *Decameron* drawings to A. G. Stephens [q.v.] who described them in the *Bulletin* as 'the finest example of pen-draughtsmanship of their kind yet produced in this country'; J. F. Archibald wrote to Norman seeking some illustrations for the paper. Julian Ashton [q.v.7] after seeing the *Decameron* drawings offered to raise £300 to enable him to study in Europe; but he rejected the proposal, recording years later that intuition advised him that such a move had been 'extremely disastrous to every Australian artist who had subjected himself to the corrupting influence of European movements in art'.

In May 1901 Lindsay visited Sydney and accepted Archibald's offer of £6 a week to join the *Bulletin* as a staff artist providing cartoons, decorations and illustrations for jokes and stories. The association was to last, with a few breaks, for over fifty years. More than any other artist, he gave visual definition to the *Bulletin*'s editorial policy, particularly its nationalism and racism—Aborigines invariably figured as comics, Jews as old-clothes dealers with hooked noses.

During his first three months in Sydney Norman stayed with Ashton. Then his family joined him and he rented a cottage at Northwood and a studio in Bond Street. As his career prospered his marriage deteriorated. Ashton introduced him to a beautiful and robust young model, Rose Soady, aged 16. Their relationship remained professional until Katie returned to Melbourne to be close to her family prior to the birth of her second son RAYMOND on 25 August 1903.

In Sydney, Lindsay's work freed itself from the decorative Art Nouveau line of his Melbourne years. A rhythmical energy emerged and he became more concerned with light and colour. The change is visible in 'Laudate O Dionysus' exhibited with the Society of Artists in September 1902. There followed a major series of drawings, 'The Scoffers' (1903), 'Pollice Verso' (1904) and 'Dionysus' (1905), in which he attacked prevailing attitudes to sex and formulated his own vitalist philosophy of the artist's role in society. Critics praised his technical achievement highly but severely criticized his subject matter. Yet his work sold well and in the years leading up to World War I he achieved a higher income than any other Australian artist.

The birth of a third son PHILIP at North Sydney on 30 April 1906 and the purchase of a home at Lavender Bay with help from the *Bulletin* did not save the marriage. Norman took to horse-riding with a group that included Rose, Paterson and (Sir) Frank Fox [q.v.8], assistant editor of the *Bulletin*. Lindsay and Fox conceived the *Lone Hand* (1907-21), a monthly devoted to literature and art, to which Norman contributed many drawings, stories and critical articles. In it he fought for an independent Australian culture and supported writers such as McCrae, whose first book of poems, *Satyrs and sunlight* (1909), he illustrated. Successful exhibitions in Sydney and Melbourne provided sufficient funds to leave for London in October 1909 with his sister Ruby and Will Dyson, recently married. With him were over 400 drawings for a projected illustrated edition of the *Memoirs of Casanova*. On Norman's departure, Katie and the three boys left for Brisbane, to be closer to her sister Mary who had married Elkington.

On the voyage Lindsay read the *Satyricon* in the Bohn translation and on visiting Pompeii, *en route*, conceived the idea of illustrating Petronius. In London he found no publisher interested in the *Casanova* drawings but Ralph Strauss, whom he had met in Sydney earlier, agreed to publish a *de luxe* edition of the *Satyricon*. Rose joined Norman and they took a studio cottage at Hampstead where he worked on the *Satyricon* drawings. The Dysons had taken a cottage nearby but the sudden appearance of Rose shattered Norman's friendship with Will. Then Hugh D. McIntosh [q.v.], an old friend, arrived and agreed enthusiastically to publish the *Casanova* drawings—in French, German, Italian and Spanish as well as English.

They went to Paris and talked to publishers, but the venture came to nothing. Lindsay first saw Post-Impressionist paintings there and was horrified—'a mob of modern Hottentots'—and became a committed opponent of modern art. At the Louvre it was Rubens he most admired but the work of Degas, Manet, Goya and Delacroix also greatly attracted him. In London he joined the Chelsea Arts Club and at the Savile Club struck up a friendship with Max Beerbohm. Although all 250 copies of the *Satyricon* sold in a few days, mainly to Americans, Lindsay was ill at ease in London: 'I hate the climate and I'm beginning to hate the people', he wrote to Archibald. So, on receiving an increased offer from the *Bulletin* (despite a somewhat better one from *Harper's Magazine*, New York) he decided to return. On the eve of his departure on 25 November 1910, he visited the Post-Impressionist exhibition organized by Roger Fry—a horrifying revelation. 'It smelt of the jungle'.

Lindsay's health suffered in London and soon after returning to Sydney he fell ill with pleurisy. Tuberculosis was suspected. Rose, highly practical and soon to be his efficient business-manager, found a cottage at Leura, then another at Faulconbridge, after which they bought the house at Springwood that became their permanent home. His energy returned and he began to diversify his talent. At the Society of Artists' exhibition of 1912 he exhibited some of his earliest paintings in oils and a model of Captain Cook's [q.v.1] *Endeavour*. While in London he had studied and made careful drawings of ship models in the Victoria and Albert Museum. But his most controversial work was 'Crucified Venus', depicting a tonsured monk nailing a naked woman to a tree, to the approval of a mob of exultant clerics and wowsers below. When shown in the All Australian Exhibition, Melbourne, in September 1913, it so outraged opinion that the management committee removed it. Only when Ashton threatened to withdraw all work from New South Wales was it rehung. Lindsay's diversity was extending to writing. He had been publishing stories in the *Lone Hand* since 1907, and in 1913 his first novel, *A curate in Bohemia*, which was based on memories of his Melbourne years, was published.

At Springwood one day a week was set aside for the *Bulletin*'s political cartoon which tended to be apocalyptic rather than amusing: the eternal forces of evil aligned against the eternal forces of good. Norman maintained that a professional cartoonist was bound to express his paper's political views, not his own. So his South African war cartoons expressed Archibald's pro-Boer attitudes when Lindsay's were, if anything, pro-British. Throughout World War I his views were at one with *Bulletin* policy and in 1918 he drew posters for Australia's last recruiting drive. The war cartoons invariably presented Germans as monsters of depravity, the allies as the children of light.

As a distraction from the war's horror he wrote *The magic pudding* (1918), his ever-popular tale for children. Encouraged by Lionel, he produced and exhibited his first etchings, in partnership with Rose who printed them, assembled the editions and cancelled the used plates. Early in 1917 Norman had heard that his brother Reginald had been killed on the Somme and he later received his blood-stained notebook. He turned to spiritualism and with the aid of Rose and a ouija board communicated, as he believed, not only with Reginald but such departed celebrities as Shakespeare and Apollo. This new interest led to a permanent rupture in his long friendship with Lionel. Rose's first pregnancy was almost fatal and the child stillborn and in 1919 his sister Ruby died of influenza. At Strathfield Norman and Rose were married with Presbyterian forms on 14 January 1920. His divorce from a reluctant Katie was made absolute on 28 January.

From this troubled time came a thorough reappraisal of his thoughts on art and life that were published first in *Art in Australia* in 1920 and more fully in *Creative effort* (1924). Based on elements drawn from Plato and Nietzsche, Lindsay sought to construct for himself a systematic philosophy of art and life that denied all social and political progress. History was eternal recurrence. The creative mind, especially the masculine, existed apart from the mass mind which, essentially feminine, constantly attacked it with the aid of such lesser breeds as Jews, Asians and Africans. Modernist art and the war were but the most recent manifestations of these unending attacks upon the creative elite. Once formulated, Lindsay's views changed little.

In 1923 he became involved in another major controversy: Sydney Ure Smith [q.v.] and Ashton arranged a large exhibition of Australian art for exhibition at the Royal Academy, London. Stimulated by a newspaper controversy, a deputation to the minister for public instruction failed to prevent the inclusion of Lindsay's works. When shown in London they attracted large crowds, but most London critics, like their Australian colleagues, praised his technique but criticized the subject-matter. Sir William Orpen, whose work Lindsay admired, was the most damning. 'His work is bad', he wrote. 'It shows no sign of art, no technique—nothing. Ignore it'. Orpen, an Irishman, confirmed Lindsay's doubts about provincials who made their reputations in London.

After completing a brilliant degree in classics at the University of Queensland, Norman's eldest son Jack returned to Sydney in 1921 and became his father's most important disciple. A brilliant and persuasive conversationalist, Norman inspired younger writers with a feeling for classical and European traditions and a belief in gaiety as a vital element in all art. The poets R. D. FitzGerald, Kenneth Slessor and Douglas Stewart acknowledged his influence—Stewart indeed eventually wrote of Lindsay as 'the fountain-head of Australian culture in our time'. Jack and Norman established a literary periodical, *Vision* (1923-24), which, though it lasted for only four issues, introduced a new generation of poets. Norman illustrated Slessor's poems, *Thief of the moon* (1924) and *Earth-visitors* (1926), and those of his son Jack: *Fauns and ladies* (1923) and *The passionate neatherd* (1926). Norman saw the possibility of a renascence in art that might spread from Australia to the rest of the world. So he lavished extravagant praise not only on his new circle of poets but also on the paintings of Elioth Gruner [q.v.9] and the musical compositions of Adolphe Beutler, and he supported the establishment of the Fanfrolico Press in London to bring his work and ideas and those of Jack and their circle to an international audience. John Kirtley and Jack, proceeding to London in 1926, set it up at Bloomsbury. There until its demise in 1930 it published *de luxe* editions of Jack's translations from the classics, illustrated by Norman, as well as work by P. R. Stephensen [q.v.], Slessor, Philip Lindsay and others.

Norman worked prolifically both as a writer and artist throughout the 1920s, producing short stories and novels, pen drawings, etchings and dry-points, water-colours and ship-models, showing his work regularly in the annual exhibitions of the Society of Artists and the Australian Water-Colour Institute, or in special exhibitions. But officialdom continued to harass him. In April 1930 Faber, London, published his novel *Redheap*, based on life at Creswick during his boyhood. In May the government prohibited the book entering Australia—16 000 copies had to be shipped back to London. The ban remained until the late 1950s, although the book was readily available in England, and in the United States of America under the title

Every mother's son (1930). An Australian edition was not published until 1959.

Disgusted, Lindsay decided to leave the country—at least temporarily. In July 1931 he sailed with Rose for New York where he found himself widely known because of the success of *Every mother's son*. But the Depression had hit and the planned exhibition of his work did not take place. Instead he completed a novel, published in 1932 as *Mr. Gresham and Olympus* in America and as *Miracles by arrangement* in England. In January 1932 they left for London where he failed to interest publishers in setting up a house in Australia to publish Australian works, but by April he was back in Sydney. Out of pocket from his travels he rejoined the *Bulletin* staff and talked the editor, S. H. Prior [q.v.], into establishing the Australian Book Publishing Co. Ltd under the imprint of Endeavour Press, with Stephensen as editor. Beginning with Norman's *Saturdee* (1933) it published twenty titles, but the interest in Australian books had been overestimated and the press closed in 1935. Meanwhile *The cautious amorist* (1932), his first attempt at a novel written twenty years before, had been published in New York. Australian Customs forbade its entry.

Lindsay now entered a period of depression—his hunchback phase he called it—when creative work seemed impossible. To recapture his energy he left Springwood in 1934 and rented a studio at 12 Bridge Street, Sydney. Here he began to paint constantly in oils for the first time, working continuously from the model. His studio became a kind of art and literary salon visited by old and new friends, the latter including the writers Kenneth Mackenzie, John Tierney ('Brian James') and Stewart. However, most of the new generation of artists and writers who began to exhibit and publish in the late 1930s and had come under the influence of modernism found Lindsay's art and writing old fashioned and its philosophy, so strongly tainted with anti-Semitism, sinister.

During the 1930s Lindsay's political cartoons expressed the *Bulletin*'s isolationist policies, but during World War II they became as ardently anti-German as they had been in World War I. Rose, fearing an allied defeat and a German occupation of Springwood, left Australia for America with her married daughter Honey Glad and her husband. Norman returned to Springwood, as did his other daughter, Jane. Rose took with her the *Casanova* drawings that McIntosh had failed to publish years before, but they were destroyed by fire in a freight train with other Lindsay drawings. Depressed by the incident, Rose returned to Springwood.

In 1945 Lindsay published *The cousin from Fiji*, his most carefully constructed novel. He continued to exhibit with the Australian Water-Colour Institute until 1952, but after that his work was mostly shown in retrospective exhibitions or with that of other members of his family. *Bohemians of the Bulletin* appeared in 1965 and *The scribblings of an idle mind* in 1966. His views had not changed substantially since he wrote *Creative effort*, but he had more to say about his belief in the lost city of Atlantis. Norman Lindsay painted his last picture, 'For King and Parliament', in September 1969. He died at Springwood on 21 November that year and was buried with Methodist forms in Springwood cemetery. He was survived by his son Jack, who had become a prolific and very distinguished writer, and by his second wife and their two daughters. His estate was valued for probate at $65 698. In 1970 his autobiography, *My mask*, was published. Norman had arranged for the State branch of the National Trust of Australia to acquire Springwood.

Norman Lindsay was a pen draughtsman and etcher of great technical brilliance, a fine water-colourist and craftsman of ship-models. His oil paintings were less successful, heavy handed both in touch and colour. Though a private man, happiest in the company of a few friends, throughout his life he enacted, in a manner unrivalled in Australia, the public role of the artist as a critic of moral and social values. In his early years he exercised a liberating force upon Australian culture but in later life his fear of modernism in literature and art and his anti-Semitism were characteristic of a generation that feared change. His portrait (1931) by Longstaff is in the Art Gallery of New South Wales.

Norman's second son Raymond (1903-1960), artist, was brought up in Brisbane by his mother. Towards the end of World War I he became a cadet reporter on the *Brisbane Courier*, but lost the job after reporting a local council meeting that did not take place. He joined his mother in Sydney in 1921 and, keen to become an artist, received free tuition at Ashton's Sydney Art School; his father provided his art materials. Ray left Ashton's, probably because of differences over painting technique, and studied for a time at the Royal Art Society's class. At the National Art Gallery of New South Wales, Ford Madox Brown's 'Chaucer at the Court of King Edward III' made a deep impression, and he aspired to become a painter of Australian history subjects.

During the late 1920s Ray painted several large canvases depicting aspects of the mutiny of 1808 and the arrest of Governor Bligh [q.v.1]. When shown at the annual exhibition of the Society of Artists in 1928, they were well received. Cecil Mann wrote in the *Bulletin* that they surpassed the work of Norman at a comparable age. Dame Nellie Melba [q.v.] purchased 'Major Johnston Announcing the Arrest of Governor Bligh, January 1808', presented it to the Geelong Art Gallery and advised Lindsay to 'get out of this country'. 'It's no good for any artist'. Rubery Bennett exhibited Ray's work at his Australian Fine Art Gallery in July 1929, and again it was favourably reviewed and sold well. On 28 December he married Loma Kyle Turnbull, the potter Loma 'Lautour'. Lindsay's success as a painter did not survive the difficult years of the Depression and he turned increasingly to freelance illustration and reading for publishers. In the mid-1930s he separated from his wife, whom he divorced in March 1941, and married Margaret Joan Skinner on 21 May. He wrote art criticism for the *Daily Telegraph* and continued to paint subject pictures occasionally, particularly of pirate themes.

Like his uncle Percy, Ray was a convivial Bohemian and lacked the driving energy of his father. After 1930, with both his brothers in England, he was solely responsible for his ailing mother. The fame of his father Norman and the reputations of his uncles Lionel and Percy did not make his success as a painter in Sydney any easier. Survived by his wife, he died of cancer on 13 June 1960 at Elizabeth Bay and was cremated.

Norman's third son Philip (1906-1958), novelist, was educated at the Church of England Grammar School, Brisbane, where his only interest lay in history and literature. At 14 he returned to Sydney with his mother and brothers and lived in rented rooms at Darlinghurst and Bondi. Also provided with free tuition at the Sydney Art School, he quickly found that art was not for him and drifted into the company of a mob of Kings Cross larrikins—graphically described in his autobiography, *I'd live the same life over* (1941). His father encouraged his early efforts at writing and lent him books, notably Trollope [q.v.6]. A short sketch of Philip's was published in *Vision* (November 1923) and some early verses appeared in the *Spinner* in 1926. In September 1929 he arrived in London after encouragement from Jack, and some of his poems and sketches were published in the *London Aphrodite* (1929).

Reading in the British Museum, Philip turned increasingly to the historical novel. His first book, *Morgan in Jamaica* (1930), and his novel, *Panama is burning* (1932), continued that interest in piracy which had obsessed his family since the 1890s. He then took to writing historical romances of the Tudor and later medieval periods. On the strength of his highly successful *Here comes the king* (1933) he became artistic director of (Sir) Alexander Korda's film, *The private life of Henry VIII* (1933).

Writing with verbal exuberance and violent colour, Philip Lindsay published a historical novel or monograph (and sometimes two) almost every year. He acknowledged the mastery of Sir Walter Scott, admired Richard III as a king and was a fellow of the Society of Antiquaries of Scotland. He wrote some sensitive studies of Australian poetry and in 1951 a biography, *Don Bradman*.

On 4 April 1933 Lindsay married a divorcee Jeanne Ellis, née Bellon; they had one daughter. After their divorce he married on 15 September 1943 another divorcee Isobel Beatrice Spurgeon, née Day. They lived in Sussex where his adopted village 'adored him in his Johnsonian chair at the Rose and Crown'. He died of a respiratory disease at Hastings on 4 January 1958, survived by his wife.

Robert and Jane Lindsay's seventh child and second daughter, Ruby, was born on 20 March 1885. She left home for Melbourne at 16 and resided for a time with her brother Percy, while attending the National Gallery School. She drew occasionally for the *Hawklet*, the *Bulletin* and regularly for the Adelaide satirical journal, the *Gadfly* (1906), illustrated books such as 'Rudd's' *Back at our selection* (1906) and William Moore's [q.v.] *Studio Sketches* (1906), and designed posters. On 30 September 1909 she married Will Dyson at Creswick and travelled with him and her brother Norman to London. In England she continued with book illustrations, particularly of children's books. Her daughter Elizabeth was born on 11 September 1911. After the war her brother Daryl took her to visit relations in Belfast and Dublin. There she caught the influenza virus then sweeping Europe and died in Chelsea a few days later on 12 March 1919.

Of shy, retiring disposition, Ruby Lindsay was described by Henry Tonks as 'the most beautiful creature I ever looked at'. Many others remarked on her unusual beauty. Haldane MacFall described her as 'one of the most remarkable women-artists with pen-line now living' in *A history of painting* (1911). Shortly after her death Will Dyson published *Poems: in memory of a wife* (1919) and Cecil Palmer produced *The drawings of Ruby Lind* (1920).

The sixth son and ninth child of Robert and Jane Lindsay, Ernest Daryl, born on 31 December 1889, joined the Ballarat branch of the English, Scottish and Australian Bank as a junior clerk at 17. About a year later Daryl became a jackeroo. He worked for two years at Yeranbah on the Narran River, south Queensland, and took part in overlanding 9000 Shorthorns from Hebel to Camooweal. Then he put in another two years at Kulki near Argoon, before becoming an overseer first at Ercildoune, then at Trawalla near Ballarat.

Daryl enlisted as a driver in the Australian Army Service Corps, served in France for almost two years and became batman to his brother-in-law Will Dyson who encouraged him to make drawings of trench life and portraits of diggers. On leave in London in 1918 his talent in drawing was noticed and he was posted with the rank of honorary lieutenant to the Australian section for wounds to the face and jaw at Queen Mary's Hospital, Sidcup, Kent. Here he met Henry Tonks, head of the Slade School of Fine Art, at whose suggestion he was given one day a week to study drawing at the Slade, his task at Sidcup being to make medical diagrams for facial surgery. Tonks and Lindsay became lifelong friends and his taste in art was largely fashioned around the work of the artists of the New English Art Club, such as Walter Sickert and Wilson Steer, and patient study of the English water-colour tradition.

Back in Melbourne in June 1919 Lindsay held an exhibition of war sketches at the Decoration Art Gallery in August. He joined Dillon's Sun Art studios and designed posters for Robur tea and Swallow & Ariel puddings, and illustrations for *Pals* magazine. Sun Art studios published his *Digger book* (1919). About 1920 he obtained a commission from the directors of the Mount Morgan Gold Mining Co. Ltd, Queensland, to make a series of drawings and water-colours of the mine. In 1921 he returned to London for further study, taking with him a letter of introduction from Sir Baldwin Spencer [q.v.] to Frank Rinder, adviser to the Felton [q.v.4] bequest committee. In London Lindsay haunted the art museums and art auction houses, laying the foundation of knowledge of the art market and connoisseurship that was to serve him so well later. Rinder introduced him to men of influence in London's art world such as Harold Wright of Colnaghi's, D. W. Cameron, Sir Charles Holmes, and (Sir) George Clausen, a former Felton adviser.

In London he married Joan à Beckett, writer and daughter of Theyre à Beckett Weigall, barrister, at the Marylebone Registry Office on 14 February 1922. On returning to Melbourne they lived at St Kilda and Toorak before making a permanent home at Mulberry Hill, Baxter. Lindsay continued to work with Dillon but developed his landscape painting, sketching often in company with George Bell [q.v.7]. In June 1924 the Fine Arts Society Gallery, Melbourne, held an exhibition of the water-colour drawings of Joan and Daryl Lindsay, and in July 1928 a second exhibition of his water-colours.

In 1930 the Lindsays returned to Europe and Daryl held an exhibition of water-colour paintings at Colnaghi's. During a visit to Ireland he painted hunters, then landscapes on the Norfolk Broads with Sir Alison Russell before returning to Australia. In June 1931 the Fine Arts Society Gallery held an exhibition of his oil paintings, and in August *Art in Australia* published a Daryl Lindsay number. It well reveals the style and range of interests from which his art never departed, clear and well-structured but unambitious water-colours of picturesque landscapes, and oil paintings in similar vein reminiscent of the late style of Gruner.

In the late 1930s Lindsay became a close friend of Sir Keith Murdoch [q.v.] and encouraged him to collect and take an active interest in art. In 1937 Lindsay and his wife again visited Europe, travelling widely on the Continent. In London he bought pictures for Murdoch, made drawings of the de Basil ballet, and was elected an associate of the Royal Society of Painters in Water Colours. In 1939, on Murdoch's advice, he applied for and was appointed keeper of the prints, National Gallery of Victoria. He was appointed director in 1941.

Under Lindsay the gallery broadened its appeal to the general public, abandoned its traditional hostility to modern art, and made notable acquisitions both of old masters and contemporary work. With Murdoch's assistance he took steps to establish the National Gallery Society of Victoria in 1947. He visited America under the auspices of the Carnegie Corporation of New York in 1952. Lindsay retired as director in December 1956 and was knighted for his services to Australian art next year. In 1960 he returned to the Northern Territory, camping with cattlemen while sketching and painting. The Legend Press later published a portfolio of reproductions of his paintings entitled 'A tribute to the men and horses of the Northern Territory'. Lindsay was a member of the Commonwealth Art Advisory Board in 1953-73 (chairman 1960-69) and founding president of the Victorian branch of the National Trust of Australia. In 1964 a book of essays was published to commemorate his services to the National Gallery of Victoria, entitled *In honour of Daryl Lindsay*. He published an autobiography, *The leafy tree*, in 1965.

Survived by his wife (d. 1984), Lindsay died on 25 December 1976 at Mornington and was cremated. His portrait by George Bell is at Mulberry Hill, which was left to the National Trust.

Pen drawings of Norman Lindsay, S. Ure Smith and B. Stevens eds (Syd, 1918); *Norman Lindsay water colour book* (Syd, 1939); Jack Lindsay, *Life rarely tells* (Melb, 1958); Joan Lindsay, *Time without clocks* (Melb, 1962); F. Philipp and J. Stewart (eds), *In honour of Daryl Lindsay* (Melb, 1964); Rose Lindsay, *Model wife* (Syd, 1967); L. B. Cox, *The National Gallery of Victoria, 1861 to 1968* (Melb, 1970); J. Hetherington, *Norman Lindsay* (Melb, 1973); R. Radford, *Percy Lindsay*, Ballarat

Fine Art Gallery exhibition cat (Ballarat, 1975); D. Stewart, *Norman Lindsay* (Melb, 1975); L. Bloomfield (ed), *The world of Norman Lindsay* (Melb, 1979); E. Hanks (comp), *Australian art and artists to 1950* (Melb, 1982), and for bibliog; Ray Lindsay, *A letter from Sydney* (Melb, 1983); R. McMullin, *Will Dyson* (Syd, 1984); *Studio* (Lond), Dec 1948; U. E. Prunster, The pagan in Norman Lindsay (M.A. thesis, Univ Syd, 1983), and for bibliog.

BERNARD SMITH

LINLITHGOW; *see* HOPETOUN

LINTON, JAMES WALTER ROBERT (1869-1947) and JAMES ALEXANDER BARROW (1904-1980), artists, were father and son. James Walter Robert was born on 14 June 1869 in London, second of eleven children of Sir James Dromgole Linton and his wife Harriet Maria, née Allen. Sir James was an academic water-colourist who fought for the recognition of British art and for water-colour as a medium. The young James was educated in the more adventurous British art schools: under Alphonse Legros at the Slade School of Fine Art in 1885-88; and, later, with Frederick Brown at the Westminster School. In both he learned the importance of drawing and to develop his powers of observation and visual memory. He was briefly articled to the architects Batterbury & Huxley; however his only known architectural work is the Leake [q.v.] memorial fountain in King's Park, Perth (1904).

In 1896 Linton's father sent him to investigate a disappointing investment in the Miner's Dream Gold Mines near Coolgardie, Western Australia. Linton established himself as a merchant in Perth and about 1899 opened the Linton School of Art. On 26 April 1902, at St George's Cathedral, he married a former pupil Charlotte Bates Barrow; they had two sons and a daughter.

That year Linton became art master at Perth Technical School. His infectious enthusiasm influenced casual and serious students alike, and a few achieved recognition in a variety of fields including his son Jamie, Kathleen O'Connor [q.v.], Hal Missingham and Leslie Rees. Linton emphasized drawing, observation, and the value of construction and introduced to Perth a serious, professional approach to art.

His first commission for craftwork had come in 1901 when he designed a casket to be presented to the duke and duchess of Cornwall and York during their visit to Western Australia. Like much of Linton's later woodwork, it was of local timbers and embellished with carved motifs based on local flora and fauna. In England in 1907-08 he studied metalwork under Harold Stabler. In 1910 the silversmith Arthur Cross joined him in a partnership and they held two joint exhibitions, in 1910 and 1913, before Cross's death in 1917. From 1921 Linton's partner was his elder son James who was born on 15 May 1904 in Perth. Following studies with his father and work with him as a silversmith, Jamie went in 1925 to attend the Central School of Arts and Crafts in London and the Académie Julian in Paris. On his return two years later he worked with his father and their silverware became well known. Often in an Art Nouveau style, it employed abstract twists and interlacings of wire with Western Australian motifs. Linton's work was more abstract than his son's; Jamie's was more representational and sculptural. Linton enjoyed experimenting with his materials, the object's utility taking second place to its artistry; while Jamie, a full-time silversmith, was more alert to function and new technologies.

For fourteen years from 1922 Linton was a trustee of the Public Library, Museum and Art Gallery of Western Australia. On his retirement from the technical school in 1931, he continued to teach at the Linton Institute of Art until 1938. He moved to Parkerville with a former student Betsey Currie (who changed her name to Linton by deed poll) and lived and worked there until his death.

Linton's water-colours and late oils are among his finest achievements. He depicted Nature through light and was fascinated by skies, the subtle nuances of atmospheric effects and their reflections on the landscape. His family holds a self-portrait.

A small, compact man with a trim Vandyke beard, Linton dressed well with a large, black, silk bow-tie. He was equable and good humoured, quietly spoken but able to hold attention with his stories. He never lowered his standards, although he was patient and persuasive and never denigrated the work of even the dullest student.

Survived by his wife, children and Betsey, Linton died on 29 August 1947 in Perth, and was cremated with Anglican rites. His work is in the Victoria and Albert Museum, London, the Australian National Gallery, State and regional galleries and many private collections. Retrospective exhibitions were held at the Art Gallery of Western Australia in 1955 and 1977.

Jamie was busy as a silversmith until his death in Perth on 9 May 1980. His wife Marguerite, née Stubbs, whom he had married on 15 December 1934, and five children, including John, also a silversmith, survived him. His silverware is owned by the Queen Mother, the Danish royal family, and the Australian government, and is held in many public and private collections.

A. Gray (comp), *James W. R. Linton 1869-1947* (Perth, 1977); L. Hunt (ed), *Westralian portraits* (Perth, 1979); *Art in Aust*, Nov 1935, p 49; *Art and Aust*, 16 (June 1979), no 4, p 364; *Milday*, 1 (Jan 1949), p 27; *West Australian*, 17 Dec 1927, 23 Feb 1929, 14 May 1980; *Daily News* (Perth), 17 July 1967; J. W. R. Linton notebook and papers (WA Museum, Art Gallery of WA and Battye Lib).

ANNE GRAY

LINTON, SIR RICHARD (1879-1959), businessman, philanthropist and politician, was born on 10 March 1879 at Palmerston North, New Zealand, son of James Linton, Scottish-born importer, and his wife Ann, née Kibblewhite. Educated locally at the Terrace End School and Kenneth Wilson's High School, he came to Australia about 1899 to work as a dispatch clerk in the Sydney firm of Henry Bull & Co. Ltd. He then joined Middows Brothers (Australia) Ltd., paper and machinery merchants, managing branches in Brisbane and Perth and, from 1907, Melbourne. He became managing director, acquiring a large interest in the firm. On 31 March 1909, at Wellington, New Zealand, Linton married Ethel Isobel Bannister.

Fulfilling a long-held ambition to devote his energies to public life, Linton retired from Middows Bros in 1924. His first and most enduring public activity was his founding, in 1924, of the Big Brother Movement, an organization combining loyalty to Empire with Australian idealization of life on the land. The movement promoted the migration of British youths or 'Little Brothers' to work on farms. On arrival each became the responsibility of an Australian 'Big Brother' who provided initial accommodation and maintained contact with the youth after he had been placed in rural employment. The 'Little Brother' remained under the movement's paternalistic guidance until the age of 21.

The idea for the Big Brother Movement grew out of Linton's own experience of arriving in Sydney from New Zealand knowing that his elder brother was already there to assist him. In 1925 and 1928 he visited Britain and proved to be an enthusiastic and successful promoter of the movement. Under the scheme 8000 youths migrated to Australia until its suspension during World War II. It was later revived in New South Wales and continued, in a modified form, until 1983.

In 1927 Linton entered the Victorian Legislative Assembly as the Nationalist member for Boroondara. In parliament his first question and maiden speech both centred on immigration. He was greatly troubled by increasing numbers of non-British migrants, principally from Italy, believing that their presence undermined the wages scale. 'It is our duty as a Parliament to encourage our own people to come from the Old Land . . . God help this country if we continue to allow foreigners to come into it'.

An active parliamentarian, Linton spoke on a wide range of issues. Although his wider economic views were conventional, the onset of the Depression saw him devise several schemes to alleviate youth unemployment: an unemployment relief stamp tax and an extension of income tax to the same purpose; a camp at Broadmeadows for unemployed single men; establishment of a jam factory to provide work for unemployed girls; and, in 1931, the setting up of the Boys' Employment Movement which encouraged boys to continue technical education and helped to place them in jobs afterwards. He described his work in this field as 'a labour of love'.

Linton was briefly appointed honorary minister in December 1929, during the final days of the McPherson [q.v.] ministry. He served as secretary to Argyle's [q.v.7] cabinet in 1932-33 and was a member of a board of inquiry into social services in 1932. He resigned from parliament in March 1933, having been appointed agent-general for Victoria in London. Linton's love for the 'Old Land' where he was well known, his business experience and promotional ability made him an obvious choice for the post and he was glad to accept it. Yet it is surprising that he was never offered a ministerial portfolio: his energetic advocacy of social service measures involving additional taxation may not have sat well with the Country Party members of Argyle's coalition ministry.

Linton's term as agent-general expired in July 1936; he was knighted in the same year. In 1940-46 he was in the Department of Defence as honorary liaison officer with voluntary organizations. Politics still tempted him: in 1940 he considered standing for the House of Representatives; in 1940 and 1948 he unsuccessfully sought pre-selection for the State seat of Toorak.

Linton was a short, solidly built man, quick in thought and movement; his motto was 'Do it now'. His extensive collection of Australian art was sold in 1933 before his departure to England; subsequently he collected antique furniture. His appreciation of tennis together with his interest in young people led him, in 1923, to initiate an interstate junior teams competition for the Linton Cup.

Linton died in the Freemasons' Hospital, East Melbourne, on 21 September 1959. Survived by his wife and two sons, he was cremated with Anglican and Masonic rites.

Table Talk, 30 Sept 1926; *Sun-News Pictorial*, 20 May 1932; *Age*, 8 Feb 1933, 22 Sept 1959; *The*

Times, 22 Sept 1959; information from Dr R. G. Linton, Fremantle, WA.   GEOFF BROWNE

LISTER, WILLIAM LISTER (1859-1943), artist, was born on 27 December 1859 at Manly, Sydney, son of John Armitage Lister and his wife Eliza Kirkby, née Bateson. In 1868 his father returned to his native Yorkshire with his family and William attended Bedford School, studying art under a Mr Rudge and later in Paris at Pont Ste Maxence for a year. His early outdoor work on the Yorkshire moors laid the foundations for his later recognition as a landscape artist of the *plein air* school. In 1876-80 he studied mechanical engineering at the College of Science and Arts in Glasgow and at the Fairfield Engineering Works, then became a ship's engineer in a Cardiff collier. During his four years at sea he voyaged to America, the West Indies and throughout the Mediterranean.

While studying engineering Lister had joined the St Mungo Art Club in Glasgow and by 1876 at 17 he had already exhibited at the Royal Scottish Academy. In 1884 he went to London to begin a new career as a professional artist and teacher. He exhibited continually with the Royal Society of British Artists, the Royal Cambrian Academy of Art, Wales, the Royal Institute of Oil Painters and the Royal Empire Society of Artists.

Returning to Sydney in 1888, Lister joined the (Royal) Art Society of New South Wales, and was vice-president in 1894-97 and president in 1897-1943. He stayed with the society when professional artists such as Tom Roberts [q.v.] and A. H. Fullwood [q.v.8] formed the breakaway Society of Artists, Sydney, in 1895. He oversaw the two societies' amalgamation and adoption of a royal charter in 1903 but could not prevent the subsequent split in 1907. In 1900 he was appointed a trustee of the National Art Gallery of New South Wales (the only professional artist on the board) and was vice-president in 1919-43. In 1937 with Sydney Long [q.v.] he refused to join the Australian Academy of Art.

In 1898 Lister was represented in the Exhibition of Australian Art in London at the Grafton Galleries, sponsored by (Dame) Eadith Walker [q.v.]. Several of his paintings, sold to Seigelmeyer, a famous European collector, fetched the highest price of any exhibiting artist. In 1898 Lister won his first Wynne prize for landscape painting with 'The Ever Restless Sea' (Art Gallery of New South Wales). At Woollahra on 17 May 1899 he married a divorcee Bessie Enid Jenkins, née Waldron; they lived at Mosman for many years. He won the Wynne prize again in 1906, 1910, 1912, 1913 ('Federal Capital Site'

which also won the Commonwealth government's £250 prize), 1917 and 1925. He exhibited regularly from 1889 with the Royal Art Society and at Anthony Hordern [q.v.4] & Sons Ltd's gallery in Sydney in 1919-40.

Recognized as a consummate craftsman, Lister Lister (as he signed his paintings) worked in both oils and water-colours, often on very large canvases, effectively mirroring the minutiae of Nature. His contemporaries nevertheless commented on the lack of emotion in his work and modern critics tend to agree. A large proportion of his massive canvases dealt with seascapes and landfalls. Even in his landscapes water was rarely far away.

Lister died at North Sydney on 6 November 1943 when knocked down by a taxi, and was cremated. His daughter survived him. Portraits by Albert Coates and Lawson Balfour [q.v.7] are in the Art Gallery of New South Wales—he was dark, with a strong profile and a bristling moustache.

Catalogue 1946 memorial exhibition (Syd, 1946); *A'sian Critic*, 1 (1890), no 1; *A'sian Art Review*, 1 (1899), nos 1-4, 6-8, 12 (1900), no 1; *Red Funnel*, 1 Aug 1906; *Lone Hand*, Sept 1915; *Art in Aust*, no 3, 1917; *Art and Architecture*, 2, Jan-Feb 1905, no 1; *Cwlth Home*, 4 Dec 1925; *Bulletin*, 7 Apr 1900; *Sydney Mail*, 6 Aug 1913; *SMH*, 5 Apr 1929; Croll papers (LaTL).   J. FENTON-SMITH

LISTON, JOHN JAMES (1872-1944), civic leader and liquor trades spokesman, was born on 21 September 1872 at Granny, Roscommon, Ireland, son of John Haire Liston, constable, and his wife Mary Ann, née McNamany. The family migrated to Victoria about 1882 and settled at Williamstown where, after education at St Mary's Parish School, young Liston became a hairdresser. A member of the Catholic Young Men's Society, he was an outstanding debater and a keen sportsman; he played for Williamstown Football Club and in 1889 joined the Williamstown Racing Club. He was to head both organizations (the Football Club in 1923-33, the Racing Club in 1939-44) and become a prominent racehorse-owner. His barber's shop in Nelson Place was remembered as 'a sportsman's bureau'.

A big, ambitious man who studied to improve himself, Liston stood for Williamstown Council in 1897, revealing 'an astonishing grasp of municipal affairs' but losing the election by two votes. Next year he was returned unopposed. He was mayor in 1901-02 (the youngest in the State) and again in 1913-14. By 1906 he was licensee of the Customs House Hotel and that year was appointed secretary of the Liquor Trades' Defence Union, based in Melbourne. He sold his hairdressing business and, on 3 August 1910 at St Mary's Catholic Church, West Melbourne, married a milliner Eva Emily Roberts (d.1928).

Williamstown was a working-class suburb whose industries were in decline. As its representative on the Melbourne Harbor Trust in 1909-13, Liston sought public works for his area, expressed strong protectionist views and urged the trust to build its own ships at Williamstown. Even before his five successive mayoral terms in the 1920s it was said that Liston ran the town. Chairman of the finance and lighting committee, he persuaded the council to light the suburb with electricity in 1917 and take over supply. The financial success of the venture led to a new town hall and the purchase of a theatre and ferry steamer. Liston's plan to charge the cost of new streets to the benefiting property-owners was implemented after a long legal battle. In 1922-27 his supporters abandoned the rotation of the mayoralty so that he might carry out his programme of public works. But towards the end of the decade Liston and his 'progressive party' lost their grip. In August 1930 'grave irregularities' were alleged. A royal commission cleared Liston of wrong-doing but he resigned from the council and, after marrying May Ward on 15 December at St Patrick's Cathedral, moved to St Kilda. He claimed at this time to have lost all his Williamstown investments.

Liston had long ceased to be a purely local man. In 1918-30 he was Williamstown's representative on the Melbourne and Metropolitan Board of Works; he was the northern and western suburbs representative on the Metropolitan Town Planning Commission in the 1920s; and in 1923-31 he was a Melbourne city councillor and for six years chairman of the traffic and building regulations committee. A supporter of a Greater Melbourne Council, in 1931 he was defeated by one vote for the position of lord mayor.

Liston worked with Montague Cohen [q.v.8] to amalgamate Melbourne's breweries and strove to thwart the prohibitionists. He led 'the wets' to victory in the 1930 and 1938 'no licence' referenda; during the first campaign a *Herald* writer called him 'the busiest man in Melbourne'.

In his rise from humble origins and in the scope of his influence Liston may be compared with his co-religionist John Wren [q.v.]. He devoted an extraordinary amount of effort to public service, bestowing patronage on sporting and charitable associations and performing unpublicized acts of kindness during the Depression. A Williamstown high school, a regional hospital at Footscray and the Friendly Societies' Association were among his causes. He was a trustee of the Port Phillip Pilots' Association and of the Melbourne Cricket Ground and president of both the Victorian Soccer and Victorian Football associations.

Liston died of heart disease at Cliveden Mansions, East Melbourne, on 12 April 1944, survived by his wife and by two sons from his first marriage, one of whom was killed on active service next year. Archbishop Mannix [q.v.] attended his funeral and J. H. Scullin [q.v.] was a pallbearer. His estate was sworn for probate at £293 481. There is a bust in the Williamstown Town Hall and the Williamstown Historical Society holds a portrait. He is also remembered by the J. J. Liston medal for the best and fairest player in the Victorian Football Association and by the J. J. Liston Stakes at Sandown.

O. Ruhen, *Port of Melbourne, 1835-1976* (Syd, 1976); Williamstown Hist Soc, *Newsletter*, no 58, July 1980; *Williamstown Advertiser*, 21 Aug 1897, 13 Aug 1898, 31 Aug 1901, 17 Aug 1907, 6 Sept 1913, 11 Oct 1919, 19 Aug 1922, 22 Mar 1924, 5 Sept 1925, 4 Sept 1926, 27 Aug 1927, 9 Aug, 29 Nov, 13 Dec 1930, 15, 22 Apr 1944; *Age*, 24 Aug 1927, 13, 22 Apr 1944; *Herald* (Melb), 11 Jan, 2 Aug, 6, 11 Dec 1930, 13 Apr 1944, 27 Sept 1946; *Argus*, 1, 26, 31 Mar, 16 Dec 1930, 10 Oct 1931, 10 Oct 1938, 13 Apr 1944; 1944; S. de Wolf, Why we did not get prohibition in Victoria (B.A. Hons thesis, Monash Univ, 1970).   DAVID DUNSTAN

LITCHFIELD, JESSIE SINCLAIR (1883-1956), Northern Territory pioneer and author, was born on 18 February 1883 at Ashfield, Sydney, second child of John Phillips, contractor, and his wife Jean Sinclair, née Reid. The family lived in various country towns until 1895 when they returned to Sydney. Jessie attended Neutral Bay Public School, where one of her teachers was Mary Cameron, later Dame Mary Gilmore [q.v.9].

On 21 January 1908 at Darwin Jessie married Valentine Augustus Litchfield, a handsome miner she had met on a ship to Darwin. They moved wherever the diamond drills were sent, first to West Arm, then to Anson Bay, Brocks Creek, the Ironblow mine, the Union reefs and Pine Creek. Conditions were isolated and crude but Jessie became committed to Territory life. She wrote in 1909 to a Victorian church publication, the *Messenger*, describing her hardships: 'Chinese and blacks my nearest neighbours', eighty miles (129 km) from town by land, twenty (32 km) by sea, three (5 km) from the nearest white woman and two (3 km) from the nearest white man. Her plea for mission stations may have influenced the establishment of the Australian Inland Mission.

When the diamond drills finished, Val found work in Darwin with Vestey's meatworks. By the time of his death in 1931, Jessie, mother of seven, had written *Far North memories* (Sydney, 1930) based on life in the diamond-drill camps. A passionate and prolific writer, she completed five books, as well as short stories, articles and verse. She advanced her career as a journalist when, desperately in need of an income, she overwhelmed objections and in 1930 captured the editorship of the *Northern Territory Times and Government Gazette*. Vigorous, self-reliant and enterprising, she edited the *Times* until June 1932 when it was purchased by its union-owned rival, the *Northern Standard*, with which Jessie, vociferously conservative and anti-communist, had fought many an ideological battle. She was Darwin press representative for several Australian and overseas papers, including Reuters for six years.

In February 1942 she was compulsorily evacuated to Sydney where she purchased a small lending library, 'The Roberta', that she reopened in self-built premises in Darwin after the war. A self-trained photographer and historian, she was something of a local expert on Territory affairs. Writing to influential people, she crusaded for Darwin, which she envisaged as 'the Great Front Door of Australia', and for Territory self-government. In 1951, when 68, she unsuccessfully contested the Territory Federal seat as an Independent, campaigning by taxi over 3000 miles (4830 km).

In 1953 Jessie Litchfield was presented with the coronation medal for outstanding service to the Northern Territory and in 1955 became its first female justice of the peace. In 1954 she helped to establish the *North Australian* monthly, serving as assistant editor and Territory correspondent. She died on 12 March 1956 at Richmond, while on a visit to Melbourne, and was cremated. Her ashes were scattered over Darwin. Like most strong figures, Jessie had her critics but the flood of tributes included Dame Mary Gilmore's; 'She was a builder, an influence and an historian. Her interest never dulled and her spirit never failed. She personified the true Territorian'.

Her manuscripts and estate of £3000 were left to the Bread and Cheese Club, Melbourne, to establish an annual Jessie Litchfield literary award for Australian literature, preferably dealing with Territory life.

J. Dickinson, *Jessie Litchfield—grand old lady of the Territory* (Brisb, 1982); *People* (Syd), 15 Aug 1951; *Bohemia*, 15, no 2 (Mar 1964); *Canb Times*, 12 Nov 1964; *NT News*, 4 Dec 1982; J. Litchfield papers (NL); MS 1424 (ML). BARBARA JAMES

LITHGOW, ALEXANDER FRAME (1870-1929), composer and bandmaster, was born on 1 December 1870 in Glasgow, Scotland, son of Samuel Lithgow, master tinsmith and his wife Agnes Alison, née Shanks. The family migrated to Invercargill, New Zealand, when Alexander was 6. He was educated at Invercargill Grammar School. His family was musical, performing as the six-member Lithgow Concert Company. Alexander, an acknowledged prodigy, was accepted by the Invercargill Garrison Band at 11 and by 16 was its principal cornet-soloist, and at 20 its bandmaster, playing also with the Theatre Royal orchestra as first violin. He won cornet-solo championships at Dunedin in 1890 and 1891 and at Christchurch in 1893, touring New Zealand as a professional soloist before moving to Tasmania. In 1894-1906 he was conductor of the Launceston St Joseph's Band, except in 1901-02 when he conducted the Woolston Band at Christchurch. On 6 June 1900 at Launceston he married Elizabeth Hill Telfer with Presbyterian forms. He earned his living as a compositor at the Launceston *Examiner* and the *Daily Telegraph* until 1927.

His virtuosity helped to foster local musical life. The St Joseph's Band was successful in competitions and its city and country concerts were immensely popular. Lithgow was associated with the short-lived Launceston Orchestral Society (1897-98), the 12th Battalion Launceston Regiment (1904-10) and the Launceston Musical Association (1909-10). He was also conductor and spontaneous composer for the silent film orchestra at the Lyceum and Princess theatres. His enthusiasm led to the founding of the Launceston Concert Orchestra which he conducted in 1923-27, presenting innovative music including symphonic jazz and the latest Lithgow compositions.

When his jaunty, patriotic marches were published in America and Europe, he was acclaimed as 'the Sousa of the Antipodes'. His first composition, 'Wairoa', was published in 1892 and his work was soon familiar to colonial bands, the Woolston Brass Band presenting a complete programme of his music in October 1901. His celebrated quick march, 'Invercargill', composed in 1909, broke phonograph sales records, and with 'Parade of the Anzacs' was heard at Gallipoli and on the European front. Lithgow produced approximately two hundred marches, as well as numerous pieces for band, orchestra, piano and voice. Some were printed by his own Commonwealth Band Music Publications and later by W. H. Paling [q.v.5] & Co., but he acquired no copyrights and many of his pieces, in his immaculate notation, were lost or unpublished.

Lithgow returned to St Joseph's in 1922 and remained until ill health forced his retirement in 1927. A fund-raising all-Lithgow concert in 1923 included two four-piece suites,

'In Sunny Australia', and 'At the Movies'. Music dominated his existence, but time for composing was scarce when after a long day's work he cycled home to change for an evening performance or a musical gathering.

Lithgow died on 12 July 1929 of cerebral haemorrhage at Launceston and was buried in Carr Villa cemetery to the sound of massed bands playing 'Invercargill' and 'Queen of the North'. His wife, son and two daughters survived him. Memorial plaques were unveiled in the Paterson Street Barracks and the rotunda in City Park, Launceston, in 1953.

Cyclopedia of Tasmania, 1 (Hob, 1900); G. H. and T. G. Stancombe (comp), *A. F. Lithgow memorial plaques erected Paterson Barracks and City Park* (Launc, 1953); R. A. Ferrall, *Partly personal* (Hob, 1974); S. P. Newcomb, *Challenging brass* (priv print, Takapuna, NZ, 1980); *A'sian Bandsman*, Sept-Oct 1960, Jan 1971; *Weekly Courier*, 12 Oct 1901, 15 Mar 1902, 8 Apr, 4, 25 Nov 1909, 29 Dec 1910, 25 Nov 1920, 18 Oct 1923; *Examiner* (Launc), 4 Nov 1909, 13 July 1929; Lithgow file (Local History Room, Northern Regional Library, Launc, Tas).

J. F. Firth
Margaret Glover

LITTLE, ROBERT ALEXANDER (1895-1918),

World War I fighter ace, was born on 19 July 1895 at Hawthorn, Melbourne, son of James Little, bookseller and importer of medical and surgical works, and his Victorian wife Susan, formerly Smith, née Solomon. He was educated at Scotch College and later joined the family business as a commercial traveller, living with his parents at Windsor. Rejected with hundreds of others for the four vacancies at Point Cook Military Flying School, he sailed for England in July 1915, at his own expense. He paid for his flying training at Hendon where he gained his flying certificate (No. 1958 Royal Aero Club) on 27 October. He entered the Royal Naval Air Service as a probationary temporary sub-lieutenant on 14 January 1916.

Posted to the relatively inactive war flight at Dover, Kent, Little suffered eye and stomach trouble in the air. He married Vera Gertrude Field at the Congregational Church, Dover, on 16 September 1916. Posting to No. 1 Wing at Dunkirk, France, in June had brought action at last—against the submarine base at Zeebrugge, Belgium. His physical troubles disappeared with the change to aircraft which did not spray him with castor oil and he quickly established a favourable reputation. The Somme offensive of the second half of 1916 imposed such strain on the Royal Flying Corps that the Admiralty created new R.N.A.S. squadrons for service on the Western Front. In October Little was transferred to the new No. 8 Squadron, 'Naval 8', equipped with Sopwith Pups. His plane, N5182, rebuilt, is now on display at the Royal Air Force Museum, Hendon. On 1 November he scored his first aerial victory and by March 1917 was credited with nine enemy aircraft shot down; he was promoted flight lieutenant in April.

In 'Bloody April' the R.F.C. suffered appalling casualties while the three naval squadrons (1, 3 & 8), re-equipped with formidable new Sopwith Triplanes, were given a wide berth by the enemy. In April-July Flight Lieutenant Little really showed his mettle, mainly in N5493 'Blymp', streaming the cardinal, gold and blue of Scotch College. 'Blymp' became the affectionate nickname of his infant son, while Little himself became 'Rikki' to the squadron, after Kipling's mongoose Rikki-Tikki-Tavi, the deadly cobra-killer. By early August 1917, when he was posted to Walmer on the Kent coast for a period of rest, he had destroyed thirty-seven enemy aircraft and damaged many more. He had been awarded the Distinguished Service Order, the Distinguished Service Cross and Bar and the Croix de Guerre; in September he received a Bar to the D.S.O.; in December he was mentioned in dispatches and he was promoted flight commander in January 1918.

Paradoxically, Little was a clumsy flyer with a record of crash landings, but in aerial combat his brilliance derived from a combination of fearless aggression, quite exceptional eyesight, superb marksmanship and close-range firing. His armourers calculated that he fired an average of forty-four rounds per aerial victory. The audacity with which he would, single-handed, attack large enemy formations brought the advantage of surprise. Twice he actually struck enemy aircraft in his eagerness to close the range. He was of average height, stocky and athletic in build. Likeable and friendly with a strong sense of fun, he was a great talker. He devoted much time on the ground to rifle and pistol practice at moving targets. In the air he was a brilliant loner rather than a leader.

At Walmer Little was able to enjoy a settled period of family life but in March 1918 he declined a desk job and volunteered to return to France where as flight commander with 'Naval 3' he flew Sopwith Camel B6318. Soon afterwards the R.F.C. and R.N.A.S. amalgamated as the Royal Air Force and he became Captain Little of 203 Squadron. The end came on the night of 27 May when he went up alone from Ezil le Hamel to intercept enemy bombers in the dark. Fatally wounded in the groin, he crashed near Norviz where he was found next morning. He was buried in the village cemetery at Norviz and subsequently in Wavans British cemetery, France. He was 22. Conforming to his wish, his widow brought their infant son to grow up in Australia.

Little is officially credited with a tally of 47 enemy planes brought down. He is Australia's World War I ace of aces: the next officially recognized 'victories' of Australians were 39 by his friend Major R. S. Dallas [q.v.8] and 29 by Captain A. H. Cobby [q.v.8]. Little ranks eighth of all British Commonwealth aces, and fourteenth of all aces from both sides of the conflict. Major (Air Vice Marshal) R. R. Collishaw, his commanding officer in 'Naval 3', wrote of him: 'Little had an outstanding character. Bold, aggressive and courageous yet he was gentle and kindly . . . his example was a tribute to the high standards of Australian manhood'.

Until very recently the achievements of Little and Dallas were neglected in their native Australia, only those who served in Australian forces being afforded official recognition, an anomaly now being rectified. Photographs, medals and mementoes of R. A. Little are held by the Australian War Memorial.

E. Haddingham, *The fighting triplanes* (Lond, 1968); K. Isaacs, *Military aircraft of Australia, 1909-1918* (Canb, 1971); L. H. Rochford, *I chose the sky* (Lond, 1977); *London Gazette*, 16 Feb, 22 June, 20 July, 11 Aug, 14 Sept, 11 Dec 1917; *Cross and Cockade* (USA), 16, no 2, 1975, p 168, *and* (Eng), 17, no 1, 1976, p 13; Dept of Defence (Canb), Australia's 'unknown' top air ace (typescript, nd, received Feb 1978; R. A. Little, War records file (British Ministry of Defence); War log of Sopwith Pup, 25 Aug 1916-24 Jan 1917, N5182, RNAS (RAF Museum, Hendon, Eng); Combat reports, 6 Apr 1917 to 26 Aug 1917, Squadron record book, Naval 8 Squadron (PRO, Lond); information from J. M. Bruce (RAF Museum, Hendon), H. Tomson, Haddenham, Bucks, and Sir G. Bromet, Littlestone-on-Sea, Kent, Eng, and E. R. Grange, Toronto, Canada.   J. C. LITTLE

LITTLEJOHN, EMMA LINDA PALMER (1883-1949), feminist, journalist and radio commentator, was born on 11 December 1883 at Double Bay, Sydney, fifth child of Richard Teece [q.v.], actuary and later general manager of the Australian Mutual Provident Society, and his wife Helena, née Palmer; R. C. Teece [q.v.] was her brother. Educated at Ascham School, Darling Point, she became active in philanthropic work through membership of the Ascham Old Girls' Union. On 5 April 1907 at St John's Church of England, Darlinghurst, she married Albert Littlejohn, a merchant and son of a director of the A.M.P. Society.

By the 1920s Linda Littlejohn was the mother of four children and a well-respected figure in the Sydney women's movement. In 1926 she was an executive-member of the National Council of Women of New South Wales and the Feminist Club. Two years later she launched the League of Women Voters to support female candidates for public office and to press for feminist reforms. While she was president the league became a foundation affiliate of the United Associations of Women, formed to co-ordinate women's groups. She chaired an industrial peace meeting but was driven from the platform by the wives of striking timberworkers. She spoke frequently on eugenics, advocated uniform divorce laws, joined the Who's for Australia? League, helped to found the Racial Hygiene Association of New South Wales and was appointed to the Board of Health in 1929.

Mrs Littlejohn was Australian delegate to the congress of the International Alliance of Women for Suffrage and Equal Citizenship in Istanbul in 1935. Next year she addressed the Assembly of the League of Nations on behalf of the Equal Rights International (Geneva), of which she became president in 1937. She lobbied the Australian high commissioner in London to promote the equal status programme of British feminists.

An ardent publicist for the feminist cause, Mrs Littlejohn broadcast for the British Broadcasting Corporation and for 2UW and 2UE in Sydney. She reported for the *Australian Women's Weekly* on the campaigns of the United Associations and the Australian Federation of Women Voters. She belonged to the New South Wales Institute of Journalists (1933-41) and the Business and Professional Women's club of Sydney. In her novel *Life and Lucille* (1933) she dramatized the need for women in parliament, divorce reform and the introduction of adequate training to enable women to be economically independent of their fathers and husbands.

From 1937 Linda Littlejohn annually toured Europe and the United States of America, lecturing on women's rights and stressing the urgent need for women to oppose Fascism and preserve democratic government through international solidarity. In 1939 she resigned as vice-president of the United Associations and president of the Equal Rights International. She worked briefly in 1941 as national director of recruiting for the Women's Australian National Services. On 21 April she divorced Albert Littlejohn and went to America next year. At Charleston, South Carolina, on 6 April 1942 she married Charles Joseph Tilden, a retired professor of engineering from Yale University, and settled in New Jersey; they returned to Sydney in 1944. She died of cancer in the Scottish Hospital, Paddington, on 21 March 1949 and was cremated. Survived by her husband, and her two sons and two daughters, she left an estate valued for probate at £42 070.

Linda Littlejohn was a talented debater and forceful speaker who commanded attention on the public platform and the airwaves. Tall and always elegantly attired, she is remembered for her charismatic personality and commitment to the international women's movement.

W. Mitchell, *50 years of feminist achievement—a history of the United Association of Women* (Syd, nd); *Ascham Charivari,* June 1903, Dec 1905, May 1906, June 1907, Sept 1908, Nov 1915, May 1916, May 1917, Nov 1920, May 1925, May 1928; *Plain Talk*, 30 Mar 1929, p 29; *SMH,* 9 Nov 1928, 18 Mar, 31 Dec 1929, 6 Nov 1931, 17 Feb, 10 Nov 1933, 21 Feb 1940, 17 July, 28 Aug 1941, 21 July 1944, 24 Mar 1949; Feminist Club records, *and* United Assn of Women records (ML); information from R. A. Littlejohn, Harden, NSW.

MEREDITH FOLEY

LITTLEJOHN, WILLIAM STILL (1859-1933), headmaster, was born on 19 September 1859 at Turriff, Aberdeenshire, Scotland, son of Wilson Littlejohn, watchmaker, and his wife Margaret, née Gordon. After local schooling he went to Aberdeen Grammar School in 1872 and then to the University of Aberdeen, where he studied classics, mathematics, science and philosophy and played Rugby. He won many prizes and graduated M.A. in 1879, having worked extremely hard and sagaciously, despite poverty and poor eyesight.

By temperament and upbringing he was a religious man, but serious doubts stopped him entering the ministry. A pointer to his rationality was his acceptance of Darwin's theory of evolution as a credible mechanism within creation. 'Surely', he wrote, 'it is no degrading view of God to superintend and govern all these activities'.

Littlejohn obtained teacher registration in 1879 and taught at Clydesdale College, Hamilton, then tutored privately. Before leaving to join his family in New Zealand in 1881, he kindled a lifelong interest in the outdoors by tramping, or riding a velocipede, great distances across Scotland. From 1882 to 1898, as an assistant master at Nelson College, he developed his teaching skills and philosophy. Friendly but firm, enthusiastic and very energetic, he succeeded in making hard work fun and put reasoning far above rote-learning. He pioneered experimental methods in science and loved geological excursions. Among his first pupils was Ernest (Lord) Rutherford. With a huge, boyish laugh, he threw his 5 ft. 11 ins. (180 cm), 12½ stone (80 kg) frame into the scrum for the school's Rugby team and batted and bowled with skill and perseverance at cricket. He studied military manuals and made the Nelson College Cadet Corps famous for its drill.

In 1885 Littlejohn proposed to Jean Berry, a teacher whom he had met during his university days. Despite a long silence she migrated and married him in Wellington on 25 December, to become the most powerful influence in his life.

Appointed principal at Nelson from 1898, Littlejohn set about transforming the school. Within five years there were four times as many boarders and twice as many day-boys. He drove staff and pupils hard, but within a humane curriculum, making English the main subject, emphasizing translation in languages, experiment in science and stressing the stimulus of the library, museum and extra-curricular activities. To increase participation, he divided the school into groups of thirty for Rugby and twenty-two for cricket.

But for his wife he might never have moved from Nelson. She organized the application which brought him the headmastership of Scotch College, Melbourne, in 1904. Before accepting, he insisted upon extensive improvements, especially the provision of laboratories. And he went on building. School enrolments (240 when he arrived) jumped by about fifty per year. In 1914, with over 500 pupils, the council decided to move from cramped quarters at East Melbourne to an extensive site among Melbourne's expanding middle class at Hawthorn, where by 1923 there were 1200 on the roll. To keep in touch, Littlejohn accepted a prodigious workload, which took a physical toll. Threatened with blindness in 1911, he had to take a year overseas and was ill for six months in 1917.

To Graham McInnes, who recalled his 'crisp white beard, curly white hair, rimless pebble-lens glasses and totally unreconstructed Scottish accent', Littlejohn seemed 'an administrative dynamo driven by evangelical Scots fervour'. He believed that a school should be large to give challenging experiences and to allow specialization across the broad curriculum. His appetite for academic success, expressed in high salaries for 'senior subject-masters and ruthless streaming, ensured that Scotch excelled at public examinations. In 1927 his boys won twelve of the eighteen exhibitions. They were prepared by three exams each term, their masters spurred on by 'Old Bill's' assiduous scrutiny of form averages and his sudden classroom visits. His deputy considered that Littlejohn could take any class in any of the twenty subjects on the curriculum. That capacity, and his knowledge of educational literature, ensured the respect of his staff. Whether standing in the 'quad', watchmaker's son's watch in hand to ensure punctuality by roaring at offenders, or 'shouting to God and at us' during morning assembly when he prayed for better performances in exams and at games and asked for better Christian lives, he effectively drama-tized his role. He lived for the school and expected his staff and pupils to be fulfilled within it.

A fellow headmaster who called Littlejohn 'a mark fiend' was probably correct about the inappropriateness of that exam factory for boys in the ruck of the school for whom, as for their masters, the system was often demoral-izing; but he may not have understood the broad, balancing humanity that made Scotch a nursery of liberal thinkers. Apart from intro-ducing a prefect system and getting boys to run the library, museum and many societies, Littlejohn founded the *Scotch Collegian* and entrusted it to student editors and poets who, true to his vision, made it a notable magazine. Many of them became prominent in journal-ism and letters.

As on all private Church schools, World War I made an immense impact. Formerly a captain in the New Zealand militia, zealous for discipline and intensely patriotic, Littlejohn supported recruitment. During the conscrip-tion controversy of 1916, 600 Scotch boys sang at one of Billy Hughes's [q.v.9] rallies. In the memorial hall of the new school, to whose original motto 'Deo et Litteris' he caused 'Patriae' to be added, mourning the dead became a ritual on Anzac and Armistice days.

With his intense focus on Scotch and edu-cation, he had little time for social life. He relaxed by walking in the bush and often fished in New Zealand with Sir John MacFar-land [q.v.]. His only club was the Old Scotch Collegians'. From 1905 to 1926 he was a very active member of the board of public exami-nations (schools board) of the University of Melbourne and from 1915 to his death was on the university council. He was a member of the faculty of education and a chairman of the Headmasters' Conference of Australia. For his services to education his old university awarded him a doctorate of laws in 1929.

Littlejohn died at the school on 7 October 1933, after murmuring, 'Kneel', to his wife and a daughter and whispering a prayer. He was cremated. His wife, two sons and three daughters survived him; three of his children became doctors. A portrait by W. B. McInnes [q.v.] hangs in the Scotch College memorial hall.

A. E. Pratt, *Dr. W.S. Littlejohn* (Melb, 1934); *The first hundred years* (Melb, 1952); G. McInnes, *The road to Gundagai* (Lond, 1965) and *Goodbye, Melbourne town* (Lond, 1968); *Melbourne studies in education*, 1982, S. Murray-Smith ed (Melb, 1983); Scotch College (Melb), *Annual Reports*; Univ Melb, *Calendar*, 1905-33, Council minutes 1915-33, Schools Board minutes 1905-26 (Univ Melb, Archives); *Argus* and *SMH*, 9 Oct 1933.

WESTON BATE

LITTLER, CHARLES AUGUSTUS MUR-RAY (1868-1916), soldier and businessman, was born on 26 March 1868 at Launceston, Tasmania, eldest child of Augustus East Littler, clerk, and his wife Hannah Sarah, née Murray. He was a cousin of F. M. Littler [q.v.], Tasmanian ornithologist. Charles was educated at Launceston High School. About 1888 he went to Devonport as a teller with the Bank of Van Diemen's Land, and by August 1891 when the bank became insolvent he had been successfully managing the Zee-han branch for two years. At Devonport on 26 January 1892 he married Helen Cotgrave Thomas (d. 1953); they had three sons.

After working as a produce merchant in 1897 Littler became manager of the North-West Farmers' Association in Devonport. He was involved with several sports clubs and served in the Tasmanian defence forces—in 1902 he was commissioned and in 1904 he became a provisional captain with the Tas-manian Rangers.

In July 1904 Littler left Tasmania for the Philippines. Living at first in a houseboat on Manila Bay, he joined his brother-in-law Edward Thomas in a stevedoring agency which Littler continued to run until 1909. During this period he served with American forces in the Philippines and was granted an honorary commission by the Russian navy in 1905 for having helped to supply three Rus-sian cruisers at Manila. He also undertook intelligence work for the British navy. In 1910 Littler became manager of a rubber and coconut company on Mindanao Island, and his extensive knowledge of East Asia was put to good use by the Tasmanian government which had appointed him as its unpaid com-mercial agent in 1904.

Owing to financial problems Littler returned to Tasmania early in 1914; he enlisted as a lieutenant in the Australian Imperial Force on 16 December. At Mel-bourne on 2 February 1915 he embarked for Egypt with the 2nd Reinforcements, 12th Battalion. He landed at Gallipoli on 25 April and soon after was promoted captain and given command of the beach parties. Respon-sible for the unloading of stores and equip-ment at Anzac, Littler and his work parties (consisting of many troublesome soldiers put on beach fatigues as punishment) worked tirelessly to ensure that supplies were con-stantly available. As beach commandant at North Beach, he played a major role during the evacuation of Anzac and was probably the last Australian to leave. Widely known as the 'Duke of Anzac', he fully earned the Distin-guished Service Order awarded a few months later. He was also mentioned in dispatches.

Following Gallipoli the A.I.F. returned to Egypt and Littler became commandant at Moascar Camp near Ismailia on the Suez

Canal. In March 1916 he was transferred to the newly formed 52nd Battalion which sailed for France in June. Despite severe ill health he led his company in its attack on Mouquet Farm at dawn on 3 September. In the half-light, as the troops approached a German machine-gun post, Littler was badly wounded, yet continued to struggle toward the gun, where he died.

According to official historian C. E. W. Bean [q.v.7] Charles Littler was 'a brave, honourable and experienced leader' whose slowness of promotion was due to an unfortunate outspokenness. This 'best known personality on Anzac Beach' was well respected by his subordinates. Two of Littler's three sons served in the war; both were wounded and were invalided back to Australia (the younger, Burnett Guy (Sam) Littler, won the Military Cross and served in World War II).

W. Tilley, *The wild west of Tasmania* (Zeehan, Tas, 1891); C. E. W. Bean, *The story of Anzac* (Syd, 1921, 1924) and *The A.I.F. in France*, 1916 (Syd, 1929), *and* Diaries, nos 58, 142, 143, 244 (AWM); L. M. Newton, *The story of the twelfth* (Hob, 1925); *Cyclopedia of Tasmania* (Hob, 1931); *Reveille* (Syd), Apr 1930; *Advocate* (Burnie), 17, 21 June, 25 July 1904; *North West Post*, 25, 28 Sept 1916; War diary, 52nd Battalion, AIF, and C. A. Littler papers, 3 DRL 3319, and S. H. Watson papers, 3 DRL 1958 (AWM); Premier's Dept records, 1/172, file 136/3/1904, 1/180, file 136/4/1905, 1/215, file 136/5/1909, 1/239, file 136/3/1911 (TA); information from Mr J. W. Littler, Devonport, Tas, Mr C. G. Littler, Palmwoods, Qld, and Mrs R. Littler, Newcastle, NSW.   MATTHEW HIGGINS

LITTLER, FRANK MERVYN (1880-1922), ornithologist, entomologist and accountant, was born on 1 January 1880 at Launceston, Tasmania, only son of Henry Charles Littler, accountant, and his wife Annie Rosina, née Horne. He was educated at Launceston Church Grammar School where he won various school prizes, was captain of the cricket team and in the football team. He followed his father into accountancy and employment at the Mount Bischoff Co. office at Launceston.

Littler's scientific interests began early. Between 1901 and 1913 he published twenty-five items listed in H. M. Whittell's *The literature of Australian birds*. In 1901 his article 'Bird protection' was published in the first issue of the *Emu*, journal of the Australian Ornithological Union. He was a founding member of the Royal Australasian Ornithologists' Union and his paper 'Notes on some birds peculiar to Tasmania' was read before its Melbourne congress in November 1902. From 6 July 1901 to 1 July 1905 he wrote a fortnightly column on Tasmanian birds for the Launceston *Weekly Courier*; it provided much

of the groundwork for his best-known work, *Handbook of the birds of Tasmania and its dependencies* published in 1910. It was well advanced for the time, written with the text arranged in a format now adopted for field guides. Entries for species had an observation section as much as two or three pages long, based on Littler's personal observations. Ornithologists still refer to this work, especially when making historical comparisons with present-day population densities and distribution and behaviour patterns.

Littler was described as both an entomologist and an ornithologist during his life, whereas he is referred to posthumously solely as an ornithologist. However, he joined the Entomological Society, London, in 1903 while attending an entomological congress in London where he had been invited to represent Australia and New Zealand. He was also a member of the Entomological Society of America and the American Association of Economic Entomologists. Anthony Musgrave's [q.v.] *Bibliography of Australian entomology, 1775-1930* credits him with four articles.

Littler made collections of bird-skins, insects and butterflies including local and other species acquired by exchange with other collectors. Though his obituary in the *Mercury* stated that he presented a splendid entomological collection to the Queen Victoria Museum and Art Gallery, Launceston, neither this donation nor that of bird-skins which his daughter believed he made to the museum can be verified. His publishing virtually ceased after 1913 and many of his papers were lost after his death.

Littler continued his sporting activity after he left school, rifle-shooting and playing cricket for several seasons with the Nil Desperandum Club. He died on 1 July 1922 at Ravenswood of meningitis and was buried at Carr Villa cemetery, Launceston, with Anglican rites. On 27 February 1908 he had married Honora Ivy Iacyanth, daughter of William Holyman [q.v.9], at Launceston. His wife survived him together with a son and a daughter who affectionately remembered her father as a gentle man of tall, slender build.

B. W. Rait, *The story of the Launceston Church Grammar School* (Launc, 1946); *Mercury*, 3 July 1922; *Weekly Courier* (Launc), 6, 20 July 1922.
                    DENNIS ABBOTT

LIVINGSTON, JOHN (1857-1935), stock-dealer and politician, was born on 19 September 1857 near Mount Gambier, South Australia, second son of the fourteen children of John Livingston, stockholder, and his wife Catherine, née Steele. His father had arrived in South Australia in 1846 and later bought

Curratum in the south-east, where he built a school and engaged tutors to educate his children and those of his workmen and neighbours; he died in Victoria in 1886. John Livingston junior was educated at Curratum and then worked as a drover, stock-dealer and station manager in New South Wales, Queensland and Victoria. He married at Mount Gambier, on 11 June 1884, Eliza Dunn Paltridge, daughter of a local grazier and granddaughter of John Dunn [q.v.4].

In 1880 Livingston and Frank Paltridge had explored the mineral and farming potential of the Gascoyne River area of Western Australia; after Frank's death Livingston returned to South Australia. About 1890 he bought and lived briefly on the property Colleringa near Bourke, New South Wales, but returned to Mount Gambier to manage Burrungil for Paltridge & Co. In the mid-1890s he was farming at Benara and was an early member of the district council there. In 1898 he opened an auctioneering business at Mount Gambier and was mayor in 1899 before being elected that year to the House of Assembly for the seat of Victoria (later Victoria and Albert). He soon sat on a select committee investigating codlin moth regulations and later was active in bringing about a railway extension from Mount Gambier to Glencoe. He was defeated in 1906 but later that year won the House of Representatives seat of Barker, which he held as a conservative until 1922 when he resigned. In 1911 he had been a member of the parliamentary party which attended the coronation of King George V in London and next year, with two colleagues, he published an account of these travels, *Three Australians abroad*. As a back-bencher he spoke occasionally on agricultural matters and consistently opposed plans to develop Canberra.

At Mount Gambier Livingston was chairman of the local branch of the South Australian Farmers' Union and president of the Stock Owners' Association. He was also an active council-member of the Mount Gambier School of Mines. He judged stock at agricultural shows and encouraged innovations that he had witnessed in Europe and America, especially with regard to production of beet sugar and the planting of pine forests, an industry developed by his sons John Malcolm and Frank, famous yachtsmen.

In 1894 as a director of the Mount Gambier Freezing Co., Livingston had prepared one of South Australia's first shipments of fat lambs; 500 were frozen at Newport, for export to London. He continued to work as an auctioneer until his retirement in 1925.

He valued his Scottish associations: a president of the Caledonian Society, later in life he had his portrait painted by John Longstaff [q.v.] in tartan kilt and cap; it is still in the family's possession. Livingston died in Melbourne on 4 September 1935. Survived by his wife, five daughters and two sons, he was buried in Lake Terrace cemetery, Mount Gambier.

R. Cockburn, *Pastoral Pioneers of South Australia*, 2 (Adel, 1927); *Border Watch*, 21 Dec 1901, 1 Aug 1903, 5, 23 Sept 1935; *Advertiser* (Adel), 7 Aug 1914, 5 Sept 1935; *Argus* and *Sun-News Pictorial*, 5 Sept 1935; *Naracoorte Herald*, 10 Sept 1935; *Australasian*, 14 Sept 1935; interviews with Mrs R. Ibbott and Mrs R. Sinclair Poyntz, Mount Gambier.   LEITH G. MacGILLIVRAY

LIVINGSTON, THOMAS (1851–1922), politician and manufacturer, was born on 12 June 1851 at Bathurst, New South Wales, son of John Livingston, shepherd, and his wife Margaret, née Brock. The family moved to Ballarat, Victoria, when Thomas was 5. In 1869 he undertook a Board of Education teacher-training course and taught at schools in the Ballarat area in 1870-78 and at Numurkah from 1879. His inspectors described him as energetic and intelligent. On 11 April 1882 at Majorca he married, with Wesleyan forms, a fellow teacher Genefor Deborah Perry.

Resigning from the Education Department in July 1883, Livingston worked as a journalist at Shepparton, became part-proprietor of the *Numurkah Standard* and then proprietor of the *Tungamah and Lake Rowan Express* which he sold in 1887 to edit the *Goulburn Valley Farmers' Gazette*. Next year he founded the Melbourne Chilled Butter Co. and became its managing director, later visiting Denmark in the firm's interests. The company pioneered the export of butter in 1889 and established seventeen creameries throughout Victoria before expanding to cheese-making and the export of frozen poultry, rabbits and fruit. Livingston ceased active involvement with the firm in 1900, although remaining chairman, and bought a farm at Agnes River, South Gippsland.

Elected to the Legislative Assembly for Gippsland South in October 1902 as a supporter of the Kyabram retrenchment movement, Livingston worked hard to secure road and rail improvements for his electorate while seeking to limit other government activities. He opposed the extension of the Factories and Shops Act to country areas and led the opposition to Swinburne's [q.v.] milk supervision bill in 1905. More sympathetic to the claims of education than to industrial or health reform, he advocated better pay and conditions for state-school teachers, referred to school inspectors as 'small Czars' and described as 'blackmail' the requirement for parents in remote country areas to pay for erection of schools. As a member of the country faction he supported the removal of Sir Thomas Bent's [q.v.3] government in December 1908. In 1909 he chaired a board of inquiry into the Small Holdings Act.

Genial, conscientious and unassuming, Livingston was a popular government whip and secretary to cabinet in the Murray [q.v.] government of 1909-12; (Sir) Harry Lawson [q.v.] regarded him as 'easily first' among party whips. Honorary minister under Watt [q.v.] in 1913-14, he served in the subsequent Peacock [q.v.] government as minister of public instruction from June 1914 to November 1915 and then as minister of mines, minister of forests and vice-president of the Board of Land and Works until November 1917. He was a cautious administrator who made more impact in mines and forests than in education. In 1917 he appointed the brown coal advisory committee whose recommendations led to the establishment of the State Electricity Commission. In 1918, believing that the state forests had been 'ruthlessly and scandalously destroyed', he altered royalty payments to sawmillers to minimize timber wastage.

Livingston returned briefly to office in 1921 as honorary minister with responsibility for agriculture in the Lawson ministry, but relinquished the post because of ill health. He was a Freemason and Presbyterian temperance advocate.

He died at Middle Park on 13 July 1922, one week after being elected deputy chairman of the parliamentary country Liberals. Survived by his wife and daughter, he was given a state funeral and was buried in Brighton cemetery.

Victoria of today (Melb, 1902); E. H. Sugden and F. W. Eggleston, *George Swinburne* (Syd, 1931); C. Edwards, *Brown power* (Melb, 1969); Education Dept (Vic), *Vision and realisation*, L. J. Blake ed (Melb, 1973); *PD* (Vic), 1906, p 110, 1908, p 1756, 1917-18, p 175, 1922, p 144; *Gippsland Farmers' J*, 17 July 1922; *Argus*, 14 July 1922; information supplied by Education History Services, Education Dept, Melb.   GEOFF BROWNE

LIVINGSTONE-LEARMONTH, FREDERICK VALIANT COTTON (1862-1945), superintendent of the Australian Agricultural Co. and soldier, was born on 6 June 1862 at Ercildoun, near Ballarat, Victoria, third son of Thomas Learmonth [q.v.2] and his first wife Louisa Maria, daughter of Major General Sir Thomas Valiant. The family returned to Scotland in 1873 and after attending Westminster School, London, Frederick graduated M.A. from Pembroke College, Cambridge. Two years on the Continent made him proficient in French and German. In 1883 he returned to Australia and managed Bringagee, his father's station on the Murrumbidgee River, and for many years he controlled Thomas Learmonth's Australasian interests. He went to Greece in 1897, acting as *The Times* correspondent during the Graeco-Turkish war and touring Turkey, Greece and Russia.

On the outbreak of the South African War Learmonth embarked as a corporal with the 1st New South Wales Mounted Rifles, fought at Osfontein and Driefontein and took part in the advance to Pretoria under Lieut-Colonel De Lisle. He saw action in the battle of Diamond Hill, and in the Orange Free State and Cape Colony. He was promoted lieutenant, awarded the Distinguished Service Order for excellence in the field and mentioned in dispatches.

On 31 October 1901, at St Mary's Anglican Church, North Melbourne, Learmonth, using the name Livingstone-Learmonth, married Riñ Aille Eidil Marie, daughter of Canon Joseph Carlisle, rector of St Mary's. Next April the Australian Agricultural Co. asked Jesse Gregson [q.v.4], its superintendent, to nominate his successor and Livingstone-Learmonth was given a trial appointment. At Newcastle, New South Wales, he worked as Gregson's assistant until the latter's departure in 1905. He then began one year as acting general superintendent at £1250, preparatory to a seven-year term.

Hebburn, an A.A. Co. colliery, had begun yielding profits in 1903 and, with Brown [q.v.7] Bros' Pelaw Main mine, it pioneered coal-cutting machines, inaugurating a new era in both extraction and industrial relations. By 1907 the Vend, a cartel which regulated prices and shared the trade between Newcastle coal proprietors, was operating. Livingstone-Learmonth spearheaded the confrontation leading to the disastrous strikes of 1909: he was secretary to the Associated Northern Collieries and secretary and, later, chairman of the Hunter River District Colliery Proprietors' Defence Association, and his conservatism and militancy contributed to deadlocked negotiations with the union leader, Peter Bowling [q.v.7]. The company ultimately withdrew from coal-mining in 1914-16.

A. A. Co. pastoral operations were mainly at Warrah where George Fairbairn's skilled management eased Livingstone-Learmonth's burden. The extension of wire netting and formation of a Border Leicester stud confirmed Warrah's prosperity. 'Forced by the iniquitous principle of resumption which is so popular under our ultra democratic government', Livingstone-Learmonth advised a voluntary Willow Tree subdivision. When State government proclaimed the Warrah Settlement Purchase Area, he protested at a 'distinct breach of faith', only to be told of a change in policy and a new bill. He was disappointed at a Court of Appeal's award in 1911 for the 45 006 acres (18 200 ha) resumed. He protested strongly against the 'crushing' 1910 Federal land tax.

To offset these losses he recommended purchase of Corona, a first-class sheep station west of Longreach, Queensland, belonging to his family's Groongal Pastoral Co. This 1911 purchase presaged a pattern of purchase and lease throughout northern and Western Australia.

His wife's sudden death in 1912 and Labor's decision to open a state-owned coal-mine confirmed Livingstone-Learmonth's decision not to continue a work-load which, though congenial, had left him 'utterly worn out and almost broken down'. He resigned on 31 March and moved his family to England. Directorships in the A.A. Co., Peel River Land & Mineral Co. and the Bank of Australasia strengthened his position as confidant to Charles Gibbs Hamilton, governor of the A.A. Co. in 1910-48 and son of E. W. T. Hamilton [q.v.4].

Livingstone-Learmonth died at Woking, Surrey, on 12 July 1945 and was buried in Brookside cemetery. He left an estate of £57 854 and was survived by two daughters.

R. Gollan, *The coalminers of New South Wales* (Melb, 1963); *Pastoral Review*, 16 May 1910, 15 Aug 1911, 16 Oct 1945; *The Times*, 14 July 1945; Blake to Gregson, 1 Apr, 12 June, 29 Nov 1902, 11 Feb, 5 Aug 1904, Gregson to Blake, 27 June 1903, 17 Feb, 13 Aug, 1, 15 Oct 1904, Learmonth to Blake, 25 Nov 1904, 10 Aug 1909, Learmonth to Hamilton, 5 June, 12 July, 17 Oct 1911, A.A. Co papers, (ANU Archives).   JOHN ATCHISON

LLOYD-JONES, SIR CHARLES; *see* JONES, SIR CHARLES LLOYD

LOCKE, HELENA SUMNER (1881-1917), author, was born on 4 July 1881 at Sandgate, near Brisbane, sixth daughter of Rev. William Locke, Anglican clergyman, and his wife Annie, née Seddon, both English born. Brought up in Melbourne from 1888 and probably educated at home, Sumner showed early promise as a writer and had stories accepted by such journals as the *Bulletin* and the *Native Companion* before the Melbourne production of her play, *The vicissitudes of Vivienne*, in 1908; it was followed a year later by the Sydney production of a one-act play, *A martyr to principle*, written with Stanley McKay. Sumner Locke's reputation was consolidated with the publication in 1911 of her collection of humorous interconnected stories, *Mum Dawson, 'Boss'*. The setting is a selection presided over by the sardonic matri-

arch Mum Dawson who battles, in the manner of 'Steele Rudd's' [q.v.8 A. H. Davis] Dad, to prosper on a small farm and maintain control over her husband and unruly children. Bert Bailey [q.v.7] produced it for the stage in 1917. The book was a New South Wales Bookstall Co. popular success and was followed by two further selection volumes, *The Dawsons' Uncle George* (1912) and *Skeeter Farm takes a spell* (1915), illustrated by Lionel Lindsay [q.v.].

In 1912 Sumner Locke left for England, where she worked as a freelance journalist and short story writer. She returned to nurse her mother through her last illness in 1915, and next year published *Samaritan Mary*, a novel set in the United States of America and focused on a kindly countrywoman; favourably reviewed in America, it confirmed Locke's ability to capture humorously the idioms of rural folk. On 23 December 1916 in Sydney she married Henry Logan Elliott, an accountant who had joined the Australian Imperial Force. She travelled to America next year, visiting New Mexico and Boston, but as the Atlantic was closed to civilians, returned to Sydney. She died there on 18 October 1917 of eclampsia the day after the birth of her son, and was buried in the Anglican section of Woronora cemetery. Short and slight of stature, she was warmly remembered for her humour, energy and vivaciousness.

One of her mourners reputedly said, 'I hope the son will be worth the sacrifice'; he was the playwright and novelist Sumner Locke Elliott. His novel, *Careful, he might hear you* (London and New York, 1963), is dedicated to 'H.S.L.'; as Sinden Marriott, 'Dear One', Sumner Locke is an important presence. Other characters are based on her sisters: Lilian largely brought up her nephew after a custody fight over his guardianship with her younger sister Jessie; and Blanche, an actress and singer, was the model for Shasta in Locke Elliott's *Water under the bridge* (New York, 1977). *In memoriam Sumner Locke* (1921) contains tributes from some of her contemporaries, including Randolph Bedford, Mary Grant Bruce [qq.v.7] and Vance Palmer [q.v.].

Her eldest sister LILIAN SOPHIA (1869-1950) was born on 6 June 1869 in Melbourne. A socialist and friend of Vida Goldstein [q.v.9], she was secretary of the United Council for Woman's Suffrage in the 1890s and, later, organizing secretary of the Political Labor Council of Victoria. An 'excellent platform speaker', she campaigned in Victoria, South Australia and Tasmania and wrote for the *Tocsin*. The 'only lady member' of the Trades Hall Council, Melbourne, she was a Tasmanian delegate at the 1905 Commonwealth Political Labor Conference. She also wrote verse. At Christ Church, South Yarra, on 6 January 1906 Lilian Locke married George Mason Burns (1869-1932), member of the Tasmanian House of Assembly in 1903-06 and of the House of Representatives for Illawarra in 1913-17. They worked as industrial organizers in Queensland until 1910 before returning to New South Wales. She died childless at North Sydney on 1 July 1950 and was cremated with Christian Science forms.

A'sian Typographical J, 1 Dec 1905, p 11, 1 Jan 1906, p 11; *Everylady's J*, 6 Jan 1915, p 58; *Aust Home Beautiful*, 1 Apr 1935, p 52; *Weekly Times* (Melb), 15 July 1905; *Tocsin*, 21 Dec 1905; *Shoalhaven News*, 2 Apr 1908; *Punch* (Melb), 25 Apr 1912; *New York Times*, 16 Apr 1916; *Sun* (Syd), 21 Oct 1917; *Bulletin* (Syd), 25 Oct, 1 Nov 1917; *Age*, 19 Oct 1917; Sumner Locke papers *and* Lilian Locke Burns, Newspaper cuttings (ML).

B. G. ANDREWS

LOCKINGTON, WILLIAM JOSEPH (1871-1948), Jesuit priest, was born on 23 February 1871 at Ross, New Zealand, eldest of eight children of Elisha Lockington, carpenter and later sawmiller from Derbyshire, England, and his wife Mary, née Canfield. Elisha had migrated to the Beechworth, Victoria, goldfields in the 1850s, moving to Ross in 1862; Mary, a milliner, had arrived in New Zealand from England in 1868.

After primary education at the Convent of Mercy, Hokitika, William at 14 became a pupil-teacher at Ross and at 18 head-teacher of the public school at Capleston; his wide reading and retentive memory, talent for music and passion for physical exercise made him a highly esteemed schoolmaster. He was also a well-known racing cyclist. On 2 June 1896 he entered the novitiate of the Society of Jesus at Greenwich, Sydney, where Aloysius Sturzo, the former superior of the Australian Jesuit communities and then master of novices, disseminated a feeling for internationalism and concern for the poor. Lockington subsequently studied at Tullamore, King's County, Ireland, in Jersey, Channel Islands, and at Stonyhurst College, Lancashire, England. He taught at The Crescent College, Limerick, Ireland, in 1902-07 and undertook his tertianship at Milltown Park, Dublin, and Poughkeepsie, New York. Ordained in July 1910, he returned to Ireland to assist at Milltown Park in the training of novices and tertians in 1911-13. A course of his lectures, published in 1913 as *Bodily health and spiritual vigour* and reprinted and translated several times, illustrates his continued emphasis on physical fitness. His admiration for Ireland resulted in his book, *The soul of Ireland* (1919).

Recalled to Australia in 1913, Lockington worked as parish priest at Richmond, Melbourne, until his appointment in 1916 as rector of St Patrick's College, East Melbourne. In 1917-23 he was superior of the eleven Australian Jesuit communities; in addition to overseeing four secondary colleges, one seminary and six parishes, he helped to establish Newman College at the University of Melbourne and a seminary at Werribee, Corpus Christi College, for the training of priests from three States.

During this period in Victoria, Lockington gained a reputation as controversialist in the tradition of William Kelly [q.v.5]. This partly sprang from his association with Archbishop Mannix [q.v.] whom he drilled in oratory, requiring him to practise declaiming from one end of the cathedral grounds to the other. Lockington was described by a colleague as 'the best platform orator in Australia'. His topics covered religion, temperance, education and the plight of working people; many of his addresses were published. He worked hard to further the growth of the Australian Catholic Federation and was regarded by the Protestant press as a principal in the 1917 anti-conscriptionist 'Jesuit scare'. In 1916 he founded the Catholic Women's Social Guild (later, Catholic Women's League). With Mannix presiding, he was a key speaker in the federation's mid-1917 lecture series which drew a Melbourne audience of thousands; his accusations of sweated labour in confectioners' establishments occasioned debate in the Legislative Assembly. In 1921 the town of Lockington was named after 'the noted author, preacher and lecturer'. His most famous panegyric was yet to come—that for Marshal Foch at St Mary's Cathedral, Sydney, in April 1929.

Lockington was headmaster of St Ignatius' College, Riverview, Sydney, in 1923-32. Despite the Depression, he resumed a massive building programme, halted since 1901, to complete the main features of the college. He promoted religious music, drama and physical vigour; open-air dormitories bear his stamp. After 1932 he undertook parish duties at Toowong, Brisbane, until 1936 and at Richmond and Hawthorn, Melbourne, until 1947. He was a committee-member of the Catholic Broadcasting Co. and, particularly on Archbishop Duhig's [q.v.8] urgings, gave numerous retreats and lectures.

On his way to one such retreat, Lockington died in Brisbane on 10 October 1948. One of the best-known Catholic priests in Australia, and to Mannix 'the friend of half a lifetime', he was buried in Nudgee cemetery.

U. M. L. Bygott, *With pen and tongue* (Melb, 1980); *Jesuit Life*, no 7, Dec 1981; Lockington papers (Society of Jesus Provincial Archives, Hawthorn, Melb).

G. J. O'KELLY

LOCKWOOD, ALFRED WRIGHT (1867-1956), journalist and newspaper proprietor, was born on 9 December 1867 at Lancefield, Victoria, second son of Matthew Lockwood (d. 1870), farmer, and his Scottish-born wife Ellen, née Kelly. His paternal grandfather, a Chartist, had brought his family to Victoria from Yorkshire, England, in the early 1850s.

Alfred left school at 13 for an apprenticeship at the *Lancefield Mercury*, but poor wages soon induced him to become a 'tramp printer'. Walking from town to town, he worked for newspapers in north-eastern Victoria until he had saved enough to return to Lancefield and buy a half-share in the *Mercury*. He sold this interest in 1899 and purchased the Natimuk *West Wimmera Mail* preparatory to his marriage on 25 August 1900 at St Alban's Anglican Church, Elaine, to Alice Ellen Francis. His wife, a former scholarship student and contemporary of E. F. (Henry Handel) Richardson [q.v.] at Presbyterian Ladies' College, Melbourne, was by 1900 schoolteacher, musician and temperance campaigner. It was she who provided the talent and drive to extend the Lockwood newspaper interests, temporarily, to Edenhope, Kaniva and Bordertown; her sisters, brother and niece worked with her in the printery which, until the late 1930s, was operated entirely with manual machinery.

The four-page, weekly *Mail*, popular and respected, carried leading reports of district social and sporting events. Lockwood was conservative and humane, concerned with the well-being of the west-Wimmera settlers rather than with money-making. He was largely responsible for the monument near Arapiles raised to the memory of Jane Duff, the child who in 1864 saved the lives of two brothers when they were lost for nine days in the bush; he influenced the change of name of the nearby rail station from Nurcoung to Duffholme. The paper also featured Lockwood's pointed denunciations of wrongdoers—town larrikins, 'flappers', 'shirkers' and 'socialists'. After Alice's death in 1913, however, the business was plunged into a financial chaos relieved only by Lockwood's marriage on 15 March 1916 to another 'good manager', Ida Dorothea Klowss. The marriage attracted some wartime anti-German sentiment despite the jingoism of the *Mail* and Ida's local birth.

Post-war competition from city newspapers and the 1930s Depression decimated rural publications. The *Mail* survived mostly because of family devotion. Lockwood's daughter and three sons from his first marriage all learned to set type and operate the job-printing plant by the age of 10. His second family of three sons continued the tradition of unpaid labour, the two younger taking over the paper on Lockwood's retirement in 1950; in 1959 a merger with the *Horsham Times* formed the *Wimmera Mail-Times*.

Lockwood served on many Natimuk committees; he enjoyed gardening, bowls and the excitement of trips to Melbourne, Sydney and Darwin. He died in Sydney on 13 September 1956, survived by his seven children, and was buried in Natimuk cemetery. Four of his sons, including Rupert who reported the Spanish Civil War and was for long a leading propagandist for the Australian Communist Party, became journalists; the eldest son Surgeon Rear Admiral Lionel was medical director-general of the Royal Australian Navy in 1955-64; Douglas (1918-1980) was a historian of the Northern Territory and author on Aboriginal affairs.

D. Lockwood, *Alfred Wright Lockwood* (Horsham, 1976); *West Wimmera Mail*, 18 Sept 1956; family information.   ALLAN W. LOCKWOOD
RUPERT LOCKWOOD

LOCKWOOD, JOSEPH (1862-1955), storekeeper and local politician, was born on 17 June 1862 at Whittlesea, Victoria, son of William Henry Lockwood, wheelwright, and his wife Naomi, née Bullock, both from England. Educated at Whittlesea, Lockwood engaged in storekeeping there for about six years and for one year in South Gippsland, where, however, conditions did not please him. In 1888 he turned to the Mallee, recently opened to selection, and bought a store at the junction of five roads at Birchip.

In 1890 Lockwood became first president of the Birchip Progress Association and in 1895 when the Shire of Birchip was inaugurated he became a councillor. Over the next sixty years he missed only four meetings and acted as president for seven terms: a world record for length of service was claimed. It was said that he 'had a beaten track to the offices of the Public Works Department in his efforts to get help for the Birchip Shire'. He was president of the North-Western Shires and Boroughs' Association of Victoria for twenty years and represented it as an executive member of the Municipal Association of Victoria for eighteen years.

Lockwood held an impressive array of local public offices. He was a guarantor of the railway, chairman of the water works trust, president of the agricultural and pastoral society and the mechanics' institute, and lifetime member of the public hall committee. Other roles such as justice of the peace (from 1889) and deputy coroner reinforced his authority. As treasurer of the Methodist Church Trust, a keen Rechabite, a member of the Masonic Lodge and the Australian

Natives' Association, he was the epitome of the nineteenth-century founding father. On 17 June 1897 at Ballarat with Wesleyan forms he married Agnes Blyth (d. 1919); they had four children.

At times, during drought or depression, Lockwood's domination of Birchip public life was challenged, especially in the 1930s when the council came under criticism for its mishandling of relief. However, his credit as 'the grand old man' carried the day and remained the basis of his appeal to ratepayers after the demands of the post World War II period had outstripped his original vision.

The tendency to identify the story of Joseph Lockwood with the story of Birchip and the Mallee is valid. As a storekeeper his fortunes were linked closely to the farming community and as a councillor his interpretation of the district's needs was central to its development. In his paper-strewn office or out in front of his store, the short, sturdy figure of 'Uncle Joe' with his white beard and pipe in hand appeared a symbol of probity and perseverance.

In 1945 Lockwood was appointed O.B.E. and was presented to Queen Elizabeth during her visit in 1954. He died at Birchip on 17 July 1955 and was buried in the local cemetery. His estate, valued for probate at £20 379, was divided between his two daughters, his surviving son and his grandchildren.

J. Smith (ed), *Cyclopedia of Victoria*, 3 (Melb, 1905); J. E. Senyard, *Birchip—essays on a shire* (Birchip, 1970); *Herald* (Melb), 28 Mar 1940.

J. E. SENYARD

LOCKYER, SIR NICHOLAS COLSTON (1855-1933), public servant, was born on 6 October 1855 at Woolloomooloo, Sydney, son of Edmund Lockyer [q.v.2] and his wife Eliza, née Colston. He was educated at Fort Street Model School and the Lyceum Academy, Sydney. When 13 he joined the civil service as a cadet and in 1870 was appointed clerk to the Treasury Department of New South Wales, where he came under the influence of (Sir) George Reid [q.v.]. In September-November 1883 he was an inspector of public revenue accounts, in December he was appointed receiver of revenue and in 1886 accountant to the Treasury. He was responsible for the reorganization of the taxation department under the Land and Income Tax Assessment Act of 1895. In 1896 he was appointed to the combined positions of collector of customs and first commissioner of taxation in New South Wales. On 22 January 1885 he had married Mary Juliet, daughter of Geoffrey Eagar [q.v.4]; she died in 1898. On 30 October 1901

he married Winifred, daughter of (Sir) Harry Wollaston [q.v.].

After Federation Lockyer transferred to the Commonwealth Public Service and in 1908 was appointed assistant comptroller-general of customs. He was by now an impressive, disciplined figure who, despite pince-nez and drawling accent, was credited with the 'penetrating power of a hundred-ton gun'. Together with C. C. Kingston [q.v.9] and Wollaston he had been responsible for framing the first Federal customs tariff. When Wollaston retired, Lockyer became comptroller-general in 1911. In 1913-20 he was a member of the Inter-State Commission empowered to monitor the commerce provisions of the Constitution. He had previously prepared reports on the meat and butter and pearling industries.

During six months furlough in 1916 Lockyer, with the honorary rank of major, was honorary comptroller of the Australian Imperial Force's garrison institutes in Australia, troopship canteens and prisoner-of-war canteens. From 1917, as first controller of repatriation, he was largely responsible for the organization of the Repatriation Department. In 1920-33 he was chairman of the A.I.F. Canteens Funds Trust and of the Sir Samuel McCaughey [q.v.5] Bequest for the education of soldiers' children.

In 1919 the Inter-State commissioners, whose powers had been invalidated by the High Court of Australia, were appointed members of a royal commission on the sugar industry. Lockyer retired from the public service in 1920. In 1926 he was appointed special representative of the Commonwealth government to inquire into the financial position of Tasmania. His candid report, described by the Launceston *Examiner* as 'packed with commonsense' and by the Hobart *Mercury* as 'hopelessly futile', revealed the serious condition of Tasmania's finances and the urgent need for assistance from the Commonwealth. In 1929-31 Lockyer was a Commonwealth representative on the board of Commonwealth Oil Refineries.

He was appointed I.S.O. (1906) and C.B.E. (1918) and was knighted in 1926. In his youth he had been a leading oarsman and shark-hunter. (Sir) Ernest Scott [q.v.] remembered 'a lithe, vigorous athletic man' who had spent one holiday cycling through the inhospitable Moreton Bay country explored by his father. Lockyer died after a long illness on 26 August 1933 at his home at Toorak, Melbourne, and was cremated. His wife, their son and two daughters of his first marriage survived him.

PP (Cwlth), 1914-17, 2, p 7, 356, 1923-24, 4, p 4, 1932-34, 4, p 182; *SMH*, 30 Jan 1885, 28 Dec 1896, 21 Sept 1933; *Australasian*, 18 Jan, 2 Nov

1901; *Argus*, 13 Aug 1913, 8 Feb 1926, 28 Aug 1933; *Brisbane Courier*, 28 Feb 1919; *Examiner* (Launc), 20, 21 Apr 1926; *Mercury*, 20 Apr 1926.   D. I. McDONALD

LODEWYCKX, AUGUSTIN (1876-1964), scholar, was born on 8 December 1876 at Booischot, Belgium, son of Joannes Lodewijckx, farmer, and his wife Maria Dymphna, née Maes. After completing his secondary education at Antwerp he studied Germanic languages, French and philology in 1897-1902 at the University of Ghent where he became deeply involved in the Flemish movement; in 1902 his doctoral thesis on the Austrian playwright Grillparzer was awarded the coveted gold medal by King Leopold II. Lodewyckx then pursued postgraduate studies at the University of Leyden, including work on the great Dutch dictionary, *Woordenboek der Nederlandsche Taal*.

In 1905-10 Lodewyckx was professor of French and German at Victoria College, Stellenbosch, South Africa. On 24 January 1910 at Simonstown he married Anna Sophia Hansen. Next year he was appointed to the Belgian colonial service in the Congolese province of Katanga, where he organized the settlement of Belgian colonists and established a system of education for children of European settlers. Concern about the adverse effect of the climate on his family prompted him to seek employment in the United States of America, sailing via Australia, in 1914. Stranded in Melbourne on the outbreak of World War I, he was advised by the Belgian consul to remain. His knowledge of European languages was utilized by the wartime censorship office and, after a year as modern language master at Melbourne Church of England Grammar School in 1915, he was appointed lecturer in German at the University of Melbourne when his predecessor, a German national, was dismissed because of wartime prejudice.

Building up his department with diligence and zeal, Lodewyckx was appointed associate professor in 1922. He soon gathered an enthusiastic German reading circle (*der Deutsche Leseverein*), a group which fulfilled a need among the German-speaking community and Australians who had learned German. But his aim was to expand his department to cover the whole Germanic field. In 1918 he was appointed instructor in Dutch in the university's continuing education programme. Eventually, urged by his own students of German and by newly arrived refugees from the Netherlands East Indies, he introduced Dutch as a university subject in 1942, writing and producing his own material

because textbooks were not available. In 1944 he published a Dutch grammar and in 1946 a literary history for his students.

Iceland's language and civilization became one of Lodewyckx's interests. Having mastered modern and ancient Icelandic, he visited the country in 1931 and again in 1937-38. In 1944 he introduced Old Icelandic as a university subject and continued to teach it at home after his retirement in 1947. In 1958 with his wife he founded the Anna Lodewyckx scholarship to enable Australian students to study in Iceland. He also donated the initial finance in 1960 for the teaching of Swedish at the university.

The time Lodewyckx spent at the University of Melbourne marked a turning point in the approach to modern languages, which hitherto had been taught as dead classical languages. As teacher and scholar he represented the European tradition of strict intellectual exactitude and with his distinguished colleague A. R. Chisholm he raised the intellectual and cultural standards of his discipline. Chisholm wrote that Lodewyckx was 'a born explorer, who wandered far afield in both the literal and metaphorical sense'; in so doing he inspired generations of students.

Lodewyckx's interests were broad and deep. They focused on philology and the history of Germanic languages within the Indo-European group and on demography and patterns of culture. His first book (1911) was a detailed study of geographical conditions in central and southern Africa. His book on Germans in Australia (1932) was the first standard work in the field and set the pattern for later research. Shortly before his eightieth birthday he published *People for Australia: a study in population problems* (1956), a book highly commended by A. A. Calwell, architect of Australia's post-war immigration programme. Altogether he published fourteen books and innumerable articles in five languages. He was decorated by the governments of Iceland (1937), The Netherlands (1952), Sweden (1963) and Belgium (1964) and in 1955 received a gold medal from the Goethe Institute in Germany.

Lodewyckx died at his Mont Albert home on 4 September 1964. He was survived by his wife, son Karel Axel, librarian of the University of Melbourne, and daughter Hilma Dymphna, translator, editor and wife of Manning Clark, historian.

A. R. Chisholm, *Men were my milestones* (Melb, 1958), and *The familiar presence, and other reminiscences* (Melb, 1966); K. A. Lodewycks, *The funding of wisdom* (Melb, 1982); *Univ Melb Gazette*, Dec 1951, p 96, Nov 1964, p 5; *AUMLA*, 5 (1956), p 4; *Skírnir*, 141 (1967), p 60; *Vlaanderen in de wereld*, 2 (1974), p 425; *Viw-Nieuws*, 25 (May-July 1977), p 4.   JOHN STANLEY MARTIN

LOFTUS-HILLS, CLIVE (1885-1967), geologist, was born on 31 March 1885 at Deloraine, Tasmania, and registered as Loftus, son of James Hills, builder, and his wife Mary, née Smith. He was educated at Launceston Church Grammar School and the University of Tasmania (B.Sc., 1907; M.Sc., 1913). In 1907-12 while a chemist, assayer and metallurgist in Launceston he was also a part-time lecturer in geology and briefly head of the mining branch of the government technical school. On 12 February 1908 he married Jessie Adelaide Dean, daughter of a Launceston stockbroker and former mayor. As assistant government geologist with the Geological Survey of Tasmania in 1912-15 he worked on mining fields including Read-Rosebery and published significant contributions to knowledge of the areas. His work on the stratigraphy structure and mineralogy of the Read-Rosebery zinc-lead ores formed the basis for their mining and treatment.

In January 1916 Hills joined the Australian Imperial Force and in May embarked as lieutenant with the 4th Australian Tunnelling Company. He transferred in France to the 1st Tunnelling Company and was appointed M.B.E. in 1919.

In 1919-23 as government geologist and director of the Geological Survey, Tasmania, Hills had much to do with the comprehensive survey of the State's coal resources. During this period he attracted criticism and encountered problems created by the clumsy administrative structure of the Department of Mines (later restructured). His discountenancing of exploration for crude oil brought him under public attack by his minister E. F. B. Blyth, director of a company involved in the venture. Though a public service commissioner's inquiry into Hills's suitability to administer the Geological Survey found in his favour, the commissioner received hostile representations from the staff of the Department of Mines. The post of director of the Geological Survey was abolished and Hills was subordinated to a non-technical departmental head, the secretary of mines. Hills resigned.

In 1924 he received the first science doctorate awarded by the University of Tasmania, and the David Syme [q.v.6] prize, University of Melbourne, for original scientific work. In 1923-37 he was a consultant geologist and occasional broadcaster. Mineral exploration took him to the Fiji goldfields and various parts of Australia. In 1938-46 he was chemist and chief chemist, Commonwealth Department of Supply, in New South Wales, Victoria and South Australia, and worked on munitions production during World War II. In this period he altered his name to Clive Loftus-Hills.

After the war he returned to Tasmania and took up mineral exploration in the west where he had made a major impact on mining in the Zeehan and Renison Bell fields; his work now led to further activity there. His estimates of ore reserves in the Read-Rosebery and Fijian goldfields, once ridiculed in the contemporary mining press as excessive, have been proved conservative. In 1946-65 Loftus-Hills was active as a consultant geologist and mining entrepreneur. He stood successfully for the Hobart City Council in 1950 and served on a number of committees. 'Of good address and physique', he was noted for his stamina, climbing Mounts Darwin and South Darwin in western Tasmania in his sixties. About 1950 he was received into the Catholic Church. He died on 13 December 1967 in Melbourne and was buried in Springvale cemetery. His wife and two sons survived him.

Loftus-Hills was a thorough, accurate, imaginative geologist who suffered at times for his integrity. He suffered also for seeming over-ambitious and would have made a greater contribution had he been more tolerant. Nevertheless he greatly advanced knowledge of the ore deposits of Tasmania.

Mercury, 16 Dec 1967; C. Loftus-Hills file (H1/144), MIN 21/2, 22/1, 23/1, 24/1 (TA); family papers held by Dr G. D. Loftus-Hills, Montmorency, Melb.   MAXWELL R. BANKS

LONERGAN, JOHN JOSEPH (1888-1938), Catholic clergyman, was born on 22 March 1888 at South Melbourne, only son of Michael Lonergan, driver, and his wife Norah, née Tobin. He was educated at the local Catholic primary school run by the Loreto Sisters, then at St Patrick's, East Melbourne, and St Patrick's College, Manly, Sydney. After ordination in November 1911, Lonergan was appointed assistant priest at Gisborne, a small town within the archdiocese of Melbourne. His first post as parish priest was at Drysdale, an even smaller rural district.

Appointed to the staff of St Patrick's Cathedral, Melbourne, in 1916, Lonergan became diocesan inspector of religious instruction in schools and, in 1924, administrator and chancellor of the archdiocese and private secretary to Archbishop Daniel Mannix [q.v.]. During Mannix's absence in the pilgrimage year of 1925, he took charge of the archdiocese. Unlike his flamboyant archbishop, Lonergan worked unobtrusively from the cathedral on a wide range of administrative tasks. He served as chairman of the tribunal for matrimonial causes and acted as spiritual director to all the main associations of Catholic Melbourne, from the Catholic Young Men's Society to the Society of St Vincent de Paul. He sat on the board of the Catholic *Trib-*

une newspaper and administered property trusts and insurance for the archdiocese. Much of the responsibility for the organization of the International Eucharistic Congress in Sydney in 1928 fell to him and earned him, with the other members of the consulting council, the rank of monsignor. Next year he was created a domestic prelate to the pope, and in 1934 was attached to the suite of the visiting papal legate, Cardinal McRory. He was prominent in the eucharistic congresses in Melbourne (1934) and Adelaide (1936).

In January 1938 Lonergan was appointed bishop elect to the diocese of Port Augusta, South Australia. But he did not live to take up his post. After a long illness he died of hypertensive heart failure on 14 July 1938 at the Convent of the Good Shepherd, Oakleigh, Melbourne. He was buried in Melbourne general cemetery after solemn office and pontifical requiem Mass at St Patrick's Cathedral.

An eloquent preacher and platform speaker, Lonergan from an early age seemed destined for leadership within the Catholic community. Respected for his 'unvarying courtesy and genial disposition', he was described by the *Age* at the time of his elevation as 'the most popular clergyman of . . . the archdiocese'. He did much to extend personal friendship to Protestants in Melbourne and to help to assuage some of the bitter animosities of the war years. He cut a fine figure in a slowly growing band of Catholic clergymen born in Australian working-class parishes, educated at Manly and sent out to minister to flocks still accustomed to Irish clergymen.

Sun-News Pictorial, 13 Dec 1934, 15 July 1938; *Age*, 18 Jan 1938; *Argus* and *SMH*, 18 Jan, 15 July 1938; *Advocate* (Melb), 21 July 1938.

CHRIS MCCONVILLE

LONG, CHARLES RICHARD (1860-1944), educationist, was born on 31 August 1860 at Wallan Wallan, Victoria, son of Henry Samuel Long and his wife Sarah, née Sayers, who had both migrated from England in 1857. After mining ventures failed, the Longs settled at Alexandra where Henry owned a shoemaking shop and set his son an example of active work in organizations such as the Freemasons, Oddfellows, Orangemen, dramatic and debating clubs, the local council and mechanics' institute. Recognizing his addiction to alcohol, Henry became a Rechabite as, in time, did Charles, though without his father's motivation.

Despite shyness, poor sight and acute self-consciousness as an albino, Charles successfully completed a pupil-teachership, begun on 1 February 1877. In August 1880 a nervous, naive but ambitious country-boy, he entered the Training Institution in Melbourne where

F. J. Gladman [q.v.4] was preparing an impressive group of young teachers to work for the reform of Victorian education. He completed the course by July 1881 with very high marks and taught for the next nine years, mainly at State School 1567, Richmond. Here he met Louisa Catherine, daughter of Louis Michel [q.v.5]. They married at North Carlton on 19 April 1886 and when she died in 1905 they had had eight children. While at Richmond Long graduated B.A. (1887) and M.A. (1889) from the University of Melbourne and, with colleagues such as Frank Tate [q.v.], attempted to improve teachers' salaries and to remedy defects in Victorian state education.

In 1890 Long was appointed an inspector of schools and next year began lecturing at the Training College. In this work and outside the college, he endeavoured to introduce some of the educational ideas and practices becoming popular in Britain; but, despite his earnestness, he had made little progress when in 1893 government retrenchments closed the college and Long had to take work lecturing to pupil-teachers.

In 1895 dissatisfaction with the *Royal readers* used in elementary schools prompted the preparation of a monthly *School Paper* similar to the *Children's Hour* established in South Australia by J. A. Hartley [q.v.4]. Long was given editorial responsibility. The first issue appeared in 1896 and from then until its replacement in 1929 by the *Victorian Readers* the *School Paper* was the official reading material in schools; and for long after 1929 it was used as supplementary reading material. Long was also foundation editor of the official *Education Gazette and Teachers' Aid*, first published in 1900. His own numerous works ranged from pamphlets on educational method to a jointly written history of Victorian state education (1922). He prepared many textbooks and, as the titles of two of them, *Stories of Australian exploration* (1903) and *British worthies and other men of might* (1912), suggest, he combined an ardent love of Britain (which, during the South African War and World War I, lent a lurid jingoism to the *School Paper*) with a strong Australian nationalism.

Long was a member of Theodore Fink's [q.v.8] royal commission on technical education (1899-1901), and though disturbed by its attacks on some senior officers of the Education Department, he supported many of its suggestions for reform. He lectured for University Extension, was a member of the Shakespeare Society and a foundation member of both the (Royal) Historical Society of Victoria and the Australian Literature Society; he also helped to popularize the work of Adam Lindsay Gordon [q.v.4]. Until 1921 his editorial work was combined with some ordinary inspectorial duties, and though these often proved irksome they enabled him to meet another teacher, Margaret Ellen Willard, whom he married on 16 December 1908 at St Jude's Church, Carlton, and by whom he had a son and daughter.

After his retirement from the Education Department in 1925, Long was asked to return to work on the *Victorian Readers*, which he did from 1 January 1927 until 30 June 1928. His second retirement left him free to work even more actively for the Church of England, of which he was a fervent member, and for other societies and groups. He died at Frankston on 14 December 1944, survived by all but one of his children, and was buried in Frankston cemetery. Through his publications Long offered Victoria's school-children a moral vision suffused with incipient Australian nationalism, an unwavering faith in the superiority of British ways and the middle-class values of thrift, industriousness, honesty, decent ambition and respect for the social order—all of which he adhered to in his own life.

E. L. French (ed), *Melbourne studies in education 1963* (Melb, 1964); Education Dept (Vic), *Vision and realisation*, L. J. Blake ed (Melb, 1973); *Education Gazette and Teachers' Aid*, 20 Feb 1926, 27 Jan 1945; *VHM*, 21 (1945), no 1; Education Dept (Vic), Records (History section, Education Dept, Melb).   R. J. W. SELLECK

LONG, CLARENCE; *see* MILERUM

LONG, GEORGE MERRICK (1874-1930), Anglican bishop and educationist, was born on 5 November 1874 at Carisbrook, Victoria, youngest son of English parents William Long, grocer, and his wife Eliza, née Merrick. On leaving Maryborough Grammar School he entered the local branch of the City of Melbourne Bank. He was encouraged to matriculate by his vicar, Canon Charles Harris, who also instructed him in public speaking and persuaded Archbishop Goe [q.v.9] to offer him the Rupertswood theological studentship at Trinity College, University of Melbourne (B.A., 1899; M.A., 1901). In 1897, after gaining first-class honours in inductive logic and mental philosophy, he was awarded a Hastie exhibition and the Trinity College Dialectic Society's medal for oratory. Long was made deacon on 28 May 1899 and priested on 10 June 1900. From 1899 he had charge of the district of Foster in Gippsland where the church and rectory had recently been destroyed by a bushfire. At Maryborough on 4 July 1900 he married Felecie Alexandra, daughter of Alfred Joyce [q.v.2].

Long returned to Melbourne as senior curate to Archdeacon Hindley [q.v.9] at Holy Trinity Church, Kew. Here he suggested the foundation of a boys' school despite opposition from the council of Melbourne Church of England Grammar School; after twelve months as a preparatory school, Trinity Grammar School accepted boys of all ages and Long became headmaster in 1904. He adopted a modern curriculum and exercised that 'mysterious gift of personality which excites the personal devotion and enthusiasm of the boys. He had dignity without stiffness, and a very approachable friendliness of manner without familiarity'. An outstanding headmaster, he declined the wardenship of St John's Theological College, St Kilda, offers of important parishes and nomination for the headmastership of Geelong Church of England Grammar School. He served on several diocesan committees and in 1910 was made a canon of St Paul's Cathedral. When in May 1911 Long was elected to the see of Bathurst, New South Wales, he became one of the few Australian-born bishops. Consecrated on 30 November 1911 in St Andrew's Cathedral, Sydney, he immediately began revising antiquated diocesan finances and ordinances and was awarded a Lambeth D.D. in 1912.

In November 1917 Long enlisted in the Australian Imperial Force as a chaplain and honorary captain. He embarked for London in January and early in April went to the Australian Reinforcement Camp in France, where his abilities were recognized by Major General Sir Brudenell White [q.v.]. Transferred to Australian Corps Headquarters, he was promoted on 1 June honorary lieut-colonel and appointed director of education with the task of organizing professional, technical and general training (particularly in agriculture).

Returning to London in September Long and his small staff by Herculean efforts set up the administrative machinery. He secured the co-operation of British (and European) universities, professional, technical, commercial and industrial institutions and many other groups and individuals, such as the British Wool Buyers' Federation, a perfume manufacturer in France and Albert Mansbridge, founder of the Workers' Educational Association. Teaching within the divisions was hampered by lack of books and paper and the movement of the men, but after the Armistice 'non-military employment' was found for many. Some 12 880 soldiers and nurses completed courses of training or work-experience and many thousands more participated. In March Long's health broke under the strain. He was promoted brigadier general on 1 January 1919, awarded an honorary LL.D. by the universities of Cambridge (1918) and Manchester (1919) and appointed C.B.E. in 1919.

In July Long returned to his diocese, where he began to expand educational opportunities. He resuscitated All Saints' College, Bathurst, on a new site; in 1925 he opened Marsden School for Girls at Kelso; he encouraged the founding in large country towns of hostels for boys and girls from bush homes attending public high schools; he supported the re-establishment of St John's Theological College at Morpeth; and he promoted the training scheme of the Brotherhood of the Good Shepherd, Dubbo, which assisted men without means to enter the priesthood. In 1920 he began the rebuilding of his crumbling cathedral to a towering design by Louis Williams; the sanctuary, choir and warriors' chapel were consecrated in November 1927. In 1920 he had become foundation president of the national council of the Church of England Men's Society and, a Freemason, was grand chaplain of United Grand Lodge in 1923-26. With the help of (Sir) John Peden [q.v.], he drafted and cogently advocated a constitution for the Church of England in Australia independent of the Church in Britain; his draft, by 1928 ratified by every diocese except Sydney, became the basis of all subsequent versions. He favoured conservative revision of the Book of Common Prayer and deplored the 'paralysis of fear' besetting both those who wanted it retained and those who deemed Australian churchmen 'intellectually incompetent' in liturgical studies. A democrat and nationalist, he advocated the White Australia policy on grounds of racial purity and industrial harmony, and as politically expedient for a 'high-spirited people' in an 'active and mobile young democracy'.

In December 1927 Long was elected bishop of Newcastle and enthroned on 1 May 1928. He had a sensitive knowledge of economic and industrial issues and was popular with the mining unions on the Newcastle coalfields. He had retained his connexion with the Australian Military Forces and in 1929 was appointed chaplain-general. In March 1930 he sailed for England to attend the Lambeth Conference in London, but suffered a cerebral haemorrhage after its opening session and died on 9 July in St Thomas's Hospital. His requiem was celebrated by Archbishop Cosmo Lang before 300 bishops, and his ashes were brought back to New South Wales and placed in All Saints Cathedral, Bathurst. He was survived by his wife, three sons and three daughters; his eldest son Gavin Merrick (1901-1968) became official historian of World War II.

Tall and dignified, with smooth dark hair and regular features, Long was a fine athlete, cricketer and tennis-player when young. Although he was a High Churchman, but not an Anglo-Catholic, his charm and administrative gifts were recognized by all Anglicans. To C. E. W. Bean [q.v.7] he was 'one of the great Australians of his generation', whose outstanding work may well have been his contribution to the 'turning of the A.I.F.'s effort from destruction to construction'. St Christopher's chapel in Christ Church Cathedral, Newcastle, is his memorial, and a window of its Tyrrell [q.v.6] chapel contains his portrait.

Aust Church Congress, *Official Report* (Melb, 1925); W. H. Johnson, *The Right Reverend George Merrick Long* (Morpeth, NSW, 1930); C. E. W. Bean, *The A.I.F. in France*, 1918 (Syd, 1937); *Melb Univ Mag*, July 1920; *Syd Diocesan Mag*, 1 Aug 1930; *The Times*, 10 July 1930; *Church Times* (Lond), 11 July 1930; *Aust Church Review*, 17, 31 July 1930; *Church Standard*, 18 July 1930.

RUTH TEALE

LONG, RICHARD HOOPPELL (1873-1948), poet and carpenter, was born on 27 November 1873 at Tue Brook, Lancashire, England, son of Richard Long, engineer, and his wife Marian, née Hooppell. The family migrated to Australia in 1879. Largely self-educated, Long worked as a carpenter and cabinetmaker and also as a ship's joiner on the Australia-New Zealand run. Apart from a brief period in Sydney, he lived with his family, and after the death of his mother in 1913 and his father in 1919, with his sister, Minnie Isabel (Belle), at Sandringham, Melbourne. Neither brother nor sister married, though Long's legatee Eric Charles Haslem was treated 'as a son'.

Throughout his adult life Long wrote topical verse, prompted to do homage to Nature and to denounce capitalism by such particular matters as bee-keeping or what he saw as the outrageous resistance of that 'faithless shepherd', the bishop of London, to an early conclusion of World War I. Many of the poems appeared in the Melbourne *Socialist* and *Fellowship*. A collection, *Verses*, was published in 1917.

Long and his sister belonged to the Victorian Socialist Party and the Free Religious Fellowship. Long's literal-minded devotion to the 'brotherhood of Man' was such that he kept a coiled chain in his workshop above the familiar injunction to 'Workers of the World'. Characteristically, his religious faith was Independent: he refused to wear a collar at fellowship gatherings, as his forefathers, he said, had worn one inscribed with the legend 'Serf'.

In 1918 Long represented the fellowship at the Australian Peace Alliance Conference at Leura, New South Wales, (afterwards walking home to Melbourne) and his period of intense and somewhat perverse public agitation began in September that year. Although critical of the Bolshevik Revolution he flew the red flag of socialism on successive Sundays on the Yarra Bank in defiance of government proclamation. He was three times imprisoned for a total of eight months between December 1918 and December 1919. After these stubborn flourishes his political activities became more sedate. In 1925 he made his only trip to England when, with his sister, he attended the War Resisters' International Conference at Hoddesdon, Hertfordshire.

During the Depression Long was forced to supplement carpentry with day-labouring. He wrote verse steadily and indulged his favourite pastime of long bush excursions, treading 'the quiet, country roads of God'. Contemporaries (among them J. Le Gay Brereton [q.v.7], Bernard O'Dowd, Nettie Palmer and Percival Serle [qq.v.]) remembered him as gentle, versatile and candid. He was of medium height and build, with blue-grey eyes, round features and a heavy beard; in later life he was bald.

Belle died in 1947. Next year Long was knocked off his bicycle by a car and died of bleeding from a peptic ulcer on 19 July 1948 in Melbourne. He was cremated. Whether or not he was 'a spiritual kinsman of St Francis and Walt Whitman', as Sinclaire [q.v.] suggested, or the 'half-satirist, half-saint' recollected by Nettie Palmer, he was a poet of limited yet determined ambition, capable of felicity within his compass:

I have had dreams and visions, but distrust Imaginations that lack strength to bear Communion with the commonplace . . .

F. T. Macartney, *Australian literary essays* (Syd, 1957); *Landfall*, 29, no 1, Mar 1975; K. J. Kenafick, The life and work of R. H. Long, Australian poet *and* R. H. Long papers (LaTL).

PETER PIERCE

LONG, SYDNEY (1871-1955), painter and etcher, was born on 20 August 1871 at Ifield, Goulburn, New South Wales, posthumous fifth child of James Long, Irish commission agent, and his native-born wife Susan, née Fletcher. He was educated at Goulburn Boys' High School, and about 1888, the date of his first extant painting, moved to Sydney where he worked for some years at Sandeman's, wine and spirit merchants in George Street. From about 1890 he studied under A. J. Daplyn and Julian Ashton [qq.v.4,7] at the Art Society of New South Wales's school. When he first exhibited with the society in 1893 he was awarded second prize in the life class and in painting, and the president's prize. Next year his first major painting, 'By Tranquil Waters', a self-consciously Impressionist study of boys bathing at Cook's River,

attracted widespread, mostly favourable critical attention, and was purchased by the National Art Gallery of New South Wales.

Becoming a full-time painter, Long supplemented his income by teaching private pupils. When the Art Society split in 1895 and the Society of Artists, Sydney, was formed by Ashton, Tom Roberts, Arthur Streeton [qq.v.] and others, Long joined them and was elected to the council of the rebel group. He was a small man of almost elfish appearance, with brown hair and light blue eyes. After he became president of the Society of Artists in 1898 he wore a top hat, partly to emphasize his status but also to conceal his lack of height. He was active in the amalgamation of the two societies to form the Royal Art Society of New South Wales in 1903. However, when it split again in 1907, he rejoined the Society of Artists.

Long's mature work evolved into a decorative symbolist style, which owed more to the English Aesthetic movement than to the more European Art Nouveau. Most of his major works from this period are in public collections: 'Pan', 'Midday' and 'Flamingoes' (Art Gallery of New South Wales); 'Spirit of the Plains' (Queensland Art Gallery); and 'The Valley' (Art Gallery of South Australia). In 1898 he became engaged to fellow artist Thea Proctor [q.v.], but she broke the engagement after she went to Europe.

By the early 1900s Long was trying to save to undertake further study in England. From 1907 he was Ashton's second-in-command in the new Sydney Art School. He finally managed to leave Australia in 1910, reaching London in October. Although Long claimed to have married in 1911, he did not actually marry Catherine Brennan, a dancer, until 1 December 1924, at Lambeth. In 1911 he enrolled at an art school at Kennington and soon associated himself with the more conservative tendencies in British art. He visited France, Belgium and Holland in 1912, but remained firmly Anglocentric. One of the continuing problems of Long's London years was his lack of financial security. He had arranged for the Sydney dealer Adolph Albers to sell works on consignment. During World War I transport of these works became irregular as did payment, and he was often impoverished.

Long achieved minor success in England, exhibiting intermittently with the Royal Academy of Arts from 1913 to 1929, but he failed to obtain the recognition which he felt he deserved, especially compared with George Lambert [q.v.9]. In 1918 Long began to learn etching at the Central School of Arts and Crafts, Holborn. His quality of line and tone had a natural affinity with the medium and he rapidly became an accomplished etcher. In 1920 he was elected an associate of the Royal Society of Painter-Etchers and Engravers and was foundation honorary secretary of the Society of Graphic Art.

In 1921 Long returned to Australia for eighteen months, held successful exhibitions in Sydney and was a founding member of the Australian Painter-Etchers' Society (later president). In 1925 he returned with his wife to settle at Lane Cove, with a caravan at Narrabeen and a studio in George Street. His pupil Donald Friend remembered him as 'a very odd man indeed: envious, jealous, professionally and emotionally very timid: no close friends, only cronies. He yearned after the young, but discouraged actual friendliness. He was a debunker and "a knocker". Very lonely I think'.

From 1912 he had been sending works to the Royal Art Society and on his return continued to favour it and taught at its school. He was a trustee of the Art Gallery in 1933-49 and strongly opposed the foundation of the Australian Academy of Art.

Long remained one of Australia's leading etchers until the collapse of the etching boom in the mid-1930s, when he turned again to painting. In 1938 and 1941 he won the Wynne prize for landscape painting. His later years were characterized by hostility to younger *avant-garde* artists and bitterness towards more successful artists of his generation. Late in life he under-stated his age by seven years. In 1952 Long and his wife left for London where he died on 23 January 1955 and was buried in Streatham cemetery.

D. E. Paul (ed), *The etched work of Sydney Long* (Syd, 1928); J. Mendelssohn, *The life and work of Sydney Long* (Syd, 1979).

JOANNA MENDELSSOHN

LONGFORD, RAYMOND JOHN WALTER HOLLIS (1878-1959), actor and film director, was born on 23 September 1878 and named John Walter, at Hawthorn, Melbourne, second surviving son of John Walter Longford, Sydney-born civil servant, and his English wife Charlotte Maria, née Hollis. The family moved to Sydney in the 1880s, his father becoming a warder at Darlinghurst gaol. Educated at St John's Parochial School, Darlinghurst, as a youth Longford was apprenticed to sail and at 18 held a third mate's ticket. He gave his occupation as ablebodied seaman and had added Raymond to his names when he married Melena Louisa Keen at St Luke's Anglican Church, Concord, Sydney, on 5 February 1900. They had one child, a son born in August.

According to legend Longford's theatrical career began in India, where he acquired a working knowledge of Hindustani. He joined Edwin Geach's Popular Dramatic Organisation in the early 1900s and as Raymond Hollis Longford toured country towns in eastern Australia and New Zealand for some ten years with the Geach, and Clarke [q.v.7] and Meynell companies. He frequently played the villain but also more sympathetic roles in melodramas such as *Camille, Her love against the world, The midnight hour* and *The power of the Cross*. He distinguished himself as the patriotic hero Mr Brown in *An Englishman's home* in 1909. Tall, long-faced, brown-haired and clean-shaven, he had a commanding presence and a resonant voice.

Lottie Lyell's [q.v.] parents entrusted the young actress to Longford's care and they featured in several plays. The most successful was *The fatal wedding*, much noticed for its famous children's 'tin can band'. A romantic attachment developed between them; his marriage with Melena had failed but she did not divorce him until 1926.

In 1910 Longford left the stage to appear in two bushranging films released in 1911, *Captain Midnight* and *Captain Starlight*, and as the convict Gabbett in *The life of Rufus Dawes* (based on Marcus Clarke's [q.v.3] novel, *For the term of his natural life*), made by Alfred Rolfe for Cozens Spencer [q.v.]. That year Longford successfully directed *The fatal wedding*, in which he and Lyell starred, and was appointed director of production for Spencer's Pictures. He completed two more films in 1911, *The romantic story of Margaret Catchpole* and *Sweet Nell of Old Drury*, featuring Lottie Lyell and Nellie Stewart [q.v.] respectively. Next year he made two melodramas including *The midnight wedding*, shot by Ernest Higgins [q.v.9]. In 1913 Longford directed *Australia calls*, a patriotic film showing a 'Mongolian' attack on Sydney, filmed by Ernest, Tasman and Arthur Higgins [qq.v.9], and reflecting contemporary fears of the 'yellow peril'. Between shooting, he and E. Higgins made a valuable documentary, the *Naming of the Federal capital*, for Spencer.

Despite his successes Longford had to seek work elsewhere after Spencer's Pictures merged with other firms to form Australasian Films Ltd. Henceforth his career as a director was seldom untroubled, but between 1913 and 1921 he made sixteen feature films for various short-lived companies. *The silence of Dean Maitland* (1914), although popular, was beset by exhibition difficulties and litigation. Denied studio facilities in Sydney, he made *A Maori maid's love* (1915) and most of *The mutiny of the Bounty* (1916) in New Zealand, but found exhibition no easier there. *The church and the woman* (1917) was the subject of an unsuccessful copyright case, and *The woman suffers* (1918), shot in South Australia, was banned without explanation in New South Wales after running for two months. Longford had nevertheless entered upon his best period, creating a screen classic in *The sentimental bloke* (1919) and directing a less effective C. J. Dennis [q.v.8] adaptation, *Ginger Mick* (1920). Then followed the honest, if exaggerated, Steele Rudd [q.v.8 A. H. Davis] dramatizations, *On our selection* (1920) and *Rudd's new selection* (1921) for E. J. and Dan Carroll [qq.v.7].

Lottie Lyell, already consumptive, was Longford's co-director for *The Blue Mountains mystery* (1921). They formed their own companies, to make *The dinkum bloke* (1923), *Fisher's ghost* (1924) and *The bushwhackers* (1925). Their partnership ended with Lyell's death in December 1925. As a director, in his creative years Longford was notable for 'his calmness and openness with actors' and the length of time he took in production, especially in choosing his cast, the writing of scenarios, and long journeys for crews and casts for the most authentic backgrounds possible. His films were praised by critics for their 'human qualities' and his blending of 'melodrama with naturalism'.

In 1923 Longford had made two immigration films for the Commonwealth government for display at the British Empire Exhibition in London. He made one more film under the Longford-Lyell name, *Peter Vernon's silence* (1926), and was then engaged by Australasian Films to complete *Sunrise*. He also made two melodramas in the expectation that he would direct *For the term of his natural life* for Australasian Films. When an American, Norman Dawn, was appointed, Longford never recovered from the blow. For the next fifteen years his life in cinema was tenuous. He went abroad to learn the new sound technology but except for one poorly received 'talkie', *The man they could not hang* (1934), he never again directed. In the 1930s he helped to produce several sound movies and was forced to accept minor acting parts. He last appeared on the screen in 1941. On 19 July 1933 he had married a 28-year-old stenographer, Emilie Elizabeth Anschutz, at North Sydney.

Over the years Longford had led a bitter and unsuccessful fight by local producers to secure an effective quota system and fair distribution for Australian feature films. He alleged that he was persecuted by Australasian Films—'the combine'. In evidence to the 1927 royal commission on the moving picture industry he claimed that 'I have been, and still am the outstanding figure in the industry, I, mainly, have been made . . . the subject of attack by Australasian Films Ltd'. However, lacking business acumen, he was genuinely bewildered about his perennial difficulties in getting his films released.

During World War II Longford found employment as a tally-clerk on the Sydney wharves, and later as a watchman. On the waterfront he was noted for his care in dress-

ing and proud independence of the pension. He died at St Leonards on 2 April 1959, survived by his son and his second wife, who arranged his burial with Anglican rites in the same grave as Lottie Lyell in Northern Suburbs cemetery.

The discovery of a print of *The sentimental bloke* in 1958 prompted some belated understanding of Longford's work, but another decade passed before the extent of his contribution to the Australian film industry was generally recognized. The Australian Film Institute's Raymond Longford award is named in his honour.

A. Pike and R. F. Cooper, *Australian film 1900-1977* (Melb, 1980); J. Tulloch, *Legends on the screen* (Syd, 1981); Cwlth of Aust, *Royal commission on the moving picture industry in Australia: Minutes of evidence* (Canb, 1928), *and* Report, *PP* (Cwlth), 1926-28, 4, p 1371; Report of enquiry into the film industry in New South Wales 1934, *PP* (NSW), 1934-35, 3; R. F. Cooper, 'And the villain still pursued her'. Origins of film in Australia, 1896-1913 (M.A. thesis, ANU, 1971); archival films and excerpts and Longford records (National Film and Sound Archive, Canb).   MERVYN J. WASSON*

LONGMAN, ALBERT HEBER (1880-1954), newspaper publisher and museum director, was born on 24 June 1880 at Heytesbury, Wiltshire, England, son of Frederick Longman, a Congregational minister of liberal views, and his wife Susan, née Passmore. Educated at Emwell House, Warminster, he was encouraged in his leanings towards botany, geology and archaeology. Because of a chest weakness he came to Queensland in 1902 and settled at Toowoomba where, on 29 January 1904, he married Irene Maud [q.v.], daughter of Congregational minister James Molineux Bayley.

Heber Longman had bought the plant of a recently defunct newspaper and produced a news-sheet, the *Downs Post*. This lively publication attracted local support and businessmen formed a small company to produce a weekly paper, named the *Rag*, from November 1904. George Essex Evans [q.v.8] became editor, Longman sub-editor and manager until ill health caused Evans to withdraw; then Longman, as editor, renamed it the *Citizen*.

Keenly interested in the plant life of the district, Longman became an assiduous collector and initiated the Field Naturalists' Club at Toowoomba. After one of its members, Dr Ronald Hamlyn-Harris [q.v.9] of the Toowoomba Grammar School staff, had been appointed director of the Queensland Museum, Longman gladly accepted his invitation in 1911 to join the staff as a scientific assistant. Although lacking formal qualifications, Longman established a considerable reputation as a scientist over the next forty years. In 1917, when Hamlyn-Harris resigned, he was appointed acting director, then director on 24 April 1918. The museum channelled his interests around zoology. He did not entirely neglect plant science, but no longer undertook any detailed tasks of botanical taxonomy.

Most of Longman's publications—some seventy papers—appeared in the Queensland Museum *Memoirs*. While the animals and insects of Queensland were included in his researches, his contributions to vertebrate palaeontology established his reputation internationally. New genera described included dinosaurs, marine reptiles, fish and a marsupial. His book, *The religion of a naturalist* (London, 1911), expressed his emancipated position as an agnostic and foreshadowed his membership of philosophical and rationalist clubs and societies.

Shortage of funds and staff, particularly during World War II, resulted in overwork and Longman's increasing ill health. He retired from the museum in 1945. Described as courteous and kindly, he had distinguished himself as president of the Royal Society of Queensland (1919, 1939) and the Queensland Naturalists' Club, as vice-chairman of the Great Barrier Reef Committee, member of the Australian National Research Council, fellow of the Linnean Society of London and of the Royal Anthropological Institute of Great Britain and Ireland, and corresponding member of the Zoological Society of London. In 1946 he received the Australian Natural History medallion and in 1952 the coveted Mueller [q.v.5] medal.

For the last six years of his life, his urbane and unpretentious column 'Nature's ways' had a wide and devoted following in the *Courier Mail*. Heber Longman died at his home at Chelmer on 16 February 1954 and was cremated. Childless, he was survived by his wife.

Qld Naturalist, 15 (1954), no 1, 2; Qld Museum, *Memoirs*, 13 (Apr 1956), pt 2; Roy Soc Qld, *Procs*, 42 (1957), no 7; State Government Insurance Office, *Insurance Lines*, 42, Oct-Dec 1959; *Courier Mail*, 1 Jan 1946, 17, 20 Feb 1954; *SMH*, 19 Feb 1954.   J. C. H. GILL

LONGMAN, IRENE MAUD (1877-1964), politician and community worker, was born on 24 April 1877 at Franklin, Tasmania, daughter of Rev. James Molineux Bayley and his wife Mary Alice, née Frencham. Her father, a Congregational minister, had moved to Queensland by 1895, his last parish being Toowoomba. Irene was educated at Sydney Girls' High School and Sydney Church of England Girls' Grammar School, obtained a kindergarten diploma and taught at Normanhurst and at the Sydney and Rockhampton Girls' Grammar schools. On 29 January 1904 at Toowoomba she married Albert Heber Longman [q.v.]; they were to be childless. She helped him to run his Toowoomba newspaper and joined him in zoological research. They moved to Brisbane in 1911 where in 1913-15 she was a supervisor and trainer of students for the recently established Crèche and Kindergarten Association.

Mrs Longman was interested in a wide range of social issues, including town planning and the preservation of native plants, but her work was principally in the field of the welfare of women and especially children—from the movement to establish baby clinics to the effects of the newly popular motion pictures on young minds. She was first secretary of the Playground Association of Queensland. She was particularly interested in the welfare of the mentally handicapped, and in 1922 led a deputation to the secretary for public instruction which brought about establishment of opportunity classes for the intellectually backward.

President of the Queensland branch of the National Council of Women in 1920-24 and subsequently honorary life member, she was nominated in 1929 by the Queensland Women's Electoral League as a candidate in the State election. The first woman ever to stand for parliament in Queensland, she won Bulimba from Labor for the Country and Progressive National Party. During her term in parliament Longman was responsible for the appointment of the first women police in Queensland, for changing the venue of the Children's Court from its meeting place in the precinct of the Police Court, and for the appointment of an advisory panel of one man and one woman in very difficult cases of juvenile delinquency. An earnest, vivacious speaker with a pleasant contralto voice and sparkling repartee on the platform, she could handle a lively meeting with ease. She was an avid reader in the parliamentary library. Her term, however, was short, for she lost her seat in the landslide which swept away the Moore [q.v.] government in 1932. It was a lasting disappointment to her that no woman succeeded in following her into State parliament during her lifetime.

Irene Longman's interest in politics, economics and social questions continued. She was vice-president of the Lyceum Club, vice-president of the Queensland Women's Peace Movement and president of the Association for the Welfare of Mental Deficients, Queensland. Her recreations were walking and bridge. She died on 29 July 1964 in Brisbane and was cremated.

Her two brothers were also parliamentarians, Percy Molineux Bayley as Farmers'

Union and Independent member of the Legislative Assembly for Pittsworth in 1915-20, and James Garfield Bayley as Nationalist member of the House of Representatives for Oxley in 1917-31 and M.L.A. for Wynnum in 1933-35.

Brisbane centenary official historical souvenir (Brisb, 1924); C. A. Bernays, *Queensland—our seventh political decade, 1920-1930* (Syd, 1931); *The first fifty years in the history of the National Council of Women of Queensland* (Brisb, 1955); *Brisbane Kindergarten Teachers' College; diamond jubilee souvenir* (Brisb, 1972); M. Sawer, *A woman's place* (Lond, 1984); *PD* (Qld), 1964-65, p 11; *Woman's World*, 1 Feb 1929, p 73; *Daily Mail* (Brisb), 30 Apr, 13, 14, 23 May 1929; *Queenslander*, 16 May 1929, 21 Jan 1932, 23 Jan 1936; *Courier Mail*, 28 1929; Aug 1924, 17 Apr, 14 May 1929, 31 July 1964.
                                    MARY O'KEEFFE

LONGMORE, LYDIA (1874-1967), infant-teacher, was born on 15 July 1874 at Little Chilton Colliery, Durham, England, daughter of Rev. Isaiah Longmore, Wesleyan home missionary, and his wife Martha Susan, née Lynax. The family migrated to South Australia in 1884, Lydia and her aunt remaining in Adelaide while her father and mother followed his calling as a bush missionary.

Longmore's career began at Kadina in 1895 after four years as a pupil-teacher and a year at the Training College. In 1906, with Elsie Claxton, she was sent to Melbourne to gain the Infant Teachers' Certificate. Two years later she was appointed by Alfred Williams [q.v.] to the newly established Observation and Practising School in Currie Street, Adelaide, before heading the State's first infant school for 5- to 7-year-olds, at Norwood in 1910; an inspector noted that she was 'very capable, intensely enthusiastic and sympathetic' and 'filled with "divine fire" '. In 1915 and 1916 she was at Blackfriars Public School in Sydney to study Dr Maria Montessori's method under Martha Simpson [q.v.]. On her return Longmore began a Montessori class at Norwood.

In January 1917 she became an inspector of schools with a special interest in infant classes. This was the first such position, for a woman, in Australia; later that year New South Wales, the leader in Australian infant education, appointed Miss Simpson as Longmore's counterpart. With the co-operation of the new director of education W. T. McCoy [q.v.], Longmore organized the flowering of infant education in South Australia. In 1920 separate infant departments, with a high degree of autonomy and headed by infant-mistresses responsible to Longmore, were established in the larger schools. That year she encouraged the formation of the Infant Mistresses' Club and the first mothers' clubs.

For both teachers and Longmore, who presided over fortnightly meetings, the club provided friendship and stimulus. The mothers' clubs, headed by infant-mistresses, grew from one in 1920 to thirty-seven in 1931 with over 20 000 mothers being involved; their Froebelian aim was to deepen both mothers' and teachers' understanding of children. The clubs' impact on school life impressed the superintendent of primary education: 'At no time . . . in South Australia has there been such living contact between the school and the home'.

Lydia Longmore opposed drill and revolutionized infant schools by fostering in them a joyous atmosphere, 'as necessary to the growing child as sunlight is to the growing plant'. She used Montessori's methods to mobilize both infant-teachers and mothers. Her own example inspired in them loyalty and self-sacrifice and, in their children, a love of school and learning. Infant-mistresses in metropolitan schools supervised infant classes in neighbouring schools and corresponded with country teachers. Mothers' clubs supported their less fortunate members, especially during the Depression. Thus Longmore demonstrated the power women could have in the community. From 1926 the new Infant Schools Mothers' Clubs Association, with Longmore as president and the director of education's wife as patron, held annual rallies, drawing 4500 from city and country in 1932. Its symbol was a bluebird in a silver circle: 'happiness is *in* unity'. The association protested to the minister of education when in 1931 press reports indicated that, as cost-saving measures, infant schools might lose their independence and infant-mistresses their status. The director of education agreed that infant-teachers had transformed schools 'from prison houses to houses of joy'.

Moved by the plight of outback children, in 1917 Miss Longmore had begun to organize a correspondence school. Also, with her close friend and colleague Dr Gertrude Halley [q.v.9], whose emphasis on a psychological approach to teaching she shared, Longmore established and supervised several playgrounds in Adelaide. She was convener of the child welfare committee of the South Australian branch of the National Council of Women. When she retired in 1934 she became secretary of the metropolitan branch of the Country Women's Association, but care of her aged aunt precluded further community service. Her Wesleyan childhood and Congregational membership influenced all that she wrote: 'To have power to create the right atmosphere the teacher must adjust her own inner life so that a spirit of peace and serenity may prevail'. In 1957 she was appointed O.B.E.

When young, Lydia Longmore had been

shy. She was warned against being 'a modest violet', and developed 'an indomitable will' while remaining warm and witty. She loved cream sponge and pretty china, but was also a pioneer camper who enjoyed motoring, photography, was clever with her hands and a skilled puppeteer. She died at Allambi Home for the Aged, Glengowrie, on 30 October 1967 and was buried in Mitcham cemetery. In 1969 the Mothers' Club Association established the Lydia Longmore Trust Fund to commemorate her work.

N. J. Mitchell (comp), *The life and work of Lydia Longmore* (Adel, 1970); Annual reports of minister controlling education, *PP* (SA), 1907-35; *Education Gazette* (SA), 1922-33; Dept of Education (SA), *Pivot*, 2, no 3 (1975); *Advertiser* (Adel), 1 Jan 1957, 16 July 1963, 31 Oct 1967; R. Naughton, Miss Longmore's place in the history of infant education in South Australia (typescript, 1969, Thiele Lib, SACAE); Assn of Junior Primary School Parents' Clubs of SA Incorporated, Records (SAA); information from Miss Ann Milne, Aldinga Beach, SA.

ELIZABETH KWAN

LONGSTAFF, Sir JOHN CAMPBELL (1861-1941), artist, was born on 10 March 1861 at Clunes, Victoria, second son of Ralph Longstaff, storekeeper from England, and his Scottish wife Jessie, née Campbell. Will Longstaff [q.v.] was his cousin. He was educated at a boarding-school at Miners Rest and at Clunes State School. Displaying an early aptitude for art, in which he was encouraged by his mother, he received drawing lessons at Clunes from a Dane named Bruhn and in 1873 won a junior division prize in the Victorian schools of design's freehand drawing competition.

By 1874 the Longstaffs had moved to Shepparton where John worked inefficiently in his father's stores and tutored himself in oil-painting technique from a popular art instruction manual. Ralph, dismissive of his son's artistic talent, next found him work as a clerk, at first locally and in 1880 with the Melbourne importers Sargood [q.v.6], Butler & Nichol. He agreed to John's entry into the art school of the National Gallery of Victoria in 1882 only after urgings from Henry Butler who had recognized the young man's true *métier*.

Under G. F. Folingsby [q.v.4] Longstaff, 'an athletic-looking husky', received a sound academic training in figure drawing and painting. An outstanding student, he won the school's first travelling scholarship in 1887 with 'Breaking the News', a figure composition depicting the tragic aftermath of a mining accident. Shortly before sailing for Europe that year he made an impetuous marriage, on 20 July at East Melbourne with Anglican rites, to a 17-year-old beauty Rosa Louisa (Topsy) Crocker; her attraction for him never

waned, but her extreme shyness accorded ill with his exuberance and later urbanity.

After only a fortnight in London, Longstaff went to Paris where, on the advice of his compatriot John Peter Russell [q.v.], he entered the liberal studio of Fernand Cormon, a painter of Oriental and Stone Age subjects and an occasional portraitist. He spent the summer of 1889 with his wife at Russell's chateau at Belle-Ile; under the influence of Russell's Impressionism he temporarily lightened his palette and loosened his technique. Next year he spent three months in Spain studying the art of Velasquez whose careful craftsmanship and subtle dark tonalities remained a major influence on his portraiture. During this period Longstaff exhibited each year at the Old Salon; a portrait of his wife and first child (National Gallery of Victoria) received a *mention honorable* in 1891 and his large-scale allegorical subject, 'The Sirens', painted under the terms of the travelling scholarship, was exhibited with success at the 1892 Salon and at the Royal Academy of Arts in 1894.

In 1893 Longstaff went to London as a portraitist, but in 1895 he returned to Australia, his wife and family having travelled home at least three years earlier. In Melbourne during the depression, he designed advertisements for a living until he established a portraiture practice. In 1898 the National Gallery of Victoria purchased his large bushfire subject 'Gippsland, Sunday Night, February 20th, 1898'.

Longstaff returned to England in 1901 to undertake a commission from the National Gallery of Victoria's Gillbee [q.v.4] bequest to depict the explorers Burke and Wills [qq.v.3,6]; the resultant huge canvas was not completed until 1907. On his arrival he enjoyed almost immediate success as a portraitist, his subjects including King Edward VII and Queen Alexandra in 1904. By 1906 he resided in the fashionable St John's Wood area and had a 'magnificent studio' at nearby Carlton Hill. A regular exhibitor at the Royal Academy in 1902-20, he also exhibited nine works with the Royal Society of Portrait Painters. In 1911 he visited Australia, ostensibly to see his ageing parents at Shepparton, though he appears to have spent considerable time painting portraits in Sydney and Melbourne. In 1918-19 he served as an official war artist with the Australian Imperial Force, executing portraits of distinguished Australian servicemen.

From August 1920 Longstaff lived permanently in Melbourne, travelling to other capital cities as his work dictated. He won the Archibald [q.v.3] prize for portraiture five times: in 1925, 1928, 1929, 1931 and 1935. In 1928 he was knighted. During this last period in Australia he held numerous official positions: at various times president of the Victorian Artists' Society and of the Australian Art Association, first president of the Australian Academy of Art in 1938-41, and a trustee of the Public Library, Museums and National Gallery from 1927.

Tall, handsome and charming, Longstaff moved effortlessly in society circles where his skills as a portraitist were eagerly sought. The constant flow of commissions impeded his ambition to paint significant subject pictures, but his portraiture left an impressive record of notable Australians, while he also painted several important figure subjects on nationalistic themes. His art was basically academic and conservative though some of his early work reveals the influence of Whistler's Aestheticism.

In later life Longstaff carried the financial burden of supporting his wife and youngest son and daughter in England where they had chosen to remain. Rosa died in 1939 and at his death in Melbourne on 1 October 1941 Longstaff was survived by his daughter and three sons; another son had been killed in World War I. Longstaff was cremated. His estate, valued for probate at £4631, bore no signs of the 'princely income' which was supposed to have been his.

N. Murdoch, *Portrait in youth of Sir John Longstaff 1861-1941* (Syd, 1948); P. Timms, *Sir John Longstaff (1862-1941), an exhibition prepared by Shepparton Art Gallery for Arts Victoria 75* (Shepparton, 1975); M. Plant and A. Galbally (eds), *Studies in Australian art* (Melb, 1978); *Lone Hand*, 1 June 1908, p 206; *Life*, 15 (May 1911), p 493; *Art in Aust*, 15 Apr 1931; *SMH*, 27 Aug 1920; Longstaff correspondence (LaTL); Tom Roberts correspondence (vols l-3, letters to Tom Roberts,ML); biog file (NL).
                                    LEIGH ASTBURY

LONGSTAFF, WILLIAM FREDERICK (1879-1953), artist, was born on 25 December 1879 at Ballarat, Victoria, son of Thomas Longstaff, pharmacist, and his wife Frederica Elizabeth, née Francis, both English born. He was a cousin of (Sir) John Longstaff [q.v.]. Will was educated at Grenville College, Ballarat, studied art at the Ballarat School of Mines, and had experience as a jackaroo. In 1900-01 he spent sixteen months as a trooper in charge of remounts with the South African Light Horse during the South African War. He later went to Europe where he continued his art studies, attending the Heatherley School of Fine Art in London in 1908. On his return to Victoria he taught art privately and in 1910-11 with Leslie Wilkie [q.v.]. Longstaff and his wife Eliza Mary lived at Eltham.

In October 1915 he joined the Australian Imperial Force, embarking as captain for Egypt in November with the 1st Australian Remount Unit. Longstaff was invalided to England in October 1917 and next year was selected for camouflage training and attached to the 2nd Division Headquarters as divisional artist under the Australian Records Section war art scheme. While in Egypt he had made pictorial records of the Anzac Mounted Division and the Desert Column. In June 1918 he was billeted with Arthur Streeton [q.v.] and on occasion they worked side by side painting such scenes as Amiens Cathedral and the salvage dump at Glisy. Longstaff, a skilful and innovative camouflage worker, took plane flights to note effects from the air. His thoroughness contributed to successful concealment of allied activity before the offensive of 8 August and probably saved many lives.

After the war Longstaff joined the group of artists who worked for the Australian War Records Section at its St John's Wood studio, London, preparing material for display in the proposed Australian War Memorial; these included paintings depicting the battle of 8 August 1918 and the breaking of the Hindenburg line (25 September). He subsequently moved to Sussex, where he lived quietly with his second wife and two children while maintaining a London studio. In 1919 he was represented in the Royal Academy of Arts annual exhibition by a water-colour 'Somme Valley'. He painted many unambitious views of the Sussex landscape, exhibiting with the Society of Australian Artists, London, in 1920. He also undertook many portrait commissions including those of David Lloyd George and Sir Granville Ryrie [q.v.].

Will Longstaff is best known for his large, popular, allegorical paintings of ghostly fallen soldiers on battlefields, such as 'Menin Gate at Midnight' ('Ghosts of Menin Gate') 1927, and the 'Immortal Shrine' ('Eternal Silence'). The former was purchased by Lord Woolavington for 2000 guineas and presented to the Australian government (Australian War Memorial) in 1928. When this painting was exhibited in 1928-29 it created a sensation and reproductions were sold in great numbers. The painting met the need of many at the time to remember those who had died and the contemporary interest in spiritualism. 'Carillon', a third allegorical picture, painted in 1934, depicting New Zealand war dead haunting the Belgian coast, is in the National Art Gallery, Wellington; and a fourth painting, of Vimy Ridge, with the spirits of the Canadian Corps, was presented to the Canadian government.

Longstaff died on 1 July 1953 at Littlehampton, Sussex.

Aust War Memorial, *'Menin Gate at Midnight'. The story of Will Longstaff's great allegorical painting* (Melb, Syd, nd); A. Gray, 'Will Longstaff's sketch-book', *J of the Aust War Memorial*, no 3, Oct 1983; *Age* and *The Times*, 3 July 1953; Bean papers, *and* files 18/1/31, 18/3/13, 449/9/96, 895/4/205 (AWM).   ANNE GRAY

LONGWORTH, WILLIAM (1846-1928) and THOMAS (1857-1927), mine-managers and industrial entrepreneurs, were the eldest and third sons of Thomas Longworth, coal-miner, and his wife Rose, née Gardiner, from Guernsey, Channel Islands. William was born on 22 November 1846 at Worsley, Lancashire, England. His father, under contract to the Australian Agricultural Co., migrated to New South Wales with his wife and son, reaching Port Stephens in the *Artemisia* on 28 December 1849. Thomas was born on 5 April 1857 at Newcastle. The boys, noted for their sprinting ability, worked with their father in coal-mines around Newcastle.

In 1878 the family opened a small coal-mine at Rixs Creek, near Singleton. At All Saints Anglican Church, Singleton, Thomas married Frances Nowlan on 14 April 1884. The death of Thomas senior and thirteen other miners in a roof collapse on 30 September profoundly influenced the brothers and forged them into a close working relationship. They combined with their brother-in-law W. W. Robinson and (Sir) Albert Gould [q.v.9], both Singleton solicitors, and another local collier Dr Richard Reed, to produce coal suitable for the railways and installed extensive coking ovens at Rixs Creek. Finding insufficient outlet for coking coal, the partners in 1890 engaged an authority on copper mining and smelting who drew their attention to the Great Cobar copper mine, idle since 1889. They began negotiations to operate the mine on tribute and with the addition of A. A. Dangar [q.v.4] formed the Great Cobar Mining Syndicate in 1894. Thomas Longworth moved to Cobar to take charge of operations, while William managed the Singleton Coal & Coke Co.

With copper prices low, Thomas introduced coke-fired blast furnaces, fitted with crucible water jackets, that lowered the reduction cost of the rich ores, which had a high gold content. By 1898 five blast furnaces were in use and electric lighting was installed in the works. Next year, improved furnaces using a hot blast were operating. The main shaft was deepened and connected to other workings by cross-cutting. With the price of copper at £70 a ton by 1899 of which £15 was paid as tribute, the syndicate purchased the mine outright in 1900.

At Lithgow, under William's direction, a refinery and electrolytic plant with an associated colliery were opened. By the electrolytic method he extracted gold worth over £20 a ton, leaving pure copper. From 1900 William and Thomas alternated as manager at Cobar. They persuaded the railway commis-sioners to supply water trains from Warren during the worst seven months of the 1902 drought to prevent closure of the mine and the dismissal of 600 men, and to reduce freight rates when copper prices fell in 1903. After rebuffing approaches from the Mount Lyell Mining and Railway Co. Ltd, in 1906 the syndicate sold to an English firm, Great Cobar Ltd, all their mines, smelters, refineries, collieries and coke works for £1 006 000 of which £800 000 was paid in cash to the six principals.

The same members of the syndicate founded Australian Woollen Mills Ltd at Marrickville in 1908, with William as a director in 1908-9 and Thomas chairman in 1908-27. Under the latter's direction the factory expanded and contained the most efficient machinery available internationally. By early 1914 judicious management had made it possible to double the plant for carding, combing and spinning operations. During World War I the mill produced enormous quantities of khaki for the Australian Imperial Force as well as adequate supplies of khaki knitting wools for regimental comforts' funds. By 1927 A.W.M. operated 200 looms, employed 700 persons and manufactured only high-grade worsted serges.

The brothers also operated a brickworks, potteries and timber-mills at Thornton and had pastoral interests; William bred racehorses at Dulwich, near Nundah. As 'W. T. Nowlan' they jointly owned and raced such winners as Blue Metal (Summer Cup 1899 and 1900, and Australian Cup 1902) and Satin Bird (Epsom Handicap 1917). At his Sydney home, Rockleigh, Point Piper, William married a 59-year-old widow Margaret Thornton, née Howard, on 1 June 1901. He soon bought Glenroy at Karuah, Port Stephens, remodelling the house and building aviaries, gardens and boatsheds. Among other benefactions, he distributed £12 000 among hospitals in the Newcastle area, built, equipped and endowed a hospital for children at Waratah at a cost of £15 000, and presented a historic building in Newcastle to the Australian Society of Patriots. After his wife died, he married a widow Mary Ellen New, née Gilligan, on 5 April 1916.

Sturdy in build, William had hooded eyes and a long spade-beard. Survived by his wife he died on 5 December 1928 at Karuah and was buried in the Anglican cemetery at Singleton. He left his estate, valued for probate at £363 363, to his sisters, nieces and nephews.

Thomas moved to Lithgow in 1902 but in 1905 bought a mansion, Woollahra House, Point Piper, from the Cooper [q.v.3] estate and built a steam yacht, *Cobar*, for use on Sydney Harbour. He died at Woollahra on 5 February 1927 and was buried in the Anglican section of South Head cemetery. Predeceased by his wife, he was survived by seven sons, including William [q.v.] and two daughters. His children inherited his estate, valued for probate at £305 582.

V&P (LA NSW), 1887-88, 6, p 683; *Textile J of Aust*, 15 Jan 1929, p 674; *Newcastle School of Arts J*, Apr 1937; Aust Railway Historical Soc *Bulletin*, 22 (Sept 1969), no 383, p 190; *Maitland Mercury*, 2 Oct 1884; *SMH*, 7 Feb 1927, 6 Dec 1928; *Bulletin*, 10 Feb 1927; *Newcastle Morning Herald*, 6 Dec 1928; information from Mr W. Clelland, Cobar, NSW, and Mr R. T. Longworth, Randwick, Syd.

JOHN ATCHISON

LONGWORTH, WILLIAM (1892-1969), swimmer and businessman, was born on 26 September 1892 at Singleton, New South Wales, son of Thomas Longworth [q.v.] and his wife Frances, née Nowlan. Bill was educated at Sydney Grammar School which he represented at swimming, athletics and Rugby.

In January 1911 the 1320 yards Australian championship at Sydney's Domain baths, although expected to prove the relative merits of (Sir) Frank Beaurepaire's [q.v.7] trudgen style and Cecil Healy's [q.v.9] Australian crawl, was won by Longworth from the Eastern Suburbs club by 30 yards in the world record time of 17 minutes, 42 seconds. He had used a perfect two-beat Australian crawl which finally proved that it was suitable for long distances. The same season he won the mile championship. Next year Longworth won all the New South Wales and Australian freestyle championships from 100 yards to one mile, a feat unequalled for thirty-seven years. He also set Australian records for 100 yards (56.8 seconds), 100 metres (65 seconds), 220 yards (2 minutes, 27.4 seconds) and three miles (1 hour, 18 minutes, 22.4 seconds). At the 1912 Olympic Games at Stockholm he qualified for the 100 and 1500 metres finals but withdrew because of illness. In 1913 and 1914 he won every New South Wales and Australian title except for the 100 yards.

Longworth enlisted in the Australian Imperial Force on 13 September 1915. Embarking in May next year, he served in France from November as a sergeant with the Anzac Entrenchment Battalion, and in supply and motor transport columns. He was commissioned in June 1917. He represented the A.I.F. in swimming, married Ellen Humphrey on 16 July 1919 in London, and returned to Sydney in November.

Longworth entered the family business ventures; he was a director of Australian Woollen Mills Ltd (later Textile Holdings Ltd), Ashtonfields Coal Mining Co. Ltd,

Bunarba Pastoral Co. Ltd, Oswald-Sealy (Overseas) Ltd, and chairman of Beare & Ley Pty Ltd.

Interested in the history of Australian swimming, Longworth contributed the article on 'Swimming' to the *Australian Encyclopaedia* in 1926. He was New South Wales amateur snooker champion in 1920 and 1921, Sydney Metropolitan billiards champion in 1937 and a vice-president of the British Billiards Control Council. A member of the Australian Jockey Club, as 'Mr W. Biey' he owned and raced horses and won the A.J.C.'s Metropolitan Stakes with Young Crusader in 1936. He was chairman of the Owners and Trainers' Association and of the Sydney Turf Club.

Longworth divorced his wife in 1946 and at St Mark's Church, Darling Point, married Irene Annie Elizabeth Ley on 5 February 1947. He died at his home at Wahroonga on 19 October 1969 and was buried with Anglican rites in Northern Suburbs cemetery. Two sons and a daughter of his first marriage and his wife and their daughter survived him. His estate was valued for probate at $271 760.

G. Inglis, *Sport and pastime in Australia* (Lond, 1912); *Forbes Carlile on swimming* (Lond, 1963); *Bulletin*, 19 Jan, 9, 16 Mar 1911, 11 Jan, 1, 8 Feb 1912, 12, 26 Aug 1915; *Australasian*, 21 Jan 1911, 13 Jan 1912; *SMH*, 13, 16 Mar 1911, 30 May 1940, 17 Aug 1943, 19 June 1944, 27 June 1945, 14 July, 25 Aug 1959, 29 Mar 1961, 31 July 1962, 20 Oct 1969.

G. P. WALSH

LORD, CLIVE ERROL (1889-1933), naturalist and museum director, was born on 6 October 1889 in Hobart, son of Octavius Lord, cashier, and his wife Ida, née Watchorn, and great-grandson of David Lord [q.v.2]. Clive was educated at Buckland's and The Hutchins schools at Hobart and after serving his articles practised as an architect. His development into the State's leading ornithologist stemmed from a keen interest in natural history pursued as a youthful foundation member (1904) of the Tasmanian Field Naturalists' Club, as its energetic 'Hon. Sec.' after 1911, and later as president. He was elected a member of the Royal Society of Tasmania in 1917 and was its secretary in 1918-33. In 1917 he was appointed assistant curator at a somewhat neglected Tasmanian Museum. In 1921 he became curator and in 1923-33 he was director of the Tasmanian Museum and Art Gallery.

Lord was a man of energy and enthusiasm, with the skills of a great organizer. He gave devoted labour to Tasmania's first 'national' park from its inception in 1916, as secretary to the Mount Field National Park Board. With E. T. Emmett [q.v.8] and G. Weindorfer [q.v.],

Lord submitted a successful proposal for the creation of the Cradle Mountain Park. He supported the idea of a game and fisheries commission to protect land and sea animals that led to the Animals and Birds Protection Act (1928) and was a foundation member of the administering board. With Sir Douglas Mawson [q.v.] and Captain Frank Hurley [q.v.9] he waged a campaign to preserve the penguins and seals of Macquarie Island that resulted in the island being proclaimed a wildlife reserve. He was a foundation member of the Tasmanian Sea Fisheries Board and the Salmon and Freshwater Fisheries Commission. As secretary of the Royal Botanical Gardens for many years, he reorganized the gardens on his return from London where he had been Tasmanian representative at the centenary celebrations of the British Association for the Advancement of Science in 1931. In 1931-32 he was president of the Royal Australasian Ornithologists' Union.

His major work, *A synopsis of the vertebrate animals of Tasmania* (1924), was written in association with H. H. Scott [q.v.], but he compiled several handbooks and contributed numerous papers to scientific societies arising from his diverse interests and knowledge of the Tasmanian environment. He also pursued an interest in history, tracing the landfalls of early navigators in his own yacht and writing *The early explorers of Tasmania* (1920).

Tall and erect, with a genial disposition and a sense of humour, Lord got on well with people as 'the companion and adviser of all seeking knowledge in the realms of natural science and early Tasmanian history'. He was a fellow of the Linnean Society, London (1922), and of the Tasmanian Institute of Architects. In 1930 he was awarded the Tasmanian Royal Society's medal. In 1927-33 he was an associate member of the Australian National Research Council, as well as local secretary of the Australasian Association for the Advancement of Science. He was active in local organizations such as the Hobart Development League and was a foundation member of the Hobart Rotary Club. On 10 February 1915 Lord had married Doris Harland Mills, whom he divorced; on 17 July 1929 he married Florence Jessie Knight. He died on 15 July 1933 at Sandy Bay of hypertensive cerebro-vascular disease and was buried at Cornelian Bay cemetery. His wife and a daughter of his first marriage survived him.

Roy Soc NSW, *J*, 68 (1934); *Examiner* (Launc) and *Mercury*, 17 July 1933.   JACK THWAITES

LORD, JOHN ERNEST CECIL (1870-1949), police commissioner and soldier, was born on 8 May 1870 at Brighton, Tasmania, one of ten children of Richard David Lord, farmer, and his wife Augusta Louisa, née Packer. Leaving school at 15 he entered the Tasmanian Civil Service and a year later was transferred as a clerk to the inspector of police whose function was to co-ordinate the many municipal and territorial police districts of Tasmania. Under the Police Regulation Act of 1898 a centralized, State-wide Police Department was created. Never a constable or a police officer, Lord spent twenty years in administrative positions until, on 1 January 1906 at the time of a royal commission into police administration, he became acting commissioner and was confirmed in office the following July. He was commissioner of police for almost thirty-five years until his retirement on 25 November 1940.

Always conspicuous in sport, Lord became president of the Royal Hobart Regatta Association, the Derwent Rowing Club and the Tasmanian Amateur Boxing and Wrestling Association. On 9 January 1901, at St George's Anglican Church, Battery Point, he married Hannah May Smith (1874-1948); they had nine children of whom five survived to adulthood. Derwentwater at Sandy Bay was the family home.

In 1908 Lord was ordered by the Tasmanian attorney-general to 'report upon the state of the Furneaux Group of Bass Strait islands, the condition and mode of living of half-castes, the existing method of regulating the reserves, and suggest lines for future administration'. Authoritarian and condescending in the light of later attitudes to minority regional and ethnic problems, his report gives, however, a fine account of early conditions in the Furneaux islands.

In Lord's era the police were the 'catch-all' of many legal and social problems: the criminal investigation and traffic branches were created, women police were recruited, constables were appointed as assistant harbourmasters and bailiffs of crown land and assigned to detect codlin moth, false weights and measures, and school truancy. They also undertook tide-watching for the Commonwealth Customs, town surveying and property valuations. The commissioner was required to be chairman of the Scenery Preservation Board, Salmon and Freshwater Fisheries Commission and the Animals and Birds Protection Board.

Lord began his military service as a private on 19 May 1898 and was commissioned lieutenant in the Tasmanian Infantry Regiment on 22 December 1899. Promoted captain in 1902, he transferred to the Derwent Regiment and commanded its 1st Battalion from 1910; he was a major from 1912. At the outbreak of war in 1914 he was in command of harbour defences in Hobart. On 10 February 1916 he joined the Australian Imperial Force as lieut-colonel commanding the 40th Battalion and embarked on 1 July. After training on Salisbury Plain, England, Lord and the 'Fortieth' were dispatched to France on 24 November. There followed two years in the trenches of France and Belgium, at Armentières, Messines, Ypres, Passchendaele, Villers-Bretonneux, the Somme and the Hindenburg line. He retained command of the 40th Battalion but between July 1918 and February 1919 held temporary commands of the 5th, 9th (in the battle of Amiens), 10th and 15th Brigades. After the Armistice he examined police administration in Britain and embarked for Australia on 20 April 1919; his A.I.F. appointment ended on 6 August. For his war service he was awarded the Distinguished Service Order and the French Croix de Guerre, was appointed C.M.G. and mentioned in dispatches three times. Until the end of 1924 he was in command of the 25th and 12th Brigades, Australian Military Forces. On 8 May 1928 he was placed on the retired list with the rank of colonel, thus completing thirty years in the Australian Army.

Lord died at Cygnet on 29 October 1949 and, after a service in St David's Cathedral, Hobart, with full military and police honours, was cremated at Cornelian Bay cemetery. In a foreword to *The Fortieth* Sir John Monash [q.v.] wrote: 'the Battalion found an officer . . . capable of setting and enforcing a high example, and of forming and guiding the soul of his command'. Survived by one son and three daughters, Lord left an estate sworn for probate at £20 500.

Cyclopedia of Tasmania (Hob, 1900); F. C. Green, *The Fortieth* (Hob, 1922); C. E. W. Bean, *The A.I.F. in France*, 1917, 1918 (Syd, 1933, 1942); R. L. Wettenhall, *A guide to Tasmanian government administration* (Hob, 1968); M. Sharland, *Once upon a time* (Hob, 1976); *Reveille* (Syd), Jan 1941; *Mercury*, 2 Jan, 2 July 1906, 31 Oct 1949; *Examiner* (Launc), 8 May 1940.

ALAN WARDEN

LORDING, ROWLAND EDWARD (1899-1944), soldier, accountant and author, was born on 20 June 1899 at Balmain, Sydney, son of Edward Ernest Lording, cycle mechanic, and his wife Elizabeth Orton, née Bennett, both Melbourne born. He was educated at Burwood Public School and later became a book-keeper.

Rowley Lording was barely 16 when he enlisted in the Australian Imperial Force on 19 July 1915, was posted to the 30th Battalion and selected for its signalling section. He embarked for Egypt on 9 November and, as a lance corporal, topped the visual signalling class at the Zeitoun School of Instruction. He served in Egypt until June 1916 when the battalion sailed for France. After a very brief tour in a quiet part of the front line he took part in the battle of Fromelles on 19-20 July. As Lording was leading his section across no man's land he was struck down by a burst of machine-gun fire which ripped across his chest and right arm. Minutes later several pieces of shrapnel lodged in his back. With both arms useless and his legs semi-paralysed by spinal injuries he was hospitalized in France and later in England. Operation followed operation and it was not until January 1917 that he was able to get out of bed for the first time. On 22 February he was invalided to Australia and was discharged from the A.I.F. on 12 October.

As a result of his wounds Lording underwent over fifty surgical procedures in the next fifteen years. Six of his ribs were removed and eventually, after many operations to save it, his right arm was amputated above the elbow. Though in constant pain he carried on with 'characteristic grit', taking up art leatherwork and accountancy. In England he had met Rosalind Mary Crowther; they were married in St John's Church, Beecroft, Sydney, on 14 June 1922 and had two sons and a daughter. On full military pension, Lording was founder of the 30th Battalion Association and for several years its honorary secretary. He was also honorary manager of the employment bureau of the Limbless Soldiers' Association. He wrote an account of his war and post-war experiences, *There and back*, published in 1935 under the pseudonym 'A. Tiveychoc'.

Lording's marriage ended in divorce and on 1 January 1943 he married Orea Moustaka; he was by then an incorporated accountant. Next year, on 1 October, he died 'in tragic circumstances' at Callan Park Mental Hospital, and was cremated with Methodist forms. His second wife and the children of his first marriage survived him. Because of his shocking wounds Lording's post-war life was 'an epic of human suffering'. An obituary in the *Limbless Soldier* stated: 'Of small build, and knocked about as he was, Rowley had the heart of a lion and the guts and tenacity of the British bulldog'. A. G. Butler [q.v.7], official medical historian of the A.I.F., considered that he deserved 'a special place (if anyone does) among the immortals of the A.I.F.'

H. Sloan (ed), *The purple and gold* (Syd, 1938); A. G. Butler, *Official history of the Australian Army Medical Services*, 3 (Canb, 1943); *Reveille* (Syd), Oct 1935; *Limbless Soldier* (Syd), Dec 1944; *Courier Mail* (Brisb), 10 Mar 1938, 7 May 1939; *Labor Daily*, 25 Apr 1938; *Sunday Sun* (Syd), 7 May 1939; *SMH*, 3 Oct 1944; *Bulletin*, 11 Oct 1944; War diary, 30th Battalion AIF (AWM).

WILLIAM A. LAND

LOTHIAN, THOMAS CARLYLE (1880-1974), publisher and publishers' representative, was born on 7 May 1880 at Newcastle-upon-Tyne, England, eldest child of John Inglis Lothian, book-keeper, and his wife Lillias Charlotte, née Smith. He arrived in Melbourne in July 1888, John having come to represent the publishing firm of Walter Scott. After attending the Brighton Road State School Thomas worked for four years at Cole's [q.v.3] Book Arcade, learning the book trade and incidentally furthering his general education.

About 1897 Lothian entered his father's business, and by 1901 was travelling to show samples and circulars (now including those of other firms beside Walter Scott) to booksellers in the capitals, in country towns of eastern Australia, and throughout New Zealand. In 1908, already appearing as agent for educational publishers, he visited the firm's principals abroad in preparation for taking over the business. In 1911 he established the Standard Publishing Co. Pty Ltd to sell direct to the public, through advertising and canvassing, the publications of the Caxton Press.

On 16 February 1912, with Congregational forms, Lothian married Effie Marian Vines, who had worked for several years in his father's office. Also in 1912, on his father's retirement, he formed the company of Thomas C. Lothian Pty Ltd to carry on the business of representation, which was to include over the years agencies for numerous well-known British and American publishers.

Lothian had become a publisher in his own right with the production, in December 1905, of Bernard O'Dowd's [q.v.] *The silent land and other verses.* There soon followed further poetry, natural history, stories, educational works, books on health, cookery and business skills. In 1907-09 he published several magazines, including titles of literary and general interest, a tri-lingual series and another on golf and motoring. His authors included E. J. Brady, J. Le Gay Brereton [qq.v.7], Henry Lawson, Walter Murdoch and T. G. Tucker [qq.v.].

Following the outbreak of war, Lothian sought to expand this branch of the business by forming the Lothian Book Publishing Co. Pty Ltd (from 1924 the Lothian Publishing Co. Pty Ltd). By 1918 he had published more than half of his total of some 230 titles, including, in 1916, his two most ambitious productions, *Elves and fairies,* illustrated by Ida Outhwaite [q.v.], and *The art of Frederick McCubbin* [q.v.].

During the 1920s and 1930s Lothian continued to operate through his three major companies and, from time to time, some smaller enterprises. His publishing consisted of re-issues of successful textbooks; verse, including the collected poems of John Shaw Neilson [q.v.] (1934); novels, including Miles Franklin's [q.v.8] *Old Blastus of Bandicoot* (1932), and items of general and sporting interest. During World War II he produced little of his own, but published in Australia titles for both Penguin Books and Robert Hale.

After the war Lothian handed over his businesses to his two younger sons. He retained his office, pursuing from there almost to the end his interest in the Melbourne Rotary Club of which he was an enthusiastic foundation member, serving as honorary secretary in 1931 and 1937, and as vice-president in 1968-69.

Thomas Lothian died, a widower, at his home at Mont Albert on 19 April 1974 and was cremated with Christian Science forms. His five children survived him. A portrait by Ernest Buckmaster is held by the family.

The house of Lothian is seventy-five (Melb, 1963); Lothian papers (LaTL).   CECILY CLOSE

LOTON, SIR WILLIAM THORLEY (1838-1924), politician, merchant and landowner, was born on 11 June 1838 at Dilhorne, Staffordshire, England, son of Joseph Loton, publican, and his wife Ann, née Gates. At 14 he left school and later joined the London firm, Copestake, Moore & Co. In 1862 he migrated to Western Australia, arriving at Fremantle on 26 March 1863. A cautious, fair businessman, he entered commerce in Perth and Geraldton and in 1867 formed a fruitful partnership with Walter Padbury. Apart from widespread mercantile activities, the firm financed and supported agricultural and pastoral development, particularly in the North-West where Loton held much land. In 1876 he bought Belvoir on the Upper Swan and in 1881 Springhill near Northam. After the sale of Padbury, Loton & Co. in 1889, Loton concentrated on the development of the two properties. He was inaugural president of the Northam Agricultural Society in 1890 and, later, four times president of the Royal Western Australian Agricultural Society. Succeeding generations of Lotons maintained the high standard of stock and property development initiated by him. Springhill remained in the family until 1936, and Belvoir till 1962.

In 1884 Loton was appointed a member of the Legislative Council. He resigned in 1887 and was elected for Greenough in the council from 1889. He represented Swan in the Legislative Assembly in 1890-97, then returned to the council, for Central province in 1898-1900 and East province in 1902-08. He was a practical, industrious politician committed to progress and development but critical of what he saw as frivolous, unintelligent planning and haphazard expenditure. He supported responsible government and granting the franchise to women, but resisted liberalization of divorce law. Although a Western Australian delegate to the Federal conventions in 1891 and 1897-98, Loton opposed the colony's entry into the Federation and believed that the issue should be decided by referendum rather than by the parliament. However in the council in 1906 he joined the minority of six who voted against the resolution that Western Australia secede. He had no fears for Western Australian progress, provided the Commonwealth gave fair treatment; meanwhile it was foolish to raise the cry of secession which would come about only with strong popular support.

In Perth he owned considerable real estate. In 1871 he had been a foundation member of the Weld Club. He was a generous benefactor of St George's Cathedral and, from 1888, a trustee of the Church of England in Western Australia. In 1882 he became a director of the Western Australian Bank and from 1909 was its chairman; he was also a director of the Colonial Mutual Life Association. Loton was mayor of Perth in 1901-02 and in 1923 he was knighted.

On 18 February 1868 in Perth he had married Annie Morris; they had three daughters and three sons of whom Ernest William (1872-1953) settled on Belvoir and Arthur George (1876-1921) on Springhill.

Loton was a forceful, able man who, while not a visionary, brought a valuable breadth of outlook to Western Australia's early years of development. He died at his Perth home, Dilhorne, on 22 October 1924 and was buried in Karrakatta cemetery. His wife (d. 1927), one son and two daughters survived him. His estate was sworn for probate at £212 122.

J. S. Battye (ed), *Cyclopedia of Western Australia*, 2 (Adel, 1913); R. Erickson (comp), *Dictionary of Western Australians*, 3 (Perth, 1979); *West Australian*, 15 Nov 1900, 23 Oct 1924; *Sunday Times* (Perth), 4 Feb 1962; PR 5663 and 8135 *and* MN 82 (Battye Lib).   PAT SIMPSON

LOUGHLIN, PETER FFRENCH (1882-1960), politician and grazier, was born on 12 December 1882 at Mongarlowe, near Braidwood, New South Wales, son of John Loughlin, policeman, of Ireland, and his wife Sarah Jane, née Ffrench, of New South Wales. He was educated at Ginninderra Public School and in 1896-97 at St Patrick's College, Goulburn; he then worked in a store at Goulburn. In 1900 he became a teacher in the Department of Public Instruction, being sent next year to Erambie Aboriginal School at Cowra,

where at St Raphael's Catholic Church on 16 April 1906 he married Louisa Davis. He taught at several country schools including Darby's Falls, Neila Creek and Blowering.

Loughlin's interest in public affairs and debating skills, honed in several societies, made him a valuable member of the Labor Party. He opposed conscription in World War I and defeated ex-Laborite G. A. Burgess for the State seat of Burrangong in 1917. By then he was an expert on rural problems and had helped to consolidate Labor's extensive country support. His social awareness was reinforced and sustained by his religion, and he joined moderate party members who won control from extremist 'industrialist' (trade union) groups headed by J. S. Garden [q.v.8] and A. C. Willis [q.v.] in 1919.

Loughlin was of medium build, with pleasant features and a receding hairline. His warm personality matched his political talents, and after he had won a Cootamundra seat in 1920 —after some conflict with J. J. G. McGirr [q.v.]—he became minister for lands and forests in J. Storey's [q.v.] government, retaining the portfolios in James Dooley's [q.v.8] 1921-22 cabinets. An active and perceptive minister, he finally abolished the role of land agents who had long imposed on credulous land-seekers; he tightened the administration of the ailing soldier settlement scheme, but lacked time to realize his vision of closer settlement. Labor lost the 1922 general election; but Loughlin had developed as one of its most sagacious parliamentarians with a firmness now refining his natural courtesy and good temper.

Factionalism remained endemic in the labour movement, with country members wary of attempts of city industrialists to dominate the party. The complexity was compounded by novel pressures from 'communists', led by Garden but not clearly defined organizationally on the radical margin until 1923, by efforts of the Australian Workers' Union, with J. Bailey [q.v.7] prominent, to maintain its influence, and by the renewed ambitions of Willis, secretary of the miners' federation. Loughlin assessed the position in August 1922 as, 'Self-confessed, the movement is full of corruption', and determined to preserve its pristine purity. Strangely sensing a kindred spirit in J. T. Lang [q.v.9], Loughlin combined with him to seek Federal party help to nullify the State executive's appointment of McGirr as leader in March 1923. The June conference justified their activity and Loughlin was mentioned as party leader, but in July he became deputy leader to Lang. Their manifesto denounced capitalism and sectarianism, and sought co-operation with the industrialists. In 1924 Loughlin responded to the tide of revulsion against communism by issuing a pamphlet, *Ten reasons why Labor should exclude the Communist Party.*

Labor won the 1925 election and Loughlin again became minister for lands and forests. His understanding with Lang crumbled as the premier's aggressiveness generated cabinet fissures, and his ambition and need to appease the industrialists forced him to appoint Willis to the Legislative Council and the ministry. Loughlin contributed to the government's social and industrial legislation, and as acting premier in May-June 1926 smoothed party dissension. But Lang's insecurity and extra-parliamentary links increased tensions. Loughlin resigned his portfolios and challenged him in September after he had refused to defend certain parliamentarians against attacks in the *Labor Daily*, and seemed about to accept the alleged plans of the industrialists to introduce new 'red' party rules to perpetuate his leadership and their control: a tied caucus vote, against a background of pressure from trade union secretaries, left Lang in charge.

Loughlin resumed the deputy leadership, and attended a large conference at Bathurst which he had organized as part of Labor's policy to regulate marketing of rural products. He resigned again on 19 November and left the party after a special conference had removed Lang from caucus control and foreshadowed the implementation of the 'red rules'; but with fellow country members V. W. E. Goodin and R. T. Gillies he unexpectedly refrained from voting in a censure motion and Lang survived, agreeing to an early election. But a pact with Goodin and Gillies helped to keep the government in office until October 1927, when Loughlin, as Independent Labor, lost his seat narrowly. A public testimonial of £3237 reflected not only much country but also city appreciation of his integrity: H. V. Evatt and T. D. Mutch [q.v.] were among its organizers.

Loughlin then became associated with the *Goulburn Evening Penny Post* and developed his criticism of party government, arguing that a 'Ministry should be representative of the main currents of political thought'. In 1930 he lost as an Independent at Young. But he held Goulburn for the United Australia Party in 1932-35, and was on that party's council in 1934-38, failing to win Goulburn and Wollondilly in 1938. He had settled on the land at Carcoar in 1934. He became discontented with the negativism of his new party, and in 1943 castigated its role in building up the Country Party and its 'present strivings for . . . mergers with other organisations'.

About 1957 Loughlin retired to Pennant Hills, Sydney. On 11 July 1960 he died in Hornsby hospital after a motor car accident. Buried in the Field of Mars cemetery, he was survived by his wife, their two sons and three of their five daughters. His estate was valued for probate at £19 788. Above all, Loughlin was a devoted and successful countryman; socially radical and politically idealistic, he sought reforms through the Labor Party and contributed much to its wide moral appeal. But, not unlike W. A. Holman [q.v.9], he came to resent the role of the extra-parliamentary component of the party. His dilemma was complicated by his loathing of communism and distrust of city trade unionists which led eventually to his rejection of Labor factionalism and the opportunism of Lang.

H. Radi and P. Spearritt (eds), *Jack Lang* (Syd, 1977); *SMH*, 12 Apr 1920, 8 June 1922, 1 Aug 1923, 16 Nov 1923, 24 Apr 1924, 11 Dec 1925, 16 Sept, 22 Nov 1926, 21 Nov 1927, 26 May 1931, 13 June 1932, 12 July 1960; *Freeman's J*, 15 Apr 1920, 18 June 1925; *Fighting Line*, 22 Apr 1920; *Aust Worker*, 27 May 1925; *Bulletin*, 22 May 1935; family information.   BEDE NAIRN

LOVE, ERNEST FREDERICK JOHN (1861-1929), physicist, was born on 31 October 1861 at Weston-super-Mare, Somerset, England, eldest son of John Henry Love, surgeon, and his wife Emily, née Serle. Later the family moved to Wolverhampton, Staffordshire, where Love and his two brothers—one of whom, Augustus E. H. Love, was to win great renown as a mathematician—attended Wolverhampton Grammar School. All three are said to have been very reserved, taking little if any part in school life outside their work.

Love matriculated at the University of Cambridge in 1879 as a sizar at St John's College and was elected a scholar two years afterwards. As an undergraduate he studied experimental physics in the Cavendish Laboratory, obtaining second-class honours in the natural sciences tripos examinations in 1883. He then worked as demonstrator in physics at Mason College, Birmingham, (later the University of Birmingham) and published several papers on experimental physics, the two most ambitious of which unfortunately attracted fairly damning criticism.

In February 1888 Love was appointed to the University of Melbourne as assistant lecturer and demonstrator in natural philosophy, a new position associated with the university's introduction of separate degrees in science. Soon after his arrival he found himself in charge of his department, Professor H. M. Andrew [q.v.3], having taken leave of absence. Following Andrew's death, Love applied for the vacant chair but lost to (Sir) Thomas Lyle [q.v.] with whom he was to share responsibility for all teaching of natural philosophy in the university for many years. Love joined the Royal Society of Victoria in

1889 and published regularly in its *Proceedings*. During the 1890s he persuaded the society to attempt a gravity survey of Australasia and himself undertook precision determinations of the gravitational acceleration at Melbourne and Sydney. He returned to geodetic questions in 1922-29 as founding secretary of the Australian National Research Council's national committee for geodesy and geophysics.

He was also active in the Australasian Association for the Advancement of Science, serving as local secretary for Victoria in 1893-1904, as a member of several specialist committees, and as president of section A at the 1907 Adelaide congress where his presidential address dealt with another lifelong interest, the thermodynamics of electrolytic processes. In 1908 the University of Melbourne awarded him a D.Sc. for his collected thermodynamical publications. An interest in astronomy had seen him elected a fellow of the Royal Astronomical Society in 1895; he was also president of the Victorian branch of the British Astronomical Association in 1899-1903. Late in life Love developed expertise in acoustics, and his advice was sought by architects responsible for several major public buildings, including the Melbourne Town Hall.

Love never married. A member of the Anglican synod, he lived in Queen's College at the university as a fellow and tutor until 1896 when he took up residence at Coburg with his unmarried sister. Recurring bouts of 'nerve fatigue and exhaustion' beginning about 1915 eventually led to a reduced teaching load. He retired in 1927, when he presented his valuable library to the university, and died at Coburg on 9 March 1929. He was buried in Fawkner cemetery.

Roy Astronomical Soc, *Monthly Notice*, 90 (1930), p 373; *Obituary Notices of Fellows of the Roy Soc*, 3 (1941), p 467; *Herald* (Melb), 9 Mar 1929; *Argus*, 11 Mar 1929; Univ Melb Archives.

R. W. HOME

LOVE, JAMES ROBERT BEATTIE (1889-1947), clergyman and missionary, was born on 16 June 1889 at Lislaird, Killeter, Tyrone, Ireland, fifth child of Rev. George Clarke Love and his wife Margaret Georgina, née Beattie. When he was five months old the family migrated to Australia and, after a short stay in Victoria, settled at Strathalbyn, South Australia, where his father ministered to the Presbyterian congregation from 1892 until his retirement in 1923. Love received his schooling at Strathalbyn and the Pupil Teachers' School, Adelaide. He taught at Strathalbyn in 1906-07 and attended the University

Training College in 1908-09 (B.A., Adelaide, 1915).

He was classified as head teacher and appointed to the school at Leighs Creek (Copley) in 1910. He began sending specimens of birds to Edwin Ashby [q.v.7] who exhibited them at meetings of the Royal Society of South Australia; one of these birds was identified as a new genus and species, and named *Ashbyia lovensis*.

Late in 1912 Love accepted an honorary commission from the board of missions of the Presbyterian Church of Australia to investigate and report on the condition of the Aborigines and possible locations for mission work among them. His report was published as a pamphlet, *The Aborigines, their present condition as seen in northern South Australia, the Northern Territory and western Queensland* (Melbourne, 1915). Two years later he took temporary charge of the Presbyterian Mission to the Aborigines at Port George IV (Kunmunya), Western Australia.

On 9 November 1915 Love enlisted in the Australian Imperial Force; he joined the 1st Light Horse Training Regiment in April 1916, transferring to the Camel Corps in May. In August 1917 he was commissioned second lieutenant in the 1st Imperial Camel Brigade (Anzac Section) and promoted lieutenant in November. He transferred to the 14th Light Horse in July 1918, was wounded in September and returned to Australia next month. He had been awarded the Distinguished Conduct Medal in February and the Military Cross in September, in both cases for 'conspicuous gallantry and devotion to duty'.

Love entered the Presbyterian Theological School in Ormond [q.v.] College, University of Melbourne, spending his first and final years at the college and the second as superintendent at Mapoon, an Aboriginal mission on the west coast of Cape York Peninsula, Queensland. After his ordination in 1922 he returned to Mapoon where, on 4 September 1923, he married Blanche Margaret Holinger of Melbourne, who was teaching in the mission school.

In 1927 the Loves moved to Kunmunya where he was superintendent until 1940. In the earlier years the missionaries (Love, his wife and children and another married couple) were dependent for communication and supplies on the mission ketch. It sailed to Broome once a month except December to February (the cyclone season). Later the installation of the pedal-radio and preparation of an airstrip enabled daily contact with the flying doctor base at Wyndham and quick transport to hospital in emergencies. Love himself dressed wounds, set broken limbs and dispensed medicine to the less serious cases.

The purpose of the mission, its methods,

and the people of the Worora tribe are described in his book, *Stone-age bushmen of today* (London, 1936). Cattle were bred for meat and goats for meat and milk. Vegetables, fruit and tropical cereals were grown. Some income was derived from the sale of peanuts and bêche-de-mer. However, the very rugged terrain and the remote location ruled out selling livestock. The intention was to train and employ the able-bodied men and women. The Aborigines were paid for working on the mission but, apart from the old and the sick, those who did not work were obliged to support themselves in their traditional ways, maintaining their dignity and self-reliance.

Love translated parts of the Bible into Worora and some Worora stories into English. His analysis of the Worora grammar was presented as a thesis to the University of Adelaide (M.A., 1933). His observations on the languages, religion and customs of the tribes among whom he lived formed the subject of at least thirty articles in scientific and religious periodicals.

During his long furlough in 1937 Love spent six months establishing a new mission at Ernabella in the Musgrave Range, South Australia. After a further three years at Kunmunya, he moved to Ernabella, where he stayed until early 1946. Sheep were run on the mission property, in the care of Aboriginal shepherds. Policies and methods were essentially the same as at Kunmunya.

Love retired from mission work in 1946 and was elected moderator of the General Assembly of the Presbyterian Church of South Australia. He accepted a call to the parish of Mount Barker-Lobethal-Woodside that year but illness prevented him from spending much time there. He died of kidney disease on 19 February 1947, survived by his wife, three sons and a daughter, and was buried in Centennial Park cemetery.

Love saw himself, and was seen by his Aboriginal parishioners, as a paternal figure. The Worora gave him and his wife names in their language meaning, not the formal 'Father' and 'Mother' but the affectionate 'Dad' and 'Mum'. He encouraged the preservation of those aspects of tribal life that were compatible with Christianity and strove for a balance between upholding tribal law and maintaining the discipline that he considered necessary for the mission's well-being. With some exceptions, unacceptable practices, while discouraged, were not overtly suppressed. The people gradually changed their ways as they came to understand more of the teaching and example of the missionaries; many of them became Church members. Preaching the gospel, teaching manual skills, educating the children and caring for the helpless were regarded as inseparable elements in a mission that aimed to give the Aborigines a

new religious faith and an introduction to modern technology that, Love believed, would make them healthier, happier and better able to survive the impact of contact with white people.

Advertiser (Adel), 26 Feb 1947; J. R. B. Love papers (PRG 214, SLSA).   J. H. LOVE

LOVE, JAMES SIMPSON (1863-1933), horse-exporter, pastoralist and philanthropist, was born on 1 February 1863 at Newtown of Fintry, Stirlingshire, Scotland, only son of John Love, provision merchant, and his wife Janet, née Simpson. During his childhood Love's father died and in 1877 his mother married the geologist Robert Logan Jack [q.v.4]. The couple moved to Townsville, Queensland, where Jack was based. James remained in Scotland to complete his schooling until 1879 when he sailed for Brisbane.

Despite youth, inexperience and parental opposition, Love immediately joined Jack's second expedition to Cape York Peninsula. The expedition involved severe privation and conflict with Aborigines, and Jack reported approvingly on the conduct of his stepson.

After employment on Woodstock and Inkerman stations, from the early 1880s Love operated a livery stable and commission agency at Townsville in partnership with Frederick Cruckshank. On 22 December 1886 at Townsville, with Catholic rites, he married Mary Jane Gordon. In the 1890s Love began exporting remount horses to the British Army in India; this enterprise extended to South Africa in 1899-1902 and Egypt in 1914, but the enduring market was India. By the 1920s there was an annual military requirement for 2000 Australian horses in India, of which he contributed up to 700; he made regular trips to Calcutta with his consignments. Horses were purchased for export throughout northern and western Queensland, and Love acquired Egera station near Charters Towers and Butcher's Hill west of Cooktown as horse-depots. The enterprise was registered as Indian Remounts Ltd in Calcutta and as Egera Pastoral Co. in Queensland. He was well known as a judge of blood horses at shows.

Between 1906 and 1933 Love had a stake in at least fourteen pastoral properties. His business enterprises included Queen's Hotel Townsville Ltd; he lived his latter years at the hotel. His share portfolio included companies in England, Singapore, Fiji, New Zealand and Australia, and in 1931-33 he purchased the cattle properties: Dunbar, Valley of Lagoons and Gainsford.

A horse-racing enthusiast, Love was secretary of the Townsville Turf Club from 1894 to 1924, then president until his death; he was also president of the Townsville Show Society. He imported stud Shorthorn bulls and numerous Clydesdale and thoroughbred stallions. He was also sometime president of the Brisbane Club and of the Townsville Golf Club.

Over six feet (183 cm) tall, well-built and of ruddy complexion, Love was a notable athlete and boxer; obituaries record his bout in Mackay with Charles Armstrong, husband of (Dame) Nellie Melba [q.v.]. Of seemingly complex character, Love was described as a man of energy, enterprise and great personal charm, as a firm friend and unforgiving enemy; elsewhere as an autocrat, an iron disciplinarian, and by Indian workers as a fearsome bully.

Love died suddenly on board ship at Jetty Wharf, Townsville, on 28 November 1933, and was buried with Presbyterian forms in Townsville cemetery. He was survived by three daughters. He left most of his estate as a perpetual trust, with income from assets to be distributed annually to approved charities. The will stipulated, however, that the Roman Catholic Church or any Catholic body could not benefit. The trustees, (Sir) Arthur Fadden and Patrick Collins, declared the Love estate at £207 166 on 30 November 1938; settlement had been complicated by the wide distribution of assets, irregularities in business records, and a successful legal challenge by Love's daughters. Queensland Trustees Ltd now review applications from Church, education, medical and general welfare organizations, and make allocations, as the will provides.

R. L. Jack, *Northmost Australia* (Lond, 1921); *North Queensland Register*, 24 Apr 1899, 14 Oct, 2 Dec 1933; *Townsville Herald*, 8 Jan 1887; *Queenslander*, 11 Aug 1906, 7 Dec 1933; A17126, Supreme Court files, 38, 38a, 38b of 1934 (QSA).
ANNE ALLINGHAM

LOVE, SIR JOSEPH CLIFTON (1867-1951), manufacturer and businessman, was born on 18 January 1867 in Brisbane, second son of Harry Clifford Love, Dublin-born storekeeper, and his English wife Ann Paton, née Bell. Educated at Brisbane and Sydney Grammar schools, he followed his father, founder of Clifford Love & Co., tea merchants, in mercantile and manufacturing pursuits. Clifton was manager of the Imperial Manufacturing Co. Ltd which joined with his father's firm in 1911 when he became manager of the new firm Clifford Love & Co. Ltd; in 1919 he became general manager. The firm, manufacturers of cereal and kindred foodstuffs (notably 'Uncle Toby's Oats', 'Wade's Cornflour' and 'Laundrena Starch'), operated throughout Australia and their establishments included oatmeal mills at Kent Street, Sydney, and large cornflour and starch mills on the Lane Cove River.

A confirmed protectionist, Love was prominent in organizations promoting manufacturing and safeguarding employers' rights. He was a founder of the New South Wales Chamber of Manufactures in 1895 (vice-president 1915-20, president 1920-22) and president of the Associated Chambers of Manufactures of Australia. In 1922 he was president of the All-Australian Exhibition of Manufactures held in Sydney. For some years he was the employers' representative in the Industrial Court in connexion with applications from milling, starch and condiment workers. He strongly opposed the 44-hour week. He was appointed government representative on the Soldiers' State Industrial Council in 1920 and on the Repatriation Arbitration Committee in 1925. Knighted that year, he was known as Sir Clifton.

Among his other activities, Love was president of the Australian division of the Chartered Institute of Secretaries in 1930, commissioner of the Government Savings Bank of New South Wales, 1931-33, and chairman of Manufacturers' Mutual Insurance Co. and Carpet Manufacturers' Ltd. In 1946 he joined the board of Joyce Biscuits Ltd.

Politically conservative, Love was prominent in the National Association of New South Wales as a vice-president and treasurer. He was a keen supporter of W. M. Hughes [q.v.9], even when he stood as an Independent Nationalist in 1929. In 1933 Love supported J. A. Lyons's [q.v.] moves to strengthen Australian defence and was appointed a vice-president of the Defence of Australia League. His consuming interest was business but he also found time for art and community service. He was president of the North Sydney district Boy Scouts' Association and of the Sydney City Mission, and chairman of the Scottish Hospital.

Love died at his home at Wollstonecraft, Sydney, on 26 August 1951, survived by his wife Maggie Drummond, née Banks, whom he had married at Balmain with Congregational rites on 3 November 1897, and by their son. His estate was valued at £99 613.

A. Pratt (ed) *The national handbook of Australia's industries*(Melb, 1934); *A'asian Insurance and Banking Record*, 75, Sept 1951, p 483; *Aust National Review*, 19 June 1925; *SMH*, 17 Feb, 11 Mar, 14 Apr, 27 Oct 1921, 25 Oct 1922, 3 June 1925, 3 Feb, 5 Oct 1927, 25 Sept 1930, 27 Aug 1951.
G. P. WALSH

LOVE, NIGEL BORLAND (1892-1979), aviator and flour-miller, was born on 16 January 1892 at South Kurrajong, New South

Wales, eldest child of native-born parents John Love, businessman, and his wife Rebecca, née Charley. On leaving Sydney Boys' High School, he joined his father's importing business, Plummer Love & Co., and in 1912-13 visited Britain on behalf of the firm.

In June 1915 Love enlisted in the Australian Imperial Force and was selected to attend the New South Wales government's flying school at Richmond. Commissioned on 11 January 1917 he embarked for Britain and was posted to several flying and gunnery schools. Promoted lieutenant (pilot) in January 1918, he served in France with B Flight, 3 Squadron, Australian Flying Corps, and, flying RE8s, was engaged in artillery co-operation and reconnaissance until May. Back in England he was attached as an instructor to No. 7 Training Squadron and served with the Royal Air Force Ferry Pool.

Love and another Australian airman W. J. Warneford joined H. E. Broadsmith, chief designer for the aircraft manufacturers A. V. Roe & Co. Ltd, who had secured the Australian agency of the Avro company. On returning to Sydney in June 1919, Love searched for a suitable airfield and, after inspecting numerous sites, leased a grazing paddock near Cooks River at Mascot, which proved ideal.

The partners, registered as the Australian Aircraft & Engineering Co. Ltd with Love as managing director, began to assemble Avro 504K aircraft at Mascot in February 1920. While Broadsmith worked on the aircraft Love tried to raise money and to create interest in aviation by joy flights and charter operations including flights over Sydney for photographic purposes and piloting the first fare-paying passenger from Sydney to Melbourne. In the first Aerial Derby of 1920 he won the handicap, and again in 1922 when he was also first man home. The company supplied Queensland and Northern Territory Aerial Services Ltd with its first passenger commercial aircraft. However, lack of orders, expenditure in designing and developing a five-seat commercial aircraft, and failure to gain assistance from the Commonwealth government forced the company into voluntary liquidation in 1923. When their lease expired the Commonwealth resumed the airfield, now Kingsford Smith [q.v.9] Airport.

At Strathfield Methodist Church on 4 June 1924 Love married Phyllis Eloise, daughter of George Arthur Davey, managing director of Edwin Davey & Sons, flour-millers. He joined the firm, becoming sales manager, and in 1928 bought the Lidcombe Bakery. In January 1935 he registered N. B. Love Pty Ltd and built a flour-mill at Enfield. He adopted the brandname 'Supreme' and introduced controls to produce a quality flour with an unusual degree of uniformity. He also developed 'Fine-Tex' flour for cake-making and an increased-protein flour 'Pro-Max', franchising bakers. He was a founding member of the New South Wales Flour Millers' Trade Council in 1942.

Appointed wing commander in the Royal Australian Air Force in August 1941, Love commanded No. 2 wing of the Air Training Corps, for boys aged 16 to 18, throughout World War II. In 1943 as a Liberal Democrat he unsuccessfully contested the Federal seat of Parkes. He was president of the State branch of the Air Force Association in 1945-46.

In 1940 Love had taken over Edwin Davey & Sons, and in 1944 acquired a flour-mill at Boggabri. In 1952 he set up Millmaster Feeds Pty Ltd to produce stock-feed pellets at Enfield, and in 1958 started to manufacture bread at Enfield, introducing a high-speed dough development technique and also manufacturing gluten and starch. That year he decided to float a public company, N. B. Love Industries Ltd, with himself as managing director; in 1962 the company was sold to George Weston (Australia) Pty Ltd. Love retired and set up two cattle properties, Urambi, near Canberra, and Glenrossal, Braidwood, where he bred Poll Herefords. He wrote an unpublished autobiography covering the years 1915-23.

Survived by his wife, daughter and three sons, Love died at Killara on 2 October 1979 and was cremated. His estate was valued for probate at $508 867. A firm, even fanatical, believer in the future of aviation in Australia, Love differed from many of his aviation contemporaries in his sound business instincts and training.

Transport Aust, 18, 1977, p 8; *Wings*, 29 Sept 1977, p 14; *Baker and Millers' J*, Nov 1979; N. B. Love Pty Ltd, *Prospectus*, 1 Jan 1959 (Registrar General, NSW); information from Ms J. Gall, Canb, and Mr John Love, Killara, Syd.   J. D. WALKER

LOVE, WILTON WOOD RUSSELL (1861-1933), medical practitioner, was born on 16 November 1861 at Hollymount, Mayo, Ireland, son of Rev. James Love, United Presbyterian minister and Hebrew scholar, and his wife Mary, née Russell, of Belfast. The family migrated to Queensland in 1862. James Love soon became founding minister of the Presbyterian Church, Wickham Terrace, Brisbane, but in 1871 entered the Anglican communion and in 1878 became the first rector of Lutwyche parish, Fortitude Valley.

Love was a distinguished student at Bris-

bane Grammar School. Dux in 1877-78, he
won the gold and silver Lilley [q.v.5] medals,
the John West [q.v.6] medal for senior public
examinations, University of Sydney, the
Queensland exhibition which he took out at
the University of Edinburgh, and the Thomson bursary. At Edinburgh in 1884 he graduated M.B., Ch.M. and then served as house
surgeon and physician at the Royal Infirmary.

Love's outstanding lifelong career in general medicine in Queensland began in 1886. A
pioneer in bacteriology, pathology and the use
of diathermy and X-rays, he also lectured in
chemistry at the Brisbane Technical and
Pharmacy colleges. He had one of the first X-
ray plants in Queensland and introduced X-
ray investigations to the Children's Hospital.
His first X-ray equipment had consisted of a
6-inch spark coil with a mercurial interrupter;
the primary current was derived from a bi-
chromate battery. Over time the apparatus
became more powerful. By 1897 Love's
radiographs were referred to in medical journals. He frequently assisted the Department
of Police in microscopic forensic work.

Love's medicine was based soundly on general medical and classical traditions. The
medical journals to which he contributed
included the *Lancet*. Conversant with ancient
Greek, he aptly illustrated his spoken and
written discourses with classical allusions. He
was a splendid raconteur and his personality
and accomplishments attracted public office.
At various times he was secretary of the
Queensland Central Board of Health and of
Australasian Medical congresses (1899,
1920); president of the Queensland Medical
Society; councillor and president of the
Queensland branch of the British Medical
Association and member of the B.M.A.'s federal committee; and foundation fellow of the
College of Surgeons of Australasia. He was a
consulting surgeon to the Brisbane Children's
Hospital, the Lady Lamington Hospital for
women and the Lady Bowen maternity hospital. He served as a foundation member of the
Senate of the University of Queensland in
1910-16, and was a member of the Queensland Club. Love's 'serene and unruffled, courteous though firm manner' helps to explain
his popularity as a children's and women's
doctor.

Love had married Lucy Davidson, daughter
of a surveyor-general of Queensland, on 8
May 1888 at Milton; she predeceased him.
He died at his historic home, Bulimba House,
on 3 January 1933, survived by two daughters
and a son, and was buried in Toowong cemetery with Church of England rites.

Love had been an enthusiastic bird-lover
and subscribed to G. M. Mathews' [q.v.] *Birds
of Australia*. On his death his family presented a bound set of these plates with an illu-

minated screed to the University of Queensland.

Alcazar Press, *Queensland 1900* (Brisb, nd); W.
Watson & Sons Ltd, *Salute to the X-ray pioneers of
Australia* (Syd, 1946); *MJA*, 25 Mar 1933, p 386;
Brisbane Courier, 4 Jan 1933; *SMH*, 5 Jan 1933;
Sunday Mail (Brisb), 19 Mar 1933; *Telegraph*
(Brisb), 20 Mar 1933; personal information from
Mrs H. Spence, Indooroopilly, Brisb.

C. A. C. LEGGETT

LOVEKIN, ARTHUR (1859-1931), journalist, was born on 12 November 1859, probably at Slough, Buckinghamshire, England,
son of Rev. Lewis James Lovekin, Anglican
clergyman, and his wife Mariann, née Ken-
yon. He was educated privately and at St
Edmund's School, Canterbury, in 1871-75.
Lovekin migrated in 1879 and worked for a
year as a surveyor in Victoria. In 1880 he
joined the Melbourne *Age* as a journalist; and
on 26 June 1882 at Ballarat he married Elizabeth Jane Letcher.

He went to the *South Australian Register*
in 1883 and with T. Harry formed a partnership as public shorthand writers in 1885. Next
year he moved to Western Australia as senior
reporter on the Fremantle *Herald*, the
colony's first radical newspaper. Almost
immediately the *Herald* was absorbed by
Stirling Bros & Co., owners of the conservative evening paper, the *Daily News*. From
1890 Lovekin was company secretary and
director; by 1894 he was editor and managing
director of the *Daily News* which, apart from a
period of eighteen months, he controlled
(after 1916 as sole owner as well as editor)
until he sold it to News Ltd in 1926 for
£86 000.

In 1893, in England, he had bought machinery which allowed the *Daily News* to install
the first rotary printing press and linotype
machines in Western Australia. Three years
later Lovekin launched the *Morning Herald* in
competition with (Sir) John Winthrop Hackett's [q.v.9] *West Australian*. Successful at
first, the newspaper, indeed the whole company, fell into trouble after Lovekin resigned
in 1900, allegedly because of 'political
wrangling at meetings'. He returned to restore the position next year. Hackett and
Lovekin were strikingly similar. In politics
both were conservative on constitutional
questions, but progressive on education, justice, health and welfare. Both exerted
influence and power through their newspapers and associates. In the 1890s Lovekin and
Hackett, with Alexander [q.v.8] and David
Forrest, were regular participants in the Sunday morning discussions at the home of Premier Sir John Forrest [q.v.8]. Much government policy resulted—with, not surprisingly,

support from the Perth press. Lovekin was a patriotic Western Australian and crusader for development, based on an expanding rural economy and the fashioning of a beautiful city: like Hackett, he was a substantial benefactor to Perth.

Through the *Daily News* Lovekin had campaigned for responsible self-government for Western Australia; he remained opposed to Federation, despite Sir John Forrest's and Hackett's eventual support for it. His relations with Forrest remained cordial—Lovekin called him 'the best friend I ever had'. Over the years Lovekin was perhaps the most ardent advocate of secession for Western Australia, and in 1930 was to publish three pamphlets recommending it; one included the draft of a bill 'to constitute Western Australia a free State'. Clarity and directness characterized his writing.

In World War I he matched the 'King's Shilling' with his own to volunteers and was an organizer of the 1916 conscription campaign. By the end of the war he was very wealthy, having stockpiled newsprint which he sold to newspapers affected by wartime shortages; this was later assessed by a subsequent chief-of-staff at the *Daily News*, F. H. Goldsmith, as akin to black-marketeering. In 1920 he attended the second Imperial Press Conference in Ottawa. He was a member of the Legislative Council for Metropolitan Province in 1919-31.

The King's Park was Lovekin's other great preoccupation. He was a foundation member of the honorary committee established in 1893 which became the King's Park Board in 1896; in 1918 he became president, a position he held as a benevolent autocrat until his death. That Perth today has, adjacent to the central city, this magnificent large park is due largely to Sir John Forrest's and Lovekin's foresight and tenacity.

Lovekin was a chairman of the Children's Hospital board of management. He also helped to set up the Children's Court, serving on the bench for nearly two decades; he published a historical commentary (1929) on the court in which he argued that 'kindness, mercy and charity invariably lead to reformation'. Other interests included economics, amateur acting, cricket and cycling. Memorials which carry his name include a prize for journalism, set up in 1928 through the University of Western Australia, and Lovekin Drive which was built in King's Park, largely at his expense.

Lovekin appeared reserved and preoccupied. He had 'a redoubtable and complex character, mixing caution and audacities'. Forrest once said, 'he's a good milkman, but has a habit of kicking over the bucket', and a fellow journalist remarked that 'Arthur Lovekin was a man who never shirked a fight'. Pre-

deceased by his wife (d. 1929) he died on 10 December 1931 and was buried in Karrakatta cemetery with Anglican rites; he was survived by a daughter.

Truthful Thomas, *Through the spy-glass* (Perth, 1905); L. W. Matters, *Australians who count in London* . . . (Lond, 1913); V. Courtney, *All I may tell* (Syd, 1956); *Western Mail* (Perth), 23 January 1914; WA Newspapers, *Q Bulletin*, 3 May 1964, no 2; *West Australian*, 11, 12 Dec 1931; *Daily News* (Perth) and *SMH*, 12 Dec 1931; *Bulletin*, 16 Dec 1931; V. Hughes, The custody of King's Park, Perth 1829 to 1931 (B.A. Hons thesis, Murdoch Univ, WA, 1978); F. H. Goldsmith papers (Battye Lib).

DONALD GRANT

LOVELL, HENRY TASMAN (1878-1958), psychologist and educator, was born on 6 January 1878 at East Kempsey, New South Wales, third child of James Haines Lovell, a New Zealand-born schoolteacher, and his Victorian wife Elizabeth, née Shepherd. His father taught in small country schools and Tasman became a pupil-teacher at Bowraville Public School in 1894. In December 1898 he won a scholarship to Fort Street Training School, Sydney, completing the course with a class 2 certificate. After a few months at Redfern, he was appointed on 26 April 1900 to Fort Street Model School where he spent six years. At St Paul's Anglican Church, Redfern, he married Alice Eleanor Arnold on 4 January 1904; they had three sons.

In 1902 Lovell had enrolled in arts as an unmatriculated evening student at the University of Sydney and also studied for and passed the matriculation examination in March 1903. He was twice awarded Professor (Sir) Francis Anderson's [q.v.7] prize for philosophy and in 1906 graduated B.A. with first-class honours and the university medal in logic and mental philosophy and first-class honours in French. He gained his M.A. in philosophy in 1908 and was awarded the graduates' prize for a philosophical thesis and the Woolley [q.v.6] scholarship. He held this scholarship at the University of Jena, Germany, where he was awarded a doctorate in 1909, his thesis being on Spencer's utilitarian theory of education. Though he began serious study of the language only in 1907, he wrote his thesis in German.

Before leaving for Jena, Lovell had been on the staff of the Teachers' College at Blackfriars which on his return he rejoined, teaching education, French and possibly German. In 1913 he was appointed assistant lecturer in philosophy at the university and during World War I was also a part-time assistant censor from 1914 for his expert knowledge of German and French. Anderson handed over to him the first-year course in logic and psychology. The psychology was markedly philosophical and in the Scottish manner. Lovell slowly gave it a more observational flavour, included some statistical method and in 1915 provided a second (half) course in experimental psychology. By 1917 this had grown into a full-course alternative to philosophy II. It consisted of abnormal (including Freudian), social and experimental psychology and in both first and second years laboratory and other observational work was required. In 1921 Lovell was appointed McCaughey [q.v.5] associate professor and given an assistant, A. H. Martin. By 1925 they provided the first Australian three-year psychology sequence leading to a pass or honours degree. Experimental psychology was replaced with psychometrics in psychology II and the new psychology III became almost exclusively experimental with extensive laboratory work.

Appointed McCaughey professor of psychology in 1929, Lovell was given charge of a separate department—the first professor and the first department of psychology in Australia. In 1938 the faculty of arts required a fourth year for the honours B.A. In psychology IV students were required to attend a seminar on theoretical psychology and a course in advanced statistics, to write a short thesis on a set theoretical topic and to report on a piece of observational work (laboratory, psychometric, social field observation or clinical case studies). Over the next decade about one-third of the honours graduates proceeded to M.A.

Lovell was a superb teacher. His speech was fluent and pleasing, he was a great user of blackboard, slides and front-bench demonstrations. An ex-student wrote that his 'integrity and sincerity, his passion for truth burned in his eyes'. He was highly innovative but once having introduced something he rarely changed it, although he added new developments deriving from his avid reading of books and journals in English, French and German. This diligence can be seen in the brief marginal notes he wrote in the journals of his day. He taught what he had learned from his reading and contributed little of his own to it beyond integration.

His position indicated background in the Scottish philosophy of common sense. The central task of psychology was the study of mental life (he added unconscious processes to the Scottish exclusive concern with consciousness). Cognition he treated as phenomenalist, adopting the representative theory of ideas. He accepted the notion of self as an agent in cognition and affection and as an entity which possessed continuity except in special states such as fugues and multiple personality. He accepted purposivism both at the instinctive level, which he placed in a firm evolutionary context, and at the voluntary and moral levels. He accepted that mind was embodied, being influenced by both neurophysiological and endocrinological states and processes. Lovell wrote two small books, *The springs of human action* (1914) and *Dreams* (1923, and greatly extended as *Dreams and dreaming*, 1938), and numerous journal articles. He was editor of the *Australasian Journal of Psychology and Philosophy* in 1927-34.

He was dean of the faculty of arts and fellow of the senate in 1937-41 and first president of the Australian branch of the British Psychological Society. Lovell was also active in the policy-making of many social services: he was chairman of the Child Welfare Advisory Council and president of the Council of Social Service of New South Wales, the Recreation and Leadership Movement, Toc H, and the Australian Council for Educational Research (1939-48), among many other offices.

Lovell retired in 1945; his wife died in 1953 and on 26 June 1954 he married a widow Alice Wood Johnson, née Younger. He died on 30 September 1958 at Parramatta and was cremated with Anglican rites. His wife and the sons of his first marriage survived him. A portrait medallion of Lovell by Andor Meszaros was struck, and may be awarded annually for the best Ph.D. thesis in psychology at the University of Sydney.

K. F. Walker, W. M. O'Neil and J. F. Clark (eds), *A'sian J of Psychology*, 10 (1958), no 1; Register of teachers, Education Dept Archives (Syd); Dept of Defence, B543, correspondence files 1911-17, file 363/4/700 (AAO).   W. M. O'NEIL

LOVELY, LOUISE NELLIE (1895-1980), actress, was born on 28 February 1895 at Paddington, Sydney, daughter of Ferruccio Carlo Alberti, Italian musician, and Elise Louise Jeanne de Gruningen Lehmann, a Swiss. Louise spoke French better than English in her early years; this helped her to win her first stage role at the age of 9 as Little Eva in *Uncle Tom's Cabin* as the producers wanted a young actress whose speech they could mould. After several juvenile parts, some in amateur productions, she joined Nellie Stewart's [q.v.] company for a New Zealand tour. Small roles there were her apprenticeship for the lead with the George Marlowe Company, which she joined in her early teens.

Her first films were made for Gaston Mervale and his Australian Life Biograph Company. In 1911 she starred in *A tale of the Australian bush, One hundred years ago, A ticket in Tatts,* and *Colleen Bawn,* and, in 1912, *Hands across the sea, A daughter of Australia, Conn, the shaughraun,* and *The ticket of leave man.* When the company collapsed in May 1912 and its assets were taken over by Universal Films (an Australian company) Louise made *The wreck of the Dunbar.* On 20 February 1912 in Sydney she married writer and actor William Harrie (Wilton) Welch, and in 1914 they left for the United States of America.

Their goal was Hollywood where Louise was noticed by Carl Laemmle, and after a successful screen test was engaged for Universal Pictures, under the 'Blue Bird' label. Louise had been known as Louise Carbasse, but Laemmle provided the stage name 'Louise Lovely'. She had a very French, demure, petite appearance and a halo of soft, bleached blonde hair. Her 'Blue Bird' pictures were very successful but she refused to renew her contract when Universal neither raised her salary nor allowed her to accept an invitation from Pathé Frères to work in France. For a year she was blacklisted by the studio but made a few films for independent producers. The ban was broken when Fox Film Corporation Ltd invited her to co-star with William Farnum. She worked for Fox in 1918-22, making with Farnum films such as *The last of the Duanes* and *The wings of the morning*, and occasional films with other leading men. In 1922 Louise returned to vaudeville with her 'studio act' in which she showed her own last film and followed it with a live performance involving the audience.

In 1924 she returned to Australia, and toured several States with her 'studio act'. In Hobart Marie Bjelke-Petersen [q.v.7] approached her with a request to produce a film of her book, *Jewelled nights.* Louise read it and set about raising the finance. Wilton Welch wrote the script and produced the film while Louise directed and starred as a Melbourne society girl who ran away from an arranged marriage and became a miner on the Tasmanian osmium fields. Outdoor scenes were shot on location in the Savage River area in Tasmania, and interiors in studios set up inside the Glaciarium and Wirth's [q.v.] Circus building in Melbourne. The film opened at Hoyts De Luxe, Melbourne, on 24 October 1925, and was well received by the public, though not by the critics. By the time of the 1927 royal commission into the moving picture industry Louise could see that the film would not recoup its cost of £8000. Her evidence to the commission stressed the need for a fully equipped Australian studio to enable Australian productions to compete in quality with imported films. Nothing came of her idea, or of the commission, and she retired from films disillusioned.

She divorced her husband in November 1928 and on 26 November married theatre manager Andrew Bertie Cowen in Melbourne. In 1949 they set up home permanently in Hobart where Cowen became manager of the Prince of Wales Theatre.

Louise Cowen died on 17 March 1980 at Taroona and was cremated. She was one of the most successful of a long line of Australian actors and actresses who entered the competitive world of Hollywood, and one of the many unable to achieve their film ambitions within Australia.

A. Pike and R. F. Cooper, *Australian film 1900-1977* (Melb, 1980); G. Shirley and B. Adams, *Australian cinema* (Syd, 1983); *Everyone's*, 11 Nov 1925, p 12; *Australian*, 20 Apr 1968; interview with Louise Lovely (MS, film pioneers oral history project, NL).   INA BERTRAND

LOVETT, MILDRED ESTHER (1880-1955), artist, was born on 13 September 1880 in Hobart Town, eldest of four children of Edward Frederick Lovett, clerk, and his wife Alice Edith, née Gibson. She attended Mrs H. Barnard's Ladies' School in 1887-93, and was trained in the domestic arts by her mother. On leaving school she worked as a retoucher at Richard McGuffie's photographic studio. In 1896-1901 she studied painting, modelling, life-drawing and china-painting at Hobart Technical School under Benjamin Sheppard; a fellow pupil was Florence Rodway [q.v.]. In 1898-99 she spent six months at Julian Ashton's [q.v.7] art school in Sydney.

Returning to Hobart Miss Lovett painted miniatures, gave private tuition and in 1906-08 taught modelling and life-drawing at Hobart Technical School. Lucien Dechaineux [q.v.8] encouraged her to start china-painting classes, and supplied her with designs from native flora. In 1909 in *Art and Architecture* Ashton praised her 'superior' china-painting. A vase she painted that year from a design by Sydney Long [q.v.] (Art Gallery of New South Wales) is one of the most characteristic examples of Australian Art Nouveau work.

Early in 1909 Miss Lovett moved to Sydney and in 1910 succeeded Long as second-in-charge of Ashton's Sydney Art School. Until the mid-1930s she exhibited regularly with the Art Society of Tasmania and the Society of Artists, Sydney, serving on the latter's committee in 1911-19.

On 19 November 1913 at the Presbyterian Church, Manly, Mildred Lovett married Stanley Livingstone Paterson, clerk; they soon moved to Brisbane where she met and painted with Vida Lahey [q.v.9] who became a close friend. In 1917 Lovett painted a full-length portrait in oils of Ashton (Tasmanian Museum and Art Gallery). She returned to Hobart in 1919, and in 1921 opened her own studio and supervised the evening students at the Technical School. In 1924 she was represented at the British Empire Exhibition and in 1926-27 exhibited in Sydney with 'A Group of Modern

Painters' (soon the Contemporary Group), founded by George Lambert [q.v.9] and Thea Proctor [q.v.]. Versatile, she painted landscapes in oils and won a considerable reputation for her portraits and elegant figure drawings.

Appointed art instructor at Hobart Technical College in 1925, Mildred Lovett took leave of absence in 1929 and with her husband went overseas. She enrolled at the Westminster School of Art, London, and at the Académie Lhote in Paris; she made copious notes about Lhote's cubist theories. She visited many galleries, finding works by Gauguin 'bonza' and Marie Laurencin 'delightful. Like a lark singing . . . (quite feminine and valuable for that reason alone)'. She was also enthusiastic about old masters, notably Memling, the Van Eycks, Mantegna, Pisanello and in Florence 'Everything'.

At Hobart Technical College in 1930-40, Mildred Lovett was 'one of a very select group of teachers in Australia . . . who had any sympathy or understanding for Cubism'. Her art department 'was recognized as one of the most enlightened in Australia'. A councilmember of the Art Society of Tasmania she made the first of her few lithographs in 1932. Quiet and unassuming, she was always open minded. With dark hair, she had a strong face and serene expression. Her students included Grace Crowley and Anne Dangar in Sydney and Jean Bellette, Joseph Connor, Edith Holmes, Amie Kingston and Dorothy Stoner in Tasmania. From 1940 she lived in Sydney but returned to Hobart in 1952 and gave some private classes. She died childless on 23 March 1955 at Sandy Bay.

D. H. Skinner and J. Kroeger (eds), *Renniks Australian artists*, no 1 (Adel, 1968); Important Women Artists (Gallery), *Mildred Lovett 1880-1955 and her students*, exhibition cat (Melb, 1980); H. Kolenberg, *Edith Holmes, Dorothy Stoner: two retrospectives*, exhibition cat (Hob, 1983); *Lone Hand*, 1 May 1913; *Illustrated Tasmanian Mail*, 29 Sept 1921, 22 Sept 1932; Hobart Technical College records (TA); Lovett letters to her family, London and Paris 1929 (pc in Tasmanian Museum and Art Gallery).   HENDRIK KOLENBERG
                                    SUE BACKHOUSE

LOW, SIR DAVID ALEXANDER CECIL (1891-1963), cartoonist, was born on 7 April 1891 at Dunedin, New Zealand, third son of David Brown Low, pharmacist from Scotland, and his New Zealand-born wife Jane Caroline, née Flanagan. The family soon moved to Christchurch where the sons attended the Boys' High School, but David's formal education ended when he was 11; his parents believed the death of his elder brother was caused by 'over study'. Inspired by such English halfpenny comics as *Chips*, *Comic Cuts* and *Larks* he started to draw, and while still in short pants sold cartoons to the Christchurch *Spectator*. At 18 he joined the staff of the *Canterbury Times*.

Low was aggressively ambitious and constantly mailed newspapers containing his cartoons to the Sydney *Bulletin*. Eventually, in 1911, the *Bulletin* offered him a temporary job in Melbourne. He joyfully accepted and only briefly once returned to New Zealand. He shared a studio at the top of Collins Street with Hal Gye [q.v.9] and provided illustrations, joke-drawings and caricatures for the *Bulletin* and *Lone Hand*. After six months his position was confirmed, but before moving to Sydney he was sent around Australia seeking subjects. A collection of these was published as *Caricatures* in 1915. Meanwhile, to his great disappointment Norman Lindsay [q.v.] remained chief cartoonist and he was not encouraged to produce full-page political cartoons; instead he was required to depict 'the personalities and the minutiae of the politics involved'.

The advent of W. M. Hughes [q.v.9] as prime minister and his visit to London gave Low his second big chance. His cartoon, entitled 'The Imperial Conference', published in the *Bulletin* on 16 March 1916, made him famous: it depicted Hughes in full cry and the Imperial War Cabinet under cover over the caption 'Asquith: David, talk to him in Welsh and pacify him'. Thereafter, Low concentrated on Hughes's 'colourful and irascible personality'. In 1918 he published *The Billy book*, a collection of satirical drawings of the imagined capers of Hughes in London. Low posted copies to English editors; Henry Cadbury, part-owner of the London *Star*, read Arnold Bennett's review in the *New Statesman*, secured a copy of *The Billy book* and in 1919 cabled Low an offer to join the *Star* at a salary of £3000.

In London, at St Paul's Church, Covent Garden, Low married Madeline Grieve Kenning of Auckland on 7 June 1920; they lived for many years at Golders Green. He was soon involved again in rowdy contention—in Melbourne he had been called a bastard to his face by Hughes—this time he resigned over the tiny space the *Star* allotted to his cartoons. A compromise followed, although there were to be unending arguments over presentation, space and position in the paper. He settled down to drawing the antics of British politicians. His double-headed ass, labelled 'Coalition', suggested the futility of going both ways at once and getting nowhere.

After eight years with the *Star*, Low accepted an offer from Lord Beaverbrook to work for the *Evening Standard* which guaranteed complete independence in choice of subjects, treatment and political viewpoint.

Low created his world-famous character 'Colonel Blimp' in 1932: 'a rotund, bald, fierce gentleman with long white moustache', Blimp was the mouthpiece of reactionary opinion and confused thinking. Low was a major propagandist for the anti-Fascist cause.

After World War II newsprint shortages led to the curtailment of cartoon space in the *Evening Standard* and in 1950 Low joined the Labour *Daily Herald* but in 1953 moved to the *Manchester Guardian*. In his long working life he drew for some forty world-wide newspapers and magazines, and published some thirty collections of cartoons in book form, as well as *Ye madde designer* (1935) and *Low's autobiography* (1956). Although a tall, 'distinguished looking, dark-bearded man with fine hands and dominating black eyebrows', Low always caricatured himself as 'an impertinent figure of fun'. He belonged to the National Liberal and Savile clubs.

Awarded honorary LL.D.s by the universities of New Brunswick (1958) and Leicester (1961), he was knighted in 1962. He died in West London Hospital on 19 September 1963. His wife and two daughters survived him and largely inherited his estate, valued for probate at £99 205.

Low's draughtsmanship was in lineal descent from Phil May [q.v.5] and, developed to a style bold and simple, never changed. Originally he drew with a pen, but after a year in Australia used a full flowing brush, with beautiful quality, expression and control, over a lightly pencilled framework. Low virtually pioneered brush-drawing in Australia, to create a vogue with succeeding cartoonists. After his death he was described in the press as 'the dominant cartoonist of the western world'—a reputation he had enjoyed for about thirty years. His books and a collection of cartoons are in the library of New Zealand House, London, as a memorial.

V. Lindesay, *The inked-in image* (Melb, 1970); *Lone Hand*, 1 Oct 1915; *People* (Syd), 24 May 1950; *Aust Letters*, 7 (Oct 1965); *Argus* (Melb), 1 Feb 1950; *The Times*, 21 Sept 1963; *Age*, 12 Dec 1931, 21 Sept 1963.   VANE LINDESAY

LOWER, LEONARD WALDEMERE (1903?-1947), humorist and newspaper columnist, was probably born on 24 September 1903 at Dubbo, New South Wales, son of Sydney Waldemere Lower, pharmacist, and Flora, née Robinson or McInerney. His alcoholic father was a member of the Dubbo Dramatic Society and the town band, and wrote music. Some time after 1910 the parents separated and his mother moved to Sydney and married a businessman C. K. Oades. The anarchic and restless individualism which characterized Lower's career appeared early.

He attended Darlinghurst Public School and enlisted for five years in the Royal Australian Garrison Artillery on 14 September 1920. In December next year he deserted and, as 'Leonard Walter Brett', joined the Royal Australian Navy on 12 April 1922. He served as a stoker in H.M.A.S. *Brisbane*, but again deserted (at Gladstone, Queensland) on 11 August 1923.

For several years Lower carried his swag through Queensland and New South Wales and, while unemployed, slept in the Sydney Domain. About 1928 he began working for Jack Lang's [q.v.9] *Labor Daily*, and later *Beckett's Budget* and the *Daily Guardian*, finally working regularly for (Sir) Frank Packer's *Australian Women's Weekly* and the *Daily Telegraph*. Sacked by Packer in 1940 for being publicly rude about Noel Coward, he joined *Smith's Weekly* for which he had written in the 1930s. On 20 February 1942 he enlisted in the Australian Imperial Force, but was discharged medically unfit on 29 April, without leaving Australia.

For many years Lower was acclaimed as 'Australia's funniest writer'. Being funny had its costs—small, dark and nervous, he was described as 'serious', 'melancholy', 'morose', a marvellous talker, but someone whom 'one could never get close to', and his drinking was legendary. He wrote in the bar of the Tudor Hotel and many other watering holes, in country hotel rooms where Syd Deamer, editor of the *Daily Telegraph*, sent him to get him away from the temptations of the city, and from newspaper offices—'head down, leaning against the typewriter, arms hanging straight down, pondering, agonisingly refining' the seemingly effortless comedy.

His one novel, *Here's luck* (1930), became a classic of Australian humour. In observing life in the eastern suburbs of Sydney, the battle of the sexes and the generations, low life and 'gimme' girls, and the anarchy of a man freed from the restraints of marriage and work, Lower expressed many of the jokes and fantasies that can be seen in the cartoons and gags of the popular press of the late 1920s. Despite the comic exaggeration, it has been suggested that the novel's hero was drawn from life, which points to Lower's genius as a journalist—his ability to distort the real into the truly comic.

In Sydney on 9 November 1929 Lower married Phyllis Constance Salter; they had no children and moved house constantly within Sydney's inner suburbs. Impulsive by nature, he led a chaotic life. A niece told how he once abandoned his wife (without her fare home) at the theatre—going for 'a quick drink' during the interval he met a ship's captain who was about to sail for Newcastle, and decided to go along. Eventually he returned to Sydney by train. 'Uncle Lennie was not what you would call a considerate husband'.

Lower died in Sydney Hospital on 10 July 1947 of cancer, wisecracking to the end, and was cremated with Anglican rites. Reaction in the press at the time was muted, but his reputation has steadily grown. In 1963 Claude McKay wrote of him that 'for genuine humour and the turns of phrase that proclaimed the artist, Lennie Lower was without peer'. *Here's luck* has remained in print. His ephemeral columns for the newspapers were collected several times during his life, and other selections were made in 1963 and 1983. His compound of 'realism, fantasy, absurdity, satire, and sardonic wit' has kept his writing from dating over the last fifty years. In 1972 the Dubbo Historical Society completed the 'Lennie Lower Memorial Room' in the Dubbo Museum; and in 1982 Barry Dickins's play *Lonely Lenny Lower* was produced in Melbourne and Sydney.

G. Blaikie, *Remember Smith's Weekly* (Adel, 1966); *Southerly*, 1958, no 2, 1961, no 3; *Sunday Telegraph* (Syd), 13 July 1947, 4 June 1972; *Smith's Weekly* (Syd), 19 July 1947; *Nation*, 14 Dec 1963, 16 Oct 1965; *Age*, 1 Feb, 29 Apr 1982; *Australian*, 29 Apr 1982; *SMH*, 9 Apr, 4 June 1983; information from Mrs D. Ceinar, Gladesville, Syd, and Mr J. T. Maskey, Hamilton South, Newcastle.

JULIAN CROFT
KEITH WILLEY*

LOWERSON, ALBERT DAVID (1896-1945), soldier and farmer, was born on 2 August 1896 at Myrtleford, Victoria, sixth child of English-born Henry Lowerson, engine driver and later farmer, and his Victorian wife Mary Jane, née McMaster. Alby Lowerson had been dredging for gold at Adelong, New South Wales, before enlisting in the Australian Imperial Force in Melbourne on 16 July 1915; he was allotted to the 5th Reinforcements of the 21st Battalion which embarked in September.

Lowerson joined his unit on 7 January 1916 and accompanied it to France in March. After a period in the quiet Armentières sector he entered the battle of the Somme, seeing heavy fighting for Pozières Heights from 25 July to 7 August. Two weeks later he was back in the front lines near Mouquet Farm where he was wounded on 26 August. He rejoined the battalion a month later and was promoted corporal on 1 November. Promoted temporary sergeant on 11 April 1917, he was again wounded during the 2nd battle of Bullecourt on 3 May. It was six months before he rejoined his unit as sergeant on 1 November. In the final allied advance in 1918 he distinguished himself on 27 August at Virgin Wood and on 28 August at Herbécourt.

Lowerson won the Victoria Cross on 1 September during the capture of Mont St Quentin. He was cited for his leadership and courage during the battle, particularly for his effective bombing of the strong point which was the centre of stern resistance: a huge crater from which machine-guns fired and stick-bombs were hurled. He inflicted heavy casualties on the Germans and captured twelve machine-guns and thirty prisoners. Although wounded in the thigh he refused to withdraw until the prisoners had been sent to the rear and the posts of his men had been organized and consolidated. He then refused to leave the battalion for two days until evacuated because of his wound. He resumed duty on 17 September in time to participate in the last Australian infantry action of the war, at Montbrehain on 5 October where he was wounded for the fourth time. He received the Victoria Cross from King George V at Buckingham Palace on 1 March 1919; a month later he embarked for Australia and was discharged on 8 July.

Between the wars Lowerson was a dairy and tobacco farmer on a Victorian soldier settlement block. He named his property, on Merriang estate near Myrtleford, St Quentin. He married Edith Larkins at St Patrick's Cathedral, Melbourne, on 1 February 1930. Re-enlisting on 5 July 1940, he served as a sergeant in various training units throughout Australia until discharged in 1944. Survived by his wife and daughter, he died of leukaemia at Myrtleford on 15 December 1945 and was buried there after a Methodist service. A memorial headstone was unveiled in 1949 and local returned servicemen make an annual pilgrimage to the grave. Myrtleford in 1966 named the A. D. Lowerson Memorial Swimming Pool in his honour.

A. R. MacNeil (ed), *The story of the Twenty-first* (Melb, 1920); C. E. W. Bean, *The A.I.F. in France*, 1918 (Syd, 1942); L. Wigmore (ed), *They dared mightily* (Canb, 1963); K. Robertson, *Myrtleford* (1973); *Mufti*, Jan 1938, May 1946, Oct 1949; *Bulletin*, 28 Dec 1945; *Reveille* (Syd), June 1969; *The Times*, 3 Mar 1919; *Age* and *Argus*, 17 Dec 1945; *Myrtleford Times*, 20 Nov 1978, 22 Nov 1982; War diary, 21st Battalion, A.I.F. (AWM).

ANTHONY STAUNTON

LOWRIE, WILLIAM (1857-1933), agricultural educationist, was born on 18 October 1857 in Selkirkshire, Scotland, son of John Lowrie and his wife Christina, née Anderson. They lived on Clarilaw, one of the largest farms in Roxburghshire, where his father was a shepherd. After attending school at Blainslie, William worked for two years as a farm servant. He returned to school at St Boswell's and then proceeded to the University of Edinburgh (M.A., 1883), maintaining himself by teaching. In 1884 he won a Highland and Agricultural Society of Scotland bursary to the same university to study agriculture and related sciences. He graduated B.Sc. in 1886 as university prizeman in mathematics with several first-class honours.

After lecturing in natural science and agriculture at Gordon's College, Aberdeen, Lowrie was appointed professor of agriculture and principal at Roseworthy Agricultural College, South Australia, in 1888. On arrival he also became a member of the Central Agricultural Bureau. His grasp of scientific principles and his practical approach to farming, as well as his formidable wit, soon won the respect of the rural community. More than once this support was mobilized when Lowrie offered to resign after his ministerial superior failed to endorse his recommendations. He was badgered by a succession of ministers who, according to one journalist, 'scarcely knew the difference between a nanny goat and a Hereford bull'. In 1897 he reported fruitlessly to the Victorian government on various aspects of agricultural education in that colony.

Lowrie resigned from Roseworthy in 1901 after a series of disputes with the government's superintendent of public buildings, architect C. E. Owen Smyth [q.v.], over the college's requirements. This time, neither public support from farmers nor the offer of increased salary and greater autonomy could induce him to stay. For the next seven years he was director of Canterbury Agricultural College (later, Lincoln College), New Zealand, where he again won respect within both his college and the rural community.

In 1908 Lowrie became director of agriculture in Western Australia, where his brother-in-law (Sir) Newton Moore [q.v.] was premier. Shortly afterwards he declined the foundation chair in agriculture at the University of Sydney. In 1912, because of his knowledge of the parasitic enemies of plants, he was appointed director of agriculture in South Australia, a position from which he resigned two years later over disputes with the minister of agriculture about the department's reorganization. The Queensland minister of agriculture then tried to obtain his services but Lowrie took up farming and the breeding of Border Leicester sheep on Battunga, near Echunga. Here he remained until his death on 20 July 1933; he was buried at St George's cemetery, Magill.

Lowrie had married twice. On 24 June 1891 he wed Mary Longbottom, who died four months later from an ectopic pregnancy. At Napier, New Zealand, on 23 March 1903, he married her sister Alice who survived him. There were no children.

A stern Presbyterian who deplored waste and inefficiency, Lowrie was always a hard worker and he expected high standards of others. His research into and energetic advocacy of bare fallowing and the use of superphosphate did much to raise yields and establish wheatgrowing on a profitable basis in South Australia. Professors A. J. Perkins and A. E. V. Richardson [qq.v.] revered him. A bust of Lowrie, sculptured by Marguerite Richardson, is at Roseworthy Agricultural College.

I. D. Blair, *Life and work at Canterbury College* (Christchurch, NZ, 1956); A. W. Black, *Organizational genesis and development: a study of Australian agricultural colleges* (Brisb, 1976); J. Daniels (ed), *Roseworthy Agricultural College: a century of service* (Roseworthy, 1983); *PD* (Qld), 1914, p 119, 2564; *Observer* (Adel), 26 Nov 1887; *Advertiser* (Adel), 30 Dec 1887, 22 July 1933; *Australasian*, 13 Nov 1909; G. C. and D. P. Vaudrey, Memorabilia of the Revd William Longbottom and descendants in Australia (SLSA); PRG 30/5/17, Way letters 1913 (SAA).   ALAN W. BLACK

LOYNES, JAMES (1862-1950), building contractor and soldier, was born on 23 December 1862 at Birmingham, England, son of Charles Henry Loynes, maltster, and his wife Charlotte, née Lawrence. He was educated at St Matthew's Church of England School, Birmingham, before migrating to Queensland at 20. On 5 November 1886 he married Edith Mary Cornelius at All Saints Church, Brisbane.

Loynes was an active member of the part-time Queensland Defence Forces and had served for thirteen years before joining the 1st Queensland Mounted Infantry Contingent in 1899 for service in the South African War. He fought during the relief of Kimberley and the capture of Johannesburg and Pretoria and was promoted sergeant major and mentioned in dispatches.

When the 5th Queensland Imperial Bushmen's Contingent was being raised in March 1901 Loynes joined as a lieutenant. He was slightly wounded at Familie Hoek on 6 December and four weeks later was part of a force which was captured by the Boers, disarmed and set free. In March 1902 the Queensland Bushmen returned to Australia. Loynes resumed work as a building contractor at Ipswich and continued in the militia as a lieutenant in the 13th Australian Light Horse (Queensland Mounted Infantry) Regiment. In 1910 he transferred to the reserve of officers.

In 1915 Loynes, aged 52, enlisted in the Australian Imperial Force and embarked for overseas service on 2 June as major in command of 'A' Squadron, 11th Light Horse Regiment. The regiment went from Egypt to Gallipoli where it provided reinforcements. Loynes's squadron was taken on strength of the 2nd Light Horse Regiment and served on the peninsula from 28 August until the evacuation in December. He rejoined the 11th L.H.R. in March 1916 upon its reorganization in Egypt and several weeks later it commenced operations east of the Suez Canal. In July he commanded an escort operating around El Mahadat and then took part in actions through Sinai. In October he commanded his squadron in the attack on Maghara.

In the Palestine campaign, on 19 April 1917, the 11th Light Horse was heavily engaged in the 2nd battle of Gaza. There Loynes's squadron was prominent in the fighting around Kirbet Sihan. Heavy artillery and machine-gun fire forced the Australians to withdraw and Loynes was severely wounded and evacuated for three months. He then resumed command of his squadron and for several months during 1918 acted as second-in-command of the regiment. He was actively involved in operations in the Jordan Valley, including the Es Salt and Amman actions and the advance to Damascus.

On 25 September 1918 at Semakh on the Sea of Galilee he led his squadron in a bold mounted charge against enemy machine-gun positions. The light horsemen came under heavy fire from the village buildings. Loynes, the 'headstrong veteran . . . swung to the left and headed for the native village'. Once there he led a dismounted bayonet charge. Later he successfully attacked the railway buildings which were the main enemy strong point. His brave action had stopped 'what might have been a repulse . . . he did great work'. He received the Distinguished Service Order and was mentioned in dispatches. The Palestine campaign concluded a few weeks later. Throughout Loynes had served with the vigour and strength of a much younger man, earning comment in the regiment for his 'fearless example' and also for his 'highly developed sense of humour'. Before embarkation for Australia in July 1919 he commanded the regiment for three months.

After the war Loynes was appointed deputy commissioner of war service homes in Queensland. Survived by five of his children, he died at the Repatriation Hospital, Greenslopes, Brisbane, on 23 October 1950, and was buried in Bulimba cemetery with Anglican rites.

Aust Defence Dept, *Official records of the Australian military contingents to the war in South Africa*, P. L. Murray ed (Melb, 1911); H. S. Gullett, *The A.I.F. in Sinai and Palestine* (Syd, 1923); E. W. Hammond, *History of the Eleventh Light Horse Regiment, 1914-18* (Brisb, 1942); James Loynes file, War records section (AWM).

PETER BURNESS

LUCAS, ANTONY JOHN JEREOS (1862-1946), Greek community leader, philanthropist and restaurateur, was born Antonios Ioannis Gerasimos Lekatsas on 18 October 1862 at Exoghi, Ithaca, Greece, second child of Ioannis Lekatsas, priest, and his wife Magdalene, née Palmos. At 17 Lucas left the poverty of the island to work in Patras, later served in the Greek army for two years and returned to Exoghi where he met an uncle who had gone to the Australian goldfields and returned with glowing accounts. Lucas sailed with two cousins, arriving in Melbourne in 1886.

On 28 February 1893 Lucas married Margaret Wilson (d. 1942), head of the fur department of Foy & Gibson [qq.v.8]. A thrifty, shrewd businesswoman, she and Lucas opened the Town Hall Café in Swanston Street, Melbourne, in 1894. It occupied two floors, accommodated 650 diners and employed a mostly Greek workforce of 70. The family lived on the top floor, later moving to Queen's Road, to Toorak and finally in 1928 to the Mornington Peninsula. Encouraged by the success of the Town Hall Café, Lucas opened two more restaurants. One, the Paris Café, a two-storey building in Collins Street remodelled at a cost of £6000, accommodated 350 diners and employed a staff of 30 under a French chef. The other restaurant, on the site of the present Hotel Australia in Collins Street, was the Vienna Café, later the Café Australia, which Lucas had renovated by Walter Burley Griffin [q.v.9]. Inspired by commercial and architectural success Lucas again commissioned Griffin to design the Capitol Building, in association with Melbourne architects Peck and Kemper, and to redesign the house and landscape the gardens of his home, Yamala, at Frankston.

One of the founders of the Greek Orthodox community in Melbourne in 1897, Lucas was many times its president. He was Greek consul-general for Australia in 1921-25 and consul in Melbourne in 1931-46. Under his guidance the Melbourne Greek community became the most influential in Australia. President of the Ulysses Philanthropic Society of Melbourne, during World War II he arranged a scheme by which Melbourne's Greeks donated a day's pay to the Greek war effort, and himself donated £10 000 to a fund which he organized for Greek and British child war-victims. From 1931 annually on his birthday he donated 100 guineas to the Lord Mayor's Hospital Appeal. He visited Greece in 1921, 1930, 1933 and 1937 and established a hospital for poor people on Ithaca. In

1939 in recognition of services to Greece and Australia he was the first Australian-Greek recipient of the Golden Cross of Taxiarchon, an order initiated by King George I of Greece. In October 1944 a special service to commemorate his birthday and the coincident liberation of Athens was conducted in the Greek Orthodox Church in Victoria Parade.

Lucas inspired the central character, Yianni, in Jean Campbell's novel, *Greek key pattern* (1935). A successful businessman, public benefactor and worker for Greek welfare, he possessed integrity and indomitable will. Compassionate and devoted to children he appreciated church music, gardens and architecture. In later life he was director of several companies. Once said to be the richest Greek in Australia, he died in Sydney on 10 August 1946, leaving an estate valued for probate at nearly £134 000. He was buried with Greek Orthodox rites in Melbourne general cemetery; his six daughters survived him.

J. Smith (ed), *Cyclopedia of Victoria*, 3 (Melb, 1905); E. C. Rowland, *Frankston portraits* (Melb, priv print, 1979); *Punch* (Melb), 14 Nov 1912; *Sun-News Pictorial*, 21 Feb 1939, 14 Aug 1946; *Age*, 12 Aug 1946; M. Tsounis, Greek communities in Australia (Ph.D. thesis, Univ Adel, 1971); Lucas family archive (held by A. E. Lucas, Panorama, Adel); information from Mr H. Gilchrist, Deakin, ACT, and Dr C. Price, Deakin, ACT.

                                                    A. E. LUCAS

LUCAS, ARTHUR HENRY SHAKESPEARE (1853-1936), schoolmaster and biologist, was born on 7 May 1853 at Stratford-on-Avon, Warwickshire, England, third son of Rev. Samuel Lucas, Wesleyan minister, and his wife Elizabeth, née Broadhead. His father was an itinerant clergyman with a small stipend and a passion for the natural sciences, especially geology. He awakened a love of Nature in Arthur, who as a boy collected seaweeds, flowers, fossils and shells.

With a scholarship, Lucas spent seven years at New Kingswood School, near Bath. In 1870-74 he was an exhibitioner at Balliol College, Oxford (B.A., 1874; M.A., 1877); but shy, poor and poorly clad, he was unable to join sports clubs or participate in social life. After a bout of pneumonia he graduated with fourth-class honours in mathematics in 1874, but was awarded the coveted Burdett-Coutts scholarship in 1876. He had won an entrance scholarship at the London Hospital in the East End and the gold medal for botany of the Society of Apothecaries.

Awarded a B.Sc. by the University of London in 1879, Lucas had sacrificed his medical career to support the three children of his widowed brother, Dr Thomas Pennington Lucas (1843-1917), who was tubercular and advised to migrate to Australia. Arthur taught at Leys School, Cambridge, for five years and was elected a fellow of the Geological Society in 1881. At the parish church of St Cuthbert, Bedfordshire, he married Charlotte Christmas on 29 July 1882.

Appointed mathematics and science master at Wesley College, Melbourne, Lucas reached Australia in January 1883. Finding the science laboratory was a shed with a few test-tubes and bottles of reagents, he introduced nature study in the field and, taking an *ad eundem* M.A., became a member of the Senate of the University of Melbourne. He was soon busy trying to improve the position of science in schools and the university. With C. A. Topp [q.v.6] he suggested a separate chair of biology, which led to the appointment of (Sir) Baldwin Spencer [q.v.]. Within the university he also tutored at Ormond [q.v.5] and Trinity colleges and was a founder and fellow of Queen's College.

In 1884-92 Lucas edited the *Victorian Naturalist*, the journal of the Field Naturalists' Club of Victoria (founded by his brother in 1882). As its president in 1887-89 he urged the government to reserve Wilson's Promontory for a national park (which came about in 1898). He was a council-member of the Royal Society of Victoria, and with Spencer, J. B. Wilson [q.v.6] and others organized its first biological survey of Port Phillip. At Spencer's suggestion Lucas wrote an *Introduction to the study of botany* (1892) with A. Dendy [q.v.8], and *The animals of Australia* (1909) and *The birds of Australia* (1911) with W. H. D. Le Souef [q.v.]. He also published numerous papers on fishes and, with C. Frost, on lizards.

Moving to Sydney, Lucas was headmaster of Newington College in 1892-98. He included French, history and natural science in the curriculum, but was frustrated by lack of funds for expansion and a system of dual control with Rev. J. E. Moulton [q.v.5] as president. In January 1899 he became senior mathematical and science master at Sydney Grammar School. Known affectionately as 'Daddy' by Sydneians, he was, according to Dr C. J. Prescott [q.v.], 'a masterly teacher, lucid, thorough, exacting, inspiring, with a surprising variety of subject. And his teaching was shot through with a human interest in everyone he taught'. In his twenty-five years at Sydney Grammar, his pupils won medals at the senior public examination in thirteen subjects, including languages. He read French, German, Spanish and Italian, taught himself Russian in order to read a book about lizards, and was well versed in English literature.

During World War I Lucas was acting head-master in 1916-19 while H. N. P. Sloman was at the front. Despite his gentle calm and the school's high morale and sporting triumphs, Lucas found these 'the bitterest days I ever experienced'—of 1740 old Sydneians who enlisted 301 did not return, and his only son was fighting in France. He was headmaster from 1920 to 1923 and after retirement was acting professor of mathematics at the University of Tasmania for two years.

A council-member of the Linnean Society of New South Wales in 1894-1936, Lucas served as president in 1907-09. In its journal he published on diverse topics with an astonishing productivity while schoolteaching. After his retirement he concentrated on the study of marine algae—he also worked as honorary curator of algae at the National Herbarium of New South Wales. His interests were not shared by other Australian botanists but he corresponded on algal matters with overseas phycologists.

After his wife's death in 1919 Lucas lived with his daughter Ida Cortis-Jones at Roseville, but spent many summer vacations at Point Lonsdale, Victoria, with the family of Herbert Brookes [q.v.7], an ex-pupil. At their instigation he wrote his memoirs, published posthumously in 1937 as *A.H.S. Lucas, scientist, his own story*. Frequently he visited Mrs George Perrin (née Florence Dawson) at Launceston, Tasmania. They visited Lord Howe Island and Low Islands in Queensland, and exchanged many letters; he called her 'his eyes' when collecting. On their last expedition Lucas, despite stormy weather, collected seaweeds from rockpools at Warrnambool, Victoria. He developed pneumonia and was taken from the train at Albury, New South Wales, where he died on 10 June 1936; he was cremated with Methodist forms. A son and three of his four daughters survived him.

After W. H. Harvey [q.v.4] Lucas was the most important earlier worker on Australian algae, publishing in Adelaide *The seaweeds of South Australia* (part I in 1936 and part II with Florence Perrin in 1947). Many of his observations have stood the test of time. The devout, shy, self-effacing, modest and unselfish man in a shiny and threadbare black suit, had a sharp wit and was happy without too many worldly possessions. With white hair and beard, 'his face had a touch of sadness' in repose. His portrait by H. A. Hanke (1935) is held by Sydney Grammar School.

D. S. Macmillan, *Newington College 1863-1963* (Syd, 1963); Syd Grammar School, *Sydneian*, Apr 1923, Aug 1936, centenary number 1957; *Wesley College Chronicle*, Aug 1936; *Vic Naturalist*, 54 (1936); Linnean Soc NSW, *Procs*, 62 (1937); *Aust Q*, June 1938; Brookes papers (NL); Perrin family papers and Lucas papers (S. Ducker collection, Univ Melb Archives).   SOPHIE C. DUCKER

LUCAS, SIR EDWARD (1857-1950), draper and politician, was born, one of twin brothers, on 14 February 1857 at Galonetra, Cavan, Ireland, son of Adams Lucas, a small farmer, and his wife Eliza, née Martin. After schooling at Ballieboro, Lucas was apprenticed to a draper and worked for Switzer, Ferguson & Co. in Grafton Street, Dublin, before migrating to South Australia in 1878.

He found employment with the Rundle Street store, John Martin & Co., but by 1882 had his own drapery at North Adelaide. Next year, with Frederick M. Edwards, he set up shop in Hindley and Rundle streets and they soon opened branches. In 1886 Lucas moved to Gawler where he established Edward Lucas & Co. He thrived and stayed fifteen years, becoming active in community affairs. He was president of the Gawler Institute and a member of the school of mines council, the school board of advice and the committee that successfully advocated the Barossa water scheme. Mayor in 1893 and 1899, he became vice-president of the Municipal Association of South Australia and of the Australasian Federation League. He invested in mining.

On 15 April 1885 Lucas married Frances Louisa Johnson; she died following the death of their first child in 1887. On 21 March 1890 he married Mabel Florence Brock, a school-teacher.

In 1900 Lucas won the North-eastern (later Midland) seat in the Legislative Council; he returned to Adelaide and bought a large tailoring business. Early parliamentary speeches covered the need for custom, precedent and 'old traditional reverence'. Lucas feared that 'the ruthless hand of a vandalic socialism' might extend the political representation of the non-propertied classes. Genial but somewhat cocksure, and fond of embellishing his rhetoric with poetry, he was once described as 'the glibbest gasser' in the council. Colleagues spoke of 'his immense fighting capacity' and the press noted his 'bull terrier reputation'.

Lucas was interested in prison reform and commercial and industrial matters. Responding to newspaper controversy, in 1904 he proposed an inquiry into 'the alleged sweating evil' and chaired the resulting select committee, which concentrated on the clothing industry. The committee was unsympathetic about the work's severity—sewing forty-eight pairs of trousers in a week—but found large-scale sweating did exist. It recommended the creation of two wages boards for the clothing trade (established by an Act of 1904) for women and juveniles; creation of a court of industrial appeal; amendments to the

Factories Amendment Act; and a system of indentured apprenticeship. In 1909 Lucas sat on a committee which recommended further wages boards, for blacksmiths, boilermakers and the confectionery trade.

Lucas was a member of the committee that in 1910 had formed the Liberal Union by amalgamating the Liberal and Democratic Union, the Australasian National League and the Farmers' and Producers' Political Union. In 1913 he became the leader of his party in the Legislative Council. He worked on the State War Council in 1914-18 and was vice-chairman of the State Recruiting Committee.

In 1918, under a new policy to harness commercial acumen, Lucas became South Australia's agent-general in London. After a second term he returned to South Australia in 1925, having been knighted in 1921. The ex-draper was a small, dapper man with a trim goatee. A Methodist and rather autocratic, he was a lay preacher and philanthropist, a strict teetotaller and temperance advocate who yet raced his own horses. In retirement he was a director of several companies and institutions, notably the District Trained Nursing Society and the South Australian Navy League. He unsuccessfully contested the 1928 Senate election as a Nationalist. Since his youth he had written verse.

Predeceased by his wife, Lucas died on 4 July 1950 and, survived by two daughters, was buried in Payneham cemetery.

H. T. Burgess (ed), *Cyclopedia of South Australia*, 1 (Adel, 1907); *Quiz and the Lantern* (Adel), 18 Sept 1903; *Critic* (Adel), 22 Nov 1905; *Mail* (Adel), 13 Feb 1915; *Observer* (Adel), 8 Jan, 2 Apr 1921, 16, 23 May 1925; *Chronicle* (Adel), 8 Aug 1929; *Advertiser* (Adel), 5 July 1950; information from Lady Barker, Hackney, Adel.

SUZANNE EDGAR

LUCAS, WALTER HENRY (1869-1954), Pacific entrepreneur, was born on 15 March 1869 at Wanstead, Essex, England, son of James Roach Lucas, police sergeant, and his wife Eliza Jane, née Ogle. Little is known of his early years but he went to sea and by 1891 was purser of the Australian Union Steamship Navigation Co.'s S.S. *Palmer*. At Townsville, Queensland, on 1 June 1891 he married Margaret Marianne Smith of Fife, Scotland. In 1893 he joined the Australian New Hebrides Co. as supercargo in the antiquated S.S. *Croydon* to compete with the French in the New Hebrides (Vanuatu) copra trade, which provided him with serviceable yarns and a baptism in ruthlessness. When the A.N.H. Co. was taken over by Burns [q.v.7], Philp [q.v.] & Co. Ltd in 1896, Lucas joined the S.S. *Titus* with the task of opening up a regular Aus-

tralian shipping service to the Solomon Islands and Papua. This challenge to the German Norddeutscher Lloyd Co. depended on a system of standard freight rates that provoked German retaliation in a contract system that excluded the Australian company in 1905.

Manifestly shrewd and inventive in the volatile mercantile rivalry of the Pacific, Lucas, after a period as ship's husband, returned to Sydney in 1901 as Burns Philp's island manager. He brought with him a petition from the white residents of the New Hebrides to be allowed to recruit their own labour and was a member of the deputation that presented it to Prime Minister Barton [q.v.7]. Beginning a strong rapport with Atlee Hunt [q.v.9] Lucas negotiated a Commonwealth-subsidized mail contract for Burns Philp in 1902, renewed in 1907, offering company land in the New Hebrides to the government to promote settlement there and counter French influence. It was Lucas who selected and escorted the first Australian settlers, accompanied by A. B. Paterson [q.v.] who helped him personally to survey their leases. When Burns Philp succeeded in gaining an indemnity from the German-owned Jaluit Gesellschaft in 1905, Lucas carried their flag back to the Marshall Islands.

The lanky and generally popular Lucas employed his acute diplomatic instincts in government interests as well as in the service of his firm. When the repatriation of Pacific islanders was decided on in 1906 Atlee Hunt left the operation to Lucas. In 1910 he argued a cogent case to Hunt for the separation of the offices of governor of Fiji and high commissioner for the Western Pacific and for the location of the latter in Australia. A persistent advocate of the monopolistic development of the Pacific with Australian capital, between 1908 and 1911 he organized copra plantation companies in the Solomons of which he was a director and shareholding managing agent.

In 1911-20 as island inspector, the lugubrious-looking troubleshooter, his long-nosed face burdened by a heavy moustache, supervised Burns Philp trade, philosophically accepting recurring attacks of malaria. During the Morocco crisis of 1911 he tinkered with the idea of putting pressure on the French to cede the New Hebrides. In 1912 Burns Philp was appointed Australian agent of the British government for the Solomon Islands; its other agencies, including the Western Pacific High Commission and the government of Tonga, were personally supervised by Lucas. When German New Guinea was surrendered in 1914 Lucas, already in the islands, immediately resumed the trading interrupted in 1905. He gave evidence to the Inter-State Commission in 1916 on shipping, and in August 1919, with Atlee Hunt and (Sir)

Hubert Murray [q.v.], he was a member of a royal commission considering the future government of ex-German New Guinea. In a majority report Hunt and Lucas opposed several of Murray's recommendations, including the amalgamation of mandated New Guinea and Papua.

In May 1920 W. M. Hughes [q.v.9] appointed Lucas technical adviser to the government on Pacific islands matters. In January 1921 he was appointed chairman of the Expropriation Board, instituted to liquidate German commercial interests under the reparations provisions of the Treaty of Versailles. Arriving in Rabaul with accountants and plantation supervisors, mostly ex-servicemen, the chairman was hailed as 'Lucas and his Twelve Apostles'. The board, with powers wider than the military or civil administration, managed the assets of German trading companies, including some 300 plantations, examined German claims against the occupation and arranged German repatriation.

Lucas resigned in 1926 and returned to live in Sydney as a company director. He died on 12 June 1954 at Canberra Hospital and was cremated. One son survived him.

F. West, *Hubert Murray* (Melb, 1968); K. Buckley and K. Klugman, *The history of Burns Philp* (Syd, 1981); *Pacific Island Mthly*, May, July 1954, Jan 1961; *A'sian*, 29 May 1920; *Punch* (Melb) 3 June 1920; *Western Argus*, 1 Mar 1921; *Bulletin*, 6 Nov 1929, 30 June 1954; Atlee Hunt papers (NL).
                                              MARGARET STEVEN

LUFFMAN{N), CHARLES (BOGUE) (1862-1920), horticulturist and writer, was born on 15 February 1862 at Cockington, Devon, England, son of George Luffman, gamekeeper, and his wife Emma, née Earl. In his early years the family moved to Knowle, Bristol. In his late twenties Luffman spent four years in the dried fruit business in Italy, France and Spain, working for two years as field manager for Delius Bros at Malaga, Spain. During his travels he had met the author Lauretta Lane [q.v. Luffman] who encouraged him to write. After returning briefly to England he published *A vagabond in Spain* (1895). He had romanticized his name to Carl B. Luffmann and his publisher John Murray was instructed to use C. Bogue Luffmann, the name by which he frequently came to be known.

Luffman's experience led to his appointment by the government of Victoria as advisory instructor on raisin culture at Mildura. He arrived in Victoria early in 1895. In late 1895 Lauretta Lane joined him and they were married on 14 December in Melbourne. He gave evidence in June 1896 before the royal commission into the Mildura settlement on the suitability of the area for growing figs, raisins, muscatels, currants and sultanas. Luffman was credited with having organized Mildura's dried fruit trade and putting it on a sound footing.

He resigned to become a roving horticulturist, giving advice, lectures and demonstrations. In 1897, however, he became the second principal of the School of Horticulture, Burnley, described as being in a 'state of confusion'. Luffman made the grounds into a school of demonstration, forming paddocks, orchards and ornamental gardens. These provided the basis for his extensive writings on garden design and management, especially in relation to orchards and farms. *The principles of gardening for Australia* (Melbourne, 1903), the product of six public lectures, underlined his approach to garden design, championing 'those gardens which come nearest to the finest expressions of nature'. He saw curving paths and shady glades as vital components of the Australian garden, with the summer garden to the south and east of the site and the winter garden, surrounded by deciduous trees, to the north and west. Examples of his designs, though now much altered, are Burnley Gardens and the Metropolitan Golf Club, Oakleigh, in 1908 one of the earliest examples of large-scale Australian native planting. Before the royal commission on technical education in 1900 he claimed 'over twenty-five years in commercial horticulture'. Proud of the achievements of his women students he told the commission, 'I do not think horticulture is an affair of sex'.

Luffman and his wife separated about 1902. Elinor Mordaunt [q.v.], the writer, who moved into the principal's house to look after the female staff and students at the school, described him as 'a short, strongly built, very dark man, like a Spaniard . . . jealous, exacting and selfish'. He resigned from the School of Horticulture in January 1908, and returned to Spain to augment his earlier notes, some of which had been published in the Melbourne *Age*. In 1904 he had forwarded notes about his experiences in Spain to Murray, to be published anonymously since he was a public servant. *Quiet days in Spain* was published in 1910.

An invitation from the United States of America to advise on diseases in oranges provided the funds to travel to Japan. In *The harvest of Japan* (1920) Luffman reported on Japanese life, although as with all his travel books there is surprisingly little material about horticulture. A. L. Sadler [q.v.], the expert on Japan, told Luffman's friend (Sir) Lionel Lindsay [q.v.] that he was greatly impressed by the book, particularly as the author knew no Japanese.

During World War I Luffman was a gardener at Wyke Regis, Dorset, England, and lectured on gardening to wounded servicemen. He died of cancer on 6 May 1920 at Babbacombe, Devon.

J. Smith (ed), *Cyclopedia of Victoria*, 1 (Melb, 1903); E. Mordaunt, *Sinabada* (Lond, 1937); *J of the Aust Garden Hist Soc*, no 2, Winter 1981; *Weekly Times* (Melb), 12 July 1902, 11 Apr 1903, 10 Mar 1906, 14 July 1906 supp, 28 Dec 1907; *Australasian*, 25 Jan 1908; correspondence between C. B. Luffman and John Murray (Publishers) Ltd, Lond (1895-1904, held by firm); information from G. W. Bell, Burnley, Melb.

J. PATRICK

LUFFMAN, LAURETTA CAROLINE MARIA (1846-1929), writer and women's activist, was born on 17 December 1846 at Bedford, England, third child of John Edward Lane, naval lieutenant, and his wife Lauretta Maude, née Bluett. A delicate child, motherless from the age of 10, she was educated at home and in France. She was a 'born reader'.

From her early twenties Laura was engaged in writing, in philanthropic work and in helping her married sister to run a boys' school. Her first full-length work, a three-volume novel, *Gentleman Verschoyle*, was published in 1875 under the name, Laura M. Lane. Between 1877 and 1894 fourteen more books appeared including a biography (1890) of Alexander Vinet, the Swiss critic and theologian. However most were stories for girls, some about young working women. She suffered a nervous illness in the early 1880s and for some years lived on the Continent. On a visit to London she helped Clementina Black, 'an ardent social reformer', to collect evidence on women in sweated industries and was 'borne to the brink of the new Socialism'.

In London in 1893 she met Carl Bogue Luffman [q.v.]. She joined him in Melbourne where they were married at St James' Church on 14 December 1895; from 1897 he was principal of the School of Horticulture, Burnley. She found Melbourne parochial but enjoyed visiting the country and shared her husband's interest in horticulture and visitors to the gardens.

Her life with Luffman ended abruptly about 1902 and she moved to Sydney where she took up journalism. In 1903-05, as 'Una', Mrs Luffman contributed articles on women to the *Daily Telegraph*. In 1903 women in New South Wales voted for the first time; while interviewing the leaders of the women's political associations, she met and became a close friend of Mrs Hilma Molyneux Parkes [q.v.], founder of the Women's Liberal League of New South Wales (Women's Reform League from 1915). In May-October 1905

Mrs Luffman edited the monthly *At Home* and gave the league much favourable publicity. In 1908 she joined its council, was organizing secretary in 1909-18, president in 1918-21, and editor of its *Monthly Record* (*Liberal Woman* from 1910 and *Woman's Voice* from 1916). She often wrote practically the whole issue and when she resigned in 1923 *Woman's Voice* ceased.

Besides editing and public speaking, Mrs Luffman visited country and suburban areas as organizing secretary, and was a delegate to the National Council of Women of New South Wales. Much of her energy was spent in educating women as voters. During World War I she campaigned vigorously for conscription, worked for the Bush Book Club and the Australian Red Cross Society, and served on the executives of the Australasian League of Honour for Women and Girls, the Racial Hygiene Association, the Women's Horticultural and Home Industries Society and, after the war, the State branch of the League of Nations Union. She now regarded socialism as a threat to Australia, advocated free trade and was a strong supporter of the Empire.

Two of the short stories Laura Bogue Luffman had contributed to the *Sydney Mail* were reprinted in *The red kangaroo* (Sydney, 1907). A children's book, *Will Aylmer: a tale of the Australian bush* (London, 1909), and a novel, *A question of latitude* (London, 1911), are both set in Australia. In the 1920s she contributed articles to the *Sydney Morning Herald* and wrote an unpublished autobiography, 'Impressions of life by a contented woman'. She was remembered as dignified and reserved in manner, especially towards those who did not know her well. She loved the bush and regularly visited her Bluett cousins at Brindabella.

She died on 7 June 1929 at Queanbeyan and was cremated with Anglican rites. The Laura Bogue Luffman literary competition was established by (Dame) Mary Gilmore [q.v.9] in her memory.

E. Mordaunt, *Sinabada* (Lond, 1937); *Woman's Voice*, 1 Sept 1918; *Daily Telegraph* (Syd), 7 Apr 1915; *SMH*, 25 Oct 1916, 22 Mar, 13 Apr, 5 Dec 1917, 6 June 1919, 18 Mar 1921, 8, 29 June, 30 July 1929.

MARGARET BETTISON

LUKIN, LIONEL OSCAR (1868-1944), judge, was born on 4 January 1868 at Condamine, Queensland, son of Tasmanian-born George Lionel Lukin, clerk, and his Irish wife Annie, née Magovern. He was a nephew of Gresley Lukin [q.v.5]. Educated at private schools in Roma, Brisbane (Brisbane Grammar, 1879-83) and Gympie, at 16 Lukin entered government service as assistant mining registrar, Gympie. In 1887 he was transferred to Charters Towers but resigned in December to study for the Bar. Admitted on 4 March 1890, he established a large, versatile practice insisting on a person's right to be defended even in the police court. On 9 September 1893 he married at All Saints Church, Brisbane, Catherine Alicia Rennick, M.A. (Melbourne), a teacher.

In 1907 Lukin joined Arthur Feez [q.v.8] and others in forming the Incorporated Council of Law Reporting for the State of Queensland, a self-supporting body that contributed to the funding of the Supreme Court Library. Next year he wrote, with A. D. Graham and T. J. Lehane, *Justices' civil jurisdiction*, a guide to the statutes and rules affecting the duties of magistrates in Queensland—for many years a standard text.

Lukin became the first Queensland-born judge of the Supreme Court: he was appointed to the central division, Rockhampton, from July 1910. In one of his more unusual judgments he gained the approval of three widows to pay medical costs to an injured Chinese man and of his own 'fatherly' thrashing of their guilty sons. In April 1922 he was transferred to the Brisbane bench. At the time he was first appointed there was no fixed retirement age and if he served fifteen years he would be entitled to retire with a half-salary pension. The Judges Retirement Act of 1921 imposed on all judges a retirement age of 70. All existing judges kept pension rights; all future judges were denied pensions. Lukin's strongly conservative outlook involved him in clashes with T. J. Ryan [q.v.] and later Labor premiers. In consequence he was passed over for the chief justiceship in 1922 and again in 1925. In 1926, at 58, Lukin resigned unexpectedly, having qualified for an annual pension of £1000.

To the chagrin of the Queensland Labor government, he took up appointment as a judge of the Commonwealth Court of Conciliation and Arbitration with an annual salary of £3000 and no fixed retirement. Labor governments in Queensland, as a result of Lukin's *coup*, remained steadfast in their refusal to reintroduce judges' pensions. Turmoil followed his judgments in the timber-workers' case, 1928-29, cutting wages and restoring a 48-hour week. Strikers burnt his effigy in public and sang 'We'll hang Judge Lukin to a sour apple tree'. In 1930 he became first Federal judge in bankruptcy, exercizing jurisdiction in Melbourne and Sydney, and introduced important innovations. In 1934 he was also the first judge sworn into the Supreme Court of the Australian Capital Territory, blankly refusing cuts in his salary during the Depression, despite example from other judges. Retaining office until ill health caused his unwilling retirement in November 1943, Lukin died in Melbourne on 1 June 1944, sur-vived by two sons and two daughters. He was buried in Lutwyche cemetery, Brisbane, after a service at St Stephen's Roman Catholic Cathedral.

Remembered by some as genial, humorous, short and beefy, with a stentorian voice, Lukin was a stickler for observance of the rules of the court. After his death Mr Justice Macrossan praised him for his 'wide experience of human nature, exceptional physical power, immense industry, a robust personality, intellectual understanding and integrity'. However, while noted for his patience and goodwill, Lukin did not hesitate to use his great abilities to manipulate circumstances to his advantage, particularly when he considered he had been unfairly used.

R. O'Dea, *Principles of wage determination in Commonwealth arbitration* (Syd, 1969); R. Johnston, *History of the Queensland Bar* (Brisb, 1979); L. McDonald, *Rockhampton*, (Brisb, 1981); *Hist Studies*, 19 (1963), no 4, p 479; *Labor Daily*, 27 Feb 1929; *SMH*, 11, 30 Apr 1929, 16 Feb 1934; *Telegraph* (Brisb), 1 June 1944; *Courier Mail*, 5, 7 June 1944; *Herald* (Melb), 7 June 1944.

J. C. H. GILL

LUMSDAINE, JOHN SINCLAIR (1895-1948), songwriter, vaudeville artist and entertainer, was born on 18 November 1895 at Casino, New South Wales, son of Herbert Sinclair Lumsdaine, native-born bank manager, and his English wife Edith, née Bentley, a music teacher who taught her son to sing and play the piano. In 1905, after his parents moved to Hunters Hill, Sydney, Jack attended St Andrew's Cathedral Choir School (also studying music and playing the organ), and in 1909-10 Sydney Grammar School. He was briefly a bank clerk but in 1911 he joined a vaudeville company, the All Blacks; for two years he toured Australia, singing and playing mostly impromptu numbers.

In September 1915 Lumsdaine enlisted in the Australian Imperial Force. He served briefly in the Middle East and for a year in France where he was reputedly gassed; hence the sobriquet 'Whispering Baritone'. In 1917 he was evacuated to England where he served as a pay sergeant and, unofficially, as an entertainer. Shortly before his return to Australia he was promoted temporary warrant officer class II and married Dorothy Rosina Staley on 7 June 1919 at Pimlico, London.

Demobilized, Lumsdaine worked for music publishers, Allan [q.v.3] & Co. Pty Ltd of Melbourne and later J. Albert [q.v.7] & Son of Sydney, advising them on what overseas sheet music to publish. Tours of Australian and New Zealand theatres, with Lumsdaine performing before the main film, were one way of promoting this music as well as his own. He composed hundreds of songs, some of which he recorded; one of the most popular was 'Every Day is a Rainbow for Me' with (Sir) Donald Bradman at the piano. Many recorded by Peter Dawson [q.v.8] were sung all over the world. Lumsdaine also conducted orchestras and was a theatre organist. On the vaudeville circuit he began as an accompanist to imported acts; he had a record run of eleven weeks at Sydney's Tivoli Theatre.

In 1923 Lumsdaine began working in radio. 'Music While You Wait' was an instant success in 1926; listeners would phone 2FC with the title for a song and within half an hour Lumsdaine would compose the words and the music. In 1932 he joined 2GB, undertaking announcing and other duties and appearing every Friday night as the 'Radio Rascal'. Later he teamed with Jack Davey in a song and gag show, 'Daffy and Dilly', and from 1936 as 'Two Jacks and a Piano'. Lumsdaine was also a commentator on the Fox Movietone newsreels, directed a weekly variety show, 'Radio Pie', and did musical work for the Colgate-Palmolive radio unit. While mostly associated with 2GB, he also worked during World War II for 2UE.

Generous and tolerant, Lumsdaine was 'ready with laughter and rude jests'. He liked to drink but never let it affect his work, followed the horses, played golf and sailed. He died of cancer at Rushcutters Bay on 28 August 1948 and was cremated with Anglican rites. 'Policemen and tramguards saluted', Kenneth Slessor wrote, 'and the traffic was stopped by the crowds in George Street' when his funeral set out from St Andrew's Cathedral. He was survived by his wife and their only child Thora, whose work in radio included plays and the 'Radio Pie' show with her father.

Wireless Weekly, 23 July 1926, 18 Oct 1935, 3 Sept 1937; *Listener In*, 26 June 1937; newspaper cuttings held by Mrs T. Twohill, Davidson, Syd.
                                         MURRAY GOOT

LUNDIE, FRANCIS WALTER (1866-1933), union official, was born on 1 March 1866 at Port Adelaide, son of John Lundie, railway labourer, and his wife Maryann Josephine, née Moran. He attended Port Adelaide and Morgan public schools before starting work at 11 as a station-hand, shearer, and bullock-puncher in western New South Wales.

Lundie joined the Amalgamated Shearers' Union of Australasia (from 1894 Australian Workers' Union) in 1887 and two years later became president of its Adelaide branch. He was its paid, full-time organizer from 1892 until 1900 when he became secretary, a posi-

tion he kept until his death. Never 'an indoor official', Lundie rode a bicycle to the shearing sheds on the Darling River and in south-east South Australia. In 1894-1900 he was also agent for the A.W.U. at Broken Hill, New South Wales, where he helped to lead the 1894 shearers' strike; and he was president of the South Australian branch of the United Labourers' Union in 1907-12. On 20 January 1891 at Brompton Lundie had married Elizabeth Margaret Battens Armstrong (d. 1907). On 20 January 1909 at Holy Trinity Church, Adelaide, he married Edith Mary Armstrong.

Lundie helped to make the A.W.U. the State's largest, most powerful union. While not a dogmatic syndicalist, he believed that direct action was better than arbitration or political action in the struggle to improve wages and conditions for unskilled workers. This philosophy often distanced him from both the more moderate State Labor men and the A.W.U.'s national leadership. A key member of the United Labor Party of South Australia, he had helped to organize the election of three Labor members to the House of Assembly in 1893. But Lundie believed that the party should be controlled by the working class in their interests and he sought to overthrow the dominant politicians and moderate craft union leaders.

He promoted several bitter industrial disputes with the Verran [q.v.] Labor government in 1910; some labour leaders hated him as the 'industrial King of Adelaide' nearly as much as the Establishment did. Throughout Verran's premiership (June 1910-February 1912), Lundie and the A.W.U. tried to capture control of the U.L.P. organization but they won rank and file support only for minor concessions. Not until the majority of the U.L.P. membership deserted the party's leadership in 1917, because of the latter's support for conscription, was Lundie able, skilfully and ruthlessly, to manipulate this resentment and take over the party. After most of the parliamentarians were effectively expelled in February, an A.W.U.-dominated executive was elected with Lundie as president. That year he became the union's national president, defeating W. G. Spence [q.v.6], but lost the position to Arthur Blakeley [q.v.7] in 1919. Lundie was also a director of Labor Papers Ltd.

His political and industrial extremism diminished, but he remained a force in the Labor Party, as State vice-president in 1924-25 and 1929-30. However, he had failed to gain election to the Senate in 1917 and 1919 and to the House of Assembly in 1905 and 1924. He sat on the royal commission on the pastoral industry in 1927.

In 1900-09 Lundie had been a member of the Port Adelaide City Council and, with A. A.

Edwards [q.v.8] and S. R. Whitford [q.v.], was a Labor member of the Adelaide City Council in 1909-31. A teetotaller, he provoked conservatives with his fiery temper and militancy.

Predeceased by his second wife, and survived by seven daughters and five sons, Lundie died on 13 July 1933. His tall, grey, angular presence was deeply missed in the movement where he had represented uncompromising socialist rectitude and humanity. About 1000 people, representing all classes, several races, and many poor people attended his burial in West Terrace cemetery. An ex-prisoners' hostel in Whitmore Square was established and named after him in 1963.

D. J. Murphy (ed), *Labor in politics* (Brisb, 1975); *Aust Worker*, 6 May 1905, 1 Feb 1917, 19 July 1933; *Mail* (Adel), 12 Oct 1912; *Advertiser* (Adel), 14 July 1933; S. Weeks, The relationship between the Australian Workers' Union and the South Australian Labor Party, 1908-1918 (B.A. Hons thesis, Flinders Univ, 1981).

STEVEN WEEKS

LUXTON, SIR HAROLD DANIEL (1888-1957), businessman and lord mayor, was born on 25 June 1888 at Kangaroo Flat, Victoria, fourth son and last of eight children of Thomas Luxton [q.v.5], sharebroker, and his wife Sarah, née Schooling. Soon afterwards the family moved to Melbourne where from 1899 Harold distinguished himself in athletics and rowing at Melbourne Church of England Grammar School.

Upon leaving school Luxton found himself in the hardware business, his father buying McLean [q.v.5] Bros & Rigg in 1907 and James McEwan & Co. in 1910. Luxton recalled that he was a 'man of affairs' at 19, and when his father died in 1911 he and his brother Tom had 'the full responsibility of running a big business at a time when I, at any rate, should have been playing tennis'. He also made an early marriage, to Doris May Lewis at St George's Church of England, Malvern, on 17 November 1909.

In February 1915 Luxton enlisted in the Australian Field Artillery as provisional lieutenant and was appointed second lieutenant when he joined the Australian Imperial Force in October; he served with the 4th Field Artillery Brigade, as lieutenant, in France. In October 1916 he transferred to the Royal Flying Corps, attended the Oxford School of Aeronautics and flew on bombing and spotting missions. He was shot down in August 1917, suffering a fractured skull, broken jaw and other injuries. During World War II he was Victorian director of the Empire Air Recruiting Committee.

After the war Luxton returned to the family business in Elizabeth Street. In 1919 he stood successfully for the Lonsdale Ward of the Melbourne City Council, intending to represent returned soldiers. He retained the seat until redistribution in 1939 when he represented Hoddle Ward, retiring in 1943. In 1928, when managing director of McEwans but still dark-featured and youthful in appearance, he succeeded Sir Stephen Morell [q.v.] as lord mayor—the youngest-ever. He was the first returned soldier so distinguished and, more remarkably, one who had not served as chairman of a committee, although he had been a member of four—licensed vehicles, finance, abattoirs and cattle markets, and public works.

Luxton declared himself in favour of more bridges over the Yarra River and of the centralization of charities in the Lord Mayor's Fund as a community chest on the American model. With three terms as mayor behind him, in 1931 he publicly regretted that the recommendations of the Metropolitan Town Planning Commission had not been implemented, or a town planning authority created. Nor was his vision of a single charity organization much further advanced. He blamed the economic Depression. Even the lady mayoress complained in 1930 that 'Debutantes are having a hard time this year. There are hardly any parties for them. People cannot afford it'. In 1932 Luxton received the standard reward for lengthy mayoral service, a knighthood.

The image of the able young community leader, 'decisive in speech and manner', carried Luxton into State parliament at a by-election in 1930 for Caulfield to join other young Nationalists such as (Sir) Wilfrid Kent Hughes, (Sir) Thomas Maltby and (Sir) Robert Menzies. He expressed a businessman's view that no solution was possible to the problem of unemployment without the restoration of profits to industry, and maintained that what the country needed was 'more millionaires'. But Luxton's impact was slight. He faced the Hogan [q.v.9] Labor administration of 1929-32 and remained a back-bencher during the Argyle-Allan [qq.v.7] United Australia Party-Country Party coalition of 1932-35. He resigned from parliament on the eve of the 1935 election after obtaining party endorsement, explaining that years of public service had affected his health.

In the 1930s Luxton extended his affiliations as a businessman. He became a Victorian director of the Bank of New Zealand and chairman of directors of the Metropolitan Gas Co., the National Mutual Life Association of Australia Ltd (1935-53) and the Fourth Victoria Building Society. A member of the Athenaeum and the Naval and Military clubs, he was a well-known breeder of racehorses at his Dandenong property and became an enthusiastic traveller abroad. In 1933 he was one of two Australian representatives on the International Olympic Committee and attended the 1949 Rome meeting which voted to give Melbourne the 1956 Olympics. Returning from the 1950 Copenhagen meeting of the international committee he urged Melburnians to prepare themselves for the influx of visitors, complaining of a lack of hotel accommodation and sophisticated night-life. He claimed that Victoria's politicians had made a grave mistake in not extending hotel drinking-hours. 'I love Melbourne', he said, 'I have lived here all my life, but it is still deadly dull'.

Deteriorating health in the 1950s forced Luxton into semi-retirement. His place on the organizing committee for the 1956 Olympics was taken by his son Lewis, although he remained the elder statesman of the movement. At his death of hypertensive cardiovascular disease, on 24 October 1957 at The Lodge, Dandenong, he was still chairman of the family business. He was cremated. His wife, three sons and daughter were the main beneficiaries of his estate, valued for probate at £98 610. A portrait by W. B. McInnes [q.v.] is at the Melbourne Town Hall.

A'sian Hardware and Machinery, 1 Sept 1910, p 293; *Punch* (Melb), 30 Oct 1919; *Age*, 10 Oct 1928, 7 July 1943, 29 Aug 1958; *Herald* (Melb), 24 Nov 1928, 10 Oct 1930, 29 Aug 1931, 25 Aug 1950, 22 July 1954, 25 Oct 1957; *Table Talk*, 29 Nov 1928; *Argus*, 29 Jan 1935, 13 Sept 1950; *Sun-News Pictorial*, 25 Aug 1950, 25 Oct 1957; *SMH*, 25 Oct 1957.   DAVID DUNSTAN

LYELL, GEORGE (1866-1951), naturalist, was born on 25 July 1866 at Ararat, Victoria, son of George Lyell, printer from Scotland, and his English-born wife Jane, née Avery. He was educated at Stawell State School. About 1883 the family moved to South Melbourne and for seven years Lyell worked at Kew for J. Bartram & Son, butter, cheese and bacon factors, progressing from junior clerk to head of the dairy machinery branch. In 1890 he accepted a partnership in the Gisborne firm of E. Cherry & Sons, manufacturers of butter-factory and dairy appliances and sole suppliers in Victoria of entomological equipment. On 21 November 1893 at Gisborne, which was to be his home for life, he married a 45-year-old widow Fanny Ould, née Freeman.

In 1888 Lyell's capture of a Caper White butterfly at Albert Park had turned his attention seriously to insect collecting and prompted him to join the Field Naturalists' Club of Victoria where he came under the influence of pioneers of Australian natural history—Frank Spry, (Sir) Baldwin Spencer [q.v.], Dudley Best, Charles French and James Kershaw [qq.v.7,8,9]. He built up an enormous collection of butterflies and moths, at first from country areas near Melbourne and then from the Gisborne area and other States. A correspondence begun with the National Museum of Victoria in 1902 resulted in his magnanimously donating the collection to the museum in 1932 and working until 1946 to amalgamate it with the museum's existing Lepidoptera holdings. Lyell continued to add to the collection until in 1951 it stood at 51 216 specimens, representing 6177 species and 534 types: not only remarkable in its extent, but 'an everlasting monument to the neatness and skill of its donor', it still forms the major part of the museum's Lepidoptera collection.

Lyell contributed papers and notes to the *Victorian Naturalist*, mainly between 1890 and 1929. In 1914 with G. A. Waterhouse [q.v.] he published *Butterflies of Australia*, the first comprehensive work on the subject and a valuable reference book for almost twenty years. He also took a deep interest in native orchids and his valuable collection of pressed orchids from all over Australia was bequeathed to the National Herbarium, Melbourne.

'Genial and likeable', Lyell was remembered as 'an excellent companion on a ramble'. At 80 he could still enjoy a walk of several miles although, after a serious illness in 1931, he had given up night collecting; he was 84 before he admitted his field days were over. A devout Presbyterian who supported many local organizations, he died at Gisborne on 19 May 1951, and was cremated. His wife predeceased him; they had no children.

R. T. M. Pescott, *Collections of a century* (Melb, 1954); *V&P* (LA Vic), 1905, 2 (10), p 309; *Wild Life* (Melb), June 1951, p 593; *Vic Naturalist*, 68 (1951-52), p 53.   A. NEBOISS

LYELL, LOTTIE EDITH (1890-1925), actress and film producer, was born on 23 February 1890 at Balmain, Sydney, younger daughter of Joseph Charles Cox, land and estate agent, and his wife Charlotte Louise, née Hancock, both native born. About 1906 she was taught 'elocution and the natural method' by the Shakespearean actor Harry Leston. Her parents then placed her in the care of Raymond Longford [q.v.], an actor with Edwin Geach's Popular Dramatic Organisation which she joined. For several years, as 'Lottie Lyell' she toured Australia and New Zealand in such romantic melodramas as *Why men love women, Her love against the world* and *The midnight wedding*. Reviews noted her enunciation, stagecraft and vivacity. She had bobbed dark hair and an oval face with large brown eyes, a straight nose and determined chin.

In 1911 Lottie Lyell joined Spencer's [q.v.] Pictures when Longford was appointed to direct its films. She repeated her stage role in his first production, *The fatal wedding* (1911). The film had great commercial success, and she played leading roles in other films made by Longford for Spencer: *The romantic story of Margaret Catchpole* (1911), *The midnight wedding* (1912) and *Australia calls* (1913). She was a capable swimmer and an accomplished horsewoman who often displayed her riding skills on the screen.

When Spencer's Pictures Ltd amalgamated with other companies to form Australasian Films Ltd, Lottie Lyell, married to Longford in all but name, stayed with him and acted only in films that he directed. These included *'Neath Austral skies* (1913), *The silence of Dean Maitland* (1914), *A Maori maid's love* (1915), *The mutiny of the Bounty* (1916), and *The church and the woman* (1917). She accompanied him to South Australia to make *The woman suffers* (1918). Her mounting reputation as a screen actress was crowned with general acclaim for her sensitive portrayal of Doreen in Longford's masterpiece, *The sentimental bloke* (1919).

Failing health and added work in production made her screen appearances less regular, but she played Doreen in *Ginger Mick* (1920) and Nell in *Rudd's new selection* (1921). She scripted and co-directed with Longford *The Blue Mountains mystery* (1921) and had 'plenty of healthy argument when their ideas about a scene differed'. With him she formed a partnership, Longford-Lyell Australian Productions, but despite popular success with *The dinkum bloke* (1923) the company failed through lack of financial backing. She had again helped to script and direct the film in which she appeared on the screen for the last time. They formed a new company, Longford-Lyell Productions, and made *Fisher's ghost* (1924) and *The bushwhackers* (1925).

Lottie Lyell died of tuberculosis on 21 December 1925 and was buried with Anglican rites in Northern Suburbs cemetery. She had made a unique contribution to the Australian film industry as its first female star and producer. She was admired for her brains and proved her capacity as a script-writer, film editor and director, although credited as Longford's assistant director in only two films.

A. Pike and R. F. Cooper, *Australian film 1900-1977* (Melb, 1980); J. Tulloch, *Legends on the screen* (Syd, 1981); *Aust Variety and Show World*, 31 May 1916; *Picture Show*, June-Oct 1919, Feb, Dec 1920, Nov 1921; *Lone Hand*, Feb, Mar 1920; *Everyone's*, 12 Aug 1925; *Cinema Papers*, June-July 1976; Longford records and archival films (National Film and Sound Archive, Canb); Emilie Longford interviews, documents (held by author, Calala, NSW).   MERVYN J. WASSON*

LYGON, SIR WILLIAM; *see* BEAUCHAMP

LYLE, SIR THOMAS RANKEN (1860-1944), mathematical physicist, was born on 26 August 1860 at Coleraine, Londonderry, Ireland, second son of Hugh Lyle, landowner, and his wife Jane, née Ranken. At the Coleraine Academical Institution Thomas excelled in work and sport. He won a sizarship in mathematics in 1879 to Trinity College, Dublin, and graduated B.A. in 1883 with the highest honours the college could bestow—the University studentship in mathematics and large gold medals in both mathematics and experimental science. His teachers included G. F. FitzGerald, one of the great figures of nineteenth-century mathematical physics.

For several years after graduation Lyle undertook private coaching for the university honours examinations. As well, he gained valuable experience in 1884 as representative of the Commissioners of Irish Lights in a famous series of experiments on the relative merits of oil, gas and electricity as lighthouse illuminants; he came down cautiously in favour of the Irish gas-burner system. In 1885-86, though not himself a Catholic, he was assistant lecturer in mathematics and mathematical physics at the Catholic University College, Dublin. After taking out his M.A. in 1887, however, he devoted himself entirely to advanced study in physics and mathematics with a view to obtaining a Trinity College fellowship. Runner-up in 1888, he was virtually assured of election next year but instead accepted appointment to the chair of natural philosophy at the University of Melbourne, unexpectedly made vacant by the premature death of H. M. Andrew [q.v.3].

In 1884 Lyle had taken up Rugby, progressing in a single season from the college second XV to the Irish international team. He played for Ireland five times in 1885-87 before suffering knee injuries that caused lameness in later life. He was also a keen cricketer and in Melbourne he became an Australian Rules enthusiast, serving for many years on the Victorian Football League tribunal.

Lyle took up his Melbourne appointment in mid-1889. A separate degree in science had been instituted only three years before and Lyle and two other outstanding arrivals, (Sir) David Masson and (Sir) Baldwin Spencer [qq.v.], were chiefly responsible for establishing this on a sound footing. A major feature of the new degree was its provision for systematic laboratory instruction, which in physics it fell to Lyle to implement; regular practical classes for second- and third-year students were begun in 1891 and practical work was included in the first-year course from 1901. With the introduction of the M.Sc. degree in 1891 research was established in the department and in due course Lyle himself embarked upon a modest research programme.

Much of the apparatus needed had to be made on the spot. Fortunately, Lyle was good with his hands. An expert glassblower, he made much of the glassware for both teaching and research. He was also an enthusiastic photographer. In February 1896, when news of Röntgen's discovery of a mysterious new form of radiation reached Melbourne, he put this combination of skills to good use, quickly assembling the apparatus needed to take what were probably Australia's first X-ray photographs. His assistance was thereafter in demand by members of the Melbourne medical community.

Lyle's own research interests lay, however, in the field of electrical power technology. Alternating currents and their associated magnetic effects became his specialty. In his earliest paper on the subject (1898) he introduced, apparently independently of Steinmetz, the complex-number representation of alternating currents that came to be widely used. Soon afterwards he showed how the method could be extended to take account of the hysteresis of an iron core. In later papers he described an ingenious 'wave-tracer and analyser' that he had developed and its use in investigations of the behaviour of iron under periodic magnetizing forces. The paper generally regarded as his masterpiece is a theoretical analysis of the alternating current generator (1909). Lyle was an active member of the Royal Society of Victoria to which he presented many of his papers. Most were also published in London. They led to the award of the Sc.D. degree of his Irish alma mater in 1905 and a fellowship of the Royal Society in 1912. 'Lyle of course', Spencer later wrote to Sir John Monash [q.v.], 'is the greatest man, scientifically speaking, that we have ever had in the University'.

Once Lyle had organized his department's affairs he began assuming responsibilities outside the university. In 1899 he investigated technical education facilities in Britain and the United States of America for the Victorian government and in 1901 was a major witness before the Fink [q.v.8] royal commission on technical education. He had already joined the board of visitors of the Melbourne Observatory in 1899; from 1903 until his death he served as chairman. In 1904-14 he represented the university on the Victorian Rhodes scholarship selection committee. In 1906, with C. Napier Hake, he inquired on behalf of the Commonwealth Department of Defence into a rash of accidents caused by the bursting of army rifles; next year he was a member of a conference that advised on the establishment of the Commonwealth Bureau of Meteorology; and in 1910-34 he was a university representative on Victoria's Council of Public Education.

On 28 December 1892 at East Melbourne, with Presbyterian forms, Lyle had married Frances Isobel Clare, daughter of a prominent Western District grazier, Thomas Millear. His marriage, prudent investments and Ranken family inheritances in the U.S.A. provided a considerable private income which enabled him to contemplate early retirement when his damaged knees left him increasingly incapacitated. He resigned in mid-1914 with effect from 28 February 1915; T. H. Laby [q.v.9] succeeded him.

The outbreak of war, however, led to new advisory and administrative responsibilities. Lyle became a member of the Federal Munitions Committee, president of the Industries Exemption Advisory Committee and scientific adviser to the Naval Board. He worked long hours with H. J. Grayson [q.v.9] to perfect the latter's superb ruling engine for producing super-high quality diffraction gratings. Following Grayson's death in 1918 Lyle purchased the machine and, using university laboratory space, kept the work going until the mid-1930s, supplying excellent gratings not only to Laby and his research students but also to overseas research workers.

In December 1915 Lyle was a member of the four-man delegation that waited on Prime Minister Hughes [q.v.9] to discuss the establishment of a national laboratory for scientific research. He was active in the affairs of the resulting Advisory Council of Science and Industry throughout that body's unsuccessful struggle to realize the scientists' early hopes and, following the establishment of the Commonwealth Institute of Science and Industry in 1919 and the appointment of a director in 1921, he provided (Sir) George Knibbs [q.v.9] with much-needed support and advice. When the institute was supplanted in 1926 by the Council for Scientific and Industrial Research he became a member of the Victorian committee.

Lyle was also a foundation member of the Australian National Research Council in 1919 and president in 1929-32. From at least 1916 he was active in the movement to establish a national system of engineering standards and was chairman of working committees of both the Australian Commonwealth Engineering Standards Association and its successor, the Standards Association of Australia. (He was never, however, chairman of the association itself.) He served on the Council of the University of Melbourne in 1916-33 and in 1929-31 on a committee which made recommendations for the establishment of a university in Canberra. In 1932 he sat on a committee of inquiry into the future of Australia's observatories. His outstanding contribution to the nation's scientific life was recognized by the A.N.R.C. when in 1931 it created the Thomas Ranken Lyle medal for distinguished Australian research in mathematics and physics.

In 1919-20 Lyle, as one of the three newly appointed part-time Victorian State electricity commissioners, chaired the meetings at which policies of far-reaching importance were broadly settled—the final commitment to La Trobe valley brown coal in preference to hydro-electricity or Altona coal and the method of its extraction; the establishment of Yallourn; plans for absorbing the existing municipal supply schemes and the Railway Department's generating plant; routes for power lines and standards for the licensing of technicians. After the institution of the State Electricity Commission with Monash as full-time chairman, Lyle continued as a commissioner. Knighted in 1922, he supported Monash in his determined defence of the commission against political attack. Lyle's contribution to the commission's success has been somewhat overshadowed by Monash's achievements but was well understood by his fellow commissioners who at his retirement in 1937 paid tribute to 'his profound knowledge, sound judgement and breadth of vision', affirming that 'neither time nor changing circumstances have made it necessary to alter the policy decisions in major matters registered during the period of his Chairmanship'.

Lyle lived for many years in a large home at Toorak and moved easily among men of influence in public affairs. He held several company directorships, most notably the Metropolitan Gas Co. He was president of the Melbourne Club in 1928. Inevitably, his political views were conservative. Extremely hard-working, he was also a man of gentle humour and considerable warmth and charm, popular with his students and later with S.E.C. workers: 'one of the nicest, kindliest gentlemen I have ever met', according to one of the latter. He was a little above medium height and physically very strong until his last years, despite his lameness. In 1940 a cerebral haemorrhage left him a semi-invalid.

Lyle died at South Yarra on 31 March 1944, survived by his wife, a son and three daughters; the eldest daughter (Dame) Mary, a Melbourne medical graduate, married (Sir) Edmund Herring and became a well-known figure in Melbourne society. Lyle's estate

was valued for probate at £79 056. His portrait by W. B. McInnes [q.v.], presented to the University of Melbourne in 1925, was later lost in a fire, but a replica hangs in the university's school of physics.

G. Blainey, *A centenary history of the University of Melbourne* (Melb, 1957); G. Currie and J. Graham, *The origins of CSIRO* (Melb, 1966); C. Edwards, *Brown power* (Melb, 1969); *Alma Mater* (Univ Melb), July 1897; *Aust J of Science*, 6 (1944), p 174; *Obituary Notices of Fellows of the Roy Soc*, 5 (1945), p 33; *Isis*, 60 (1969), p 5; *Hist Records of Aust Science*, vol 2, no 3 (1972), p 18, vol 5, no 3 (1982), p 41; Monash papers (NL); Lyle papers (held by Mr T. R. Lyle, Gunnedah, NSW); State Electricity Commission of Victoria Archives, Melb; Univ Melb Archives; W. R. Armstrong, History of State Electricity Commission of Victoria (MS, SEC Lib, Melb).   R. W. HOME

LYNAS, WILLIAM JAMES DALTON (1886-1947), miner and soldier, was born on 20 December 1886 at Auckland, New Zealand, son of Irish-born Thomas Reid Ward Lynas, engineer, and his wife Ellen Kate, née Dalton, born in Paris. After his father was appointed manager of a Western Australian sawmill about 1901 William was educated at Busselton. On leaving school he worked in grocery and briefly managed a store at Brookton. He probably moved to the Marble Bar district following a tin rush in 1906; in 1910 he was employed as a storeman on a mine at Moolyella.

In September 1914 Lynas enlisted in the 16th Battalion, Australian Imperial Force, and sailed for Egypt in December. He served throughout the Gallipoli campaign as a signaller, and was promoted lance corporal, then second lieutenant in January 1916. He was engaged in Egypt until June, then went with his battalion to France. A lieutenant from April he won the Military Cross in August near Pozières for a dangerous reconnaissance as intelligence officer and the capture of thirty prisoners. Later that month at Mouquet Farm, his work in preparing an attack and leading stretcher parties won him a Bar to the M.C. Promoted captain in April 1917, he spent six months with a training battalion in England but, on hearing that his unit was in action again, illegally rejoined it. In June and July 1918, although wounded, he distinguished himself near Hamel when his management of a very successful raid brought a second Bar to his M.C. and his leadership in a major attack won him the Distinguished Service Order. In December he was mentioned in dispatches.

Lynas sailed for Australia in February 1919 and when his A.I.F. appointment ended in June was placed on the reserve of officers, Australian Military Forces, as a captain. He returned immediately to Moolyella. While overseas he had investigated mining developments and, backed by English money, took up tin-dredging in partnership with W. Atkins. He also became an agent for Copley's Bank of London in buying base metals and mined for asbestos. As the post-war boom in metals subsided, so did Moolyella. Lynas sought concessions from the State government in 1924 and when the application failed altered his occupation on the electoral roll from miner in 1926 to philosopher in 1928: he was so designated for the rest of his life. Friends who knew him at this time described him as 'a wild spirit' and 'a terrible tease' with 'a touch of larrikinism'.

In June 1940 Lynas was recalled to full-time military duty and went to the Middle East in April and May as an A.I.F. troopship adjutant. During a second voyage in September and October he was injured on board and his appointment was terminated on medical grounds in April 1942. On 4 August 1944, in the Perth registry office, he married a divorced saleswoman, Enid Kathleen Coates, née Mawkes.

Lynas and his wife settled at Nullagine in the Pilbara district and on 1 September 1945 he was appointed part-time secretary of the local roads board. Survived by his wife, he died of coronary vascular disease at Nullagine on 12 January 1947 and was buried there. C. E. W. Bean [q.v.7] wrote that 'Bill' Lynas was 'one of the finest fighting leaders that Australia produced . . . a man whose name was constantly coupled with those of Harry Murray [q.v.], Percy Black and Albert Jacka' [qq.v.7,9]. The combination of military decorations he won is extremely rare.

C. Longmore, *The old Sixteenth* (Perth, 1929); C. E. W. Bean, *The A.I.F. in France*, 1918 (Syd, 1942); *Reveille* (Syd), Aug 1931; *Pastoralist & Grazier*, July 1963; *Pilbara Goldfields News*, 12 May 1906, 10 June, 22 July, 5, 12 Aug, 28 Oct 1919, 2 Mar, 21 Sept, 5 Oct, 16 Nov 1920, 3, 27 Sept, 11 Oct 1921, 25 July, 19 Sept 1922; W.A. Mines Dept, file 535/24, 1924 *and* Nullagin Roads Board, district minutes, Acc.1278/6 (Battye Lib).

H. J. GIBBNEY

LYNCH, ANNIE (1870-1938), religious and hospital administrator, was born at Virginia, Cavan, Ireland, daughter of a grazier, and his wife Annie, née O'Reilly. Educated by the Sisters of Mercy at nearby Ballyjamesduff, she joined the Little Company of Mary, a congregation devoted to the care of the sick and the dying, on 1 April 1887. She spent seven years at the congregation's mother house in Rome as a postulant and novice under the immediate care of Mother Foundress Mary Potter. Her novitiate completed, she took the religious name Mary Xavier.

Accompanied by three other 'Blue Sisters' (the title deriving from their blue veils), she was sent in 1894 to establish a hospital in Malta.

Recalled from Malta, Mother Xavier was dispatched to Sydney where the congregation ran Lewisham Hospital and Mount St Margaret psychiatric hospital; strains were developing among the Sisters and between them and the archdiocesan authorities. She arrived on 21 August 1899 on a six-month term as visitor-general. Years later she wrote: 'At Sydney things were at first very precarious, but within three months everything was right again and Cardinal Moran [q.v.] was a staunch friend of the Little Company of Mary'. By 31 December she had been apppointed superintendent.

Among the twenty-eight successful candidates at the Australian Trained Nurses' Association's examination for registration in 1906 were Mother Xavier and thirteen other religious from Lewisham. During her years as superior at Lewisham the small hospital for women and children became one of Sydney's leading general hospitals (male patients were admitted in 1912) and nurses' training schools. At least one surgeon S. H. Harris [q.v.9], impressed by the skilled and dedicated nursing of the Sisters, did much of his operating there. A stern but just disciplinarian at Lewisham, Mother Xavier was selflessly solicitous for the welfare of those in her charge.

In November 1899 she had acquired a hospital at North Adelaide, staffed by five Sisters from Lewisham, and in 1904 she sent four Sisters to establish a hospital in South Africa. Early in 1914 she took four Sisters to establish a house at Christchurch, New Zealand, returning next year for the laying of a foundation stone for a congregation hospital. In between she attended the congregation's first general chapter in Rome and visited hospitals in England, Ireland and the United States of America. In 1922 the Little Company of Mary was constituted into four provinces—Italy, England, Ireland and Australasia—and Mother Xavier was first provincial of Australasia for two three-year terms. She retired as superior at Lewisham to devote more time to provincial affairs, visiting New Zealand and Rome in 1924, and oversaw the establishment of hospitals at Wagga Wagga in 1926 and Wellington, New Zealand, in 1927.

Slightly above medium height, with graceful carriage and a hearty laugh, Mother Xavier loved music and dance and had a notable mezzo-soprano voice. Visitors to the hospital were impressed with her brilliance and charm. In 1929 she retired to the congregation's rest-home at Wollongong where she died on 7 June 1938; she was buried in Rookwood cemetery. Her memory rests on her achievements as one of Australia's most noted hospital and nursing administrators and in extending the work of the Little Company of Mary in the Southern Hemisphere.

D. Wordley, *No-one dies alone* (Syd, 1976); *Aust Catholic Hist Soc J*, 4 (1973), pt 2; *Catholic Press*, 16 June 1938; Archives, Little Company of Mary, Lewisham Hospital, Syd.   J. C. H. DEWDNEY

LYNCH, ARTHUR ALFRED (1861-1934), rebel and polymath, was born on 16 October 1861 at Smythesdale, Victoria, fourth of fourteen children of Irish Catholic John Lynch (1828-1906), surveyor and civil engineer, and his wife Isabella, née MacGregor, from Scotland. John Lynch had migrated in the early 1850s, worked as a gold digger, was one of Peter Lalor's [q.v.5] captains at Eureka and was imprisoned but released for want of evidence. His reminiscences in *Austral Light* in 1893-94 were later republished as *The story of the Eureka Stockade*. A lover of poetry who would spout 'Rabbie' Burns by the hour, he was first chairman of the Browns and Scarsdale municipality and in 1870 a leading founder of the Ballarat School of Mines and examiner in mathematics.

Because the family was so large Arthur spent some of his childhood with his MacGregor grandparents. Several of his siblings died of diphtheria. In retrospect he considered his early schools thoroughly bad, but was happier at Grenville and Ballarat colleges. Voraciously reading Adam Smith, Locke and Herbert Spencer, and 'entranced' by the differential calculus, he determined to pursue education in his own way: 'If I were to live at all I would live with the utmost effectiveness and with entire dauntlessness of spirit'. Quinsy troubled him throughout his youth; nevertheless, exulting in his physical prowess, he became an outstanding runner in a period when Smythesdale was a centre for athletics.

From 1878 Lynch took the 'certificate' course in civil engineering at the University of Melbourne. He was delayed by twice failing in elementary natural philosophy, but after award of the exhibition in second year he finished in February 1882 with second-class honours. After engineering employment and teaching mathematics, he completed his B.A. in 1885 and took third-class honours in logic and mental and moral philosophy in February 1886 (M.A., 1887). But for W. C. Kernot [q.v.5], to whom he was devoted, he found his teachers to be mediocre—'no great mind . . . no great soul'; Professor Nanson [q.v.] was 'chilling'.

Seeking to 'further explore . . . the realms of thought', Lynch left for Europe, never to return. He studied physics, physiology and psychology at the University of Berlin in 1888-89, acquiring respect for German science and especially for the physicist Helmholtz. In Berlin he met an Irish student Annie Powell whom he was to marry in 1895. In London in the early 1890s he worked as a freelance writer, publishing verse which owed much to Byron and *Our poets* (1894), a verse-satire which earned him enmity. Prominent in Irish circles, he stood unsuccessfully for the House of Commons for Galway, and later was commissioned to voyage to the United States of America to attempt to reconcile two Irish factions. He became a powerful journalist for the *National Reformer*, then the *Daily Mail* for which by 1898 he was Paris correspondent. Having travelled widely, Lynch was now fluent in several languages and wrote well in French and German.

Sent to report on the South African War, he immediately made contact with Botha and agreed to help form a second Irish 'brigade'; Kruger appointed him colonel in command of the motley band of about seventy volunteers of diverse nationalities. Republican anti-monarchism was one of his basic principles. Under its amateur commander the 'brigade' performed creditably but was disbanded after six months. Lynch was sent to America to promote the Boer cause before returning to Paris. Meanwhile he had been elected for Galway as a Nationalist and, after announcing his intention of taking his seat in a letter to *The Times*, set off for London and was arrested at Dover on 11 June 1902. Next January, calmly protesting that he was an Australian, he was tried for treason and sentenced to be hanged, but immediate commutation to life imprisonment followed. After mass petitioning and intervention by King Edward VII he was released a year later and pardoned in 1907. Lynch took up medical studies at St Mary's, Paddington, graduated from the University of London (M.R.C.S., L.R.C.P., 1908) and practised at Haverstock Hill. He later found time to graduate in Paris with a diploma of electrical engineering. In 1909 he was elected to parliament for West Clare. During World War I he fought for freedom as ever, he believed. After informal work in France, aiding communication between British and French leaders, late in the war he was appointed colonel in order to encourage recruiting in Ireland; he had little success. By now he was a close ally of Lord Northcliffe.

Lynch did not stand at the general election in 1918 and returned to medicine, controversy (such as attacking the notions of Dr Freud) and prolific authorship. He wrote nearly thirty books in all, including five volumes of verse and two novels. Perhaps his most important contributions were in psychology and ethics and his critical writings on science, though his *Case against Einstein* (1932) did not long survive scrutiny. He published his entertaining *My life story* in 1924.

A hefty man, strikingly handsome, of charm, courtesy and even temper, Lynch was one of the most picturesque figures of his time. He was erratic in his grasp of public affairs but was generally respected for his integrity and extraordinary range of knowledge, and was on friendly terms with many great contemporaries. He had no doubt that his was one of the outstanding minds of the age. Survived by his wife, childless, he died at Paddington, London, on 25 March 1934.

J. G. Roberts, *Smythe's Creek and Smythesdale* (Ballarat, 1930); *DNB*, 1931-1940; V. Palmer (ed), *A. G. Stephens* (Melb, 1941); R. L. Wallace, *The Australians at the Boer War* (Canb, 1976); B. Lewis, *Our war* (Melb, 1980); *British A'sian*, 29 Mar 1934; *People* (Syd), 4 July 1962; *Argus*, 19 June 1909, 27 Mar 1934; *The Times*, 26 Mar 1934; *Ballarat Courier*, 27 Mar 1934; *Canb Times*, 7 July 1979; Lynch papers (LaTL).   GEOFFREY SERLE

LYNCH, PATRICK JOSEPH (1867-1944), politician, was born on 24 May 1867 at Skeark, Meath, Ireland, son of Michael Lynch, farmer, and his wife Bridget, née Cahill. Patrick was educated at Cormeen National School and Ballieborough Model School, Cavan, continuing casual schooling while working on his father's farm.

In 1886 he migrated to Queensland, hewing railway sleepers in the north, then trekking 900 miles (1450 km) from Charleville in the south-west to the newly discovered Croydon goldfield. At Port Darwin in 1888 when he learned that his next destination, the Cossack goldfield in Western Australia, was a failure he became a stoker on coastal and island ships. During seven years at sea he qualified as a marine engineer and won a Royal Humane Society award for a life-saving attempt at night in shark-infested waters near Fiji. Lynch then worked as an engineer on a Fijian sugar-plantation, and in the gold mines at Kalgoorlie, Western Australia. A picturesque orator with a musical brogue, Paddy Lynch was one of the founders and then general secretary of the Goldfields & Enginedrivers' Association in 1897-1904. He served on the Boulder City Council in 1901-04 and won a reputation as a lucid and forceful advocate for various labour groups before the Western Australian Arbitration Court. On 21 November 1901 at Boulder he had married Annie Cleary.

In June 1904 Lynch was elected unopposed to the Legislative Assembly as Labor member for the new seat of Mount Leonora. He became minister for works for two months from June 1905 but the Daglish [q.v.8] government fell; in November 1906 he was elected to the Senate. He was a member of the royal commission on the fruit industry in 1912-14 and vice-chairman of the newly created Joint Standing Committee on Public Works (October 1914-November 1916). He was also first chairman of the River Murray Commission in 1916. At the same time he farmed 2500 acres (1000 ha) at Three Springs, jointly owned with his brother.

As the first Federal Labor parliamentarian to advocate conscription, Lynch followed W. M. Hughes [q.v.9] out of the Labor caucus on 14 November 1916. When the North Coolgardie district council sent him to the Labor interstate conference in Melbourne on 4 December he was refused admission, with two other Western Australian conscriptionist delegates. He was expelled from the State Labor party in March 1917. Lynch served briefly as minister of works and railways (November 1916-February 1917) in the Hughes ministry but then had to make way for an ex-Liberal.

With Henry Gregory [q.v.9] he reported to Prime Minister Bruce [q.v.7] in March 1922 on the possibilities of settling migrants on lands in Western Australia. He was again a member of the Public Works Committee in July 1923-June 1926 and served on a Senate committee on the standing committee system in 1929-30. He was president of the Senate from August 1932 to June 1938. Defeated at the 1937 election, he unsuccessfully contested the State seat of Geraldton in 1939.

The neatly bearded but generally dishevelled Irishman was an avid reader and an artless and friendly companion. A fiery advocate for those causes he supported, he doubtless contributed, with Archbishop Clune [q.v.8] to the strong 'Yes' vote in Western Australia in the conscription referenda; but he was overshadowed for ministerial appointment by his State colleague (Sir) George Pearce [q.v.]. On 1 May 1933 Lynch had married Mary Brown at Narrogin. He was appointed C.B.E. in 1936. He died on 15 January 1944 at Mount Lawley and after a state funeral was buried in the Catholic section of Karrakatta cemetery. His wife and two daughters and a son of his first marriage survived him.

J. S. Battye (ed), *Cyclopedia of Western Australia*, 1 (Adel, 1912); *Punch* (Melb), 23 Nov 1916; *British A'sian*, 18 Jan 1917; *To-day* (Melb), 1 Apr 1934; *West Australian*, 20 Oct 1905, 16 Jan 1944; *Kalgoorlie Miner*, 10 Oct 1916; J. R. Robertson, The Scaddan government and the conscription crisis 1911-1917 (M.A. thesis, Univ WA, 1958); E. S. Buttfield, The Daglish ministry 1904-05 (M.A. thesis, Univ WA, 1979).   DAVID BLACK

LYNCH, THOMAS (JOSEPH) (1860-1921), soldier, was born on 11 September 1860 at Coolamatong near Cooma, New South Wales, son of Thomas Lynch, store-keeper, and his wife Ellen, née Kane, both from Ireland. After attending St Patrick's College, Goulburn, he enlisted in the New South Wales Artillery on 18 January 1879. By 1885 he had been promoted sergeant and served during the Sudan War with the field battery of the New South Wales Contingent. After training on 9-pounder guns issued in Suakin the battery moved to Handoub on 17 April and until returning to Suakin on 14 May provided mounted men to accompany the 20th Hussars on patrol. On 17 May the contingent left for Australia and at Colombo Lynch was disembarked for treatment of enteric fever.

In 1886 Sergeant Lynch topped the first course at the newly established School of Gunnery at Middle Head, Sydney. From February to July 1887 he was an assistant instructor there and qualified as master gunner, 3rd class. He married Louisa Maria Johnson at Watson's Bay on 14 February 1888; they had no children. On 1 January 1894 he was promoted master gunner, 1st class (warrant officer) and was appointed assistant fire-master, New South Wales Field Artillery Regiment.

After the outbreak of the South African War Lynch was commissioned second lieutenant in the New South Wales Citizens' Bushmen and on 1 April 1900 was promoted lieutenant. The regiment landed at Biera, Mozambique, on 11 April then moved to Marandellas in Rhodesia and Lynch's detachment marched as a convoy escort for over 300 miles (483 km) to Bulawayo. On 13 July he was transferred to the New Zealand Battery of the Rhodesian Field Force. He was invalided home in October but in April 1901 returned to rejoin the Citizens' Bushmen. Allotted to the Royal Army Service Corps, he was promoted captain and appointed transport officer of Colonel St George Henry's column. In August he was invalided home again and on 14 January 1902 became assistant fire-master, and in October regimental sergeant major, Royal Australian Artillery (New South Wales). From 1 June he was quartermaster, with the rank of honorary lieutenant, on the Administrative and Instructional Staff. Promoted honorary major on 8 May 1913, from July he was adjutant, 6th Field Artillery Brigade.

When World War I began Lynch was appointed brigade major, 2nd Light Horse Brigade, Australian Imperial Force, on 17 September 1914. The brigade embarked from Egypt on 16 May 1915 for service on Gallipoli; on 10 June Lynch was seconded for duty as camp commandant, 1st Division Head-

quarters, but on 23 June he was admitted to hospital with conjunctivitis. He remained on Gallipoli, through the heavy fighting in August, until the evacuation to Egypt in December. Suffering from general debility, Lynch embarked for Australia on 3 March 1916 and on 14 April was discharged from the A.I.F. He then resumed the appointment of adjutant, 6th Field Artillery Brigade, Australian Military Forces and from 1 January 1918 he was temporarily brigade major, 5th Infantry Brigade Area. He was promoted major in 1919 and retired in 1920 as an honorary lieut-colonel.

Lynch died of pernicious anaemia on 30 November 1921 and was buried in the Catholic section of Randwick cemetery. He is remembered for his leadership, training and administrative qualities in war and peace and for active service spanning Australian involvement in three wars.

History of the origin and formation of the field artillery of New South Wales (Syd, 1895); J. Green, *The story of the Australian bushmen* (Syd, 1903); (Staff officer at Victoria Barracks), *Historical record of the New South Wales Regiment of Royal Australian Artillery* (Syd, 1903); Aust Defence Dept, *Official records of the Australian military contingents to the war in South Africa*, P. L. Murray ed (Melb, 1911); R. Sutton, *For Queen and Empire* (Syd, 1974); R. L. Wallace, *The Australians at the Boer War* (Canb, 1976); R. Cubis, *A history of 'A' Battery, New South Wales Artillery (1871-1899), Royal Australian Artillery (1899-1971)* (Syd, 1978); W. St. P. Bunbury, Beginning of the School of Gunnery at Middle Head (MS, RAHS, Syd); Records, Dept of Veterans' Affairs (Canb), and AWM; information from Prof S. E. Livingstone, Maroubra, Syd, and Roy Aust Artillery Hist Soc, Syd.

R. SUTTON

LYNE, CHARLES EMANUEL (1850-1910), newspaperman and public servant, was born on 12 October 1850 at Cheapside, London, son of Emanuel Lyne, warehouse-man, and his wife Mary Ann, née Jordan. The family came to Australia, via California, when he was 7. He attended schools in Brisbane and Sydney before joining the *Evening News*. Transferring to the *Sydney Morning Herald*, he had become by the mid-1880s chief of its parliamentary reporting staff. In November 1884 he accompanied Commodore (Sir) James Erskine [q.v.4] in H.M.S. *Nelson* as the *Herald*'s 'special commissioner' at the proclamation of the protectorate over Papua. His reports were republished in 1885 as *New Guinea: an account of the establishment of the British Protectorate*.

When the Parliamentary Standing Committee on Public Works was established in 1888 Lyne was appointed secretary at a salary of £700. The committee was set up by Sir Henry Parkes [q.v.5] to report upon proposals for public works, apart from defence works, estimated to cost more than £20 000, probably as a means of escaping responsibility for a form of ministerial patronage which was losing its usefulness. At least two men who served on it, John Haynes [q.v.4] and J. C. Watson [q.v.], believed that Lyne's efficiency contributed greatly to its success in forcing governments to think out their proposals, thereby saving the colony much money. Certainly he rapidly became known as a most efficient public officer. He acted as official secretary to (Sir) Francis Suttor [q.v.6] at the Colonial Conference, Ottawa, 1894, and on his return to Sydney next year was appointed secretary to the new Public Service Board. The pressure of reclassifying the whole public service led to ill health, and after twelve months he was transferred at his own request back to the Public Works Committee, with his salary reduced to £600.

In 1899, when a proposal for a salary increase of £95 came before the Legislative Assembly, John Norton [q.v.] alleged that Lyne, while still a newspaperman, had 'had pickings from the public service in the way of special shorthand-writing jobs on commissions . . . from which he made thousands and thousands of pounds', enabling him to lend large sums to Parkes in return for which he had received his secretaryship. The allegations had no more truth in them than most of Norton's statements. Lyne had been, however, a close friend of Parkes, as is shown not only by his hagiographic, if occasionally touching, *Life of Sir Henry Parkes, G.C.M.G.* (1896), but also by his willingness to represent Parkes's interests when the old man was disputing with his son Varney [q.v.].

The Public Works Committee declined in importance as its membership came to reflect the balance of forces in the Legislative Assembly and it tended to become a rubber stamp for government proposals; Lyne's work was consequently much less onerous. He died of cancer at his home at Ashfield on 11 February 1910 and was buried in the Church of England cemetery, Enfield. His wife Louisa Jane, née Witherspoon, whom he had married in the Wesleyan Methodist Church, Newcastle, on 11 August 1881, and their three sons and four daughters survived him.

V&P (NSW), 1899 (1), p 477; *PD* (NSW), 1899 (102), 3238; *A'sian*, 7 July 1888, 19 Feb 1910; *Daily Telegraph* (Syd), 12 Feb 1910; *SMH*, 12 Feb 1910; Parkes correspondence (ML).

W. G. McMinn

LYNE, Sir WILLIAM JOHN (1844-1913), politician, was born on 6 April 1844 at Great Swan Port, Van Diemen's Land, eldest son of John Lyne, farmer, later member of the Tasmanian House of Assembly, and his first wife Lillias Cross Carmichael, née Hume. John had arrived in Hobart Town in 1826 from Gloucestershire, England. William was educated first by a tutor, Rev. Andrew Mackersley, then at Horton College, Ross, in 1851-59 and finally by Rev. H. P. Kane [q.v.2] at Rostella. Robust, adventurous and an excellent horseman, at 20 he went with a cousin to western Queensland, then took up a sheep-station, Merton Vale, near Burketown on the Gulf of Carpentaria. But hardship, illness and his cousin's death drove him back to Tasmania, where in August 1866 he became council clerk with Glamorgan Municipality. Responsibilities included those of superintendent of police and town surveyor. He also became rector's warden of All Saints Church for nine years and captain of the local cricket club. On 29 June 1870 at Swansea he married Martha Coates 'Pattie' Shaw.

In 1875 Lyne moved to New South Wales. His brother Bishop took up land near Germanton (Holbrook). William leased Bowna, near Albury, a sheep-run of about 5000 acres (2020 ha), part of Cumberoona station. Again he quickly became a community leader— playing in the cricket team, joining the committee of the Albury and Border Pastoral Agricultural and Horticultural Society and officiating at local races. He became chairman of the Albury district's sheep directors and his Lincoln rams won prizes at the 1878 local show.

Free selectors had heavily settled in the Riverina during the 1870s. Lyne involved himself in the growing agitation for amendment of the Land Acts. In July 1880 he was appointed a delegate to a free selectors' conference to meet in Sydney in October, by which time he had become a candidate for the Legislative Assembly seat of the Hume. In November, supporting pro-selector policies, he topped the poll.

Lyne immediately aligned himself with the Opposition to the Parkes-Robertson [qq.v.5, 6] coalition, supported the unsuccessful attempt to remit interest on conditional purchases and opposed the pro-squatter ringbarking on crown lands regulation bill. But in 1881 he had himself become a squatter, buying Tyrie, a run of about 60 000 acres (24 300 ha) in central New South Wales, with two partners. An infrequent attender in parliament in 1882, he did not vote in the division in November which unexpectedly overturned the government. At the ensuing election he urged moderate reform of the land laws and was re-elected unopposed. Generally supporting the Stuart [q.v.6] ministry, Lyne was prominent in the long session which framed J. S. Farnell's [q.v.4] Crown Lands Act, 1884, and his sympathy with squatter interests became evident. A persistent advocate of water conservation, in May 1884 he became president of a royal commission whose only practical outcome was the establishment of a water conservation and irrigation branch in the Department of Mines.

His strong parliamentary performances and ambition marked Lyne as increasingly important in the anti-Parkes faction during the 1880s. A hardened bushman, bearded, 6 ft. 2 ins. (188 cm) tall, he had an impressive physical presence. In the first Dibbs [q.v.4] ministry on 2 November 1885 he succeeded H. S. Badgery [q.v.3] as secretary for public works. The government lasted only until 21 December. In early 1886 Lyne acted temporarily as leader of the Opposition, but stood aside in favour of Sir Patrick Jennings [q.v.4] on 10 February. From February 1886 to January 1887 he was secretary for public works in the Jennings cabinet.

Despite being occasionally laid up with gout, Lyne was a hard-working minister. Faced with a financial deficit, he dismissed hundreds of fettlers. Yet he continued his predecessors' railway expansion, pushing ahead with the Culcairn-Corowa line in his own electorate. His government railways bill, proposing a board of commissioners, was later implemented by Parkes in an altered form.

In his 1880 election manifesto Lyne had 'entirely agreed with the principle of free trade' and condemned the 'influence of protection as unsound and delusive'. But in March 1886 he suggested reciprocal duties against Victoria, especially on cereals—a policy popular in his border electorate. In the election of February 1887 Lyne was returned unopposed, now advocating outright protection, as he was to do for the rest of his career. Prominent in the opposition to Parkes, in December Lyne was a founder of the protectionist journal, the *Australian Star* (in 1890 chairman of directors). He was secretary for lands in the brief Dibbs ministry (January-March 1889). On 23 October 1891 he became secretary for public works under Dibbs, supported by protectionist Labor members. Though criticized for lacking 'bold ideas of a national policy' by the *Review of Reviews*, and for continuing with costly railway expansion, Lyne was generally adjudged to be successful in his portfolio. The government resigned on 2 August 1894.

Lyne had moved his family to Sydney by about 1887, and for some time also had a residence at Katoomba. Later he lived at North Sydney. He relinquished Bowna in May 1893. In the depression of the 1890s he was rumoured to have faced the possibility of bailiffs. In 1895 he was a director of the Citizens Life Assurance Co. Ltd. He continued to run Tyrie, selling it in 1908. In 1912 he purchased the family property, Gala, in Tasmania.

In 1895 he held aloof from a frail alliance between Parkes and Dibbs, who lost his seat in the snap election held in July. Lyne became leader of the Opposition. It was difficult to counter wily (Sir) George Reid [q.v.], who exploited his opponent's slow thought processes and tendency to bluster through difficulties; but Lyne responded with persistence and pugnacity. Late in 1895 he reformed the party organization, founding the National Protection Union. For the next three years he withstood attempts to make the party reactionary and shrugged off rumours of Dibbs's return to depose him.

The Federation question posed problems for Lyne. He was a delegate to the 1897-98 Australasian Federal Convention and a member of its finance committee, but argued strongly that sections of the draft bill disadvantaged New South Wales. He particularly objected to equal representation of States in the Senate. In the June 1898 referendum he opposed acceptance of the Constitution bill. But most Protectionists supported Federation, and Lyne was forced to stand aside when (Sir) Edmund Barton [q.v.7] became leader of the National Federal Alliance for the July election and was elected parliamentary Protectionist leader in October. In the June 1899 referendum Lyne, after hesitating, again opposed the bill.

With Federation assured, Barton's lack of support from radical Protectionists re-emerged and on 23 August he resigned. In a series of subterranean moves, Lyne again became Opposition leader, and Labor withdrew support from Reid. Opponents alleged that these changes were orchestrated by the *Daily Telegraph* which, despite its free-trade policy, now supported Lyne, whose ministry was sworn in on 14 September.

In detaching Labor from Reid Lyne had promised specific reforms, and achieved an astonishing list of important legislation: early closing of retail shops, coal mines regulation and miners' accident relief, old-age pensions, graduated death duties and Sydney municipal reform. In July-December 1900 no fewer than 85 Acts were passed. Unlike Reid's, Lyne's progressive legislation passed the Legislative Council. Important industrial arbitration and woman's suffrage legislation, enacted in 1901-02, had been introduced in his term. He also acted promptly to send military forces to the South African War and to combat the plague in Sydney. In June 1900 he was appointed K.C.M.G.

On 19 December 1900 Lord Hopetoun [q.v.9] invited Lyne to form the first Commonwealth government. Although this was eventually described as 'the Hopetoun blunder', Lyne's political strength and New South

Wales's position as the senior colony explain the governor-general's action. But Lyne was unable to form a ministry when Barton declined to serve and Alfred Deakin [q.v.8] persuaded leading Victorian and South Australian politicians also to refuse. Barton was sworn in as first Australian prime minister on 1 January 1901 and Lyne became minister for home affairs.

He immediately had to set up the machinery for the first Commonwealth elections. He resigned his New South Wales seat on 20 March and on 29 March was elected for the Federal seat of Hume. Retaining the home affairs portfolio, he was responsible for the Commonwealth Electoral Act (enfranchising women) and for establishing the Commonwealth Public Service. On 7 August 1903 he became minister for trade and customs. Next month Deakin replaced Barton as prime minister after Lyne failed to secure enough party support for the leadership; he remained minister for trade and customs until April 1904.

Upon the defeat of J. C. Watson's [q.v.] government in August, Lyne and (Sir) Isaac Isaacs [q.v.9] joined Labor in a formal alliance. In June 1905 Labor caucus rejected a proposal for a coalition with Protectionists under Lyne. Again minister for trade and customs in Deakin's second ministry, he had charge of its New Protection legislation, which linked 'encouragement to Australian industry . . . with measures to prevent the growth of injurious monopolies and ensure fair prices . . . and fair wages'.

In 1907 he visited England with Deakin for the Colonial Conference, where he bluntly urged preferential trade upon the unresponsive British government, and was Australia's chief delegate at the conference on merchant shipping legislation. Acting prime minister during Deakin's illness in June-September, he ably handled the wire-netting controversy with (Sir) Joseph Carruthers [q.v.7]. In July 1907 he became treasurer and was responsible for Australia's first truly protectionist tariff. In presenting his well-judged 1908 budget Lyne suggested 'a government bank of issue, a treasury note system and a local coinage, which it was left for Labour to achieve'. His term as treasurer, ending in October, set the pattern for Australian financial arrangements for the second decade of the Commonwealth.

In April he had made another effort for the highest political office. Deakin offered to resign if Lyne could re-form the government as a coalition with Labor. Again he failed, again he accepted failure calmly in public. But in May 1909, when Deakin withdrew support from the Fisher [q.v.8] government, overriding Lyne's protests within the party, the old man's composure finally broke. In parlia-

ment he attacked Deakin angrily, accusing him of the treachery of Judas. With Australia's political map now totally recast, Lyne was left in bitter isolation. Close to Labor, which did not oppose him in Federal elections for Hume, he never joined the party, though his brother Bishop was a member. In 1910 Lyne was re-elected as a pro-Labor Independent. Next year, nominated by Fisher's government, he attended the coronation of George V in London.

Expert at managing his difficult electorate, 'Old Bill' would tour it at election time 'with the boot of his buggy filled to the gunwales with liquid refreshment'. Unable, through illness, to campaign in May 1913, he was narrowly defeated. His wife had died in 1903. Lyne died at his Double Bay home on 3 August 1913 and was buried in South Head cemetery with Anglican rites. He was survived by three daughters and a son, and by his second wife Sarah Jane Olden (1869-1961) and their daughter. His estate was sworn for probate at £17 862.

Lyne was one of the key political figures in a crucial thirty-year period of Australia's history. His career began in the years of faction politics and land agitation of the early 1880s, spanned the period of fiscal grouping under free traders and protectionists, and was enmeshed in the great national questions of Federation and the accession to power of the Labor party. A home-loving man, 'he liked the races. He was fond of a first-class concert. He occasionally went to the theatre . . . When he read anything it was usually a magazine'. He was neither an orator nor an intellectual and his reputation has, like Reid's, suffered from the predominantly Deakin-inspired political history of Australian Federation. Deakin's biassed description of Lyne—'a crude, sleek, suspicious, blundering, short-sighted, backblocks politician'—has stuck.

In 1907 the *Catholic Press*, often unfairly critical of him for an alleged leaning towards 'Orangeism', recalled Parkes saying that Lyne 'looked around him when he entered a room like a policeman seeking clues'. In 1927 the Melbourne *Age* remembered him as having 'courage and mental pertinacity' and 'a rugged, semi-articulate vein of common sense'; he was 'broad-shouldered, erect as a flagstaff, and 17 st. [108 kg] in weight, without corpulence . . . In the Parliamentary Chamber . . . his laugh was the loudest, his interjection of dissent was the most emphatic. His full blue eyes danced with merriment or gleamed like incandescent lights in anger'. A 'great personality . . . courageous, openhanded, cheery, boyish-spirited', he was 'a hard fighter, who displayed much grit and great shrewdness'.

A portrait of Lyne by W. H. Gocher [q.v.9] is at the National Library of Australia, and a marble bust by Theo Cowan [q.v.8] at Parliament House, Canberra.

H. V. Evatt, *Australian Labour leader* (Syd, 1945); W. M. Hughes, *Policies and potentates* (Syd, 1950); G. Sawer, *Australian Federal politics and law, 1901-29* (Melb, 1956); A. Deakin, *The Federal story*, J. A. La Nauze ed (Melb, 1963); P. Loveday and A. W. Martin, *Parliament factions and parties* (Melb, 1966); B. Nairn, *Civilising capitalism* (Canb, 1973); L. Nyman, *The Lyne family history* (Hob, 1976); Report of a conference . . . merchant shipping legislation, *PP* (GB), 1907 (Cd 3567); *Express* (Syd), 10 Dec 1885; *SMH*, 11 Feb 1886, 4 Aug 1913; *Evening Echo* (Ballarat), 26 Sept 1903; *Catholic Press*, 5 Sept 1907; *Daily Telegraph* (Syd), 4 Aug 1913; *Age*, 14 May 1927; H. S. Evans, Sir William Lyne and the Australian Constitution (M.A. thesis, UNE, 1984); Barton *and* Deakin *and* Lyne papers (NL); information from Mrs D. Brown, Green Point, NSW.   CHRIS CUNNEEN

LYNN, ROBERT JOHN (1873-1928), shipowner and businessman, was born on 14 March 1873 at Stockton, Newcastle, New South Wales, third son of Richard Lynn, an American shipwright and marine surveyor, and his wife Mary, née McKindley, from Scotland. He was educated at public schools at Newcastle and at 14 began work as a clerk with a Newcastle wholesale firm and became chief salesman.

Lured by the gold discoveries in Western Australia, in 1895 Lynn went to the Coolgardie fields where he spent a year prospecting unsuccessfully. Disillusioned, he returned to Fremantle and joined the shipping firm of McIlwraith, McEacharn [qq.v.] & Co. as a clerk. He soon became junior partner in the shipping firm of Denny Bros & Lynn and joined a business partnership with H. E. Mofflin. In 1906 he acquired a fleet of five small ketches and schooners and formed R. J. Lynn & Co.; with these craft and agencies the firm was involved in shipping on the Western Australian coast for the next fifteen years.

In 1919 Lynn amalgamated his firm with that of Walter Johnson, trading as Johnson & Lynn Ltd. They bought and operated run-down coal-mining leases at Collie, which were in need of capital and entrepreneurship. In 1920 Johnson & Lynn set up Amalgamated Collieries of Western Australia Ltd; in the next five years this company bought and incorporated nearly all the operative leases at Collie. With Lynn and Johnson as joint general managers and alternate chairman of directors, Amalgamated Collieries monopolized the coalfields' output for the next decade. A royal commission of 1931-33 on the production costs of coal reported that Amalgamated Collieries paid abnormally high wages to its miners; and it was severely critical of the firm, which it concluded had been making unfair profits at the expense of the government.

Eventually Lynn was managing director of six companies and a director of three others, their interests including banking, insurance, timber, cement, roads, printing and tanneries. He was also a Fremantle councillor in 1904-09 and served on the Municipal Tramways Board, Fremantle, in 1903-18. In 1912 he was elected to the West Province seat of the Legislative Council; a Liberal and later National Party representative, he retired in 1924.

Lynn was generous and kind and without any apparent desire for reward or recognition: he endowed scholarships to schools of any denomination. Parliamentary colleagues respected his common sense and practicality and his ability to acknowledge publicly his mistakes. He had a lifelong interest in fishing and boating and his name is perpetuated in a trophy of the East Fremantle Football Club of which he was a revered patron for seventeen years.

Lynn died of nephritis on 12 September 1928 at his Perth home and was buried in the Congregational section of Karrakatta cemetery. He had married at Fremantle on 13 June 1901 Ada Turton who survived him with a daughter and two sons. Lynn's estate was valued for probate at £35 999.

J. S. Battye (ed), *Cyclopedia of Western Australia*, 1-2 (Adel, 1912); G. Wilson (ed), *WA centenary 1829-1929* (Perth, 1929); *PP* (LA WA), 1930-31, 3 (21); *West Australian*, 14 Sept 1928; L. W. Johnson, A history of the Collie coal mining industry (M.A. thesis, Univ WA, 1956).

ALAN BONDS

LYON, JOHN LAMB (1835?-1916), stained-glass painter and art decorator, was born in Glasgow, Scotland, son of James Lyon, clerk, and his wife Janet Lang, née Thorburn. On leaving school he was apprenticed to Kearney & Co., glass painters, where he learned to mix and grind his own colours. He worked in London for six years with Ward & Hughes, stained-glass painters to Queen Victoria. In Glasgow on 24 June 1857 he married Jane Clark who died childless. He married Elizabeth Gillespie Pearson in Glasgow on 3 December 1860 before sailing for Melbourne; they arrived on 20 March 1861. His father, a storekeeper at Maldon, had migrated some years earlier. John worked for Ferguson & Urie and by 1866 had become a partner. In 1870-71 he visited Britain.

Moving to Sydney in 1873, he set up in business as Lyon, Cottier & Co. with his old friend and fellow apprentice Daniel Cottier (d. 1891), now a peripatetic leading London decorator with a branch in Fifth Avenue, New

York. Prominent architects were invited to inspect the Pitt Street premises, decorated in the latest London style. In addition to painting and firing domestic, religious and heraldic stained-glass, Lyon imported 'paper-hangings', Venetian gasoliers, Indian rugs and carpets, and 'art furniture'. He was soon commissioned by James Barnet [q.v.3] to decorate the new General Post Office, Government House and rooms in Parliament House.

Working for such prominent architects as Barnet, Horbury Hunt, W. W. Wardell [qq.v.4,6], (Sir) John Sulman and W. L. Vernon [qq.v.], Lyon carried out many commissions for commercial buildings and decorated clubs and private houses. Among the most notable were Cranbrook for James White [q.v.6] and Woollahra House for (Sir) William Cooper, and in Collins Street, Melbourne, the English, Scottish and Australian Chartered Bank with Sir George Verdon's [q.v.6] residence above. By 1879 Lyon had moved to 179 Liverpool Street and retained the site for his office and glassworks when he moved to Balmain in 1884. Overseas in 1886, he found Cottier's in New York 'sumptuous' and saw the red and gold satin, patchwork bedcovers being made for the Vanderbilts. He also visited Britain and Europe. Late that year he was joined in Sydney by Andrew Wells. For ten years the firm traded as Lyon, Wells, Cottier & Co. and in the late 1880s had an office in Melbourne run by Wells. Other talented artists and experienced foremen were sent out by Cottier.

Over the years Lyon received many awards for his distinctive stained-glass. At the Victorian Intercolonial Exhibition in 1875 his window portraying Captain Cook [q.v.1] was bordered with native fauna and flora motifs. He made stained-glass windows for St Saviour's Cathedral, Goulburn, and All Saints Cathedral, Bathurst, and for numerous churches throughout New South Wales and in Tasmania, Victoria and Queensland. He won gold medals for windows at the New Zealand International Exhibition at Christchurch in 1906 and the 1908 Franco-British Exhibition in London when he was again in Britain. Assisted by two of his sons from about 1900, he opened a large glassworks at Rushcutters Bay in 1910.

Lyon had exhibited with the Art Society of New South Wales from 1880 and served on its committee in the early 1880s. He mainly painted portraits, often of his family, but he presented his portrait of John Young [q.v.6], building contractor, to the City Bowling Club of which they were fellow members.

Lyon died at his Balmain home on 14 June 1916 and was buried with Presbyterian forms in Waverley cemetery. His wife, three sons and three daughters survived him. Through Cottier's standing as a leading decorator and close connexions with the English Aesthetic movement, Lyon could satisfy his clients' desire to follow the latest decorative fashions. Although he was involved in the management of his firm until 1912, 'a long and active life brought no diminution in either [his] enthusiasm or skill as a practical, artistic craftsman'.

His bust by Achille Simonetti [q.v.6] is held by a descendant.

S. Forge, *Victorian splendour* (Melb, 1981); I. Evans, *The Australian home* (Syd, 1983); M. Stapleton (ed), *Historic interiors* (Syd, 1983); J. Zimmer, *Stained glass in Australia* (Melb, 1984); *A'sian Painter and Decorator*, Aug 1909, 1 July 1916; *Leichhardt Hist Soc*, July 1973; *Hist Houses J*, Mar 1982; information from and papers held by J. L. Lyon, Cottesloe, Perth.

MARTHA RUTLEDGE

LYONS, HERBERT WILLIAM (1888-1958), farmer, politician and company director, was born on 30 September 1888 at Wild Horse Plains, South Australia, son of Henry Alexander Lyons, storekeeper and farmer from Ireland, and his wife Margaret, née Crothers. He was educated at the local school and in Adelaide, and then returned to work on the family farm.

With an elder brother Charles he formed a partnership, Lyons Bros, which after farming initially at Wild Horse Plains, extended its activities to Long Plains, Inkerman, Mallala and Avon in the Adelaide Plains area, the South Australian Mallee and the Western District of Victoria. They became one of South Australia's biggest wheat-growers. Later the partnership split, with Charles taking over the Victorian property and Herbert carrying on locally.

In 1929 Herbert Lyons became a director of 'The Farmers' Own Company', Cresco Fertilizers Ltd (formerly South Australian Fertilizer Co. Ltd), and chairman in 1930-31. Australia's rural industries were then in crisis because of the Depression: prices on international markets had plummeted, with grim consequences for the fertilizer industry, heavily dependent at one remove on these export markets, particularly for wheat. Disagreement about appropriate policies in the continuing slump led to a vigorous contest for directorships in 1932; Lyons retained his seat. Next year the board, still under his chairmanship, sacked the founding managing director. Lyons became joint managing director for a period, and in 1939 sole managing director. He retained this post and the chairmanship until his death. He was a director also of associated companies—Cresco Fertilizers (W.A.) Ltd, Sulphuric Acid Ltd, Nairne

Pyrites Ltd, Fertilizer Sales Ltd and Albany Superphosphate Co. Pty Ltd, W.A.

As chairman for twenty-eight years and managing director for twenty-five, Lyons played a major role in piloting Cresco through the economic troubles besetting rural industries, and their linked suppliers, in the 1930s to secure first a share of shrinking demand and later a healthy position in the expanded post-war market. Substantial plant modernization and expansion undertaken in the post-war decade, along with receptiveness to ideas arising from agricultural research, improved product, output levels and profits.

Lyons entered the House of Assembly in 1933 for the seat of Barossa; an elder brother, John Alexander, was already member for Stanley. Although he remained in parliament until 1938, Herbert Lyons spoke seldom in debate after his first year: his responsibilities with Cresco probably left him little time for a large involvement. He usually restricted himself to the interests of primary producers and hardly influenced proceedings, although his remarks suggest sound commercial acumen and practical knowledge of farming. A member of the Liberal and Country League, he retired in 1938. In 1952-54 he was on the Unley City Council.

Lyons attended Methodist and Congregational churches. He had married a schoolteacher, Vera Adelaide Rinder, on 14 March 1925 at Manthorpe Memorial Congregational Church, Unley; they had one son and one daughter. Tennis was his favourite relaxation. He died on 1 September 1958 of hypertensive heart disease.

South Australian, 9 Dec 1926; *Advertiser* (Adel), 3 Sept 1958; Business records, Cresco Fertilizers Ltd (BRG 90, SAA); information from Mr C. H. Lyons, Adel.   ERIC RICHARDS
JOAN HANCOCK

LYONS, JOSEPH ALOYSIUS (1879-1939), schoolteacher, premier and prime minister, was born on 15 September 1879 at Stanley, Tasmania, son of Irish-born parents Michael Henry Lyons and his wife Ellen, née Carroll. His early education was at St Joseph's Convent School, Ulverstone. Michael Lyons had little success as a hotelkeeper, farmer, butcher and baker. In 1887 he lost all of the family's money speculating on the Melbourne Cup. He suffered a breakdown and became unable to care for his wife and eight children. When 9 young Joe helped to support the family by working as errand boy, farm labourer and printer's devil for the *Coastal News* at Ulverstone. He was saved from drudgery by two aunts, the Misses Carroll, who supported him when he returned to school at 12.

Guided by a sympathetic teacher at Stanley State School, John Scott, Lyons was appointed a monitor, assisting with the education of younger children at an annual salary of £15. He became a pupil-teacher in 1895 and qualified in 1901, teaching at small country schools. At Smithton, Lyons took up debating and developed quickly as a platform speaker. Much influenced by the Irish radicalism of his mother, and perceiving the strength of the Protestant landholders in the small communities of northern Tasmania, he joined the North-West League of the Workers' Political League, the forerunner of the Australian Labor Party in Tasmania. But the Education Department warned him against engaging in politics. It was the first of many clashes between Lyons and the department, but he soon resumed political activity as a critic of the education system.

In 1907 Lyons became one of the pupils at Tasmania's first teacher training college. He taught in Launceston and Hobart, then resigned to contest the State seat of Wilmot for Labor in 1909. He campaigned vigorously. Horsewhipped by a local landholder whom he had criticized, Lyons was awarded damages and believed that the incident enabled him to win the election. In parliament he at first was inclined to talk too much and seemed to take himself too seriously. The Labor caucus lacked talent, and Lyons took a lead, concentrating on educational issues such as the need for post-primary state schools and equal pay for women teachers. He urged the breaking up of big estates, factory legislation, free education and medical treatment for children, a state-controlled medical scheme, aid for small farmers and reform of the Legislative Council.

In 1912 Lyons was elected president of the State branch, and in January 1914 became deputy leader of the Parliamentary Labor Party. From April 1914 to April 1916 he was treasurer, minister for education, and minister for railways in the Earle [q.v.8] Labor government. He was able to reform the Education Department, abolishing school fees and improving pay and conditions for teachers, although he failed to effect equal pay. He authorized the building of several schools, including the first high schools in Hobart and Launceston.

Lyons married Enid Muriel Burnell on 28 April 1915, after a short courtship. He was 35 and minister for education, she was an 18-year-old trainee teacher. His request raised some problems for Enid's father, who pointed out that if the suitor had not been Mr Lyons there would have been objections on the grounds of age and religion. Enid became an enthusiastic convert to Catholicism.

Lyons always abhorred violence, opposing capital punishment and refusing to participate in wartime recruiting, although he respected volunteers. He campaigned strongly for a 'No' vote in the conscription referenda of 1916-17, arguing that there was no moral right to vote away another's life. The war years rekindled his Irish nationalism. He became vice-president of the Hobart United Irish League in 1916, describing the leaders of the Easter Rising as misguided heroes and urging immediate Home Rule. When the A.L.P. split over conscription, Lyons replaced Earle as leader on 2 November 1916.

After he had matriculated from the Teachers' Training College in 1907, Lyons's intellectual development had been largely based on his reading. He concentrated on nineteenth-century English poets, Dickens [q.v.4], Henry Lawson [q.v.] and Australian nationalist writers. He was a member of a Labor Party discussion group of Fabian hue formed by Lyndhurst Giblin [q.v.8]. Between 1909 and 1922 Lyons described himself as a socialist, establishing a reputation as a firebrand. Despite his rhetoric, he did not have a distinctive political ideology and his socialism was thoroughly reformist and ethical. His revulsion at the carnage of World War I, which he blamed on 'the pernicious capitalistic system', spurred him to passionately advocate a new social order through 'revolution ... by peaceful means'. After the war Lyons became more cautious and pragmatic, influenced by his prospects in a conservative electorate. The Labor Party was defeated in the 1919 State election. Lyons himself was further badly beaten in December when he stood for the Federal seat of Darwin.

As leader of the Opposition, Lyons strongly criticized the finance policies of Sir Walter Lee's [q.v.] Nationalist government. His development as a consensual politician was demonstrated in 1922 when he described himself as a friend of all members of the Legislative Assembly. In 1923 he argued that the A.L.P. was not sectional, and was the only party capable of developing comprehensive State policies. These attitudes made him more acceptable to many Nationalists than their own leaders.

In October 1923 several Nationalists revolted and brought down Lee's government. Lyons became leader of a minority Labor government with their support. He proceeded cautiously and impartially. With the advice of economists such as Giblin and (Sir) Douglas Copland, and the approval of the Opposition and businessmen, he worked to reform Tasmania's financial structure, pruning expenses, imposing new taxes, reducing loan expenditure, and presenting the State accounts honestly. His successes and the approval of the State Nationalists gave him greater access to the Bruce [q.v.7]-Page [q.v.] government and also to the Commonwealth Treasury.

Lyons's tactful skills helped in the return of his government in 1925. He sought new industries such as wood pulp and mining. He referred to the Opposition leader (Sir) John McPhee [q.v.] as his 'colleague and mate' and cultivated the press, but was chagrined when the Nationalists reverted to hard party politics in 1928 and attacked him for rising unemployment and economic stagnation. In the 1928 elections Labor won a slender majority of the vote, but the Nationalists won sixteen of the thirty seats. McPhee became premier, praising Lyons for his statesmanship and offering to serve under him should he leave the A.L.P.

Lyons had antagonized sections of his party, particularly the small Left group centred on Hobart trade union leaders, which considered his brief espousal of the 'One Big Union' and the socialization objective in the early 1920s as insincere, and his consensual politics as a betrayal. In 1924 he had contemplated moving to the Federal parliament, 'the better to fight for just treatment' for Tasmania there. Losing the premiership and offside with sections of his party, Lyons was undecided about his future. He made soundings for appointment as a Federal arbitration commissioner. With the backing of the influential Hobart *Mercury*, he considered standing for the Senate, but at the request of the Federal A.L.P. leader, James Scullin [q.v.], he stood for the Federal seat of Wilmot and won convincingly at the elections in October 1929. Scullin appointed him postmaster-general and a senior member of cabinet. Lyons was an established figure in the labour movement, and apart from Edward Theodore [q.v.] was the only minister with administrative experience.

Lyons found the Federal Parliamentary Labor Party uncongenial. Accustomed to the parochial Tasmanian Labor Party, he felt little kinship with the machine politics of the Sydney and Melbourne trades halls. He was content to administer his department and made no comment or interjection in parliament unrelated to his portfolio or Tasmania. This preoccupation with administrative and State matters did not save him from caucus critics who felt that his policies were too orthodox.

Imbued with respect for conventional economics and orthodox finance, like most Australians of his era, Lyons equated government debt with personal debt and insisted that all commitments had to be fully honoured. He opposed inflation and stressed the importance of balanced budgets and strict loan repayments. He was aware of Keynes's doctrines, probably through Giblin, but felt that, even if they were correct, experiment was inappropriate for the small Australian economy. Lyons became acting treasurer in August

1930, after Theodore had stood aside, and attended the meeting of Federal and State leaders which adopted the Melbourne Plan, designed to adjust the Australian economy to the impact of the Depression. The British financier Sir Otto Niemeyer described Lyons and Scullin as 'entirely at sea . . . like a couple of rabbits popping their heads out of the hole'. Despite lack of experience in Federal fiscal administration, Lyons assumed responsibility for implementing the Melbourne Plan which hinged on budgetary restraint. In the absence of Scullin in London, Lyons and the acting prime minister, James Fenton [q.v.8], took the full brunt of criticism within caucus. Lyons was forced to defend orthodox policies against the radicalism of Theodore and those caucus members who supported the New South Wales Labor leader, J. T. Lang [q.v.9].

Because of temperament and Tasmanian experience Lyons was susceptible to the cautious advice of economists such as Giblin, Copland and (Sir) Leslie Melville, and the orthodox banking principles of Sir Robert Gibson and (Sir) Alfred Davidson [qq.v.8]. He believed that significant inflation would bring economic and political chaos, although he was prepared to accept a degree of controlled credit expansion to stimulate industry. Lyons proposed to balance the budget, and to reduce government spending, wages and possibly pensions. A sequence of tumultuous caucus meetings began on 28 October 1930. Lyons presented a plan prepared by the Treasury, proposing the unpegging of exchange rates, stabilization of internal prices through monetary control, reduction of interest rates, and provision of Commonwealth Bank credit for industry. His mildly adventurous proposals were rejected in favour of Theodore's more sweeping proposals for credit creation. Lyons secured an adjournment of the House of Representatives to give the government a chance to devise a compromise. When the whip gagged Opposition expressions of jubilation at cabinet's embarrassment, Lyons voted with the Opposition. He returned to cabinet and threatened resignation if the salaries of senior public servants were not reduced. He won on this issue, but the larger conflict over economic policy was not resolved. Against the advice of Lyons and Theodore, caucus voted to postpone repayment of an overseas loan falling due on 15 December. Lyons said that he would not implement this decision, threatened resignation and went ahead with plans to convert the loan. Scullin endorsed his actions in cables and publicly praised him, enabling him to defy caucus, which deferred further debate.

Lyons's protracted struggle with caucus and his successful defiance gave him national prominence. With assistance from committees of businessmen and non-Labor politicians, the loan was over-subscribed. Lyons spearheaded the successful campaign. But his stature deteriorated within the A.L.P. On 4 December 1930 the Opposition leader, (Sir) John Latham [q.v.], called for national unity to fight the Depression. Lyons agreed, but caucus rejected Latham's proposal. Lyons was shouted down and rumours were spread that he wanted a coalition government. He vehemently denied it, and challenged his opponents to move a motion of no confidence against him.

Lyons's co-operation with a loan conversion committee in Victoria had brought him into association with Melbourne businessmen, civic leaders and non-Labor politicians. A small body, known simply as 'the Group', was formed to sponsor him as a national political leader and to secure his defection from the A.L.P. Its principal members were the financier Staniforth Ricketson, a former journalist whom Lyons had known in Tasmania, and (Sir) Robert Menzies. Through Menzies Lyons obtained access to National Party networks, including the influential National Union which was the party's principal financial sponsor. Other members of 'the Group' promoted him to powerful business and press interests.

Lyons had remained in the government out of loyalty to Scullin, and to resist the radical proposals of Theodore and the increasingly militant Lang. When Scullin returned in mid-January 1931 he affirmed Lyons's policies, but rejected his pleas to take over as treasurer. Scullin restored Theodore as deputy prime minister and treasurer on 26 January, although Theodore had not then been exonerated on the Mungana allegations. Lyons was affronted, believing that Theodore should clear his name before returning to cabinet. With his close supporter Fenton, Lyons resigned from cabinet on 29 January, although both remained in the caucus. Lyons consulted closely with 'the Group' and other supporters in Melbourne. He likened his circumstances at this time to Mahomet's coffin, suspended between heaven and earth and with no true home. Powerful citizen movements emerged, opposing party politics and promoting the tenets of 'sane finance', looking to Lyons to provide non-party leadership.

The moves which precipitated his departure from the A.L.P. are obscure, but 'the Group' and the National Union were principal factors. Lyons agonized for some weeks, but after caucus accepted Theodore's proposals for a fiduciary note issue, he sounded out his few Labor supporters and prepared to defect. Early in March he went to Melbourne and informed 'the Group'. On 13 March he voted for a motion of no confidence in the Scullin government, vindicating his action in a powerful speech, in many ways the finest of his long political career. With four other defectors he formed a 'little band' which had no electoral support; but he shrewdly cultivated the citizen groups with an eye to forming a base, while continuing negotiations with the National Party. By the end of March there was tacit acceptance that Latham would step down for Lyons in a new political movement embracing the citizens' groups. In April these called on Lyons to serve as their leader, and the Nationalists agreed to pursue the unity of all opponents of the Scullin government. Lyons was unwilling to supplant Latham who, however, was forced to step aside by Nationalist pressure. A United Australia Movement was formed which ultimately incorporated the National Party and the principal citizens' groups. In the Federal parliament, the Lyons group merged with the Nationalists to form the United Australia Party with Latham as Lyons's deputy. Lyons announced the changes in parliament on 7 May amid a torrent of denunciation and recrimination from his former colleagues.

Lyons was absorbed in organizing the U.A.P., particularly at the electoral level, leaving much of the parliamentary leadership to Latham. Lyons's indifferent parliamentary performance aroused criticism but his leadership was firmly entrenched by a decisive victory in the elections of December 1931. The U.A.P. won an absolute majority and he formed a government after negotiations with the Country Party had broken down. His immediate task as prime minister was to counter Lang who had sought to repudiate overseas loan payments. In a series of skilful manoeuvres largely devised by Latham and pursued vigorously by Lyons, Lang was forced into increasingly desperate reponses which led to his dismissal by the governor, Sir Philip Game [q.v.8]. The U.A.P. won convincing victories in New South Wales and Victoria in 1932: Australian politics lost much of the turbulence of 1930-32, and Lyons governed for seven years in a climate of relative stability, buttressed by gradual economic improvement. He easily won the 1934 elections, but the U.A.P. lost its absolute majority and he negotiated a coalition with the Country Party under (Sir) Earle Page [q.v.] who became deputy prime minister. The coalition was re-established after Lyons's convincing victory in the 1937 elections.

Lyons was content to apply the orthodox economic policies embodied in the Premiers' Plan. He also sought to rekindle the development and welfare objectives of the Bruce-Page government of the 1920s. He tried without success to develop Northern Australia by charter companies, and sought expansion of public works programmes with emphasis on

housing and urban infrastructure. He was frustrated in introducing welfare policies by lack of funds and from the opposition on constitutional grounds of Menzies, deputy leader since the 1934 elections. Lyons sponsored a national insurance scheme which parliament approved in 1938, but the Act was never proclaimed. He took few initiatives in foreign affairs, contenting himself with the reiteration of Imperial sentiments and stressing the primacy of the British navy in Australia's defence. He maintained his opposition to conscription as pressure for rearmament grew in the late 1930s, imposing it on his cabinet colleagues in a rare assertion of policy. Latham's earlier enthusiastic efforts to prosecute communists, and the vigorous censorship and restrictive immigration policies applied by some ministers had given the Lyons government a repressive tinge.

In his early years as prime minister, Lyons relied on experienced colleagues such as Latham, Bruce and (Sir) Walter Massy-Greene [q.v.]. These ministers had left the cabinet by 1934 and Lyons depended on Page and on younger colleagues from his own party, notably Richard (Lord) Casey. His relationship with Menzies was ambivalent. There are hints in Lyons's correspondence with his wife that he expected to make way for Menzies after the 1934 elections, but was persuaded to remain by the National Union which considered Menzies immature.

Lyons's skills as a consensual politician and co-ordinator were fully deployed in the management of a difficult cabinet. He acted largely as chairman, using his abilities to present decisions in the best light. This approach led him into errors of judgement, notably over the trade diversion controversy of 1936-37 and the exclusion from Australia in 1936 of a British passport-holder, Mrs Mabel Freer, apparently on moral grounds. For the most part, Lyons was able to contain tensions and avoid political mishaps. His touch with his parliamentary party was just as sure although he sustained occasional rebuffs, notably over tariff adjustments and the timing of the 1937 elections. Much of his energy was devoted to co-ordinating and administering the loosely organized U.A.P. He spent considerable time publicizing his government, holding frequent press conferences and briefing journalists, editors and newspaper proprietors. He sought the assistance of private enterprise groups in economic reconstruction.

Lyons won three successive elections convincingly, a performance then unmatched by any other prime minister. His victories in 1931 and 1934 were certainly assisted by bitter divisions within the A.L.P., but he overcame formidable difficulties, including his own declining health and disillusionment within the electorate and the U.A.P., to defeat a rejuvenated Labor Party under John Curtin in 1937. Lyons innovatively made extensive use of air travel and placed emphasis on radio broadcasting. His parliamentary skills were outstanding, Menzies describing him as the finest parliamentarian he had seen in action.

Despite increasing exhaustion, Lyons maintained the stability of his government until the final months before his death, but his increasing desperation was revealed in letters to his wife. He wrote in May 1938: 'It is just dreadful to come back to what always awaits me here [Canberra] but I suppose one day it will come to an end'. He found solace and relief in official visits to Europe and the United States of America in 1935 and 1937. Menzies, who accompanied him in 1935, effusively praised his extempore speeches and public performance, although he noted with distaste the relish of Lyons and his wife for official travel, observing that both were 'over-inclined to extract the last drop of juice from the orange'. Lyons was deeply affected by his visits to Australian war cemeteries in France and Belgium, which reinforced his pacifist and anti-conscription convictions.

His final months were miserable as his government became increasingly unstable. Apart from Menzies, there were other threats, particularly from Charles Hawker [q.v.9]. According to Enid Lyons, Hawker was on his way to Canberra to challenge Lyons when he was killed in a plane crash in October 1938. Lyons lost the support of (Sir) Henry Gullett [q.v.9] to whom he had been extremely loyal during the trade diversion controversy, and he came to doubt even Casey's loyalty. Although Menzies never issued a direct challenge, he made pointed public comments about lack of national leadership; through 1938-39 his claims were advanced in the newspapers of Sir Keith Murdoch, previously an enthusiastic supporter of Lyons. He retained the support of the National Union, the U.A.P. State branches and most federal parliamentarians, and was able to thwart the implicit Menzies challenge in the final months of 1938. On 14 March 1939 Menzies resigned from cabinet because of the deferment of the national insurance scheme. Sensing that a direct challenge to his leadership was inevitable, Lyons urged Bruce to return from London to take over, but he insisted on impossible conditions, including a national government. Despite these pressures there were signs in this period that Lyons was emerging as a more assertive and decisive figure, ready to confront his opponents. There is evidence that he would not have submitted to Menzies without a struggle.

Lyons died in Sydney Hospital on 7 April 1939 from coronary occlusion. After memorial services in Sydney and Canberra, his body was conveyed in state by an Australian navy vessel to Devonport in Tasmania where he was buried. He was survived by (Dame) Enid, six daughters and five sons of whom Kevin became deputy premier of Tasmania in the Liberal ministry of Angus Bethune. Lyons's estate amounted to £344.

Lyons was the first prime minister to use the official lodge in Canberra as a family home. The large family was often split, with Lyons looking after three or four of the children at the lodge with the assistance of domestic staff. He was often photographed in the grounds flanked by his children. His closest political ally and adviser was his wife, who became a minister in the post-war Menzies government. His devotion to her emerges in the tender letters of their courtship, one of the few surviving documentations of the intimate relationships of an Australian prime minister. His first act as prime minister in January 1932 was to write to Enid, 'because whatever honours or distinctions come are ours, not mine'. His letters through the 1930s reflected his distress at frequent family separations and his bouts of despair: 'I wish they would defeat us and we'd be out of our misery and get a little happiness'. Other letters display a vulgar touch: 'Foll says the Country Party are like copulating cats, getting all they want and crying out all the time'. Above all, the correspondence shows his spirit of resignation and his firm belief that he had done his duty: 'Neither you nor I can put everything right and we saved Australia from ruin. Think of the homes that are happy because of what we did and realise that no-one is unhappy because of what we did'.

Lyons was plump, of medium stature, upright in bearing, with blue eyes and an unruly mop of blond hair. Caricatured as a koala, he had a thin, longish nose and a high forehead, and in his later years walked with a marked limp, the legacy of a car accident. His voice was a little high pitched. He was an enthusiastic sportsman in his youth, playing cricket and football, cycling, and running in the Burnie Gift. He attributed his physical durability to the residue of fitness built up when young. A portrait by W. B. McInnes [q.v.] hangs in Parliament House. In later years Lyons sought relaxation with occasional games of golf and billiards, and visits to the cinema with his driver. As prime minister he attended Mass each Sunday at Manuka parish church in Canberra. He was a moderate drinker, usually of Scotch.

Despite his apparent simplicity and the conventional stereotype of 'Honest Joe', Lyons had an enigmatic and elusive personality. The New South Wales premier, (Sir) Bertram Stevens [q.v.], who admired and respected him, felt that there was a studied aspect to his populism, although it was fundamental to his nature. (Dame) Mary Gilmore [q.v.9] emphasized his populist appeal, describing him as 'deeper and wider than party'. Charles Hawker, who opposed his leadership, described his conservatism as that 'of the man with small savings, a home of [his] own'. Lyons's critics stressed his plebeian qualities and their manifestation in his political leadership. According to the Labor newspaper, the *World*, Lyons was the victim of a suburban personality, 'an eminently well-meaning dullard'. Perhaps the greatest tribute to his political skills was the rapid disintegration of the U.A.P. after his death. His major achievements were reform of the Tasmanian financial structure and the stability of government he brought to Australian society during the difficult years of the Depression and the drift to World War II.

E. M. Lyons, *So we take comfort* (Lond, 1965), and *Among the carrion crows* (Adel, 1972); P. Hart, J.A.Lyons: a political biography (Ph. D. thesis, ANU, 1967); C. J. Lloyd, the formation and development of the UAP, 1929-37 (Ph. D. thesis, ANU, 1984); J. A. Lyons, Official papers (AAO) *and* personal papers (NL); A. Clark, Taped interviews with Dame Enid Lyons (copies held by C. J. Lloyd, Canb); Dame Enid Lyons, Personal papers (NL).

P. R. HART
C. J. LLOYD

LYONS, THOMAS (1861-1938), businessman, was born on 3 January 1861 at Hobart Town, son of William Henry Lyons, master mariner, and his wife Charlotte, née Priest. He was educated at The Hutchins School. In 1882 he was appointed accountant to the Hobart Gas Co. and next year joined the Bank of Van Diemen's Land, becoming inspector of branches before the bank was forced to close in 1891.

Lyons suggested that much freehold property to which the bank held title be disposed of by lottery. The necessary legislation was passed in September 1893 and George Adams [q.v.3], who had conducted sweeps in New South Wales and Queensland, agreed to organize the lotteries. In January 1894 Lyons accepted a position with Adams and played an important part behind the scenes in persuading members of parliament, despite intense public opposition, to support further legislation in 1896 that allowed the establishment of Tattersall's in Tasmania. He remained 'a confidant, advisor and close friend' of Adams, taking an active part in the management of the business. Lyons purchased a seat on the Hobart Stock Exchange in February 1896 and for a short period carried on a commission agency with Peter Facy. In 1900 he became a committee-member of the stock exchange.

Mining interested Lyons greatly and he worked leases for tin, nickel, gold and other minerals, particularly in the north-east and on the west coast. When Adams died in 1904 he left Lyons a share of the annual net proceeds of Tattersall's sweeps. In 1907 Lyons left the firm and entered into partnership with H. W. Bayley, whose old-established stockbroking company had several overseas agencies, as Bayley & Lyons. He became a director of many enterprises including the Derwent & Tasman Assurance Co. Ltd and Perpetual Trustees & National Executors of Tasmania Ltd and a trustee and general manager of Tattersall's in 1927-38.

Another important facet of Lyons's life was his involvement with horse-racing, both as breeder and owner. His horses won many classic races including six Hobart Cups. His interest began with the purchase of Oakdene in 1912 from whom he bred many notable winners including Talisman and Prince Viol. A committee-member of the Tasmanian Racing Club since 1900, he was chairman or deputy chairman in 1915-38 and a life member. An annual handicap race and a grandstand bear his name.

Lyons was a tall man, dignified and dapper. He was patriarchal with his family but popular in public, credited with being as shrewd a judge of men as of horses and with a deserved reputation for generosity. From 1908 until his death he was president of the Athenaeum Club and from 1920 either patron or president of the Sandy Bay Regatta Association; he was also foundation president of the Autocar (later, Royal Automobile) Club of Tasmania.

He worshipped in turn at Presbyterian, Anglican and Congregational churches, abandoning St Stephen's Church of England following an attack from the pulpit on lotteries. He had married Maud Beatrice Stanfield (d. 1890) on 13 March 1889 at Rokeby, then on 28 June 1899, in Hobart, Elizabeth Turnbull Robertson Riordan. Lyons died on 6 July 1938 at St Vincent's Hospital, Sydney; as an expression of regret there was no morning call on the Hobart Stock Exchange. He was cremated in Hobart. His wife and their five children, to whom he largely left his estate sworn for probate at £77 639, survived him.

T. Wilson, *The luck of the draw* (Melb, 1980); R. Ferrall, *The Hobart Stock Exchange* (Hob, 1982); D. A. Denholm, 'Tattersall's in Tasmania', *PTHRA*, 13 (1966); *Mercury*, 4 Aug 1891, 8 Sept 1893, 1 Feb 1894; Harvey Bayley & Co., A brief history of this firm (typescript, 1981, held by firm and Tasmanian collection, SLT); Hob Stock Exchange, Minutes, Feb 1896-May 1900 (Hob Stock Exchange); Tas Racing Club, Minutes and records, 1915-38 (held by club, Glenorchy, Hob); Dept of Mines (Tas), Records of leases, 1913-1930 (TA).

JAMES G. COOPER

LYSAGHT, ANDREW AUGUSTUS (1873-1933), politician and barrister, was born on 8 August 1873 at Fairy Meadow, Wollongong, New South Wales, sixth child of ANDREW LYSAGHT (1832-1906). His father, who had also been born at Fairy Meadow, became a well-known local sporting identity, and managed and later acquired the Queen's Hotel at Wollongong. Closely identified with every movement to further the development of the region, he represented Illawarra in the Legislative Assembly in 1885-87 and 1891. His refusal to take seriously the Free Trade-Protectionist divisions and factions led to his eclipse as a parliamentarian. On 6 September 1860 Lysaght had married Irish-born Johanna Carroll at Appin. He died at Fairy Meadow on 3 September 1906, survived by his wife and children; two daughters became nuns, rising to superior positions in their convents.

Andrew junior received his early schooling at Wollongong and on 30 January 1891 was articled to N. W. Montagu, a Sydney solicitor. He was admitted as a solicitor on 30 May 1896. Practising in Sydney, he began specializing in workers' compensation cases and industrial law, soon becoming well known. In 1902-03 he represented the miners before the royal commission on the Mount Kembla colliery disaster. He developed a close and mutually affectionate relationship with members of the mining lodges of the South Coast and represented miners at two other royal commissions. He briefed counsel to defend Andrew Gray in the famous Bowling [q.v.7] conspiracy trial before Mr Justice Pring [q.v.] in 1910. By the time he was admitted to the Bar in May 1923, he was widely recognized as an expert on mining and industrial legislation.

In 1905 Lysaght had made an extended tour of Great Britain, Ireland and Europe, and for several months he studied art in Paris and Rome. On 22 January 1907 at Nowra he married Margaret Ellen O'Dwyer, a milliner; they established a family home at Wollongong, moving later to Campbelltown.

Inheriting his father's commanding physique and presence, Lysaght was over 6 ft. 5 ins. tall (196 cm). Well-read and a fluent platform speaker, he soon attracted a following from those sections of the community which had supported his father, and from the growing labour movement. In 1900-02 he served as an alderman on North Illawara Municipal Council and was mayor in 1902. After twice standing unsuccessfully for Labor pre-selection, he was elected to the Legislative Assembly in 1925 for Wollondilly, and in May 1927 he became attorney-general and minister of justice when J. T. Lang [q.v.9] reconstructed his ministry. He won Illawarra in September.

In November 1930 Lysaght won Bulli and was reappointed attorney-general by Lang, although he had been unsuccessful in the caucus ballot for ministers. A stormy relationship soon developed in cabinet between Lysaght and those with more extreme views. He was criticized for proposing a law reform bill which might provide a powerful tool of repression in the hands of any future anti-Labor government: the left thus added its weight to the public condemnation of the bill by the legal profession as 'impracticable' and he failed to carry his proposals in caucus. When key government legislative initiatives—such as the newspaper tax and the attempt to abolish the Upper House—were declared to be unconstitutional, it was suggested that Lysaght should have provided suitable legislation. He apparently lost Lang's personal favour when he gave only passive attention to the premier's unsuccessful attempts to institute proceedings against the leader of the Opposition (Sir) Thomas Bavin [q.v.7] and (Sir) Bertram Stevens [q.v.], who were blamed for causing the collapse of the Government Savings Bank of New South Wales by their propaganda.

Suffering from a disease of the nervous system, Lysaght became increasingly erratic and irascible. According to Lang, he developed the habit of offering his resignation frequently in 'temperamental outbursts' and when he resigned on 16 June 1931 over a trivial incident in parliament, the premier accepted—'to his utter consternation'. Lysaght held Bulli in 1932, but experienced increasing difficulty in carrying out his parliamentary duties. He died at Campbelltown on 3 May 1933 and was buried in the Roman Catholic cemetery behind St Bede's church at Appin, a township in his electorate for which he had particular affection. His wife, son and two daughters survived him.

[Ex MLA], *Our present parliament* (Syd, nd [1886]); J. T. Lang, *The turbulent years* (Syd, 1970); *Aust Worker*, 6 Sept 1906, 27 May 1925, 10 May 1933; *Freeman's J* (Syd), 8 Sept 1906; *Catholic Press*, 13 Sept 1906; *Punch* (Melb), 20 Aug 1925; *SMH*, 11, 16, 17 June 1931, 4 May 1933; *Illawarra Mercury*, 12, 19, 26 June, 10 July 1931, 5 May 1933.   FRANK FARRELL

LYSAGHT, HERBERT ROYSE (1862-1940), manufacturer, was born on 15 December 1862 at Clifton, near Bristol, England, son of Thomas Royse Lysaght, architect, and his wife Emily Sophia, née Moss. He was educated at Bristol Public Grammar School. Migrating to Sydney, he joined the Commercial Banking Co. of Sydney in September

1883. After working mainly at head office and at Bathurst in 1885-89, he went as manager to Berrigan in October 1891 and to Maclean in September 1896. At All Saints' Cathedral, Bathurst, on 26 October 1892 he married Ellen Zoe Lydiard. Lysaght resigned from the bank on 15 April 1899.

His uncle John Lysaght (1832-1895), manufacturer of Bristol, had in 1880 set up the Victoria Galvanized Iron & Wire Co. in Melbourne, with branches in the other colonies, to take advantage of the demands of the building and pastoral industries. In 1899 this importing firm was replaced by Lysaght's Galvanized Iron Pty. Ltd, with Herbert as a director, Sydney manager and Queensland supervisor of the new firm, which was the largest customer of the English organization. By 1913 Lysaght's was supplying 70 per cent of the entire Australian demand for galvanized products. In 1918 Herbert became chairman and managing director of John Lysaght (Australia) Ltd, a new company formed to deal with the business of the parent company. Australia had been almost entirely cut off from supplies of galvanized and black iron sheets during World War I and Lysaght devoted his entire energies to the setting up of sheet mills and galvanizing works and transforming Lysaght's from an importing into a manufacturing company. This was effected on 4 April 1921 when Lysaght's Newcastle Works Ltd, of which he was chairman, opened. In 1937 another plant began operating at Port Kembla.

His great administrative ability contributed much to the success of other business enterprises with which Lysaght was associated. He was chairman of the Australian Bank of Commerce and a director of the Perpetual Trustee Co., Broken Hill Proprietary Co. Ltd, Australian Iron and Steel Ltd, Commonwealth Rolling Mills Pty Ltd, Nettlefolds Pty Ltd, the Royal Insurance Co. Ltd, Anthony Hordern [q.v.4] & Sons Ltd and J. Meloy Ltd. Politically conservative, Lysaght saw the Employers' Liability Act, the 44-hour week and like measures as detrimental to the national interest, and in the early 1920s tried to get increased protection for Australian galvanized products. He had a kindly personality outside business affairs, and a wide circle of friends; golf and gardening were his main leisure interests. In 1920 he had been appointed O.B.E. for his work on the executive of the Australian Comforts Fund during the war and in 1930-40 he was a director of Sydney Hospital. He was a member of the Australian and Union clubs in Sydney.

One of the chief pioneers of the Australian iron and steel industry, Lysaght died suddenly at his Darling Point home on 28 June 1940. Survived by his son Douglas Royse, he was cremated after a service at St Mark's Angli-can Church, Darling Point. His personal estate was sworn for probate at almost £150 000.

John Lysaght (Aust) Pty Ltd, *Lysaght's silver jubilee 1921-1946* (priv print, Syd, 1946), and *Lysaght venture* (Syd, 1955); *V&P* (LA NSW), 1894-95, 4, 164; *B.H.P. Review*, 17 (Aug 1940), no 5; *SMH*, 16 Oct 1920, 25 Feb 1922, 24 Feb 1927, 28 Mar 1930, 22 Nov 1933, 5 Nov 1935, 30 May, 29 June 1940; information from National Australia Bank Archives, Pyrmont, NSW.   G. P. WALSH

LYSTER, JOHN SANDERSON (1850-1930), soldier, was born on 31 August 1850 at Beaumaris, Anglesey, North Wales, son of George Fosbery Lyster, civil engineer, and his wife Martha Eliza, née Sanderson. Educated at Guernsey, Channel Islands, where his father was engaged in building harbour works, and later tutored in England by the Wimbledon army coaches Brachenbury and Wynne, Lyster undertook the regulation course at the Royal Military College, Sandhurst. Commissioned ensign (by purchase) in the 71st Highland Light Infantry in 1869 he was stationed during the next eight years at Gibraltar, Malta and Inverness, Scotland; he was promoted lieutenant in 1871.

In 1877 on his return to London from a tour of military stations in Europe, Lyster met (Sir) Thomas McIlwraith [q.v.5] who encouraged him to migrate to Queensland; he sold his commission that year. On arrival in Brisbane he had intended to establish a cheese factory but he soon joined a survey expedition to the Gulf of Carpentaria. After returning to Brisbane in 1881 he was appointed clerk to the Legislative Assembly. With the development of colonial military forces he decided in 1884 to resume permanent military service and was appointed captain and chief staff officer with the Queensland Defence Force in 1885. He was promoted major in 1886 and lieut-colonel in 1894. From December 1899 to January 1902 he was acting commandant of the Queensland Defence Force and oversaw the training of troops and dispatch of contingents to the South African War.

Late in 1901 the 1st Battalion of the Australian Commonwealth Horse was formed with units from New South Wales, Queensland and Tasmania and Lyster was appointed commanding officer. It was quickly deployed to Durban, South Africa, where it arrived in March 1902; the unit proceeded by rail to Klerksdorp in western Transvaal. As part of Colonel de Lisle's column its tasks were to clear the districts north of Klerksdorp and then take part in the drive to the Kimberley-Mafeking railway blockhouse line. After successful operations the unit returned to

Klerksdorp where it remained until the end of the war.

The good standard of discipline maintained by Lyster's troops in South Africa was not displayed on the transport *Drayton Grange* during its voyage to Australia. Influenza and measles broke out among the 2043 troops on board and 17 men died. A royal commission later found that the epidemic was aggravated by overcrowding, deficient hospital accommodation and neglect of some routine discipline. Despite this setback Lyster was appointed commandant of Commonwealth land forces in South Australia in 1902-03 and in Queensland from 1906 to December 1911 when he was placed on the retired list; he was promoted colonel in 1905. During World War I he was inspector of equipment.

Lyster played an important part in the development of the Commonwealth Military Forces. He had demonstrated an outstanding capacity to train officers, and among those senior officers of the Australian Imperial Force who received their early training from him were Generals Sir Brudenell White [q.v.], C. H. Brand, T. H. Dodds and C. H. Foott [qq.v.7,8]. Survived by his wife and daughter, Lyster died on 5 January 1930 at St Peter Port, Guernsey.

G. B. Barton, *The story of South Africa*, 2 (Syd, 1901); J. J. Knight and R. S. Browne, *Queensland* (Brisb, 1900); Aust Defence Dept, *Official records of the Australian military contingents to the war in South Africa*, P. L. Murray ed (Melb, 1911); R. L. Wallace, *The Australians at the Boer War* (Canb, 1976); L. M. Field, *The forgotten war* (Melb, 1979); *Argus*, 21 Feb 1930; *Bulletin*, 26 Feb 1930; MP 78, 207/1/20 (AWM).   DARRYL MCINTYRE

M

McALPINE, DANIEL (1849-1932), vegetable pathologist, was born on 21 January 1849 at Saltcoats, Ayrshire, Scotland, third son of Daniel McAlpine, schoolmaster, and his wife Flora, née Nicol. His father, a noted Gaelic scholar and staunch Presbyterian, taught at the Ardeer School where the young McAlpine received his early education. After teaching there himself he matriculated at the University of London in 1873 and attended lectures at the Royal School of Mines, South Kensington, in biology by T. H. Huxley [q.v.1], in botany by (Sir) William Thistleton-Dyer, in geology by (Sir) Archibald Geikie and in paleontology by R. Ethridge. In these subjects he excelled and was appointed professor of natural history at the new Veterinary College, Edinburgh, and, in 1877, lecturer in biology and botany at the Watt-Heriot College. He also lectured in the pharmaceutical department at the Edinburgh School of Medicine. While in Edinburgh he prepared a biological atlas (1880), a zoological atlas (1881) and a two-volume botanical atlas (1883) as well as a booklet on elementary physiology and physiological anatomy (1883).

On 24 December 1878, at Govan with Wesleyan Methodist forms, McAlpine married Isabella Jamieson Williamson. Deciding to migrate to Australia after the death of their infant son, they arrived in Melbourne in 1884. Next year McAlpine was appointed to a lectureship in biology at Ormond [q.v.5] College, University of Melbourne, and in 1886 became visiting lecturer in botany at the Melbourne College of Pharmacy, a position he held until 1911, reportedly never missing a lecture and never a minute late. He also lectured at the School of Horticulture, Burnley Horticultural Gardens, and examined for technical schools and the Melbourne Veterinary College. On 12 May 1890 he was appointed to the Victorian Department of Agriculture as vegetable pathologist 'to attend to all diseases of plants that might form the subject of inquiry'. This was reputedly the first full-time appointment of its kind in the British Empire and was undoubtedly a consequence of the devastating epidemic of wheat rust in 1889; immediately prior to his appointment McAlpine had joined a committee of the Australasian Association for the Advancement of Science to investigate the problem.

During his period with the Victorian government McAlpine helped to organize four intercolonial conferences on rust in wheat, being chairman of the last in 1896, and co-operated very closely with the wheat experimentalist William Farrer [q.v.8]. He produced the first monographs published on plant diseases in Australia: *Fungus diseases of citrus trees in Australia* (1889); *Fungus diseases of stone-fruit trees in Australia* (1902); *Rusts of Australia* (1906) including a general discussion of rusts which was extolled at the time as 'by much the best account . . . available in the English language'; *Smuts of Australia* (1910); and *Handbook of fungus diseases of the potato in Australia* (1911). They were all profusely illustrated by photographs, an art at which he excelled. His *Systematic arrangement of Australian fungi* (1895) was considered a masterpiece. He also published prolifically in government and scientific journals.

McAlpine's work, according to his daughter, was 'all absorbing and his hobby', occupying him 'far into the night and at weekends'. All work was done from a small room of his home at Armadale until offices were provided by the government in 1906. His correspondence was written in longhand from his expertly drafted shorthand notes; he provided his own microscopes and equipment. An assistant, G. H. Robinson, was appointed in 1900, followed in 1908 by C. C. Brittlebank, a farmer and microscopist who eventually became McAlpine's successor.

In 1911 McAlpine was assigned to the Commonwealth and State governments for four years to undertake researches into bitter pit of apples, a disease he had reported in 1900. Realizing the difficulties such an investigation posed, he was reluctant to accept the post but did so 'for the credit of Australia'. He made detailed observations of the disease and published five reports but, unable to discover the cause, found himself arrayed against the Victorian government botanist Professor A. J. Ewart [q.v.8], who mistakenly attributed bitter pit to traces of poison in the soil.

McAlpine was an honorary member (from 1894) of the Caesarian Leopold-Caroline Academy of Natural Phenomena, Germany, and a corresponding member (from 1902) of the Linnean Society of New South Wales. During a Victorian royal commission on fruit, vegetables and jam in 1915 attention was drawn to his lack of university qualifications: he had in fact refused an honorary LL.D. from the University of Edinburgh before migrating, considering it would be an embellishment unnecessary in his new country. Representations were made to the commission by J. H. Lang on behalf of fruit-growers urging McAlpine's reappointment as bitter pit investigator and the expansion of his research brief, but his services were dispensed with from July 1915 and he retired, greatly disappointed and without a pension, first to Croydon and later Leitchville.

McAlpine's relationships with fellow scientists had always been cordial. At the Pan Pacific Congress held at the University of Melbourne in 1923 the meeting regretted McAlpine's absence and expressed 'its deep appreciation of the value of his contribution in plant pathology'. An originator of his discipline, he was, with N. A. Cobb [q.v.8], a pioneer of its application in Australia. He died at Leitchville on 12 October 1932 and was buried in Cohuna cemetery, survived by his wife and five daughters, one of whom, Constance, was married to James MacDougall [q.v.]. The Daniel McAlpine memorial lectures were initiated in 1971 by the Australian Plant Pathology Society.

PP (LA Vic), 1901, 3 (36), p 236, 1915, 2 (58), p 426; Vic Naturalist, 66 (1949-50); Aust Plant Pathology Soc, A.P.P.S. Newsletter, 5 (1976), no 1; Hunt Inst biogs (Basser Lib, Canb); McAlpine papers (LaTL); letters from W. J. Farrer to McAlpine (ML); letters held by and information from Mrs E. Wedge, Mont Albert, Vic.

NEVILLE H. WHITE

MACANDIE, GEORGE LIONEL (1877-1968), public servant and naval administrator, was born on 26 June 1877 at South Brisbane, fifth child of Scottish parents William Macandie, clerk, and his wife Catherine, née Kennedy. He was educated at Brisbane Grammar School and qualified as an associate of the Federal Institute of Accountants on 29 April 1903. On 18 August 1896 he had joined the Queensland Public Service as a clerk in the Marine Defence Force Office.

After Federation Macandie transferred to the Commonwealth Department of Defence and in 1903 joined Captain (Sir) William Creswell [q.v.8] in setting up the Navy Office in Melbourne. On 24 February 1904, at Park Church, South Brisbane, he married Alice Hood with Presbyterian forms; they had three children. He served with Creswell as a senior clerk through the wilderness years while Australia sought to establish a firm naval policy, and he rejoiced in 1909 in the decision to create a substantial fleet. He laboured on the development and administration of the Royal Australian Navy, playing his part backstage; he controlled the office, conducted correspondence, devised and watched over systems for administering the fleet; in short he was an enabler—advising and guiding the navy on how best to achieve its manifold aims. He was secretary of the Australian Naval Board, holding this post from 1914 to 1946. He was given honorary rank—pay-

master in 1912 and fleet paymaster (equivalent to commander) in 1916.

Macandie was the secretary of the first Department of the Navy from March 1919 until the Navy Office was again merged into the Department of Defence in 1921. After having received some criticism from a 1918 royal commission on deficiencies in naval administration he was belatedly accorded the benefit of a years experience at the British Admiralty from June 1920—while surviving attempts by lesser men to oust him from office. In October 1920 he was appointed C.B.E. for his wartime services. He guided the R.A.N. through the financial reductions of the 1920s and 1930s and saw the brief revival of naval aspirations under the Bruce [q.v.7]-Page [q.v.] government with the acquisition of H.M.A.S. *Australia* and *Canberra* in 1928-29. He was one of the unseen architects of the naval part of the defence development programme of the mid-1930s, when *Sydney*, *Perth* and *Hobart* were added to the fleet. He assisted a succession of naval leaders from the Royal Navy until R.A.N. officers acquired necessary experience and seniority.

When, by 1941, World War II brought again the need for a separate department to administer the navy, Macandie was 64 and the government wanted a younger man at the helm. A. R. Nankervis, who was appointed secretary, was well served by Macandie as secretary of the Naval Board. He remained until May 1946, beyond his formal retirement from the public service in June 1942. Subsequently he compiled *The genesis of the Royal Australian Navy*, published in 1950.

Macandie's private interests were dominated by his Presbyterianism; he was an elder of the Frank Paton [q.v.5] Memorial Church, Deepdene, Melbourne, its session clerk in 1923-34 and superintendent of its Sunday school in 1935-39. Survived by his wife, son and two daughters, he died at Canterbury on 30 April 1968 and was cremated. He was a large likeable man, calm in a crisis, with a controlled geniality and a sometimes impish sense of humour. If Creswell was the father of the R.A.N., Macandie was its benign and watchful uncle.

R. Hyslop, Australian naval administration, 1900-1939 (Melb, 1973); Hist Studies, May 1954, no 22; Reveille (Syd), Aug 1963; Sun-News Pictorial, 22 Mar 1924; Argus, 11 Feb 1950; Federal Inst of Accountants, list of members, Dec 1930; Roy Com on navy defence administration, Report, PP (Cwlth), 1917-19, 4 (105); Navy Office files, B1127, and Dept of Defence files, B413 (AAO, Melb).

ROBERT HYSLOP

McARTHUR, JOHN (1875-1947), soldier, was born on 6 April 1875 at Bannockburn,

Stirling, Scotland, son of John McArthur, engineman, and his wife Elizabeth, née Baird. The family migrated to Queensland and young John was educated at Helidon and Ipswich.

McArthur's military career began when at 19 he joined the Queensland Mounted Infantry (militia). In November 1899 he sailed for South Africa as a sergeant with the 1st Queensland Mounted Infantry Contingent, and saw action at the relief of Kimberley and at Driefontein before being invalided back to Australia in September 1900. At Toowoomba on 23 September 1903 he married Isabella Agnes Bruce; they had five children. Two years earlier McArthur had joined the instructional staff of the new Commonwealth (permanent) Military Forces as a squadron sergeant major and in 1911 he was transferred to Melbourne. He was a warrant officer when war broke out in 1914. In August 1915 he was seconded to the Australian Imperial Force as a lieutenant and on 10 November he embarked for Egypt as a captain and adjutant of the 29th Battalion.

In July 1916, during the abortive battle of Fromelles, McArthur played a part in the informal truce which permitted the recovery of many wounded from no man's land. Soon after he was promoted major and given command of 'D' Company. Several months later the battalion was on the Somme; McArthur later reflected that the Somme winter of 1916-17 was 'the most trying time' of the entire war. In March 1917 he commanded the battalion's forward companies during the German counter-attack on the village of Beaumetz. From October to December he attended the senior officers' school at Aldershot, England, and was made lieut-colonel, with command of the 29th Battalion, in March 1918.

On the night of 28 July the battalion attacked German trenches on a ridge south of Morlancourt, France. McArthur personally reconnoitred the position and moved his headquarters into the front line. Despite heavy German artillery fire he went out to the captured position as soon as it was consolidated and remained continuously on duty for forty-eight hours, ensuring the success of the operation. His gallantry and able leadership won him the Distinguished Service Order. Twelve days later McArthur led the battalion's attack on Vauvillers. Disregarding heavy machine-gun fire he again went forward and when the advance was temporarily checked personally conducted operations, being severely wounded in the neck while doing so. The village was captured. For his leadership, gallantry and initiative he was awarded a Bar to his D.S.O.

McArthur was evacuated to England but returned to the front in October. Until early December he commanded the 31st Battalion before taking command of the 32nd (with which the 29th merged). In March 1919 he became commandant of the Convalescent Training Battalion at Tidworth, England. He returned to Australia in November and his A.I.F. appointment ended in January 1920. He had been twice mentioned in dispatches.

In 1921 McArthur resumed duty with the Australian Instructional Corps. He held positions with various militia units and was appointed O.B.E. in June 1933 for his long and distinguished military service. Two years later he was placed on the retired list as an honorary colonel and during the next few years worked in the circulation department of the Melbourne *Age*. After the outbreak of World War II he re-entered the army and was a general staff officer at Army Headquarters, Melbourne, from 1940 until his final retirement in 1942. Survived by two sons and three daughters, he died on 22 July 1947 at his East Kew home and was buried in Melbourne general cemetery.

C. E. W. Bean, *The A.I.F. in France*, 1916-18 (Syd, 1929, 1938, 1942), and *Anzac to Amiens* (Canb, 1946); R. Clark, *First Queensland mounted infantry in the South African War 1899-1900* (Canb, 1971); *London Gazette*, 25 Dec, supp 28 Dec 1917, 5 Nov, supp 7 Nov, 27 Dec, supp 31 Dec 1918; *Argus*, 3 June 1933; *Age*, 23 July 1947; C. E. W. Bean, Diaries, nos 145, 191, *and* War diary, 29th Battalion, *and* 29th Battalion brief record, *and* Biographical details of Lieut-Colonel McArthur J., *and* AIF nominal roll, 29th Battalion, *and* Honours and rewards, 5th Australian Division, 13-31 July, 5-12 Aug 1980 (AWM).

MATTHEW HIGGINS

McARTHUR, SIR WILLIAM GILBERT STEWART (1861-1935), judge, was born on 18 September 1861 at Meningoort station, Camperdown, Victoria, third son and one of ten children of Scottish parents Peter McArthur, grazier, and his wife Margaret, née McLean. His father had migrated from Islay, Argyllshire, and settled in the Western District in 1839. His mother was the sister of Captain John McLean, a mariner of some note in the early settlement of Port Phillip. Educated at Geelong College, Stewart McArthur was a talented sportsman, excelling at football, cricket and athletics. In 1879, while still at school, he played in the Geelong football and cricket teams and completed the first year of the University of Melbourne's arts degree. Next year he entered Trinity College at the university on the understanding that he would transfer to Ormond [q.v.5] College on its opening. This he did in 1881 becoming the first undergraduate on its roll, a matter of lifelong pride; he was later first president of the Old Ormond Students' Association. While at the university he played for Essendon Football Club, captaining the team for part of the 1881 season.

McArthur graduated LL.B. in 1882, read with J. B. Box and was admitted to the Bar in 1884. On 17 December 1890 at Scots Church, Melbourne, he married Margaret Rutherford, daughter of grazier Ewen MacPherson. During the 1890s he practised principally in the County Court and by the end of the decade was its undoubted leader. However he declined a County Court judgeship and turned his attention to Supreme Court and later High Court work. He took silk in 1912. He was admired at the Bar not so much for his oratory as for his sincerity, calmness and ability to persuade a jury, patiently, that right was on his side. When he was appointed to the Supreme Court bench in 1920 the Bar was delighted. As a judge he was noted for a deep-seated sense of justice and sincere humanity. When occasion demanded he could be forceful, even stinging, yet he conveyed impartiality; his unfailing courtesy, natural dignity and well-considered industry, together with his sound understanding of court practice, greatly benefited both Bar and bench. He retired in 1934 on account of ill health and was knighted the following year.

A tall, spare man, long-faced, quiet and kindly, McArthur in maturity achieved a reputation as a most accomplished whip, driving four in hand. He was a founder and sometime president of the Bohemian Club, for many years driving its coach to the Melbourne Cup and other major meetings. He was later a prominent member of the Melbourne Club (president, 1924).

McArthur died on 5 July 1935 at Meningoort which he had inherited in 1917. Survived by his wife, two daughters and son (Sir) Gordon Stewart, later president of the Legislative Council, he was buried in Camperdown cemetery.

The eldest McArthur brother JOHN NEIL (1857-1917), pastoralist and racing identity, was born on 20 June 1857 at Meningoort. After attending Geelong College he entered the University of Melbourne in 1877 but did not graduate. Instead, he leased Lawrenny station from his father and managed it until on the latter's death in 1897 he inherited the northern part of Meningoort. Like his brother he had a 'gentle face and . . . quiet manner'. He was a Warrnambool shire councillor in 1894-1900 and captain of the Western District Company of Colonel Tom Price's [q.v.] voluntary mounted rifle regiment. In 1896-1900 he represented Villiers and Heytesbury in the Legislative Assembly.

A member of the Melbourne Club and master of the Hamilton Hunt Club, McArthur was a gifted polo player and horseman. It was as a

breeder and owner of racehorses, 'a straight-goer in the fullest acceptation of the term', that he was best known. He was never a betting man but horses in his colours (sapphire blue, pink sash) won many races throughout Australia; Marmont, his most famous horse, won the Victoria Racing Club Grand National Hurdle and the Victorian Amateur Turf Club Australian Hurdle in 1903 and the Australian Cup in 1904. McArthur was a member of the V.A.T.C. committee and a founder of the Camperdown Turf Club.

McArthur's wife Elizabeth Margaret, née McLean, whom he had married on 24 March 1897 at Mortlake, died in 1900. On 10 June 1915 he married Henrietta Thompson Fergusson, who survived him when he died in Melbourne on 13 March 1917. He had no children.

J. Smith (ed), *Cyclopedia of Victoria*, 2 (Melb,. 1904); A. Henderson (ed), *Early pioneer families of Victoria and Riverina* (Melb, 1936); E. Scott, *Historical memoir of the Melbourne Club* (Melb, 1936); A. Dean, *A multitude of counsellors* (Melb, 1968); *Pastoral Review*, 16 Apr 1917, p 355; *Aust Law J*, 15 July 1935; Geelong College, *Pegasus*, May 1920, Sept 1935; *Argus*, 14 Mar 1917, 6 July 1935; *Camperdown Herald*, 14 Mar 1917; J. N. McArthur diaries (LaTL).

J. McI. YOUNG

MACARTHUR-ONSLOW, JAMES WILLIAM (1867-1946), soldier, grazier and politician, **GEORGE MACLEAY** (1875-1931), soldier and grazier, and **FRANCIS ARTHUR** (1879-1938), grazier and businessman, were born at Camden Park, Menangle, New South Wales, sons of Arthur Alexander Walton Onslow [q.v.5] and his wife Elizabeth (1840-1911), daughter of James Macarthur and granddaughter of John Macarthur [qq.v.2].

Arthur Onslow died in 1882 and in 1887 their mother took her surviving six children to Europe for their education. She studied dairying in southern England and the métayage share-farming system in Italy and, on returning to Australia in 1889, founded the dairying complex on the Camden estate and installed a relation A. J. Onslow Thompson as manager in 1889-1915. In the 1890s the model dairies and creameries were served by twelve co-operative farms and forty leased farms—the milk and butter were sold on the Sydney market. In 1899 Elizabeth converted the estate into a private company with her children as shareholders and directors. In 1928 the Camden Vale Milk Co., which had been established to produce a special milk for children and invalids, merged with the Dairy Farmers' Co-operative Milk Co. Ltd.

James Macarthur-Onslow was born on 7 November 1867. Educated at Sydney Grammar School and Trinity College, Cambridge (B.A., LL.B., 1890), he returned to Australia in 1891 and in February 1892 was commissioned captain in the Camden squadron of the New South Wales Mounted Rifles. In 1894-95 he was selected by Major General (Sir) Edward Hutton [q.v.9] for special training in India with the 11th Hussars, the Royal Artillery, and the 1st Battalion, King's Royal Rifle Corps, with which he served in the relief of Chitral expedition including the storming of Malakand Pass and the action at Khar. For these actions he received the Chitral medal with the Malakand clasp. Back in Australia he was promoted major in February 1896 and in 1897 accompanied a detachment of Mounted Rifles to England for Queen Victoria's diamond jubilee celebrations. In April 1898 he was promoted lieut-colonel.

During the South African War he went as a special service officer to Cape Town at his own expense, arriving on 11 April 1900. After a period on the staff of the 7th Division he served as aide-de-camp to Hutton from June to October, visited England and returned to Australia in March 1901. He took the 5th Battalion, Australian Commonwealth Horse, to Durban in July 1902 as its commanding officer, but the war had ended and on arrival back in Sydney in August the unit was disbanded. For service in the South African War he received the Queen's medal with four clasps and was mentioned in dispatches; in 1902-09 he was A.D.C. to the governor-general. He commanded the 2nd Light Horse Regiment from July 1903 and in December 1907 was promoted colonel in command of the 1st Light Horse Brigade. From January 1910 he was on the unattached list. Between August 1915 and February 1917 Colonel Macarthur-Onslow made several voyages in the Sea Transport Service of the Australian Imperial Force between Australia, the Middle East and Britain. He was A.D.C. to the governor-general again in 1917-20 and on 7 November 1925 was placed on the retired list with the honorary rank of major general.

Macarthur-Onslow, who had been a prominent supporter of the National Federal Party of (Sir) Edmund Barton [q.v.7], represented Waverley in the New South Wales Legislative Assembly in 1907-13, Bondi in 1913-17 and Eastern Suburbs in 1920-22. Claiming to represent the Liberal interest and later the National Party, he opposed socialism, the Saturday half-holiday and the abolition of capital punishment. In usually short, forthright speeches, he was fond of airing his learning by adverting much to English history. He told the House: 'I shall vote according to my convictions irrespective of party or whip'. In 1922 he was nominated to the Legislative Council where he was usually inactive or on leave; he did not seek election to the council when it was reconstituted in 1933. He was a member of the Australian and Union clubs

(Sydney) and the Travellers' Club in London. Gardening and fly-fishing were his chief recreations.

James Macarthur-Onslow, who was for many years chairman of directors of Camden Park Estate Pty Ltd, did much to promote the dairy industry through the breeding and showing of dairy cattle. He lived at Gilbulla, Menangle, and, after exchanging houses with his sister Sibella [q.v.] in 1931, at Camden Park. He also inherited Elizabeth Bay House, Sydney, from his great-uncle Sir William Macleay [q.v.5].

He died at Camden Park on 17 November 1946, survived by his wife Enid Emma, née Macarthur and granddaughter of Hannibal Macarthur [q.v.2], whom he had married at St John's Church, Darlinghurst, on 15 December 1897, and by a son and two daughters. He was buried in the family cemetery at Camden Park. His elder daughter Helen Maud (d. 1968) married Major General Sir Reginald Stanham and inherited Camden Park; after her death it passed to her son Brigadier Richard Quentin Macarthur-Stanham.

George Macarthur-Onslow was born on 2 May 1875 and was educated at Rugby School, England. He was commissioned in the New South Wales Mounted Rifles on 5 April 1895 and promoted lieutenant next year. In July 1903 he was made a lieutenant in the reorganized 2nd Light Horse. Promoted captain in 1911, next year he was appointed commanding officer of the 9th Light Horse Regiment. In February 1914 he was promoted major and, in December after joining the Australian Imperial Force, was appointed second-in-command of the 7th L.H.R. under Lieut-Colonel J. M. Arnott.

The 7th reached Egypt in February 1915 and after completing its training at Maadi saw service as a dismounted unit at Gallipoli between May and December. After a period of illness which necessitated return to Egypt, Macarthur-Onslow took command of the 7th Light Horse in October. On 17 December he organized the famous cricket match at Shell Green two days before the final evacuation of Anzac Cove.

On 5 August 1916 he was severely wounded in the counter-attack at Romani which put him out of action for three months. For outstanding work he was awarded the Distinguished Service Order and mentioned in dispatches. Returning to duty with his regiment he played a conspicuous part in all the subsequent operations at Gaza, Beersheba, the pursuit up the Philistine Plain and the raids across the Jordan into Amman and Es Salt, displaying outstanding leadership. He was rewarded with the temporary command of the 2nd Light Horse Brigade from May to August 1918 during the absence of Brigadier General (Sir) Granville Ryrie [q.v.].

In September he was promoted colonel and temporary brigadier general commanding the 5th Light Horse Brigade for the advance on and capture of Damascus. In January 1919 he contracted typhoid fever and four months later was invalided back to Australia. For his war service since December 1916 he was twice more mentioned in dispatches, awarded the Order of the Nile (3rd class) and appointed C.M.G.

After the war Macarthur-Onslow held appointments in various light horse militia units. In 1920-23 he was an honorary A.D.C. to the governor-general and in 1927-31 temporary colonel-commandant of the 1st Cavalry Division. In addition to military matters he was general manager and a director of Camden Park Estate Pty Ltd, and took a close interest in local affairs, being a councillor of the Wollondilly Shire, alderman of Camden Council and four times mayor of Camden.

George Macarthur-Onslow was a genial, fresh-faced six-footer who loved wit and good company and was respected and beloved by many. Though quick-tempered, he soon forgave and forgot. As befitted a countryman he had a shrewd sense of ground; according to General Sir Harry Chauvel [q.v.7], 'He was a born cavalry leader, full of dash and initiative, quite fearless, at the same time possessing the entire confidence of his men'.

He died of pneumonia on 12 September 1931 at his residence, Murrandah, Camden, and was buried in the family cemetery. He had married at Manar, near Braidwood, Violet Marguerite Gordon on 16 October 1909. She and their daughter survived him.

Francis Arthur Macarthur-Onslow, known as Arthur, was born on 7 June 1879 and was educated at Rugby and Exeter College, Oxford. On 29 April 1897 he was commissioned in the New South Wales Mounted Rifles and in July 1899 promoted lieutenant. He served in the South African War in 1900-01 where he was attached to the 7th Dragoon Guards. He saw active service in Cape Colony, the Orange Free State and the Transvaal including the actions at Johannesburg, Diamond Hill and Belfast for which he received the Queen's medal with five clasps. He returned to Australia in 1902 after recuperating in London from rheumatic fever. In 1907 he transferred to the reserve of officers and in 1919 was placed on the retired list with the rank of lieutenant.

Engaged at first in sheep-raising, from 1916 at Macquarie Grove, he became a director of Camden Park Estate Pty Ltd, Camden Vale Milk Co. and the Dairy Farmers' Co-operative Milk Co. In 1924 the herd became the only one in the State tested for tuberculosis. He was three times mayor of Camden. After a time as managing director of the estate he retired to the city and became involved with real estate. A keen racing man he had his own track and stud at Camden. He was a member of the Australian Jockey and Australian clubs and a leading Freemason. He travelled extensively overseas.

Arthur Macarthur-Onslow died suddenly of cerebral haemorrhage in Sydney on 3 March 1938 and was buried in the family cemetery. He was survived by his wife Sylvia Seton Raymond, née Chisholm, whom he had married on 16 May 1903 at Goulburn, and by three sons and a daughter. The eldest son, later Major General Sir Denzil, carried on the family's military tradition and dairying activities.

Camden Park Estate: Australia's oldest pastoral property (Syd, nd); Cyclopedia of N.S.W. (Syd, 1907); Aust Defence Dept, Official records of the Australian military contingents to the war in South Africa, P. L. Murray ed (Melb, 1911); H. S. Gullett, The A.I.F. in Sinai and Palestine (Syd, 1937); Reveille (Syd), 30 Sept 1931, 1 Feb 1940; Pastoral Review, 16 Oct 1931, 16 Mar 1938; Daily Telegraph (Syd), 12 Sept 1907; T&CJ, 8 Jan 1908; SMH, 14, 15 Sept 1931, 23 Dec 1932, 4, 5 Mar 1938, 18 Nov 1946; information from Miss Annette Macarthur Onslow, Camden, NSW.

G. P. WALSH

MACARTHUR ONSLOW, ROSA SIBELLA (1871-1943), charity and church worker, was born on 4 June 1871 at Camden Park, Menangle, New South Wales, third of eight children and only surviving daughter of Captain Arthur Alexander Walton Onslow, R.N. [q.v.5], and his wife Elizabeth, daughter of James Macarthur [q.v.2]. Brought up at Camden Park, she was educated by her mother and later by an elderly German tutor. She enjoyed singing, dancing and acting: musical evenings and a choir were organized at Camden Park by Miss Woolley and Miss Pedley [q.v.].

After her father died in 1882, Sibella assumed considerable responsibility for her brothers, as her mother was the proprietor and very much in control of Camden Park with some 20 000 acres (8100 ha). In August 1899 Camden Park Estate Pty Ltd was registered as a private company with Elizabeth managing director and her six surviving children directors. The right for Elizabeth and her issue to use the surname Macarthur Onslow had been granted by royal licence on 12 March 1892.

While her brothers were being educated in England, Sibella was overseas in 1887-90, 1892-94 and 1902, when she helped to form the Ladies' Empire Club in London. At home, when her brother George [q.v.] founded the People's Reform League of New South Wales, to raise the standard of morality in public life, she joined him and spoke to women to awaken them to the importance of their vote. Her mother died in London in 1911, bequeathing Camden Park, the surrounding 963 acres (390 ha) and £20 000 for its upkeep to Sibella for life. This was a great compliment to her capabilities over those of the heir, her brother James William [q.v.].

Saddened by the deaths of her brother William and of her cousin A. J. Onslow Thompson during World War I, Sibella, an Anglican, turned to the Church. She took a generous and discerning interest in the welfare of the local parish, belonged to the Mothers' Union and the Ladies' Home Mission Union, taught once a week at the Camden school and during the 1919 influenza epidemic fearlessly organized relief hospitals. She was a member of the Australian Board of Missions and chaired its Sydney Diocesan Women's Auxiliary.

Meanwhile in 1914 Miss Onslow had joined the central executive of the New South Wales division of the British Red Cross Society and was secretary (president from 1930) of the Camden branch. She was a founder and deputy president in 1924-43 of the Victoria League in New South Wales; president of the Queen's Club, Sydney, in 1920 and 1922-25; and active in the Bush Book Club of New South Wales and the National Council of Women of New South Wales, representing the latter at the 1927 biennial conference of the International Council of Women at Geneva. In 1930 she was appointed C.B.E.

Camden Park was her life: there Sibella entertained such distinguished visitors as the duke and duchess of York in 1927. In 1914 she published *Some early records of the Macarthurs of Camden*, which her mother had begun. She was a caring and erudite gardener and loved animals; as well as her dogs she kept tame Australian birds and animals. Tall and good-looking, Sibella had charm and a great presence, but was in no way intimidating. Ill health bothered her at times and her normally reliable temperament could become very excitable. She once admonished a gentleman caller anxious to sketch the house, and much to her chagrin Camden Park was a notable omission from Hardy Wilson's [q.v.] *Old colonial architecture.*

In 1931, aware of her mother's testamentary wishes that Camden Park remain in the family in perpetuity, she exchanged houses with her brother James, moving to nearby Gilbulla. She died there on 16 July 1943 and was buried in the family cemetery at Camden Park; a memorial service was held at St Andrew's Cathedral, Sydney. Her estate was valued for probate at £80 326, and was left mainly to her nephews and niece.

G. N. Griffiths, *Some houses and people of New South Wales* (Syd, 1949); *London Gazette*, 22 Mar 1892; *SMH*, 1 Jan, 1 Feb 1930, 25 Feb, 11 Sept 1933, 6, 24 Aug, 14 Dec 1938, 25 May 1939, 17, 24 July 1943; *Camden News*, 22 July 1943; Camden Hist Soc Archives; Macarthur papers (ML); information from Annette Macarthur Onslow, Camden, NSW.

CAROLINE SIMPSON

MACARTNEY, CHARLES GEORGE (1886-1958), cricketer, was born on 27 June 1886 at West Maitland, New South Wales, son of Joseph Belton Macartney, Victorian-born house painter and later motor mechanic, and his wife Mary Ann, née Moore. Mary's father George, an intercolonial cricketer in the 1870s, bowled to his young grandson. In 1898 the Macartney family moved to Sydney; educated at the Woollahra Superior and Chatswood Public schools and at Fort Street Model School, Charles began work in a produce store in 1902. That year he joined North Sydney Cricket Club, transferring to Gordon on its foundation in 1905; he remained with Gordon until 1934, scoring 7648 runs and taking 547 wickets. Macartney made his Sheffield Shield début for New South Wales in 1905-06, topped the Sydney first-grade batting and bowling averages in 1906-07, and played his first Test against England in Sydney in December 1907. One of his opponents, noting Macartney's confidence at the wicket, dubbed him the 'Governor-General', a nickname that stuck.

In 1909 Macartney toured England with the Australian team and took 7 wickets for 58 in the third Test at Leeds. Primarily an all-rounder, he hit hard in the middle order, bowled left-arm spin and fielded with verve in front of the wicket. His emergence as an outstanding batsman dates from the refusal of Clem Hill [q.v.9], Victor Trumper [q.v.], whom he revered, and others to tour England in 1912. He consolidated his reputation on tour with 2207 runs at 45. Enlisting in the Australian Imperial Force on 4 January 1916, he served in France, as temporary warrant officer, from July 1917 with the 3rd Division artillery. He was awarded the Meritorious Service Medal for gallantry in June 1918. The death of his father that year caused him to seek early repatriation and prevented his joining the Australian Services side.

Macartney resumed his Test career for the 1920-21 series and apart from 1924-25, when he had a nervous illness, was a regular Australian player until he retired in October 1927. His most memorable performances were on the 1921 and 1926 tours of England. In 1921 he scored 345 in under four hours against Notts, which has remained the highest score by a batsman playing for Australia; he also led the tourists' batting with 2335 at 58 and was named one of *Wisden*'s cricketers of the year. In 1926 he scored centuries in three Tests; his 151 at Leeds included a famous century before lunch.

Of short stature, strongly featured with a square jaw, his cap characteristically set firmly over his eyes, Macartney was a pugnacious batsman who attacked with an audacious range of shots. In 35 Tests against England and South Africa he scored 2131 runs at just under 42, with seven centuries; in all first-class matches the figures were 15 050 runs at 46, 49 centuries and 419 wickets at 21. With something of Trumper's inventiveness and Bradman's ruthlessness, he was a player whose impertinence captured the imagination of Australian spectators. Macartney received a benefit in February 1927 which yielded over £2500. He also toured Canada and the United States of America in 1913, New Zealand in 1924, Malaya in 1927 and India in 1935.

On 28 December 1921 Macartney had married Anna Bruce at Chatswood Presbyterian Church and henceforth described himself as a civil servant. He also wrote for several Sydney newspapers, in 1936-42 regularly for the *Sydney Morning Herald*; in 1930 he published *My cricketing days* (London). In World War II he was a lieutenant in the amenities service, and afterwards was a personnel officer at Prince Henry Hospital. Predeceased by his wife and childless, he died of coronary occlusion on 9 September 1958 and was cremated with Congregational forms.

N. Cardus, *Good days* (Lond, 1937); R. Barker and I. Rosenwater, *England v Australia . . . 1877-1968* (Lond, 1969); *London Gazette*, 17 June 1918; *Wisden Cricketers' Almanack*, 1922, p 276; NSW Cricket Assn, *Year Book*, 1973-74; Gordon District Cricket Club, *Annual Report*, 1975-76; *SMH*, 1 Dec 1924, 31 Dec 1925, 16-26 Feb, 22 Mar, 19 Oct 1927, 10, 11 Sept, 11 Nov 1958; *Table Talk*, 14 Jan 1926; *Sydney Mail*, 16 Feb 1927; *Sun-Herald*, 14 Sept 1958.   B. G. ANDREWS

MACARTNEY, SIR EDWARD HENRY (1863-1956), solicitor and politician, was born on 24 January 1863 at Holywood, Down, Ireland, youngest son of William Isaac Macartney, formerly commissioner of police, Ceylon, of a prominent Northern Ireland family, and his wife Henrietta, née Dare. Educated at Holywood, Enniskillen, Gracehill and Dublin, Edward had over four years of commercial experience at Belfast.

Arriving in Brisbane in March 1883 on the *Bulimba* with his brother, the ship's surgeon, he apparently went jackarooing briefly as a 'new chum', then worked for the Queensland National Bank at Maryborough, Ipswich, Normanton and Townsville till 1885. He took up articles with the solicitors Thynne [q.v.] & Goertz. On 4 July 1888 he married Caroline Tottenham Lucas Cardew, daughter of a police magistrate, at St Andrew's Church of England, South Brisbane. In 1891 Macartney was admitted as a solicitor and, after the dissolution of the firm, became Thynne's partner in 1893; they developed a strong practice, especially in commercial matters.

Entering politics through local government, Macartney was a wardsman of Ithaca Shire in 1899-1903 (president, 1900) and played a role in the Local Authorities' Association of Queensland. In 1900 he won the Assembly seat of Toowong as an independent Ministerialist against Labor's concerted efforts. He was then espousing what some saw as 'progressive liberal' ideas such as state aid for the aged and needy and divorce reform. Yet he strongly endorsed the Philp [q.v.] government's policy allowing private railway construction and condemned the Labor Party for the 'undemocratic control' exerted over it, he claimed, by the Trades Hall and Mat Reid [q.v.]. Defeating Reid in 1904, Macartney held Toowong until 1908 when in a snap election he was replaced while overseas.

Although not a good orator and extremely sensitive to criticism, Macartney was seen to be politically powerful from 1902, often acting as chairman of committees. He took a keen interest in electoral redistribution, argued for one vote one value, and successfully introduced legislation against juvenile smoking in 1905. He became deputy leader of the Philp Opposition in 1907. In 1909-11 Macartney was the junior member for Brisbane North and in 1911 regained Toowong which he held until 1920. He was secretary for public lands (1911-12) in Denham's [q.v.8] government while the department was trying to tackle the prickly pear problem. He piloted through the Public Service Superannuation Act of 1912. On 11 December he resigned over an auditing disagreement with the home secretary, J. G. Appel [q.v.7], about police administration.

Between 1915 and 1920 Macartney was locked in combat with the Labor government; a personal and professional dislike developed between him and Premier T. J. Ryan [q.v.]. Macartney denounced the government's policies of state regulation of the economy, state enterprises and abolition of the Legislative Council; spoke out ardently for private enterprise and freedom of contract, and against the nationalizing tendencies of Labor's socialist policies; and turned his invective against Labor Speakers. Labor saw Macartney as a conservative reactionary, 'the Hercules of toryism in this State'. Mindful of the 1912 strike, the government criticized him as the representative of monopolies and the money power, and his legal firm was likened to big American corporation lawyers; he was accused of fusing his political and professional roles, was called 'the emissary of the Colonial Sugar Refining Company', 'elected by the commercial magnates of the State'. Macartney and Ryan also crossed swords in legal cases, such as *Fowles* v. *The Eastern and Australian Steamship Company*, and Macartney accused Ryan of profiting from legal cases while he was attorney-general. In 1916 Labor introduced a constitutional bill, popularly dubbed the 'Thynne and Macartney disabling bill', designed to disqualify solicitors who acted 'for monopoly companies or alien companies' from being members of parliament. Macartney supported conscription for overseas military service.

Reluctantly, briefly in 1915 and in 1918-20, he led the Opposition. Not nearly as astute a tactitian as Ryan and dogged by ill health, Macartney gave up politics and resumed legal practice in 1920. He became chairman of directors of Swift Australian Co. Pty Ltd and of the local board of the National Bank of Australasia Ltd, and a director of Finney Isles & Co. Ltd, Queensland Newspapers Pty Ltd and British Traders' Insurance Co. Ltd. In 1929-31 he was agent-general in London for the Moore [q.v.] government, and was knighted in 1930.

Macartney was the university's solicitor from 1913 and a committee-member of the Queensland Club for six years. He was a keen golfer, sometime president of the Brisbane Golf Club. He died on 24 February 1956 in Brisbane, where he was cremated after an Anglican service. His wife and their two sons predeceased him.

C. A. Bernays, *Queensland—our seventh political decade, 1920-1930* (Syd, 1931); D. J. Murphy et al (eds), *Prelude to power* (Brisb, 1970); D. J. Murphy, *T. J. Ryan* (Brisb, 1975); *Pugh's Almanac*, 1914; *Brisbane Courier*, 15-20 Mar 1883, 19-28 Nov 1900, 22 Mar 1907, 29 Jan 1920; *Patriot* (Brisb), 4 Aug 1906; *Queenslander*, 5 June 1930; *Courier Mail*, 25 Feb 1956; Brisb City Council Archives (Town Hall, Brisb).

W. ROSS JOHNSTON

MACARTNEY, HENRY DUNDAS KEITH (1880-1932), regular soldier, was born on 1 February 1880 at Waverley station, Broadsound, Queensland, eighth child of Irish-born John Arthur Macartney [q.v.5] and his English wife Annie Flora, née Wallace-Dunlop. His father, who held extensive grazing and pastoral properties throughout Queensland, had taken up Waverley in 1857. His grandfather was the Most Rev. Dean Macartney [q.v.5] of Melbourne; one of Henry's cousins was (Sir) Edward Macartney [q.v.]. Educated at Geelong Church of England Grammar School, Henry served for six years in the Victorian Cadet Corps.

On 9 March 1900 he joined the Queensland Defence Force and was commissioned lieutenant in the militia field artillery. On 20 June 1901 he was appointed lieutenant in 'A' Battery, the permanent component of the Queensland Regiment of the Royal Australian Artillery, Commonwealth Military Forces. In 1902 he was attached to 'A' Field Battery, New South Wales, and during this appointment was aide-de-camp to the general officer commanding, Major General G. A. French [q.v.8]. Next year Macartney obtained a first-class certificate in the short gunnery course, Sydney, and in 1906 was transferred to Victoria as a company officer in the R.A.A.

In 1908-10 he was on exchange duty in Britain, and on returning to Australia in 1911 was promoted captain and appointed instructor of artillery in Victoria. In December he was attached to the instructional staff of the newly founded Royal Military College, Duntroon, where he remained until 1916, from 1914 in the rank of major. At St Peter's Anglican Church, Mornington, Victoria, he married Alexandrina Vans Zichy-Woinarski on 18 December 1912; they had no children.

In January 1916 Macartney was appointed to the Australian Imperial Force as a major attached to No. 1 Squadron, Australian Flying Corps, and embarked for overseas service. In June he was transferred to the 2nd Divisional Artillery, where he initially commanded the 15th Field Battery which served in July-August on the Somme in France and at Ypres, Belgium, in September. On 2 October he was promoted temporary lieut-colonel in command of the 7th Field Artillery Brigade, 3rd Division. A fellow officer in the 7th F.A.B. later praised 'his ability to rapidly and accurately size up any situation, his shrewd common-sense, his boundless energy, [and] his adherence to the highest standards of conduct'. With the 7th F.A.B. he saw action at Armentières, Messines and Passchendaele. On 17 January 1918 he was appointed general staff officer, grade 2, Headquarters, Australian Corps, and on 8 October he became commander of the 3rd Army Brigade of the Australian Field Artillery. In January-March 1919 he was temporary commander Royal Artillery, 3rd Division, with the temporary rank of colonel. He embarked for Australia on 13 April. For his war service he was appointed C.M.G., awarded the Distinguished Service Order, and mentioned in dispatches four times.

After demobilization Macartney was appointed director of drill at the Royal Military College and in October 1920, after temporary command of the 3rd Battery, A.F.A., he was appointed to the Staff Corps. In 1921 he commanded XVIII Brigade, A.F.A., and in August 1922 transferred to the unattached list; five years later he was placed on the reserve of officers. He retired to Rimbanda, his property near Kentucky, New South Wales, and was a grazier until his death following a car accident at Cleveland, Queensland, on 24 October 1932. He was buried in Toowong cemetery, Brisbane, and was survived by his wife. Tributes following his death, both from his superior officers and those who served under him, made special reference to his kindly and considerate nature, as well as to his professional competence.

Reveille (Syd), Dec 1932, Feb 1933; Queenslander, 27 Oct 1932; SMH, 25 Oct 1932; Age, 9 Nov 1932; H. D. K. Macartney file, war records section (AWM).   DONALD H. JOHNSON

MACARTNEY, SIR WILLIAM GREY ELLISON (1852-1924), governor, was born on 7 June 1852 in Dublin, eldest son of John William Ellison (from 1859 Ellison-Macartney, having inherited from a maternal uncle) and his wife Elizabeth Phoebe, née Porter. The father's chief estate was in Tyrone which he represented in parliament in 1874-85. His son attended Eton and Exeter College, Oxford, taking a first class in modern history (1875). Law and politics became his dominant interests. Already grand secretary of the Grand Orange Lodge of Ireland, he became Conservative member for South Antrim in 1885. Next January he convened a meeting which inaugurated the parliamentary Ulster Unionist Party, and duly served as whip. His speeches in the Commons concentrated on Irish matters in predictable style.

Macartney was a competent secretary to the Admiralty from 1895 until a ministerial reshuffle ousted him in 1900. A consolation was admission to the Privy Council. Resigning from parliament in 1903, he became deputy master of the Royal Mint where his work won official commendation. On 5 August 1897 at Holcombe, Somerset, England, he had married Ettie Myers Scott who bore him a son and two daughters. Her brother was Robert Falcon Scott whose career Macartney helped: 'you have been a brick', the explorer wrote, awaiting death in Antarctica.

In December 1912 Macartney was appointed K.C.M.G. and governor of Tasmania. Irish Nationalists protested that his Orange links would offend Tasmanians sympathetic to Home Rule. Secretary of State (Lord) Lewis Harcourt averred that the Tasmanian government had approved the choice, but there was some local criticism.

The Tasmanian sojourn was made eventful by a constitutional dispute. In April 1914, with Labor and Liberal parties near deadlock, Macartney agreed that John Earle [q.v.8] form a Labor ministry, on condition *inter alia*

that an election follow. Earle became premier but, under pressure from all sides, sought no dissolution. Macartney had to suffer the mortification of having his procedure repudiated by the secretary of state while his pertinent dispatches, argued with learning and vigour, were not published.

Macartney's comments on Tasmanian affairs were often acid. 'Any comprehensive criticism . . . appears to be beyond the capacity of either of the Legislative Houses', he wrote of budget debates in October 1915. Politicians he saw as concerned to hold their well-paid seats, profligate with public moneys and subject to narrow interest groups. His view of the State at large was more generous, and he discharged public duties with due form. Perhaps he was happiest as grand master of the Grand Lodge of Tasmania.

In April 1917 Macartney transferred to the governorship of Western Australia where, during his two years and nine months term, he witnessed three changes of political leadership. Government, however, remained in conservative hands. The governor avoided public skirmishes with his ministers but, as in Tasmania, he seems never to have regarded them highly. Toward the end of 1917 he secretly advised Whitehall that State administration was 'a monument of inefficiency, incompetence and waste'. He travelled extensively within his domain and in Perth continued to participate in Freemasonry, replacing Archbishop Riley [q.v.] as grand master in 1918.

On returning to the United Kingdom in 1920, Macartney gave his name and leadership to educational and philanthropic good works before dying at Chelsea, London, on 4 December 1924. He stands a cold and remote figure whose abilities were real but somewhat sterile.

A. B. Keith, *Responsible government in the Dominions*, 1, 2nd ed (Oxford, 1928); R. Huntford, *Scott and Amundsen* (Lond, 1979); *Irish Hist Studies*, 12 (1960-61); *Bulletin*, 11 Dec 1924; *The Times*, 6 Dec 1924; Governor's dispatches (TA).

MICHAEL ROE

McAULAY, ALEXANDER (1863-1931), mathematician and physicist, and ALEXANDER LEICESTER (1895-1969), physicist, were father and son. Alexander was born on 9 November 1863 at Luton, Bedfordshire, England, son of Samuel McAulay, a Scottish Wesleyan minister, and his wife Jane Annie, née Sowerby. The famous mathematician Francis Sowerby McAulay was an elder brother. Alexander was educated at Kingswood School, Bath, Somerset; Owens College, Manchester, where he commenced an engineering course; and Gonville and Caius

College, University of Cambridge (B.A., 1886) to which he was drawn by growing interest in mathematics. In 1888 he was appointed lecturer and tutor in mathematics at Ormond [q.v.5] College, University of Melbourne (M.A., 1889), and in 1893 first lecturer and from 1896 first professor of mathematics and physics at the newly established University of Tasmania. On 6 February 1895 at the Hobart Registry Office, he married IDA MARY (1858-1949), daughter of Charles Butler, a Hobart solicitor, and his wife Georgine Jane, née Wilmot. Ida was an aunt of C. E. W. Bean [q.v.7] and her family was prominent in Hobart society.

McAulay was a lifelong advocate of the quaternion as a mathematical instrument in vectorial analysis. Introduced by the great Irish mathematician Sir William Hamilton in the 1840s, quaternions were important in the development of three-dimensional algebra. By the 1890s when the methods of modern vector analysis were displacing quaternions, there was much bitter debate. McAulay was at the centre of it, with his impassioned writings and his strong advocacy of the quaternion description of the physical world, in fields such as electro-magnetism, hydrodynamics and elasticity. This controversy never left him. He commented in 1924 that a referee had recommended against acceptance of a paper in which he used quaternion notation on the grounds that he might as well address his audience in Sanskrit. He had contributed the article on quaternions to the eleventh edition of the *Encyclopaedia Britannica* (1910-11) and earlier articles had appeared in mathematical journals. He had already published *Utility of quaternions in physics* (1893) and *Octonions: a development of Clifford's biquaternions* (1898).

With Professor E. G. Hogg, McAulay carried out a magnetic survey of Tasmania in 1900-01. He compiled a pocket volume, *Five-figure logarithmic and other tables* (London, 1909), remarkable for the amount of information it contained, that was used by scientists and engineers for the next fifty years. In his later years he published several papers on relativity. When failing eyesight hampered his research he adapted the Braille system to include his complex mathematical notation.

Perhaps his most lasting memorial was his pioneering interest in hydro-electric power development in Tasmania, about which he wrote to the Hobart *Mercury* in 1905. On the family property, Kanna Leena, at Shannon in central Tasmania, he studied the flow and fall of water from Great Lake. As a consequence of his advocacy the first major hydro-electric station was completed at Waddamana, close to their property, in 1916.

McAulay was a tall, gaunt figure, seen by his children as rather remote and forbidding, but always ready to enter into serious discussion with them on a range of topics. His wife enjoyed entertaining, and their country house at Shannon was often full of visitors. However, he shunned company and would disappear for days to a remote shack on the property, returning only for fresh supplies. In his later years he became even more of a recluse.

Incipient blindness caused him to cease teaching in 1924 and he was appointed research professor until his retirement in 1929. He died on 5 July 1931 of cerebral haemorrhage at home at Sandy Bay, and was buried in Hobart. His wife, their son and two daughters survived him.

Ida McAulay, born on 23 January 1858, was a feminist who rejected the argument of intrinsic differences in 'the mind-stuff of the sexes' and advocated higher education for girls, sex education and family planning. In 1899 she dismissed the claim that women would be drawn out of their sphere by the franchise: 'a woman's sphere is just that which she chooses to make it'. She was active in women's clubs and was president (1903-05) of the Tasmanian Women's Suffrage Association (later the Women's Political Association), resigning after a controversy. An active horsewoman, she was also a keen rifle-shot, admitting its cruelty—'but it is glorious'. She died at Sandy Bay on 15 October 1949.

Alexander Leicester McAulay was born on 15 November 1895 at Bellerive, Hobart, and educated at The Hutchins School, the University of Tasmania (B.Sc., 1916), Gonville and Caius College, Cambridge (B.A., 1921, M.A., 1926) and the University of Manchester (Ph.D., 1921). During 1917-18 he had been employed by the British Air Ministry and the Ministry of Munitions. In 1922 he was appointed lecturer in physics at the University of Tasmania, and professor in 1927 when a separate chair of physics was created. On 1 January 1932 he married Margaret Kathleen Hogarth who drowned a week later on their honeymoon. On 14 December 1934, at Campbell Town, he married Joan Paige Oldrey (d. 1949).

During his term as professor the physics department grew into one of the most active in Australia. In appearance, Leicester McAulay stood out in a profession not renowned for conventionality. He was tall and thin with hawk-like features, long untidy hair and shabby clothes. His trousers were just prevented from responding to the pull of gravity by a three-inch belt (or occasionally a piece of string). When he was the only member of staff and student numbers were small, his teaching was very informal, often conducted around a pot of coffee. His lecturing style was unconventional, not liked by those students expecting to take notes with a minimum of thought and effort. He would pace up and down while he talked, flexing a metre stick through what appeared to be impossibly large angles. Then he would step to the blackboard where he might lose his way through a mathematical derivation. Yet many of his students found inspiration in his lectures, particularly those in which he discussed his ideas on the concepts of physics which excited him most—time and space, relativity, matter and energy, the uncertainty principle, and man's interaction with the environment. Some of his graduates made notable contributions to physics in Australia and overseas.

His unusual abilities were probably more evident in research. He had studied under (Lord) Rutherford and had many of the qualities of that giant of experimental physics. His experiments were always simple, aimed directly at the basic problem; his students learned to think carefully about the aims and underlying principles of their work because any limitations were quickly exposed by his searching questions. The breadth of his interests was reflected in the number of research groups in the physics department. The topics of particle physics, cosmic radiation and metal surface electrochemistry were included among his early publications. He became interested in biophysics in the 1930s at a time when most physicists felt that their field of study did not extend beyond the inanimate world. He encouraged the establishment of experimental stations in Antarctica, Macquarie Island, New Guinea and around Tasmania.

The optical industry established in Hobart resulted from McAulay's judgement and confidence during World War II. In 1940 when Australia had no optical industry and was desperately short of components for military equipment the physics departments in all universities were consulted for optical experience. Though his department had none, Leicester built up a team which short-cut procedures and within months was producing precision prisms and lenses for gun-sights and cameras. He and co-workers developed an entirely new method of lens design.

In his later years he became fascinated by the physics of mental processes, believing that a flaw in deterministic theories lay in the uncertainty principle. Just before he retired he conducted some experiments in psychokinesis and parapsychology. He was a fellow of the Institute of Physics, London. His main recreations included bushwalking, flying, skiing and acting. In later years he took up painting and was a skilled gardener.

Failing health caused him to retire in 1959. McAulay died of coronary vascular disease on 10 April 1969 at his home at Sandy Bay, and was cremated. He was survived by his third wife Bettina Nancy, née Morgan-Jones, whom he had married on 25 October 1951 at Chatswood, Sydney, and by a daughter of his second marriage.

M. J. Crowe, *A history of vector analysis* (Nelson, British Columbia, Canada, 1967); A. McAulay bibliography in Univ Tas, *Calendar*, 1931, 1952, 1958; *Hecate*, 2, no 2, July 1976; *Togatus* (Univ Tas student newspaper), 23 Apr 1969; *Mercury*, 6 July 1931, 11 Apr 1969; *SMH*, 7 July 1931; Ida McAulay papers (TA); Univ Tas Lib Archives; private papers and letters (held by Miss I. McAulay, Mount Nelson, Tas).   BRUCE SCOTT

McBEATH, SIR WILLIAM GEORGE (1865-1931), merchant, was born on 17 April 1865 at Fitzroy, Melbourne, son of David Francis McBeath, a Protestant draper from Belfast, and his Melbourne-born wife Elizabeth, née Blay. He was educated at Nelson College, New Zealand, returning to Melbourne to become a commercial traveller. On 10 January 1889 he married Annie McHutchison at St Kilda. Next year he became Melbourne agent for the London silk firm of M. Makower & Co. When they opened a Melbourne branch he became manager, then partner, and finally managing director of Makower, McBeath & Co. Pty Ltd. A constant traveller, McBeath built the firm into a leading wholesale warehouse with branches in Sydney, Adelaide, Brisbane and New Zealand. In 1925 he resigned in favour of his son George to become chairman of directors.

McBeath was involved in local government as a councillor of Boroondara Shire and Camberwell City in 1890-1917, being four times president or mayor. Appointed in 1911 to the board of commissioners of the State Savings Bank of Victoria, he became its chairman from 1918 until his death. Under his leadership the bank made housing loans widely available and established its own building department to design and supervise the erection of low-cost housing, including forty-five acres (18 ha) as a 'garden city' at Fishermen's Bend, Port Melbourne. In 1927 a 'bank where you work scheme' was introduced.

During World War I McBeath was a principal business adviser to the Commonwealth Department of Defence. Public pressure after some spectacular pay-embezzlement scandals, as well as obvious overspending on defence equipment, forced the Hughes [q.v.9] government to appoint a royal commission on navy and defence administration in July 1917. McBeath was chairman, with Sydney retailer J. Chalmers and Adelaide merchant F. A. Verco the other members. Their report was presented in four parts between December 1917 and March 1918. Though recognizing the extreme stress under which the Defence

Department had been operating, the report found 'muddle, waste and fraud' and 'chaos in pay offices', and drew attention to a lack of accountancy and business training. Its main recommendations, adopted by the government, involved a complete restructure of defence supply and support, removing them from military control and establishing a three-member central board of business administration. During the reorganization McBeath acted as an honorary member of this board.

Financial adviser to the Commonwealth during the demobilization of the Australian Imperial Force in 1919 and chairman of the A.I.F. Disposals Board in London in 1919-20, McBeath was appointed C.B.E. in 1918 and K.B.E. in 1920. In 1924 the Bruce [q.v.7]-Page [q.v.] government sent him as delegate to the League of Nations in Geneva, and he advised the government in 1925 on revision of income tax.

Behind the scenes, McBeath became a powerful figure in the National Party during the 1920s as a member of the National Union, the financing body. He had probably been a member of the Constitutional Union, a predecessor from 1910, and was one of the select inner group of fund-raisers listed by the National Union's founder Herbert Brookes [q.v.7]. By 1925 McBeath was chairman of the union and a highly respected figure in the party. Reverses in the 1924 Victorian elections caused him to launch a 'revival' under the slogan 'Insurance against Bolshevism', seeking members, funds and new branches to secure the re-election of Prime Minister Bruce.

This successful campaign encouraged McBeath to apply pressure on Bruce for the deportation of Tom Walsh [q.v. Pankhurst] and Jacob Johnson of the Australian Seamen's Union. When the High Court ruled against deportation, McBeath is said to have cut short his Hawaiian holiday to press Bruce to draft amending legislation. Bruce, however, refused even to let him see the draft bill, with-standing McBeath's threats of reprisals. This tendency of the National Union and its leaders to play a more conspicuously dominating role was manifested in Victorian politics in the same period. According to a rare article on this secretive body, in *Smith's Weekly* in 1926, McBeath was the leading member of the four-man executive of the National Union, whose policies and personnel came to dominate the supposedly independent National Federation between 1925 and 1928. In 1928 the National Union favourite Sir William McPherson [q.v.] became premier of Victoria; the *Age* asserted that the 'Big Four' in the National Union were running Victorian politics.

McBeath's business success was reflected in his large houses at Canterbury and later at Toorak and Mount Macedon; his membership of the Melbourne, Australian, Yorick, Royal Melbourne Golf and Victoria Racing clubs; and his frequent travel overseas. He was an honorary consul for Japan, director of some minor firms and chairman of directors of the Bankers and Traders' Insurance Co. of Victoria. He made occasional benefactions and was credited with 'surreptitious generosity'.

McBeath died on 2 April 1931 of empyema and was cremated with Presbyterian forms. His funeral was impressively attended by Nationalist and business associates headed by Bruce. McBeath's wife, son and two daughters survived him. His estate was sworn for probate at £54 304 and he also held substantial property in New Zealand.

T. Craddock and M. Cavanough, *125 years* (Melb, 1967); Roy Com on navy defence administration, Report, *PP* (Cwlth), 1917-19, 4 (105); *Argus*, 5, 16, 22 Feb 1918, 4 Apr 1931; *Smith's Weekly* (Syd), 20 Feb, 6 Mar 1926; *Age*, 18 Apr 1927, 10 Nov 1928; M. Vines, The instability of governments and parties in Victoria in the 1920s (M.A. thesis, Univ Melb, 1975).   MARGARET VINES

McBRIDE, SIR PETER (1867-1923), politician, was born on 9 February 1867 at Dunolly, Victoria, third son of Peter McBride, storekeeper, and his wife Catherine, née Hazle, both from Scotland. After attending Dunolly State School and Wesley College, Melbourne, he went into his father's St Arnaud timber and general hardware store. He became a successful local trader with a reputation as an enlightened employer, and a mining investor. On 26 October 1892 at East Melbourne, with Wesleyan forms, he married his cousin Mary Isabella Lawson.

In 1897 McBride was elected to the Legislative Assembly for the seat of Kara Kara. As a back-bencher he took an informed interest in mining, forestry and river development, serving on the royal commission on State forests in 1900 and for five years on the standing committee on railways. Never one for oratory, he preferred the written word, corresponding prolifically with constituents, ministers and government departments. He also collected statistical detail on the primary and extractive industries. He became best known in the precincts of Spring Street at theatres and restaurants and in racing and yachting circles; he was very much the country squire in town, complete with cigar, bountiful table and unaffected amiability. He belonged to the Royal Melbourne Yacht Squadron and Tennis Club as well as the Athenaeum, Commercial Travellers' and West Brighton clubs. His popularity probably helped his appointment as minister of mines and of forests and vice-president of the Board of Lands and Works in the Murray [q.v.] Liberal government of 1909.

Following the financial collapse of the Korumburra-Outtrim coal-mines—to the advantage of the New South Wales coal cartel—and increasing trade union unrest in the interstate coal and maritime industries, the Murray ministry promised to establish a reliable source of black coal for the railways and manufacturing industries. McBride was wary of disturbing the sanctity of private ownership of mining in Australia, but a New South Wales miners' strike lasting four months late in 1909 forced him to introduce legislation for an 'emergency' government coal-mining operation near the Powlett River. The Mines Department took immediate control to operate Australia's first modern state coal-mine, at what was to become Wonthaggi.

McBride shielded the scheme from concerted attacks from private mining interests, the Melbourne press and members of his own party. In 1910-11 he demonstrated clearly Wonthaggi coal's competitive price and value to the railways. He accused a 1910 select committee of inquiry of self-interest and disparaged its members as 'patriots who might be spared for their country's good'. The government was forced to transfer control of the mine to the railway commissioners but it remained state run until its closure in 1968.

As forests minister McBride was responsible for the establishment of the Creswick Forestry School in 1910. In April to October 1911 he was acting chief secretary. Next year in the Watt [q.v.] ministry, with railways added to his portfolios, he oversaw the electrification of the metropolitan railway system. In mines, building on the success of the State Coal Mine, he protected the brown coalfields from private mining ventures and expanded the Department of Mines' boring on the brown coal reserves.

In January 1913 McBride was appointed Victorian agent-general in London. Taking up his post in April, he voiced his belief in increased preference to British manufacturers. His office spanned the war period and he and his wife were unstinting in their work for servicemen in London; their dedication was undoubtedly influenced by the enlistment of their two sons, one of whom was killed in action.

Knighted in 1915 and also decorated by the Belgian and Serbian governments for his wartime efforts, McBride remained in London after his retirement in 1922. The Royal Thames Yacht and the Royal Automobile were among the nine clubs to which he belonged. Perhaps remembering Australian summers, he chased the winter sun at Cannes, France, where he died suddenly on 3

March 1923. His wife, son and daughter survived him. His political career had not been spectacular; but he ably served Victoria in the orderly development of natural resources and his role in the establishment of state mining of black coal established an important precedent for the public ownership and mining of the brown coalfields under the authority of the State Electricity Commission.

A. Sutherland et al, *Victoria and its metropolis*, 2 (Melb, 1888); Y. S. Palmer, *Track of the years* (Melb, 1955); J. M. Coghlan (ed), *The State coal mine and Wonthaggi, 1909-1968* (Wonthaggi, Vic, 1979); *V&P*(LC Vic), 1910 (A1); *Punch* (Melb), 18 May 1911, 13 Apr 1916; *Argus*, 11 Jan 1913, 6 Mar 1923; *The Times*, 7 Mar 1923; *Dunolly and Betbetshire Express*, 9 Mar 1923; A. D. Spaull, The origins and rise of the Victorian brown coal industry, 1835-1935 (M. Com. thesis, 1967, Univ Melb).   ANDREW SPAULL

McBRYDE, DUNCAN ELPHINSTONE (1853-1920), businessman and politician, was born in 1853 probably at Whitehaven, Cumberland, England, son of Robert McBryde, engineer, and his wife Mary, née Ashbridge. Arriving in Australia in 1872, he became lessee of Mount Poole station (formerly Depot Glen) north of Broken Hill, New South Wales. Gold was discovered near the property in 1880 and may have aroused McBryde's lifelong interest in mining. In 1883 or 1884 he moved to Melbourne where he married Ellen Menzies, sister of the owner of Menzies Hotel, on 2 August 1883.

In 1885 McBryde was among the first public buyers of shares in the Broken Hill Proprietary Co. Ltd. Elected a director in December, he remained on the board until his death, one of three Melbourne directors whose constant attendance at weekly meetings provided steady leadership not only for the development of the mine at Broken Hill and the smelting facilities at Port Pirie, South Australia, but for the opening of large-scale iron-ore mining in the South Australian Middleback Ranges, and the move into steel. He was chairman twice, from 1 February 1895 to 11 February 1897 and from 22 January 1915 to 9 March 1917, presiding over the official opening, in June 1915, of what was then Australia's largest steelworks at Newcastle, New South Wales.

In 1888-1916 McBryde chaired the Silverton Tramway Co. which, connecting the Broken Hill mine with the South Australian railway system, paid out over £1 million in dividends before 1908. McBryde was also a director of the Broken Hill Proprietary Block 10 Co. Ltd, floated by B.H.P. in 1888, and in 1892 with Bowes Kelly, William Knox [qq.v.9] and H. H. Schlapp [q.v.] invested in the rich Mount Lyell Mining Co. Ltd. His interests in silver and copper were extended to lead and zinc when he became B.H.P.'s representative on the boards of Broken Hill Associated Smelters in 1915 and the Zinc Producers' Association in 1916.

Outside mining, McBryde was a director of the Commercial Bank of Australia Ltd from 1903 and of the National Trustees Executors & Agency Co. Ltd from 1910. In 1891-96 he represented North-Western Province in the Victorian Legislative Council and in June 1901 succeeded William Knox as member for South-Eastern Province, retaining the seat until June 1919 when he retired from politics. He had been minister of public health, commissioner of public works and vice-president of the Board of Lands and Works in the Bent [q.v.3] ministry of 31 October 1908 to 8 January 1909.

McBryde was a large man with light eyes and a walrus moustache. A Presbyterian and a justice of the peace in both Victoria and New South Wales, he had as his main recreational interest the Melbourne Rifle Club; he was president for ten years and donated the United Service Shield for annual competition.

About 1918 McBryde moved from Brighton to Kamesburgh, Wallace Avenue, Toorak. He died there in his sleep of heart disease, still holding a book, on 24 November 1920. His wife had died in 1914 and he was buried with her in Brighton cemetery, survived by their two daughters to whom he left an estate valued for probate at £55 494. His obituaries were restrained, but one comment, that McBryde was 'a sound and able' politician, echoes the solid progress made by the commercial organizations to which he had devoted many years of quiet attention.

J. Smith (ed), *Cyclopedia of Victoria*, 1 (Melb, 1903); R. Bridges, *From silver to steel* (Melb, 1920); G. Blainey, *The peaks of Lyell* (Melb, 1954); P. Mawson, *A vision of steel* (Melb, 1958); *Table Talk*, 25 Apr 1901; *Argus*, 10 Jan 1914, 26 Nov 1920; *Age*, 26 Nov 1920; Broken Hill Proprietary Co. Ltd, Half yearly Reports, 1894-1918, Minutes of Board of Directors, 1885-1920, Minutes of shareholders' meetings, 1887-1893, Register of directors' shareholdings, 1889-1952 (BHP Archives, South Melb). DOREEN WHEELER

McBURNEY, MONA MARGARET (1862-1932), composer, pianist and teacher, was born on 29 July 1862 at Douglas, Isle of Man, youngest of six children of Isaiah McBurney LL.D., teacher and classical scholar, and his wife Margaret, née Bonnar, art and music teacher. She was educated in Edinburgh, where she also received her first formal musical training from (Sir) Alexander Mackenzie, who was later to become the principal of the Royal Academy of Music.

Migrating to Victoria probably early in 1881, the family lived at Geelong, where Mona attended the Ladies' College, of which her brother Samuel McBurney [q.v.5] was principal. She matriculated to the University of Melbourne in 1881 and in 1892, after the appointment of the first Ormond [q.v.5] professor of music G. W. L. Marshall-Hall [q.v.], enrolled as a music student. She was awarded general exhibitions for the first and second years of her course and in 1896 became the fourth bachelor of music graduate, and the first such woman graduate from an Australian university.

Distinction as a composer and performer came early in Mona McBurney's career, and continued throughout her life. In 1902 her 'Ode to Dante' was awarded an honourable mention by the Società Dante in Rome, and was subsequently performed throughout Australia and New Zealand. By 1905 she had composed an opera, *The Dalmatian*, the libretto adapted from a popular novel by F. Marion Crawford, *Marietta: A maid of Venice*; excerpts were performed in December 1910. Produced in its entirety in 1926, it was the first performance of an opera by a woman composer in Australia. In 1907 she conducted Una Bourne [q.v.7] and a women's orchestra in her 'Northern Ballad', which had been commissioned for the Exhibition of Women's Work. It was included in the 1908 season of Marshall-Hall concerts, and later published as a two-piano arrangement.

Throughout her career Mona McBurney contributed actively to musical and literary societies, as a composer and performer. For over three decades her songs and piano works were a regular feature of the Musical Society of Victoria concerts. She was also prominent in the British Music Society from its inception in 1921, the Queen's Hall concerts, the Melbourne Music Club, choral societies and private music and literary groups. Her noted 'at homes' and soirées provided a forum for young musicians and composers and gave a lead to women professionally committed to music.

Mona McBurney was appointed a teacher of Italian and French at the university conservatorium in 1918, and of Italian at the Albert Street Conservatorium in 1921, continuing in both positions until her death. In 1926 she was elected an honorary life member of the Lyceum Club.

All Miss McBurney's major works—an opera, a concerto for piano and orchestra, a string quartet, two choral odes, her piano works, and most of her thirty songs and part-songs—were performed during her lifetime. Recognition continued after her death, with several public performances, radio broadcasts and private recitals.

A shy, retiring woman, Mona McBurney

possessed a driving enthusiasm and a capacity to inspire her students, who regarded her with affection. She died of pneumonia at her Hawthorn home on 4 December 1932 and was buried in the Presbyterian section of Kew cemetery. Her most famous pupil, the composer Margaret Sutherland, described her as 'one of the most sensitive, gentle, yet vital persons I ever knew'.

F. Fraser and N. Palmer (ed), *Centenary gift book* (Melb, 1934); J. M. Gillison, *A history of the Lyceum Club* (Melb, 1975); A. Lubbock, *People in glass houses* (Melb, 1977); *Southern Sphere*, 1 Dec 1911; *Woman's World*, 1 June 1926; *Aust Musical News*, 2 Aug 1926, 28 Feb, 4 May, 9 June 1933; *A'sian*, 25 Apr 1925, 19 June 1926; *Herald* (Melb), 5 Dec 1932; *Argus*, 6 Dec 1932.   FAYE PATTON

McCABE, STANLEY JOSEPH (1910-1968), cricketer, was born on 16 July 1910 at Grenfell, New South Wales, third son of native-born parents William McCabe, hairdresser, and his wife Harriet, née Glynn. Educated locally and in Sydney at St Joseph's College, he was a promising schoolboy cricketer who achieved recognition in country carnival matches. Chosen to represent New South Wales in 1928 at a time of team reconstruction, he was selected to tour England in 1930 before he had scored a century in first-class cricket. He was only 19 when he played in his first Test match at Nottingham in June. Thereafter, he was a member of every Australian Test team—thirty-nine in all—up to World War II.

McCabe showed more potential than performance in the early series against England, South Africa and the West Indies. Indeed, his 20 wickets were almost as useful as his 607 runs. But on 2-3 December 1932 in Sydney, against the fury of England's 'bodyline' attack, Stan McCabe came into his own. Scoring 187 not out in an innings of high courage and adventure, he inscribed his name in cricket history.

His reputation vindicated, McCabe topped the tourists' first-class averages in England in 1934. At Johannesburg in the 1935-36 season he produced a classic innings of 189 not out in 195 minutes, including a century before lunch. McCabe made runs when needed against England in Australia in 1936-37. He capped his Test career with a chanceless 232 in 230 minutes at Nottingham in 1938. (Sir) Donald Bradman and the English bowler S. F. Barnes, great cricketers of different generations, agreed that it was the finest innings they had seen.

McCabe hit 2748 runs in Tests at 48 an innings, 3031 in the Sheffield Shield competition at 55 and 11921 runs at 49 in all first-class matches. It was an impressive tally

but, in a period of very high scores, not outstanding. What was remarkable was the way he made them—thirty runs from Stan McCabe were more memorable than a hundred by most batsmen. He seemed to lack the inclination to score unnecessary runs or to assume that each century had to be doubled. He played with superb grace and had every shot in the book, but was never a mere accumulator of runs. Neville Cardus observed in his brilliant stroke play 'a certain courtliness': in spirit and approach, McCabe belonged to an earlier, golden age of batsmen.

In his earlier years an agile fieldsman, he was always a reliable medium-pace bowler. With Australia's attack based largely on spin, he was sometimes required to take the new ball. His 39 Test wickets were valuable: he dismissed Walter Hammond four times.

From the 1935-36 South African tour, McCabe was Australia's vice-captain. He captained New South Wales with success, especially in the triumphant 1939-40 season. Thereafter, foot trouble restricted his wartime appearances to occasional matches. Captaincy in no way affected McCabe's popularity with his team-mates. He was still 'Napper'—his shortish, somewhat plump figure and his prematurely receding hairline gave him a fancied resemblance to Napoleon.

At St Mary's Cathedral, Sydney, McCabe married Edna May Linton on 5 February 1935. In 1939 he opened a sports store in George Street, which he conducted for the rest of his life. He was appointed to the Sydney Sports Ground and Cricket Ground Trust in 1963: many people thought that he should have been given more scope as an administrator. On 25 August 1968, while trying to dispose of a dead possum, he died in a fall from a cliff near his home at Beauty Point, Mosman. He was buried in Northern Suburbs cemetery, after a requiem Mass attended by many friends and admirers. His wife, son and daughter survived him.

G. Tebbutt, *With the 1930 Australians* (Lond, 1930); A. G. Moyes, *Australian batsmen* (Syd, 1954); N. Phillipson, *The Australian cricket hall of fame* (Melb, 1979); *NSW Cricket Year Book*, 1968-69; *Wisden Cricketers' Almanack*, 1969; *SMH*, 14 June 1938, 5 Jan 1957, 26 Aug 1968.
                                                K. J. CABLE

McCALL, SIR JOHN (1860-1919), medical practitioner, politician and agent-general, was born on 10 August 1860 at East Devonport, Tasmania, son of John Hare McCall, pharmacist, and his wife Johanna, née Shanahan. He was educated at Don and the University of Glasgow (M.B.; C.M., 1881), Scotland. On 4 May 1880 he had married a Glaswegian, Mary Cluckie (d. 1896). McCall returned to

Tasmania to practise at Waratah where he was also medical officer for the Mount Bischoff mine. He settled at Ulverstone about 1885 where his practice developed and he became a large landowner.

He was soon active on many local bodies, including the Forth Road Trust, the Leven Municipal Council and the Leven licensing bench. In his work on the Leven Marine Board and the Leven Harbour Trust he did much to further the development of Ulverstone's port. Both McCall and his father were elected to the Tasmanian parliament in 1888, McCall senior to the Legislative Council for Mersey and his son to the House of Assembly for West Devon, vacated by (Sir) Edward Braddon [q.v.7]. McCall's hold on this seat was linked closely with Braddon's career. In the 1893 election he stood aside for the returning agent-general who was soon to become premier, but in 1900 he came within eight votes of defeating Braddon, and in 1901 he won back the seat after Braddon moved to the House of Representatives. McCall held the seat until 1909, during which time he vigorously promoted development of the rapidly growing north-west coast.

McCall was chief secretary and minister for agriculture in the Propsting [q.v.] government of April 1903-July 1904. A particular interest in health and local government matters lay behind his introduction of a new Public Health Act (1903) that consolidated and reformed existing legislation, while many of his ideas were embodied in a new local government bill. The bill had not been passed before the government fell, but the Evans [q.v.8] government accepted its proposals and eventually asked McCall to pilot them through the House. In 1905 Glasgow University awarded him an M.D. for his thesis on the management of smallpox.

According to the Hobart *Mercury* McCall 'found his place' when he was appointed as Tasmania's seventh agent-general in 1909. A competent administrator and an enthusiastic spokesman for his State, he worked hard to attract capital to Tasmania. Mount Lyell mines, Launceston white lead works and the encouragement of hydro-electric power generation were among the developments influenced by his activity. He was also a director of several companies floated in London for Tasmanian ventures. He was knighted in 1911.

McCall made a brief visit home in 1913, and on the outbreak of World War I the former Tasmanian Volunteer (from 1897) was appointed medical officer in charge of the Australian Auxiliary Hospital, London, with the rank of major (August 1915). As president of the Australian Natives' Association in London, he was largely responsible for the Anzac Buffet which entertained Australian and New Zealand servicemen. Many Tasmanians expressed their gratitude for his attention to their needs and for the welcome he and Lady McCall gave soldiers on leave. McCall was chairman of the Australian Voluntary Hospital at Wimereux, France, and he helped to organize a convalescent home for Belgian soldiers in France, for which he was awarded the Belgian Order of the Crown. He was appointed K.C.M.G. in 1919.

On 27 June 1919 McCall died in London of pneumonia and was buried in Putney Vale cemetery. He was survived by his second wife, Claire Pearson, née Reynolds, whom he had married on 20 November 1900 in Hobart, by their two sons and by a son and a daughter of his first marriage.

A member of the Church of England, McCall was a man of great energy and a fine orator. *The Times* described him as 'a virile character of much integrity and sympathy, whose help and counsel were always at the disposal of a fellow-Australian'.

Mercury, Examiner (Launc), and *The Times*, 30 June 1919.   SCOTT BENNETT

McCALLUM, ALEXANDER (1877-1937), bookbinder and politician, was born on 28 October 1877 in Adelaide, son of Hugh McCallum, labourer, and his wife Margaret, née McPhee. At 14 he was apprenticed to a bookbinder. In 1898 he left for Perth where he worked in the Government Printing Office. A member of the Bookbinders and Paper Rulers' Industrial Union, McCallum spoke for printing industry employees in general, sometimes so vehemently that his job was at risk. He married Elizabeth (Bessie) Ferres with Baptist rites at Fremantle on 1 January 1902.

McCallum became a radical Labor politician; his party pledge was paramount. He was a forceful early leader of Western Australian trade unionism, an energetic and innovative cabinet minister, and finally a compassionate bank commissioner. Serious and intense, he abhorred fools and was trenchant in attack. He was also systematic, persistent and slow to delegate. Considered 'bossy' by parliamentary colleagues, he was nicknamed 'Musso' (Mussolini). In other company 'Alick' was known as kindly, even sentimental, gregarious and a good listener. Although abstemious, he enjoyed smoke socials at the Fremantle Workers' and Leisure Club. A stocky, sturdy man, with pigeon-toed gait, McCallum had square jowls, large eyes and dark hair with a cowlick. In his youth he excelled as a runner and was later a keen gardener and bird-fancier.

By 1905, when he stood unsuccessfully for South Fremantle, McCallum was president of the Coastal Trades and Labour Council, and secretary of the metropolitan division and the South Fremantle branch of the Political Labor Party. He first worked in a galvanized iron lean-to described as a 'corner of Hades'. Mainly through his efforts, the Perth Trades Hall was built in 1911. He failed to win election to the House of Representatives in 1913 and 1914 but that year was appointed general secretary of the Australian Labor Party in Western Australia. His early reputation as a 'red ragger' was probably exaggerated. Despite his relish for the cut and thrust of bargaining, he was a conciliator: 'the ordinary trades union official is busy enough and has sufficient anxiety without a strike'.

A skilled arbiter, in court and on the job, he defused the potentially explosive 'Battle of the Barricades' on Fremantle wharf in May 1919, when Premier (Sir) Hal Colebatch [q.v.8] intervened in the *Dimboola* dispute. Likewise in December 1924, through McCallum's perspicacity, and despite their president's objections, Fremantle waterside workers withdrew support from the national Seamen's Union in favour of arbitration by the A.L.P. disputes committee. This culminated in George Ryce's expulsion from the union and the defection from the Labor Party of T. J. Hughes, who was unforgiving; he aimed to 'get McCallum'.

McCallum had suffered a nervous breakdown in May 1916 and, helped by unionists' contributions, went to Adelaide to recuperate. At its triennial conference in June the Western Australian Labor Party refused to commit itself against conscription. On 6 November, in response to a telegram from Perth, McCallum left Adelaide for Melbourne to attend a national executive meeting and a special interstate conference. Following his brief, though not from personal conviction, he voted against the non-conscription motion. In Perth next year he printed his speech attacking his former hero W. M. Hughes [q.v.9] whom he accused of 'dictatorship' for defying caucus and precipitating Labor's conscription split. McCallum toured the goldfields to appease the disaffected but in September failed to wrest the Yilgarn seat from a Labor defector.

But McCallum's power was growing. As a director of the restructured *Westralian Worker*, he was close to the new editor John Curtin. The paper's declared policy was to support any campaign undertaken for the improvement of labour, politically or industrially. McCallum had been a member of the royal commission into the alleged shortage of artisans (1911) and was treasurer from 1914 of the Workers' Education Association (W.A.). He was union representative at discussions in 1917 with employers, employees and educationists on training apprentices, which paved the way for the Apprenticeship

Board he was to set up in 1926. In 1918 he was appointed to the Western Australian Repatriation Board.

McCallum won the South Fremantle seat in the Legislative Assembly in 1921. He was minister for public works, labour, water supply and state trading concerns in 1924-30 in Philip Collier's [q.v.8] cabinet and deputy leader of the Opposition from 1930, until he resumed his previous portfolios (except trading concerns), with the added status of deputy premier, in April 1933. McCallum was acting premier during Collier's absence for two months in 1934-35. Next March he resigned to become chairman of commissioners of the reconstituted Agricultural Bank.

In debate McCallum vigorously presented the Labor case. He simultaneously led the parliamentary party's resistance to the State executive's attempt to influence government unduly. It was enough, he argued, for parliamentarians to honour the pledge; government must make its own decisions. He created a Department of Labour—the culmination of his long career in labour relations. Despite an obstructive Legislative Council and resentment from the industrial sector, he amended the Arbitration Act, established the Court of Arbitration in 1926 and appointed its first president (Sir) Walter Dwyer [q.v.8], thereby shifting a backlog of disputes. Legislation for a 44-hour-week, a State basic wage award, the formation of the State Government Insurance Office, and workers' compensation was passed. He instituted a major reorganization of the Public Works Department (1926), development of the metropolitan water-sewerage scheme, expansion of the water supply and construction of Canning Dam, and administered Federal funding for extended State roads. Perhaps his most creative legislation was a Town Planning Act (1928) and the Swan River reclamation scheme (1925); a riverside park in Perth bears his name.

In 1932 McCallum was strongly criticized for abandoning his union constituents by voting for bulk-handling of wheat at a time of low employment. But he was so concerned about unemployment and monopolies that he called for and sat on a select committee of investigation on which he was the sole dissenter. McCallum never lacked detractors; the most persistent was T. J. Hughes, who accused him of dishonesty and political expediency. The two had fought over the One Big Union concept in 1918-20 (McCallum promoted the Australian Workers' Union plan); and in parliament Hughes attacked McCallum about his farm, Koojarlee, at Muntadgin, the licensing court, and his part-ownership, with Senator E. B. Johnston's [q.v.9] wife, of the Captain Stirling Hotel. McCallum was exonerated by a royal commission in 1937. The conservative *West Australian* said: 'he lived long enough and performed ably enough to survive the distrust of his political opponents . . . a prodigious worker; a fair, if forceful fighter; a zealous industrial reformer, a trusted colleague and opponent'.

He suffered from exhaustion in 1912, dengue fever in 1921, and nervous breakdowns in 1916 and 1928. After two years poor health he died of chronic nephritis on 12 July 1937 and, following a state funeral, was buried in the Methodist section of Fremantle cemetery. McCallum's photograph was hung in the Perth Trades Hall and his probate was sworn at £13 836. His wife and son survived him.

G. C. Bolton, *A fine country to starve in* (Perth, 1972); R. Pervan and C. Sharman, *Essays on Western Australian politics* (Perth, 1979); C. T. Stannage (ed), *A new history of Western Australia* (Perth, 1981); *West Australian*, 16 Oct 1905, 4 Mar, 11, 13, 27 May 1921, 6 Dec 1929, 4, 19 Oct 1934, 20 Apr 1935, 13, 14 July 1937; *Westralian Worker*, 20 Oct 1905, 22 Dec 1911, 23 May 1913, 19 July 1937; Metropolitan District Council, Minutes, 1910-1920, 1933-1935 (Battye Lib); State Executive, ALP, Minutes (Battye Lib); information from Mr F. J. S. Wise, Cottesloe, Perth.

WENDY BIRMAN

MacCALLUM, Sir MUNGO WILLIAM (1854-1942), educationist, scholar and administrator, was born on 26 February 1854 at Glasgow, Scotland, son of Mungo MacCallum, merchant, and his wife Isabella, née Renton. Educated at High School, Glasgow, and the University of Glasgow, he graduated M.A. in 1877, well versed in classics, philosophy and literature. The influence of Edward Caird, professor of moral philosophy, was lasting: MacCallum asserted in 1933 that 'I don't think the critical Idealism of my young days superseded'. Elected to the Luke fellowship in humanities, he studied in Glasgow and at the universities of Berlin and Leipzig: in Germany he concentrated on medieval literature and published several articles in the *Cornhill Magazine* in 1879-80. The full range of his research appeared in 1884 as *Studies in Low German and High German literature*.

In 1879 MacCallum had become professor of English literature and history at the University College of Wales, Aberystwyth. Despite few resources he worked hard to build up an effective department. By 1886 he was seeking a change. A committee, which included Matthew Arnold and Leslie Stephen, selected him out of forty-five candidates to be the foundation professor of modern language and literature in the University of Sydney. With his wife Dorette Margarethe, née Peters, of Hanover, whom he had married on 28 June 1882, and two children, MacCallum

sailed for Australia, arriving in February 1887.

At a time when the university was branching into professional and scientific training and expanding the faculty of arts with the prospect of the munificent Challis [q.v.3] bequest, MacCallum was faced with a major task. French and German had been taught for their language utility; despite the championship of Professors Badham and Woolley [qq.v.3, 6], English literature was a visitor to the curriculum. All three had to be presented as scholarly subjects. Teaching much of the three literatures himself, though English was his direct responsibility, MacCallum gradually built up a reputable department, and delegated the organization of the French department to G. G. Nicholson [q.v.] and, notwithstanding his own fluency, most of the teaching of German eventually to Christopher Brennan [q.v.7]. By 1892 honours schools existed. MacCallum sought to encourage young Sydney scholars to enter academic work and to undertake postgraduate studies overseas. By early in the century, this policy had taken effect: E. R. Holme [q.v.9] was the first such recruit and became his loyal coadjutor in English language teaching.

MacCallum and his fellow professors believed it their duty to take the university to the general community and impress its traditions on the student body. Extension lectures were their stock in trade: MacCallum's English literature courses were justly celebrated. In 1897 he became president of the Sydney University Union and characteristically gave his inaugural address on the university spirit. In 1898 he became dean of the faculty of arts, an office that he held (with one interval) until 1919, and *ex officio* a fellow of the senate. He had become a major academic figure and was involved in passionate debate with members of other faculties over the distribution of scarce resources.

In his earlier years at Sydney, MacCallum had scant leisure for research. He published a major book in 1894, *Tennyson's Idylls of the King and Arthurian story from the XVIth century*, which acknowledged only one local helper, his friend and fellow Scot J. T. Wilson [q.v.], professor of anatomy at Sydney. Though not a Celtic scholar, MacCallum now traced the Arthurian story from its 'Brythonic' origins through Malory and beyond and up to its final phase in Tennyson. Hoping to redress recent neglect of the *Idylls*, he stressed their 'true allegorical character'. Focusing on Tennyson, MacCallum was turning from his original medieval interests to the nineteenth century. He had already published a lecture on Meredith, whom he championed; later he wrote a lively account of an interview. He continued this line of work, producing pamphlets on Swinburne, Browning, Walter

Scott, and, in his 1924 Warton lecture to the British Academy, on *The dramatic monologue in the Victorian period* (1925).

The centre-piece of undergraduate studies in English literature was Shakespeare. A. R. Chisholm, one of MacCallum's students, later wrote:

'Mac' was a little man with a big personality. He had a rather scrubby beard and moustache, spoke with a broad Scotch accent . . . and wrote a dreadful hand, which on the blackboard began in one corner and finished somewhere diagonally opposite. But his lectures were extraordinarily good, and when he talked about Shakespeare he kept his audience spellbound.

In this field MacCallum was not only an expositor but an original scholar. His first interest was in *Hamlet*. His published extension lectures were followed by a piece (he later disavowed its conclusion) on the authorship of the early *Hamlet* in a 1901 miscellany presented to J. S. Furnival. The appearance of A. C. Bradley's magisterial work on Shakespearian tragedy three years later seemed to inhibit further study, but MacCallum was already using David Scott Mitchell's [q.v.5] Elizabethan books to research those tragedies with a classical setting. The result is *Shakespeare's Roman plays and their background* (1910, reprinted 1925, 1935, 1967) in which he made an exhaustive analysis of the sources of the three principal Roman plays and a searching analysis of their leading characters.

MacCallum was an ardent supporter of the Empire and its ideals of service. During the South African War his belief that the university should uphold this position involved him in public argument with George Arnold Wood [q.v.], professor of history, over the latter's criticisms of the British treatment of the Boers. Yet the senate's censure of Wood was not to MacCallum's liking and the two men carried on a bitter controversy, though without the ugly rancour that marred many of Wood's critics. In World War I he wholeheartedly supported Australia's involvement: as president of the Universal Service League in 1915-17 he vigorously campaigned for conscription and in 1918 was a founder executive-member of the 'King's Men', formed to promote loyalty. Yet he deplored the prevalent anti-German hysteria and tried to help some of its victims.

The war obliged MacCallum to remain in his chair; indeed his colleagues' absence on government duties added to his burden. Permitted to retire in 1920 MacCallum, now emeritus professor, became honorary professor of English literature and continued to lecture within the combined English department.

MacCallum was called upon to act as warden of the university in 1923 and again in 1924. Late that year he was appointed warden and, in December, to the now salaried position of vice-chancellor, while on a visit to England. Aged 70, he took on fresh and larger administrative responsibilites for the major expansion of the university made possible by the McCaughey [q.v.5] bequest. Although MacCallum regarded his vice-chancellorship as an annual appointment, he took his office very seriously. The university's finances had been over-strained by the growth of teaching facilities, student numbers and buildings. While benefactions, especially in medicine and science, permitted further developments, due economy had to be observed. With the help of some decline in student enrolment, he kept on a steady course. His discipline was firm, his concern for the morale of the institution paternalistic.

In 1925 he regretfully but decisively upheld the majority decision of the senate requiring the resignation of Brennan, to whom his attitude had always been ambivalent for he admired his literary work and scholarship but not his mode of life. MacCallum was no less emphatic when the proposal for a war-memorial carillon, a project which he warmly supported, became complicated by the activities of a powerful rival committee. Believing his authority to be at risk, he publicly denounced the alternative scheme and even threatened resignation. He did resign at the end of 1927. Awarded an LL.D. by the University of Glasgow in 1906 and an honorary D.Litt. by Oxford for his Shakespearian studies in 1925, he was appointed K.C.M.G. next year.

In April 1928 MacCallum was elected deputy chancellor. After annual reappointments to that office, he was chancellor in 1934-36. In the 1930s he helped the university to ride out the Depression and to weather the criticisms made in parliament and the press on the alleged unpatriotic utterances of Professor John Anderson [q.v.7]. He had little patience with his fellow-Glaswegian's empiricist philosophy and style of teaching, although they shared an almost old-fashioned reverence for a classical education, but outside and intemperate attacks on the university had always aroused his ire.

In the 1890s MacCallum had enjoyed conversation at the Athenaeum Club and later belonged to the Australian Club. In the wider community he had been first president of the Shakespeare Society of New South Wales which had grown out of his extension lectures. He was a trustee from 1890 of the Public Library of New South Wales (chairman, 1906-12), a member of the advisory committee of the Commonwealth Literary Fund in 1917-29, president of Sydney Repertory Theatre Society and the Turret Theatre Dramatic Club, and chairman of trustees of Sydney Grammar School in 1929-32. Foundation president of the Sydney branch of the English Association in 1923, he published six of his lectures to it; the association became an important promoter of English studies and Australian literature. In 1927 he chaired a Commonwealth committee appointed to report on the provision of university facilities for residents of Canberra. In 1930 MacCallum published his last work of considerable size, *Queen Jezebel*, 'fragments of an imaginary biography in dramatised dialogue'. It was received with respect but little enthusiasm.

MacCallum died on 3 September 1942 at his home at Edgecliff, and was cremated with Anglican rites after a crowded memorial service in St Andrew's Cathedral where a memorial tablet was placed.

His elder son Mungo Lorenz (1884-1933), Rhodes scholar of 1906, lawyer, scholar and journalist, and his daughter Isabella Lightoller predeceased him. MacCallum was survived by his wife and younger son Walter Paton, physician, who served with the Australian Imperial Force, ending the war as a major with the Distinguished Service Order and Military Cross. Lady MacCallum was a founder of the National Council of Women of New South Wales and president in 1919-28. She also worked for the Infants' Home, Ashfield, the Sydney Day Nursery and Nursery Schools' Association, the Australian Board of Missions, the New Settlers' League of Australia, the Royal Society for the Welfare of Mothers and Babies and the Sydney University Women's Society (Settlement). An expert cook, she entertained frequently and loved gardening.

Mungo MacCallum served the University of Sydney for so long that he appeared, in his later years, to be an institution in himself. The small, spare figure was a familiar sight to generations of undergraduates. Although he was not a forceful orator, his unfailing choice of the right word and the telling phrase made him a most effective speaker, and his lectures were illumined by his 'cheerfulness of spirit and quick sense of humour'. Immensely energetic, he could debate with passion and criticize with vigour but his natural sense of fairness and moderation usually triumphed.

A portrait by John Longstaff [q.v.] is held by the University of Sydney, whose MacCallum Building was named after him.

H. E. Barff, *Short historical account of the University of Sydney* (Syd, 1902); A. R. Chisholm, *Men were my milestones* (Melb, 1958); R. M. Crawford, *'A bit of a rebel'* (Syd, 1975); A. Clark, *Christopher Brennan* (Melb, 1980); *Sydney Tatler*, 25 Jan 1923; *Southerly*, 3, 3 Dec 1942, 5, 2 Sept 1944; Univ Syd Union, *Union Recorder*, 10 Sept 1942; *SMH*, 4 Sept 1942; Univ Syd, Senate minutes 1886-1942 *and* MacCallum papers (Univ Syd Archives).

K. J. CABLE

McCANN, Sir CHARLES FRANCIS GERALD (1880-1951), agent-general and trade commissioner, was born on 10 June 1880 at Jamestown, South Australia, son of John Henry McCann, an Irish-born farmer, and his native-born wife Catherine Alice, née Morris. He was educated at Hornsdale State School and Christian Brothers' College, Adelaide.

At 18 McCann became a cadet with the Produce Export Department in Adelaide, and enjoyed remarkable promotion: by 1900 he was clerk-in-charge at the Dry Creek depot; six years later he became works manager at Port Adelaide; and in 1910 sub-manager of the department. That year he went to Western Australia to advise on the proposed construction of abattoirs and meat-export works. He was also chief inspector of wheat for South Australia and examining officer for export rabbits and meat. The detailed expertise which he accumulated, along with his rural family background, underpinned his career in the international marketing of primary produce.

From 1911 McCann deputized in London for the South Australian trade commissioner, succeeding to the position in 1914. In World War I he co-operated with the War Office's food supply department, organizing the import and distribution of frozen and chilled meat. Having developed both his commercial reputation and his trade contacts, in 1919 he became general manager in Argentina for the British-owned Smithfield & Argentine Meat Co. His eleven years with one of Australia's great trading rivals spanned labour troubles, a major plant enlargement and modernization programme, and the so-called 'meat war' within the cartel of overseas packing companies controlling Argentinian meat exports.

In 1930 McCann returned to London as a director of Minear, Munday & Millar Ltd, wholesale fruit-merchants with South Australian connexions. During the prolonged illness of South Australia's trade commissioner R. M. K. Lewis, McCann gave unpaid help to the agent-general, Sir Henry Barwell [q.v.7]. When Lewis died in 1931 McCann resumed the trade commissionership for a five-year term. Although he resigned all his English and Argentinian appointments, his whole-hearted commitment to South Australia was briefly questioned in State parliament in July 1932; but the government and primary producers' organizations believed McCann was ideally qualified to represent the State's export marketing needs.

Barwell's successor in 1933, former Labor premier L. L. Hill [q.v.9], in early dispatches referred to McCann's 'splendid services'. But there was soon serious discord and friction in the London office, arising partly from petty misunderstanding, and partly from Hill's trespass into McCann's territory. In October McCann contemplated resignation; the government tried to resolve the conflict by making the trade commissioner responsible directly to the minister of agriculture. Hill accepted this, yet continued to interfere in trade matters, withheld McCann's correspondence, and instituted an audit of his activities. With relations at breaking-point, McCann visited Adelaide next June, ostensibly for discussions about marketing South Australian produce in Britain. In ten weeks he addressed over sixty meetings throughout the State, offering advice to fruit-growers, butter-manufacturers, dairymen, poultry-farmers, cattlemen, lamb and pig breeders, wine-makers and cereal-growers, urging them to study precise market requirements and to tailor quality and type of output to meet those demands. He also conferred in Melbourne and Sydney with the Graziers' Federal Council of Australia, advocating formation of an exporting authority similar to the recently established New Zealand Meat Board. He appreciated the need to sharpen Australia's competitive edge against South American export companies, whose sophisticated marketing organization gave them dominance in the British market.

In August 1934 McCann told the premier that he would not return to England as trade commissioner while Hill was agent-general. Unwilling to lose McCann, the government gave Hill the choice between recall and resignation. McCann replaced Hill, while retaining his post as trade commissioner, and assumed the combined position on 21 September.

Throughout the 1930s McCann sought to promote South Australian products in Britain by improving quality, packaging, distribution and publicity. To this job he brought extensive knowledge of the production and marketing of perishable goods, sound judgement and indefatigable energy. In 1938 he was knighted. Apart from a brief visit to South Australia, he remained in England in World War II, again assisting government food supply authorities. In 1943 he became a member of the International Wool Secretariat, and later its chairman. In the post-war years 'Charlie' cordially received streams of South Australian visitors in London, many of them taking up his time with requests for social calls, garden parties, and advice on accommodation, employment and personal matters.

He helped Australian jockeys in the British racing industry, answered queries about horse-breeding and bloodstock, facilitated arrangements for migrants, and remitted detailed reports on trade prospects, marketing strategies and the condition of the State's produce on arrival. His advice, practical and to the point, was often reported to farmers in the South Australian *Chronicle*.

In 1950 McCann visited South Australia, and again crusaded at producers' meetings, speaking some seventy-five times. On his return to London he underwent an abdominal operation, his first experience of hospital, but died in office three months later of cancer, on 5 June 1951, after almost two decades of service as agent-general.

His greatest contribution had been as an export promoter. In the 1930s he had been an important advocate of international trade agreements: indeed their growth in the post-war years eventually reduced the scope for State promotion. He remained a key link in the economic relations between Australia and Britain. Combining vitality, hard experience, practical business expertise and many personal contacts, McCann was one of Australia's most effective representatives in London.

A Catholic, he had married Eileen Florence Hammond, a nurse from Strathalbyn, on 22 February 1909; they had a daughter and a son. His chief recreation was the racecourse.

PP (SA), 1908 (20); *Public Service Review* (SA), Feb 1909, Aug 1911, June 1914, Oct 1919; *Advertiser* (Adel), 4, 13, 16 June, 13, 16, 21 Aug 1934, 1 Jan 1938, 7, 8 June 1951; *Adel Stock and Station J*, 19 Apr 1950; *Chronicle* (Adel), and *The Times*, 7 June 1951; papers relating to Agent-General and Trade Commissioner (GRG 20/3, 20/6, 55, SAA).

ERIC RICHARDS
JOAN HANCOCK

McCANN, EDWARD JOHN (1888-1973), musician and radio executive, was born on 18 April 1888 in Hobart, son of James Robert McCann, musician, and his second wife Frances Amelia, née Revis, shopkeeper. Educated at Thomas Mitchell's and N. F. Mulhall's schools, Hobart, Ted became an apprentice jeweller with Taylor & Sharp and, rejected by the army as physically unfit, was involved from 1917 in the jewellers, Finlater & McCann.

His family was devoutly Catholic (one of his sisters became a nun) and overwhelmingly musical. His father, stepbrother, elder brother and five of his six younger brothers were musicians. McCann's father was born on 28 May 1854 in Hobart Town, son of James McCann, bricklayer, and his wife Mary Ann, née Mulhall, who, it is said, brought the musical gift into the family. After spending 1872-81 in Melbourne James established himself in Hobart as music teacher, accompanist, organist of St Mary's Cathedral and pianist with the Theatre Royal orchestra. He died on 28 October 1916. His son by his first wife Margaret Jane, née Keating, James Robert junior (1878-1938), was a Hobart music teacher and wartime conductor of the Hobart Symphony Orchestra.

Ted's elder brother ARTHUR FRANCIS (FRANK) (1887-1966), also a jeweller's apprentice, born in Hobart on 7 March 1887, was a silent-film pianist before forming and conducting His Majesty's Theatre orchestra. He succeeded his father as St Mary's Cathedral organist in 1916, spent 1925-35 in Sydney as organist and musical director at the Lyceum and State theatres, and returned to Hobart as official accompanist with the Australian Broadcasting Commission. For many years secretary and treasurer of the Tasmanian branch of the Professional Musicians' Union, he died on 29 October 1966.

By 1920 Ted was a violinist in Frank's orchestra. Soon afterwards he established and conducted the Vice-Regal Orchestra at the Prince of Wales Theatre, and later gave performances between film screenings when the 'talkies' threatened the group with extinction. In the late 1920s he moved his orchestra into radio, broadcasting the romantic 'Golden Hour' session from the Tasmanian Broadcasters Company's 7ZL. In 1931 McCann managed 7ZL for the Australian Broadcasting Co. and next year became controller of programmes under the company. From 1946 until his retirement in 1953 he was manager of the A.B.C. in Tasmania, apart from interludes in 1946 and 1947 when he was acting manager in South Australia and Queensland and assistant controller of programmes in Sydney. Hard-working, modest and enthusiastic, he was able at a pinch to combine the roles of manager, conductor, director and producer. One of his unusual broadcasts was that of the opera *Maritana* performed at the Bush Inn, New Norfolk, where Vincent Wallace [q.v.2] actually wrote the aria, 'Scenes that are Brightest'.

McCann undertook other local musical duties. Conductor of St Mary's Cathedral choir in 1915-22, he was eisteddfod adjudicator, organizer of the annual music week in the 1930s and president of the Musical Association in 1945-50. In retirement he continued his customary charitable work and acted as adviser to the radio station 7HT. He was appointed O.B.E. in 1962. He died at Lenah Valley on 18 July 1973, survived by his wife Kathleen Ila, née Tracey, whom he had married in St Mary's Cathedral on 11 September 1920, and by their son.

BERNARD ALOYSIUS (1892-1961), fourth son of James and Frances McCann, was born in Hobart on 26 October 1892. He began work as a bass player in Frank's orchestra and like Frank was secretary of the Musicians' Union. The family entrepreneur, he established McCann Bros' music warehouse about 1923 and in 1937 helped to found Metropolitan Broadcasters' 7HT of which he became chairman of directors. He took over the Theatre Royal when it was threatened with conversion into business premises and later sold it to the National Theatre and Fine Arts Society. He had mining interests, particularly at Mount Victoria and Black Bluff, was a city alderman in 1948-56 and a generous benefactor to the Catholic Church. He died in Hobart on 23 October 1961, survived by his wife Ethel Irene, née Sawford, whom he had married on 26 July 1945 at New Town, and by two sons. His estate was valued for probate at £232 255.

After Bernard's death his youngest brother Leonard Charles (1902-1974), a double-bass player, took over McCann Bros. Following family tradition, he was a life member of the Musicians' Union, organist at St Mary's and a director of 7HT.

Professional Musicians Union of Aust, *Tasinotes*, July 1974; *Mercury*, 30 Oct 1916, 1 July 1957, 24 Oct 1961, 31 Oct 1966, 20 July 1973, 22 May 1974; *Tas Mail*, 2 Nov 1916; NS 864/3 (TA).   TOM PICKERING

McCANN, PETER (1828-1908), builder, quarrymaster and cement manufacturer, and WESLEY BURRETT (1874-1961), cement manufacturer, were father and son. Peter was born on 18 September 1828 at Parramatta, New South Wales, son of Nicholas McCann (1803-1880), stonecutter, and his wife Catherine, née Johnson. His mother died in 1831 shortly after the family moved to Georgetown, Tasmania, and his baby sister Ann, adopted by a Launceston couple, was taken to England. About 1836 Peter accompanied his father to Port Fairy, Port Phillip District, helping him in whaling and squatting pursuits until 1841 when Nicholas moved to Geelong and returned to the building trade. In 1850 Peter, now in partnership with his father, went to England to bring back his sister and returned with a wife Elizabeth, née Begley, whom he had married on 26 September at the Wesleyan Methodist Chapel, Grantham, Lincolnshire. In 1854 he established home at Ceres in the Barrabool Hills where he and his father opened a sandstone quarry.

Peter became a member of the Ceres Roads Board and a justice of the peace. With his eldest son John Nicholas he opened a limestone deposit at Waurn Ponds and in

1888 purchased 1200 acres (486 ha) at Batesford, seeking to exploit the limestone deposit there, with clay from the flood plains of the Moorabool River, for the manufacture of Portland cement. He registered the Australian Portland Cement Co. Ltd in 1889 with Geelong and Melbourne builders as shareholders; Richard Taylor, an English-trained cementmaker, was appointed company secretary and a works was established at Fyansford.

The technology employed was based on six shaft kilns flued to a common stack; it was labour intensive, expensive and difficult to adapt to the local raw materials. Operation was spasmodic and, following reduced prices for imported cement, unprofitable. The company was liquidated in 1895, but McCann, indefatigable, immediately set up another company and after a second liquidation in 1904 next year formed the Australian Portland Cement Co. Pty Ltd. At his death on 19 June 1908 at Ceres he left an estate valued for probate at £16 166 and a viable company.

Wesley was born on 21 October 1874 at Ceres, the sixteenth and last child. Educated at Ceres State School and Geelong College, he joined Australian Portland Cement straight from school and became secretary-manager in 1905, remaining in this position when a further restructuring of the company in 1911 gave control to a group of investors led by T. J. Noske. Further changes saw the company floated on the stock exchange in 1925 as Australian Cement Ltd. In 1928, acting for several leading cement companies, it bought out the Tasmanian-based National Portland Cement; the following year, after an amalgamation with Kandos Cement Co. Ltd, New South Wales, a new parent company, Australian Portland Cement Co. Pty Ltd, was registered. McCann was chairman, and also general manager (managing director from 1946) of Australian Cement Ltd until shortly before his death.

'W.B.', like his father, was determined to persevere with a struggling organization. He supervised modernization of the plant, including installation of the company's first rotary kiln in 1912 and of a second, using the superior 'wet' process, in 1914. Horse-drawn transport of raw materials gave way to an aerial ropeway in 1912 and to a company railway in 1928. McCann continued his expansion and upgradings until in 1961 plant capacity stood at 500 000 tons a year compared with an output of 2000 tons in 1905.

McCann's other activities displayed his vitality. With interests in the pastoral and farming industries he was a councillor and a president of the Shire of Corio, president of the Geelong Chamber of Commerce and Manufactures, a director of the Chamber of Manufactures Insurance Co. and a council-

member of the Building Industry Congress (president, 1933). He served the Cement and Concrete Association as councillor and president, was a councillor of the Gordon Institute of Technology, and belonged to the Geelong and Melbourne Rotary clubs and the Barwon Heads Golf Club.

McCann died on 20 January 1961 at Geelong and was cremated. His wife Zeta, née Manchester, whom he had married at Coburg, Melbourne, on 5 July 1905 with Methodist forms, predeceased him by a few weeks. He was survived by two daughters and a son.

W. B. McCann, *History of the descendants of Peter McCann who landed in Australia in 1799* . . . (priv print, copy LaTL); A. Sutherland et al, *Victoria and its metropolis*, 2 (Melb, 1888); *Land and Transport*, 1 (Sept 1917), no 5, p 16; Inst of Engineers, Aust, *J*, 6, 1934, p 412; *Age*, 28 Sept 1946; *Geelong Advertiser*, 24 Jan 1961; W. B. McCann, History of Australian Cement Ltd (1927, Aust & Kandos Cement Holdings, Sth Melb, archives); VPRS 932, file 2376/1,18 3046/1,13,14 3936/1,4,13,17 (PRO, Vic).

PHILIP McKAY

McCANN, WILLIAM FRANCIS JAMES (1892-1957), soldier and lawyer, was born on 19 April 1892 at Glanville, Adelaide, son of John Francis McCann, engine driver, and his wife Eliza, née Francis. Educated at Adelaide High School, he qualified in 1913 as a teacher with the Education Department and was appointed to Ethelton Public School; he later taught at Malvern and Glanville.

McCann enlisted as a private in the 10th Battalion, Australian Imperial Force, on 24 August 1914 and, already a sergeant, embarked in October. On 25 April 1915 he landed at Gallipoli as a company sergeant major and because of outstanding service between 6 May and 28 June was mentioned several times in routine orders. On 4 August he was commissioned second lieutenant and was promoted lieutenant on 14 November. His early postings were in signals and intelligence.

As scouting, sniping and intelligence officer McCann accompanied the 10th Battalion to France and was promoted captain on 16 April 1916. He distinguished himself at Pozières on 23 July when commanding the battalion's leading company in the first stage of the attack; for his gallantry and leadership he was awarded the Military Cross. He was severely wounded in the head at Pozières and after convalescence in England rejoined his unit in mid-November. On 8 April 1917 he was wounded in the neck during a night attack on Louverval Wood; refusing for several hours to leave the line he was an inspiration to his men. He resumed duty at Ribemont in late May and from September had several postings which kept him away from the unit until June 1918. He was awarded a Bar to his Military Cross after action at Mont de Merris on the night of 29 July when he led one of the attacking companies with great dash in a daring operation. He received the Distinguished Service Order after, on 10 August at Crépey Wood, 'his courage and fine leadership prevented an important position falling into the hands of the enemy'. Crépey was 'under an inferno of enemy fire', but he directed his men with 'the greatest coolness and resource'.

On 23 September McCann was promoted temporary major and was confirmed in rank on 21 October; that day he was seconded to the School of Tactics, Camberley, England, and returned to the battalion as second-in-command on 7 December. From early January 1919 until the unit was disbanded in March, he was commanding officer. He was mentioned in Earl Haig's final dispatch that month and led the 3rd Brigade in the victory march through London on Anzac Day 1919. Returning to Australia in June he spent three months in Keswick Hospital, Adelaide, before his A.I.F. appointment ended on 8 September. Few members of the A.I.F. had risen from private to battalion commander. Two of McCann's brothers, one of whom was killed in action, had also served in the A.I.F.

McCann took up farming in the Truro and Manoora areas, but his war injuries proved too great a handicap. On 20 August 1921, giving his occupation as 'clerk', he married Mildred Southcott (d. 1948) at St John's Church, Adelaide. He became an articled clerk and entered the law school of the University of Adelaide in March 1922. Admitted to the Bar in 1925, he formed a partnership with A. S. Blackburn, V.C. [q.v.7]. McCann began soldiering again in 1927 as company commander in the 10th Battalion, Australian Military Forces, transferred to the 43rd Battalion that year and became its commanding officer in December with the rank of lieut-colonel. In 1930 he was placed on the unattached list and in 1935 on the reserve of officers. In 1939 he briefly became officer commanding the special constabulary of men over 45, South Australian Emergency National Defence League. He was appointed O.B.E. in 1935 and C.M.G. in 1956 for his activities on behalf of ex-servicemen. In 1938-54 he was State and deputy Commonwealth prices commissioner. He was State vice-president of the Returned Sailors' and Soldiers' Imperial League of Australia in 1921-23 and president in 1924-29, resigning to unsuccessfully contest as a Nationalist the seat of Boothby in the House of Representatives.

'Bill' McCann was an able speaker and a keen debater with a pleasant and tenacious personality. Survived by two sons and a daughter he died of coronary vascular disease at his Tusmore home on 14 December 1957 and was buried in North Road cemetery.

C. E. W. Bean, *The story of Anzac* (Syd, 1921, 1924), and *The A.I.F. in France*, 1916-18 (Syd, 1929, 1933, 1937, 1942); C. B. Lock, *The fighting 10th* (Adel, 1936); *Reveille* (Syd), Oct 1931; *News* (Adel), 19 Sept 1924; *Examiner* (Adel), 15 Sept 1928; *Bulletin* (Syd), 1 Jan 1958; War diary, 10th Battalion A.I.F., and records (AWM).

H. J. ZWILLENBERG

MacCARTHY, CHARLES WILLIAM (1848-1919), medical practitioner, was born on 31 March 1848 at Fethard, Tipperary, Ireland, son of John MacCarthy, merchant, and his wife Elizabeth, née Fitzgerald. He showed great musical ability as a child and was educated at the local National school and at Castleknock School near Dublin. After a wild and adventurous boyhood and youth, during which he excelled at most sports, he entered the Catholic University School of Medicine, Dublin.

In 1870 MacCarthy interrupted his studies to join an ambulance unit attached to a regiment of *franc-tireurs* in the Franco-Prussian War. After working as resident clinical assistant at the Mater Misericordiae Hospital, Dublin, he received the licentiate of the King and Queen's College of Physicians in Ireland in 1872. He practised briefly at Manchester, England, before returning to Fethard where he married Anastasia Theresa Cantwell on 24 September 1873. By 1877 he had moved to Clonmel, Tipperary, where he had an extensive practice. After his wife's death he married Marion Cuddihy, a contralto, in Dublin on 25 June 1881. In 1884 he graduated M.D. at the University of Brussels and was admitted a fellow of the Royal College of Surgeons in Ireland.

In poor health, MacCarthy migrated to Sydney late that year with his family and an introduction from the archbishop of Cashel to Cardinal Moran [q.v.]. He soon established a wide practice in Elizabeth Street, became an honorary physician and surgeon at St Vincent's Hospital and personal physician to Moran, and was known as 'a gentle and skilful surgeon'. In the 1890s he belonged to the Royal Society of New South Wales and investigated psychic phenomena.

Prominent in the Catholic and Irish communities, he was chairman of the '98 Centenary Celebration Committee and designed the monument erected over the grave of Michael Dwyer, 'the Wicklow Chief', self-exiled to Australia in 1805. An ardent constitutional Home Ruler and supporter of the Redmonds [qq.v.6], he was chairman of the New South

Wales Home Rule executive. He deplored the 1916 Easter rebellion.

MacCarthy had a natural talent for music, painting and sculpture. He composed several comic operas including *Lady Nora* which was staged at Her Majesty's Theatre, Sydney, wrote patriotic war-songs including 'The Toast is "Anzac!" Gentlemen', lectured and wrote on music and in 1912 helped to establish the Tom Moore concerts at which he was an accompanist. His paintings were mainly on religious themes; however, Sarah Bernhardt sat for him for a portrait as Cleopatra in 1891. Although entirely self-taught, he excelled as a sculptor: marble portrait-busts of violinist Mischa Elman, the statuette, 'Ils ne Passer-ont pas', embodying the spirit of France, and the bas-reliefs at the Waverley monument were among his best works. His life-size bust of Napoleon was exhibited in the 1915 Panama-Pacific International Exposition, San Francisco.

Charles MacCarthy, genial, ever-generous helper of the poor and friend of struggling artistic talent, died at his Elizabeth Street home on 7 June 1919 and, after a requiem Mass in St Mary's Cathedral, was buried in Waverley cemetery near the '98 memorial. He was survived by a son and daughter of his first marriage and by his wife and their daughter Maude, a celebrated violinist, who were both living in England.

E. Digby (ed), *Australian men of mark*, 2 (Syd, 1889); *Proceedings of the third A'sian Catholic Congress . . . 1909* (Syd, 1910); *MJA*, 28 June 1919; *Freeman's J* (Syd), 9 Apr, 28 May 1898, 2 Mar 1901, 12 June 1919; *SMH*, 8 Aug 1891, 29 Sept 1892, 9 June 1919, 28 Mar 1979; *A'sian*, 6 Mar 1915; *T&CJ*, 11 June 1919; *Bulletin*, 12 June 1919; G. M. Tobin, The sea-divided Gael: a study of the Irish Home Rule movement in Victoria and New South Wales, 1880-1916 (M.A. thesis, ANU, 1970).   G. P. WALSH

McCARTHY, DAME EMMA MAUD (1859-1949), nursing sister and army matron-in-chief, was born on 22 September 1859 at Paddington, Sydney, eldest child of William Frederick McCarthy, solicitor, and his Sydney-born wife Emma Mary, née à Beckett, niece of Sir William and Thomas Turner à Beckett [q.v.3]. Maud was educated at a school run by Lady Murray, wife of Sir Terence Murray [q.v.2], known as Springfield College, Sydney, and passed with honours the University of Sydney's senior examination. After her father's death in 1881 she helped her mother to rear her brothers and sisters.

By 1891 she was in England and on 10 October, giving her previous occupation as 'companion' and her age as 28, she entered London Hospital, Whitechapel, to begin general nursing training as a probationer.

Hospital records state that 'she had an exceptionally nice disposition' and was 'most lady-like and interested in her work' though 'she found it hard to control others, or to take firm action when necessary'. She was promoted sister in January 1894.

Maud McCarthy was sister-in-charge of Sophia women's ward at the outbreak of the South African War and was one of the six sisters selected from London Hospital by Princess Alexandra to go to South Africa as her own 'military' nursing sisters. Resigning from the hospital on 25 December 1899, McCarthy served with distinction throughout 1899-1902 with the Army Nursing Service Reserve, receiving the Queen's and the King's Medal and the Royal Red Cross. Returning to England in July 1902, she was awarded a special decoration by Queen Alexandra. She then became involved in the formation of Queen Alexandra's Imperial Military Nursing Service, was promoted matron within the service in February 1903 and during the next seven years was successively matron of Aldershot, Netley and Millbank military hospitals. In 1910 she was appointed principal matron at the War Office, a position she held until the outbreak of World War I.

Matron McCarthy sailed in the first ship to leave England with members of the British Expeditionary Force, arriving in France on 12 August 1914. In 1915 she was installed at Abbeville as matron-in-chief of the B.E.F. in France and Flanders, taking charge of the whole area from the Channel to the Mediterranean, wherever British and allied nurses worked; she was directly responsible to General Headquarters. In August 1914 the numbers in her charge were 516; by the time of the Armistice they were over 6000. She was responsible for the nursing of hundreds of thousands of casualties in the years 1914-18. An indefatigable leader and administrator, she visited field units, casualty clearing stations, hospital trains, hospital ships and stationary and general hospitals. The constant shortage of trained nurses, continual postings of staff, and personnel requirements of individuals were handled with tact and skill. She was the only head of a department in the B.E.F. who remained in her original post throughout the war, although she was off duty with appendicitis in March-August 1917. She was appointed G.B.E. in 1918, received a Bar to her Royal Red Cross and was awarded the Florence Nightingale Medal, the Belgian Medaille de la Reine Elizabeth, and the French Légion d'honneur and Medaille des Epidémies. When she left France on 5 August 1919, representatives from the French government and the medical services saw her off. The meticulous records kept since her arrival in France were taken to England with her.

Describing the matron-in-chief during the

war, one general said: 'She's perfectly splendid, she's wonderful . . . she's a soldier!. . . If she was made Quartermaster-General, she'd work it, she'd run the whole Army, and she'd never get flustered, never make a mistake. The woman's a genius'. A contributor to the *Sydney Morning Herald* in 1914 referred to her as a 'slight, delicately-organised woman' with 'an absolutely wonderful gift for concentrated work, and a power of organisation that has made her invaluable in army hospital work'.

She was matron-in-chief, Territorial Army Nursing Service, from 1920 until her retirement in 1925. Dame Maud McCarthy died at her home at Chelsea, London, on 1 April 1949. A pastel portrait by Austin Spare is in the Imperial War Museum.

J. Piggott, *Queen Alexandra's Royal Army Nursing Corps* (Lond, 1975); *SMH*, 16 Dec 1914; personal record of E. M. McCarthy (London Hospital, Whitechapel, Lond); personal information.

PERDITTA M. McCARTHY

McCARTHY, LAWRENCE DOMINIC (1892?-1975), named at birth Florence Joseph, soldier, commercial traveller and building superintendent, was born probably on 21 January 1892 at York, Western Australia, son of Florence McCarthy of Cork, Ireland, and his wife Anne, née Sherry. His parents died when he was very young and he was brought up in Clontarf Orphanage, Perth, and educated in Catholic schools.

McCarthy was working as a contractor when he enlisted in the Australian Imperial Force on 16 October 1914; he was posted as a private to the 16th Battalion and sailed for Egypt in December. On 26 April 1915 'Fat'—the appropriate and affectionate nickname earned by his 'ample frame'—landed at Gallipoli with 'C' Company. Appointed lance corporal on 13 May, he was promoted corporal on 19 July and sergeant on 1 September. That month he was evacuated because of illness, returning to duty in November. On 20 December he left Gallipoli with the last party of his battalion.

The 16th Battalion reached France in June 1916 and took part in heavy fighting around Pozières and Mouquet Farm in August. On 8 March 1917 McCarthy was appointed company sergeant major and on 10 April was commissioned second lieutenant. Next day he was wounded at Bullecourt and evacuated to England, rejoining his unit on 9 July. A lieutenant from 1 November, he received the French Croix de Guerre at Beaumetz two days later. From 31 January 1918 he was posted to the 13th Training Battalion, Tidworth, England, returning to the 16th in time for the offensive of 8 August.

Near Madam Wood, east of Vermandovillers, France, on 23 August McCarthy performed what the official war historian rated as 'perhaps the most effective feat of individual fighting in the history of the A.I.F., next to Jacka's [q.v.9] at Pozières'. The 16th Battalion, with McCarthy commanding 'D' Company, had attained its objectives but the battalion on the left was unable to make headway. Accompanied by Sergeant F. J. Robbins, D.C.M., M.M., McCarthy attacked the German machine-gun posts which were preventing its advance. They raced into the enemy trench system, shooting and bombing as they went, destroying three machine-gun positions. When his mate fell wounded, McCarthy pressed on, picking up German bombs as he continued to fight down the trench 'inflicting heavy casualties'. Coming upon another enemy pocket, he shot two officers and bombed the post until a blood-stained handkerchief signalled the surrender of the forty occupants.

This feat of bravery, which resulted in the award of the Victoria Cross, had an extraordinary conclusion. As the battalion historian records, 'the prisoners closed in on him from all sides . . . and patted him on the back!' In twenty minutes he had killed twenty Germans, taken fifty prisoners and seized 500 yards (460 m) of the German front. This jovial hero believed that there was 'a V.C. in everybody if given a chance'.

On 21 November 1918 McCarthy was again evacuated, ill, to England. He returned home on 20 December 1919 and his A.I.F. appointment ended on 6 August 1920. In England, on 25 January 1919, he had married Florence (Flossie) Minnie Norville, at Weston-super-Mare, Somerset. Their only child Lawrence Norville was killed in action on Bougainville in 1945.

'Mac' moved from Western Australia to Victoria in 1926 where he joined the staff of the Sunshine Harvester Works. He remained with the company, mostly as a traveller in the Mallee, until the Depression forced staff reductions in 1934. From 1935 until his retirement in 1969 he was superintendent of the Trustees, Executors & Agency Co. Ltd building, Melbourne.

He attended the V.C. centenary celebrations in London in 1956 and was present at the opening of V.C. Corner at the Australian War Memorial, Canberra, in 1964. A most popular, generous and unassuming man, he took a keen interest in community affairs.

Laurie McCarthy died at Heidelberg Repatriation Hospital, Melbourne, on 25 May 1975 and was cremated with full military honours. He was survived by his wife who donated his V.C. and medals to the Australian

War Memorial, which also holds his portrait by Charles Wheeler [q.v.].

C. E. W. Bean, *The A.I.F. in France*, 1918 (Syd, 1942); C. Longmore, *The old Sixteenth* (Perth, 1929); L. Wigmore (ed), *They dared mightily*(Canb, 1963); *Reveille* (Syd), Jan, Mar 1931; *Freeman's J* (Syd), 26 July 1917; *Herald* (Melb), 26 May 1975; War diary, 16th Battalion A.I.F. (AWM); information from Mrs F. McCarthy, Melb.   W. H. CONNELL

McCASH, JOHN McDONALD (1897-1962), soldier and railwayman, was born on 12 February 1897 at Pitlochry, Perthshire, Scotland, son of James McCash, vanman, and his wife Isabella, née McDonald. A sailor in his youth, he enlisted in the 22nd Battalion, Australian Imperial Force, in Melbourne on his eighteenth birthday. On 10 May 1915 Private McCash embarked with 'D' Company for Gallipoli where he served from 5 September until the evacuation.

On 22 July 1916 McCash transferred to the 60th Battalion at Rouge de Bout in the Armentières sector, France. He rose rapidly through the ranks, being promoted lance corporal on 8 August, corporal on 28 August, sergeant on 25 October and company sergeant major on 22 February 1917. He was brought to the notice of his corps commander for gallant conduct during the 2nd battle of Bullecourt.

Back in Britain, McCash joined the 15th Training Battalion in August 1917 and the 14th Training Battalion in April 1918 before returning to the 60th Battalion on 3 May. He was wounded in action but remained on duty on 18 June near Méricourt. During the battle of 8 August his conspicuous gallantry and devotion to duty led to the award of the Distinguished Conduct Medal and Bar when, in charge of two platoons, he assisted his company commander in the early advance through fog. Next day at Harbonnières he organized the advance of the right half-company under heavy fire and enabled it to proceed; then, at Péronne on 2 September, by his coolness and good judgement under heavy fire, many casualties were avoided.

Transferred to the 59th Battalion on 25 September, McCash took part in operations against the Hindenburg line. He embarked for Australia in May 1919 and was discharged from the A.I.F. in Melbourne in August. On 22 November, describing himself as a railway conductor, he married Doris Elizabeth Malmsbury Jarvie at St Michael's Anglican Church, North Carlton; they had two daughters. In the inter-war period he remained in Melbourne, living at East Malvern, North Carlton and Albert Park—pursuing a career as a traffic officer. During World War II he served again, as a lieutenant in the Australian

Army Employment Service from December 1942 and transferring to the Australian Army Labour Service in July 1944. He was placed on the retired list from the 8th Australian Employment Company in February 1945 and returned to his Albert Park home and his civilian career. In the 1950s he was a commissionaire and market inspector.

Survived by his wife and daughters, McCash died of coronary occlusion at the Repatriation General Hospital, Heidelberg, on 21 July 1962 and was cremated. Although about 1754 D.C.M.s were awarded to Australians in World War I, McCash was one of only 27 who were awarded the D.C.M. and Bar.

M. S. C. Smith, *Australian campaigns in the Great War*(Lond, 1919); A. D. Ellis, *The story of the Australian Fifth Division* (Lond, 1920); *London Gazette*, 5 Dec 1918, 1 Jan 1919; *Sun-News Pictorial*, 23, 24 July 1962; War diary, 22nd, 59th and 60th battalions, AIF (AWM).
                                    W. M. CHAMBERLAIN

McCATHIE, HARRIETTE ADELAIDE (1842?-1912), retailer, was born in Dublin, daughter of Mr Colgan, landed proprietor, and his wife Alicia. In Dublin she probably married a Mr Seybourne and bore him two children. In 1863 she married Christopher Bailey (d. 1906); they migrated to New Zealand arriving at Auckland in the *Ganges* on 12 October. He farmed near Auckland where their son, the actor Albert Edward (Bert) Bailey [q.v.7] was born in 1868. By 1871 Harriette was living in Sydney. Divorced by Bailey, she married a Scottish accountant David Henderson McCathie on 11 September 1879 at the Redfern Registry Office. McCathie worked for John Vicars [q.v.6], tweed manufacturer, and died on 13 October 1882, survived by their three children and leaving an estate valued for probate at £400.

Next year Mrs McCathie bought a house at Ashfield, where the family remained for some ten years. After working as a milliner at Farmer [q.v.4] & Co. Ltd, in September 1886 she obtained a mortgage, probably using the money to found her business—by 1888 Mrs McCathie's Hat Shop, in King Street, Sydney, was a substantial concern.

Of medium height and build, with dark hair pulled back austerely from her stern face with its hooked nose, this astute and hard-working woman built up a thriving retail outlet. She possessed considerable fashion flair (she reputedly always wore a bonnet) and shrewd judgement on matters of business and investment. In the 1890s the stock lines were increased from millinery alone to women's clothing, necessitating several extensions to the premises. When no further alterations could be accommodated, the store, now a general drapery as well as ladies' outfitter, was relocated in 1905 in spacious premises in Pitt Street, next to the Strand Arcade. Mrs McCathie Ltd was registered as a limited company on 13 July that year. She retired from active participation in the firm; however, the carefully worded memorandum of the company and her share-ownership ensured her continued power, if not control.

The company after 1905 was headed by her son David McCathie and son-in-law Ernest Edward Brown. Mrs McCathie lived in a separate residence on the Browns' estate, The Highlands, at Gordon. She was remembered by a descendant as being 'a very severe grandmother'.

Mrs McCathie died on 11 April 1912 at St Kilda, Melbourne, while on a visit to her daughter Florence Manisty; she was buried in the Presbyterian section of Gore Hill cemetery, Sydney, her grave bearing the simple inscription 'Our Mother'. The Pitt Street emporium, 'the busiest shop in Sydney', was draped in crêpe and closed for trading. Her estate was valued for probate at over £50 000. Alone and without means, she had achieved financial and social success for herself and her children in a climate ungenerous to women.

SMH, 14 Oct 1882, 13, 15 Apr 1912; *Evening News* (Syd), and *Sun* (Syd), 12 Apr 1912; *Daily Telegraph*, 13, 15 Apr 1912.

JENNIFER MACCULLOCH

McCAWLEY, THOMAS WILLIAM (1881-1925), public servant and chief justice, was born on 24 July 1881 at Toowoomba, Queensland, sixth of eight children of Irish-born James McCawley, drover, and his wife Mary, née Stenner, from Prussia. Educated at the Sisters of Mercy's Hibernian Hall and at a state school, at 14 he became a clerk with the local solicitors, Hamilton & Wonderley. He also studied shorthand at the technical college. In 1898 he joined the Queensland Government Savings Bank, Brisbane, as a clerk on probation and was promoted to positions with the Public Service Board in 1899 and the Department of Justice in 1900. After hours he studied law and followed the Toowong Football and Viking Cricket clubs.

McCawley worked with the attorney-general (Sir) James Blair [q.v.7] on several important, successful appeals by the Crown, and with Blair and Thomas Macleod [q.v.] published *The Workers' Compensation Act of 1905*. From May 1907 he was joint editor, with Macleod, of *The Queensland Justice of the Peace and Local Authorities' Journal*, a monthly publication. Admitted to the Bar on 7 May 1907, he was appointed first clerk of the Justice Department and certifying barrister, and admitted to the professional division of the public service. He then acted as master of titles and as legal adviser to the stamp commissioner (1908), and was confirmed as crown solicitor in November 1910 after six months acting. It was a controversial appointment, made by Attorney-General T. O'Sullivan [q.v.].

The Labor victory in 1915 added to the considerable volume of crown business. McCawley's advice was sought in many successful appeals. He instructed T. J. Ryan [q.v.] before the Privy Council in the so-called Eastern case and before the High Court of Australia in the stock embargo case. He played a key role in drafting the government's industrial arbitration and workers' compensation bills, and prepared a comprehensive memorandum on workers' compensation and insurance. He had also revised W. G. Cahill's [q.v.7] *The policeman's manual—Royal Irish Constabulary* (Brisbane, 1913). In 1915 he was rewarded by the dual appointment of under secretary for justice and crown solicitor. He was also a member of the Workers' Dwellings Board.

Objections were raised in vain—on political grounds and his lack of experience as a barrister—against McCawley's appointments in January 1917 as first president of the Queensland Court of Industrial Arbitration (from January) and puisne judge of the Supreme Court of Queensland (from October). The Supreme and High courts held that his appointment to the Supreme Court was invalid, but the Privy Council upheld it. McCawley took his place on the bench in May 1920. Subsequently, on 1 April 1922, while retaining his position with the arbitration court, he became the youngest chief justice in the British Empire.

McCawley's most significant contribution as a judge was in the field of industrial law and industrial relations. He knew precisely the aims and intentions of the government. As president of the arbitration court he knew that his function was not merely to conciliate and arbitrate but was also in part legislative in so far as it involved determining—and improving—wages and conditions of workers. He had read the Fabian tracts and was familiar with the work of Mr Justice H. B. Higgins [q.v.9]. During his presidency of the court, unions were granted preference, thus allowing them to be brought in as a fundamental part of industrial law which in turn led to a rapid increase in their membership.

Several significant decisions readjusting wages for workers were handed down by McCawley. In 1917, for the first time, he framed an award for all railway employees; he was responsible for consolidating award wages in many industries. In 1921, again for the first time, he fixed a minimum wage for the State after a review of the methods of wage-fixing throughout Australia: the minimum wage was fixed on the basis of what industries of average prosperity could afford to pay. At the time of his death, he was working on a redetermination of the basic wage with the object of freeing a married man with a family from economic disability or inequality. He also hoped that a uniform system of industrial arbitration to avoid disputes between the States and the Commonwealth could be established.

McCawley published several pamphlets and articles on industrial arbitration as well as a pamphlet on criminal punishment and a short book, *Industrial arbitration* (1924). He also left unpublished fragments, including the beginnings of what was designed to be a critical study of 'industrial arbitration, its success and failure'. Notes containing a plan for a biography of Sir Samuel Griffith [q.v.9], whom he revered, are among his papers.

A member of the Senate of the University of Queensland from 1919, McCawley advocated the study of Australian literature and economics and encouraged industry and the public service to employ graduates as a way of raising standards. He supported establishment of a law school and took an active part in the formation of the local economic society. He belonged to various Brisbane clubs, including the Royal Queensland Golf Club.

McCawley was described as virile and athletic, as a man of wide culture with a genial and entertaining personality. He died suddenly of coronary vascular disease on 16 April 1925 at Roma Street railway station, Brisbane, survived by his wife Margaret Mary, née O'Hagan, whom he had married at St Stephen's Cathedral on 29 November 1911, and by four sons and a daughter. A staunch Catholic, he was given a state funeral at St Stephen's Cathedral before the burial at Toowong cemetery. Parliament was asked to provide for the education of his children and the *Brisbane Courier* launched an appeal for his family. On 13 December 1927 a bronze bust of McCawley was unveiled at the Board of Trade and Arbitration, Brisbane.

D. J. Murphy, *T.J. Ryan* (Brisb, 1975); R. Johnston, *History of the Queensland Bar* (Brisb, 1979); *Qld State Reports*, 1917, p 62; *Univ Qld Law J*, 9 (1976), no 2, p 224; *Brisbane Courier*, 9, 23 Mar, 6 Apr, 23 Aug 1918, 17, 22 Apr 1925; *Daily Mail* (Brisb), 27 Apr 1918; *Punch* (Melb), 26 Jan 1922; *Daily Standard*, 16, 17 Apr 1925; *SMH*, 17, 18, 22 Apr, 7 May 1925, 13 Dec 1927; M. Cope, A study of Labour government and the law in Queensland, 1915-1922 (B.A. Hons thesis, Univ Qld, 1972).

MALCOLM COPE

McCAY, ADAM CAIRNS (1874-1947) and **DELAMORE WILLIAM** (1877-1958), journalists, were born on 27 December 1874 and 8 January 1877 at Castlemaine, Victoria, fifth and sixth sons of Rev. Andrew Ross Boyd McCay, Presbyterian minister, and his wife Lily Ann Esther Waring, née Brown. They were educated at Castlemaine Grammar School where Adam, after graduating from the University of Melbourne (B.A., 1894; M.A., 1896), succeeded his eldest brother (Sir) James Whiteside McCay [q.v.] as principal. He married Edina May Malcolm at Castlemaine on 12 May 1899. On completing school Delamore worked for twelve years as an accountant and married Frances Eva Macpherson at Port Fairy on 18 June 1911.

Both brothers, who like others in their family had a love of literature and a talent for writing verse, frequently contributed to weekly papers. In 1903 Adam joined the Melbourne *Argus*, as a crime reporter, to be followed by Delamore in 1906. In the column 'The Passing Show' Adam, as 'Oriel', wrote satirical paragraphs and topical verse and in 1907-12 leading articles. Delamore reported the inauguration ceremonies of the Union of South Africa in 1910.

In 1912 Monty Grover [q.v.9] recruited Adam and Delamore McCay to work on (Sir) Hugh Denison's [q.v.8] Sydney daily *Sun*. As the first 'Peter Persnerkus', an identity later assumed by Delamore, Adam wrote its satirical column 'The Moving Picture Show' and leading articles distinguished by their polish, clarity, brevity and 'punch'. As 'Hugh Kalyptus' he wrote on various subjects with the 'brilliant literary grace that distinguishes the natural-born journalist from the tailor-made reporter'. Adam was appointed editor of the *Sun* in 1916, while Delamore, news editor from 1915, was associate editor in 1917-19.

After touring eastern Asia and the United States of America in 1919, Adam McCay became literary editor of the new *Smith's Weekly* while Delamore succeeded him as editor of the *Sun*. Adam spearheaded *Smith's* attack in 1920 on the by then ineffectual premier, W. A. Holman [q.v.9], who subsequently lost office and his seat.

Adam McCay continued, as he said, 'bucketing about', serving as editor of the *Sunday Times* in 1920-23 and of the *Daily Guardian*, 1924-27. After a brief spell with *Truth*, he rejoined the *Guardian* until Sir Joynton Smith [q.v.] sold it in 1930, when he returned to *Smith's*. Rejoining the *Sun* in 1933, he was transferred to the *Daily Telegraph* as associate editor and leader-writer until it was taken over by Consolidated Press Ltd in 1936. He returned to the *Sun*, retiring in August 1940.

It was a turbulent career. Adam's satirical

pen provoked politicians and fellow writers alike. Goaded by leading articles in the *Sun*, J. T. Lang [q.v.9] asked in the Legislative Assembly on 14 March 1916 whether it was true that Adam had been dismissed from the *Argus* for 'an attempt to blackmail members of Federal Parliament'. When a denial from the *Argus* was ignored by the premier, Holman, the Australian Journalists' Association, of which McCay was a member, expressed 'disgust and indignation' at the 'slanderous attack'. Next year Adam retaliated by revealing Holman as author of a damaging memorandum advocating unfair methods of recruitment. In 1927 Adam's scathing comments about newspaper personalities, made during a private conversation and exaggerated in the *Sunday Times*, led to his dismissal and a public apology to Joynton Smith. Scepticism may have hardened into cynicism. Norman Lindsay [q.v.], bitter about Adam's tendency to 'make a joke of all serious values', described him as 'one of the five worst men in Australia'.

Delamore's career was more conventional. He served as London manager and editor of the Sun-Herald Cable Service in 1921-24, returning as editor of the *Sun* in March 1924. Appointed editor-in-chief of Associated Newspapers Ltd in 1934, next year he led the Australian delegation to the Imperial Press Conference in South Africa. From 1937 he was London representative of the *Sydney Morning Herald*, returning to Australia in 1939 to become secretary of the Australian Newspaper Proprietors' Association (1939-48), and of the Australian Newspapers' Council until he retired in 1950.

Both brothers earned reputations as outstanding journalists. Kenneth Slessor considered Adam 'the greatest of all Australian newspapermen' of his time. He was widely respected for his wit, versatility, editorial skills and command of six languages; his facility with words enabled him to turn out vast amounts of high-quality prose and verse. Delamore was recognized for his political commentaries and editorials as well as for his verse, marked by 'delicacy of perception' and 'incisive wit'.

The bespectacled and conventional appearance of the brothers belied their strong, aggressive and colourful personalities. Only Adam's humorous mouth and the gleam in his eyes behind his glasses suggested his gifts as a prankster, raconteur, bon vivant, composer of bawdy verse and originator of extravagant escapades. While working at *Smith's Weekly* he 'held court' at the Assembly pub next door where, according to Douglas Stewart, 'anything could happen and, very often, did'. He argued the classics with and gave money to Christopher Brennan [q.v.7]; he was celebrated in Slessor's poem 'To a Friend'. The

Sun referred to him as 'the last of the Bohemians' and on his death recorded that the 'man who loved life' had died. From childhood he was known as 'Dum', a contraction of Lewis Carroll's aggressive Tweedledum. Delamore ('Del') too was remembered by a colleague as 'an explosive personality' with 'an inexhaustible fund of quite original expletives'.

As flamboyant in his personal as in his professional life, Adam McCay was divorced by his first wife for adultery in 1916. He married the co-respondent Violet Mary, née Watson, with Presbyterian forms at St Stephen's, Phillip Street, on 1 June 1916. Although reputed in 1919 to be the highest-paid journalist in the Southern Hemisphere, he over-committed himself in purchasing a large property at Randwick; forced to sell at a heavy loss in 1923, he lived with his second wife in boarding-houses until he left her in 1924 for Maideau Elizabeth Françoise Stokes, daughter of F. J. Broomfield [q.v.7]. In 1930 Adam McCay declared himself penniless and in debt. Divorced again in 1927, he married Maideau, now divorced, on 22 October 1930 at Mosman. Much loved by the McCay family, she sought, before her death in 1935, to temper Adam's alcoholism and bring some financial order into his life. In retirement he contributed articles and reviews to the *Bulletin* and other periodicals. He died at Camden on 31 August 1947, survived by a son of each of his first two marriages, and was buried in the Presbyterian section of Northern Suburbs cemetery.

Delamore McCay retired to Casterton, Victoria, where he died on 19 May 1958 and was buried with Anglican rites. His wife and four daughters survived him.

Four brothers, as well as James Whiteside, were notable: Campbell Ernest (1867-1943), who published verse, was W. L. Baillieu's [q.v.7] private secretary and later worked for the Melbourne City Council; Hugh Douglas (1870-1953), deputy master of the Royal Mint both in Melbourne and London; Andrew Ross (1873-1958), senior officer in Tasmania of the Bank of Australasia; and Walton (1879-1963), chairman of the Rural Bank and director of land settlement in Western Australia.

Sun Newspapers Ltd, *The Sun, 1910-1929* (Syd, 1929); J. T. Lang, *I remember* (Syd, 1956); G. Blaikie, *Remember Smith's Weekly?* (Adel, 1966); K. Slessor, *Bread and wine* (Syd, 1970), and *Selected poems* (Syd, 1975); D. Stewart, *A man of Sydney* (Melb, 1977); *Aust Literary Studies*, 2, no 3, Oct 1984; *Journalist*, July 1916, Aug, Dec 1919, Nov 1947; *Associated Newspapers Ltd*, Sept 1940; *Newspaper News*, 2 Sept 1940, 1 Sept 1947; *VHM*, 31, no 1 (1960); *Punch* (Melb), Nov 1920; *Smith's Weekly* (Syd), 25 June 1921, 7 May 1927; *Daily Guardian* (Syd), 24 May 1927; *Bulletin*, 16 Sept 1931, 3 Sept 1947; *SMH*, 28 Jan, 7, 11 Feb 1935,

17 Feb, 25 May 1937, 20 May 1958; *Argus, Sun*
(Syd), and *Daily Telegraph* (Syd), 1 Sept 1947; *Age*,
20 May 1958; Deakin *and* O'Malley papers (NL);
information from Mr H. Grover, Blairgowrie, Vic,
and Mrs J. Smythe, Downer, ACT.

DIANE LANGMORE

McCAY, SIR JAMES WHITESIDE (1864-
1930), soldier, politician and lawyer, was born
on 21 December 1864 at Ballynure, Antrim,
Ireland, eldest of ten children of Rev. Andrew
Ross Boyd McCay (1837-1915), Presbyterian
minister, and his wife Lily Ann Esther
Waring, née Brown. Adam Cairns and Delamore William McCay [qq.v] were brothers.
The family pronounced the name to rhyme
with sky; for much of his life James signed
himself M'Cay. After migrating to Victoria in
1865, Boyd McCay accepted a call to Castlemaine where he remained minister for
twenty-five years. He taught church history
to theological students, graduated M.A. at the
University of Melbourne in 1882 and had an
Irish D.D. conferred on him in 1887. Esther
McCay 'spoke seven languages fluently'.

James attended Castlemaine State School
and when 12 won a scholarship to Scotch College, Melbourne. He passed the matriculation
examination next year and was dux of the
school in 1880 when at the public examinations he won the classics and shared the
mathematics exhibition with J. H. Michell
[q.v]. He entered Ormond [q.v.5] College,
University of Melbourne, and in 1881 and
1882 took exhibitions in classics, logic and
English, with second-class honours both
years. In 1883 he interrupted his course in
order to teach privately and at Toorak Grammar School. He learned to read French, Italian and Spanish.

In 1885 McCay bought the Castlemaine
Grammar School. As its principal he made a
reputation as a good teacher, a firm disciplinarian who birched freely and, influenced by
his mother who taught at the school, a supporter of higher education for women. McCay
was tall with a wilting moustache and was
generally referred to as Jim. In 1892 he completed his degree, concentrating on mathematics (M.A., 1894). He won two exhibitions
in law in 1893 and in February 1895 finished
with first-class honours and the Supreme
Court prize (LL.M., 1897). Still teaching at
Castlemaine, he reputedly had not attended a
single lecture. He put up his shingle as a solicitor in Barker Street and installed the first
telephone in the town. On 8 April 1896 he
married Julia Mary O'Meara, daughter of the
Catholic police magistrate at Kyneton; they
had two daughters.

On 29 October 1886 McCay had been commissioned in the 4th Battalion, Victorian
Rifles, and was promoted captain in 1889,

major in 1896 and lieut-colonel in 1900. A
practical soldier, he did not encourage practice of 'pretty parade-ground movements' or
adoption of 'gold-lace' uniforms.

He was a member of the Castlemaine Borough Council in 1890-93, president of the
mechanics' institute and treasurer of the
school of mines. He became something of a
'political boss' of the radical faction opposing
the sitting parliamentarian (Sir) James Patterson [q.v.5]. When Patterson died in 1895,
McCay won the November by-election by ten
votes. He had declared himself a collectivist
rather than an individualist, in support of (Sir)
George Turner's [q.v.] Liberal government.
His radical tendencies soon withered and with
other bright young Liberals he was prominent
in the intrigue which led to Turner's defeat by
Allan McLean [q.v.] on 5 December 1899.
McCay described Turner's as 'a Government
that cannot be followed because it does not
lead'. He was appointed to the ministry, but
was defeated in the ministerial election at
Castlemaine by the young football hero (Sir)
Harry Lawson [q.v.], one of his former pupils
who eventually became a staunch friend.
McCay's questioning of the wisdom of sending a Victorian contingent to the South African War—for surely England did not need
assistance—cost him votes. At the elections
in November 1900 he could not even win the
second seat.

McCay had worked for Federation and in
March 1901, as a protectionist supporter of
(Sir) Edmund Barton [q.v.7], won the Federal
seat of Corinella; he was unopposed in 1903.
He made his mark in parliament by hard work,
but cutting and satirically witty remarks
about fellow members reduced his popularity,
which he always scorned to seek. Hungry for
office, he harried the Watson [q.v.] Labor government of 1904, carrying a vital amendment
to its arbitration bill which eventually led to
Watson's resignation. He became minister for
defence from 18 August to 5 July 1905 in the
Reid [q.v.]-McLean ministry. McCay had
earned a reputation as a defence specialist,
especially in modifying Major General Hutton's [q.v.9] reform proposals in the Defence
Act of 1903. He entirely supported Hutton's
basic plans for a citizen soldiery (though not
for their service overseas) but represented a
moderate nationalist consensus (supported by
Labor) in eliminating many of Hutton's proposals regarded as militarist, Imperialist or
extravagant. As minister, he was capable,
cool and lucid. Amendments to the Defence
Act late in 1904, without consultation with
Westminster, led to establishment of a Council of Defence and military and naval boards
with strong civil representation, confirming
ministerial control of defence policy. At the
first meeting of the Council of Defence,
McCay brusquely rejected recommendations

for naval expansion in preference to military.

In 1906 McCay's electorate was eliminated and, unwisely choosing to stand in Corio against R. A. Crouch [q.v.8], he was soundly defeated. Disillusioned with politics, he stood only once more, for the Senate in 1910, and was swept away in the Labor landslide, though he could still stir Labor supporters to fury. About 1900 McCay had taken William Thwaites into legal partnership; about 1905 they opened a Melbourne office. He turned to further self-education as a soldier. As minister he had supported Lieut-Colonel (Sir) William Bridges's [q.v.7] pleas for additional staff for the Intelligence Department. On Bridges's recommendation McCay was appointed on 6 December 1907 to command the new Australian Intelligence Corps, a militia body, and promoted colonel. Because of alleged abrasiveness of personality, the appointment was not widely welcomed. Recognition of the total inadequacy of national mapping speeded development, and research on conditions in neighbouring countries and on local transport proceeded. McCay worked closely with his commandant in Victoria (Sir) John Monash [q.v.]. The corps was infiltrating into staff work and McCay was irritating his permanent-officer superiors. In 1911 he lectured on 'The true principles of Australia's defence' (published in the *Commonwealth Military Journal*). By 1912 he was on bad terms with the Military Board and the corps was removed from militia control; his appointment was terminated on 31 March 1913. He had taken a prolonged trip to Europe.

On the outbreak of war McCay was immediately given charge of censorship, diligently applying the prepared plan, establishing district offices in the capital cities. However, on 15 August 1914 he was appointed to command the 2nd Infantry Brigade, Australian Imperial Force. At a function in his honour he surprised many by asserting that 'This titanic struggle cannot end early, nor easily'. The first contingent reached Egypt early in December. McCay trained his command exhaustingly, 'drawing his own orders, and sometimes training his own platoons', and became unpopular as a martinet. According to the 5th Battalion historian, after some playing-up on New Years Eve he paraded the brigade and let loose 'a torrent of invective [which] deeply wounded the decent-minded men who were in the majority'. He had brushes with Major General Bridges who considered relieving McCay of his command because of his 'tendency to regard all orders from the point of view of the lawyer and to argue about them'. But Bridges became more than satisfied.

Bridges chose the 2nd Brigade to follow close behind Colonel Sinclair-MacLagan's [q.v.] 3rd Brigade in the landing at Gallipoli on 25 April. The 2nd was intended to extend left to the north, but the misjudged landing led to utter confusion. Soon after McCay landed about 6 a.m., he found MacLagan and accepted his request, although MacLagan was his junior and it was against orders, to come in on the right where for the next few days the brigade concentrated on 400 Plateau. In those first hours McCay was shot twice through his cap and once through his sleeve. By midday he had made contact with three of his four battalions, many of whose men, however, had pushed on out of control. Bridges ordered digging in on Second Ridge but by late afternoon a dangerous gap at Lone Pine was evident: McCay requested support from the last reserve battalion, Bridges agreed and the position was held. McCay was not consulted that night about possible evacuation and later said he would have opposed it. The brigade lost half its strength in the first two days, and was relieved on the 29th and 30th.

On 3 May General Sir Ian Hamilton demanded reinforcements at Cape Helles. Believing that McCay's leadership was enhanced by his week's experience, Bridges sent the 2nd Brigade. On the 8th it was brought in at thirty-five minutes notice, more than half a mile behind the line, to make a futile open attack on Krithia. McCay could do little more than rip out an order to his battalions. Reaching 'Tommies' Trench' under a tempest of fire, McCay said to C. E. W. Bean [q.v.7], 'This is where I suppose *I* have to do the damned heroic act' and scrambled on to the parapet shouting, 'Now then, Australians! Which of you men are Australians? Come on, Australians!' ('I said in effect to them', he wrote home, '"Come and die", and they came with a laugh and a cheer'.) Urging on his senior officers, McCay advanced to probably the most forward position occupied by an A.I.F. brigade headquarters during the war, and realized the attack was hopeless: the rest of the line was held up. They had made 'the only worthwhile advance in the entire battle of Krithia', but suffered more than 1000 casualties. The brigade dug in: at 2 a.m., while arranging for stretcher-bearers and rations, McCay had his leg broken by a bullet. He suffered unjust blame for the attack which was not his responsibility.

After evacuation to Egypt, he returned to Anzac on 8 June 1915 with his leg not properly healed. He was outraged by the appointment of Major General Legge [q.v.] to succeed Bridges; 'McCay talks far too much', Bean remarked. Lieut-General Sir William Birdwood [q.v.7] and Legge chose McCay to take command of the new 2nd Division but on 11 July his leg snapped.

In hospital in Malta he endured several operations and dangerous wastage of weight before being invalided home. Meanwhile his wife had died on 13 July and his father on 1 September. He reached Melbourne on 11 November to a hero's welcome. On 29 November he was promoted temporary major general as inspector general of the A.I.F. in Australia; he had also been appointed C.B. and awarded the Légion d'honneur. In December he quelled a near-riot among troops at Liverpool, New South Wales.

Birdwood recommended to the Australian government that McCay take command of the 3rd Division forming in Australia. However, the government insisted on Australian command of one of the two new divisions in Egypt. So, escaping a medical board, McCay was appointed to the 5th Division and took command on 22 March 1916. Bad luck continued to dog him. II Australian Corps had to march across open desert to replace I Anzac Corps at Suez Canal. McCay objected, but was ordered to carry on. His 14th Brigade finished the march in 'utter exhaustion . . . like the remnant of a broken army'; McCay sacked Brigadier General Irving [q.v.9] for his defective arrangements. Rigorous training continued until June when the 5th was the last of the four divisions to transfer to France but the first to see serious action, at Fromelles.

In support of the Somme offensive the division, under the tactical control of the British XI Corps, was intended to eliminate a German salient. Planning was hurried and indecisive, the experienced opposing German division expected the attack, the troops were heavily shelled while assembling and the British barrage was ineffective. The Australians reached their first objectives but the third line which was their aim turned out not to exist, and they were forced back in disarray. In a few hours the division suffered over 5500 casualties. McCay had made only one conspicuous mistake in ordering his men to vacate the first trench after clearing it. He also had Colonel Pope [q.v.] sent back to Australia for alleged drunkenness; Pope was probably merely totally exhausted. Once again McCay was widely blamed by his men for the defeat, but the A.I.F. commanders knew the responsibility was not his.

The division was crippled for weeks, but in September and October often raided successfully at Fleurbaix. It was then transferred to the Somme where rain and mud held up an intended attack at Flers and the 5th Division was relieved by the 2nd.

In January 1917 McCay was relieved of his command, probably because of his lameness and uncertain health during the winter, his general unpopularity and in particular his unsatisfactory relations with his staff; officially he was invalided out. Lieut-Colonel J. P.

McGlinn [q.v.] disliked his 'priggish pedantic mannerism'. On 1 May the government appointed him to command the base depots in England, against the advice of Birdwood who would have preferred his appointment to administrative command at Horseferry Road. Brigadier General Griffiths [q.v.9], commandant there, found co-operation with McCay so difficult that he pleaded to be allowed to return to France.

McCay in 1917 and until May 1918 was the senior A.I.F. officer in the area, and nearly all the other senior commanders dreaded the possibility of his appointment either to the Corps or to administrative command if Birdwood were to leave the A.I.F. Birdwood warned the minister of defence of McCay's unsuitability as general officer commanding. His old friend Monash in July 1917 wrote home that Jim 'declares he has become an old man and will be able to see no more active service [but] he showed all his old clearness of grasp and power, and was as nice and amiable and friendly as it was possible for any one to be'. McCay nevertheless still fruitlessly strove for either the fighting or administrative command. For almost two years at Salisbury Plain he efficiently and loyally trained and supplied reinforcements and controlled movements during demobilization. He was appointed K.C.M.G. in 1918 and K.B.E. in 1919.

Lieut-General Sir Brudenell White [q.v.] later remarked that McCay was 'one of the greatest soldiers that ever served Australia . . . greater even than Monash'. In intellect and military education he was indeed comparable with Monash. But whatever his potential he had no opportunity to excel at high command; and he had little of Monash's capacity to work harmoniously with staff or to earn essential trust in his leadership. And he had none of Monash's luck: as Bean concluded, the popular verdicts against him following the charge at Krithia, the desert march and Fromelles were grossly unjust. But they wrecked his military career.

McCay was demobilized in August 1919 and had to attempt to live down his reputation as a reckless commander; he never deigned to defend himself. He abandoned his legal practice and was appointed as business adviser to the Commonwealth government, which he remained until 1922, and, on Lawson's nomination, chairman in 1919 of a Victorian royal commission on high prices on whose recommendation a Fair Profits Commission was established. He had been a commissioner of the State Savings Bank of Victoria since 1912 and now became deputy chairman. During the police strike McCay acted for several months in 1923-24 without pay as commander of the Special Constabulary Force. He frequently wrote for the *Argus* leading articles and essays on political and economic subjects, sometimes under pseudonyms. He retired from the army as honorary lieut-general in 1926. In his later troubled years he was in constant pain from his wound.

McCay died on 1 October 1930 of hypertensive renal disease and was buried in Box Hill cemetery; he had long been a trustee of the Castlemaine Presbyterian Church. His daughters survived him: Beatrix Waring, LL.M., married (Sir) George Reid, Q.C., attorney-general of Victoria in 1967-73; Margaret Mary, M.A., became a teaching nun. McCay's portrait by Marion Jones is in the Castlemaine Art Gallery of which he had been a trustee.

A. W. Keown, *Forward with the Fifth* (Melb, 1921); C. E. W. Bean, *The story of Anzac* (Syd, 1921, 1924), and *The A.I.F. in France, 1916-18* (Syd, 1929, 1933, 1937, 1942); N. Meaney, *A history of Australian defence and foreign policy, 1901-23*, vol I (Syd, 1976); C. D. Coulthard-Clark, *The Citizen General Staff* (Canb, 1976); G. Serle, *John Monash* (Melb, 1982); D. McCarthy, *Gallipoli to the Somme* (Syd, 1983); *VHM*, 31 (1960-61), no 1; *V&P* (LA Vic), 1919, 2, p 431; *Table Talk*, 13 Dec 1895; *Punch* (Melb), 21 Jan 1909, 14 Mar 1912, 2 Sept 1914; *Argus*, 7 July 1915, 2 Oct 1930; *Castlemaine Mail*, 3 Oct 1930; L. D. Atkinson, Australian defence policy. A study of Empire and nation 1897-1910 (Ph.D. thesis, ANU, 1964); Monash papers (NL); information from Sir G. Reid, Warrandyte, Melb.   GEOFFREY SERLE

McCLELLAND, DAVID JOHN (1873-1962), engineer, was born on 31 March 1873 at Buninyong, Victoria, eldest child of Irish-born David Caldwell McClelland, goldminer and schoolteacher, and his Victorian-born wife Mary, née Magor. When 13 David won the open competition against adults for violin at the Ballarat (South Street) eisteddfod and played in a local orchestra. He was educated at Ballarat College, holding a state scholarship for three years, the Ballarat School of Mines and the University of Melbourne (B.C.E., 1896; M.C.E., 1898) where he was at Ormond [q.v.5] College. He gained honours in second and third-year engineering and at his final examinations won second-class honours and shared the *Argus* scholarship. He later acquired qualifications as a surveyor and a municipal, mining and hydraulic engineer.

After completing his first degree McClelland worked as a surveyor on a Melbourne sewerage contract, with Mephan Ferguson [q.v.4] as a design draughtsman, and as a mining and land surveyor in Western Australia. On returning in 1899 he spent six months with the Victorian Railways on line construction before being appointed engineer to Kerang Shire and eventually to eleven irrigation and water-supply trusts.

He began private practice in Melbourne about 1906 but soon took up contracting. His major construction work was the main western channel for the State Rivers and Water Supply Commission; he also built an irrigation canal in the Riverina, the Moorabool reservoir, a railway line in South Australia and reinforced concrete bridges.

In the 1920s, in partnership with the English firm Armstrong Whitworth, McClelland carried out the civil engineering work on the Sugarloaf-Rubicon hydro-electric power stations of the State Electricity Commission of Victoria, also hydro-electric works on the Shannon River, Tasmania, and the Clarence River, New South Wales. In 1932-41 he was an S.E.C. commissioner and in 1936 an able and amiable chairman of a royal commission to investigate the affairs of State Rivers. About this time he was also an active member of the Foreshore Erosion Board, and designed and installed a hydro-electric power plant for mining companies in the Wau-Bulolo area, New Guinea. In 1940-41 he was a member of a royal commission enquiring into the operations of the Tasmanian Hydro-Electric Commission. He was increasingly in demand as an arbitrator, advocate and technical witness in disputed engineering cases.

McClelland also developed business interests, being sometime chairman of directors of the Civil Engineering Construction Co. Pty Ltd, Cork Industries (Aus.) Pty Ltd which he conducted for some twenty-five years, Steelite Pty Ltd and Damman Asphalt (Vic.) Ltd, and managing director of Kingsville Quarries Pty Ltd.

He was a member of the faculty of engineering at the University of Melbourne and honorary lecturer and examiner in the economics of engineering. His published lectures, *Civil engineering estimates and contract costs for contractors or engineers* (Melbourne, 1931), became a standard text. McClelland was elected to full membership of the Institution of Civil Engineers, London, in 1918 without having been an associate, and was a member of the Institution of Engineers, Australia, from its foundation and of the Institution of Mining and Metallurgy, Australasia. He was a Freemason.

As consulting engineer to the Melbourne Cricket Club he supervised construction of new stands in the 1930s and 1950s and the regrading of the ground for the 1956 Olympic Games: in his later years he was honorary treasurer of the club. A shooter and footballer who played a season with Melbourne in his youth, he also followed racing and played bowls and golf.

McClelland's childless first marriage had ended in divorce. On 13 January 1923 he married Nellie Kathleen Fotheringham at South Melbourne. Survived by one son and four daughters, he died on 11 March 1962 at Windsor and was buried in Brighton cemetery. His estate was sworn for probate at £39 644.

His younger brother WILLIAM CALDWELL McCLELLAND (1875-1957) was born at Buninyong and educated at Brighton Grammar School and the University of Melbourne (B.A., 1899; M.A., 1901; M.B., B.S., 1905). He was medical officer to the Brighton City Council for over forty years. A brilliant centre half back for the Melbourne Football Club and its captain in 1901-04, he became president of the Victorian Football League in 1926-55 and of the Melbourne Cricket Club in 1944-57. McClelland was appointed C.B.E. in 1955. He did not marry.

J. Smith (ed), *Cyclopedia of Victoria*, 3 (Melb, 1905); K. Dunstan, *The paddock that grew* (Melb, 1962); *Age*, 31 May 1957, 13 Mar 1962; *Sun-News Pictorial*, 2 Aug 1932, 10 Jan 1936, 13 Mar 1962; MS autobiographies (held by Mr D. J. McClelland, Menora, Perth, and Mrs K. Truex, Caulfield, Melb); information from Sir Ronald East, Mount Waverley, Melb.   GEOFFREY SERLE

McCLELLAND, HUGH (1873-1958), farmer and politician, was born on 27 December 1873 near Smeaton, Victoria, fourth son of Andrew McClelland, farmer and selector, and his wife Jane, née McGowan. McClelland attended Cope Cope State School and in 1892 took up land in the Mallee shire of Berriwillock. He later moved to Sea Lake, where he acquired a large wheat property. On 14 June 1904 he married Janet Crothers at Birchip. For twenty-seven years he served on Wycheproof Shire Council, becoming further involved in rural politics as chairman of the Victorian Wheat Growers' Corporation Ltd, president of the Victorian Chamber of Agriculture, councillor of the Royal Agricultural Society and chairman of the Bendigo Co-operative Freezing Co. Considered an expert on marketing wheat, he attended the International Co-operative Wheat Pool Conference in 1929.

McClelland narrowly won the Federal seat of Wimmera in December 1931, entering parliament in the aftermath of the Scullin [q.v.] government's 'grow more wheat' campaign and a world-wide slump in the price of the commodity. As the representative of an important wheat district, McClelland ventilated the plight of growers, showing in November 1932 that the price in 1930 was already less than half the cost of production. Following his call for an investigation of the industry, the Lyons [q.v.] government in January 1934 set up a royal commission on the wheat, flour and bread industries, under the chairmanship of Sir Herbert Gepp [q.v.8]. It

reported in 1934-36, recommending a home consumption price for flour, the establishment of a Commonwealth Wheat Board to direct overseas sales, and a plan for debt adjustment for wheat producers. At a conference convened by (Sir) Earle Page [q.v.] in October 1935 to discuss the industry, where McClelland represented the Wheat Growers Corporation of Victoria, he called for more consideration of the recommendations of the wheat commission, requesting in particular a ballot of growers on a compulsory pool which he strongly advocated. He supported several Wheat Growers Relief Acts in 1933-36 but cautioned against 'placing farmers on what may be called the dole'.

He spoke against the Commonwealth Land Tax Act as the 'most obnoxious' on the statute book. In December 1934 he believed that the problem of employment was linked to a 'solution of the difficulties confronting the wheat industry' and advocated the imposition of a wheat tax, continually emphasizing the employment-creating value of the industry.

McClelland's infrequent contributions to debates led one journalist to observe, in 1934, that he was 'retiring enough to be forgotten on occasions in the rush and bustle of the political struggle'. That year, with many of his Federal colleagues, McClelland refused to sign the United Country Party pledge to follow caucus decisions and, forfeiting U.C.P. support, barely held his seat. In 1937 he was defeated by the endorsed Victorian Country Party candidate. He tried unsuccessfully to regain Wimmera in 1940.

In 1948 McClelland retired from farming and settled in Melbourne. He died on 14 December 1958 at Caulfield and was cremated. Three daughters and two sons survived him.

Sun-News Pictorial, 5 June 1929, 13 Jan 1934; *Age*, 1 Apr 1932, 16 Dec 1958; *Star* (Melb), 14 Mar 1936; *Herald* (Melb), 15 Dec 1958.
                                          CHARLES FAHEY

McCLINTOCK, ALBERT SCOTT (1880-1968), librarian, estate agent and Labor stalwart, was born on 28 January 1880 at Balmain, Sydney, youngest son of Scottish-born Robert McLintock, accountant, and his wife Jeanie Scott, née Duff. His schooling at Balmain was cut short when his father was retrenched. Albert worked as a law clerk and at the University of Sydney library until he was appointed in 1900 secretary, librarian and editor of the *Ormond* at the Melbourne Working Men's College. He belonged to the Victorian Labour Federation and wrote for *Labor Call*.

In 1903 McClintock went to a post as secretary of the Kalgoorlie Miners' (Mechanics' from 1905) Institute, Western Australia, becoming foundation president of the Goldfields Clerical Workers' Union of Workers in 1907. In 1911 the *Kalgoorlie Miner* described him as a 'fetch and carry Joey for Scaddan' [q.v.]. Next year he compiled the *Western Australian goldfields souvenir.* He was an active anti-conscriptionist in 1917. A long-term representative of the Goldfields Trades and Labour Council (eastern industrial district) on the State executive of the Australian Labor Party, he was a delegate in 1933 at the special Labor conference in Sydney. As a director of the *Westralian Worker* he helped to bring John Curtin to Perth. Although he constantly campaigned for others, he missed pre-selection for Senate and State seats himself.

McClintock was a self-taught, able, bookish man, who expanded and popularized his libraries where he created a club-like atmosphere. Mainly because of his efforts, the first secretaries' and librarians' conference took place at Perth in 1904; an Institutes Association resulted, which advocated, fruitlessly, free public lending libraries.

Moving to Perth in 1913, McClintock became the librarian ('Boan's [q.v.7] Book Bonaparte') and advertising and real-estate manager at Boan's Emporium. In the 1920s he established McClintock & Co., estate agents. He invested in suburban properties, two country hotels and, with his brother Robert, a farm at Naraling. In 1926 he was appointed a Licensing Court magistrate. A past State president of the Australian Natives' Association, he was its overseas tour organizer in 1934 and 1937; on tour he lectured and promoted Australian products. Afterwards he managed his hotel at Denmark until, having been found guilty of a homosexual offence in 1946, he retired to Sydney.

Wherever he lived McClintock identified with the community's cultural, religious, Masonic, educational, sporting and political life. Convinced that 'progress means the remorseless removal of the obsolete', he served local government at Kalgoorlie, South Perth and Denmark. He produced glossy publications about all three municipalities and annual Boan's family albums (1914-19), packed with information and homilies. He was commodore of South Perth Yacht Club and president of the Perth Amateur Swimming Club. In 1935 he secured leases at Meier's Find, Yilgarn, for London principals, and when 86 he published *Information and protection for shareholders and companies* (Canberra, 1967).

McClintock, or 'Sinto', was bespectacled, prematurely bald and always well attired; a wit, he was respected for his business acumen and open-handedness to relatives and political colleagues. On 21 November 1906, at St Andrew's Presbyterian Church, Kalgoorlie, he had married Gertrude Williams, a teacher of voice production. At home, although he was demanding, domineering and ungenerous, his wife remained steadfast through adversity. They had a son and a daughter, 'Ray' (Ruby Gertrude) Oldham, landscape architect and author. McClintock died at Manly, Sydney, on 5 July 1968 and was buried in the Anglican cemetery, Frenchs Forest. His estate was sworn for probate at $152 232.

J. S. Battye (ed), *Cyclopedia of Western Australia*, 2 (Adel, 1913); *South Australian Institute J*, 1, 24 Sept 1904; *WA Librarians Institute J*, Nov 1904; *Western Mail* (Perth), 19 Jan 1917; *West Australian*, 4, 5 Nov 1904, 12 Apr 1946; *Westralian Worker*, 18 Oct 1912; Kalgoorlie Mechanics' Institute, 1903-1913 (PR 3995, Battye Lib); McClintock papers held by, and information from, Mrs R. Oldham, Swanbourne, Perth.
WENDY BIRMAN

McCLOUGHRY, WILFRED ASHTON (1894-1943) and **EDGAR JAMES** (1896-1972), airmen, were the first and second sons of James Kingston McCloughry, draper, from Larne, Northern Ireland, and his Australian-born wife Charlotte Rebecca, née Ashton. Wilfred was born on 26 November 1894 at Knightsbridge, Adelaide, and Edgar on 10 September 1896 at Hindmarsh. Wilfred later changed his surname to McClaughry and Edgar became Kingston-McCloughry.

Wilfred was educated at Queen's School, North Adelaide, University of Adelaide and the Adelaide School of Mines. Commissioned into the Australian Military Forces in 1913, he transferred to the Australian Imperial Force in 1914 and went overseas with the 9th Light Horse Regiment. On Gallipoli from May to August 1915 he was wounded twice. Seconded to the Royal Flying Corps in March 1916, after flying training he served in a home defence squadron operating against German airships. He joined No. 100 Squadron, the R.F.C.'s first night bomber unit, on its formation and in March 1917 accompanied it to France as a flight commander. He was awarded the Military Cross in July.

One of the experienced Australians in the R.F.C. selected to strengthen the expanding Australian Flying Corps, Wilfred joined the Second Squadron and accompanied it to France as a flight commander in September 1917. In October he was recalled to England to command the Fourth Squadron and took that overseas in December. Quiet but firm, he led one of the most efficient Sopwith Camel squadrons on the Western Front in 1918. He flew frequent daylight missions and undertook several risky night sorties against enemy heavy bombers in Camels not equipped for night flying. Credited with three victories, he was awarded the Distinguished Flying Cross and the Distinguished Service Order and was mentioned in dispatches three times.

On General Birdwood's [q.v.7] recommendation Wilfred obtained a permanent commission in the Royal Air Force in August 1919 as squadron leader. In 1922 he attended the first R.A.F. Staff College course and graduated from the Imperial Defence College in 1931. Promoted group captain in July 1934, he was posted to Egypt and in July 1936, as acting air commodore, he was appointed air officer commanding Aden Command. On 27 April 1940 he married Angela Grace Maria Segalir; this was his second marriage, the first having been dissolved.

During the battle of Britain Wilfred commanded No. 9 Fighter Group and in 1942, appointed C.B. and air vice marshal, became Air Officer Commanding, Egypt. On 4 January 1943 he died in an aircraft crash near Heliopolis and was buried in Cairo war cemetery. Electric chimes in the Congregational Church, Brougham Place, Adelaide, were later dedicated to his memory and his portrait by Cuthbert Orde is in his widow's possession.

Edgar was educated at Adelaide University and the South Australian School of Mines. Commissioned into the A.M.F. in May 1915, he transferred in December to the A.I.F. After service in Egypt and France with the Australian Engineers he was seconded to the R.F.C. in December 1916 for training as a pilot, graduated in August 1917 and was posted to No. 23 Squadron, R.F.C., in France. He was soon invalided to hospital in England after a serious crash. He was a flying instructor in the Sixth Training Squadron, A.F.C., then was posted in June 1918 as a flight commander and temporary captain to Wilfred's Fourth Squadron in France. Within four months Edgar was credited with shooting down nineteen enemy aeroplanes and four balloons and was awarded the Distinguished Service Order and Distinguished Flying Cross and Bar and mentioned in dispatches. A few fellow airmen, however, considered that some of his claims were over-enthusiastic. He was twice wounded. On leaving the A.F.C. in August 1919, Edgar, now known as Kingston, graduated M.A. at Cambridge in mechanical science, worked in the engineering industry, then joined the R.A.F. with a short service commission in December 1922, obtaining a permanent commission on 1 January 1926. His later postings included staff courses at Andover and Camberley.

Good-looking and ambitious, Kingston was reserved but at times outspoken. His closeness to leading political figures caused some displeasure to his service chiefs. In 1940, while an air commodore, he drew the atten-

tion of various prominent people to what he considered false information about Britain's effective aircraft strength presented to Cabinet by the R.A.F. This unconventional action was damaging to his career; he later attributed to it his failure to achieve the rank of air marshal and a knighthood. Of his several responsible positions, the most important was chairman of the Allied Expeditionary Air Force Bombing Committee which produced the tactical and strategic bombing plans for the invasion of Europe. He retired, as air vice marshal, in 1953, his last posting being chief air defence officer, Ministry of Defence. He had been appointed C.B.E. in 1943 and C.B. in 1950.

Kingston was the author of *Winged warfare* (1937) and five books on air and defence strategy in 1947-64. He was an associate fellow of the Royal Aeronautical Society. On 16 January 1924 in London he had married Freda Elizabeth Lewis. They had two daughters, and were later divorced. Kingston-McCloughry died on 15 November 1972 in Edinburgh. He willed his body to medical research and his papers and manuscripts to the Imperial War Museum.

E. J. Richards, *Australian airmen. History of the 4th Squadron, A.F.C.* (Melb, nd); F. M. Cutlack, *The Australian Flying Corps . . . 1914-18* (Syd, 1923); I. Jones, *Tiger squadron* (Lond, 1954); A. Morris, *Bloody April* (Lond, 1967); K. Isaacs, *Military aircraft of Australia 1909-1918* (Canb, 1971); S. Zuckerman, *From apes to warlords* (Lond, 1978); A. H. Cobby, *High adventure* (Melb, 1981); Written records section 1914-18 (AWM); Air Hist Branch papers (PRO, Lond); Kingston-McCloughry papers (Imperial War Museum, Lond); family papers held by Mrs A. McClaughry and Mrs S. Harvey, Lond, Mrs P. Maclean, Vancouver, and Miss A. McQueen, Adel.   ALAN FRASER

McCOLL, JAMES HIERS (1844-1929), politician and legal manager, was born on 31 January 1844 at South Shields, Durham, England, son of Hugh McColl [q.v.5] and his first wife Jane, née Hiers. The family arrived in Melbourne in January 1853, but Jane had died just before the ship berthed; Hugh remarried in 1856. James was educated at the Model School, Sandhurst (Bendigo), and briefly at Scotch College, Melbourne, leaving to work in a general store at Sandhurst in 1857. Intending to be a mechanical engineer, he served an apprenticeship in fitting and turning at the iron foundry of J. Horwood & Sons. On 1 January 1867 he married Emily Boyle (d. 1898) at Sydney Flat, Bendigo. In 1873 James became an insurance agent and legal manager of companies with R. A. Rankin in the firm McColl & Rankin, which his father started in 1871.

Hugh McColl was a fervent supporter of

irrigation and closer settlement and James took up these causes after his father's death in 1885. He won the Legislative Assembly seat of Mandurang in 1886 by a huge majority. In 1889 the seat was subdivided and McColl successfully contested the new seat of Gunbower. He was minister of mines and of water supply in the Patterson [q.v.5] ministry (January 1893-September 1894) and commissioner of crown lands and survey, minister of forests and president of the Board of Land and Works in the McLean [q.v.] ministry (December 1899-November 1900). Regarded as 'one of the soundest authorities in Victoria on agricultural and mining questions', he pressed for closer settlement under irrigation and dry farming conditions, taking pride in the fact that as minister for lands he purchased the first Victorian estates to be divided for closer settlement. He was also determined to eliminate abuses connected with mining law.

A strong supporter of Federation, in March 1901 he won the Federal seat of Echuca and soon became known as one of the 'solid, able men of the Liberal party'. In 1907-14 he sat in the Senate where he was admired for his vigorous debating and 'unshrinking honesty of purpose'. He was vice-president of the Executive Council in the Cook [q.v.8] ministry (June 1913-September 1914) and a temporary chairman of committees in 1907-12.

Believing that Victoria's permanent prosperity lay in agricultural and mining development, McColl attended a dry farming congress in the United States of America in 1909 at his own expense and presented a report to the Deakin [q.v.8] government. He was among the first to expound the virtues of dry farming in Australia but his support of the prickly pear as a 'fine stand by for stock' proved misguided. Defeated in 1914, McColl purchased an irrigation property at Gunbower, north of Bendigo, in 1917 and lived there for some years before retiring to Deepdene, Melbourne.

A Presbyterian and a Freemason, he taught at St Andrew's Sunday school, Bendigo, for fifty-five years. McColl died on 20 February 1929 in Melbourne and was buried in Bendigo cemetery. On 29 January 1900 he had married Sarah Ann Thomas at Stawell. She survived him with two sons and a daughter and two daughters of McColl's first marriage. His son Hugh had been killed in France in World War I.

J. Smith (ed), *Cyclopedia of Victoria*, 1 (Melb, 1903); *Aust Mining Standard*, 6 May 1893, p 245; *Punch* (Melb), 4 Jan 1906, 28 Dec 1911, 20 Nov 1924; *Age*, 21 Feb 1929; *Argus*, 21, 22 Feb 1929; *Bendigo Advertiser*, 22, 25 Feb 1929.

AMANDA M. ROLFE

McCOMAS, ROBERT BOND WESLEY (1862-1938), merchant, was born on 2 August 1862 at Collingwood, Melbourne, fourth of nine children and second son of Scots-Irish Protestant parents JOHN WESLEY McCOMAS (1819-1906), auctioneer, merchant and inventor, and his wife Jane Isabella, née Addey.

McComas senior, born into a Dublin commercial firm, had moved from a classical education designed to fit him for the Church into medical and scientific studies at Trinity College. In 1851 ill health prompted his migration to Victoria. After working on the goldfields he dabbled in a succession of enterprises before establishing in the 1860s the Melbourne auctioneering firm which developed into McComas & Co., factors and importers. The 1864-68 drought destroyed his Riverina squatting ambitions, but his invention, patenting and manufacture of McComas's Prize Water Lifter underwrote his commercial success. His later invention, the McComas Wool Press, continued to be manufactured into the 1930s. A member of the Church of England Assembly and of the Victorian auxiliary of the British & Foreign Bible Society, McComas was over 70 when he retired. He died at his Toorak home on 1 November 1906, leaving his family a legacy of Christian faith and love of learning.

Robert, like all but the youngest of his siblings, was privately educated. He entered McComas & Co. in 1875, moving to the New Zealand Loan & Mercantile Co. in 1880 and in 1882 to William Haughton & Co., formed to take over the general merchandising side of his father's company. A quiet man, McComas engaged little in social activities but his business acumen was acute; as a partner in Haughton & Co. from 1887 and as sole proprietor from 1890 he developed the firm as wool and skin brokers and shipping agents with branches throughout Australasia and in London and Canada. He also had charge of McComas & Co. by 1893 and later became principal of Wilson, Canham & Co. On 27 December 1893, at Hawthorn with Wesleyan forms, he married Ethel Jane, daughter of Dr William Henry Cutts [q.v.3]; she died in 1904 and he did not remarry.

In November 1916 McComas was appointed wool-buyers' representative on the Commonwealth Central Wool Committee set up to manage the wartime supply of Australian wool to Great Britain. At other times he headed the Victorian, Adelaide and Tasmanian Wool Buyers' associations. His expertise and influence were of utmost importance in the post-war expansion of the Australian woollen textile industry. McComas was also chairman of directors of the General Accident, Fire & Life Assurance Co. Ltd and in 1924-35 a director of the Commonwealth

Bank of Australia (acting chairman in 1927). He was appointed C.M.G. in 1936.

McComas amassed considerable wealth. As well as valuable Melbourne real estate, he owned a weekend farm near Drouin and a Queensland sheep and cattle property. His philanthropy was almost entirely private and directed towards education. Publicly, he was a conscientious member of the council of the Working Men's College from 1917 (the wool school at the Royal Melbourne Technical College was named after him) and a devotee of the Melbourne Cricket Club.

McComas died at his Hawthorn home, Gresford, on 19 August 1938 and was buried in Boroondara cemetery. His estate, valued for probate at £110 822 in England and £774 244 in four States, was left principally to his two daughters. From 1935 his nephew R. G. McComas had been assistant manager of William Haughton & Co., by then one of the largest individually directed businesses in Australia.

JANE ISABELLA (1864-1960), Robert's younger sister, was born on 26 September 1864 at Footscray. She had a notable career as principal of Glamorgan Preparatory School for Boys from 1893. Established in 1887 by her sister Annie Wilhelmina Wesley next door to the family home at Toorak, the school was taken over by Geelong Church of England Grammar School in 1947 when Miss McComas retired. S. M. (Viscount) Bruce [q.v.7] was a former pupil as were the sons of Sir Robert Garran [q.v.8] and Sir Frederick Mann [q.v.]. Isabel's interests reflected her father's: she was treasurer of the Toorak branch of the British & Foreign Bible Society, a parishioner of St John's Church of England, Toorak, for seventy years and a member of the Classical Association of Victoria. She died at Colac on 14 October 1960.

A. Sutherland, *Victoria and its metropolis*, 1 (Melb, 1888); *Who's who in the world of women* (Melb, 1934); E. Scott, *Australia during the war* (Syd, 1936); *Australasian*, 3 Nov 1906; *SMH*, 7 Oct 1924, 2 Jan 1936, 20 Aug 1938; *Age*, 20 Aug 1938; information from Sir R. Southey, Mount Eliza, Vic.   ANN G. SMITH

McCORKINDALE, ISABELLA (1885-1971), temperance worker, was born on 5 January 1885 at Rutherglen, Lanarkshire, Scotland, eldest daughter of Archibald McCorkindale, wholesale ironmonger, and his wife Barbara, née Brown. In 1886 the family migrated to Brisbane where Isabel was educated at Junction Park State School and at a business college.

Interested in temperance reform from youth, Isabel began in 1911 her sixty-year association with the Woman's Christian Temperance Union, serving in its Queensland branch as associate in the department of anti-gambling, then State organizer and in 1917 organizing secretary. In 1920-24 she was also director of the women's section of the Queensland Temperance Alliance. In 1924-27 she travelled overseas, lecturing with the British Women's Temperance Association in 1925 and with the Canadian Temperance Federation in 1926 as well as studying at the University of Edmonton and touring extensively through the United States of America.

On returning to Australia Miss McCorkindale was appointed national director of education and research for the W.C.T.U. (1927-56, 1959-69). Based in Adelaide and later returning to Brisbane, she travelled widely throughout Australia and in 1928-29 launched an extensive education campaign in New Zealand. Her programme in Australia was organized under the slogan: 'Enrol the babies, educate the children, enlist the youth, equip the members, enlighten the public'. Besides her lectures and study groups she prepared and presented radio programmes, trained temperance workers and organized campaigns against liquor licences and extension of drinking hours.

In 1934 Isabel McCorkindale and Ada Bromham [q.v.7] attended as Australian delegates the world W.C.T.U. convention in Stockholm, also the British Commonwealth League Conference and the World Congress against Alcoholism. After visiting Switzerland, Austria and Russia—whose progressive social welfare policies impressed Miss McCorkindale—they returned via China and Japan to Australia where she resumed her work for the W.C.T.U. From 1948 she edited its monthly magazine, the *White Ribbon Signal*. Her publications include, besides temperance pamphlets and study books, *The Frances Willard centenary book* (1939), *Pioneer pathways* (1948) and *Torch-bearers* (1949). In her later years she promoted the use of fruit juices as an alternative to alcohol, and campaigned for road safety, advocating use of the breathalyser. In 1958 she helped to establish an Australian committee of the International Commission for the Prevention of Alcoholism. She was national president of the W.C.T.U. in 1963-66.

A prominent figure in the international W.C.T.U., Isabel McCorkindale served as world vice-president in 1947-59 and president in 1959-62. She represented Australia at international conventions in England (1950), Canada (1953), West Germany (1956), Mexico (1959) and India (1962). In 1963 she was appointed M.B.E.

Slight, dark and bright-eyed, Isabel McCorkindale appears in photographs a rather elfin figure beside some of her strong-jawed, sturdy temperance colleagues, who appreciated her charm, leadership capacity, sense of humour and eloquence. In her speaking and writing she used scientific rather than emotive arguments against alcohol. Like that of many of her colleagues her commitment was part of a wider concern for the status of women. A member of the League of Women Voters, she served as a committee-member for the 1946 Australian Women's Charter conference, and defended the charter against attack from other women's organizations. In 1950 she was a member of the Australian delegation to the United Nations' Status of Women Commission in New York. A lifelong member of the Coorparoo Methodist Church, she felt challenged to 'make the world a better place'. She died unmarried at her home at Holland Park, Brisbane, on 24 February 1971 and was cremated.

A. G. Lather, *A glorious heritage* (Brisb, 1968); Woman's Christian Temperance Union, Victoria, *Forward in faith* (Melb, 1975); *White Ribbon Signal*, 80, no 5, Apr-May 1971; *Herald* (Melb), 24 Sept 1927; *SMH*, 10 May, 30 Aug 1927, 9 Jan, 11 Apr 1929, 30 Oct 1930, 11 Dec 1931, 8 Mar 1934, 1 May, 13 June 1935, 22 June 1946, 11 Oct 1951; information from Miss E. McCorkindale, Holland Park, Brisb.   DIANE LANGMORE

McCORMACK, WILLIAM (1879-1947), miner, trade union organizer and premier, was born on 27 April 1879 at Purnam near St Lawrence, central Queensland, fourth of six children of Melbourne-born Patrick McCormack, carrier, and his Irish wife Mary, née Brennan. Educated at the local state school, McCormack worked on his parents' small grazing property before turning prospector in the Mount Morgan district. In 1904 he departed for the North Queensland base-metal fields and was engaged by the Stannary Hills Mines & Tramway Co. There he experienced the hardships of working underground for low wages in high temperatures and along poorly ventilated drives where safety regulations were virtually ignored.

In 1906 McCormack met a young Irvinebank miner E. G. (Ted) Theodore [q.v.], who extolled the benefits of organization. Largely on their initiative members for the Amalgamated Workers' Association of North Queensland were recruited from September 1907. Six months later McCormack became inaugural vice-president. Local conditions augured well for the A.W.A.'s success: as managers had cut wages, many miners joined the union. By July McCormack was general secretary. With a successful conclusion to the Etheridge railway dispute in September, the A.W.A.'s penetration of non-mining occupations was almost as spectacular as its record

for winning strikes in mining areas. Forced to leave Stannary Hills and find employment at Nymbool, McCormack was elected full-time secretary at the first A.W.A. conference at Chillagoe in February 1909; he was paid £200 a year after victimization by his employers. With Theodore aspiring to State parliament, McCormack increasingly shouldered the A.W.A.'s organizational responsibilities and championed amalgamation proposals to incorporate rural workers, miners, smelterers, sugar-workers, railway navvies and town labourers. He also steered the union towards political action 'to secure direct representation of Labour in Parliament'.

In 1910-12 McCormack was North Queensland's most influential industrial leader. He achieved an amalgamation in December 1910 of several smaller unions including the Amalgamated Sugar Workers', and six months later, 'to justify ourselves', orchestrated a sugar strike which lasted over three months. The settlement terms on pay, hours, bonuses and employment conditions were vindicated by the 1912 royal commission on the sugar industry. McCormack's health, however, was seriously impaired by strain and a subsequent recurrent coronary condition. With A.W.A. headquarters now at Townsville, McCormack predicted that 'we are not likely to have a great deal of peace in the future'. Within a month the 1912 general strike had been called, much to his consternation.

Although McCormack supported the strike initially, he considered the pretext flimsy and, detecting signs of impending defeat, ordered the A.W.A. back to work. His intuitive pragmatism thus ensured that the A.W.A., unlike some other unions, emerged from the dispute largely intact. With the labour movement rudderless after the strike, McCormack made new amalgamation proposals. By 1913 McCormack and Theodore had engineered the modern Australian Workers' Union, following a series of conferences with interstate non-craft unions. McCormack accepted the A.W.U.'s vice-presidency in 1913. Meanwhile, politics had captured his imagination. He narrowly won the Legislative Assembly seat of Cairns in April 1912, and from the back-bench concentrated on industrial relations and the sugar industry.

After T. J. Ryan's [q.v.] electoral victory in 1915, he seemed certain to enter the ministry, having bowed out of union affairs; however, he was defeated in caucus by parliamentary experience and intrigue. A consolation was his election as Speaker. Maintaining his strong links with the Labor machine, McCormack was blatantly partisan in his rulings from the chair. He served on the party executive, was a delegate to conferences, attended caucus meetings and chaired party sub-committees. In the assembly he regularly prejudiced debate, passing notes to ministers and arbitrarily invoking standing orders against the Opposition. During the 1916 anti-conscription campaign he often addressed rallies while parliament was in session, ruling out of order subsequent questioning of his behaviour. In November 1917 McCormack devised tactics to expose censorship of Labor leaders' anti-conscription addresses. By 1919, however, he was anxious to relinquish the Speakership. He nominated for a Federal seat but withdrew during a reshuffle which culminated in Ryan's entry into Federal politics.

McCormack became an efficient home secretary in the Theodore ministry until 2 July 1923. Few reforms were introduced, because of the nature of the office and because ill health necessitated his absence on 46 of the 126 sitting days. During his subsequent twenty-eight months as secretary for public lands, however, he introduced nineteen bills and emerged as the cabinet strongman. In Theodore's absence he was acting treasurer.

When Theodore stepped down in February 1925, McCormack was favoured over the deputy premier W. N. Gillies [q.v.9] but, to his surprise, was narrowly beaten, having made many enemies in caucus; he became deputy leader. However, Gillies' leadership was found wanting in the settlement in September of the week-long railway unions strike. By-passing the State arbitration court, the government met the union's demands in full, despite economic ramifications. On 22 October Gillies retired and McCormack was elected leader, and thus premier. His troubled inheritance included financial difficulties and conflict with militant unions. Appreciating these electoral liabilities he was determined to assert firm leadership from the outset.

McCormack's relations with the Trades Hall unions had been deteriorating since July 1917, when he condemned Townsville strikers for defying the arbitration court. In 1921 he clashed with militants over Labor's socialization objective, and two years later at the Emu Park Labor-in-Politics convention he abused advocates of direct action, claiming that workers had obtained significant material gains under Labor's arbitration legislation. Sniping continued at the central executive level and mutual intolerance was reflected in the February 1925 leadership ballot. In one of his first actions as Labor premier, McCormack manoeuvred the exclusion of militant union delegates from the central executive and ultimately the party, for failing to sign the anti-communist pledge. The ruthlessness with which he cynically exploited this ideological issue for sectional and personal advantage rebounded upon him

later in his premiership, when his critics had remustered their forces. Meanwhile, he led Labor to a handsome electoral victory in May 1926.

The barren legislative period from 1926 to 1929 reflected the government's realistic handling of State finances. Drought, losses on state enterprises and accumulated deficits obliged McCormack, as treasurer (and chief secretary), to introduce stringent economies. Unprofitable state undertakings were shut down, taxation increased, government expenditures pruned. Probably one of the most significant initiatives was taken in May 1927 when McCormack, in London raising loans, agreed to concessions which permitted the development of Mount Isa. The 1928-29 budget showed, however, that McCormack had achieved his economic goals, and could finance attractive election promises after the May 1929 poll. But his government was in deep trouble.

McCormack's show-down with the unions had come in August 1927 on his return from overseas. A strike at the South Johnstone sugar-mill had snowballed, with railwaymen being suspended for refusing to handle 'black' sugar. To uphold the railway commissioner's authority, and that of the government, McCormack dismissed all railway workers, insisting on a signed undertaking to abide by the commissioner's rulings as a condition of reinstatement. The lock-out provoked a storm of protest from the labour movement but applause from the press, Opposition and general public. The unions capitulated twelve days later, after which many officials pledged themselves to a campaign to discredit the premier.

He retained his seat but his administration was swept from office in May 1929. McCormack contributed heavily to Labor's defeat by a restrictive financial policy, a negative policy speech, the abandonment of state enterprise, opposition to wage claims, roughshod treatment of many union leaders, and there was also the taint of corruption. Despite self-justifications he resigned from the leadership on 16 May.

For many years allegations of his involvement with the Mungana Mining Co., which sold properties to the State for £40 000, had circulated in North Queensland. Challenged by his opponents, he persistently denied any connexion. In late 1929 he was exposed for misrepresenting his shareholdings in Mount Isa; in February 1930, the month that he resigned from parliament, a royal commission was set up to investigate Mungana. Its report was a political bombshell: it declared not only McCormack to be 'guilty of fraud and dishonesty', but also Theodore, then Commonwealth treasurer. Although the Crown failed in a subsequent civil prosecution, the damage was done, ruling out a return to political life.

Only 52, McCormack retired to his Annerley home, financially comfortable from investments from which he supported his spinster sisters. He entered business in Sydney and, in later years frequently visited the Queensland parliamentary gallery. Following months of ill health, McCormack died, unmarried, of hypertensive heart disease, on 21 November 1947 at Annerley, and was buried in Toowong cemetery with Catholic rites. He was remembered by his contemporaries as a warm, but not colourful personality, strong-willed and dogmatic. Within his party, he was not a popular premier, although cabinet loyalty was a feature of his term in office. To the public, however, the spectre of political corruption remained; his name evoked recollections of the railway lock-out of 1927, and his unswerving friendship with Theodore.

Queensland and Queenslanders (Brisb, 1936); I. Young, *Theodore* (Syd, 1971); D. J. Murphy, *T. J. Ryan* (Brisb, 1975); K. H. Kennedy, 'William McCormack: forgotten Labor leader', in D. J. Murphy and R. B. Joyce (eds), *Queensland political portraits 1859-1952*, and for bibliog, and *The Mungana affair* (both Brisb, 1978), and 'The South Johnstone strike and railway lockout, 1927', *Labour Hist*, Nov 1976, no 31, and 'Theodore, McCormack and the Amalgamated Workers' Association', *Labour Hist*, Nov 1977, no 33; *Aust Q*, June 1929; Whips of the Queensland Parliamentary Labour Party 1893-1981 *and* Executive members of the ALP (Qld branch) PLP 1893-1981 (typescripts, Queensland Parliamentary Library, 1981).   K. H. KENNEDY

McCORMACK, WILLIAM THOMAS BARTHOLOMEW (1879-1938), civil engineer and public servant, was born on 1 January 1879 at Heathcote, Victoria, son of Thomas McCormack, Irish-born publican and his wife Emily, née Ewen, of Sydney. Educated at the local state school and privately, he worked as a clerk in the shire office at Seymour before being appointed in 1902 secretary and shire engineer at Mirboo, Gippsland. On 27 September 1904 at Mirboo Catholic Church, he married Margaret Muirhead. Certificated as municipal surveyor, hydraulic engineer and municipal clerk (Victoria) and engineer (New South Wales), he worked as shire engineer at Lockhart, New South Wales, and Korumburra, Victoria, before being appointed in 1909 to the Public Works Department as assistant engineer, engaged in constructing roads and levees and reclaiming swamps. He was an honorary lecturer in engineering at the University of Melbourne in 1913-15, a foundation member of the Institution of Engineers, Australia, and a member of the Institution of Civil Engineers, London.

In March 1913 McCormack was appointed one of the three foundation members of the Country Roads Board of Victoria. In 1913-15 they travelled widely, frequently on horseback, to lay the foundation of the State's road network. McCormack's knowledge of local government, his diplomatic skills and quiet, equable personality made him a successful ambassador for the board in its negotiations with sometimes fractious shire councils.

A lieutenant in the Australian Intelligence Corps in 1911-14, McCormack enlisted in the Australian Imperial Force in January 1916 and in June embarked as major commanding the 10th Field Company, Engineers. In 1917 he acted as commanding royal engineer, 3rd Division, under his mentor Major General (Sir) John Monash [q.v.]. Following the battle of Messines he was mentioned in dispatches and in August 1918 was awarded the French Croix de Guerre. After the war he briefly studied British road construction, town planning, sewerage and water-supply.

Returning to Australia in April 1919 McCormack resumed his work with the Country Roads Board, taking charge of the construction, initially by returned soldiers, of the Great Ocean Road which reached Eastern View in 1922 and, eventually, Apollo Bay in 1932. Acting chairman of the board during William Calder's [q.v.7] visit to Europe and the United States of America in 1924, he was appointed chairman upon Calder's death in March 1928. During his decade in office about 11 000 miles (17 700 km) of roadway were under his jurisdiction and in that time much of its macadam surface, suitable for horse-drawn vehicles, was replaced with more durable bitumen and gravel. He also established the board's research laboratory. In 1937 McCormack visited North America to study advances in road-building and published a report on his return.

Contemporaries observed that McCormack spoke of roads with poetic eloquence, insisting that they should 'follow the lines of Nature' for aesthetic as well as practical reasons. He was committed to providing 'a road to every farmer's gate' and urged the use of local materials wherever possible.

A pianist and composer of dance music, McCormack was also a member of Victoria Golf Club and donor of the McCormack cup to the Melbourne division of the Institution of Engineers. He died in Melbourne from pneumonia on 23 January 1938 and was buried with Catholic rites in Brighton cemetery. His wife, daughter and two sons survived him. Memorials to him include an archway at Eastern View, opened by General Sir Harry Chauvel [q.v.7] in 1939.

Inst of Engineers J, 11, no 12, Dec 1939; *Aust Road Research*, Sept 1963; *Herald* (Melb), 27 Feb

1913, 15 Mar 1928, 24 Jan 1938, 2 Nov 1939; *Age*, 3, 24 Jan 1938; *Argus*, 24 Jan 1938; information from Road Construction Authority, Kew, Melb.

DIANE LANGMORE

MacCORMICK, SIR ALEXANDER (1856-1947), surgeon, was born on 31 July 1856 at North Knapdale, Argyleshire, Scotland, son of Archibald MacCormick, farmer and coastal trader, and his wife Mary, née Campbell. He was educated at Lochgilphead School and studied medicine at the University of Edinburgh (M.B.,Ch.M.,1880) with (Sir) Thomas Anderson Stuart, Robert Scott Skirving [qq.v.] and (Sir) Arthur Conan Doyle. He spent a year at Liverpool, England, as house surgeon to E. R. Bickersteth, one of the first surgeons to adopt Lister's methods.

When Anderson Stuart came to Sydney to found the medical school at the university in 1883, MacCormick joined him in July as demonstrator in anatomy and physiology. In 1885 he was awarded an M.D. and gold medal by the University of Edinburgh for his thesis on the musculature of the native cat. That year he was appointed an honorary assistant surgeon at Royal Prince Alfred Hospital and in 1890 senior surgeon and lecturer at the university in the principles and practice of surgery. His skills as a surgeon and outstanding diagnostician, as well as his introduction of Listerian antiseptic methods, led to rapid success and wide recognition. Reputedly the first man in Sydney to wear a white coat while operating, he was dubbed by his colleagues 'The Hokey Pokey Man'. Taciturn by nature, he did not enjoy lecturing and was not good at it, but taught by example and was always ready to answer questions. Physically very strong and apparently tireless, he worked through long lists.

At All Saints Church, Woollahra, MacCormick married Ada Fanny Hare, sister of C. W. Cropper [q.v.8], on 26 February 1895. He served in the South African War as an honorary major with the New South Wales Medical Corps from January 1900 and was mentioned in dispatches in September 1901. He was president of the New South Wales branch of the British Medical Association in 1905, and between 1884 and 1915 published over thirty articles in the *Australian Medical Gazette* and other journals. He was elected an honorary fellow of the Royal Colleges of Surgeons, England, in 1900 and Edinburgh in 1905, and was knighted in 1913. That year he retired from Royal Prince Alfred Hospital and was appointed honorary surgeon to St Vincent's Hospital, which he remained until 1931.

On the outbreak of war in 1914 MacCormick went to England and joined the British Expeditionary Force in November. As a colonel and consulting surgeon he served in France at the Boulogne base. He took with him a supply of Thomas knee splints and in vain urged their use by field ambulances. Also commissioned in the Australian Army Medical Corps, he was sent to Lemnos where he was '*unable to do any operating at all*'. Frustrated, he returned to Sydney in February 1916 but after the death in action in October of his eldest son he rejoined the A.I.F. in May 1917: in France his talents were again largely wasted. Back in Sydney in February 1918, he had become a consultant at Prince Henry Hospital and the Military Hospital, Randwick.

From 1903 MacCormick had owned a private hospital, The Terraces, at Paddington; he also built a seven-storey block of flats and consulting rooms in Macquarie Street and in 1912 a house, Kilmory, on Point Piper, where he lived quietly. He was a director of the Australian Mutual Provident Society in 1919-31 and the Bank of New South Wales in 1930-31, president of the Central District Ambulance Committee and an executive-member of the Navy League. In 1926 he gave The Terraces with an endowment of £25 000 to the Presbyterian Church in memory of his son; it became known as the Scottish Hospital. He was appointed K.C.M.G. that year and in 1927 was a foundation vice-president of the College of Surgeons of Australasia.

Sailing was MacCormick's great pleasure. He bought the yacht, *Thelma*, and successfully raced her in the 1890s. Joining the Royal Sydney Yacht Squadron in 1893, he was commodore in 1897-1900 and in 1913-20. In 1913 he had built a cutter, *Morna*, for cruising. He was a founder and first commodore of the Prince Edward Yacht Club in 1920. In 1927 he visited Scotland to supervise the building of a schooner, *Ada*. With four others he sailed her through the Panama Canal reaching Sydney after a four-month voyage. He was made a member of the Royal Yacht Squadron at Cowes and became the only yachtsman on Sydney Harbour privileged to fly the white ensign.

Rugged and sunburned, with a bristling moustache, MacCormick had 'a heavy physique without anything soft in it . . . large square hands and keen bright blue eyes'. With a Scot's 'canny sense of humour he smiled more with his eyes than his mouth'. He never spared himself in the case of the sick and even in old age would rarely delegate responsibility.

MacCormick retired to the Channel Islands in 1931 and sailed in Scotland in the summers. He dramatically escaped from Jersey in his yacht crammed with refugees only hours before the Nazis arrived. He lived in London for the rest of the war but died at St Brelade, Jersey, on 25 October 1947, survived by his wife, son and two daughters. His portrait by

John Longstaff [q.v.] is held by the University of Sydney.

A. G. Butler (ed), *Official history of the Australian Army Medical Services . . . 1914-18*, 2, 3 (Canb, 1940, 1943); P. R. Stephensen (ed), *Sydney sails* (Syd, 1962); G. N. Griffiths, *Point Piper, past and present* (Syd, 1970); J. A. Young et al, *Centenary book of the University of Sydney Faculty of Medicine* (Syd, 1984); *MJA*, 24 Jan 1948; *Scottish A'sian*, 21 Nov 1923, 21 Feb 1928; *SMH*, 15 May 1917, 20 May, 3 July 1926, 30 Mar 1927, 30 Jan 1928; MacCormick, small war diary 1915 and 1917 (Archives, Roy A'sian College of Surgeons, Melb); letters from MacCormick 1913-19 (held by author, Syd).   Douglas Miller

McCORMICK, PETER DODDS (1834?-1916), schoolteacher and songwriter, was born at Port Glasgow, Scotland, son of Peter McCormick, seaman, and his wife Janet, née Dodds. After completing his apprenticeship to a joiner, he migrated and reached Sydney on 21 February 1855. He pursued his trade and became involved in musical societies.

In 1863 McCormick attended Fort Street Model School for a month before being appointed teacher-in-charge at St Marys National School. On 16 July he married Emily Boucher, who became sewing teacher at her husband's schools. They taught at schools closer to Sydney in 1865 but she died in March 1866; on 22 December he married Emma Elizabeth Dening. McCormick was appointed to the Presbyterian denominational school at Woolloomooloo in 1867 and to Dowling (Plunkett) Street Public School in 1878 where he remained until he resigned in 1885.

McCormick was an elder of St Andrew's Presbyterian Church, Woolloomooloo, and later of the Grahame Memorial Church at Waverley. In 1896 he published a moral tale, *Four school mates*. He gave religious instruction in public schools until 1916 and was remembered by A. R. Chisholm as 'a white-haired man with a red face . . . [who] remained imperturbable amid the tumult of the class-room, and was extraordinarily laconic'.

Both ultra-Scottish and ultra-patriotic, McCormick was honorary secretary of St Andrew's Benevolent Society, a founder of the Caledonian Society and, after its merger, of the Highland Society of New South Wales and of the Burns Anniversary Club. His greatest interest, however, was music: he was precentor of the General Assembly of the Presbyterian Church of New South Wales and organized many church choirs. He conducted very large choirs such as the 10 000 children and 1000 teachers at the 1880 Robert Raikes Sunday school centenary demonstration, and

15 000 schoolchildren at the laying of the foundation stone of Queen Victoria's statue.

McCormick published about thirty patriotic and Scottish songs; 'The Bonnie Banks o' Clyde', 'Advance Australia Fair' and others became very popular. 'Advance Australia Fair' was first sung (by Mr Andrew Fairfax) at the St Andrew's Day concert of the Highland Society on 30 November 1878: the *Sydney Morning Herald* described the music as bold and stirring, and the words as 'decidedly patriotic'—it was 'likely to become a popular favourite'. As 'Amicus' he later had the music and four verses published by W. H. Paling [q.v.5] & Co. Ltd. It was sung by a choir of 10 000 voices at the inauguration of the Commonwealth and played by massed bands at the naming of the Federal capital celebrations in Canberra. In 1907 the Carruthers [q.v.7] government awarded McCormick £100 for his patriotic composition.

On 1 August 1913 McCormick described how he came to write the song: after attending a concert at which national anthems were sung he 'felt very aggravated that there was not one note for Australia. On the way home in a bus, I concocted the first verse of my song, & when I got home I set it to music. I first wrote it in the Tonic Sol-fa Notation, then transcribed it into the Old Notation, & tried it over on an instrument next morning, & found it correct . . . It seemed to me to be like an inspiration, & I wrote the words & music with the greatest ease'. On 3 September 1915 he formally registered his copyright.

Survived by his wife, McCormick died childless at his home at Waverley on 30 October 1916 and was buried in Rookwood cemetery. His estate was valued for probate at £52.

After his death sporadic attempts to have 'Advance Australia Fair' proclaimed Australia's national anthem succeeded in 1974. Subsequently a descendant of John Macfarlane (d. 1866) claimed that Macfarlane had originally composed the music and written the first verse. Some musicologists consider the tune to be based on a typical 'wandering melody', a theory given some credence by McCormick's ease and method of composition. It seems, however, that there is little doubt that McCormick was responsible for 'Advance Australia Fair'—certainly his contemporaries accepted his bona fides.

A. R. Chisholm, *Men were my milestones* (Melb, 1958); *Messenger* (Presbyterian, NSW), 22 Feb, 21 Mar 1907, 24 July 1913; *Scottish A'sian*, 1 Mar 1912, p 867, Jan 1917, p 5221; *SMH*, 27 Nov, 5 Dec 1878, 31 Oct 1916, 10 May 1942, 20 July, 7 Aug, 20, 30 Nov, 1, 6, 7, 8 Dec 1943; *Canberra Times*, 19 May 1984, 26 Jan, 7, 23 Feb 1985; Applications for employment, 1/373, *and* in-letters, 1863, St Marys National School, 1/421,

Bd of National Education (NSWA); P. D. McCormick letter, 1 Aug 1913 (NL); information from Prof W. Bebbington, Brisb.　　　　　JIM FLETCHER

McCOURT, WILLIAM JOSEPH (1851-1913), newspaper proprietor and parliamentarian, was born in March 1851 in Monaghan, Ireland, son of James McCourt, farmer, and his wife Bridget, née Smith. Aged 2 he was brought to New South Wales by his parents who settled at Wollongong. He was educated at Wollongong National School and at 13 entered the office of John and Thomas Garrett [q.v.4], before being apprenticed as a printer with the *Illawarra Mercury*. He read avidly, played cricket with the Illawarra team and enjoyed shooting.

Soon after completing his articles, McCourt founded the Moss Vale *Scrutineer and West Camden Advocate* in 1874 and made a local reputation before selling it in 1886. He was vice-president of the Berrima District Cottage Hospital board, a director of the Berrima District Butter Co. and, a Freemason, was worshipful master of the Bowral lodge. At Holy Trinity Church, Berrima, on 18 May 1882 McCourt married Emily Elizabeth Galbraith, daughter of a storekeeper; later they lived at Berrima. He travelled extensively in Australia, speculated in land in New South Wales and Western Australia and in 1887-1913 was chairman of the Intercolonial Investment, Land, and Building Co. Ltd.

Defeated in 1880, McCourt had been elected to the Legislative Assembly for Camden in 1882. He did not contest the 1885 election, but represented that seat in 1887-94, Bowral in 1894-1904 and Wollondilly in 1904-13. A strong if conventional Free Trader, he supported Sir Henry Parkes [q.v.5] and became a close follower of (Sir) George Reid [q.v.]. He foresaw financial problems in Federation, opposed payment of members and life appointments to the Legislative Council, was suspicious of squatters and financial institutions and supported female suffrage. His interventions in debate were few and short, largely confined to local matters. Elected chairman of committees in 1894, McCourt resigned his seat in February 1895 when the calling in of a bank guarantee forced him into bankruptcy. Although he was not discharged until July, the by-election was uncontested and he was re-elected chairman of committees in March, holding this position until elected Speaker in June 1900, with the support of (Sir) William Lyne's [q.v.] Protectionist government.

His remarkable achievement was to be elected to the two presiding positions of the assembly over sixteen years without having his candidature contested. Faced with certain defeat by the Labor candidate J. H. Cann [q.v.7] McCourt did not stand for the Speakership in November 1910. More than any other presiding officer before or since, he expressed the tradition, often notable by its entire absence, of an impartial Speaker enjoying support from all sides of the House. With thick, dark eyebrows and walrus moustache, he owed his success more to a dignified geniality than to intellectual distinction. W. A. Holman [q.v.9] thought that McCourt's 'amiability of temperament made him disposed rather to overlook offences than pursue them with any rigour'.

About 1907 McCourt moved to Sydney; he was an alderman on the Vaucluse Municipal Council in 1908-11 and in 1912 served on the royal commission into legalising and regulating the use of the totalisator, which he favoured. On 22 June 1913 he died of intestinal obstruction at Darlinghurst and was buried in the Church of England section of Berrima cemetery. His estate was valued for probate at £2592. He was survived by his wife (d. 1923), two sons, and three daughters including twins Myall and Mallee; the elder son William Rupert was clerk of the Legislative Assembly in 1930-47.

Cyclopedia of N.S.W (Syd, 1907); R. A. Arnold (comp), *Decisions of Honorable William McCourt* (Syd, 1910); G. N. Hawker, *The parliament of New South Wales, 1856-1965* (Syd, 1971); *Illustrated Express*, 27 Apr 1887; *Daily Telegraph* (Syd), 6 July 1894; *T&CJ*, 25 Dec 1907, 25 June 1913; *SMH*, 23 June 1913; *Fighting Line*, 19 July 1913; Bankruptcy file 9317 (NSWA); Parkes papers (ML).
　　　　　　　　　　　　　　　　　G. N. HAWKER

McCOY, WILLIAM TAYLOR (1866-1929), educationist, was born on 13 October 1866 in Sydney, son of James Smith McCoy, bootmaker and prominent Methodist, and his wife Eliza, née Wilson, a schoolteacher. William was educated at Cleveland Street Public School and in 1881 began as a pupil-teacher at Ultimo Public School. He attended Fort Street Training School for a year in 1885; several brief appointments followed. Teaching at Redfern in 1890-93, he also studied at the University of Sydney (B.A., 1894). He married Rachel Armstrong, a teacher, on 27 December 1894 with Presbyterian forms. McCoy was head teacher in schools at Glen Innes, Armidale and Burwood and in 1905 became inspector for the Lismore district of 120 schools.

During McCoy's career as inspector his most noted contributions concerned in-service work for teachers and a drive to gain more parental and public interest in schools' activities. Both were part of a campaign to advance the reformist 'New Education' cause, associated with the director of education Peter Board [q.v.7]. When controversy forced W. L. Neale [q.v.] to resign as Tasmania's director of education in 1909, McCoy replaced him next year.

Neale had laid the foundations of administrative reorganization and curricular innovation, but there was still much to do. Tasmanian public education fell short of that on the mainland, especially in the infant and post-primary sectors, facilities for remote areas, and teacher training. McCoy's challenge was to improve the system while placating the community and teaching service. Early salary increases and a system of classification to regularize promotion made teachers receptive to other sweeping changes. McCoy convened and addressed meetings of teachers throughout the State, explaining his changes to the regulations and primary school syllabus. He accompanied the 1910 revised syllabus with copious notes of advice. Both the method and the substance of such innovation owed much to Board's example. There was an adherence to the psychological concept of transfer of training; and an emphasis on morality, respect for property and social stability, and national pride. McCoy's pedagogic reforms did not reflect deep theoretical knowledge or originality, but he implemented others' ideas effectively. His skill in mobilizing the inspectorate as a means of curricular change was crucial. This showed in his new policy of recruiting inspectors on grounds of intellect and personality rather than seniority, and in his use of inspectors more as diagnosticians and less as assessors.

A notable achievement was the establishment of post-primary education. Persuading the University of Tasmania to relax the subject requirements of the junior public examination, he encouraged larger primary schools to develop 'super-primary' classes. The first two state high schools were opened in 1913 in Hobart and Launceston; intermediate high schools followed at West Devonport and Burnie in 1915 and a new system of bursaries helped country children seeking secondary schooling. McCoy also directed attention to educational goals for working-class children. The Tasmanian government was planning hydro-electric expansion and growth of electrolytic zinc works and advocated technical education for these purposes. But the form it took grew from McCoy's ideas: technical education was brought under the Education Department and in 1918 a system of junior technical schools was introduced.

Teacher training was transformed. In his professionalization of the teaching service McCoy was assisted by the establishment in 1911 of the Philip Smith Training College near the university. The state secondary schools enabled the teachers' college to shift from completing a secondary education to the professional preparation of standard recruits; for those recruits for small schools who had customarily by-passed the college, a short intensive training course was established at East Launceston School in 1913. By 1919 public education in Tasmania resembled the centralized systems on the mainland.

In October 1919 McCoy became director of education in South Australia, where morale was low and a sense of educational stagnation was reflected in the press. Initially he impressed teachers by a reclassification scheme that removed major promotion barriers, a liberalization of the inspectorial system and an increase in salaries. He reformed the primary school syllabus in 1920 with an emphasis on social-moral goals and an increased dose of patriotism. In 1921 he supported a bill to introduce religious instruction into state schools, but it was opposed in parliament and by teachers; on its defeat, and during later attempts to revive the issue in the 1920s, McCoy was silent.

The changes most clearly associated with McCoy in South Australia related to vocational and teacher education. In 1925 he introduced central schools, primary school annexes offering post-primary courses in commercial, junior technical and home-making work. Faced with conflicting assessments of the venture, McCoy defended it as a suitable compromise between the technical school's vocationalism and the academic emphasis of the high school. In teacher education a scheme introduced in 1920 raised entry qualifications and attacked the old notion of apprenticeship by insisting that training be completed before the commencement of teaching.

McCoy's decisions on innovations (such as Montessori's experiments in infant education, the use of radio in schools or specialist guidance for school leavers) were cautious rather than radical. But once convinced, his implementation of reforms demonstrated energy and tact. He produced two centralized, smooth-running school systems between 1910 and 1929. He made a mark with ideas and discussion at the Imperial Education conferences in London in 1923 and 1927, but his contribution had been mainly within Australia. McCoy died suddenly of hypertensive cerebro-vascular disease in Adelaide on 12 August 1929 and was buried in North Road cemetery; his wife, daughter and son survived him. He was remembered for his idealism, efficiency and justice; the president of the Public Teachers' Union said 'union and teachers had lost the best friend they ever had'.

B. K. Hyams, 'W. T. McCoy, Director of education, Tasmania, 1910-19; South Australia 1919-29', in C. Turney (ed), *Pioneers of Australian edu-*

cation, 3 (Syd, 1983); *Advertiser* (Adel), 13 Aug 1929; D. V. Selth, The effect of poverty and politics on the development of Tasmanian State education, 1910-1950 (M.A. thesis, Univ Tas, 1969); W. G. Richards, W. T. McCoy and his directorship of education in South Australia 1919-1929 (M.Ed. thesis, Univ Adel, 1973).   B. K. HYAMS

McCRACKEN, ALEXANDER (1856-1915), brewer and sportsman, was born on 7 May 1856 in Melbourne, second son of Robert McCracken [q.v.5] and his wife Margaret, née Hannah. He was educated at Scotch College and then joined his father's brewery firm, R. McCracken & Co., becoming a junior partner in 1884. In 1888 he became managing director after McCracken's was purchased and floated as a public company by B. J. Fink [q.v.4]. The company lost heavily in 1892 when Fink was declared bankrupt; the continuing depression took further toll. In June 1896 McCracken went to London to negotiate concessions on the interest payments to debenture holders. Some accommodation was achieved but only after an English representative had investigated the company's affairs and strongly criticized the board of directors. The company was saved from liquidation, but trading did not improve and in May 1907 McCracken's and five other brewing firms were merged into Carlton & United Breweries Ltd. McCracken was made a director.

Though the shareholders had suffered, McCracken's City Brewery had never ceased to project a large and popular image. McCracken himself had a reputation for genial management and honest dealing. He became a powerful figure in the organization of the brewing industry, and its favourite spokesman. He was an early president of the Brewers' Club of Melbourne (1891), and first chairman of the Brewers' Association of Victoria (1901), the Manufacturers' Bottle Co. of Victoria (1903) and the Liquor Trades Defence Union (1903). He was president of the Royal Agricultural Society in 1909-15 and a director of the Trustees Executors & Agency Co. Ltd and of the Victoria Insurance Co.

A good speaker and an easy mixer, McCracken was a man made for the public appearance and the social occasion. His enthusiasm for team-games amounted to a passion. He was the first secretary and later president of the Essendon Football Club; his portrait hangs in their rooms. He was founder and president of the Essendon Rowing Club. Local cricket, tennis, golf, bowling, athletics, baseball, cycling, rifle-shooting and lacrosse were all indebted to his generous patronage; trophies bearing his name became commonplace. He was also president of the Essendon Poultry, Dog, Pigeon and Canary Society, the Essendon Town Fire Brigade and the Essendon Literary and Debating Society.

Outside Essendon he was first president of the Victorian Football League (1897-1915) after the breakaway from the Victorian Football Association, and a founder of the Oaklands Hunt Club. He raced a number of horses with modest success, winning the Caulfield Grand National Steeplechase in 1893 with Knight of the Garter, and served as chairman and vice-chairman of the Victoria Racing Club.

In 1894 McCracken stood against Alfred Deakin [q.v.8] for the Legislative Assembly seat of Essendon and Flemington. Soundly defeated, he did not attempt to enter politics again. He died of cirrhosis of the liver at his home, North Park, Essendon, on 25 August 1915 and was buried in Melbourne general cemetery, leaving an estate valued for probate at £175 358. The main beneficiaries were his wife Mary Elizabeth, née Peck, whom he had married on 19 September 1884 at Pascoe Vale, and his two sons and three daughters. The Essendon Presbyterian Church received a small legacy.

A. Henderson (ed), *Australian families*, 1 (Melb, 1941); A. D. Pyke, *The gold, the blue: a history of Lowther Hall* (Melb, 1983); *Aust Brewers' J*, 8 (1889); *Essendon Gazette*, 27 Nov 1913; *Argus*, 26 Aug 1915.   G. H. GELLIE

McCRAE, HUGH RAYMOND (1876-1958), poet, was born on 4 October 1876 at Anchorfield, Hawthorn, Melbourne, second son of George Gordon McCrae [q.v.5], Scottish-born civil servant and poet, and his Tasmanian wife Augusta Helen, née Brown; Georgiana McCrae [q.v.2] was his grandmother. He was educated at Hawthorn Grammar School and brought up in literary circles, which he later vividly portrayed in *My father and my father's friends* (1935).

Briefly articled to an architect, McCrae was soon emboldened by his friends Lionel and Norman Lindsay [qq.v.] to attempt to make a living by freelance writing and drawing: his first poem was published in the *Bulletin* in 1896. He lived a Bohemian existence and belonged to the artists' club, the Prehistoric Order of Cannibals.

At Christ Church, Hawthorn, on 4 May 1901 McCrae married Annie Geraldine (Nancy), daughter of William Anderson Adams, grazier. They went at once to Sydney and later shared a house at Lavender Bay with the Norman Lindsays; McCrae derived an exiguous income by contributing verses and drawings to the *Bulletin, Lone Hand, Worker, Bookfellow, Trident* and *Clarion*. He was encouraged to write poetry by the warm appreciation of A. G. Stephens [q.v.] and Norman Lindsay, who later wrote that McCrae's 'personality and his poetry have both become interwoven through the years with my progression through art and life . . . his imagery was so much in key with mine that the urge to illustrate his poetry was irresistible'. He illustrated McCrae's first volume of poetry, *Satyrs and sunlight: silvarum libri* (1909, 1911). Lionel Lindsay described him at this time: 'Tall, and apparently robust, impetuous in movement, nervous, and capable of intense happiness or suffering, there is in the set of Hugh McCrae's shapely head that bespeaks the man apart'. All his life McCrae stood aside from public ferment. Like Norman Lindsay's, his world was full of satyrs, centaurs, unicorns, fauns and nymphs. He drew on 'Greek myth, the medieval past particularly through the Scottish border ballad and the French middle ages', the eighteenth century and 'his own kind of chinoiserie or japonaiserie'.

In May 1914, 'broke and with no work', McCrae went to the United States of America, but nearly starved in New York. He managed to get work on the stage, playing minor parts in *Androcles and the lion* and *The man who married a dumb wife*, both produced by Granville Barker, and in *The garden of paradise*. Returning to Melbourne McCrae played the lead in a silent film, *The life's romance of Adam Lindsay Gordon* (1916), acted in Shakespearian productions under Ian MacLaren and with Gregan McMahon's [q.v.] Repertory Theatre Company, and was employed as a decoder in the wartime Censor's Office.

A limited edition of *Colombine*, a book of McCrae's poems, was published by *Art in Australia* in 1920 and later that year by Angus [q.v.7] & Robertson [q.v.] Ltd with eleven illustrations by N. Lindsay, who also published fifteen of McCrae's poems, with five of his own etchings, in a limited edition, *Idyllia* (1922). It was described by H. F. Chaplin as 'one of the most beautiful books ever produced in Australia'.

In 1922 McCrae returned to Sydney with his family where, except for a few years at Camden in the early 1930s, he lived for the rest of his life. The *Du Poissey anecdotes* (1922), light-hearted annals written in an eighteenth century manner, illustrated by himself, is a dish relished by scholars with a fine taste for satire and the oddities of life, but not generally palatable. Before returning to Sydney McCrae had begun, and continued thereafter, the verse-drama, 'Joan of Arc', that he hoped to make his masterpiece. Three scenes entitled 'Orlando and Isabelle' were included in his collected poems, *Satyrs and sunlight*, again illustrated and decorated by Lindsay and published in London by the Fanfrolico Press in 1928.

Unworldly and perennially hard up, McCrae received a Commonwealth Literary Fund pension of £52 a year from 1926, except for 1928 when with Ernest Watt [q.v.] he was joint editor (at £7 a week) of the *New Triad*: in 1941 his pension was increased to £2 a week. Otherwise he scraped a meagre living by contributing theatre criticisms, prose sketches, pen drawings and cartoons to Melbourne *Punch*, the *Bulletin*, *Art in Australia*, *Home* and other journals, and poems to the *Sydney Morning Herald*. His musical fantasy, *The ship of heaven*, with music by Alfred Hill [q.v.9], was produced by Doris Fitton at the Independent Theatre on 7 October 1933 and published with his own illustrations in 1951. He edited and published his grandmother's diaries, as *Georgiana's journal*, in 1934. In 1938 his fantastical poem, *The Mimshi maiden*, appeared. R. G. Howarth made selections of McCrae's poems—*Forests of Pan* (1944), *Voice of the forest* (1945), a collection of his prose writings, *Story-book only* (1948), and a posthumous volume, *The best poems of Hugh McCrae* (1961), which included the whole of the incomplete 'Joan of Arc'.

A man of great charm and attractiveness, enhanced by his classical good looks, McCrae was a rare human being with a 'Rabelaisian sense of humour'. He delighted his family and friends with innumerable letters and notes, written in beautiful calligraphy and adorned with marginal drawings of 'striking boldness and clarity of line'; they constitute a major part of his claims to fame. His prose was distinguished by fastidious choice of words, invention, humour and irony. A collection of his letters, edited by R. D. FitzGerald, was published posthumously in 1970.

McCrae's wife had died in 1943. At Mosman on 4 July 1946 he married Janet Le Brun, née Brown, widow of the composer Horace Keats [q.v.9], but the marriage was dissolved on 22 July 1948. Appointed O.B.E. in 1953, McCrae died at Wahroonga on 17 February 1958 and was cremated. His three daughters, Dorothea Huntly Cowper, Marjorie Francesca McWilliam and Georgiana Rose Morris, survived him. Intestate, he left only books, pictures and manuscripts, valued for probate at £133.

Admired as a poet in his generation, he was honoured in a special Hugh McCrae number by *Art in Australia* in 1931 and by *Southerly* (No. 3, 1956) subtitled 'A birthday garland for Hugh McCrae'. In the words of Vivian Smith 'McCrae seemed to his admirers to stand like a peak above the tepid swamps of provincial versifying of his day'. His poetry was joyful, sensuous, full of colour and delightful verbal arabesques, but it showed no development, lacked coherent structure and was often incomplete. He shunned any kind of philosophy and earnestness about poetry or life;

nevertheless he was one of the most influential Australian poets, notably on Kenneth Slessor and to a lesser extent on Douglas Stewart, R. D. FitzGerald, Kenneth Mackenzie and A. D. Hope. H. M. Green described him as 'a prince of lyricists' and many of his poems were set to music—by Arthur Benjamin, Frank Hutchens [qq.v.7,9], Dorian le Gallienne, Alfred and Mirrie Hill and Keats. For Judith Wright, McCrae's 'real importance lies in those early years of the century, when he broke through the self-congratulatory parochialism of Australian literary life . . . The fact that he was a singer, not a thinker, freed the notion of poetry from the portentousness of the Nationalist and radical schools'.

A bust of McCrae by C. Web Gilbert [q.v.9] is in the Art Gallery of New South Wales.

T. I. Moore, *Six Australian poets* (Melb, 1942); N. Palmer, *Fourteen years* (Melb, 1948); G. Dutton (ed), *The literature of Australia* (Melb, 1964); George Mackaness, *Bibliomania* (Syd, 1965); H. F. Chaplin (comp), *A McCrae miscellany* (Studies in Aust bibliog, no 16, Syd, 1967); N. Lindsay, *My mask* (Syd, 1970); K. Slessor, *Bread and wine* (Syd, 1970); L. Kramer (ed), *Oxford history of Australian literature* (Melb, 1981); *Lone Hand*, 1 Jan 1909; *Meanjin Q*, 30, no 3, Sept 1971, p 353; *Bulletin*, 24 Apr 1924; Mackaness papers (NL); Commonwealth Literary Fund, Minutes of meetings (A3753, item 72/2760, 2766) *and* Dept of Defence corresp. files 363/4/700 (AAO).   NORMAN COWPER
MARTHA RUTLEDGE

McCUBBIN, FREDERICK (1855-1917), painter and art teacher, was born on 25 February 1855 at 165 King Street, Melbourne, third son of Alexander McCubbin, baker from Ayrshire, Scotland, and his English wife Anne, née McWilliams. Educated at William Willmott's West Melbourne Common school and St Paul's School, Swanston Street, at about 14 he was placed in a solicitor's office. He soon joined the family business and drove a baker's cart before being apprenticed to a coach-painter.

In 1869 he enrolled at the Artisans' School of Design, Carlton, and later studied drawing under Thomas Clark [q.v.3] at the school of design, National Gallery of Victoria. He completed his coach-painting apprenticeship in 1875 but next year his hopes for furthering his studies at the gallery were curtailed by the death of his father and the need to assist with the family business. McCubbin continued in the school of design under O. R. Campbell [q.v.3], and joined the school of painting as well under Eugen von Guerard [q.v.4] in 1877. Tom Roberts and Mackennal [qq.v.] were fellow students. He remained at the art schools on the appointment of G. F. Folingsby [q.v.4] in 1882 and next year was awarded the

trustees' first prize in the first of the annual students' exhibitions. He also studied and exhibited at the Victorian Academy of Art, showing in their annual exhibitions of 1876 and 1879-82, selling his first painting, 'View Near Fisherman's Bend', from the 1880 exhibition. In 1882 he was awarded a silver medal for figure drawing in the academy life-class and was elected an associate.

When Roberts returned from overseas in 1885, he and McCubbin went on painting trips, camping at Housten's farm at Box Hill, at Mentone on Port Phillip Bay and later in the Heidelberg area. Here they were joined by Arthur Streeton [q.v.], Charles Conder [q.v.3] and others, these first camps marking the beginning of what came to be called the Heidelberg school. Nicknamed 'The Proff' because of his philosophizing, McCubbin was a strong advocate of the particularly national element in the work of the school, drawing his inspiration both from the earlier traditions of colonial art and the growing sense of nationalism of the time.

In 1886 he was appointed drawing master of the school of design and held this position for the rest of his life. A group of professional artists led by McCubbin, Roberts, John Ford Paterson [q.v.5] and others broke away from the Victorian Academy of Art in 1887 and formed the Australian Artists' Association. A committee-member, McCubbin participated in the association's exhibitions until it amalgamated with the academy in 1888 as the Victorian Artists' Society. McCubbin served as a councillor of the society from the beginning and was president in 1903-04 and 1909. He contributed regularly to its annual exhibitions until 1912, when he resigned to join with seven other artists to form the Australian Art Association as its first president.

In 1889 he had joined Roberts, Streeton, Conder, C. Douglas Richardson [q.v.], R. E. Falls and Herbert Daly in the exhibition of 9 x 5 impressions at Buxton's Galleries. He occasionally participated in the Society of Artists' exhibitions of the late 1890s in Sydney, was represented in the 1898 Exhibition of Australian Art, Grafton Galleries, London, and held one-man shows in Melbourne from about 1904. He had married Annie Lucy Moriarty at St Ignatius Church, Richmond, on 5 March 1889. In the following years they lived in the Melbourne suburbs of Auburn, Blackburn, Brighton and Carlton, then for several years in the cottage named Fontainebleau at Macedon, and finally at Carlsburg, South Yarra. On the death of Folingsby in 1891 McCubbin was acting director of the National Gallery until the appointment of Bernard Hall [q.v.9] in 1892, and was so again in 1903 and 1905. He did not find Hall a congenial superior. He visited Tasmania in 1899, and in 1907 was given leave from the gallery to visit England and Europe, staying with his old friend Roberts and visiting numerous galleries and art schools. He was given further leave in 1916 owing to ill health and he died of heart disease on 20 December 1917 at South Yarra, and was buried in Brighton cemetery. His wife, four sons including Louis [q.v.] and two daughters survived him.

McCubbin's first work to be acquired for a public gallery was 'Feeding Time', purchased by the National Gallery of Victoria in 1894 and exchanged for 'A Winter Evening' in 1900; 'The Pioneers' was also acquired in 1906. The Western Australian and New South Wales galleries made purchases in 1896 and 1897; 'A Bush Burial' was bought by public subscription for the Geelong Art Gallery in 1900; and the Art Gallery of South Australia purchased paintings in 1900 and 1912.

McCubbin, as one of the founders of the Heidelberg school, was a major figure in the development of the Australian school of landscape and subject painting that emerged at the close of the nineteenth century. His early interest in the portrayal of national life was illustrated in his large subject pictures of recent history, extolling the virtues and quiet heroism of the pioneers. His work was directly influenced by the earlier traditions of Australian colonial art, late-Victorian subject pictures of a high moral tone, Folingsby's interests in heroic history pieces, and the young colony's emerging sense of national identity. Other influences included Louis Buvelot [q.v.3], Roberts and *plein air* realism, combined with the example of Bastien-Lepage and his humble peasants. In later years McCubbin turned increasingly to landscape painting, portraying the lyrical and intimate beauty of the bush. The early influence of Corot gave way to that of J. M. W. Turner, as he turned from the quiet poetry of the shaded bush to the brilliant impressionistic effects of light and colour of his final manner. He was also a portrait painter.

A warm and gregarious personality and a gentle and intuitive teacher, Frederick McCubbin contributed greatly to the art world in Melbourne by his activities in various societies, through the conviviality of the McCubbin house which was always a focus for artists and students, and as a teacher of several generations of artists. He was a member of the Savage Club.

An early self-portrait is in the Art Gallery of New South Wales and a later one in the Art Gallery of South Australia. A retrospective exhibition to mark the centenary of the artist's birth was held at the National Gallery of Victoria in 1955.

E. La T. Armstrong, *The book of the . . . National Gallery of Victoria, 1856-1906* (Melb, 1906) and . . .

1906-1931 (Melb, 1932); J. S. MacDonald (ed), *The art of Frederick McCubbin* (Melb, 1916); Bernard Smith, *Australian painting, 1788-1960* (Melb, 1962); A. Galbally, *Frederick McCubbin* (Melb, 1981); K. Mangan, *Daisy chains, war, then jazz* (Melb, 1984); *Meanjin Q*, 15 (1956) no. 3; *Art and Aust*, 7 (June 1969); Cttee of the National Gallery to the trustees of the Public Lib, Museums and National Gallery of Vic, *Reports*, 1870-86; *LaTL J*, 6, no 24, Oct 1979; Minute-books of the Vic Academy of the Arts, Aust Artists' Assn and Vic Artists' Soc (SLV); personal information.

DAVID THOMAS

McCUBBIN, LOUIS FREDERICK (1890-1952), artist and gallery director, was born on 18 March 1890 at Hawthorn, Melbourne, eldest of seven children of Frederick McCubbin [q.v.] and his wife Annie Lucy, née Moriarty. He was educated privately and at the National Gallery School, Melbourne, under Bernard Hall [q.v.9] and his father in 1906-11. In May 1916 he enlisted in the Australian Imperial Force, 14th Battalion, and served in France from November 1917 as a stretcher-bearer with the 10th Field Ambulance. Appointed an official war artist under the Australian Records Section scheme to the 3rd Division, he visited scenes of battles with Wallace Anderson and C. Web Gilbert [q.v.9] after the war to collect data for proposed dioramas.

In 1920 McCubbin returned to Australia and joined the staff of the Australian War Museum, then located in the Exhibition Building, Melbourne, to paint backgrounds for dioramas and murals until 1930. He was awarded the Crouch [q.v.8] prize for landscape in 1928 and in 1931 was commissioned by the Australian National Travel Association to paint a series of pictures of the Barrier Reef. He was president of the Victorian Artists' Society in 1933-35. During 1935 he was senior instructor in drawing and painting at Swinburne [q.v.] Technical College, Melbourne, and in 1935-36 he undertook further work on the dioramas for the War Memorial. On 27 April 1936 he married the widowed Stella Elsie Mary Jackson (d. 1939), née Abraham, at Christ Church, South Yarra.

McCubbin was director of the Art Gallery of South Australia in 1936-50, and revitalized it through his many innovations. He renovated the displays, rewrote the catalogue to the collection, initiated weekly lectures for schoolchildren, introduced the quarterly *Bulletin* containing articles on outstanding works of art in the collection, and organized touring exhibitions to country districts. He also made significant acquisitions, placing particular emphasis on Australian art, including Conder's [q.v.3] 'How We Lost Poor Flossie' and 'Feeding the Chickens', Streeton's [q.v.] 'Road to Templestowe' and Drysdale's 'Woman in a Landscape'. Moreover, he was prominent with other directors of State galleries in endeavouring to bring important exhibitions to Australia.

During World War II McCubbin was deputy director of camouflage, South Australia (1941-43), and was a member of the art committee of the Australian War Memorial. Among those artists he supported were Ivor Hele, Donald Friend, Stella Bowen [q.v.7] and Murray Griffin. He was a member of the Commonwealth Art Advisory Board in 1945-52. In 1947 he was appointed O.B.E. He retired through ill health in 1950 and returned to Melbourne. In 1946 he had refused the offer of directorship of the National Art Gallery of New South Wales because of inadequate salary.

Louis McCubbin worked under the influence and the shadow of his father, who depicted him as a child in his paintings; and before World War I they occasionally exhibited together. Louis continued to paint works of some charm; however, gallery administration increasingly absorbed his time. He always maintained an open mind to the work of other artists, especially encouraging the young, and his taste 'at once so fine and so catholic' was respected. Tall and rather heavily built, McCubbin, though equable in manner and friendly and modest, was yet responsible and forceful. Intensely human, with a joyous outlook on life, he had a delightful sense of humour and a generous nature.

McCubbin died, childless, on 6 December 1952 at the Royal Melbourne Hospital of cerebral haemorrhage and was cremated. His work is represented in several Australian public collections.

Bulletin of the National Gallery of South Australia, 11, no 4, Apr 1950, 14, no 3, Jan 1953; *Advertiser* (Adel), 8 Dec 1952; Bean papers (AWM); Louis McCubbin papers (SLV).   ANNE GRAY

McCULLOCH, ALLAN RIVERSTONE (1885-1925), ichthyologist and field naturalist, was born on 20 June 1885 at Concord, Sydney, son of Herbert Riverstone McCulloch, barrister, and his wife Ella Maude, sister of Alfred Backhouse [q.v.7], both Australian born. At 13 he joined the Australian Museum, Sydney, as an unpaid volunteer and on 1 July 1901 became mechanical assistant to E. R. Waite [q.v.] who introduced him to systematic ichthyology and with Charles Hedley [q.v.9] encouraged his obvious artistic talent. He later studied drawing under Julian Ashton [q.v.7]. On 1 July 1906 he was appointed a scientific assistant and in October accompanied W. A. Haswell [q.v.9] in the *Woy Woy* carrying out dredging operations thirty-five miles (56 km) off Port Jackson. His paper on

the fishes and crustaceans found at 800 fathoms was the first of many in the *Records* of the Australian Museum and other scientific journals. On Waite's departure in 1906 he was appointed in charge of vertebrates.

At first interested in decapod crustacea, on which he became a recognized authority, McCulloch soon turned his attention to the formidable task of ordering the Australian fish fauna, the nomenclature of which, owing to much careless earlier work, was in a disorganized state. In this painstaking work he described many new species but the unravelling of a difficult piece of synonymy always gave him acute pleasure. In 1908 he published in the *Records* the first of an eight-part series, 'Studies in Australian fishes', and in 1911 and 1914-16 completed extensive reports on fishes obtained around the Australian coast by H. K. Dannevig [q.v.8] in the ill-fated fisheries' investigation ship, *Endeavour*. In 1919 he began publishing his most important work, 'Check-list of the fish and fish-like animals of New South Wales', in the *Australian Zoologist*, which was later issued separately as *Australian Zoological Handbook No 1* (Sydney, 1922). He also contributed numerous entries on Australian fishes for the *Australian Encyclopaedia* (Sydney, 1925-26).

As an ardent field naturalist McCulloch carried out work on the whole east coast of Australia, including several expeditions to the Great Barrier Reef and various Pacific islands; in 1922 with Frank Hurley [q.v.9] he undertook an adventurous journey into Papua-New Guinea. Not physically robust (though he had succeeded in finally joining the Australian Imperial Force in September 1918), he worked indefatigably, often far into the night; lack of recreation seriously undermined his health physically and mentally. Unable to resist his 'naturalists' paradise', he spent much time recuperating from ill health on Lord Howe Island.

Granted a years sick leave, McCulloch went to Hawaii in mid-1925 where he conferred with fishery specialists and was involved in planning a fisheries conference of the Pan-Pacific Union. He was found dead in his room at the Colonial Hotel, Honolulu, on 1 September 1925 with a self-inflicted gunshot wound to the head. His ashes were interred in a tall granite column on Flagstaff Hill on his beloved Lord Howe Island. He was unmarried.

McCulloch was of a retiring disposition, but a genial nature underlay his reticence. He was an expert photographer and cinematographer, an accomplished musician and excellent lecturer. A consummate artist, apart from illustrating his own papers and some of the illustrations in G. Lyell's and G. A. Waterhouse's [qq.v.] *Butterflies of Australia* (Sydney, 1914), his pencil and brush were always at the disposal of his junior and less gifted colleagues. He was prominent in training the younger members of the zoological staff and never failed them in help and advice. He was a council-member of the Linnean and Royal Zoological societies of New South Wales, and edited the latter's journal, the *Australian Zoologist*, for some years.

The noted American ichthyologist David Starr Jordan regarded McCulloch as 'one of the most accurate workers in systematic ichthyology' and though he won similar praise from his contemporaries, history's verdict is less enthusiastic. According to Ronald Strahan some of his efforts were misdirected: 'Like most self-taught naturalists, he was a "species-splitter"with an inordinate respect for the written word', and rather than let sleeping dogs lie, 'would upset accepted nomenclature by resurrecting obscure names'.

In 1929-30 *Check-list of fishes recorded from Australia* was prepared and edited from material left by McCulloch by his successor Gilbert P. Whitley and published as *Memoir* 5 of the Australian Museum.

A. Musgrave, *Bibliography of Australian entomology 1775-1930* (Syd, 1932); R. Strahan (ed), *Rare and curious specimens* (Syd, 1979); Linnean Soc NSW, *Procs*, 51 (1926), p vi; *Aust Zoologist*, 4 Apr 1926, p 227; Aust Museum, *Records*, 15 (1926-27), p 141, and for publications; *SMH*, 7 Sept, 9 Oct 1925.   G. P. WALSH

McCUTCHEON, ROBERT GEORGE (1841-1918), printer and politician, was born in 1841 at Omagh, Tyrone, Ireland, son of John McCutcheon, farmer, and his wife Margaret, née Bothwell. He arrived in Melbourne with his family in 1858 and next year travelled to India, working for twelve months as a printer in Calcutta. Returning to Victoria, he worked as a journalist and printer at Ballarat and at Port Fairy. On 13 December 1867, in Melbourne, he married Mary Ann Ebblewhite with Wesleyan forms.

In 1873 McCutcheon joined the Melbourne printing firm of Mason, Firth & McCutcheon Pty Ltd, succeeding his brother John in 1876 and becoming sole proprietor by 1878. The firm printed the catalogue for Melbourne's first international exhibition in 1880-81 and expanded to become one of the largest printing and lithography businesses in Australia. A former employee (Sir) John Mackey [q.v.] described him as 'a generous and fair employer'.

In October 1902 McCutcheon won the Legislative Assembly seat of St Kilda. He was an enthusiastic supporter of (Sir) William Irvine [q.v.9] and of the 'economy in government' ideals of the Kyabram movement.

Although McCutcheon usually supported the non-Labor governments of the day, breaking ranks only in 1908 to vote for the no confidence motion against Sir Thomas Bent [q.v.3], he remained an independently minded back-bencher who 'always said what he thought'. Only near the end of his political career did he attain office, serving as minister without portfolio in the Peacock [q.v.] government from November 1915 until November 1916.

Described as 'the most conservative member of the Assembly', McCutcheon believed that 'the functions of a Government were to look after the peace and well-being of the people, to see that the expenses of the State were obtained from legitimate sources, and apart from this, and from the defence of the people, to let the people alone as much as possible'. He gave practical effect to his concerns for economy by serving on the Public Accounts Committee in 1904-12 and by his departure from the Peacock ministry over its alleged failure to curb expenditure.

McCutcheon disapproved of free secondary education and opposed pensions on the grounds that it was an 'evil principle' for any government to 'dispense directly money to any class in the State'; he was deeply suspicious of public servants who, as dependants of the State, would be 'anxious for . . . as much socialistic legislation as possible'. Yet, like most Victorian conservatives, he was prepared to give qualified approval to some aspects of 'State Socialism'. He admired the work of Frank Tate [q.v.] as director of education, believed in the extension of technical education and supported teachers' claims for higher pay.

Dour in character, McCutcheon was an active Methodist; chess was his principal hobby and he was president of the Melbourne Chess Club in 1908-18. He retired from parliament in October 1917 and died at his St Kilda home on 20 October 1918. Survived by his wife, who was a prominent member of the Australian Women's National League, and by five sons and three daughters, he was buried in Melbourne general cemetery.

PD(Vic), 1918, p 1782; *Cowans*, June 1904; *Age* and *Argus*, 21 Oct 1918; K. Rollison, Groups and attitudes in the Victorian Legislative Assembly, 1900-1909 (Ph.D. thesis, La Trobe Univ, 1972).
                                         GEOFF BROWNE

McDONAGH, ISABELLA MERCIA (1899-1982), PHYLLIS GLORY (1900-1978) and PAULETTE DE VERE (1901-1978), film-makers, were born on 3 January 1899, 7 January 1900 and 11 June 1901 at

Macquarie Street, Sydney, the eldest of seven children of Dublin-born John Michael McDonagh, medical practitioner, and his Sydney-born wife Annie Jane (Anita), née Amora. They were educated as weekly boarders at the Convent of the Sacred Heart, Elizabeth Bay. Isabel worked as a nurse in her father's hospital at College Street, founded a photographic parlour with Rennie Pardon and modelled for Thea Proctor [q.v.].

As the daughters of the honorary surgeon to J. C. Williamson's [q.v. 6] theatrical companies they grew up familiar with show business circles, and showed an early interest in film. Known professionally as 'Marie Lorraine', Isabel made her first acting appearances in *Joe*, and *Painted daughters*, two films made in 1925. That year Paulette worked as an extra on Arthur Shirley's *The mystery of a hansom cab*. Next she attended a film-acting school run by P. J. Ramster whom she later hired to help with the sisters' first production. Paulette's talents proved superior to Ramster's and she learned more from her close study of Hollywood film-making devices. With cameraman Jack Fletcher she learned to use camera and editing techniques to build the emotional rhythms which she so admired in American films.

Together the McDonaghs made three silent feature films: *Those who love* (1926), *The far paradise* (1928) and *The cheaters* (1930). Working in close collaboration, Paulette as director and Phyllis as production manager wrote scenarios which showed Isabel to great advantage. Providing a more interesting heroine than those found in most melodramas, they showed her breaking and entering, and cracking safes, as well as in a lover's arms. They were able, therefore, to give her more screen time than was usual. At a time when over-acting was still the norm, Isabel was praised for her natural and subdued performances achieved under Paulette's careful direction. Made on small budgets, these films were entertaining society melodramas of romance, sacrifice and parental opposition, set against an urban background: a contrast to the bush emphasis in contemporary Australian films. The sisters used the family's colonial home, Drummoyne House, and its antique and elaborate furnishings, to give their films great style at little expense.

The first two films earned great critical acclaim, and the press made much of the fact that Governor de Chair [q.v. 8] was moved to tears at the première of *Those who love*. Yet *The cheaters* proved a victim of the widespread enthusiasm for the new talkies. Just before its release in 1930 the sisters added some synchronized sound sequences. The result sadly disappointed them: even the tapping of an egg sounded like the 'Anvil Chorus'!

The unsophisticated quality of the sound greatly detracted from the impressive script, performances and cinematography.

Despite the Depression, the sisters made several short sporting documentaries with financial backing from Standardtone Film Production Co., including *Australia in the swim* with 'Boy' Charlton [q.v. 7] and the Olympic swimming team, (Sir) Donald Bradman in *How I play cricket* and Phar Lap in *The mighty conqueror*. Only the last survives. The McDonaghs' fourth and final feature, *Two minutes silence* (1933), was based on Leslie Haylen's stark anti-war play. In strong contrast to their early melodramas, its theme of serious social realism was praised by critics but failed to please audiences craving romance and comedy.

Meanwhile on 14 September 1932 at St Mary's Cathedral Isabel had married Charles Stewart (d. 1955), a Scottish-born rubber broker who had served in the Australian Imperial Force. They went to London where her eldest child was born in 1933. She refused a contract offered by (Sir) Alexander Korda before returning to Sydney in 1935 to be near her family. In 1959 she and her three children played in Tennessee Williams's *Orpheus descending* at the Ensemble Theatre and next year in *Time remembered*. She returned to London in 1965 and, survived by her children, died there on 5 March 1982.

Phyllis also retired from film-making and became editor of *New Zealand Truth*. On 15 October 1941 at Wellington she married a salesman, Leo Francis Joseph O'Brien. She returned to Sydney as a freelance journalist and short-story writer and from 1960 worked as social editor on the *North Shore Times*. Survived by her husband, she died childless on 17 October 1978.

Paulette was less than eager to follow their example. In 1934 she worked without remuneration on a romantic epic based on the life of Rev. John Flynn [q.v.8]. Unable to raise the necessary budget, Paulette found it difficult to carry on alone as an independent film maker. Her film career over, she continued to live with her younger sisters until 1940, when she moved to Kings Cross. She died in Sydney on 30 August 1978.

At the height of their careers, family ties and inexperience led the sisters to reject Hollywood offers. A decade later their work was all but forgotten until the rescreening in the early 1970s of prints of *The far paradise* and *The cheaters* (now held in the National Film and Sound Archive). Shortly before her death Phyllis flew to Perth in August 1978 to receive on behalf of the sisters the Australian Film Institute's Raymond Longford [q.v.] award for their significant contribution to Australian film-making. Today the McDonagh sisters are remembered as 'the most talented of the late silent era film-makers in Australia' and the most courageous of the early talkies era.

A. Pike and R. Cooper, *Australian film, 1900-1977*(Melb, 1980); J. Tulloch, *Legends on the screen* (Syd, 1981); G. Shirley and B. Adams, *Australian cinema* (Syd, 1983); *Cinema Papers*, June/July 1976; *Film News*, Dec 1978; information from Mr A. B. J. Stewart, Lond.   ANDRÉE WRIGHT

McDONALD, ARTHUR STEPHEN (1891-1955), radio engineer, was born on 6 March 1891 at Swan Hill, Victoria, son of Victorian-born parents John McDonald, boot-maker, and his wife Eliza Mary, née Stevenson. Educated at Swan Hill until 8 and later at primary and secondary schools at Ararat where he boarded with relations, McDonald worked without any formal training as a general mechanical engineer for three years before joining the Postmaster-General's Department in 1910 as a junior instrument setter in the engineering branch. Erection engineer for the Coastal Radio Service from 1911, he transferred with the radio service to the Department of the Navy in 1916 where he was appointed assistant engineer for equipment and in 1918 radio engineer. In 1920 he returned to the P.M.G.'s department.

In 1922, when many of the Commonwealth government's radio activities were taken over by Amalgamated Wireless Australasia Ltd, McDonald left to become A.W.A.'s radio engineer. He became chief engineer, assistant general manager to (Sir) Ernest Fisk [q.v.8] in 1930, and in 1945-46 assistant general manager (engineering) to Fisk's successor.

McDonald was prominent in establishing broadcasting; as an engineer he was soon to become 'as well known as the AWA tower'. He helped to construct radio stations, including 2FC, and was responsible for experiments carried out with the Marconi company. These resulted in the opening, in 1927, of the beam wireless service between Australia and Britain and, in 1930, of the first commercial use of two-way radio telephone links with other countries. In 1946, when the Overseas Telecommunications Commission was established, McDonald became chief engineer.

He was a foundation member of the Institution of Radio Engineers, Australia, in 1932 serving on its council and as president in 1943-45; he wrote a paper, '1913-1938: A Quarter Century of Radio Engineering in Australia', for the World Radio Convention in Sydney in 1938. In 1922 McDonald became a fellow of the Institute of Radio Engineers, United States of America, and was elected vice-president in 1949. He was also a member of the Acoustical Society of America, an associate member of the Institution of Engineers, Australia, sometime vice-president of the Radio & Telephone Manufacturers Association and a member of the electrical section committee of the Standards Association of Australia.

A big man 'both in stature and mind', McDonald was also described in 1924 as 'a typical constructional engineer—somewhat sparing in words but abundant in action'. His recreations were shooting and motor yachting; in 1939-46 he was commodore of the Royal Motor Yacht Club of New South Wales.

McDonald had married Edith Roseina Ethell on 27 January 1915 at Geraldton, Western Australia; in the late 1930s and early 1940s she worked as a milliner, opening a shop in Rowe Street, Sydney. McDonald died of hypertensive cerebro-vascular disease on 23 April 1955 at Longueville and was cremated with Presbyterian forms. He was survived by his wife, son and daughter Patricia Ethell, a radio and television actress. Most of his estate, valued for probate at £31 498, was left to his wife.

Wireless Weekly, 27 June 1924; Inst of Radio Engineers, *Procs*, Aug 1955; *Bulletin*, 4 May 1955.   MURRAY GOOT

MACDONALD, BENJAMIN WICKHAM (1853-1920), company manager, was born on 15 March 1853 at Elgin, Morayshire, Scotland, son of Alexander Macdonald, flesher, and his wife Jessie, née Urquhart. He was schooled at Elgin Academy, then worked for a local law firm, Fife, Duff, Robertson & Skinner, from 1866. At 19 he entered the service of A. & J. Inglis, shipbuilders, Glasgow, and seven years later joined the staff of Mackinnon, Mackenzie & Co., managing agents for the British India Steam Navigation Co., first at Karachi, then at Calcutta.

For reasons of health, in 1884 Macdonald moved to Brisbane and the subsidiary Queensland Steam Shipping Co., next year to the newly incorporated British India & Queensland Agency Co., and in 1887 to the Australasian United Steam Navigation Co., recently formed by London interests associated with B.I.S.N. He became travelling inspector, then agent, at Rockhampton (1887-90), Cooktown (1890-96) and Adelaide (1896-1900). In 1900 James Lyle Mackay (later Lord Inchcape) visited Australia to reorganize A.U.S.N.'s affairs and Macdonald was transferred to Brisbane as general manager of both A.U.S.N. and B.I.Q.A.

In 1902 Macdonald was a leading negotiator in the formation of the 'Collins pool', the first all-embracing agreement between the major coastal shipping companies. By both co-operation and competition he and his arch-rival Ernest Northcote of the Adelaide Steamship Co. built up the impressive Australian coastal fleet. In 1915 the chairman of B.I.Q.A., Lord Inchcape, wound down the company and established an agency for A.U.S.N., named after its first two senior managing partners, Macdonald, Hamilton & Co. Macdonald's influence now extended far beyond the Queensland coast.

His firm was an agent for a number of shipping, insurance and trading companies and he was chairman of directors of E. Rich & Co. Ltd, the Lymington Collieries Ltd (Sydney), and Blackheath Collieries Ltd (Brisbane). In 1907-17 Macdonald was Russian consul for Queensland.

While not unsympathetic to the legitimate aspirations of workers, Macdonald refused to co-operate with the premier's request to re-employ union labour during the 1917 maritime strike. His tact nevertheless kept A.U.S.N.'s labour relations generally above average.

A 'big and genuine' man, a keen observer and cheery companion with a fine tenor voice, Macdonald was an active member of the Brisbane Liedertafel in his middle years. With dwindling time for golf, cricket, bowling and yachting, he retained membership of the Queensland, Brisbane, Royal Queensland Yacht, Stock Exchange and Commercial Travellers' Association clubs.

Macdonald had married Letitia Amelia Rendall in Brisbane on 19 April 1888 with Presbyterian forms. Predeceased by her, he died on 22 October 1920 and was buried in Toowong cemetery with Church of England rites. He was survived by his four daughters and son Rodney Wickham, who in turn became managing partner of Macdonald, Hamilton and who fathered Benjamin Wickham, currently its managing director. Macdonald's estate was sworn for probate at £39 218.

Newspaper Cartoonists' Assn of Qld, *Queenslanders as we see 'em* (Brisb, 1915); N. L. McKellar, *From Derby round to Burketown* (Brisb, 1977); *PD* (Qld), 1917, p 1036; Commercial Publishing Co. of Syd Ltd, *Annual Review of Qld*, 1 (1902), no 1; *Sea, Land and Air*, 3, 1919-20, p 589; *RHSQJ*, 6, 1974-75, p 13; *Queenslander*, 30 Oct 1920.

N. L. McKELLAR

McDONALD, CHARLES (1860-1925), watchmaker and politician, was born on 25 August 1860 in North Melbourne, son of Charles Thomas Young McDonald, confectioner, and his wife Harriet, née Pape. The family moved around four colonies and McDonald left the public school at Mudgee, New South Wales, to become an apprentice printer. He later transferred to watchmaking, and worked as a tradesman in New South Wales before establishing his own business at Charters Towers, Queensland, in 1888.

McDonald energetically organized local goldminers and shop-assistants into trade unions. He was famous as a cyclist and on one campaign reportedly rode over 3000 miles (4800 km). In 1890 he was the Charters Towers delegate to the first general council of the Australian Labor Federation in Brisbane which launched the Labor Party in Queensland, and was elected president (1890-92). Despite the enthusiasm of McDonald and other delegates its socialistic political platform was rejected by the majority of member district councils. As president of the A.L.F. he attended the Intercolonial Trade Union Congress at Ballarat in 1891. During the 1891 shearers' strike, he was sent to Barcaldine as an emissary of peace, but when negotiations failed he organized support for the strike among the central Queensland trade unions. In 1893 'Fighting Charlie' won the seat of Flinders and entered the Queensland parliament with fifteen other Labor members including Andrew Fisher, Andrew Dawson [qq.v.8], John Hoolan [q.v.9] and Mat Reid [q.v.]. On 11 October 1892 he had married Mary Ann Tregear with Wesleyan forms at Charters Towers.

McDonald was a small, wiry, athletic man, with a drooping moustache, whose oratory, 'persistent as a summer fly', made up for his lack of size. He gained a reputation for his knowledge of standing orders, which he was reputed 'to sleep with . . . under his pillow'. One challenge to the chair's ruling, during debate on the peace preservation bill in 1894, saw him suspended with other Labor members. McDonald was a delegate to the Queensland Labor-in-Politics conventions of 1898, 1901 and 1905, a federal conference delegate in 1900 and 1905, and a member of the central political executive of the Queensland Labor Party from 1898 to 1903.

He opposed Federation 'as a middle-class device for diverting the needs of Labour', but with the issue decided, he resigned from the Queensland parliament and in 1901 successfully contested the outback Federal seat of Kennedy, holding it until his death in 1925. *Hansard* reveals his concern for the working class on such issues as pensions, taxation and monopolies. He was chairman of committees in 1906-10 and Labor's first Speaker from July 1910 to June 1913 and again from October 1913 to June 1917. As a noted republican he abandoned the traditional Speaker's wig and gown and had the mace removed from the table of the House. An anti-conscriptionist, he remained with Labor after the 'split' of 1916, serving the remainder of his parliamentary life on the back-bench.

In visibly declining health for many years with paralysis agitans, despite a recuperative voyage in 1924 to Britain McDonald died in Melbourne of cerebro-vascular disease on 13 November 1925. After a state funeral, he was buried in Boroondara cemetery. His wife and daughter survived him. His portrait by Josephine Muntz-Adams is in Parliament House, Canberra.

G. C. Bolton, *A thousand miles away* (Brisb, 1963); D. J. Murphy (ed), *Labor in politics* (Brisb, 1975); D. J. Murphy et al (eds), *Prelude to power* (Brisb, 1979); *Queenslander*, 14 Aug 1897, 21 Nov 1925; *Daily Standard*, 13 Nov 1925.

T. MORONEY

MACDONALD, DONALD ALASTER (1859?-1932), journalist and Nature writer, was born probably on 6 June 1859 at Fitzroy, Melbourne, elder son of Donald Macdonald and his wife Margaret, née Harris. His father farmed near Keilor, but after their mother died Donald and his brother lived with an aunt in the town. He was educated at the local state school, becoming a pupil-teacher in 1876 before joining the *Corowa Free Press* and in 1881 the Melbourne *Argus*. On 26 February 1883 at Scots Church, Melbourne, he married Jessie Seward; their only daughter was born two years later.

As 'Observer' he soon made his mark as a cricket and football commentator; his vivid accounts, without tiresome detail, revolutionized cricket reporting. For some forty years he travelled overseas with every Australian team. He sometimes signed himself 'D.M.' in the *Argus*, and in the *Australasian* 'Gnuyang' (a gossip) and for his weekly column 'Woomera'.

Sent by the *Argus*, Macdonald was the first Australian war correspondent at the South African War during which he was beseiged at Ladysmith. His delayed dispatches were carried on the same steamer that returned him to Australia, suffering from dysentery. Published in the *Argus*, they were 'discussed in every home and hotel bar' and reprinted as *How we kept the flag flying* (1900). The response to a lecture in the Melbourne Town Hall led to a years leave to tour Australia, New Zealand and Britain. In 1909 and 1910 Macdonald repeated his lecture, 'Scenes and sensations of battle', at the Portsea summer schools for teachers.

His early sketches of country life and his Nature reflections in the *Argus* and *Australasian* were easy, unstudied reveries, tinged with humour. Pieces on subjects as diverse as the red kangaroo, life in the Riverina and Sunday in Sydney were seen by the author as 'moments of respite from the duties of daily journalism'. A selection published as *Gum*

boughs and wattle bloom (1887) had a remarkable success.

On his return from South Africa he established a weekly column in the *Argus* called 'Nature Notes and Queries'. It was extended to 'Notes for Boys' in 1909 and suggested his next work, the *Bush boy's book* (1911), enlarged in four more editions in 1927-33. In 1922 a Nature book for children, *At the end of the moonpath*, was published, and his daughter made a selection of his writings in *The brooks of morning* (1933). Macdonald had also compiled the *Tourists' handbook of Australia* (1905) and written a novel, *The warrigal's well* (1901), in collaboration with J. F. Edgar.

A 'big man, with shrewd and pleasant features', he 'retained that grace and charm of style in his writings which revealed, as clearly as talking with him did, his rare personal qualities'. In ill health for many years, Macdonald died of emphysema on 23 November 1932 at Black Rock, and was buried in Fawkner cemetery. His wife and daughter survived him. A fountain memorial, designed by Stanley Hammond, is in Macdonald Park, Beaumaris.

Macdonald was 'about the most versatile man on the Melbourne Press' and one of the best-known journalists in Australia. As a writer on Nature he influenced a whole generation. According to the *Argus*, many children 'who first saw their own country through the eyes of Donald Macdonald have learned to know it and to love it through their own'.

C. Barrett, *Wanderer's rest* (Melb, 1946); C. McKay, *This is the life* (Syd, 1961); A. H. Chisholm, *The joy of the earth* (Syd, 1969); F. K. Norris, *No memory for pain* (Melb, 1970); Education Gazette (Vic), 20 Feb 1909; *Newspaper News*, 1 Dec 1932; *Labor Call*, 30 Aug 1923; *Argus*, 24, 26 Nov 1932; *SMH*, 24 Nov, 3, 10 Dec 1932.

HUGH ANDERSON

McDONALD, EDGAR ARTHUR (1891-1937), professional cricketer, was born on 6 January 1891 at Launceston, Tasmania, son of Arthur McDonald, tinsmith, and his wife Jane, née McBean. He was educated at Charles Street School and played cricket for Tasmania in 1909-10 and 1910-11. Then he moved to Victoria, where he played pennant cricket for Fitzroy, swapped his early reputation as a batsman for that of fast bowler, and was included in the Victorian team before the outbreak of World War I. McDonald was picked for Australia in the 1920-21 series against England, when he had three undistinguished if unlucky Tests, and first partnered J. M. Gregory [q.v.9] with the new ball.

On the tour of England in 1921 McDonald was the outstanding Australian bowler with

150 wickets, including 27 in the Test series which Australia won 3-0. With Gregory, McDonald formed the first great fast-bowling combination in Test cricket history. His Test batting average of 46 (assisted by not outs) was just behind C. G. Macartney's [q.v.]. After three more Test matches in South Africa, McDonald ended his Australian career by deciding to play in England on pitches that he had found more responsive. A qualifying season in Lancashire League in 1922 was followed by a highly successful career with the county in 1924-31. When he retired McDonald had taken 1053 wickets for Lancashire, made a maiden first-class century and played much of his finest cricket. On a trip back to Australia, he turned out again for Fitzroy. In 1932 he rejoined Lancashire League and on retirement became a licensed victualler.

Few bowlers have attracted such thoughtful superlatives as 'Ted' McDonald. A. G. Moyes rated him as 'the most gifted fast bowler' and Ian Peebles as 'the most perfect of fast bowlers', confirming the endorsement of Warwick Armstrong [q.v.7], McDonald's captain in 1921. In his account of the 1921 tour, Ronald Mason said that McDonald 'harboured in a not very approachable personality a genuine vein of genius'. He performed best when the opposition was strongest; was until Larwood's advent the fastest bowler in England; and in his fortieth year bowled (Sir) Donald Bradman for nine. McDonald's speed was complemented by an ability to move the ball either way (so far that out-swingers and leg-cutters often missed off stump, Armstrong remembered) and to reduce his pace to bowl off-cutters on slow pitches.

McDonald was tall, slim, powerful, with black hair and a deeply bronzed complexion. T. C. F. Prittie described him as 'the most impressive figure of his day on the cricket field'. His approach to the wicket attracted special notice because of its effortless, gliding motion—'his silent run of sinister grace', (Sir) Neville Cardus called it. To Sir Robert Menzies, McDonald's action suggested silk running off a spool. His feats for Lancashire prompted some of Cardus's most lavish praise: 'A Lucifer of his craft', 'a satanic bowler, menacing but princely'.

On 22 July 1937, McDonald was killed when struck by a car near Bolton, Lancashire. He was survived by his wife Emily Myrtle, née Hamill, whom he had married on 10 April 1920 at Holy Trinity Church, East Melbourne, and their two sons.

N. Cardus, *The summer game* (Lond, 1929); T. C. F. Prittie, *Cricket north and south* (Lond, 1955); A. G. Moyes, *Australian cricket* (Syd, 1959); R. Mason, *Warwick Armstrong's Australians* (Lond, 1971); E. W. Swanton (ed), *Barclay's world of cricket* (Lond, 1980); J. Pollard, *Australian cricket* (Syd, 1982); *The Times* and *Argus*, 23 July 1937; *SMH*, 23, 24, 28 July 1937. PETER PIERCE

McDONALD, GEORGE ROY WILLIAM (1883-1951), politician and businessman, was born on 29 January 1883 in Sydney, son of George McDonald, Canadian-born contractor, and his wife Margaret Amy, née McNamara, from Brisbane. Known as Roy, he entered the public service in April 1898 and was deposition clerk, Broken Hill, before serving in Sydney and then as assistant clerk of petty sessions at Goulburn, Albury and Bathurst. In 1908 he resigned to become a land agent at Tamworth, and in 1911 moved his business to Sydney. In 1910, as Labor candidate, he was elected to the Legislative Assembly for Bingara, defeating the secretary for lands, S. W. Moore [q.v.]. He proved to be highly critical of the Labor government's land legislation: a move in 1914 to bar land agents from election to parliament seems to have been directed at him.

In 1915 McDonald stated his support for conscription but, unwilling to give his reasons for not enlisting, had avoided participating in recruitment campaigns. He frequently condemned strikes where arbitration was available to workers. When he resigned his seat and Labor Party membership in 1916, R. J. Stuart-Robertson said he had never been a Labor man. McDonald held Bingara as an Independent at the subsequent by-election and as a Nationalist in 1917. He was nominated to the Legislative Council in 1920.

McDonald had repeatedly protested at attempts to dismiss from public office persons of German descent. In 1914 he had defended Dr August Scheidel, naturalized since 1890, from critics seeking his internment; Scheidel had reported slate and limestone deposits near Rylstone in which McDonald acquired an interest. When Kandos Cement Co. Ltd was formed in 1919 to take over the cement works and colliery, McDonald became a director and ceased to act as a land agent. He was also a director of Western Australian Portland Cement Co. Ltd and of the Southern Union General Insurance Co. of Australasia, and chairman of Carroll [q.v.7] Musgrove Theatres Ltd and the New Caledonian Meat Co. Ltd. A founding vice-president of the National Roads and Motorists' Association in 1924, he was a director of N.R.M.A. Insurance Ltd. He was later associated with several blue-metal quarrying enterprises, including the Brisbane Metal Quarries Ltd in which J. C. Watson [q.v.] also invested. By 1928 Kandos Cement had extended its activities to New Zealand, but excess production led to its amalgamation with Australian Cement Ltd in 1929. As returns from cement and blue metals fell, he formed a company to buy the Imperial and Mount Victoria hotels.

Granted nine months leave from the Legislative Council in 1923, McDonald married May Camille Dezarnaulds, from New Caledonia, on 4 September at Woollahra. As well as overseeing his business interests, he studied law and on 26 August 1927 was admitted to the Bar. His political views narrowed to protection of his own business interests and he opposed most of Labor's reforms. In 1930 he resigned and stood unsuccessfully for Barwon; later he contested the Federal seats of Wentworth (1940) and Gwydir (1946). When a quota system for Australian feature films was introduced in 1935 he led the oppposition from distributors. On 12 August 1937 he was admitted as a solicitor and established the firm, G.R.W.McDonald & Co.

On 28 July 1951 McDonald died of cerebrovascular disease at his Bellevue Hill residence and was cremated with Anglican rites. His wife and son survived him and inherited his estate, valued for probate at £28 588.

Roy Com on the purchase of the Boorabil estate and adjoining improvement leases, Report, *PP* (NSW), 1914-15, 5, p 91; *Millions Mag*, 1 Mar 1920; *SMH*, 17 Oct 1910, 30 Apr 1916, 14 Feb 1920; A. Wilkinson, The N.R.M.A. story (typescript, 1964, held by NRMA, Syd).

HEATHER RADI

MacDONALD, JAMES STUART (1878-1952), art critic and gallery director, was born on 28 March 1878 at Carlton, Melbourne, son of Hector MacDonald, Victorian-born solicitor, and his American wife Anna Louisa, née Flett. He hated his time at Kew High School and Hawthorn Grammar School where he was often in trouble. As a child, through his father's partner William Lynch, an art collector, MacDonald met many painters and in the mid-1890s studied at the National Gallery of Victoria's school; he was also apprenticed to a printer and was taught lithography.

MacDonald went to London in 1898 to the Westminster School of Art, then for five years to Paris where he shared a studio with Hugh Ramsay [q.v.] and attended the Julian and Colarossi schools; he exhibited at the Royal Academy of Arts, London, and the Old Salon, Paris. Having returned to Melbourne, on 4 August 1904 he was married to an American art student Maud Mary Keller by Rev. Charles Strong [q.v.6]. They moved to New York where he taught art until 1910 at a high school. Back in Australia he painted some portraits and landscapes and turned to drawing in charcoal and to lithographic portraits.

On 9 September 1914 MacDonald enlisted in the 5th Battalion, Australian Imperial Force. At Gallipoli, as a private, on 26 April 1915 he was seriously wounded in the abdomen and was classified unfit for active service on 27 October. He served as a pay sergeant in 1916-17, mainly in England. In June-August 1918 he worked as a camouflage artist with the 5th Division in France. The effects of his wound required hospital spells both before his departure from England in October 1918 and after his discharge in Melbourne the following April; he was granted a war pension.

In 1916, in his absence, MacDonald's *The art of Frederick McCubbin* [q.v.] had been published; similar studies followed in 1920 of Penleigh Boyd, David Davies and George Lambert [qq.v.7,8,9]. Having given up painting, from 1923 he was art critic for the Melbourne *Herald*. In *Art in Australia* and elsewhere MacDonald wrote prolifically and well, from deep knowledge, but he was blindly hostile to nearly all twentieth-century painting and much before. He profusely praised the work of his friend John Longstaff [q.v.] and especially, articulating a weirdly extreme racial nationalism, that of Arthur Streeton [q.v.]. His works pointed to 'the way in which life should be lived in Australia, with the maximum of flocks and the minimum of factories . . . If we so choose, we can yet be the elect of the world, the last of the pastoralists, the thoroughbred Aryans in all their nobility'.

In October 1928 Jimmy MacDonald was appointed director of the National Art Gallery of New South Wales. He chafed at his limited authority and having to act as secretary as well as director. Sydney Ure Smith [q.v.] found him 'narrow and biased' but he satisfied most of the conservative trustees. MacDonald held more exhibitions of Australian work than was customary and added workshops and storerooms to the gallery. He confided to his powerful friend (Sir) Robert Menzies his ambition of becoming director of an Australian national gallery.

In 1936 MacDonald applied for the directorship of the National Gallery of Victoria, stressing to an extraordinary degree his conviction that only painters were fit to be critics or advisers, while deriding scholars and connoisseurs. The trustees' recommendation to appoint W. Hardy Wilson [q.v.] was overturned by the government after strong lobbying on MacDonald's behalf. The omens were unpropitious, for one trustee was Sir Keith Murdoch [q.v.], a modernist patron. MacDonald made useful progress in cataloguing, bought Australian paintings including major works by McCubbin, and aimed to fill gaps in the European collection. But in doing so he rudely attacked overseas advisers. 'We have bought names . . . We bought for an enormous price a canvas [self-portrait] which Rembrandt was too disgusted to finish; a Raeburn hardly worth looking at; the world's worst Watteau'. He later correctly doubted an alleged Uccello and a Claude Lorraine purchased in the 1940s, but he did not query the 'van Eyck' Madonna. He supported Menzies in founding the Australian Academy of Art and reviled George Bell [q.v.].

MacDonald reported vehemently on the 1939 *Herald* exhibition of contemporary French and English painting, sponsored by Murdoch (now president of trustees). 'They are exceedingly wretched paintings . . . putrid meat . . . the product of degenerates and perverts . . . filth'. But the gallery purchased paintings by van Gogh, Vallotton and Derain.

Early in 1940, following a mild stroke, MacDonald was away from work for three months. In September the trustees recommended against his reappointment. E. R. Pitt [q.v.], the chief librarian, officially reported and expressed agreement despite the 'qualities of integrity, knowledge and fearlessness which . . . endear him to his friends'. MacDonald fought to the end, reapplying for the advertised directorship, and was granted a retiring sum of £100 a year for five years.

In later life MacDonald displayed his frequent inability to express aesthetic disagreement without libellous denigration and accusations of commercial, often Jewish, conspiracy to promote certain artists for market advantage. In 1943 he was first witness on behalf of those who brought an action against the award of the Archibald [q.v.3] prize to William Dobell for his portrait of Joshua Smith: MacDonald described it as a 'pictorial defamation of character'. In 1943-47 he was art critic for the *Age* and he was appointed to the Commonwealth Art Advisory Board (chairman 1949-52). He made little progress with a survey of the development of Australian painting for which the Commonwealth Literary Fund provided a grant. He lived at Montrose and joined the Liberal Party. A convivial drinker at the Savage Club, he was a man of charm, tactlessness and combativeness.

MacDonald died in Melbourne on 12 November 1952 and, survived by his wife and their son and daughter, was cremated. In 1958 a collection of his writings, *Australian painting desiderata*, was published with a foreword by Menzies. His portrait by Hugh Ramsay is held by the University of Melbourne.

Bernard Smith, *Place, taste and tradition* (Syd, 1945) and *Australian painting 1788-1960* (Melb, 1962); L. B. Cox, *The National Gallery of Victoria 1861 to 1968* (Melb, 1970); A. Bradley and T. Smith (eds), *Australian art and architecture* (Melb, 1980); R. Haese, *Rebels and precursors* (Melb, 1981); *People* (Syd), 12 Sept 1951; MacDonald papers (NL).   GEOFFREY SERLE

McDONALD, LEWIS RICHARD (1881-1936), printer and Labor Party administrator, was born on 22 December 1881 at Auchterhead, Lanark, Scotland, son of Lewis McDonald, farmer, and his wife Isabella, née Lyon. With his parents he migrated to Victoria in 1883, moved to Fiji and arrived in Queensland in 1886. Educated at the Brisbane Central School and at university extension classes, McDonald became an apprentice printer but fell ill and in 1905 moved to Mourilyan, North Queensland, where he helped to organize the Amalgamated Sugar Workers' Union.

Returning to Brisbane in 1908, he resumed printing and became an organizer of the Queensland Typographical Union. He joined the Fortitude Valley Workers' Political Organisation as secretary and, a protégé of Albert Hinchcliffe [q.v.9], became assistant secretary to the central political executive of the Queensland Labor Party on 30 August 1909. McDonald was its first paid full-time secretary from 1 October 1910. He attended all subsequent State Labor conventions, every interstate Labor conference after 1912, except one, and was a Queensland representative on the federal executive from 1915 until his death. McDonald inherited Hinchcliffe's mantle but lacked his innovatory skills and political feel. He faithfully served the Queensland conventions and executives which, after 1916, were increasingly dominated by the Australian Workers' Union and its chiefs E. G. Theodore and W. McCormack [qq.v.].

Secretary of the Queensland anti-conscription campaign committees in 1916-17, McDonald used his considerable administrative abilities to facilitate a 'No' vote both times. He was also a pamphleteer and prominent in the Brisbane Workers' Educational Association. Appointed to the Legislative Council in 1917, he remained until its abolition in March 1922 but spoke infrequently and contributed little except to organize government business. He unsuccessfully contested Toowong in 1912, the Brisbane mayoralty in 1921 and the Senate in 1934.

An extrovert, McDonald enjoyed a beer, could tell a good story and liked old-time musical comedies. While he used his secretarial skills in the interests of the A.W.U. faction, he was never personally self seeking, but he certainly facilitated the growth of an 'official' machine which, with its complaisant politicians, ultimately controlled the movement at the expense of the grass roots and the militant unions. Ernest Lane [q.v.9] saw him as 'a faithful servant of the reactionary section of the Movement', the key-cog in that well-oiled, purged, and successful oligarchy which politically ran Queensland in 1915-29 and 1932-57.

McDonald's conciliatory and manipulative powers helped to heal rifts in the federal Labor movement during the Depression. But his declining health caused questioning of his administrative efficiency and J. S. Collings [q.v.8] took increasing responsibility for the State executive. In his last days McDonald tired visibly and lost the confidence of Forgan Smith [q.v.] and C. G. Fallon.

John Curtin called him 'an admirable officer with sound judgement and resolute decision [whose] capacity for makeshift endeared him to all'. Others, excluded from office and influence, were less charitable about this gentle, persistent, rule-mongering functionary. McDonald's early craft-union radicalism and personal political hopes were submerged by those structures, rules and manipulations endemic in that Queensland Labor establishment which he had done so much to construct, refine and facilitate.

McDonald died suddenly of cerebral haemorrhage at Highgate Hill, Brisbane, on 18 September 1936. He had married Alexandra McDonald Hunter at Corinda on 16 January 1911 with Presbyterian forms; she survived him with three sons. Although cremated with Anglican rites, McDonald had long maintained no formal creed.

J. Larcombe, *The Labor government in Queensland* (Brisb, nd, [1915]); E. H. Lane, *Dawn to dusk* (Brisb, 1939); D. J. Murphy, *T. J. Ryan*, and (ed), *Labor in politics* (Brisb, 1975), and et al (eds), *Labor in power* (Brisb, 1979); *PD* (LA Qld), 1919-20, p7; *Daily Standard*, 11, 12 Oct 1917, 8, 9 July 1921, 10 July 1934; *Worker* (Brisb), 9 June 1921, 22 Sept 1936; *Telegraph* (Brisb), 18 Sept 1936; *Courier Mail*, 19 Sept 1936; *Truth* (Melb), 20 Sept 1936; information from Mr F. Waters, Brisb.

D. B. WATERSON

MACDONALD, LOUISA (1858-1949), educationist, was born on 10 December 1858 at Arbroath, Forfarshire, Scotland, seventh daughter and eleventh child of John Macdonald, town clerk and lawyer, and his wife Ann, née Kid (d. 1860). In this prolific and prosperous family, she was educated by elder sisters and a tutor, beginning Latin aged 7 and Greek at 12. After two years at a finishing school in London, she and her sister Isabella prepared for the Edinburgh Local Examinations by correspondence; Louisa headed the list of candidates in 1878. As the University of Edinburgh did not admit women to degrees, they matriculated at the University of London and, as students of University College, were among the first residents in College Hall. Bella became one of the first women doctors; Louisa graduated B.A. in 1884 with first-class honours in classics and M.A. in classics in 1886.

In 1887 Louisa Macdonald visited the United States of America and New South Wales to see a brother J. M. L. Macdonald of Wallabadah. On returning to London in 1888 she became a fellow of University College. In addition to teaching and research in classical antiquities at the British Museum, she pioneered educational projects for women outside the university and travelled widely in Europe.

In 1891 Miss Macdonald was chosen from sixty-five applicants as first principal of the Women's College, University of Sydney. The college opened on 21 March 1892, in rented premises, with one student; a week later there were four. Though Louisa Macdonald described the early years as a 'golden picnic', she faced difficult and pressing problems, especially financial. In contrast to Britain there was no urgent demand for women's education and a university education for women seemed to many 'not only unnecessary but unsuitable'. The Women's College was seen as a white elephant. Established as a non-denominational college of equal status to those provided for men, Women's College had from its inception a specific ideology of social and intellectual equality. Louisa Macdonald chose its motto, 'Together', taken from Tennyson's *The Princess*:

The woman's cause is man's; they rise
　and sink
Together, dwarfed or godlike, bond
　or free.

The building and decoration of the Italianate-style college, opened in May 1894, and its carefully designed garden, reflected her belief that gracious surroundings were part of a liberal education.

For twenty-seven years Miss Macdonald, assisted by her lifelong friend and companion Evelyn Dickinson, built up student numbers and placed the college on a sound financial basis, while forging its academic and corporate traditions. Numbers rose slowly in the depressed 1890s to 13 students in 1897, 24 in 1906, and suddenly doubled during World War I. In 1916 the college received the same financial endowment as the men's colleges, which allowed all debts to be liquidated. Extra accommodation was provided by building and purchase.

In the 1890s Louisa Macdonald was active in the Womanhood Suffrage League of New South Wales and the Women's Literary Society, and was a committee-member of the Australian Economic Association. She was a founder and committee-member of the Sydney University Women's Association (Union) and the University Women's Society (Sydney University Women's Settlement from 1906). She lectured, catalogued the Greek vases in the Nicholson [q.v.2] Museum of Antiquities, and in 1907 was the first woman to stand for the university senate, but was defeated. She attempted to introduce teacher-training courses and student exchange programmes with European universities. She recognized and encouraged the importance of social life within the college by debates, sport and dances and through intercollegiate contacts. Moving easily in Sydney's social life, she strove to make the college part of the university and the wider community. To celebrate the college's twenty-first birthday in 1913 she designed and directed *A mask*, the words composed for her by Christopher Brennan and John Le Gay Brereton [qq.v.7]. In 1914-15 she was vice-president of the Classical Association of New South Wales—and during the war studied Russian.

When Louisa Macdonald resigned in June 1919 she left behind her a flourishing institution. She returned to London and was appointed to the council of College Hall. She purchased and restored the twelfth-century Abbot's House at Arbroath, which she donated to Scotland. She corresponded with old students and entertained numerous Australians, frequently at Ballintuim, Perthshire. One of her last actions was to write a small history of the college in aid of its building fund. She died on 28 November 1949 at her London home. A staunch Presbyterian, she was no 'bluestocking', although formidable and determined 'to guide and direct the studies of young women'. Imbued with tolerance and a ready sense of humour, she believed higher education should be accessible to all.

W. V. Hole and A. H. Treweeke, *The history of the Women's College* (Syd, 1953); *Cosmos Mag*, 29 June 1895; *Sun* (Syd), 20 Apr 1913; *Daily Telegraph* (Syd), 28 Apr 1915; *T&CJ*, 14 May 1919; *The Times*, 14 Dec 1949; *Union Recorder*, 22 Sept 1960; letters and papers of Louisa Macdonald *and* Council minutes (Women's College, Univ Syd, Archives); Brereton papers *and* Louisa Macdonald letters 1892-98 (ML).   H. ALEXANDER

McDONALD, SYDNEY FANCOURT (1885-1947), paediatrician and army doctor, was born on 18 November 1885 at Rocklea near Brisbane, youngest son of George Thomas McDonald, a Scottish surveyor, and his wife Amelia Margaret, daughter of Sir William Mitchell [q.v.5]. Sydney was educated at the Normal School, Brisbane, and at Brisbane Grammar. As a medical student, resident at Trinity College, University of Melbourne, he won prizes and exhibitions (M.B., 1909; B.S., 1910; M.D., 1913) and was prominent in student affairs. After staff appointments at the Queen's Memorial Infectious Diseases and Alfred hospitals, McDonald was assistant senior resident surgeon at

the Children's Hospital (1912-14). He undertook further studies as a resident medical officer at Queen Charlotte's Hospital, London (1914).

His military involvements began in 1904 when he was commissioned second lieutenant in the Australian Militia Engineers. From 1910 he was the first officer commanding the Melbourne University Rifles, and was promoted major in 1913. In London he enlisted on 4 August 1914 as captain in the Royal Army Medical Corps and was posted to the 4th (British) General Hospital, Versailles, France. He served as an anaesthetist and radiographer and was mentioned in dispatches. McDonald also served with the 33rd and 51st Casualty Clearing stations and the 46th Stationary Hospital. On 11 October 1916 he married Marjorie Caroline Peck (d. 1940) in London. For a time he was chief lecturer at the R.A.M.C. school at Bethune, France. In 1919 he became a member of the Royal College of Physicians, London.

Returning to practise in Brisbane, McDonald was appointed out-patient physician to the Hospital for Sick Children in 1920, succeeding Colonel A. G. Butler [q.v.7] as senior in-patient physician in 1923. A secretary to the Hospital Clinical Society, McDonald also became a councillor of the British Medical Association (Queensland branch) in 1923-44 (president, 1930), and a councillor of the Medical Defence Society of Queensland from 1928. He became chief medical examiner for the Department of Civil Aviation (Queensland) that year. He was president of the section on paediatrics at the Australasian Medical Congress, Hobart, in 1934, and a foundation fellow of the Royal Australasian College of Physicians in 1938.

His principal contributions to medical knowledge were in the field of clinical paediatrics, with particular emphasis on differential diagnosis and the natural history of certain childhood disorders. McDonald wrote major papers on nephritis, lead poisoning in children, poliomyelitis and pink disease. His name is the most frequent in the index of the *Medical Journal of Australia* in 1920-46. He was the first Queensland doctor, and probably the first Australian paediatrician, to be elected a fellow of the Royal College of Physicians, London (1940).

McDonald had remained involved with the armed services as medical examiner to the Royal Australian Air Force and, in 1923, as physician to Rosemount Military Hospital; he was a consultant physician at Greenslopes Repatriation Hospital in 1940-47. He was commissioned wing commander, R.A.A.F., in 1937 and became group captain, medical branch, in 1941. As Jackson [q.v.9] orator, McDonald spoke on 'Some debts of medicine to the fighting services' (*M.J.A.*, 1940), and wrote the official text, 'Tropical and sub-tropical fevers', for army medical manuals in World War II. He delivered the Stawell [q.v.] oration on 'The mosquito: a teacher of medicine' (*M.J.A.*, 1943). Having a sympathetic interest in ex-servicemen suffering from neuroses, he wrote extensively about anxiety neurosis and nephritis, with major papers on the problems of the pensioner and on nervous and neurological disorders.

Meanwhile from 1925 McDonald was a foundation member of the Queensland postgraduate committee of the B.M.A. (chairman 1930-47). In 1938 he was the first (part-time) clinical lecturer in paediatrics appointed to the faculty of medicine within the University of Queensland, from 1944 a member of the faculty board, and from 1946 chairman of its advisory committee on paediatric studies.

McDonald married Annie Emilie Jane Darvall, née Goertz, on 18 December 1941; he was very fond of children but childless. A tall, powerful figure with a diffident, shy and intellectual demeanour, he was a person who was 'very proper, very correct and formal, who lived his professional life in the tradition of the highest ideals of clinical medicine'. A scholar with extensive knowledge of the classics and of literature, he also left many clinical photographs and scenes of Queensland town and marine life.

Survived by his wife, McDonald died of cardio-renal failure at his Brisbane home on 8 August 1947 and was cremated after a funeral with full military honours at St John's Cathedral.

J. Pearn, *A worthy tradition—the biography of Sydney Fancourt McDonald* (Brisb, 1985); *MJA*, 2, 1947, p 502; *Bulletin*, 20 Aug 1947; family information.   J. H. PEARN

MACDONELL, DONALD (1862-1911), shearer, trade unionist and politician, was born in January 1862 at Stuart Mill, Victoria, son of Alexander Macdonell, Scottish migrant of Catholic Highland extraction, and his wife Christina, née McMaster. His parents were hard working, industrious and frugal and imparted these virtues to Donald and his brother and sisters. From boyhood he accompanied his father through shearing sheds and mining camps in search of regular income to supplement the uncertain returns from the family's small farm. He became an accomplished woodsman and shearer, moving 'up the track' to the far west of New South Wales when 23. He briefly visited New Zealand before returning to Australia early in 1890.

At the outbreak of the maritime strike of 1890 Macdonell was shearing at Tinapagee on the Paroo River in north-western New South Wales. He had been a founding member of the shearers' union in 1886 and soon became prominent as a rank-and-file leader of the strike. He also defended arrested shearers in court and later was active in dealing with scabs—his immense physical strength and wiry 6 ft. 3 ins. (191 cm) frame probably helping to persuade recalcitrant workers to accept the union's point of view. During the 1891 Queensland shearers' strike he led a party from the Bourke sheds to assist the strikers, narrowly escaping arrest after an assault on a 'blackleg'. Yet he was widely respected for his kindness and generosity to complete strangers. As a 'ringer' he sheared 214 sheep with hand-shears in a day at Belalie station in 1892.

In 1893 Macdonell was elected secretary of the Bourke branch of the Amalgamated Shearers' Union of Australasia and was prominent in bringing about its merger with the General Labourers' Union; he moved the resolution which adopted the name, Australian Workers' Union, at its first convention at Albury in January 1895. When the 1896 A.W.U. convention decided to suspend publication of the *Worker* he persuaded the Bourke branch to continue publication until the union's finances had improved. He succeeded Arthur Rae [q.v.] as general secretary of the union in 1899.

With other A.W.U. figures, such as W. G. Spence and Hector Lamond [qq.v.6,9], Macdonell began to exert increasing influence in the Labor Party. He had lost a Legislative Assembly by-election for Bourke in December 1891, and was defeated for the Barwon (as an independent Labor candidate) in 1894, and in 1895 and 1898. He had been a delegate to the first Labor Party conference of 1892 and emerged at the 1897 conference as perhaps the most outspoken opponent of the socialists. He argued that while 'it is one thing to capture a conference' for socialist policies, 'it is quite another to get electors to vote the ticket'.

When Spence moved to the House of Representatives in 1901 Macdonell was elected unopposed for his seat, Cobar, in the Legislative Assembly and held it until 1911. He was a delegate to the Labor Party's federal conference in 1902 and 1905 and a member of its New South Wales executive in 1901-10. In parliament he was primarily concerned with trade union affairs. Following the passage of the Arbitration Act of 1902 the A.W.U. sought registration in the State court but was frustrated by registration of the bogus Machine Shearers' and Shed Employees' Union. Macdonell chaired a select committee into its evasion of the Arbitration Act in 1903 and persuaded the government to appoint a royal commission. He successfully fought a defamation case against the new union's newspaper, the *Shearer*, and eventually succeeded in having the A.W.U. formally registered. However he strongly favoured a Federal award for the pastoral industry and battled for years to overcome the legal obstacles to the presentation of a case.

When the first Labor government took office in New South Wales in October 1910, Macdonell became colonial secretary and minister for agriculture. However, plagued by increasing illness over sixteen years, he suffered a complete breakdown of health in January 1911. In February he moved to Melbourne for rest, but went into hospital immediately and remained there. He retained his portfolio as chief secretary but relinquished agriculture in September, when his seat was formally declared vacant because of his absence from parliament. He was re-elected unopposed but died of cancer on 26 October 1911. Unmarried, he was survived by two sisters. Widely honoured by unionists and parliamentarians from both sides of the House, he was buried at Stuart Mill after a state funeral with Catholic rites. Among the many tributes accorded him was the naming of Macdonell House, the headquarters of the A.W.U. in Sydney.

Of all the A.W.U. leaders in 1886-1910, Macdonell was the only one to conform to the mythical standards of the eastern Australian countryman. His experience, combined with his physical attributes, intelligence, compassion and political skills, set him apart from his several union colleagues who were also elected to the New South Wales parliament up to 1910: as Henry Lawson [q.v.] said of him in 1899, he was 'the tallest, straightest, and perhaps the best of the Bourke-side bush-leaders'. But his early death prevented the fulfilment of his great potential.

W. G. Spence, *Australia's awakening* (Syd, 1909), and *History of the A.W.U.* (Syd, 1911); P. Ford, *Cardinal Moran and the A.L.P.* (Melb, 1966); B. Nairn, *Civilising capitalism* (Canb, 1973); D. J. Murphy (ed), *Labor in politics* (Brisb, 1975); *Daily Telegraph* (Syd), 22 July 1901; *Catholic Press*, 24 Dec 1902; *SMH*, 27 Oct 1911; *Worker* (Syd), 22, 29 Oct 1951.

FRANK FARRELL

McDONNELL, FRANCIS (1863-1928), draper and politician, was born on 24 January 1863 at Ennis, Clare, Ireland, son of James McDonnell, farmer, and his wife Elizabeth, née Bradish; his father died when Francis was 7. At 13 he began work in a factory, then returned to school to the Christian Brothers at Ennis. In 1879 he was apprenticed as a draper to Gallagher Bros of Ballina, a fellow employee being T. C. Beirne [q.v.7]. Accompanied by his only sister, McDonnell arrived in Brisbane in 1886. On 31 December 1890 he married Mary Heffernan at St Stephen's Cathedral.

He worked as a drapery assistant with Finney, Isles & Co., then with T. J. Geoghegan and, in 1889-96, with Edwards & Lamb. In 1901 he established the drapery firm McDonnell & East in partnership with Hubert East [q.v.8], backed financially by Peter Murphy [q.v.]. He remained with the firm, alternating the managing directorship with East who balanced McDonnell's extroverted public-mindedness with quiet backroom efficiency. They thought highly of each other.

In 1888 McDonnell, as secretary, organized the Shop Assistants' Early Closing Association and the publication of the *Early Closing Advocate* with leading articles by William Lane [q.v.9]. His zeal for industrial reform led to appointment in 1891 to the royal commission on shops, factories and workshops. Its findings formed the basis of a bill (rejected in the Legislative Council) and the less than satisfactory Factories and Shops Act of 1896.

As Labor candidate McDonnell unsuccessfully contested the Fortitude Valley seat in 1893, but as the 'clerks' hero' was victorious in 1896 on a large personal vote. He introduced the shops early closing bill unsuccessfully in 1897 but saw his cause finally successful in the 1900 Factories and Shops Act. That year he passed a resolution to establish a wages board. In 1899 he was party whip for the short-lived Dawson [q.v.8] Labor government, a member of the central political executive of the Queensland Labor Party in 1898-1903 and treasurer in 1901-03. He emphatically opposed Federation in the belief that it would increase unemployment.

McDonnell was a strong advocate of improvement of conditions for the police and teachers. In 1899 he secured the extension of the grammar school scholarship system to other approved schools; taking effect from 1901, this measure was of particular benefit to Catholic schools and firmed the Catholic-Labor bond.

Not seeking re-election to the Legislative Assembly in 1907, McDonnell was immediately appointed to the Legislative Council. He continued to interest himself in Queensland's industrial development, seeking especially to promote the cotton industry. In 1915 he bought the entire crop, initiating a mattress and quilt-making industry.

McDonnell was an executive member of committees promoting Home Rule and sponsoring Irish Parliamentary Party visitors. In 1910 he was a founder and first director of the Hibernian Newspaper Co. Ltd which, in 1911, launched the *Catholic Advocate*. He attended the Irish National Convention in Melbourne (1919) but withdrew from further involvement in Irish politics on the establishment of the Irish Free State. He was one of the first trustees of the Brisbane Trades Hall, a member of the committee of management of the Queensland Blind, Deaf and Dumb Institution and an original member of the Senate of the University of Queensland (1910-22).

McDonnell died at Mater Misericordiae Hospital, South Brisbane, on 26 November 1928 and was buried in Toowong cemetery after a funeral at St Stephen's Cathedral. His wife, four sons and three daughters survived him. His estate was sworn for probate at £21 843. Some years after his death the Christian Brothers' Old Boys' Association established the Frank McDonnell medal for the highest State scholarship pass in Catholic schools.

J. O'Leary (comp), *A Catholic miscellany* (Brisb, 1914); C. A. Bernays, *Queensland politics during sixty (1859-1919) years* (Brisb, nd, 1919?); R. Lawson, *Brisbane in the 1890s* (Brisb, 1973); *Queensland Shop Assistant*, 11 Jan, 1 Mar 1929; *Worker* (Brisb), 1 Mar 1890, 28 Nov 1928; *Telegraph* (Brisb), 27 Nov 1928; *Daily Standard*, 28 Nov 1928; *Catholic Advocate*, 29 Nov 1928; J. Hunt, Church and State in education in Queensland (B.A. Hons thesis, Univ Qld, 1959); family information.

M. R. MacGinley

McDOUGALL, CHARLES EDWARD (1865-1923), studmaster and cattle-breeder, was born on 4 December 1865 at Texas, Queensland, fourth of eight sons and two daughters of Malcolm Septimus McDougall, pastoralist, and his wife Blanche Eliza, née Weston. The family settled on Lyndhurst estate near Warwick in 1875. Charles was educated at Warwick and at Toowoomba Grammar School and when his father died in 1882 assumed the managership of Lyndhurst. In 1886 he bought the Australian thoroughbred stallion Archie, and founded what was to be Queensland's leading thoroughbred stud for much of the next century.

McDougall quickly distinguished himself by his energy, decisiveness and ability, at Lyndhurst and in local affairs. An inaugural councillor of Rosenthal Divisional Board in 1889, he was later to become its chairman, as with many other organizations. Noxious weeds, irrigation and local government finance were preoccupations. Less predictably, in the late 1880s he owned several top coursing dogs. In 1890 he set up a stock and station business with two partners at Warwick. In later years he withdrew from active participation in the business in favour of his brother Andrew Septimus (Jim) and other partners.

A beef Shorthorn stud was established at Lyndhurst in 1893. McDougall's initial stock was Australian, but as the stud progressed he increasingly sought expensive imported bulls, looking particularly to promote early maturity in his cattle. The breaking of the 1890s drought and pastoral depression saw McDougall steadily growing in standing and prosperity. Acquiring other properties, in 1905 he established studs at Dulacca West, near Yuleba, managed by his brother Jack (John Graham, *c.*1875-1955). In 1905 Charles bought Lyndhurst's first imported thoroughbred sire, Ladurlad, which was an immediate success; similar successes followed with the importation of Syce, sire of Molly's Robe, and Seremond, sire of Mollison. His most famous Shorthorn bull, Lyndhurst Royal Peer, was champion at the Brisbane Exhibition in 1912-15 and 1917, at a time when Shorthorns were numerically the strongest breed in the State.

McDougall was a strong supporter of the conservative parties in Queensland politics, though never a candidate for parliament. A forthright public speaker, during World War I he was vice-president of the Reinforcement Committee of Queensland, and was on the platform when Billy Hughes [q.v.9] was struck by the notorious Warwick egg.

From 1917 McDougall was president of the (Royal) National Agricultural and Industrial Association of Queensland. He was renowned for his energetic and direct supervision of Lyndhurst's affairs, and showed a pride and delight in his foals that was almost paternal. Unmarried, he was devoted to his family, particularly his mother and his unmarried sister Julia May.

Charles McDougall died at Warwick of gallbladder disease on 16 May 1923 and was buried in Warwick cemetery with Anglican rites. His mother died ten days later. His estate was sworn for probate at £76 960. In 1924 the Queensland Turf Club established the C. E. McDougall Stakes, still so named, in his memory.

McDougall was succeeded at Lyndhurst by his brother Jack, who also remained unmarried. The latter is most noted for his importation in 1931 of The Buzzard, who sired winners of more prize-money than any preceding stallion in Australia.

M. J. Fox (ed), *The history of Queensland*, 1 (Brisb, 1919); J. McKey, *The Warwick story* (Warwick, 1972); *Pastoral Review*, 33 (June 1923), p 476; *Warwick Daily News*, 17 May 1923, 1 Aug 1955.

S. J. Routh

McDOUGALL, DUGALD GORDON (1867-1944), professor of law, was born on 28 March 1867 at Hawthorn, Melbourne, second son of Irish-born Dugald McDougall, stationer and later head of the printing firm Sands [q.v.6] & McDougall, and his wife

Mary Allott, née Chisholm, of Melbourne. McDougall was 17 when his father died. He was educated privately at St Leonards-on-Sea, Sussex, England, at Hawthorn Grammar School and at Trinity College, University of Melbourne (B.A., 1888; M.A., 1890), where he proved a brilliant student, taking exhibitions in most subjects, the Wyselaskie [q.v.6] scholarship in modern languages in 1886 and scholarships in the schools of classics, philosophy, and English, French and German in 1888. In 1888-92 he attended Balliol College, Oxford (B.A., 1892), where as Williams exhibitioner he took first classes in classical moderations, the final school of jurisprudence and the postgraduate course in civil law. He was called to the Bar at the Inner Temple in 1892 and next year returned to Melbourne where he worked with the solicitors Blake & Riggall and in 1895-97 read in the chambers of T. à Beckett Weigall [q.v.]. Graduating LL.B. in 1894 and LL.M. in 1896 from the University of Melbourne, he was admitted to the Victorian Bar in 1895 and practised to 1900.

A tall, well-proportioned and handsome man, McDougall was a keen tennis and billiards player, captain of the Oxford lawn tennis IV and Oxford billiards cue in 1892. Although his father had been a founder of the Hawthorn Presbyterian Church, McDougall had been a devout Anglican since early youth. In 1900 he was appointed professor of law and modern history at the University of Tasmania. He took up the post next year after his marriage on 23 February at St Paul's Church, Ipswich, Queensland, to Helen Ione Atkinson. In 1902 he graduated M.A. and B.C.L. from Oxford and in 1909 LL.D. from Melbourne.

McDougall made a special study of Federal law. In 1905, when he was acting professor of law at the University of Sydney, he published *Self-governing colonies*, followed by *Commonwealth and States* in 1907. His major achievement, however, over three decades as Tasmania's sole full-time law academic, was to produce the State's law graduates and consequently its judges and magistrates. In his lecturing, covering an astonishing ten subjects, great intellectual talents were combined with a teaching skill that still commands the admiration of former students. His scholarship went beyond the law: he remained well learned in history, Greek, Latin, French and German. After his wife became mentally ill about 1910, his enormous teaching load was combined with the responsibility of bringing up their six sons. He retired from the university in June 1933 as emeritus professor.

In retirement McDougall lived on Norfolk Island and later in Sydney on a yearly government grant of £100. His unsuccessful application for a Commonwealth Literary Fund pension in 1937 drew attention to his drinking problem. He died in hospital at Kogarah, Sydney, on 19 June 1944 and was cremated. Of his sons, Archibald was a Tasmanian Rhodes scholar and a lawyer, four became accountants and one a service station proprietor.

Univ Melb, *Calendar*, 1900; *Mercury*, 21 June 1944; CSR A 3753 item 72/2760 (AAO); family papers held by and information from Mr Q. McDougall, Hob.
R. W. BAKER*

McDOUGALL, FRANK LIDGETT (1884-1958), public servant and economist, was born on 16 April 1884 at Greenwich, Kent, England, third son of (Sir) John McDougall, miller and later chairman of the London County Council, and his second wife Ellen Mary, née Lidgett. Educated at Blackheath Proprietary School and the University of Darmstadt, Germany, he spent two years in South Africa on an uncle's wattle farm.

At 25 McDougall joined his half-brothers and sisters in South Australia where he took up a fruit block at Renmark. On 4 September 1915 in Adelaide he married Madeline Joyce, sister of F. M. Cutlack [q.v.8]. In May he had enlisted in the Australian Imperial Force. He was commissioned second lieutenant in the 27th Battalion in September and served in Egypt and France with the 1st Anzac Cyclist Battalion until late 1918.

Back in Australia Captain McDougall joined the board of the Australian Dried Fruits Association in which he had long been active. In 1922 he went to Britain with W. B. Chaffey [q.v.7] and C. E. D. Meares [q.v.] to seek a larger share of the British dried fruit market, and to promote their cause through 'judicious propaganda'. This was to be McDougall's forte. From 1923 he was closely associated with Prime Minister S. M. (Viscount) Bruce [q.v.7] who encouraged his advice and later observed that McDougall 'brings me a new idea every morning'. Bruce summoned him back to the Prime Minister's Department in Melbourne in 1924, then arranged for him to return in January 1925 as part-time secretary of the London agency of the Dried Fruits Control Board with the direction: 'in your more uplifted moments you can call yourself the confidential representative of the Australian Prime Minister, when less inflated a secret service agent!'

In England McDougall cultivated politicians of all parties and leading newspaper editors. He wrote *Sheltered markets* (1925) and many pamphlets and articles, often anonymous, for *The Times* and *Manchester Guardian*. McDougall represented both the Commonwealth Development and Migration Commission and the Council for Scientific and Industrial Research, maintaining constant correspondence with his close friend (Sir)

David Rivett [q.v.] and actively establishing interchange of scientific ideas and personnel. He attended the Imperial Conference of 1923, the Imperial Economic Committee (1926) and the Ottawa Conference (1932), as a diligent apostle of Imperial preference. In 1926 he was appointed C.M.G.

A member of the Empire Marketing Board in 1926-32, during the Depression he preached that governments should increase food consumption and improve diets and that Australia should produce more food to feed the hungry. At the International Economic Conference in Geneva in 1927 and as a member of its economic consultative committee he extended his horizons, stressing the need to reactivate trade in Europe and substitute 'a reasonably fat Germany for a desperately lean one'. McDougall was a regular adviser to Australian delegations at the League of Nations in Geneva from 1928 until its demise in 1940. At the 1935 assembly Bruce and McDougall evolved the slogan 'Marry health and agriculture', promoted so effectively by Bruce that a permanent committee (including McDougall) was set up to report back to the assembly on nutrition in relation to health and economics.

In 1941-42 he worked with Australian economic missions in Washington, won the support of Eleanor Roosevelt and dined at the White House with the president and Harry Hopkins. McDougall was a member of the Australian delegation to the Hot Springs (Virginia) Conference, summoned by Roosevelt early in 1943, that laid the foundations of the United Nations' Food and Agriculture Organisation, set up in Rome after World War II. McDougall worked increasingly for F.A.O.: though he could have been its director-general he preferred always to work through others, as a counsellor. He was its liaison officer with the United Nations and worked closely with Sir John (Lord) Boyd-Orr and Dag Hammarskjöld.

McDougall was extremely vigorous, a lifelong golfer and mountain walker, a host who enjoyed good company, good wine and good food. Beneath the astringent surface of his quick, dry wit there was a warm humanity. While not conventionally religious, as an Anglican he retained, along with profound beliefs, an exceptional memory for the Cranmer Prayer Book and King James Bible. Their language often appeared in his speeches and memoranda, and sometimes also in Bruce's. The British diplomat Lord Gladwyn testified to 'his ability to recite all the Collects, an accomplishment equalled by few other economists'.

McDougall died from a burst appendix on 15 February 1958 in Rome, and was buried near the poet Shelley in the Protestant cemetery. A son and daughter survived him.

There is a portrait in the 'Australia' room of F.A.O.

E. Hill, *Water into gold* (Melb, 1937); C. Edwards, *Bruce of Melbourne* (Lond, 1965); *The memoirs of Lord Gladwyn* (Lond, 1972); A. Stirling, *On the fringe of diplomacy* (Melb, 1973), and *Lord Bruce* (Melb, 1974); R. Rivett, *David Rivett* (Melb, 1976); P. G. Edwards, *Prime ministers and diplomats* (Melb, 1983); W. J. Hudson and W. Way, *Letters from a 'secret service agent'* (Canb, 1985); Aust Dried Fruits Assn, Minutes (Melb).

ALFRED STIRLING*

MacDOUGALL, JAMES (1858-1942), manufacturer, was born on 9 July 1858 in Glasgow, Scotland, son of James McDougall, master pastry baker, and his wife Agnes, née Malcolm. He was educated at Glasgow High School and began his business career in 1874 with the Clydesdale Bank in Glasgow, later becoming a teller. In 1881 he migrated to Victoria where he opened a wine and spirit importing business in Melbourne. On 28 March 1883 at Clinker Hill, Castlemaine, he married Elizabeth Brydie McRobbie with Presbyterian forms.

In 1889 MacDougall established the Austral Nail Co. in South Melbourne, next year forming it into a limited liability company with himself as managing director. The undertaking flourished and in 1896 he sold his importing business. From making nails the company expanded into barbed wire in 1905 and wiredrawing in 1911. MacDougall's three sons, all of whom served in World War I, joined him in the business.

During the war Prime Minister W. M. Hughes [q.v.9] requested MacDougall to establish a mill to meet Australia's wartime wire requirements. After negotiations with Broken Hill Proprietary Co. Ltd, for the supply of wire rods, MacDougall agreed. By 1919 the company was producing 300 tons of wire per week and that year opened a second plant at Newcastle, New South Wales. In 1921 Austral amalgamated with an English company to become Rylands Bros (Australia) Ltd. MacDougall relinquished the managing directorship in 1925 when the new company merged with B.H.P.

After retirement MacDougall played a major role in the Victorian Chamber of Manufactures. A member of the executive since 1920, he was president in 1927-32. Following his election he helped to revitalize the Associated Chambers of Manufactures of Australia which had not met for two years; he initiated a new constitution, re-ordered the finances and served as president in 1927-29 and 1931-32. MacDougall presented the employers' case to Nationalist and Labor governments persuasively and directly. At the same time, like many employers, he believed that management and labour had common interests and that their differences could be reconciled. With the agreement of S. M. (Viscount) Bruce [q.v.7] he convened the Commonwealth Industrial Conference in Melbourne on 6-9 December 1928. As an attempt at national reconciliation the conference failed, achieving little but an exchange of platitudes. However, it is a measure of the respect in which MacDougall was held by both the government and the labour movement that he was successful in arranging the meeting at all.

MacDougall was a director of several public companies. He also served on the council of the New Settlers' League of Victoria, on the Kew City Council and in 1933-41 on the Council of the University of Melbourne. He belonged to Melbourne Rotary Club. A small man, he had regular features, a goatee beard and a benign expression which belied the determination he brought to his business activities. His wife died in 1929 and on 3 March 1932 at Scots Church, Melbourne, he married Constance Jamieson, daughter of Daniel McAlpine [q.v.].

MacDougall died on 8 April 1942 at Cliveden Mansions, East Melbourne, and was cremated, survived by his second wife and his sons. He left an estate valued for probate at £20 475.

Vic Chamber of Manufactures Gazette, 27 June 1927; *BHP Review,* Feb 1937; *Argus,* 9 Apr 1942.   WARREN FRIEND

McDOUGALL, JOHN KEITH (1867-1957), politician, farmer, poet and Labor propagandist, was born on 10 August 1867 at Learmonth, Victoria, eldest child of Donald McDougall, farmer, and his wife Margaret, née Keith. Educated at Rossbridge Common School, McDougall was a bright pupil but left at 13 to assist on his parents' farm. The local schoolmaster and a Presbyterian minister encouraged further informal education and kept the young McDougall supplied with books—the classics, the English poets, ancient history—whose influence on his writing is readily apparent. He contemplated training for the Presbyterian ministry, but soon rejected all religion and channelled his zeal for social reform into politics, concluding that 'church and state were for the rich/And Labor stood alone'.

He formalized his commitment to Labor, joining the Ararat branch of the Political Labor Council on its formation in 1903; he was its first secretary and president in 1904. Involved in agitation to break up the large land holdings in western Victoria, McDougall stood for the Ararat Shire Council, succeeding on his second attempt in 1904. In 1906 he won the Federal seat of Wannon for Labor,

despite a disastrous campaign-opening at Hamilton when he suffered acute stage fright and was unable to speak. His two terms in parliament were, by the usual criteria, undistinguished. 'J.K.' rarely participated in debate, and critics dubbed him 'the Silent Member', but he was an assiduous worker for his constituency. He was a member of King O'Malley's [q.v.] 'torpedo brigade' and, like O'Malley, was later to claim that that group had forced the Fisher [q.v.8] ministry to implement Labor's pledge to establish a Commonwealth Bank. His defeat in the 1913 election was largely attributable to a general swing against Labor, compounded by an unfavourable electoral redistribution in Wannon. McDougall returned to his farm at Maroona, near Ararat, reappearing unsuccessfully as Labor candidate for Flinders in 1914, and for the Grampians in 1915 and 1917.

In countless contributions to the Labor press over four decades, McDougall used verse, letters, articles, and regular columns to denounce capitalism and castigate its adherents. He was equally outspoken in criticizing Labor's pragmatists and backsliders: Fisher [q.v.8], Watson, Theodore, Scullin [qq.v.], and Labor 'rats' like Hughes [q.v.9] and Lyons [q.v.] were all, in their time, victims of his scathing pen. His political verse was, if anything, more biting than his prose, but he also wrote what one admirer described as 'poetry of pure and delicate lyricism'. Five books of his verse were published, but his work remained largely unknown.

Temporary notoriety came when, in their 1919 election campaign, the Nationalists used reworded verses of his anti-war poem 'The White Man's Burden', written in 1900, as 'evidence' of Labor's contempt for the 'digger'. Stirred on by shameful publicity, a gang of returned soldiers dispensed rough justice, luring McDougall from his home to be tarred and feathered and dumped in an Ararat street. An openly partisan judge later fined the six men charged a paltry £5 each.

'J.K.' had married Margaret Ellen McGennisken on 3 March 1908 at Richmond. On his wife's death in 1952, McDougall retired to his daughter's Portland home to write his memoirs. A radical of a later generation, Brian Fitzpatrick, found him in 1955 to be 'an hospitable teetotaller and conserving iconoclast . . . still, at 88, physically and intellectually fit and active'. He died at Ararat on 11 April 1957 and was cremated. Two sons and a daughter survived him.

P. Hay (ed), *Meeting of sighs* (Warrnambool, 1981); *Recorder,* Oct 1976, p 5, Dec 1976, p 17; *Overland,* Aug 1979, p 43; T. King, 'The tarring and feathering of J. K. McDougall', *Labour History,*

Nov 1983; McDougall papers (held by M. Luers, Portland, Vic); S. Merrifield collection (LaTL).

TERRY KING

McDOUGALL, STANLEY ROBERT (1889-1968), soldier and forester, was born on 23 July 1889 at Recherche, Tasmania, son of John Henry McDougall, sawmiller, and his wife Susannah, née Cate. Educated locally, he took up blacksmithing and served his time at this trade. He was an excellent horseman, an expert marksman, a competent bushman and an amateur boxer.

Illness prevented him from enlisting in the Australian Imperial Force until 31 August 1915 when he was posted to the 12th Reinforcements to the 15th Battalion. In Egypt, on 3 March 1916, he was drafted into the 47th Battalion and embarked for France in June. The battalion fought at Pozières Heights in August and in the battles of Messines and Broodseinde in 1917. Appointed lance corporal on 5 May 1917, McDougall was promoted corporal in September; he became temporary sergeant in November and was confirmed in that rank next January.

McDougall was awarded the Victoria Cross for his actions at Dernancourt on 28 March 1918. He was on watch at a post on the 47th's right flank when he heard Germans approaching. When a Lewis-gun team was knocked out by an enemy bomb McDougall snatched up the gun, attacked two machine-gun teams and killed their crews. He turned one of the captured machine-guns on the enemy, killing several and routing one wave of their attack. Meanwhile about fifty Germans had crossed a section of railway which the Australians had held. McDougall turned his gun on them and when his ammunition was spent he seized a bayonet and charged, killing four men. He then used a Lewis-gun, killing many Germans and forcing the surrender of the remaining thirty-three.

Eight days later, in the same location, McDougall won the Military Medal. During a heavy enemy attack he got a gun into position and enfiladed the Germans at close quarters. When the gun was hit he crawled some 300 yards (275 m) under fire to get a replacement; he then took command of the leaderless platoon for the rest of the action. He was posted to the 48th Battalion on 28 May. At Windsor Castle on 19 August he was invested with the Victoria Cross by King George V and shortly afterwards returned to Australia where he was discharged from the A.I.F. on 15 December 1918.

McDougall entered the Tasmanian Forestry Department and in the early 1930s became an inspector in charge of forests in the north-western part of the State. He several times performed outstanding organizational and rescue work during bushfires. He was living at Scottsdale before visiting London for the V.C. centenary in 1956. McDougall died on 7 July 1968 at Scottsdale, survived by his wife Martha, née Anderson-Harrison, whom he had married in 1926; they had no issue.

The uniform he wore and the Lewis-gun he used at Dernancourt are displayed in the Australian War Memorial Hall of Valour with his Victoria Cross and Military Medal. The memorial also has a portrait of him by Frank Crozier.

C. E. W. Bean, *The A.I.F. in France*, 1918 (Syd, 1937); L. Wigmore (ed), *They dared mightily* (Canb, 1963); *London Gazette*, 30 Apr, 12 July 1918; *Reveille* (Syd), June 1934; *Militia Mthly*, Mar 1935; records (AWM).
J. G. WILLIAMS

McDOWALL, ARCHIBALD (1841-1918), surveyor and public servant, was born on 2 December 1841 at Moonee Ponds, near Melbourne, son of Archibald McDowall of Logan, Bothwell, Van Diemen's Land, and his wife Charlotte, née Gill. Educated privately in Hobart Town and at Campbell Town Grammar School, he studied surveying under J. E. Calder [q.v.1] and moved to Queensland in 1861. He joined the Surveyor-General's Department on 13 May 1862. Appointed commissioner of crown lands, West Maranoa, in addition to his surveying duties, he carried out the first town-survey of Roma in 1862. On 7 December 1863 he became commissioner for the Maranoa, then for the Warrego in 1867-68. After a brief term as commissioner for the Kennedy district, he worked for seven years at Toowoomba, being variously Darling Downs commissioner for crown lands, land commissioner, first-class surveyor and district surveyor. He was at Maryborough as district surveyor in 1875-85. Returning to Toowoomba, he served as district surveyor until appointed surveyor-general on 23 February 1891, remaining in that office till retirement on 30 June 1902. He served on the 1900 royal commission into railway extensions in Queensland.

McDowall was a conscientious public servant and a thoroughly professional surveyor. In 1877 he introduced to Queensland the standard steel tape for ground measurement, in place of the chain. In 1883 he supervised the vital field-work involving the establishment of the Jondaryan base line, the foundation of the triangulation survey of south Queensland. Once appointed surveyor-general, he took every opportunity to modernize survey practice, eliminating the use of magnetic compass and chain in favour of the theodolite, steel tape and careful astronomical observation. Advocating survey before land selection and careful planning of access roads, his evidence to the 1897 royal commission on land settlement had a constructive effect on consequent legislation. In 1892 he supported the initial intercolonial surveying conference in Melbourne, stressing the need for reciprocity of training and qualifications. Chairman of the Queensland surveyors' board of examiners from 1892, McDowall became first president of the rejuvenated Queensland Institute of Surveyors in 1899.

His impact as surveyor-general, although impressive, was weakened by the depression of the 1890s which reduced staff numbers and capital expenditure to bare survival level. He inaugurated the use of telegraphic time-signals for accurate longitude observations; supported increased use of photo-lithography in map-production; introduced strict adherence to surveys on the true meridian; rationalized the parish and county boundaries of Queensland; introduced parish maps to promote land settlement; and set up a time-standard system, using carefully controlled clocks, telegraphic time-signals and a time-ball on the Brisbane observatory building.

McDowall commented on the wastefulness of Queenslanders in destroying stands of native timber and pioneered reafforestation experiments on Fraser Island in 1882 with kauri pine. He speculated on 'the hard things the future generation will certainly say of the present inhabitants', accurately forecasting the ecological menace of prickly pear and water hyacinth.

McDowall enjoyed a comparatively untrammelled public career, earning a high reputation for impartiality. He married Annie Coutts with Presbyterian forms on 26 May 1871; they had three sons and one daughter, but Annie died on 18 April 1878 and their daughter the following year. Risking the disapproval of the Anglican and Catholic establishments, he married his sister-in-law, Ada Sarah, on 2 June 1880 at Maryborough. Their son Valentine [q.v.] became a prominent Brisbane radiologist. McDowall died at Middleton, Tasmania, on 13 May 1918.

Alcazar Press, *Queensland,1900* (Brisb,nd); S. E. Reilly, *The profession of surveying in Queensland* (Brisb, 1970).   PAUL D. WILSON

McDOWALL, VALENTINE (1881-1957), medical practitioner and wireless and television pioneer, was born on 14 February 1881, at Maryborough, Queensland, son of Archibald McDowall [q.v.], and his wife Ada Sarah, née Coutts. He attended Brisbane Grammar School in 1895-99, then entered the University of Sydney medical school in 1900, graduating M.B. in 1905 before serv-

ing as a resident medical officer at the Royal Prince Alfred Hospital, Sydney. On 12 January 1906 he married Janet Laurence Crombie, a grazier's daughter, at St Andrew's Presbyterian Church, Brisbane. Moving to Laidley in 1907, McDowall employed a battery-powered X-ray unit in his general practice. In 1915 he joined the Australian Imperial Force as captain, Army Medical Corps, and served in Egypt with the 1st Australian General Hospital, the 2nd and 14th Field Ambulance and from June 1916 with the 1st Australian Dermatological Hospital. He returned to Australia in May 1917 and his A.I.F. appointment ended in August.

Having taken his Ch.M. degree in Sydney in 1917, McDowall returned to Brisbane in 1919 and practised as a specialist in radiology and dermatology. After six months study in the United States of America in 1926 at the Rochester Clinic and elsewhere, he was reputedly the first doctor in Queensland to use radium in treatment. In the 1930s he worked as a radiographer and radiotherapist from Wickham Terrace and was senior honorary radiologist at the Brisbane General Hospital in 1919-34.

During World War II McDowall was temporary lieut-colonel, A.I.F., commanding the 117th A.G.H. early in 1942. He continued service as a visiting specialist in radiology at Greenslopes Repatriation General and other Brisbane hospitals.

Meanwhile he had been president of the Queensland branch of the British Medical Association in 1925, a founding fellow of the Royal Australasian College of Physicians, a fellow of the faculty of Radiologists of England and a foundation fellow of the College of Radiologists of Australasia (president, 1947). He advised on the founding of the Queensland Radium Institute and was a foundation member of the Biophysics Standing Advisory Committee (Queensland). He published in the *Medical Journal of Australia* and the *British Journal of Ophthalmology*.

From 1921 McDowall (with Thomas Elliot) pioneered regular programmes of recorded music on 4CM, his radio station at Preston House, Brisbane; they claimed the first live broadcast in Queensland from the stage of His Majesty's Theatre. In the 1930s they shifted 4CM to the old windmill on Wickham Terrace to experiment with low-resolution television broadcasting, and in October 1935 transmitted a legible page of the *Courier Mail*. Experiments continued until the war. Part of the equipment is preserved in the collection of the Royal Historical Society of Queensland, of which McDowall was a member. He also belonged to the Royal Society of Queensland and the Queensland Club.

Kind and courteous to his patients, McDowall was always a keen sportsman who had been captain of his school's cricket team and a Sydney university rowing blue; in later life he went shooting with his brother Dr Sandy McDowall and took his family yachting and deep-sea fishing. Enthusiastic about machinery, he had one of the first cars at Laidley and served on the committee of the Royal Queensland Aero Club in 1935-41, while securing a private pilot's licence. He was a competent woodworker and manufactured and demonstrated excellent fireworks.

McDowall died at Ascot of cardiac disease on 22 October 1957, survived by his son and daughter. He was cremated after a Presbyterian service.

MJA, 21 Dec 1957, p 920; *RHSQJ*, 6 (1961-62), no 4, p 750; *Telegraph* (Brisb), 23 Oct 1957; information from Roy Qld Aero Club, Brisb, Mr E. Wixted, Queensland Museum, and Mr W. V. McDowall, Toowoomba, Qld.   D. J. ROBINSON

McEACHARN, SIR MALCOLM DONALD (1852-1910), businessman and politician, was born on 8 February 1852 in London, son of Malcolm McEacharn, master mariner, and his wife Ann, née Gay, both from the Isle of Islay, Scotland. His father died when his ship, *Brahmin*, was wrecked near King Island, Bass Strait, in 1854; his mother remarried in 1863. As the child of a dead Scottish sailor, Malcolm was cared for and educated at the Royal Caledonian Schools, Islington, from about 1859 until 1866 when he joined the London shipping office of Rucker, Offor & Co. At 21, having risen to a senior position, he began his own shipbroking business and was for a time a member of Lloyds.

In February 1875, with Andrew McIlwraith [q.v.], McEacharn founded the shipping firm McIlwraith, McEacharn & Co. Within a year the partners had contracted to carry cargo and migrants to Queensland and had begun to build up a fleet of ten ships sailing under the name of the Scottish Line. Success encouraged them to develop a mercantile export and import department; visiting Australia themselves, they were quick to appreciate opportunities for further investment and for intercolonial shipping. Both men had relations in Australia; McIlwraith's brothers John and (Sir) Thomas [qq.v.5] were established in Victoria and Queensland respectively, John acting as the firm's Melbourne agent in 1875-78; McEacharn's uncle Neil McEacharn (d.1881) was an early Melbourne shipmaster and another uncle Archibald McEacharn (d.1905) had been in business in the Australian colonies since 1847.

On 10 January 1878 McEacharn married Anne Peirson, a landowner, in the parish church, Pickering, Yorkshire. After her death

in December, he arrived in Queensland next year to launch the Australian trade in refrigerated meat. A new Glasgow steamer, *Strathleven*, had been chartered and equipped to carry the meat and butter which McEacharn selected personally and accompanied back to London from Sydney. The *Strathleven*'s arrival, with its cargo sound, was a great *coup* for the partners even though they lost money on this and a subsequent voyage.

Unlike McIlwraith, McEacharn settled in Australia. In 1881 he purchased for the company the Rockhampton business of Walter Reid [q.v.6] & Co. He also secured Queensland pastoral properties for himself and a share in a Mackay sugar-mill. On 4 July 1882 at Sandhurst (Bendigo), Victoria, with Presbyterian forms, he married Mary Ann Walton, daughter of the mining millionaire J. B. Watson [q.v.6].

A decline in the migrant trade and, from 1881, competition from the British India Steam Navigation Co. saw McIlwraith, McEacharn progressively withdraw its sailing ships from the Queensland run. Two steamers were built to maintain the trade, but new affiliations were made (notably with (Sir) James Burns [q.v.7] in the Queensland Steam Shipping Co.) and the company also extended itself south by shipping coal under contract to the Melbourne Metropolitan Gas Co. In 1887 McEacharn moved to Melbourne to set up the head office; by 1891, when the firm became a limited liability company, it was established as an intercolonial business distinct from its London parent. The maritime strike of 1890 had slowed progress but in 1893 McIlwraith, McEacharn latched on to another boom in the form of passenger and cargo trade to the Western Australian goldfields with voyages to Java, Singapore and India during the slack period. The identification with far-flung Australasia was seen in the nomenclature of the ships—*Cloncurry, New Guinea, Coolgardie* and *Kalgoorlie*. By World War I the company was one of the seven major Australian coastal shipping concerns.

In March 1893 McEacharn succeeded Matthew Lang [q.v.5] as Melbourne city councillor for Lonsdale Ward and a member of the Melbourne Harbor Trust. He quickly made his mark in the council and after serving as mayor in 1897-1900 was knighted; in 1903 he served another term, as lord mayor. As chairman of the electric supply committee he consolidated corporation control of supply to the metropolis, his defence of the economic role of local government earning him a reputation as a 'municipal socialist'. He also supported the idea of a Greater Melbourne Council and helped to incorporate North Melbourne, Flemington and Kensington into the council in 1905. Although by no means a doctrinaire radical, he was probably more progressive and astute than most of his fellow councillors. But the real reason for his rapid rise is perhaps best explained by the *Argus* when, in 1903, it noted: 'It has become the rule to pick none but rich men . . . Wealth and the occupation of the Mayor's or Lord Mayor's chair have become the easiest of passports to knighthood'.

McEacharn was a director of the limited companies Burns, Philp [q.v.], Walter Reid, National Trustees Executors & Agency, North Queensland Insurance, South Australian Brewing, Brisbane Tramways and Bellambi Coal. He helped to amalgamate the Tokyo tramway companies in 1902-03 and became consul-general for Japan in Melbourne. He was involved in the Queensland Chillagoe mines and the Brisbane *Daily Mail*, was a vice-president of the Melbourne Chamber of Commerce, a fellow of the Royal Geographical Society and a member of the council of the (Royal) Zoological and Acclimatisation Society of Victoria. As president of the (Royal) Caledonian Society of Melbourne, he took special interest in the formation of the Victorian Scottish Regiment which he commanded with the rank of major until 1905.

A Federationist, McEacharn had ambitions beyond local government. In 1901 he stood for the House of Representatives seat of Melbourne, in support of the Barton [q.v.7] ministry, his object being 'to get Home in some representative capacity'. Endorsed by the *Age* and, albeit grudgingly, by the free-trade *Argus*, he defeated William Maloney [q.v.]. McEacharn identified strongly with the interests of employers but retained an independent outlook. He favoured conciliation and arbitration and wanted the Federal government to take over the Victorian railways, but he did not enhance his popular appeal by opposing female suffrage and defending the use of Melanesian labour on the Queensland cane-fields. Tom Roberts [q.v.] considered he had 'the best business and mercantile head of all the members'. He was, in fact, one of the few to have much financial or mercantile experience, but he never quite came to grips with the new milieu. The *Argus* noted late in 1903 that 'as Mayor and councillor he is clear, direct, decided; in Parliament no one quite knows where he is to-day or will be to-morrow'.

In the elections of December 1903 McEacharn defeated Maloney only narrowly and the election was declared void on a technicality. The subsequent poll on 30 March 1904 attracted great attention; McEacharn's meetings were rowdy battles as the dapper plutocrat sought to win support from increasingly hostile, class-conscious, inner-city residents. He lost, and the seat became a Labor stronghold. McEacharn's decision to abandon poli-

tics after one defeat was widely regarded as a mistake, but, true to his stated intentions, he abandoned not only politics but Australia. He left Melbourne in 1905 and purchased the ancestral home of the earl of Galloway in Wigtownshire, Scotland.

He died suddenly, of heart failure brought on by pneumonia, at Cannes, France, on 10 March 1910. McIlwraith was with him at the time and he was survived by his wife, two daughters and a son. His estate was valued for probate at over £200 000.

McEacharn was a self-made man, a capitalist of almost archetypical qualities. In Melbourne he had lived in style in a mansion, Goathlands, surrounded by, among other things, art works he had brought back from Japan. He had ambition, ability, energy, dash and flair, and perhaps a deep-seated insecurity. Vain and obsessively neat, he slept with a pistol by his bed. McEacharn was always on the look-out for the main chance; but he was also a builder who contributed materially to the many enterprises in which he was involved.

A. Sutherland et al, *Victoria and its metropolis*, 2 (Melb, 1888); J. Smith (ed), *Cyclopedia of Victoria*, 1 (Melb, 1903); R. H. Croll, *Tom Roberts* (Melb, 1935); G. Blainey, *The tyranny of distance* (Melb, 1966); B. Pemberton, *Australian coastal shipping* (Melb, 1979); *A'sian Shipping Record*, Nov 1975; *Outpost* (Melb), 25 May 1900; *Argus*, 22,23, 28 Mar 1901, 10 Nov, 11, 14 Dec 1903, 31 Mar 1904, 12 Mar 1910; *Table Talk*, 25 Apr 1901, 17 Mar 1910; *Punch* (Melb), 10 Sept 1903; *Age*, 12 Mar 1910, 4 Jan 1936; *Herald* (Melb), 21 Oct 1932; Palmer-McIlwraith papers (Oxley Lib, Brisb).

DAVID DUNSTAN

McEACHERN, WALTER MALCOLM NEIL (1883-1945), singer, was born on 1 April 1883 at Albury, New South Wales, sixth of thirteen children of Archibald Hector McEachern, miner, and his wife Rebecca Mary, née Tubman. Malcolm was educated at Albury Public School where he had his first singing lessons from Howard Tracey. Over six feet (183 cm) tall with an immense, well-proportioned frame, he was fond of sport, especially Rugby, boxing, billiards and riding. In 1904 his family moved to Sydney where he worked as a salesman and undertook casual singing engagements, his leisure allegedly embracing sport, gambling, social outings and good times. His engagement in 1913 to pianist Hazel Hogarth Doyle, who became his accompanist, provided musical direction and discipline and he soon established himself as one of the most promising singers in Sydney. They were married on 2 February 1916 at Willoughby Congregational Church.

During World War I McEachern toured with the Melba [q.v.] Concert Company; he performed often later with Melba as well as with other leading artists, including Ella Caspers, Ada Crossley [q.v.8], and Marie Narelle. In 1918-20 the McEacherns toured Asia and North America. From Chicago they went to England in 1921 where McEachern was hailed as one of the finest bass singers of his day and as an outstanding oratorio singer. He appeared with orchestras under Sir Henry Wood and (Sir) John Barbirolli, in Shakespearian productions and in Gilbert and Sullivan operas. His voice was an unusually resonant *basso cantante* with a range of three octaves: the registers were always perfectly blended and weight of tone even. The voice was always sonorous without being ponderous. A pioneer of both radio and television for the British Broadcasting Corporation he was often chosen for royal command performances.

Early in 1926 he joined Bentley Collingwood Hilliam (1890-1965), a Yorkshire pianist with a flair for composing witty topical songs. As 'Flotsam and Jetsam' they became an enduring light entertainment act. McEachern made his film début in *Chu Chin Chow* in 1933.

During World War II he did considerable stage and radio work, including a West End revival of *Show boat* in 1944. He was a member of the Savage Club. He died on 17 January 1945 in London after an operation for cancer of the oesophagus. Of his death Peter Dawson [q.v.8] said, 'The world has been robbed of a master of song'. He was survived by his wife and a son who was killed in action three months later.

McEachern was a cultured and convivial musician who disliked pretension, especially in music. The sole aim of his singing was to give enjoyment. His size, jovial nature and booming voice gave him great presence. He recorded 187 studio performances, including opera, operetta, oratorio, art songs, and popular compositions of which 88 were made for the Vocalion Company (1921-27) and 99 (including 53 'Flotsam and Jetsam' duets) for Columbia Graphophone (1927-41). On his centenary in 1983 all his solo recordings for Columbia were issued by EMI (Australia).

B. and F. Mackenzie, *Singers of Australia* (Melb, 1967); *The Times*, 18, 19 Jan 1945; *SMH*, 18 Jan 1945.   PETER BURGIS

MACFARLAN, SIR JAMES ROSS (1872-1955), judge, was born on 30 April 1872 at Glenlyon, Victoria, son of James Macfarlan, storekeeper and postmaster, and his wife Mary, née Nairn, both from Scotland. Of Presbyterian upbringing, he attended Wesley College, Melbourne, and after winning the Walter Powell [q.v.5] scholarship, became a student at Queen's College, University of Melbourne. He graduated B.A. with first-class honours in 1893 and taught as senior classics master at Geelong Church of England Grammar School before obtaining his LL.B. and M.A. in 1896. He was admitted to the Bar that year, reading with (Sir) Leo Cussen [q.v.8].

In 1898-99 Macfarlan was acting professor of law and modern history at the University of Tasmania, and then went into practice at the Victorian Bar. He was elected a fellow of Queen's College in 1901. On 23 December 1902 at St George's Church, Hobart, he married Hilda Charlotte, daughter of W. G. Gibson, member of the Legislative Council of Tasmania; they had five children.

His first legal success came at Bendigo, where he built up a considerable practice in common law and commercial cases. He was known for hard fighting, handling his opponents and their witnesses roughly but fairly. In 1913 he stood unsuccessfully for Liberal preselection for the newly created Federal division of Henty, then continued to work for the Liberal party at Sandringham, and later at St Kilda; in November 1917 he stood, again unsuccessfully, as an Independent Nationalist for the State seat of St Kilda.

Macfarlan took silk in 1920 and in January 1922 was appointed a justice of the Supreme Court of Victoria, following the resignation of Sir Joseph Hood [q.v.9]. He was appointed senior puisne judge in 1935 and was knighted in 1938. As a judge, he was considered an outstanding exponent of common law, known for the care with which he watched the interests of the accused in criminal trials. However, he had a reputation for a short temper with counsel, his keen perception of the points of an argument arousing his impatience with those of slower comprehension. Frequent complaints came to a head when Macfarlan fined a barrister who persisted in trying to establish his point. The Bar advised (Sir) Robert Menzies, the attorney-general, that Macfarlan should be removed from the bench for misbehaviour. The crisis was averted, and matters generally improved, after a personal visit by the attorney-general to Macfarlan whose irascibility on the bench was in marked contrast to his charming manner on social occasions.

A keen golfer, Macfarlan was a member of the Royal Melbourne (for which he played pennant) and Barwon Heads golf clubs. He was also a member of the Melbourne Club where he resided from 1935. He enjoyed shooting and was fluent in French and Italian.

In 1949 Sir James resigned from the Supreme Court bench and in 1950 had the unusual experience of reading of his own death in *Debrett's Peerage*—an error which he took in good humour. He died on 12 July 1955 at South Yarra, survived by four sons and one daughter, and was cremated. Macfarlan's younger brother Ian was briefly premier of Victoria in 1945.

A. Dean, *A multitude of counsellors* (Melb, 1968); P. Joske, *Sir Robert Menzies 1894-1978* (Aust, 1978); *Punch* (Melb), 1 Nov 1917; *SMH*, 23 Dec 1920; *Bulletin*, 13 Jan 1921; *Argus*, 17, 18 Jan 1922, 9 June 1938, 21 Dec 1949, 13 July 1955; *Age*, 9 June 1938, 21 Dec 1949; *Herald* (Melb), 15, 19 July 1950; *Sun-News Pictorial*, 19, 20 July 1950.   ELISE B. HISTED

MacFARLAND, SIR JOHN HENRY (1851-1935), educationist and churchman, was born on 19 April 1851 at Omagh, Tyrone, Ireland, elder son of John MacFarland, draper, and his second wife Margaret Jane, daughter of Rev. William Henry, a famous Covenanting Church minister. Both parents were devout Presbyterians, well educated, with strong intellectual interests.

John attended the local National school until he was 13 when he moved to the Royal Academical Institution, Belfast. He proceeded to Queen's College, graduating B.A. with first-class honours in mathematical science in 1871 and M.A. by examination next year. On the way he had won junior and senior scholarships and every possible mathematical honour. He went on to St John's College, Cambridge, for three more years undergraduate study of mathematics and physics (B.A., 1876; M.A., 1879). He took his first class as 25th wrangler; he had been expected to do better, but was hindered by a skating accident. MacFarland passed the next four years pleasantly, teaching at Repton School, Derbyshire, where he started a physics laboratory, made a special study of the telephone, formed a natural history society and proved himself a gifted teacher.

The emissaries of the provisional council of Ormond College, University of Melbourne, were impressed. Francis Ormond [q.v.5] himself reported: 'MacFarland is just the man we want. He is a first-class scholar, Maths, Science, etc, an English university man, of high personal character, and a staunch Presbyterian. [He is] fresh, healthy, strong, looks less than his age, a gentleman, a scholar, has good appearance and pleasing manners'. MacFarland negotiated a salary of £600 plus the profit from 'farming' the college. On 18 March 1881 the boyish-looking master passed the opening-day ordeal in the presence of 440 Presbyterian grandees, clergy and their ladies. Dr Alexander Morrison [q.v.5],

headmaster of Scotch College, coached him in local Presbyterian and education politics, and his Belfast friend Rev. J. L. Rentoul [q.v.] also helped him to settle in.

MacFarland soon won a free hand from his council, appointed outstanding tutors, taught incisively himself in mathematics and physics, and developed bitter rivalry with Alexander Leeper [q.v.] of Trinity College. In 1892 he named his own terms to the college council; he gave up 'farming' but accepted £1000 a year plus capitation fees and free accommodation—higher payment than any professor's. His tutors included (Sir) Thomas Dunhill [q.v.8], (Sir) John Latham, Daniel McAlpine and (Professor) Darnley Naylor [qq.v.]. MacFarland's mastership was already legendary: he was brusque and stern, but above all just; 'he thought of the students as boys and treated them as men'; he made few rules of conduct but insisted they be observed; he encouraged self-government by a students' club. His discipline did not offend: his 'Yes' and his 'No', with little if any explanation, were famous. He knew everything that was happening, though never inquisitorial, but perhaps became rather too awesome for troubled men to seek him out. Ormond graduates were proud of the frank and manly tone of the college. The students referred to MacFarland as 'Mac', later 'The Doctor', and eventually 'Snapper'.

In 1886 MacFarland began a 49-year stint on the university council and was quickly prominent, radical in supporting provision of state scholarships and the propriety of professorial representation on council. By 1900 he had moved to the centre of educational affairs. He was a member in 1899-1901 and often acting chairman of Theodore Fink's [q.v.8] innovative royal commission into technical education, and formed a productive alliance with Frank Tate [q.v.], later director of education. MacFarland took the lead when in August 1901 major defalcations by the university accountant were exposed. He was appointed to an emergency committee to reorganize management of the university offices and then became chairman of the finance committee, initiating stringent reforms. The financial situation was desperate but in 1904 MacFarland's negotiations with Premier Bent [q.v.3] led to some relief. In 1910 he became vice-chancellor, in effect commencing a period of twenty-five years as unpaid chief university executive. In 1913 he chaired the council committee whose comprehensive proposals for reform eventually led to revision of the university Act ten years later.

MacFarland resigned the Ormond mastership in February 1913, but continued through 1914; he probably now saw his university duties as more satisfying. He had published

266

nothing as mathematical scholar or educationist, but was a practised, pithy speaker at graduations and school speech-nights. He very likely considered his Church work to be of greatest importance. He was manager at Scots Church from 1892, elder from 1896 and 'ever the affectionate comrade of the ministers of this parish, and indeed of all his fellow-officers'. He was regularly elected to assemblies at which he rarely spoke and never on doctrinal matters; but according to well-founded legend he and his friend Dr W. S. Littlejohn [q.v.], headmaster of Scotch College, used to settle much of the business beforehand. (After church on Sundays he dined regularly at the Littlejohns', taking Glenlivet and 'watter' with the meal and enjoying his pipe afterwards.) He became the Church's leading financial executive, probably the most important Presbyterian layman in Victoria. For some thirty years he sat on the councils of Scotch College and Presbyterian Ladies' College, as chairman from 1919 and 1920; he believed it the councils' duty to make financial policy and to trust their headmasters.

On Sir John Madden's [q.v.] death in 1918 MacFarland became chancellor of the university and was knighted in 1919. He presided over a period of considerable expansion, working closely with Sir John Monash [q.v.], vice-chancellor from 1923, and Sir James Barrett [q.v.7]. MacFarland was immensely and properly proud of his careful financial management, but the erstwhile reformers were hardly tender enough in balancing economy with humanity. The professors became increasingly restive about the limited responsibility for academic matters and allocation of resources council allowed them; MacFarland's close alliance with the innovative but authoritarian Barrett was widely seen as a basic problem. When in 1928 the issues came to a head, however, MacFarland's prestige was too much for the professoriate who, anyway, had great respect for his administrative capacity, humanity and reasonableness. Even in his eighties he would not retire as chancellor, probably wisely concluding that his likely successor Barrett would prove to be too divisive.

MacFarland's reputation as a business manager led to his directorship from about 1905 of the National Mutual Life Association (chairman from 1928) and of the Trustees Executors & Agency Co. Ltd. From 1913 he represented the Trustees Executors on the Felton [q.v.4] Bequests Committee. He was also the popular chairman from its foundation in 1908 of the Alexandra Club Co.; the members of the leading female social club preferred men to control their finances.

Latham reckoned MacFarland the best committee-chairman Melbourne had known, with such capacity to go to the root of a matter he might have been a gifted judge. He habitually refused to make up his mind until he had heard all arguments; once sure of his ground, he acted swiftly. In public he spoke briefly, emphatically, unambiguously.

MacFarland was broadly liberal in politics, a close friend of H. B. Higgins [q.v.9]. Although of course a staunch Imperialist, who spoke at a counter-demonstration against Archbishop Mannix [q.v.] in 1918, he also helped to tone down a Presbyterian General Assembly resolution condemning Catholics for disloyalty. His community standing was such that, as the Depression deepened, he was called on to chair the Melbourne Town Hall meeting of February 1931 which founded the Australian Citizens' League, though he took no part in the subsequent All for Australia League and United Australia Party.

In his younger days MacFarland was a vigorous cyclist and walker in the Australian Alps, Tasmania and New Zealand. By the age of 40 he was spending a month each summer trout-fishing in the South Island of New Zealand. He was also a regular golfer at Royal Melbourne and belonged to the Melbourne Club.

MacFarland died on 22 July 1935 and after a service at Scots Church was cremated. The university council minuted:

> Few men in any community, and almost no man in this community, can have won such universal esteem. No evil was ever spoken of him, or could be thought of in connection with him; before him evil quailed. The greatest disciple of the greatest of the Greeks called his dead master 'our friend whom we may truly call the wisest, and the justest, and the best of all men we have ever known'. And many of us can sincerely say that of John Henry MacFarland.

The simplicity of his mode of life, his evident entire unselfishness, and the charm and courtesy so easily detected behind the gruff exterior made him widely loved.

During his life MacFarland had given away large sums of money; he had recently presented £8200 for scholarships at Ormond. Apart from pensions to relations and small bequests he left his estate, valued for probate at over £78 000, to the Presbyterian Church (89 per cent including 37 per cent to Ormond), the Lord Mayor's Fund (7 per cent) and the university (less than 4 per cent). He may best be judged as one who devoted his life primarily to his Church as a celibate lay priest.

G. Serle, 'Sir John MacFarland', in S. Macintyre (ed), *Ormond College centenary essays* (Melb, 1984); *VHM*, 25, no 4, June 1954.

GEOFFREY SERLE

McGAW, ANDREW KIDD (1873-1956), company agent and manager, was born on 5 October 1873 at Foveran, Aberdeenshire, Scotland, son of John McGaw, a dentist turned evangelist with the Christian Brethren Church, and his wife Margaret, née Findlay. McGaw was educated at Gordon's College, Aberdeen. He became a chartered surveyor and worked on estates in Scotland and England. In 1902 he was appointed chief agent and manager of the Van Diemen's Land Co. and associated companies, taking up his duties in Burnie on 1 February 1903. On 5 March 1902 he married Elsie Pringle Wotton at Ludlow, Shropshire, England.

'Probably the most unfortunate of all capitalist ventures in early Australia', the V.D.L. Co. through poor selection of land, mismanagement, and bad luck (the rich Mount Bischoff tin-mine was later discovered just outside its boundaries) had been a continual drain on shareholders' funds. However, a degree of prosperity was attained towards the end of the nineteenth century. Under McGaw, a diligent manager who paid close attention to detail, the company's agricultural interests were extended and developed, and land sales (a major source of income) placed on a regular basis. Much of the original grant was gradually sold, farmland cleared, orchards created, and activity concentrated on stock and crops. Some of the company's land was farmed by tenants, while other small properties had been purchased from the company on mortgage. A sawmill was erected at Burnie in 1905 to process company timber and the Burnie Brick & Timber Co. was established as a subsidiary in 1907, with a brickworks at Cooee.

McGaw's greatest contribution to the development of Burnie and north-west Tasmania may have been his work for the Marine Board of Burnie of which he became a warden in 1907, the year after a long, acrimonious legal battle between the board and the company had been settled. He was elected master warden in 1910, defeated in 1914, re-elected in 1924 and held the position until 1945, a record period. McGaw was a tireless champion of the development of Burnie as a port. He guided the Marine Board, initiated construction and expansion including a pier and breakwater, and attracted shipping. McGaw Pier was named in his honour in 1930. He encouraged the establishment of a pulp and paper industry and is credited with playing 'the greatest part of any individual' in the emergence of Burnie as an industrial centre.

McGaw was very active in business and civic organizations. He was the first president of the Agricultural Bureau of Tasmania, chairman of the Tasmanian Timber Organization and the Northwestern Sawmilling Association, a member of the Tasmanian committee of the Council for Scientific and Industrial Research, and he chaired a government board of inquiry into the operations of the Agricultural Bank of Tasmania in 1935. President and later patron of the Burnie Agricultural Show for many years, he was an elder in the Christian Brethren Church and chairman of the Bible Society and the Burnie Benevolent Society (which was very active during the Depression). He was appointed C.M.G. in 1937.

McGaw retired on 31 March 1947 in failing health. He was appointed local director of the V.D.L. Co., but he soon resigned because of illness. He moved to Mont Albert, Melbourne, and after his departure the company gradually sold off its property and closed its offices. It retained its Woolnorth estate in the north-western corner of Tasmania.

McGaw was an energetic, friendly man, but not gregarious. He was respected for his honesty and fairness, though he was never quick to forgive those who had failed him. Tall, slender and prematurely grey, he dressed fastidiously. His main recreation was running a small farm at Ridgley. McGaw died on 11 January 1956 in Melbourne and was buried in Box Hill cemetery. His wife, two daughters and a son survived him.

P. G. Mercer, *Burnie* (Burnie, 1965), and *Gateway to progress* (Burnie, 1969); H. J. W. Stokes, 'The Van Diemen's Land Co.', *Tasmanian Year Book 1971* (Hob, 1971); *Advocate* (Burnie), 8 Feb 1949; *Mercury* (Hob), and *Examiner* (Launceston), 12 Jan 1956; Records of the Van Diemen's Land Co. (TA).   JIM KITAY

McGEE, LEWIS (1888-1917), railway engine driver and soldier, was born on 13 May 1888 at Campbell Town, Tasmania, son of John McGee, labourer and later farmer, and his wife Mary, née Green. McGee left for posterity virtually no record of his pre-war days. He married Eileen Rose Bailey at Avoca on 15 November 1914. When he enlisted in the 40th Battalion, Australian Imperial Force, on 1 March 1916 he was living at Avoca and was employed by the Tasmanian Department of Railways as an engine driver.

The 40th Battalion, known as the 'Fighting Fortieth', was raised as a Tasmanian unit, under the command of Lieut-Colonel J. E. C. Lord [q.v.], to encourage recruitment in that State. Soldiers attached to it were trained at the Claremont military camp near Hobart before sailing for England and eventually the French-Belgian border, which they reached on 24 November 1916. McGee quickly developed a reputation as a reliable and fearless soldier. He had been promoted lance corporal only twenty-two days after enlistment and on

4 December, when the battalion was operating near Armentières, he rose to corporal; on 12 January 1917 he was promoted sergeant.

The 40th Battalion took part in the battle of Messines in June after which it joined in the 3rd battle of Ypres. From September conditions were appalling with soldiers battling in a 'sea of mud and water'. On 4 October the battalion was engaged in the attack on Broodseinde Ridge. McGee's platoon was 'suffering severely' from machine-gun fire coming from a German pill-box. Single-handed, McGee rushed the post across open ground armed only with a revolver and, descending upon the garrison, shot some of its crew and captured the rest. His action enabled the advance to proceed. Afterwards he reorganized the remains of his platoon and was 'foremost' in the rest of the advance. He was awarded the Victoria Cross for his 'coolness and bravery', but the decoration was posthumous for on 12 October he had been killed in the fighting at Passchendaele. He was buried there in Tyne Cot cemetery.

McGee had been 'respected by all'. However his comrades and family were not the only ones to suffer from his loss. The Launceston *Examiner* commented that his death marked the fourteenth young man from Avoca who had paid 'the supreme sacrifice' which was a 'heavy toll' for a small community. McGee was survived by his wife and a daughter; in 1929 Eileen remarried but remained in Avoca. She and her daughter attended the unveiling of a memorial plaque to McGee at the town's cenotaph in 1984.

L. Broinowski, *Tasmania's war record* (Hob, 1921); F. C. Green, *The Fortieth, a record of the 40th Battalion* (Hob, 1922); L. Wigmore (ed), *They dared mightily* (Canb, 1963); *Examiner* (Launc), 8 Nov 1917; *Mercury*, 19 Mar 1984.

QUENTIN BERESFORD

MACGEORGE, NORMAN (1872-1952), artist and art patron, was born on 8 July 1872 in Adelaide, son of Alexander Macgeorge, prosperous draper and later land agent, and his second wife Rachel Elizabeth, née Luxmoore. Educated at the Collegiate School of St Peter, he studied art at the Adelaide School of Design under Harry Gill [q.v.9] and the National Gallery School, Melbourne. After being placed third in 1899 for the gallery's travelling scholarship, behind Max Meldrum and Hugh Ramsay [qq.v.], he travelled independently to Britain and Europe.

Drawing master at Wesley College, Melbourne, in 1902-06, Macgeorge introduced 'freehand drawing and perspective as a regular form subject throughout the school', a study that was closer to his heart than the regions of 'strict geometry'. He also taught at Melbourne Teachers' College and, in 1902-32, at Melbourne Church of England Grammar School. Tall, athletic, clean-shaven and well-groomed, he belied the conventional artist's image; his students derived pleasure from counting 'the number of his new suits'.

On 25 January 1911 at Holy Trinity Church, East Melbourne, Macgeorge married May Ina Hepburn, granddaughter of the pioneering pastoralist Captain John Hepburn. On the unanimous advice of his painter friends, he engaged Harold Desbrowe Annear [q.v.7] to design a house for him at 25 Riverside Road, Ivanhoe, at the junction of the Yarra River and Darebin Creek. The formal garden layout was the work of Blamire Young [q.v.]. Here Macgeorge lived until his death, journeying to Europe on occasion and absorbing new developments. He used his financial security to aid the course of art and artists, and his area of interest was broad, encompassing literature and ballet. With his wife he welcomed his contemporaries and the young to the relaxing ambience of his home, Fairy Hills, with its talk-filled dinners and summer punting-parties.

Just too late to be part of the Heidelberg movement, Macgeorge painted lyrical and contemplative landscapes—yet his personal stance accommodated the new developments in Europe. But although seen by contemporaries as leaning towards the *avant garde* and with an understanding of the modern movement, Macgeorge was never entirely at ease with the German Expressionists, the Cubists or Picasso and his contemporaries. In an article contributed from London to *Art in Australia* in 1930 he said of the German salon at the Biennial International Exhibition at Venice, 'Germany has entirely cast aside the trammels of convention and tradition at the risk of becoming neurotic and even repulsive'.

Macgeorge was active in art education and politics. He was second president of the Australian Art Association, founded in 1912. He wrote for the Melbourne *Herald*, lectured to university extension classes, and exhibited. One of the group that opposed (Sir) Robert Menzies' dream of an Australian Academy of Art (1937-46), he helped to establish the Contemporary Art Society in 1938 in opposition to it. He delivered the society's third lecture, largely on the artistic bankruptcy of commercial painters. At his own expense he published two works which showed his wide understanding of the continuous fabric of all art: *Borovansky Ballet in Australia and New Zealand* (1946) and *The arts in Australia* (1948).

Norman Macgeorge died, childless, on 2 September 1952 and was cremated. His estate of £11 867 was bequeathed, after the death of his wife in 1970, to the University of Melbourne. They wished their home to continue to be a centre for encouragement of the arts, especially to benefit students. The university established the Macgeorge Bequest and set up a committee of management for the property. Successive artists-in-residence at the university have lived there.

Macgeorge is represented in several collections of major institutions. The National Gallery of Victoria has the oil painting for which he is best known, a 'large, delicately high-keyed work', 'Mother of Pearl'. The University of Melbourne has significant examples of his oil landscapes and a large collection of his water-colours. It also holds the major portrait in oils of him, by his friend Napier Waller [q.v.]. In 1979 Macgeorge was one of 'Five Artists from Heidelberg', a retrospective exhibition at the Banyule Gallery by the National Gallery of Victoria.

Melb C of E Grammar School, *Liber Melburniensis* (Melb, 1937); *Wesley College Chronicle*, Apr 1902; *Art in Aust*, no 2, Nov 1922, no 42, Feb 1932, no 76, Aug 1939; Melb Teachers' College, *Trainee*, 1965; Aust Art Assn cats (SLV); ms collection relating to N. and M. Macgeorge (LaTL); Macgeorge papers (Univ Melb Archives).

RAY MARGINSON

McGILL, ALEC DOUGLAS (1886-1952), barrister, was born on 2 January 1886 at Newtown, Ipswich, Queensland, twin son of James McGill, an ironmonger from Scotland, and his Irish wife Elizabeth, née Watson. He was educated at Newtown State School and, by scholarship, at Ipswich Grammar School. Dux in 1904, he won the Lewis Thomas [q.v.6] exhibition to the University of Sydney (St Andrew's College), where he graduated (B.A., 1907) with honours in classics. He then became resident classics master at Cooerwull Academy, Bowenfels. Returning to Queensland in 1910, he read for the Bar in the chambers of P. B. McGregor and was admitted on 6 June 1911. On 26 September 1914 he married Eva Minnie Grace Hardwicke at Bald Hills Presbyterian Church near Brisbane.

McGill's practice grew, but he was also attracted by politics. President of the Country and Progressive National Party from 1925 until its demise in 1935, he contested unsuccessfully the South Brisbane State seat in 1926. With the advent of the Moore [q.v.] government in 1929, he received much crown work—too much in the eyes of the Labor Opposition. McGill prepared the crown submission for the royal commission of 1930 on the Mungana-Chillagoe mines. On 15 June 1934 he was appointed K.C. Active in the Law

Council of Australia, in 1939 he presided over the 4th Australian Law Convention in Brisbane. That year he was offered a judgeship, but declined it.

Figuring in many notable cases, McGill appeared for Hancock [q.v.9] & Gore Ltd during the Commonwealth royal commission (1948-49) into timber rights in Papua-New Guinea. He defended Rylance Collieries Pty Ltd when the Queensland government sued civilly for the refund of moneys paid for coal short-delivered under a contract to supply the railways. He appeared for Archbishop (Sir) James Duhig [q.v.8] in the Holy Name Cathedral case in which the architect J. F. Hennessy [q.v.9] sued for professional fees, and for Golden Investment Pty Ltd during the royal commission into alleged malpractices in the conduct of the lottery. McGill's tenacity and adroitness in the 1950 Bulimba election appeal on behalf of the defeated Liberal candidate J. Hamilton were largely responsible for exposing forged votes, which resulted in a fresh election.

From 1935 until his death McGill was a member of the University of Queensland law faculty and of the university senate, and became deputy chancellor from 1946. In the immediate post-war period he was acting professor of law and dean of the faculty. A member of the Queensland Turf Club, the Queensland Club (from 1929) and the Johnsonian Club, he held directorships with the Roseberry Sawmilling Co., the Timber Corporation Ltd and Hancock & Gore Ltd.

McGill died suddenly from hypertensive heart disease on 6 July 1952 in a bus at South Brisbane and was cremated after a Presbyterian service. His wife and two daughters survived him; his son John had been killed in 1944 on active service with the Royal Australian Air Force.

McGill had a powerful, resonant voice. Courteous to witnesses, he distinguished himself at the Bar by his ability to maintain a broad strategic plan of conduct of a case. His cross-examination of notable figures like Randolph Bedford [q.v.7] and C. G. Fallon in two celebrated defamation cases in Queensland was an education to any young lawyer.

K. H. Kennedy, *The Mungana affair* (Brisb, 1978); R. Johnston, *History of the Queensland Bar* (Brisb, 1979); *PP* (Cwlth), 1948-49, 4, p 1153; *Univ Qld Gazette* 1945, p 2, 1952, p 7; *Aust Law J*, 26 (Aug 1952), no 4, p 211; *Courier Mail*, 7 July 1952.

J. C. H. GILL

McGIRR, JOHN JOSEPH GREGORY (1879-1949), pharmacist, land dealer and politician, was born on 21 October 1879 at

Parkes, New South Wales, second son and third child of John Patrick McGirr, miner, and his wife Mary, née O'Sullivan, both Irish born. John Patrick (1847-1925) migrated with his brother to New South Wales in 1868 to join their uncle Fr J. McGirr, parish priest at Parkes. John Patrick dug unsuccessfully for gold, and after his marriage in 1873 began to acquire dairying and town properties, gradually becoming wealthy and founding a family that was to achieve prominence in the mid-western district and in the Labor Party.

Greg McGirr was educated at St Joseph's Convent, Parkes, St Stanislaus College, Bathurst, and at the University of Sydney where in 1902-03 he qualified in pharmacy. He soon opened a chemist shop at Peak Hill, later extending to Parkes, Orange, Narromine and eventually Sydney; with managers operating them, they proved profitable investments, specializing in veterinary products and vermin poisons. McGirr himself concentrated on land and stock trading and built up his business to a turnover of £100 000 annually. Despite his increasing affluence he retained a radical streak, and joined the increasing flow of Catholics into the Labor Party as Protestants became a mainstay of the Liberal Party. In 1910 McGirr ran unsuccessfully for the seat of Orange, but won Yass at a by-election in 1913. On 14 November 1914 in Brisbane he married Rachel Rittenburg Miller, B.A., a schoolteacher.

By then McGirr had adopted an ebullient, populist style, tending to be overbearing and insensitive, with a sledge-hammer eloquence. But, if something of a stormy petrel, he was good company and generous, of medium build, good-looking with reddish hair. The split in the Labor Party in 1916 over conscription for overseas service in World War I resulted in the expulsion of twenty-three parliamentarians, of whom five were Redmondite [q.v.6] Catholics, and the formation of a Nationalist government by W. A. Holman [q.v.9]. As whip in 1916-17, McGirr reflected the rising influence of the radical Irish element in the enlarged Catholic group in the Labor Party. He did not attend parliament regularly but his aggressiveness, especially his enmity with T. J. Ley [q.v.], maintained his prominence, and in the 1920 elections he won a Cootamundra seat, playing a significant part in Holman's defeat there.

McGirr had not been active in the development of Labor policy on child endowment, but he espoused it vigorously and was minister for public health and motherhood in J. Storey's [q.v.] 1920 government, becoming known as 'Mother McGirr'. Next year he opened a baby health clinic at Woolloomooloo, but the belief that he was not devoting sufficient time to his portfolio was justified when he took over a year to bring down the motherhood endowment bill; although it did not become law, it restored his popularity. When Storey died in October 1921, J. Dooley [q.v.8] became premier and McGirr his deputy; they were an antipathetic pair. McGirr was also minister for labour in October-December.

The fall of the government in 1922 aggravated Labor's factional strife. McGirr had manoeuvred to gain the support of New South Wales elements of the Australian Workers' Union which, under J. Bailey [q.v.7], dominated the State executive but were at odds with the Federal branch of the union. This tactic enabled him to gain pre-selection for a Sydney seat in 1922 although he continued to live at Parkes; but it resulted in the defeat of a popular Laborite M. Burke and McGirr alienated some of his caucus support. He exacerbated his estrangement at the party conference in June when he attacked his former cabinet colleagues J. T. Lang [q.v.9], C. C. Lazzarini, P. F. Loughlin, T. D. Mutch [qq.v.] and (Sir) W. J. McKell. But he retained the party machine's backing and, when Dooley was expelled in March 1923, McGirr was made leader by the executive. The resulting crisis was settled by the intervention of the federal party executive, on which the federal A.W.U. was influential; it appointed W. F. Dunn [q.v.8] stopgap leader pending a caucus vote, at which Lang was elected in July.

McGirr was now distrusted by all Labor factions, including most of his co-religionists. He seemed to lose his political judgement, resigned from the Labor Party on 31 July, founded the Young Australia Party in 1925 and lost his seat that year. Thereafter he concentrated on his business interests, which now included hotels in country towns, though in 1940 he contested the Federal seat of Calare for the State (Hughes-Evans) Labor Party. He died of coronary vascular disease on 23 March 1949, survived by his wife and eight of his nine children. He was buried in the Catholic section of Northern Suburbs cemetery. His estate was sworn for probate at £215 226.

McGirr's elder brother Patrick Michael (1875-1957) was a businessman and grazier. A Labor member for Macquarie in 1917-20 and of the Legislative Council in 1921-55, he was western lands commissioner in 1932-33. His youngest brother James (1890-1957), a pharmacist and investor, was Labor premier and treasurer in 1947-52.

M. Dixson, *Greater than Lenin?* (Melb, 1977); H. Radi and P. Spearritt (eds), *Jack Lang* (Syd, 1977); *PD* (NSW), 1923, p 132, 147; *Freeman's J* (Syd), 15 Apr 1920, 13 Oct 1921, 21 May, 26 Nov 1925; *SMH*, 19 June 1922, 10 Mar, 3 Aug, 1 Nov 1923, 9 May 1925, 24 Mar 1929, 5 Sept 1940; *Aust Worker* (Syd), 14 Mar 1923.

BEDE NAIRN

McGLINN, JOHN PATRICK (1869-1946), soldier and electrical engineer, was born on 11 April 1869 in Sydney, son of John Joseph McGlinn, gun-maker, and his wife Bridget Bergin, née O'Connor, both from Tipperary, Ireland. He attended St John's School, West Maitland, becoming a junior telegrapher in the New South Wales Postmaster General's Department on 29 January 1883. With the telegraph branch he worked at Tamworth, Bathurst, Wagga Wagga and West Maitland.

On 27 November 1893 McGlinn was commissioned second lieutenant in the 4th Infantry Regiment, New South Wales Military Forces, and in 1898 was promoted lieutenant. In the South African War he served as adjutant, 1st New South Wales Mounted Rifles, which disembarked in Cape Town in February 1900. Promoted captain, he was awarded the Queen's South Africa Medal with six clasps: Cape Colony, Driefontein, Johannesburg, Diamond Hill, Wittebergen, and South Africa 1901. In March 1901 the regiment returned home.

After Federation McGlinn was transferred to the Commonwealth Public Service, resuming work with the P.M.G. at West Maitland, and on 10 July married Olivia Paton at Bathurst. He was promoted captain in the Australian Military Forces in 1905, brigade major, 1st Infantry Brigade, next year and lieut-colonel in 1911; he was awarded the Colonial Auxiliary Forces Long Service Medal and Officers' Decoration.

In September 1914 Colonel John Monash [q.v.] selected McGlinn, then a P.M.G. lines engineer, as brigade major, 4th Infantry Brigade, Australian Imperial Force. During training in Egypt in March 1915 Monash described him as 'a tower of strength on the administrative side' who took 'a great burden of detail off my shoulders'. The portly pair became very close friends.

After landing on Gallipoli the 4th Brigade suffered very heavy casualties. In May Monash wrote: 'McGlinn is . . . calm, cool, collected and a man of sound judgement. He works late and early and nothing is too much trouble for him'. During Monash's absence on leave McGlinn temporarily commanded the brigade from 17 October to 8 November while out of the line. On 17 December, during the evacuation of Gallipoli, he took out 800 men from 4th Brigade without loss. He was twice mentioned in dispatches and was appointed C.M.G.

On 12 March 1916 McGlinn became assistant adjutant and quartermaster general on 5th Division Headquarters, and after training in Egypt the division reached Armentières, France, in June. On 25 June it relieved the 4th Division and in the battle of Fromelles on 19/20 July suffered 5000 casualties. During operations up to October McGlinn and his staff effectively maintained resupply of the division from the railhead at Bac St Maur. In October the division moved to Flers and Gueudecourt on the Somme and on 9 November he was evacuated ill; he did not return to the division. In November he was mentioned in dispatches again.

McGlinn was appointed commandant of No. 4 A.I.F. Depot at Codford, England, in April 1917 and in October commandant of No. 2 A.I.F. Depot at Weymouth. He was promoted colonel on 8 December. On 17 March 1918 he was promoted temporary brigadier general and became deputy adjutant and quartermaster general on Headquarters, A.I.F. Depots, in England. In January 1919 he was appointed C.B.E. From September 1919 to January 1920 he was liaison officer in England for the Department of Repatriation and Demobilisation. He was president of a court martial in November 1919 which acquitted the Australian Catholic chaplain, Father O'Donnell [q.v.]. Returning to Sydney in March 1920, in July he was transferred to the unattached list as honorary brigadier general.

At Monash's instigation, McGlinn was appointed a commissioner of the Commonwealth Public Service Board in June 1923, having become deputy State engineer (lines) in the P.M.G. He retired on 10 March 1930. Later he was chairman of the Commonwealth (A.I.F.) Canteens Trust Fund, the Sir Samuel McCaughey [q.v.5] A.I.F. Bequest and the Sir John Monash Memorial Fund. In 1935-42 he was a member of the State War Council of Victoria. He died on 7 July 1946 and after a requiem Mass at the Sacred Heart Catholic Church, Kew, was buried with full military honours in St Kilda cemetery. His wife, two sons and a daughter survived him. His younger son Eric Paton, a lieutenant in the 2/29th Battalion, A.I.F., was a prisoner of war on the Burma Railway.

McGlinn was a citizen force staff officer with exceptional skills and a devotion to the service overall, to the troops whom he served and, most of all, to Monash, whom he regarded as a 'national possession'.

Aust Defence Dept, *Official records of the Australian military contingents to the war in South Africa*, P. L. Murray ed (Melb, 1911); A. D. Ellis, *Story of the Fifth Division* (Lond, c.1920); C. E. W. Bean, *The story of Anzac* (Syd, 1921, 1924), and *The A.I.F. in France*, 1916 (Syd, 1929); T. A. White, *The fighting Thirteenth* (Syd, 1924); G. Serle, *John Monash* (Melb, 1982); *London Gazette*, 5 Nov 1915, 2 June, 11 July 1916, 2 Jan 1917, 31 Dec 1918; *SMH*, 25, 29 Nov, 1, 2 Dec 1919, 9 May 1921; *Age*, 8 July 1946; McGlinn collection, 3/DRL/632 (AWM); information from Mr E. P. McGlinn, Kew, Vic.   R. SUTTON

McGOWEN, JAMES SINCLAIR TAYLOR (1855-1922), boilermaker and politician, was born on 16 August 1855 on the *Western Bride*, 'three weeks sail from Melbourne', son of James McGowan, boilermaker, and his wife Eliza, née Ditchfield, both from Lancashire, England. McGowan senior came to Victoria with an agreement with the government to work on bridges. The family moved in 1867 to New South Wales where McGowen helped his father on bridges at Yass, Bathurst and Aberdeen.

After some schooling McGowen was apprenticed in 1870 as a boilermaker in Sydney to P. N. Russell [q.v.6] & Co. and was involved in the 1873-74 iron trades strike; he joined the United Society of Boilermakers and Iron Shipbuilders of New South Wales on its formation in 1873, and was its secretary intermittently from 1874 to 1890. After employment at the Atlas Foundry & Engineering Works and FitzRoy Dock, in 1875-91 he worked at the railways' workshop at Eveleigh. McGowen became a devoted trade unionist; a delegate to the New South Wales Trades and Labor Council, he was on its executive in 1888-91 when he was also president of the Eight Hours Demonstration Committee. As an executive-member of the Trades Hall Committee he played a major role in the erection of the Sydney Trades Hall in the late 1880s. In 1884 he represented his union at the second Intercolonial Trades Union Congress in Melbourne. On 18 April 1878, at Redfern with Wesleyan forms, he had married Emily Towner.

McGowen served the boilermakers' well, helping to gain the closed shop without any major dispute, and by 1890 he was well known, respected and liked in working-class circles. Of medium height, he was heavily built and dark, with an overflowing moustache, abundant cropped hair, a large nose and protruding ears. He conveyed an air of ponderous and amiable integrity. But his appearance was deceptive: he had been a good cricketer, and helped to form a district competition in Sydney, replacing the old, and often exclusive, clubs—later he became a keen lawn bowler, and was playing in Redfern Park in January 1903 when Victor Trumper [q.v.] scored 335 runs in an afternoon and hit several balls out of the adjoining oval on to the bowling-green. And McGowen's deliberate speech and apparent slow thinking fitted his invulnerable honesty, adherence to principles and loyalty to individuals that more than counterbalanced his lack of brilliance. He was a religious man, active in the relief of distress in Redfern where he lived; he was superintendent for thirty-five years of the Sunday school at the local St Paul's Anglican Church, and sat in the diocesan synod in his later years.

The Labor Electoral League (Labor Party) was founded by the Trades and Labor Council in 1889-91 without any notable contribution by McGowen. But from its first electoral successes in 1891 he believed it should be independent and 'a distinct power in the House'. He won a Redfern seat and held it until 1917; 21 of the 35 elected were under 40 years, and McGowen was the most experienced trade unionist among them. His steadfastness proved invaluable in parliament in 1891-94 when the party split twice on the question of free trade or protection and discipline was almost lost. His speech on 10 December 1891, when he declared that although he was a protectionist he had been elected 'as what is called a Labour man', helped to set the basis of the party's survival and of his own accession to its leadership. However, (Sir) Joseph Cook [q.v.8] became the first official leader in October 1893. By March next year the Labor conference's demand for the adherence of parliamentary members to its form of pledge had been accepted only by McGowen and two others.

At the 1894 elections the Labor Party nominated 74 'solidarity' candidates for 125 seats; 14 won, including only J. H. Cann, T. M. Davis [qq.v.7,8] and J. Kirkpatrick, as well as McGowen, of the original 35. The 'non-solidarities' won 13 seats, but were soon absorbed by the old fiscal parties. In Labor's electoral success McGowen's indefatigable and increasingly skilful work in the Legislative Assembly had complemented J. C. Watson's [q.v.] role in the non-parliamentary structure. Watson and W. M. Hughes [q.v.9] were among the members who elected McGowen unanimously as leader in August. At 39 he was the second oldest Labor parliamentarian. He always looked older than he was, and even then was known as often as 'Old Jim' as 'Honest Jim'.

He agreed with W. S. Landor's ideal of a government that would provide for honest and humane living. But that was a distant objective for Labor in the 1890s. McGowen led a novel and complex mass party with a detailed programme for radical social and political reform, subject to constant non-parliamentary as well as parliamentary pressures. Some very talented and restless young men were colleagues; as he exerted authority he convinced them of the need to come to terms with a cautious electorate. The Labor Party was on probation, but McGowen was not a probationary leader. He was wary of what he saw as the links between social unrest and socialism.

McGowen was pleased with the party decision to keep the reformist Reid [q.v.] free-trade government in office. Some legislative concessions, including land taxation, were gained, and some administrative changes, notably the gradual employment of day in place of contract labour on public works. McGowen remained active in parliament, and in 1896 he claimed that Labor was 'the propellor in the legislative machinery'. But in 1895-99 Federation slowly became the dominant political issue; Labor was officially committed to a Federal system, but in practice was ambiguous about it, being fearful of its obvious conservative aspects and anxious to continue the party's mission to reform New South Wales. In 1897 Labor nominated a bunch of ten candidates for the Federal convention: they all lost, with McGowen polling best.

After the 1898 elections Reid's majority was precarious. But the orderly and quick acceptance of Federation by New South Wales depended chiefly on him. McGowen, with help from Watson, persuaded the Labor Party to maintain its support of the government at least until the formalities of founding the Commonwealth had been completed. Early in March 1899, with the executive's backing, he and Watson spearheaded an agreement between the party and Reid to have four Labor men appointed to the Legislative Council as part of the plans of the premier to submit to a referendum the final form of the Federal Constitution. Despite strong opposition from Hughes and W. A. Holman [q.v.9] the appointments were made and the referendum was held. McGowen adhered to party policy and opposed the acceptance of the Constitution, but the colony approved it.

Reid, however, had lost his reforming impetus, and several Labor parliamentarians wanted to depose him in favor of (Sir) William Lyne [q.v.] who was prepared to make further concessions to the party. McGowen was in the minority of eight to eleven when caucus finally decided to vote Reid out. But, as the sole party speaker in the censure motion in September 1899, he announced the decision and paid a sincere tribute to Reid.

McGowen narrowly lost the election for the Federal seat of South Sydney in 1901. Back in the State parliament he was on the Public Works Committee in 1901-04 and the State Children Relief Board in 1900-08. As Labor gradually became the official Opposition in New South Wales he found that honesty and loyalty were not enough for a modern political leader. Holman's election as deputy party leader in 1905 reflected the feeling that McGowen needed guidance. But he remained popular and was on the party executive in 1906-09. His presence reassured voters that progress with the party would be judicious and safe. His leadership was an important factor in Labor's win at the 1910 State elections. But he soon revealed that he could not control let alone inspire his ministry of individualistic and talented men.

His premiership of 1910-13 saw much reforming legislation, but Holman, with some difficulty, ran the government. Cabinet problems and vacancies resulted in McGowen also being treasurer in 1910-11, colonial secretary in 1911-13 and minister for labour and industry in 1913-14. He enjoyed his six-month trip to the British Isles in 1911 for the coronation of George V, travelling widely, addressing the Derby Boilermakers' Society, breakfasting with Lloyd George, and interviewing John Burns.

During Holman's absence in England in 1913 McGowen tried to settle a strike of gas-workers by warning them that he would allow 'free workers' to take their jobs: a decision that went against the grain of his whole career, reflecting his weakened health and failing concentration, and appalled the labour movement. Holman returned on 6 June and replaced McGowen as premier on 30 June; R. D. Meagher [q.v.] defeated him for the Speakership.

During World War I McGowen had three sons at the front; one was killed at Gallipoli in 1915. He saw the war as a struggle for civilization between the British Empire and Germany; and when in 1916 the Labor conference decided to oppose conscription for overseas service he disagreed and was expelled with many others from the party. At the elections in March 1917 he stood as independent Labor, but spent the campaign in hospital in Hobart with a broken leg and lost to (Sir) William McKell. Holman had him appointed to the Legislative Council in July, and prevailed on him to be president of the National Association in 1917-18.

McGowen's style as 'a Labour man' endured and was reflected in his speeches and votes in the council. J. T. Dooley [q.v.8], Labor premier, in 1922 appointed him 'vigilance officer in connection with moving pictures', after the abolition of the Housing Board of which he had been chairman since 1912. McGowen died of heart disease on 7 April 1922, and was buried in the Anglican section of Rookwood cemetery, survived by his wife, five of their seven sons, and two daughters. Dooley spoke with genuine regret: 'we all loved and respected him [because of his] honesty and integrity'. A cenotaph for McGowen was dedicated at St Paul's Church in November.

H. V. Evatt, *Australian Labour leader . . . W.A. Holman* (Syd, 1942); B. Nairn, *Civilising capitalism* (Canb, 1973); *British A'sian*, 6 July 1911; *Daily Telegraph* (Syd), 3 June 1891; *SMH*, 22 Oct 1910, 10 Nov 1916, 15 Mar 1917, 8 Apr 1922; *Punch* (Melb), 31 Oct 1912; *Freeman's J* (Syd), 15 Mar 1917; *Aust Worker*, 12 Apr 1922.

BEDE NAIRN

McGRATH, DAVID CHARLES (1872-1934), storekeeper and politician, was born on 10 November 1872 at Newtown, Scarsdale, Victoria, son of Irish-born David McGrath, miner, and his wife Evelyn, née Horsefield, from England. Educated at Newtown State and Creswick Grammar schools, he joined the family store at Allendale where he came to share his father's interest in politics, although they later joined opposing parties. He claimed to have enrolled some 700 members while secretary of the Allendale branch of the Australian Natives' Association. A keen sportsman, McGrath made a name for himself as a stocky, energetic rover in the South Ballarat football team during the 1890s. On 24 May 1898 he married Elizabeth Johnstone Gullan at the Talbot Street Presbyterian church, Ballarat. They moved to Pitfield Plains in 1900 to open another McGrath store.

In 1902 he helped to establish the Hollybush Social Democratic Club and in 1904 won the Legislative Assembly seat of Grenville for Labor. He took a close interest in the mining industry, often speaking on behalf of mineworkers and small, independent operators who were threatened by larger capitalist enterprises. Outside the House, 'Bull' McGrath worked to expand the Labor Party's organization in country areas, undertaking an extensive tour of Gippsland with Frank Anstey [q.v.7] in November 1904. 'We pedalled or pushed our bikes into country far remote from the railway lines'.

He won the Federal seat of Ballarat in May 1913 after a close tussle with H. V. McKay [q.v.]. In October he was suspended for the rest of the session after refusing to apologize for his allegations against the Speaker. In 1914 he held his seat with an increased majority and constantly pressed the government to improve soldiers' conditions. In March 1916 McGrath enlisted, embarking as a staff sergeant with the 22nd Army Service Corps, Australian Imperial Force. Promoted warrant officer in December 1916 and appointed to Australian Imperial Headquarters, he was transferred to No. 1 Company, 1st Army Service Corps, France, in 1917. Following a serious illness, he returned to Australia in April 1918 and was discharged as medically unfit.

Although re-elected during his absence in 1917, McGrath was narrowly defeated at the 1919 poll. On appeal, the result was declared void and he was returned at a by-election in July 1920. During the early post-war years McGrath was a pugnacious advocate of repatriation benefits for servicemen and a stern critic of the means by which Imperial honours were awarded. He was a member of the joint committee on public works in 1926-29. In the Scullin [q.v.] government McGrath

was chairman of committees (1929-31) and, ironically enough, deputy Speaker. However, as the Depression overwhelmed that singularly luckless government, he was increasingly drawn towards Sir Otto Niemeyer's orthodox solution to the nation's financial crisis, and in March 1931 followed Lyons [q.v.] out of the Labor Party. At the subsequent election he retained his seat as a United Australia Party candidate, serving until 1934 in failing health. On 31 July 1934 he died at his home in Ballarat. Mourned by the many ex-servicemen he had served so well, he was buried with military and Masonic honours in the Ballarat old cemetery. His estate was valued for probate at £944. He was survived by his wife, two daughters and two sons, one of whom (Sir) Charles became chairman of Repco Ltd.

M. M. McCallum, *Ballarat and district citizens and sports at home and abroad* (Ballarat, 1916); *Hist Studies*, 18, no 72, Apr 1979; *Tocsin*, 19 May, 15 Dec 1904; *Punch* (Melb), 27 Nov 1913; *SMH*, 18 Oct 1919, 10 July 1925, 5, 17 Mar 1931; *Aust Worker*, 4 Dec 1929; *Ballarat Courier*, 31 July 1934; *Age*, 31 July, 1 Aug 1934; *Argus*, 1 Aug 1934; F. G. Anstey papers (NL).   PETER LOVE

McGREGOR, GREGOR (1848-1914), labourer and politician, was born on 18 October 1848 at Kilmun, Argyllshire, Scotland, son of Malcolm McGregor, gardener, and his wife Jane. In 1854 the family went to Ireland where Malcolm became chief gardener to Sir Gerald Aylmer and Gregor attended the National School, Tyrone, before joining his father. Travelling through England on foot for two years as an agricultural labourer furnished experience of rural poverty. At the Clyde shipyards, Scotland, where he worked in 1869-76, he participated in successful agitation to reduce the working week.

In 1877 McGregor worked his passage to South Australia. Short, sturdy and thickset he became an itinerant farm labourer in the mid-north of the colony. An accident in 1878 while felling trees permanently and seriously impaired his sight, but McGregor was to reduce the burden of his disability by developing a prodigious memory. On 10 April 1880 in Adelaide he married Julia Anna Steggall who died within the year. On 17 June 1882 he married the widowed Sarah Ann Brock, née Ritchie, at the Flinders Street Baptist Church, Adelaide.

When employment became scarce McGregor spent 1885-91 in Victoria as a stonemason. On his return to South Australia and navvying, he immersed himself in the trade union movement, becoming secretary, then president of the United Builders' Labourers Society. He was several times president of the United Trades and Labour Council of South Australia and in 1893 president of the United Political Labor League. As a radical agitator and spirited fighter he helped materially to organize the Labor Party. McGregor was elected to the Legislative Council for the Southern District in May 1894. A fervent protectionist who espoused the sanctity of White Australia, he gave his main attention to workers' compensation and conciliation and arbitration. He derided the South African War and opposed any South Australian contribution.

Though initially suspicious of Federation he was the State's first Labor representative elected to the Senate in March 1901. From May he was deputy chairman of the parliamentary party and first leader in the Senate. He was vice-president of the executive council in the three pre-war Labor ministries and a regular delegate to Commonwealth Labor conferences. He came to dominate the Senate through his tactical shrewdness. A wrestler in his youth, he enjoyed a political fight, leading the Labor-controlled Senate in 1913-14 against the Cook [q.v.8] government; a double dissolution followed in June 1914.

McGregor supported compulsory arbitration, age pensions, land taxes on large estates, the formation of the Commonwealth Bank and nationalization. A democratic individualist he campaigned against inappropriate reverence for British forms and traditions, facetiously urging British aristocratic candidates to refuse any offer of the governor-generalship as a gesture of solidarity with Lord Hopetoun [q.v.9]. He believed that the High Court of Australia rather than the Privy Council should ultimately determine any Australian legal issue. Himself a devout and teetotal member of the Church of Scotland, he opposed the reading of prayers in parliament as a distasteful and hypocritical 'parade of religion'.

His speeches were usually short and spontaneous with a calculated vulgarity that led him to be accused of 'a coarse brutal directness'. They could however be inexorably logical, fortified by the pages of figures he could recite from memory. Devoted to his party and its principles, McGregor relished election opportunities for the stump-oratory that returned him a large personal vote. The practicality rather than the theory of issues concerned him. When Labor held the balance of power in the House of Representatives in 1901 he announced that his party was 'for sale, and we will get the auctioneer when he comes, and take care that he is the right man'. Powerful, dour and bitter-tongued in debate, outside politics he was genial and good natured, one of the most temperate and widely trusted Labor leaders. He enjoyed travelling and was a member of the South Australian Caledonian Society and the Democratic Club, Adelaide.

Increasing physical disabilities reduced his effectiveness, and in mid-1914 he was unable to perform his parliamentary duties. He died of a heart condition at home at Unley on 13 August 1914 and was buried in West Terrace cemetery after a state funeral. His wife and stepson survived him. He left an estate valued for probate at £734. McGregor was a widely esteemed figure in early Federal politics: after his death the *Bulletin* described him as 'a rough-hewn old man' who commanded 'universal respect'.

H. T. Burgess (ed), *Cyclopedia of South Australia*, 1 (Adel, 1907); G. F. Pearce, *Carpenter to cabinet* (Lond, 1951); G. Souter, *Lion and kangaroo* (Syd, 1976); *Who was who, 1897-1916*; *Advertiser* (Adel), 22 May 1894, 10 Dec 1903, 14 Aug 1914; *Register* (Adel), 22 May 1894, 14 Aug 1914; *Daily Herald*, 14 Aug 1914; *Bulletin*, 20 Aug 1914; J. Scarfe, The Labour wedge: the first six Labour members of the South Australian Legislative Council (B.A. Hons thesis, Univ Adel, 1968).

G. C. GRAINGER

MACGREGOR, LEWIS RICHARD (1886-1973), agriculturalist and public servant, was born on 4 May 1886 at Hardway, Alverstoke, Southampton, England, son of Scottish parents Thomas Macgregor, corporal in the Royal Marines, and his wife Mary Anne (Polly), née Bartholomew. When Lewis was 2 his father died on military service. His mother took him to Scotland to live with relations, who were devout members of the Free Presbyterian Church, while she pursued her nursing career. Educated at a Glasgow primary school, Glasgow High and the Glasgow and West of Scotland Technical College, Lewis was forced by ill health to leave college prematurely to recuperate in a rural environment.

After working as an agricultural labourer at Aberfeldie, Macgregor was indentured to a lawyer, Colonel Munro of Murthly, in 1901 and was trained in banking, insurance, local government, estate factorship, and stock and crop marketing in the management of various estates. In 1909 he became assistant general manager of the Gairkhata Estates, Bengal, India, attending to housing-construction, water-supply, roads, drainage, cultivation and manufacturing. He joined the Northern Bengal Mounted Rifles. In 1912 Macgregor followed the estates' chief engineer to Western Australia and became secretary and accountant to Hawter's orchards and nurseries near Bunbury, mastering every aspect of fruit-growing.

Describing himself as a 'typically impetuous, quick-tempered emotional Highland rebel', he married the calm Mary Hannah

White, from Yorkshire, England, on 11 April 1914 at Kwelkan. That year he enlisted for military service but was declared medically unfit from past malaria.

'Mac' took up wheat-growing on his own account and became involved in rescuing co-operative companies from financial ruin by implementing effective marketing and management plans. After managing the developing co-operative scheme, he became chief inspector at Northam, then manager of Westralian Farmers Ltd, Perth. In 1917 Macgregor succeeded in securing sole wheat-acquisition rights for that organization. As secretary to the Western Australian Grain Growers' Co-operative Elevators Ltd, he originated the scheme of bulk wheat-handling. After he was sent to Europe in 1919 as representative of the Westralian Farmers' Co-operative Co. to inquire into the marketing of agricultural products, his reports were made available to the Australian Wholesale Co-operative Federation and the Commonwealth government.

In 1922 Macgregor became Queensland's highest-paid public servant as director of the Queensland Producers' Association, a body concerned with inaugurating marketing schemes based on primary producer control. With confidence and brusque common sense he collaborated with A. E. J. C. K. Graham [q.v.9] in proposing and executing co-operative legislation, largely instigated by E. G. Theodore [q.v.]. Among others, the Primary Producers' Organisation and Primary Products Pools Acts of 1922 established the Council of Agriculture and the Department of Agriculture and Stock. He viewed his Primary Producers' Co-operative Associations Act of 1923 as 'in advance of the South African legislation . . . hitherto . . . the best in the British Empire'.

Next year Macgregor assisted the Western Australian government in the preparation of its marketing legislation, a task which he also performed for the Tasmanian government. His confidential report in 1925 to the Western Australian minister for agriculture was based on his examination of the progress and impact on agriculture of the recent Queensland legislation. He cautioned against the multiplicity of Acts for different schemes and products (in 1923 Queensland had at least fourteen such Acts).

Despite initially vehement farmer opposition and the *Brisbane Courier*'s editorial warning of a 'foretaste of the compulsion of Sovietism' in the proposed fruit-marketing legislation of late 1923, Macgregor managed to smooth the path for further primary producers' organization and marketing legislation in 1923-26. As director of marketing from 1926, he supervised all primary producer organizations, distinguishing himself with his ability to act as intermediary between farmer and consumer. His first published report (1928) set out some principles of agricultural marketing which still hold today. According to the historian A. A. Morrison, Macgregor's agrarian reforms profoundly influenced contemporary Queensland politics by undercutting support for the Country Party. Queensland's schemes for agricultural marketing were adapted in the United States of America and Britain.

On 31 March 1930 Macgregor was appointed trade commissioner to Canada by the Federal government. He was an adviser to the Australian delegation to the Imperial conferences in London (1930) and Ottawa (1932), negotiated the first commercial treaty between Canada and Australia, and led trade missions to Newfoundland (1932), British West Indies (1933) and the Union of South Africa (1937). Appointed C.B.E. in 1938, in 1938-41 was Australian trade commissioner in North America.

During World War II he was director-general of the Australian War Supplies Mission in Washington and Ottawa. In 1945-49 he was Australian minister to Brazil. He led special missions for the United States government during the Korean war and to Western Europe in 1954.

In his remaining years Macgregor was engaged in private business in the U.S.A., attended Imperial and international conferences and continued to give advice on agricultural development. He reputedly had worked for ten Australian prime ministers and seven State premiers, with thirty-two governments and in fifty countries or territories; his autobiography *British Imperialism; memories and reflections* (New York, 1968), written for private circulation, lists his achievements, honours, associations and 'famous' contacts. He died on 1 March 1973 in Barbados, West Indies, survived by his wife, a son and a daughter.

D. J. Murphy et al (eds), *Labor in power* (Brisb, 1979); *Govt Gazette* (Qld), 29 July 1922; *Qld Producer*, 8 Dec 1926; *Qld Agr J*, Aug, Oct 1922; *Economic Record*, Feb 1928; *Qld Heritage*, 2, no 5 (1971); *Brisb Courier*, 21 July 1922; *Daily Mail* (Brisb), 26 Aug 1922, 3 Dec 1926, 6, 12 Mar 1930; *Daily Standard*, 16 Sept 1922; Dept of Agr and Stock, L. R. Macgregor, personnel file *and* Director, Qld Council of Agr, Confidential report (Perth, 23 Mar 1925), *and* Director of Marketing, Report 1928 (QA).   DENISE K. CONROY

McGREGOR, MARTIN ROBERT (1859-1936), farmer and politician, was born on 22 February 1859 in Hobart Town, son of Duncan Robert McGregor, clerk and later wine merchant, and his wife Betsy, née Roberts. He came to Melbourne as a baby with his family and was educated at St Peter's Common School, Eastern Hill. For eighteen years he served in the Chief Secretary's Department, spending some time on the administrative staff of the Sunbury Mental Hospital. He followed pastoral activities in Queensland for a further seven years before returning to Victoria and taking up a farm at Narracan, near Moe, Gippsland. He faced years of work clearing away the huge trees and fallen logs but his farm, named Skye for his Scottish background, eventually became a model potato-growing and dairying property. On 14 September 1902 at the East Melbourne Presbyterian manse he married Agnes Marshall, and in the same year became secretary of a movement to build a hall in his community.

In 1908 McGregor was elected a councillor for the East Riding of the shire of Narracan; he held this seat until his death, frequently unopposed at elections. He was shire president in his first year, when he led the movement to shift the shire seat from Moe to Trafalgar, and also in 1917-18 and 1929-30. He was a justice of the peace and served on the Narracan Shire Repatriation Committee; the Returned Soldiers' and Sailors' Imperial League of Australia awarded him its highest honour, the certificate of merit, for this work. A founder of the Gippsland Shire and Boroughs Development Association, in 1918 he became an executive member of the Municipal Association of Victoria, serving as vice-president in 1922-30 and as treasurer in 1931-36.

McGregor represented Gippsland Province in the Legislative Council from May 1922 until his death. A Nationalist, he was for a time vice-president of the National Federation. He was honorary minister in the third Lawson [q.v.] and the third Peacock [q.v.] governments in 1924 and in the Allan [q.v.7] government from November 1924 to May 1927. In 1928-31 he was a member of the Railways Standing Committee, serving as chairman for a time. Described as an exceptionally friendly man, 'a good mixer', he was a forthright speaker on rural matters, always keen to promote the interests of Gippsland; in particular he supported inclusion on the local electoral rolls of the State Electricity Commission employees at Yallourn.

McGregor was founding chairman of the Trafalgar Water Trust (1926) and of the Trafalgar Meadows Drainage Trust, holding both posts until his death. He was also a director of the Trafalgar Co-operative Butter Factory, president of the Central Gippsland Agricultural Society and a member of the Chamber of Agriculture.

He died at his home at Narracan on 17 August 1936, survived by his wife; they had no children. Before his cremation his body lay in state at the new Narracan shire hall at Traf-

algar, which he had striven for years to see built. McGregor Park in Trafalgar commemorates his many years of service to the district.

J. D. Adams, *So tall the trees* (Trafalgar, Vic, 1978); *Age* and *Argus*, 19 Aug 1936; *Narracan Shire Advocate*, 21 Aug 1936; *Trafalgar and Yarragon Times*, 24 Aug 1936.   J. D. ADAMS

MACGROARTY, NEIL FRANCIS (1888-1971), barrister and politician, was born on 1 May 1888 at South Brisbane, eleventh child of Daniel Cannon Macgroarty, inspector of schools, and his wife Anna Maria, née Kearney, both Irish born. Educated by the Christian Brothers at Gregory Terrace and Nudgee, Brisbane, he entered into articles of clerkship with Patrick Alban O'Sullivan and was admitted as a solicitor of the Supreme Court of Queensland on 19 August 1911. After practice for eight years in partnership with his former master, Macgroarty transferred to the Bar and was admitted on 6 May 1919; he practised from the old Inns of Court building, Adelaide Street. On 21 December 1929 he married Doreen Mary Joseph at St Mary's Catholic Church, South Brisbane; they had five children.

Macgroarty became interested in politics and as candidate for the Country and Progressive National Party in 1929 was elected to the Legislative Assembly for South Brisbane. He was well known in the area by reason of long residence; moreover he was president of the Queensland Irish Association in 1924-32 and, in his younger days, had been a Rugby player of note and subsequently an executive-member of the Queensland Rugby Union.

He achieved immediate prominence by going straight into the Moore [q.v.] ministry as attorney-general—unprecedented for a newly elected member in Queensland. He shared this distinction with Ernest Albert Atherton, secretary for mines. His three-year term—often in stormy conflict with the Labor Opposition—was filled with action. His maiden speech attracted considerable controversy when, in reply to an interjection, Macgroarty stated that the Queensland Court of Industrial Arbitration would be 'ring-barked' at an early opportunity.

On 30 April 1930 Macgroarty opened the crown submissions to the royal commission into the purchase of the Mungana mines and Chillagoe smelters by the Queensland government from E. G. Theodore, W. McCormack [qq.v.], P. L. Goddard and F. Reid. After the commissioner, J. L. Campbell [q.v.7], found the transaction had been fraudulent, Macgroarty on 22 July 1931 led A. D. McGill [q.v.] and G. Seaman for the Crown, in an attempt to recover the purchase money from the four defendants, before Chief Justice Sir James Blair [q.v.7] and a jury of four in a civil action. The jury, however, found in favour of the defendants.

Important legislation introduced by Macgroarty included the Companies Act of 1931. His controversial Judicial Proceedings (Regulations of Reports) Act of 1931, allegedly an attempt to protect public morals, was seen by Labor as a personal vendetta against Brisbane *Truth*. By the 1932 election Macgroarty had fallen out with important Catholic elements and, bitterly pursued by the Labor Party seeking vengeance, was defeated by V. C. Gair.

Disillusioned by his political experiences, Macgroarty resumed his law practice until retirement. He was a member of the Johnsonian Club and a golfer. He died on 10 August 1971, survived by his wife, two sons and two daughters, and was buried in Toowong cemetery after a requiem Mass at St Ignatius' Church, Toowong. An officer of the Queensland Bar Association said of him that he was 'a singular personality. Humorous, warm, intolerant of hypocrisy, he became a legend during a lifetime which covered 60 years in the legal profession'.

C. Lack (ed), *Three decades of Queensland political history, 1929-1960* (Brisb, 1962); K. H. Kennedy, *The Mungana scandal* (Brisb, 1978); *PD* (Qld), 1930, p 589, 1931, p 2331; Roy com into Mungana, Chillagoe mines, *PP* (Qld), 1929-30, 2nd Session, 6, p 1345; *Courier Mail*, 11 Aug 1971.

K. E. GILL

McGUIGAN, BRIGID (1842-1923), Sister of Charity, was born on 16 January 1842 at Braidwood, New South Wales, second of ten daughters of John McGuigan, native-born grazier, and his wife Ellen, née Foran. She was educated as a boarder by the Benedictine nuns at Subiaco Convent, Rydalmere, in 1856-59. On 22 July 1861 she entered the Sisters of Charity at St Vincent's Convent, Darlinghurst, and was trained as a teacher at its certified Victoria Street Roman Catholic School (later St Vincent's College). She took the religious name Mary Francis and was professed on 21 April 1864. Her teaching proficiency was noted and in 1869 she became headmistress of the Victoria Street school, with 173 girls and 68 boys. In 1872 she applied to the Council of Education for promotion which was granted in 1874 when her salary was increased to £108.

In 1882 Mother McGuigan was elected superior general and became responsible for all the institutions run by the Sisters of Charity, including St Vincent's Hospital and seven schools. Her election coincided with the abolition of state aid but, several trained

teachers such as the Brutons and Mother M. Berchmans Daly [qq.v.7,8] having entered the congregation, she was able to staff four new schools in 1883 and seven more in New South Wales and two in Victoria by 1903. She oversaw the building of the Sisters' residence in 1882 and new wings to St Vincent's Hospital in 1888 and 1892, St Joseph's Hospital for consumptives at Parramatta (1886, transferred to Auburn in 1892), St Anne's Orphanage at Liverpool (1888), the Sacred Heart Hospice for the Dying at Darlinghurst (1890), St Vincent's Hospital, Melbourne, in 1893 and private hospitals in Sydney (1909) and Melbourne (1913).

Mother Francis visited Ireland in 1895 and studied educational centres; the doctors of St Vincent's Hospital, Dublin, paid tribute to the high standards of the hospital in Sydney. On her return she oversaw the foundation of the teachers' college and music centre at St Vincent's Convent.

A gracious countenance enhanced the stately deportment of the tall Mother McGuigan. Tact allied with common sense and business ability made her perceptive and a methodical correspondent. Deeply spiritual with a grasp of the principles of justice, she aimed at preserving the integrity of her congregation with its central system of authority; its work was more complex than that of diocesan communities engaged in only one field. When she celebrated her golden jubilee on 21 April 1914, she was honoured by three bishops and fifty-two priests, six from Victoria: the Sisters gave a Gothic marble altar and pipe-organ to the Mother House chapel. There had been 44 Sisters in 1882; there were 403 when she retired in 1920. She died in St Vincent's Hospital on 27 October 1923 and was buried in the Lady Chapel, St Vincent's Convent, Potts Point.

Dublin Times, 28 June 1895; *Freeman's J* (Syd), 2, 16 Apr 1914; *Catholic Press*, 11 June 1914; Records of the Denominational School Bd, *and* Council of Education (NSWA); Sisters of Charity Archives (St Vincent's Convent, Potts Point, NSW); Sisters of Charity records (box 1, 2, Syd Diocesan Archives, St Mary's Cathedral, Syd).

CATHERINE O'CARRIGAN

McGUINNESS, ARTHUR (1878-1970), schoolteacher and union leader, was born on 28 January 1878 at Auckland, New Zealand, son of Arthur McGuinness, boilermaker, and his wife Elizabeth, née Kirkpatrick. His parents returned to Scotland, leaving Arthur with grandparents in Sydney, but they soon returned to settle at Bathurst where he went to school. McGuinness became a teacher-pupil at Lucknow in 1896, but failing the examinations was transferred to Kelso where he completed the four years training. He began as an assistant teacher on probation at Mount Hope on £90 a year, was transferred to Crown Street Public School, Sydney, in 1904 and promoted in 1909. In Sydney he organized Rugby competitions for primary schools. At St Stephen's Presbyterian Church he married Constance Jemima McManus on 8 January 1906.

In 1910-24 McGuinness was teacher in charge of small country schools: Araluen, Matong, Kangaroo Valley and Bombo. He returned to Sydney in 1925 to Caringbah on £507 a year and was moved in 1931 to Blakehurst where he remained until final retirement in 1945. He did not seek promotion to the highest levels of the service. He was much liked at Blakehurst, organizing a parental campaign to obtain a new school and then moving tons of rock and soil to improve the site.

McGuinness threw himself into teachers' politics and trade unionism and in 1928-45 served on the executive of the New South Wales Teachers' Federation. While he was president in 1929-32 the federation continued its aggressive defence of teachers and public education, and resisted suggestions of pay cuts and dismissal of women teachers as the Depression deepened. McGuinness became president in 1930 of the Crown Employees' Protection Committee which aimed to represent all State public servants, and caused Premier Lang [q.v.9] to describe him as 'a tough negotiator, a hard hitting blunt public speaker, . . . a born politician'. By late 1932 McGuinness had begun to reflect the rising mood of caution and passivity among teachers and refused to call mass meetings to oppose government legislation to cut salaries and dismiss married women teachers. He did not stand for the presidency in 1933 and was defeated in 1934 by a moderate, but he returned for the next two years when teachers were more optimistic.

In his final term as president in 1940-45 McGuinness led vigorous and imaginative campaigns for better conditions, for teachers' professional and civil rights and for a strong war effort against Japan. In 1943 the federation achieved a new system of classifying schools and teachers which recognized professional qualifications, and its affiliation with the Labor Council of New South Wales and the Australasian Council of Trade Unions. During the war some able communists rose to prominent positions in the federation, but they never challenged McGuinness who believed he retained effective control.

A remarkably popular teachers' leader, McGuinness drew general support because he was seen as a fearless critic of political and departmental complacency and authoritarianism, and a defender of teachers' exercise of

professional integrity. Although they had many clashes, he earned the respect of D. H. Drummond [q.v.8] and was praised by Frank Tate [q.v.] for a public attack on timid departmental administrators. He was awarded a Carnegie scholarship to travel abroad in 1938.

In retirement McGuinness lived at Penshurst. A widower, he died at Kogarah on 15 March 1970 and was cremated with Presbyterian forms. Two sons and two daughters survived him.

B. A. Mitchell, *Teachers, education and politics* (Brisb, 1975); *SMH*, 17 Mar 1970; information from Arthur McGuinness, 1968; Dept of Education, NSW, Teachers' records (Syd).

BRUCE MITCHELL

McHALE, JAMES FRANCIS (1881-1953), footballer and coach, was born on 12 December 1881 at Botany, Sydney, son of John Francis McHale, police constable, and his wife Mary, née Gibbons, both from Ireland. McHale's ironic nickname 'Jock' originated in a caricature of him in a kilt by the *Herald* cartoonist Wells during the 1920s. After coming to Melbourne as a young boy, he received primary schooling at St Bridget's, North Fitzroy, and St Paul's, Coburg, and in 1894-96 attended Christian Brothers' College (Parade), East Melbourne. Upon leaving school, he was employed at the McCracken [q.v.] Brewery; he became a leading hand and on his retirement in 1947 was supervising the brewing process at the Carlton Brewery, Bouverie Street.

Despite a common misconception, McHale was not the first coach employed by the Collingwood Football Club; his several predecessors had included Dick Condon. But he established a Victorian Football League record by coaching the team for 38 years (1913-50), during which the club won eight premierships (1917, 1919, 1927-30, 1935-36), including a record four in a row, and was runner-up ten times.

McHale's fame as 'Prince of Coaches' has overshadowed an equally illustrious playing career (1903-18) as a centreman for Collingwood to which he graduated from the Coburg Juniors (1899-1902). He played 262 league games, including a contemporary record consecutive 191 in 1906-17, and in the opinion of the club historian was one of the greatest players ever for Collingwood. McHale played in two premiership sides (1910, 1917), was captain twice (1912-13), players' representative (1911-19), committee-man (1921-38) and vice-president (1939-53).

McHale's success as a coach sprang from his love of the club and his uncanny ability to know when players were fit. Reputation and

talent meant little to him; players were selected on the basis of form and willingness to
'run through walls for Collingwood'. He was
not a great teaching coach: the McHale
method, which never changed over forty
years, inculcated machine-like team-play, the
main objective of each player being to beat his
individual opponent. Although McHale
believed in fitness above all, his half-time
addresses were inspirational; he did not
rehash the first half, but 'could get inside' the
players by instilling club 'spirit' into them. A
man who could never abide losing, he perpetuated the Collingwood tradition of insatiable will to win.

McHale was 'a Collingwood six-footer',
5 ft. 11 ins. (180 cm) tall, of 12 stone (76 kg)
playing weight, with curly, dark brown hair
and grey, penetrating eyes. He remained
active at the Collingwood Football Club until
his death on 4 October 1953 at Coburg.
McHale's initial heart attack occurred the day
after Collingwood's grand final victory of 26
September 1953; he had played a vital role in
the selection of the side. He was survived by
his wife Violet Mary Angel, née Godfrey,
whom he had married on 28 April 1909 at
Brunswick, and by his son John, who played
for Collingwood in 1941 and 1943-44; a
daughter and son predeceased him. A portrait
by Paul Fitzgerald hangs in the Collingwood
Social Club. He was buried in Coburg cemetery with Catholic rites.

P. Taylor, *Collingwood Football Club 1892-1948*
(Melb, nd, 1950?); L. Richards, *Boots and all* (Melb,
1963); E. H. Buggy, *The real John Wren* (Melb,
1977); Collingwood Football Club, *Annual Reports*,
1903-53, Records and Statistics, 1897-1981, and
Cash Outward, 1897-1928; *Argus*, 14 Aug 1950;
Advocate (Melb), Oct 1953; information from J. J.
McHale (Kew), Harry Collier (Preston), and Leo
Morgan (Collingwood).   R. STREMSKI

McHARDIE-WHITE, JESSIE; *see* WHITE,
JESSIE McHARDIE

McILRATH, SIR MARTIN (1874-1952)
and **WILLIAM** (1876-1955), merchants and
philanthropists, were born at Banbridge,
Down, Ireland, sons of Robert McIlrath,
farmer, and his wife Mary, née Urey. Martin,
born on 9 July 1874, arrived in Victoria in
1889 and spent some time in the Wimmera
district. In 1892 he joined his brother Hugh in
a grocery business in Sydney; this developed
into McIlraths Ltd and McIlrath Holdings
Ltd, a State-wide grocery and provisions business with thirty-six chain stores in the Sydney
metropolitan area.

McIlrath acquired pastoral properties
including Merribindinya, a 6000-acre (2430
ha) Hereford and merino station at Bethungra. His company directorships included
the Bank of New South Wales in 1940-52
(president, 1950-52). Though he shunned
publicity he spoke out when his business
interests were involved: in 1944 he criticized
tea and sugar rationing; in 1950 the trade
union movement; and in 1952 high taxation,
the 'costly' welfare state and the structure of
the Commonwealth Bank of Australia which
he averred was 'not conducive to the unbiased
leadership of the banking system'. In 1941 he
had been elected president of the Australian
National Service League.

His interests extended beyond the field of
business and McIlrath became well known for
his philanthropy. The full extent of his generosity is not known but in 1937 he endowed a
new ward at the Royal North Shore Hospital
of Sydney and in 1940 he and his wife gave
£10 000 to the Commonwealth government
for the war effort. His largest single donation
was £50 000 to the University of Sydney for
medical research in 1950; he also gave
£20 000 to the Presbyterian Ladies' College,
Pymble, of whose council he was chairman for
many years. In 1945 he gave Merribindinya,
valued at £58 000, to the State government
for soldier settlement on condition that the
government pay the approximate value of the
property into a trust to endow scholarships in
agriculture and veterinary science at the university. In recognition of his generosity the
university conferred on him an honorary
LL.D. in 1952.

A kind and gentle personality, Martin
McIlrath was as modest and shy as he was
successful and wealthy. Though of a retiring
nature, he was no recluse: he was a foundation
member and president of the Avondale Golf
Club, Pymble, and a prominent member of the
New South Wales and Tattersall's clubs. He
died of cancer at his home Ingleholme, Turramurra, on 20 December 1952—his knighthood was announced posthumously—and was
cremated with Presbyterian forms. He was
survived by his wife Ada Maitland, née
Eldridge, whom he had married at West Maitland on 5 September 1906, and by three
daughters and an adopted son. His estate was
sworn for probate at £524 018.

William arrived in Victoria in 1890 and
worked with Martin in the Wimmera before
joining his elder brothers in the grocery firm
in Sydney in 1897. After Hugh's mysterious
disappearance in Shanghai, China, in 1909
William became joint managing director with
Martin. On 12 October 1910 at St David's
Presbyterian Church, Haberfield, he married
Catherine McLeod. In 1928 he made a 'motor
expedition' through New South Wales and
central and western Queensland to Darwin.

Managing director of Town & Country Lands Pty Ltd, in the 1930s he set up the Windsor Hereford stud at Myall Creek, Delungra, so named after its foundation sire Windsor Matchless, imported from the Royal stud in England. He became well known in Australia and overseas as a successful breeder of beef cattle and won a record number of first prizes at the Sydney show.

Like his brother, William was a generous benefactor. In 1938 he gave £10 000 to the Prince Henry Hospital and £10 000 to the Commonwealth government for the war effort in 1941. Elected to the board of the Royal Prince Alfred Hospital in 1939, in addition to £2500 donated in 1936 he gave an undisclosed but substantial sum to the hospital to establish visiting 'guest professorships' for 'men of high academic standing in the world of medicine and the allied sciences'. In 1953 he gave £50 000 to the Commonwealth Scientific and Industrial Research Organization for animal husbandry research. He was a foundation member of the council and a benefactor of Knox Grammar School.

William was a member of the Australian and New South Wales clubs and his private annual dinner at the latter to Hereford breeders was a notable show-time event. His main recreation was bowling at the Warrawee club.

McIlrath died suddenly of heart disease while addressing directors of his city office in Pitt Street on 20 June 1955, survived by his wife and a daughter. His only son and a daughter had been killed in an aircraft accident overseas. He was cremated with Presbyterian forms. His estate was valued for probate at £588 747.

Pastoral Review, 19 Jan 1953, 16 July 1955; *SMH*, 21 Aug 1928, 20 Dec 1938, 17 May 1940, 10 Mar, 19 May 1941, 3 Aug 1945, 17 Nov 1948, 6 Jan, 20 Apr, 2 May, 25 Nov 1950, 29 Nov, 22, 28 Dec 1952, 19 Mar, 22, 25 Oct 1953, 21 June 1955.
       G. P. WALSH

McILWRAITH, ANDREW (1844-1932), shipowner and frozen-meat trade pioneer, was born on 11 July 1844 at Ayr, Scotland, fourth son of John McIlwraith, plumber and shipowner, and his wife Janet Hamilton, née Howat. Educated at Ayr Academy, he joined his father's business in 1868; he supervised the family's Scottish Line and established close commercial relationships with his brothers, John and (Sir) Thomas [qq.v.5], in Melbourne and Brisbane. On 30 November 1871 at Staveley, Derbyshire, England, he married Mabel Eliza Stephenson, daughter of an engineer James Campbell. In 1875, with (Sir) Malcolm McEacharn [q.v.], he established the London-based shipping and mercantile firm McIlwraith, McEacharn & Co. When he visited Queensland on business in 1875-76, his connexion with Thomas, then premier, resulted in a royal commission. This followed allegations (finally deemed unfounded) that the McIlwraiths had conspired to obtain lucrative government contracts and, through speculating in steel rails, had unduly profited at the expense of the colony.

In 1879 Andrew, capitalizing on his own business acumen and his father-in-law's mechanical aptitude, organized the chartering and fitting out with a freezing plant of the steamer *Strathleven*, the first ship to successfully land a cargo of frozen meat in London from Australia (on 1 February 1880). Earlier Andrew had met T. S. Mort [q.v.5], inspected his vessel *Northam* at Sydney and instigated extensive trials at Glasgow of Bell & Coleman's freezing plant.

In 1887 a branch of McIlwraith, McEacharn was established in Melbourne; by 1895 the firm, in which Andrew had a quarter-interest, was returning a regular profit of 8 per cent on capital of over £500 000. Following a bitter family struggle—'Andrew', said John, 'would never make a gentleman although he tries it hard'—McIlwraith purchased his brothers' interest in the business next year. He also had shares in the Australasian United Steam Navigation Co. and associated British lines. The last of McIlwraith's several trips to Australia was in 1912-13 following his successful reorganization of the Tokyo tramways. A progressive Liberal, he was a close friend of Andrew Fisher [q.v.8], an important relationship in view of Labor's attempts to regulate the coastal shipping business and to control both foreign and British intrusions.

Andrew McIlwraith was large, handsome and red bearded, with an outwardly affectionate nature. Friendly with Brunel and Paxton, he was made an associate of the Institute of Naval Architects in 1887. Abstemious, but never refusing large draughts of medicinal brandy and scrumpy, he retired, after residing at St Albans, Hertfordshire, to Salcombe, Devon; he died there on 19 October 1932 and was buried with Church of England rites, although originally a Presbyterian. His family life had been unhappy. His first marriage ended in separation and his second, to an American, Holte Leichenburgh, in 1895, also failed. Two sons died in the South African War and a third also predeceased him. Survived by two daughters from his first marriage and another from his second, he left an estate valued for probate at £107 200. A portrait is in the possession of his granddaughter

Jean Scott of New Zealand, and another hangs in Salcombe House.

N. L. McKellar, *From Derby round to Burketown* (Brisb, 1977); D. B. Waterson, 'An Ayrshire family, 1526-1900, the McIlwraiths of Auchenflower, Ayr and Australia', *Ayrshire Collections*, 12 (1978), no 3; *A'sian Pastoralists' Review*, 15 Nov 1894; *Argus*, 3, 4, 6, 8 Dec 1879; *Brisbane Courier*, 30 Mar 1880; *Age*, 21 Oct 1932; *Ayrshire Post*, 21 Oct 1932; *The Times*, 24 Oct 1932; John McIlwraith & Co records (ANU Archives); Palmer-McIlwraith papers (Oxley Lib); family information.

D. B. WATERSON

McINNES, WILLIAM BECKWITH (1889-1939), artist, was born on 18 May 1889 at St Kilda, Melbourne, son of Malcolm McInnes, clerk, and his wife Alice Agnes, née Beckwith. McInnes was a delicate child and, although not from an artistic family, was encouraged to draw by his mother; he painted his first still life at 8. When 14 he entered the Melbourne National Gallery School to study drawing under Frederick McCubbin [q.v.], later graduating to painting under Bernard Hall [q.v.9]. Hard-working and probably the ablest student of his time, he none the less failed twice to win the travelling scholarship, in 1909 and 1911. Soon afterwards, however, he held a successful show at the Athenaeum Gallery with F. R. Crozier and left for Europe in 1912.

Billy McInnes travelled and painted in France, Spain, Morocco and Britain, spending time in his ancestral Scotland (including a bitterly cold winter in the Hebrides when he lived on boiled potatoes). He discovered the work of Rembrandt, Velasquez, Hals and Raeburn, who were to be his lifelong masters. He exhibited his landscapes in London at the Royal Institute of Oil Painters in 1913 and after his return to Melbourne that year held a sell-out exhibition at the Athenaeum. On 24 February 1915 at the Presbyterian Manse, Armadale, he married the still-life painter Violet Muriel Musgrave. They settled at Alphington; still largely farmland, the locality and nearby Yarra valley provided many of McInnes's subjects.

In 1916 he stood in at the National Gallery School while McCubbin was on leave and after McCubbin's death in 1918 was appointed drawing master. He revisited Europe in 1925, returning to great demand as a portrait painter. He won the Wynne prize in 1918, the Archibald [q.v.3] seven times (in succession 1921-24) and exhibited at the Royal Academy of Arts, London, in 1928. In 1927 he was commissioned by the Federal government to depict the opening of the first parliament in Canberra by the duke of York; in 1933 he went overseas again to paint the duke's portrait. In 1934 McInnes was acting director of

the National Gallery of Victoria and on Bernard Hall's death that year became head of the gallery school. Although president of the Australian Art Association in 1923-24 and a member of the other leading art societies (including the Australian Academy of Art), he was not active in art politics.

In a spectacularly successful career McInnes was lauded as the heir to Streeton [q.v.]. Stockily built and described as affable but having little conversation and no hobby outside his work, he had no intellectual interest in art. To him art was craft and his love was for the qualities of naturalistic vision, to which he brought a virtuoso technique in oil—a crisp, vigorous and unerring use of the square brush in depicting air and sunlight. His nearest contemporaries were Penleigh Boyd and Elioth Gruner [qq.v.7,9]; although more conservative than either, he was not dogmatic or reactionary and was regarded with some affection even by the most radical of his students.

'A nice modest fellow', a worrier, McInnes suffered from poor health all his life. His troubles were added to when in a motoring accident in November 1937 he fatally injured a pedestrian; he settled the ensuing civil action out of court. He resigned his position in July 1939. Suffering from a congenital cardiac disorder, he died at East Melbourne on 9 November; he was cremated. His wife, four sons and two daughters survived him. A memorial exhibition of his work was held in Melbourne and Sydney in 1940. A self-portrait is held by the Art Gallery of New South Wales.

Argus, 2 Dec 1937, 5 Apr 1938; *SMH*, 18 Dec 1937; *Herald* (Melb), 9 Nov 1939; P. Serle, Autobiography (MS, LaTL).

RICHARD HAESE

McINTOSH, HAROLD (1868-1917), grazier and soldier, was born on 14 June 1868 at Bathurst, New South Wales, eighth child of John Nepean McIntosh, solicitor, and his wife Mary Ann, née Black, both Australian born. He was educated at All Saints' College, Bathurst, where he was a good student and a gifted sportsman; in his final year, 1885, he was school captain. After graduating from the University of Sydney (B.A., 1889) he served his articles with his father's firm, McIntosh & Co., before going on the land at Rockley, near Bathurst.

When a half-company of the New South Wales Mounted Rifles was raised at Bathurst in 1895 McIntosh was one of the local horsemen to join. In 1897 he accompanied a privately funded detachment from the regiment to England to compete in military tournaments and to train with British Army regiments. The tour culminated in the military celebrations for Queen Victoria's Diamond

Jubilee. He was a sergeant two years later when he joined the regiment's special service squadron raised for active service in South Africa.

'A' Squadron, New South Wales Mounted Rifles, embarked from Sydney in November 1899 and was one of the first Australian units to arrive at the front. Sergeant McIntosh took part in all its major operations including the relief of Kimberley, the action around Paardeberg, the entry into Bloemfontein and the capture of Pretoria. He was commissioned lieutenant while on service and returned to Sydney in January 1901. He went back to South Africa as a lieutenant in the 2nd New South Wales Mounted Rifles in April. This regiment served for one year, mostly in the Transvaal, during which time McIntosh was promoted captain.

On 5 October 1904 he married Florence May Lee at All Saints' Cathedral, Bathurst. Returning to his family's property, Bunnamagoo, which he managed, in 1907 he was elected a local shire-councillor and was three times president. He was also active in his school's old boys' activities.

McIntosh enlisted as a captain in the Australian Imperial Force on 4 May 1915 and on 1 June was appointed to command 'B' Squadron of the 12th Light Horse Regiment with the rank of major; he embarked for Egypt that month. On 29 August the regiment landed at Gallipoli where it was broken up to serve as reinforcements for other light horse units. Next day he was wounded in the thigh and evacuated and eventually sent to England to recuperate. The 12th L.H.R. was being reformed in Egypt when McIntosh rejoined it. He was appointed second-in-command in February 1916 and commander in June; his promotion to lieut-colonel was confirmed on 11 August. The regiment operated in Egypt and Sinai and in October took an active part in the sharp action against the Turks at Maghara.

Early in 1917 the 12th L.H.R. became part of the reorganized 4th Light Horse Brigade and prepared for action on the Gaza-Beersheba front. McIntosh led his regiment in the 2nd battle of Gaza where on 19 April it was heavily committed at Atawineh Redoubt. During the battle the diminished 4th Brigade captured an enemy position at Two Tree Farm and soon afterwards came under heavy fire while advancing dismounted. In the face of increasing shell and machine-gun fire the 11th and 12th Regiments were forced to halt and flatten themselves in barley crops gay with red poppies. McIntosh was hit by shrapnel, a pellet severing an artery in his groin. He was evacuated for treatment but on 24 April his wound reopened as he lay in a hospital train at El Arish and he was found dead in the morning.

A leader in civic affairs, Harold McIntosh was also an outstanding soldier who had risen through the ranks to command a regiment on active service. He 'was a daring leader, much loved by his men' and his death 'cast a gloom over the whole of Bathurst district'. He was buried in Kantara war cemetery and was survived by his wife.

Aust Defence Dept, *Official records of the Australian military contingents to the war in South Africa*, P. L. Murray ed (Melb, 1911); H. S. Gullett, *The A.I.F. in Sinai and Palestine* (Syd, 1923); W. A. Steel and J. M. Sloman, *The history of All Saints' College, Bathurst, 1873-1934* (Syd, 1936); *Bathurst Times*, 28 Apr 1917; information from Bathurst District Historical Soc.

                                    PETER BURNESS

McINTOSH, HUGH DONALD (1876-1942), sporting and theatrical entrepreneur and newspaper proprietor, was born on 10 September 1876 in Sydney, son of Hugh McIntosh, Scottish-born policeman, and his Irish-born wife Margaret, née Benson. His father died in 1880, leaving his family in poverty. Hughie later claimed he attended the Marist Brothers' St Mary's Cathedral School and ran away, aged about 7, as assistant to an itinerant jeweller. He became an ore-picker at Broken Hill, returning after two years to Sydney, where he worked for a doctor and is said to have attended night school.

In the early 1890s McIntosh moved about the colony and Victoria working as farm labourer, engine driver, baker's boy, tarboy, stage-hand, chorus-boy, pie-seller and waiter. On 10 November 1897, at Newtown, giving his occupation as barman, he married with Independent Baptist forms Marion Catherine Elizabeth Backhouse, teacher of painting. In 1899 he took over Thomas Helmore's catering company, supplying pies to race-tracks and prizefights from the Masonic Hall, North Sydney, where he lived; here he also ran a physical-culture club and managed a few boxers.

An erratic racing cyclist in 1900-01, in 1903-07 McIntosh was secretary of the League of Wheelmen of New South Wales. In November 1903 he had become a justice of the peace. He sold the catering business to Charlotte Sargent's [q.v.] company in 1906 and invested in hotels at National Park and other resorts, including The Creel, near Jindabyne. Now living in Park Street, Sydney, in December he ran unsuccessfully for the municipal council.

The prospective visit of the American fleet in 1908 stirred McIntosh's commercial instincts. In an audacious *coup*, he brought out world heavyweight boxing champion Tommy Burns to fight Australian Bill Squires at an open-air stadium hastily erected in a leased Rushcutters Bay paddock. The fleet stayed away from the fight, but McIntosh had tapped into Sydney's new-found passion for mass spectator sport. He persuaded Burns to defend his title against American Negro Jack Johnson on Boxing Day 1908 at the Sydney Stadium. McIntosh refereed the bout and 20 000 people saw Johnson crush Burns. McIntosh made a huge profit. Even more lucrative was his film of the fight, which in January 1909 he took to Europe and the United States of America. He returned in November and had success with boxer Bob Fitzsimmons's [q.v.8] tour and a sortie into John Wren's [q.v.] patch, Melbourne.

Again leaving for America in June 1910, McIntosh was for a time based in London, staging boxing contests at the Olympia annexe and in Paris. He returned to Sydney in September 1911 keen to finalize a deal he had been pursuing for three years—the purchase of Harry Rickards's [q.v.] Australasia-wide Tivoli circuit. In August 1912 he bought it for £100 000 and embarked upon a new career as a vaudeville producer. He sold his stadium interest for £30 000 to a syndicate headed by R. L. Baker [q.v.7] in December. That month McIntosh was trounced in a Sydney municipal election.

Very short, slightly stooped but thickset and muscular, McIntosh had a tanned face, blue eyes, short, black hair and for much of his life a close-clipped moustache. To Melbourne *Punch* he was a 'hustler', positively bristling with 'energy and nervous force'. Not averse to a 'stoush', he had a reputation for coarse language and unscrupulousness; but his open, attractive personality aided a vaunting ambition to force his way into respectable society. His generosity and extravagance quickly became legendary. He contributed liberally to hospitals and other charities. With a fleet of three Pierce-Arrow motor cars, his coat of arms emblazoned on the sides, by 1913 he lived at Darling Point. He collected fine books; his friend Norman Lindsay [q.v.] designed his book-plates.

McIntosh also befriended Labor politicians W. M. Hughes and especially William Holman [qq.v.9], whose trip to England in 1912 he financed. Holman described him at this time as 'flamboyant and unreliable . . . an adventurer'. As early as 1911 McIntosh, who never joined the party but probably contributed to its election fund, was promised by Holman a seat in the Legislative Council. This was blocked within the party. From August 1915 (until 1920) McIntosh was local president of the British Empire League—his predecessor Sir William McMillan [q.v.] accused him of 'jumping' the position and 'packing' the league.

In May 1916 McIntosh bought the controlling interest in the *Sunday Times* company, which also published the *Referee* and other papers. Elected president of the local Returned Soldiers' Association in August, he soon resigned after criticism that the position belonged to a returned soldier. When Holman was expelled from the Labor Party over conscription in October, McIntosh and P. T. Taylor [q.v.] negotiated on his behalf for the ensuing Nationalist coalition; he was probably a member of the party's consultative committee. In May 1917 McIntosh was finally nominated to the Legislative Council; but he attended infrequently and spoke rarely. His connexion with railway contractor Henry Teesdale Smith [q.v.] embarrassed the government and contributed to Holman's defeat in the 1920 election.

McIntosh was president of the Weekly Newspapers' Association of New South Wales, executive member of the Empire Parliamentary Association, and life member of the Royal Australian Historical Society. As theatrical producer he had most success with revues (the Tivoli Follies) and built a new theatre in Brisbane, opened in May 1915. In 1919 he had success with *The lilac domino* and with *Chu Chin Chow*, a lavish musical comedy which opened in Melbourne in December 1920. Claiming ill health and a desire to concentrate on his newspaper interests, he withdrew from theatrical production in March 1921.

In 1919 McIntosh had bought Bellhaven, a mansion at Bellevue Hill which he extensively renovated. But he craved a still rarer atmosphere. In August 1923 he leased Lord Kitchener's Broome Park, near Canterbury, England, re-laying its cricket pitch with soil from Bulli, New South Wales. He now divided his time between England and Australia. In April his wife had been invited to the wedding of the duke of York. In 1928 he attended a private party at Buckingham Palace. Contesting a Scottish seat in the House of Commons for Labour in May 1929, he lost. In England he continued to entertain lavishly. Having sold Bellhaven, when in Sydney McIntosh now lived at the Astor, Macquarie Street.

Always one to cultivate leading politicians, he drew increasingly closer to Labor leader J. T. Lang [q.v.9], whom he persuaded to fund the cenotaph in Martin Place (1927). McIntosh voted with Labor for abolition of the Legislative Council. He even claimed to have helped Lang to defeat a leadership challenge from Peter Loughlin [q.v.] in 1926.

By the mid-1920s McIntosh's luck was running out and his finances sliding into disorder. The *Sunday Times* was losing money and when he sold it in 1927 he was heavily indebted to the company. Plunging back into vaudeville production, in 1928 he bought the Tivoli Theatre, Sydney, but in 1930 debts forced the company into liquidation. A scheme to sell Angora rabbits from Broome Park and a Derby sweep project run by T. J. Ley [q.v.] also failed. In December 1930 bankruptcy proceedings commenced. Though he fought hard his estate was sequestrated in 1932 and consequently in May he lost his Legislative Council seat. Attempts to recapture luck at formerly successful ventures—a cake shop, boxing promotion for Sydney Stadium, managing a guest house—came to nothing.

In August 1935 'Huge Deal' McIntosh again justified his nickname: he opened the Black and White Milk Bar in Fleet Street, London. Soon its success led to an over-ambitious scheme for a chain, which foundered in November 1938. Reputedly he then began a timber business. But he was once again penniless when he died in London on 2 February 1942; he was cremated. He was survived by his wife (d. 1959) of whom John Hetherington wrote: 'Their life was chequered by his insatiable appetite for both commercial and concupiscent adventures, but her loyalty to him never wavered'. She had been president of the New South Wales Ladies' Amateur Swimming Association in 1915-16. The marriage had been childless but throughout his life McIntosh had supported several nephews and nieces.

H. V. Evatt, *Australian Labour leader* (Syd, 1940); J. T. Lang, *I remember* (Syd, 1956); J. A. Hetherington, *Australians* (Melb, 1960); R. Cashman and M. McKernan (eds), *Sport in history* (Brisb, 1979); R. B. Walker, *Yesterday's news* (Syd, 1980); *Triad* (Syd), 2 Feb 1925; *People* (Syd), 27 Aug 1951; *Daily Telegraph* (Syd), 13 June, 9 July 1903, 3 Dec 1906, 7 Sept 1915, 24 Oct 1919, 26 Mar 1932; *Sydney Sportsman*, 3 Feb 1904; *Arrow* (Syd), 30 Sept 1905; *Truth* (Syd), 7 Apr 1907, 14 Dec 1930; *Referee* (Syd), 24 Mar, 21 Apr, 10 Nov 1909, 6 Sept 1911, 24 May 1916; *Sun* (Syd), 30 Aug 1912, 8 Sept 1916, 24 Oct 1919, 3 Feb 1942; *Argus*, 31 Aug 1912, 2 Mar 1921; *Punch* (Melb), 12 Sept 1912; *Sunday Times* (Syd), 6 Aug, 22 Oct 1916; *Daily Guardian* (Syd), 19 Apr, 15 Sept 1926; *Smith's Weekly* (Syd), 27 June 1931, 19 Jan, 3 Aug 1935, 25 July 1936, 27 Aug 1938; *Daily Mirror* (Syd), 3 Feb 1942; Ada Holman papers (ML); Bankruptcy files 149/1931, 100/32 (NSWA).

CHRIS CUNNEEN

MACINTYRE, RONALD GEORGE (1863-1954), Presbyterian clergyman, was born on 30 August 1863 in Melbourne, youngest son of Angus Macintyre, a Scottish-born Roman Catholic pastoralist descended from the Macdonalds of Tulloch, and his wife Catherine, née Cameron, a Presbyterian. After his father's death in 1864, Macintyre returned with his mother to Fort William, Scotland, where he was raised a Presbyterian. He was educated at the Public School, Fort William,

and then spent three years in a solicitor's office undertaking preliminary training in law.

In late adolescence Macintyre experienced a 'great spiritual change' and, offering himself for the Free Church ministry, attended New College, University of Edinburgh (M.A., 1886; B.D., 1889; D.D., 1919). He held pastorates at Birkenhead, England (five years), and Dumfries, Scotland (eight years). In Edinburgh on 1 August 1895 he married Christina Cromb; they were childless. In 1903 Macintyre accepted nomination to become minister of St Columba's Presbyterian Church, Woollahra, Sydney. He was appointed in 1909 professor of systematic theology and apologetics at the Theological Hall, St Andrew's College, University of Sydney. He was also a council-member of St Andrew's College and chairman of the Scots College council.

An astute politician, prolific fund-raiser, and respected theologian, writer and orator, Macintyre was convener of the business committee of the General Assembly of Australia for forty years, and at various times of almost every assembly committee. His admirers pointed to his sagacity and deep commitment to the Presbyterian Church, but those who found themselves the butt of his sometimes Machiavellian diplomacy referred to him, in his absence, as 'King Ronald' or 'the Cardinal'. Macintyre displayed a shrewd capacity to align himself with popular causes within the Church. In 1904-09 he promoted the cause of 'Australian ministers for an Australian Church', and raised funds to finance a third professorship at the Theological Hall, filled by Rev. Samuel Angus [q.v.7]. In 1912, at a time of marked enthusiasm for mass evangelistic missions, he chaired the organizing committee of the Chapman-Alexander mission. In 1916-18, while moderator-general of the Presbyterian Church of Australia, he served at the same time as chairman of the State Recruiting Committee. He was appointed O.B.E. in 1918 for his organizing ability and stirring oratory in the cause of recruitment, and C.M.G. in 1926. Next year he retired from the Theological Hall and in 1927-34 was managing director of the Burnside Presbyterian Orphan Homes.

After the war Macintyre had turned his attention to the Church Union movement, and assumed increased responsibility for the financial basis of the Church. Through his influence, Presbyterian institutions received generous bequests from Sir Samuel McCaughey [q.v.5]. In 1934 Macintyre chaired a three-man commission, with powers to 'do anything' to check the deteriorating financial position of the Church.

In his Theological Hall lectures, public speeches and writings Macintyre defended evangelical theology against the assaults of rationalism and liberal theology. In 1911 he declared that the 'so-called Liberal Theology' stood bankrupt and victory lay with orthodox scholarship. After the war, however, his examination of the doctrine of Christian eschatology and his wartime experiences caused him to recognize the need for a degree of theological restatement. His defence of a doctrine of potential, or conditional, immortality in *The other side of death. A study of Christian eschatology* (1920) gained him a D.D. from the University of Edinburgh, and the censure of conservative churchmen, who questioned his orthodoxy and 'loyalty to Christ'. He resolutely denied the charge. Macintyre's critical review of Angus's scholarly work, *Religious quests of the Graeco Roman World* (*Sydney Morning Herald*, 9 November 1929) started public debate about Angus. At first Macintyre took a conciliatory role in the controversy, eschewing the potentially divisive effects of a heresy case. After the publication of Angus's polemic *Truth and tradition* in 1934, however, he became a resolute opponent and that year published a pamphlet, *The theology of Dr. Angus: a critical review*.

Following the death of his first wife, Macintyre married a widow Alice Mary Parkinson, daughter of Rev. Dr J. N. Manning, on 12 February 1935. In retirement he lived at Springwood where he enjoyed gardening and bowls. He died on 22 June 1954 in the Scottish Hospital, Paddington, and was cremated. At his funeral service Rev. Victor Clark-Duff described him as 'the brightest luminary in the ecclesiastical firmament of our Church since the days of John Dunmore Lang' [q.v.2]. Macintyre was survived by his wife and two stepchildren.

C. A. White, *The challenge of the years* (Syd, 1951); *Scottish A'sian*, Nov 1916; *NSW Presbyterian*, 26 May 1927, 2 July 1954; Angus papers (Ferguson Memorial Lib, Presbyterian Assembly Hall, Syd); Minutes, The Heretics (held by K. J. Cable, Univ Syd).   SUSAN E. EMILSEN

MACK, MARIE LOUISE HAMILTON (1870-1935) and AMY ELEANOR (1876-1939), writers, were born on 10 October 1870 in Hobart Town and on 6 June 1876 at Port Adelaide, daughters of Rev. Hans Hamilton Mack (d. 1890), Wesleyan minister from Downpatrick, Ireland, and his wife Jemima (d. 1930), née James, from Armagh, whom he had married in Sydney in 1859. Louise, the eldest girl in a family of thirteen, was registered as Mary Louisa. The family, moving from circuit to circuit, left South Australia in 1878, and after three years at Morpeth and Windsor, New South Wales, settled in Sydney in 1882. The sisters were educated by their mother and a governess and at the Sydney Girls' High School, where Louise and her friend Ethel Turner [q.v.] edited rival papers; she drew on her school memories for her books *Teens* (1897) and *Girls together* (1898), published by Angus [q.v.7] & Robertson [q.v.].

After briefly working as a governess Louise became a regular contributor to the *Bulletin* in the late 1880s, encouraged by J. F. Archibald [q.v.3] and A. G. Stephens [q.v.]. On 8 January 1896 she married John Percy Creed (d. 1914), a barrister from Dublin; there were no children. The same year Louise's first novel, *The world is round*, was published in London. In 1898 she joined the *Bulletin* staff, writing the 'Woman's Letter' under the pen-name of 'Gouli Gouli'. In 1901, shortly after she had gone abroad without her husband, the *Bulletin* published her poems, *Dreams in flower*.

In England she lived close to starvation while writing her novel, *An Australian girl in London* (1902). The book was very well received and she became a protégée of W. T. Stead, writing for his *Review of Reviews*. She was engaged by Alfred Harmsworth (Lord Northcliffe) as a journalist on the *Daily Mail* and in 1904 published another novel, *Children of the sun*, set in Sydney. She wrote many successful serials, later published in book form, for Harmsworth Press publications, a retrograde literary step from which she made a great deal of money, all of which she quickly spent. She travelled widely, published several popular novels, and for six years lived at Florence, editing the *Italian Gazette* in 1904-07.

Back in England in 1914 Louise managed to get to Belgium as the first woman war correspondent, reporting for the *Evening News* and the *Daily Mail*. Her eye-witness account of the German invasion of Antwerp and her adventures—*A woman's experiences in the Great War*—was published in 1915.

In 1916 she returned to Australia and in 1917-18 toured the country, speaking on her war experiences and raising money for the Australian Red Cross Society. From 1919 to the early 1930s she lectured in the Pacific islands and New Zealand and, in association with the Department of Education and the Good Film League of New South Wales, toured Australia with travel talks and films for schools.

When in Melbourne on 1 September 1924 Louise married 33-year-old Allen Illingworth Leyland (d. 1932), a New Zealand Anzac, she claimed to have one living child. These years were very difficult for Louise but she met misfortune with her usual courage and vitality, working as a freelance journalist and publishing two more novels, *Teens triumphant*

(1933) and *Maiden's prayer* (1934). She died on 23 November 1935 at Mosman of cerebrovascular disease, and was cremated with Presbyterian forms. Described by Le Gay Brereton [q.v.7] as fluffy, like a chicken, Louise was fair, pretty, extroverted, audacious, unpredictable, a genuine Bohemian who chose a life of adventure and insecurity. She died possessionless.

Amy Eleanor was dark, less temperamental than Louise and lived more sedately. Soon after leaving school she began work as a journalist and in 1907-14 was editor of the 'Women's Page' of the *Sydney Morning Herald*. On 29 February 1908 she married Launcelot Harrison [q.v.9]; there were no children. She soon published two collections of essays, *A bush calendar* (1909) and *Bush days* (1911) which had previously appeared in the *Sydney Morning Herald*, and two very popular children's books, *Bushland stories* (1910) and *Scribbling Sue, and other stories* (1915).

With her husband she left in 1914 for England where Launce did postgraduate work at Cambridge. While he served in Mesopotamia, she worked in London as publicity officer for the ministries of munitions and food. The Harrisons returned to Sydney in 1919 and lived at Gordon in a house full of books, antique furniture and Persian carpets. From 1922 Launce was professor of zoology at the University of Sydney. That year Amy published *The wilderness*. She regularly contributed to the literary page of the *Sydney Morning Herald*, was honorary secretary in 1920-23 of the National Council of Women of New South Wales and accompanied her husband on scientific expeditions. Though she continued to publish occasional articles after he died in 1928, the impulse to write faded as her health declined and on 4 November 1939 she died of arteriosclerosis in St Vincent's Hospital. She was cremated with Presbyterian forms.

J. Colwell (comp), *The illustrated history of Methodism, Australia* (Syd, 1904); N. Phelan, *A kingdom by the sea* (Syd, 1969); P. Poole (comp), *The diaries of Ethel Turner* (Syd, 1979); A. W. Barker (ed), *Dear Robertson* (Syd, 1982); B. Niall, *Australia through the looking glass: children's fiction 1830-1980* (Melb, 1984); *Cosmos Mag*, 31 Oct 1895; *Bulletin*, 20 Apr 1901, 24 Jan 1903; *Lone Hand*, May 1907, Dec 1913; *SMH*, 26, 30 Nov 1935, 7, 8 Nov 1939; Angus & Robertson papers *and* Louise Mack scrapbooks (ML).

NANCY PHELAN

MACKANESS, GEORGE (1882-1968), educationist, author and bibliophile, was born on 9 May 1882 at Blue's Point, Sydney, eldest of eight children of native-born parents George Mackaness, printer and lithographer, and his wife Annie Ellen, née Barnett. He was educated at Drummoyne Public School, where he began as a probationary pupil-teacher in July 1897. Next January he was transferred to Balmain Superior Public School, where he completed the four years training in December 1901. He spent 1902 at Fort Street Training School on a half-scholarship and began teaching at Fort Street Public School in January 1903 at £96 a year. At St Thomas's Anglican Church, Balmain, he married Alice Matilda Symons on 19 December 1906.

Meanwhile he had studied part time at the University of Sydney, graduating B.A. with first-class honours in English and half the James Coutts scholarship in 1907 and M.A. with first-class honours in English in 1911. From 1912 he was master of English and deputy headmaster of Fort Street Boys' High School. To the boys he was known as 'Creeping Jesus', because his rubber-heeled shoes enabled him to surprise wrongdoers.

At Fort Street Mackaness was encouraged by the headmaster A. J. Kilgour [q.v.9] to develop a new approach to teaching English. Although he expected the boys to read the classics, he deplored the lack of appreciation of Australian literature. With Bertram Stevens [q.v.] he edited *Selections from the Australian poets* (1913), which ran through many editions and was revised with his daughter Joan as *The wide brown land* (1934). To develop self-expression he introduced 'magimaps' of imaginary islands drawn by the boys, who wove stories about the people and places associated with their individual islands. He pioneered the 'Play day movement' in New South Wales: Fort Street became noted for its annual days in which every class acted scenes from Shakespeare or other writers. His book embodying his methods, *Inspirational teaching* (London, 1928), won international recognition.

In 1924-46 Mackaness was lecturer-in-charge of the department of English at Teachers' College, Sydney, where Bernard Smith found his conductor-like gestures, while demonstrating how to teach primary school-children the significance of poetic metre, 'wholly ludicrous'. He was also examiner in English for the intermediate certificate, a university extension lecturer and acting lecturer in English at the university in 1909, 1915-18 and 1927-30. He published several textbooks, an anthology, *Australian short stories* (London, 1928), and a selection of Henry Lawson's [q.v.] prose works (1928).

By the 1930s Mackaness was a major figure in Sydney literary circles: he was an active foundation member of the Sydney branch of the English Association from 1923, an early member of the Sydney P.E.N. Club and president of the Fellowship of Australian Writers in 1933-34. He resigned when despite his protests Egon Kisch attended a luncheon for John Masefield. In 1938 with (Dame) Mary Gilmore [q.v.9] and others he tried to found a new literary society excluding journalists. Still involved in amateur dramatics, he was president of the Junior Theatre League and of the Impressionist Theatre, which staged Continental drama. He revered Norman Lindsay [q.v.] and became a close friend of Hugh McCrae [q.v.], who frequently addressed him as 'Joyous Jarge'. From 1937 he served on the advisory board of the Commonwealth Literary Fund and in 1942-65 was a trustee of the Public Library of New South Wales. In 1946 he published an anthology, *Poets of Australia*. Over the years Mackaness corresponded with many writers. He chided Miles Franklin [q.v.8] for sending him typewritten letters: 'You know I save them up for posterity . . . That's why Kipling's letters to me don't have the imprimatur of his personality as I should have liked'.

Encouraged by Professor (Sir) Ernest Scott [q.v.], Mackaness became absorbed in historical research. In 1931 he published *The life of Vice-Admiral William Bligh*, for which he was awarded a D.Litt. by the University of Melbourne in 1932. Like Ida Lee [q.v.] earlier, he compiled massive documentary material, but he failed to 're-create the man or his times' and offered few general insights. H. M. Green found the life of Bligh 'verbose and repetitive and full of journalistic clichés', pitfalls which Mackaness largely avoided in his second major biography, *Admiral Arthur Phillip* (1937).

A prolific contributor to newspapers and journals, Mackaness edited and had privately printed in limited editions a series of thirty-nine Australian historical monographs. He also published lighter sketches such as *Lags and legirons* (1944) and bibliographies of the works of James Bonwick, C. J. Brennan [qq.v.3,7] and Lawson. A Freemason, he wrote with K. R. Cramp [q.v.8] *A history of the United Grand Lodge* (1938). He was a council-member, fellow from 1940 and president in 1948-49 of the Royal Australian Historical Society. Appointed O.B.E. in 1938, he was awarded an honorary D.Sc. by the University of Sydney in 1961.

His interest in historical research led Mackaness and his wife into the by-ways of book-collecting. With limited money (he was earning £960 a year when he retired in May 1946), he built up probably the largest private collection of Australiana by the 1960s. In seventeen articles in the *Amateur Book Collector* (Chicago) in 1951-52 he described some of his finds including a leatherbound copy of the pirated edition of Charles Dickens's [q.v.4] *The Pickwick Papers* published in Launceston by Henry Dowling [q.v.1] in 1839, and the journals of the Canadian patriots transported to New South Wales in 1838. He traced the Australian descendants of one, Joseph Moreau, and found a mint copy of Leon (Léandre) Ducharme's *Journal d'un exilé politique aux Terres Australes* (Montreal, 1845), which he translated and produced in 1944. Another find was the manuscript of George Augustus Robinson's [q.v.2] account of his journey into south-eastern Australia in 1844. He also published two collections of his articles and essays in the field, *The art of book-collecting in Australia* (1956) and *Bibliomania* (1965).

In 1966 Mackaness asked Angus [q.v.7] & Robertson [q.v.] Ltd to dispose of his huge library at his Drummoyne home on a share basis. He died at Five Dock on 3 December 1968, and was cremated with Anglican rites. His wife and daughter survived him and inherited his estate, valued for probate at $46 119. A large man, balding in his later years, Mackaness was tireless but inclined to be pernickety. He made notable contributions in three fields—as a teacher of English, as a historian who made available quantities of documentary material, and as a bibliophile who made the collecting of Australiana popular.

E. Kisch, *Australian landfall* (Lond, 1937); C. Morris, *The school on the hill* (Syd, 1981); *Age*, 19 Mar 1960; *SMH*, 23 Nov, 11 Dec 1934, 26 June 1966, 4 Dec 1968; *Daily Telegraph* (Syd), 23 Nov, 11, 13 Dec 1934, 4 Dec 1968; Mackaness papers (NL and ML); ML printed cat; Miles Franklin *and* Mary Gilmore papers (ML); Teachers' records (Education Dept Archives, Syd).

BRUCE MITCHELL
MARTHA RUTLEDGE

MACKAY, DONALD GEORGE (1870-1958), explorer, was born on 29 June 1870 at Yass, New South Wales, son of Alexander Mackay, owner of Wallendbeen station, and his wife Annie, née Mackenzie, both Scottish born. Major General James Alexander Kenneth Mackay [q.v.] was a brother. Donald was educated at Wallendbeen Public School and at Oaklands School, Mittagong. After a brief engineering apprenticeship he worked as a jackaroo for his father until he died in 1890; his inheritance provided a substantial private income. In 1890-99 Mackay travelled extensively throughout the world and tried prospecting for gold in western New South Wales.

In July 1899 he and Alec and Frank White left Brisbane to bicycle round Australia. Though the Whites had to abandon the attempt Mackay returned to Brisbane in March 1900 in a record-breaking time of 240 days after an 11 000 mile (17 700 km) ride through scarcely known areas.

Mackay married Amy Isabel Little on 16

April 1902 at Homebush, Sydney. Their home at Port Hacking was a base for fishing, motoring, sailing and further travel. He led and financed an expedition to Papua in 1908 to investigate the headwaters of the Purari River. During the following decade he sailed a yacht in the South Pacific and visited New Zealand and the Dutch East Indies.

In 1926 Mackay financed and accompanied the first of several expeditions to the Northern Territory when, with the anthropologist Dr Herbert Basedow [q.v.7] he went into the Petermann Ranges by camel. In 1928 they explored in Arnhem Land. In 1931, 1933, 1935 and 1937 Mackay supervised aerial surveys of Central Australia, the first of which in 1931 discovered the large lake that the Commonwealth government named after him. The surveys produced far more useful maps than had previously existed. Copies of all Mackay's maps and reports were donated to the Commonwealth government and the Mitchell [q.v.5] Library, Sydney.

Criticism by Mackay of the harsh treatment of Aborigines, reported in the British press in July 1933, caused official denials; Prime Minister Lyons [q.v.] and S. M. (Viscount) Bruce [q.v.7] expressed concern at the harm done to Australia's reputation. Mackay offered to withdraw his comment if Lyons could prove that the treatment of Aborigines had been humane.

Appointed O.B.E. in 1934 and C.B.E. in 1937, Mackay in his old age won deserved recognition as 'the last Australian explorer'. While his journeys lacked the significance of some earlier ones they did much to increase knowledge of remote areas. A powerfully built man, he was well known for his generosity, physical fitness and qualities of leadership.

Mackay died on 17 September 1958 at Sutherland Shire Hospital and was cremated after a Presbyterian service. A widower, he had no children.

H. Basedow, *Knights of the boomerang* (Syd, 1935); F. P. Clune, *Last of the Australian explorers* (Syd, 1942); M. Durack, *Sons in the saddle* (Lond, 1983); A'sian Assn Advancement of Science, *Report of meeting 1911* (1911); *Home,* Jan 1928, Jan 1929; *New Nation Mag,* June 1928; *Land, Farm and Station Annual,* 1938; *SMH,* 1 Feb 1937; *Daily Telegraph,* 18 Sept 1958; *Northern Territory News,* 12 Nov 1983; D. Mackay papers (ML).

DAVID CARMENT

MACKAY, GEORGE HUGH ALEXANDER (1872-1961), politician and Speaker of the House of Representatives, was born on 20 March 1872 at Copperfield, near Clermont, Queensland, son of Hugh Mackay, carpenter, and his wife Jane, née Baird, both Scottish migrants. He was educated at Clermont and Bundaberg state schools and after a brief apprenticeship as a chemist joined the *Peak Downs Telegram* as an apprentice printer in 1887. He became foreman printer in 1894, then managing editor. On 23 September 1896 he married Edith Ann Heard at the Wesleyan Church, Clermont. Mackay then conducted a newsagency and bookselling business at Clermont with his sister Barbara. In 1899 he was elected to the Clermont Town Council and in 1900-02 was mayor.

In 1902 Mackay moved his family to New South Wales, where he ran a newsagency briefly at Lismore, then leased a dairy farm at McLean's Ridge. In 1905 the family joined settlers from the Richmond River at Gympie, Queensland, where dairying and fruit-growing were developing around the goldfield. In partnership with Ray King, Mackay opened an auctioneering and real estate business there and in March 1906 was honorary secretary of the committee that established the Wide Bay Dairy Co-operative Association. He was elected to the Gympie City Council in 1911 and became mayor in 1917.

In 1912 Mackay was elected as a Liberal to the Legislative Assembly for Gympie, a seat which he had unsuccessfully contested in 1909. He was defeated in 1915. In 1917, standing as a Nationalist, Mackay won the Federal seat of Lilley, which then stretched from north of Gympie to Breakfast Creek in Brisbane, and held it easily in six subsequent elections. Mackay conscientiously represented the concerns of the farmers and small businessmen who elected him. He was a competent public speaker and a careful speech-writer with a fondness for quoting figures. He served on the Joint Committee on Public Works (1920-28) and as its chairman in 1926-28 was involved in building the Australian War Memorial and in the development of Canberra. Mackay was a moderate man who had 'no time for extremists or muddlers', and was little attracted to the Country Party.

In recognition of his long experience in parliament, his work as temporary chairman of committees in 1929-31 and his service to the National and United Australia parties, he was elected Speaker on 11 February 1932. In March 1934 he announced his intention to retire at the end of the parliamentary session, saying only that 'one may remain in parliament too long'. In retirement Mackay pursued his interest in bowls and was president of the Gympie Bowling Club in 1936-39.

Tall and well-built, Mackay was a good runner and rifle shot in his youth. Described as 'rational and without malice', he had a calm disposition, modesty, a dry wit and cautious but sound judgement in financial matters. He was a devout Presbyterian and wrote 'A summary of the history of the Gympie Presbyterian Church' (1952). A Freemason, in 1955 he was awarded the fifty years long-service jewel.

Mackay died on 5 November 1961 at Gympie and after a state funeral from the Presbyterian Church was buried in Gympie cemetery. Predeceased by his wife, he was survived by a son. His portrait by A. E. Newbury is in Parliament House, Canberra.

Gympie Times, 9 Feb, 17 Mar 1917, 7 Nov 1961; *Courier Mail*, 20 Mar 1934; family information.

ELAINE BROWN

McKAY, HUGH VICTOR (1865-1926), manufacturer, was born on 21 August 1865 at Raywood, Victoria, fifth of twelve children of Nathaniel McKay (pronounced to rhyme with day) and his wife Mary, née Wilson, from Monaghan, Ireland, and adherents of the Free Church of Scotland who arrived in Victoria in 1852. After mining at Ballarat, Stawell and north of Bendigo, the McKays settled at Raywood, moving to a selection at Drummartin in the early 1870s.

The older children had little formal schooling, but Nathaniel and Mary read them the Bible, sermons, the works of John Bunyan and other improving literature. All eight sons became successful businessmen, tradesmen or farmers, and four of them were closely associated with Hugh Victor's enterprise. Nathaniel Breakey (1859-1924) became a schoolteacher, journalist and founded the *Mildura Cultivator*; John (1861-1936) built an extensive provisioning business in northern Victoria; George (1867-1927) was a coachbuilder; Samuel (1871-1932) became a storekeeper with John. Hugh Victor was educated briefly at the Drummartin school and under his brother Nathaniel in north-eastern Victoria, until recalled at 13 to help on the farm.

On the edge of the northern plains harvesting depended on the horse-drawn South Australian stripper and the manual winnower. Government prizes stimulated attempts to produce a harvester combining stripping, threshing, winnowing and bagging. At Drummartin in October 1883 Hugh Victor's attention was caught by J. L. Dow's [q.v.4] article in the Melbourne *Leader* describing the mechanization of Californian wheat-farming by giant 'combination harvesters'. With his brother John and his father, McKay assembled a stripper-harvester from existing implements and machines, work which they always claimed was done in total ignorance of other experiments. Their prototype was completed in January 1885, tried in the field and patented for 'Improvements in and connected with harvesting machines' on 24 March. Hugh Victor persuaded the ploughmakers McCalman, Garde & Co. of North Melbourne

to manufacture this machine, which was exhibited at the National Agricultural Society Show in August. Several were sold and gave good service. McKay's boast that they were the first successful stripper-harvesters on the market was later inflated by company propaganda into the claim that he had invented the first machine. In fact James Morrow [q.v.5] had perfected, patented and exhibited a stripper-harvester more than a year earlier, had won a prize at the government trial in December 1884, and had narrowly taken the honours from McKay in the 1885-86 field trials.

McKay's first harvesters were made under contract in Melbourne, Sandhurst (Bendigo) and from 1888 at Ballarat, where he opened an office. The McKay Harvesting Machinery Co., established in 1890, purchased McKay's patents and the rights to manufacture, and traded profitably until it fell victim to the economic crisis of 1892-93. The family held more than a quarter of the shares. McKay, recently married on 11 March 1891 to Sarah Irene Graves, was left with only £25 to his name. Assisted by a small syndicate, he snapped up the company assets, traded as The Harvester Co., in 1893 built an improved harvester, tested it in two successive harvests, and marketed it as the 'Sunshine'. Though he purchased the business and established formal independence, his erstwhile partners were rural businessmen who gave essential financial backing over the next decade.

The business expanded phenomenally during the long drought at the end of the century. The 'Sunshine' cut costs, encouraging wheatfarmers to sow more extensively. 12 were built in 1895, 50 in 1896, and production almost doubled annually to 500 in 1901. McKay established agencies in the capital cities and employed demonstrators throughout the inland grain belt. In 1901-02, urged by his brother Sam who had become sales manager since his return from the South African War, he followed his chief competitor Nicholson & Morrow overseas. 'Sunshine' harvesters were dispatched to South Africa, and in 1901 Sam and three Ballarat experts went to the Argentine where they demonstrated 'La Australiana' on a variety of crops so effectively that they soon threatened the trade in North American reaper-binders and headers. Sam superintended South American operations, and established the business throughout north Africa. By mid-1904 McKay's overseas trade had earnings of £70 000, making him the largest manufacturing exporter in the Commonwealth.

Soaring production (1023 machines in 1903-04, 1916 in 1905-06) encouraged McKay to install mechanized plant and streamlined assembly. Innovations included a revolutionary new steel foundry, moulding by machine, a bolt-manufacturing department, and a sawmill and woodworking department using McKay timber. George McKay was works manager. In declining Ballarat the Sunshine Harvester Works was the great success-story. Year-round production guaranteed employment to some 500 loyal workers by 1905. The works fielded cricket teams, the 'Sunshine' choir sang in the South Street competition, and the employees marched as a body on Eight Hours' Day. McKay's meteoric rise made his success seem fortuitous, but few observers could have been aware of the nervous energy required to sustain what was really a risky and fragile business. McKay's profits were substantial and rising, from around £3000 in 1898, to £39 000 in 1905. But competition, local and overseas, was cutthroat, the weather exposed the business to sudden slumps, and the short harvest demanded absolute reliability of his harvester and of replacement and repair services. Generous warranties and extended credit terms for machines, together with the rapid expansion of the works, meant that McKay operated on substantial bank overdrafts and loans. His triumph was almost as much financial as one of manufacturing and supply.

Sea and rail supply-lines for fuel, raw materials, subcontracted parts and finished machines made a seaboard location imperative. In 1904, alerted by his brother William, manager of the Commercial Bank at Footscray, McKay acquired the well-equipped works of the Braybrook Implement Co. at Braybrook Junction. At the northern and western rail-junction this site had an additional advantage. Being within a shire and requiring an Order in Council to bring it under a wages board determination, it offered shelter from a system to which McKay was implacably opposed. He had stated before the royal commission on factories and shops laws that market forces should determine wage levels, through individual bargaining. In 1901-02 he had helped to form the Ballarat Chamber of Manufactures which campaigned against wages boards, and when a board was mooted in his industry he threatened variously to replace workers by machines, to move his business interstate, and to send his patterns to America and assemble his machines from imported parts. When the Ironmoulders' Wages Board's determination restricted the number of juveniles and improvers in 1904, McKay appealed to the government, obtained a secret undertaking from premier Bent [q.v.3] that the determination would not be extended to Braybrook, and moved his works there. McKay's evasion of the wages board did not endear him as a high tariff protectionist to his Victorian competitors or to the union movement. Business rivals accused him of hypocrisy; Laborites, including Tom Mann [q.v.], branded him a free trader in humans.

McKay argued that the low Federal tariff left him vulnerable to unfair competition from overseas manufacturers supplying larger markets and enjoying cheaper labour, raw materials and freight. Further, he asserted that the stripper-harvester, pirated by Americans, was being dumped below cost in Australia in an attempt to destroy the local industry. In 1904-05 he launched a highly emotive campaign against the 'American Octopus Trust', the International Harvester Co. of Chicago. Workers and protectionists formed the Harvester Defence League to demand a higher tariff, but critics suspected that McKay was taking refuge in patriotism to disguise his fear of competition from fellow-Britishers Massey Harris of Canada, who appear to have been exporting machines copied from Morrow's Union Harvester, not only to Australia but to South America. McKay put the case for higher duties in April 1905 to the Tariff Commission appointed by the Reid-McLean [qq.v.] government.

The commission's reports of August 1906 recommended increased duties, and a doubling of those on stripper-harvesters, subject to the outlawing of combines, and the suspension of duties where manufacturers made unwarranted price increases or failed to pay 'a fair and reasonable rate of wages'. The Deakin [q.v.8] government responded with its New Protection legislation, designed to spread the benefits of tariff protection to workers and consumers. Despite legal advice that the Excise Tariff (Agricultural Machinery) Act was unconstitutional, McKay applied for exemption from excise duties, and Justice Higgins [q.v.9] selected his as the test case. In his celebrated Harvester judgment of November 1907, Higgins, while praising the Sunshine Harvester Works as 'a marvel of enterprise, energy and pluck', decided that 'the normal needs of the average employee, regarded as a human being in a civilized community', dictated that an unskilled labourer should be paid a minimum of seven shillings a day of eight hours, and that as some wage rates at Sunshine were below this McKay could not be exempted. The government looked for a compromise, but McKay determined on confrontation, forcing the government into the role of debt-collector. He challenged the constitutionality of the Excise Act, which was declared *ultra vires* by the High Court of Australia in 1908.

The Harvester judgment made McKay an instant convert to the Victorian wages board system, but his behaviour boosted unionism and strengthened worker interest in Federal conciliation and arbitration. In 1911 the agricultural implement makers' union called a strike, ostensibly to enforce the closed shop but as part of a strategy to bring the industry under a Federal award. Led by McKay the employers responded with a lockout of all unionists, striking or not. McKay refused Prime Minister Fisher's [q.v.8] offer to mediate. The Harvester dispute lasted thirteen weeks, affected 2500 workers, left the union defeated, demoralized and bankrupt, and poisoned industrial relations for decades. McKay's detestation of Labor and unionism was expressed in his support for the free (non-union) labour cause and in his own campaign for the Ballarat seat at the election of 1913. Labor won the seat in a tough and close fight.

Initially McKay's promotion of worker residence at Braybrook had been speculative, appreciating that as land values rose 'we can sell it by the foot instead of by the acre'. But the 1911 dispute set him thinking about the possibility of creating at Sunshine, as the Braybrook Junction township was known from 1907, a model community of worker freeholders opposed to militant unionism. He drew inspiration from overseas company towns, notably those of Cadbury and Lever brothers in England. His own estate department built stores, a public hall and library, and a coffee palace, provided land for a technical school, supplied electric light and public gardens, and initiated tree planting. If there were an element of idealism, Sunshine was nevertheless an investment in industrial peace. McKay anticipated that married men, preoccupied with family, mortgage repayments and their gardens, would prove a loyal, diligent, and politically moderate workforce. At Ballarat he had introduced generous holiday leave, a contributory accident fund and a personal loan scheme; these were extended at Braybrook under the management of worker committees. Hugh Victor, Sam, Nathaniel and George McKay and their families lived at Sunshine, and exercised a pervasive influence. Critics saw not so much philanthropy as subtle social and industrial controls.

The Sunshine Harvester Works was for many years the largest factory in Australia, and it grew prodigiously to cover 30 acres (12 ha), employ 2500 workers and in 1926 distribute £600 000 in wages and salaries. McKay had initiated full-line production. Under J. B. Garde, who adapted the stump-jump principle to the American-derived disc plough, the tillage department produced an array of successful implements from 1905-06. McKay experimented with self-propelled harvesters from 1902, and in 1912 Sunshine commenced the manufacture of internal combustion engines for farm use. A severe challenge to his stripper-harvester from the Massey Harris reaper-thresher was met when McKay bought the rights to Headlie Shipard Taylor's

[q.v.] header-harvester. Taylor's header was available for the 1916-17 harvest, and it met the Massey Harris challenge and also rapidly outpaced the stripper-harvester, especially after spectacularly successful work on storm-damaged crops in 1920-21. This was a most opportune development, for McKay was never to regain the South American markets lost on the outbreak of war in 1914. Otherwise, war and business had combined naturally for him. War materials were produced on a considerable scale and McKay initiated the production of drawn steel shafting and brass and copper tubing, supplying the latter widely to industry. He and Sam were members of the Federal Munitions Committee, and McKay served on the board of business administration formed in 1918 to advise the contract and supply board of the Department of Defence. While in London during 1919 he chaired the Australian War Materials Disposal Board. For these services he was appointed C.B.E.

The war and post-war years saw a widening range of Sunshine machines: engine-functioned harvesters from 1916, combined seed and fertiliser drills and cultivators (after R. A. Squire) from 1917, reapers and binders from 1921, and Taylor's self-propelled auto header from 1925. McKay's own motor tractor of 1917, like his self-propelled harvester of 1908-09, was suspended as not commercially viable. The survival and prosperity of the McKay enterprise depended on the inventiveness of practical farmers and specialist engineers around the country, attracted by McKay's reputation and wealth to sell him their patents and expertise. Surveying the agricultural implement industry, and finding it littered with enterprises which had collapsed on the deaths of their founders, McKay yet refused to relax his personal control. When H. V. McKay Pty Ltd was created in 1921, he became governing director for life with absolute power. Sunshine was plagued by industrial disputation, despite McKay's institution of pensions and retirement allowances in 1921, a sick-pay scheme in 1922 and a mortuary fund in 1924. In 1922 he founded with G. D. Delprat [q.v.8] and others the Single Purpose League devoted to the abolition of compulsory arbitration. He told Prime Minister Hughes [q.v.9] that he favoured collective bargaining by industrial tribunals composed of equal numbers of employers and employees.

McKay left his Sunshine home in 1922 when he achieved his long-held ambition of owning Rupertswood at Sunbury. Not finding the move or the social life to her taste, Sarah McKay lived apart until McKay's health deteriorated in 1925. Extensive tests in London confirmed terminal cancer. McKay received the verdict with great courage, continuing his business and public duties to within days of his death. In his last weeks he summoned his old friend Hume Cook [q.v.8], to whom he told his life-story of the humble farmer's son who had invented the stripper-harvester, converted a suspicious farming community, defended Australian interests against American industrial pirates and triumphed single handed over immense odds, including interfering socialist unions and governments, to create the greatest manufacturing enterprise Australia had ever seen. The power of this legend was apparent in the response to his death at Rupertswood on 21 May 1926. The press vaunted the most widely known industrialist in Australian history as 'McKay of Sunshine' and the 'Inventor of the Harvester'. The *Argus* thought him a character of towering strength and tenacity; the *Age* eulogized him as 'a man with an intense faith in his own vision, and with a determination of character and bigness of heart that enabled him to take all obstacles in his stride'. Hundreds of his employees swelled the congregation at his funeral service and led the procession with the Sunshine pipe band to the Sunbury cemetery for a Presbyterian and Masonic burial. The moderator-general drew this lesson from McKay's life: 'Success came to him through his own splendid strength and manful endeavour . . . He was an inspiration to Australian youth, and stood for what a man could accomplish by determination'.

McKay was survived by his wife, a daughter and two sons. He left an estate of £1 448 146, and a codicil vested the income from 100 000 shares in the H. V. McKay Charitable Trust, chaired by George Swinburne [q.v.] and designed to encourage rural settlement, improve country life, and assist charitable objects at Sunshine. The Museum of Victoria houses a bust by Wallace Anderson and the farm smithy in which McKay conducted his first experiments. On several putative anniversaries of his 'invention in 1884 of the harvester', memorials to McKay were unveiled in the city of Sunshine.

Sam was managing director until his death on 12 November 1932 in Sydney while returning from the Ottawa Conference, where he had been an adviser to the Australian delegation. He had presided over the merger with the Australian interests of Massey Harris in 1930. H. V. McKay's son Cecil Newton (1899-1968) was managing director of H. V. McKay Massey Harris Pty Ltd from 1937 and chairman from 1947. The McKay name disappeared when Massey Harris purchased the remaining family interests in 1955 and renamed the business Massey Harris Ferguson, subsequently Massey-Ferguson (Australia) Ltd.

J. Smith (ed), *Cyclopedia of Victoria*, 2 (Melb, 1904); V. Palmer, *National portraits* (Syd, 1940); A. R. Callaghan and A. J. Millington, *The wheat industry in Australia* (Syd, 1956); J. Rickard, *Class and politics* (Canb, 1975); G. R. Quick and W. F. Buchele, *The grain harvesters* (Michigan, 1978); D. McNeill and the McKay family, *The McKays of Drummartin and Sunshine* (Melb, 1984); Roy Com on the operation of the factories and shops law of Vic, Minutes of evidence, *PP* (LA Vic), 1902-03, 2, (31); Roy Com on the Cwlth tariff. Progress reports: no 5, agricultural machinery and implements, no 6, stripper harvesters, *PP* (Cwlth), 1906, 4, Minutes of evidence 1906, 5; Roy Com on stripper harvesters and drills, *PP* (Cwlth), 1909, 2; *A'sian Hardware and Machinery*, 1 Sept 1905; *Aust Farming*, 16 Dec 1921; *Aust Home Builder*, 15 Apr 1925; *Vic Chamber of Manufactures Gazette*, 25 May 1926; *Aust Manufacturer*, 26 Nov 1932; *Leader* (Melb), 6 Oct 1883, 28 Oct 1899; *Ballarat Star*, 22 Oct 1897, 30 July 1898, 28 Jan 1901; *Ballarat Courier*, 23 Oct 1897, 26 Jan 1901; *Punch* (Melb), 23 Mar 1911; *Age*, 22 May 1926, 14 Nov 1932; *Argus*, 22, 24 May, 6 Aug 1926, 14, 16 Nov 1932; *Weekly Times* (Melb), 4 Dec 1974; G. S. Cope, Some aspects of the metal trades in Ballarat, 1851-1901 (M.A. thesis, Univ Melb, 1971); I. W. McLean, Rural outputs, inputs and mechanisation in Victoria, 1870-1910 (Ph.D. thesis, ANU, 1971); J. F. Lack, Footscray: an industrial suburban community (Ph.D. thesis, Monash Univ, 1976); Bavin *and* Deakin *and* Hume-Cook *and* Groom *and* Aust Industries Protection League papers (NL); H. V. McKay Archives (Museum of Vic); information from Mrs J. Alexander, Malvern, Melb.

JOHN LACK

MACKAY, JAMES ALEXANDER KENNETH (1859-1935), soldier, author and politician, was born on 5 June 1859 at Wallendbeen, New South Wales, son of Scottish-born parents Alexander Mackay, squatter, and his wife Annie, née Mackenzie; Donald George [q.v.] was his brother. He was educated at home and at Camden College and Sydney Grammar School. In his mid-twenties he extended his education by attending H. E. Southey's college at Mittagong. He was a good athlete and an outstanding horseman, well-known in country districts as an amateur jockey. He also rode at Randwick and Rosehill.

In 1885, while at Mittagong, Mackay raised a volunteer cavalry troop called the West Camden Light Horse and was appointed captain in command. Shortly afterwards he returned to the family property to assist his ageing father. He spent his quieter moments writing short stories and ballads. Several were published in newspapers and popular journals before his first book, *Stirrup jingles* (1887). Similar publications in Sydney, *A bush idyll* (1888) and *Songs of a sunlit land* (1908), followed. He also wrote the novels, *Out-back* (London, 1893) and *The yellow wave* (1895), which imagined a Chinese invasion of Australia. On 13 March 1890 he married Mabel Kate White at the Presbyterian manse, North Melbourne.

Mackay was elected as a Protectionist to the Legislative Assembly for Boorowa in 1895; he held the seat for (Sir) Edmund Barton's [q.v.7] National Federal Party in 1898. Vice-president of the Executive Council in (Sir) William Lyne's [q.v.] ministry from 15 September 1899, he was nominated to the Legislative Council in October to represent the government. He held the same position under (Sir) John See and Thomas Waddell [qq.v.] in 1903-04 and remained in the council until its reconstitution in 1933.

In 1897 the unpaid volunteer component of the New South Wales Military Forces was being revived. Mackay raised the 1st Australian Horse, a regiment of cavalry recruited entirely from country districts, was appointed to command and in 1898 was promoted lieut-colonel. A composite squadron from the regiment was sent to the South African War but Mackay was too senior in rank to accompany it. Instead, resigning his portfolio, he was given command of the New South Wales Imperial Bushmen's Contingent which sailed from Sydney in April 1900. The Bushmen were sent to Rhodesia and placed under the command of Sir Frederick Carrington.

They moved to Mafeking in July and into the western Transvaal. In the next three months Mackay rode over 550 miles (885 km), lived in the open with his men and was several times under fire. It was an unhappy period in his life: he was frustrated by Carrington's poor command, he quarrelled with his brigadier, and he was deeply shocked by the death in action of his wife's young brother who was serving with him. Finally, outside Zeerust, he was injured when his horse fell. He was sent to Cape Town and in November 1900 was appointed chief staff officer for the various Australian contingents. While in South Africa he unsuccessfully stood for election to the first Australian Senate. He returned to Sydney in July 1901 and for his war service was appointed C.B., mentioned in dispatches and granted the honorary rank of colonel.

In 1906-07 Mackay was chairman of a royal commission covering the administration of Papua; its report was presented in 1907 and in 1909 his personal account *Across Papua* was published. He retained his interest in military matters and in 1912 was given command of the 1st Light Horse Brigade. As colonel he supervised its reorganization into the 3rd Light Horse Brigade. He commanded the military parade at Canberra in 1913 for the setting of the foundation stone and the naming of the capital.

Too old for active military service during World War I, he was appointed to raise an Australian Army Reserve from returned soldiers and was its first director-general from 1916. He was appointed O.B.E. in 1920. That year he retired from the Australian Military Forces with the honorary rank of major general.

Throughout his life Mackay had maintained a close interest in primary industry and the bush and its people. His own property, Wallendoon, was part of the land which his father had occupied since 1842. He was living there when admitted to Cootamundra District Hospital where he died on 16 November 1935; he was cremated. His wife and two daughters survived him.

Cyclopedia of N.S.W. (Syd, 1907); J. Stirling, *The colonials in South Africa, 1899-1902* (Edinb, 1907); Aust Defence Dept, *Official records of the Australian military contingents to the war in South Africa*, P. L. Murray ed (Melb, 1911); P. V. Vernon (ed), *The Royal New South Wales Lancers, 1885-1960* (Syd, 1961); R. L. Wallace, *The Australians at the Boer War* (Canb, 1976); L. M. Field, *The forgotten war* (Melb, 1979); *SMH*, 18 Nov 1935; Mackay family papers held by, and information from, Mrs K. Jacobs, Wallendbeen, NSW.

PETER BURNESS

MACKAY, JOHN HILTON (1877-1952), engineer and grazier, was born on 2 May 1877 at Everton, Victoria, fourth child and second son of George Edward Mackay, squatter, and his wife Jane Frances, née Howe. Educated at the University of Melbourne (B.C.E., 1901; M.C.E., 1903), Mackay won the final year exhibition in engineering and a Trinity College scholarship in 1897 and in 1899 the Dixson scholarships in civil engineering and architecture and in hydraulic engineering, mining and metallurgy. From 1899, when he joined the Victorian Institute of Engineers, until 1903, when the University of Tasmania offered him a twelve months lectureship, he was associated with L. H. Reynolds, George Higgins and the Australian Gold Dredging Co. Ltd in the design and construction of minerals and harbour dredging machinery.

On 27 June 1903 at St Peter's Church of England, Melbourne, Mackay married Fanny Mildred, daughter of a former commissioner of railways, William Henry Greene. Although reluctant to sever connexions with Higgins, with whom he was working as chief draughtsman on the Adelaide Outer Harbour works applying cutting machinery to dredging, Mackay left for Hobart in August. His lectureship was confirmed and reclassified from mining to engineering next year when the professor of mining resigned. But students were very few.

For the next sixteen years Mackay battled constantly against poor conditions, eking out his low salary by taking fees for testing plant and by practising privately in vacation. He was appointed to the chair of engineering in

1912 after being offered the directorship of the Charters Towers, Queensland, School of Mines. In 1916 he was refused leave of absence to join the army and in 1920 he resigned. The university council, on which he had sat since 1918, acknowledged that 'from small beginnings and with inadequate assistance [he] raised the School of Engineering to a worthy place among the Universities of Australia'.

Having an adventurous spirit and a love for the land Mackay, in 1906, had bought a heavily timbered property at Roger River for sawmilling. During university vacations he and his wife travelled back and forth to Mill Farm by means of a smart tandem, spending several nights *en route*. Ever busy supervising, Mackay expanded the enterprise to a chain of six sawmills. The blackwood to line Parliament House in Canberra was shipped out from his estate. In 1935 he introduced Romney Marsh and Border Leicester sheep to the property which, by the 1980s, still in the hands of the family, was reputed to have achieved one of the highest outputs per man in Australia. Mackay also had an interest in a 22 000-acre (8900 ha) Queensland property which he acquired for his son in 1925.

A tall, well-built man, always immaculately dressed, Mackay died on 5 May 1952 at Port Sorell and was buried at the Don. He was survived by his wife and son and left an estate valued for probate at £80 589.

Univ Tas Archives; family information.

C. J. GREGORY

MacKAY, WILLIAM JOHN (1885-1948), police commissioner, was born on 28 November 1885 in Glasgow, Scotland, son of Murdoch MacKay, police inspector, and his wife Isabella, née MacKay. He joined the Glasgow police in 1904 and was promoted detective constable two years later. On 2 December 1909 he married Jennie Ross Drummond in Glasgow, before migrating to Sydney; he joined the New South Wales Police Force in April 1910. His knowledge of shorthand led to his appointment in the administration section where he worked as chief clerk.

Early in World War I with Detective N. Moore [q.v.] MacKay attended meetings in the Domain of the Industrial Workers of the World to make shorthand reports to assist the prosecution of speakers. MacKay was made sergeant in 1922 and thereafter gained rapid promotion, partly as a result of the publicity he obtained in being credited with suppressing the Darlinghurst 'razor gangs'. By 1928 he was detective inspector in charge of the Criminal Investigation Branch and was sent to Britain for eight months to study police methods.

With the onset of the Depression the police became increasingly involved in political surveillance as unemployment and dissent became more widespread. MacKay was often in the forefront of such events as at Rothbury in December 1929 when police, guarding the mine, fought against locked-out miners and a young miner was shot dead. By the time the Old Guard, the New Guard and the All for Australia League had become organized to fight against J. T. Lang [q.v.9], he had inserted policemen into these groups, as well as the Communist Party of Australia. MacKay repudiated New Guard claims that its main cause of existence was to come to the aid of the police when the trade unionists and communists tried to seize power, and dealt firmly with a New Guard demonstration outside the Liverpool Street Court on 1 April 1932. The New Guard leader Eric Campbell [q.v.7] condemned MacKay for not welcoming the proffered assistance and publicly impugned him for not having enlisted during the war.

With the dismissal of Lang and the election of the new premier, (Sir) Bertram Stevens [q.v.], MacKay was instructed on 7 June 1932 to increase surveillance of the Communist Party; his officers that year produced much of the material for the Lyons [q.v.] government and its attorney-general (Sir) John Latham [q.v.] to launch proceedings to have the Communist Party declared an unlawful association under the Crimes Act. MacKay was awarded the King's Police Medal in 1932 and appointed police commissioner in 1935.

In April 1936 he again left for an eight-month tour of Britain, Germany, Italy and the United States of America. MacKay was impressed by J. Edgar Hoover and the Federal Bureau of Investigation. Even more impressed by the efficiency of the German police and the discipline of Nazi society, he praised their labour youth battalions because, he said, they 'subordinate the individual to the welfare of the nation'. On his return he established in April 1937 the first of the Police Boys' clubs and next year a federation, now known as the Federation of Police-Citizens Boys' Clubs.

By 1938 MacKay was becoming unwell under the strain of inquiries and royal commissions into matters involving illegal off-course betting and police officers, and was nearly retired because of ill health. The Police Association of New South Wales outspokenly criticized his arbitrary methods of promoting officers in the force and he turned on the association in January 1942 by posting all seventeen members of its executive to country stations. The premier, (Sir) William McKell, took over the administration of the Police Department and had the seventeen returned to their original positions. Another clash between MacKay and his force occurred over an incident on 9 January 1943 when two constables arrested a man, late at night in a public urinal, who turned out to be the editor of the *Daily Telegraph* for whom the proprietor, (Sir) Frank Packer, interceded. The two constables were dismissed from the force because of their alleged extensive arrest pattern for this type of offence although one was later reinstated after active Police Association lobbying and disgruntlement in the force.

In April 1942 MacKay had been appointed by the Curtin Federal government director of the revamped Security Service, established to work with the army to maintain surveillance of enemy aliens and communists and to issue security clearances. He had already established in 1938 a combined police and military intelligence unit in his own force. He sought to expand the Security Service, envisaging it as an F.B.I.-style organization, but offended Military Intelligence, which dominated security work, and returned to the Police Force in September. However, he continued to expand the force's work in maintaining surveillance of local communists and radicals.

During his commissionership MacKay set up the police cadet system, and the vice, drug, motor and pawnbrokers squads which all modern police forces were then establishing. Known in the force as 'Big Bill', he was 6 ft. (183 cm) tall and weighed 15 stone (95 kg): he had a reputation when young for smashing down doors. While he continued to push aside opposition to his administrative schemes he developed a more guileful style of using information in his possession to place possible opponents in his debt. He spoke with a strong Scottish accent and was proud of his ancestry. His strong ego led him to convert the police military band into a Scottish pipe band dressed in the MacKay tartan; and he established a police air wing by purchasing an obsolete and uneconomical aeroplane rather than continue to hire aircraft.

By 1946 MacKay was becoming unwell again and on 22 January 1948 he died suddenly at his Edgecliff home while entertaining senior police colleagues; he was buried in the Presbyterian section of Randwick cemetery. He was survived by his wife and son and left an estate valued for probate at £13 892.

F. Cain, *The origins of political surveillance in Australia* (Syd, 1983); *SMH*, 21 July 1928, 12 Mar 1935, 23 Sept 1936, 22 Jan 1942, 23 Jan 1948; NSW Police Dept, Special bundle, 10/1829 (NSWA); MP 72916, CRS A373 (AAO).   FRANK CAIN

MACKELLAR, SIR CHARLES KINNAIRD (1844-1926), physician, politician and businessman, was born on 5 December 1844 in Sydney, only son of Frederick MacKellar (d. 1863), physician, from Dundee, Scotland, and his wife Isabella, née Robertson, widow of William McGarvie [q.v.2]. Educated at Sydney Grammar School, Charles moved with his family to the Port Macquarie district about 1860. He spent several years on the land before proceeding to Scotland to attend the University of Glasgow (M.B., Ch.M., 1871). Returning to Sydney he registered with the Medical Board of New South Wales on 25 March 1872. In 1873-77 he was honorary surgeon at the Sydney Infirmary and Dispensary (Sydney Hospital from 1881) where his father had been first salaried medical officer; (Sir) Henry Normand MacLaurin [q.v.] also joined the staff in 1873 and cemented one of the most important friendships of Mackellar's life. He was a physician at the hospital in 1882 and a director in 1884-1903. He was also a director of Royal Prince Alfred Hospital 1886-1917. He worked 'stupendously' at general practice in early years.

In September 1881 Mackellar joined the board, led by Dr Alfred Roberts [q.v.6], which was appointed to control the first serious smallpox epidemic in New South Wales, and was gazetted as the Board of Health on 6 January 1882. In July Mackellar became government medical adviser, health officer for Port Jackson, chairman of the Immigration Board, and an official visitor to the hospitals for the insane at Gladesville and Parramatta. He was also *ex officio* emigration officer for Port Jackson, and a member of the Board of Pharmacy and the Medical Board. In July next year he campaigned for a federal quarantine system and was appointed president of the Board of Health in August. Contemporaries believed that Mackellar was solely responsible for the organization of the department but he deferred to Roberts: 'it is rather . . . that I doggedly and persistently followed his lines than that I formulated any original scheme of my own'—the Mackellar motto was *Perseverando*.

Persuaded by the attorney-general W. B. Dalley [q.v.4], a private patient, Mackellar resigned his official appointments in August 1885 and was nominated to the Legislative Council to promote public health legislation he had helped to draft, but which lapsed with the resignation of the Stuart [q.v.6] government in October. He was an ordinary member of the Board of Health until 1925. In 1886-87 as vice-president of the Executive Council and briefly secretary for mines Mackellar represented the Jennings [q.v.4] government in the Legislative Council. He introduced the Dairies Supervision Act of 1886 which helped to reduce infant mortality. Except for October-November 1903, when he was appointed to the Commonwealth Senate, he remained in the council until 1925. In 1903-

04 he chaired the royal commission on the decline of the birth-rate, dominating its proceedings in a manner uncharacteristic of his usually careful approach to scientific enquiry.

In 1882-85 Mackellar had been a member of the State Children Relief Board. In 1902-14 he was president, and was identified with the Neglected Children and Juvenile Offenders Act (1905), which created children's courts and the probationary system. He was soon at loggerheads with his under-secretary Peter Board [q.v.7], largely over the extension of the board's activities into areas not envisaged by its Act. Criticism, muted while Mackellar remained in office, became public not long after his departure.

Until at least 1912, Mackellar had been convinced that environmental factors determined the development of the young. Enquiries abroad leading to his report as royal commissioner on the *Treatment of neglected and delinquent children in Great Britain, Europe, and America* (1913) caused him to modify his views. With Professor D. A. Welsh [q.v.], he published an essay, *Mental deficiency* (1917), advocating better training and care of the feeble-minded, and suggesting their sterilization on eugenic grounds. Mackellar consistently lectured and published pamphlets to propagate social reform. He was admired for his reluctance to align himself with any political faction, and for his unselfish devotion to the public interest. Knighted in 1912, he was appointed K.C.M.G. in 1916.

On 9 August 1877 Mackellar had married Marion (d. 1933), daughter of Thomas Buckland [q.v.3]. He acquired considerable pastoral interests and in 1896 succeeded his father-in-law as a director of the Bank of New South Wales, of which he was president in 1901-23 apart from absences abroad in 1904-05 and 1912-13. Mackellar was chairman of the Gloucester Estate Co. in its later years and succeeded MacLaurin as chairman of the Mutual Life & Citizens' Assurance Co. Ltd; he had been a trustee in 1911-14. He was also a director of Pitt, Son & Badgery [qq.v. 5, 3] Ltd, the Union Trustee Co. of Australia Ltd, United Insurance Co. Ltd, Royal Insurance Co. Ltd, Colonial Sugar Refining Co., Australian Widows' Fund, and Equitable Life Assurance Co. Ltd of which he was medical director. He was surgeon in the Volunteer Rifles from 1872; chairman of the medical section of the Royal Society of New South Wales in 1881; founding councillor and in 1883-84 president of the New South Wales branch of the British Medical Association; examiner in medicine at the University of Sydney in 1889-1901; vice-president and in 1907-14 president of the Sydney Amateur Orchestral Society; inaugural vice-president of the Royal Society for the Welfare of Moth-

ers and Babies in 1918; and a member of the Australian and Athenaeum clubs, Sydney.

By 1923 Mackellar had resigned most of his business appointments as health and memory deserted him. He died at his residence, Rosemont, Woollahra, on 14 July 1926 and was buried in the Anglican section of Waverley cemetery. His estate, valued for probate at £39 205, was left in trust to his wife and upon her death in 1933 to their surviving children Eric, Malcolm and Dorothea [q.v.]. His eldest son Keith Kinnaird had been killed in action in South Africa in 1900.

Testimonials in favour of Charles K. Mackellar (Syd, 1973, copy Roy Aust College of Physicians); J. H. L. Cumpston, *The health of the people* (Canb, 1978); N. Hicks, *This sin and scandal* (Canb, 1978); *V&P* (LA, NSW), 1883, 2, p 953; *PP* (LC & LA, NSW), 1920-21, 4, p 451; *NSW Medical Gazette*, Mar 1873; *Scottish A'sian*, May 1918; *MJA*, 7 Aug 1926; *RAHSJ*, 63, no 3, Dec 1977; *SMH*, 10 Sept 1881, 12 Oct 1912, 15 July 1926; *Daily Telegraph* (Syd), 21 Apr 1888; Mackellar papers (ML).   ANN M. MITCHELL

MACKELLAR, ISOBEL MARION DOROTHEA (1885-1968), writer, was born on 1 July 1885 at Dunara, Point Piper, Sydney, third child and only daughter of native-born parents (Sir) Charles Kinnaird Mackellar [q.v.], physician, and his wife Marion, daughter of Thomas Buckland [q.v.3]. She was educated at home and travelled extensively with her parents, becoming fluent in French, Spanish, German and Italian, and also attended some lectures at the University of Sydney. Her youth was protected and highly civilized. She moved easily between the society of Sydney's intellectual and administrative elite, life on her family's country properties, and among their friends in London.

Dorothea began writing while quite young and surprised her family when magazines not only published but paid for her verses and prose pieces. On 5 September 1908 a poem, 'Core of My Heart', which she had written about 1904, appeared in the London *Spectator*. It reappeared several times in Australia before being included as 'My Country' in her first book, *The closed door, and other verses* (Melbourne, 1911). She published *The witchmaid, and other verses* in 1914 and two more volumes of verse (1923 and 1926), also a novel, *Outlaw's luck* (London, 1913), set in Argentina. With Ruth Bedford, a childhood friend, she wrote two other novels (1912, 1914). During World War I and as a result of its frequent inclusion in anthologies, 'My Country' became one of the best-known Australian poems, appealing to the sense of patriotism fostered by the war and post-war nationalism.

Photographs of Dorothea in her twenties

show her to have been then an ideal image of the Australian girl, pretty, sensitive, and fashionable. She was said to be a strong swimmer, a keen judge of horses and dogs. Her verse shows that she was cultivated and spirited, her novels that she was hopelessly romantic. Between 1911 and 1914 she was twice engaged. The first engagement she broke because the man was over-protective; the second lapsed through misunderstanding and lack of communication after the outbreak of war. Her writing, once the product of youthful passions and enthusiasms, became increasingly souvenirs of travel or dependent on Nature for inspiration. She was unable to write of her disappointment in love except in powerful translations from little-known Spanish and German poets.

Despite her 'loathing *all* restrictions and meetings', Dorothea Mackellar was honorary treasurer of the Bush Book Club of New South Wales and active in the formation in 1931 of the Sydney P.E.N. Club. She became responsible for her ageing parents, and apparently wrote little after her father's death in 1926. Her mother died in 1933 and Dorothea, 'a not particularly robust dormouse', was frequently in poor health, spending ten years in a Randwick nursing home. Yet she outlived her younger brothers and was able to keep both Cintra, Darling Point, and a house at Church Point on Pittwater. She was appointed O.B.E. just before she died on 14 January 1968 in the Scottish Hospital, Paddington, after a fall at home. She was cremated after a service at St Mark's Anglican Church, Darling Point, and her ashes laid in the family vault in Waverley cemetery. Her estate was valued for probate at over $1 580 000.

H. M. Green describes her as a 'lyrist of colour and light' in love with the Australian landscape. She herself 'never professed to be a poet. I have written—from the heart, from imagination, from experience—some amount of verse'. Privileged and unusual, she was also typical of many Australian women of her generation in the contrast between the inspired vigour of her youth and the atrophy of her talent and vitality through lack of use.

A. Matzenik, 'Dorothea Mackellar. A memoir', in *The poems of Dorothea Mackellar* (Adel, 1971); *Aussie*, 42 (Aug 1922), p 37; *Spinner*, vol 1, no 9 (June 1925), p 143; *Aust Woman's Mirror*, 1 Nov 1927, p 11, 54; *Sth Australiana*, 8, no 1 (1969), p 11; P. O'Harris, Notes on Dorothea Mackellar (MS) *and* John Le Gay Brereton papers (ML); G. Mackaness collection (NL).   BEVERLEY KINGSTON

McKELLAR, JOHN ALEXANDER ROSS (1904-1932), poet, was born on 9 December 1904 at Dulwich Hill, Sydney, son of Neil Cal-

man McKellar, Victorian-born stock, station and land agent, and his wife Valentine Irene, née Machattie, from Bathurst. He was intensely proud of his parents' Highland origins and later developed Jacobite sympathies. Educated at Sydney Boys' High School, he surprisingly did not learn an ancient language.

In 1920 McKellar joined the Bank of New South Wales and took to banking with the same zest and application that he did everything. Promoted to head office in 1930, he worked on the amalgamation with the Australian Bank of Commerce. He was an ardent cricketer and Rugby footballer, captaining a successful Randwick reserve grade fifteen in 1929 and playing with the firsts next year. He also coached Sydney High's crews.

Throughout the 1920s he read omnivorously. While the Jacobean and Caroline dramatists and poets and the later eighteenth-century novelists were his English favourites, and the Roman satirists and the Greek anthology were his classical choice, his interest in French literature was catholic and deep. His poetic development was rapid. Early imitations of Housman changed to a distinctive style in his three poems in the *New Triad* in 1928. He met Hugh McCrae [q.v.] and began to impress his fellow craftsmen. When Frank Johnson began the Jacaranda Tree series of Australian poets, McKellar wrote the introduction, stressing the continuity of local poetry with overseas tradition. He helped to edit Kenneth Slessor's contribution with (as the author admitted) salutary effect. For all his enthusiasms, McKellar was a realist and a practical critic. His own volume, *Twenty-six*, appeared as the first in the series early in 1932. 'It must not be presumed that because this poet is young he has little to say or little skill in self-expression', said the *Sydney Morning Herald* reviewer.

McKellar was working on 'The fourth Napoleon', his most ambitious venture, when, unmarried, he died on 8 March 1932 of pulmonary embolism and pneumonia at Mosman; he was cremated with Anglican rites. Many of his new poems were published by *Southerly* in 1944, with a perceptive memoir by J. W. Gibbes. In 1946 his *Collected Poems* finally appeared.

McKellar was an attractive, many-sided man. His poetic form was conventional but his imagery and turn of phrase could be strikingly original. Like other Australian poets of his generation, he often tried to relate the European heritage to Australia, not only the Rome of Petronius or the France of Voltaire, but also his boyhood memories of Anzac and of Australia at war. With these he joined a lively perception, as in 'Pigeons in the City' and 'Oxford Street—The Five Ways', of the urban present. H. M. Green, whose radio broadcast in 1942 began renewed interest in McKellar's work, later asserted that 'the four leading intellectual poets [Hope, McAuley, Slessor and FitzGerald] might have been five but for the cutting short of one of the most promising of all Australian youthful poetic talents'.

Meanjin Q, 1, no 11, 1942; *Southerly*, 5, no 4, 1944; Univ Syd Union, *Union Recorder*, 7 June 1945. K. J. CABLE

McKELVEY, SIR JOHN LAWRANCE (1881-1939), surgeon, was born on 9 February 1881 at Ravenswood, Queensland, second child of John Lawrance McKelvey, hotelkeeper, and his wife Catherine Ellen, née Kerfoot, both Irish born. Educated at Townsville Grammar School, he resided at St John's College while studying arts in 1899, then medicine at the University of Sydney (M.B., 1905; Ch.M., 1911). He was resident medical officer at Royal Prince Alfred Hospital in 1905, becoming acting medical superintendent in 1906; next year he was demonstrator in anatomy at the university. He spent 1908 as medical superintendent at (Royal) Melbourne Hospital before returning in 1909 to the same position at Royal Prince Alfred.

McKelvey was appointed an honorary assistant surgeon there when he went into private practice in 1911, and at St Vincent's Hospital in 1913. At St Patrick's, Church Hill, on 8 January that year he married Jane Trigg Lane, adopted daughter of Dr R. H. Treloar and somewhat publicized as 'a beauty' in the newspaper columns; their only child died in infancy.

By the early 1920s McKelvey was an honorary surgeon at Royal Prince Alfred and St Vincent's hospitals and a consultant at South Sydney Women's and Canterbury District Memorial hospitals. He succeeded to a considerable practice from Sir Herbert Maitland [q.v.] in 1923 and was generally regarded as a skilful and deft operator who modelled himself on Sir Alexander MacCormick [q.v.], but he published little, lacked originality and made no contributions to surgical progress. Surgical tutor for ten years, he lectured in clinical surgery at the university from 1926 and was an entertaining teacher, a good raconteur and enjoyed the company of willing listeners. A foundation fellow in 1927, McKelvey became a council-member in 1937 and a vice-president in 1939 of the Royal Australasian College of Surgeons. He served on the New South Wales Post-Graduate Committee in Medicine and the advisory council of Prince Henry Hospital and was a fellow of St John's College. Knighted in 1933, he was a well-known and forceful figure in the medical

world at a time when the profession had recognized leaders.

Although McKelvey liked to use classical references and had a very good memory, he was not deeply learned. He had many admirers and sycophants, but also many detractors. He was of medium build, thickset, with a square jaw and had a rather determined expression except for a charming smile, reserved for children and a few friends. Despite his professional success, his way of life was simple; he was charitable to patients and uninterested in making money. He belonged to the university club, and enjoyed music, golf, fishing and above all racing. He was a member of the Australian Jockey Club from 1918 and was elected to its committee in 1938. Knowledgeable about thoroughbred breeding, in 1938 he had the rare experience of winning at the first attempt with his first racehorse, Marengo.

Early in 1939 McKelvey suffered a severe stroke, becoming hemiplegic and aphasic; he died of heart disease at his home at Potts Point on 7 July 1939 and, after a service at St Mary's Cathedral, was buried in South Head cemetery. His wife survived him, and inherited his estate, valued for probate at £17 947.

MJA, 2 Sept 1939; *SMH*, 2 Jan 1933, 25 Apr 1938, 8 July 1939. DOUGLAS MILLER

McKENNA, BERNARD (JOSEPH) (1870-1937), educationist, was born on 6 June 1870 at Warwick, Queensland, son of Patrick McKenna, labourer and later farmer, and his wife Ellen, née Minton, both Irish. 'Barney' enrolled, about 1876, at Warwick West State School under head-teacher J. A. Canny, and in 1884 he began four years pupil-teacher training at Allora State School under head-teacher C. L. Fox; both Canny and Fox became district inspectors. On 5 July 1894 McKenna married Edith Kezia Warwick in the Baptist Tabernacle, Brisbane.

While he was teacher and head-teacher at six south-east Queensland schools in 1889-1908, his teaching aptitude and excellent early training bore fruit and inspectors described him as industrious, skilful and progressive. He easily accommodated to the utilitarian, child-centred 'New Education' trends in the 1900s. Following service as head-teacher at Enoggera (1909-10) and Sandgate (1911-13) in Brisbane, he became district inspector (1914-21) in north and central Queensland, where his sympathy for the isolated deepened his conviction of the need for a utilitarian (especially rural) orientation in education. In 1917 he travelled some 10 000 miles (16 000 km) and inspected 109 schools. McKenna became the Department of

Public Instruction's acting chief inspector (January 1922) and acting under secretary (January 1923).

McKenna's choice as under secretary (April 1923) was judicious. Conscientious, determined and basically progressive, but not an original thinker and still less a rebel, he could be trusted to extend the initiatives of J. D. Story [q.v.], a close friend and former under secretary, who retained a powerful influence on education. In common with Story, and the then Labor governments, his educational philosophy emphasized egalitarianism, utilitarianism and agrarianism. He saw good (socially efficient) citizens as the basic goal of education, but recognized equal opportunities for individuals of all aptitudes and skills, and responsiveness to current socio-economic needs, as prerequisites. Consequently, he attacked excessively academic syllabuses which disadvantaged 'different' children and obscured the basic socio-economic need, highlighted by the 1930s Depression, for 'a sturdy and intelligent rural peasantry'.

This philosophy permeated the initiatives personally associated with McKenna—the Primary Correspondence School (1922), intermediate schools (introduced in 1928 as a cautious step in reorganizing post-primary education) and, together with L. D. Edwards [q.v.8], the new primary syllabus (1930). Additionally, he extended his predecessor's initiatives, including vocational railway schools, rural schools, the home project club scheme, opportunity schools and reorganization of the Gatton Agricultural College. Departmental medical services, especially ophthalmic services for rural children, were another special interest. A full-time ophthalmic surgeon was appointed in 1927 and Wilson Ophthalmic Hostel for bush children opened in 1929.

Under McKenna the education system remained centralized and authoritarian, largely untempered by personal warmth from the system's head. A big man with large, strong features, he had a stern, sometimes abrupt, administrative style. He demanded loyalty and could be obstinate and defensive, equating criticism with disloyalty and dismissing outside criticism as interference. Though he regularly attended conferences of State directors of education, and accepted the Australian Council for Educational Research established in 1930, his attitude to such groups was guarded. This parochialism was highlighted in 1936 in his opposition to the planned New Education Fellowship conference.

McKenna retired officially on 31 December 1936, but was retained to rewrite syllabuses and associated textbooks for primary, intermediate and rural schools. This task was incomplete at his death at Eagle Junction, following a stroke, on 2 June 1937. Survived by his wife and two sons, he was buried in Toowong cemetery with Presbyterian forms.

Men of Queensland (Brisb, 1929); Secretary for Public Instruction, *Annual Report*, 1914, 1921, 1923, 1933; *Courier Mail*, 9 Oct, 9, 31 Dec 1936, 3 June 1937; *Telegraph* (Brisb), 9 Oct 1936, 2 June 1937; B. J. McKenna staff card (Dept of Education Archives, Brisb); Register of teachers, *and* St Helen's State School file, *and* Public Service Bd, Staff file no 2629 (QA); information from Mr B. J. McKenna, Hamilton, Brisb.   G. N. LOGAN

MACKENNAL, SIR EDGAR BERTRAM (1863-1931), sculptor, was born on 12 June 1863 at Fitzroy, Melbourne, second son of John Simpson Mackennal (1832-1901) and his wife Annabella, née Hyde, both Scottish. He was educated at the Melbourne Model School and King's College. His initial training was undertaken by his father, a locally prominent architectural modeller and sculptor, and was reinforced by studies at the National Gallery School of Design under O. R. Campbell [q.v.3] from 1878.

Advised in 1881 to study in Europe and promised employment by the visiting English sculptor Marshall Wood, Mackennal left Australia in 1882. Upon arrival in England he found that Wood had died. Mackennal then shared a studio with student friends Charles Douglas Richardson and Tom Roberts [qq.v.]. Disillusioned after a few months instruction at the Royal Academy of Arts schools, he went to Paris where he obtained tuition by visiting the studios of artists and sculptors. Securing a commission for a bust of a British army officer in 1884, Mackennal returned to London where he married Agnes Spooner. They then visited Italy and returned to Paris. In extreme poverty, early in 1886 Mackennal was appointed head of modelling and design at the Coalport Potteries, Shropshire. His relief, 'The Five Foolish Virgins', was accepted that year for the Royal Academy's summer exhibition.

Commissioned to design the relief panels on the façade of Parliament House, Melbourne, Mackennal returned and set up a studio in Swanston Street where, as Arthur Streeton [q.v.] recalled, on the last Friday of each month he entertained at his Bohemian supper-table two or three favourite guests. Despite commissions (1888) for the spandrels of the Mercantile Chambers, Collins Street, and some for busts, he lacked sufficient clients. When his model for the monumental group 'The Triumph of Truth' only received second prize (the first prize was not awarded) in a National Gallery competition, Mackennal, following the advice of the visiting Sarah

Bernhardt and obtaining a loan from Frank Stuart [q.v.], returned to Paris in 1891.

In 1892 he exhibited two sculptures at the Old Salon and next year his life-size figure 'Circe' was awarded an honourable mention. In need of funds, in 1893 he briefly became an assistant to the Scottish sculptor William Birnie Rhind in Edinburgh. However, at the 1894 Royal Academy summer exhibition 'Circe', with its pedestal concealed for the sake of modesty, caused enough of a stir to make his name. Another major sculpture in the Symbolist style, 'For she Sitteth on a Seat in the High Places of the City' (sometimes called 'Rahab'), exhibited at the Royal Academy in 1895, confirmed his position in London as an important young sculptor. Private commissions were followed by others from public bodies for statues of Queen Victoria in England, India and Australia. In 1900, when Mackennal visited Victoria to supervise the installation at Ballarat of his statue of the Queen, he failed to gain the commission for Melbourne's royal monument. In 1901 he was involved in another skirmish with the trustees of the National Gallery over their offer for the full-size bronze cast of 'Circe', eventually sold to Carl Pinschof [q.v.] but later bought for the gallery.

In 1907 Mackennal's marble group, 'The Earth and the Elements', and in 1908 his 'Diana Wounded' were bought by the Chantrey bequest and placed in the Tate Gallery, London. He produced the medals for the Olympic Games held in London in 1908 and next year was elected an associate of the Royal Academy. In 1910 he designed the coronation medal, the currency, postage stamps and military honours for King George V and received the commission for the tomb of King Edward VII, St George's Chapel, Windsor. He produced commemorative monuments for Melbourne and Adelaide, as well as an equestrian statue of Edward VII for London and two marble statues of George V for India. Mackennal was appointed M.V.O. in 1912 and knighted in 1921—the first Australian-born artist to be so honoured. In 1922 he was elected R.A.

His bronze pedimental group, 'Phoebus Driving the Horses of the Sun' for Australia House, London, was erected in 1923. In 1926 he visited Australia and New Zealand, exhibiting at Macquarie Galleries, Sydney, in October. His proposal for a sailor's memorial on the Sow and Pigs Rocks, Sydney Harbour, was rejected, but he was offered a commission for the Cenotaph, Martin Place. On his return to England he continued his usual strenuous production schedule with monumental figures of Cardinal Moran [q.v.] and Archbishop Kelly [q.v.9] for St Mary's Cathedral, Sydney, and the Cenotaph figures, along with the Lord Curzon memorial monu-

ment and a design for the Port Said War Memorial.

Sir Bertram Mackennal died suddenly on 10 October 1931 from rupture of abdominal aneurysm and was buried in Torquay cemetery, Devon. His wife and daughter survived him. In 1933 the Royal Academy honoured Mackennal and George Lambert [q.v.9] with a retrospective exhibition.

Mackennal was strongly built, slightly above medium height, with blue eyes. Edmund Fisher was reminded of 'a fighting curate', observing that 'Mackennal has the strong artistic brain in the hard, business head'. Although he was seen as a conservative academic sculptor by London art circles in the late 1920s, in the 1890s his Symbolist-style sculpture, influenced by Auguste Rodin, was thought to be extremely 'French' and very advanced. Mackennal's work is widely represented in British and Australian collections.

M. Spielmann, *British sculpture and sculptors of today* (Lond, 1901); L. Taft, *Modern techniques in sculpture: Scammon lectures for 1917* (Chicago, 1921); W. K. Parkes, *Sculpture of today*, 11 (Lond, 1921); *DNB*, 1931-40; N. Hutchison, *Bertram Mackennal* (Melb, 1973); G. Sturgeon, *The development of Australian sculpture 1788-1975* (Lond, 1978); K. Scarlett, *Australian sculptors* (Melb, 1980); S. Beattie, *The new sculpture* (New Haven, Connect, 1983); *Bulletin*, 13 Apr 1901; *Argus* and *The Times*, 13 Oct 1931; *Herald* (Melb), 12 Oct 1931; *Age*, 8 Apr 1933; family information.

                                    NOEL S. HUTCHISON

McKENZIE, HUGH (1853-1942), politician and stock and station agent, was born on 13 December 1853 at Rogart, Sutherlandshire, Scotland, elder son of John McKenzie, game warden, and his wife Elizabeth, née Clark. He came to South Australia in 1855 when his father was appointed manager of Glencoe station in the Mount Gambier district; the family moved to (Sir) James MacBain's [q.v.5] Wyuna station, near Kyabram, Victoria, in 1865.

Educated at the Murchison local school and Scotch College, Melbourne, Hugh was an overseer at Wyuna from 1869 until the early 1870s. In 1877, with Laurence Kickham, he opened a profitable general store at Undera, south-east of Echuca, on land he had earlier selected with his father. McKenzie was a staunch Presbyterian but on 15 January 1878 at Echuca he married a Catholic, Margaret Jane Mitchell; their six children were raised as Catholics. Following his marriage McKenzie opened a livery stable at Echuca with his brother-in-law Edward Mitchell, but he soon joined J. M. Chanter [q.v.7] in a stock and station agency. The Murray River Stock Station & Agency Co., formed by a merger in 1889, was forced into liquidation in 1892, but

McKenzie, undaunted, immediately joined the Echuca auctioneer, Thomas Copp, to form the Echuca stock and station agency, McKenzie & Co. He, and later his sons, managed the business until its acquisition by Younghusband Ltd in 1939.

McKenzie's political life began in 1882 when he joined the Echuca Borough Council; he served fourteen years as councillor, with two terms as mayor (1883-84, 1903-04). In 1904 he won the Legislative Assembly seat of Rodney as a Liberal and represented the electorate (usually polling about 70 per cent of the Echuca vote) until his defeat by the Victorian Farmers' Union candidate John Allan [q.v.7] in 1917. He was president of the Board of Lands and Works and commissioner of crown lands and survey in the Murray and the Watt [qq.v.] governments (1909-13) and minister of railways and of water supply and vice-president of the Board of Lands and Works in 1915-17 under Peacock [q.v.].

McKenzie was important in developing closer settlement policy. In May 1910 he headed an overseas mission in an attempt to attract 6000 settlers skilled in irrigation. Ironically, his defeat in November 1917 was largely caused by his steadfast support for the controversial clause 69 of the Closer Settlement Act (1912) which made title to the land conditional upon residence. In Echuca, however, it was widely considered that he had revealed 'true greatness' by sacrificing 'place and position for a principle'.

McKenzie's involvement in community affairs included membership of the Farmers & Citizens Trustee Co., Bendigo, the Echuca Agricultural Society, the board of management of the Echuca Presbyterian Church and the technical college council. A justice of the peace, he founded the Echuca branch of the Australian Natives' Association in 1886 and was a captain in the Echuca volunteer militia. He also served terms as president of the Echuca Gentlemen's Club, Fathers' Association and Hospital Board and as chief of the Caledonian Society.

A tall, distinguished-looking man, McKenzie was noted for his 'kindly, sympathetic and understanding nature'. When he died at Echuca on 4 August 1942 the town hall flag was flown at half mast while the town mourned the passing of its 'Grand Old Man'. Survived by three sons and a daughter, he was buried in Echuca cemetery.

L. G. Houston, *Ministers of water supply in Victoria* (Melb, 1965); S. Priestley, *Echuca, a centenary history* (Brisb, 1965); *PD* (Vic), 1912, p 3136; *Riverine Herald*, 3 Oct 1916, 7 Aug 1922, 12 Nov 1924, 22 July 1940, 5, 6, 12 Aug, 11 Sept 1942; *Argus*, 5 Aug 1942; A. M. Rolfe, Echuca in the twentieth century: aspects of its social history (M.A. thesis, Univ Melb, 1979).

AMANDA M. ROLFE

MACKENZIE, RODERICK (1891-1961), sailor and soldier, was born on 28 January 1891 at Applecross, Ross, Scotland, son of Roderick Mackenzie, merchant seaman, and his wife Catherine, née Kennedy. After serving in the British Army (Territorials) he migrated to Australia and enlisted as a private in the Australian Imperial Force at Liverpool, New South Wales, on 22 June 1915 with reinforcements for the 18th Battalion; he was a sailor at the time of enlistment. He joined his unit at Gallipoli on 11 October and served there until the evacuation.

On 23 March 1916 Mackenzie was promoted lance corporal and two days later his unit reached France; he was wounded at Pozières on 1 August. After a period with the 5th Training Battalion he rejoined the 18th Battalion on 5 August 1917 with the rank of corporal. Chosen as a leading battalion in the battle of Menin Road, the first of a series of heavy assaults towards Passchendaele, the 18th commenced the advance at dawn on 20 September. During the assault Mackenzie dashed forward to keep his men close to the creeping barrage. He captured several shell-hole outposts before the battalion reached its final objective, and during the period of consolidation 'showed absolute disregard for his personal safety' as he helped in the laying out and construction of defences. He took out several patrols, gaining information and bringing in wounded, often under heavy machine-gun and sniper fire. For outstanding bravery and leadership which did much to maintain the morale of his men under heavy shell-fire, he was awarded the Distinguished Conduct Medal. He was promoted sergeant on 30 September.

The 18th Battalion fought in the battles of Amiens and Mont St Quentin before the battle of the Hindenburg line in October 1918, the action in which Mackenzie, promoted to company sergeant major on 4 April, was to win a Bar to his D.C.M. The 18th was on the right of the 2nd Division in a major assault planned to capture German positions on 3 October. The wire of the Beaurevoir line across the battalion's front was found to be extremely thick, averaging six belts in depth: the whole was raked with machine-gun fire. Mackenzie's company commander and two officers were early casualties. Under heavy fire Mackenzie cut a path through the wire and led his platoon through the gap. With other companies unable to advance, he was the first to reach the objective where he personally directed the mopping-up and consolidation. When all the battalion objectives were taken he organized a small party and rushed a pill-box where he bayoneted two enemy and captured the remaining four. His exemplary performance earned him his Bar.

Mackenzie embarked for return to Australia on 3 April 1919 and was discharged in Sydney on 25 July. On 4 February 1928, describing himself as a sailor, he married Jemima Wilson, a tailoress, at Randwick. Survived by his wife, a son and a daughter, he died on 2 December 1961 at the Repatriation Hospital, Concord, and was cremated with Presbyterian forms.

C. E. W. Bean, *The story of Anzac*, 2 (Syd, 1924), and *The A.I.F. in France*, 1918, 5, 6 (Syd, 1937, 1942); *London Gazette*, 16 Nov 1917, 11 Mar 1919; War diary, 18th Battalion, AIF (AWM).

I. G. McNEILL

MacKENZIE, SEAFORTH SIMPSON (1883-1955), public servant, was born on 9 August 1883 at Timaru, New Zealand, son of Scottish parents Eneas Simpson Mackenzie, clerk, and his wife Jennie Hogg, née Purves. He was educated at Timaru High School and Victoria University College, Wellington (LL.B., 1905), winning the Macmillan-Brown prize for original literary work. He joined the legal department of the Public Trust Office. On 28 February 1905 he was admitted as a solicitor and on 29 July 1907 as a barrister. At the end of 1909 he moved to Melbourne and for two years was editor of the monthly *Southern Sphere*; his poems appeared there as well as in anthologies such as *New Zealand Verse* (London, 1906). On 4 May 1912 he married Joyce Delbridge at the Presbyterian manse, Warrnambool. In February 1914 he joined the Commonwealth Attorney-General's Department as a clerk in the professional division.

On 16 March 1915 Mackenzie, who had a knowledge of German, was commissioned with the rank of major in the Australian Naval and Military Expeditionary Force to relieve the assistant judge-advocate-general in German New Guinea. On 3 April he took up duty at Rabaul as deputy judge-advocate-general and legal adviser to the administrator, Colonel S. A. Pethebridge [q.v.]. Mackenzie lost no time in translating into English the German ordinances, which continued in force. As civil judge he was also registrar-general, registrar of land titles and registrar of births, deaths and marriages. He had no trained counsel in court. Moreover the district officers, who functioned as magistrates, were without legal training. Mackenzie had no legal assistance until a crown law officer was appointed at the end of 1915 and took over the Department of Justice.

He took the terms of capitulation to their logical conclusion when he recommended the granting of freehold land titles to which the German administration had been committed. Pethebridge would not agree. Mackenzie also drew up a scheme to grant freehold land to Australian settlers as a means of establishing British interests before the end of the war. Pethebridge again dissented, contending that this was beyond the rights of the occupying power. Mackenzie was promoted brevet lieut-colonel on 1 July 1916; his rank was made substantive on 1 January 1918. He had made a success of his appointment; German businessmen had no hesitation in taking their litigation to the Central Court.

When the ailing Pethebridge left Rabaul, he named the judge as his successor and in January 1918 Mackenzie was appointed acting administrator. He instituted a Department of Agriculture and appointed its first director. To encourage the villagers to make copra, he tried to prevent purchase of their coconuts. Trading regulations to the Gazelle Peninsula and the Duke of York Islands were reapplied. In a submission to Melbourne he made another unsuccessful attempt to provide for Australian settlers on small freehold plantations. Otherwise he conformed to Pethebridge's established policies. When the new administrator Brigadier General G. J. Johnston [q.v.9] arrived at Rabaul on 21 April 1918, Mackenzie resumed his duties as legal adviser and was appointed judge of appeal.

In January 1921 he returned to the Attorney-General's Department, Melbourne, as legal assistant and in June 1922 was appointed principal registrar of the High Court of Australia. From 1921 he worked also on volume X of the official war history, *The Australians at Rabaul* (1927). C. E. W. Bean [q.v.7] had difficulty in extracting his drafts, but the eventual volume was a substantial study.

In 1926 Mackenzie had purchased three over-valued, expropriated coconut plantations in the Mandated Territory, borrowing heavily for the deposit. By 1932, with eight court judgments for debt against him, he owed £19 000 to the Commonwealth for the plantations and another £7000 for money lent and accumulated losses. On 28 August 1936 he appeared in court in Melbourne on charges of forging and uttering seals of the High Court in his custody. At his trial he averred that his interests tended towards literature and that he had never been a businessman. He was convicted and sentenced to four and a half years imprisonment; his appeal was dismissed. He was released in February 1940. Divorced by his wife in 1937, he married Mary Elizabeth Hanna on 27 October 1944. Survived by his wife and three sons and two daughters of his first marriage, Mackenzie died in Melbourne on 20 October 1955 and was cremated.

In his prime Mackenzie was described as suave with an engaging manner; others found him flamboyant. He evidently had a good deal of charm. His performance as judge in New Guinea, considering his almost entire lack of experience, had been creditable, and he was an adequate acting administrator.

M. P. Hansen and D. McLachlan, *An Austral garden* (Melb, 1912); *Report by the Minister of State for Defence on the military occupation of the German New Guinea possessions* (Melb, 1921); C. D. Rowley, *The Australians in German New Guinea, 1914-1921* (Melb, 1958); *Smith's Weekly* (Syd), 11 June 1932; *Age*, 4, 5, 9, 26, 29, 30 Sept, 1 Oct 1936.   RONALD McNICOLL

McKENZIE, WILLIAM (1869-1947), Salvation Army officer and military chaplain, was born on 20 December 1869 at Biggar, Lanarkshire, Scotland, eldest of seven sons of Donald McKenzie, ploughman, and his wife Agnes, née Callan. He claimed to have been brought up on 'porridge, the shorter catechism and plenty of lickings' but his parents, strict Presbyterians, probably provided for his education. In 1884 the family migrated to Queensland. His father purchased a sugarcane farm near Bundaberg and prospered, employing all his sons and Melanesians as well. McKenzie loved the outdoor life and worked as a jackeroo and on a dairy farm, intending to go on the land. In 1887, however, he attended a Salvation Army meeting and found the practical Christianity on display much to his liking. In 1889, following study at the training college in Melbourne, McKenzie became a commissioned officer. His first posting was to Newcastle, New South Wales—'a tough place', he described it. The Salvation creed 'meant giving up things— drink, tobacco and much else—and facing scorn and derision . . . it meant living with the lowest and the worst; it meant fighting with the devil himself for the souls of men . . . I said to myself "Here's the true religion for a fighting man" '.

McKenzie was posted throughout Australia, marrying Annie Dorothy Hoepper, a fellow Salvationist, at Horsham, Victoria, on 21 June 1899. In 1914 he was Australian delegate to the World Congress of the Salvation Army in London. On the outbreak of war McKenzie applied for a chaplaincy immediately and was selected. He joined the Australian Imperial Force on 25 September 1914, was attached to the 4th Battalion, and sailed on 20 October.

McKenzie soon made his presence felt on the transport. He was a very big man with a big voice to match. He conducted the usual church parades but also organized concerts and sports. Unlike many chaplains he participated in the men's recreations, taking particular delight in the boxing contests. His long reach, jarring upper-cuts and dangerous half-hooks left some of the A.I.F.'s best fighters dazed.

At Mena Camp, Egypt, McKenzie worked hard to improve physical conditions and was diligent in the provision of 'comforts'. The legend sprang up that, incensed that the venereal diseases camp had taken on the appearance of a prison, he helped the men to pull down the barbed-wire fence. This is unlikely because in his diary McKenzie shows a distinct lack of sympathy for venereal sufferers. His earliest A.I.F. nicknames were 'Holy Joe', 'Salvation Joe', then 'Padre Mac', but he was soon to become famous as 'Fighting Mac'.

McKenzie was one of the first chaplains ashore at Gallipoli; he lumped stretchers and carried water for months on end as well as tending the wounded and burying the dead. Observing that water carriers had difficulties on part of the track, he spent most of a night cutting out a series of steps. McKenzie enjoyed the company of all types of Australians and, with a relaxed manner and broad sense of humour, encouraged men to talk freely to him. Many other chaplains seemed comparatively aloof and rigid in their views. As one soldier remarked: 'I'm not religious, but your damned religion'll do me every damned time'.

'Fighting Mac' soon became renowned as a soldier as well as a chaplain. These stories may well have been exaggerated for chaplains were prevented by their calling from joining in the fight. Unlike John Fahey [q.v.8], another reputed soldier-chaplain, McKenzie did not deny these stories. Reports abound that he led charges at Gallipoli, often armed only with a shovel.

In France and Belgium he continued to live in the front line with the troops. He was at Pozières, Bullecourt, Mouquet Farm, Polygon Wood and Passchendaele. With the men he endured that terrible 1916-17 winter on the Somme and tried to help with coffee stalls and other comforts. By this time McKenzie had become famous, both in the A.I.F. and at home. He had lost five stone (32 kg) at Gallipoli but not his enthusiasm and certainly not his powerful singing voice. He was forever writing songs; one, 'Goodbye Cairo!', became the battalion's rallying cry.

In late 1917 McKenzie was released from active service, his health shattered, not surprising for a man of 48. He had been awarded a Military Cross in June 1916 for 'distinguished services in the field', and it was rumoured that he had three times been recommended for the Victoria Cross. He was farewelled officially from the battalion—a most unusual gesture.

7000 people crowded Melbourne's Exhibition Building to greet him on his return early in 1918; other welcomes followed in every State. But the war had profoundly affected him. He said he was 'completely unstrung and unnerved—I had seen so many fine chaps killed . . . I had buried so many, too—that I had to ask myself again and again, is it worthwhile living?'

Even after the war's end McKenzie remained famous and much in demand. He resumed Salvation Army work in several States until in 1926 he took charge of the Salvationists' work in North China. He spent more than three years in China and 'lost his heart to the country'. Again, practical Christianity dominated his approach during an appalling four-year drought with millions dying of starvation. McKenzie returned to Australia with some reluctance in 1930.

The Salvation Army promoted him to command of the 'southern territory' (Victoria, Tasmania, South Australia and Western Australia), 1930-32, then as commissioner to command of the 'eastern territory' (New South Wales and Queensland), 1932-39. He was appointed O.B.E. in 1935.

McKenzie, the most famous man in the A.I.F., as some dubbed him, was prominent in Anzac day celebrations in Sydney from 1933. With W. M. Hughes [q.v.9], he was the man every digger wanted to greet.

On 1 March 1939 McKenzie retired from active work and was farewelled quietly in accordance with his wish. He died on 26 July 1947 in Sydney, survived by his wife, three sons and daughter, a Salvationist medical missionary in Rhodesia, and was buried in Rookwood cemetery.

'Lieut-Col' Bond, *The army that went with the boys* (Melb, 1919); *London Gazette*, 2, 3 June supp 1916; *Reveille* (Syd), 1 Mar 1933; Journal of Chaplain Major William McKenzie MC, 4th Battalion, AIF *and* newspaper cuttings file (AWM); information from Dr M. Mortimer, Claremont, WA.

MICHAEL McKERNAN

MacKENZIE, SIR WILLIAM COLIN (1877-1938), orthopaedist, comparative anatomist and philanthropist, was born on 9 March 1877 at Kilmore, Victoria, youngest of six children of John McKenzie, draper, and his wife Anne, née McKay, both Scottish born. His formal education began at Kilmore State School and was continued, thanks to a three-year scholarship, at Scotch College, Melbourne, from which he qualified for matriculation, with honours in Greek, in December 1893. He entered the medical school at the University of Melbourne next year and graduated M.B. in December 1898, obtaining first-class honours in surgery, obstetric medicine and diseases of women and children in February 1899. (He did not take out his B.S. degree until 1902.)

A year as resident surgeon at the (Royal) Melbourne Hospital was followed by two years as senior resident surgeon at the (Royal) Children's Hospital during which he obtained his M.D. (1901, by examination) and began publishing in professional journals. At the Children's he came under the influence of Peter Bennie, who was well known for his management of the tuberculous hip-joint, and whom he greatly admired. He then went into general practice at the Hay Market, conveniently close to the university and the Melbourne and Children's hospitals. He was also in 1902 appointed honorary demonstrator in anatomy at the university, thereby beginning a long association with the department of anatomy, later as senior demonstrator and lecturer in applied anatomy.

In 1903 MacKenzie went to Europe for further study. He sat the examinations for the Royal College of Surgeons, Edinburgh, in October and was elected fellow on 15 December 1903, having been proposed by Richard Berry [q.v.7], then lecturer in anatomy at the college, later to be his professor at the University of Melbourne. He also visited two outstanding orthopaedic centres to study their methods; one, headed by O. Vulpius, at Heidelberg, Germany, and the other by Robert Jones, at Liverpool, England. This interest in orthopaedics was possibly connected with the severe epidemic of poliomyelitis which had broken out in Australia, beginning in Sydney in the summer of 1903-04 and spreading widely over four States.

When MacKenzie returned to Melbourne many people in need of orthopaedic skills became his patients, and the number was increased by a further extensive epidemic in 1908. He developed a systematic method of treatment which as a whole was his own, although its major elements were due, as he acknowledged, mainly to H. O. Thomas, Jones, Bennie and Vulpius. The treatment was published, as he developed it, in his journal articles, and in the pamphlet, circulated within the profession at home and abroad, *The treatment of infantile paralysis: a study on muscular action and muscle regeneration* (Melbourne, 1910). His methods were simple and today are common practice, but at that time were novel and controversial. By their means he was able to promote optimum use of the remaining muscle power, to prevent much deformity, and even to improve longstanding cases which had not had early treatment by his methods. His concern for his patients and their families is evident in his writings. Eventually, he moved to Collins Street as an orthopaedic consultant.

During World War I MacKenzie spent three years in England (1915-17) at the Royal College of Surgeons, where he assisted (Sir) Arthur Keith to catalogue specimens of war wounds for the army and to bring out a new edition of Treves's *Surgical applied anatomy*. At the same time he continued research begun in Melbourne on the comparative anatomy of Australian fauna, using specimens he had brought with him. In 1917 he had a chance to test his principles of muscle rest and re-education on patients of a different kind, when Robert Jones, now inspector of military orthopaedics, asked him to set up a unit at the Military Orthopaedic Hospital, Shepherd's Bush. As a result, he was commissioned by the War Office to write a paper on 'Military orthopaedic hospitals' (*British Medical Journal*, May 1917). During these years, too, he was writing his best-known book, *The action of muscles: including muscle rest and muscle re-education* (London, 1918), and became a council-member of the Anatomical Society of Great Britain and Ireland.

MacKenzie returned to Melbourne early in 1918, took a house at 612 St Kilda Road, converted part of it into a laboratory and museum, which from 1919 he called the Australian Institute of Anatomical Research, and thereafter devoted much time to research on Australian animals. His first results appeared in four volumes published in 1918 and 1919, which were sometimes collectively known as *The comparative anatomy of Australian fauna*, and were illustrated in part by Victor Cobb [q.v.8]. In 1920 MacKenzie was granted permissive occupancy of almost 80 acres (32 ha) of bushland at Badger Creek, Healesville, by the State authorities, as a field station for his research. At his own expense he fenced the land, built a six-roomed house for a curator, a cottage for visiting scientists, a workshop and animal pens; and employed technical assistants. When he vacated this land towards the end of 1927 he suggested that the reserve be enlarged to 500 acres (202 ha) and become a national park. The Sir Colin MacKenzie Sanctuary was eventually officially opened in May 1934, along the lines he had suggested.

The extensive collection of specimens that he and his staff and co-workers had built up as the result of work at St Kilda Road and Healesville became well known, and large sums were offered for it from the United States of America. However, in 1923 he offered it as a gift to the Australian government and, in October 1924, an Act was passed setting up the National Museum of Australian Zoology, to consist of MacKenzie's gift and future additions to it, with MacKenzie as its first director and professor of comparative anatomy. It was to be housed in Canberra but, in the meantime, was to remain at St Kilda Road, and the work was to continue there and at Healesville. MacKenzie now retired from surgical practice.

The museum naturally had low priority in the building programme attendant on the removal of the seat of government to Canberra, but in 1928 responsibility for it was transferred to the Department of Health and preliminary steps were taken which led to its completion in 1930, together with an auxiliary research station and reserve for native animals. It was renamed the Australian Institute of Anatomy. Sadly, no sooner had the institute moved to Canberra than drastic cuts in its funding were made, because of the Depression. In 1928 MacKenzie outlined the ideas which lay behind his work at the institute in his presidential address to section D of the Australasian Association for the Advancement of Science, 'The importance of zoology to medical science', and, later, in the Bancroft [q.v.3] lecture in Brisbane, 'Functional anatomy and medical practice'. That year the Commonwealth accepted his offer of £1000 for an annual oration on preventive medicine in memory of his mother.

On 22 December 1928 MacKenzie married in Melbourne his assistant, Winifred Iris Evelyn (M.B., B.S.), daughter of Arthur N. Smith, a journalist. MacKenzie was knighted in 1929. In his Canberra years he served as a member of the Medical Board, and in 1933 became second president of the Canberra-based Royal Society of Australia. He had been a fellow of the Royal Society of Edinburgh since 1905. Ill health forced him to retire in November 1937 and he and his wife returned to Melbourne. MacKenzie died of a cerebral haemorrhage on 29 June 1938 at his home in Studley Park Road, Kew, and was cremated. His wife survived him; there were no children.

MacKenzie had red hair which earned him the sobriquet 'Bricky'. He had a great affection for children, which seems to have been reciprocated; his friends spoke of his modest, retiring nature and essential kindness, but he clearly also had great energy and determination. He disliked controversy but was often involved in it. He was inclined to jump to theoretical conclusions with great conviction on little evidence. This can be instanced by his ideas on the importance of Australian fauna for the understanding of human health and disease, on which the institute was founded, and by his controversy, with Wood Jones [q.v.9], Elliot Smith [q.v.] and others, on the antiquity of the Jervois skull, which he considered to pre-date Peking Man. On the other hand, he was a pioneer in orthopaedics in Australia and a dedicated practitioner. He energetically espoused the conservation of Australian fauna and was very generous with his time and money, both in his efforts to advance Australian science and in the care of his poorer patients. Former students have spoken with warmth and gratitude of the personal help and inspiration he gave them. He had a love of things Australian including Australian Rules football, which he considered the best form of human exercise. His wife borrowed Wren's epitaph for the commemorative plaque in the institute: 'Si monumentum requiris, circumspice'. A portrait by W. B. McInnes [q.v.] is held by the Museum of Australia; a pencil portrait by Victor Cobb is in the Anatomy Department, University of Melbourne.

A. Pratt, *The call of the koala* (Melb, 1937); *MJA*, 1 Oct 1938, p 576, 27 Jan 1973, p 194; *J of Bone and Joint Surgery*, 32B, no 4 (Nov 1950), p 601; *Age*, 16 July 1938; *Argus*, 28-31 July 1931, 6, 7, 10, 14, 17, 19, 20, 22, 28 Aug, 10 Dec 1931, 30 June 1938; Inst of Anatomy, Canb, records, 1925-79 (AAO, Canb); Dept of Conservation, Vic, Correspondence with W. C. MacKenzie; personal information.   MONICA MACCALLUM

MACKENZIE, WILLIAM KENNETH SEAFORTH (1872-1952), lawyer and soldier, was born on 7 January 1872 in Sydney, son of Walter Fawkes Mackenzie, surgeon, and his wife Frances, née Usill, both English born. He was educated at Sydney Grammar School, the University of Sydney and in 1891-95 at St John's College, Oxford (B.A., 1894). He was called to the Bar at the Inner Temple, London, on 18 November 1895, and admitted to the New South Wales Bar on 2 March 1897. He practised in Sydney with Bowman & Mackenzie in 1898-1900, specializing in divorce and tenancy consultations. He was author of *The practice of divorce in New South Wales* and wrote several papers on the Landlord and Tenant Act. In 1901-14 he was in chambers at Phillip Street, Sydney.

Mackenzie's interest in soldiering extended over thirty years, commencing in 1898 when he was commissioned in the New South Wales Military Forces in the 5th Infantry Regiment (Scottish Rifles). He rose steadily through the ranks (lieutenant 1900; captain 1903; major 1907; lieut-colonel 1911), occupying staff and regimental appointments in the 5th Regiment and then in the 1st Battalion, New South Wales Scottish Rifles. He commanded the latter from 1909 and from 1912 the 25th (City of Sydney) Infantry.

On 26 April 1915 Mackenzie joined the Australian Imperial Force as lieut-colonel commanding the 19th Battalion. Embarking for Egypt in June, he landed at Anzac on 21 August and after a few weeks in which the 19th was used either in reserve or to close the dangerous gap between the Gurkhas at Susak Kuyu and the British operating from Suvla Bay, took command at Pope's Hill. For the next three months the battalion was mainly engaged in improving and extending trenches and on ration and water-carrying fatigues. His men suffered from dysentery, and Turkish

broomstick bombs caused casualties. He remained at Anzac until the evacuation.

After employment in the Suez Canal defences from January 1916, on 18 March the 19th Battalion embarked for France. On 15 April it entered the front-line trenches in the Armentières sector and from 23 May was shelled daily. On 25 July the battalion entered the forward trenches covering Pozières—a 'shockingly bad relief', according to Mackenzie. 'Companies got mixed. Too many men in front-line'. Next day Mackenzie drew back one company and thinned out the line. Pozières was subjected to dreadful bombardment and casualties were severe; but for Mackenzie, they would have been worse.

Early in September the battalion moved to Ypres, Belgium, and in November entered the front line at Flers, where the trenches were in a 'dreadful state' with mud knee deep and almost waist deep in places. On 14 November, in appalling conditions, the battalion participated in an attack on The Maze. Mackenzie commanded the 19th on the Somme during the winter of 1916-17, but in February fell ill and was evacuated to England. He returned to France on 15 March but went back to England to take command of the 61st Battalion in a projected A.I.F. 6th Division. The division was never formed and in November Mackenzie was appointed to command the 2nd Australian Division Base Depot. Next month he took command of the Australian Infantry Base Depot at Le Havre. He relinquished command in June 1918 and on 23 July was attached to the 23rd Battalion. Until the Armistice he carried out legal tasks, including supervision of the conduct of field general courts martial. On 19 February 1919 he sailed for Sydney and on 6 June was demobilized.

Slightly below average height and of slim build, Mackenzie was a dignified and learned leader, well served in the 19th Battalion by a group of outstanding young officers. He felt deeply the hardships and dangers to which his men were exposed and did his utmost to alleviate them. He won the Distinguished Service Order at Pozières, 'never sparing himself during the whole time and scarcely allowed himself time for ordinary rest'. He was also awarded the (Russian) Order of St Stanislaus, 3rd class, and was thrice mentioned in dispatches.

Mackenzie resumed legal practice in 1921 in Denman Chambers, Sydney, and until 1952 was associated with leading barristers. From 1920 he was retained by the Law Book Co. as legal reporter and in 1942-51 edited the *N.S.W. State Reports* and *Weekly Notes*, establishing an unequalled record for meticulous interpretation. He was for fourteen years honorary secretary of the New South Wales United Service Institute.

Mackenzie died unmarried on 3 June 1952 at the Royal Prince Alfred Hospital, Camperdown, and was cremated. A stained-glass window to his memory is in the Sailors' and Soldiers' Memorial Church of St Luke, Clovelly.

Oxford University roll of service (Oxford, 1920); *London Gazette*, 29 Dec 1916, 2 Jan, 13 Feb, 1 June 1917; *Aust Law J*, 19 June 1952; *Reveille* (Syd), June 1953; W. K. S. Mackenzie, Personal diary, Mar 1915-Mar 1919, *and* Biog file, War records section (AWM).   A. J. SWEETING

McKEOWN, KEITH COLLINGWOOD (1892-1952), entomologist, naturalist and author, was born on 6 November 1892 at Burwood, Sydney, second son of George Maurice McKeown, agriculturalist, and his wife Emmeline Mary, née Mayhew. His early years were spent on the Wollongbar Experimental Farm, between Lismore and Ballina, where his father was officer in charge. At 3 'with a cicada in both fists and a dead field mouse in his pocket' he began his lifelong interest in natural history. In November 1897 his father became manager of the experiment farm at Wagga Wagga where Keith received his schooling and taught himself entomology in his spare time; in the school holidays he delighted in visits to the Australian Museum, Sydney.

In September 1915 he was appointed to the Water Conservation and Irrigation Commission at Leeton as a clerk. He joined the Linnean Society of New South Wales in 1917 and next year published, in the *Australian Naturalist*, his first paper, which dealt with the habits of the Carpenter bee of the grass trees (*Lestis bambylans*). In 1920 at the request of (Sir) John Cleland [q.v.8] he reported on the presence of the anopheline mosquito in the Murrumbidgee Irrigation Area. Other notes and papers followed and in January 1927 he was appointed entomological research officer in the commission to work in conjunction with the Department of Agriculture on the various insect pests in the M.I.A. In June 1929 he was appointed scientific assistant (second class) to Anthony Musgrave [q.v.] at the Australian Museum, at a salary of £368; he later became assistant curator of insects. On 29 December 1932 he married Marie Julia Matthew at the Registrar General's Office, Sydney.

McKeown popularized Australian nature studies through numerous articles in the *Sydney Morning Herald* and *Australian Museum Magazine* and especially through his very readable and popular books. His *Insect wonders of Australia* (1935) and *Spider wonders of Australia* (1936) both ran to several editions. These were followed by the *Land of Byamee, Australian wild life in legend and fact* (1938), based on his observations of the Aborigines of the Wiradjurie tribe in the Riverina district (regarded by Dame Mary Gilmore [q.v.9] as 'one of the most important books written on the aborigines'); an *Alice in Wonderland*-type children's fantasy, *The magic seeds: Tessa in Termitaria* (1940); *Australian insects: an introductory handbook* (1942), published by the Royal Zoological Society of New South Wales of which he was a fellow and council-member; and *Nature in Australia* (1949).

As well as his popular writings McKeown published specialist scientific papers on the orders Coleoptera, Neuroptera and Orthoptera including the authoritative *Catalogue of the Cerambycidae, Coleoptera, of Australia* (1947). He also turned his attention to the economic aspects of entomology and published his observations on the food of birds and fish. He was a member of the scientific advisory committee to the Mount Kosciusko State Park Trust and a keen amateur photographer.

McKeown collapsed during the Australian and New Zealand Association for the Advancement of Science conference in Sydney and died of heart disease on 21 August 1952, survived by his wife and young son who shared his father's love of natural history. He was cremated after an Anglican service.

A. Musgrave, *Bibliography of Australian entomology 1775-1930* (Syd, 1932); *PP* (NSW), 1922, 1, p 181, 1927, 3, p 447; *Aust Museum Mag*, 15 Sept 1952, p 371; Roy Zoological Soc NSW, *Procs*, May 1954, p 6; *Daily Telegraph* (Syd), 10 Dec 1949; *SMH*, 23 Aug 1952.   G. P. WALSH

MACKEY, SIR JOHN EMANUEL (1863-1924), teacher, lawyer and politician, was born on 7 August 1863 at Sandhurst (Bendigo), Victoria, son of David Mackey, horse-dealer, and his wife Mary Anne, née Moore, both Irish born. Little is known of his boyhood, part of which was spent at Ararat. He is said to have hardly ever attended school, starting to earn a living when about 10 and teaching himself to read and write. He served an apprenticeship as a compositor at Stawell and by about 1882 was lodging with C. R. Long [q.v.] in East Melbourne with the parents of Frank Tate [q.v.], who became a lifelong close friend; the three of them often 'planned to set the world to rights'. Rough in manners and appearance, Jack Mackey matriculated when almost 20 in June 1883 after at least one failure. He joined the South Yarra Presbyterian Literary Society.

After failing first-year arts his record at the University of Melbourne (B.A., 1887; M.A.,

1889; LL.B., 1890) was extraordinary. Supporting himself by work at the Government Printing Office and by coaching, he entered Ormond [q.v.5] College and concluded his arts course with first-class honours in history, political economy and jurisprudence, with the Wyselaskie [q.v.6] prize in political economy, the Bowen [q.v.3] prize for his essay on 'The limits of legislative interference with the liberty of the individual', and the Cobden Club medal. He then attempted medicine but lost interest and failed his examinations in October 1887. In the same month he was awarded the Wyselaskie scholarship for English constitutional history, and next February he was awarded first-class honours in the school of logic and mental and moral philosophy, with another scholarship. He was chairman of the Melbourne University Union in 1888.

After completing his law degree Mackey was admitted to the Bar; he subsequently lent his lecture notes to his friend (Sir) John Monash [q.v.]. From 1890 he was briefly an inspector of schools. Over the next few years he was lecturer in classics and history at the Working Men's College and occasional lecturer, tutor and examiner at the university; in 1895 he was acting professor of logic and mental and moral philosophy while Henry Laurie [q.v.] was on leave. His Bar practice developed little. In 1899-1900 he was a member of an inquiry into the operation of the Melbourne and Metropolitan Board of Works.

Mackey had set himself for a political career. He stood as a liberal free trader for Melbourne South in 1894 and for Ripon and Hampden in 1897. After attempting West Gippsland in 1900 he won the seat in 1902 and became so popular and respected that he was opposed only once in the following twenty-two years. On 18 December 1902 he married Zella Watson, daughter of the politician William Bates; they had two daughters and three sons.

Mackey became a key member of the Bent [q.v.3] government of 1904-09. Initially he was only minister without portfolio, but from 17 August 1906 until October 1908 he was lands minister and, as well, solicitor-general from 28 February to 8 September 1908. From 31 October 1908 to 8 January 1909 he was chief secretary and minister of labour. He was a constructive, common-sense reformer, who concentrated on legal and social issues, 'one of those men who are essential in any government to give form, consistency and legal verbiage to the ideas of practical politicians'; he was adept at speedily drafting amendments at the table of the House. He had introduced and passed the 'Flos Greig [q.v.8] enabling bill' in 1903; he carried legislation establishing children's courts (1906), indeterminate sentences (1907), and the Court of Criminal Appeal (1914). In 1905, against great opposition by David Gaunson [q.v.4] and others, he was staunch in support of Tate in forcing through legislation enabling promotion of teachers by merit, as he did later with other education reforms. From 1905 he arranged for work on consolidation of the criminal law, then from 1908 for (Sir) Leo Cussen's [q.v.8] massive consolidation of the statutes, published in 1915. He mastered the land problem, but his bold and systematic legislation for compulsory purchase in the Western District was lost in the Legislative Council. No one, perhaps, contributed more to establishing the Country Roads Board (1912), for which his constituents were enormously grateful. He was an able negotiator in conferences over conflicts between the Houses.

After loss of his ministerial positions, Mackey was chairman of the royal commission on railways and tramways in 1911, was a member of the public accounts committee (chairman, 1914) and sat on several select committees. He was often mentioned as a possible premier, but for no clearly discernible reason was not a member of the Murray, Watt and Peacock [qq.v.] ministries in 1909-17. He was chairman of committees from 1914 and, though prominent in the 'National and Economy' group in 1917, was content to become Speaker when (Sir) John Bowser [q.v.7] became premier. He was a strict, fair and courteous Speaker, ruling over an unusually orderly assembly. He was knighted in 1921. He seems to have lacked the ultimate drive to reach the top.

Mackey had been a staunch friend of his university. He was lecturer in Equity from 1900, after the accountant's defalcations took a leading part in the financial rescue by the Bent government in the amending Act of 1904, and joined the council in 1913. He was chairman of the trustees of the Melbourne Cricket Ground from 1907, a trustee of the Public Library, Museums and National Gallery of Victoria from 1912, and a member of the board of visitors to the Melbourne Observatory. He was also a member of the Wallaby Club.

A square-jawed, determined man, solid and serious, a hesitant rather than eloquent speaker, Mackey was highly regarded for his clarity of mind, sincerity, forbearance and good humour. He was popular and conciliatory, a friendly conversationalist with wide cultural interests. He lived at Brighton and was a member of the Presbyterian Church.

Mackey died suddenly at Nayook of angina pectoris on 6 April 1924 and after a state funeral conducted by Rev. Dr Sugden [q.v.] was buried in Brighton cemetery. His intestate estate was valued at £2037. To provide for her young family, Lady Mackey opened a florist's shop in Flinders Street which she conducted for some thirty years.

E. H. Sugden and F. W. Eggleston, *George Swinburne* (Syd, 1931); H. Copland, *The path of progress* (Warragul, Vic, 1934); E. L. French (ed), *Melbourne studies in education 1963* (Melb, 1964); R. J. W. Selleck, *Frank Tate* (Melb, 1982); G. Serle, *John Monash* (Melb, 1982); *Punch* (Melb), 8 June 1905, 13 Dec 1917, 23 Sept 1920; *Argus*, 7 Apr 1924.   GEOFFREY SERLE

MACKIE, ALEXANDER (1876-1955), educationist, was born on 25 May 1876 in Edinburgh, son of William Mackie, master grocer, and his wife Margaret, née Davidson. He was educated at Daniel Stewart's College, and in 1893 became a pupil-teacher at Canonmills Public School. In 1897 he entered the Edinburgh Training College, Moray House, on a two-year scholarship and concurrently attended the University of Edinburgh under Professor Simon Somerville Laurie. Graduating M.A. with first-class honours in philosophy in 1900, he spent only two years as a schoolteacher before, in December 1902, he became an assistant lecturer in education at University College of North Wales, Bangor.

In 1906 Mackie was appointed principal of the new Teachers' College, Sydney, which had been established by the Department of Public Instruction in response to widespread critical review of the education system and the decision to abolish pupil-teachers. At the request of Professor (Sir) Francis Anderson [q.v.7], he acted in 1908 as professor of philosophy at the University of Sydney while the former was on leave. In 1910 Mackie was appointed professor of education, while remaining Teachers' College principal. Despite the difficulties of the years to 1920 it was a time of development, achievement, promise and personal satisfaction. He married Anne Burnett Duncan, a young Australian teacher, on 4 June 1913 at North Sydney, forged his college into a tertiary institution with well-qualified staff, including his vice-principal P. R. Cole [q.v.8], and saw some progress towards his ideal of the teacher as a well-educated professional. He was fully supported by Peter Board [q.v.7], director of education in 1905-22.

By 1912, after the establishment of a state system of secondary education, the Intermediate and Leaving certificates became the examinations for the award of teacher-education scholarships and for entrance to the college for the one-year 'short course' and two-year 'long course'. Initially the short course was a major step forward, doubling the previous training of entrants seeking appointments to small rural schools. However, the one-year course was thrust upon many students by the department and, despite Mackie's protests, was not finally abandoned by a department often desperately short of teachers until 1937. The Leaving certificate gradually became the necessary requirement to secure a scholarship and hence gain admission. Under arrangements fostered by Mackie and approved by Board, those students who qualified for admission to the university could take Mackie's courses in the history and theory of education, and later experimental education, as second or third-year B.A. subjects and proceed to the graduate diploma in education.

During Mackie's training the educational world was enlivened by the 'New Education'. His own stance, as evidenced in his addresses and publications, was in essence a well-considered although not especially distinctive or distinguished expression of the 'New Education', which incorporated as an obviously influential component some of the views expressed by Plato; there is considerable compatibility between Mackie's views and those of John Dewey. In *Groundwork of teaching* (1919) and *Studies in education* (1932) Mackie expounded his view that the function of schooling was 'to secure and promote the welfare and happiness of children' to prepare them for the future and for community life, but also to be critical of the social order in a context where schooling was 'enjoyable and absorbing'. Equally important was his concept of teachers as well-educated professionals who should be accorded professional freedom in the exercise of their responsibilities.

Under Mackie, the Teachers' College soon became a centre of educational activity and discussion and a college distinguished for the quality of its academic staff, where men and women who were to become eminent in Australian education began their careers. In his first year Mackie organized the Education Society, which was to produce over forty monographs. In 1917 Mackie established the journal *Schooling*, a publication he was forced to abandon in 1933 for financial reasons. He himself wrote fairly extensively, often with members of the college staff as co-authors and these publications in education, if not always significant in themselves, were important as Australian ventures into this field. He also encouraged research and experiment by members of his staff and the staff of nearby demonstration schools. Mackie encouraged students to accept responsibility for their own affairs, instigating the establishment of a student representative council, and organizing the timetable to provide for student clubs and activities. He also tried to create a physical environment appropriate to a tertiary institution, placing considerable emphasis upon the library and the acquisition of works of art.

In 1920 the college moved at last to its new building in the university grounds. In 1922 Board retired and was replaced by S. H. Smith [q.v.] as director; and almost immediately there was a shift to educational conservatism. Ignoring Mackie's protests, Smith insisted upon impressing his will upon the college. Thus in 1923 its courses were revised by a departmental committee to ensure that during their course primary students studied the content of the primary school subjects. Mackie and Smith also held very different views on the value of a university education for teachers. Smith imposed severe restrictions upon the number of students granted university scholarships. In 1927 Mackie was required to assist in implementing an emergency scheme whereby a group of students were placed for continuous practice in school for a year to alleviate a teacher shortage. Mackie even protested directly to the minister against Smith's actions and attitude. Their antagonism culminated in a clash which resulted in Mackie being suspended by Smith from 9 to 15 November 1927 until an objectionable letter was withdrawn. Further disappointments followed. The university's professorial board rejected Mackie's proposal that he parallel college courses with university courses and that college students be permitted to sit for university examinations; the reciprocal arrangements between the university and the college remained confined to candidates for the university's diploma in education. In 1927 the State Superannuation Board excluded Mackie from participating in the State Superannuation Fund on a technicality related to his professorial status when this could have been simply overcome as it was for his successor in 1940.

During the Depression, student intake to the college was reduced; college staff were sent back to the schools, and supplies and equipment were curtailed. Never a man to be silent on issues affecting his college, Mackie several times publicly criticized government and departmental policies and both G. R. Thomas, who in 1930 replaced Smith, and D. H. Drummond [q.v.8], minister for education, reprimanded him for such utterances. However, amid all the difficulties of the 1920s and 1930s Mackie continued his efforts on behalf of the college and of Australian education generally. Much of his writing was done at this time. With Professor Tasman Lovell and Frank Tate [qq.v.], he helped to found the Australian Council for Educational Research in 1928 and was a member of its executive until 1940. In 1933 he was a member of the committee appointed to inquire into the system of examinations ·and the secondary school course.

Mackie became ill suddenly and his career concluded abruptly in 1940. He then faced a long period of illness and depression during which he made only a few visits to the college which had been his life for so long. He died of cerebral haemorrhage on 23 October 1955, and was cremated with Presbyterian forms. His wife, son and daughter, both of whom followed careers in tertiary education, survived him.

The *Sydney Morning Herald* linked Mackie with Board and Francis Anderson in its obituary, describing their influence upon Australian education as lasting and profound. Mackie was specifically identified by the *Herald* as an outstanding educator who had effectively raised the status of teacher education. To his colleagues he had become almost a legendary figure for his insistence that teaching be accorded the status of a profession, that teachers must have both a sound general and a sound professional education, and his insistence that his staff be accorded academic freedom, especially from any arbitrary and inappropriate restraints by the Public Service Board or the department.

A fine portrait painted by George Lambert [q.v.9] in 1926, funded by public subscription, hangs in the Alexander Mackie library of the Sydney Institute of Education, Sydney College of Advanced Education. The Mackie medal was established for award to outstanding Australian educators by the Australian and New Zealand Association for the Advancement of Science.

L. A. Mandelson, 'Alexander Mackie', in C. Turney (ed), *Pioneers of Australian education*, 3 (Syd, 1983); *Kookaburra*, 18 Dec 1926; *Forum of Education*, 14, no 3, Apr 1956; *SMH*, 15 Dec 1926, 25 Oct 1950; A. J. Baillie, Alexander Mackie (M.Ed. thesis, Univ Syd, 1968).   L. A. MANDELSON

MACKINNON, DONALD (1859-1932), politician, was born on 29 September 1859 at Marida Yallock, Boorcan, Victoria, eldest son of Daniel Mackinnon [q.v.5] and his wife Jane, née Kinross. He was educated at Geelong Church of England Grammar School and Trinity College, University of Melbourne. A family friend (Professor) H. A. Strong [q.v.6] introduced him to New College, Oxford, where his first tutor and later friend was W. A. Spooner (famed for 'Spoonerisms'). Mackinnon's first impression of Oxford was that 'the young men here seem to be very effeminate, they are painfully fond of laughing at nothing and talk in a very affected way'. He studied classics and jurisprudence; a serious student, he had hopes of second-class honours but took a 'good' third-class B.A. in 1883. At 5 ft. 11 ins. (180 cm) and 11½ stone (73 kg) he rowed, was on the fringe of the university cricket team as a round-arm bowler, and learned French and German in long vacations on the Continent. He was called to the Bar at the Middle Temple in 1883 and admitted to the Victorian Bar next year.

In Melbourne Mackinnon built a modest Bar practice while writing for the *Argus* and *Australasian*. He joined the Melbourne and Bohemian clubs, and went in for amateur theatricals but regretted having to 'waste' many evenings on 'dinners, routs, dances and fool-playing generally' at the height of the boom. In 1889 Chief Justice George Higinbotham [q.v.4] selected him to assist in his massive consolidation of the Victorian statutes; they worked together far into the night for many months. Higinbotham later commended his fidelity, industry, skill and exact knowledge.

On his father's death in 1889 Mackinnon inherited Marida Yallock, which his brother William Kinross (1861-1943) managed for most of his life. On 19 August 1891 at All Saints Church of England, St Kilda, he married Hilda Eleanor Marie, daughter of B. F. Bunny [q.v.3] and sister of Rupert [q.v.7].

Despite his pastoral background and wealth, Mackinnon became a radical liberal politician. Although wide reading had induced well-informed, liberal and tolerant views, in the late 1880s he was considering standing for Western District constituencies in the pastoral interest and was perturbed by the rise of the Shearers' Union. It is likely that his association with the great popular tribune Higinbotham so changed his outlook that he accepted the traditions of radical Victorian liberalism as expounded also by Alfred Deakin and H. B. Higgins [qq.v.8,9]. The collapse of the boom and the subsequent terrible depression further shaped his mind.

After standing unsuccessfully in 1897 for Prahran, where he was president of the Australian Natives' Association branch, Mackinnon was narrowly elected in 1900 as 'the next best thing to a Labor man'. Supporting the Turner and Peacock [qq.v.] ministries in 1900-02, he served usefully on royal commissions into the University of Melbourne and local government. After losing office to (Sir) William Irvine [q.v.9] the Peacock Liberals provided only weak opposition. Early in 1904 Peacock passed the leadership to Mackinnon and the Progressive Liberal Association, linked with the Federal Deakinites, was formed.

Mackinnon condemned both government and railway strikers in 1903 for class hatred. He had strongly opposed Irvine's constitutional reform measures, holding that the Legislative Assembly must predominate over the Legislative Council whose veto power should be reduced to one of delay. He supported direct taxation, raising the threshold of income taxation to £200 a year, and religious instruction in schools; he opposed gambling which should be kept 'as disreputable as possible'. He favoured extension and strengthening of the Factories Act: the state had a duty to protect the weak. Above all he was a land reformer, supporting closer settlement and compulsory acquisition. 'The history of all countries shows that the occupying peasantry or yeomanry are the very salt of the country'. According to (Sir) Frederic Eggleston, Mackinnon was full of 'zeal to reform his own class and interest'. He 'remains an aristocrat, but some of Higinbotham's democracy hangs about him still', the *Bulletin* conceded.

The Mackinnon Liberals polled much better at the June 1904 election, but won fewer seats in the smaller reformed House, becoming generally known as 'the Victorian XI'. They sympathized with the Labor Party and often voted with it, but could not stomach Labor's extra-parliamentary organization and the pledge. Moreover Labor's fast-growing support threatened them. By early 1907 the government of (Sir) Thomas Bent [q.v.3], who had succeeded Irvine, was losing support and Mackinnon as Opposition leader agreed to a fusion or coalition. The Liberals gained little other than further factory legislation. The vital issues were the land valuation bill (the basis for a future land tax), under Mackinnon's control as minister without portfolio, and the Western District land scheme. Bent withdrew both pieces of legislation and in October 1908 Mackinnon, Peacock and George Swinburne [q.v.] resigned in disgust. Bent soon lost office and an election, and John Murray [q.v.] formed a ministry. Mackinnon claimed a victory for land reform, but it was a dying issue. During 1909, as fusion proceeded, his group lost its identity in a broadened Liberal Party.

Mackinnon remained a back-bencher until 22 December 1913 when, after a seven-month overseas trip, he became attorney-general, solicitor-general, minister of railways and vice-president of the Board of Land and Works in the Watt [q.v.] and subsequent Peacock ministries. He took particular satisfaction in presiding over (Sir) Leo Cussen's [q.v.8] further consolidation of the statutes and, on the outbreak of war, carrying anti-profiteering measures.

When Peacock was forced to reconstruct his ministry in November 1915, Mackinnon was content to withdraw and concentrate, with conspicuous success, on chairmanship of the Victorian recruiting committee. From May 1916 he was also chairman of the State War Council, primarily concerned with repatriation. After the failure of the conscription referendum, on 29 November Mackinnon was appointed Commonwealth director-general of recruiting, without pay. He set up a structure of central recruiting committees in every Federal electorate and local government area, and recruiting officers in towns. He travelled constantly to speak and confer, and himself wrote many propagandist pamphlets and articles. His policy was that recruiting must be persuasive and conciliatory, not offensive to anyone.

Mackinnon was perhaps the sanest man in the country on the issues which were bitterly dividing the nation. He criticized the British Army Council's demand in mid-1916 for 175 000 additional troops within a year as an 'over-estimate' and 'a hindrance and discouragement to recruiting'. He often asserted that those still advocating conscription were wrecking recruiting; he reprimanded hecklers of Labor speakers who shared his platform. The second referendum of December 1917 made his task even more difficult. He fought for increased allowances for soldiers' dependants, criticized unrealistically high medical standards for recruits, condemned the conscriptionist Melbourne press for belittling the voluntary movement, attacked the censorship for not permitting the people to know how serious the war situation was. He recognized how extraordinary it was that so many had volunteered. Mackinnon chaired the governor-general's almost useless conference on recruiting in April 1918 and earned J. H. Scullin's [q.v.] tribute that 'he had acted throughout in an absolutely impartial way'. His elder sons had been serving with the British Army; the younger died from illness in August. In November the government formally thanked him for his 'sturdy optimism' and 'unfailing perseverance'.

Early in 1919 he took a long holiday in Tasmania but had energy enough to write articles describing the State. On return he chaired the soldier settler qualification committee, then on 5 June his friend Premier (Sir) Harry Lawson [q.v.] called on him to take over soldier settlement as minister without portfolio. Still a yeoman idealist at heart, Mackinnon threw himself into the work, searching crown lands all over Victoria for possible new farms and negotiating for purchase and compulsory acquisitions. The number of intending settlers and the speed of their repatriation was unexpected, but in fifteen months he settled some 4000 ex-servicemen. He was now, rather than a social reformer, an exponent of 'Australia Unlimited', a 'wholehogger' on immigration with visionary hopes of thickly settling the Riverina by joint planning with New South Wales and extending Victorian railways to the Northern Territory and western Queensland. But, to wide distress, he lost Prahran at last at the October 1920 election to Labor.

In twenty years as a parliamentarian Mackinnon had been a minister for five years. He never quite lived up to popular expectations. He was too much an intellectual, too principled, too conciliatory, suspect because of his background, insufficiently a demagogue, to be adequately equipped as a political leader. In his early days he was widely regarded as being an idealistic crank. But his integrity and unpretentiousness gave him moral authority; his manner displayed him as 'a sensible man talking plainly and tolerantly to sensible people'.

From June 1923 to November 1924 Mackinnon was Australian commissioner in the United States of America, promoting trade and closer relations; he believed he did something to put Australia on the map. He knew Franklin Roosevelt and foretold his greatness. On his return he unsuccessfully sought National Party pre-selection for the Federal seat of Henty, stood as an Independent Nationalist and lost decisively to (Sir) Henry Gullett [q.v.9]. In the next few years he travelled extensively by motor in the outback.

In his later years Mackinnon's chief interest was Geelong Grammar School whose council he had joined in 1909 and of which he was chairman from 1922. He took the lead in the appointment as headmaster from 1930 of (Sir) James Darling with whom he then worked in close co-operation. His other favourite activity was his active presidency, since 1906, of the Victorian Cricket Association. He continued as chairman of directors of the Equity Trustees, Executors & Agency Co., the Victorian Insurance Co. and the Talbot Colony for Epileptics. He was also president of the Victorian Scottish Union and chairman of trustees of Scots Church, Melbourne; his Christian faith was central to his philosophy. Like his great Victorian exemplars, he refused any honour (except a French decoration). In 1931 Herbert Brookes [q.v.7] described him as 'one of the finest democrats this country has thrown up from the native soil' and recalled that both of them had imagined when young that Australia could be made a paradise.

Mackinnon died in Melbourne of cardiac disease on 25 April 1932, and was cremated. His wife and three sons and two daughters survived him. His son Donald (1892-1965) was a pastoralist and ambassador to Brazil; Ewen Daniel (1903-1983) was a grazier, Federal Liberal member of parliament and ambassador to the Argentine, Peru and Uruguay; and Kenneth Wulsten, Q.C. (1906-1964), was prominent at the English Bar. Mackinnon's estate was sworn for probate at £142 262. In his will he had provided for the statue of Higinbotham which stands adjacent to the Treasury Building, Melbourne. Mackinnon's portrait by Rupert Bunny is at Marida Yallock.

His brother JAMES CURDIE (1865-1957) was educated at Geelong Grammar and Trinity Hall, Cambridge. In his youth he managed the family property, Marion Downs, in western Queensland. In partnership with W. T. [q.v.] and E. Manifold and his brother William, he purchased Wyangarie station on the Richmond River, New South Wales, and by 1916 had managed its subdivision into one hundred dairy farms. He became chairman of directors of the Union Trustee Co. of Australia, Strachan [q.v.2] & Co. Ltd, and Trufood of Australia Ltd. He did not marry.

J. Smith (ed), *Cyclopedia of Victoria*, 3 (Melb, 1905); E. H. Sugden and F. W. Eggleston, *George Swinburne* (Syd, 1931); A. Henderson (ed), *Early pioneer families of Victoria and Riverina* (Melb, 1936); E. Scott, *Australia during the war* (Syd, 1936); L. L. Robson, *The first A.I.F.* (Melb, 1970); J. R. Darling, *Richly rewarding* (Melb, 1978); *Bulletin*, 24 Mar 1904; *Argus*, 13 Apr 1904, 31 Jan, 2 Dec 1918, 18 Nov 1920; *Table Talk*, 4 Nov 1926; *Punch* (Melb), 7 Feb 1907, 4 Jan 1917; Mackinnon papers (LaTL); H. Brookes papers (NL); K. Rollison, Groups and attitudes in the Victorian Legislative Assembly, 1900-1909 (Ph.D. thesis, La Trobe Univ, 1972); family information.

GEOFFREY SERLE

MacKINNON, ELEANOR VOKES IRBY (1871-1936), Red Cross leader, was born on 8 February 1871 at Tenterfield, New South Wales, only daughter and sixth of thirteen children of Glentworth Walsh Fraser Addison, police magistrate, and his Sydney-born wife Ellen, née Campbell. Her father, from Manchester, England, was directly descended from Joseph Addison, the essayist. The family moved to Sydney in 1882 and Eleanor attended the Clergy Daughters' School, Waverley, and Sydney Girls' High School with Louise Mack and Ethel Turner [qq.v.]. On 16 September 1896 at Paddington she married with Presbyterian forms Roger Robert Steel MacKinnon (d. 1935), physician. They lived at Warialda where their two sons were born.

Settling at North Sydney in 1903, Eleanor studied painting under Lister Lister [q.v.] and wrote verse, but soon became involved in charitable and political activities. A life-member of the Royal Society for the Prevention of Cruelty to Animals, she was first president of King Edward's Dogs' Home. In 1909 she succeeded Mrs Molyneux Parkes [q.v.] as president of the Women's Liberal (Reform) League of New South Wales. She was on the board of the Royal Alexandra Hospital for Children and the committee of the Bush Book Club.

On 11 August 1914 Eleanor MacKinnon became foundation honorary secretary to the State division of the Australian branch of the British Red Cross Society; she was a member of the State executive and finance committees and a delegate to the central council until her death. Conceiving 'the idea of using the idealism and generosity of young people to relieve suffering and distress', she founded the world's first Junior Red Cross division, provided its motto, 'The Child for the Child', and was honorary director until 1935. By 1918 the movement was established in fifty-two countries. She was a member of the State council for Voluntary Aid Detachments; director of the Red Cross Produce Depot; honorary publicity officer; and a house committee-member of Graythwaite Convalescent Home, North Sydney. She founded (and edited for twenty-one years) the *Red Cross Record* in December 1914 and the *Junior Red Cross Record* in 1918, and compiled the *Red Cross Knitting* and *Cookery* books.

President of 17th Battalion Comforts Fund and founder and co-editor of the *War Workers' Gazette*, she worked for the Citizens' War Chest. In 1916 she became a vice-president and executive member of the National Association of New South Wales, the National Council and the National Women's Club (later holding similar positions in the United Australia Party). An 'eloquent and forceful' platform speaker, in the 1920s she occasionally broadcast on politics.

Appointed O.B.E. in 1918, next year Mrs MacKinnon raised funds for the Peace Loan. During the pneumonic influenza epidemic she helped to organize emergency hospitals and as honorary director oversaw the whole nursing service. Anxious about servicemen's children, particularly those suffering from tuberculosis, Mrs MacKinnon obtained for their use two houses in the Blue Mountains and one by the sea at Ramsgate, which were used as 'preventoria' as well as sanitoria. In 1925-26 she worked tirelessly to reconstruct the Red Cross, touring the country to form new branches, and to divert it to peacetime activities and to the care of civilians.

In 1924-29 she was a government representative on the Senate of the University of Sydney. She gave the proceeds of her slender volume of verse, *The golden land* (1924), to the university's 'Memorial Carillon' fund. A substitute delegate to the sixth general assembly of the League of Nations at Geneva, Switzerland, in 1925, she was invited to speak from the tribune for her work in helping to found the Australasian Armenian Relief Fund in 1922. She also visited the headquarters of the League of Red Cross Societies in Paris.

In 1929 Mrs MacKinnon was appointed to the first Hospitals Commission of New South Wales. She helped to form many hospital auxiliaries, convened three large conferences of hospital matrons in Sydney and arranged regular regional conferences in the country. She was also responsible for publicity and promoted immunization against diphtheria. Long an admirer of Sister Elizabeth Kenny [q.v.9], in 1934 she helped to set up her clinic for poliomyelitis cases at Townsville, Queensland. Mrs MacKinnon was awarded King George V's Silver Jubilee Medal in 1935. Survived by her sons, she died on 31 January 1936 in Royal North Shore Hospital and was cremated with Anglican rites.

Junior Red Cross Record, 1 Mar 1936; *Red Cross Record* (NSW), 1 Mar, 1 Apr 1936; *Daily Telegraph* (Syd), 24 Feb 1915; *Aust National Review*, 17 July 1925, 26 May 1927; *SMH*, 31 Jan, 1 Feb 1936, 15 Mar 1973.   JACQUELINE ABBOTT

MACKINNON, SIR LAUCHLAN CHARLES (1848-1925), newspaper proprietor and manager, was born on 12 April 1848 at Broadford, Skye, Scotland, eldest son of Rev. Alexander Kenneth Mackinnon and his wife Barbara, née Reid. His education at private schools was provided for by his wealthy cousin Lauchlan Mackinnon [q.v.5], co-proprietor of the Melbourne *Argus* and *Australasian*, who chose him as his successor.

In his youth Mackinnon worked in the offices of the London *Times* and the Edinburgh *Scotsman* and with the publishers W. H. Smith & Co. In 1870 he moved to Melbourne to gain administrative experience with the *Argus*. On 23 January 1873 he married a widow Elizabeth Anketell-Jones (d. 1875), daughter of William Learmonth [q.v.5]. On 13 December 1876 at Plympton, Devon, England, he married Emily Grace Bundock, adopted daughter of his cousin Lauchlan.

After three years as *Argus* representative in London where he developed the paper's joint cable-service with the *Sydney Morning Herald* and the South Australian *Register* (which eventually became the Australian Press Association), Mackinnon became general manager in 1881. He was sole trustee and representative of the Mackinnon interest in the company after his cousin's death in 1888. During his thirty-nine years as general manager, Mackinnon was a key Establishment figure, preserving the *Argus* as a rigidly conservative organ and developing a highly profitable enterprise; in his time circulation grew from 11 000 to 123 000. He is said to have always presided, in later years at least, over meetings of Australian newspaper proprietors. A 'benevolent disciplinarian', he rewarded merit among his staff and gave opportunities of work overseas to his senior journalists. He was knighted in 1916.

Engrossed in his work, Mackinnon had few outside interests. He was a devout member of Scots Church, and belonged to the Melbourne Club (president, 1903), Australian (Melbourne) and Reform (London) clubs. He was a founder of the (Royal) Melbourne Golf Club and occasionally enjoyed shooting. He retired in 1919 and settled at Crediton, Devon, England. Predeceased by his wife, Mackinnon died on 3 December 1925, survived by a son and two daughters. His estate in England and Victoria was sworn for probate at about £50 000.

His son LAUCHLAN (1877-1934) was born on 28 September 1877 at Hawthorn, Melbourne, and educated at Uppingham College, England, and Cumloden, St Kilda, Melbourne. After some training on the *Scotsman* he worked on the managerial side of the *Argus* until 1915-18 when he served in France with the Royal Army Service Corps. Captain Mackinnon succeeded his father in 1920 as general manager of the *Argus* and representative of the Mackinnon interest. He rode to hounds, was an outstanding polo player and a prominent racehorse owner; he was a member of the Melbourne Club.

On 16 November 1904 in Scotland Mackinnon had married Hilda Law, daughter of the general manager of the *Scotsman*. She and three sons survived him when he died suddenly in Melbourne on 9 October 1934. His estate was sworn for probate at £24 545. The Mackinnon interest in the *Argus* was sold in 1937.

LAUCHLAN KENNETH SCOBIE MACKINNON (1861-1935), Lauchlan Charles's second cousin, was born on the Isle of Skye, migrated to Melbourne in 1884 and from 1888 was a partner in Blake & Riggall, solicitors. He was a company director and in 1935 chairman of the Victoria Racing Club; the L. K. S. Mackinnon Stakes is named after him.

Argus, 5, 7 Dec 1925, 10 Oct 1934; Men who made the *Argus* and *Australasian*, typescript, C. P. Smith papers (LaTL).   GEOFFREY SERLE

McKINNON, THOMAS FIRMIN (1878-1953), journalist, was born on 9 June 1878 at Yass Plains, New South Wales, second son of Scottish-born Laughlin McKinnon, farmer, and his wife Margaret, née Faulder. Firmin spent some boyhood years on his uncle's property, then worked for the *Yass Courier* and subsequently as a journalist in Sydney (receiving his basic training with the *Daily Telegraph* from 1903) and as editor of a Lismore newspaper. He achieved some notoriety by assisting Bennet Burleigh in 1904-05 to cover the Russo-Japanese war and dispatching the news of the Russians' naval defeat.

McKinnon joined the Brisbane *Telegraph* about 1907, the year that his future wife, Rockhampton-born Emma Louise Powell—the only woman journalist on its staff—joined the paper. On 20 January 1911 Firmin and Emmie became foundation members, and he secretary, of the Queensland Journalists' Association. His brief secretaryship of the Australian Journalists' Association, Queensland district, led to a lifelong friendship with R. Spencer Browne [q.v.7]. McKinnon was then appointed editor of the *Darling Downs Gazette*, a post formerly held by Emmie's uncle, Rev. J. H. L. Zillman. Emmie's father, Rev. William Powell, married the couple in his South Brisbane parsonage on 30 March 1912 with Methodist forms.

In 1913 McKinnon joined the Brisbane *Courier* as parliamentary reporter and in 1919, under R. S. Taylor as editor, was appointed associate editor, principal leader-writer and literary columnist. His colleagues nicknamed him 'the Encyclopaedia'. In 1925-42 he was Queensland correspondent for *The Times*, London. In 1928 he wrote the introduction for the memorial edition of George Essex Evans's [q.v.8] *Collected verse*. He corresponded increasingly with authors like (Dame) Mary Gilmore [q.v.9], the Palmers [qq.v.] and H. M. Green and among Queensland writers he singled out William Baylebridge [q.v.7]. The McKinnons participated actively in Brisbane's cultural life. Emmie was State president (1927) and later a life vice-president of the Lyceum Club and a founding member (1921), honorary general secretary and later president of the Queensland Bush Book Club. Firmin, recognized as a tireless literary lecturer and mentor of many young writers, was also honorary secretary and later a life member of the (Royal) Historical Society of Queensland, and vice-president (1941) of the Queensland Authors' and Artists' Association.

On Taylor's death in June 1932, McKinnon was appointed the *Courier*'s last editor before its merger with the *Daily Mail* in August 1933. Sir Keith Murdoch [q.v.] by-passed him for the editorship of the *Courier Mail* but, because he had acted in the position in August-December until the arrival of Tingey Foster, folklore has endowed McKinnon with the reputation as first editor. In 1935 he attended the Empire Press Conference in South Africa. North of Sydney, McKinnon was perhaps the most formidable reviewer of Australian books. In 1940 he assisted E. Morris Miller [q.v.] with the chapter 'Poets and poetry: Queensland' in *Australian literature from its beginnings to 1935*. His Anglocentric conservatism, however, allowed little sympathy for certain literary trends. In his reviews of Rex Ingamells's *Jindyworobak anthology, 1938* and of C. B. Christesen's first

issue of *Meanjin Papers* McKinnon concluded that it was not a good period for Australian poetry.

In the 1940s and early 1950s he was also a regular *Courier Mail* art reviewer who fought on behalf of art groups and institutions and sought increased financial backing for them. He succeeded Spencer Browne as part-time editor of *Queensland Trustees' Quarterly Review* in 1943 till his retirement on 14 June 1946, after which he edited Queensland Newspapers' *House News* from August 1947 to mid-1951.

Slightly built, meticulously dressed and an inveterate pipe-smoker, McKinnon was conservative and reserved, but with a dry sense of humour: a gentle, likeable and respected man. He died from cancer at his home at Highgate Hill, Brisbane, on 11 March 1953 and was cremated with Anglican rites. Childless, he was survived by his wife and three sisters.

Qld Newspapers Pty Ltd, *House News*, 16 Dec 1949, 20 Oct 1950, 2 Apr 1953; *RHSQ Bulletin*, 108, Apr 1953; *Journalist*, Apr 1953; *Southerly*, 15, no 3, 1954; *Courier Mail*, 30 Apr 1935, 3 Dec 1938, 28 Dec 1940, 24 June 1946, 12 Mar 1953, 16 Jan 1964; H. J. Summers, History of the Australian Journalists' Association, Queensland (1952, typescript at A.J.A., Brisb); McKinnon materials (in various MS collections) *and* Bush Book Club papers (Fryer Lib, Univ Qld); Oxley Cttee minutes (Oxley Lib, Brisb); information from H. J. Summers, Ashgrove, and J. Cossey, Clayfield, Brisb, R. T. Foster, Waverley, Syd, and R. Whitehurst, Yass, NSW.

DESMOND MACAULAY

McKIVAT, CHRISTOPHER HOBART (1879-1941), footballer, was born on 27 November 1879 at Burrawang, New South Wales, fifth surviving of ten children of Edward McKivat, Irish-born farmer, and his Tasmanian wife Susan, née Bellette. By 1897 McKivat was playing senior grade Rugby Union with Bowen Bros Tannery's team at Orange. He performed well for country against city in 1901 and next year was selected to tour New Zealand, but had to decline. Moving to Sydney in 1905, he joined Glebe (called the 'Dirty Reds' for their maroon guernseys) which won the premiership in 1906 and 1907. McKivat played either as scrum-half or five-eighth.

He represented New South Wales against New Zealand in 1907 and next year captained Glebe. In August 1908, selected for the first Wallaby tour of Britain and the United States of America, he was presented by fellow workers at the Farmers' & Dairymen's Milk Co. Ltd with an inscribed gold watch. An unselfish player, he scored eight tries on tour. As captain H. M. Moran [q.v.] and vice-captain Freddy Woods were frequently injured,

McKivat led the Wallabies seventeen times, including the match against Cornwall at the London Olympic Games when the Australians won gold medals.

On returning to Sydney in September 1909, fourteen of the Wallabies played a series against the Rugby League Kangaroos. McKivat, allegedly paid £150, was expelled with the others from the amateur code. In 1910 he played for Australasia in all three Tests against the touring British (Rugby League) team. In 1911-12 he led the second Kangaroos' tour of Britain; although older than his colleagues, he played in 32 of the 36 matches, scoring 41 points from 13 tries and 1 goal. The Australasians won all three Tests. McKivat played no more representative matches, but continued to captain Glebe Rugby League team until 1914.

At St Benedict's Catholic Church on 6 February 1915 he married Ada Glynn, a tailoress. His occupation then was storeman; earlier he had been a labourer and engine driver, later a weigh-clerk. He was also a successful football coach, taking North Sydney to premierships in 1921 and 1922.

Sturdily built, 5 ft. 8½ ins. (174 cm) tall, weighing about 12 stone (76 kg), McKivat had thick, dark, curly hair, rugged features and a wide mouth. Reputedly Australia's finest halfback in either Rugby code, to G. V. Portus [q.v.] he gave 'the impression of strength rather than agility. But his feet and hands worked in perfect combination with his eyes, and behind them all was a quick-thinking brain . . . His passes were accurate, well-timed and . . . he was a deadly tackler'. Adept at stealing from the scrum-base, he was very quick off the mark without straightening up and was master of the high short kick. His screw-punting was handy in defence. 'A born captain . . . of equable temperament—never rattled', according to Claude Corbett [q.v.8], he constantly snapped out orders to his players on the field; off it he was a quiet humorist.

All his life he enjoyed going to the football on Saturdays and having a few beers with mates after the game. He was not a churchgoer. McKivat died on 4 May 1941, survived by his wife and son, and was buried in the Catholic section of Botany cemetery.

G. V. Portus, *Happy highways* (Melb, 1953); *NSW Rugby League Annual*, 1928; *Leichhardt Hist J*, no 8, 1979; *Sydney Mail*, 20 June 1906; *Referee*, 5 Aug 1908; *Sun* (Syd), 5 May 1941; information from Mr C. A. McKivat, West Ryde, Syd.

CHRIS CUNNEEN

MACKNESS, CONSTANCE (1882-1973), teacher and author, was born on 17 June 1882 at Tuena, New South Wales, second child of James Mackness, goldminer, and his native-born wife Alice, née Brown. James was born in Buckinghamshire, England, in 1838. In 1851 he ran away to sea, came to Australia as a cabin boy, was shipwrecked near Williamstown, Victoria, and worked his way to the Ballarat goldfields in time for the Eureka stockade. He wrote a diary in verse of his adventures on various fields and eventually settled on the Tuena goldfields.

Constance's childhood was later reflected in her first novel, *Gem of the Flat*, (Sydney, 1915), which described a young girl's life on a smallholding in a family which lived by goldfossicking, rabbit-shooting and small crops. Life was Spartan in the wattle-and-daub house on 'Needy Flat' but, her heroine declared, 'she meant to be a lady some day, cultured, capable, charming, and she educated herself to that end'. She often sighed because she was unlovely and was a very unmusical child but, with coaching in school and out and help from philanthropic friends and relations, she was able to go to a Sydney school.

Constance became the first female dux of the Fort Street Model School, matriculating in 1898 with honours in French, and winning one of only three university bursaries available to girls. In 1902 she graduated B.A. from the University of Sydney with first-class honours in English, French and history and a prize for physiography, taught by Professor (Sir) Edgeworth David [q.v.8], who also gave her the grounding for her retirement hobby, conchology.

Entering the teaching profession, Constance was the main financial support of her ailing family for the next fifty years. At the Presbyterian Ladies' College, Croydon, she dedicated herself to the principles and practice of Presbyterian education for girls. She taught her pupils to reconcile *Genesis* and evolution: 'God made the world . . . such wonders are beyond man's making'. She went from Croydon to the new Presbyterian Ladies' College, Pymble, in 1916 as househeadmistress.

In 1917 the Church, wisely guided as was said in retrospect, selected Miss Mackness as founding headmistress of the Presbyterian Girls' College, Warwick, Queensland. For the next thirty years she devoted herself to the school, building a reputation for herself as zealous, beneficent and firm and earning for P.G.C. a highly respected name. She gave the school the McInnes clan motto, *'E labore dulcedo'*, and wrote her most popular book about *The glad school* (Sydney, 1927), a record of the happy, healthy and morally sound environment for which she strove so successfully. As her niece wrote: 'a PGC girl smiled a lot and walked with head high and back straight'. In *Gem of the flat* a teacher's craft was explained: 'she always looked at children as though she knew they meant well and would do well, and somehow they tried unconsciously to live up to her expectations'.

Constance Mackness published ten books, all of them about young people, and wrote 'pars', articles and short stories for the *Bulletin* and local papers. In later years she compiled *Clump Point and district: an historical record*. Her brothers had settled there, south of Innisfail, and it is the setting for her book, *The young beachcombers* (London, Melbourne, 1934). E. Morris Miller [q.v.] described her work as 'the fun and frolic of schoolchildren delightfully told'.

In 1949 Miss Mackness retired from the school, amid all the honours which a grateful Church and her devoted pupils could lavish. Appointed M.B.E. in 1959, she lived in the northern family home until failing health brought her to Hopetoun, the Presbyterian home, Corinda, Brisbane, where her old girls were constant visitors. She died there on 13 December 1973, and was cremated.

H. M. Saxby, *A history of Australian children's literature, 1841-1941* (Syd, 1969); *Presbyterian Outlook* (Brisb), 1-2 (1918-19); Presbyterian Girls' College, Warwick, Twenty-seventh annual report, Dec 1944; Presbyterian Church of Qld Archives (Brisb); Qld Women's Hist Assn records (Brisb); family papers (held by Mrs P. Wilbe, Helensburg, NSW).   NANCY BONNIN

MACKRELL, EDWIN JOSEPH (1878-1965), politician, was born on 16 December 1878 at Strathbogie, Victoria, fifth of eight children of George Mackrell, farmer from Ireland, and his Victorian-born wife Mary Ann, née Perkins. Mackrell was educated at Strathbogie State School. While a schoolboy he assisted his cousin George Mackrell at Mansfield Butter Factory and later built a smithy on his parents' farm to repair machinery. This mechanical bent brought him the post of manager at Fish Creek Butter Factory when he was 18 and later management of the Buln Buln factory near Warragul.

In 1901 Mackrell prospected unsuccessfully at Kalgoorlie, Western Australia, then became a mine carpenter and engine driver. In 1906, back home, he was engaged by Bartram & Sons of Melbourne to sell and install Alfa Laval separators. He travelled the northeast of Victoria and the Riverina until transferred to Johannesburg, South Africa, in July 1908. After further travelling he became butter factory manager at Senekal, Orange Free State, briefly resuming Bartrams' Johannesburg agency after his marriage at Durban, on 15 July 1910 with Methodist

forms, to an Australian, Elsie Flora Harris. He set up his own butter factory but his leadership of Senekal loyalists under Botha during the Afrikaner rebellion of 1914 lost him his business.

Mackrell returned home in 1916, bought land at Boho near Violet Town, but exchanged this for the old Strathbogie station pre-emptive right, adding adjacent land. In 1920 he was elected as Victorian Farmers' Union candidate for Upper Goulburn in the Legislative Assembly. Within the V.F.U. he was conservative, supporting Premier (Sir) Harry Lawson [q.v.] against the more radical wheat-growers in the 1921 wheat-pool dispute. In 1922-36 he was secretary of the Victorian Parliamentary Country Party, and minister without portfolio, contributing mainly to railway planning, in the 1924-27 Allan [q.v.7]-Peacock [q.v.] administration. He moved to Canterbury, Melbourne, in 1927.

Mackrell achieved a large electoral majority in 1935 and was unopposed for ten years. In the Dunstan [q.v.8] ministry, sworn in on 2 April 1935, he was honorary minister in charge of sustenance and the labour exchange, and continued to deal with these matters when he became minister for labour on 28 July 1936. On 23 June 1941 he was given charge of post-war reconstruction. 'I . . . know something of how men get out of work', he commented, 'and therefore I should know something of how to put them back into work'. The portfolio of public health was added to his responsibilities next January. A conscientious minister, though without parliamentary brilliance, Mackrell pushed through necessary Depression and wartime legislation and worked hard for his rural constituents.

When on 9 September 1943 the Dunstan government fell and was eventually succeeded by a Dunstan-Hollway coalition Mackrell, who had offered to step down, was not included in the cabinet. As a back-bencher he supported Dunstan until 30 August 1945; angered then by Dunstan's refusal to resign over the redistribution issue, he joined a disaffected Country Party coterie to support a Labor censure motion. Expelled from the party, he helped to bring down the government on 25 September. Minister of water supply and of decentralization in the brief Liberal administration of Ian Macfarlan, Mackrell was defeated in the November elections when he stood as an Independent Country Party candidate for the new seat of Goulburn.

Mackrell was a Presbyterian and a Freemason. He was a justice of the peace for Victoria and for New South Wales where he owned a 1608-acre (651 ha) property, Burraboi. He died at Canterbury on 24 March 1965 and was cremated. His three daughters survived him.

B. D. Graham, *The formation of the Australian Country Parties*(Canb, 1966); *Argus*, 28 July 1938, 24 June 1941, 17 Sept 1943, 6, 19, 20, 22, 24, 25 Sept 1945: *Sun-News Pictorial*, 29 July 1936, 20 Sept 1945; *Age*, 25 March 1965; Mackrell reminiscences (MS, LaTL); information from Miss D. Mackrell, Balwyn, Melb.   DON CHAMBERS

MACKY, WILLIAM MARCUS DILL; *see* DILL MACKY

McLACHLAN, ALEXANDER JOHN (1872-1956), lawyer, businessman and politician, was born on 2 November 1872 at Naracoorte, South Australia, son of Alexander McLachlan, grazier, and his wife Mary, née Patterson. He was raised in the atmosphere of a Gaelic-speaking family and workforce, and educated privately at Hamilton Academy, Victoria, and Mount Gambier High School, South Australia.

In 1890 he was articled to Davison & Daniel of Mount Gambier, subsequently transferring his indenture to E. B. Grundy of Adelaide. McLachlan completed the Final Certificate in Law at the University of Adelaide and was admitted to the South Australian Bar in 1895 (and to the Victorian Bar in 1929). After practice at Gladstone and Petersburg (Peterborough), he entered into partnership with C. C. Kingston [q.v.9] in 1897. Owing to Kingston's political involvements, McLachlan effectively conducted the business until the partnership was dissolved in 1905. He subsequently took several partners including W. J. Vandenburgh and (Sir) Mellis Napier. His professional career was marked by success in several leading cases, but Chief Justice Sir George Murray [q.v.] refused to nominate him for silk. With E. W. Benham, he revised the *Magistrates' guide* (1906). On 1 June 1898 he had married Cecia Antoinette Billiet (d. 1941) at St Andrew's Church, Adelaide.

McLachlan was chief of the Caledonian Society in 1899-1902 and lieutenant in command of a South Australian Scottish Corps in 1901. For some years he was legal adviser to a small company, Hume [q.v.9] Bros., and when the Hume Pipe Co. (Aust) Ltd was formed in 1920 he joined the board and became its second chairman.

Between 1896 and 1922 McLachlan unsuccessfully contested six parliamentary elections: for the House of Assembly districts of Victoria in 1896 and Adelaide in 1912; the Legislative Council (Southern District) in 1905; the Federal electorate of Adelaide in 1908 and 1910; and the Senate in 1922. He was a founding organizer and second president (1913-16) of the South Australian Liberal Union, forged from several non-Labor groups. Following the 1916 Labor split he was involved in merging the new National Party into the S.A.L.U., to form the Liberal Federation.

McLachlan was eventually elected to the Senate in 1925. In the normal course of events he would have occupied his seat in July 1926; however, following the resignation of Senator Benny, McLachlan was appointed to fill the casual vacancy in January. In August he was appointed honorary minister (to discharge the functions of the absent attorney-general) in the Bruce [q.v.7]-Page [q.v.] government. On the return of Attorney-General Latham [q.v.] he continued to serve as 'a sort of offsider to the prime minister', doing the work of any ill or absent minister. In 1928 he led the Australian delegation to the League of Nations, where he defended Australia's tariff policy and signed the Kellogg-Briand Pact on behalf of Australia. He lived mainly in Melbourne from about 1930.

In the Lyons [q.v.] government McLachlan was vice-president of the Executive Council (1932-34). As minister in charge of development and scientific and industrial research (1932-37) he promoted the Council for Scientific and Industrial Research's work in the fishing industry, salinity control in the Murray, and coal hydrogenation. When postmaster-general (1934-38) he permitted extensive commercial licensing of wireless stations. In 1937-38 he was leader of the government in the Senate.

Throughout this period McLachlan advocated greater preparations for war, including the formation of an Empire naval fleet to supplement the Royal Navy. His advocacy at public functions, he recalled, was 'received with a dumb silence'. Nor were his opinions on defence supported by Lyons, with whom his relationship was deteriorating. McLachlan's public support of sanctions against Italy made him unpopular in cabinet. Lyons's procrastination over the national health and pensions insurance bill of 1938, which McLachlan pressed through the Senate and which he was anxious to have proclaimed, further strained relations. On 3 November 1938 a parliamentary question was asked which implied that the postmaster-general had misused his position to influence the letting of contracts to the Hume Pipe Co. Although no evidence was adduced and the claim was denied by McLachlan, Lyons was less than fulsome in his defence. McLachlan's resignation the same day ('one's personal honour is dearer than all the pelf on earth') caused a sensation.

He remained on the Senate back-bench until June 1944 and was disappointed not to be appointed a privy councillor. In 1943 he failed to secure pre-selection for a further Senate term. His autobiography, *McLachlan: an F.A.Q. Australian* was published in 1948. Tall, burly and genial, he enjoyed golf and bridge, and was chairman of the South Australian Football League (1920-25).

McLachlan died childless on 28 May 1956 at the Mercy Hospital, East Melbourne, and was cremated after a state funeral. His estate, sworn for probate in Victoria at £127 161, was left largely to his nephews.

M. Farr, *Origins of the Liberal Party and Country League of South Australia* (Adel, 1969); *Advertiser* (Adel), 12 Sept 1913, 10 Sept 1915, 26 Apr 1922, 7 Sept 1925, 4, 11 Nov 1938, 30 May 1956; *Argus*, 4 Nov 1938; *SMH*, 30 May 1956.

GRAHAM LOUGHLIN

McLACHLAN, DUNCAN CLARK (1853?-1929), public service commissioner, was born probably in 1853 in Glasgow, Scotland, son of Donald McLachlan, joiner, and his wife Margaret, née Cowan. His parents migrated about 1857 to Sydney where his father opened a general store at Redfern. Duncan was educated at a school attached to St Paul's Church of England, Redfern, at W. A. Yarrington's private school and under the tutorship of Rev. James McSkimming. He joined the New South Wales Railways as a clerk in 1869. On 13 November 1879 at Darlinghurst he married Emily Matilda (d. 1929), daughter of Obediah West, owner of the Barcom Glen estate on which sections of Darlinghurst and Paddington were eventually built.

McLachlan's 'alertness and capacity for rapid administration' enabled him to pass quickly through all grades to become chief clerk in 1886, acting occasionally as secretary to the railway commissioners. When the enterprise was converted to public corporation status in 1888, he became chief clerk and secretary to the tender board in the Department of Public Works which retained the railway construction function. In this position he successfully reorganized the several semi-autonomous branches into one ministerial department. In March 1896 he was appointed under secretary of the Department of Mines and Agriculture. This position broadened his administrative experience, bringing him in contact with the colony's leading producers and with complex technical matters.

He had found time to play cricket and lead the movement for free libraries in Redfern and in Paddington, where he lived after 1890. An alderman of the Paddington Municipal Council, in 1899 he was a founder and first president of the local Masonic Club.

In May 1902 McLachlan was appointed the first Commonwealth public service commissioner. His departure from the New South Wales service was almost a canonizing event. The *Public Service Journal* declared there had been 'no more popular Under-Secretary . . . and none who better deserves his popularity'. However, the numerous eulogies were not to last long, and they perhaps contributed to the formation in McLachlan of an almost God-like view of his new mission, for his second career was far less peaceful, and more controversial, than his earlier one.

Of course the task was immense. McLachlan had to mould into a single integrated Federal service the transferred elements from six colonial services, with widely differing employment conditions. This job was well done, the outcome being a model public service for its day. McLachlan began a second seven-year term in 1909, and was appointed I.S.O. (1903) and C.M.G. (1909). He visited England in 1912 to inspect civil service conditions, and stated on return that, comparatively, Australian civil servants were better off. He retired in May 1916.

McLachlan was a man of high ideals, and his annual reports to parliament, carrying, like his correspondence with department heads, a large and beautifully crafted signature, suggest a man taking himself very seriously as 'father of the public service'. In his 1906 report he quoted:

We live in deeds, not years; in thoughts, not breaths;
In feelings, not in figures on a dial . . .

'Each official', he had reported in 1904, 'will be expected to show evidence of a strenuous official life, to work diligently and conscientiously, and legitimately earn the salary he receives . . . The stamp of officer . . . who arrives unpunctually, does little, gossips much, takes no personal interest in his work, and leaves with scrupulous promptness . . . is utterly useless'. Later reports urged the development of initiative and the payment of bonuses for outstanding service, and condemned 'moonlighters', loiterers and those who put personal before official benefit.

The Littlejohn reforms of the mid-1890s had given New South Wales the most advanced system of public personnel administration in Australia. McLachlan brought to the Commonwealth a firm belief in the concept of an impartial, neutral public service, and in the accompaning requirement for economical, efficient and incorruptible administration. Subjected to much pressure, seeing himself as trustee of the general public interest, he refused to compromise. Increasingly he came into collision with Labor politicians, the developing staff associations, and other manifestations of the radicalism of the early twentieth-century Commonwealth. He did not endear himself to radicals, and came to be seen not only as paternalistic but also as an opponent of change. His increasing conservatism probably reflected a fear that the substantial gains already made under his early leadership would be jeopardized, rather than any real inclination to defy the radicals.

Fissiparous tendencies worried him: notably public servants' access to the Commonwealth Court of Conciliation and Arbitration, the exempting of large areas of defence employment from the public service commissioner's jurisdiction, and the possibility, latent in a long-running royal commission and a business leader's inquiry, that the Postmaster-General's Department might be turned into a public corporation. McLachlan often criticized these tendencies in his annual reports. He returned to the charge after being called back from retirement in September 1918 as royal commissioner to advise the Hughes [q.v.9] government on the system of public service personnel management and on the proposed overhaul of the Public Service Act. His wide-ranging, pungent and controversial report, prepared in under four months, was released in 1920, coinciding with legislation before parliament resulting from the so-called 'Economies' royal commission.

Increasingly parliament was establishing statutory authorities outside the public service to undertake urgent tasks of government. McLachlan reported that 'the exercise of influence both direct and indirect is bound to be attempted in regard to appointments, fixing of salaries, and tenure of office, which will be most prejudicial to the interests of the Commonwealth'. He also wanted final arbitral powers vested in the public service commissioner to halt the 'weakening of constituted authority, the reduction of efficiency, and the general disorganization of departmental management' which he believed had followed the gaining of access to the Arbitration Court in 1911.

In 1920 legislation transferred arbitral powers from the general court to a special public service arbitrator, not back to the commissioner as McLachlan had wanted. Further legislation in 1922 followed his recommendation that Commonwealth public servants should have their own superannuation scheme. A major revision of the Public Service Act, also in 1922, converted the office of commissioner into a three-member Public Service Board, as had been suggested by the 'Economies' commission but opposed by McLachlan. However, his views were influential in the staffing sections of the Act, for example in organizing the service into four divisions, in appointment and promotions procedures, and in granting the right of appeal against departmental decisions on punishments and promotions.

What McLachlan facilitated after 1902, and whose full integrity he sought to restore in his 1920 report, was a strong executive government able to marshal the administrative resources of the state in the service of the public good, as defined by parliament, and made possible through a co-ordinated subsystem of personnel management. In his repeated criticism of the inroads being made into the integrated system by use of statutory authorities, public corporations and other 'exempted' agencies, he defined the parameters of a debate since carried on in many parts of the world, between advocates of integrated, homogeneous departmental systems and advocates of heterogeneous systems providing room for flexible and autonomous agencies to carry out a wide variety of public functions.

After his retirement McLachlan returned to Sydney from Melbourne to embark on, in the opinion of the *Bulletin*, 'the toughest job in his life' when he joined the board of the Civil Service Co-operative Society of New South Wales. 'Then all the troubles in the world seemed to fall upon him'. He was elected a director in 1923 and subsequently chairman of directors of the co-operative society, which among other things operated a large store in Pitt Street, Sydney. McLachlan had visited England and the Continent with the manager of the stores in 1922, to inspect the operation of similar commercial houses. The business decline of the later 1920s frustrated an expansionist decision by the directors in 1925 to purchase more city property in the expectation of benefits from the opening of the harbour bridge and the city underground railway. McLachlan resigned because of ill health in 1928.

In retirement he played golf and was president of the Warringah Bowling Club. On 20 April 1929 the *Sydney Morning Herald* published his article on the 'Old Sydney water mill', an early enterprise of his wife's family. He died on 18 October 1929 at his Mosman home and was buried in St Jude's Church of England cemetery, Randwick. His three sons and three daughters survived him. The new building for the Public Serice Board in Canberra was named after him in 1980 when the board acknowledged that McLachlan had been responsible 'for the consolidation of advanced personnel practices based firmly on the career service concept and the structuring of the federal Public Service into departments'. No other single individual had made such a mark on the shape and practices of the Commonwealth service in its formative period.

McLachlan's brother Hugh (1856?-1909) also joined the New South Wales Railway service: the *Bulletin* described him in 1929 'as probably the most brilliant secretary the Railway Department ever had'.

Roy Com on public service administration, *Report* (Melb, 1920); G. E. Caiden, *Career Service* (Melb, 1965); Public Service Bd, *The Public Service Board 1923-73* (Canb, 1973), and *Annual Report*, 1980; R. L. Wettenhall, *Architects of departmental systems* (Canb, 1984); B. Juddery, *White collar power* (Syd, 1980); *Public Service J* (NSW), 10 Apr 1902; *Transmitter* (Syd), 17 May 1902; Public Service Commissioner, *Annual Reports*, 1904-16; *Public Administration* (Syd), 22, no 2, June 1963; *T&CJ*, 21 Mar 1896; *SMH*, 21 Oct 1929; *Bulletin*, 23 Oct 1929; *Canb Times*, 30 Nov 1980.

R. L. WETTENHALL

MACLAGAN; *see* SINCLAIR-MACLAGAN

McLAREN, CHARLES INGLIS (1882-1957), psychiatrist and missionary, was born on 23 August 1882 in Tokyo, younger son of Samuel Gilfillan McLaren [q.v.] and his wife Marjory Millar, née Bruce. He was educated at Scotch College, Melbourne, and Ormond [q.v.5] College, University of Melbourne (M.B., 1906; B.S., 1907; M.D., 1910). In 1907-08 he was resident medical officer at the (Royal) Melbourne Hospital and next year worked at the Children's Hospital. From schooldays he was active in the Australasian Student Christian Union and the Student Volunteer Movement for Foreign Missions; as Australasian chairman of the latter, in 1910 he toured Australian and New Zealand universities and colleges.

On 22 August 1911 at Alma Road Presbyterian Church, St Kilda, McLaren married Jessie Reeve, a missionary's daughter and travelling secretary of the Christian Union. In September, as missionaries of the Presbyterian Church of Victoria, they sailed for Korea where McLaren was assistant superintendent and in 1915-22 superintendent of Paton Memorial Hospital, Chinju. In 1917, following the death of his brother Samuel Bruce [q.v.], he enlisted in the Royal Army Medical Corps, serving as medical officer to the Chinese Labour Battalion, France. In 1922-39 he was professor of neurology and psychological medicine, Union Christian Medical College, Severance Hospital (later medical faculty, Yonsei University), Seoul, undertaking postgraduate study in Vienna in 1929. He worked again at Chinju Hospital in 1940-41.

Furloughs provided opportunity to revisit Melbourne. In July 1927 McLaren lectured there on the relationship between body and mind, publishing his paper in the *Austral-*

asian Journal of Psychology and Philosophy, 1928. In introducing him (Sir) Richard Stawell [q.v.] referred to his 'great intellectual ability . . . exceptionally fine character, steadfast and earnest . . . high purpose in life . . . [and] exceedingly pleasant temperament'. In 1934 McLaren lectured for the Melbourne University Student Christian Movement and delivered the Beattie Smith [q.v.] Lecture on Insanity, taking as his subject the interpretation and treatment of psychoneurosis and psychoses (published in the *Medical Journal of Australia*, 1936). In 1941 he wrote 'The Principle of Health' as the Sir Richard Stawell oration. He contributed to British, Chinese and Japanese medical journals and discussed the Japanese Shinto shrine issue in religious journals.

During the 1930s McLaren argued against Japan's enforcement of emperor-worship. On Japan's entry into World War II he was imprisoned for eleven weeks, interned and later repatriated to Melbourne, arriving in November 1942. He gave talks throughout Australia for the Army Education Service and to church audiences on Japan and Korea and on the basis of peace being reconciliation. In 1943-44 he published *Preface to peace with Japan, Eleven weeks in a Japanese prison cell* and *They kept the faith*. Chairman-editor of a Presbyterian report on communism and the church, he also wrote *Christianity, communism and the world situation* (Melbourne, 1952).

In 1949 McLaren stood as an Independent for the Federal seat of Melbourne against the minister for immigration Arthur Calwell in protest at 'the provocative, and dangerous administration' of the White Australia policy; he expressed his views in *The Christian faith and the White Australia policy*. He was first chairman of Friends of Vellore, a Victorian support group for the medical college and hospital in South India. In 1951 he organized the John Fisher Williams Memorial Foundation in memory of the Melbourne psychiatrist.

Tall and trim, McLaren had as his most striking aspects alert, attractive eyes and a disarming smile. He was a man of compassion, courage and ceaseless intellectual activity, a pioneer of psychiatry and a lifelong explorer of the New Testament. He was revising a manuscript on the life of Jesus when he died at Kew on 9 October 1957. He was buried in Box Hill cemetery, survived by his wife and daughter.

E. W. New, *A doctor in Korea* (Syd, 1958); K. Fitzpatrick, *PLC Melbourne* (Melb, 1975); *MJA*, 21 Dec 1957; Aust Student Christian Movement, *A'sian Intercollegian*, 1910, 1911; C. I. McLaren's personal 'Medical and general Record' (typescript held by Mrs R. Human, Kew, Melb); McLaren letters held by, and information from, Mrs M. Miller, Forest Hill, Melb.   FRANK ENGEL

McLAREN, JOHN (JACK) (1884-1954), writer, was born on 13 October 1884 at Fitzroy, Melbourne, eldest of five children of Rev. John McLaren, Presbyterian minister, and his wife Mary, née Brown (or Bow), Scottish migrants. McLaren entered Scotch College on 8 October 1896, but ran away four years later and carried a swag for a year. He then worked for ten months as cabin boy and seaman on a windjammer which sailed from Adelaide to Port Elizabeth, South Africa, and back to Newcastle, New South Wales. This voyage is recorded in his *Blood on the deck* (London, 1933).

Working his passage to North Queensland, McLaren in 1902-11 engaged in various romantic occupations in tropical places. He worked as a miner, mule-driver and rabbit-poisoner. He searched for pearl-shell out from Thursday Island, for bêche-de-mer and tortoise shell on the Barrier Reef, and for sandalwood on Cape York. In Malaya, the Solomon Islands and Fiji he worked as an overseer, and sometimes a labour-recruiter, on coconut plantations. He visited Java and the Ellice Islands, and was shipwrecked in the Gulf of Papua. In New Guinea he ran trade stores, prospected, transported copper overland to Port Moresby, and hunted birds of paradise. *My odyssey* (London, 1923) tells part of the story of these years.

On 6 October 1911, tired of wandering, McLaren landed at Simpson's Bay on the west coast of Cape York. Alone except for the tribe of Aborigines whom he paid to work for him, he built a house and established a coconut plantation. Writing under the pseudonym, 'McNorth', he sent a stream of paragraphs to the *Bulletin* in Sydney, and also completed his first novel, *Red mountain* (1919). Some of his experience on Cape York is recounted in *My crowded solitude* (London, 1926).

After selling the plantation, McLaren journeyed to Sydney early in 1919, hoping to earn a living from writing. Receiving a small sum from the New South Wales Bookstall Co. for his first two novels, he also found work as a laboratory assistant. By March 1924 he was living at Northcote, Melbourne, where he enjoyed Bernard O'Dowd's [q.v.] friendship and financial support. On 19 August 1924 he married a fellow novelist, Ada Elizabeth Moore, née McKenzie; the marriage seems to have been childless.

In 1925 McLaren settled in London where his address changed with his fortunes. London remained his base for nearly thirty years, though according to his last autobiography, *My civilised adventure* (London, 1952), he made trips to Corsica and France, and even returned briefly to Thursday Island and New Guinea. He seems never to have been financially secure. He broadcast and wrote scripts for the British Broadcasting Corporation and during World War II was in charge of the section of the Ministry of Information responsible for publicity about the Empire. McLaren's first wife died in 1946 and on 21 February 1951 he married Dorothy Norris of Chelsea. Among his few literary acquaintances in London were Thomas Burke, J. M. Barrie, Guy Howarth and Philip Lindsay [q.v.]. McLaren died of myocardial infarction on 16 May 1954, while on holiday at Brighton.

Authenticity of background, derived from his experience in the tropics, is the only merit of most of McLaren's twenty-one volumes of fiction. In *Sun man* (London, 1928) he nevertheless succeeded in commenting implicitly on the genre of the romantic adventure novel, by overturning the expected ending; and *A diver went down* (London, 1929) is a genuine thriller in an exotic setting. His literary reputation must rest on his autobiographies, and principally on *My crowded solitude*. This work offers sensitive observations on the small fauna inhabiting McLaren's retreat, and anecdotes and insights about his rare visitors, and especially about his Aboriginal companions. McLaren observes the tribe from the platform of European civilization, and derives humour and occasionally satire from contrasting expectations and values. This theme is constant in his writings, all of which reflect the journeys between civilization and the wild which prevailed in his life and gave it its particular quality.

T. Burke, Preface to J. McLaren, *My South Sea adventure* (Lond, 1936); *All About Books*, 18 July 1929, p 253; *Meanjin Q*, 13, no 2 (1954); *Sydney Mail*, 5 May 1920; *The Times*, 18 May 1954; *Age*, 21 May 1966.
                                                    CHERYL TAYLOR

McLAREN, SIR JOHN GILBERT (1871-1958), public servant, was born on 15 October 1871 at Parramatta, New South Wales, son of William Burness McLaren, stonemason, and his wife Mary, née Gilbert, both born at Parramatta. He was educated at Sydney Boys' High School and the University of Sydney (B.A., 1895). He had joined the Postmaster-General's Department, New South Wales, in January 1888, as a clerk, and transferred with his department to the Commonwealth service in 1901.

McLaren was Commonwealth electoral officer for New South Wales in 1904-19 and a member in 1911-12 of the commission that redistributed electoral boundaries for the State. In July 1919 he was appointed assistant secretary, Prime Minister's Department, and in 1921-28 was secretary of the Department of Home and Territories. He visited Darwin in 1925 to report on and recommend staff reorganization in the Northern Territory, and in 1927 he examined the government of the Mandated Territory of New Guinea as a preliminary to its revision.

In June 1928 McLaren was appointed a commissioner of the Public Service Board. However, when S. M. (Viscount) Bruce [q.v.7] reshuffled the Commonwealth Public Service in December, McLaren replaced Percy Deane [q.v.8] as secretary to the Prime Minister's Department (1929-32) to which the administration of the territories of Papua and New Guinea was transferred. At the request of Prime Minister Scullin [q.v.] he reviewed the functions of the External Affairs Branch to bring it more closely within the departmental structure. (Sir) Keith Officer observed that although McLaren was very friendly he was 'almost too well informed of affairs in the office and asked such embarrassing questions'. He was chairman of the Australian Tobacco Investigation in 1931-32 and chairman of the Commonwealth advisory committee on employment (1932).

During his appointment as official secretary, High Commissioner's Office, London (January 1933-October 1936), on a salary reduced by a quarter under the Financial Emergency Act, McLaren represented Australia at International Labour Organization conferences (1933, 1934) and annually at meetings of the Permanent Mandates Commission, Geneva. As deputy high commissioner he attended the London Naval Conference in 1935-36 and the Council of Accession (1936). The financial responsibilities of the high commissioner were attended to by Bruce during McLaren's term, but pressures for economy led McLaren to suggest that all State agents-general should be located in Australia House.

During his early career McLaren had been active in literary and debating circles and was an attractive and well-informed speaker. On 8 February 1904 at Annandale, Sydney, he had married with Catholic rites Emily Frances Sarah Wynn (d. 1941), oratorio and concert soprano, and on his transfer in 1927 he became prominent in the nascent cultural life of Canberra. He was the first president of the Canberra Musical Society (1928-30) and of the Canberra Repertory Society (1932), and a member of the Canberra Society of Arts. In August 1927 he was a member with (Sir) Robert Garran [q.v.8] and (Sir) David Rivett [q.v.] of a committee calling for the establishment of a university and was a government nominee to the council of Canberra University College (1930-32) and acting chairman (1930).

McLaren was appointed C.M.G. in 1925 and knighted in 1935. When he retired in 1936 and returned to Sydney it was rumoured that he might seek a political career. He took an active interest in immigration and in work for the League of Nations and for over twenty years was a member of the Millions Club of New South Wales and its president in 1951-58. He died on 27 July 1958 at Strathfield, and was cremated. McLaren had married on 1 October 1949 at Mosman, a widow Lucie Adela Nash, née Sparrow, who survived him together with three daughters of his first marriage.

P. G. Edwards, *Prime ministers and diplomats* (Melb, 1983); *SMH*, 13 Feb 1904, 15 Sept 1925, 2 Sept 1927, 8 Dec 1928, 2 Aug 1930, 7 June 1951, 29 July 1958; *Canb Times*, 27 Sept 1927, 17 Feb, 11, 25 Apr, 22 May 1928, 18 Jan, 1 Feb, 13 Sept 1933; Officer papers (MS 2629, items 1/86, 1/102, 8/82, NL); Dept of Home and Territories, Univ Canb: proposed establishment, 1927, A1 27/17321 (AAO).

D. I. McDONALD

McLAREN, SAMUEL BRUCE (1876-1916), mathematician and mathematical physicist, was born on 16 August 1876 at Yedo, near Tokyo, elder son of Rev. Samuel Gilfillan McLaren [q.v.] and his wife Marjory Millar, née Bruce. Arriving in Melbourne with his parents in 1886, he was educated at Coburg State School, Brighton Grammar School and Scotch College where he was dux. He attended the University of Melbourne on an Ormond [q.v.5] College scholarship and graduated B.A. in 1897 with first-class honours in mathematics and the Wyselaskie [q.v.6] and Dixson scholarships. He then went to Trinity College, Cambridge; graduating B.A. with first-class honours in 1900, he received the Isaac Newton studentship in astronomy and physical optics in 1901.

In 1904 McLaren was appointed lecturer in mathematics at University College, Bristol. He transferred to Birmingham University in 1906 and in 1913 accepted the chair in mathematics at University College, Reading, a position for which he was a last-minute candidate, impressing the interviewers as a man 'who breathed freshness and fullness of life and vigour'.

McLaren's career took a path common in Australian mathematics before World War II; while J. H. Michell [q.v.] returned to Melbourne in 1890 and lectured to McLaren, the latter was kept in Britain by the revolution in mathematical physics of which, along with Jeans, Einstein, Planck, Laue and Abraham, he was part. Attracted by fundamental ideas, McLaren published only on them—120 pages, concentrated in the period 1911-13, and summarized posthumously, with memoirs, as *Scientific papers* (Cambridge, 1925). His written work was characterized by 'originality and a fine boldness of conception', its paucity no measure of his diligence and interest. In 1913 he shared the Cambridge

Adams prize with J. W. Nicholson who commented that McLaren 'undoubtedly anticipated Einstein and Abraham in their suggestion of a variable velocity of light, with the consequent expressions for the energy and momentum of the gravitational field'.

To his friends McLaren appeared a man of inner reserve, powerfully built, active in sport, genial and singularly modest about his work. His intellectual pursuits brought him to the fringes of the Bloomsbury group. At the peak of his powers at Reading, he was popular with his colleagues and worked hard to establish the new institution and its reputation. In June 1914 he visited Australia for the meeting of the British Association for the Advancement of Science. War was declared as proceedings began in Perth and the September return journey was traumatic: while his stern sense of duty wrestled with his loathing of bloodshed, McLaren received news of his father's death. Finally resolving to serve in an active capacity, he learned signalling during the trip.

Commissioned as lieutenant in the Royal Engineers he was attached to an infantry brigade near Abbeville, France. 'Absolutely fearless and intrepid to an extent which made him both an anxiety to his brother officers and an inspiration to his men', he was wounded in July 1916 when clearing bombs out of a burning ammunition dump and died in hospital on 13 August. Unmarried, he was buried at Abbeville.

History of Scotch College, Melbourne, 1851-1925 (Melb, 1926); *Beiblätter zu den Annalen der Physik*, 35 (1911), 37 (1913), 38 (1914); Lond Mathematical Soc, *Procs*, 16 (1916-17); *Nature* (Lond), 97, 31 Aug 1916; *Reading Univ College Review*, no 25, Dec 1916; *Scotch Collegian*, Dec 1916; *The Times*, 18, 24 Aug 1916; information from Miss R. Graham, Trinity College, Cambridge, and from Mr G. M. C. Bott and Mr H. E. Bell, University of Reading, Eng.   J. J. Cross

McLAREN, SAMUEL GILFILLAN (1840-1914), missionary and educationist, was born on 17 September 1840 at Gask, Perthshire, Scotland, son of Peter McLaren, head gardener of the Gask estate, and his wife, née Carmichael. An apt pupil, he wished to become a minister but, reluctant to put his parents to the expense, he served articles with a legal and banking firm, studying mathematics and modern languages at night. After four years he became a legal clerk with Tods, Murray & Jamieson in Edinburgh.

In 1870 McLaren's firm sent him to the United States of America in connexion with the missing earl of Aberdeen: McLaren was to establish the earl's brother as heir by proving that the earl was one and the same George Osborne who, childless, had died

while serving as first mate on a ship bound for Melbourne. His successful handling of the case opened up excellent professional prospects but, spurning these, McLaren entered the University of Edinburgh, graduating M.A. in 1884. Then followed three years study at the Presbyterian Theological College and postgraduate work at Leipzig and Heidelberg, Germany. After ordination McLaren married Marjory Millar Bruce and went as missionary to Japan, becoming professor of history and biblical literature at the Presbyterian Union Theological Seminary, Tokyo. Eight years later 'lung troubles' drove him back to Scotland and, with health unimproved, he migrated to Melbourne in 1886.

For two years McLaren served as minister at Coburg and as chaplain at Pentridge gaol. Then in 1889 he received a call to succeed Andrew Harper [q.v.9] as principal of Presbyterian Ladies' College, Melbourne. He proved a born teacher and his wife 'a real helpmate in the work of the school'. He astutely saw the college through the penny-pinching days of the 1890s, accepting substantial financial restrictions while simultaneously conducting an advertising campaign to attract much-needed pupils. After the depression the school expanded and prospered.

Believing in equality of educational opportunity, McLaren stated in 1899 that as a result of giving girls as good an education as boys 'the listless anaemic female of the Lydia Languish type is being replaced by the active, healthy new woman of real life'. He had in charge the last generation of girls to be educated in the classical tradition, among them such gifted scholars as Enid Derham [q.v.8] and Marion Phillips [q.v.]. He was exceptionally supportive of his headmasters, first J. P. Wilson, then James Bee [q.v.7] whose modernization of the science curriculum produced a stream of medical women including (Dame) Jean Macnamara [q.v.].

'Perhaps the greatest of the Principals of PLC', McLaren retired in 1911 and died on 20 September 1914 at Ferntree Gully. He was survived by his wife, his sons Samuel and Charles [qq.v.] and his daughters Mary and Marjory, both of whom graduated from the University of Melbourne and, until marriage, taught at P.L.C.

K. Fitzpatrick, *PLC Melbourne* (Melb, 1975); *Argus*, 22 Sept 1914.   Ann G. Smith

McLAUGHLIN, CLARA JANE (1856-1931), Sister of the Good Samaritan, was born on 25 January 1856 at Sodwalls, New South Wales, sixth daughter of John McLaughlin, innkeeper, and his wife Mary Clare, née Loftus, both from Ballina, Mayo, Ireland. Clara was educated by the Sisters of

Mercy at Bathurst and entered the Sisters of the Good Samaritan of the Order of St Benedict at the House of the Good Shepherd, Pitt Street, Sydney, on 2 February 1876, taking the religious name Mary Berchmans. The congregation had been founded in 1857 by Archbishop Polding [q.v.2] to assist needy women but its members soon became involved in education. Sister Berchmans was professed on 25 March 1879 and taught at various schools in New South Wales. She was appointed superior of St Patrick's Convent, Campbelltown, in 1890 and of Rosebank Convent in 1893.

On 21 December 1898 Mother Berchmans was elected superior general of the congregation. She initiated a great expansion in the work of the Good Samaritans—in 1890 there was only one community outside New South Wales, at Port Pirie, South Australia. Over the next eighteen years she provided Sisters for remote outback missions in Queensland, crowded suburbs in Melbourne and new ones in Brisbane, and farming settlements in Victoria. The number of communities increased from 19 to 39 and of Sisters from 167 to 373.

When the Pitt Street convent was demolished in 1901 Mother Berchmans found Toxteth Park at Glebe, which she transformed into a mother house, St Scholastica's Convent, and there opened a secondary school in 1901 and St Scholastica's Training College in 1906. She introduced changes in Catholic education in line with current trends and procured teachers of science such as Sarah Brennan [q.v.7] and of art and music. In 1911 she moved the novitiate to Randwick. She strongly influenced her congregation and set in motion the process for the full approbation by the Vatican of the congregation and its constitutions.

Retiring as superior general in 1916, Mother Berchmans was assistant general to her successor in 1916-28. She planned and oversaw the building of a new four-storey novitiate, Mount St Benedict, at Pennant Hills where she was superior in 1926-31. She died there on 3 August 1931 and was buried in Rookwood cemetery. She had 'a large heart and a great fund of common sense, which allied to a remarkable ability in administration, spelt success for everything she touched'.

Sisters of the Good Samaritan, *The wheeling years* (Syd, 1957), and *Annals*, 1968, and Archives (Glebe Point, NSW); *Catholic Press* and *Freeman's J* (Syd), 13 Aug 1931. PAMELA PULLEN

MacLAURIN, SIR HENRY NORMAND (1835-1914), physician, company director and university administrator, was born on 10 December 1835 at Kilconquhar, Fife, Scot-

land, son of James MacLaurin, schoolmaster, and his wife Catherine, née Brearcliffe. Always known as Normand, he was educated at home and at the University of St Andrews (M.A., 1854), where he achieved distinguished results despite assisting his father to run the parish school. Both parents died before he was 19. With help from his only brother Rev. James MacLaurin and some tutoring fees, he enrolled in medicine at the University of Edinburgh (M.D., 1857).

James contracted tuberculosis in 1857 and with Normand went to Malaga, Spain, but died on 3 January 1858. Normand wound up his brother's affairs and was commissioned as assistant surgeon in the Royal Navy on 3 August. Of the eight ships in which he served, the *Marlborough* based at Malta in 1861-64 was his favourite; he also spent two years at Greenwich Hospital.

MacLaurin had thought of migrating to Australia in 1853; on 4 February 1868 he reached Port Phillip with the training ship, *Nelson*. He transferred to the *Challenger* just prior to its association with the Sydney visit of Alfred, duke of Edinburgh [q.v.4]. Disenchanted with his prospects in the navy, MacLaurin registered with the Medical Board of New South Wales on 1 October 1868 and met Dr Charles Nathan [q.v.5] and his family. He was obliged to return to England with his ship late in 1870, and meantime was promoted surgeon in December. In London, he gained one months midwifery experience at Queen Charlotte's Lying-in Hospital and in May 1871 obtained twelve months leave on half-pay. He returned to Sydney where he married Nathan's daughter Eliza Ann at St James' Church on 6 October 1871. He was dropped from the navy list in January 1873.

MacLaurin went to Parramatta and soon succeeded to the practice and official appointments of his partner Dr George Hogarth Pringle (d. 1872). MacLaurin moved to Macquarie Street after Nathan's death in September 1872. He was appointed examining medical officer to the Police Department in 1873, and also to the new post of ophthalmic surgeon to out-patients at St Vincent's Hospital. He resigned the latter when appointed honorary physician (1874-76). At the Sydney Infirmary and Dispensary he was honorary physician from February 1873, surgeon from 1874 and again a physician in 1882; he retired from the active staff in January 1884.

By now MacLaurin was well established in his profession. He remained in practice until about 1905 and was reputed to have been among the last doctors in Sydney to take a medical apprentice. He was a member of the Royal and Linnean societies of New South Wales and of the British Medical Association; a medical witness at numerous public enquiries; and a somewhat unlikely president of the royal commission (1888) into schemes for the extermination of rabbits in Australasia. From 1882 MacLaurin was a member of the Board of Health and succeeded (Sir) Charles Mackellar [q.v.] as chairman in 1885-89; for the same period he was government medical adviser and chairman of the Immigration Board. He was a justice of the peace from August 1886. In January 1889 he was a section president at the Intercolonial Medical Congress of Australasia, Melbourne. He spent much of that year and 1892 in Europe with his family.

Nominated to the Legislative Council on the advice of (Sir) George Dibbs [q.v.4] in February 1889, MacLaurin resigned all other official appointments. Between April 1893 and August 1894 he was vice-president of the Executive Council under Dibbs, and was credited with a decisive role in the passing of the Bank Issue Act (1893) although there is little evidence to support the beliefs of his admirers. In the 1890s he became known for sound financial judgement. His association with E. W. Knox [q.v.9] began at the Board of Health and later extended to the University of Sydney and Sydney Grammar School; he was a director of the Colonial Sugar Refining Co. Ltd in 1896-1914. Knox supported MacLaurin's vigorous anti-Federation campaign of 1899-1900, when one observer judged MacLaurin to be 'far and away the ablest, as he is the most trusted' of Protectionists opposed to the Constitution bill. A unificationist, MacLaurin foresaw the inevitable conflict when financial relationships were ill defined and the States retained sovereign powers. When Knox and the C.S.R. board refused to co-operate with the royal commission into the sugar industry in 1912, MacLaurin's was the test case for the court proceedings that followed, leading to a fine for contempt, later overruled by the High Court of Australia and the Privy Council (1914).

MacLaurin was chairman of the Mutual Life Association of Australasia, and after its amalgamation with the Citizens' Life Assurance Co. became chairman of the Mutual Life & Citizen's Assurance Co. Ltd, 1908-14. He was also a director of the Commercial Union Assurance Co. Ltd, Gloucester Estate Ltd (founded 1903), and the Bank of New South Wales (1900-14) of which he was president in 1904-05 and 1912-13. He undertook research into his family history, was active in the Highland Society of New South Wales (president, 1895-1901) and was a member of the Australian Club.

Best known for his association with the University of Sydney, MacLaurin was an examiner in medicine from 1876 and in January 1882 was offered the first chair of an-

atomy and physiology. The circumstances are obscure. MacLaurin was an experienced morbid anatomist, but the senate offer was made without advertisement and provoked such a storm of protest that MacLaurin pleaded ill health and withdrew his claim. After advertisement (Sir) Thomas Anderson Stuart [q.v.] was appointed in October. MacLaurin was elected a fellow of the senate in 1883; was vice-chancellor in 1887-89 and 1895-96; and from October 1896 became one of the longest-serving chancellors at a time when the honorary post carried a heavy burden of executive responsibility. Anderson Stuart's ambitions for the medical school would not have been realized without MacLaurin's support.

Despite significant changes wrought in the buildings and curricula, particularly in professional studies, MacLaurin's most important contribution was to preserve private funds by shrewd investment policies. The university acquired numerous neighbouring properties and in the heart of the city, including the land in Martin Place on which Challis [q.v.3] House was built in 1907 and Wigram (later University) Chambers in Phillip Street in 1912. The chancellor also persuaded the government to pay for the Fisher [q.v.4] Library building, completed in 1910. When the University (Amendment) Act (1912) effected sweeping changes in the constitution of the senate and reduced the life tenure of its fellows to five-year terms, exceptions were made for MacLaurin and his vice-chancellor Alfred Backhouse [q.v.7]. The chancellor was *ex officio* a director of the Royal Prince Alfred Hospital, and a trustee of the Sydney Grammar School and of the Public Library of New South Wales. He was also a trustee of St Andrew's College. Knighted in 1902, he received honorary LL.D.s from the universities of St Andrews (1888) and Edinburgh (1903).

MacLaurin's quick perceptions made him a formidable fixer, in and out of the committee room. He was an earnest speaker, lacking a light touch but with a flair for communicating financial detail in a compelling way. University students complained of prolixity in later years and often gave him a hard time during Commemoration Day celebrations. Described in his maturity as 'spare rather than robust, with a slight stoop of the shoulders, and . . . a well-shaped head', he had learned to conceal the impetuosity of his youth and his manner was formal, courteous and, to most people, severe. He was generally tolerant and fair minded (as in the George Arnold Wood [q.v.] South African War affair); however, personal loyalties did occasionally lead him astray. If any of his sons were a disappointment to him, it was not something he would admit.

Lady MacLaurin died on 7 January 1908 and Sir Normand's health failed in 1913. He rallied after surgery in July 1914 but died on 24 August and was buried in Waverley cemetery with Presbyterian forms. His five sons survived him and inherited his estate, valued for probate at £68 890.

The university holds portraits of MacLaurin by Ronald Gray (1902) and Ethel A. Stephens (1911); a fine bronze-relief medallion by Dora Ohlfsen (1919); and a stained-glass panel by A. K. Nicholson (1920-21). Another portrait of him by Gray is in the Mitchell [q.v.5] Library.

Of his sons, Charles (1872-1925), M.B., B.S., F.R.C.S. (Edinburgh) was notable for his pioneering essays on the clinical histories of the famous, *Post mortem* (1923) and *Mere mortals* (1925); and Henry Normand (1878-1915), barrister and colonel-in-command of the 1st Infantry Brigade, Australian Imperial Force, was killed on MacLaurin's Hill at Gallipoli by a sniper on 27 April 1915.

K. M. Brown, *Medical practice in old Parramatta* (Syd, 1937); J. A. Young et al (eds), *Centenary book of the University of Sydney faculty of medicine* (Syd, 1984); *A'sian Medical Gazette*, Feb, Mar, Dec 1882; *Scottish A'sian*, Dec 1909, p 7, Sept 1914, p 3060, June, Sept 1915, p 3739, 4012; *MJA*, 9 May 1925, p 497, 7 Dec 1963, p 966; *JRAHS*, 21 (1935), pt 4, p 209, 54 (1968), pt 3, p 265; *SMH*, 2 Aug 1883, 24 Apr 1893, May-June, 5 Oct 1912, 15 Jan, 25-27, 29 Aug 1914; *Australasian*, 24 June 1899; *Daily Telegraph* (Syd), 25, 27 Aug 1914; Mackerras papers *and* MacLaurin papers (ML); Senate minutes *and* MacLaurin papers (Univ Syd Archives); student record, 1854-57 (Edinburgh Univ Archives).   ANN M. MITCHELL

McLEAN, ALLAN (1840-1911), stock and station agent and politician, was born on 3 February 1840 at Oban in the Highlands of Scotland, son of Charles McLean and his wife Anne, née McLellan. According to Allan his parents 'were practically frozen out of Scotland' by 'an exceptionally severe winter'. In 1842 Charles, his wife and son, and his brother Angus migrated to Sydney, where Charles was offered the management of Captain MacAlister's sheep-runs in newly discovered Gippsland. Indeed, Mrs McLean was said to be the first white woman to cross the Glengarry River into north Gippsland. By 1848 the brothers had, with Simon Gillies, established their own Glenaladale station on the Mitchell River, originally estimated at 105 640 acres (42 750 ha).

Allan McLean grew up in the relative isolation of a settlement whose only communication with Melbourne was by sea. Although he had no memories of Scotland, McLean always spoke with something of a Highland burr. He was educated at home and at the Tarraville

school, and brought up in the Catholic faith of his ancestors. By 16 he was said to have graduated as a bushman, a 'dashing young station hand [who] could tame a warrigal, put a mob of cattle over a river, dance a reel, play the bagpipes until the skirl came screaming back from the hills, or sing a Scottish ballad in broad Gaelic with the fire and pathos of an ancient minstrel'. McLean recalled the Aborigines as being 'very troublesome'; he also had a 'vivid recollection' of the bushfires of Black Thursday, 1851, when the smoke turned day into night. His uncle Angus wrote two novels which drew on the McLeans' pioneering experiences—*Lindigo, the white woman, or the Highland girl's captivity among Australian blacks* (Melbourne, 1866), based on the 'White Woman of Gippsland' legend, and *Harry Bloomfield or the adventures of an early Australian squatter* (1888). McLean himself dabbled in verse: in 1888 his *Rural poems* were published locally at Sale.

On 12 July 1866 he married Margaret Badalia Shinnick (d. 1884) at Stratford. In 1865 McLean and his brother Norman had taken up the lease on the Lowlands station, near Sale; seven years later he formed A. McLean & Co., stock and station agents, Maffra, in which Norman joined him. Branches were later established in Traralgon, Bairnsdale, Warragul, Mirboo and Melbourne. The success of the enterprise owed much to McLean's inimitable reputation as an auctioneer. He became a councillor of Avon Shire in 1873, and three times president of Maffra Shire. He was also active in helping to form the Municipal Association of Victoria.

It was a natural transition for him, therefore, to be elected to the Legislative Assembly for Gippsland North in 1880. He first gained office in the Munro [q.v.5] and Shiels [q.v.] governments (November 1890-January 1893) as president of the board of land and works and commissioner of crown lands and survey throughout, chief secretary from April 1891, and minister of agriculture briefly. He was minister without portfolio in the Turner [q.v.] government from September 1894 until April 1898, when he resigned in opposition to the proposed Federal constitution. In November 1899 he successfully moved a motion of no confidence in the government whereupon he became premier and chief secretary, retaining office until his ministry lost its majority in the November 1900 election.

In his early years McLean described himself as a constitutionalist, but his advocacy of protection, in particular the stock tax, seemed to identify him increasingly as a liberal. He was a friend and associate of William Shiels, serving in his government and supporting his claims for liberal leadership in 1894. Shiels in turn helped to manage

McLean's own bid for power in 1899 and became treasurer in his government.

Liberal or not, McLean was always very conscious of representing the rural interest. He was one of the few Victorian politicians to oppose the draft constitution in 1898-99, but his reasons for doing so were essentially provincial. He criticized the provision for senators being elected by the entire State, arguing that this would give too much power to the cities. He regretted the abrupt abolition of colonial tariffs, his particular concern being the effect of Victoria giving up the stock tax to which he was so attached. He also complained that the State would be losing the power to encourage new industries. McLean's involvement at this time in the development of the sugar-beet industry at Maffra gave him a particular reason for being suspicious of the economic effects of Federation.

McLean's devotion to rural interests was also evident in his accession to power in 1899. He became the spokesman for a group of country liberals who were dissatisfied with the water-supply advance relief bill, and the makeshift alliance with the conservative Opposition and a few discontented radicals that emerged was sufficient to oust the long-lived Turner government. McLean's cabinet included a notable conservative newcomer, (Sir) William Irvine [q.v.9], whose appointment as attorney-general was seen by some as belying the claim that the government was a liberal one.

In fact, McLean's policies differed little from his predecessor's. Perhaps the new premier's greatest success was the re-enactment of the Factory Act in 1900. The bill which had been proposed by Turner's chief secretary, (Sir) Alexander Peacock [q.v.], gave the governor-in-council power to create a board for any trade carried on in a factory. The Legislative Council objected, and demanded parliamentary control of the creation of new boards by requiring a resolution of both Houses, thus giving the council a veto. A conference between the Houses took place at a time when, with the onset of Federation, many thought it prudent to avoid a constitutional confrontation. McLean proposed an ingenious compromise, namely that a board could be created on the resolution of either House; it was sufficient to break the impasse, and it made possible the rapid expansion of the wages board system.

Although at the time it was seen as 'a mere shuffling of the political cards', as H. G. Turner [q.v.6] put it, the overthrow of the Turner government signalled the end of the old liberal coalition of manufacturers, trade unions and farmers. The political alliance which sustained McLean was to be developed by Irvine into Victoria's particular brand of anti-Labor ascendancy. The organizing of the country liberals also foreshadowed the emergence, some twenty years later, of the Country Party.

Following the defeat of his government in November 1900 McLean entered the new Commonwealth parliament as member for Gippsland. Elected in the protectionist interest, he supported the Barton and Deakin [qq.v.7,8] governments, but when Labor briefly took office in 1904 McLean was among the conservative protectionists who joined with the free traders, led by (Sir) George Reid [q.v.], to defeat the government in August. Both Turner and McLean served in the ensuing coalition government, but Turner, pleading ill health, ceded the leadership of the cabinet protectionists to McLean, who became minister for trade and customs and Reid's deputy. The Reid-McLean government passed the Arbitration Act which had triggered the defeat of both the Deakin and Watson [q.v.] governments, but itself had only a precarious majority. After a long parliamentary recess a new alliance between Deakin and Labor brought about the government's defeat in June 1905. Although the Reid-McLean coalition was a political failure it foreshadowed the anti-Labor Fusion of 1909; once again McLean had played an important part in shaping the new political order.

In the 1906 election McLean was surprisingly defeated in his Gippsland homeland. Ill health, especially rheumatism, had prevented him from fighting an active campaign and was blamed for his defeat, but in an era of increasingly sectarian politics it is also possible that his Catholicism was a disadvantage. If so, this was an irony because McLean was an ardent Imperialist and hardly part of the colonial Irish Catholic mainstream; religion seemed to play little part in his politics.

As a politician McLean very much identified with his region. The early settlers, it was said, 'almost worshipped him', and as a pioneer and a 'character' he was part of Gippsland's history. According to Reid he 'united the best qualities of a Highlander with the best qualities of an Australian colonist'. But if his Scottish background endowed him with a colourful image, McLean's political manner eschewed emotion and embraced the values of homely common sense. Like many an advocate of rural interests he believed that 'a large peasant population would lead to a sound form of Government'; similarly, he welcomed female suffrage as promoting 'a more solid family vote'.

On 8 September 1885 McLean had married a widow Emily Macarthur, née Linton, at Port Melbourne. He died on 13 July 1911, after several months illness, at his Melbourne residence at Albert Park. His body was taken to Sale, where Bishop Corbett [q.v.8] officiated at the burial. His wife and seven children of his first marriage survived him. His estate was valued for probate at £53 573.

G. H. Reid, *My reminiscences* (Lond, 1917); H. H. Peck, *Memoirs of a stockman* (Melb, 1957); J. W. Leslie and H. C. Cowie (eds), *The wind still blows* (Sale, 1973); J. Rickard, *Class and politics* (Canb, 1976); P. Loveday, A. W. Martin and R. S. Parker (eds), *The emergence of the Australian party system* (Syd, 1977); R. Spreadborough and H. Anderson, *Victorian squatters* (Melb, 1983); *PD* (Vic), 1883, p 41, 1897, p 586, 1899, p 1147; *Punch* (Melb), 4 Feb, 25 Aug 1904; *Argus*, 28 Jan 1905, 14 July 1911; *Maffra Spectator*, 17 July 1911; information from Mr P. Morgan, Churchill, Vic.

JOHN RICKARD

McLEAN, MARGARET (1845-1923), temperance advocate and feminist, was born on 7 April 1845 at Irvine, Ayrshire, Scotland, eldest child of Andrew Arnot, builder and carpenter, and his wife Agnes, née Russell. The family migrated to Port Phillip, settling at East Melbourne, in 1849. Margaret's father became treasurer of the Melbourne Total Abstinence Society and she was enlisted early in the town's first Band of Hope. In 1859, after primary school education, she became a pupil-teacher at the United Methodist Free Church School, Fitzroy. She attended the new Melbourne Training Institution for teachers in 1862-64 and then worked as an assistant at Common School no.557 (St James' Cathedral School) until 1869. On 10 March that year at Fitzroy she married William McLean [q.v.5]. At first the McLeans lived at Kew. Later, as William's hardware firm prospered, they built the handsome Torloisk, East Melbourne. Both became active members of Collins Street Baptist Church.

With the object of 'doing all that women can do, when inspired by the love of Christ, to rescue those who are enslaved by strong drink', in 1887 Margaret McLean became a founding member of the Woman's Christian Temperance Union of Victoria. Initially in charge of its Melbourne branch, in 1891 she became acting president of the colonial body; she was president in 1892-93 and from 1899 until 1907 when she retired with failing health. The W.C.T.U. members had early perceived the need for political influence and Mrs McLean became one of their foremost advocates of votes for women. Her pamphlets *Womanhood suffrage* (1890) and its sequel *More about womanhood suffrage* were circulated throughout Victoria via the W.C.T.U.'s branch-network. Their author also helped to organize the women's petition for the franchise, presented to parliament in 1891.

Endowed with keen intelligence and strong personality Mrs McLean contrived to combine an energetic public career with devotion to her large family; she had five sons, one

dying in infancy, and six daughters. She was noted for her hospitality, whether as hostess to temperance missionaries or as organizer of 'drawing-room meetings' for recruitment. She saw clearly how the W.C.T.U. was itself an agent of women's emancipation, providing a much-needed *esprit de corps*, developing women's 'minds, faculties, and gifts' and teaching them 'that we *are* citizens, that we have responsibilities as such, and ought to have privileges corresponding thereto'. She often spoke for the W.C.T.U. in deputations to government and in 1900 was Australian delegate to the World's W.C.T.U. Convention in Edinburgh where she also conducted a service in St Giles' Cathedral. In 1902 she helped to found the National Council of Women of Victoria which, with the W.C.T.U., pressed for women's suffrage, juvenile courts, police matrons, and other reforms.

For her 'long and distinguished services' Margaret McLean was made honorary vice-president of the W.C.T.U. of Victoria in 1907. In retirement she continued working for temperance, social reform and the Baptist Church. Survived by eight of her children, she died at Malvern on 14 February 1923 and was buried in Melbourne general cemetery.

Mrs McLean's six daughters together reflected the several aspects of their mother's career. While the two youngest Eva (1886-1962) and Jessie (1888-1964) led domestic lives, the eldest Ethel (1873-1940) was for many years head of staff at Lauriston Girls' School, Melbourne. Lucie (1877-1944) took up nursing and Hilda (1879-1938) spent her life as a Baptist missionary in Bengal. The fourth daughter Alice (1884-1949) graduated in medicine in 1906 and practised for many years in Bengal where her husband, Rev. Lorraine Barber, was likewise a missionary. She also helped to run the Women's Hospital, Melbourne, during World War I and later practised psychotherapy, making an influential contribution to its establishment in Melbourne.

Historical Cttee of the Women's Centenary Council (comp), *Records of the pioneer women of Victoria, 1835-1860* (Melb, 1937); I. McCorkindale (ed), *Pioneer pathways* (Melb, 1948); W.C.T.U. of Victoria, *Annual Report*, 1888; *Alliance Record*, 29 Nov 1890; *White Ribbon Signal* (Melb), Aug 1895, Sept 1896, March 1923; *Age* and *Argus*, 17 Feb 1923; H. Carnegie (comp), The Barber family chronicle, with the related families of Napier, McLean, Wright, Nicholls and Reynolds (MS, privately held); Education Dept (Vic), Records (History Section, Education Dept, Melb).

ANTHEA HYSLOP

McLEISH, DUNCAN (1851?-1920), pastoralist and soldier, was born probably on 20 July 1851 at Yea, Victoria, son of Duncan

McLeish, grazier, and his wife Catherine, née Cameron. Educated privately, he followed grazing pursuits, becoming part-proprietor of Glenmore station, Yea. He was one of the original officers of the Victorian Mounted Rifles, being commissioned lieutenant on 1 April 1887 and promoted captain in 1889.

On the outbreak of the South African War in 1899 McLeish was depicted as a fit, mature officer with a full moustache. He was appointed captain in command of the 1st Company of Victorian Mounted Rifles which, with an infantry company specially recruited, constituted Victoria's first military contingent dispatched on overseas service. The partly trained men were enrolled quickly from existing forces and embarked on 28 October for Cape Town. The Victorians were attached to the force on the Modder River front and, when the Australian Regiment was formed, served in the Colesberg district. Captain McLeish's company took part in the first major invasion of enemy country when, under Major General J. M. Babington, it reconnoitred into the Orange Free State towards Jacobsdal from 9 January 1900. McLeish found the seizing and burning of civilian property distasteful.

Impressed with the V.M.R., Babington suggested that all the Australians be mounted: McLeish and Colonel J. C. Hoad [q.v.9] offered to mount the Australian Regiment which was fully horsed by 6 February. A week later the Victorians suffered severe casualties as the Boers advanced at Bastard's Nek and Pink Hill, the V.M.R. carrying out of danger men of the dismounted Wiltshire Regiment. The Australian Regiment then crossed into the Orange Free State and pushed northwards to Bloemfontein by 4 April. There the regiment was disbanded, the Victorians becoming part of the 4th Mounted Infantry Corps, participating in actions leading to the capture of Johannesburg and Pretoria in the Transvaal and thereafter advancing to the Portuguese East African border by September. On 30 April, at Karee Kloof, McLeish was pulled from the saddle while rescuing a man of the Cornwall Regiment. General Clements admired him as a good officer. Major W. T. Reay [q.v.], war correspondent, indicated that other commanding officers could have learned from him the art of managing horses and caring for men. McLeish was promoted major on 25 October 1900. The V.M.R. embarked for home from Cape Town on 5 November.

On 22 January 1902 he was promoted lieut-colonel commanding the 2nd Battalion, Australian Commonwealth Horse, and returned to South Africa for operations in Natal and the last drives in the Transvaal. Hostilities ended on 31 May and by August the A.C.H. had returned to Australia. For his war service

McLeish was mentioned in dispatches, appointed C.M.G., and awarded the Queen's South Africa medal with six clasps and the King's medal with one clasp. He resumed grazing activities at Glenmore and from July 1903 also commanded the 7th Light Horse Regiment, Australian Military Forces; in 1906 he was commander of the 3rd Light Horse Brigade, A.M.F., and was promoted colonel in December 1907. In World War I, despite his age, he served as a colonel with the Australian Imperial Force in command of remount units in Egypt in 1915-19 and was appointed C.B.E. and twice mentioned in dispatches. His A.I.F. appointment ended on 16 February 1920.

McLeish died unmarried on 18 April 1920 at Brighton, Melbourne, and was buried in Brighton cemetery. His estate of £22 610 was distributed among numerous relatives and charities. A Presbyterian, McLeish was described by Donald MacDonald [q.v.] as 'a typical Australian rider, bronzed, lean and sinewy, a man of strong character and few words, a crack rifle shot, well versed in bushcraft, and caring nothing for the pleasures of town life'.

W. Harding and D. MacDonald (eds), *War in South Africa* (Melb, 1899); W. T. Reay, *Australians in war* (Melb, 1900); G. B. Barton and J. C. Ridpath, *The story of South Africa*, 2 (Syd, 1901); Aust Defence Dept, *Official records of the Australian military contingents to the war in South Africa*, P. L. Murray ed (Melb, 1911); *London Gazette*, 16 Apr 1901, 6 July 1917, 31 Dec 1918, 1, 22 Jan 1919.
W. M. CHAMBERLAIN

McLEOD, DONALD (1837-1923), politician, was born in 1837 at Caithness, Scotland, son of Rev. Roderick McLeod of the Free Church of Scotland, and his wife Christina, née McKay. He arrived in Victoria in 1847 with his father, sent out to Gaelic-speaking Highlanders. McLeod senior took up land near Kilmore where Donald grew up before completing an apprenticeship to a Melbourne chemist. Leaving Melbourne to try his luck on the Jim Crow Diggings (Daylesford), he turned bullocky, hauling machinery to neighbouring goldfields, and eventually settled on a small farm at Wombat Flat. On 19 September 1861 at Coburg, Melbourne, he married Annie Rennie.

Appointed town clerk of Daylesford in 1872, McLeod held the position for twenty-eight years, becoming 'a virtual dictator' to the Daylesford Borough Council. He was a leading light in many other local institutions—secretary of the water trust for twenty-eight years, president of the hospital (thirty years) and president of the committee which established Daylesford Technical School. These activities gave him an excellent local base when, in 1900, aged 63, he resigned as town clerk, to be elected with a large majority to the Legislative Assembly for Daylesford. He retained many of his local interests—in the hospital, St George's Masonic Lodge of which he was a founder, and Daylesford Woollen Mills.

As a new M.L.A., McLeod gravitated towards the country liberal faction led by Allan McLean [q.v.] and (Sir) William Irvine [q.v.9], and supported by the Kyabram movement. When in 1902 this group, together with the conservative faction, formed a government led by Irvine, McLeod became an honorary minister. In the subsequent Bent [q.v.3] ministry (1904-09) he was minister of mines and of forests with additional short stints as minister of water supply and acting treasurer.

By 1912 McLeod had established himself as leader of a country faction in the Liberal Party, with policies favouring irrigation and water-supply development, and closer settlement. In 1913 the country liberals defeated Premier Watt's [q.v.] proposed redistribution, which threatened them both as individuals and as an interest group, and brought down his government, although Watt survived with a reconstructed ministry.

In the Peacock [q.v.] ministry of 1915-17, McLeod was chief secretary and minister of public health. From this peak in his career, his fortunes declined with those of the Peacock government, although the loyalty of his constituents ensured that he survived its November 1917 electoral disaster. He sat on the corner benches with the Peacock-Lawson [q.v.] group through the Bowser [q.v.7] ministry of 1917-18 but was not included in the 1918 Lawson government. Melbourne *Punch* in 1919 placed him first among the 'men not wanted in the ministry', disqualified by both age and the performance of the Peacock government.

When Donald McLeod died on 8 July 1923 at Middle Park, he was still in harness, the leader of the country liberals and the oldest member of the assembly. Known as the 'Grand Old Man of Daylesford' he was the prototype of the local identity whose career culminated in a distinguished contribution to politics. He was buried in Daylesford cemetery. His wife and seven of their ten children survived him; one son was killed at Pozières in 1916 while serving with the Australian Imperial Force.

Punch (Melb), 31 July 1919; *Argus,* 9 July 1923; *Daylesford Advocate,* 10 July 1923.

MARGARET VINES

McLEOD, DONALD NORMAN (1848-1914), farmer, pastoralist and politician, was born on 10 June 1848 at Borhoneyghurk station on the Moorabool River, Port Phillip District, second son of JOHN NORMAN McLEOD (1816-1886), pastoralist, and his wife Agnes, née Paterson. Donald's parents were typical Scottish pioneers of Victoria's Western District. John Norman, whose father Major Donald McLeod had taken up a land-grant in Van Diemen's Land in 1820, took sheep to Port Phillip in 1837 and formed Borhóneyghurk station. In 1849-50 he sold out and bought runs on the Wannon River which, in turn, he sold and moved to Portland where he built the mansion, Maretimo. Eventually he bought Castlemaddie at Tyrendarra where he established an estate of 1500 acres (610 ha).

A devout Anglican, McLeod was active in evangelistic, charitable and public works. He represented Portland in the Legislative Assembly in 1859-60 and was actively concerned with Aboriginal welfare. He died on 18 April 1886 at Tyrendarra and was buried in South Portland cemetery. His wife and seven children survived him.

Donald was educated at Portland and at Scotch College, Melbourne. At 16 he was sent to his uncle Hugh McLeod's station Benyeo, near Apsley, to learn about sheep-farming; he eventually became overseer. In 1872, with John Hancock of Ashburton Plains, McLeod shipped stock to Nicol Bay, Western Australia, near where Roebourne now stands, and, after exploring the hinterland, successfully established and managed Chiritta station; the bushman's skills learned from his father enabled him to prosper in the dry, isolated territory. On 24 February 1879 at the Church of St Mary, Busselton, he married Charlotte Harriet, daughter of Alfred Pickmore Bussell [q.v.3].

Donald sold his Nicol Bay run in 1883 and returned to Portland to establish a dairy-farm, Yannarie, near his father's property, which became well known for his innovative approaches to farming. McLeod used rollers to clear the thick tea-tree scrub, imported judiciously to produce a breed of Ayrshire cattle, and was the first Victorian farmer to make ensilage on a large scale. His most remarkable advances were made in the techniques of butter and cheese-making: well before the factory system was introduced he had a steam-driven cream separator; and he adopted the Cheddar method of cheese production, receiving the highest award for cheese at the 1888 Intercolonial Dairying Exhibition. Yannarie, which McLeod sold in 1892, was occasionally opened to visitors, as in 1888 when Alexander Crawford [q.v.8] used McLeod's plant and staff to demonstrate butter-making techniques.

For many years a justice of the peace and a councillor of Portland Shire and Borough, McLeod represented Portland in the Legislative Assembly in 1894-1900. In 1895 he was appointed to a board to enquire into the best methods of exporting perishable goods and in 1897-98 he was a member of the royal commission on old age pensions. Towards the end of his parliamentary career he was chairman of the Society for the Protection of Aborigines and vice-president of the Zoological and Acclimatisation Society. He held a commission in the Victorian Mounted Rifles under Colonel Tom Price [q.v.] and when the first Bushmen's contingent was recruited for the South African War he examined candidates for their ability as bushmen and roughriders.

In 1899 McLeod severed his Victorian connexions and took up Minilya station in the Carnarvon district of Western Australia. He died in Perth on 25 October 1914, survived by his wife, six daughters and five of his six sons, and was buried in the Congregational section of Karrakatta cemetery. Represented at the funeral were the Pastoralists' Association of Western Australia, the Clan McLeod Society of Australia, the Caledonian Society of Perth and the Narrogin Masonic Lodge.

J. Smith (ed), *Cyclopedia of Victoria*, 1 (Melb, 1903); A. Henderson (ed), *Early pioneer families of Victoria and Riverina* (Melb, 1936); *PD* (Vic), 1859-60, p 645, 706, 793, 1169; *Portland Guardian*, 20 Apr 1886; *Table Talk*, 17 Aug, 8 Sept 1894. L. LOMAS

MACLEOD, THOMAS (1881-1963), barrister, aviator and grazier, was born on 5 June 1881 in Brisbane, eighth child of Thomas McLeod, Brisbane Grammar School master, and his wife Blane, née Robertson. His father died when he was 4. Thomas attended Leichhardt State School and Brisbane Grammar School by scholarship in 1895. After employment at Charters Towers with Watson & Dowden, assayers, he returned to Brisbane to study law and was admitted to the Bar on 2 September 1902.

Macleod established a reputation as an author and editor of legal publications. With (Sir) James Blair [q.v.7] he revised and edited R. A. Ranking's [q.v.] *Queensland police code and justices' manual* in 1905. In 1906 with Blair and T. W. McCawley [q.v.] he edited with annotations *The Worker's Compensation Act of 1905*. Macleod and McCawley began editing the *Queensland Justice of the Peace and Local Authorities' Journal* in 1907; and in 1913 Macleod published both *Queensland criminal reports 1860-1907* and *The liquor law of Queensland*, and in 1915 a *Queensland criminal code supplement*.

A yachting and flying enthusiast, Macleod built and launched his auxiliary yacht *Brynhild* in 1909 and next year helped to found the first Queensland Aero Club and a State branch of the Aerial League of Australia. In July he helped to build a biplane glider, the first heavier-than-air apparatus built in Queensland, and made the State's first officially observed flight in a bat's wing monoplane glider, which he had constructed, on 11 October 1910 near Brisbane. The biplane glider's first flight was made on 22 December. A wooden rail was used along which the glider slid, on a cradle, before becoming airborne. Experiments continued, and Macleod met and became a firm friend of Bert Hinkler [q.v.9].

In November 1914 Macleod formed the Queensland Volunteer Flying Civilians to train at Hemmant for aerial warfare in a reconstructed Caudron aircraft. He and eight Volunteers sailed for England where the Royal Flying Corps accepted them. Commissioned second lieutenant, Macleod was appointed temporary captain on 22 December 1916. He served with No. 13 Squadron, with a period in command, and was awarded the Croix de Guerre avec Palme for his work as an aerial observer in the 1st battle of Arras and at Vimy Ridge. In 1918 he was appointed O.B.E. Transferred to the Australian Flying Corps, he was demobilized in 1919 as major. On his return to Brisbane he was a founder of the (Royal Queensland) Aero Club. In December 1922 he was appointed a commissioner of the World's Board of Aeronautical Commissions.

Macleod married Ruby Margaret Shannon (d. 1923) on 5 January 1921 at St Luke's Church of England, Toowoomba. A war-inflicted disability forced him to abandon his legal practice in 1923. He published *The High Court on the interpretation of statutes* in 1924, then took up Firshot, a grazing property at Longreach, renamed Wingalong. As a director (1925-29) of the Queensland and Northern Territories Aerial Services Ltd, he helped to establish its involvement in the flying doctor service. In the 1926 election and a 1928 by-election, Macleod was the unsuccessful Country and Progressive National Party candidate for Mitchell.

In England Macleod had known Lady Aurea Frederswyde Wace, daughter of the 9th earl of Carlisle; he married her on 2 June 1928 at St Andrew's Presbyterian Church, Longreach. Because of his health they settled in England, where he bred sheep. During World War II he trained Local Defence Volunteers as a lieutenant-colonel in the Home Guard. Macleod died at Par, Cornwall, on 24 September 1963 and was cremated after a service at Tywardreath Methodist Church. His wife survived him.

The Thomas Macleod Aviation Archives, Queensland Museum, established in 1973, is named after him.

S. Stephenson (comp), *Annals of the Brisbane Grammar School, 1869-1922* (Brisb, 1923); E. P. Wixted, *Queensland aviation, no 1, From the ground up 1910-1912* (Brisb, 1972), and (comp), Queensland Museum History and Technology leaflet no 9 (Brisb, 1976), and personal aviation files (Queensland Museum); *Queenslander*, 2 Dec 1922, 14 Apr 1923; *The Times*, 28 Sept 1963; Qld Supreme Court Library cat.   J. C. H. GILL

MACLEOD, WILLIAM (1850-1929), artist and businessman, was born on 27 October 1850 in London, son of William Macleod, cordwainer, and his wife Juliana, née Exness (or Esner). The family followed the gold rush to Victoria and after her husband's death in 1855 Julia settled in Sydney, where she married the portrait painter James Anderson. His drinking excesses caused Macleod to seek work from the age of 12; trained by Edmund Thomas at the Sydney Mechanics' School of Arts and known first as William Macleod Anderson or James Anderson junior, he had his first artistic contribution published in 1866 in the *Illustrated Sydney News*. Over the next decade he travelled widely and won a reputation as a painter of portraits and cattle, a designer of stained-glass windows, and as illustrator with a strong line for such journals as the *Sydney Mail*, the *Australian Town and Country Journal* and *Sydney* and *Queensland Punch*. On 29 January 1873 he married Emily Collins at St Mary's Cathedral, Sydney.

In January 1880 Macleod illustrated the first lead-story of the new Sydney *Bulletin*. In March he and another artist, Samuel Begg, jointly secured a third share in the journal but relinquished it when the financial affairs of J. F. Archibald and John Haynes [qq.v.3,4] improved. A prominent freelance contributor of robust cartoons to the *Bulletin* and the designer of its new pink cover in 1883, Macleod purchased part of Haynes's holding in April 1884. After extensive involvement in the *Picturesque atlas of Australasia* (1886) project—he executed many of the portraits used and was chairman of its publishing company—Macleod joined the *Bulletin* full time in 1886 in response to a plea from Archibald following the departure of W. H. Traill [q.v.6]. They became joint owners in 1887; Macleod was the *Bulletin*'s manager or managing director for the next forty years.

'He sits there like a dob of mud' was Victor Daley's [q.v.8] oft-reported comment on Macleod at the *Bulletin*. The comment suggests Macleod's settled stoutness, but is more generally cited as evidence of a stolidness and lack of imagination which is contrasted with Archibald's nervy, sensitive flair. Yet Macleod's sobriety complemented Archibald's editorial brilliance: while the one was the 'literary cobbler', the other cautiously and conscientiously controlled business affairs. Macleod also contributed much to the *Bulletin*'s artistic successes through his friendship with Livingston Hopkins [q.v.4] and his encouragement of talents such as David Low's [q.v.]; and despite his renowned lack of interest in poetry and fiction he supported the publishing activities of A. G. Stephens [q.v.]. It was Stephens who provided the proper corrective to Daley: 'Without Archibald, after Traill left, there would have been no *Bulletin*. Without Macleod, there would have been no *Bulletin* long'.

If Macleod presided over the *Bulletin*'s most famous years, he also presided over the start of its decline, particularly after the departure of Archibald in 1903 and Stephens in 1906. In 1910 he resigned as manager in favour of his son Norman; another son Ronald became manager of the Melbourne office. The deaths of his daughter Ada and of Norman from influenza in 1919 affected Macleod greatly; his involvement in the *Bulletin* declined and in 1927 he sold out his major shareholding to the next *Bulletin* family of significance, that of S. H. Prior [q.v.].

Macleod was of medium height, thickset, brown eyed, round faced and bearded. He worked in a variety of art forms from stained glass to black-and-white drawing, oils, watercolour, engraving, lithography, clay modelling and sculpture. His strength was as an illustrator in the days of wood-engraving, but he possessed the adaptability and keen commercial sense to succeed even before his management of the *Bulletin*; his estimated annual income was £1500 in the late 1870s and his eventual estate was valued for probate at over £232 000.

In later life Macleod lived at Dunvegan, Mosman, where he painted, played bowls with zeal, and was a genial and kindly host. He possessed a fine collection of Australian art, including John Longstaff's [q.v.] 'Breaking the News'. He died on 24 June 1929 and was cremated with Anglican rites. He was survived by a son and two daughters, and by his second wife Agnes Conor O'Brien, whom he had married on 10 April 1911 at Pymble Catholic Church. She was a *Bulletin* journalist who wrote the highly sympathetic *Macleod of 'the Bulletin'* (1931). Samples of his stained glass work include the memorial window to Robert Campbell [q.v.1] in the Anglican Church of St John the Baptist, Canberra, and he is represented in the Art Gallery of New South Wales and the Australian National Gallery.

G. A. Taylor, *Those were the days* (Syd, 1918);

M. Mahood, *The loaded line* (Melb, 1973); P. Rolfe, *The journalistic javelin* (Syd, 1979); S. Lawson, *The Archibald paradox* (Melb, 1983); *Scottish A'sian*, 1 Apr 1911; *Newspaper News*, 1 July 1929; *Bowyang*, 7, 1982; *Daily Telegraph* (Syd), 21 June 1924; *Bulletin*, 26 June 1929; MS cat under Macleod (ML).   B. G. ANDREWS

McMAHON, GREGAN (1874-1941), actor and theatrical producer, was born on 2 March 1874 in Sydney, elder son of Irish-born John Terence McMahon, clerk, and his wife Elizabeth, née Gregan. He was educated at Sydney Grammar School, St Ignatius' College, Riverview, and the University of Sydney (B.A., 1896). He went to work for a Sydney law firm and on 4 October 1899 in St Mary's Cathedral married Mary Kate, daughter of Thomas Hungerford [q.v.4]. However he had already set his mind on an acting career and in 1900 joined the Robert Brough [q.v.3] company for a tour of some fifteen months in Australia, India and China. On his return to Sydney in 1901, McMahon was immediately offered leading parts with the William Hawtrey company and by 1906, when it disbanded, had firmly established himself as a 'character actor'. Over the next few years he appeared for various other managements, including J. C. Williamson [q.v.6]. Like most actors of his day he was virtually an itinerant worker.

In 1906 McMahon considered going to London, but his responsibilities as a husband and father of two children held him back. What particularly beckoned him were the Court Theatre productions, beginning in 1904, of such playwrights as Shaw, Hauptmann, Maeterlinck, Schnitzler, Yeats and Granville Barker, who had broken away from the conventions and clichés of the late Victorian era. Even while professionally occupied in frivolous farce and bombastic melodrama, McMahon kept an eye on developments abroad, especially plays written, as he later put it, 'to illustrate an idea, social, moral, poetic, fantastic or even utilitarian', and in which characters were 'true to life instead of to the idiosyncrasies of individual actors'. He recognized opportunities for himself in directing such plays on the stage. Distrustful of the star-virtuoso system then in vogue, he saw ensemble acting, co-ordinated and guided by a regisseur, as the way of the future. The burgeoning repertory movement in provincial Britain, notably in Manchester, gave him an organizational model for this fusion of new approaches in writing, acting and production.

McMahon set up the Melbourne Repertory Company in 1911 and it first performed in public at the Turn Verein Hall, East Mel-

bourne, on 26 June, with a double bill—act 2 of Sheridan's *The critic* and St John Hankin's *The two Mr Wetherbys*. This alternated with Ibsen's *John Gabriel Borkman*. During 1911-18 he introduced Melbourne audiences to a wide range of modern English and European drama, together with thirteen Australian plays. It was ironic that, dependent on the well-to-do for patronage and talent, McMahon produced plays which were in some sense portents of social change and ferment.

Nevertheless, he still maintained his commercial connexions and occasionally undertook outside engagements. When the Melbourne venture folded in 1918, he moved to Sydney and entered into an arrangement with J. C. Williamson's, then coming steadily under the control of the Tait [q.v.] brothers. McMahon contracted to work for 'ordinary companies' as well as towards the presentation of 'special repertory plays'. Two years later he founded the Sydney Repertory Theatre Society, with 700 subscribers. But the Taits held the purse-strings. In the choice of plays he was now more willing to compromise with West End and Shaftesbury Avenue trends. It also indicates a certain withdrawal from creative risk-taking that in 1920-27 he staged only four Australian plays.

All this time McMahon's frustration with amateurism had been growing. His own professionalism was widely respected, especially by the visiting overseas stars he directed for J.C.W's, but among his subscribers there was uneasiness about his pact with the Taits. In 1928 he put forward a proposal for one full-time professional repertory company to serve Sydney and Melbourne (where he had resumed directorship in 1926). It was intended to be a joint McMahon-J.C.W. enterprise, with the societies guaranteeing a basic audience but excluded from business or artistic participation. Rejection of the proposal was swift, the parting bitter.

The Gregan McMahon Play Company opened at the King's Theatre, Melbourne, on 12 May 1928, entirely under J.C.W. sponsorship. But despite a repertoire of good, substantial plays, critical and box-office reception was lukewarm, often hostile. 'The company is dreadful', wrote Louis Esson [q.v.8] to Vance Palmer [q.v.], 'a mixture of duds and derelicts . . . I can't see any hope for it'. After a calamitous Sydney season later in the year, it disintegrated. Ever resilient, McMahon signed on with the Fuller [q.v.8] management in Melbourne. He also began circularizing for subscribers and in 1929 was able to form the Gregan McMahon Players on a mixed professional-amateur basis. He began with a few productions each year, first in J. C. Williamson playhouses, later at the Garrick. In 1935 he capitulated yet again to the Taits, who from then until his death became his sole protectors and kept him on a tight financial rein. Although he had over 2000 subscribers, the profit from his much-praised 1937 production of Pirandello's *Henry IV* amounted to only £32. His income had always been erratic, varying from comfortable to barely above subsistence level. From 1917 he lived apart from his wife, but continued to send her money and even financed his daughter's trip to England and the Continent—a journey which he himself never made.

Among McMahon's productions in the late 1930s were Walter Greenwood's *Love on the dole*, Auden and Isherwood's *The ascent of F6*, Thornton Wilder's *Our town*, Obey's *Noah*, and Giraudoux' *Amphitryon 38*. Although scarcely *avant-garde* or revolutionary, his selections accurately reflected high-culture fashion in London and New York. The C.B.E. awarded him in 1938 was scant recognition for so many years of struggle. Towards the end he seemed tired and somewhat disillusioned, wondering whether he had really advanced since his great breakthrough in 1911. He died suddenly of hypertensive heart disease at his Jolimont home on 30 August 1941, and was buried in the Catholic section of Melbourne general cemetery. Only about twenty people stood at the graveside. His son and daughter survived him.

To have known McMahon during this final phase of his life was perhaps not to have experienced him at his best. Stockily built and nearly always soberly dressed, he was a low-key personality outside the theatre. Except that his blue eyes twinkled elfishly, his face resembled a cartoonist's Humpty-Dumpty. Only the bald, high-domed head betokened his formidable capacities. Despite his proclaimed belief in naturalistic acting, his own methods derived fundamentally from the nineteenth-century larger-than-life school. He was most admired in fey, fanciful roles, like Lob in Barrie's *Dear Brutus*, yet even here his portraits were too fussy, the outlines blurred with irrelevant detail and excessive comic energy. But he brought to all his acting a quite unusual intelligence, as though he were not so much impersonating as making a critical comment on the character. It was this analytical ability that also gave him authority as a director. In early twentieth-century Australian theatre he was unique in his combination of technical proficiency, careful craftsmanship and intellectual insight.

S. E. Napier, *The Sydney Repertory Society* (Syd, 1925); V. Palmer, *Louis Esson and the Australian theatre* (Melb, 1948); H. Porter, *The watcher on the cast-iron balcony* (Lond, 1963); *Lone Hand*, Aug 1916; *Home*, June 1923; D. Douglas and M. M. Morgan, 'Gregan McMahon and the Australian theatre', *Komos*, 2, no 2, Nov 1969, 2, no 4, (nd), 3, no 1-4, 1973; A. Ashbolt, 'Courage, contradiction and compromise: Gregan McMahon 1874-1941', *Meanjin*, 37, no 3, 1978; *T&CJ*, 3 Nov 1909; *Age* and *Argus*, 1 Sept 1941; McMahon papers (ML); personal information.   ALLAN ASHBOLT

MacMAHON, JAMES (1858?-1915) and CHARLES (1861?-1917), theatre and cinema entrepreneurs, were born at Sandhurst (Bendigo), Victoria, sons of Patrick MacMahon, contractor, and his wife Mary Ann, née Delany, and two of four brothers who all became noted theatrical managers. At 17 James, after interludes as a lawyer's clerk and journalist, pioneered the family business by becoming a Bendigo theatrical agent, staging a disastrous pantomime at Christmas 1875; but two years later the visiting actress Mrs Scott Siddons was impressed enough to engage him as manager of her company. For six years James toured North America and the British Isles as manager and freelance journalist, and in the early 1880s worked for a time for Henry Irving's company. Meanwhile Charles and his brother Joseph Francis (1863?-1918) had established themselves as managers and agents in the Bendigo-Ballarat-Castlemaine area.

On James's return in 1884, the brothers formed a partnership with the actor-manager George Leitch which lasted, apart from a rift in 1887-88, until about 1890, and toured productions such as Leitch's *His natural life* (1886) through Australia and New Zealand. The MacMahons also had a long association with the actor Grattan Riggs from 1882 until the 1890s, and managed the tours of performers such as John F. Sheridan, Dion Boucicault [q.v.3], George Darrell, Alfred Dampier [qq.v.4], the Majeronis and Wybert Reeve. James oversaw the general running of the firm, while Charles and Joseph travelled with the companies.

In 1887 the brothers expanded their activities into Queensland with a presentation of *The Mikado*; in 1888 their company opened Her Majesty's Opera House in Brisbane. Next year Charles and James took a long lease on the Melbourne Opera House, presenting such successes as the Nellie Stewart [q.v.] Opera Company in *Paul Jones*, and John F. Sheridan's *Fun on the Bristol*. Concurrently they presented variety entertainments in the Exhibition Building and Wirth's Circus in a marquee in Swanston Street. While in the United States in 1890 James recruited the famous Evangeline Burlesque Company and the retired champion boxer, John L. Sullivan, but financial difficulties, compounded by a court case for debt, forced the closure of the Sydney season and the Opera House lease at the end of 1891.

During the 1890s the brothers' theatrical activities were greatly reduced but, always interested in the latest technology, they made several trips to the United States in search of 'novelties'. In 1890 James displayed a model of Edison's phonograph and obtained a new model for the Sydney Tivoli in 1899. Charles exhibited an electric weighing machine in 1891, and in 1895 toured a demonstration 'kinetoscope'. In 1896-97 James opened the Salon Cinématographe in Pitt Street, Sydney, introducing a new cinématographe with special colour effects and a coupon system of payment. From this time the brothers' interest in cinema grew; their last major Australian theatrical venture, a twenty months' tenancy of the Sydney Lyceum in 1897-99, initially presented films before the melodrama main bill.

In 1907 Charles made the first of his two silent feature films, *Robbery under arms*, 5000 feet (1524 m) long and costing £1000, with Jim Gerald, later a noted vaudeville star, as the Aborigine, Warrigal. After a première in Melbourne it was screened at the Oxford Theatre, Sydney, where eager patrons 'stormed' the ticket office. Next year Charles, in conjunction with E. J. Carroll [q.v.7], made a 2000-feet (610 m) film of *For the term of his natural life*, shot in the ruins of Port Arthur, Tasmania, at a cost of £7000. The film broke records with an eight-week run at the Queen's Hall in Sydney in 1908. The MacMahons now branched into film distribution, in 1910 setting up the Dominion Picture Theatres Co. in New Zealand, and in 1910-15 opening cinemas in Auckland and Wellington. Charles's last film, a travelogue entitled *London by day and night*, was made and released in 1914. Both James and Charles died of pneumonia, James at Ashfield, Sydney, on 29 April 1915 and Charles in Melbourne on 27 June 1917; they were buried with Roman Catholic rites in Waverley and Brighton cemeteries. Charles left his estate of £585 to the actress May Granville who was widely accepted as his wife.

The brothers and their two sisters were an affectionate and close-knit family, and there were many tributes to their business integrity and enterprise. James, a 'genial and companionable man' known as 'Mighty Atom', was the innovator and driving force before 1900, after which 'Charlie' seems to have become the leading partner. Although he seemed a 'hard-bitten showman' to the young entrepreneur Claude Kingston, his sunny nature, his love of practical jokes, his legendary generosity and the perpetual flower in his button-hole made him a colourful and endearing personality.

F. Reade, *Australian silent films* (Melb, 1970); C. Kingston, *It don't seem a day too much* (Adel, 1971); A. Pike and R. Cooper, *Australian film, 1900-1977* (Melb, 1980); *Theatre* (Syd, Melb), 1 Aug 1917; *Table Talk*, 11 May, 28 Sept 1888, 15 Aug 1890; *T&CJ*, 3 Aug 1889; *Evening Post* (Wellington, NZ) and *New Zealand Times*, 18 Apr 1911, 30 June 1917; *Bendigo Independent*, 1 May 1915, 29 June 1917; *Bendigo Advertiser*, 1 May 1915, 29 June 1917, 27 Nov 1918; *Argus*, 3 May 1915, 28 June 1917; *Auckland Weekly News*, 28 Nov 1918; Leitch papers (ML).

MARGARET WILLIAMS

McMASTER, SIR FERGUS (1879-1950), grazier, businessman and airline founder, was born on 3 May 1879 at Morinish near Rockhampton, Queensland, sixth and youngest son of Scottish parents William McMaster, mine manager, and his wife Jessie, née Scott. Fergus attended Morinish Provisional School in his early years, but was largely self educated. His father was killed in a mine accident in 1885 and his brother William was drowned in 1888.

The McMaster brothers took up Kelso grazing lease in 1891, a 10 000 acre (4050 ha) resumption from Wellshot station, Longreach. When Fergus was 12 he assisted his brothers in droving 4000 sheep from Logan Downs (Clermont) over the Drummond Range and western plains to Kelso. Other western grazing leases selected by McMaster Bros were: Leswalt (1894), Siberia (1895), Moscow (1902), Edkinson (1908), Devoncourt (1910), Oban (1910), and El'Rita. Some, including Kelso, were waterless, so Fergus and his brothers built dams with horses and scoops and sank wells. In early manhood Fergus managed both Moscow (Winton) and Devoncourt (Cloncurry). He married Edith May Scougall (d. 1913) with Presbyterian forms on 29 August 1911, at Townsville. Having previously been rejected on medical grounds, McMaster enlisted in the Australian Imperial Force on 13 January 1917 and served in France in 1918 as a gunner and dispatch rider.

After a chance meeting at Cloncurry with P. J. McGinness, McMaster was invited to assist him and another Australian Flying Corps pilot (Sir) Hudson Fysh [q.v.8] to secure aircraft for operation in the bush areas of Queensland. His enthusiasm following a meeting in Brisbane in August 1920 prompted the formation of Queensland and Northern Territory Aerial Services Ltd (QANTAS). Registered in Brisbane on 16 November, with McMaster as chairman of directors (1920-23, 1927-34), the company took delivery of an Avro Dyak aircraft on 21 January 1921. The Dyak, piloted by McGinness, and a borrowed plane flown by Fysh landed at Barcaldine a few days later for a pre-arranged meeting with McMaster who, aided by 'a good smoke', guided the planes over gidyea stumps to a claypan. McGinness then flew McMaster on a promotion flight to Longreach and Winton. Occasionally, during that first year of business, no wages could be paid until McMaster 'had taken the hat around' among his friends.

In November McMaster led a deputation to Prime Minister W. M. Hughes [q.v.9] seeking government support for the Charleville to Cloncurry air service; Hughes told him to come back in ten years. As company chairman McMaster then issued a prospectus, offering 15 000 ordinary shares at £1 to shires, western towns, businessmen and graziers. According to Fysh, he was a 'strong man of unshakable integrity'. On 21 June 1922 he married Edna Faulkner in Brisbane with Presbyterian forms.

That year, after much negotiation, McMaster announced that QANTAS had secured the Federal government contract for the Charleville to Cloncurry service; the inaugural flight left Charleville on 2 November with McGinness as pilot. This was the first regular airmail service in Queensland and the second in Australia. McMaster was at Longreach to welcome it. Next day Fysh piloted the plane to Winton, while McMaster drove his car 128 miles (206 km) over bush tracks to greet the first passenger.

McMaster's drive and determination between 1929 and 1933 led to a successful outcome for QANTAS, following a legal challenge from three other airlines, in the bid to provide an airmail service from Australia to Singapore, to be linked with the Imperial Airways service from London. Qantas Empire Airways was registered in Brisbane on 18 January 1934 with McMaster as chairman of directors, which he remained until the Commonwealth government acquired the airline in 1947. In May-June 1935 he was the first return passenger on the regular airmail service between Australia and England. By 1931 he was also managing director of McMaster Bros, graziers and woolscourers.

In 1941 McMaster was knighted. A director of Tasman Empire Airways Ltd, he was also the founding director of North Australian Worsted & Woollen Mills Ltd, and the Electric Supply Co., Charters Towers. He was a foundation member in 1936 and later treasurer of the Queensland Country Party, but in 1941-43 was president of the Country-National Party; he had stood for a State seat as a Nationalist in 1923.

Sir Fergus McMaster died in Brisbane on 8 August 1950 and was cremated. His estate was sworn for probate at £32 398. The daughter of his first marriage and two sons of his second survived him; another son had died in 1944 while serving as a Royal Australian Air Force pilot. McMaster's portrait by William Dargie hangs in the QANTAS board room in Sydney.

M. J. Fox, *The history of Queensland*, 3 (Brisb, 1923); *Remember—by air Q.A.N.T.A.S. Ltd* (np, nd, c.1925); *The 'Qantas' airway* (np, nd, c.1928); H. Fysh, *Qantas rising* (Syd, 1965?); *Men of Queensland* (Brisb, 1937); QANTAS Ltd, *Australia and Australians in civil aviation*, 1 (Syd, 1971); J. S. Fysh (ed), *Rambling memories of Sir Fergus McMaster* (Warwick, Qld, c.1978); *Morning Bulletin*, 28, 29 Sept, 3 Oct 1885; *Galloway Advertiser* (Stranraer, Wigtown, Scotland), 10 Feb 1944; *Courier Mail*, 9 Aug 1950; letters to author from Mrs J. S. Fysh, Wavell Heights, Brisb, and information from Mr T. G. McMaster, Rockhampton, Qld.

LORNA L. McDONALD

McMASTER, SIR FREDERICK DUNCAN (1873-1954), pastoralist, was born on 9 July 1873 at Surry Hills, Sydney, second son of Duncan McMaster, Scottish-born pastoralist from Cooma, and his native-born wife Christina, née Cox. On leaving Sydney Grammar School in 1891 he took over the management of Dalkeith station at Cassilis, purchased for him by his father, and in 1899 assumed ownership. On 20 November 1901 at the Wesleyan Methodist Church, Manilla, he married Muriel Evelyn Clair Sherlock, daughter of a Cooma pastoralist.

McMaster developed a reputation as a leader in pasture management and soil conservation, especially on the black-soil country of which Dalkeith was typical, based on judicious and conservative stocking and on the control of rabbits rather than on pasture improvement. He described his system as 'reserve stocking' as distinct from 'understocking'; it involved the practice of always having a reserve of natural pasture in each grazing paddock. A born experimenter and an amateur engineer, he actively sought and practised the most advanced scientific knowledge available.

At first McMaster continued to buy Merino rams from Tasmania, but soon introduced Boonoke ewes and rams bought from F. S. Falkiner & Sons [qq.v.4,8] Ltd. A notable studmaster, he bred the champion ram at the 1936 Sydney Sheep Show. He also had a purebred herd of Hereford cattle. He was a council-member and later vice-president of the New South Wales Sheepbreeders' Association and of the Royal Agricultural Society of New South Wales, which he served in the beef-cattle section for many years, patron of the Standard Stock Dog Association and an honorary life-member of the Royal Agricultural Society of England from 1943. A keen tennis-player until the age of 70, he was a director and trustee of the New South Wales Lawn Tennis Association and president of the Sydney Lawn Tennis Club. He was also a vice-president of the Royal Empire Society and an honorary life-member of the English-Speaking Union. He belonged to the Australian and Australian Jockey clubs.

In an address to the Sheepbreeders' Association in 1929, Prime Minister S. M. (Viscount) Bruce [q.v.7] challenged graziers to share with the government the burgeoning cost of rural research. A few weeks later McMaster, a foundation member of the State committee of the Commonwealth Council for Scientific and Industrial Research from 1926, gave £20 000 to build an animal health research laboratory in the grounds of the University of Sydney, the Commonwealth government meeting the cost of staff and equipment through C.S.I.R. The F. D. McMaster Animal Health Laboratory was opened in August 1931 with (Sir) Ian Clunies-Ross as its first director; it quickly earned a world-wide reputation as a centre of research, especially on internal and external parasites of sheep. McMaster also assisted in the provision of field facilities for the laboratory. He was knighted in 1934.

In November 1954 McMaster made a further gift of £50 000 to the Commonwealth Scientific and Industrial Research Organization to add a wing to the McMaster laboratory in memory of his son Ian Frederick, M.C., who in 1942 was killed in the battle of El Alamein. The McMaster generosity was also frequently demonstrated in less public ways: in 1930 he gave 500 stud rams to the State government to distribute to needy settlers. He often quoted:

> We lose what we keep,
> We have what we share
> And what we have given
> We find everywhere.

His contemporary Alan Tory described McMaster as 'an almost legendary figure whose mind and vision match his dominating physique . . . a figure of acknowledged authority who moves among his peers with a youthful curiosity and quiet assurance that the destiny of Australia rests upon the broad shoulders . . . of farmers, graziers and stud owners'. He was a man of action—in a sense a benevolent despot. He was also a generous host to the steady stream of visitors to his property, including members of the royal family, Davis Cup tennis players and other public figures.

McMaster died at Dalkeith on 28 November 1954 and was cremated after a service at St Stephen's Presbyterian Church, Sydney. His estate was valued for probate at £216 403 for eventual bequest to C.S.I.R.O. He was survived by his wife and unmarried daughter Thelma, who founded a Hereford stud at Dalkeith and managed the property until she died in 1981.

A. Tory, *Harbour in heaven* (Syd, 1949); *J of the CSIR*, 2, no 4, Nov 1929, p 193, 4, no 4, Nov 1931, p 201, 6, no 3, Aug 1933, p 214, 9, no 3, Aug 1936, p 239; *Pastoral Review*, 16 Dec 1931, p 1187, 16 June 1934, p 556, 16 Dec 1954, p 1489; *Aust J of Science*, 1, no 5, Apr 1939, p 142; *Aust Veterinary J*, 57, May 1981, p 249; *J of the Soil Conservation Service of NSW*, 11, no 1, Jan 1955, p 1; *Farmer and Settler*, 4 Dec 1941; *Country Life*, 5 Dec 1941, 3 Dec 1954; *SMH*, 26, 29 Nov 1954; CSIRO Archives (Canb).   KEITH O. CAMPBELL

McMILLAN, ROBERT (1848?-1929), journalist and author, was born in Edinburgh, son of Robert McMillan and his wife Margaret, née York. At 14 Robert ran away to sea, and some of his experiences are told in his adventure story, *Voyage of the 'Monsoon'* (1900). For a time he lived in the United States of America, working on a Boston newspaper. Later he moved to England, joined the staff of the *Liverpool Mercury*, and married Chrissie Walker or Ingle.

Ill health took McMillan to New South Wales about 1890. He lived at Katoomba, becoming editor and proprietor of the *Blue Mountains Express*. In 1892 he was approached by William Brooks [q.v.7], owner of the *Stock and Station Journal*, to relieve the 'array of trade matter' by writing a weekly article. McMillan accepted, and soon became editor and a shareholder. He remained in Sydney with the journal until 1917.

McMillan wrote bright and informative columns and features, often under the pseudonyms, 'Gossip' and 'Globe Trotter'. He discussed 'in simple language, but with the highest regard for accuracy' such topics as the earth's motion and the law of gravitation. Selections were published in *Australian gossip and story* (1895), *There and back* (1903), *No breakfast* (1905), *The origin of the world* (1913) and *Story of a microscope* (1914). His books were often dedicated to children (especially boys), and his beloved *Stock and Station Journal* readers.

Representing the New South Wales Country Press Association, in 1902 McMillan went to Melbourne to protest against Federal taxes on paper, ink and type. In 1908 he published a pamphlet, *An infamous monopoly*, vigorously attacking the United Cable (Australian Press) Association's monopoly of press cables. Next year he gave evidence to the Senate select committee on press cable service and, as a director of the Independent Cable Association of Australasia Ltd, continued his campaign at the first Imperial Press

Conference in London in 1909. The monopoly was broken in 1910 when the Fisher [q.v.8] Labor government subsidized an independent cable service. On his way to London in the *Pericles*, McMillan had been shipwrecked on 31 March: his graphic account of the disaster was published in the Sydney *Daily Telegraph*.

Quiet and unobtrusive, with a kind face, luxuriant moustache and Vandyke beard, in 1907 McMillan was a foundation committee-member of the New South Wales Institute of Journalists. He was also a member of the Institute of Journalists, London, and of the Royal Colonial Institute. In 1917 he went to Brisbane to become editor of the *Queensland Grazier* and in 1920 was a founder and honorary secretary of the Queensland Press Institute. From 1921, back in Sydney and again editor of the *Stock and Station Journal* (*Country Life* from 1924), he actively encouraged the foundation of the Country Women's Association of New South Wales.

After several years of failing health McMillan died on 18 February 1929 at Little Bay and was cremated. Childless, he was survived by his wife.

J. Loney, *Wrecks in Australian waters* (Melb, nd); Country Women's Assn of NSW, *The silver years* (Syd, 1947); *Cosmos Mag*, 31 Jan 1896; *British A'sian*, 13 Mar 1902, 28 July 1910, 12 Dec 1914; *SMH*, 1 Apr 1910, 23 July 1926, 20 Feb 1929; *Australasian*, 2 Apr 1910; *Queenslander*, 21 Feb 1929; NSW Inst of Journalists, *Annual Report*, 1913, 1917.   MARION CONSANDINE

McMILLAN, SIR ROBERT FURSE (1858-1931), chief justice, was born on 24 January 1858 at Camden New Town, London, eldest son and third of nine children of John McMillan, barrister and West India merchant, and his wife Mary, née Furse. He was registered as John, but when baptized on 2 June he was named after his maternal grandfather. The family lived in London but also had a country home.

At 13 Robert went to Westminster School where two years later he became a Queen's scholar. He attended Trinity Hall, University of Cambridge, where in 1879 he became a scholar and, in 1880, a fellow. Completing the law tripos, first class (bracketed senior), in 1879, and his LL.B. next year, he was called to the Bar in 1881, having been admitted to the Inner Temple where he had been a scholar and an Inns of Court student. He earned a reputation at the Bar for thoroughness and, unlike his father, avoided participation in politics or business. On 2 August 1887 at St Paul's Church, Hampstead, London,

McMillan married Margaret Aitchison Elder, daughter of a Victorian pastoralist.

In 1902 he was invited to apply for appointment to a vacant judgeship in Perth. He did so, was appointed and, with misgivings, arrived at Fremantle early next year. On 18 March he sat for the first time as a member of the full court. In 1914 McMillan became chief justice. He was knighted in 1916 and appointed K.C.M.G. in 1925. Lieutenant-governor from 1921, he acted as administrator of the State in 1922, 1924 and 1929.

His influence on the laws and legal system was substantial. He did not spare himself as a judge; the number of his reported judgments (828) far exceeds that of any other Western Australian judge, certainly in the first half of the century. Few of his judgments were taken on appeal, and in most of those that were his opinion prevailed. Speaking in 1961, Sir Owen Dixon praised him as 'an ornament to the judiciary; one who struck the imagination of any young judge as a man of the highest refinement and character, representing the best traditions of the judiciary in the English-speaking world'.

McMillan had great charm. Clean-shaven and handsome, though stern-looking and reserved, he was eloquent, witty and courteous. When he was first appointed there had been resentment that the government had not filled the vacancy from the local profession. But this soon evaporated and he was widely esteemed, not only by lawyers. Sir John Northmore [q.v.] said of him, he was 'not a man who courted popularity. On the contrary he was of a reserved disposition. But [popularity] came to him unsought in full measure . . . no man at the time of his death held such a high place in the regard of the people of the State and no other held a higher place in the affection of those who called him friend or in the respect of those who . . . knew him only as Chief Justice'.

Like many of his peers, McMillan believed that socially a judge should remain aloof, and he adhered to this strictly. Shortly after his arrival in Perth he had a house built at View Street, Peppermint Grove, where he lived for the rest of his life. He was a member of the Weld Club. His hobbies were collecting china and old books, gardening and music; he regularly took early morning swims in the Swan River near his home. He was a member of the board of governors of Perth High School and a trustee of the Public Library of Western Australia and of the Western Australian Museum and Art Gallery.

Sir Robert collapsed and died on 23 April 1931 at the opening of St George's College at the University of Western Australia, having just, in a typically humorous, appropriate and well-received speech, thanked the governor for his address. He had been a devout Anglican and his remains lay in state in St George's Cathedral before his burial in Karrakatta cemetery. His wife, two daughters and two sons survived him.

Univ WA Law Review, 6, no 2, Dec 1963; *Brighton Times* (Eng), 24 Sept 1880, supp; *West Australian*, 1 Dec 1902, 24, 25 Apr 1931; *The Times*, 24 Apr 1931; personal information.

ERIC J. EDWARDS

McMILLAN, SAMUEL (1859-1931), coachmaker, wheelwright, blacksmith and inventor, was born on 12 December 1859 at Mansfield, Victoria, eldest son of Thomas McMillan, farmer, and his wife Margaret, née Maclure; his grandparents Samuel and Janette McMillan had migrated to Victoria from Scotland in 1840 and eventually acquired the Logan Falls farm near Mansfield. The young Samuel attended Mansfield Common School which his father, determined that his children should have the schooling which he himself had been denied, had helped to establish. A bright, inventive boy, Samuel used his spare time making tools and toys and, noting this, his father apprenticed him to William Carey, a skilled local blacksmith and coachbuilder; he continued his training under Michael Ridge of Jamieson and at Johnstone's Foundry, Melbourne, where he perfected his skill as a wheelwright.

Returning to Mansfield, McMillan joined William Rundel, blacksmith, wheelwright and coachbuilder, in his business. The pair built a splendid reputation, winning over one hundred awards at country and town shows in Victoria. They early used a four-horse-power steam engine to increase production and they employed an artist, named Wells, to decorate their coaches, buggies and jinkers. When Rundel retired McMillan continued the business with increasing success.

He put his inventive ability to good purpose. Where the window-light was strongest in his big smithy in High Street, he set up a large blackboard and on this drew designs of possible inventions to the interest of customers, passers-by and children going home from school. He invented a rabbit-poisoning machine known as 'The Ringer' which, though difficult to use in the hilly country of Mansfield, was most successful in New South Wales and Western Australia. In 1885 McMillan became the first Mansfield exporter when the machine was sold in the United States of America. He patented a self-closing spring gate fastener and designed an improved clothes peg. In later years he spent much time designing an aeroplane. He was one of the first in Mansfield to fly as a passenger over Mount Buller; he was also one of

the first to own and drive a motor car, an early model known as 'The Little'.

McMillan lent generous support to many public activities and despite increasing deafness never lost interest in his town. He was a member of the Mansfield Hospital committee and a commissioner of the waterworks trust. He was a Freemason and Oddfellow and won many competitions with the Mansfield Gun Club. A skilled horseman, he was famed for his fast but safe driving of his four-in-hand team. He was unmarried. He suffered from diabetes and died at Mansfield on 22 March 1931 and was buried in the local cemetery. No man, it was said, had more true friends. Years before, at a dinner given by the people of Mansfield to honour McMillan, the chairman in proposing the toast had declaimed, 'Longfellow wrote that men do not go to Paradise in coaches but I'd be proud to go in one of Sam's!'

J. Gillison, *Colonial doctor and his town* (Melb, 1974); RHSV, *J*, 43 (May 1972), no 2; *Mansfield Courier*, 5 Oct, 25 Nov 1885, 6 Jan 1890, 18 Jan 1893, 8 June 1895, 27 March 1931; family papers held by G. Friday and A. McMillan, Mansfield, Vic.

JOAN GILLISON

McMILLAN, SIR WILLIAM (1850-1926), merchant and politician, was born on 14 November 1850 in Londonderry, Ireland, third son of Gibson McMillan, Wesleyan minister, and his wife Eliza, sister of Alexander McArthur [q.v.5]. He was educated at St Stephen's Green (the Wesleyan Connexional School), Dublin, with H. B. Higgins [q.v.9], and at Tulse Hill School in London. Although initially intended for the Bar, at 17 he went into the London office of his uncles' merchant business, W. and A. McArthur Ltd. Sent out in 1869 to join A. H. C. Macafee, a Sydney partner, he worked as traveller in New South Wales and spent several years in Melbourne in the McArthurs' Flinders Lane warehouse. At the Wesleyan Church, South Yarra, he married Ada Charlotte Graham, aged 16, on 8 March 1878. On Macafee's death in 1878 he returned to Sydney to become partner and manager of the firm's Australian operations.

On first arriving, McMillan had joined the Sydney School of Arts Debating Club where he met budding politicians like (Sir) George Reid [q.v.] and (Sir) Edmund Barton [q.v.7], developed his talent for public speaking and sharpened his already considerable knowledge of literature and economics. By the 1880s, through his lectures, articles and letters to the press, he was recognized as an authority on commercial matters and spokesman for the interests of Sydney importers. Elected president of the Sydney Chamber of

Commerce in 1886, he attended in London the Congress of the Chambers of Commerce of the British Empire. As the tariff issue became important in the colony's politics he played a leading part in setting up the Free Trade Association of New South Wales, urging men of 'wealth, intelligence, and influence . . . to show some patriotic interest in the country to which they owe their all'.

Under pressure from the chamber and 'a large number of businessmen', he agreed to stand for East Sydney at the general election of 1887. The *Bulletin* dubbed him 'Patriotic MacMillion', champion of the 'calico-jimmy' interest, and cartoonist Livingstone Hopkins [q.v.4] sketched him as the would-be rescuer, armed with a 'freetrade' blunderbuss, of a 'softgoods pup' doomed to be gobbled up by the crocodile, 'protection'. But McMillan won effortlessly, was chosen by the new Parkes [q.v.5] ministry to move the address-in-reply, and settled into the Legislative Assembly as leader of a small Free Trade ginger group which leavened Parkes's faction followers. As such he headed a party revolt when Parkes resigned in pique in 1889 on trivial Opposition charges of corruption. After a narrow Free Trade victory at a consequent general election, Parkes was forced to reconstruct the ministry as an unequivocal Free Trade combination: McMillan became treasurer and deputy leader.

Parkes was not an easy chief to follow. His refusal to consult ministers brought cabinet dissension and several plots to unseat him in favour of McMillan or J. N. Brunker [q.v.3]. Though incapacitated with a broken leg, Parkes refused during the maritime strike to surrender control of the police to his deputy and after the Circular Quay 'riot' of September 1890 publicly rebuked McMillan, who 'in the unfortunate absence of my chief' had provocatively committed the government to putting down 'disorder and anarchy'. McMillan offered his resignation but the governor Lord Carrington [q.v.3] persuaded him to withdraw and, with ruffled tempers smoothed, the treasurer remained at his post until pressure of private business forced him to resign in July 1891. In McMillan respect—even affection—for Parkes in fact ran deep.

Though, like most doctrinaire free traders, initially nervous at the possible tariff implications of Federation, McMillan became under Parkes's tutelage a keen Federationist. He was a delegate at the 1890 Australasian Federation Conference and at the 1891 National Australasian Convention where, in La Nauze's words, he 'usefully insisted on discussing practical issues'. Elected to the 1897 Australasian Federal Convention, he spoke of the financial arrangements for the future Commonwealth as an 'insoluble conundrum' and was chosen to chair the difficult finance

committee. He was appointed K.C.M.G. in 1901 primarily in recognition of this work.

McMillan represented Burwood in the Legislative Assembly in 1894-98. His early hostility to Reid waned as the latter consolidated the Free Trade party and proved himself a shrewd and capable leader. Reid's radicalism and his readiness to work with the Labor Party were however not entirely to McMillan's taste and he was as much the government's 'candid critic' as its supporter. He particularly deplored Reid's attacks on the Upper House, disliked his establishment of an income tax and kept a sharp eye on all financial measures. He was either not asked, or refused, to serve in Reid's cabinets, though the two came more happily together in the first Federal parliament, to which McMillan was elected for Wentworth. In May 1901 the Free Trade members of the House of Representatives elected Reid as leader and McMillan as deputy. Reid, obliged by professional engagements to spend much time in Sydney, thought McMillan's acting leadership always 'zealous and efficient'. But McMillan's career in the Federal house was short: business cares forced his retirement in 1903, and, unexpectedly, his political career was at an end.

McMillan's business interests were wide ranging and took him on frequent visits to England. In the 1890s he was Sydney director of the National Bank of Australasia, chairman of Associated South Coast Collieries and the Metropolitan Coal Trust Co. of Sydney Ltd and a director of the limited companies, Westinghouse Brake, Phoenix Assurance and E. Rich. He lectured on public finance to the Institute of Bankers of New South Wales and, though a political opponent, was consulted by Sir George Dibbs [q.v.4] on banking legislation during the crisis of 1893. The McArthur firm was reconstructed in 1907 and conditions for such importers worsened during and after World War I. Though McMillan's financial fortunes waned he remained interested in public affairs. He was defeated for the State seat of Willoughby in 1913, but was an active member of the British Empire League in Australia and the Proportional Representation Society of New South Wales, served for twenty years on the Council of Women's College, University of Sydney, and was in demand as a public speaker for a variety of patriotic and charitable causes. He also maintained his active membership of the New South Wales, Australian, Union and Melbourne clubs, and the Devonshire Club, London.

On 15 November 1888 McMillan had been granted a judicial separation from his wife and custody of his four children, and on 3 September 1891 a decree absolute. In Glasgow, Scotland, on 19 August 1892 he married a widow

Helen Maria O'Reilly, née Gibson and grand-daughter of Rev. William Boyce [q.v.3]. She was president of the National Council of Women of New South Wales in 1918-19 and was involved in several charitable organizations. McMillan died at his home, Althorne, Bellevue Hill, on 21 December 1926 and was buried with Wesleyan forms in the Anglican section of Waverley cemetery. A son and two daughters of his first marriage and his second wife and their two daughters survived him; Lady McMillan married A. W. Munro [q.v.] in 1930. McMillan's portrait by Norman Carter [q.v.7] is at Parliament House, Canberra.

Alfred Deakin [q.v.8] saw McMillan as the prototype of the 'thoughtful, educated businessman, narrow and cold after the manner of the Manchester School . . . business-like in manner and incisive in debate'. An enlightened conservative, in his public life he did his best to vindicate the uses in government of good management and probity. A handsome figure with eyes 'intensely and vividly blue', his dour exterior hid, if Lady McMillan is to be believed, 'a great love of fun . . . quick and ready wit and gift for repartee'. His letters to Parkes, especially those written at the time of his divorce, reveal a man of great sensitivity and inner resourcefulness.

A. Deakin, *The Federal story*, H. Brookes ed (Melb, 1944); J. A. La Nauze, *The making of the Australian Constitution* (Melb, 1972); P. Loveday et al (eds), *The emergence of the Australian party system* (Syd, 1977); A. W. Martin, *Henry Parkes* (Melb, 1980), *and* 'William McMillan: A merchant in politics', *JRAHS*, 40, pt iv (Mar 1955); *Review of Reviews for A'sia*, 20 July 1894; B. Nairn, 'A note on the colonial treasurer's resignation', *Hist Studies*, 13, no 49 (Oct 1967); Helen McMillan, Brief record of William McMillan, K.C.M.G. (typescript held by Mr P. M. Gunnar, Portland, Oregon, USA); Parkes papers (ML).   A. W. MARTIN

MACNAGHTEN, CHARLES MELVILLE (1879-1931), solicitor and soldier, was born at Rhutenpore, India, on 18 November 1879, eldest son of (Sir) Melville Leslie Macnaghten and his wife Dora Emily, daughter of Rev. R. E. Sanderson. He spent his early life in East Bengal where his father managed family estates but in 1888 the family returned to England and his father began a distinguished career at Scotland Yard. Charles went to Eton in 1893 and in 1898 entered Trinity College, Cambridge (B.A., 1901).

Arriving in Sydney from India about 1903, he married Yorkshire-born Annetta Nina Thirza ('Nettie') Hopcroft at the New Unitarian Church, Pitt Street, on 30 December 1904. In June he had commenced his solicitor's articles with T. J. Hughes, transferring to A. W. Hyman [q.v.9] in December 1905;

illness delayed his examinations and he was finally admitted to practice in November 1908. It was said that 'the close and concentrated study of those years adversely affected a highly-strung, sensitive temperament'. He began practice on his own account but in 1913 joined the law firm of Dodds & Richardson.

Macnaghten was interested in military affairs. In May 1909 he was appointed second lieutenant in the 1st Battalion, New South Wales Scottish Rifle Regiment, and in November 1910 was promoted lieutenant and appointed temporary area officer for Woolloomooloo district in anticipation of the introduction of universal military training. He was transferred to the 25th Infantry Regiment in July 1912 and to the 26th a year later. In December 1913 he was promoted major.

Described by C. E. W. Bean [q.v.7] as 'distinguished by a vigorous impetuosity', Macnaghten threw himself into his work, training senior cadets in a half-slum district 'in which the bane of area-officers, the larrikin, was probably strongest'. He taught drill to unit officers on the flat roof of the University Club's premises in Castlereagh Street and his cadet battalion became known as the best in Sydney. Twenty years later a colleague recalled 'Macnaghten in his Glengarry, tight-fitting short tunic, plaid breeches, and dark blue puttees, with his masterful face, heavy shoulders, and slim legs, striding on to parade, and his . . . vibrant compelling voice ringing out the command "Par-r-rade, 'shun" '.

With the raising of the Australian Imperial Force, Macnaghten was appointed second-in-command of the 4th Battalion on 15 August 1914. According to the official war history, Macnaghten and Colonel H. N. MacLaurin, in command of the 1st Brigade, 'working together, largely influenced the choice of officers throughout this brigade'. On Gallipoli on 26 April 1915, when a verbal order for a general advance was mistakenly received, it was Macnaghten's impulsive advice to Lieut-Colonel A. J. Onslow Thompson ('I'll take the right, Colonel, if you'll take the left') which sent the 4th Battalion on an unplanned attack without objective against Lone Pine. Macnaghten was shot twice in the chest and throat, and a note written from his stretcher was the first hint received by the staff that the sole unit of the 1st Division intact after the landing had been decimated. He returned to the unit in June and on 14 July was appointed to command with rank of lieut-colonel. During the Turkish counter-attack on Lone Pine on 7 August Macnaghten was wounded in the knee, and evacuated to England. He resumed command in December in time for the evacuation of the peninsula. In January 1916 he was appointed C.M.G. and mentioned in dispatches for his Gallipoli service. Appointed camp commandant at Tel-el-Kebir, Egypt, in February he was hospitalized next month and returned to Australia, his A.I.F. appointment being terminated in September.

Ordered to the Royal Military College, Duntroon, as a member still of the Australian Military Forces, Macnaghten became restive and attempted to return to the war but was refused permission on medical grounds. Reportedly disguising his limp and altering his appearance, and without telling even his family, he went to Queensland and re-enlisted in October as a private in reinforcements for the 9th Battalion as 'Ciam MacMilville'. He embarked for England and was sent to France in April 1917 as a second lieutenant in the 13th Battalion. Next month his identity was discovered; no action was taken apart from amending his name in orders, though back in Australia army authorities were seeking him and preparing to declare him a deserter. He was wounded in action in June but remained on duty. In July he was again in hospital and briefly returned to duty, but was discharged from the A.I.F. in England on 10 October as permanently unfit.

Macnaghten remained in England for a time and then went to Canada, drifting to Montreal in 1924 where he was employed by the Canadian Pacific Railway Co. as an accountant until 1930. On 4 February 1931 he died of pneumonia in his rooms at Notre Dame de Grace and was cremated. He left no children.

C. E. W. Bean, *The story of Anzac*, 1, 2 (Syd, 1921, 1924); *London Gazette*, 11, 28 Jan 1916; *Scottish A'sian*, Aug 1916; *Reveille* (Syd), 28 Feb 1931; *The Times*, 24 Feb 1912, 30 Mar 1914, 13, 17, 19 May 1921, 7 Feb 1931; *SMH*, 4, 5 Apr 1912, 13 Feb 1931; *Gazette* (Montreal) and *Montreal Daily Star*, 6 Feb 1931; *Herald* (Montreal), 7 Feb 1931; *Argus* (Melb) and *Globe* (Toronto), 9 Feb 1931; *Bulletin*, 11 Feb 1931; records (AWM).

C. D. COULTHARD-CLARK

MACNAMARA, DAME ANNIE JEAN (1899-1968), medical scientist, was born on 1 April 1899 at Beechworth, Victoria, second daughter of Victorian-born parents John Macnamara, clerk of courts, and his wife Annie, née Fraser. She was brought up in her mother's Presbyterian faith, but it was probably from her Catholic father, impetuous and forthright, that she inherited her determined spirit.

After the family moved to Melbourne in 1907, Jean attended Spring Road State School, Malvern. A scholarship took her to Presbyterian Ladies' College where she became editor of the school magazine, *Patchwork*, and at 15 won the prize for general excellence. The war years strengthened her seriousness of purpose and she felt obliged 'to be of some use in the world' when she entered the University of Melbourne on an exhibition at 17. She graduated M.B., B.S., in 1922 (as part of a brilliant year which included (Dame) Kate Campbell, Lucy Bryce [q.v.7], Jean Littlejohn and (Sir) Macfarlane Burnet) with exhibitions in surgery and anatomy and the Beaney [q.v.3] scholarship in surgery. She became a resident medical officer at the (Royal) Melbourne Hospital.

In May 1923 Jean, with high recommendations, was appointed resident at the (Royal) Children's Hospital. She remained until 1925 when, having graduated M.D., she became clinical assistant to the Children's outpatients' physician and entered private practice with a special emphasis on poliomyelitis. In 1925-31 she was consultant and medical officer responsible to the Poliomyelitis Committee of Victoria led by Dr John Dale [q.v.8] and in 1930-31 honorary adviser on polio to official authorities in New South Wales, South Australia and Tasmania. In 1928-51 she was honorary medical officer to the Yooralla Hospital School for Crippled Children.

The 1925 polio epidemic prompted Dr Macnamara to test the use of immune serum in the treatment of patients at the pre-paralytic stage. Convinced of the value of the method, she published and defended her results in Australian and British journals in 1927-35, notably with F. G. Morgan in the *Lancet* of 27 February 1932. The therapy, difficult to administer properly, was damned by the discouraging findings of W. H. Park in New York in 1931, even though Jean was quick to pin-point vital weaknesses in his procedures. The efficacy of the treatment was in fact never disproved and although its general adoption was 'wrecked', she believed, 'on the rocks of carelessness' in America, she continued to use it privately. Her discovery, in collaboration with Macfarlane Burnet, of the existence of more than one strain of polio virus (reported in 1931 in the *British Journal of Experimental Pathology*) has, however, been acknowledged as an early step towards the development of the Salk vaccine.

From September 1931 to October 1933 Dr Macnamara travelled in England and North America on a Rockefeller fellowship. Conflict with 'John Dale and his crew' over the development of immune serum therapy firmed a resolve to concentrate on orthopaedics. An admirer of Dame Agnes Hunt whom she met at the Shropshire Orthopaedic Hospital, she wrote to her mother on 3 February 1932, 'my best chance of real happiness is to hitch onto some ideal like she did and go for it'. Typically she added, 'I'd like to come [back] to Australia while this Government is in power for with Mr [Viscount] Bruce [q.v.7], Mr [Sir John] Latham [q.v.] and Mrs Lyons all friendly I would get a good spin'. Although research still appealed, and she worked part-time at the Walter and Eliza Hall [q.v.9] Institute in Melbourne in 1933-37 on serum and psittacosis, her special field remained conservative orthopaedics.

While overseas she preached the necessity for adequate after-care of disabled persons, met President Roosevelt, ordered Australia's first artificial respirator, and armed herself with new ideas for splinting and rehabilitation. She also wrote to health departments around the world canvassing the possibility that the polio virus was transmitted through milk.

On 19 November 1934, at the Presbyterian Church, Gardenvale, Jean married Joseph Ivan Connor, a dermatologist. They acquired Springfield, South Yarra, the former home of the pioneer woman doctor Lilian Alexander.

Only 5 ft. (152 cm) tall, plump, rather shabbily dressed, quick-witted and blunt in manner, Jean Macnamara (who rolled her own and had a smoker's cough) won great renown for her orthopaedic work, being appointed D.B.E. in 1935. Moving from Collins Street to larger premises at Spring Street, she often worked through week-ends and went without fee. During the 1937-38 polio epidemic she supervised patient care at both the Children's and Fairfield hospitals. She had little time for the unco-operative, but her remarkable ability to inspire confidence in her patients, mostly children, filled her clinics with families prepared to wait hours for her attention.

Her method was to splint the paralysed part of the body until the damaged nerve had recovered and patiently re-educate the muscles. She spent much time not only with her patients but with her splint-maker, devising ingenious restraining devices. She organized a system of itinerant physiotherapists and almoners and a volunteer chauffeur service; in 1938 she established a clinic at Carlton where thirty children were treated daily, being driven there and back and given a hot midday dinner. Dame Jean also conducted country clinics and administered the Arthur Marsden Whiting Sympathy Fund. She belonged to the Consultative Council for Polio in 1937-42 and 1946-47 and served on the 1935 Queensland royal commission investigating Sister Elizabeth Kenny's [q.v.9] treatment. Wisely, she supported the establishment of an experimental Kenny treatment centre at Brighton (Hampton), at the same time acquiring improved hospital facilities for herself. Her work extended to victims of lead poisoning and cerebral palsy and to healthy people with poor posture. The first centre for spastic children in Australia was opened on her recommendation at the Children's Hospital in 1940.

From girlhood Jean had an affinity with the land, farm holidays impressing upon her the effects of rabbit and drought in destroying 'the children's inheritance'. In 1933 at Princeton University her introduction to Richard Shope, who was trying to combat myxomatosis in rabbits, had given her the idea of deploying myxomatosis to eradicate the rabbits in Australia. She was unaware that H. de B. Aragao had advocated the same solution years earlier and that a Brazilian strain of the virus had been held in Melbourne since 1919. When the virus sample she dispatched to Melbourne in 1933 was destroyed, Jean elicited the support of Stanley Bruce in London and arranged that tests for the safety of domestic animals be carried out in Cambridge by Sir Charles Martin [q.v.]. Lionel Bull of the Council for Scientific and Industrial Research then tested Australian animals at Werribee, Victoria, in 1937 and until 1944 ran a series of field trials on rabbits, using mosquitoes and fleas as vectors, in the Spencer Gulf area and the dry north of South Australia: the virus failed to spread.

Convinced that the experiments had been abandoned prematurely, Dame Jean revived the cause in a letter to the Melbourne *Herald* on 11 May 1949 and conducted a heated newspaper exchange with Bull and other scientists. Having worked for the election and appointment of a sympathetic minister for lands, (Sir) Rutherford Guthrie, she lobbied producers' organizations and co-opted the support of entomologist G. W. Douglas. Testing was resumed, in a more favourable location along the Murray River, in 1950, initially without success. Then, by chance, at the end of the year the virus became epizootic.

The aspersions Dame Jean had cast upon the professionalism of Commonwealth Scientific and Industrial Research Organization officers rankled. But in 1952-53 'myxo' was reputed to have augmented the wool cheque by at least £30 million—the 'conspicuous gadfly' had been vindicated. The woolgrowers gave her £800 and a clock.

With her husband, who died in 1955, Jean had a hobby farm in the Romsey district. She belonged to the Compost Society and fought against indiscriminate use of pesticides. In a bitter campaign she also thwarted the plans of Francis Ratcliffe, head of the wildlife division of C.S.I.R.O., to protect breeders' rabbits against myxomatosis. In 1964 the animal house at the Keith Turnbull Research Station, Frankston, was named in her honour. The University of Melbourne awarded her an honorary LL.D. in 1966.

Neglectful of her own health, Dame Jean continued to treat victims of paralysis until her death from heart disease on 13 October 1968. Many former patients attended her funeral which, it was said, resembled a scene from Lourdes. According to her wishes, her ashes were buried under a mossy rock at Beechworth. She was survived by her two daughters.

D. Zwar, *The Dame* (Melb, 1984); Macnamara papers, MS 2399 (NL).   ANN G. SMITH

McNAMARA, DANIEL LAURENCE (1876-1947), politician, was born on 28 March 1876 at Pomborneit, near Camperdown, Victoria, son of Michael McNamara, farmer, and his wife Mary, née Taff, both Irish born. The family moved to Kooweerup, some fifty miles (80 km) south-east of Melbourne, when Daniel was 6. After education at local state schools he became involved as a young man in local co-operative ventures and trade union work. Later he was elected to the Berwick Shire Council, and was president in 1906-07.

McNamara moved to Melbourne in 1906 and was almost immediately prominent in the labour movement. An organizer of the Victorian Rural Workers' Union, he was for a time its secretary before it was absorbed by the Australian Workers' Union in 1913. He also made many appearances for unions before arbitration authorities. On the more directly political side, he was a delegate to the Australian Labor Party's Victorian annual conference from 1906 and a member of the central executive from 1909 and of the office staff of the party from 1910. From that position he used his great talent as an administrator to become assistant secretary (1910-22), organizing secretary (1922-25) and then general secretary in Victoria in 1925-47.

Appointed secretary of the federal executive of the party in 1925, McNamara held the position until 1946. He was therefore at the centre in the stormy years when the federal executive was fighting to establish its authority over the State branches, especially in New South Wales in 1927 and 1931-36 against J. T. Lang [q.v.9]. As both federal and a State secretary McNamara was very fortunate that in his time Victoria was not in conflict with the federal organization. He was a staunch supporter of the Premiers' Plan at both State and federal levels.

McNamara had for long been much interested in Federal-State relations and this led to his appointment as a member of the royal commission on the Constitution in 1927-29. He was one of the three who presented dissenting reports and his views were later published in a booklet, *Constitution of the Commonwealth: proposals for amendment* (1938); his major themes were the replacement of State parliaments with a number of regional councils, and, generally, the concentration of power and responsibility in the national government. His report influenced the official party approach to the question for several decades.

McNamara stood unsuccessfully for the Legislative Assembly in 1907, 1908, 1909 and 1911. He was elected unopposed for Melbourne East Province in the Legislative Council in 1917 and held a seat in the council continuously until his death. He was a minister in three short-lived Labor governments: for mines and forests in 1924, honorary minister in 1931-32, and in 1943 commissioner of crown lands and minister of forests and water supply. In all he held ministerial office for less than sixteen months.

His parliamentary career was long but not distinguished. He was a conscientious member but he did not speak often and it seems that his salary, time and energy were consumed in his two party secretarial posts. In them he earned distinction by his efficient administration, quiet manner and his total, unremitting dedication to the Labor Party and gained his reputation as a quiet but effective wielder of influence in its internal affairs.

'Danny' McNamara married Florence Spinks at St Ignatius' Church, Richmond, on May Day 1915, with John Curtin as best man. He died of coronary vascular disease at his home at East St Kilda on 28 December 1947, survived by his wife, a daughter and two sons. After a state funeral and requiem Mass he was buried in the new Cheltenham cemetery.

PD (Vic), 1961-62, p 593; *Labor Call*, 20 Aug 1936, 20 Feb 1947; *Argus* and *Herald*, 29 Dec 1947.   PETER COOK

McNAMARA, DAVID JOHN (1887-1967), footballer and racehorse trainer, was born on 22 January 1887 at Boosey, near Yarrawonga, Victoria, sixth son of Melbourne-born Michael McNamara, farmer, and his wife Mary, née Quinlan.

Educated at local schools, as a youth Dave engaged in Australian Rules football, playing for Benalla, and horse-racing. In 1905 he joined St Kilda Football Club and in his senior début helped the side to an unexpected victory with four of the team's five goals. By 1907 his goalkicking exploits had helped St Kilda to reach their first finals series, and he was already widely regarded as the finest footballer in the Victorian Football League. Next year he was St Kilda's captain and at the inaugural National Football Championships in Melbourne was adjudged best player of the series.

On 20 October 1909 he married Florence Mary Dobson at St Francis' Church, Melbourne; they had a son and a daughter. Midway through that year McNamara crossed to the Victorian Football Association. With

Essendon Association he played in premiership teams in 1911-12, when he kicked 81 and 107 goals. The 1912 total included 18 in one match; he was the first player in Australian senior football to kick over the century in one season. Refused a clearance to return to St Kilda in 1913, he stood out of football until his clearance was granted in 1914. After St Kilda went into recess in 1915, he resumed on its return in 1918. Captain throughout this time, in 1923 he became playing coach. From 1924 he played with the amateur side, Ormond, until well past his fortieth birthday. In the 1930s he returned to St Kilda as a committeeman, was voted life membership, served as vice-president, and in 1938 was elected president.

McNamara's league playing career, mostly at full-forward or centre-half forward, spanned 148 games. He kicked some 600 goals in the V.F.L., the great majority by left-footed place kick. The distances he set with this kick were legendary: 89 yds. 2 ft. (Sydney, in a long-kicking competition with 'Dally' Messenger [q.v.], 1914); and a world-record 93 yds. (85 m) (St Kilda, 1923). His kicking ability, as well as his physique, earned him the nickname 'Long Dave'.

At 6 ft. 3 ins. (191 cm) and 14 stone (89 kg), McNamara was an ideal size for a key position player. A fine team man, he held that true footballers could never be fully professional: only a player who loved the game for itself could play to its real potential. In *Football* (Melbourne, 1914) he outlined his thoughts on the game, mainly 'to combat the pernicious effects' of the game's detractors, many of whom were then highly critical of football and football administrators over McNamara's clearance problems of that year.

After retirement, McNamara devoted himself to horse-racing; he established himself through the 1930s as a trainer of many winners at city and country meetings. In the 1940s he served in various posts, including president, with the Victorian Trainers' Association. He continued training horses until about 1958.

In later life McNamara was a busy worker on behalf of many benefactory appeals and held several hospital life governorships. On 15 August 1967 he died at his Caulfield home. Survived by his daughter, he was buried in Brighton cemetery with Catholic rites.

M. Fiddian, *The pioneers* (Melb, 1977); St Kilda Football Club, *Year book*, 1967, 1969; *People* (Syd), 11 Oct 1950; *Sun-News Pictorial*, 27 Oct 1938, 17 Apr 1965, 16 Aug 1967; *Herald* (Melb), 5 Sept 1950.
PAUL R. BARTROP

McNAMARA, FRANK (FRANCIS) HUBERT (1894-1961), airman, teacher and administrator, was born on 4 April 1894 at Rushworth, Victoria, son of William Francis McNamara, an officer of the Department of Lands, and his wife Rosanna, née O'Meara, both Victorian born. Educated at Rushworth local school and Shepparton Agricultural High School, he was appointed a junior teacher in the State Education Department in March 1911 and in 1913-14 studied at the Teachers' Training College, Melbourne, for a diploma. After graduating he was a temporary teacher in 1915 at four schools.

McNamara had joined the senior cadets while still at school and in 1913 was commissioned in the 46th Infantry Battalion (Brighton Rifles). He was mobilized on the outbreak of World War I and carried out garrison duty at Queenscliff and Point Nepean fixed defences before attending the Officers' Training School, Broadmeadows, in December 1914. He was then an instructor at the Australian Imperial Force's training depot, Broadmeadows, until August 1915, when he was selected for the military aeronautics course at Point Cook Flying School. He graduated as a pilot in October and after attending an advanced officers' course was posted to No. 1 Squadron, Australian Flying Corps, as adjutant when that unit was being formed in Melbourne as part of the A.I.F. The squadron sailed for Egypt on 5 January 1916 but McNamara went on to England where he was attached to No. 42 Squadron, Royal Flying Corps, from May to July. He qualified at a course at the Central Flying School, Upavon, and returned to Egypt as an instructor with No. 22 Squadron, R.F.C., before rejoining No. 1 Squadron, A.F.C., later that year. While serving with this unit he became the first Australian airman to receive the Victoria Cross.

In March 1917 the allies were planning an attack on Gaza and an important Turkish supply centre known as Junction Station was subjected to repeated air attacks by No. 1 Squadron, and No. 14 Squadron, R.F.C. On 20 March an Australian aircraft from No. 1 Squadron, piloted by Captain D. Rutherford, was forced to land after being hit by ground fire. Although his aircraft, a BE-2C, was a two-seater, he was flying solo at the time. A large body of enemy cavalry which was close by had seen the aircraft land and galloped towards it. McNamara, who had been on the same raid and had been wounded after encountering heavy anti-aircraft fire, was on his way home. He saw what was happening and despite a severe leg wound decided to attempt a rescue. He was able to make a safe landing beside Rutherford who at once climbed aboard McNamara's aircraft. However, this was a Martinsyde, a single-seater, and he could only stand on the wing and hold on to the struts. His weight made the aircraft very lop-sided and his presence in the airstream added extra drag to one side. Owing to his wound, and these extra problems, McNamara was unable to control his machine on the rough ground and crashed it badly on attempting to take off.

The two airmen, who were uninjured, set fire to McNamara's aircraft and returned to Rutherford's machine, which by this time was close to capture by the Turkish cavalry. Also, by then, the enemy had begun firing at the escaping airmen, and with bullets kicking up the sand nearby, McNamara managed to climb into the pilot's seat while Rutherford went to work on the engine. While McNamara provided what covering fire he could with his revolver and with the enemy almost upon them, Rutherford swung the heavy four-bladed propellor. Fortunately the engine fired at the first attempt and Rutherford jumped into the observer's seat as McNamara gave the aircraft full throttle.

Despite some damage to the struts and fuselage, and with McNamara fighting pain and close to unconsciousness from loss of blood, he managed to get them off the ground safely. He then flew them back a distance of some seventy miles (122 km) to their home base at El Arish where he carried out a safe landing but lost consciousness from loss of blood and an allergic reaction to an injection. For this brilliant rescue, carried out under extremely hazardous conditions and under heavy enemy fire, McNamara received the only V.C. awarded to an Australian airman in World War I. A painting by Septimus Power [q.v.], depicting the dramatic escape of the two pilots, is in the Australian War Memorial collection.

In April 1917 McNamara was appointed flight commander and promoted captain but was invalided to Australia in September and demobilized in January 1918. However, he was reappointed to the A.F.C. on 9 September, as lieutenant (honorary captain), as a flying instructor, an appointment which was then with the army and known as the Aviation Instruction Staff. When the (Royal) Australian Air Force was formed in March 1921 he transferred with the rank of flight lieutenant. He served at R.A.A.F. Headquarters, Melbourne, as staff officer, Operations and Intelligence, until July 1922, when he was appointed officer commanding, No. 1 Flying Training School, at Point Cook; he was promoted squadron leader in March 1924. On 29 April, at St Patrick's Cathedral, Melbourne, he married Hélène Marcelle Bluntschli of Brussels whom he had met in Egypt during the war; his groomsman was Squadron Leader A. Murray Jones [q.v.9]. McNamara was posted to Britain in 1925 on exchange duty with the Royal Air Force, returning to Australia in November 1927 and a re-posting

to No. 1 Flying Training School, initially as second-in-command, and then as commanding officer in October 1930. He was promoted wing commander in October 1931 but remained in command of No. 1 Flying Training School until February 1933, when he was posted to command of No. 1 Aircraft Depot and R.A.A.F. Station, Laverton, Victoria.

McNamara was promoted group captain three years later and in 1937 was sent to the United Kingdom to attend the Imperial Defence College; he was then posted to Australia House as the Australian air liaison officer with the Air Ministry. On the outbreak of World War II he was promoted air commodore and in 1942 was appointed air officer commanding R.A.A.F., London, with the rank of air vice marshal. He was later attached on loan to the R.A.F. where he was air officer commanding British forces at Aden in 1942-45. On returning to London he became R.A.A.F. representative at the British Ministry of Defence, and, in 1946, director of education at headquarters, British Occupation Administration, Westphalia, Germany. He retired from the R.A.A.F. that year, and was a member of the National Coal Board, London, in 1947-59. Survived by his wife, a son and a daughter, he died of hypertensive heart failure at Amersham, Buckinghamshire, on 2 November 1961; a large congregation attended his funeral at St Joseph's Priory, Austin Wood, Gerrard's Cross.

McNamara was a genial, 'cheery, unruffled soul', unassuming and perennially courteous. Air Vice Marshal A. T. Cole, who had served with him in Egypt, described him as 'quiet, scholarly, loyal and beloved by all . . . the last Officer for whom that high honour [the V.C.] would have been predicted'. He was appointed C.B.E. in 1938 and C.B. in 1945. In 1928 he had resumed studies interrupted by war service and graduated B.A. from the University of Melbourne in 1933.

F. M. Cutlack, *The Australian Flying Corps. . . 1914-1918* (Syd, 1923); Univ Melb, *Record of active service* (Melb, 1926); L. Wigmore (ed), *They dared mightily* (Canb, 1963); *Reveille* (Syd), June 1966; *Herald* (Melb), 28, 29 Apr 1924, 26 Dec 1933, 8 Mar 1969; *Argus*, 27 Dec 1939, 10 Aug 1940; *SMH*, 12 Nov 1961.   A. D. GARRISSON

McNAMARA, MATILDA EMILIE BERTHA (1853-1931), socialist agitator, feminist and bookshop-owner, was born on 28 September 1853 at Posen, Prussia (Poland), daughter of Karl Frederick Kalkstein, civil servant, and his wife Paulina Wilhelmina, née Berndt. Economic difficulties broke up the Kalkstein home and Bertha migrated to Victoria, via England, in 1869. After six months with an uncle in Melbourne she went to

Bairnsdale as governess to the children of her aunt Mrs Drevermann. There she married Peter Hermann Bredt, a 34-year-old Prussian-born accountant, on 26 February 1872 at St John's Church of England. Bertha was diminutive, with strong facial features, an aquiline nose and twinkling blue eyes. While Bredt worked as Bairnsdale's shire secretary, she reared their three surviving sons and three daughters; three children died in childhood.

Bredt's death in 1888 left Bertha with few resources; moving to Melbourne, she provided for the children by working as a travelling saleswoman, selling mainly jewellery and sewing machines. At this difficult time in her life, she turned to radical politics. In Hobart in 1891, though her English was still imperfect, she published *Home talk on socialism*, one of the earliest socialist pamphlets produced in Australia.

On 9 July 1892 she married William Henry Thomas McNamara [q.v.] at Collingwood Registry Office. She returned with him to Sydney, where they opened a bookshop in Castlereagh Street that became a famous gathering-point for radicals. Bertha ran a boarding-house in conjunction with the shop. Practical and kind, she fed and housed many new migrants from Europe until they found employment. The back room and the reading room above the shop were scenes of almost constant activity and discussion by socialists, feminists, anarchists, rationalists, Laborites and literary Bohemians. In this milieu two of her daughters met their husbands—in 1896 Bertha married Henry Lawson [q.v.] and Hilda married J. T. Lang [q.v.9]; the Langs lived with the McNamaras for a time. Bertha McNamara was herself producing a second family: a son in 1895 and a daughter in 1899.

In the 1890s Bertha was a leading member of the Social Democratic Federation of Australasia and of the Womanhood Suffrage League of New South Wales. In 1894 she published three pamphlets: *Commercialism and distribution of the nineteenth century, Forgery* and *Workingmen's homes*. In the first she advocated a decentralized form of socialism, where working-class people would create a better society by assuming control of their immediate environment, as producers and as consumers. Only when socialism had already been built up from below would it be safe to direct the state to nationalize the means of production, distribution and exchange—Labor politicians could not be trusted.

In 1897 she campaigned vigorously for imprisoned labour-movement activists in Spain. Using the bookshop as a command centre, she organized protest meetings in the Domain, collected money for the prisoners' families and wrote angry letters to the press. During the South African War she and

William faced hostile crowds when voicing their opposition. She always spoke with a pronounced German accent. She was a founder of the Labor Women's Central Organizing Committee and was a frequent delegate to State Labor Party conferences. After William died in 1906 Bertha conducted the bookshop on her own, and published more pamphlets, *How to become rich beyond the dreams of avarice* (1908) and *Paper money* (1910). During World War I the shop was more than ever in demand as an organizing centre for radical activity. Bertha assisted in many ways, especially by selling banned anti-militarist literature.

In 1920 Bertha McNamara wrote another pamphlet, against money-power, called *Shylock exposed*. In the early 1920s she devoted much energy to the launching and support of the *Labor Daily*. In 1922 the bookshop was demolished, but Bertha and her son William ran two bookshops in Park and Oxford streets for four years and were back in Castlereagh Street in 1926-29. She worked relentlessly within the Labor Party, hoping to win it to the cause of socialism, and often led women's deputations to Premier Lang, her son-in-law, who reputedly was afraid of her.

One wet and cold Sunday in 1931, suffering from a severe cold, Bertha visited the Domain to confront her former friend Adela Pankhurst [q.v.] with her apostasy. She contracted pneumonia and died at North Sydney on 1 August 1931. Her eight children survived her. Hundreds of leading Labor, radical and literary figures attended her cremation after a Rationalist service. The Bertha McNamara Hostel was opened at Miller's Point, and a sculptured portrait plaque by Lyndon Dadswell in her honour as 'The Mother of the Labour Movement' still adorns the entrance foyer of the Sydney Trades Hall. It reads:

Kindly and gracious in her splendid way
She knew no nationhood
And her religion each and every day
Was that of doing good.

ALP Golden Jubilee Committee, *50 years of Labor* (Syd, 1940); J. T. Lang, *I remember* (Syd, 1956), and *The turbulent years* (Syd, 1970); M. Dixson, *Greater than Lenin?* (Melb, 1977); V. Burgmann, *'In our time'* (Syd, 1985); *SMH*, 3 Aug 1931, 28 Mar 1932; *Bulletin*, 5 Aug 1931; *Herald* (Melb), 28 Mar 1932; family information from Mrs Wilma McKeown, Canb.   VERITY BURGMANN

McNAMARA, WILLIAM HENRY THOMAS (1857-1906), socialist agitator and bookshop-owner, was born on 18 March 1857 at Taradale, Victoria, son of James Macnamara, digger, and his wife Ann, née O'Bryan, both from Ireland. An enthusiastic secularist as a young man, he decided in 1886-87 that 'mere bible-smashing' was inadequate, and became the leading figure in the group of eight men who founded the Australian Socialist League on 4 May 1887 in Sydney. He later worked as an organizer of the Amalgamated Shearers' Union of Australasia.

Within the A.S.L., which contained socialists of widely differing viewpoints, in the late 1880s McNamara espoused 'Modern Socialism': the belief that socialism could and should be achieved by workers voluntarily forming co-operatives, and gradually wresting control of society from private capitalists. An imposing figure, with dark hair and a large black beard, he became the league's most accomplished orator. His colourful rhetoric was characterized by satire and sarcasm. The industrial militancy of the early 1890s convinced McNamara that the way forward to socialism was now through the ever-expanding union of workers, with community control of production, distribution and exchange, 'thus doing away with, for ever, the inevitable starvation, crime and destitution'. McNamara organized the Amalgamated Navvies and General Labourers' Union of New South Wales, represented it on the Trades and Labor Council of New South Wales and was a director of the council's newspaper, the *Australian Workman*.

In 1891 McNamara left the Socialist League because it had adopted reformist state socialism as its official ideology and was supporting the new Labor Electoral League. He turned his attention to improving the morale and fighting spirit of the unemployed, by forming an unemployed executive committee which functioned both as an agitational and welfare organization. In Melbourne in 1892 he worked as a correspondent for John Norton's [q.v.] *Truth*, but not to Norton's satisfaction. He considered that McNamara wrote 'in too fiery a style' and that his work teemed with libels. At Collingwood Registry Office on 9 July 1892 McNamara married a widow Matilda Emilie Bertha Bredt, née Kalkstein [q.v. McNamara].

On returning to Sydney, William and Bertha established in 1893 a bookshop in Castlereagh Street. Advertised as a 'Democratic Rendezvous', it became an unofficial headquarters for varied socialist and radical activity. They sold 'Socialistic and all kinds of advanced Literature', mainly from European and American publishers; the works of A. B. Paterson and Henry Lawson [qq.v.] ('splendidly bound'); 10 000 novels by writers such as Dickens [q.v.4], Defoe, Rider Haggard, Balzac, Zola, Wilkie Collins, Twain, Hugo and Dumas; and stationery and tobacco. The 'Cosmopolitan Lending Library' contained 2000 volumes; and the 'International Reading Room' filed hundreds of newspapers, especially European and American socialist papers,

which could be consulted for a penny. In the wake of the 1893 bank crashes, McNamara was imprisoned for six months for selling a newspaper, *Hard Cash*, produced by Arthur Desmond [q.v.8], which allegedly criminally libelled a financial corporation.

Late in 1892 McNamara had formed another socialist organization, the Social Democratic Federation of Australasia, which held daytime propaganda meetings in Parramatta Park and Sunday evening meetings on the corner of Bathurst and George streets. At the 1898 elections he stood for Sydney-Bligh as Independent Labor, using the opportunity to make socialist propaganda and attack the Labor Party for its conservatism, rather than to win votes.

On 11 May 1906 in the Sacred Heart Hospice for the Dying, McNamara died of phthisis; he had suffered from it and from heart problems for some time. He was buried in Waverley cemetery with Unitarian forms. His wife, his son William who later helped his mother to run the bookshop, and a daughter, Alice, survived him.

Social Democratic Federation, *Manifesto* (Syd, 1895); V. Burgmann, '*In our time*' (Syd, 1985); *Socialist J of the Northern People*, 19 Feb 1898; *Aust Radical* (Hamilton, NSW), 11 Aug 1888; *Aust Workman*, 1, 8 Nov 1890, 10 Jan 1891, 19 Mar 1893; *Worker* (Syd), 4 Nov 1893, 24 Aug 1895, 16 May 1896, 17 May 1906; *Socialist* (Syd), 11 July, 29 Aug 1896; J. N. Rawling papers (ANU Archives).
                                    VERITY BURGMANN

MACNEIL, NEIL HARCOURT (1893–1946), headmaster, was born on 17 April 1893 at Sandringham, Victoria, fifth child and second son of Rev. John MacNeil, Scottish-born Presbyterian minister and evangelist, and his Victorian wife Hannah, née Thomas. He was educated at Scotch College where he was a member of the rowing eight and cricket team and dux in classics. He entered the University of Melbourne in 1912 with exhibitions in Greek and Latin and a scholarship to Ormond [q.v.5] College, and was selected Victorian Rhodes Scholar for 1914.

In England on the outbreak of World War I, MacNeil was commissioned in the 12th Battalion, Highland Light Infantry, on 27 November. In France from July 1915, he was awarded the Military Cross for 'conspicuous gallantry' near Loos on 25 September and was severely wounded next day while rallying men of other units; he was also mentioned in dispatches. He returned to France in September next year and was promoted acting captain in December. Seconded to the Royal Flying Corps in October 1917, he was commissioned in No. 16 Squadron, Royal Air

Force, and served in France from April 1918.

From January 1919 MacNeil read modern history at Balliol College, Oxford (B.A., 1920; M.A., 1926). He rowed in the Oxford eight at Henley in 1919 and gained his 'blue' in 1920. His teachers included A. L. Smith and Kenneth Bell who reinforced his ideals of community service. From July to October 1920 he was in Poland with the Relief Services. Intended for the ministry from childhood, he studied divinity at the University of Edinburgh for a session in 1920-21 but turned to teaching. In 1921 he was awarded a teacher's diploma by the University of London and taught at Cheltenham College in 1922-23.

Late in 1923 MacNeil was appointed first headmaster of Knox Grammar School, Sydney, founded at Wahroonga by a group of Presbyterian ministers and laymen, including (Sir) Robert Gillespie [q.v.9] and William McIlrath [q.v.]. The school opened in February 1924, the council promising a liberal education, Presbyterian religious instruction and encouragement in 'all manly sports'. MacNeil gathered a diverse and well-educated staff of whom half came from England. On 16 December 1924 at Scots Church, Melbourne, he married Jean Isobel Hamilton; they had no children.

The school grew steadily to 1930 when enrolments reached 320. The curriculum was classical and traditional. MacNeil used out-of-class activities—debating, singing, drill, sports—to develop the self-discipline and co-operative effort he valued. Despite a decline in enrolments and financial difficulties in the early 1930s, he established a technical branch. The Depression, he said, should teach us 'the dignity of work with our hands'. He took a public stand against the examination system, and dropped the Intermediate certificate at Knox: parents and employers were suspicious of the move. He was a founder and honorary secretary of the Fairbridge [q.v.8] Farm Schools of New South Wales in 1936-38.

In March 1939 MacNeil accepted the invitation of the council of Wesley College, Melbourne, to become headmaster from January 1940. Convinced of laxness, he at once made changes and earned unpopularity in much of the school community. But his staunchness and optimism won admiration when—its buildings occupied by the army—the school spent two years in shared quarters at Scotch College (March 1942-February 1944). The council unanimously reappointed him at the end of 1944.

On an overseas visit in 1932 MacNeil had been seriously ill with rheumatic fever. At Wesley he remained active and coached the crew in 1941-45, but he was overstrained. On 1 August 1946 he collapsed and died from cardiovascular disease, and was cremated after a service in the school chapel. His wife survived him. MacNeil's bearing was erect, his manner severe and aloof, obscuring the humanity of his educational ideals and relations with individuals. He kept the piety of his parents but put the emphasis on practical religion.

Univ Melb, *Record of active service* (Melb, 1926); G. Blainey et al, *Wesley College. The first hundred years* (Melb, 1967); B. Mansfield and F. Richardson, *Knox. A history of Knox Grammar School, 1924-1974* (Syd, 1974); Univ Melb, *Calendar*, 1912-15; *London Gazette*, 4 Nov 1915; *Knox Grammarian*, May 1939; *Reveille* (Syd), 1 Aug 1939; untitled typescript by Mrs N. H. MacNeil (Knox Grammar School); Knox Grammar School records.   BRUCE E. MANSFIELD

McNEILL, JOHN JAMES (1868-1943), union official and politician, was born in 1868 at Tantanoola, South Australia, son of John McNeill, farmer, and his wife Jane, née McBride. Educated to primary level, McNeill worked on the family farm and as a shearer before becoming a selector at Woosang, Victoria, in the 1890s. He sold out to join the gold rush to Coolgardie, Western Australia, and on his return settled at Macarthur. On 9 February 1896, at the Roman Catholic Church, Hamilton, he married Mary Ann Mills (d. 1905). An active member of the Shearers' Union (later the Australian Workers' Union) in its campaigns to improve conditions, he was an organizer for the Victoria-Riverina branch of the A.W.U. for six years, and contested the Victorian Legislative Assembly seat of Glenelg for Labor in 1906.

In 1908 McNeill went to Roma, Queensland, as a settler and when defeated by conditions organized the Charleville branch of the A.W.U., and became its secretary. In 1913 he succeeded John Barnes [q.v.7] as secretary of the Victoria-Riverina branch of the A.W.U., holding the post until 1922, when he narrowly won the Federal seat of Wannon. President of the Ballarat Trades and Labor Council, he was a director of the Ballarat *Evening Echo*, a Labor daily. On 11 January 1915 at St Patrick's Cathedral, Ballarat, he married Catherine, sister of J. H. Scullin [q.v.]. In 1923-24 he was president of the Victorian branch of the Australian Labor Party. He was defeated for Wannon in 1925, but held it again in 1929-31.

McNeill spoke infrequently in parliament. He was a staunch proponent of White Australia, advocating the development of the north and a self-reliant defence policy. A supporter of closer settlement and a critic of large-scale commercial enterprise, he was concerned for the poverty-stricken wheatfarmers. On 3 March 1931 he was appointed minister for health and minister for repatriation. Previously an occasional opponent of Scullin in caucus, in cabinet McNeill supported his Depression financial policies.

From 1933 until his death, McNeill was general secretary of the New South Wales branch of the A.W.U. and from 1938 federal general president, having been vice-president since 1930. During World War II he was a member of the Commonwealth Wool Board and A.W.U. representative on the Trades Union Defence Advisory Panel. He died on 14 June 1943, at Coogee, Sydney, of coronary occlusion and, after a state funeral and service in St Patrick's Cathedral, was buried in Melbourne general cemetery. His wife and their two sons, and his two sons and a daughter of his first marriage, survived him.

His cheerful and kindly nature belied by his dour appearance, McNeill was widely respected for his experience and integrity. He opposed conscription in 1916-17 and admired Australian servicemen, praising in March 1943 the soldiers opposing the Japanese in New Guinea as 'men of pure British race'. He was a staunch nationalist who enjoyed bush literature and kept his pact with Barnes and Andrew McKissock to plant Cootamundra wattles on their graves.

PD (Cwlth), 1923, 102, p 118, 1924, 105, p 25, 108, p 2799, 1929-31, 131, p 4008, 425l, 1940-43, 175, p 3; *Argus*, 30 Oct 1929, 12, 14 Dec 1931, 16 June 1943; *Aust Worker*, 1 Jan 1930, 4 Mar 1931, 10 Mar, 16 June 1943; *Herald* (Melb), 14 June 1943; *Labor Call*, 17 June 1943.

J. R. ROBERTSON

McNESS, SIR CHARLES (1852-1938), ironmonger and philanthropist, was born on 26 March 1852 at Saint Benedicts, Huntingdon, England, son of James Mackness, shoemaker, and his wife Mary, née Moss. He began work as a child, was apprenticed to a tinsmith, and in 1875 moved to London where he traded in scrap metals; there he married Maude Metherall. Hard work and frugal living enabled him to save and invest in property. In 1876 he migrated to Western Australia under a colonial scheme which encouraged 'small capitalists'. He built a warehouse for rental on the outskirts of Perth, and leased a corner of Hay and Barracks streets, where he built five shops of galvanized iron and opened business as a tinsmith and ironmonger under the name of Charles McNess. The firm prospered, and in a letter of 1881 he said he was 'coining money'.

In the late 1880s he made the first of four visits to England. In London he was again married, to Mrs Annie Elsie Poncy. They returned to Perth where their only child, a son, was born in 1893. McNess made the most of the gold rush of the 1890s, moving his ironmongering business to Wellington Street and expanding into mortgage brokerage. He continued to invest in property, buying the Royal Arcade Building in 1896.

A sober and retiring man, McNess and his wife lived simply and quietly. He retired in 1915 to enjoy travel and philanthropy, distributing much of his fortune to public and charitable institutions. During World War I he supported war loans and patriotic funds. He assisted the Presbyterian Church, donating funds for McNess Hall, other Protestant denominations, and hospitals, charities and institutions that cared for young people.

The Depression elicited further benefactions. In June 1930 he gave £6200 to the State government: £1200 was for the upkeep of the State War Memorial while the remaining £5000 formed the basis of the McNess Housing Trust. This provided low-cost housing—four-roomed wood and iron cottages costing about £250—for impoverished families. Later gifts to this trust amounted to £90 000. He also gave £1365 to the mayor for an emergency clothing fund, £4000 to the State Gardens Board to provide work for the unemployed, and £3000 to the Perth Public Hospital. These benefactions, made unobtrusively, were generally directed through Louis Shapcott [q.v.], under-secretary to the premier.

McNess was knighted in 1931 while in London; his visits to the Dominions Office there resulted in queries to Western Australia, the suburb of Holloway being considered an unlikely address for a future knight. His appearance also excited comment; with snowy hair and moustache, 'he looked like a down and out swaggie'. On returning home McNess gave the State a further £20 000, which provided employment in developing a national park at Yanchep. In 1932-37 gifts totalling £16 500 were made to the Young Men's Christian Association, Legacy Club of Perth, the Returned Sailors' and Soldiers' Imperial League of Australia, the Blind Institution, the St John Ambulance Association and the Presbyterian, Wesleyan and Congregational churches.

Lady McNess, a partner in this philanthropy, died in 1937 and Sir Charles donated £11 500 to construct the Lady McNess Memorial Drive in the Darling Ranges. Next year, on 22 June, McNess died at his son's Mount Lawley home. He was buried in the Anglican section of Karrakatta cemetery, leaving an estate of at least £200 000. Aside from relatives and friends, provision was made in his will for bequests totalling £32 000 to charities, institutions and Churches and for three further public memorials to himself and his wife. It was estimated in 1938 that between £150 000 and £200 000 had been distributed by this benefactor during his life, in New South Wales and Queensland as well as his home State.

G. C. Bolton, *A fine country to starve in* (Perth, 1972); *West Australian Times*, 29 Sept 1876; *Herald* (Melb), 3 June 1931; *Smith's Weekly* (Syd), 13 June 1931; *West Australian*, 21 Mar 1936, 4 Feb 1937, 23 June, 27 Sept 1938, 15 June 1940, 30 May 1941; *Sunday Times* (Perth), 14 Mar 1937; *SMH*, 27 June 1938; *Daily News* (Perth), 28 June 1938; McNess family papers (Battye Lib); Premier's Dept, acc 1496, file 809/1932, file 169/32, file 162/36, file 74/37; Dept of Lands and Surveys file, acc 553 (Battye Lib).   WENDY BRADY

McNICOLL, SIR WALTER RAMSAY (1877-1947), schoolmaster, soldier and administrator, was born on 27 May 1877 at Emerald Hill, Melbourne, son of William Walter Alexander McNicoll, photographer, and his wife Ellen, née Ramsay. He was educated at state schools. In 1893 he joined the Victorian Education Department as a monitor, becoming a pupil-teacher in 1895. He studied at the Teachers' Training College under the direction of Frank Tate [q.v.] in 1900-01 and obtained the Trained Teacher's Certificate. In 1905 he joined the staff of the newly opened Melbourne Continuation (High) School where he taught drawing and commanded the cadets. On 10 June at St John's Church, Heathcote, he married another teacher, Hildur, Victorian-born daughter of Oscar Wedel Jarlsberg, a Norwegian migrant. Appointed founding headmaster of the future Geelong High School in 1911, he gained his diploma of education in 1912. He divided his spare time between the military forces, in which he was a major, and yachting on Port Phillip Bay.

On the raising of the Australian Imperial Force in August 1914 McNicoll was appointed second-in-command of the 7th Battalion. He sailed with his unit in October, trained with it in Egypt, and in April 1915 was given command of the 6th Battalion. He led the 6th in the landing at Anzac Cove on 25 April, and for his work then and during the following night he received one of the first awards of the Distinguished Service Order in the A.I.F. His battalion, with others, was moved to Cape Helles to attempt the capture of the Achi Baba heights: there, on 8 May, it took part in the costly and unsuccessful second battle of Krithia. In the attack McNicoll was severely wounded in the abdomen, and he might not have survived had not the war correspondent Charles Bean [q.v.7] made a note of where he lay, and brought stretcher-bearers after nightfall. In hospital at Alexandria efforts failed to extract the bul-

let, and it was not until McNicoll reached London that an operation was successful. He was invalided to Australia late in 1915.

By February 1916 he was fit enough to be appointed to command the newly raised 10th Infantry Brigade, a component of the 3rd Division commanded by Major General (Sir) John Monash [q.v.]. The brigade reached England in July. During the winter of 1916-17 it was in a quiet sector of the line in Flanders. In June 1917 it took part in the battle of Messines. In October it was engaged in the third battle of Ypres where it achieved great success at Broodseinde but failed (as did others) in the fight for Passchendaele. The brigade was in reserve in March 1918 when the Germans broke through the front farther south: it was rushed to the Amiens sector and took a major part in stabilizing the line.

Monash's appointment to command the Australian Corps in May left the command of the 3rd Division vacant. He favoured McNicoll. However, the appointment went to Brigadier General (Sir) John Gellibrand [q.v.8].

The 10th Brigade was heavily engaged in the battle of Amiens, and for the last six days of August it was almost continuously in action. Its final battle took place at the end of September, on the Hindenburg line. For his work on the Western Front McNicoll was appointed C.M.G. and then C.B., and he was four times mentioned in dispatches. As a brigade commander he had been intensely loyal to Monash, whose plans, sometimes faulty, he never questioned in public. He had shown himself to be over sanguine on occasions, but courageous, determined, and an able leader of men.

After the Armistice McNicoll was appointed inspector-general (from April 1919 director) of education, controlling the civil education and training of the soldiers waiting for ships to take them home. He returned to Australia late in 1919. Although his university studies had been interrupted by the war he was granted in 1920, while headmaster of Coburg High School, a B.A. 'in view of his distinguished military services'. But without further qualifications his prospects in the Victorian Education Department were limited, and he resigned to become principal of the new Presbyterian Ladies' College at Goulburn, New South Wales.

In that small provincial city he was prominent as a returned soldier, a Freemason, and musical director of the very active choral society, and during the founding years of the school he was content. Thereafter growth slowed and the job became tedious. From 1929 the school was hard hit by the Depression.

During 1931 McNicoll began to take an active interest in politics. After the Scullin [q.v.] government was defeated in November, McNicoll was chosen as the Country Party candidate for the Federal seat of Werriwa, and the United Australia Party decided to support him. At the election in December McNicoll won on preferences against the sitting Lang [q.v.9] Labor member, H. P. Lazzarini. In parliament McNicoll concerned himself largely with defence, war pensions, and the interests of servicemen. During the winter recess of 1933 he visited Papua and the Mandated Territory of New Guinea. He had already sought an appointment to an administratorship, having found parliamentary temporizing distasteful, and conscious that his seat was not safe. Appointed administrator of the Mandated Territory of New Guinea in August, he assumed office on 13 September 1934 in succession to Brigadier General T. Griffiths [q.v.9]. He was described at the time as 'a slightly built man, rather above middle height' with the 'pale face of the ascetic', a 'keen and sharp' expression and 'a charming though reserved manner'.

McNicoll established a pattern of regular visits to all the outlying districts, paying particular attention to the economically important Morobe goldfield. As administrator he held a balance between the many conflicting interests of planters, missionaries, miners and prospectors. Funds were always short, and desirable initiatives such as native education were restricted. McNicoll was given a fairly free hand by most of the nine ministers under whom he served: these ranged from the sagacious Sir George Pearce [q.v.] to the vain and capricious W. M. Hughes [q.v.9].

When the volcanoes at Rabaul erupted on 29 May 1937 the administrator was on the mainland. He flew back—the first aircraft to land at Rabaul—and took over from Judge Phillips [q.v.] who had organized the evacuation. He decided upon the early reoccupation of the town. His appointment to K.B.E. headed the special honours list for the Rabaul emergency.

As the threat of war grew in 1939 McNicoll became increasingly concerned about the Territory's vulnerability, now viewing its mandate status as a liability rather than a strength. When war broke out in September he interned many of the German missionaries, and more in May 1940. It was not until January 1941 that he was relieved of responsibility for defence.

Rabaul's larger volcano erupted again in June 1941, making the town almost uninhabitable. McNicoll decided to transfer the seat of government to Lae and, in order to speed construction, moved there himself with several departments, leaving H. H. Page [q.v.] at Rabaul as deputy administrator. The entry of Japan into the war increased McNicoll's concern over the vulnerability of

the territory and of Rabaul in particular, and he pressed for reinforcements, but without success. On 20 January 1942 Lae was destroyed in an air raid. Two days later Rabaul fell to the Japanese, and McNicoll, suffering from malaria, was flown from Lae to Wau. He made his way south, still a sick man, hoping to see his minister; but it was evident that the Mandated Territory was substantially lost.

He retired from office at the end of 1942, having served as administrator for more than eight years. He died in Sydney on 24 December 1947 and was cremated. He was survived by his wife and four sons of whom Ronald became a major general, Alan a vice admiral and David a prominent journalist.

His record is that of a conscientious, energetic and somewhat conventional man, disinclined to compromise, not tactful, but considerate; a firm believer in the virtues of discipline and loyalty; and, in New Guinea, more liberal than was usual at the time.

A portrait by John Longstaff [q.v.] is in the Australian War Memorial.

R. McNicoll, *Walter Ramsay McNicoll 1877-1947* (Melb, 1973), and for bibliog; G. Serle, *John Monash* (Melb, 1982); K. Fewster (ed), *Gallipoli correspondent* (Syd, 1983); information from Education History Services, Vic Education Dept, Melb; McNicoll papers (NL, *and* UPNG Lib).

RONALD McNICOLL

McPHEE, SIR JOHN CAMERON (1878-1952), businessman and politician, was born on 4 July 1878 at Yan Yean, Victoria, son of Donald McPhee, storekeeper from the Isle of Skye, Scotland, and his Victorian-born wife Elizabeth, née McLaughlin. Educated at state schools until 14, after a time on the family farm John was apprenticed to a printer. A period on a Bairnsdale newspaper, reporting, advertising and typesetting, was followed by work as a compositor in the Government Printing Office, Melbourne. At night-school McPhee learned shorthand, typing and business principles. As a keen temperance worker (once a trainee for the Presbyterian ministry), a debater in the Australian Natives' Association and a shorthand reporter studying the orators of the day, he laid the basis for his political career.

In 1908 McPhee moved to Hobart where he bought Hedley Button's Central Business College, conducting it for fifteen years as the Remington Business College and relinquishing his interest only in the 1940s. He also established a stationery and office equipment company, J. C. McPhee Pty Ltd, became co-proprietor of the *Huon Times* and was a director of several Tasmanian firms. On 17 April 1911 at Christ Church, Longford, he married Alice Bealey Crompton Dean. About this time he became an Anglican and was subsequently a lay reader and a member of the Tasmanian synod.

Supported by temperance interests, McPhee contested Denison in the 1916 State elections and in a 1917 by-election. He lost, but won a Denison seat as a Nationalist in 1919, holding it until 1934. In August 1922 he entered J. B. Hayes's [q.v.9] ministry as chief secretary and minister for railways but resigned, for business reasons, next June. In October 1923 W. H. Lee [q.v.], Nationalist premier since August, was overturned by National and Country Party dissidents, and Joseph Lyons [q.v.] formed a Labor government. McPhee was one of seven Nationalists whose vote on 31 October helped to defeat an Opposition motion of no confidence in the new ministry; as leader of the Opposition from 1925 he continued to work with Lyons in co-operative rivalry.

In June 1928 McPhee led the Nationalists into government. As well as premier he became treasurer, minister for forests and minister controlling the Hydro-Electric Department. His personal austerity, as teetotaller and virtual non-smoker, made him an appropriate leader in a period of national belt-tightening, and in the 1931 elections he won the greatest victory over Labor since the full implementation of Hare-Clark [q.v.3] voting—the sole Australian premier to triumph electorally during mid-Depression. Albert Ogilvie [q.v.], leading Labor, had campaigned on an expansionist policy, while McPhee accepted the expenditure cuts required by the subsequent Premiers' Plan.

In March 1932 McPhee exchanged the portfolio of hydro-electricity for that of agriculture. Troubled by persistent heart problems during the following two years, he resigned the premiership to Lee in March 1934 and retired from politics. He was appointed K.C.M.G. in June.

Short and stocky, identifiable by his black Homburg and pince-nez, McPhee, in contrast to the aggressive Ogilvie, was a low-key political figure. An infrequent parliamentary speaker, cautious in decision, he inspired confidence through modesty and sincerity. Conservative in economics, he rejected state industrial ownership in favour of free enterprise with minimal government control. He believed, however, that Tasmania's indissoluble Legislative Council should be forced to election if in disagreement with the Lower House.

McPhee failed in an attempt at a political comeback in 1937 when he was defeated for the Federal seat of Denison. But in 1941, amid a landslide victory for Labor under Robert Cosgrove, he narrowly won a Franklin seat in the House of Assembly. He retired in 1946 to concentrate on business and charit-

able interests. His humanitarian work for the Tasmanian Institution for the Blind, Deaf and Dumb, the Tasmanian Sanatorium, the Temperance Council, Red Cross Society and war loans organizations was substantial. A justice of the peace and a council-member of the University of Tasmania, McPhee belonged to the Royal Autocar Club, the Tasmanian Club and Hobart Rotary. A cyclist as a youth, he played bowls in retirement.

McPhee died in his sleep of coronary vascular disease in Hobart on 14 September 1952 and was cremated. His wife, five daughters and the second of his two sons survived him.

SMH, 12 Aug 1922, 22 Feb, 8 May 1923, 29 June 1928, 19 May 1932; *Herald* (Melb), 4 June 1934, 27 July 1937, 30 May 1931; *Mercury* (Hob), 1 Nov 1923, 14 May 1925, 15, 17 Sept 1952; information from Mr J. C. McPhee, Berriedale, Hob.

R. P. DAVIS

McPHERSON, SIR CLIVE (1884-1958), pastoralist and businessman, was born on 13 January 1884 at St Arnaud, Victoria, second son of Victorian-born parents William George McPherson, bank-manager, and his wife Alice Gertrude, née Mogg. His mother, a gifted pianist, belonged to the pioneering family of nearby pastoral Swanwater. Clive derived from his father a sense of humour and an interest in finance; from his mother, a strong disciplinarian, came his love of independence, order, punctuality and neatness.

In 1890 the family embarked on a grand tour of Europe but on returning to Victoria found its fortunes diminished by the financial crisis. Clive was educated at Caulfield Grammar School, Melbourne, of which he remained intensely proud. At 13 he took up a career in banking. Finding the work too confining, he left to work on his uncle's property, Yallock Vale near Ballan. In 1899 he combined the position of overseer at Bungeeltap with his work at Yallock Vale. During these years he acquired an intimate knowledge of and love for the Victorian countryside. About 1901 McPherson decided to move to Queensland to escape the cold of central Victoria. As a step in the right direction he became book-keeper on a Riverina property. Not satisfied with purely clerical responsibilities, he worked on the property by day and on the books at night.

In 1903 he became office-manager of McNamara & Co., auctioneers, at Yarrawonga in northern Victoria. His quick analytical mind and powerful memory attracted attention and Jack Thom invited him to join in an auctioneering business, McPherson, Thom, Kettle & Co., with Clive as the managing partner. Formed at a time of large-scale subdivision in the Murray valley, the business prospered and McPherson began to acquire property.

On 7 July 1915 he married Sidney Marion Isabel Orme Wolfenden. The family homestead, Boomanoomana, at Mulwala, New South Wales, and some 4500 acres (1820 ha) was bought in 1920 and in the interwar years McPherson acquired five properties in southern New South Wales and one in Victoria.

In the 1920s McPherson emerged as a leader of the rural community in Victoria. His emphasis on loyalty, trust, obedience, discipline and fiscal frugality marked him as a conservative; his benevolent paternalism kindled the affection of his peers and subordinates alike. Self-confidence and mastery of his own emotions enabled him to resolve conflict with remarkable facility. Six feet (183 cm) tall, handsome and with a capacity to convey understanding and warmth, he attracted as much attention in Melbourne as in the country.

With the growth of government regulation of rural industry his public responsibilities multiplied. In 1927-46 he was Australian government representative on the British Phosphate Commission. He was also a government representative on the Dairy Produce Export Control Board, and served on the Victorian Unemployment Council. His knowledge of closer settlement problems in the Murray valley led to his appointment as a member of the Victorian royal commission set up in 1930 to investigate complaints of British migrant settlers. Then from 1933 to 1938 McPherson was chairman of the Closer Settlement Commission in Victoria. At the nadir of the Depression, with many small settlers ruined financially, the commission was responsible for the reconstruction of farms and for such restoration of financial stability as was possible. The family moved to Melbourne in 1933. He was appointed C.B.E. in 1925 and was knighted in 1941.

McPherson was managing director and chairman of the pastoral house, Younghusband Ltd, from 1938. He joined the board of the National Bank of Australasia Ltd in 1949, following the death of Sir Ernest Wreford [q.v.], and was a director of the Commonwealth Bank in 1940-45. He served on the board of Royal Melbourne Hospital and offered valuable advice to the finance subcommittee; he had a long association with the Royal Agricultural Society of Victoria. He was a friend and admirer of Sir Robert Gibson [q.v.8]; among the many friends of his own age were Sir Harold Clapp, Harold Darling [qq.v.8], Sir Albert Ellis, (Sir) Leslie McConnan, C. N. McKay and (Sir) Robert Menzies. McPherson was honorary chairman of the

Australian Wheat Board, set up hastily on the outbreak of World War II. Its responsibilities were to acquire compulsorily, store and market the entire Australian crop, previously handled by voluntary pools and private merchants. There was much accumulated bitterness in the conflicting interests of the representatives of growers, merchants, shippers and governments on the board, but due largely to McPherson's strength of character, tact and negotiating skill it was welded into an effective marketing agency. After McPherson relinquished his chairmanship of the Wheat Board in 1945 and was replaced by the Labor government on the Commonwealth Bank Board and British Phosphate Commission, he concentrated on the management of Younghusband Ltd. Annual addresses to shareholders reflected the central themes of his life: the crucial role of the wool industry in the national economy, the need to reduce costs, the dangers of idleness and the value of stability. He condemned excessive taxation and denounced the spread of communist influence. In everything he attempted he strove for excellence, his symbol of perfection being the legendary racehorse, Carbine; his interest in racing was an extension of his devotion to the land. As a member of the Peninsula Golf Club, he enjoyed an occasional round.

Late in life McPherson was serenely untroubled. His portrait, painted in 1950 by William Dargie and in the possession of his daughter, depicts an open countenance, eyes without pain or hardship, skin barely wrinkled and aglow with health, and an aura of benevolence and personal fulfilment. He was able to combine strict self-discipline with regulated gaiety and a keen interest in the younger generation. As an elder on the board of the National Bank, he advised and encourged younger members such as Sir Rupert Clarke.

McPherson's life was dominated by his public obligations and commitment to primary industry, work and success. Although not a regular church-attender, he was a man of practical Christian principles. Predeceased by his wife in 1946, he died on 10 November 1958 having suffered from coronary sclerosis. Following an Anglican service at Christ Church, South Yarra, he was cremated. His daughter survived him. His estate was valued for probate in Victoria at £95 224.

C. J. Perrett, *Australian Wheat Board 1939-65* (Melb, nd); *Smith's Weekly* (Syd), 22 Jan 1944; *Age*, 11 Nov 1958; Younghusband Ltd papers (Univ Melb Archives); family and business information.

C. B. SCHEDVIN

McPHERSON, JOHN ABEL (1860-1897), printer and politician, was born on 28 January

1860 at Aberdeen, Scotland, son of Ann McPherson, domestic servant. Educated at St Paul's Street School and the mechanics' institute, he was apprenticed with the *Free Press* Printing & Publishing Co. In 1881 he married Mary Ann Wight. McPherson belonged to the Scottish Typographical Association and in 1882 he and his wife migrated to Adelaide where he joined the South Australian Typographical Society, of which he was president in 1893-95. He worked for J. H. Sherring & Co., printers, and later joined the composing staff of the *South Australian Register*. In 1889 McPherson left the newspaper during a strike over the right of employees to join the union. He was unemployed for some time before finding work with Vardon & Pritchard.

In 1890 he became honorary secretary of the United Trades and Labour Council. McPherson organized the building and management of the Trades Hall (opened 1896) and was an effective conciliator in disputes between employers and butchers, drivers, tanners and carriers, and maritime workers over shorter hours and wage regulation. In 1891 he was at the U.T.L.C. meeting which formed an elections committee; this became the United Labor Party and McPherson was its founding secretary.

Next February he won a by-election for East Adelaide and became the first Labor member of the House of Assembly, proudly noting the part taken by typographical societies in all colonies in achieving wage-earners' election to parliament. In his maiden speech McPherson deplored coloured immigration, noted the hundreds of unemployed in city and country, and advocated opening up the land to smallholders and a progressive land tax. He accused Chief Secretary C. C. Kingston [q.v.9] of conservatism and threatened to withdraw support, saying that he would pursue Labor policy whichever side of the House introduced bills that approximated to it. Re-elected in 1893, McPherson chaired the growing Parliamentary Labor Party with tact and scrupulous attention to detail.

In 1892 he had sat on the shops and factories commission that recommended consolidation and simplification of the Health Act and new laws to cover factories and working conditions. But he was unsuccessful as a dogged presenter of petitions and spearhead of pressure for an early closing law. One of the first secretaries of the Working Women's Trade Union (formed 1890), in 1893-94 he supported moves that gave women the vote.

McPherson's recognition of the need for a labour newspaper dated from the *Register* strike; he was on the managing committee of the company that from 1894 produced the *Weekly Herald*. From 1896 he was a member of the State Children's Council. Next year he spoke frequently in the House on Federation, to which he gave characteristically cautious support, from a democratic standpoint; he feared the power of the Senate. McPherson was admired by peers and colleagues of all views for his honest, broad-minded approach. He disliked ostentation and lived plainly, with little leisure, but he loved poetry.

By August 1897 he was ill, with cancer. In early December he called for his boyhood friend James Hutchison [q.v.9]. 'I never truckled to anyone', he said, 'Tell the boys to pull together'. He died on the thirteenth. One thousand mourners, led by members of the typographical society and the W.W.T.U., followed his coffin to West Terrace cemetery. A memorial fund to assist his wife, three daughters and son collected £600. An oil portrait by Mrs E. Anson was presented to the Trades Hall and an inscription from Robert Browning carved on his tombstone:

'One who never turned his back but marched breast forward . . .'

D. J. Murphy (ed), *Labor in politics* (Brisb, 1975); *A'sian Typographical J,* Mar 1890, Feb, Nov 1892, Dec 1897, Jan, May 1898; *Quiz and the Lantern,* 5 Feb 1892, 26 Mar 1896, 16 Dec 1897; *Advertiser* (Adel), 14, 15 Dec 1897; *Weekly Herald* (Adel), 17 Dec 1897; *Observer* (Adel), 18 Dec 1897; SA Typographical Soc, Minute-book (deposit E92 series 1/2, 1/3, 1/5, ANU Archives); Arch. 1348, p 72 (SAA).   SUZANNE EDGAR

MACPHERSON, MARGARET (1875-1956), pharmacist and benefactress, was born on 20 February 1875 at Gundagai, New South Wales, second daughter of native-born parents Alexander MacPherson, surveyor and later grazier, and his wife Delicia Anne, née Vyner. She was brought up on her father's station, Umbango, near Tarcutta. After passing a preliminary examination, she was indentured for three years to Josiah Parker, chemist, of 221 William Street, Sydney. She was registered by the Board of Pharmacy on 11 August 1904, having gained first place in the final examination; at the same time she was granted her poison licence. With a gentleman assistant, she was managing one of Parker's branches in William Street.

In September 1908 Miss MacPherson was appointed dispenser at the Royal Hospital for Women, Paddington, at a salary of £62 a year; by January 1912 it had reached £156. In March 1911 she had joined the Pharmaceutical Society of New South Wales. She left the hospital in December 1916 and worked briefly at Dixon's pharmacy in King Street.

The family property, Umbango, was sold in 1918 after the death of her father in 1917 and next year of her brother Alister. A good linguist, Margaret MacPherson was fluent in French and Italian. With her younger sister Elizabeth (1878-1953), a schoolteacher, she travelled overseas and lived for a time at Florence, Italy; on their return they settled at Darling Point, then at Double Bay. In April 1933 the sisters approached W. H. Ifould [q.v.9], principal librarian of the Public Library of New South Wales, about establishing some memorial collection. After negotiations it was decided that it should consist of 'books of pure literature and fine arts' known as the 'Donald MacPherson Collection of Art and Literature'. This was in memory of their grandfather who had migrated from Scotland in 1838, been a schoolteacher of some renown and a prominent member of Scots Church, Sydney. During their lives the sisters gave money for the purchase of books (the first were bought in 1945).

Margaret MacPherson died in the Scottish Hospital, Paddington, on 27 October 1956 and was cremated after a service at St Mark's Anglican Church, Darling Point. Both sisters, in almost identical wills drawn up in November 1937, after life interests bequeathed the residue of their estates to the library: Elizabeth's was valued for probate at £13 423 and Margaret's at £16 354. When the deed of release af all monies was made in April 1970, the library received $113 914. The Donald MacPherson Collection of Art and Literature forms part of the special collections in the State Library of New South Wales.

A'sian J of Pharmacy, 30 Nov 1964; Estate of M. and E. MacPherson (Office file, SLNSW).

JEAN F. ARNOT

McPHERSON, SIR WILLIAM MURRAY (1865-1932), businessman, premier and philanthropist, was born on 17 September 1865 in West Melbourne, ninth child and third surviving son of Thomas McPherson, iron merchant, and his wife Jessie, née Fulton, both Scottish born. He was educated at West Melbourne State School. After an apprenticeship with James McEwan, he entered his father's firm. Thomas's death in 1888 left William and his brother Edward in charge; after Edward's death (1896) William became sole proprietor. When McPherson entered politics in 1913, he established a private company, McPherson's Pty Ltd. On 19 April 1892 he had married Emily, daughter of the Sydney merchant W. M. Jackson, at St Andrew's Cathedral.

McPherson was a shrewd, successful and sometimes enterprising businessman. His inherited concern with engineering supplies and imported machinery broadened in 1900 when he and others set up the Acme Bolt Co. to protect local manufacturers from exploitation by overseas bolt producers. The other

backers lost confidence; McPherson bought them out in 1905 and made the company profitable. During World War I he produced machine tools, previously imported, but he was no war profiteer: it was 1917 before his profits, as a percentage on capital (and without allowing for inflation), matched those of 1911. At the end of the short post-war boom the machinery side of the business was being carried by the bolt works, which ultimately profited greatly from a Sydney Harbour bridge contract. After a visit to the United States of America in 1924 McPherson decided to convert his under-utilized machine capacity to manufacturing pumps.

McPherson always saw arbitration courts and wages boards as unnecessary and their operations as uninformed, claiming that judges and politicians knew nothing of industrial needs. He himself could be a peremptory employer who could sack a difficult employee out of hand, or stump through the office after hours emptying to the floor the contents of untidy desk-drawers. But the Boss's presence on the annual works picnic at Port Phillip Bay symbolized a highly intelligent goodwill. No one seeking work was ever refused an interview; McPherson would not add humiliation to the pain of unemployment. Bonuses instituted in 1896 were paid every year except 1931 when there was no dividend. In 1901-21 they represented 8 per cent of profits and were sometimes much higher, in days when expansion was largely financed from profit.

In 1923 employee shares, paid for from dividends, were introduced for managerial staff, then for all employees. A works canteen (with washable calico covers on the chairs) was a novelty in 1927, for which the board was told that the chairman would personally pay if the company could not afford it. McPherson even surrendered a lifelong conviction that retirement was a personal responsibility, and introduced a company superannuation scheme. In 1927 a Labor opponent reluctantly described him as 'the best private employer in Australia'. His will left, as well as separate legacies for directors, £5000 for division among his employees, strikers alone excluded. But he never faced a strike.

Even in the 1920s, all this was somewhat old fashioned, as were the business principles unvaried from 1898: tell the truth, *always* meet a contract, never denigrate a competitor. McPherson had something to give to public life, but he was not a natural politician, and only partially a successful one.

In 1902-13 McPherson represented importers on the Melbourne Harbor Trust, and in 1909 was elected president of the Melbourne Chamber of Commerce. When in 1913 George Swinburne [q.v.] resigned the Legislative Assembly seat of Hawthorn, his friend McPherson succeeded him, holding it effortlessly thereafter. He tried to bring to politics the 'business commonsense' which had served him as merchant-manufacturer. In 1917 an 'anti-extravagance' campaign, spearheaded by the *Age*, brought down the Peacock [q.v.] government. McPherson became treasurer (1917-23), briefly under (Sir) John Bowser [q.v.7] and then (Sir) Harry Lawson [q.v.]. He became National Party leader in 1927 and, with the fall of the Hogan [q.v.9] government (November 1928), premier and treasurer. Defeated at the 1929 general election, and in failing health, he retired in August 1930.

In the turbulent faction-ridden Victorian politics of the 1920s, with growing imbalance between city and country, a weak Labor Party, an ambitious Country Party, division on the right and a conservative Upper House, McPherson's qualities were valuable, if limited. He had little charisma and no talent for political in-fighting, nor for long-term strategy. He did have unchallengeable integrity, a zest for careful management and a personal gift for conciliation. He inspired affection. His own beliefs that soldier settlement and railway expansion needed subsidy and could not show quick profits, that economic progress required low taxes, that good government was thrifty, and that thinly populated rural electorates deserved special electoral consideration attracted considerable, if rather motley, support.

Six successive budget surpluses had him labelled as 'the threepenny Treasurer', but he did have flashes of imagination: he backed both the State Electricity Commission and (Sir) Harold Clapp's [q.v.8] railways appointment. His resignation of Treasury office on 20 November 1923, because (he said) the government could not honour its promises without tax increases it was pledged to avoid, showed his principle and his inflexibility. (Sir) Frederic Eggleston [q.v.8], whose political career he had encouraged but who became paranoiacally estranged from him, later attacked him bitterly, alleging that he knew nothing of public finance, balanced his budgets accidentally through inflation, and financed soldier settlement by irresponsible borrowing. In fact, McPherson valued Victoria's good overseas credit, which kept loan interest low, and disapproved of heavy debt. His penny-pinching did not preclude a few liberal concepts like town planning, and he could even, if pushed, unexpectedly squeeze out a badly needed university grant. But in 1928-29, he still thought the State should 'pay its way' within a minimal budget, avoiding increased taxation that might discourage the private enterprise essential for prosperity. He did not grasp the increasing need for public expenditure to meet the needs of an increasingly complex and urbanized com-munity. He became premier by default, rather than by ambition, with an outlook which prohibited a search for new policies.

McPherson used his own wealth as he believed wealth should be used, to help fill the gaps necessarily left by economical government. In 1909 he became a foundation councillor and permanent benefactor of Swinburne's new technical college. His Treasury resignation was followed by a gift of £25 000 for the domestic science college which the government could not afford, and career opportunities for girls became wider: the Emily McPherson College of Domestic Economy produced dietitians as well as efficient housewives. He gave freely to the Congregational Church, and his unpublicized generosities were innumerable. After a friend's wife, a Queen Victoria Hospital committee-member, persuaded him of the need for a community hospital for women unable to afford private hospital fees, he quietly handed her an envelope—'Well, Nan, there's your hospital!' Inside was a personal cheque for £25 000 but its donor insisted on remaining anonymous until *after* the 1929 election. At the opening of the Jessie McPherson Community Hospital in December 1931, he was delighted that its fittings had supplied employment by being Australian made.

McPherson had been appointed K.B.E. in 1923. He died suddenly on 26 July 1932 of a heart attack and was buried in Boroondara cemetery. A son and two daughters survived him. His estate, valued for probate at £466 628, provoked argument with the Federal tax commissioners; it was a bad time for a private company to face death duties (it became a public company in 1944). Nevertheless, one unprofitable section of his company's operations still escaped a Depression cutback, because its female staff were family breadwinners. Such a humane policy was McPherson's legacy.

A. Henderson (ed), *Australian families*, 1 (Melb, 1941); G. Serle, *John Monash* (Melb, 1982); *Table Talk*, 26 June 1928; *Age, Argus* and *Herald* (Melb), 27 July 1932; M. Vines, The instability of governments and parties in Victoria in the 1920s (M.A. thesis, Univ Melb, 1975); Eggleston papers (NL); F. W. Eggleston, Confidential notes: the Victorian parliament as I knew it (Menzies Lib, ANU); McPherson papers (LaTL); press cuttings in possession of McPherson Ltd, Melb; personal information.
ALISON PATRICK
BARBARA HAMER

McPHILLAMY, VERANIA (1889-1961), superintendent of soldiers' canteens, was born on 1 November 1889 at Croydon, Sydney, second child of Charles Smith McPhillamy, grazier, of Warroo, Forbes, and his wife Alice Kate, daughter of Henry Halloran [q.v.4]. She was educated at Warroo Public School and as a boarder at Ascham School, Sydney, where she succeeded academically and captained the cricket team. At 18 she visited Britain and France.

Joining a Voluntary Aid Detachment, Miss McPhillamy left for Egypt in October 1915. Next year she joined (Dame) Alice Chisholm [q.v.7] at the newly opened soldiers' canteen at Kantara, on the Suez Canal. At their own expense and initially without official sanction, they soon catered for thousands of Empire troops. 'Trooper Bluegum' [O. Hogue q.v.9], described this 'refreshing oasis', where even showers were available and soldiers found 'rest and comfort, and a cheery Australian welcome'.

Mrs Chisholm and Rania, as she was affectionately known, cheerfully contended with heat, sand, wind, flies and scarcity of water. No man was ever refused a meal and wastage was minimal. For some time 'iced tongue and salad' appeared on the menu, when Rania cornered the Cairo tinned-tongue market. Profits were used to reduce prices and improve accommodation.

General Allenby considered their work 'heroic', and with his approval and assistance Rania opened a branch canteen in Jerusalem in summer 1918. Ignoring the sound of heavy artillery, she was soon providing many meals daily and, as at Kantara, refreshments were taken to hospital trains passing through. When she took over the next-door house of a wealthy German she created a 'home away from home', with curtains, tablecloths, comfortable chairs and a piano. She inspired great loyalty among her staff. After the Armistice she moved her canteen to the Anzac Mounted Division camped in the desert at Rafa; she found it 'heavy work', but also ran open-air picture shows. Two months later she was forced to leave at short notice when the Egyptians rebelled.

Slim, with large blue eyes, a lively expression and a quirkish sense of humour, Rania was beloved by the Australian desert troops, who presented her with a jade necklace; (Sir) Michael Bruxner, (Sir) Charles Bickerton Blackburn and (Sir) Henry Gullett [qq.v.7,9] became her friends for life. She was appointed M.B.E. in 1918 and O.B.E. in 1920.

In the troopship returning to Australia she met a physician, Lieut-Colonel Clive Vallack Single, D.S.O., of the 4th Light Horse Field Ambulance; they were married at Warroo on 21 June 1920. He became government medical officer at Moree, where two of their children were born. She was a founding member of the local branch of the Country Women's Association of New South Wales in 1922, and they both helped to establish a baby health centre in 1925. After visiting Europe together in 1927 Single practised in Macquarie Street, Sydney. Mrs Single was left with four children when he died at their Woollahra home in 1931. With her daughters attending Ascham, her friendship with the headmistress, Margaret Bailey [q.v.7], grew; she was a member of the first school council. She also served on the council of the Australian Mothercraft Society, worked for returned soldiers and in World War II entertained pilots on leave.

She inherited her father's love of horse-racing and entertained at the Queen's Club. She was an avid reader and, denied a university education herself, encouraged her children to acquire one. Survived by her son and three daughters, she died at Woollahra on 3 February 1961 and was cremated with Anglican rites.

H. S. Gullett, *The A.I.F. in Sinai and Palestine* (Syd, 1923); *London Gazette*, 12 Mar 1918, 1 June 1920; *MJA*, 15 Aug 1931; *Reveille*, 31 Aug 1931, 1 Mar 1961; *Ascham Charivari*, June 1961; *SMH*, 14 July 1917, 5 Jan 1918, 4 Sept 1919, 3 Dec 1927, 6 Feb 1961; *Bulletin*, 11 Sept 1919; *Moree Gwydir Examiner*, 15 June 1922, 13 July 1931; family papers held by, and information from, Mrs R. Murray, Woollahra, Syd. GILLIAN FULLOON

McRAE, CHRISTOPHER JOHN (1863-1924), storekeeper and primary industry organizer, was born on 27 June 1863 at Stroud, New South Wales, second of four sons of Christopher McRae, Scottish-born store-keeper, and his English wife Maria, née Farley. He was educated at Stroud and entered his father's business. In 1886 he was employed by F. G. Crofton of Lismore and in 1888 joined him in partnership in a general store at Coraki. There, on 22 January 1890, McRae married Florence Eliza Mobbs. Crofton and McRae had dissolved their partnership in 1889, but McRae carried on as McRae Bros & MacIntyre and in 1907 became sole proprietor. Active in local affairs, he was an alderman on Coraki Municipal Council in 1891-96 and 1908-10, and mayor in 1909-10; he also worked for a railway from Kyogle via Casino to Coraki. Commissioned first lieutenant in 1892 in the New South Wales Lancers, he was promoted captain and transferred to the 5th Light Horse in 1903, joining the reserve in 1910.

McRae acquired a wide experience of agricultural districts whose land use was changing rapidly from sugar-cane to dairying. A chairman of the Coraki Co-operative Butter Co. Ltd and president of the Northern Rivers Associated Butter Factories, he was deeply respected by dairy farmers and all operators of co-operative factories. He was a prominent founder and first president in 1916-24 of the Primary Producers' Union, presiding over its

Richmond district council until he moved to Sydney in March 1919 to assume official duties. He was largely responsible for the union's constitution and for building up membership to over 14 000, with some 300 branches, within five years.

In World War I McRae was a producer representative on the Necessary Commodities Control Commission in 1914-20, the Australian Dairy Council, the State Butter Advisory Committee and various post-war committees preparing stabilization schemes for dairy products. He was also employer representative on the State Board of Trade in 1918, and was appointed to the Commonwealth Board of Trade in 1923.

In a paper to the 1918 jubilee conference of the Royal Agricultural Society of New South Wales, McRae pointed to dairying as the one organized primary industry, the success of which lay in being largely producer controlled. He argued strongly against the desire of government, especially Federal, to continue control of primary industry after the war. His consciousness of cost factors and tenuous profitability was allied with a vision of overseas market expansion. As P.P.U. leader he combined the judicial temperament, clear thought and wide outlook of a man with an absorbing interest in the business aspects of primary production. He strove to keep the union out of politics and there was some criticism when in August 1923 he accepted nomination to the Legislative Council by Sir George Fuller [q.v.8].

An active Freemason and Presbyterian, McRae belonged to the New South Wales Club and lived at Eastwood in Sydney. On 3 September 1924 he died suddenly in a railway carriage near Yass. He was buried in the Field of Mars cemetery after a funeral service at St Stephen's Presbyterian Church, Sydney. His wife, a son and six daughters survived him.

Roy Agr Soc (NSW), *Procs of jubilee conference of primary producers* (Syd, 1918); W. A. Bayley, *History of the Farmers and Settlers' Association of N.S.W.* (Syd, 1957); *PD* (LC NSW), 1925, p 1774; *PP* (NSW), 1908, 2nd S, 3, p 703; *Sydney Tatler*, 18 Jan 1923; *Aust National Review*, 20 Aug 1923; *SMH*, 3, 21 Aug, 3 Sept 1923, 5, 6 Sept 1924.

JOHN ATCHISON

McRAE, JAMES (1871-1939), educationist, was born on 19 November 1871 at Ascot, Victoria, tenth child of Scottish parents Christopher McRae, farmer, and his wife Mary Ann, née McDonald. He attended the local state school and Creswick Grammar School, matriculating in 1888. That year he joined the Education Department as pupil-teacher at Coghills Creek State School and subsequently taught in other rural schools. At the Presby-terian Church, Avoca, on 5 May 1898 he married Margaret Louisa Tuck.

Although at Coghills Creek he had been poorly rated by the local inspector, 'Jock' McRae proved a capable teacher with real affection for his work and pupils. Later inspectors' reports described him as 'a schoolmaster of striking merit' who did 'full justice . . . to every pupil'. In 1904 while at Glenpatrick he was selected as one of twenty outstanding rural teachers to attend evening classes at the University of Melbourne. He graduated B.A. in 1907 and M.A. in 1909, sharing the 1908 exhibition in logic and philosophy. At the Teachers' Training College, where he had obtained his diploma of education in 1906, he was impressed by J. Smyth's [q.v.] emphasis on the educational virtues of the small school and on the child as the centre of the learning process. He also formed a friendship with Frank Tate [q.v.] whose children were McRae's pupils at Kew East Rural Practising School.

In 1908 McRae was appointed master of method at the Training College and in 1909 second lecturer. He was a brilliant exponent of classroom practice and teacher of philosophy and experimental education and proved, in 1913-22, a loyal and effective vice-principal. A district inspector from 1910, he was appointed chief inspector of primary schools in 1922 and chief inspector in 1925.

McRae had pioneered school correspondence lessons in 1914; in 1922-32 he initiated vocational guidance programmes, junior farmers' clubs and the platoon classroom system (on a limited basis) and helped to establish special classes for backward children. He also encouraged W. J. Elijah to publish *Principles and methods of teaching* (1924), the 'teachers' bible' for the next twenty-five years. McRae gleaned many of his ideas as Education Department travelling scholar in 1926. His report reveals keen observation of British and North American practices; but his loyalty to the basic Victorian education system remained firm, an attitude well demonstrated by his rejection of the North American vogue for small-school consolidation. His views unfortunately helped to maintain another two decades of poorly trained teachers and teacher shortages in city schools.

In 1932 McRae became acting-director and then director of education, succeeding M. P. Hansen [q.v.9]. He provided his department with much-needed stability, healing the rifts between the department and ministry and between those authorities and the teachers. He publicly supported the teachers' union claims for salary restoration and a tribunal, but could make little headway against government Depression policies. Conscious of his own first teaching days, he fought a brave, losing battle to reconcile school inspector and teacher. Having helped to prepare the 1911 and 1922 primary school curriculum revisions, he presided over the introduction of its major revision in 1934, only to see it flounder because of lack of funds and misunderstanding of its progressive intentions. He retired, disappointed with his efforts, in 1936.

A tall, gaunt man with trim moustache and piercing eyes, McRae had a biting wit which found occasional expression in official publications. Always a hard worker, enthusiastic and idealistic, he reserved his greatest passions for his demonstration of classroom techniques, his support of Carlton football team, and for gardening. Widowed in 1926, he married a divorcee, Mabel Irma Donald, née Williams, former acting secretary of the Victorian Teachers' Union, on 31 March 1934.

McRae died in Melbourne of cancer on 13 June 1939 and was cremated. His wife and his son and three daughters of his first marriage survived him.

A. D. Spaull, 'John Smyth, principal Melbourne Teachers College 1902-1927', C. Turney (ed), *Pioneers of Australian education*, 3 (Syd, 1983); Education Dept (Vic), *Vision and realisation*, L. J. Blake ed (Melb, 1973); R. J. W. Selleck, *Frank Tate* (Melb, 1982); *Herald* (Melb), 27 Nov 1934, 16 Feb 1935, 19, 28 Nov 1936, 13 June 1939; James McRae career outline (comp by Education History Services, Education Dept of Vic, Melb).

ANDREW SPAULL

MacRORY, MARGARET (1862-1931), religious Sister, was born on 18 December 1862 at Ballygawley, Tyrone, Ireland, daughter of Francis MacRory, farmer, and his second wife Rose, née Montague. Her brother Joseph, older by a year, became a cardinal and primate of all Ireland. Margaret had her early schooling with the Sisters of Mercy and from 16 as a boarder at the Convent of the Sacred Heart, Armagh. She entered the novitiate of the Society of the Sacred Heart of Jesus at Roehampton, London, in August 1881. Before completing her noviceship she was sent to Le Mans, France, to work in the school of the congregation as an assistant-teacher until recalled briefly to London in 1884.

Margaret arrived in Sydney on 4 November 1885. She taught at the Convent of the Sacred Heart, Rose Bay, in 1886-94 and was professed there on 2 July 1889. In Melbourne in 1894-1902 she taught at the congregation's boarding school in Burke Road, Malvern, and returned as headmistress to the nearby day school in 1907-10, after spending the intervening years at the new and short-lived school in Bourke Street, Sydney.

This tall, slender and fair Irishwoman was a dynamic teacher who gained the confidence of her students by her love for and interest in each one. In 1910 she was appointed headmistress of Rose Bay and under her guidance the school grew in numbers. She brought the school curriculum into line with requirements for registration and invited government inspection. From 1915 the students were prepared for public examinations. She founded an ex-students association in 1912 and by her personal contacts created the strong bonds that still characterize that association.

In 1923 Mother MacRory was chosen to open a house in City Road, Darlington, for Catholic women at the University of Sydney. Her time there was broken by a call to Rome to attend a retreat for English-speaking superiors of the congregation. She visited England, Scotland and Ireland where she strengthened her bonds with her brother Joseph, then a bishop, and travelled through the United States of America, inspecting liberal arts colleges run by the congregation.

On her return Mother MacRory was responsible for the building of the residence within the university for Catholic women on part of the land of St John's College. She established its independence from St John's, whose rector had seen the new foundation as simply an extension of his college. She could not prevent the foundation stone from bearing the inscription 'In honorem St Joannis Evangelistae'—but the new hall, which opened in 1926 with Mother MacRory in charge, became Sancta Sophia. Under her guidance the number of students increased and a wing of twenty-four rooms was added in 1927.

When in 1929 legislation established Sancta Sophia as a college within the University of Sydney, the council appointed her as its first principal. She chose the crest of the college with its symbols of truth and wisdom. Her own wisdom and understanding with her readiness to listen to others and to learn from them tempered her slightly authoritarian nature and won her students' respect and confidence. She died of septicaemia on 23 May 1931 at Sancta Sophia and was buried at Rose Bay. In five years she had established a tradition of scholarship based on Christian values following the motto of her choosing— 'Walk in Wisdom'.

L. Barlow, *Living stones* (Syd, 1982); Provincial Archives of the Society of the Sacred Heart, Rose Bay, Syd, including D. Loughnan, Life of Margaret MacRory.   MARY SHANAHAN

MACROSSAN, HUGH DENIS (1881-1940), judge and politician, was born on 20

February 1881 at Lutwyche, Brisbane, son of John Murtagh Macrossan [q.v.5] and his wife Bridget, née Queely, both Irish born. He was educated privately and in state schools until 12, when he attended Nudgee College for five years. Academically gifted, in 1898 he passed the New South Wales senior public examination. An accomplished student of the University of Sydney and resident at St John's College, Macrossan graduated B.A. in 1902. For three years he returned to Nudgee as a teacher.

Turning to the law in August 1904 as associate to Mr Justice Real [q.v.], on 22 October 1907 Macrossan was admitted to the Bar. He married a widow Lydia Cremin Hall (d. 1922), née Woodhouse, on 12 June 1912 at St Patrick's Church, Sydney. Although unsuccessful when he stood as a committed Liberal Senate candidate in 1910, in 1912 he was chosen by Premier Denham [q.v.8] as a Ministerialist candidate for the Legislative Assembly seat of Windsor and won easily against W. R. Crampton [q.v.8]. Once in parliament he found himself uncomfortable with party ties; he urged politicians to 'be free of party bias and prejudice, and free of the party machine'. He espoused a wide range of social reforms, looking to New Zealand's advanced social and industrial legislation, yet he condemned the Labor Party and policies of nationalization, and opposed trade unions asserting political, rather than social and industrial, power. Seeing himself as a true, 'sane' liberal and democrat, while asserting that socialism was contrary to human nature, he was critical of the system which had made him 'a mere automaton' and declined Denham's endorsement in the 1915 election. He stood as an Independent Liberal.

Impressed by Switzerland's political system he argued against party government, favouring a government responsible to the people through elective ministries, referenda and proportional representation. He also sought an elective Upper House. His battery of proposed social reforms included control over trusts and combines; prohibitions on speculation in food; unemployment insurance; compulsory profit sharing; town planning; quinquennial parliaments; regulation of private enterprise in the best interests of the public; nationalization of public utilities (he was critical of the handling of the 1912 general strike); Federal borrowing on account of the States; protection for Australian workers. He lost to the Labor candidate H. G. McPhail.

Despite clashes in parliament with the Labor leader T. J. Ryan [q.v.], an increasing bond between them led to Macrossan's identification by some Liberals as crypto-Labor. Having established himself as a leader at the Bar, with fluent and witty command of language, he appeared with Ryan in leading cases

such as the Mooraberrie case, the McCawley [q.v.] case and on behalf of George Cuthbert Taylor. He also appeared for Ryan when W. M. Hughes [q.v.9] prosecuted him for 'seditious and false statements', and in a libel case against the Melbourne *Argus* in 1919. He held a retainer from the Crown and appeared, for example, with the solicitor-general on behalf of the commissioner for income tax. In 1924 he appeared as counsel before the Privy Council for the Brisbane Tramways Trust. Much of his early Bar work was in criminal cases but later he was frequently called on in matters of constitutional law.

On 23 July 1926 Macrossan was sworn in as a justice of the Supreme Court of Queensland, succeeding L. O. Lukin [q.v.], and on 1 December he was commissioned as senior puisne judge. On 2 December he married Gladys Mildred Trenfield at Fortitude Valley, with Catholic rites; they formally separated ten years later. He was an official host to the papal legate at the laying of the foundation stone of Holy Name Cathedral, Brisbane, in 1928; next year Pope Pius XI appointed him knight of St Gregory the Great.

Despite a public difference of opinion with, and a rebuke by, Premier W. Forgan Smith [q.v.] in 1934, arising from a comment by Macrossan in court about 'restless pretensions of bureaucracy', his legal career continued to flourish. He was a master of cross-examination, as barrister and judge a prodigious worker who meticulously prepared cases, summings-up and decisions; and he had a sympathy for the genuine underdog. Barristers respected his 'tongue of silver and steel' and his acute, speedy judgments.

Macrossan was appointed chief justice on 17 May 1940, but died on 23 June at Scarborough of coronary thrombosis, having suffered for years from acute asthma. Survived by the two children of his first marriage, he was buried in Nudgee cemetery after a public funeral. His younger brother Neal William became chief justice in 1946.

D. J. Murphy, *T. J. Ryan* (Brisb, 1975); R. Johnston, *History of the Queensland Bar* (Brisb, 1979); *Univ Qld Gazette*, Dec 1956, p 5; *Courier Mail*, 1 Jan, 13 Mar 1910, 22 Mar, 29 Apr 1912, 27-30 Mar 1915, 16, 26 Apr, 20, 25 May 1915, 22, 23, 24 July, 2, 3 Dec 1926, 23, 28 Feb 1934, 13, 18 May, 24-26 June 1940.   W. Ross Johnston

McSHARRY, TERENCE PATRICK (1880-1918), soldier, was born on 9 August 1880 at Curracuringa, Townsville, Queensland, son of Irish-born Matthew McSharry, contractor, later accountant, and his Queensland-born wife Margaret, née Pottinger. Known as 'Jockey Jim' within the family, for his love of horses, after attending Christian

Brothers' St Joseph's College, Gregory Terrace, Brisbane, Terry was a book-keeper in Brisbane in 1903-08, joined the Metropolitan Water and Sewerage Board, and was a surveyor by 1912. That year, on 25 March, he was commissioned in the Australian Intelligence Corps and in February 1914 was appointed a staff officer (Queensland District).

Enlisting in the Australian Imperial Force on 21 August 1914, McSharry was commissioned lieutenant in the 2nd Light Horse Regiment and embarked on 24 September. The regiment landed at Gallipoli on 12 May 1915. He was permanent post adjutant and works' officer at Quinn's Post, where during the critical Turkish break-in of 29 May, although senior officers were present, it was McSharry who, 'with his thorough knowledge of the post and eminent coolness and decision, most fully grasped and controlled the situation'. Early in the attack, rallying men with the call 'Come on, Australia!', he led a party which halted infiltrating enemy with crude 'jam-tin' bombs. He received a bullet through his 'Irish hat with the little brim', an example of the irregularities of the Anzac uniform—most of its brim was cut off. For his 'exceptional bravery and resource', especially in this action and that of 4 June, he was awarded the Military Cross. He had been promoted captain and transferred as adjutant to the 15th Battalion in June.

In Egypt McSharry was promoted major in January 1916 and in June sailed with the battalion to France. He was promoted temporary lieut-colonel and took command of the 15th on 30 August.

McSharry was one of the notable A.I.F. battalion commanders in France. To Bean 'there was no wiser head in the force'. Except when detached to temporarily command the 4th Brigade from 13 to 25 July 1918, he led his battalion for almost two years, an exceptionally long period. He commanded it in the battles of Stormy Trench (January-February 1917), 1st Bullecourt (April), Messines (June), Polygon Wood (September) and in 1918 at Hamel. Four times mentioned in dispatches, he was awarded the Distinguished Service Order in June 1917 and was appointed C.M.G. in June 1918. While helping a wounded man to shelter in a bombardment at Vaire-sous-Corbie, on the Somme, McSharry was mortally wounded and died on 6 August 1918. He was buried near Corbie. He was posthumously awarded a Bar to the D.S.O.

McSharry was remembered as 'a lovable comrade . . . a gallant and intellectual soldier . . . cheery and energetic'. With hair parted in the middle, and an upturned nose, he was short, described by the battalion historian as 'of jockey weight . . . with a small voice with more than its share of biting sarcasm if matters did not go his way . . . Outspoken to a degree of bluntness that at times was most alarming, intermingled . . . with a caustic wit . . . There are hundreds of stories relating to his contempt for danger . . . he could tell and appreciate a good joke'. He was unmarried. A portrait by W. B. McInnes [q.v.] is held by the Australian War Memorial.

C. E. W. Bean, *The story of Anzac* (Syd, 1921, 1924), and *The A.I.F. in France*, 1916-18 (Syd, 1929, 1933, 1937, 1942); T. P. Chataway, *History of the 15th Battalion A.I.F.* (Brisb, 1948); *Queenslander*, 14 Aug 1920; information from Hugh J. McSharry, Marburg, Qld. MERRILYN LINCOLN

MACTIER, ROBERT (1890-1918), soldier and farmer, was born on 17 May 1890 at Tatura, Victoria, son of Scottish-born Robert Mactier, farmer, and his Victorian wife Christina, née Ross. Seventh child in a close-knit Presbyterian family of ten, he was educated at Tatura State School and later worked on his father's properties at Tatura and Caniambo. Stocky and athletic, he excelled at football and shooting; his 'irrepressible sense of humour' and 'gentlemanly disposition' made him popular among the locals.

Mactier enlisted as a private in the Australian Imperial Force on 1 March 1917 and embarked for England with the 19th Reinforcements for the 23rd Battalion. After training he joined the battalion in France on 23 November. Allotted to 'B' Company, in April 1918 he was in heavy fighting around Albert on the Somme and was gassed. In May he was a scout at company headquarters. He fought in the battle of Hamel in July and in the August offensive and on 22 August wrote his last letter home. Victory was in sight: 'if our side only keep going I think the war [will] be over by next spring'.

On 1 September, north of Péronne, Mactier won his battalion's only Victoria Cross. The 23rd was moving into position for the early morning assault on Mont St Quentin. With only twenty minutes left until zero hour, it was stopped by an enemy machine-gun behind a barbed-wire barricade. Two similar posts could be seen further on. An attack on the first position failed and Private Mactier, his company's runner, was sent to investigate. Armed with bombs and a revolver, he ran forward, sized up the situation and dashed to the barricade. He threw a bomb, climbed over the wire and toppled the machine-gun out of the trench. His comrades then advanced, found the eight-man gun-crew dead and saw Mactier capturing all occupants of the next post. He charged the third post, bombing and killing the garrison and discovered yet another obstacle. To avoid wire in the trench he ran into the open and was rushing in for his fourth attack when shot by a gunner on his flank, though one of his friends said that he was 'killed by concussion from a hand grenade'. Through his actions the assaulting companies filed into position just as the barrage fell on Mont St Quentin.

Mactier was buried nearby but was re-interred in the Hem Farm cemetery, Hem-Monacu. In noting his posthumous award the London *Times* praised his 'exceptional valour and determination', describing him as 'a fine type of the wiry Colonial'. His mates, in their battalion newspaper, remembered him as 'only one of the boys' while his letters home are those of a genial unpretentious man. A radio series on V.C. winners, broadcast in 1936-37, ably summed him up: 'Bob Mactier was typical of his kind, the countryman who became a soldier . . . a healthy man . . . well-behaved . . . quiet and unassuming; he had nothing spectacular in his make-up'. In 1983 his family donated his V.C. to the Australian War Memorial. His name is commemorated in a soldier's club at Watsonia Barracks, Melbourne, which also holds a bronze bust by Wallace Anderson. Mactier was unmarried. His brother David served in the 37th Battalion, A.I.F.

C. E. W. Bean, *The A.I.F. in France*, 1918 (Syd, 1942); L. Wigmore (ed), *They dared mightily* (Canb, 1963); *London Gazette*, 14 Dec 1918; *The 23rd* (France), 15 Sept 1918, 1 Jan 1919; *Herald* (Melb), 14 May 1935; *Canb Times*, 26 Sept 1983; Mactier collection, *and* War diary, 23rd Battalion, AIF (AWM); diary and letters of R. Mactier, 1917-18 (held by Mr P. J. Mactier, Tatura, Vic).

MERRILYN LINCOLN

McVICARS, JOHN (1877-1958), coal-miner and union secretary, was born on 9 December 1877 at Ipswich, Queensland, son of John McVicars, a migrant Scottish collier, and his wife Jane, née Beveridge. He began work at 14 as a trapper at the Mount Kembla colliery, on the Illawarra River, New South Wales, where his family had moved seeking employment. In 1893 he accompanied his father to the newly opened Victorian coalfield at Korumburra, in south-west Gippsland. Here McVicars worked for the Coal Creek Mining Co., becoming secretary of the Victorian Coal Miners' Association lodge at that mine.

In 1903-04 an attempt by local mine-owners to reduce wages precipitated a seventy-week lockout. When organized resistance ceased, the union had been destroyed and its members dispersed. McVicars travelled to Queensland, but soon returned to Gippsland to act as secretary of the South Gippsland Miners' Association, a recently formed competitor to the reviving V.C.M.A.

But after 1909 miners at the newly established Wonthaggi State Coal Mine held the key to the recognition of competing Victorian mining unions, and here the V.C.M.A. reasserted its strength. In 1910 McVicars sought work at Wonthaggi, becoming a V.C.M.A. branch committee-man the following year. In 1913 he was elected to the joint office of branch and Victorian district secretary, a position he retained until his retirement in 1946.

For McVicars, the defeat of 1903-04 exemplified the catastrophes that could overtake mining communities. It determined his industrial philosophy throughout his career as a union official. Conciliation was preferred to confrontation, negotiation to strike action. In a newly established mining community conscious of the opportunities offered by economic expansion, such an attitude accurately reflected a consensus among the workforce. McVicars stood aloof from the wave of syndicalism that swept Australian coalfields after World War I, and it was due to his influence that the Victorian district continued to support arbitration in contrast to the Miners' Federation's preferred policy of direct action.

Depression destroyed Wonthaggi's fragile security. Mass retrenchments from the State mine after 1932 eroded support for the conciliatory tactics which McVicars espoused. His opposition in February 1934 to a branch decision to strike in defence of victimized mineworkers undermined his 'constitutionalist' position. Branch elections held during this strike returned a majority of communists or their supporters. McVicars alone among constitutionalists held his position, but from 1934 until his retirement twelve years later he lacked his former political influence within the union.

McVicars was at the height of his influence during Wonthaggi's optimistic years, when miners and entrepreneurs alike anticipated its becoming a 'Newcastle of the South'. These were also years of Labor Party ascendancy. Active in the party since his years in Korumburra, McVicars was also a leading member in Wonthaggi, serving for a decade as a borough councillor and twice as mayor. He was also a trustee of the Union Theatre and the Miners Co-operative Dispensary. On retirement he became a caretaker at the State mine.

McVicars had married Ethel Louise Dobell at Korumburra on 10 January 1901. Predeceased by her and survived by seven of their nine children, he died at Wonthaggi's district hospital on 8 July 1958. He was buried in the local cemetery.

E. Ross, *A history of the Miners' Federation of Australia* (Syd, 1970); *Sentinel* and *Powlett Express*

(Wonthaggi), 10 July 1958; A. P. Reeves, *Industrial men: miners and politics in Wonthaggi 1909-1968* (M.A. thesis, La Trobe Univ, 1977).

ANDREW REEVES

McVILLY, CECIL LEVENTHORPE (1889-1964), sculler, soldier and public servant, was born on 3 August 1889 in Hobart, son of Joseph Henry McVilly, press reader and later newspaper editor, and his wife Marion Jane Thompson, née Smith. Educated at Queen's College, Hobart, he was a member of the senior cadets and a noted sculler. In 1910, 1911 and 1914 he won the Australian sculling championship and in 1913 the Diamond Sculls at Henley-on-Thames, England. For four years he served with the Derwent Infantry, and reached the rank of sergeant. He married Kathleen Agnes Williams in Hobart on 28 August 1915.

On 9 December 1915 McVilly was commissioned second lieutenant in the Australian Imperial Force and was posted to 'B' Company, 40th Battalion; his occupation on enlistment was commercial traveller. He was promoted lieutenant on 1 May 1916 and in July embarked for England for training.

McVilly landed in France on 23 November, was promoted captain in December and was engaged in training raiding parties at the Ecole Professionale, Armentières, in early 1917. He commanded 'B' Company, 40th Battalion, at the battle of Messines, 6-7 June, and was awarded the Military Cross for leadership under intensive enemy bombardment as his troops moved to their assembly position. During the 3rd battle of Ypres, at Broodseinde on 4 October, he was severely wounded and did not rejoin his unit until 20 December.

Selected for special service in Mesopotamia, on 29 January 1918 McVilly embarked in England for Basra at the head of the Persian Gulf. He joined Dunsterforce on 28 March, and took part in the defence of Baku on the Caspian Sea in August. Returning to England in January 1919, he embarked for Australia in March; he was mentioned in dispatches on 21 February for special service in Mesopotamia.

McVilly's A.I.F. appointment ended on 3 June and he became a captain on the reserve of officers, Australian Military Forces. In 1919-29 he worked for the Repatriation Commission in Tasmania. He was appointed inspector of charities in Victoria in 1929 and in 1948 became chairman of the Victorian Hospitals and Charities Commission. When he retired in 1953 he was living at Brighton, Melbourne. He later moved to Cowes, Phillip Island, where he died on 4 November 1964.

Cremated with Anglican rites, McVilly was survived by his wife and twin daughters.

F. C. Green, *The Fortieth, a record of the 40th Battalion* (Hob, 1922); C. E. W. Bean, *The A.I.F. in France* 1916-17 (Syd, 1929, 1933); *London Gazette*, 24 Aug 1917, 21 Feb 1919; *Herald* (Melb), 19 Aug 1929, 14 June 1930, 18 June 1953; *Weekly Courier* (Launc), 28 Aug 1929; records (AWM).

J. G. WILLIAMS

McWHAE, SIR JOHN (1858-1927), stockbroker, businessman and politician, was born on 22 June 1858 at Ballarat, Victoria, son of Scottish parents Peter McWhae, goldminer, and his wife Grace, née Wilson. He attended Dumfries Academy when the family visited Scotland after his father's mining success and, on their return in 1871, Ballarat Grammar School. He was a clerk in the Union Bank of Australia for eight years before starting the business of John McWhae & Co. on the Ballarat Stock Exchange, and establishing it by investment in Broken Hill, New South Wales, in 1886-87. An active Ballarat citizen he was a captain in the militia, captain of the rowing club and secretary of St Andrew's Presbyterian kirk.

Transferring his firm to Melbourne in the late 1880s, he guided it sagaciously through the near-panic speculation over the new West Australian goldfields, enhancing his growing reputation for imperturbability and the 'Midas touch'. In March 1893 he persuaded the Victorian treasurer to negotiate what proved to be a short-lived and limited agreement among the banks for mutual assistance in an attempt to avert financial disaster. McWhae was a leading member of the Stock Exchange of Melbourne for twenty years, including a record six as chairman (1893-94, 1898-1901).

After unsuccessfully contesting the Legislative Assembly seat of Melbourne in 1894 he was elected to the Legislative Council for Melbourne Province in 1910. McWhae was appointed by the Defence Department as complaints officer for the forces, and was then commissioner of public works in the Bowser [q.v.7] ministry (November 1917-March 1918) and honorary minister in the Lawson [q.v.] government from March 1918. As acting minister for health he dealt with the influenza epidemic of 1919 when the Exhibition Building was transformed into an emergency hospital and volunteer helpers recruited. He resigned in November 1921.

In 1912 he had relinquished his exchange seat to his son John (who died at Ypres) to concentrate on his expanding interests in Philippines gold-mining, Gippsland forestry and pastoral properties in Queensland and the Western District of Victoria. He was a director of fifteen companies including the Colonial Mutual Life Assurance, Duke and Orr's Amalgamated Dry Docks, Jumbunna Coal Mining and George Stirling & Sons.

Genial and popular but not given to wasting words, McWhae was agent-general for Victoria in London from February 1922 to September 1924. He vigorously promoted Victorian manufactures and produce through exhibitions and displays, and wooed British migrants, attracting publicity by statements about Australia's empty spaces and the dangers of an influx of aliens and a polyglot population. He was knighted in 1924.

Widely travelled, McWhae died suddenly on 17 September 1927 at Yokohama, Japan, on a holiday cruise and was buried with Masonic honours on 27 October in Boroondara cemetery, Melbourne. He was survived by his wife Elizabeth Henderson, née Douch, whom he had married on 19 April 1883 at Williamstown, and by two sons and two daughters. His estate was sworn for probate at £69 737.

A. R. Hall, *The Stock Exchange of Melbourne and the Victorian economy 1852-1900* (Canb, 1968); A. T. Stirling, *Gang forward* (Melb, 1972); *PD* (LC Vic), 1927, p 1484; *A'sian Pastoralists' Review*, 15 Oct 1927; *Punch* (Melb), 20 Dec 1917, 8 May 1919, 21 July 1921; *Age* and *Argus*, 20 Sept, 27 Oct 1927.   H. A. and E. M. FINLAY

McWILLIAM, JOHN JAMES (1868-1951), vigneron and wine and spirit merchant, was born on 17 June 1868 at Denison, near Sale, Victoria, fourth of ten children of Samuel McWilliam (1830-1902), Irish-born farmer, and his wife Martha (d. 1889), née Steele, a native of Geelong. Samuel purchased 480 acres (194 ha) near Corowa, New South Wales, in 1877 and established Sunnyside vineyard of 80 acres (32 ha). J. J. McWilliam was educated at Denison State and Corowa Public schools, leaving at 13 to work in various outback occupations. He returned in 1891 to manage Sunnyside and the wineshop. On 20 July 1892 he married at Beechworth, Victoria, a Scottish migrant, Elizabeth Aitken Dewar (1868-1943).

Moving to Junee late in 1895, McWilliam obtained a colonial wine licence and opened a wine-saloon near the railway junction, before establishing his Markview vineyard and winery nearby. A model farmer and vigneron, he ambitiously took up colonial wine licences at Goulburn (1907) and Sydney (1910) and bought a dwelling at Manly; but in a district of low rainfall he was unable to stimulate the growing of wine-grapes sufficiently to support the expansion of his business.

On 2 August 1913 McWilliam successfully applied for two fifty-acre (20 ha) farms for his son Jack and himself on the Mirrool No. 1 Area, Murrumbidgee Irrigation Area. He planted a cash crop and about 35 000 vine-cuttings from Junee as a nursery from which he planted a vineyard in 1914 and offered cuttings to other settlers; he began constructing a winery in 1917. His son Douglas joined the partnership in 1922 when construction began on a second winery at Yenda to process the grapes of soldier settlers. McWilliam's example, his market for wine-grapes and his demonstration that the M.I.A. could produce both fortified and light wines from the classic European varieties tilted the balance of plantings in the area towards wine-grape vines.

Despite competition from other companies in the 1920s McWilliam became the principal purchaser of local wine-grapes but, insisting that their long-term prosperity depended on the success of his firm in the market-place, he refused to give contracts to grape-growers and negotiated prices annually. He obtained the Water Conservation and Irrigation Commission's permission to defer payments (1925) and eschewed the Commonwealth schedule prices and the wine export bounty, giving his business a competitive edge.

In a period threatening over-supply J. J. McWilliam & Sons marketed aggressively from their Sydney cellars (managed from 1928 by the third son Keith), established branches at Goulburn, Orange, Brookvale, Melbourne, Brisbane and in New Zealand, and acquired colonial wine licences and premises for direct sales. On 6 July 1931 McWilliam's Wines Ltd was registered with nominal capital of £200 000. Next year McWilliam's Wines Ltd established, with the trustee of the O'Shea estate, Mount Pleasant Wines Ltd at Pokolbin in the Hunter valley and at Newcastle. When he sold his shares in 1945 to his four sons, McWilliam had presided over an expansion of production to more than 1.5 million gallons (6.8m litres) a year; assets including subsidiary distributing companies were valued at £665 215 and combined annual turnover exceeded £1 million.

The rise of McWilliam's Wines to one of Australia's top five wine-companies was due to sound technology, to which the founder contributed outstanding viticultural practice and expertise in ferro-concrete construction for small vat fermentation and extensive storage; to his vision of a nation-wide enterprise and his example of self-denial as a first principle of capital accumulation; and to his marketing skills. He also bequeathed to his sons remarkable force of character which they presented in their own areas of responsibility.

McWilliam was a large-framed, good-humoured man with a booming voice. A native son, he had the energy and vision of a pioneer and a deep affection for the bush. He despised sloth and his travel letters (1934) reveal the pride and prejudices of Australians of his time. Survived by his four sons and four daughters, he died at Manly on 25 May 1951 and was cremated with Presbyterian forms. He left his personal estate, valued for probate at £36 679, to his daughters.

Irrigation Record, 1913-17; J. J. McWilliam, Travel letters, 1934 (held by Mrs J. Sheidow, Fairlight, NSW); L. Evans, The house of McWilliam (MS, held by author, Camberwell, Melb); McWilliams Wines Pty Ltd, Company records, 1912-45; Water Conservation and Irrigation Com, Records 1912-45 (NSWA).   LLOYD EVANS

McWILLIAMS, WILLIAM JAMES (1860?-1929), journalist and politician, was born probably in 1860 in southern Tasmania, youngest of eleven children of Thomas Cole McWilliams and his wife Sarah, both Irish born. Although officially recorded as a Church of England farm labourer, Thomas was a bounty immigrant of 1855 who with his wife was recruited to take charge of the Franklin school. Trained for the teaching profession, William at 20 became a journalist on the *Tasmanian Mail*, then joined the *Examiner* as parliamentary reporter. On 19 October 1893 at Christ Church, South Yarra, Melbourne, he married a widow Josephine Fullerton, née Hardy.

At 27 McWilliams was editor of the relatively radical Launceston *Telegraph*, advocating unimproved land taxes and reduced custom duties. Elected to the House of Assembly for the northern rural seat of Ringarooma in December 1893, he supported Sir Edward Braddon [q.v.7] at the 1897 election but became a member of the 'Corner Group', which opposed the encroachment by the Legislative Council on the rights of the assembly.

McWilliams always had a ready appreciation of the needs of his constituents, particularly those in rural areas, such as a water-supply for Scottsdale and a railway extension to Ringarooma. He was a member of select committees on railway issues and unemployment, a possible sugar-beet industry, a meteorological bureau and the 1896 education bill. McWilliams advocated voting and electoral reforms, including universal suffrage, opposed legalization of Tattersalls, and introduced unsuccessful bills for a referendum of women on their franchise and to limit salaries of all government employees except judges, ministers and the governor, to £500 annually. He argued against Federation as premature, resisted any suggestion of the Commonwealth having power to affect the appointment of State governors, and raised other constitutional issues concerning royal assent.

On 4 May 1897 McWilliams and T. Ryan convened a meeting at which the Southern Tasmanian Football Association (Australian Rules) was formed. By adopting new rules following those of the newly formed Victorian Football League (eighteen men to a team and six points for a goal), the meeting ensured the survival of the game in Tasmania as part of the national code.

Having bought the Hobart evening *Tasmanian News* in 1896, McWilliams abandoned Ringarooma for Glenorchy in 1900 but was defeated. However, he won the Federal seat of Franklin in 1903 and, three times unopposed, held it until defeated in 1922. In the early Commonwealth parliaments he opposed Federal expenditures: establishment of the High Court of Australia, the Transcontinental Railway, a Federal department of agriculture, the Inter-state Commission, 'the capital in the bush' and acquisition of the Northern Territory. Described as a 'geographical protectionist' because he supported the Free Trade group in the early parliaments, McWilliams was particularly active on behalf of the fruit, potato and timber industries, but opposed bounties for butter, cotton and sugar. He resisted the navigation bill but supported a proposal requiring shipping companies to insure freight. In 1906 he opposed preferential voting but later became a strong supporter.

Although advocating a time-limit on speeches he affirmed the rights of the parliament against the ministry. Strongly pro-British he urged Imperial preference and British immigration and favoured White Australia. He embraced country issues, urging better pay for non-official postmasters and opposing the charging of guarantees for remote telephone extensions.

McWilliams was a member of select committees on Tasmanian customs leakage (1910-11), powellising of timber (1913) and sea carriage (1920); of the royal commissions on the pearl-shelling industry (1912) and Cockatoo Island dockyard (1921); and was prominent on the Parliamentary Recruiting Committee during World War I.

When the Federal Country Party was formed in 1920 McWilliams was appointed its first leader, according to (Sir) Earle Page [q.v.] 'because of his Parliamentary background, his knowledge of procedure and the habits and characteristics of political friends and enemies'. To the *Tasmanian Mail* his choice was 'an indication that the Country Party will not always be content to keep the Hughes [q.v.9] Ministry in power'. In his first speech as leader McWilliams stressed that 'there has been no collusion, we crave no alliance, we spurn no support but we intend drastic action to secure closer attention to the needs of primary producers'. In the 1920 censure motion against the Hughes government McWilliams supported the Labor Party whereas most of his party supported Hughes. According to Page, who replaced him as leader in April 1921, 'he had shown an increasing tendency to vote against the majority'. Narrowly defeated at the 1922 and 1925 elections he won back his old seat in 1928, 'with the quiet support of the Labor Party', as an Independent Nationalist. He was one of the dissidents, marshalled by Hughes, who cast a crucial vote against the Bruce [q.v.7]-Page government on the arbitration bill, and in the consequent 1929 election he was returned with the active support of Labor.

After suffering from angina pectoris McWilliams died suddenly on 22 October 1929, in Hobart, within hours of the declaration of the poll. He was survived by his wife, a son and two daughters. He had been a member of the Anglican Synod. McWilliams was a man of independent mind and political skill with considerable communication abilities.

Cyclopedia of Tasmania, 1 (Hob, 1900); E. C. G. Page, *Truant surgeon*, A. Mozley ed (Syd, 1963); R. K. Pinchin, *A century of Tasmanian football, 1879-1979* (Hob, 1979); *V&P* (HA Tas), 1895, p 40, 60, 171, 218, 1896, p 33, 45, 139, 283, 1897, p 155, 1898, p 41, 1899, p 204, 235, 259; *Mercury*, 8 Nov 1905, 23 Oct 1929; *Punch* (Melb), 25 July 1912, 26 Aug 1920; *Tas Mail*, 26 Feb 1920; *Aust Worker* and *SMH*, 23 Oct 1929; information from Miss J. Read, Battery Point, Tas.

W. A. NEILSON

MADDEN, SIR FRANK (1847-1921) and WALTER (1848-1925), politicians, were born on 29 November 1847 and 16 December 1848 at Cork, Ireland, third and fourth sons of John Madden, solicitor, and his wife Margaret Eloise, née Macoboy, and younger brothers of (Sir) John Madden [q.v.]. The brothers were educated in London, where their father set up practice in 1850, and at Beauchamps, Normandy, France. In January 1857 the family arrived in Melbourne where the brothers continued their education at St Patrick's College, East Melbourne.

After a stint as a jackeroo at St Enoch's station near Skipton, Frank Madden prepared for a career as a solicitor. He attended law lectures at the University of Melbourne as a non-matriculated student in 1865-67 and was admitted as attorney in 1869. Practising in Collins Street, he supplemented his early income by selling pen-and-ink sketches, particularly of horses for which he and Walter both had a lifelong passion. Founder of the legal firm of Madden & Butler, he served a

term as president of the Law Institute in 1886-87 and also as chairman of the board of examiners for attorneys. On 10 October 1874 at St Peter's, Eastern Hill, he married Annie Eliza, daughter of James Goodall Francis [q.v.4].

Walter Madden, who was intended for the navy, served as a midshipman in the man-of-war, *Victoria*, and studied marine surveying. In 1866 he joined the survey department of the Lands Office, becoming in 1873 district surveyor for Horsham. He returned to Melbourne in 1879 to set up in business as a surveyor, valuer and financial agent. Elected to the Legislative Assembly for Wimmera in 1880, he was president of the board of land and works and commissioner of crown lands and survey in the O'Loghlen [q.v.5] ministry of 1881-83. Representing the concern of his constituents at the rabbit plague and the 'desolation' of the Mallee, he carried the Land Acts Continuation and Amendment Act to facilitate prompt occupation of the Mallee country. For the remainder of his parliamentary career until his defeat in 1894 he was a conservative back-bencher and a leader of one of the country groups in the assembly. He spoke on issues affecting his constituency (after 1889 Horsham), especially irrigation, land settlement, railways, rabbits and agricultural education. He served as a member of royal commissions on land titles and surveys (1884), water supply (1885) and the extension of Melbourne westward (1887), and was vice-president of the vegetable products commission (1885), set up at his instigation.

In May 1894, a few months before the close of Walter's parliamentary career, Frank Madden entered the Legislative Assembly as member for Eastern Suburbs (after 1904 Boroondara). He had unsuccessfully contested a Mornington by-election as a Constitutionalist in 1886. Forthright, angular, tactless and pugnacious, he soon earned a reputation, even in his 'Corner', as 'impossible'. Frock-coated and waistcoated, his 'sturdy, deep-chested figure, his full, round head and firm jaw told of his fighting spirit'. His opinions were extremely conservative and laissez-faire: he believed that the state was bound to impart only the 'rudiments of education'; he opposed women's suffrage on the grounds that female voters would support the minimum wage and the eight-hour day, and abolish 'soldiers and war', 'racing, hunting, football, cricket and all such manly games'.

Frank Madden's extremism helps to explain why he never held ministerial office and why, perhaps, some of his conservative colleagues sought to escape political embarrassment by acquiescing in his long term as Speaker of the Legislative Assembly (1904-17). As Speaker he was regarded as 'firm, impartial and urbane', but his combative personality ensured that the traditional Speaker's detachment did not muzzle entirely his forthright opinions. In 1915 *Punch* observed that Madden 'does not woo his electors. He tells them to vote for him or not, but not to mistake his views'. Liberal-minded candidates sought to unseat him; he survived the 1908 election by a mere eleven votes and there were bitter recriminations at the declaration of the poll. To many of his opponents he was a renegade who had repudiated his Catholic heritage and opposed Irish nationalism. An outspoken supporter of conscription, Madden commented after the Easter uprising of 1916 that 'it was a pity that the authorities could not shoot a few [Sinn Feiners] in Australia', and he urged the deportation of Archbishop Mannix [q.v.]. He paid dearly for his hysterical outbursts: his parliamentary career ended in 1917 when he was defeated at the polls.

Like his brother Walter, Frank Madden took a keen interest in the land. For some years he owned properties in the Curdie's River district where he experimented in growing grasses, and in 1895 he published a pamphlet, *Grass lands of Victoria*. An enthusiastic hunter, he followed, with his wife, the Waldock and Melbourne hounds. Although opposed to the totalizator and not himself a betting man, he served for many years on the Victoria Racing Club committee. A member of the Field Naturalists' Club from 1902 and foundation president of the (Royal) Historical Society of Victoria, he was knighted in 1911. Sir Frank Madden died at his mansion home on the heights of Kew on 17 February 1921 and was buried in Boroondara cemetery with Anglican rites. His wife, son and five daughters survived him; his estate was valued for probate at £10 464.

After his parliamentary defeat in 1894 Walter Madden continued as managing director of National Trustees, Executors & Agency Co. to which he had been appointed in 1889, and was a board-member of the National Mutual Life Association of Australasia Ltd from 1897. Genial and phlegmatic, a man of strict integrity, he had few enemies and many friends. He had remained a loyal Catholic. He died unmarried at his brother Henry's home, Travancore, at Flemington on 3 August 1925 and was buried in Melbourne general cemetery; his estate was valued at £6358.

A. Sutherland et al, *Victoria and its metropolis*, 2 (Melb, 1888); A. Henderson (ed), *Australian families*, I (Melb, 1941); E. Dunsdorfs, *The Australian wheat-growing industry 1788-1948* (Melb, 1956); N. Brennan, *Dr. Mannix* (Adel, 1964), and *John Wren, gambler* (Melb, 1976); V&P (LA Vic), 1891, 1 (4); *Vic Naturalist*, 37, no 11 (Mar 1921); *VHM*, 3, no 2 (May 1921); *Argus*, 7 July 1869, 16 Aug 1888, 18 Feb 1921, 4 Aug 1925; *Punch* (Melb), 25 May 1905, 20 July 1911, 22 Aug 1915; *Age*, 18 Feb 1921, 4 Aug 1925; *A'sian*, 26 Feb 1921; *Bulletin*, 13 Aug 1925.   S. M. INGHAM

MADDEN, SIR JOHN (1844-1918), chief justice, was born on 16 May 1844 at Cloyne, County Cork, Ireland, eldest surviving of seven sons of Catholic parents John Madden, attorney from 1848, and his wife Margaret Eloise, née Macoboy. Madden senior was manager of Ark Life Insurance Co. in London for three years before the family migrated to Melbourne, arriving in January 1857. He was admitted as attorney in the Supreme Court of Victoria on 9 April. A great racing man, although he never placed a bet, he contributed hunting notes to the *Australasian* for many years before his death in 1902.

John junior attended preparatory school in London and the Marist College at Beauchamps, France; he mastered the French language and learned some Italian and German. In Melbourne the Madden brothers attended St Patrick's College. John later recorded fond memories of this school but confessed that, in his early years, he preferred outdoor activity to study. He matriculated at the University of Melbourne in 1861, graduating B.A. with third-class honours in 1864 and LL.B. with the Billings medal as one of the first four law graduates in 1865.

After serving articles with (Sir) Edward Holroyd [q.v.4], Madden was called to the Bar on 14 September. He failed his LL.D. examination in 1868 but persevered and was the first admitted to that degree, in 1869. He had early success at the Bar (helped by having a father and two brothers, David and (Sir) Frank [q.v.], in practice as solicitors) and on 27 August 1872 at St Mary's Church of England, Caulfield, he married Gertrude Frances Stephen, a great-niece of Sir Alfred Stephen [q.v.6]; they had six daughters and one son.

In 1871 Madden unsuccessfully contested West Bourke for the Legislative Assembly. A conservative and free trader, he won the seat in 1874 but was defeated next year, after accepting the office of minister of justice in the McCulloch [q.v.5] administration. His reactionary stance in October in favour of the retention of property qualifications for Legislative Council electors, coupled with his condemnation of the bulk of mankind as too stupid to be entrusted with 'the rights of property', led to fierce onslaughts against him by the Catholic *Advocate* and the *Age* and helped to lose him his seat. He remained a member of the ministry, however, and after winning Sandridge (Port Melbourne) in a by-election in July 1876 held that seat until 1883. He was again minister of justice in the Service [q.v.6] ministry (March to August 1880).

Madden disliked the concept of a labour bureau, believing that men should 'go about the country' seeking work themselves. He opposed loans to selectors in 1878 and lent uncritical support to the felons' apprehension bill, to enable the Kellys [q.v.5 E. Kelly] to be shot down like kangaroos. In 1880, however, convinced that a miscarriage of justice had taken place, he pressed in the assembly for the prerogative of mercy to be extended to J. F. Laurence, then under sentence of death. In August 1882 Madden and his brothers William and Walter [q.v.] were named by the *Age* as partners in a land and railway fraud. Vigorous denials in the House by Madden met the allegations, and it seemed that the newspaper had blundered.

Madden was enormously busy in the decade after 1883. In his early years he had specialized in Equity but he soon moved into general law. Many qualities were attributed to him as a barrister: learning, meticulous preparation, mastery of practice, grasp of facts and forthright common sense. These, along with his polished diction, persuasive voice, pleasing smile, good humour, courtesy and self-confidence, helped to make him 'a brilliant advocate and formidable legal gladiator'. (Sir) Frederic Eggleston [q.v.8], however, summed him up as a man 'able to conceal the shallowness of his mind very successfully'.

The doyen of the Bar for many years, along with J. L. Purves [q.v.5], Madden in 1890 engaged in 150 of the 506 cases heard in the Supreme Court and undertook about the same number in the Full Court. *Table Talk* criticized barristers of his kind who made 'most of their money by accepting so many briefs that they cannot possibly stay in Court all the time a case lasts'. Madden's annual income at the height of his career has been estimated as between £7000 and £20 000, hence his refusal of two offers of a puisne judgeship. He vehemently opposed legislation for the amalgamation of the professions of solicitor and barrister, arguing that barristers, as potential judges, should remain aloof from the public (though he never observed this dictum himself) and that amalgamation would make law more costly. His assault on the implementation of the Legal Profession Practice Act (1891) rendered it largely abortive. *Table Talk* maintained that barristers like Madden and Purves fought the Act from fear that it would expose them to well-deserved charges of negligence.

When 48 Madden accepted the chief justiceship, at £3500 a year, and was sworn in on 10 January 1893. This occasioned much astonishment, (Sir) Hartley Williams [q.v.6] having been tipped to succeed Higinbotham [q.v.4]; Williams wrote a furious letter to the *Argus* slating the appointment. Perhaps Mad-

den's political outlook and experience contributed to his success, as well as his general presence: 'that dapper man with good manners and charm', Dame Mabel Brookes recalled. The *Bulletin* later suggested that the appointment was a gift from Premier Shiels [q.v.] to his friend.

Madden's obituarists did not see him as a great judge. The *Argus* wrote that 'his application of legal rules to the issues found was not always as clear and precise as the acuteness of his mind would have led one to expect'. His old enemy the *Age* said that 'his decisions did not always carry conviction in the minds of his brother jurists'. Certainly many of his decisions were reversed by the Full Court. His colleague Holroyd was openly disturbed by the uncritical manner in which the new chief justice paved the way for the reconstruction of the Commercial Bank in 1893. Nor was Madden without critics that year when his decision freed F. Millidge and Sir Matthew Davies [q.v.4], two fraudulent 'land-boomers'. Madden's judgment in Wollaston's [q.v.] case (1902), concerning income tax, was described by Andrew Inglis Clark [q.v.3] as 'full of false history, bad political science, bad political economy, bad logic and bad law'. Some of his judgments were laced with humour and others with pontification; his concern for women was frequently apparent. The loquacity of Madden 'the garrulous' was underlined in a judgment lasting eight hours, reputedly the longest on record in the Supreme Court.

Madden was appointed lieut-governor in 1899, having acted as governor with great aplomb at various times from 1893. His most publicized action in this capacity was his signing of the proclamation which declared the week beginning 1 May 1893 a 'banking holiday'. He adhered strictly to constitutional usage, refusing to grant Sir George Turner [q.v.] a dissolution in December 1899.

Madden preserved links with the University of Melbourne. In 1864 he had been acting-registrar for five weeks; in the early 1870s he helped to administer matriculation examinations and in 1873 he applied unsuccessfully for a lectureship. In 1875-82 he was warden of the senate. He was a member of the council from 1879, though he was removed for non-attendance for a period in 1885. In 1889 the council elected Madden unpaid vice-chancellor, despite the justified qualms of H. B. Higgins [q.v.9] that he would not devote the requisite time to the job. He resisted most proposals to modernize university government, though he favoured the scheme for a paid full-time vice-chancellor. In this context, a well-publicized confrontation took place in 1890-91 with the youthful Professor Edward Jenks [q.v.9]. Madden succeeded Sir Anthony Brownless [q.v.3] as chancellor in 1897. He was noted for his eloquent speeches, his skill in chairing committees, and his unwillingness to interfere with departments. A traditionalist, he did, however, in 1911 urge the retention of Latin in the law course.

Knighted in 1893, Madden was appointed K.C.M.G. in 1899 and G.C.M.G. in 1906. Lady Casey spoke of his 'wide Irish face' and his 'moustache stiffly waxed in points'; sometimes he wore pince-nez. A keen sportsman, though illness forced him to abandon strenuous effort after 1903, he had been a foxhunter, boxer and rower. He had also correctly and profitably dreamed the winner of the 1887 Melbourne Cup. He was fond of functions where he could exercise his pleasing wit, and enjoyed being patron of the Victorian Lacrosse Association and president of the Victorian Amateur Athletic Association, the Olympic Sporting Federation and the Savage Club (1911-18). He was a loyalist and Imperialist and deemed it proper, while chief justice, actively to support recruitment for the South African War and conscription during World War I. His Catholicism was not much evident and 'he never took any interest in the doings of his compatriots'.

In 1887-1913 Madden lived at Cloyne, a splendid St Kilda mansion where lavish entertainment abounded. He was an indulgent father. Leisure periods saw the family at their country property Yamala, Frankston, where Madden produced hay and dairy goods, and enjoyed his farming, gardening, carpentry and house-painting. He spent the last five years of his life at Cliveden Mansions, East Melbourne. He died, suddenly, on 10 March 1918 at South Yarra, survived by his wife and children and leaving an estate valued for probate at £29 082; he was buried in the Catholic section of Melbourne general cemetery. Lady Madden, president of the Bush Nursing Association and the Austral Salon, died in 1925.

J. L. Forde, *The story of the Bar of Victoria* (Melb, 1913); P. A. Jacobs, *Famous Australian trials and memories of the law* (Melb, 1944) and *A lawyer tells* (Melb, 1949); P. S. Cleary, *Australia's debt to Irish nation-builders* (Syd, 1933); G. Blainey, *A centenary history of the University of Melbourne* (Melb, 1957); M. Casey, *An Australian story, 1837-1907* (Lond, 1962); M. Brookes, *Riders of time* (Melb, 1967); A. Dean, *A multitude of counsellors* (Melb, 1968); R. Campbell, *A history of the Melbourne Law School, 1857 to 1973* (Melb, 1977); H. Rutledge (ed), *A season in India* (Syd, 1976); *Age*, 27 Oct 1875, 5, 6 Jan 1893, 11 Mar 1918; *Argus*, 28 Oct 1875, 9 Jan 1893, 11, 12 Mar 1918; *Table Talk*, 13 Jan 1893, 13 June 1901; *Weekly Times*, 14 Jan 1893; *Bulletin*, 20 Jan, 21 Apr 1900; *Punch* (Melb), 3 Sept 1903, 20 Apr 1905, 1 June 1911; F. W. Eggleston, Confidential notes (Menzies Lib, ANU).   RUTH CAMPBELL

MADDOCK, SARAH (1860-1955), cyclist, was born on 29 October 1860 at Wolumla, near Eden, New South Wales, daughter of James Porter, stockman, and his wife Mary, née Sullivan. Raised on a dairy farm and educated locally, she became a competent horsewoman. A childhood accident left her blind in one eye. On 22 February 1886 at St James' Church, Sydney, she married Ernest Alfred Maddock (d.1935), a solicitor's clerk, and by 1890 had three children.

Encouraged by her husband, who had begun cycling in England before migrating, Sarah Maddock began riding a bicycle in 1893, and after several months accompanied him on a 300-mile (483 km) ride from Sydney to Bega, averaging 60 miles (97 km) a day. Her trip was reported as the first long-distance ride by an Australian woman. Next year this achievement was eclipsed by a 574-mile (924 km) ride from Sydney to Melbourne, accomplished in nine days, their progress monitored by local bicycle clubs. Mrs Maddock rode a 30 lb (14 kg) Conqueror safety machine with dropped frame, gearbox and pneumatic tyres. The first woman to attempt such a feat, she was escorted into the city with her husband by members of the Melbourne Bicycle Club.

Despite poor roads, bushfires, tropical downpours and creeks which had to be forded, the Maddocks completed a 1600-mile (2570 km) round trip to Brisbane in 1895; she rode an imported New Rapid machine. The return, through New England, took 9½ days, averaging 80 miles (129 km) a day. The Sydney Bicycle Club, of which she had been made an honorary member, presented her with a gold medal.

At a time when woman cyclists provoked heated controversy, Sarah Maddock disarmed critics by her grace, style and 'sweet womanliness'. Described by one commentator as 'a graceful light-weight with a poetically pale visage', she was tall, slim and fine featured, with a quiet, reserved and self-effacing manner. Unlike some other female enthusiasts, she rejected 'rational dress', asserting that the most suitable costume for cycling was a skirt, worn with 'black satin under knickerbockers', which allowed it to 'fall gracefully into place after each stroke of the knee'. While recognizing the 'extreme folly and danger of riding tightly dressed about the waist', she advised that 'stays should by no means be discarded'.

Inspired by Sarah Maddock's example and reassured by journals and magazines as to the popularity of cycling among their counterparts in Europe and America, many women in Victoria and New South Wales took to their bicycles. A women's club was formed in Melbourne shortly after her visit and in February 1895 seven women met at Quong Tart's [q.v.5] tea-rooms to form the Sydney Ladies' Bicycle Club with Mrs Maddock as captain. Next year she estimated that there were 1000 women cyclists in New South Wales. In 1897 she formed a second women's club, the Stanmore Wheelers. About forty women also joined her as members of the new and predominantly male Cyclists' Touring Union. Writing in its *Cycling Gazette*, Sarah Maddock assured readers that such associations encouraged 'platonic friendships', a sound basis for marriage.

Sarah Maddock's life did not follow her convictions. From 1914 she lived apart from her husband, devoting herself to her family and furthering her skills as a golfer, embroiderer and woodcarver. Active still, she died on 9 September 1955 at a daughter's home at Double Bay, Sydney, and was cremated with Anglican rites; her son and two daughters survived her.

F. G. C. H. Hanslow, *Australian Cycling Annual*, 1896 (Syd, 1897); J. Fitzpatrick, *The bicycle and the bush* (Melb, 1980); *NSW Cycling Gazette*, 19 Nov, 5 Dec 1896, 2 Jan, 10 Apr, 14 Aug 1897; *SMH*, 4 Dec 1935; information and newscuttings from Mrs D. Mane, Bellevue Hill, Syd.

DIANE LANGMORE

MADIGAN, CECIL THOMAS (1889-1947), geologist and explorer, was born on 15 October 1889 at Renmark, South Australia, son of Thomas Madigan, contractor and fruit-grower, and his wife Mary Dixie, née Finey. Cecil was the eldest of two sons and two daughters. Family associations with the pioneer William Chaffey [q.v.7] were close. Thomas Madigan died on the Kalgoorlie, Western Australia, goldfields so the children were raised by their mother who worked as a teacher. Cecil attended Adelaide High School and, on a scholarship, Prince Alfred College before studying mining engineering at the University of Adelaide (B.Sc., 1910, surrendered 1932 for B.Eng.), where he graduated as an exhibitioner, and the South Australian School of Mines and Industries. In 1911 Madigan went as a Rhodes scholar to England, but deferred the appointment when he was selected by (Sir) Douglas Mawson [q.v.] as meteorologist for the Australasian Antarctic Expedition.

Madigan was to install and read the meteorological instruments during the two-year project. He made several exploratory sledge journeys from the base camp at Denison Station, Adelie Land; on one, his party reconnoitred the ice plateau in winter, experiencing record cold and wind. In the summer of 1912-13 Madigan led the eastern sledging party which traversed the sea-ice and coastline of King George V Land, a round journey of 500 miles (805 km), which took two months. Overcoming many near-disasters, the party collected significant data on the ice, and discovered a coal-bearing rock formation. His account is in his chapter of Mawson's *The home of the blizzard* (London, 1915). Madigan's journey had coincided with Mawson's southern sledging party during which his two companions perished and Mawson struggled back alone to base camp only to miss the relief ship. Madigan led the group which had remained behind to wait for Mawson's return or to mount a search for him. Madigan received the King's Polar Medal in 1914 and published *The meteorology of Cape Denison, Adelie Land* in the records of the expedition (1929).

After one term at Oxford in 1914 he joined the Royal Engineers, 76th Field Company, Guards Division, becoming captain in 1916. He served in France and was twice mentioned in dispatches. 'A fine looking, broad-shouldered fellow' of 6 ft. 3 ins. (191 cm), on 20 August 1915 in London Madigan had married Wynnis Knight Wollaston of Adelaide; he returned to the front immediately, was wounded, and after recuperating went back to France in May 1916. Their first son was born in July.

After demobilization he returned to Magdalen College, Oxford (B.A., 1919; M.A., 1922; D.Sc., 1933), taking first-class honours in geology and winning blues in rowing and boxing. In 1920 he went as assistant government geologist to the Sudan where he first encountered deserts and the use of camels in geological field operations. He returned in 1922 to the University of Adelaide as lecturer in geology, a post he held until his death.

A renewed friendship with Mawson, now professor of geology and mineralogy, coloured Madigan's academic career; both were heroic exploration geologists, of striking stature, vigour and personality; keen to succeed scientifically, they divided fields of interest—Madigan's arid central Australia, Mawson's the Antarctic and Precambrian South Australia. They influenced each other importantly. Their pupils regarded them with awe and affection. Madigan supported the students' union and the graduates' association and founded the Tate [q.v.6] Society for students of the natural sciences whom he led in the field during vacations.

His initial South Australian research centred on Fleurieu Peninsula; the results appeared in papers published in the Royal Society of South Australia's *Transactions* in 1925-28. In 1929 he won the support of the State branch of the Royal Geographical Society of Australasia and its president A. A. Simpson, and the co-operation of the Royal Australian Air Force for aerial reconnaissance of Central Australia and northern South

Australia. This was the first time that systematic aerial strip-photography had been attempted in Australia and aeroplanes used for geological work. The surveys, in August, took nineteen days. The first covered the mines at Broken Hill, New South Wales, followed by a traverse across Lake Frome to Marree, then over the other dry salt-lakes—Callabonna, Blanche, Gregory, Torrens and Eyre, all in South Australia. The next flight ran north-easterly to Birdsville, Queensland, and the margin of what Madigan named the Simpson Desert. Three flights were then made over it, the first from Birdsville to Alice Springs, the second across the northern end to Lake Caroline and the Hay River, and the third south from Alice Springs, traversing the desert's length near its western margin. The party then ran several traverses across the vast, dry, salt bed of Lake Eyre and attempted to analyse the lake surface.

The aerial reconnaissance of Lake Eyre aroused Madigan's curiosity about this lowest area of the Australian continent, the focus of a vast drainage system bounded by the Mac-Donnell Ranges and the Queensland coastal ranges, a watershed of almost 500 000 square miles (1 295 000 km²). It seemed that the lake-bed might be accessible to a motor vehicle, so in December he made a ground survey and several auger holes were sunk in the lake surface. The results of the aerial reconnaissance and the Lake Eyre (ground) exploration were published in the local Geographical Society's *Proceedings*, 1929, and in the *Geographical Journal*, 1930. Madigan calculated that the whole lake-floor could never be covered by water; he would have been astonished and delighted by several total floodings since his death.

In mid-1930 he journeyed by camel through the MacDonnell, James and Waterhouse ranges and established their geological succession and structure. The results of this and earlier work were published in a series of papers and he wrote a popular account, *Central Australia* (London, 1936). Commissioned in 1932 by Sydney newspapers, Madigan had reported adversely on an alleged major gold discovery at the Granites, Central Australia. About 1933 he began to describe meteorites and their craters. He visited the Henbury and Boxhole craters in the Northern Territory and recovered and described the Huckitta meteorite, now in the South Australian Museum.

The Simpson is a sand-ridge desert extending 200 miles (320 km) west to east, the ridges running parallel from north to south at roughly quarter-mile intervals, some reaching as high as 100 feet (30 m). Madigan planned a ground crossing in the winter of 1939. A party of nine, including a biologist, a botanist, a photographer and a radio operator, with nineteen camels, made the exhausting crossing from Andado station in the Northern Territory to Birdsville in twenty-five days. It verified Madigan's previous conclusions that the area was a wasteland. This last classic Australian exploration adventure pioneered the use of mobile radio communication; national broadcasts were made through the Australian Broadcasting Commission from desert camps. The scientific results were published and also a popular account, *Crossing the dead heart* (Melbourne, 1946). He saw the 'Dead Heart' as a land of everlasting sand-ridges and salt-encrusted clay-pans; while his conclusions seemed correct then, within twenty years the area was criss-crossed by petroleum explorers.

In 1940 Madigan became chief instructor in the School of Military Field Engineering at Liverpool, New South Wales, attaining the rank of lieut-colonel. Later he reported on water resources. He retired from the army in 1943 and returned to the University of Adelaide.

Madigan was a fellow of the Geological Society of London; president of the Royal Society of South Australia (1936), a council-member and its Verco [q.v.] medallist (1945); president of the geographical section of the Australian and New Zealand Association for the Advancement of Science (1937); and Clarke [q.v.3] memorial lecturer to the Royal Society of New South Wales (1938). He received the Murchison grant of the Royal Geographical Society in 1941 and was a local councillor of the Royal Geographical Society of Australasia in 1939-46. He was State chief commissioner of the Boy Scouts' Association from 1934 and also worked for the Legacy Club and the National Co-ordinating Council for Physical Fitness.

He died in Adelaide of coronary vascular disease on 14 January 1947 and was buried in Centennial Park cemetery; his wife, two daughters and three sons survived him.

Madigan bridged the period between the era of intrepid endeavour and that of modern transport and communications; his work in the MacDonnell Ranges, the Simpson Desert and Lake Eyre made him an authority on central Australian geology and geography. In teaching he concentrated on practical geology and, at a time when the discipline was mainly academic, introduced students to its mining, engineering and economic implications, which later became major preoccupations. In 1962 at Birdsville a cairn was erected to commemorate his 1939 crossing of the Simpson Desert.

Roy Soc SA, *Trans*, 71 (1947), p 1; *Nature* (Lond), 15 Mar 1947; *PRGSSA*, 48 (1947), p 67; *News* (Adel), 14 Jan 1947; *Advertiser* (Adel), 15 Jan

1947; PRG 43 (SAA); information from Sir R. Madigan, Melb.   L. W. PARKIN

MADSEN, SIR JOHN PERCIVAL VAISSING (VISSING) (1879-1969), physicist and engineer, was born on 24 March 1879 at Lochinvar, New South Wales, eldest of six children of Hans Frandsen Madsen, Danish surveyor, and his native-born wife Annie, née Bush. Educated at Sydney Boys' High School and the University of Sydney, he graduated B.Sc. in 1900 with the University medal in mathematics, and B.E. in 1901 with first-class honours and the University medal.

In 1901 Madsen was appointed lecturer in mathematics and physics at the University of Adelaide, where he came under the influence of Professor (Sir) William Henry Bragg [q.v.7] with whom he co-operated and became a lifelong friend. His early studies with Bragg related to radioactivity and X-rays. He was awarded a D.Sc. in 1907, but in 1909 his interest in the practical application of science led him to accept a lectureship in engineering at the University of Sydney, where he became assistant professor in 1912. He had married Maud Foster Molesworth (d. 1932) at Newtown, Sydney, on 24 August 1904.

Commissioned in the Australian Military Forces in April 1915, from 1916, as captain, Madsen was chief instructor and, promoted major in August 1917, officer commanding the Engineer Officers' Training School at Moore Park, and later Roseville, Sydney, until 1918. He was remembered as 'a tiger for regular physical exercises' and commended for the energy and distinction with which he carried out his duties.

Returning to the university, he was foundation professor of electrical engineering in 1920-49. At various times he was dean of the faculty of engineering, chairman of the professorial board and a fellow of the senate. He directed the development of the electrical engineering course in accord with his firm belief that its success in practice depended on a solid base of physical science. He encouraged students to take double degrees in science and engineering, which became mandatory in most cases for those attempting the honours course. Many of those students achieved prominence in research, the development of major industries and government organizations.

Madsen's lectures were unconventional but effective. He wasted little time in retailing information readily available from books and periodicals, but concentrated on relating practical applications to the fundamental principles on which they were based. His students remember his frequent reference to 'costs and losses' even in the middle of an erudite theoretical dissertation. His appreciation of the mutual interaction between teaching and research led him to develop in his department a strong group of engineers and physicists engaged in basic research, mainly in what came to be known as communication engineering. This activity did not always endear him to more conventionally trained engineers in the power-supply industry, who accused him of 'playing with toys', but he persisted and later developments more than justified his determination. Madsen foresaw the rapid growth of the communications industry and fostered it by providing in Australia a solid background of relevant research.

From its foundation in 1926, Madsen began a long and fruitful association with the Council for Scientific and Industrial Research. At its meeting in November he proposed the establishment of the Radio Research Board under the general aegis of C.S.I.R. and supported by the Australian Post Office; he was the board's chairman in 1927-58. Its purpose was to encourage and support research in the universities and provide a link between 'freewheeling' academic research and the more industrially oriented research of C.S.I.R. Although this policy inevitably came under attack by those advocating the central control of research, Madsen persisted in his view that independent research in the universities was an essential component of the national effort. His energy and diplomatic acumen won his point and the independence of the R.R.B.

At the same time Madsen had unsuccessfully proposed the establishment and maintenance of national standards of weights and measures, a function allocated to C.S.I.R. under its Act. In 1936-37 he was a member of the Commonwealth Committee on Secondary Industries Testing and Research, chaired by Sir George Julius [q.v.9]. When, as a result of the committee's recommendations, the National Standards Laboratory was established in the grounds of the university Madsen served as its chairman in 1938-44. Building began in 1939 and the laboratory, after the diversion of its efforts to many wartime activities, proceeded on its prescribed course in 1945.

When World War II broke out, Madsen led Australia's contribution to the allied development of radar and was first chairman of the Radiophysics Advisory Board in 1939-41. The C.S.I.R. radiophysics laboratory was established and its staffing was helped greatly by the existence of suitably trained personnel. Madsen recognized the importance of rapid interchange of information with allied countries, not only in radar but in many diverse fields, and he initiated the establishment of offices in London and Washington, making several overseas visits for this purpose.

After the war Madsen maintained his

active interest in radio research and standards. He had become a member of the C.S.I.R. council in 1944 and when it was reconstituted in 1949 he was a member of the State committee and of the advisory council of the Commonwealth Scientific and Industrial Research Organization. He was first chairman of the National Association of Testing Authorities and of the Electrical Research Board (1945-66), established with the co-operation of the Electricity Supply Association of Australia. He was also chairman of the Australian National Research Council, president of the Australian branch of the Institute of Physics, a member of the Royal Society of New South Wales from 1909 and a fellow of the Institution of Engineers, Australia, and of the Australian Academy of Science.

Madsen, who always sought recognition of the work of his colleagues but never of himself, was knighted in 1941, and awarded the (Sir) Peter Nicol Russell [q.v.6] memorial medal of the Institution of Engineers, Australia, in 1944, and an honorary D.Sc. by the University of Sydney in 1954. Survived by two sons and a daughter, he died on 4 October 1969 at Chatswood and was cremated with Anglican rites. Almost to the day of his death he remained a father figure and wise counsellor to many scientific colleagues. His energy, imagination, persistence and power of persuasion had a profound and lasting effect on many aspects of Australian life.

D. P. Mellor, *The role of science and industry* (Canb, 1958); *Records of the Aust Academy of Science*, 2, no 1, Nov 1970; *SMH*, 5 May 1954; Madsen papers (Basser Lib, Canb).

D. M. MYERS

MAGRATH, EDWARD CRAWFORD (1881-1961), printer, trade unionist and politician, was born on 5 February 1881, at Whitehaven, Cumberland, England, one of nine children of Carleton Magrath, mariner, and his wife Elizabeth, née Trohear. The family migrated to Sydney about 1889 and settled at Balmain where Magrath attended Balmain Superior Public School. At 15 he was apprenticed as a compositor to Turner & Henderson, general printers. He became a journeyman compositor in 1901 and over the next decade worked regularly for several major firms, and as a part-time instructor at Sydney Technical College. On 14 December 1903 he married Gertrude Mary Lodge at the Congregational Church in Pitt Street.

His political education began at home in discussions between his conservative father and his radically inclined mother. Magrath associated with mates who 'borrowed' but 'always returned' light reading matter from W. M.

Hughes's [q.v.9] bookshop, frequented the Balmain Workingman's Institute, developed a voracious appetite for knowledge and soon made his mark in debate. In 1901 he joined the Labor Party and, becoming a shop steward at 22, began to advocate the interests of printing tradesmen and especially apprentices.

In 1908 Magrath was elected to the board of management of the New South Wales Typographical Association. A strong critic of its narrow craft outlook, he was vice-president and president of the union in 1914, organizer in 1914-16, and then secretary of the State branch and vice-president of the Federal council of the Printing Industry Employees' Union of Australia, which absorbed the Typographical Association. The new union was registered in 1916 and was widely publicized as 'the One Big Union of Printers'. Despite his resort to militant phraseology, Magrath was also one of the most businesslike and hard-headed union leaders and disliked the trend towards extremism in the affairs of the Labor Council of New South Wales. He was trade union advocate before the living wage inquiry in 1920, contributed to the apprenticeship inquiry conducted by the Board of Trade, and served as a member of the printing trades advisory committee of Sydney Technical College. In 1924-27 he helped to compile, and successfully pursued in court, the union's complex claim for a Federal award covering the newspaper and printing industry throughout Australia. As a result he was the union's general advocate in 1927-31. He was enthusiastic about the arbitration process but accepted the need for industrial power in reserve.

Magrath was a member of the State central executive of the Labor Party in 1920-22, party vice-president in 1923-25 and State president in 1925-26; he was also a delegate to federal conference in 1926-27. His power base in the Labor Party was firmly established in 1923 when he became president of the Trade Union Secretaries' Association, which operated as a moderate influence on trade unionists, countering the left-wing leadership of the New South Wales Labor Council. With O. Schreiber and T. J. Tyrrell [q.v.] he provided a strong industrial support-base for J. T. Lang's [q.v.9] rise to dominance of the party. He was a director of the *Labor Daily* in 1924-28 and remained a supporter of Lang until they clashed over the future of the *Labor Daily* in 1936.

Magrath was appointed to the Legislative Council in July 1925 and was elected to the reconstituted council for nine years in December 1933. He resigned from the P.I.E.U.A. in 1931 when appointed deputy president of the Industrial Commission of

New South Wales; when the post was abolished in December 1932, Magrath sued the government and was awarded £2900 damages. In 1933 he became federal secretary of the P.I.E.U.A. and resumed his old position as its general advocate. Failing eyesight finally forced him to retire in January 1952. For much of his working life Magrath was separated from his wife. In his quiet retirement he cultivated roses at Maroubra and later Cronulla, before settling in a unit at Brighton-le-Sands. Survived by his wife, three daughters and two sons he died at Kogarah on 7 March 1961. He willed his body to the University of Sydney for medical research.

J. Hagan, *Printers and politics* (Canb, 1966); H. Radi and P. Spearritt (eds), *Jack Lang* (Syd, 1977); *A'sian Printer*, Jan 1952; *Printing Trades J*, Apr 1961; *Aust Worker*, 13 June 1923; *Daily Telegraph* (Syd), 10 July 1925; *SMH*, 25 Sept 1931; information from Mrs Jean Bow, Connells Point, Syd, and Mrs H. Longfield, Hurstville, Syd.

FRANK FARRELL

MAGUIRE, JAMES BERNARD (1895-1951), soldier, was born on 18 August 1895 at Killesher, Fermanagh, Ireland, son of Terrence Maguire, farmer, and his wife Cassie, née Credden. He came to Australia, probably when 14, and was cared for by an uncle. He completed his schooling in Sydney.

Maguire was working as a drapery salesman when he joined the Australian Imperial Force at Randwick on 21 August 1914; he embarked for Egypt in October as a private in the 4th Battalion. He landed at Gallipoli with the battalion on 25 April 1915 and fought there until he was admitted to hospital and evacuated to Malta on 20 October. From there he was sent to England.

The 4th Battalion was serving in France when Maguire rejoined it as a sergeant in August 1916. He distinguished himself next year on 15 April in an action near Demicourt. In command of one of the battalion's posts, which was attacked by a strong enemy force and surrounded, Maguire 'kept his head and by his courage and devotion to duty set such a fine example that few of the enemy escaped' and the attack was repulsed. He was awarded the Distinguished Conduct Medal. At Bullecourt, on 10 May 1917, he was wounded.

Next year at Merris Maguire won a Bar to his D.C.M.: in an attack on enemy positions on the night of 9-10 July 1918, he led a party against a machine-gun post that was harassing his platoon. The gun and two prisoners were captured. Later that night he led a fighting patrol against an enemy party which was forming up to attack; the Germans withdrew under heavy grenade and rifle-fire. His divisional commander reported that 'throughout the action he displayed great courage under very trying circumstances and his personal example was of great value to his platoon'.

Sergeant Maguire returned to Australia with other selected '1914 men' in November and was discharged on 23 January 1919. He established a grocery business at Rushcutters Bay, Sydney. On 17 April 1920 he married Kathleen Lurline May O'Neill at St Mary's Cathedral; this marriage was dissolved on 20 December 1938 and on 28 February 1940 he married Constance Ann Manley at the Sydney Registrar General's Office.

During World War II Maguire enlisted in the Australian Military Forces on 8 July 1940 and was posted to the Small Arms School at Randwick. Too old for overseas service, he became an instructor with the 5th Infantry Training Battalion and, later, the 1st Australian Machine-gun Training Battalion. He attained the rank of warrant officer, class II, before discharge on 27 October 1945.

After the war Maguire was employed as a clerk for a manufacturing company. He died on 13 August 1951 at Sydney Hospital from a cerebral haemorrhage after injuries 'feloniously inflicted' at the Gallipoli Legion Club two days earlier. His wife and four sons from his first marriage survived him. After a service at All Hallows Catholic Church, Five Dock, he was buried in Northern Suburbs cemetery. His portrait by John Longstaff [q.v.] is in the Australian War Memorial.

C. E. W. Bean, *The A.I.F. in France*, 1918 (Syd, 1942); file 749/61/28, War Records Section (AWM); information from Mrs C. Dargan, Tumut, NSW.

PETER BURNESS

MAHOMET, FAIZ (1848?-c.1910), camel-owner and carrier, son of Habbib Allah, was said to be of a wealthy and aristocratic Afghan family. The amir of Afghanistan was his wife's first cousin. He arrived in Australia about 1870 and managed Elder Smith [qq.v.4,6] & Co.'s camel station at Hergott Springs (Marree), South Australia. In 1880 he bought the station and operated it; the firm remained his friends and advisers. Nine years later he took his younger brother Tagh into partnership.

They left for Western Australia in 1892, bringing three steamers of camels from Adelaide and two from India, hoping to capitalize on the demand for camel transport following gold discoveries in the colony's driest regions. Trading as Faiz and Tagh Mahomet, they set up camel stations and shops in Coolgardie, Geraldton, Cue, Day Dawn and Mullewa. The largest was at Coolgardie where they had stores in Bayley Street, the town's main thoroughfare. They performed large government contracts. Faiz often staked miners by providing rations, shared the proceeds from any gold found, and saved the lives of many suffering from thirst and starvation.

He was prominent in civic affairs and both European and Afghan communities respected him. In 1895 he petitioned for the protection of his countrymen's lives and property against threats from hostile Europeans. Two years later Faiz applied for Muslim religious leaders to be allowed to migrate to minister to the growing Islamic community. He even assisted the chief inspector of stock by reporting on camels with lung complaints. Despite his civic usefulness his 1896 request for naturalization was refused.

On 10 January, while praying in the Coolgardie Mosque, Tagh was murdered by fellow Muslim Goulah Mahomet, who claimed to have been threatened by Tagh. Goulah was hanged at Fremantle Prison. Tagh's remains were later sent to Karachi, India, where he left a wife and four children.

Faiz bought out Tagh's estate, but he had a run of bad luck: many of his camels died; some of his best workers left; his new manager Sultan Raz Mahomet cheated him of substantial funds. Faiz tried to recoup by going to Karachi and importing camels from Quetta and Baluchistan in 1900. But the animals were refused entry to Western Australia because of fears of introducing foot and mouth disease and phobia about their Indian handlers. The set-back reduced his finances drastically and cost him his good name in Karachi. A 1902 select committee urged the government to take responsibility for misleading Faiz Mahomet by granting him permission to import, and then withdrawing it.

He became a merchant in Perth and in 1904 organized fellow Muslims to build a mosque there. He contributed heavily from his declining funds and travelled around the State collecting donations. He set the foundation stone on 13 November next year and soon retired, returning to India where he died.

The brothers' work benefited Western Australia; they brought supplies and water to the desolate outback, helping other pioneers to develop the interior.

V&P (WA), 1901-02, 4 (A24), 1902, 2 (A6); *Morning Herald* (Perth), 13 Jan 1896.

A. J. KOUTSOUKIS

MAHON, HUGH (1857-1931), journalist and politician, was born on 6 January 1857 at Killurine, near Tullamore, King's County, Ireland, thirteenth child of James Mahon, farmer, and his wife Anna, née McEvoy. Educated by the Christian Brothers, he was taken to the United States of America with his family in 1867, where, in hard conditions, he learned printing from 'Yankee bloodsuckers'.

Mahon returned to Ireland about 1880 and worked as a reporter at New Ross, Wexford. A political activist, he spent two months in Kilmainham gaol, Dublin, in 1881 with Irish National Land League leaders including Charles Stewart Parnell, but was released with suspected tuberculosis. He fled to London when imprisonment threatened again unless he left the country, and in March 1882 sailed for Australia under an alias as a paid agent of the league. He was one of the managers of a fund-raising tour of the eastern colonies by John and William Redmond [qq.v.6] until September 1883. Mahon edited newspapers in Goulburn, was a political reporter for the Sydney *Daily Telegraph* and briefly owned a paper at Gosford. On 24 September 1888, at Manly, he married Mary Alice L'Estrange of Melbourne. When his wife went to Melbourne for the birth of their second son he sold out, followed her and worked as a freelance journalist. In 1895 he left to edit a paper at Coolgardie, Western Australia. His family temporarily stayed in Melbourne.

Mahon settled at Menzies as the publicly active proprietor of the *Menzies Miner* and in 1897, after a campaign which left him discredited, stood unsuccessfully against his rival H. Gregory [q.v.9] for the new North Coolgardie seat. Driven out by the collapse of the goldfield, as editor of the Kalgoorlie *Sun* in 1899 he persistently denounced the Forrest [q.v.] government and its supporters for corrupt practices and became notorious after a series of libel actions. Active, though not prominent in the Separation for Federation movement, he won the Federal seat of Coolgardie as a Labor candidate in 1901.

Mahon's talent for invective and reputation as an Irish-Catholic patriot made him a useful acquisition to the struggling Labor Party. He was a member of royal commissions on ocean shipping services in 1906 and the pearling industry in 1912-13. As postmaster-general in the Watson [q.v.] ministry in 1904 and minister for home affairs in the Fisher [q.v.8] ministry of 1908-09, he was a competent but routine administrator. Caucus refused by one vote to re-elect him to the ministry in 1910, some preferring Charles Frazer [q.v.8]. Some partisans openly questioned Mahon's record as a Labor man. The *Westralian Worker* found him 'professedly . . . a democrat whose snobbish coldness of demeanour would make a snake shudder'. His electorate having been abolished in a redistribution, Mahon lost the new seat (Dampier) to Gregory in January 1913, but when Frazer died in November he won Kalgoorlie without opposition. Mahon was appointed honorary minister in the 1914

Labor government and, on the death of J. A. Arthur [q.v.7] in December, became minister for external affairs. In an administration again marked by unnecessary antagonisms he had a cool relationship with his departmental head Atlee Hunt [q.v.9], savagely persecuted former prime minister Alfred Deakin [q.v.8], but supported his friend (Sir) Hubert Murray [q.v.] unequivocally in New Guinea. Mahon's hopes of becoming treasurer in 1915 were disappointed.

As managing director of the Catholic Church Property Insurance Co. in 1912-31, he was influential in the Catholic Church and the Irish national movement, and was close to Archbishops Carr [q.v.7] and Mannix [q.v.] as an adviser. He reluctantly joined the radical majority to expel W. M. Hughes [q.v.9] from the Labor party over conscription in 1916 and lost his seat in the 1917 general election. He regained Kalgoorlie for Labor in 1919. Late in 1920, after the death of Terence McSwiney, lord mayor of Cork, Ireland, in a hunger strike, Mahon savagely attacked British policy and the Empire, referring to 'this bloody and accursed despotism', at an Irish Ireland League open-air meeting in Melbourne on 7 November; a motion for the establishment of an Australian republic was passed. The speech created a sensation and led to hostile demonstrations in Melbourne. Citing 'seditious and disloyal utterances', on 11 November Hughes introduced a motion in parliament calling for Mahon's expulsion. Though he contested the details Mahon refused to defend himself in parliament, and, after an extended and passionate debate, he was formally expelled from the House in a procedure unique in the history of the Commonwealth parliament. He then unsuccessfully contested the ensuing by-election.

In 1921 Mahon travelled to Europe and Ireland, returning to Australia in June 1922. Survived by his wife and four children he died on 28 August 1931 at Ringwood, Victoria, and was buried in Box Hill cemetery. He was a 'political conundrum' to contemporaries, who deplored his bitterness and lack of humour, but his absorption with Catholic and Irish affairs was his great consistency.

A. A. Baker, Hugh Mahon's expulsion from parliament (B.A. Hons thesis, ANU, 1967); R. G. Dryen, The significance of the expulsion of Hugh Mahon, M.H.R., from the Federal parliament, 12 November 1920 (B.A. Hons thesis, Univ NSW, 1967); H. J. Gibbney, Hugh Mahon: a political biography (M.A. thesis, ANU, 1970); Mahon papers (NL).   H. J. GIBBNEY

MAHONY, DANIEL JAMES (1878-1944), scientist, was born on 25 March 1878 in East Melbourne, son of Irish-born Daniel Mahony,

formerly mayor of Fitzroy, and his wife Catherine, née Finnigan. Educated at Downside School, Somerset, England, and Xavier College, Melbourne, he entered Ormond [q.v.5] College at the University of Melbourne in 1898 and graduated B.Sc. (1904) and M.Sc. (1906), specializing in geology under Professors J. W. Gregory [q.v.9] and E. W. Skeats [q.v.]. During Gregory's absences in 1902-04 he demonstrated in geology, and in 1912 deputized at the University of Adelaide for (Sir) Douglas Mawson [q.v.] during his Antarctic expedition.

One of the first specialists with a higher degree in the Mines Department of Victoria, Mahony was temporarily appointed in 1906 to the vacancy caused by the resignation of (Sir) Albert Kitson [q.v.9], as petrologist. He was permanently appointed on 23 February 1915. His major contribution to petrology was his study with H. J. Grayson [q.v.9] of the Mount Elephant and Camperdown district (*Memoirs of the Geological Survey of Victoria*, no.9). As editor of departmental publications he completed several bibliographies, which remain unpublished but for the one accompanying biographical sketches of the founders of the Geological Survey of Victoria, published in 1910.

Mahony went to England in 1915, enlisted as second lieutenant in the Royal Artillery and saw service on the Western Front until 1919. He was promoted acting captain in August 1917. Following discharge, he spent some months in petrological research at Sedgwick Museum, Cambridge, and resumed duty in Melbourne in March 1920.

On 14 April 1931 Mahony became director of the National Museum of Victoria following the retirement of J. A. Kershaw [q.v.9]. He fostered research and scholarship in the museum by encouraging the existing staff, depleted through government cutbacks in the Depression, by pressing for new appointments and the filling of long-standing vacancies, and by re-establishing publication of the *Memoirs of the National Museum of Victoria*. He initiated use of honorary staff to assist in the work of the museum. Mahony actively promoted its public image with a new display programme, following modern American methods demonstrated in Australia in 1937, for which he raised funds from private individuals and through a grant from the Carnegie Corporation; he also made a personal benefaction.

In 1937 Mahony was one of the founders of the Art Galleries and Museums Association of Australia and New Zealand and was elected first president. A member of the Royal Society of Victoria from 1901, he was president in 1939-40. In addition to his geological interests on which he contributed several scientific papers and reports, Mahony was keenly interested in Australian ethnology, particularly the question of the antiquity of man in Australia on which he published major papers.

Mahony was a quiet, unassuming bachelor, with a kindly nature and a keen sense of humour; his enthusiasm for the museum transformed it from a gloomy place to one of enlightenment and entertainment. He retired on 31 July 1944, and had been residing in the Melbourne Club when he died of peritonitis complicating diverticulitis on 27 September 1944. He was buried in Melbourne general cemetery. A memorial plaque, subscribed to by forty-one friends, was unveiled in the museum in May 1945.

R. T. M. Pescott, *Collections of a century* (Melb, 1954); *Wild Life* (Melb), 6, no 11, Nov 1944, p 323, 348; *Vic Naturalist*, 61, no 8, Dec 1944, p 148; Roy Soc Vic, *Procs*, 57 (1945); *Memoirs of the National Museum of Vic*, 14, no 2, 1946; *Herald* (Melb), 10 Mar 1931, 27 Sept 1944; *Argus*, 28 Sept 1944.

THOMAS A. DARRAGH

MAHONY, FRANCIS (1862-1916), artist, was born on 4 December 1862 in Flinders Lane, Melbourne, third surviving child of Timothy Mahony, Irish-born contractor, and his Cornish second wife Elizabeth, née Johns. Christened Francis, Mahony later added 'Prout' and generally signed his work 'Frank P. Mahony'; a brother, William Henry (1856-1918), was a solicitor and represented Annandale in the New South Wales Legislative Assembly (1894-1910).

Brought to Sydney aged 10, Mahony began work in an architect's office and studied under Giulio Anivitti [q.v.3] at the New South Wales Academy of Art. His emergence as an artist dates from his employment on the *Picturesque Atlas of Australasia* (1886); two of his contributions, the spearing of Edmund Kennedy [q.v.2] and E. J. Eyre's struggle along the coast with the faithful Wylie [qq.v.1,2], became part of the legendry of Australian exploration. From the centenary until Federation Mahony was one of the best-known Australian artists and illustrators, specializing in horses, which he studied assiduously, and in action scenes which stimulated—and reflected—national sentiment. His oils included 'Rounding up a Straggler' (1889), which possibly influenced Tom Roberts [q.v.], and 'The Cry of the Mothers' (1895); both were bought by the National Art Gallery of New South Wales. More significant was his black-and-white work contributed to such journals as the *Sydney Mail*, the *Bulletin* and the *Australian Town and Country Journal*. In 1893 he illustrated A. B. Paterson's [q.v.] poem 'The Geebung Polo Club' for the *Antipodean*; later in the decade his illustrations

were a prominent feature of several popular books, notably Henry Lawson's [q.v.] *While the billy boils* (1896) and *In the days when the world was wide* (1900) (which includes a sketch of Lawson as swagman), Barcroft Boake's [q.v.3] *Where the dead men lie* (1897), and Ethel Pedley's [q.v.] *Dot and the kangaroo* (1899).

Tall, dark, hospitable but temperamental, Mahony was a founding council-member in 1895 of the breakaway Society of Artists, Sydney, an instructor for the Art Society of New South Wales, and a member of the Dawn and Dusk Club. On 20 January 1897, at St Patrick's Church, Sydney, he married Mary Tobin, a barmaid from Yass, and left with her for London in late 1901. But Mahony's time had passed; although he joined the Langham Sketch Club and was in contact with other expatriate painters, he received only limited commissions. After he died of cancer in Kensington Infirmary on 28 June 1916, a memorial to 'our first Australian born artist' was erected 'by Australian admirers' at Mahony's grave in Hanwell cemetery, Middlesex. The other major memorial to his part in fashioning the 'legend of the nineties' is the original illustrations for *While the billy boils* and other works, now held at the Mitchell Library, Sydney. His son Francis William (Will) was also a successful cartoonist.

G. A. Taylor, *Those were the days* (Syd, 1918); R. Holden introd, *Frank P. Mahony (1862-1916) colonial artist*, exhibition cat, Josef Lebovic Gallery (Syd, 1983); *Bookfellow*, 25 Mar 1899; *ISN*, 28 Nov 1889; *Bulletin*, 26 June, 14 Aug 1924; pictures cat under Mahony (ML).   B. G. ANDREWS

MAIDEN, JOSEPH HENRY (1859-1925), botanist and public servant, was born on 25 April 1859 at St John's Wood, London, eldest son of Henry Maiden, china dealer and later accountant, and his wife Mary Elizabeth, née Wells. He was educated at the City of London Middle Class School where he excelled in scientific subjects, was taught chemistry by Professor F. Barff and even while at school acted as his assistant. Ill health which prevented his accepting a scholarship to Christ's College, Cambridge, and completing a science degree at the University of London, led him in 1880 to sail for Sydney.

The committee of the Technical or Working Men's College invited Maiden to deliver a course of lectures. He later contacted a friend of Barff, Professor Liversidge [q.v.5], who offered him the post of curator of the new Technological Museum. Maiden agreed, although intending to return within a year to England. However, he enjoyed the work and on 30 November 1883 at Holy Trinity Church, Kew, Melbourne, married Eliza Jane

Hammond. In 1885 Maiden began to study at the University of Sydney but again his health failed.

He threw himself into his work in the museum with gusto, despite set-backs. In 1882 the Garden Palace, which housed the collection, was destroyed by fire. Maiden and his small staff started again. Although the museum was badly housed in a tin shed until moved to Ultimo in 1893, he made it a centre of applied scientific research and popular education. His regular afternoon lectures were well attended.

Interested in Australian flora and helped by the director of the Botanic Gardens Charles Moore and by Rev. William Woolls [qq.v.5,6], Maiden quickly established himself as an expert in economic botany and encouraged research into the properties of Australian timbers and essential oils. He began writing on botanical subjects in 1887 and in 1889 published *The useful native plants of Australia*. A smaller work, *Wattles and wattle-barks*, followed next year. In 1890 he was indignant when passed over for the position of botanist in the new Department of Agriculture. Next year he was appointed consulting botanist to the department's forestry division. Early in 1894 he became superintendent of technical education and in May 1896 director of the Botanic Gardens and government botanist.

Maiden was a small man with a trim beard and lively features. He had an exceptionally methodical mind and working habits and an easy fluency in writing and speaking. He rose early and did most of his writing before breakfast; evenings were taken up with meetings. He sought to make the gardens a centre for public education as well as recreation and aesthetic enjoyment. Supportive with regard to the working conditions of his staff, he delegated easily and in return won hard work and respect bordering on reverence. He produced regular and voluminous annual reports. His major achievement was the creation of the National Herbarium of New South Wales, with a museum and library, opened in March 1901. Most of his holidays were spent on collecting expeditions throughout Australia. In Europe in 1900 he visited botanical gardens, attended conferences, and returned with a collection of portraits of famous botanists to adorn the herbarium and nearly 600 botanical specimens collected by Banks [q.v.1] in 1770 and hitherto stored in the British Museum.

Maiden continued his massive output of botanical research and publication. He maintained his interest in economic botany: the useful and the dangerous qualities of various plants. But this expanded into a taxonomic project: identification and classification of major Australian genera. His major works were *A critical revision of the genus Eucalyptus*, appearing in over seventy parts from 1903, in which he recognized 366 species, and his *Forest flora of New South Wales*, in seventy-seven parts from 1904. Many other books and articles for journals and newspapers flowed from his pen, occasionally in collaboration, including 45 papers in the *Journal and Proceedings* of the Royal Society of New South Wales, 95 in the *Proceedings* of the local Linnean Society and over 100 in the *Agricultural Gazette of New South Wales*. He lectured at the university in forestry in 1913-21 and in agricultural botany in 1914-21. He encouraged farmers to use herbarium staff to identify grasses and bushes grazed by their stock.

A long-term council-member of many learned societies in Sydney, Maiden was president of the Linnean Society in 1901-02, the Royal Society in 1906 and 1911, the (Royal) Australian Historical Society in 1905 and 1907, the Horticultural Society in 1904-17, the Horticultural Association for eighteen years, and the Field Naturalists' Society. He was also secretary of the Geographical Society of Australasia in 1884-85 and the Australasian Association for the Advancement of Science in 1907-21, and a foundation member of the Australian National Research Council in 1919. He published articles on early botanists and on the history of the Botanic Gardens, including a life of Banks in 1909. A corresponding member of societies in the United States of America, France, Switzerland, Chile, Algeria and Czechoslovakia, Maiden was always willing to provide seeds, specimens and information. He was, for example, an honorary member of the Netherlands Society for the Promotion of Industry and a fellow of the Linnean, Chemical, Royal Geographical and Royal Horticultural societies of London.

Awarded the gold medal of the Linnean Society of London in 1915, he was elected a fellow of the Royal Society and appointed I.S.O. in 1916. He also received the A.A.A.S.'s Mueller [q.v.5] medal (1922) and the local Royal Society's (W.B.) Clarke [q.v.3] memorial medal (1924). His name is commemorated in two generic, thirty-five specific and three infra-specific botanical names.

Active in the movement to retain large areas of native forests, Maiden also published important work on the use of plants to stabilize sand drift and on the essential role of trees in flood mitigation. A leading member of an important group of urban improvers, he ardently advocated more parks and trees to soften urban landscapes, dispatching thousands of seeds and cuttings from the gardens to local councils and schools. He wanted protection for trees endangered by urban development, and popularized the palms which became a feature of Edwardian Sydney. As well as the Botanic Gardens, the State nursery and several vice-regal residences, Maiden was in charge of the Outer Domain and Centennial Park. He fought hard (not always successfully) to make and maintain his various domains safe for public perambulation, day and night. In 1909 he helped to found Wattle Day 'with the view of stimulating Australian national sentiment'. For many years he was president of the State branch of the Australian Wattle League and in 1922 was elected national president.

Maiden retired in 1924 and moved to Turramurra. He had suffered from rheumatoid arthritis following an accident while collecting in 1911, but he continued to work at a prodigious rate and his wit still sparkled. He was an active Anglican. He died of heart disease on 16 November 1925 at Turramurra and was buried in St John's Anglican cemetery, Gordon. His wife and four daughters survived him; his only son had been lost at sea twenty years earlier. Funds were collected to erect a memorial pavilion in the Botanic Gardens. His portrait (1916) by Norman Carter [q.v.7] is held by the Royal Botanic Gardens.

J. Roe (ed), *Twentieth century Sydney* (Syd, 1980); *Public Service J* (NSW), 9 Feb 1901, 10 June 1915, 15 Nov 1924; *A'sian J of Pharmacy*, 1 June 1924; Linnean Soc NSW, *Procs*, 51 (1926), 55 (1930); Roy Soc NSW, *J and Procs*, 60 (1926); *Sydney Mail*, 20 June 1891; *T&CJ*, 23 May 1896; *SMH*, 18 Nov 1925; *Australasian*, 28 Nov 1925; J. H. Maiden papers (Roy Botanic Gardens Lib, Syd).   MARK LYONS
C. J. PETTIGREW

MAILEY, ALFRED ARTHUR (1886-1967), cricketer, cartoonist and journalist, was born on 3 January 1886, at Zetland, South Sydney, third son of John Hambleton Mailey, Melbourne-born carpenter, and his wife Jane Charlotte, née White, of Sydney. At 13 Arthur left Waterloo Public School, and at 16 became a glassblower which helped to strengthen his lungs and fingers. Later he worked for the Metropolitan Board of Water Supply and Sewerage. On 5 May 1913 at St Philip's, Church Hill, he married Maud Gladys Hinchcliffe (d.1937).

Like many Sydney boys devoted to cricket he gravitated to the Domain where he discovered the trick of bowling the 'bosie' or 'wrong un' which he practised to perfection. After a few seasons in lower grades he made his first-class début with Redfern and later joined the Balmain club. Rejected by the army, he became first-grade captain and excelled in assisting underprivileged players including A. Jackson [q.v.9]. His record 102 wickets in 13 matches in 1915-16 enabled Balmain to win

its first premiership. He later played for Waverley, Manly and Middle Harbour clubs. In 1913 he toured North America and, early in 1914, New Zealand.

Between 1921 and 1926 Mailey played twenty-one Tests for Australia taking 99 wickets at 33.9 runs apiece. He twice toured England where in all matches he captured 287 wickets for less than 20 runs each. In 1920-21 in Australia, bowling in only four Tests, he took 36 wickets at 26.27 runs, a record for an England-Australia series that stood for fifty-seven years. In all first-class and Sheffield Shield (1913-28) matches he took 779 and 180 wickets respectively at 24.1.

One of the greatest right-arm, leg-spin bowlers, Mailey spun the ball considerably, gave it much air and was always cheerfully prepared to 'buy' his wickets. One of his colleagues described his bowling as a mixture of 'spin, flight and sheer fun'. Like most wrist spinners, he was subject to lapses in length, but was always dangerous. His slight physique did not prevent him from bowling long spells.

Mailey was also a talented cartoonist and journalist and had attended J. S. Watkins's art class. He drew cartoons and caricatures for the Sydney *Arrow* and *Bulletin* and the London *Bystander*: in 1921 he joined the staff of the Sydney *Sun* as sporting cartoonist and cricket writer, later transferring to the *Daily Telegraph*. He frequently visited England, South Africa and New Zealand with Australian teams and organized many successful 'Arthur Mailey's' touring teams in Australia and a successful official Australian tour of North America in 1932. He covered the 'bodyline' tour in 1932-33 and wrote *And then came Larwood* (London, 1933) as well as several booklets of anecdotes and sketches.

In World War II Mailey vigorously supported the Federal government's austerity campaign. During his later years he ran a mixed business at Burraneer Bay, Port Hacking, where he enjoyed writing, painting in oils, fishing and golf. The title of his delightful autobiography, *10 for 66 and all that* (London, 1958), was inspired by his second-innings bowling figures against Gloucestershire in 1921. Survived by three sons and a daughter, Mailey died at Kirrawee on 31 December 1967 and was cremated with Anglican rites.

Quiet, unassuming, with a dead-pan, mock-angry style of humour, Mailey was one of cricket's most lovable and gentle characters. To him cricket was fun: he abhorred statistics, players taking themselves too seriously or not 'having a go'. Neville Cardus wrote that he 'bowled like a millionaire'. Satirical humorist though he was, Mailey wrote one of the most touching vignettes in the literature of cricket. Bowling as a young man for the first time against his great idol, he had Victor Trumper [q.v.] stumped off his third ball. 'There was no triumph in me', wrote Mailey, 'as I watched the receding figure. I felt like a boy who had killed a dove'.

A. G. Moyes, *Australian bowlers from Spofforth to Lindwall* (Syd, 1953); J. Pollard, *Australian cricket* (Syd, 1982); D. Frith, *The slow men* (Syd, 1984); *People* (Syd), 6 Aug 1950; *Wisden Cricketers' Almanack*, 1968; *SMH*, 22 Dec 1924, 31 Dec 1925, 16 Feb 1932, 9 Dec 1940, 12 Sept, 12, 29 Oct 1942, 14, 15 Jan, 20 Mar 1956, 15 Nov 1967, 2, 4 Jan 1968, 10 Oct 1970; *The Times* (Lond), 1 Jan 1968; *Advertiser* (Adel), *Mercury* (Hob), *Courier Mail* (Brisb), 2 Jan 1968; *Australian*, 4 Jan 1968.   G. P. WALSH

MAIN, HUGH (1883-1961), pastoralist and politician, was born on 27 August 1883 at Saltcoats, Ayrshire, Scotland, son of Hugh Main, salmon-fishing leaseholder, and his wife Mary, née Sim. The family migrated to South Australia next year, but his father died at Medindee in 1885. Young Hugh was educated in England at Tonbridge School, Kent, and in Adelaide at the Collegiate School of St Peter and Roseworthy Agricultural College where he was champion athlete and gained his diploma in 1902. In 1903 he took up orcharding at Clare; three years later, with his brother George, he purchased a wheat and wool property at Bethungra, New South Wales, where they bred racehorses including Hem which won the Australian Jockey Club Doncaster handicap (1919) and Salitros, winner of the A.J.C. Derby (1920). Main enlisted in the Australian Imperial Force at Cootamundra in October 1916 and served in France with 2nd Division supply and motor transport units, rising to the rank of sergeant. Upon discharge in May 1919 he returned to Bethungra where he resided until his death.

In 1920, standing as a Progressive, Main was the third member elected to the Legislative Assembly for Cootamundra, ahead of the sitting member and premier, W. A. Holman [q.v.9]. In his first campaign speech, Main emphasized that his party represented country interests which, hitherto, had relied upon 'the scant mercies of city lawyers and other nominees of Sydney'. He supported private enterprise and insisted that primary producers must be free of government direction in developing their markets. Although a champion of soldier settlers, he argued that they must stand on their own feet.

In December 1921 he joined the 'True Blues' led by (Sir) Michael Bruxner and D. H. Drummond [qq.v.7,8] who opposed a coalition with the National Party, and who upheld rural interests in 1922-25 during the ministry led by Sir George Fuller [q.v.8] with W. E. Wearne [q.v.] and other Progressives. Main's support was crucial in ensuring that objectives of the 'True Blues' were not ignored. Although the principles espoused by him in 1920 were tempered by time and experience, they remained the basis of his political philosophy.

Holding Cootamundra in 1922 and 1925 (for the renamed Country Party), Main represented Temora in 1927-38. He served as minister for agriculture from 16 May 1932 until 1 April 1938 in the Stevens [q.v.]-Bruxner ministries. *Ex officio* chairman of the Water Conservation and Irrigation Commission, he did much to revise and update the legislation administered by his department. Nevertheless, he was often adversely criticized by interest-groups such as the Agricultural Bureau of New South Wales which were unwilling to accept reductions in expenditure as part of governmental economy. Probably his most significant achievement was the enactment of legislation to reduce Murrumbidgee Irrigation Area settlers' rents and debts owing to the Irrigation Commission. However, R. A. Struck of Leeton, a returned serviceman who had benefited from that legislation, unsuccessfully petitioned the governor for the cancellation of Main's appointment after he had denied wild assertions that Struck and other ex-servicemen had been victimized by the Irrigation Commission.

In 1938 Main retired from politics although he continued to take an interest in the Country Party of which he was a councillor in 1934 and 1956-57. In parliament, despite his shyness, he had been 'both acute in argument and lucid in exposition', rarely indulging in point-scoring at the Opposition's expense and respected by colleagues regardless of their political affiliations.

Main died on 27 August 1961 at Cootamundra where he was buried with Presbyterian forms. He was survived by his wife Joan Helen, née Tregarthen, whom he had married in St Mark's Church, Darling Point, Sydney, on 30 January 1923, and by two daughters and a son. He was a life member of the Farmers and Settlers' Association and a member of the Union and Australian clubs. In retirement, much of his time was devoted to his grazing property and family.

U. R. Ellis, *The Country Party* (Melb, 1958); D. Aitkin, *The colonel* (Canb, 1969); *PD* (NSW), 1961-62, p 478; *Cootamundra Herald*, 18 Feb, 19, 29 Mar 1920, 28 Aug 1961; *SMH*, 12, 13 Oct 1937, 4 July, 9 Oct 1940; B. D. Graham, The political strategies of the Australian Country parties from their origins until 1929 (Ph.D. thesis, ANU, 1958).
D. I. McDONALD

MAIR, ALEXANDER (1889-1969), farmer, businessman and politician, was born on 25 August 1889 at North Carlton, Melbourne, eldest child of Victorian-born parents Alexander Mair, ironmonger, and his wife Florence, née Hunter. Educated at Wesley College, he became a keen amateur boxer and wrestler on leaving school and was apprenticed to a blacksmith at Thoona, near Wangaratta. After completing his indentures he returned to Melbourne to study commerce at Bradshaw's Business College and to work in the family firm, Alexander Mair & Co., timber, iron and steel merchants. A devout Presbyterian and active member of Scots Church, Melbourne, Mair married Grace Shoolbread Lennox there on 29 October 1913.

On his father's death that year Mair took over the family firm, which moved into hardware. He several times visited overseas suppliers, but a bout of influenza in the 1919 epidemic and subsequent asthma led him gradually to withdraw from business. In 1922 he sold the steelyard to Eliza Tinsley Pty Ltd and in 1925 the company's other assets to James McEwan & Co. Pty Ltd, serving as a director of the latter until 1927. Next year he bought Rockwood near Albury, New South Wales, a mixed grazing property that included a Corriedale stud. A solidly built, clean-shaven man, Mair began to go bald in his mid-twenties; by 1930 he looked an experienced and mature businessman.

In 1932 Mair won the State seat of Albury for the United Australia Party in a nasty campaign, during which New Guard members burnt the word 'Red', with lead nitrate, on to the forehead of one J. T. Lang [q.v.9] sympathizer. Calling for the people to deliver themselves from 'ruin and disaster' and opposing protection, Mair defeated the sitting Labor member with United Country Party preferences.

His particular brand of Presbyterian idealism emerged when he proposed that wealthier people should help the State in its financial crisis by paying their income tax in advance. Unlike most politicians Mair put his rhetoric into practice: in June he decided to distribute his parliamentary salary, less expenses, to the suffering in his electorate, a gesture he continued until 1938. A capable back-bencher, he promoted local issues, spending most of his time in his electorate, but retained his business links through membership of Tattersalls Club, Sydney, and the Athenaeum Club in Melbourne.

In 1937 Mair and his wife visited Britain for the coronation of King George VI. He also attempted an extraordinary expedition to the Soviet Union, signing on as a seaman in a Norwegian trader only to be stopped at a northern Russian port.

In April 1938 Mair joined (Sir) Bertram Stevens's [q.v.] reconstructed cabinet as an assistant minister. Ten weeks later he became minister for labour and industry and had to cope with several industrial disputes. He admired (Sir) Michael Bruxner [q.v.7] and was seen as a 'Country Party man' by U.A.P. malcontents such as J. R. Lee [q.v.]. In October Stevens, whose hold on the coalition was slipping, transferred the treasury to his protégé Mair. Confronted with a growing deficit in 1939, Mair proposed drastic cuts in public works expenditure while E. S. Spooner [q.v.], who controlled unemployment relief through his portfolios of public works and local government, urged increased government spending. In July cabinet approved Mair's proposal to channel unemployment expenditure through a subcommittee of four. Spooner on 1 August carried a motion in the assembly calling for a new financial policy. Stevens resigned. When Bruxner refused to continue the coalition with Spooner, the leadership of the U.A.P. devolved on Mair, who was sworn in as premier on 5 August.

On the declaration of war Mair backed the 'Mother Country'; both his sons enlisted in the second Australian Imperial Force. In December his cabinet refused to register German refugee doctors and in June 1940 he attacked the Menzies government for its failure to intern aliens. He committed his own resources to Britain's defence—in May 1940 he lent the Commonwealth £4000 interest free for the duration of the war and secretly paid the life insurance of sundry servicemen—but could not galvanize his government.

When attacked by the new Labor leader (Sir) William McKell, Mair could neither point to the elimination of unemployment nor a concerted war effort. In the May 1941 elections he made the war effort the first plank of government policy, only to be stymied by his old rival, Spooner, now a Federal parliamentarian and chairman of the Commonwealth Manpower Committee, who declared that State governments were hindering the war effort. McKell won a landslide victory. Mair remained leader of the U.A.P. until February 1944; in May he held Albury as a Democratic candidate. In November 1945 he accepted leadership of the new Liberal Party although he had only played a minor part in its formation, and joined the anti-Communist crusade. He resigned in August 1946 to contest unsuccessfully the Federal Senate election.

Mair returned to Rockwood, but sold the property in 1948 and departed for Melbourne, where he accepted a number of directorships, was elected to the boards of various charitable institutions, and became involved in horse-racing and the management of Scots Church. One of the least colourful of all New South Wales premiers, Mair was no power broker. Ingenuous and generous, he was more businessman than politician. Survived by his wife, two sons and a daughter, he died on 3 August 1969 at his St Kilda home and was cremated. His estate was valued for probate at $439 423.

D. Aitkin, *The colonel* (Canb, 1969); C. Hazlehurst (ed), *Australian conservatism* (Canb, 1979); *United Aust Review*, July 1932, Sept 1938, Mar 1941; *Albury Banner*, 20-27 May, 3, 24 June 1932, 11 Aug, 15 Sept, 3 Nov 1939, 24 May 1940; *SMH*, 13 June 1932, 14 Apr 1938, 26 July, 13 Sept, 7, 8 Dec 1939, 27 Mar, 4 Apr, 24 July, 17 Aug, 3 Oct, 11 Nov 1940, 5 Feb, 23 Apr 1942, 3 Sept, 5-6 Dec 1945, 4 Aug 1969; information from Mr J. Mair, Double Bay, Syd.   PETER EWER
PETER SPEARRITT

MAITLAND, ANDREW GIBB (1864-1951), geologist, was born on 30 November 1864 at Birkby, near Huddersfield, Yorkshire, England, son of George Maitland, bookkeeper, and his wife Margaret, née Gibb, both of Scottish ancestry. He qualified as a civil engineer at the Yorkshire College of Science, Leeds, where he was influenced by A. H. Green, professor of geology. From Green, pre-eminently a field geologist, Maitland derived his lasting enthusiasm for geological survey work.

He was appointed second assistant geologist to the Geological Survey of Queensland and on 17 December 1888 reported at Townsville to R. Logan Jack [q.v.4] who set him to survey rough country in the Mackay district. Maitland's maps and reports, published as parliamentary papers for 1889, satisfied Jack that his latest recruit was a capable geologist who had mastered quickly the ways of the bush. Assignments in remote mineral fields added to Maitland's reputation. In 1891 Sir William MacGregor [q.v.5] engaged him on secondment, to undertake a geological examination of British New Guinea. His reports and maps are among the first accounts of the geology of Papua. Maitland resumed his varied survey work in Queensland but became increasingly involved with study of the intake beds of the Great Artesian Basin.

When H. P. Woodward (1858-1917) resigned as government geologist of Western Australia to join the mining rush, Maitland accepted the offer to succeed him in July 1896. He completed field-work in the gulf country before leaving Queensland in October, reaching Perth to find he had been gazetted government geologist from 1 November. He had no professional staff but received a ministerial direction from (Sir) Edward Wittenoom [q.v.] to prepare a plan for a geological survey. Maitland's report of 15 May 1897 envisaged a largely self-sufficient system capable of producing topographical maps for the geologists who, in turn, would have the support of a chemist/assayer and office staff. These services, as well as a mining record office and a public museum of geology, were to be under the government geologist, answering directly to the minister. By the time an under secretary came between him and his minister, Maitland had set a lasting style for the Geological Survey of Western Australia.

He saw his survey's role in terms of systematic field-mapping, necessarily related to particular social and industrial needs, and publication. While leading the survey from the field, by example, he did not neglect office work. His still-useful *Bibliography of the geology of Western Australia* (1898) was the first of ninety-one survey bulletins issued under his direction. An acknowledged authority on underground water, Maitland had early successes in the West such as locating bores between Geraldton and North West Cape that still supply water. His predictions of artesian water resources, for instance beneath the Nullarbor Plain, likewise proved valuable. Water and gold were then crucial to prosperity in the West and Maitland and his staff inevitably devoted much attention to the goldfields. He himself spent several long and arduous seasons from 1903 in the Pilbara region, mapping a vast area and seeking geological order among its ancient rocks. In 1901 he had worked in unknown parts of the Kimberley division as geologist to an expedition led by F. S. Drake-Brockman [q.v.8]. Maitland's extensive knowledge of the State was epitomized in his *Summary of the geology of Western Australia* (1919). E. C. Andrews [q.v.7] regarded him as 'the last of the pioneer geologists of Australia', much of whose work in the West 'partook of the nature of exploration'. By November 1926 when Maitland retired about half the State had been geologically mapped, at least in reconnaissance. Behind the achievement lay extraordinary efforts and feats of endurance by men, horses and camels, hardly credible to a modern geologist.

Maitland was an original member of the Mueller [q.v.5] Botanic Society of Western Australia, forerunner of the Royal Society of Western Australia which he practically founded; and of which he was twice president (1915, 1925) and recipient of its Kelvin memorial medal (1937). Maitland served for many years as local secretary of the Australasian Association for the Advancement of Science and was awarded its Mueller memorial medal in 1924. He was an honorary member (1915) of the Royal Society of New South Wales which awarded him its (W.B.) Clarke [q.v.3] memorial medal (1927).

On 20 March 1895 at Sandgate, near Brisbane, Maitland had married Alice Maud Brumfitt with Anglican rites. He died on 27 January 1951 at Subiaco, Perth, and was buried in the Anglican section of Karrakatta cemetery. Two sons and two daughters survived him. His elder son Brigadier George Brumfitt Gibb had a distinguished medical career. Gibb River and Maitland Range, in the Kimberley division, commemorate Maitland and recall that he was generally known as Gibb Maitland. Several species of invertebrate fossils have been named in his honour; the mineral called maitlandite by E. S. Simpson [q.v.] in 1930 is now known to be thorogummite.

R. K. Johns (ed), *History and role of government geological surveys in Australia* (Adel, 1976); Dept Mines (Qld), *Annual Report*, 1888-96; Geological Survey (WA), *Annual Progress Report*, 1897-1926; *Aust Mining Standard*, 14 Oct 1897, p 2307; Roy Soc NSW, *J and Procs*, 76 (1942), p 109, 113, and 86 (1952), p xv; Roy Soc WA, *Procs*, 36 (1952), p 111; *T&CJ*, 22 Aug 1896; *West Australian*, 1 Feb 1951.

T. G. VALLANCE

MAITLAND, SIR HERBERT LETHINGTON (1868-1923), surgeon and sportsman, was born on 12 November 1868 at Surry Hills, Sydney, son of London-born Duncan Mearns Maitland, civil engineer, and his native-born wife Emily, née Dalgety. Educated at Newington College and the University of Sydney (M.B., Ch.M., 1892), young Bert was more distinguished for athletic than academic achievements. His professional life focused on Sydney Hospital where he was resident medical officer in 1892 and senior R.M.O. next year. In 1894 he left to begin private practice in Elizabeth Street but in December 1895 was appointed honorary assistant surgeon. On 8 July 1897 at Marrickville he married Mabel Agnes Cook (d. 1950). He lived and worked at 6 Lyons Terrace and about 1914 moved to a house he renovated at 147 Macquarie Street.

Maitland matured quickly at surgery of the head and neck for which he became famous. At Sydney Hospital he worked with W. H. Goode, then past his prime. Within four months of appointment, Maitland performed a rhinoplasty (nose reconstruction) which was rare enough to warrant presentation to his peers; the patient's family believed they had witnessed a miracle. By the time he was appointed to the senior staff in December 1902 his practice was almost entirely surgical. He lectured to Sydney Hospital nurses in 1900-09, and was an early medical member of the Australasian Trained Nurses' Association from 1899 and on its first board of examiners (1906-08). He was first lecturer in clinical surgery when Sydney Hospital became a clin-

ical school of the university in 1909. Students and young doctors were attracted to the hospital for the sole reason that Maitland was there. He and his colleague Robert Steer Bowker operated in the very large main theatre at the same time on Thursday afternoons. Their rivalry was exhilarating for visitors but a strain for staff responsible for the smooth flow of patients. Maitland preached the gospel of hard work and not uncommonly continued an operating session far into the night. His generosity to the sick poor was proverbial.

Maitland did not have much time for writing, but his several articles in the *Australasian Medical Gazette* between 1898 and 1912 were distinguished, as were his lectures, by their clarity and common sense. One of these, 'A radical method of extirpating malignant growths in the neck secondary to mouth carcinoma' (20 October 1906), was noticed in J. F. Binnie's *Manual of operative surgery*. Maitland later contributed to a collection of papers on specialist surgery edited by Binnie and published in Philadelphia in 1917. He was honorary secretary of the Medical Benevolent Association of New South Wales almost continuously in 1900-23; a councillor of the local branch of the British Medical Association in 1904-16 and president in 1911-12; a consultant surgeon at the Women's Hospital, Crown Street, from 1905; at South Sydney Women's Hospital from 1915 and at the Coast (Prince Henry) Hospital from about 1914.

A confidant of politicians including James McGowen [q.v.], he was knighted in 1915. In 1915-19 Maitland was on the active list of the Australian Army Medical Corps as surgeon and temporary lieut-colonel at the 4th Australian General Hospital, Randwick. Here he applied his talents to over one thousand repair, grafting and plastic operations with a 'skill and quickness so phenomenal that he would frequently complete as many as fifteen in a single morning'.

In 1916 Maitland's obligations to Sydney Hospital were increased at 'considerable personal sacrifice' when he became a director and was put on the house committee. His influence was soon apparent. Among other things he initiated improvements in business procedures, waged a vigorous campaign to obtain better facilities for patients, and promoted the interests of medical students. At his suggestion a lecture hall was built on the flat roof of the Renwick [q.v.6] Pavilion in 1920. The board named it after him.

'Handsome Bertie' had a 'mobile face lit with dark eyes which his enthusiasms kindled like live coals'. He was of medium height, gap toothed, prematurely grey, good humoured, gregarious, charming, kindly, immensely popular—and much given to smoking and swearing. He had been a member of the New-town Rugby Union team in 1888 and from the mid-1890s boxed regularly at the Sydney Amateur Gymnastic Club. When his friend Hugh D. McIntosh [q.v.] opened the Rushcutters Bay Stadium in 1908, Maitland was honorary surgeon. To the end he was renowned for his impromptu demonstrations of floor exercises and 'the best bloody biceps of the lot'. He also swam daily, played cricket, was a good shot and keen fisherman with his own boat, the *Idler*. He was president of the New South Wales Anglers Casting Club and winner of competitions in fly-casting and big-game fishing. He was a Freemason and member of the Australian Club. Well-known in theatre circles, he was a friend of the entrepreneur Hugh Ward [q.v.]. Sporting men reputedly named their houses after him and one named a horse Sir Maitland, which did quite well at Randwick.

Maitland was visibly aged by the heavy work of the war years and a bout of influenza during the 1919 pandemic. Late on the afternoon of 23 May 1923, feeling unwell, he rested in his rooms and died of coronary vascular disease. Hundreds of doctors, medical students and nurses, and scores of citizens processed from his home to Queen Victoria's statue near St James' Church. He was buried with Anglican rites in Waverley cemetery near his youngest son who had died of influenza in 1910. He was survived by his wife and two sons who were still medical students. His estate, valued for probate at £61 209, was left to his wife.

Sydney Hospital launched an over-ambitious memorial fund and the Maitland Theatre Suite was completed in 1930. The hospital's medical alumni also established the Maitland oration in 1935 which is still given at irregular intervals. Perhaps the memorial that would have pleased him most was the Sir Herbert Maitland Stakes, a weight-for-age event at the Victoria Park Racing Club, whose president was another Sydney Hospital director, Sir Joynton Smith [q.v.]. The hospital holds a cartoon by Lionel Lindsay [q.v.] and a posthumous portrait by John Longstaff [q.v.] was presented to the National Art Gallery of New South Wales by Lady Maitland in 1944. That year she married Sir Frederick Edward French.

A. Garenne, *L'amour vainqueur poésies* (Paris, 1957); Syd Hospital, *Annual Reports*, 1891-1923; Royal Sth Syd Hospital, *Annual Report*, 1915, 1923; *MJA*, 8 Apr 1916, 23 June 1923, 1 Dec 1928; *Syd Univ Medical J*, 12, no 2, Oct 1917, p 128; *Australian Bystander*, 21 June 1923; *Sydney Mail*, 23 June 1888, 4 Dec 1907, 30 May 1923; *Sun* (Syd), 24, 25 May 1923; *SMH*, 26 May 1923; *Referee*, 30 May 1923; *Smith's Weekly*, 2, 16 June 1923; A'sian Trained Nurses' Assn, Council minute-books, 1899-1923 (ML); Syd Hospital House Cttee Minutes, 13 Mar 1916, 20 Oct 1919, 8, 22 Mar 1920; Syd Hospital Bd, Minutes, 21 Sept 1920, 28 Feb 1921; Maitland papers (Roy A'sian College of Physicians, Syd *and* ML); Maitland family Bible (RAHS); information from Mrs E. Duncan, Mrs L. Hancock and Dr C. E. Winston.

ANN M. MITCHELL

MALE, ARTHUR (1870-1946), pastoralist and businessman, was born on 2 March 1870 at Bridport, Dorset, England, second son of Thomas Male, accountant, and his wife Martha, née Guppy. After attending Bridport Grammar School he worked in the family rope-works. About 1890 he migrated to Perth where he worked on a farm at Guildford. In 1894 E. W. Streeter, a London jeweller with pearling interests in south-east Asia and at Broome, visited Male's employer. Streeter's vessels had been on the west coast since 1884; he had a pastoral station at Roebuck Plains and a general trading business and a butcher shop at Broome where pearling boats spent the 'lay-up' season. Male was taken on to manage E. W. Streeter's Broome pearling business with Streeter's son George. A partnership was later formed—Streeter & Male Ltd—and when George Streeter returned to London, Male became sole manager; he was a harsh employer. On 18 January 1900 at Albany he married Constance Cox from Bridport.

The pearling trade grew following the success of Japanese divers and Male was joined by his youngest brother Archie (1877-1923). By 1912 Male's partner had only a half-interest in the pastoral station and the original Broome businesses. The Male brothers also owned Hill station, between Broome and Beagle Bay; Arthur later bought Ida Valley station, between Menzies and Leonora, where cattle from the north were fattened for sale at Kalgoorlie, Coolgardie and Perth. The firm was agent for Dalgety [q.v.4] & Co. Ltd, and the Blue Funnel Line. In 1905-14, every alternate year, Male and his wife visited England where their three eldest children were educated.

After 1918 economic conditions became less favourable; demand for pearl-shell fell and Japanese divers were staying away. Two incidents further affected Male's pastoral interests. For years he had shipped cattle to Java where a reciprocal trade developed in sugar and rice to provision the Asian indentured labour. In 1921 the Federal government prohibited importation of sugar and rice, to protect the Australian industries, so the Javanese merchants refused to purchase Male's cattle and sheep. In 1929, after an outbreak of 'pleura' among cattle in the North-West, a 'pleura line' was established running eastwards from La Grange to the Northern Territory border. Since no cattle north of this line could be sent overland to southern markets, Male could not sell his stock.

In 1905-17 he had represented the Kimberley district in the Legislative Assembly. A Liberal, he spoke infrequently in the House but showed his knowledge of the North-West; he resisted the migration of Japanese or Asians, except divers, to the area. In 1910-11 he was a minister without portfolio. From 1919 he was a member of the Broome Road Board and honorary consul for Japan from 1928.

The management of Male's Broome interests was taken over after 1930 by his eldest son A. S. (Sam) Male; Arthur retired to Perth and the Weld Club. Predeceased by his wife and survived by two daughters and four sons, he died on 20 January 1946 and was cremated with Anglican rites. His estate was sworn for probate at £29 116.

J. S. Battye (ed), *Cyclopedia of Western Australia*, 1 (Adel, 1912); Dalgety and NZ Loan Ltd (Perth), *Dalgety's Review*, 18 Apr 1963, p 12; M. A. Bain, *Full fathom five* (Perth, 1983); *Western Mail* (Perth), 24 Sept 1910; *West Australian*, 22 Jan 1946; Deakin papers (NL).

MARY ALBERTUS BAIN

MALLALIEU, HENRIETTA; see WILL-MORE

MALONEY, WILLIAM ROBERT (NUTTALL) (1854-1940), humanitarian and politician, was born on 12 April 1854 at West Melbourne, son of Jane Maloney, née Dowling, then and later being supported by her brother-in-law W. J. T. 'Big' Clarke [q.v.1]. Jane had married Denis Maloney in Sydney in 1847 and they later joined the Californian gold rush. Maloney was entered in the baptismal register as William's father, but he and Jane had parted. Many people came to assume that Clarke was the father and he provided for the boy in his will.

William attended a primary school in West Melbourne and the Errol Street National School. After a year in New Zealand he joined the Colonial Bank of Australia, left to spend a year or more at Scotch College, then rejoined the bank. At the Turn Verein he became an accomplished gymnast and was introduced to socialist ideas by German migrants. About 1874 he and his mother took up a selection at Longwarry, Gippsland, and over several years cleared 100 acres (40 ha).

Returning to Melbourne, Maloney attended night-school, matriculated, and in 1880 began a medical course at St Mary's Hospital, London (L.S.A., M.R.C.S., 1885). He became resident obstetric physician at St Mary's and later house surgeon at the Lock Hospital; London's poverty horrified him. He spent much time in Paris and in 1883 joined Tom Roberts and J. P. Russell [qq.v.] on a walking tour in France and Spain; throughout his life he enjoyed associating with artists. Russell painted a fine portrait of him, now in the National Gallery of Victoria. Maloney adopted a Bohemian style: cream silk suit, red or yellow tie or bow-tie, panama hat, waxed moustache and goatee beard. He continued to travel widely all his life, eventually to Russia when 83.

He returned to Australia in 1887 and took a medical post on a Western Australian railway-construction works. Settling in North Melbourne next year he opened a general practice, and in March 1889 he was elected to the Legislative Assembly for West Melbourne on behalf of the Workingmen's Political League, largely on the railwaymen's vote. Thus he began his fifty-one-year stint as a Labor parliamentarian. Partly bound by the Trades Hall Council's programme, Maloney added woman's suffrage, old-age and invalid pensions and republicanism. That year he introduced reputedly the first bill in the Empire for woman's suffrage; in 1908, when the Victorian parliament belatedly complied, 20 000 women signed an address of gratitude to him.

Maloney's philosophy was always misty but he was essentially an international socialist in the European social democratic tradition. In the 1890s he threw himself indiscriminately into the activities of radical groups such as the Social Democratic and Single Tax leagues and the Knights of Labor, presided over May Day celebrations, and was active in the Australian Natives' Association. Then and later he was often an executive member of the Progressive Political League, the Political Labor Council and the Victorian Labor Party. A butt of the press, seeming too extreme and eccentric to be taken seriously, he was indeed rash, tending to make wild accusations which he would graciously withdraw; in January 1891 a duel with Lieut-Colonel Tom Price [q.v.] seemed imminent.

Old-age pensions was his chief cause, the anti-sweating movement next; in 1898 he chaired a royal commission on the Melbourne tramway employees' grievances, attempting to remedy outrageous working conditions, and later was president of the tramwaymen's union. On 2 November 1892 at the Melbourne Registrar's Office he had married Minnie Grace Pester (d.1934) of Ballarat; although agnostic, he insisted on Catholic baptism of their two children.

About 1896 'the Little Doctor' established

at the Queen Victoria Market the North Melbourne District Medical Club (later, the Maloney Medical Institute, which continued until about 1950). In this refuge he treated for the most part a 'pathetic assortment of human wreckage'. From about 1907 he retained assistants but continued to regularly counsel the distressed. He reportedly lost his M.R.C.S. in 1897 for internationally sponsoring an 'electric healer'. He fell foul of the local branch of the British Medical Association for advertising 'advice and medicine, 3s. 6d', and probably also for his support for Mrs Bessie Smyth's [q.v.] campaign for birth control.

In 1901 Maloney stood for the Federal electorate of Melbourne and was soundly beaten by Sir Malcolm McEacharn [q.v.]. In 1903 he stood again and lost narrowly; on appeal a new election was granted and in March 1904, amid intense excitement, he defeated McEacharn by 810 votes; Sir Rupert Clarke [q.v.8] was prominent on his platform. Maloney held the seat until his death, blocking the ambition of A. A. Calwell, who however greatly admired him. He was one of the 'torpedo brigade' which aimed to found the Commonwealth Bank; King O'Malley [q.v.] and Andrew Fisher [q.v.8] were both his good friends. He was temporary chairman of committees (1910-17), a member of royal commissions on the pearling industry (1913) and the electoral laws (1914), of the joint committee on public accounts (1914-17) and of caucus executive (1914-31). He supported the White Australia policy and became obsessed with the Japanese threat. He was an anti-militarist, however, who vehemently resisted participation in the South African War, but joined the Australian National Defence League in 1906. He unhappily took more than his share of recruiting campaigning in World War I, but was a staunch anti-conscriptionist.

Maloney was often regarded as a lightweight politician and was never a serious contender for ministerial rank. Passing crazes such as bimetallism and Douglas Credit attracted him. Yet he was long before his time as campaigner for pensions, the maternity allowance and child endowment. He was essentially a social worker, not a class hater; he loved humankind, fought inequality and pressed the rights and needs of the poor.

He continued his fund-raising and his care for children, the aged, the unemployed and returned soldiers; he was president of the League of Child Helpers and, in the Depression, of the Melbourne Unemployed Committee. He gave away much of his income. In 1935 he made a film, as an appeal for milk for crèches and free kindergartens. About one thousand people of diverse backgrounds attended the eightieth birthday celebration in the town hall of one of Melbourne's best-loved

citizens. In 1940 Maloney led the eight-hour day procession as the senior Labor pioneer. He died at St Kilda on 29 August that year and, after a state funeral, was cremated. His son and daughter survived him.

M. Clarke, 'Big' Clarke (Melb, 1980); Australasian, 16 Jan 1897; Punch (Melb), 19 Sept 1912, 1 Jan 1925; Herald (Melb), 2 Aug 1924; R. B. Cutting, The little doctor. A biography of Dr William Maloney (B.A. Hons thesis, Monash Univ, 1974), and for bibliog; S. Merrifield collection (LaTL).

GEOFFREY SERLE

MANIFOLD, SIR WALTER SYNNOT (1849-1928), pastoralist and politician, was born on 30 March 1849 at Grasmere, Warrnambool, Port Phillip District, second son of Thomas Manifold [q.v.2] and his wife Jane Elizabeth, daughter of Captain Walter Synnot. Educated in Germany and at Melbourne Church of England Grammar School, Manifold signed the roll as a solicitor in 1875 but did not practise. With his elder brother James, he bought Pine Grove West station, near Echuca.

After again visiting Europe, Manifold toured Queensland and, impressed by the splendid grazing country, bought Sesbiana (some 700 square miles (1800 km²), part of a larger run, Werna), entering into partnership with his uncle Peter Manifold [q.v.2] and others. He managed Sesbiana in 1878-84, then sold out and returned to Warrnambool to take up his inheritance of Wollaston. On 23 April 1885 he married Fanny Maria, daughter of Commander Alexander Smith, R.N. Though childless, the union linked him with the Reads of Tasmania where he already had extensive connexions through the Synnots, and with the Officer and Chomley families in Victoria.

Manifold bred cattle at Wollaston, but turned most of the property over to dairy farming, run on a share and tenant basis. It left him time to devote to his favourite hobbies, cattle and machinery—by 1904 he had installed an electrical plant. After World War I, Wollaston was broken up for soldier settlement.

His father had been the first of the family to enter politics (briefly, in 1861), and Walter was elected to the Legislative Council for Western Province in June 1901. Reputed to have refused a portfolio in the Bent [q.v.3] ministry in 1908 (and on several other occasions), he was unofficial leader of the council in 1910-19, becoming noted for the thoroughness with which he examined legislation, and for his amiable temperament. When Sir John Davies [q.v.4] retired as president of the council in 1919, Manifold was elected narrowly over A. O. Sachse [q.v.]. His speech of acceptance was marked by a disarming humility; emphasizing that he was the first native-born president, Manifold vowed that he would aim 'to show that an Australian-born man can fill a high office without—well, making a mess of things'. Knighted in 1920, he presided until 1923 when ill health forced him to retire. He resigned his seat in January 1924. Both sides of the House praised his work and character, singling out his dignity, impartiality, simplicity and gentlemanliness.

President of the Melbourne Club in 1908, Manifold was a trustee of the Guardian Assurance Co., and a council-member of the University of Melbourne in 1923-28. A widower, he died on 15 November 1928 at Toorak and was buried in St Kilda cemetery. His estate was sworn for probate at £83 356. Like his cousins at Purrumbete, Manifold had undertaken public work as a duty, imposed by his position as a leader of society and member of the pre-gold upper-class.

A. Henderson (ed), *Early pioneer families of Victoria and Riverina* (Melb, 1936); W. G. Manifold, *The wished-for land* (Geelong, Vic, 1984); *PD* (Vic), 1919, p 66, 1923-24, p 797, 1928, p 2938; *Punch* (Melb), 21 Jan 1904; *Argus*, 8, 10 July 1919, 16 Nov 1928.   P. H. DE SERVILLE

MANIFOLD, WILLIAM THOMSON (1861-1922), JAMES CHESTER (1867-1918) and EDWARD (1868-1931), pastoralists and philanthropists, were the second, fourth and fifth sons of John Manifold [q.v.2] and his wife Marion, née Thomson. John Manifold died in 1877 and, during the minority of his children, his half-share of Purrumbete (where his sons had been born) was administered by his brother and joint-owner Peter [q.v.2] who left his share to the brothers in 1885.

William Thomson, born on 5 January 1861, was educated at Geelong Church of England Grammar School and Jesus College, Cambridge. On 5 August 1886 he married his first cousin once removed, Alice Mary Cridland (d. 1920) of Papanui, New Zealand. Their first child was born at Gnarpurt, near Lismore, which William had acquired, but after the Purrumbete estate was divided between the four then surviving brothers, W.T. moved to the homestead portion, which as eldest surviving son he had chosen. The house was virtually rebuilt and Walter Withers [q.v.] commissioned to paint murals celebrating the pioneering exploits of the Manifolds.

The rich soil of Purrumbete, traditionally cattle country, was well suited to dairying. Manifold let much of it to dairy-farmer tenants, and some to a few share-farmers. On his own portion he established the Lake Purrumbete Butter Factory, entirely supplied with milk from his farms. Its butter was exported to England under the brand name 'Pelican'. W.T. also built up a herd of milking Shorthorn cattle and bred Clydesdales. About 1916 he withdrew from dairying and sold most of the Shorthorn stud, and at the end of World War I part of Purrumbete was acquired by the government for soldier settlement. His other pastoral interests included North station, Mortlake; Milangil, Camperdown; and, in partnership with his brothers and a cousin J. E. Bostock, Sesbiana station in Queensland (sold in 1923).

Although Manifold did not enter public life, he supported Anglican and local institutions, making considerable donations, often with his brothers. The Church of England cathedral and chapter house at Ballarat, Queen's College and Ballarat Grammar School benefited from their generosity. W.T. was vicar's warden of St Paul's, Camperdown, a member of the synod and of the bishop's council, Ballarat. In 1911-23 he was chairman of the council of Geelong Grammar during the period of its move to Corio. He contributed to the cost of rebuilding, endowed a scholarship in memory of his son William Herbert who was killed in France in 1917, and gave £10 000 to establish a masters' superannuation fund. He left a large sum, in his estate of some £280 000, to Trinity College, University of Melbourne, part of which was used to build the Manifold Wing at Janet Clarke [q.v.3] Hall.

A keen polo player, 'a typical public school boy, blessed with this world's goods', Manifold was a member of the Melbourne and Bohemian clubs. He died of a heart condition on 20 October 1922 and was buried in Camperdown cemetery. Two sons and two daughters survived him.

James Chester was born on 10 February 1867. After attending Geelong Grammar School he went to England with his family in 1881, but returned because the climate did not agree with his health. Chester completed his schooling at Melbourne Church of England Grammar School. When he came into possession of his portion of Purrumbete, named Talindert, he subsequently let much of it to dairy farmers, who later bought the land on generous terms. He was a director of the Camperdown Cheese and Butter Factory, established in 1891, and its chairman from 1907. A keen sportsman, he captained the Camperdown polo team.

Chester Manifold entered public life as a member of the Hampden Shire Council in the 1890s and was twice president. In 1901 he was elected as the first member for the Federal seat of Corangamite, sitting as a Protectionist, but retired because of ill health in 1903. He was persuaded to oppose the sitting member J. H. Scullin [q.v.], and defeated him at the 1913 elections. A 'very popular man of the unobtrusive sort', he retained the seat until his death. While visiting England during World War I, Chester volunteered to report on conditions in military camps and hospitals, and to investigate rehabilitation schemes in Canada and the United States of America. He died unexpectedly on 30 October 1918 of pneumonia, a day out of San Francisco, and was buried at sea. By his wife Lilian Eva, née Curle, whom he had married on 11 March 1891, he left a son (Sir) Thomas Chester and a daughter. One of his last gifts had been a property in the Richmond River district, New South Wales, made available for local returned soldiers. Manifold was hailed by conservative newspapers as a model of the second-generation pastoralists: a good sport, public-spirited (a parliamentarian who disliked 'politics'), and generous in benefactions to his country, Church and district. His estate was valued for probate at some £400 000. A statue by Nelson Illingworth [q.v.9] was unveiled in Camperdown by S. M. (Viscount) Bruce [q.v.7] in 1921.

Edward was born on 15 November 1868 and educated at Geelong and Melbourne Grammar schools and at Trinity Hall, Cambridge (B.A., 1891). He chose the Danedite portion of Purrumbete, and on the death of his bachelor brother Thomas Peter (1863-1895), after a hunting accident, took over his allocation, Wiridgil. He also owned Boortkoi, near Hexham. On these properties he ran merino sheep, a Lincoln stud which dated back to 1870 and Shorthorn cattle; 3000 acres (1200 ha) were leased to dairy farmers.

Edward was a member of Hampden Shire Council in 1909-31, and three times president. Camperdown, largely bordered by Manifold land and partly dependent upon the local pastoral dynasties, benefited from the family's interest. Though an offer to build public baths to commemorate the Queen Victoria Jubilee in 1897 was not proceeded with, the town acquired a hospital, a reserve on Mount Leura, a clock tower and a cricket pavilion, as well as notable donations to St Paul's Church and the grammar school.

A polo player and a keen racing man, Edward was a successful owner of steeplechasers. He was a committeeman of the Victoria Racing Club for many years and a member of many Western District racing clubs. He died following an operation on 14 February 1931. On 16 July 1900 he had married his cousin Beatrice Mary Synnot Anderson by whom he had three sons. His estate was valued for probate at nearly £500 000.

The Manifolds were prepared to give time, money and leadership to district, church and state. Generous, horsey and conservative, they adapted the role and duties of an English country gentleman to Australian conditions,

and gave back to the country much of the wealth acquired by their pioneering predecessors. One journalist wrote in 1913, when Chester unwillingly prepared to return to parliament: 'A few families made the Western District of Victoria. At the same time the Western District made them'.

A. Henderson (ed), *Early pioneer families of Victoria and Riverina* (Melb, 1936); R. A. McAlpine, *The shire of Hampden, 1863-1963* (Hampden, Vic, 1963); W. G. Manifold, *The wished-for land* (Geelong, Vic, 1984); *Pastoral Review*, 15 Mar, 16 Apr, 15 June 1909, 15 July 1915, 16 Nov 1922; *C of E Messenger* (Vic), 26 Oct 1922; Geelong Grammar School, *Corian*, Dec 1922; *VHJ*, 46, no 1, Feb 1975; *Punch* (Melb), 2 Oct 1913; *Argus*, 31 Oct 1918, 21, 23 Oct 1922, 16, 17 Feb 1931.

P. H. DE SERVILLE

MANN, EDWARD ALEXANDER (1874-1951) chemist, politician and broadcaster, was born on 11 August 1874 at Mount Gambier, South Australia, son of Gilbert Hill Cheke Mann, telegraph stationmaster, and his wife Sophia Charlotte, daughter of Rev. John Ramsden Wollaston [q.v.2]. (Sir) Frederick Mann [q.v.] was an elder brother. Edward was educated privately and at the University of Melbourne. In 1890 he was appointed assistant to the chief inspector of explosives, Melbourne, then in 1895 government analyst in Western Australia and, in 1902, agricultural chemist. He was a member of the advisory committee under the Health Act and responsible for setting up the government laboratory in Perth; as chief inspector of explosives he established the magazine depot at Fremantle. A member of royal commissions on the ventilation and sanitation of mines (1904-10) and miner's phthisis (1911), he produced many technical publications that had industrial or agricultural application. He became a fellow of the Institute of Chemistry of Britain and Ireland (1914). On 11 September 1901 he had married Estelle Frances Léonie Hicks at South Yarra, Melbourne.

In 1916 Mann enlisted in the Australian Imperial Force but while in training at an officers' instructional school was asked by the Western Australian government to withdraw in favour of membership of the Commonwealth Advisory Council for Science and Industry (1916-20). When he failed to get larger representation for Western Australia he took little part in the proceedings, partly because of distance. In 1921 he resigned his post as agricultural chemist, technically over its amalgamation with another, but probably because as president of the Civil Service Association he had been prominent in the public service strike of 1920.

In 1922 he was elected Federal member

for Perth as a Nationalist. As an advocate of the duty of all members of a democracy to exercise their responsibility to vote, he steered through parliament the Electoral Act (1924) which established compulsory voting. He was temporary chairman of committees in 1925-28. Mann did not fit into the party system: he strongly supported State rights and was a highly efficient member for Perth. He argued for a reduction in tariffs, joining the Town and Country Union for that purpose, and publicly criticized his prime minister S. M. (Viscount) Bruce [q.v.7], even resigning from the party briefly in 1926. In 1929 he joined W. M. Hughes [q.v.9] in attacking the Bruce-Page government's failure to prosecute coal-owner John Brown [q.v.7]. Excluded from party meetings as a consequence, they joined three others and brought down the government when it attempted to abolish the Commonwealth Court of Conciliation and Arbitration. Although Mann failed to gain a seat as an Independent in the 1929 election, he had the satisfaction of seeing Bruce and the Nationalists rejected by the electorate.

After a brief experience in insurance Mann, under the pseudonym of 'The Watchman', became the 'nearest thing Australian radio had in the 1930's to an oracle'. As the Australian Broadcasting Commission's chief commentator, he had a daily news session, 'At home and abroad', and a weekly programme, 'The news behind the news'. His clarity and fluency created interest; some listeners were attracted because he seemed sincere and independent but others objected to his dogmatism and anonymity. A huge popular following helped to preserve his outspokenness. The government of J. A. Lyons [q.v.], offended by his criticism of its trade diversion policy, put pressure on the A.B.C. to muzzle him. His comments on the Spanish civil war and Neville Chamberlain's appeasement policy, especially at Munich, also aroused opposition.

From September 1939 Mann was subject to censorship on the orders of the R. G. Menzies cabinet. His identity was exposed in parliament late in the year. His services were reduced, and he resigned in October 1940 while contesting Flinders, which he failed to win by a narrow margin, as an Independent. Although he returned to the A.B.C. he resigned bitterly when he was deprived of his regular session. His booming voice was then heard on commercial stations; he still held a following in 1943. In 1944 he published *Arrows in the air: a selection from broadcasts by 'The Watchman'*.

Mann died on 15 November 1951, on a tram in Melbourne, from a heart attack and was cremated. On 2 August 1949 he had married Gladys Alice Kubale at Melbourne and was survived by her and a son and two daughters of his first marriage.

L. F. Fitzhardinge, *The little digger* (Syd, 1979); G. Currie and J. Graham, *The origins of CSIRO* (Melb, 1966); K. S. Inglis, *This is the ABC* (Melb, 1983); *Politics*, 13, no 2 (1978), p 286; *SMH*, 19 Aug, 11 Dec 1925, 29 July, 2 Aug, 11, 23 Sept 1926, 19 Sept, 2 Nov 1928, 23, 24, 28, 31 Aug, 3, 5, 11, 14, 17, 19, 21, 27 Sept 1929, 10 Nov 1938, 26 Aug, 4, 10, 12, 15, 16, 19 Oct 1940, 16 Nov 1951; CSIRO Archives (Canb).

E. M. ANDREWS

MANN, SIR FREDERICK WOLLASTON (1869-1958), chief justice, was born on 2 May 1869 at Mount Gambier, South Australia, son of Gilbert Hill Cheke Mann, chief telegraphist, and his wife Sophia Charlotte, daughter of Rev. John Ramsden Wollaston [q.v.2]. E. A. Mann [q.v.] was his younger brother. After attending Christ Church Grammar School and the state school at Mount Gambier, Mann studied at home before moving to Melbourne in 1887. That year he worked as a tally clerk and also matriculated to pursue degrees in arts and law at the University of Melbourne. While at the university he worked as a clerk in the Crown Law Department. He graduated B.A. in 1894, M.A., LL.B. in 1896 and LL.M. in 1898 but, although admitted to the Bar in 1896, remained with the department until 1900.

During the South African War Mann was commissioned as lieutenant in the 4th Victorian (Australian Imperial Regiment) Contingent and saw sixteen months active service; he was wounded in the shoulder at Hartbeesfontein on 16 February 1901. He returned to Melbourne on 1 November and, having lost his departmental seniority, next year set up as a barrister in Selborne Chambers.

Mann quickly built up a large practice, undertaking both common law and Equity cases and specializing to some extent in patent law. He became known for his careful cross-examination technique, later likened by (Sir) Robert Menzies to the actions of a man picking his way across a swamp. In these years he was also a well-known yachtsman and an enthusiastic member of the Melbourne Hunt Club. On 8 April 1911 at All Saints Church of England, East St Kilda, he married Adeline Mary Raleigh; they made their home at South Yarra and had five children.

On 22 July 1919 Mann was appointed to the bench of the Victorian Supreme Court. Chairman of the Court of Industrial Appeals in 1931-33, he was knighted in June 1933. On various occasions between 1923 and 1934 he was acting chief justice and when Sir William Irvine [q.v.9] retired on 1 October 1935 Mann succeeded him.

Nicknamed the 'Little Gentleman' (he was 5 ft. 6 ins. (168 cm) tall), Mann was unfailingly courteous in court and helpful to young barristers. He had a reputation for deep learning and was remembered as a patient, careful judge with a strong sense of what the justice of a case required. His pronouncements, always delivered with entire confidence, were invariably clear and precise. On 12 May 1936 he became lieutenant-governor of Victoria, the office imposing a heavy burden of social duties in addition to his legal work. On his appointment the Melbourne *Sun* described him as 'lucid, fearless, cold, crisp, alert, analytical, unostentatious and retiring . . . dignified and decorous'. He was appointed K.C.M.G. in 1937.

In 1941 Mann suffered a great personal loss when his elder son, James Gilbert, was killed in action in Crete. Having been chosen as Victorian Rhodes Scholar for 1935, James won brilliant firsts and the Vinerian Scholarship at Oxford, and was regarded as the outstanding young lawyer of his generation. He was a lieutenant in the Royal Australian Artillery when he gave up his life raft to an exhausted man after the ship evacuating his men was bombed. Rather than overload other rafts, he swam out to sea.

Sir Frederick carried on as chief justice until January 1944 when he decided to retire while his faculties were still at their best. At his farewell, tributes were paid by W. L. Ham [q.v.9], E. L. Piesse and Sir James Macfarlan [qq.v.]. He retired as lieutenant-governor in May 1945.

Always a lover of Nature, Mann in his later years found great pleasure in the study of Australian plant and bird life and was a trustee of the Melbourne Botanical Gardens Maud Gibson Trust. With this interest and his attendance at the Melbourne Club, of which he had been president in 1935-36, he spent an otherwise quiet retirement at South Yarra. He died there on 29 May 1958, and was cremated. His wife had died the previous year and he was survived by three daughters and a son. A portrait by Charles Wheeler [q.v.] hangs in the Supreme Court of Victoria.

F. H. Bradshaw, *Selborne Chambers memories* (Melb, 1962); A. Dean, *A multitude of counsellors* (Melb, 1968); *Aust Law J*, 15 Oct 1935, p 240; *Law Inst J*, July 1958, p 184; *Herald*, 27 Oct 1933; *Age*, 16 Nov 1934, 18 Sept 1935, 30 May 1958; *Sun-News Pictorial*, 13 May 1936.

ELISE B. HISTED

MANN, GOTHER VICTOR FYERS (1863-1948), artist, architect and gallery director, was born on 8 October 1863 in Sydney, younger twin son and fourth child of John Frederick Mann [q.v.5], English-born surveyor and explorer, and his Sydney-born wife Camilla Victoria, daughter of Sir Thomas Mitchell [q.v.2]; she died eight days later. Educated at Sydney Grammar School, in 1882 Mann was apprenticed to the architect Thomas Rowe [q.v.6] and attended lectures in architecture at the University of Sydney. In 1885 he met Charles Conder [q.v.3]; they became close friends, attended classes under Julian Ashton [q.v.7] and made painting trips together to the Hawkesbury River. In 1886 Mann was elected an associate of the Institute of Architects of New South Wales and next year he was awarded the president's gold medal for draughtsmanship and design. In 1888-91 he practised in Brisbane in partnership with E. J. F. Crawford.

Returning to Sydney, Mann practised as an architect in Bridge Street, studied art under Tom Roberts and Arthur Streeton [qq.v.] and regularly visited their camp at Sirius Cove. He was secretary of the Art Society of New South Wales in the mid-1890s and exhibited with that society in 1892, the Queensland Art Society in 1896 and the Society of Artists, Sydney, in 1898. On 3 April 1902 he married Mabel Beatrice, daughter of the noted photographer J. H. Newman; they lived at Neutral Bay.

In 1905 Mann was appointed secretary and superintendent of the National Art Gallery of New South Wales and from 1912 director and secretary. He organized an important loan exhibition of Australian art in 1918 and visited Europe in 1914 and 1926 to buy for the collection. In 1926 he acquired works by Corot, Boudin and Conder, attended the Venice Biennale, and visited Holland with Lionel Lindsay [q.v.] to whom he confessed that 'it was hard work to buy pictures for laymen . . . with a miserable few hundreds'. Fundamentally conservative in his tastes and a champion of Australian Impressionism, he declared his opposition to modernism on his return in 1926. He was a member from 1912 and chairman in 1918-48 of the Commonwealth Art Advisory Board, established to advise the Historic Memorials Committee; from 1914, at Mann's behest, it began to acquire the nucleus of a national collection. Although as an administrator he exerted considerable influence, he chose to remain in the background of the art establishment. In 1928 he retired and was awarded the Society of Artists' medal; next year he was appointed C.B.E.

As a painter Mann was almost entirely unknown until he held his first and only one-man show at the Macquarie Galleries in May 1930. This retrospective exhibition included many scenes of Sydney Harbour and records of his visits abroad; William Moore [q.v.] noted the freedom and breadth of the work. The few examples of his work in public collections reveal that Mann's painting style was as modest and as undemonstrative as his character. In 1932-36 he was director of Sydney's Macleod [q.v.] Gallery attached to the *Bulletin*, and in 1938 he published a local history, *The municipality of North Sydney*. He belonged to the Australasian Pioneers' Club.

Survived by his wife and daughter, Mann died on 12 November 1948 in Royal North Shore Hospital and was cremated with Anglican rites. His portrait by W. B. McInnes [q.v.] is in the Art Gallery of New South Wales.

J. Mollison and L. Murray (eds), *The Australian National Gallery* (Canb, 1982); Art Gallery of Sth Aust, *Bulletin*, July 1968; *SMH*, 20, 29 Oct 1926, 3 June 1929; Mann papers *and* Lindsay family papers (ML).   RICHARD HAESE

MANN, THOMAS (1856-1941), trade unionist and socialist, was born on 15 April 1856 at Foleshill, Warwickshire, England, son of Thomas Mann, book-keeper, and his wife Mary Ann, née Grant. After three years schooling he began work at 10 in the claustrophobic underground passages of the Victoria Colliery. His only positive memories of childhood were of weekly church and Sunday-school attendance. In 1870 the family moved to Birmingham where he completed an engineering apprenticeship and embraced self-improvement, temperance and radicalism, while intensifying his religious commitment.

In 1877 Mann left Birmingham for London and, arriving during the 'great depression', experienced unemployment, poverty and loneliness. On 2 October 1879 he married Ellen Edwards. Finding regular work at his trade in the early 1880s, he began his career as a labour activist, his growing involvement with unionism, socialism and political action reflected in his membership of the Amalgamated Society of Engineers (1881), the Social Democratic Federation (1885), and the Independent Labour Party of which he was secretary in 1894-97. He was an ardent eight-hours advocate, and his pamphlet, *What a compulsory eight hour day means to the workers*, was published by H. H. Champion [q.v.7] in 1886. Mann's concern to unionize the unskilled led in 1889 to his achieving international prominence as a leader of the London dock strike.

During the next decade Tom Mann vacillated between unionism, Labour parliamentarianism (standing unsuccessfully three times), liberal reformism, Fabianism, S.D.F. socialism and religion. In 1893 he contemplated ordination to the Anglican priesthood. After the breakdown of his marriage and the failure of his Workers' Union to meet his high expectations, Mann sailed in December 1901 for New Zealand, where he worked as organizer for the New Zealand Socialist Party. In September 1902 he arrived in Australia to undertake a lecture tour, bringing with him Elsie Harker, singer and fellow socialist, who remained his lifelong companion.

Mann travelled widely throughout Australasia, demonstrating the oratorical powers and organizational skills for which he was famed in England. He visited New South Wales and South Australia in 1902, Tasmania in 1903 and 1906, Western Australia in 1904, Queensland in 1905 and New Zealand again in 1908. His greatest influence was in Victoria where in 1903-04 he worked as organizer for the Political Labor Council, helping to expand it from a small, beleaguered Melbourne-based party to a State-wide organization with significant parliamentary representation. But he failed to persuade it to adopt a socialist platform.

Impatient with parliamentary laborism, in March 1906 Mann founded and became secretary of the Victorian Socialist Party, a development anticipated in his pamphlet *Socialism* (1905). Funded in part by his wealthy friend J. P. Jones [q.v.9], it grew to a membership of 1500 by August and produced its own weekly, the *Socialist*, edited initially by Mann, who also threw himself into its educational, social and political activities. During the winter of 1906 the V.S.P. led agitation on unemployment and in November Mann and other members were imprisoned in a campaign for free speech.

Unable to gain acceptance for the V.S.P. by the broader labour movement, or to prevent factionalism in its own ranks over issues such as co-operation with the Labor Party, Mann turned to industrial activism, lecturing and writing on 'revolutionary unionism'. His activities culminated in participation as industrial organizer for the Broken Hill (New South Wales) Combined Unions Committee in the prolonged, bitterly fought dispute in 1908-09 between the miners and the Broken Hill Proprietary Co. Ltd. In January 1909 he was arrested on charges of sedition and unlawful assembly but was acquitted in April after trial in Albury. Unsatisfactory settlement of the dispute through arbitration and continuing contact with international socialism convinced Mann of the need for militant industrial action, a belief expounded in his pamphlets of 1909, *The way to win* and *Industrial unionism*.

In December, perhaps disheartened by the parochialism of the Australian labour movement and its resistance to his industrial advocacy, Mann sailed with his family for Britain via South Africa, where he worked briefly for the Johannesburg miners. He arrived in London in May 1910 with a new sense of direction forged from his Australian experience. With the journalist Guy Bowman, he launched the

Industrial Syndicalist, which urged concerted, direct industrial action, and resumed his role of organizer of strikes and union activities. He was elected general secretary of the Amalgamated Society of Engineers in 1919 and of the Amalgamated Engineering Union in 1920. A member of the British Socialist Party from 1916, he became a founder-member of the Communist Party of Great Britain in 1920. In 1924-32 he chaired the National Minority Movement which sought workers' control of industry. He made four trips to Russia and also visited North America, China and Sweden. He died on 13 March 1941 at Grassington, Yorkshire.

Punch (Melb), 5 July 1906; *Bulletin,* 5 Jan 1905, 22 Jan 1920; *The Times,* 14 Mar 1941; C. G. W. Osborne, Tom Mann: his Australasian experience, 1902-1910 (Ph.D. thesis, ANU, 1972) and for bibliog.   GRAEME OSBORNE

MANNING, FREDERIC (1882-1935), novelist and poet, was born on 22 July 1882 in Sydney, fourth son of native-born parents (Sir) William Patrick Manning [q.v.], financier and politician, and his wife Honora, née Torpy, both of Irish descent; his elder brother was (Sir) Henry [q.v.]. A lifelong asthmatic, Frederic was educated privately except for six months at Sydney Grammar School. Aged 15 he went to England with his tutor Rev. Arthur Galton, a friend of Matthew Arnold and Lionel Johnson, who had come to Australia as private secretary to Governor Sir Robert Duff [q.v.8]. Some two years later Manning returned to Sydney, but, uninterested in business or the professions, pursued a literary career in England from 1903. He lived with Galton, from 1904 at the vicarage at Edenham, near Bourne, Lincolnshire.

With occasional visits to London (where all his works were published), Manning lived a retiring, leisured and scholarly life, steeping himself in the classics and assisted by a small allowance from home and later an interest in a Queensland sheep-station run by a brother. Through Galton he had the entrée to select literary circles, including that of Olivia Shakespeare, friend of W. B. Yeats and mother of Ezra Pound's wife Dorothy. He published a narrative poem, *The vigil of Brunhild,* in 1907 and *Poems* in 1910, and was principal reviewer for the *Spectator* in 1909-14.

Manning's first prose work, *Scenes and portraits* (1909), a collection of short historical fictions in dialogue or monologue form, explored the idea that there are 'only two religions . . . [that] of the humble folk, whose life is a daily communion with the natural forces and a bending to them; and the religion of men like Protagoras, Lucretius and Montaigne, a religion of doubt, of tolerance and agnos-

ticism'. Manning's theme sprang from a deep sense of isolation, suffering and transience of human lives. The book won him considerable attention from such writers as Max Beerbohm, E. M. Forster, T. E. Lawrence and Pound.

After failing an officers' course, Manning enlisted as a private in the King's Shropshire Light Infantry in 1915 and served in France on the Somme. On 30 May 1917 he was commissioned second lieutenant in the Royal Irish Regiment of Foot, but ill health prevented further active service. That year he published a third volume of poetry, *Eidola,* which included some war poems. After Galton's death in 1921 he lived much in Italy. He published a commissioned biography of Sir William White, designer of the first dreadnought, in 1923, and an edition of Walter Charleton's *Epicurus's morals* in 1926. His friend (Sir) William Rothenstein described him as having 'the worn look, as of carved ivory, due to constant ill-health . . . and the sensitive intelligence one finds in men of fastidious habits'. His only hobbies were horse-racing and book-collecting. Friends, including Lawrence and T. S. Eliot, found his conversation 'extraordinary for its learning and charm'.

His sensitively speculative cast of mind underlies Manning's most enduring work, the war novel published anonymously under the pseudonym, 'Private 19022', in 1929 as *The middle parts of fortune* and the abridged version next year as *Her privates we.* It was regarded as one of the outstanding English war novels by Forster, Lawrence (who discerned Manning's authorship), Arnold Bennett, Ernest Hemingway, Peter Davies (his friend and publisher) and Eric Partridge [q.v.]. The novel concerns the life of men in the ranks of an English battalion in France, both in and out of action, and is based largely on Manning's own experiences as a 'ranker'. It depicts a temporary release from isolation through a heightened form of comradeship and is a kind of acceptance of war, despite its suffering and horrors, as a heightened form of the reality of all human lives.

Soon after returning from an eighteen months visit to his siblings in Australia, Manning died on 22 February 1935 at Hampstead, London, and was buried in Kensal Green cemetery beside his lifelong friend and literary hostess, Mrs Alfred Fowler. He died a Catholic, albeit an unorthodox one. Eliot wrote that Manning lacked the prerequisites for a reputation in his own time, 'a considerable body of writing and a range of acquaintance', not only because of his ill health and lack of ambition, but because his passion for perfection could be self-destructive. Nevertheless his aesthetic perfectionism, combined with his humanism, earned him posthumously a distinguished place in English and Australian literature, for he can be seen as belonging to both.

A pencil sketch of Manning by Rothenstein is in the Mitchell Library.

W. Rothenstein, *Men and memories* (Lond, 1932), and *Since fifty* (Lond, 1939); H. Klein (ed), *The First World War in fiction* (Lond, 1976); *London Gazette*, 29 June 1917, p 6495; *Aust Q*, June 1935, p 47; *Criterion*, Apr 1935; *Reveille* (Syd), 1 Apr 1935; L. T. Hergenhan, 'Frederic Manning: a neglected Australian writer', *Quadrant*, Spring 1962, *and* 'Novelist at war: Frederic Manning's *Her Privates We*', *Quadrant*, July-Aug 1970, *and* 'Two expatriates: Frederic Manning and James Griffyth Fairfax', *Southerly*, 29, no 1, 1979, *and* 'Ezra Pound, Frederic Manning and James Griffyth Fairfax', *Aust Literary Studies*, with checklist, May 1984; *J of Cwlth Literature*, 12, no 2, 1977; *London Mag*, Dec 1983-Jan 1984, p 54; *SMH*, 8, 12 Jan 1938, 25 Oct 1978; Manning papers (ML).

L. T. HERGENHAN

MANNING, SIR WILLIAM PATRICK (1845-1915), financier and politician, and **SIR HENRY EDWARD** (1877-1963), barrister and politician, were father and son. William was born on 18 November 1845 at Chippendale, Sydney, eldest son of Irish parents John Manning, baker, and his wife Mary, née Hourigan, who had reached Sydney in the *Moffatt* in 1841 and later married. Educated at St Mary's Cathedral School, about 1862 he entered the counting-house of P. N. Russell [q.v.6] & Co., engineers, and laid the foundations of his financial and administrative skills, becoming chief accountant. When the firm closed in the mid-1870s, he set up as a public accountant and broker. On 8 August 1868 he had married Honora (Nora) Torpy (d.1940) at St Mary's Cathedral.

In 1887-1902 Manning represented Bourke Ward on the Sydney Municipal Council and was mayor in 1891-94. An excellent chairman, he was responsible for remodelling the Belmore market and the formation of Moore Street, and initiated the scheme for building the Queen Victoria Market. He chaired the royal commission on alleged Chinese gambling and immorality and charges of bribery against members of the police force in 1891-92, and served on the royal commission into the military service of New South Wales in 1892. In 1893-94 he also represented South Sydney in the Legislative Assembly and as a Protectionist supported Sir George Dibbs [q.v.4]. In the financial crisis of 1893 his calm good management of the City and in the city were alike remarkable. On 2 May in the House he spoke frankly of the deficiences of colonial banking as a whole. Dibbs in 1895 acknowledged his assistance in drafting the Bank Issue Act of 1893. During his unsuccessful electoral campaign of 1898 Manning strongly advocated Federation and reform of the Legislative Council, attacked (Sir) George Reid [q.v.] and pledged support for (Sir) Edmund Barton [q.v.7]; in 1901, however, he was defeated for the Senate.

Knighted in 1894, Manning was a director of the Citizens' Life Assurance Co. in 1896-1908 and remained on the board, after (Sir) John Garvan [q.v.8] had engineered its merger to form the Mutual Life & Citizens' Assurance Co. Ltd, until 1915. He was also local chairman of the Sun Insurance Office of London in 1894-1915. In 1910 he carried through the reconstruction of the Australian Joint Stock Bank (later the Australian Bank of Commerce) and was chairman in 1911-15. He managed the Australian financial interests of Lord Rosebery [q.v.5 Primrose], the duke of Manchester, Lord Carnarvon and Lord Sherbrooke [q.v.2 Lowe], and attended to the details when Russell in 1896 and 1904 made gifts totalling £100 000 to the University of Sydney to found a school of engineering.

'A commanding figure' standing 'fully six feet' (183 cm), Manning dressed immaculately and was hardly ever 'seen without a silk hat and a frock coat'. He was a notable Roman Catholic layman, a fellow of St John's College within the university in 1893-1915 and a papal chamberlain from 1903. Archbishop Kelly [q.v.9] publicly acknowledged in 1915 his contributions to the building of St Mary's Cathedral. He was president of the Sydney Philharmonic Society in 1891-1914.

Manning died of heart disease at his Woollahra home on 20 April 1915 and was buried in South Head cemetery. He was survived by his wife, five sons, including Frederic [q.v.], and three daughters, who inherited his estate, valued for probate at £28 027.

His second son Henry was born on 18 December 1877 at Darlinghurst. He was educated at St Ignatius' College, Riverview, and the University of Sydney (B.A., 1900; LL.B., 1902). At the university he was a prominent debater and won blues for cricket and rowing. Admitted to the Bar on 28 July 1902, he practised on the Western Circuit and in 1904 became associate to Justice R. E. O'Connor [q.v.] of the High Court of Australia. In 1904-05 he reported High Court cases in Queensland, South Australia, Western Australia and Tasmania. Witnessed by Barton, on 19 January 1905 he married Nora Antonia (d.1962), youngest daughter of Sir James Martin [q.v.5] and god-daughter of Anthony Trollope [q.v.6], at St Mary's Cathedral. When he resumed practice, most of his work was in common law and in Admiralty. In 1927 he represented the owners in the proceedings that followed the running down of the ferry *Greycliffe* in Sydney Harbour with the loss of forty-two lives. He took silk in 1929.

Defeated as a Liberal for the Legislative Assembly seats of Phillip in 1910, King in 1913 and, standing for the United Australia Party, King in 1932, Manning was nominated to the Legislative Council and joined (Sir) Bertram Stevens's [q.v.] reconstructed ministry as attorney-general on 17 June 1932. From the early 1920s Manning had been interested in reform of the council which he believed should be a House of review, neither constituted nor operating on party lines. With drafting assistance from (Sir) Thomas Bavin [q.v.7], his friend (Sir) John Peden [q.v.] and others, he drew up a scheme for an Upper House of sixty members, elected by the two Houses as a single electorate, with provision for settling deadlocks. His system, adopted by parliament and approved at a referendum in 1933, ensured that there could not be a Labor majority in the council for fifteen years and that no government could alter the situation without amending the constitution.

Elected to the new council for twelve years in 1934 and 1946, Manning remained attorney-general, vice-president of the Executive Council and government representative in the Legislative Council, in the Stevens-Bruxner [q.v.7] and Mair [q.v.]-Bruxner ministries until 1941. In 1935 he attended an interstate conference called by the Commonwealth government on ways of amending section 92 of the Constitution. Next year he went to London, briefed to represent New South Wales and Queensland in the dried fruits appeal case (F. A. *James* [q.v.9] v. *The Commonwealth*) before the Privy Council. He was appointed K.B.E. in 1939.

After Labor regained power in 1941, Manning was unofficially regarded as leader of the non-Labor members but refused the title and perquisites of leader of the Opposition in the council, when offered to him. He was 'a prolific writer of memoranda', and in 1950 opposed a suggestion that the Liberals should form a disciplined party in the Upper House. In 1957-58 he had to defend his concept of the council from strong attacks within the Liberal Party and from Labor plans to abolish it. He retired from the council in April 1958.

Manning was chairman of the M.L.C. in 1945-61, a local director of the Union Trustee Co. of Australia Ltd and the Commercial Union Assurance Co. Ltd, and a member of the Australia Club. In 1934-48 he was a fellow of the Senate of the University of Sydney: in 1941 he resigned in protest at the filling of chairs in law while many possible candidates were serving overseas, but was promptly re-elected. Survived by his two daughters, Manning died at Randwick on 3 May 1963 and was buried in the Catholic section of Northern Suburbs cemetery.

Cyclopedia of N.S.W. (Syd, 1907); *Arrow* (Syd), 20 Jan 1896; *Catholic Press,* 17 Dec 1903; *Freeman's J* (Syd), 22 Apr 1915; *T&CJ,* 28 Apr 1915; *SMH,* 20 May, 7, 10 Aug, 18 Oct 1935, 1 Apr 1936, 2 Jan 1939, 10 May 1958, 4 May 1963.

JOHN M. WARD

MANNIX, DANIEL (1864-1963), Catholic archbishop, was born on 4 March 1864 at his father's substantial tenant farm Deerpark, Charleville (Rathluirc), Cork, Ireland, son of Timothy Mannix and his wife Ellen, née Cagney. He was born in the year of the Syllabus of Errors, six years before Vatican Council I. When celebrating his last Mass on the opening day of Vatican II (11 October 1962) he drank from a gold copy of the fifteenth-century de Burgh chalice presented by his friend President de Valera of Ireland, and wore a handwoven replica of the vestments presented by the Empress of Austria to St Patrick's College, Maynooth, and worn by the archbishop of Dublin at Mannix's own ordination (8 June 1890).

His parents were scrupulously devout and ambitious; three other surviving sons went into medicine, farming and law, and a sister finished her education in France. All but one were similarly long lived although Daniel was anaemic and non-insurable as a student. His domineering mother steered him from Sisters of Mercy and Christian Brothers' primary schools into Latin-teaching academies, thence through St Colman's, Fermoy, to Maynooth in 1882. Later, in Australia he would have one cousin, Daniel Foley, as suffragan bishop of Ballarat, and six others as religious, five of them nuns. In 1889-90 he continued his outstanding scholastic success at Dunboyne Establishment, qualifying for a doctorate of divinity (awarded 1895) and proceeding directly to a lectureship in philosophy and the chair of moral theology at Maynooth (1895).

Sources are too exiguous for a well-rounded appreciation of his character and standing in Ireland. He burned documents, wrote letters sparingly and kept no diaries so that posterity could not 'analyse my soul'. His answers and notes in the *Irish Ecclesiastical Record* upholding Rome's authority and disparaging gallicanism, together with aloof austerity, led to his being called 'a lonely frigid theologian'. However, his letters show a glimmer of disdain for canon law and, in Melbourne, he largely ignored it, ultimately advocating abolition of its 'irritative' penalties because 'you can't make people good by punishment'. Mannix discouraged note-taking in class, relied on a single text, but was a lucid, free-ranging expositor. As inaugural secretary (1896-1903) of the Maynooth Union he promoted discussion of 'urgent' socioeconomic questions such as temperance, co-operatives and housing, advocated free-enterprise economic nationalism as more vital to Irish self-respect than Home Rule, and delivered (1901) a cogent if unoriginal 6000-word paper on the land question. This paper advocated freehold for tenant-farmers such as his family and, unlike Parnellites, protection and alliance with the Tories. It was the only substantial article he ever wrote. He assisted his relatives in land negotiations and ultimately, with £1000, tried to salvage the family farm which his brother Timothy wasted in drink and mismanagement.

Mannix travelled abroad in vacations, belonged to the exclusive Papal Household Club in London, rode with the other professors to hounds but, although tolerant of conviviality, was a conspicuous leader of the Pioneer temperance movement. His probity, care for rubrics, discipline and deference to the hierarchy led to appointment as vice-president and then, rapidly, president of Maynooth (1903) by unanimous election. Henceforth he rode only in a brougham. Rome appointed him monsignor in 1906.

Mannix's major tasks were to remove 'the finger of scorn from priests' and, as senator of the moribund Royal University of Ireland, to press acceptance of Maynooth, against Orange opposition, as a recognized college of the new (1909) National University of Ireland. Whereas in 1903 only 11 of 80 Maynooth entrants had qualified for matriculation studies, all priests now met degree requirements. Mannix was awarded an honorary doctorate of laws. Maynooth, once described by Canon P. Sheahan as a 'rude cyclopean [institution] . . . without one single aspect of refinement', became a 'West Point'. Among those sent down for smoking were Kevin O'Higgins and a future bishop. Mannix introduced the *Manual of etiquette and good manners*, and improved salaries and domestic welfare. Books on the Index were removed from the library, Maynooth was screened for tinges of 'modernism' and speculation in the *Irish Theological Quarterly* discouraged. Mannix contemptuously repelled student protests but was esteemed for his holiness and personal care of the sick; 90 per cent of students emerged teetotallers. However liberal he may have wanted to be, he was compelled, if he wished to join the hierarchy, to satisfy his narrow episcopal trustees. His former students were surprised to learn that their magisterial, tall, gaunt and handsome president was regarded in uptown drawing-rooms as a man of wide culture.

Certainly he appeared oblivious of the Gaelic revival: his opposition to compulsory Irish—he was never known to use a word of it—as being useless to diasporic clergy led to intemperate criticism from its propagandist Professor Michael O'Hickey. Mannix became the 'Mephistopheles' who allegedly engineered O'Hickey's dismissal from Maynooth. The 1916 martyr Padraig Pearse asked: Is Mannix an enemy to Irish nationalism? In 1926 John Devoy was still condemning him to 'sackcloth and ashes'. He must have been desolated to be seen as a 'castle Catholic' but he had eschewed politics and had cordially entertained King Edward VII (1903) and King George V (1911) in loyal displays at Maynooth. This was 'toadyism' even to Redmondites. Later Mannix and his adulators would gloss over these visits.

Through antagonizing nationalists and, probably, important hierarchs, Mannix seems to have forfeited his chance of a major Irish see. He was appointed to Melbourne (1 July 1912) soon after O'Hickey's embarrassingly protracted appeal to Rome was discontinued by the Rota. Archbishop Thomas Carr [q.v.7] had for years wanted him as a coadjutor and with Carr's age, Cardinal Moran's [q.v.] demise (1911) and Archbishop Michael Kelly's [q.v.9] dullness, a formidable leader was needed in the struggle for state aid. Ultimately, Mannix was not consulted about his appointment and, as he had insisted that his students obey Rome unquestioningly, he did not demur. He was consecrated titular bishop of Pharsalus on 6 October 1912, taking the motto *Omnia Omnibus* ('all things to all men'). He then fell seriously ill with pneumonia and, ignoring a prearranged student valediction, dispiritedly slipped out of his beloved Maynooth, never to return.

He arrived in Adelaide on Easter Saturday 1913. The autumn heat made him wonder how he could persevere, but the enthusiastic reception next day at St Patrick's Cathedral, Melbourne, where he was hailed as a world-class theologian and educationist, must have assuaged his loneliness. He said he hoped to be a good Australian and to see Catholics share in 'the good things in private and public life'. By 1918 St Kevin's central secondary and Newman tertiary colleges were opened as pledges of this. Even the *Argus* looked forward to some brilliant contribution to the community but was startled to hear his immediate aggression against 'the one great stain on the statute books'—no state aid for church schools. Within a year he was linking this deprivation to Cromwellian persecutions and convict floggings which he believed had been inflicted less than fifty years before for not attending Anglican services.

Moran's more amiable leadership of the Church gave way to deliberate confrontation. Mannix advised the 100 000-strong Australian Catholic Federation 'to twist the political screw', particularly against Labor, in balance-of-power tactics, while being gratified that 'to wince and smart' under 'the unjust burden' would enhance Catholic solidarity. He encouraged infiltration of the Labor Party although Catholics like James Scullin and Joseph Lyons [qq.v.] stressed the benefits to workers from Labor governments and predicted an inevitable sectarian backlash. But Mannix was naïve about political processes and was insensitive to the rationale for 'godless' state education. Catholic voters generally ignored him; A.C.F. members were barred from the Labor party.

Mannix approved of Britain's declaration of war in 1914 but did not preach the heroics of holy war or take part in recruiting. Rather he used Catholic voluntary participation to press for state aid and denounce 'race suicide' (contraception). Throughout 1915 sectarianism became more virulent; Catholics were falsely alleged not to be doing their share. 'Apparently not enough nuns are joining', retorted Mannix. This exasperation did not prevent his deploring the 1916 Easter Rising, but he quashed Kelly's proposed episcopal protest against it because he held England culpable. He wept over Pearse's execution, became convinced of England's irremediable perfidy and patronized the raising of relief funds. He rebuffed W. M. Hughes's [q.v.9] overtures to support conscription but entered the first referendum campaign only twice to emphasize that Australia was already doing enough. Philosophically his stance was not clear. Conscription was somehow both a purely political question, as the apostolic delegate insisted, and yet an 'evil' in itself. Victoria voted 'Yes' but afterwards Hughes scapegoated Mannix for his narrow defeat. Mannix responded by deriding this 'sordid trade war' and with 'wilful ambiguity' proclaimed he was simply putting Australia before the Empire while following the Pope's call for an honourable peace and Woodrow Wilson's plea for self-determination—which would have to be applied to Ireland.

His noble panegyric on Carr, whom he succeeded as archbishop on 6 May 1917, stressed the synonymity of Irish and Catholic in Australia, although at Maynooth he had told his levites not to hang green from their steeples overseas. Mannix now became a workers' hero, denouncing inequality of sacrifice, endorsing the justice of strikes and declaring that a vote for Hughes in the 1917 election would be a vote for conscription. When, in November, the Exhibition Building trustees refused him access, he drew possibly 100 000 people to John Wren's [q.v.] Richmond racecourse with the scathing laconic oratory he had carefully practised under William Lockington [q.v.] in the cathedral grounds. The trustees could not run 'a punch and judy show'; their supporters had the 'backbone . . . of boiled asparagus'; Australians without knowing it were really Sinn Feiners; for Ireland, England's plight meant NOW

or NEVER. In the second conscription referendum Victoria voted 'No' but again Mannix's role was hardly decisive.

Mannix dismissed contemptuously those 'self-styled leading' middle-class Catholics who expressed outrage at his 'disloyalty': Charles Heydon [q.v.9] was a 'second or third class' judge. Boycotted by such people at St John's College, Sydney University, in March 1918, he told the 'real' Catholics who mobbed him that one could search in vain for frontrank, university-educated Catholics who had not denied their faith. He returned to Melbourne for the St Patrick's Day procession where he did not doff his biretta at the National Anthem. Demands for his deportation climaxed in a mass demonstration led by Herbert Brookes [q.v.7] who for years financed fables of the 'Scarlet Woman'. However, Mannix relished being 'the lightning-rod' for Protestant bigots and slept peacefully, although Catholics were refused jobs or lodgings. Yet most Catholics probably felt a surging ethnic morale and righteous indignation rather than despair.

Mannix's scorn for his chaplain-general's uniform was reported to King George V who suggested he be transferred to Rome: 'God forbid', replied Cardinal Gasquet. The Vatican did try to silence him but was fearful of a schism. Mannix solved any church-state dilemma by simply claiming to speak *qua* citizen. What non-Catholic clergy 'could say in a pulpit, he could say in a paddock', but the 'paddocks' were usually church grounds and functions. At a 1918 episcopal conference the threat of Vatican discipline obliged him to propose a motion deprecating divisive publicity by bishops, but as the laity was not informed he did not lose face. He had become arguably the most revered and reviled figure in Australian history. Wren financed a climactic vindication when, on St Patrick's Day 1920, fourteen Victoria Cross winners on white chargers led the march, the Union Jack was obscured, and for their farewell concert a few days later 1500 Christian Brothers' students sang 'God Save Ireland'. Odes were written to Mannix, medallions struck, busts and portraits adorned Catholic homes.

In May 1920 friendly crowds organized by Wren delayed Mannix's boarding a train to begin his *ad limina* visit to Rome via the United States of America and Ireland. He had declined a £50 000 testimonial initiated by Wren, as he did all personal gifts, but Wren's adapted lyric 'Come back to Australia [Erin]' was meant to augur that he would not be refused re-entry or accept an Irish see. Sydney held a mayoral farewell. Though he said he had not corresponded with de Valera, mass meetings were organized in America. He was, to his surprise, an international figure. He said America had been the only ally with 'clean hands' and that England had been, was and always would be America's enemy; in New York he was given the freedom of the city. He came to accept the austere, pious, machiavellian de Valera as the greatest Irish leader ever.

In August the British government decided not to allow Mannix to disembark in his insurgent, Black-and-Tan-ridden homeland, and landed him at Penzance, Cornwall. 'The greatest victory the Royal Navy has had since Jutland', he quipped, 'without the loss of a single British soldier'. Lloyd George looked foolish, Mannix victimized. He refused to visit Ireland on terms or have Lloyd George bring his octogenarian mother to England. Forbidden to visit Liverpool, Manchester or Glasgow, he drew crowds outside their environs and throughout England and Scotland. In Rome he expected reproof and perhaps recall from Australia but, after three audiences, Pope Benedict XV donated 20 000 lire to Irish relief and had Mannix draft a letter of sympathy—the first Vatican censure of British conduct in Ireland. He would not allow the pontiff to intervene to get him to Ireland. In August 1921 Mannix returned to Australia to the chagrin of loyalists and the well-organized joy of his flock.

Aside from four visits to New Zealand and one to the Chicago Eucharistic Congress in 1926, Mannix made only one other overseas tour. During Holy Year 1925 he led an Australian pilgrimage to Rome, Lourdes (France) and Ireland. He was now the only episcopal supporter of de Valera in Ireland and Australia. The New York *Irish World* later called him *Mannix contra mundum Britannicum tyrannicum, et Black and Tannicum*. As a moral theologian he probably eased some republican consciences following the pro-Free State strictures of the Irish hierarchy, and he did not see perjury in de Valera's signing 'under duress' the oath of allegiance to the Crown in order to break it. As he (Mannix) was not infallible, so neither was the hierarchy!

In Ireland he was ostracized; only one bishop visited him—after dark, 'like Nicodemus in the night', Mannix said. Biding his time he stepped out of Charleville to accept officially the freedom of towns conferred on him in 1920; he was hallowed in torchlight processions and republican rallies. Declaring that he came in reconciliation, he derided leading Free Staters as placemen and the recent Senate election as a fiasco. The Free State was not 'a stepping stone' to liberation. 'I'll never set foot in Ireland again', Mannix vowed. 'Dan never understood Ireland', his clericalist mother had said before she died earlier in 1925. He saw himself as prescient when de Valera did come to power in 1932, though the Free State was accepted and par-

tition remained. He continued to comment on Irish affairs. The apostolic delegate censured him in 1933 for jibing at General O'Duffy and his semi-fascist 'blueshirts'; during World War II Mannix defended Irish neutrality, rationalizing that Germany would have overrun her otherwise; he took the St Patrick's Day salute till his death.

But Melbourne was now utterly his home. He considered there was 'no country in the world where there was a stronger bond between hierarchy and people . . . Catholics should stand against the world'. He loved the city and people. Some saw a rebuff in Sydney being granted the International Eucharistic Congress in 1928 but Mannix's triumphalist oration, 'The winter has passed . . . the flowers have appeared in our land', was an acknowledged highlight: two things mattered, the Mass and the papacy. His National Eucharistic Congress for the Victorian centenary in 1934, the greatest of his mass demonstrations, culminated in 80 000 people passing to benediction before Mount St Evin's hospital reportedly before half a million watchers.

At the accompanying conference Mannix promoted lay Catholic Action against the narrow clericalism of Kelly and other bishops. He had founded the Catholic Central Library with William Hackett [q.v.9] in 1923, fostered the Catholic Evidence Guild and, after pressure from the Jesuits, a Catholic Hour on radio 3AW (1932), but he refused to have a Catholic radio station. He was indulgent of Catholic businessmen's response to Freemasonry, the Knights of the Southern Cross. The autonomous, intellectual Campion Society (1931) was 'the flower and fruit of his higher educational efforts', dedicated to the study of papal social encyclicals and Chesterbellocian distributism. Its offshoot, the monthly *Catholic Worker* (1936), was selling 55 000 copies by 1942; other journals also flourished. The Young Christian Workers, National Catholic Girls' Movement and Young Christian Students were founded on European models and, together with the National Catholic Rural Movement, were mandated by the hierarchy as official Catholic Action and co-ordinated by a National Catholic Secretariat for Catholic Action (1937).

In spite of a vast library and subscriptions to numerous journals there is little evidence, other than the awe he inspired, to suggest that Mannix was deeply versed in political or socio-economic questions. Basically he was a social democrat. While he could praise Mussolini to an immigrant Italian audience in 1943 as 'the greatest man living today', he had been critical of the invasion of Abyssinia, and had condemned Nazism and especially anti-Semitism. He was fervently pro-Franco, and hostile to Stalin except as expedient ally, but in 1943, being sceptical that Australians could be fooled, thought communists should not be excluded from the elections. Until then capitalism was the major enemy. He enjoyed cordial relations with Labor governments. Arthur Calwell treasured a filial relationship with him and helped to arrange exemptions from wartime regulations for persons serviceable to the Church. Mannix corresponded with H. V. Evatt on constitutional safeguards for religion, approved his 1944 powers referendum, humoured him when he complained of *Catholic Worker* criticism, approved bank nationalization provided co-operative banks were allowed, and supported Evatt's stand against the Big Powers at San Francisco in 1945.

Mannix condemned the Hiroshima bombing as 'immoral and indefensible', but later complained that General MacArthur had been sent to Korea to make war but forbidden to win it. However, he mustered the other bishops behind B. A. Santamaria's Catholic Social Studies Movement (1941) which from 1945 became a secretive, ambiguously authorized form of Catholic Action although, theologically, it should have been simply 'action of Catholics', not involving the hierarchy and thus not enjoining the consciences of Catholics. Later he denied the 'secrecy' and justified using the same tactics as communists. Mannix could not distinguish between ecclesial and civil roles or understand why a party could not accept outside manipulation. Although, unlike Santamaria, he personally voted against dissolving the Communist Party in the referendum of 1951, he affirmed with increasing obduracy that Australia was in the gravest danger from communism, even after 1956 when the party was shattered.

Controversies in the Church following the 1954 Labor split elicited from the Vatican a condemnation of 'the Movement' as impolitic and theologically unsound. Mannix tried to obscure the ruling and backed the National Civic Council and the Democratic Labor Party. 'Rome has blundered again', he said; 'Santamaria is the saviour of Australia'. He intervened in subsequent elections, allowing his auxiliary bishop to pronounce that no Catholic could vote in conscience for Labor, although in 1960 three of the four Federal Labor leaders including Calwell, a future papal knight, were Catholics.

While Mannix was politically naïve and, in spite of his quick-wittedness, intellectually shallow, this was not crucial to his spiritual constituency, the clergy and faithful. Folklore asserted he was one of the four cleverest men in the world. Certainly he was God's warrior in the breastplate of St Patrick smiting bigots with apparent logic and ridicule and edifying the Church militant. Over fifty years the diocesan faithful increased from 150 000 to 600 000; churches from 160 to 300; students in Catholic primary schools from 21 792 to 73 695; secondary pupils from 3126 to 28 395; priests increased by 237, brothers by 181, nuns by 736; 10 new male and 14 female orders were introduced; 10 seminaries and 7 new hospitals, 3 orphanages, homes for delinquents, the blind and deaf, hostels for girls . . .

During the Depression, with Catholics hard hit, he continued building with Keynesian aplomb. He finally crowned Eastern Hill in 1939 with cathedral spires, an event he celebrated coincidentally with the centenary of the first Mass in Victoria in a pageant, *Credo*, at the Melbourne Cricket Ground. This was attended by 60 000 people, including an English author whom he had personally invited to record the spectacle of Mannix *in excelsis* giving the final benediction. Entering the portals of St Patrick's for High Mass, with the Vienna Mozart Boys' Choir which he had saved from wartime internment intoning Palestrina's 'Tu es Petrus', Mannix with steepled hands majestically evoked the numinous mediaeval Church. Ceremony was one source of his undisputed charisma.

Increasingly venerable and dignified, he would spend up to five hours a day in strenuous prayer. Basically an Ignatian formalist, he was neither speculative, mystical nor innovative in liturgy. Sodalities flourished, he sponsored popular devotions such as the Fatima statue and rosary crusades, and adhered to meatless Fridays and morning Mass for fear of 'protestant' indiscipline. Each Saturday he confessed humbly at St Francis' Church, then shrived penitents for long hours at the cathedral, never stinting his homilies. He was accessible to all at Raheen palace, comforting the troubled and dependent with his solicitude and charming the curious and eminent with his wryness of mind. He performed a perpetual round of communion breakfasts, confirmations, bazaars, requiems, corporal works of mercy, laying foundation stones and blessing new buildings. He kept his patronage for his own people and, unlike Archbishop James Duhig [q.v.8], never attended levées or official garden parties. (Nor did he ask if Queensland Catholics were better off without 'confrontation').

He thought hatred of Catholics by Protestants, with their unfilled churches and babel of doctrines, was inevitable. With tridentine disdain he never entered their churches; he offered courtesy, never fraternization. In 1916 he defended Lutheran schools against closure; but Luther himself was 'a distasteful subject . . . impossible to quote in decent surroundings'. He enforced the ne temere decree deploring mixed marriages. The wife of a divorced Catholic, Marcel Dupré, the French organist, who paid a courtesy call, found Mannix the rudest man she ever met. Mannix ignored his apostate brother Patrick (1865-1962) when in England. Such attitudes in a diffused plural society entrenched subcultural divisions but for Mannix Catholics would come into their own on their own terms. Teaching orders were inspired to more exacting efforts to notch government scholarships while they successfully subsidized Catholic upward mobility through celibacy, poverty and obedience. Their schools did not grasp the chance for divergent curricula; they conformed to the state syllabi plus doctrine and apologetics. Mannix applied himself to wording rigorously the penny catechism; he was hardly an educationist. Before the public subscription for his diamond jubilee was converted into the Mannix travelling scholarship (1950) for aspiring Catholic academics, he had to be briefed on the need for them to gain higher degrees.

Mannix's cathedral administrator was also his personal secretary and vicar-general; he preferred a single conduit however overburdened but, in time, there were mitres for assiduity. With minimum effort he controlled policy and patronage; aspiring bishops did the work. Filing systems were a mystery to him; he marvelled at speedy retrievals. He avoided canonical visitations to parishes and schools: his overawed but trusty clergy were left to themselves to minister, raise funds and build. Amateurish planning led to the bungled seven-figure impost on parishes for a new seminary at Glen Waverley (1959) which added to the onerous Schools Provident Fund. This inglorious pile—aesthetics was not Mannix's forte—was soon cheaply sold for a police college. At his death diocesan administration needed serious overhauling. He started a Catholic Education Office (1932) with one priest, one room and no staff. He was parsimonious even with the reliable Jesuits to whom he entrusted Newman College, his relatively liberal Corpus Christi seminary at Werribee (1923) and the encouragement of lay action. Among secular clergy and suffragan bishops he felt more comfortable with intellectual mediocrity.

Considering that Mannix was too dominant in episcopal councils and influenced preferment for Irish clergy, the apostolic delegate (1935-48), Archbishop Panico, who declined ever to stay at Raheen, appointed the first Australian-born archbishop, Justin Simonds of Hobart, coadjutor to Mannix without consulting either party. It was a slight to Mannix's competence. He gave Simonds only peripheral duties; awkward relations were aggravated by Simonds's disapproval of 'the Movement'; Mannix's longevity crippled Simonds's career. In 1945 Australia's cardinalate went to circumspect Norman Gilroy of Sydney; there followed graciously mordant

congratulations from Mannix but a noisy protest from Calwell, and disapproval from Duhig. Mannix was unacceptable to Rome. His recalcitrance on 'the Movement' brought Cardinal Agagianian of Propaganda Fide to Melbourne in 1959 to see if he was senile. The cardinal was bluntly reassured but a local attempt in 1962 to get Mannix a red hat, Newman-fashion, was futile.

Mannix has been praised for 'inflexible liberalism'. On matters such as lay participation, non-confessional universities, sex education, capital punishment (in 1953 he pleaded with President Eisenhower for the Rosenbergs) and socio-economic issues, he was usually more progressive than other bishops. However, his diocesan weeklies were restricted, manipulated and jejune. In 1919 he forced its lay proprietors to sell the *Advocate* to him at his own low valuation or face extinction; the clericalist *Tribune* criticized him by implication only once—over his attitude to Irish republicanism in 1923. An admirer of Charles Maurras, Denys Jackson, dominated the diocesan political columns from the 1930s. Santamaria, while still in his twenties, became Mannix's major political adviser, ultimately seeing him three times a week. In 1955 the *Catholic Worker* was banned from the cathedral for saying that Catholics could conscientiously vote for the Labor Party. As Mannix foresaw, most parishes followed his lead and sales dropped catastrophically; yet he claimed never to have banned anything. Errant clergy were offered kindness and reformation but those who challenged his judgement had the full rigour of canon law. He listened and opined but never deigned to argue. His dignity and authority were sacrosanct. Although he generated bitterness and lack of charity among his followers, he rarely attacked people by name, even in conversation, but he often found intimidating sarcasm and jibes irresistible. His clergy generally admired and feared him although, in earlier days, there were unpublicized critics among them and later the young curates did not know him.

Mannix was painstaking about his appearance. His top hat was carefully poised, using a mirror, before he strode with frock coat and stick from Raheen through Collingwood to St Patrick's, dispensing shillings to the needy. He cut his own hair and at 97 bought an electric razor because he could not bear to be touched. He always wore a biretta, never the zucchetto. He disliked 'ecclesiastical millinery' and tried not to appoint monsignors. Not even Hackett or Jeremiah Murphy [q.v.] were addressed by first name. Though personally monastic, he did not live in the cathedral 'palace' as did his predecessors but had Raheen, formerly Sir Henry Wrixon's [q.v.6] mansion, purchased for him in 1918 from diocesan funds. His hospitable table carried crystal and silverware though he only picked at food (indeed, fainted at Mass in 1930). He never owned but always hired a chauffeur-driven car and very rarely spoke on the telephone. He rarely officiated at marriages, baptisms, extreme unction, or at personal, rather than mass, confirmations. During speeches there was some restrained theatricality, especially wearing his Maynooth cloak with velvet collar and chain. His accent was cultivated and neutral, with neither blarney nor brogue. The pungent lines were carefully memorized but delivered as if impromptu with a shorthand writer to transcribe them; Mannix would personally 'sub' them for publication, making, as expedient, textual changes.

Admirers were encouraged to believe that he wrote an article, 'The Australian Commonwealth and the States', published under his name in *Twentieth Century* in 1954 though drafted by Santamaria; he was alleged to have constitutional expertise through his (honorary) doctorates of law. His birthday greetings were received in courtly fashion during annual holidays at Queenscliff and Portsea. As a prince-bishop he was the delight of portraitists such as John Lavery, Max Meldrum [q.v.], John Longstaff [q.v.], Clifton Pugh, Jack Cato and Helmut Newton. His friendship with Wren was publicly compromising; although he banned liquor at Catholic functions, he detested wowsers and sabbatarians. He was shocked by Frank Hardy's *Power without glory*. Though a neighbour, he said he had never visited Wren's mansion; Wren was a pious and loyal philanthropist, that was enough. As for Billy Hughes, a letter of condolence on the death of his daughter led to a visit to Raheen and respectful communication till Hughes died.

Mannix ceased his daily walks on his ninetieth birthday, but in 1961 he was still able to give a memorable television interview. Three days before his death Santamaria called to tell him that (Sir) Robert Menzies would announce limited aid to independent schools as part of his election promises. Mannix imagined that the existence of the splinter Democratic Labor Party brought about this aid. It was deeply gratifying; perhaps he did not see that Catholic schools were accepted now by the 'Ascendancy's' heirs as a buttress and were no longer a challenge. On Melbourne Cup Day, 1963, after his annual domestic sweepstakes 'flutter', he collapsed at racetime and died with dignity next afternoon, 6 November, with a loyal court, including Calwell and Santamaria, at his bedside. The cathedral bell tolled ninety-nine at minute-intervals. Mannix had broadly welcomed Vatican II, without anticipating the radical changes it would bring, and wished ruefully he had been more like John XXIII. He expected a

long purgatory. Menzies praised his unsurpassed 'power of persuasive speech'; de Valera eulogized on Radio Eireann; Simonds in his panegyric said his 'incursions into the affairs of state were not his greatest contribution to Australian life' and that he was 'primarily a man of God'. No one asked whether his political interventions and pro-Irish statements had arrested the integration of Catholics into the Australian community, or if his support for 'the Movement' had undone some of the unifying effects of World War II. A leitmotif of his career had been: 'I am unchangeable and unrepentant'. Age and obduracy had made him venerable.

Mannix had asked for simple obsequies with no public procession. The bugler of Southern Command honoured its chaplain-general—a position he declined to relinquish to Gilroy of Gallipoli—with the 'Last Post' and 'Reveille', and a 13-gun salute was fired. He had lived long enough to learn of the assassination of President Ngo Diem—whom he had honoured at Raheen—but not to pronounce on conscription for Vietnam. As he rarely distinguished his own from diocesan funds, his will was brief: small bequests to his servants and two hunter-type gold watches worth £150 and a £5 mantel clock inscribed with 'God Save Ireland'.

W. McDonald, *Reminiscences of a Maynooth professor* (Lond, 1925); J. Murphy and F. Moynihan (eds), *The national Eucharistic Congress, Melbourne, Australia, December 2nd-9th 1934* (Melb, 1936); F. Murphy, *Daniel Mannix, archbishop of Melbourne 1917-1963* (Melb, 1972); P. Ormonde, *The Movement* (Melb, 1972); W. Ebsworth, *Archbishop Mannix* (Melb, 1977); G. Cresciani, *Fascism, anti-fascism and Italians in Australia, 1922-1945* (Canb, 1980); M. M. McKernan, *Australian Churches at war* (Syd, 1980); B. A. Santamaria, *Daniel Mannix* (Melb, 1984); M. Gilchrist, *Daniel Mannix, priest and patriot* (Melb, 1982) and for bibliog; G. Henderson, *Mr Santamaria and the bishops* (Syd, 1983); C. Kiernan, *Daniel Mannix and Ireland* (Morwell, Vic, 1984); *Catholic Worker*, Aug 1944, Feb, Sept 1945, June 1950, Apr 1955, July 1959, Dec 1963; *Twentieth Century*, 8, no 3, autumn 1954; *J of Religious History*, 10, no 4, Dec 1979; *Advocate*, 13, 20 May, 23 Sept 1916, 3 Feb, 15 Mar, 23 June, 10, 24 Nov, 1, 8 Dec 1917, 5 Jan, 9, 16 Mar 1918, 20, 27 May 1920, 30 Sept 1928, 19 May 1929, 1 Oct 1947, 20 May 1948, 11 May 1950, 28 July 1954, 28 Apr, 22 Sept 1955, 7, 14, 21 Nov, 12 Dec 1963, supp Feb 1968; [Catholic] *Tribune* (Melb), 23 Nov 1916, 13 Aug 1921, 24 Sept, 12 Nov, 10, 17, 24 Dec 1925; *Argus*, 29 Jan 1917; *Herald* (Melb), 28 July 1920; *Bulletin*, 10 May 1961; *The Times*, 7 Nov 1963; J. Griffin, Daniel Mannix and the cult of personality (forthcoming publication, MS held by author, Canb), and for bibliog; Hackett papers (Society of Jesus Provincial Archives, Hawthorn, Melb); Mannix papers (including Murtagh notes and materials for Mannix biog, MDHC Archives).

JAMES GRIFFIN

MANSOUR, SYLWANOS (1854-1929), Melkite priest, was born on 24 February 1854 at Ras-Ba'albeck, Syria (Lebanon), and baptized Youssef Elias Assaad, one of four sons of Elias Assaad Mansour, carpenter, and his wife Sadie, née Ajubl. Entering the Shuweirite monastery of St John the Baptist at Khensharra in January 1875, he continued his studies at Ain-Traz clerical college, was ordained priest, with the religious name Sylwanos, on 14 January 1880 and took charge of the parish at Ras-Ba'albeck. He was secretary to Bishop Atta of Homs in 1886 and in 1887 parish priest at Ramle, Palestine. Moving to Beirut, he acquired repute for his strength and became known as 'the fighting priest'— when taunted by ruffians on one occasion, 'His patience being eventually exhausted he raised his stick, asked God's forgiveness, and slashed into them right and left'.

In the 1880s 'Syrians', overwhelmingly Christians from what is now Lebanon, migrated to New South Wales, often working as hawkers before acquiring capital to set up shops in inner Sydney. Following numerous petitions from the Melkite community, which included some of Mansour's relations, Patriarch Gregory Joseph appointed Father Sylvanos parish priest to Australia. After a short time in France, he arrived in Sydney in 1891. The census that year recorded 116 Syrian-born residents of the colony. Mansour ministered at first to the three Christian communities (Melkite, Maronite and Orthodox). A temporary church and school was set up in Redfern. He travelled extensively throughout the colony to visit his scattered flock, collecting money to build a church. In 1893 at Waterloo, Sydney, the foundation stone of the first Lebanese Church in Australia was laid. Originally planned for the three communities, when completed and consecrated as St Michael's by Cardinal Moran [q.v.] in 1895 it became exclusively Melkite.

Lebanese migration to New South Wales grew rapidly in the 1890s—in 1901 the census recorded 739 Lebanese born. They had come to settle: Father Sylwanos performed 37 baptisms in 1893-99. From 1900 assisted by another priest, he was able to continue his fund-raising travels to pay off the church debt.

Although restricted after 1901, Lebanese migration was not completely curtailed— there were 850 Lebanese-born residents of the State by 1921. Mansour learned to speak English but always conducted services in Arabic. In 1929 a second Melkite church was consecrated, in Brisbane. Archimandrite Sylwanos was visiting that community when he died on 18 November 1929. He was buried in Rookwood cemetery, Sydney, and was survived in Australia by a cousin and at least four nephews. Strong but not tall, Mansour was a man of 'unfailing courage, strong faith, and adamant energy'. Photographs show him with a full but trimmed, white beard and a dignified and distinguished face alive with intelligence and humour.

A. N. Jureidini (comp), *Souvenir of the visit of Right Reverend Monseignor Clement Malouf. . . to the 29th International Eucharistic Congress, September 6-9, 1928* (Syd, nd); A. T. Yarwood, *Asian migration to Australia* (Melb, 1964); A. and J. Batrouney, *The Lebanese in Australia* (Melb, 1985); *ISN*, 19 Nov 1892; *SMH*, 19, 23 November 1929; information from Monsignor A. Haddad, Darlington, Syd.
H. L. N. SIMMONS
CHRIS CUNNEEN

MARCH, FREDERICK HAMILTON (1891-1977), soldier and adventurer, was born on 6 August 1891 at Bowning near Yass, New South Wales, son of George Henry March, fettler, and his wife Jane, née Gurnett, both from Gundaroo. Fred claimed that after running away from home he stowed away on a ship sailing from Sydney to San Francisco and that in the United States of America he worked with General Motors at their Cadillac plant, Detroit. Certainly his mechanical skills led to a lifelong association with motor cycles, cars and machinery. He returned to New South Wales before World War I, ran hire cars at Moss Vale, and also worked as a picture show man.

Giving his occupation as chauffeur, March enlisted as a private in the Australian Imperial Force in September 1915. He served in the Middle East with the 7th Light Horse Regiment, attained the rank of sergeant and was discharged in Egypt in 1919. He never returned to Australia. In Cairo he was chauffeur to the governor-general of Sudan, Sir Lee Stack, who was fatally wounded on 19 November 1924 in an assassination attempt. Although wounded himself, March by skilful driving evaded a second hail of bullets. King George V awarded him the medal of the civil division of the Order of the British Empire (the Empire Gallantry Medal—later translated into a George Cross). With compensation money he had received for his injuries March bought a garage in Cairo.

In World War II he worked on military road-building projects in Sinai and Palestine. He spent the rest of his working life with the Sudanese Ministry of Agriculture—mainly supervising excavation of remote water-storage catchments. Appointed M.B.E. on his retirement in 1957, he was awarded the Queen's Silver Jubilee Medal in 1977. But for his longevity he would have been totally forgotten in Australia, having lost contact with his family after his mother's death in 1948.

March outlived his capacity to provide for himself and his wife Teresa Bongi, an Eritrean refugee whom he had married in Khartoum on 2 September 1967. His residence overseas precluded a normal Australian pension but strenuous activities by friends, diplomatic staff in Cairo and Khartoum and the Returned Services League of Australia finally resulted in the granting of an act of grace pension in 1973. Through this campaign Australians became aware of claims about March's alleged exploits, such as swimming ashore ahead of the Gallipoli landing and chauffeuring Colonel T. E. Lawrence during the victorious drive into Damascus.

None of these claims can be verified, nor can they all be totally dismissed. In the small European community in Khartoum legends about colourful characters such as March flourish; they lost nothing in the re-telling in Australian newspapers. Survived by his wife, he died on 30 October 1977 and was buried in the Christian cemetery, Khartoum. Next year he was reinterred in the adjacent Commonwealth War Graves Commission cemetery at the insistence of the R.S.L.

P. Sekuless, *Fred: An Australian hero*, (Brisb, 1981); records (AWM); information from Mrs T. March, Malawi.   PETER SEKULESS

MARCHANT, GEORGE (1857-1941), manufacturer and philanthropist, was born on 25 November 1857 at Brasted, Kent, England, son of Richard Marchant, licensed victualler, and his wife Sarah, née Mills. George, a farm labourer, arrived in Brisbane in the *Ramsey* on 9 June 1874. 'Friendless and practically penniless', he worked in the country as a gardener and station-hand and, on returning to Brisbane, as a carter for an aerated waters factory. He married Mary Jane Dwyer, a dressmaker, on 1 September 1877 with Presbyterian forms.

Marchant bought the ginger beer manufacturing business of John R. Palmer in Elizabeth Street, Brisbane, before building his own factory in Bowen Street, Spring Hill, in 1886. With his wife he expanded his hop beer, soft drink and cordial business to include factories in Sydney, Newcastle, Melbourne and Adelaide. He invented and patented a bottling machine which came to be used all over the world. Marchant retired from his Brisbane business on 10 May 1913 and was succeeded as managing director by his adopted son Christopher John, who ran the company until its registration was abandoned in October 1917. However, Marchant retained remote control over the Sydney company.

He built a large fortune from these undertakings. Originally a staunch anti-unionist, he later believed in social equality and frater-

nized with labour thinkers including William Lane [q.v.9]. Saved by Edward Bellamy's Utopian novel *Looking backward 2000-1887* (1888) from 'hopeless scepticism', Marchant in 1890 founded a Bellamy Society. During the 1890 shipping strike he chaired several public meetings which raised funds to support the strikers. Though described by the Labor press as 'one of the smartest profitmongers in Queensland', he practised profit-sharing. He took an annual dividend of 10 per cent on a capital of £18 000 and remaining profits were distributed among his employees. Women workers in his factory earned more than the average female wage in the food industry.

His religious leanings were unconventional. A follower of the theology of the eighteenth-century philosopher Swedenborg, who held that Scripture should be interpreted spiritually, Marchant conducted services for the New Church in Brisbane and donated money to establish Swedenborgian churches in all Australian capitals and to ministerial training colleges in England and America. He had long been an opponent of the liquor trade. He donated £41 000 of the cost of the Queensland Prohibition League's Canberra Hotel (opened 1929) in Brisbane and became a director; the building houses his portrait. He was treasurer of the league during the 1920s and was its patron after 1931.

Marchant's wide-ranging philanthropy during his life included the gift of his home, Montrose, at Taringa to the Queensland Society for Crippled Children, which became his chief beneficiary. These premises became the Kingshome centre for the care of ex-servicemen and Marchant bought another house for a new Montrose Home at Corinda. Other benefactions included another children's home, a kindergarten, the Garden Settlement for the aged, Chermside, and the donation of 100 acres (40 ha) of nearby land, known as Marchant Park, to the Kedron Local Authority. His estate of £48 660 was divided between these and other charities.

Predeceased by his wife, Marchant died childless from heart disease on 5 September 1941 and was cremated after a New Church service.

W. O. Lilley, *Reminiscences of life in Brisbane and reflections and sayings* (Brisb,1913); *Queensland and Queenslanders* (Brisb,1936); *V&P* (Qld), 1891, 2, p 1244; *Qld Digger*, 1 Oct 1941, p 31; *Worker* (Brisb), 1 July, 7 Aug, 1 Sept, 1, 18 Oct 1890; *Boomerang* (Brisb), 27 Sept, 4 Oct 1890; *Queenslander*, 16 July 1931; *Sunday Mail* (Brisb), 7 Sept 1941; *Courier Mail*, 8 Sept 1941; S. A. Rayner, The evolution of the Queensland Labor Party to 1907 (M.A. thesis, Univ Qld, 1947); S. W. Jack's cutting-book, no 41 (Oxley Lib); Company files, COM/1, 1863-88, and company registration, A/11849 (QA).   HELEN GREGORY

MARCONI, JOSEPH CORNELIUS (1876-1922), goanna oil manufacturer, was born probably on 21 April 1876 in London, son of Cornelius Joseph Mahoney, cooper, and his wife Eunice Clara, née Proud. The family arrived in Australia about 1886 and Joseph worked with his father in Sydney as a dealer in building materials; from about 1900 they spelt their surname Marney. He became a member of a marionette show in a travelling vaudeville troupe, then traded briefly as a dealer in Newcastle, and later joined the sideshow circuit, adopting the name Marconi and using Brisbane as his home base. As manager of Lyn Vane's snakebite act, and through association with 'Professor' James Morrissey, he learned of plants to which goannas were thought to resort when bitten, and of the Aborigines' belief in the healing properties of goanna fat.

From about 1910 Marconi manufactured and sold liniments and salves, the ingredients including oils distilled from herbs and goanna fat; sufferers from ills ranging from arthritis to varicose veins attested to his products' efficacy. Entrepreneur as well as showman, he skilfully used comic advertising and especially testimonials: in his delightfully illustrated *Modern nursery rhymes* (Brisbane, 1921) the rhymes were interspersed with testimonials, and his ubiquitous goanna trade marks were seen along every bush road and railway line. The Queensland government proclaimed the goanna a protected species in certain areas in 1918 and he was refused a patent application, but Marconi's sales throughout Australia and New Zealand continued to increase. He opened a shop in inner Brisbane in 1920 and in May 1922 the Marconi Curative Institute, offering massage, hydropathic and herbal treatment. He was particularly interested in the treatment of children suffering from poliomyelitis.

With his carefully cultivated Italianate appearance, Marconi was one of the most picturesque and best known figures in Brisbane. His hospitality was a byword: the small factory under his home, Astra, at Bulimba was a Mecca to local children. He topped the poll in the erstwhile strongly Labor ward of Bulimba in the Balmoral Shire Council's 1921 election as a Nationalist candidate, and proved an energetic and effective councillor.

Marconi's skull was fractured when he intervened in a fracas in Elizabeth Street on 21 October 1922, and he died a few hours later in Brisbane General Hospital. After a largely attended funeral service he was buried in the Roman Catholic section of Bulimba cemetery. He had married Mary Teresa O'Neill in Newtown Registry Office, Sydney, on 27 September 1904. She predeceased him but he was survived by three of their four daughters and three sons, of whom

Norman Charles (1905-1959) was a pioneer of aviation in Queensland. His father was remembered by Bulimba schoolchildren in their chant: 'Old Marconi's dead, knocked on the head/Goannas are glad, children are sad/Old Marconi's dead'.

Marconi's 'Australian bush remedy' became part of folklore. The business remained in family hands until 1982 when the rights of manufacture were sold, Astra was demolished and a large collection of goanna memorabilia was destroyed.

National Trust of Qld J, 7 (Nov 1983), p 13; *Brisbane Courier*, 25 Oct, 1, 3 Nov, 5 Dec 1922; *Truth* (Brisb), 29 Oct 1922; *Bulletin*, 16 Oct 1984; SCT/CG202, 15/20 (QA); information from J. C. Marconi & Co, Salisbury, Brisb.

BETTY CROUCHLEY

MARDEN, JOHN (1855-1924), headmaster, was born on 9 April 1855 at Prahran, Melbourne, fifth child of John Marden, butcher, and his wife Catherine, née Murphy, both English born. He attended Geelong College and the University of Melbourne (B.A., 1883; M.A., 1885; LL.B., 1887). At Cape Clear he married a schoolteacher, Jane Armstrong, on 20 December 1883. While completing his law degree Marden taught at Geelong College under George Morrison [q.v.5], commanding the school cadet corps, and at the Methodist Ladies' College, Melbourne.

In 1887 Marden was appointed first headmaster and principal of the Presbyterian Ladies' College, Sydney. He opened the school with Miss M. McCormick as lady superintendent in 1888 in a leased house at Ashfield; there were thirty pupils including fifteen boarders. In 1890, after examination in jurisprudence, the University of Sydney conferred on him the degree of LL.D. That year the Presbyterian Church in New South Wales bought Anthony Hordern's [q.v.9] house at Croydon. There Marden consolidated the school and, keenly interested in horticulture, laid out beautiful gardens and playing fields.

In 1916, under Marden's guidance, the Presbyterian Church bought fifty acres (20 ha) at Pymble for £15 000 and established a sister school, administered until 1929 by a single council. Marden was headmaster of both schools. At Pymble he had greater opportunity to plan and develop buildings, gardens and playing areas, and Pymble soon outgrew Croydon.

A man of strong will, Marden administered his schools with firm discipline, tempered with kindness, understanding and generosity, and, winning the respect and affection of his pupils, strongly influenced them. He firmly believed that women should share fully in opportunities for secondary and tertiary education and also hold high Christian ideals. Although trained as a lawyer, he gave physics, chemistry and biology a prominent place—at a time when few schools included much science in the curriculum. He instituted the house system in both schools. In his later years he was assisted by a prominent educational innovator, Dr E. Neil McQueen, a scientist and an ardent advocate of the Dalton plan for education, who later succeeded him at Croydon.

Marden was a tall man, with luxuriant white hair and a large dark moustache. He bought a residence at Wentworth Falls where he spent his leisure time and holidays and exercised his horticultural skills, and where in 1919, after a visit to a daughter in Western Australia, he retired. There also he became friendly with Peter Board [q.v.7], director of education. Marden was active in the Presbyterian Church, serving as an elder at Ashfield for twenty-eight years and for his last six years at Wentworth Falls. He died at Randwick on 29 October 1924 and was buried in South Head cemetery. His wife, son and three daughters survived him. There is a memorial library at Croydon and his son established a memorial scholarship at Pymble.

J. Cameron, *Centenary history of the Presbyterian Church in New South Wales* (Syd, 1905); H. D. Mackie (ed), *John Marden* (Syd, 1925); C. A. White, *The challenge of the years* (Syd, 1951); G. C. Notman and B. R. Keith (ed), *The Geelong College, 1861-1961* (Geelong, Vic, 1961); Presbyterian Church of NSW, *Minutes of the Proceedings of the General Assembly*, 1886-1925 (Reports of PLC Council); *SMH*, 30 Oct 1924; papers held by W. M. Nolan, Syd.   ALAN DOUGAN*

MARGOLIN, ELIEZER (1875-1944), soldier and businessman, was born on 26 March 1875 at Belgorod, Russia, son of Murdochy Joseph Margolin, merchant, and his wife Llata Freida, née Carlin. When Eliezer (known as Lazar) was 17 his family migrated to Palestine. At night Lazar and others from his village, Rehovot, patrolled their orchards on horseback to fight marauders from neighbouring Arab villages. After his parents died within a week of each other, Lazar, as sole breadwinner, worked the family vineyard and almond orchard and other orchards as well, to supplement a meagre income. During 1902, in depressed conditions, he was one of many Palestinian Jews who sold their land to seek capital elsewhere in the hope of eventual return.

Margolin found suitable homes for his sister and brother and sailed for Australia. He worked as a navvy and teamster and, after learning some English, opened a small medical supplies factory in Sydney before moving to the mining town of Collie, Western Australia, where he ran a cordial factory. He was naturalized in 1904. He now found the opportunity to indulge his passion for soldiering. In 1911 he was commissioned as a second lieutenant and formed the Collie Company of the 1st Battalion, Western Australian Infantry Regiment, Australian Military Forces. Although 39 in 1914, he belonged in spirit to that generation that welcomed war as the chance of a lifetime. On 1 October he joined the 16th Battalion, Australian Imperial Force, as a lieutenant; in December he was promoted captain.

On 25 April 1915 Margolin, leading 'B' Company, was among the first of his battalion to land on Gallipoli. His troops knew him affectionately as 'Margy'—a disciplinarian, taciturn, quick-tempered but fair and courageous, who always showed great concern for their welfare. He was tall and dark and had a low voice with a Russian accent, also noticeable when he spoke Hebrew and Arabic. On 18 September 1915 Major Margolin took temporary command of the battalion and commanded its rear party during the evacuation. He was awarded the Distinguished Service Order.

In France Margolin was wounded several times in 1916-17. From June to September 1917 he was temporary lieut-colonel in command of the 14th Battalion, then returned to the 16th until he was evacuated with an injury. In September he was mentioned in dispatches. Later that month while recovering from a knee injury in a London hospital, he accepted command of the 39th Battalion, Royal Fusiliers, one of three volunteer Jewish battalions of the British Army formed to fight the Turks in Palestine. On 18 March 1918, as a lieut-colonel, he took command of his battalion, telling his troops that 'our aim is to participate in the fighting on the front of Eretz Israel and the liberation of our homeland'. Later at Rehovot he persuaded friends to organize another fighting unit which within a few weeks became the 40th Battalion, Royal Fusiliers. In September these raw, somewhat ineffectual Jewish battalions under General Allenby joined the Anzac light horse which drove the Turks from northern Palestine.

After the Armistice when most Jewish volunteers had left for their homes, Margolin remained in Palestine. During the summer of 1919 he organized a new unit, 'The First Jewish Battalion of Judea', with its own uniform and insignia—with Hebrew the language of command but remaining part of and financed by the British Army. In May 1920 without British authority Margolin intervened with about 300 of his soldiers in Arab-Jewish riots in Tel-Aviv. British commanders threatened to court-martial him but after hearing his case they gave him an honourable discharge and ordered him to leave the country.

Margolin felt no remorse, believing that Jews had to fight for Israel with their own army. He became a hero of the Palestinian Jews who knew him as the first commander of Judea and appointed him governor of Jerusalem. On his return to Western Australia in 1921 he bought a service station at Nedlands, Perth. He became vice-president of the local Returned Sailors' and Soldiers' Imperial League of Australia, a foundation member of the Perth Legacy Club, and president of the Naval and Military Club and of the 16th Battalion Association. On 24 July 1926 in a civil ceremony he married Hilda Myrtle England. They had no children.

On 2 June 1944 Margolin died of cerebral haemorrhage and was cremated after a nondenominational ceremony at Karrakatta cemetery. In December 1949 his widow, as requested in his will, took his ashes, ceremonial sword, medals and decorations to Israel. A military guard of honour met her at Haifa and led a procession through the village of the Jewish Legion, Avichail, including the Eliezer Margolin Square, to Tel-Aviv, Sarafand and to Rehovot, where his ashes were buried next to his parents' graves. Among the mourners was Israel's prime minister, David Ben Gurion, a former officer in Margolin's Jewish battalion. In 1956 a memorial to Lieut-Colonel Margolin was unveiled at Rehovot.

H. S. Gullett, *The A.I.F. in Sinai and Palestine* (Syd, 1923); C. Longmore, *The old Sixteenth* (Perth, 1929); Y. Biber, *Commander of Judea* (Israel, 1978, text in Hebrew translated in part by A. Troy in his A. G. Korunski memorial lecture, Perth, 1982); *Mail* (Fremantle), 19 Nov 1931; *Bulletin* (Syd), 28 June 1944; *Reveille* (Syd), Aug 1944; Signaller E. Silas, Diary Oct 1914-Sept 1916 (AWM); interview with Mrs Hilda Margolin, Perth, 1984.   SUZANNE WELBORN

MARKS, ALEXANDER HAMMETT (1880-1954), medical practitioner and soldier, was born on 6 August 1880 in Brisbane, son of Dr Charles Ferdinand Marks [q.v.], and his wife Elizabeth Gray, formerly Dods, née Stodart. He was educated at Brisbane Grammar School and Trinity College, Dublin (M.D., 1905).

On returning to Brisbane in 1904 Marks became a general practitioner with a special interest in obstetrics and gynaecology and established his practice at Wickham Terrace. On 6 April 1907 at St Philip's Anglican Church, Sydney, he married Annie Georgina Rhodes. At various periods between 1919 and 1930 he was an honorary radiologist, junior physician and junior and subsequently senior gynaecologist at the Brisbane General Hospital; he was also a member of the honorary staff of the Lady Bowen Hospital. He had a breezy manner and impressed his junior colleagues with his practical skill.

Marks also held executive positions in local medical associations. A foundation fellow of the (Royal) Australasian College of Surgeons, he served on the council of the Queensland branch of the British Medical Association in 1909-27 (president, 1914), and was president of the Medical Defence Society of Queensland in 1931-46 and of the Australasian Trained Nurses' Association in 1923-34. Although he retired from active practice in 1945, he continued his work as a senior medical officer to the Australian Mutual Provident Society until 1950.

Marks had a distinguished military record. On 20 March 1911 he was appointed to the honorary rank of captain in the Australian Army Medical Corps and was attached as medical officer to the 2nd Brigade; before World War I he held appointments with the 1st Military District. He enlisted in the Australian Imperial Force on 20 August 1914 and was posted as regimental medical officer to the 3rd Field Artillery Brigade. A month later he embarked for Egypt and was at Gallipoli from the landing until the evacuation. He was promoted major on 6 September 1915.

On 20 February 1916 Marks was appointed deputy assistant director of medical services of the 4th Division. The division moved to France in May and Marks served with it until December when he was promoted lieutcolonel commanding the 2nd Australian Field Ambulance. He was invalided to England in February 1917 and in March was appointed to form and command the 16th Australian Field Ambulance attached to the 16th Brigade in England.

In October Marks returned to France to command the 1st Australian Casualty Clearing Station and served with this unit until September 1918 when he was appointed colonel and A.D.M.S. of the 1st Division. For his war service he was awarded the Distinguished Service Order in 1916 and the French Croix de Guerre in 1918, and was appointed C.B.E. in 1919; he was also twice mentioned in dispatches.

Marks returned to Australia in 1919 with his wife and four children. He continued part-time service with the army as deputy director of medical services of the 1st Military District in 1921-38 and during World War II was chairman and Queensland controller of the Voluntary Aid Detachment. Renowned for a keen sense of humour, he was a popular personality with both the Brisbane medical fraternity and the A.A.M.C. His hobbies were collecting antique furniture and farming near Brisbane.

Marks died on 18 January 1954 of hypertensive heart disease at his home at Auchenflower, Brisbane, and was cremated. He was survived by his second wife, Charlotte, née Watson, whom he had married on 11 July 1945 at Toowong, and by one son and two daughters of his first marriage. His son Charles Ferdinand was decorated for service with the Royal Australian Army Medical Corps in World War II.

A. G. Butler (ed), *Official history of the Australian Army Medical Services in the war 1914-19*, 1 (Melb, 1930), 2 (Canb, 1940); C. E. W. Bean, *The A.I.F. in France*, 1916 (Syd, 1929); *MJA*, 13 Mar 1954; A. H. Marks file, War Records Section, and personal narrative of A. H. Marks (A. G. Butler Collection, AWM).   DARRYL MCINTYRE

MARKS, CHARLES FERDINAND (1852-1941), medical practitioner and politician, was born on 8 September 1852 at St Leonards-on-Sea, Sussex, England, son of Alexander Hammett Marks, medical practitioner, and his wife Emily, née Smyth. After education at Epsom College and in Switzerland, he studied medicine at Queen's College, Galway, Ireland, graduating M.D. (Queen's University) in 1874. Additional qualifications included M.R.C.S. (Eng., 1875) and F.R.C.S. (Ire., 1902).

After practice in Ireland, New Zealand and England, Marks migrated to Queensland in 1879. On 23 September at St Mary's Church of England, Kangaroo Point, Brisbane, he married a shipboard companion, a widow, Elizabeth Gray Dods, née Stodart, mother of Robin Dods [q.v.8]. After a short period at the district hospital, St George, the couple returned to Brisbane in 1880 where a house was built for them at 101 Wickham Terrace. After Robin Dods supervised alterations in the early 1890s this villa residence had three storeys and twenty rooms.

Marks soon built up a busy practice and achieved eminence in many fields of medicine. He was visiting surgeon to the (Royal) Brisbane Hospital from 1883 to 1904 and the Lady Bowen Hospital. In 1882-94 he was a member of the Central Board of Health and in 1882-1912 of the Queensland Medical Board, being president in the last three years. In his retiring address as president of the Queensland branch of the British Medical Association in 1897 he advocated a state salaried medical service. Despite colleague opposition he favoured the entry of women to medicine. Other appointments included membership of the Immigration Board, surgeon major in the Queensland Defence Force and commandant of the 6th Australian General Hospital, Brisbane, during World War I.

A member of the Legislative Council in 1888-1922, he helped to guard the status of the profession whenever it was threatened by proposed legislation. He strongly supported the indecent advertisements bill in 1892. He advocated a higher priority for arts and agriculture than for medicine while a member of a commission enquiring into a proposed university for Queensland in 1891.

Marks accumulated property and was one of five partners who formed the Rubyanna Sugar Co., Bundaberg. During financial difficulties in 1891-92 he bore the full brunt of the company's liquidation after his partners had entered separate negotiations. He lost heavily but the Wickham Terrace house was saved. Resigning his official positions he was reappointed to all, including the Legislative Council, almost immediately.

Well-built, of average height, blue-eyed, with full beard early and moustache only later, Marks was a presentable figure. He had a fine sense of humour and was beloved by patients and family even though his word was law. Fond of old and new devices, he was among the first to own a motor car and a refrigerator and often tinkered with his crystal radio. In 1927 he became a foundation fellow of the (Royal) Australasian College of Surgeons.

Marks had retired to his property, Cushleva, Camp Mountain, Samford, in 1920 and died there from cerebral ischaemia on 28 March 1941; he was cremated with Anglican rites. Of the three sons and one daughter who survived him, two sons, including Alexander Hammett [q.v.], were medical specialists.

T. W. H. Leavitt (ed), *Australian representative men* (Brisb, 1888); R. Lawson, *Brisbane in the 1890s* (Brisb, 1973); *V&P* (LA Qld), 1891, 3, p 881; *A'sian Medical Gazette*, 16 (1897), p 87; *MJA*, 16 Aug 1941, p 187; *Brisb Courier*, 26 Jan, 2 Feb 1892; personal information from Dr E. N. Marks, Camp Mountain, Samford, Qld.   ROSS PATRICK

MARKS, DOUGLAS GRAY (1895-1920), soldier, was born on 20 March 1895 at Junee, New South Wales, son of Montague Marks, storekeeper, and his wife Elizabeth Caroline, née Plunkett. He attended Fort Street Boys' High School, Sydney, becoming a bank clerk, and studied mining engineering part time at Sydney Technical College.

In June 1914 Marks was commissioned second lieutenant in the 29th Infantry (Australian Rifles). He joined the Australian Imperial Force on 20 November and was appointed a second lieutenant in the 13th Battalion which sailed for Egypt in December; on 25 March 1915 Marks was promoted lieutenant. After landing at Gallipoli on 26 April his battalion moved to Quinn's Post and Pope's Hill with the task of clearing Russell's Top. In its first week of action the 'Fighting Thirteenth' suffered very heavy casualties. On 2-3 May, in the attack on Baby 700, the battalion temporarily captured the Chess Board and Dead Man's Ridge. Marks's personal knowledge of the enemy dispositions assisted his commanding officer Lieut-Colonel Burnage [q.v.7] significantly. Having been acting adjutant, on 20 July he was promoted temporary captain but on 7 August he was wounded in the left foot and evacuated. For outstanding service on Gallipoli he was awarded the Serbian Order of the White Eagle.

In Egypt, on 20 January 1916, Marks was promoted captain and on 1 February was appointed adjutant of his battalion which sailed for France in June. Following the unit's two operations at Pozières in August Marks was awarded the Military Cross for his consistent and energetic work as adjutant; he had rendered 'conspicuously valuable service frequently under the heaviest shell fire'. He was promoted major on 11 November and appointed second-in-command to Lieut-Colonel J. M. A. Durrant whom he assisted in planning the attack on Stormy Trench near Gueudecourt on 4-5 February 1917. At Bullecourt, when a shell hit battalion headquarters, he suffered a bad chest and lung wound; coughing up blood he struggled through the snow to the casualty clearing station and was eventually evacuated to England. In late August he rejoined his unit and on 5 December was promoted lieut-colonel, replacing Durrant. Aged 22 he was one of the youngest commanding officers in the A.I.F. For his work from September 1917 to February 1918 (including the Ypres Salient operations) he was awarded the Distinguished Service Order.

In March 1918 Marks's battalion led the 4th Brigade advance to halt the reported German breakthrough at Hébuterne; the town was secured and the enemy thrust halted. Brigadier General C. H. Brand [q.v.7], commanding the 4th Brigade, informed Marks that 'The Corps Commander is afraid to let the defence of Hébuterne out of your hands.'. Following the Villers-Bretonneux operations in April the battalion took part in the assault on Monument Wood and in July in the attack on Hamel where its success owed much to Marks's detailed planning and rehearsals. In the allied offensive on 8 August and operations on 23 August the unit captured many prisoners near Morcourt and at Vauvillers; in the assault on the Hindenburg line on 18 September it took its objective near Hargicourt—this was its last major battle. Marks returned to Australia via North America and his A.I.F. service terminated on 20 February

1919. He was accepted for law at the University of Sydney in 1920 but deferred for twelve months to study Latin; meanwhile, he was employed as manager of the Continental Paper Bag Co.

In a heavy surf at Palm Beach, on 25 January 1920, Marks, an indifferent swimmer, was drowned in an unsuccessful attempt to rescue a drowning stranger; his body was never recovered. An overflowing congregation, made up mainly of ex-members of his battalion, attended a memorial service at St James' Church, Sydney.

During his service in the A.I.F. Marks was mentioned in dispatches four times. In his planning he was consistent, resourceful and thorough; under fire he was cool, capable and courageous, and took every care to ensure the safety of his men. According to Durrant 'He was loyalty itself to his commanders, and he governed with universal fairness and humanity'; and Lieut-Colonel H. W. Murray [q.v.] said: 'We loved Douglas Marks for his high indomitable spirit, his dash and daring . . . no truer comrade ever lived'.

C. E. W. Bean, *The story of Anzac*, 1, 2 (Syd, 1921, 1924), and *The A.I.F. in France*, 1916-18 (Syd, 1929, 1933, 1937, 1942); T. A. White, *The fighting Thirteenth* (Syd, 1924); *London Gazette*, 29 Dec 1916, 13 Feb, 1 June, 28 Dec 1917, 28, 31 May, 27 Dec 1918; *Reveille* (Syd), Nov 1936; *SMH*, 29 Dec 1916, 23 Dec 1918, 26, 28 Jan, 9, 26 Feb 1920, 10 Sept 1921; Records (AWM) and Dept of Veterans' Affairs (Syd); D. G. Marks personal diary 1914-19 *and* letters (ML); information from Mrs M. Drake, Balmoral Beach, NSW.   R. SUTTON

MARKS, GLADYS HOPE (1883-1970), university lecturer, was born on 14 December 1883 in Brisbane, fifth child of Benjamin Francis Marks, Tasmanian-born merchant, and his wife Jane Matilda, née Cohen, from Sydney. She was privately educated by governesses and tutors. Despite opposition from her father, in 1905 she enrolled in arts at the University of Sydney (B.A., 1908) and won the MacCallum [q.v.] prize for English essays and the Garton scholarships for French and German. After teaching in private schools for girls in 1908-13, she travelled extensively in Europe and studied phonetics at the Sorbonne in Paris, and at University College, London.

Escaping from Belgium on the outbreak of World War I, she worked in London for Belgian refugees and the Soldiers' and Sailors' Families Association before returning to Sydney in 1915. She became an active assistant honorary secretary of the Universal Service League, organizing and addressing meetings.

Recruited as an acting lecturer in French at the university by Professor G. G. Nicholson [q.v.] in 1916, Gladys Marks was appointed lecturer in 1921. First-year students in her classes on phonetics and prose found her rigorous discipline somewhat daunting. They regarded with awe this slim, elegant woman whose large, dark eyes compelled their attention, and remembered her pursuit of excellence, moral integrity and illuminating sidelights on French culture. In 1929 and 1936 she was acting head of the department—the first female acting-professor at the university. In 1934 she was appointed officier d'Académie by the French government when awarded les Palmes Académiques.

In 1907-12 Miss Marks had been a committee-member of the various university women students' and graduates' organizations that preceded the reconstituted Sydney University Women's Union, of which she was vice-president in 1919-21. Later she was a vice-president of the Sydney University Women Graduates' Association and in 1930-34 president of the Australian Federation of University Women. Long involved with the National Council of Women of New South Wales, she was international secretary in 1921-26 and became an honorary life vice-president in 1934. She attended congresses of the International Council of Women in Rome in 1914 and Copenhagen in 1924. She was also a council-member of the local League of Nations Union and a founder and executive member of the Business and Professional Women's Club of Sydney. Throughout her life she spoke out against inequality and for the advancement of women.

For many years Gladys Marks lived with her family on the waterfront at Potts Point. Devoted and generous to her conservative Jewish family, she faced problems in maintaining a balance between her life at home and at the university and suffered bouts of illness and nervous depression. She retired in 1943. Her keen wit, penetrating mind and unobtrusive kindness gained her many friends. In the 1920s she was a vice-president of the Sydney University Dramatic Society and the house committee of the Sydney Repertory Theatre Society. A talented amateur violinist, she was a discerning concert-goer and a foundation member of the executive of the Musica Viva Society of Australia. She also supported the Friends of the Hebrew University in Jerusalem, and of the Israel Philharmonic Orchestra.

Gladys Marks died in the Scottish Hospital on 6 January 1970 and was cremated with Jewish forms. She left the bulk of her estate, valued for probate at $196 494, to her three nieces, and $10 000 to the University of Sydney's department of French, to which she had already given £8000 for a travelling scholarship. The State branch of the Australian Federation of University Women established the Gladys Marks memorial fund to assist mature women to complete courses at the university.

P. Thompson and S. Yorke (eds), *Lives obscurely great* (Syd, 1980); Univ Syd Union, *Union Recorder*, 3 May 1934; *National Council of Women News*, Aug 1967; NSW Assn of University Women Graduates, *Newsletter*, Mar 1970; *SMH*, 5 Apr 1921, 8 Jan 1970; *Aust Jewish Times*, 12 Feb 1981; G. Marks papers *and* Aust Federation of Univ Women, NSW, papers (Univ Syd Archives); Business and Professional Women's Club papers *and* National Council of Women (NSW), papers (ML).
MARGARET MAXWELL

MARKS, PERCY (1879-1935), jeweller, was born on 6 July 1879 in Wellington, New Zealand, son of London-born John Marks, jeweller, and his New Zealand-born wife Eliza Jane, née Levy. The family moved to Sydney about 1880 and Percy was educated at Paddington Superior Public School. At 14 he was apprenticed to R. H. J. Jenkins, jeweller, and also studied at Sydney Technical College. On 7 March 1899 he married Eliza Robinson Barton with Congregational forms, and that year started his own business in Market Street. He advertised his appointments as a vice-regal jeweller from 1908.

In 1907, impressed by samples of dark opal from Walangulla (Lightning Ridge), Marks obtained a miner's right. Although winning only 'shin-crackers' himself, he recognized the opal's market potential, and bought all available. Captivated by its 'flashing splendour', he described it as 'the orchid of gems' and named it black opal to distinguish it from the more common pale form. Promoting it as Australia's national gem, he discounted the superstition that opal was unlucky, and made a collection for public display. He won the grand prix at the 1908 Franco-British Exhibition in London and at the 1915 Panama-Pacific International Exposition in San Francisco.

In 1919 the State government commissioned him to inquire into the marketing of opals in Europe and North America. He exhibited his collection at the Foire Internationale de Lyon, France, and in Paris, and presented collections of rough and cut opal to eight French museums and mining schools. Believing the opal trade was being hampered by miners demanding excessive prices, he suggested in his report that a small advisory board be appointed by the government to protect and harmonize the respective interests of miner, jeweller and the public. In 1925 the French government appointed him officier d'instruction publique.

With a 'courtly manner' and a 'clear-cut', 'polished' appearance, Marks had a boyish whimsicality. He delighted in presenting jewellery of his own design to celebrities. At a dinner in honour of Pavlova each female guest was presented with a silver-papered 'chocolate', in reality a black opal. Others to receive gifts were Dame Nellie Melba, Elsa Stralia [qq.v.], the American bandmaster J. P. Sousa and Amy Johnson. The opal presented to the duke of Gloucester in 1934 by the Federated Retail Jewellers' Association of the Commonwealth was selected and mounted by him. Marks also made a miniature opal casket for Queen Mary's Doll's House. He donated sports trophies and charity appeal prizes, as well as presenting opal collections to the Mining and Geological and Technological museums, Sydney, and to twelve high schools.

Marks was awarded King George V's Silver Jubilee medal in 1935. He had a wide range of other interests: golf, billiards, swimming, yachting, fishing, gardening and Freemasonry. He was a director of the New South Wales Sports Club Ltd and a member of the (Royal) Motor Yacht Club and of the Amateur Billiards Association. Survived by his wife and four sons, he died of cancer in hospital at Moore Park on 23 September 1935 and was cremated. His estate was valued for probate at £21 420.

Millions Mag, 1 Mar 1921; *Cwlth Jeweller and Watchmaker*, 1 May 1934, 2 Sept, 1 Oct 1935; *Sun* (Syd), 21 Dec 1919, 27 July 1920; *SMH*, 18 Feb, 14 July 1921, 2 May 1923, 4 Apr, 7 Nov 1925, 19 June 1926, 23 Feb 1932, 21 Nov 1933, 12 Apr, 8 Sept, 15 Nov 1934, 6 May, 24 Sept 1935; *Daily Telegraph* (Syd), 22 Feb 1934; *Aust Worker*, 2 Oct 1935; family papers held by, and information from, K. R. Marks, Syd.   GILLIAN FULLOON

MARKS, PERCY JOSEPH (1867-1941), solicitor and historian, and ERNEST SAMUEL (1871-1947), woolbuyer, politician and sportsman, were born on 12 November 1867 and on 7 May 1871 at West Maitland, New South Wales, eldest sons of Joseph Marks, London-born storekeeper, and his native-born wife Elizabeth, daughter of Samuel Benjamin [q.v.1]. Their father became a woolbuyer and the family moved to Sydney in 1882; the brothers were educated at Royston College, Darlinghurst. Percy attended the University of Sydney (B.A., 1887), was articled to Creagh & Williams and, admitted a solicitor on 6 June 1891, set up in practice.

Active within the Jewish community, the brothers worshipped regularly at the Great Synagogue and were early supporters of Zionism. Neither was to marry. Percy was associated with (Sir) Daniel Levy [q.v.] on the *Australasian Hebrew* in 1896, sometime honorary secretary of the Board of Jewish Edu-

cation and honorary solicitor for sundry communal institutions. In 1908 he was a founder and first president of the Sydney Zionist Society and later of the local section of the Friends of the Hebrew University in Jerusalem. Ernest was associated with the Jewish Girls' Guild, the State branch of the Anglo-Jewish Association, and the New South Wales Jewish Association and Jewish War Memorial.

From 1912 Percy acted as unofficial historian of Australian Jewry. He was a council-member of the (Royal) Australian Historical Society in 1912-18 and published many articles and pamphlets including two bibliographies, *Australasian Shakespeareana* (1915) and *Australian Judaica* (1930, 1936). He was a committee-member of the Australian Ex-Libris Society, the Society of Australian Genealogists and the Numismatic Society, and a fellow of the Royal Colonial Institute.

In 1888-90 Ernest won over forty trophies as an athlete. He was a founder and executive-member of the New South Wales Amateur Athletic Association, the Amateur Athletic Union of Australasia and the International Amateur Athletic Federation; vice-chairman of the New South Wales Olympic Council and the Australian Olympic Federation and chairman of the Australian division of the British Empire Games. As touring manager, he attended the Olympic Games in London (1908), Stockholm (1912), and Los Angeles (1932) where he was awarded the Veterans' medal. He also founded sporting clubs and institutions such as the Darlinghurst Harriers, North and East Sydney Amateur Swimming clubs, Manly Surf Club; and the New South Wales Amateur Swimming Association, Sports Club Ltd, Amateur Billiard Championship committee and National Coursing Association. (As 'Messrs Hadles' he won many coursing events.) For fifty years he was a council-member of the New South Wales Rugby Union.

Ernest had joined his father's woolbuying firm, Joseph Marks & Co., in 1889 and in 1919 became managing director; he was also a director of the National Association Properties Ltd. During World War I he was a member of the State Recruiting Committee and of the Citizens' War Chest Fund committee. He became a life governor of Royal Prince Alfred Hospital in 1917 and was sometime chairman of the United Charities Fund. He joined the State executive of the Australian Red Cross Society in 1927 and became a vice-president of the St John Ambulance Association in 1938.

In 1920-27 Ernest Marks represented Lang Ward on the Sydney Municipal Council for the Citizens' Reform Association. He was vice-chairman of the health and by-laws committee and campaigned for more children's playgrounds and the preservation of parks. Defeated in 1922 and 1925 as a Nationalist, he was elected to the Legislative Assembly for North Sydney in 1927, but was defeated in 1930. He was a council-member of the National Party in 1923-28. In 1930 he was re-elected to the reconstituted Sydney Municipal Council for Gipps Ward, which he represented until 1947. When he was lord mayor from July to December 1930, his sister Hilda Violet (d. 1948) acted as lady mayoress. He was also president of the Noise Abatement Society and a member of the State Council for Physical Fitness. He was appointed C.B.E. in 1938.

The brothers shared many cultural activities: they were involved with the Jewish Literary and Debating Society, were founders and office-bearers of the Shakespeare Society and Percy, with Ernest's backing, was the moving force behind the formation of the Australian Jewish Historical Society; he was first president in 1939-41, followed by Ernest in 1944-47. Percy collected coins, on which he was a recognized authority; and his valuable collection of Australian Judaica was left by Ernest to the Mitchell [q.v.5] Library, as well as his own notable collection of books on sport.

Percy Marks died at his Kirribilli residence on 22 June 1941; Ernest died in St Luke's Hospital, Darlinghurst, on 2 December 1947; both were buried in Rookwood cemetery. The City of Sydney Athletic Field is a memorial to Ernest.

Jewish Chronicle (Lond), Mar 1922; Aust Jewish Hist Soc, *J*, 1 (1941), no 6, p 203, 2 (1947), no 8, p 454; *RAHSJ*, 27 (1941), p 306; *T&CJ*, 29 July 1908; *SMH*, 25 June 1930, 2 Dec 1947; Life of E. S. Marks, CBE: autobiographical notes, *and* Council Minute, 11 Dec 1947 (Aust Jewish Hist Soc Archives, Great Synagogue, Syd); E. S. Marks biographical material (Syd Municipal Council Lib, Syd); E. S. Marks, papers and newspaper cuttings (ML).   SUZANNE D. RUTLAND

MARKS, THEODORE JOHN (1865-1941), architect, was born on 4 June 1865 at Terragong, Jamberoo, New South Wales, elder son of John Marks [q.v.5], farmer from Ireland, and his Sydney-born wife Elizabeth Preston, daughter of William Moffitt [q.v.2]. In 1876 his father moved to Sydney and bought Glenrock, Darling Point. Theo was educated at C. T. Norton's school at Double Bay and at Sydney Grammar School, before being articled to the architect G. A. Mansfield. Completing his apprenticeship in 1890 he travelled overseas for two years.

On his return Marks, with G. B. Robertson, formerly managing clerk for Mansfield Bros, set up in practice in 1892, establishing the architectural firm, Robertson & Marks, in O'Connell Street. He helped to plan and construct important commercial premises including the original Challis House (1908, now demolished), buildings for the *Daily Telegraph* (1916), the Perpetual Trustee Co. (1917), Farmer [q.v.4] & Co. and Prouds Ltd (1920), the head office of the Bank of New South Wales, Martin Place (1924-29), the Prince Edward Theatre (1925) for E. J. and Dan Carroll [qq.v.7], the Mercantile Mutual building, Pitt Street (1929), and additions to Sydney Hospital. He also designed private houses, such as Llanillo, Bellevue Hill (1902), for his friend (Sir) Colin Stephen [q.v.], which featured stained glass round the front door. He visited country friends to plan alterations to their houses.

His wide business interests brought commissions to the firm—Marks was a director of Carroll, Musgrove Theatres Ltd, the Mercantile Mutual Insurance Co. Ltd, the Australian General Insurance Co. Ltd, City Freeholds Ltd, and W. H. Paling [q.v.5] & Co. Ltd, and chairman of Timberlands Woodpulp Ltd and of the Australian board of Whakatane Paper Mills Ltd.

Much of his architectural work was connected with racing. Marks was a member of the Australian Jockey Club from 1893, an original shareholder in the Victoria Park Racing and Recreation Grounds Co. Ltd for pony-racing, and chairman of the Rosehill Racing Club in 1919-41. He designed many of the buildings and alterations suggested by C. W. Cropper [q.v.8] at Randwick, Warwick Farm Racecourse for the A.J.C. in 1922 and the Leger Stand (now demolished) at Rosehill (1920). In 1922 he was commissioned by the Western India Turf Club to design three stands and improvements (estimated to cost over £500 000) to its courses at Bombay and Poona. He was also responsible for Canterbury Park Race Course and stands at Moorefield and Victoria Park, as well as at Moonee Valley and Flemington racecourses in Melbourne. As 'Mr A. Fuller' he first registered his colours, purple with white cap, in 1909. Later his horses were trained by Fred Williams at Randwick. His winners included Pixie Ring (a brilliant two-year-old), Herilda (imported), Tom McCarthy, Leura, Brank and Newry. Always poker-faced he was a well-known punter and 'as a racing commissioner, handled colossal sums for other people'.

Tall and spare, with dark hair and beautifully waxed moustache, Marks was regarded by many as the most handsome man of their acquaintance. Well-liked by both women and men, on 14 January 1913 at the King's Weigh House, London, he married a divorcée Dorothea Mary, née Mair, former wife of D'Arcy Osborne; they lived at Woollahra. Before his marriage and after her death Marks lived much at the Australian and Union clubs. He died childless at Potts Point on 23 November 1941 and was cremated with Presbyterian forms. His estate was valued for probate at almost £22 000.

Cyclopedia of N.S.W. (Syd, 1907); *SMH*, 20 Nov 1922, 25 Nov 1941; I. G. Little, The practice of Robertson and Marks, architects 1892-1941 (B.Sc. (Arch) Honours thesis, Univ NSW, 1975); information from Robertson & Marks Pty Ltd, Syd.

MARTHA RUTLEDGE

MARKS, WALTER MOFFITT (1875-1951), lawyer, yachtsman and politician, was born on 6 June 1875 at Culwulla, Jamberoo, New South Wales, son of Sydney-born James Marks, farmer, and his wife Sarah Jane, daughter of William Moffitt [q.v.2]. John Marks [q.v.5] was an uncle and T. J. [q.v.] a cousin. Walter was educated at Sydney Grammar School and after serving his articles was admitted as a solicitor·in 1902. On 25 September 1901 at Darlinghurst he married Florence Sandford.

Inheriting substantial wealth in 1912, Marks partly financed the twelve-storey Culwulla Chambers in Castlereagh Street (the highest in central Sydney for more than forty years), which included his own chambers. He won most major Australian trophies in his yachts *Culwulla I-IV*, and in 1914 participated in the trials of Sir Thomas Lipton's America's Cup challenger, *Shamrock IV*. When war broke out he joined the Royal Navy Volunteer Reserve, served as a lieutenant in a drifter in the North Sea and English Channel, and later commanded a gunnery school in Wales. He returned to Australia in March 1918 and made a recruiting tour. In 1919 he won the Sydney Federal seat of Wentworth for the National Party.

Marks caused a sensation when in an extraordinary parliamentary speech on 3 November 1921 he predicted that Armageddon would be fought in 1934 when the British navy would collect the Jewish people to form a great nation in Palestine. Under more pressure from rumours that Marks might acquire the navy portfolio, W. M. Hughes [q.v.9] deftly created him honorary under-secretary in December, to assist the prime minister especially in the administration of the mandated territories and shipping. His salary was to be paid by the ministers and, though he answered questions in the House, Marks was not a member of Cabinet. S. M. (Viscount) Bruce [q.v.7] abolished the post in February 1923.

Tall and athletic, Marks was called 'Douglas Fairbanks' by his parliamentary colleagues. He visited Hollywood several times on his frequent overseas trips. In 1924 he attended a session of the British parliamentary committee on foreign affairs and visited Germany and Japan, but was frustrated in his intention of going to Russia. He devoted himself to defence and promoted aviation, suggesting a detailed scheme for air force equipment and training in 1924. In 1927 he was chairman of a select committee and then of a royal commission in 1927-28 into the Australian film industry, negotiating references of powers between the Commonwealth and States for film policy, which along with his other recommendations were never taken up.

Marks voted unexpectedly with Hughes in 1929 to defeat the Bruce-Page [q.v.] government. He attacked Bruce for a 'form of Mussolini Government' and cited the John Brown [q.v.7] case and arbitration as issues for which Bruce had 'no mandate'. But he also linked these issues with the government's unpopular amusement tax which vitally affected the film industry. Without National Party endorsement, Marks easily retained his seat at the October election. He joined the Australian Party in November but resigned in September 1930 after a quarrel with Hughes. When the United Australia Party was formed in May 1931 Marks was admitted as a member. He returned to his law practice when defeated in December by (Sir) Eric J. Harrison after the U.A.P. endorsed both.

Reputedly a member of forty-two clubs, Marks had extensive investments in city property and the coal industry. He was first chairman (1937) of the Papuan Apinaipi Petroleum Co. Ltd. During World War II he took a vigorous part in recruiting and victory loan campaigns. Commodore of the Royal Prince Alfred Yacht Club for seven years, he was a member of the Royal Sydney Yacht Squadron, the Sydney Amateur Sailing Club and the Royal Sydney Golf Club. In his later years he led several State bowling teams.

Marks died following surgery on 31 March 1951 at Paddington and was buried in Waverley cemetery after a state funeral. A son and a daughter survived him.

A. Wildavsky and D. Carboch, *Studies in Australian politics* (Melb, 1958); *Cyclopedia of N.S.W.* (Syd, 1907); *PD* (Cwlth), 1921, p 12406; *British A'sian*, 4 June 1914, p 9, 25 June 1914, p 12, 28 Jan 1915, p 10; *SMH*, 4, 21 Nov, 22 Dec 1921, 27, 31 May, 19, 24 Sept 1929; Marks scrap-books (NL).

C. J. LLOYD

MARLOWE, MARGARET MARY (1884-1962), actress, author and journalist, was born on 18 February 1884 at St Kilda, Melbourne, only child of Victorian-born parents John Shanahan, grazier, and his wife Margaret, daughter of Sir John O'Shanassy [q.v.5]. Brought up in Melbourne after the death of her father in 1885, Mary was educated by a governess and at the Presentation Convent, Windsor. Despite the family's financial losses, she was also taught music, singing and dancing.

Determined from childhood to go on the stage, about 1907 she joined Julius Knight's company as 'Mary Marlowe', the name she was known by thereafter. Soon she 'was taken on tour because she could sing enthusiastically and knew every part in every play in the repertoire'. Although unprepared for the fierce competition, she went to England in 1910 and, after playing soubrette roles in the provinces, made her London début late that year as Sally in *The man from Mexico*. Later she toured with Derwent Hall Caine's company.

In March 1912 Miss Marlowe joined Bert Bailey and Edmund Duggan's [qq.v.7,8] company in Sydney. In *The squatter's daughter* 'her acting in the various exciting and strenuous episodes' was praised. On 4 May she was the original Kate Rudd in the famous dramatization of *On our selection*. She was 'always graceful' with a haunting, melodious voice. Zora Cross [q.v.8] recalled: 'Her dimple was adorable. She had hazel-green eyes, sleek black hair and exquisite teeth'.

Next May Mary Marlowe sailed for England and from November toured Canada under Louis Meyer's direction. She left the company in 1914 to try her luck in New York. She played two seasons with (Sir) Ben Greet's Shakespearian company, including Katharina in *The taming of the shrew* and Adriana in *The comedy of errors*, toured the southern states under Oliver Morosco's management and did some film work with Pathé Frères.

Returning 'broke' to London in 1916, Marlowe nursed full time for two years as a member of the Voluntary Aid Detachment at the Quex Park Territorial Red Cross Hospital, Kent. She had begun to write while in America and in 1917 published a novel, *Kangaroos in King's Land*, drawing on her experiences as a struggling young actress, and in 1918 a propagandist war novel, *The women who wait*.

She returned to Australia in 1920 and soon joined the staff of the Sydney *Sun*. From being 'a general dogs-body' she became dramatic editor and from 1921 as 'Puck' wrote a weekly theatrical column for the *Sunday Sun*. She interviewed performing seals as well as such notable actresses as Nellie Stewart [q.v.], Irene Vanburgh and (Dame) Sybil Thorndike. By 1934 Mary Marlowe had published seven more romantic novels, several of which were serialized in the *Australian Woman's Mirror*. Always moral and often didactic, they were popular and well reviewed. She also wrote freelance short stories and articles and was Sydney representative on the Melbourne *Woman's World* for seven years.

In the 1930s Miss Marlowe began to broadcast for Associated Newspapers Ltd and from 1934 gave a regular weekly talk, ' A woman's view of the news', on 2UE. She also broadcast film coverage and gossip, and claimed to have introduced the informal radio interview in Sydney, usually with visiting stage and film stars. Uncompromisingly professional herself, she stressed the domestic virtues in interviews and was quick thinking and imperturbable. An avowed anti-feminist, in December 1937 over 2UE she debated with Muriel Heagney [q.v.9]. During World War II she regularly passed St John Ambulance Association's first aid and home-nursing examinations and National Emergency Services courses. She continued to run a 'Dorothy Dix' column after she retired from the *Sun* in 1946, to live in her cottage at Newport Beach with her menagerie of cats and dogs.

Mary Marlowe died at Rooty Hill on 19 February 1962 and was buried in Mona Vale cemetery. A devout Catholic, she strove to maintain an untarnished reputation for virtue while on the stage and behaved with 'unfailing courtesy under all circumstances'.

D. Campbell, 'From theatre to radio', P. Spearritt and D. Walker (eds), *Australian popular culture* (Syd, 1979); *Aust Woman's Mirror*, 17 July 1928; *All About Books*, 10 Oct 1935; *SMH*, 1, 22 Apr, 4, 6 May 1912, 3 Dec 1927; *Splashes Weekly*, 4, 25 Apr, 9 May 1912; *Daily Telegraph Sunday Pictorial*, 27 Nov 1927; *Bulletin*, 22 Dec 1927; Mary Marlowe papers *and* newspaper cuttings (ML).
                                                    MARTHA RUTLEDGE

MARMION, WILLIAM EDWARD (1845-1896), merchant and politician, was born on 22 October 1845 at Fremantle, Western Australia, son of Patrick Marmion (1815-56), merchant, and his wife Charlotte Stone. Educated in Fremantle and Perth, he started work at 16. At 21 a master in the mercantile service, he began his own business at Fremantle; W.E. Marmion & Co. in the next twenty years expanded interests in pastoral, pearling and maritime activities. He jointly leased millions of acres of pastoral land, was an early station-owner in the Kimberleys, and conducted large shipping operations. Following the discovery of gold in the Yilgarn, he formed mining companies and later helped to fit out prospecting parties headed for desert regions. On 28 December 1870 in the Catholic Church, Fremantle, he had married Anna Mary Gibbons; they had three sons and six daughters.

On the introduction of representative government in 1870, Marmion was defeated for the Fremantle seat but was appointed an unofficial nominee member of the Legislative Council. He was elected for Fremantle in 1873 and until his death remained its member, from 1890 in the Legislative Assembly. Premier (Sir) John Forrest [q.v.8] appointed him commissioner of crown lands and minister for mines in 1890. Under Marmion the gold-mining industry became the economic vehicle which transformed a quiet backwater into a colony attracting enormous international interest. He had financial acumen and understood the infrastructure requirements needed to service rapidly increasing trade and population. He was a member of the finance committee of the Legislative Council and of the National Australasian Federal Convention of 1891 in Sydney where he took no prominent part.

Marmion sat on nearly one hundred select committees and royal commissions covering a wide range of topics. In the Londonderry claim-jumping case of 1894, goldfields editors accused him of conflicts of interest as minister and leading investor. However, his resignation as minister that year took many by surprise, some seeing it as consistent with his integrity.

Marmion's progressive public works policy and his voluble promotion of Fremantle's interests gave him a reputation for being honest and clear sighted, but lacking in tact. In his support for Sir John Coode's [q.v.3] plan to develop Fremantle's harbour, he evidently criticized and bullied engineers who supported C. Y. O'Connor's [q.v.] alternative plan. As a Catholic member of the Central Board of Education from its inception in 1871 to its abolition in 1895, he earned the respect of J. T. Reilly [q.v.] for his 'splendid efforts' to obtain justice.

Marmion's sudden death from liver disease on 4 July 1896 caused widespread grief. It was reported that more people attended his funeral than any other in the colony at that time and that the streets of Perth were lined with thousands of citizens. He was buried in the Catholic cemetery, Fremantle. He died intestate with his affairs in some confusion. A monument, a huge Celtic cross, was erected in Mayor's Park, Fremantle, by public subscription.

W. B. Kimberly, *History of West Australia* (Melb, 1897); J. T. Reilly, *Reminiscences of fifty years residence in Western Australia* (Perth, 1903); M. Tauman, *The Chief, C. Y. O'Connor* (Perth, 1978); R. Erickson (comp), *Dictionary of Western Australians*, 3 (Perth, 1979); *PD* (WA), 1883, p 70, 1887-88, p 15, 180, 1888, p 16, 1889, p 19; T. Manford, A history of rail transport policy in Western Australia, 1870-1911 (Ph.D. thesis, Univ WA, 1976).   R. T. Appleyard

MARQUET, CLAUDE ARTHUR (1869-1920), cartoonist, was born on 8 May 1869 at Moonta, South Australia, son of Charles Frederick Marquet, workman painter of French descent, and his wife Mary, née McArthur. When the family moved to Wallaroo, Claude attended Taplin's Grammar School there. His first job was in the mines but later, as a printer's compositor, he acquired a sound knowledge of newspaper work including process engraving. By the time of his marriage to Ann Jane Donnell on 16 June 1891 at St Mary's Church, Wallaroo, he was a proficient, self-taught black-and-white artist. In 1897 he was appointed cartoonist to the Adelaide weekly magazine, *Quiz*.

By 1900 Marquet was having work accepted by the *Bulletin* and in 1902 he left Adelaide for Melbourne. Next year he submitted a cartoon comment on the Victorian rail strike to *Tocsin*. This radical Labor newspaper was loaded with debts and libels; nevertheless the cartoon was purchased and, as Frank Anstey [q.v.7] recorded, 'another, and another, and the last was better than the one before'. During this period, when Marquet also drew for *Table Talk* and Melbourne *Punch*, he signed some of his work 'C.M.' or 'QUET'. Other later, shortened signatures were 'Claude' and 'C.A.M.'.

His big opportunity came when he was invited to Sydney as staff cartoonist on the *Australian Worker*. The first of his *Worker* cartoons appeared on 25 October 1906 and in the years before his death Marquet was delivering up to four very detailed cartoons each week. He also produced drawings and illustrations, even one comic strip, for various *Worker* publications such as *Vumps*, a failed comic paper experiment, and *Our Annual*.

Marquet drew with pen and ink in the traditional three-dimensional style; unusually, his work reveals no influences from other artists. That he could draw well cannot be questioned, although on occasions his line work appears somewhat hard. His bold style, however, ensured that his work reproduced well at a time when newspaper printing was frequently rough and ready. When the occasion called for it his political cartoons were presented in the fashionable 'Grand Manner' with allegorical figures and symbols representing not only Australia but nations the world over. A Laborite from actual experience, Marquet perpetuated the Australian cartoonists' symbol for capitalism: 'Fat', a paunchy, bloated figure in a top hat. His most memorable cartoon was that drawn with the verse by W. R. Winspear [q.v.], 'The Blood Vote'; reprinted on a million leaflets it served the 1916 anti-conscription campaign.

On 17 April 1920 Marquet and a companion Harry Palmer were drowned returning to Marquet's Kurnell home from Botany when his sailing boat was caught in a sudden squall. The bodies were never recovered. Marquet was survived by his wife. A memorial volume of his *Worker* cartoons was published in 1920 together with tributes from his friends Henry Lawson [q.v.], C. J. Dennis, Mary Gilmore [qq.v.8,9] and others, who recorded the artist's enormous popularity, his genial, obliging nature and his loyalty to the working man. The Mitchell Library, Sydney, holds seventy-five of Marquet's original *Worker* cartoons.

V. Lindesay, *The inked-in image* (Melb, 1970); M. Mahood, *The loaded line* (Melb, 1973); *Aust Worker* (Syd), 19 Aug 1920; Heagney papers (LaTL).   VANE LINDESAY

MARR, SIR CHARLES WILLIAM CLANAN (1880-1960), engineer, soldier and politician, was born on 23 March 1880 at Petersham, Sydney, son of Hobart-born James Clanan Marr, boot manufacturer, and his Irish wife Ellen, née Nilson. He was educated at Fort Street Model School, Newington College and Sydney Technical College, and played Rugby, and cricket and baseball for Petersham. He joined the New South Wales Public Service in 1896 and was appointed junior assistant in November 1899 in the Postmaster-General's Department, transferring in 1901 to the Commonwealth. On 20 September 1905 he married Ethel May Ritchie at Lewisham. Marr supervised the erection in 1912 of the first of Australia's chain of wireless telegraphy stations at Pennant Hills.

After seven years in school cadets, Marr had joined the volunteer forces in 1898 and served in an electrical company. In 1912 he commanded a signals troop, and by 1914 was a lieutenant with the Royal Australian Navy Wireless Radio Service. He enlisted in the Australian Imperial Force in the Australia and New Zealand Wireless Signals Squadron in April 1916 and in May embarked for Mesopotamia where he was acting commander and major from September until the end of the campaign. The difficulties he had with the Arabs, 'the meanest, dirtiest, most treacherous lot', strengthened his convictions of racial superiority. Twice mentioned in dispatches, he was awarded the Military Cross (1917) and the Distinguished Service Order (1918). He remained in the militia after the war, commanding the signals of the First Cavalry Division.

After his return to Australia in mid-1918, Marr won the Sydney Federal seat of Parkes as a Nationalist in December 1919. He was

government whip (1921-22) and parliamentary secretary to the Nationalists in 1921-25. In the Bruce [q.v.7]-Page [q.v.] government he was honorary minister (1925-27) and minister for home and territories (1927-28). He was again honorary minister from February 1928 until the defeat of October 1929. At the head of the Australian delegation to the League of Nations in Geneva at the time, Marr made frantic but unsuccessful efforts to return for the election campaign, even seeking the assistance of (Sir) Charles Kingsford Smith [q.v.9] to fly back. (Sir) Edward McTiernan defeated him, but after he was appointed to the High Court of Australia, Marr won the by-election in January 1931, campaigning against the financial policies of the Scullin [q.v.] and Lang [q.v.9] governments. He was vice-president in 1924-25 and 1929-31 of the National Association of New South Wales and vice-president of the Australian National Federation in 1928-31.

In the Lyons [q.v.] United Australia Party government, Marr in 1932-34 held the portfolios of health, repatriation and territories. Having served on the committees that organized the visits of the prince of Wales (1920) and the duke and duchess of York (1927), he was given charge of the duke of Gloucester's tour in 1934 and was appointed K.C.V.O. in 1935, when he was dropped from the ministry. In 1941-42 he was deputy chairman of the joint committee on broadcasting. He was defeated in 1943 when a heart ailment restricted his campaigning.

Marr was a tenacious watchdog over the development of Canberra where he lived after 1927. An enthusiastic supporter of the territories of Papua and New Guinea, Marr saw them as 'definitely white man's country', denying he had seen 'even one mosquito' during a visit to Rabaul. He hoped Papua would 'become one of the bright jewels in the Empire which the creator intended it to be'. He promoted the New Guinea Legislative Council, personally opening it in May 1933. Substantial land holdings he bought near Madang were acquired in 1929 by Amalgamated Coffee Plantations (New Guinea) Ltd, a company he founded with (Sir) Walter Carpenter [q.v.7] and others. Marr held several company directorships, including Tatua Gold, New Zealand Forest Products Ltd, Papuan Apinaipi Petroleum Co. Ltd and W. R. Carpenter & Co. Ltd, and he was chairman of Mineral Development Ltd and Gold Development Ltd.

Marr died on 20 October 1960 at Pymble and was cremated after a state funeral at the Methodist Church, Gordon. His wife, two sons and two daughters survived him. Charlie Marr's amiability and ability were widely admired among politicians; Lang described him as 'highly personable . . . an energetic local member and popular with all sections of the community, leaving politics aside'.

Reveille (Syd), Jan 1935, Dec 1960; *Pacific Island Mthly*, Nov 1960; *Table Talk*, 18 Apr 1929; *Bulletin*, 26 Oct 1960; *SMH*, 21 Oct 1969; Marr papers (NL).   C. J. LLOYD

MARRIOTT, IDA LOUISE; *see* LEE, IDA

MARRYAT, CHARLES (1827-1906), Anglican clergyman, was born on 26 June 1827 at Clarence Terrace, London, eldest son of Charles Marryat, West Indian merchant, and his wife Caroline, sister of Augustus Short [q.v.6], bishop of Adelaide. He was a nephew of Captain Frederick Marryat, R.N., novelist, and his sister Augusta Sophia married Sir Henry Edward Fox Young [q.v.6], governor of South Australia. Educated at Dr Deane's School near Twyford, Hampshire, and at Eton, Charles graduated from The Queen's College, Oxford (B.A., 1851; M.A., 1854). He was ordained priest in 1852 and served a curacy in Kent before sailing for Sydney as chaplain on an emigrant ship in 1852. After a brief chaplaincy to penal establishments at Darlinghurst and Cockatoo Island he proceeded next year to Adelaide where he became assistant curate to the Very Rev. James Farrell at Holy Trinity Church.

In 1857 Marryat was appointed canon and became incumbent of St Paul's, Port Adelaide, a church whose size he doubled in two years; by 1864 when it was consecrated, the building debt had been liquidated. In June 1868 he was made rector of Christ Church, North Adelaide, and archdeacon of Adelaide. Some of the congregation objected to his appointment which was made on the casting vote of the bishop, who was his uncle. The dissentients obtained an injunction to restrain Marryat from preaching, but in July it was dissolved and he assumed his duties. At North Adelaide he renovated and added to the church and parsonage and built a day school. Marryat was a remarkable parish priest; the secret of his success was his consistent and systematic visiting on foot.

As examining chaplain to the bishop and as archdeacon he served on synod's standing committee and its financial board. After his appointment as dean of Adelaide in 1887, Marryat twice administered the diocese during the absence overseas of Bishop Kennion [q.v.5]. He took a leading part in establishing The Cottage Homes (Inc.) for the Aged and Infirm, Poor and Widows.

Bishop Harmer [q.v.9] described Marryat as a 'man of strong opinions'. An example of his outspokenness was his 1894 press protest against 'our most beautiful hymns . . . desec-rated by their inappropriate use on the Melbourne scaffold'. In 1896 he condemned the government for giving way to the greed of local settlers and closing the Aboriginal reserve and mission at Poonindie. Another contemporary admired his 'transparent honesty . . . and energy'. When Kennion returned to England in 1894, some leading clergymen wished to nominate Marryat to the bishopric but he refused; praised for his administration of the diocese in the interregnum, he said laconically, 'I have always tried to do my duty. No man can do more; I hope I shall never do less'. Although concise and clear, he was not a brilliant speaker. He administered the diocese again when Harmer resigned from May 1905.

Marryat became the doyen of the clergy. He was devout in a way that needed few of the externals of worship, was prominent in framing synodical regulations, and active in establishing the General Synod of the Church of England in Australia and Tasmania.

On 8 August 1854 in Trinity Church, Adelaide, he had married Grace Montgomery, daughter of Rev. Charles Beaumont Howard [q.v.1]; they had six daughters and three sons. Marryat died at North Adelaide on 29 September 1906 and was buried in North Road cemetery.

A. C. Fox-Davies, *Armorial families* (Lond, 1906); G. H. Jose, *Annals of Christ Church, North Adelaide* (Adel, 1921), and *The Church of England in South Australia*, 2, 1856-1881 (Adel, 1954); *Church News*, 7 Feb 1896; *Year Book of the Church of England in the Diocese of Adelaide*; S. J. Way, letter-book, 1904 (SAA).   T. T. REED

MARSHALL, NORMAN (1886-1942), grazier and soldier, was born on 10 February 1886 at Callander, Scotland, sixth son of Rev. Alexander Marshall, D.D., and his wife Jean Crawford, née Hay. Alexander Marshall was called to Scots Church, Melbourne, in 1888, so Norman grew up as an Australian. He was educated at Scotch College. Tall, powerful and strikingly handsome, he excelled at games and became amateur welterweight boxing champion of Victoria.

Marshall was manager of a paper mill near Geelong when war broke out in 1914. Enlisting as a private in the 5th Battalion, Australian Imperial Force, on 17 August, he was a sergeant at the Gallipoli landing and was commissioned on 28 April 1915. 'Darkie' Marshall was soon recognized as a fearless and daring leader. At Lone Pine he destroyed a troublesome sniper with a bomb of his own making and led bombers who cleared the Turks from the communication trenches with jam-tin bombs. For his work on Gallipoli he was awarded the Military Cross.

As a company commander in the 57th Battalion Marshall led the first trench raid of the 5th Division in France. On the morning after Fromelles he was observed running with another officer, half-way between the opposing lines, hunting for wounded soldiers. Marshall was for a few months second-in-command of his battalion until 10 April 1917 when he was promoted lieut-colonel to command the 60th Battalion. He had risen rapidly under the stern eye of Brigadier General H. E. Elliott [q.v.8] and now became an outstanding unit commander with the distinction, unique in the A.I.F., of the Distinguished Service Order and two Bars. He was also mentioned in dispatches four times. The first D.S.O. was for his skilful and fearless handling of his own and other battalions at Polygon Wood, 25-26 September 1917, when he was largely responsible for the 15th Brigade's success. When Elliott visited him at a critical moment and Marshall indicated the source of the trouble, Elliott said, 'Come on, Marshall, you and I can fix that pill box'—and they did.

In the famous night counter-attack at Villers-Bretonneux, 24-25 April 1918, Marshall took control of the attacking battalions of the 15th Brigade at their forming-up position and 'got the whole brigade straightened up and moving forward on the right lines'; the operation was a brilliant success. He was awarded a Bar to the D.S.O. for his part in the battle.

Marshall led the 54th Battalion from May 1918 until the A.I.F. was withdrawn from operations in October. He again distinguished himself in the great battles beginning on 8 August and, for his part in the capture of Péronne on 1-3 September, was awarded a second Bar to his D.S.O. Against fierce resistance, he personally organized 'the attack on the ramparts and the mopping up of the town. Through his splendid energy and example . . . the town was held and three guns and about 600 prisoners captured by his battalion'.

In battle Marshall usually wore a short-sleeved khaki shirt and he liked to be 'here, there and everywhere'; this sometimes troubled superiors who wished to communicate with him. Nevertheless his presence and his evident disregard of danger greatly strengthened his battalion in many a battle. He was 'a natural leader who would be followed and obeyed without question anywhere'. Out of the line his energy was unflagging; he played football in the unit and brigade teams, organized and took part in boxing and exhibited 'a strong vein of merry mischief'.

After the Armistice Marshall was appointed to the Sports Control Board of the A.I.F.; he went to England to coach the A.I.F. No. 1 crew which won the King's Gold Cup at Henley in 1919. Before embarking for home Marshall spent about three months investigating paper manufacture in London. He had married Kathleen Elsie Black of Melbourne at the Scottish National Church, Chelsea, on 24 February 1917; they had four children.

After demobilization Marshall went into partnership with his brother-in-law W. G. Davies, on a grazing property near Barraba, New South Wales, but in 1924 he took up his own station, Mount Malakoff, near Stanthorpe, Queensland.

Marshall did not serve in the Citizen Forces but in 1939 he was given command of the 11th Light Horse Regiment. In May 1940 he took command of the 1st Cavalry Brigade as a brigadier but relinquished the rank to become commanding officer of the 2/25th Battalion, A.I.F. In October 1940 he again became a brigadier, commanding the 27th Brigade. Increasing ill health forced him to relinquish command in July 1941 and he retired next January. Marshall died of cancer at Toorak, Melbourne, on 12 September 1942 and was cremated. His wife and three children survived him. Both his sons served in the 2nd A.I.F.; Lieutenant Archibald Marshall killed in action at Tobruk and Major Alexander Marshall won the Military Cross. Two of Marshall's brothers had served in the 1st A.I.F., Lieutenant L. B. Marshall winning the M.C.

C. E. W. Bean, *The story of Anzac*, 1 (Syd, 1921), and *The A.I.F. in France*, 1916-18 (Syd, 1929, 1933, 1937, 1942); *London Gazette*, 16 Nov 1917, 13 Sept 1918, 1 Feb 1919; *Reveille* (Syd), Dec 1931; information from Mr A. Marshall, East Kew, Melb.

A. J. HILL

MARSHALL-HALL, GEORGE WILLIAM LOUIS (1862-1915), composer, conductor and professor of music, was born on 28 March 1862 in London, son of Marshall Hall and his wife Mary Eliza, née Mammatt; he was a grandson of the physiologist Marshall Hall, discoverer of the principle of reflex action, and a great-nephew of Samuel Hall, engineer and inventor. George's father, a barrister, did not practise but used his inheritance to further an interest in natural science. He apparently in later life hyphenated his name to Marshall-Hall, the form used by his sons.

George was educated at Mr Creak's school, The Wick, Brighton, and the Blackheath Proprietary School, London. He studied the organ under Mr Lees, organist at St Margaret's Church, London, and also learned the violin. His interest in music, initially encouraged by his paternal grandmother, never waned, despite parental disapproval and a childhood illness which left him temporarily deaf and with tone sense distorted (possibly for life).

In 1878 he attended King's College, London, before moving to Switzerland with his family. Returning to London next year, he abandoned studies for the Civil Service and an intended career in the colonies when in 1880 he was appointed organist and assistant master in French and German at Oxford Military College. To prepare for the post he journeyed to Berlin to study privately under Carl August Haupt, director of the Royal Institute for Church Music there. In December 1882, however, he resigned his college position.

Marshall-Hall attended the Royal College of Music, London, in the latter part of 1883, studying organ with Walter Parratt, composition with (Sir) Hubert Parry and counterpoint with (Sir) Frederick Bridge; the director (Sir) George Grove regarded him highly, despite the brevity of his stay. On 5 April 1884 in St Matthew's Church, Bayswater, he married May Hunt and in August he became organist and choirmaster at Newton College, Newton Abbot, South Devon.

College work left Marshall-Hall no time to compose and at Christmas 1886 he and his wife left for London where they lived in poverty; it was later said that Marshall-Hall's father had cast him off as 'a damned fiddler'. He eventually found work as assistant to A. Gray at Wellington College and by February 1888 was director of the orchestra and choral society at the London Organ School and College of Music where he also taught composition and singing. He published articles in *Musical World, Magazine of Music* and *School*.

To this English period belong the operas *Dido*, written when Marshall-Hall was 15 and later reworked as the music-drama *Dido and Aeneas* (first performed 11 October 1899, Melbourne); *Harold*, written prior to February 1888; and the lost *Leonard*. Other works include the *Harold overture* (1888), the sextet *Die Blumen* (1886) and the *Soliloquy from Tennyson's 'Maud'*, written in 1890 for voice and orchestra (first performed 6 July 1896, Melbourne).

Marshall-Hall arrived in Melbourne on 7 January 1891 to take up the University of Melbourne's new chair of music established by Francis Ormond [q.v.5] with a gift of £20 000, though without an attendant practical school. Tall, dark, bluff-mannered and idealistic, the new professor was not the expected standard organist-pedagogue, but rather a largely self-educated, flesh and blood Bohemian, who believed passionately in Art and in God not at all. The views he soon expressed in articles and lectures were considered outrageous. Opposed to pedantry, he spoke extravagantly of the power of emotive discipline—not a popular cause among strait-

laced Melburnians; he expounded his socialist theories and declared his atheism. His wild public behaviour and loud speech made enemies; but his exuberant nature often redeemed lost ground in private.

In 1892, with George Allan's [q.v.3] support, Marshall-Hall founded the Marshall-Hall Orchestra. It inherited standards, scores and some of its personnel from the Cowen [q.v.3] 1888 Centennial Exhibition (later, Victorian) Orchestra which had disbanded the previous year. Over the next twenty years Marshall-Hall established a body of players recognized by visiting musicians as equal to the general order of those in Europe; he introduced much orchestral music new to the colony and gained a reputation as a conductor of the first rank. Until 1902, when a committee took over, Marshall-Hall met the orchestra expenses himself; eventually, in 1908, (Sir) James Barrett [q.v.7] organized the Permanent Orchestra Trust Fund under the patronage of Lady Northcote. Marshall-Hall also paid the rent for the Melbourne University Conservatorium which, with W. A. Laver [q.v.], he established on 28 February 1895 in the Queen's Coffee Palace, Carlton; it was later housed in the Victorian Artists' Society premises, Albert Street, East Melbourne. The music course Marshall-Hall devised was centred on interpretative sensibility built on a basis of technical efficiency, stressing emotional response as opposed to the prevailing emphasis on pure technique. He abhorred examination systems and at various times tried to have those existing for music abolished.

Soon after his arrival in Melbourne Marshall-Hall formed close friendships with Arthur Streeton [q.v.] and other Heidelberg painters. There was clearly an exchange of ideas about current European Symbolism and Wagnerianism and mutual encouragement to creativity. Poet as well as musician, Marshall-Hall dedicated his *Hymn to Sydney* (1897) to Streeton.

In July 1898 Marshall-Hall published the fourth of his volumes of verse, *Hymns ancient and modern*. About the same time he spoke publicly in favour of war. On 5 August the *Argus* launched a full-scale attack on the book and on its author's morals, accusing Marshall-Hall of lewdness, animalism, lasciviousness and anti-clericalism, and asking the university why he should be permitted to 'lecture to the Young, especially the young Women, of Victoria'. On 12 August Marshall-Hall presented to the university council a written declaration on individual independence and the right to free speech: 'There is no toleration and no freedom when men must echo conventional views of life, religion and politics or hold their peace'. This widened the argument, enraged his opponents and resulted in petitions, for and against him, from musical and educational bodies, and in student demonstrations. Before the council came to a decision, however, Marshall-Hall recanted, asking for twelve months leave of absence and promising then to resign. He withdrew his resignation when the university made it a condition that he abstain from teaching in Victoria. In the two years of public debate which followed, Rev. Dr Alexander Leeper [q.v.] became Marshall-Hall's chief opponent: Marshall-Hall in 1898 had unwisely ridiculed Leeper, before and during the Trinity College play, *Alcestis*, whose full score by the composer outshone Leeper's production.

During the 1890s Marshall-Hall's wife spent much time in England where she died in 1901. In 1899 a whispering campaign suggested immoral conduct with female students by the music professor. His friends Lionel and Norman Lindsay [qq.v.] retaliated with lampoons and satirical verse-plays in *Outpost*; but debate on the South African War fuelled the hysteria and on 25 June 1900 Marshall-Hall's tenure was not renewed. On 6 March 1902, with Australian Church forms, he married Kathleen Hoare who for some years had passed as his wife.

As the conservatorium lessee, Marshall-Hall was able to stay on, with loyal staff and students, in East Melbourne, renaming his institution the Conservatorium of Music, Melbourne (later known as the Albert Street and later still as the Melba [q.v.] Conservatorium). The university was obliged to begin again, using Australian Music Examinations Board funds and abandoning Marshall-Hall's teaching curriculum. The break in local musical life caused by the rivalry never mended.

Marshall-Hall spent August 1906 to May 1907 in Europe, possibly for eye surgery. His reports on musical events there were widely published in Australia. From this time the demands of the Musicians' Union that professionals refrain from playing in orchestras using amateurs (usually female) undermined the financial structure and morale of the Marshall-Hall Orchestra. Though he conducted *Lohengrin* in Sydney on 30 September 1911 for the J. C. Williamson [q.v.6]-Melba company, Marshall-Hall refused permanent work with Williamson. His orchestra's last performance was on 5 October 1912. On 21 February next year he left Australia to pursue the production of his operas in London. His conservatorium passed into the hands of Fritz Hart [q.v.9] who, with Melba, later consolidated its musical gains when her school of singing was founded there.

To Marshall-Hall's Australian period belong his overture *Giordano Bruno* (1891; dedicated to Streeton), the *Symphony in C* (1892), *La belle dame sans merci* for violin and orchestra (c. 1894), *Idyll* (1894), *Choral ode* (1898), *Alcestis* (1898; first performed Melbourne, 1898), *An Australian national song* (1900), the opera *Aristodemus* (1902), the *Symphony in E flat* (1903; first performed London, 1907), *Phantasy for horn* (1905), *Bianca capello* (a play published in 1906), two *Violin fantasies* (1907), *Caprice* for violin and orchestra (1910), the *String quartett in F* (1910), the lost *String quartett in D minor* and the operas *Stella* (1910; first performed Melbourne, 1912) and *Romeo and Juliet* (1912).

When the Ormond chair of music again became vacant on the death of F. S. Peterson [q.v.] in June 1914, a new campaign was mounted in Melbourne involving Laver, a contender for the post, and Marshall-Hall. The argument this time centred on open competition for public posts on the one hand and the need to redress the injustice done to Marshall-Hall on the other. The position was eventually offered to Marshall-Hall, who accepted and arrived back in Melbourne in January 1915.

The future looked promising as the public furore died down and an uneasy truce was called with Fritz Hart at Albert Street. Then, suddenly, on 18 July 1915 at Fitzroy, Marshall-Hall died from complications of appendicitis. He was buried in the Baptist section of Brighton cemetery survived by his wife, their son and his daughter Elsa, also a composer, of his first marriage. His scores and literary output were purchased from his widow by Percy Grainger [q.v.9] in 1934-38 and were housed in the Grainger Museum, University of Melbourne, together with a 1901 portrait by Tom Roberts [q.v.]; a portrait by Streeton is in the National Gallery of Victoria; and another by Roberts (1898) is in the Performing Arts Museum, Melbourne.

As a conductor Marshall-Hall educated a whole generation of concert audiences through the high standards he achieved. His compositions, nearly all performed during his lifetime, have been revived by Richard Divall in Australian Broadcasting Commission recordings and his influence as composer has continued through his pupils, notably Margaret Sutherland. But Marshall-Hall has been remembered mainly for his ability to provoke controversy; attitudes to the role of music and the arts, freedom of speech, the meaning of academic responsibility and the purpose of the university were hammered out in Melbourne through argument which he generated.

T. Radic, *G. W. L. Marshall-Hall*, music monograph 5, Univ WA (Perth, 1982); *British A'sian*, 22 July, 12 Aug 1915; *Table Talk*, 16 Jan 1891; *Evening Standard*, 28 July 1894; Marshall-Hall papers (Univ Melb Archives); Univ Melb central registry letter files box 1890/30; T. Radic, Catalogue to the Marshall-Hall collection (Grainger Museum, Univ Melb).   MAUREEN THERESE RADIC

MARTIN, CATHERINE EDITH MAC-AULEY (1848?-1937), writer, was born on Skye, Scotland, seventh child of Samuel Nicholson Mackay, crofter, and his wife Janet, née MacKinnon. They migrated to South Australia in 1855 and with other impoverished Highland families went to Robe and later to Naracoorte in the south-east. Catherine's father had taught children on the voyage to Australia and he probably taught her too at Naracoorte. She acquired a love of German language and literature. By the early 1870s she was helping her sister Mary to run a school at Elm Cottage, Crouch Street, Mount Gambier.

From 1872 Catherine's poems and translations of German poetry appeared in the *Border Watch*. As 'M.C.' she published *The explorers and other poems* (Melbourne, 1874), which included translations from French and German, as well as a long poem about the Burke and Wills [qq.v.3,6] expedition. She moved to Adelaide about 1875, tried to make a living by journalism and became a friend of Catherine Spence [q.v.6]. Miss Mackay was a clerk in the Education Department from 1877, where she experienced discrimination financially and in her failure to gain promotion to the permanent list. She was dismissed in 1885. On 4 March 1882 she had married Frederick Martin, accountant, of whom Spence noted: 'His bent was rather towards literature than business; but business was what his father set him to'. They had no children. Catherine was now sister-in-law to Annie Montgomerie Martin, who ran a progressive school, and to Henry Maydwell Martin, vigneron, of Stonyfell Wines. The Martins were Unitarians. She lived for a time near Waukaringa where her husband was accountant at a gold-mine. In 1890 she published anonymously in London a novel, *An Australian girl*, which was well received in Australia and reprinted next year. The action moves between Australia and Europe as the bluestocking heroine decides between two suitors, a German intellectual and a rich but insensitive pastoralist. Under the pseudonym 'Mrs Alick Macleod', Catherine Martin published another novel *The silent sea* (London, 1892), which drew upon her mining experience.

In 1890-94 she and her husband travelled in Europe; Catherine continued writing, while Frederick contributed a series, 'Life and labour in other lands' to the Melbourne *Age*. In 1906 she published anonymously *The old roof-tree*: impressions and thoughts while abroad. In 1904 she and Frederick had been in Europe again, but they returned to Adelaide in 1907 when his health deteriorated; he died from tuberculosis in 1909. Catherine spent long periods in Germany. She published, under her own name, *The incredible journey* (London, 1923) which, written very effectively from an Aboriginal woman's point of view, was about a desert journey to recover her son, taken by a white man. H. M. Green found it a most interesting and realistic novel. Martin last visited Europe in 1928 when 80, returning to Adelaide in 1932. She died there on 15 March 1937 and was cremated.

Catherine Martin published essays, stories, poems and serialized novels in the Australian press. Scattered through her work were many literary references, especially to Goethe and Heine. She conveyed sympathy to Aborigines and Germany's and Britain's urban masses, and her female characters were drawn from a feminist point of view. All her books except the last were published anonymously or under a pseudonym. Criticism of her work has varied, but many have praised her lyrical descriptions of Australian landscape. Spence admired her writing but Miles Franklin [q.v.8] saw *An Australian girl* as a 'trying rigmarole'. Paul Depasquale, however, has judged that with this book's focus 'on the inner workings of the human mind' the South Australian novel reached its highest point.

C. H. Spence, *An autobiography* (Adel, 1910); P. Depasquale, *A critical history of South Australian literature 1836-1930 with subjectively annotated bibliographies* (Adel, 1978); *Voice*, Dec 1892, p 2; *Aust Letters*, 3, no 4, June 1961, p 11; *Observer*, 8 May 1909; Education Dept (SA), correspondence file, minister of education and agriculture, GRG 18/1/1877/1100, inspector general of schools, GRG 18/3/1883/4265, 1884/2802, 1885/4660; information from Miss J. B. L. Cook, Millswood, Adel.   MARGARET ALLEN

MARTIN, SIR CHARLES JAMES (1866-1955), physiologist and pathologist, was born on 9 January 1866 at Hackney, London, son of Josiah Martin, actuary, and his wife Elizabeth Mary, née Lewis. Both parents had been married previously and mustered eleven children between them before Charles, the eldest of three more, was born. The family in his own words 'was a Nonconformist middle class one characteristic of the period, with lots of children, a fading flavour of piety and a small revenue'. Educated at a boarding school at Hastings, Charles started work as a junior clerk at 15. A new-found interest in medical science was not encouraged by his family, so he enrolled in evening classes at Birkbeck and King's colleges, London, matriculating in 1883. Entering St Thomas's Hospital, he took his B.Sc. in 1886 with a gold medal in physiology and a university scholarship which enabled him to work for six months under Carl Ludwig at Leipzig. In 1887-91 he was a demonstrator in biology and physiology and lecturer in comparative anatomy at King's College, completing his medical studies at St Thomas's (M.R.C.S., L.S.A., 1889; M.B., 1890). He later received doctorates of science from London and Melbourne, and several honorary degrees. In 1891 at St Stephen's Church, Hampstead, Martin married Edith Harriett Cross; they had one daughter.

That year Martin was appointed demonstrator in physiology at the University of Sydney where he became an intimate friend of J. T. Wilson [q.v.], professor of anatomy. Together they led a distinguished band of researchers into Australia's native fauna, self-styled 'the Fraternity of Duckmaloi', which included J. P. Hill [q.v.9] and (Sir) Grafton Elliot Smith [q.v.]. Martin did impressive work on snake venom, especially that of the black snake, for which he was awarded the medal of the Royal Society of New South Wales and in 1901 a fellowship of the Royal Society, London. He also studied monotremes and marsupials and in 1902 published the first paper on their internal heat regulation and respiratory physiology.

From 1897 Martin was lecturer in physiology at the University of Melbourne, raised to the title but not the full salary of acting professor in 1900. Pragmatic and imaginative, he made much of his own apparatus, always using precise research methods. A severe but inspiring teacher, he established in Melbourne 'a legend of wisdom, integrity and good fellowship'.

Australia suited Martin profoundly: the people, climate, freedom from constraint and the camaraderie of young scientists channelling new grooves. But because his wife was homesick he returned to London as director of the Lister Institute of Preventive Medicine (1903-30). In 1912 he was also appointed professor of experimental pathology at the University of London. His own chief work was on bubonic plague, typhoid fever, the mechanics of disinfection, heat coagulation of proteins and their nutritional value, vitamins and vitamin deficiency diseases, and on internal heat regulation in man and animals. Martin made the Lister Institute a magnet for young Australians with an interest in medical research, among them (Lord) Florey, the future knights Cairns [q.v.7], Dunhill [q.v.8], N. Hamilton Fairley, Macfarlane Burnet, G. R. Cameron and Alan Newton [q.v.], C. H. Kellaway [q.v.9] and W. J. Young [q.v.].

Martin was recruited as a pathologist with the rank of major on 19 July 1915, to the Australian Army Medical Corps, one of the few permitted enlistment in the Australian Imperial Force outside Australia. He improvised a pathological laboratory at the 3rd Australian General Hospital, Lemnos, where he found that the prevalent enteric fever at Gallipoli was not caused by the typhoid bacillus, against which the victims had been vaccinated, but by the related organisms paratyphoid A and B. He then made a vaccine giving immunity against all three bacilli (T.A.B.) which the Lister produced in quantity. The Australian government 'against bitter and persistent opposition and prejudice' was the first to introduce compulsory inoculation. To counteract vitamin deficiency in troop rations the Lister Institute produced a vitamin 'soup cube' for use in the Middle East. In the 3rd A.G.H., Cairo, as lieut-colonel from February 1916, Martin organized the integration of decentralized pathology services into the A.A.M.C. In August he was sent to the Sinai to deal with an outbreak of cholera which threatened disaster to crowded Egypt. Recalled to London in November to investigate an outbreak of cerebro-spinal meningitis in troops arriving from Australia, he organized a central A.I.F. pathology laboratory in the Lister Institute. In April 1917 he went to France to set up the pathology laboratory at 3rd A.G.H. at Abbeville and late in 1917 he was seconded as assistant adviser in pathology to the British Expeditionary Force, to take control of hospital laboratories in the Paris, Rouen, Trouville area. Twice mentioned in dispatches and in January 1919 appointed C.M.G., he was demobilized on 29 September 1919.

Knighted in 1927, Martin retired from the Lister in 1930 to accept, at the request of (Sir) David Rivett [q.v.], the leadership of the division of animal nutrition of the Council for Scientific and Industrial Research in Adelaide, where he was also appointed professor of biochemistry and general physiology. He returned to England in 1933 and settled at Cambridge. For C.S.I.R. in 1934-35 he initiated experimental study of the myxoma virus at Cambridge and on a rabbit-infested island in Pembrokeshire. In retirement he continued research in animal nutrition with colleagues at the Lister Institute. He died at Cambridge on 15 February 1955.

Martin spent only fifteen years in Australia, yet his influence on Australian science was so distinct that it was dubbed 'the Martin spirit' and commemorated by the National Health and Medical Research Council of Australia, which created in 1951 two Sir Charles James Martin fellowships in medical science.

A portrait by M. Lewis is in the possession of the family, and a copy of a drawing by A. J. Murch is in the Basser Library, Canberra.

A. G. Butler (ed), *Official history of the Aus-*

tralian Army Medical Services . . . 1914-18, 2, 3 (Canb, 1940, 1943); F. M. Burnet, *Walter and Eliza Hall Institute 1915-1965* (Melb, 1971); H. Chick et al, *War on disease; a history of the Lister Institute* (Lond, 1971); K. F. Russell, *The Melbourne Medical School 1862-1962* (Melb, 1977); J. A. Young et al (eds), *Centenary book of the University of Sydney faculty of medicine* (Syd, 1984); *The Times*, 17 Feb, 14 Mar 1955; *MJA*, 28 May 1955; *Biographical Memoirs of Fellows of the Roy Soc*, 2 (1956); *Hist Studies*, no 82, Apr 1984; A. G. Butler collection (AWM); Sir C. J. Martin *and* J. T. Wilson papers (Basser Lib, Canb); CSIRO Archives (Canb); information from Mrs L. H. H. M. Hutchinson, Gordon, Syd.

PATRICIA MORISON

MARTIN, DAVID (1841-1927), public servant, was born on 1 June 1841 at Clonmel, Tipperary, Ireland, son of Robert Martin, railway surveyor, and his wife Eliza, née Paxton. Two years later the family moved to England where, at Preston and Southampton, Martin received his early education. In 1855 he accompanied his father to Victoria and promptly secured employment as assistant to a government survey party. However, with the arrival of his mother in 1857, he resumed his schooling, spending eighteen months at Scotch College, Melbourne.

On 1 January 1859 Martin joined the Department of Crown Lands and Survey as a clerk and over the next decade proved himself a careful, diligent worker. In 1874, as part of J. J. Casey's [q.v.3] reform of the chaotic Lands Department, he was appointed relieving officer and inspector of country offices, in which capacity he travelled the colony. It was an arduous assignment, so much so that early in 1877 his health broke; he took leave in Europe, studying agriculture, viticulture and forestry. He returned in January 1878 and on 1 July was made land officer at Horsham with responsibility for the important Wimmera survey district. His duties were further expanded when on 16 January 1880 he was commissioned a crown land bailiff.

In September 1881, at the insistence of the secretary for agriculture, A. R. Wallis, Martin was seconded to the Department of Agriculture as chief clerk but following Wallis's unexpected dismissal on 25 March 1882, found himself *de facto* secretary; he assumed control not only of Victorian agricultural development but also of such difficult problems as forestry management and the fight against *Phylloxera vastatrix*. In 1885 he was appointed treasurer and unofficial secretary of the Council of Agricultural Education, overseeing the establishment and subsequent operation of agricultural colleges at Dookie (1886) and Longerenong (1889), while in 1889 administration of a £233 000 rural industries bonus scheme was placed solely in his hands. With generous incentives Martin extended the network of local milk factories and significantly increased the volume of dairy-product exports.

Such responsibilities, however, only served to emphasize his anomalous position: unlike other departmental heads he was not a first-division officer of the public service and technically remained a member of the Lands Department. Persistent press and parliamentary complaints finally persuaded the government to resolve the matter; on 21 November 1890 Martin was promoted to the first division and gazetted secretary for agriculture, effective from 5 November. With characteristic efficiency he quietly used that enhanced status to broaden the scope of his department, most notably through the absorption of the Burnley School of Horticulture (1891), the foundation of a viticultural college at Rutherglen (1899) and the steady addition of scientific personnel.

On 17 May 1895 Martin's work-load grew considerably when, following a decision to amalgamate ministerial control of the departments of agriculture and public works, he was also named acting-secretary of the latter. In that role, routine administration was blended with direction of the flood-abatement measures carried out along the Yarra River, and the controversial land-reclamation and levee-construction works on the Murray and Goulburn rivers. When in 1901 the two departments were again separated, the now overburdened Martin chose to relinquish agriculture; consequently, on 1 November he was appointed secretary for public works. Although entitled to retire in 1906 the government prevailed upon him to remain until 1 August 1908.

Martin's commitment to sound administration was coupled with an equally thorough involvement in community affairs. At Horsham he sat on the boards of both the mechanics' institute and the district hospital, and later served as chairman of the Richmond Parks' Board and as a commissioner of the Supreme Court. Among many official duties, he was a member of the Board of Advice for Horticulture, the Metropolitan Parks and Gardens Board, and several royal commissions. In 1905 he was appointed I.S.O. And yet the very strength of Martin's administrative expertise—a precise, literal mind—was ultimately limiting for it sometimes led to narrow interpretations of legislative intent.

Of medium height, clear complexion, prematurely grey hair and with a trace of Irish accent, Martin enjoyed the reputation of a courteous, reserved man fond of the arts; when younger he was an active member of the Melbourne Garrick Club, and also sang in the choir of St John's Church, Toorak. He married twice; after the death of his first wife in 1876 he married on 30 June 1879 at Castlemaine, Julia Amherst Mary Stacey, who bore him eight children. He saw out his days as a government pensioner until on 27 February 1927 he died at his home in St Kilda, and was buried in the Anglican section of St Kilda cemetery.

J. Smith (ed), *Cyclopedia of Victoria*, 1 (Melb, 1903); Roy Com on technical education, Report, *PP* (Vic), 1901, 3 (36); Roy Com on the butter industry, Report, *PP* (Vic), 1905, 2 (10); *Table Talk*, 22 Nov 1895; *Australasian*, 4 Dec 1897; *Weekly Times*, 8 July 1905; *Argus*, 31 July 1908, 28 Feb 1927; *Age*, 28 Feb 1927.   R. WRIGHT

MARTIN, EDWARD FOWELL (1875-1950), soldier, accountant and public servant, was born on 22 August 1875 at Launceston, Tasmania, son of Edward Martin, pastoralist, and his wife Harriet Alice Louisa, née Fowell. The family moved to New South Wales after Edward's birth and he was educated at King's College, Goulburn. He worked as a bank accountant for three years before joining a woolbroking firm. In Sydney on 6 April 1898 he married Lilian Mary Davies; they had three children.

Martin's voluntary military service began that year when he joined the Australian Army Service Corps. He was commissioned in 1903. A major when war broke out in 1914, he immediately joined the Australian Naval and Military Expeditionary Force to New Guinea and was made a company commander. The force sailed for Rabaul on 19 August. On 14 September Martin led the advance guard of a contingent that marched on Toma, New Britain, headquarters of the German acting governor. Following the German surrender, Martin was placed in command of the garrison at Madang and acted as administrator of Kaiser Wilhelm's Land until February 1915. Given an independent role by the A. N. & M.E.F. commander, Colonel William Holmes [q.v.9], he discharged his duties responsibly.

On return to Australia, Martin joined the Australian Imperial Force on 29 March 1915 and was appointed second-in-command of the 17th Battalion. He embarked for Egypt on 12 May. The unit reached Gallipoli in August and on the 27th suffered many casualties during the attack on Hill 60. In early September the battalion occupied Pope's Post and Quinn's Post. During the evacuation in December Martin led the first draft of the unit out of the trenches.

In January-February 1916 the 17th manned posts on the Suez Canal and in March sailed for France; in April Martin was promoted lieut-colonel in command. The bat-talion served in the Armentières sector before moving to the Somme in July. At Pozières it spent a cruel eleven consecutive days in the line and fought an exhaustive bombing attack in Munster Alley. For his indefatigable efforts and organizational ability here and at Armentières, Martin was awarded the Distinguished Service Order.

The unit fought at Flers, saw action in the Butte de Warlencourt sector in February-March 1917 and again at Noreuil in April where Martin's headquarters was caught in the fighting. On 20 September the 17th fought in the battle of the Menin Road; when the forward platoons reached their objective Martin immediately moved his headquarters into the front line despite shell-fire. His battalion was recognized as an efficient and dependable fighting unit and in early 1918 he was appointed C.M.G.

In May Martin was given command of the 5th Brigade and in June was promoted colonel and temporary brigadier general. On 8 August the great allied offensive began and his brigade played an important role. On 31 August, tired and under strength, it attacked the vital position of Mont St Quentin. It took the hill and, though pushed off the summit by a counter-attack which was in turn repulsed next day by the 6th Brigade, Martin and the 5th were singled out for special praise for their stunning feat. The advance continued to the Hindenburg line and on 3 October the brigade helped to capture the Beaurevoir line, the Germans' last complete line of defence. For his part in these closing months of the war Martin was appointed C.B. and he had been mentioned in dispatches six times.

Martin returned to Australia in July 1919. The death of his son Edward in 1920 caused severe distress; Martin and his wife separated and about 1924 he went to Perth where he became an accountant with West Australian Newspapers. In 1932 he was appointed sergeant-at-arms of the Legislative Assembly and he carried the mace for the next eighteen years.

Though reticent about his wartime experiences, Martin was an active member of the Returned Sailors' and Soldiers' Imperial League of Australia and Legacy, and was a custodian of the Perth war memorial. During World War II he helped to organize the Volunteer Defence Corps in Perth. After the death of his wife he married Evlyn Lucy Haslam at Cannington in 1947. He remained sergeant-at-arms until a few days before he died on 22 September 1950 at the Repatriation General Hospital, Hollywood, survived by his wife and a daughter of his first marriage.

Martin's wartime comrades remembered him as being of a reserved, even retiring disposition, yet a man who weighed problems carefully and resolutely stuck to a course of action. He 'zealously maintained' the welfare of those who served under him.

C. E. W. Bean, *The story of Anzac* (Syd, 1921, 1924), *The A.I.F. in France, 1916-18* (Syd, 1929, 1933, 1937, 1942); S. S. Mackenzie, *The Australians at Rabaul* (Syd, 1938); K. W. Mackenzie, *The story of the seventeenth Battalion A.I.F. in the Great War, 1914-1918* (Syd, 1946); *London Gazette*, 29 Dec 1916, supp 1 Jan 1917, 2 Jan, supp 4 Jan 1917, 1 June 1917, 25 Dec, supp 28 Dec 1917, 28 Dec 1917, supp 1 Jan 1918, 24 May, supp 28 May 1918, 27 Dec, supp 31 Dec 1918, 30 May, supp 3 June 1919, 8 July, supp 11 July 1919; *Listening Post*, 22 July 1932; *Mail* (Fremantle), 21 July 1932; *Reveille* (Syd), Nov 1950; *West Australian*, 23 Sept 1950; *Bulletin*, 4 Oct 1950; War diary, 17th Battalion, *and* War diary, 5th Brigade, *and* AIF nominal roll, 17th Battalion, *and* Biographical details of Brigadier General E. F. Martin, *and* Honours and awards, 2nd Aust Division, 27 July-6 Aug 1916, 23 Feb-28 Mar 1917, 1 Feb-7 Mar, 3-6 Oct 1918 (AWM); CRS A457, item 650/31 German New Guinea administration: central applications for appointment as administrator (AAO, Canb); information from Mr S. Macqueen, Castle Cove, and Mrs J. Hawksford, Pymble, Syd. MATTHEW HIGGINS

MARTIN, FLORENCE (1867-1957), physicist, was born on 25 December 1867 at Clarens, Potts Point, Sydney, eleventh child of Sir James Martin [q.v.5], premier of New South Wales and later chief justice, and his native-born wife Isabella (d. 1909), sister of William Long [q.v.5]. She received her early education from a governess and later attended Madame Gilder's school, Campbell Lodge.

Her father died in 1886 but through Lady Martin's standing and large fortune, her children moved in the highest social circles. Not content with the life of idleness prescribed for young ladies of her class, Florence enrolled in arts at the University of Sydney in 1891. After completing the first year with honours in physics, she re-enrolled in 1892 but during the year began working instead as an unpaid research assistant in the university's physics department under a family friend, Professor (Sir) Richard Threlfall [q.v.].

This was no mere whim. During the two years Martin spent in Threlfall's laboratory she proved a reliable and accurate observer whose 'most constant assistance' Threlfall valued very highly. When her mother and most of her sisters left for Europe in early 1893, she remained behind to complete the chief piece of research on which she had been engaged, an attempt to verify experimentally some of the conclusions of Maxwell's electromagnetic theory concerning forces acting in magnetic circuits. A report written jointly with Threlfall was read to the Royal Society of New South Wales in July 1893 and was published in London in the *Philosophical Magazine*. Martin then sailed for Europe, preceded by a letter of recommendation from Threlfall to (Sir) J. J. Thomson, director of Cambridge's renowned Cavendish Laboratory.

She appears to have been only the second Australian research student to work at the Cavendish, then rapidly becoming the Mecca for every aspiring experimental physicist. Few Australian women have ever done so. She spent about eighteen months there, attending the advanced undergraduate practical classes as well as pursuing her own tidy but fairly inconsequential research on the expansion of the gas between the plates of a capacitor when the capacitor was discharged. Returning to Sydney in 1896, Martin immediately resumed her collaboration with Threlfall, publishing two more joint papers. Two years later, however, he returned to England, and Martin's career in physics was over. For six months during 1899 she acted as the university's tutor to women students, then she became housekeeper for her mother, now hopelessly senile.

In 1905 Martin met a wealthy young American explorer, William Cooke Daniels, and shared her home with his fiancée Cicely Banner during his sixteen-month absence on an expedition to New Guinea. The couple married next year and Martin went to live with them, chiefly on their English and French estates but also travelling the world until the outbreak of war in 1914.

Daniels died unexpectedly in 1918. When his widow succumbed to the influenza epidemic shortly afterwards, Martin found herself heir to a large income for life from the Daniels estate based on the Daniels & Fisher department store at Denver, Colorado. She settled there in 1919 and soon became prominent in local society. For much of the 1920s she and her sister Emily spent their summers at Florence's spectacular mountain-top residence outside Denver and their winters in London. Florence became a patron of the arts, endowing the Cooke-Daniels lectures at the Denver Art Museum. She also gave parkland to the city as a memorial to William and Cicely Daniels.

Florence Martin continued to travel widely until her last years. She died at Denver on 27 October 1957, leaving an estate of over $US200 000 to her niece.

E. Grainger, *Martin of Martin Place* (Syd, 1970); *SMH*, 27 Dec 1867; *Denver Post*, 9 Sept 1920, 25 Feb 1925, 12 July 1927, 7 Jan 1935, 8 Feb, 23 Aug 1936, 28 Jan 1937, 27 Jan 1938, 26 Jan 1955, 28 Oct, 1 Nov 1957; *Rocky Mountain News* (Denver), 28 Oct 1957; Martin family papers (ML); Threlfall correspondence (Univ Syd Archives); J. J. Thomson correspondence (Univ Cambridge Lib). R. W. HOME

MARTIN, LEWIS ORMSBY (1870-1944), solicitor, farmer and politician, was born on 16 May 1870 at Lower Jordan, Victoria, second son of Irish parents Robert Martin, miner and later clergyman, and his wife Antoinette Louisa, née Ormsby. He came to New South Wales at an early age and was educated privately by a tutor, W. Compton. In 1889 he was articled to C. Way, and matriculated at the University of Sydney (B.A., 1893; LL.B., 1895). Transferred to C. R. A. Smith in 1893 he was admitted as a solicitor on 1 June 1895.

Martin established a legal practice at Taree and soon became prominent in legal circles on the north coast where he specialized in the problems of primary producers. At St James Anglican Church, O'Connell Plains, on 5 April 1899 he married Lucy Danvers Maund, daughter of a grazier. An alderman on Taree Municipal Council in 1906-28, he served as mayor in 1911-13 and in 1920-21. With dairying and grazing interests, he was a member of the Farmers and Settlers' Association and became a councillor of the Liberal Party in 1913. He was defeated for the State seats of Gloucester twice in 1917 (as a Nationalist) and of Oxley in 1922 (as a Progressive).

In October 1927 Martin was elected to the Legislative Assembly for Oxley as a Nationalist. He became a spokesman for dairy interests and rural producers generally and in 1928 promoted the Marketing of Primary Products (Amendment) Act. He quickly became known as an able debater, easily survived J. T. Lang's [q.v.9] sweeping victory in the 1930 election and in June 1932 was returned as a United Australia Party supporter, becoming minister of justice in (Sir) Bertram Stevens's [q.v.] 'Ministry of Reconstruction'. He oversaw the passage of the revised Moratorium Act of 1932 (after party colleagues had toned down its provisions), and in 1935 introduced the Legal Practitioners (Amendment) Act, designed to safeguard funds held in trust by solicitors. The Companies Act of 1936, which greatly improved the code of operation for companies, was the crown of his legislative achievement.

Martin's aspirations for leadership of the U.A.P. were thwarted in 1935 when E. S. Spooner [q.v.] defeated him for the deputy leadership. During the ministerial crisis of August 1939 Martin supported Stevens and then Alexander Mair [q.v.]. He relinquished the justice portfolio in favour of the younger (Sir) Vernon Treatt and accepted the posts of secretary for public works and minister for local government. He lost Oxley to an Independent at the May 1941 election which saw the government thrown from office by a re-united Labor party under (Sir) William McKell.

The Martins lived in style at Ormsby House, near Taree, often entertaining distinguished guests. Lucy Martin was 'famed as a hostess'. Of small build, Martin was quick witted and well suited to public affairs. From 1936 he practised in partnership with two of his sons. Survived by his wife, seven sons and only daughter, he died at Taree on 17 April 1944 and was cremated after a service at St James' Church, Sydney. His estate was valued for probate at £18 473.

SMH, 10 Oct 1927, 18 June 1932, 1 Feb 1933, 3 Aug 1939, 18 Apr 1944; *Aust National Review*, 28 June 1932; *United Aust Review*, 22 Mar 1934; family information.   PETER SPEARRITT

MARTIN, WILLIAM CLARENCE (1890-1970), horseman, soldier and pastoralist, was born on 28 December 1890 at Jarrahdale, Western Australia, son of George Kersley Martin, labourer, and his wife Rose Sarah, née Markwell. He attended Kelmscott Primary School until he was 14, then went as a jackaroo to a station in the Murchison district.

Martin enlisted in the Australian Imperial Force on 13 July 1915 and in October embarked at Fremantle with the tenth reinforcements for the 10th Light Horse. Too late for Gallipoli, they landed in Egypt in November and joined their unit next month. Early in 1916 the regiment took part in the Egyptian Expeditionary Force's advance across Sinai into Palestine. Martin joined the 3rd Light Horse Brigade scouts during 1916 and as early as September 1917 was recommended for an award. In November he was promoted lance sergeant.

By April 1918 the British had reached the Jordan. During a difficult and ultimately unsuccessful raid on 29 April on Es Salt, across the Jordan, Martin led an advanced section of the brigade scouts. He and another scout crept on a Turkish observation post, captured two of the enemy and killed the rest. Martin was awarded the Distinguished Conduct Medal.

After the failure to secure Es Salt the troops spent four months in the Jordan valley in oppressive heat. In September the British planned to take Damascus. On the night of 27-28 September, the 10th Light Horse, to which Martin had returned in June, forced the Jordan crossing above Jisr Benat Yakub in the face of heavy machine-gun and rifle fire. Martin was riding close to his troop commander when the latter was wounded. He took command and pushed on with the charge. The ground was impossible for horses, so the men dismounted in the semi-darkness and, with Martin in the lead, rushed at the enemy with bayonets and engaged in hand-to-hand fighting. Over fifty prisoners and two machine-guns were captured. Martin was awarded a Bar to his D.C.M. and promoted sergeant on 6 November. In the opinion of his commanding officer, Martin was not only 'exceptionally brave', but possessed a 'rare intelligence and cool judgment which did not . . . impair his brilliancy and dash'; his guide work was 'really wonderful'.

In April 1919 Martin was invalided to Western Australia with malaria and discharged from the A.I.F. on 25 October, after which he went droving in the Kimberleys. Later, using money earned from droving and his entitlement under the repatriation land settlement scheme, he bought the major share in Mount Padbury Pastoral Co. near Meekatharra. He lived there until selling out about 1969. He had married Nellie Cooree Francisco at St Mary's Anglican Church, West Perth, on 25 January 1923. They had a son but the marriage ended in divorce.

Bill Martin was a rugged character, about 5 ft. 9 ins. (175 cm) tall, and a good horseman and buckjumper who loved mustering and camping out. He died of leukaemia in Sir Charles Gairdner Hospital, Perth, on 29 January 1970, leaving an estate of $72 154, and was cremated with Anglican rites. On the basis of his appearance and performance in the field Martin had been chosen in 1920 to represent light horsemen in a series of paintings of the A.I.F. commissioned by the Australian War Museum Committee. Two portraits by Frank Crozier are in the Australian War Memorial.

Distinguished conduct medals to Australia - from 1915-20, 3 (Melb, 1982); A. C. N. Olden, *Westralian cavalry in the war* (Melb, 1921); H. S. Gullett, *The A.I.F. in Sinai and Palestine* (Syd, 1941); H. P. Bostock, Diaries and letters, 1914-18 and War diary, 10th Light Horse Regiment, AIF (AWM); information from Mr A. H. Bell, Karrinyup and Mrs M. G. Nation, Wembley, WA.

MARGARET BROWNE

MARTYN, ATHELSTAN MARKHAM (1881-1956), military engineer, was born on 5 June 1881 at Armidale, New South Wales, eldest son of Sydney-born John Griffin Martyn, licensed surveyor, and his wife Hope, daughter of Thomas Markham, medical practitioner of Armidale. He was educated at The Armidale School and the University of Sydney (B.E., 1905).

Early in 1901 he had enlisted in the Sydney University Scouts and by 1903 was a second lieutenant. In 1906 he was commissioned in the permanent Australian Engineers and as a subaltern served in the Royal Australian Engineers in Victoria and Queensland. In 1911 he was promoted captain.

Soon after the outbreak of war in August 1914 Martyn, then serving in Western Australia, was commissioned in the Australian Imperial Force as captain in the 2nd Field Company. He was soon appointed to command. He embarked with his unit in October, supervised its training in Egypt, and landed with it at Anzac Cove, Gallipoli, on 25 April 1915. During the next three months he shared his company's hardships, suffering from chronic dysentery but retaining his characteristic cheerfulness. He was acting commander of the 1st Divisional Engineers for a fortnight in May, and in July was appointed commanding royal engineer although his lieut-colonelcy was not gazetted until shortly before the evacuation. For his work in the Gallipoli campaign he received the Distinguished Service Order and the French Croix de Guerre, and was mentioned in dispatches.

The 1st Divisional Engineers moved from Egypt to France in March 1916. After some months in Flanders they were engaged in the Somme sector, taking part in the battle of Pozières in July and in actions about Mouquet Farm in August. Then there was a period out of the line and Martyn was able to take some leave. On 21 October 1916, at St Mary Abbot's Church, Kensington, London, he married Stella Godfrey, only daughter of Frank Swifte of Tasmania; the bride had journeyed from Australia.

The 1st Divisional Engineers were engaged in the 1917 battles known as '3rd Ypres' at Menin Road in September and Broodseinde in October. At the end of the year Martyn was appointed C.M.G. In April 1918, after nearly two years as C.R.E., 1st Division, he was posted to command the A.I.F. Engineer Training Depot at Brightlingsea, Essex. In July he returned to the Australian Corps on the Western Front as C.R.E., Corps Troops, an appointment which he held during the 3rd battle of Amiens and the breaching of the Hindenburg line. A week after the Armistice he relieved C. H. Foott [q.v.8] as chief engineer of the Australian Corps with the rank of colonel. He embarked for Australia in April 1919. He had been mentioned in dispatches five times.

Once more a lieut-colonel, now in the Australian Military Forces, Martyn was in 1920-24 instructor in military engineering and surveying at the Royal Military College, Duntroon. He then served for eight years in a succession of appointments outside of the Royal Australian Engineers. Early in 1932 he was appointed commandant in Western Australia, as colonel and with the temporary rank of brigadier, and in 1936 took up the corresponding appointment in South Australia. He was awaiting retirement when World War II broke out but was retained in the service and appointed to administer the numerous training camps in New South Wales. He retired in June 1941, as a brigadier, to Adelaide.

'Tin' Martyn was a cheerful, gregarious man, fond of the countryside, and a keen rifle shot. In his youth he was an able engineer and showed himself a capable administrator in his later years when his early slightness of figure had been succeeded by a ruddy corpulence. He died in Adelaide of heart failure on 4 November 1956, survived by two daughters, and was cremated.

R. McNicoll, *The Royal Australian Engineers 1902 to 1919, 2, Making and breaking* (Canb, 1979).   RONALD MCNICOLL

MARTYN, NELLIE CONSTANCE (1887-1926), businesswoman, was born on 12 June 1887 at Charlton, Victoria, daughter of James Martyn (1855-1924) and his wife Lucy, née Partridge, both Ballarat born. James had been a schoolteacher and a draper before he purchased in 1900 a steelworks at Brunswick, Melbourne, which he renamed the Steel Co. of Australia. He became twice president of the Victorian Chamber of Manufactures and in 1923 represented Australian employers at the International Labor Conference, Geneva.

Nellie became a hospital masseuse. After many unsuccessful attempts to persuade her father to allow her to join the firm, he eventually submitted, some time before World War I, after she had become proficient in shorthand and typing and engineering drawing. She soon displayed an acute financial brain and when her father went overseas in 1923 he left her, not his son, with his power of attorney. On his death next year she took sole charge as managing director of what was claimed to be the 'largest steel founders in the Commonwealth', specializing in manganese and chrome steel, with well over 100 employees. She mastered all aspects of the business and began converting the buildings into a new model factory.

A Methodist, Nell Martyn had for long been active in the Young Women's Christian Association, especially in its industrial clubs. After a term as State treasurer, she became president in 1924 and was closely involved with the move of the association's national headquarters to Melbourne. She was first president of the Business and Professional Women's Club (1925) and a committee-member of the Queen Victoria Memorial Hospital. In 1925 the Australian Women's National League supported her preselection as Nationalist candidate for the State seat of Brunswick, but the male party majority forbade it.

Highly capable in business matters, a good public speaker and a constructive committee member, Miss Martyn was led by her Christian perspective to interest in social service and workers' rights. She did not seek publicity for herself. Her view of woman's position was quite simple: the basis of women's equality was that the sexes were of equal mentality—she asked no more than to compete on the same terms as men and to represent the interests of the whole community and not just women.

Knowing she was mortally ill, Nell Martyn spoke at Y.W.C.A. gatherings and others almost to the end. She died from cancer on 28 November 1926 at her family's Camberwell home and was buried in Box Hill cemetery. She was unmarried. More than 1000 mourners, including the leaders of the iron and steel industry, were at the graveside where hundreds of wreaths from business firms were laid. Her obituaries reflected widespread anguish at the loss of one so young, so admired and who promised so much. The Steel Co. of Australia Pty Ltd was carried on by the family.

Woman's World, Jan 1924, July 1925, Jan 1927; *Adam and Eve*, 1 June 1926; Young Women's Christian Assn, *Association News*, 11 Dec 1926; *Argus*, 21 Apr 1924; *Herald* (Melb), 29 Nov 1926; *Australasian*, 4 Dec 1926.   ŒNONE SERLE

MASHMAN, ERNEST JAMES THEODORE (1895-1964), potter, was born on 19 August 1895 at Willoughby, Sydney, elder son of Henry Mashman (1856-1922), potter, and his second wife Elizabeth Simpson, née Wieland, a widow. Theo, as he was known, represented the second generation of Mashmans in Australia. His father and uncles William (1851-1912), John (1858-1918) and George (1869-1951), sons of James Mashman, a potter at Doulton's Lambeth works, and his wife Harriet Frances, née Baker, had been born in London within the smell of Doulton's kilns. Familiar from birth with the business of salt-glazed bottles and jars, drain pipes, conduits, sewers and water pipes, they were apprenticed to various specialities in the firm. William, after his marriage to Charlotte Bundock in 1876, moved to her home at Leigh-on-Sea, Essex, and worked at the small Victoria pottery. Her relatives had been in Victoria during the gold rushes: after her death in 1880, he persuaded Henry to migrate with him to Australia. They reached Sydney on 10 July 1883, worked at the Fieldsend pottery, Maitland, and then, in partnership with James Sandison, took over a pottery at Willoughby in 1885.

Despite primitive equipment, this Victoria pottery flourished, producing hand-thrown household stoneware, pipes, junctions, traps and chimney-pots for the North Shore building boom. In 1887 William's mother, sons and brothers joined them. In 1889 John established a redware plant, the Carrington, at Auburn and in 1892 bought Sandison out of the Victoria. More relatives from Leigh, the Days and the Sachs, all skilled potters, arrived and the family business grew on the solid basis of housebuilding necessaries, although their early venture into art-ware was a commercial failure. Another pottery at Kingsgrove was established in 1910 by William's son, Frederick Albert (1879-1964).

Theo had practically grown up with the business. Trained at Sydney Technical College after schooling at a convent in Archer Street and Chatswood Public School, he enlisted in the Australian Imperial Force on 5 October 1915, joining the Australian Army Medical Corps. Fibrosis of the lungs saw him in and out of hospital during service with the 2nd Field Ambulance in France. He returned to Australia in June 1918, and married Ruby Millicent Eason on 19 May 1922 at St Jude's Church, Randwick.

Henry, the last potter of his generation, died that year and Theo became chairman and managing director of Mashman Bros Ltd. The Victoria works were small and old-fashioned. By 1926 the directors realized the need to restructure them. The firm, therefore, became a limited liability company, although it remained a close-knit family business. Mashman visited the United States of America and in 1927 a new factory with imported American machinery was constructed. He spearheaded the struggle to prevent the substitution of concrete for stoneware pipes for sewerage purposes. He helped to found the Clay Products Association of Australia with branches in every State, to represent pottery interests to the government and to publicize the trade, which it did with some success. In November 1933 Mashman and Thomas Campbell (managing director of R. Fowler [q.v.4] Ltd) founded its magazine the *Clay Products Journal of Australia* (now *Australian National Clay*). Mashman was president of the association in 1937-38 and remained an outstanding member for most of his life, being largely responsible for expanding the membership which eventually included brick and ceramics manufacturers.

In the 1930s Theo Mashman was presented as the model, go-ahead, Australian manufacturer, patriotic returned serviceman and sportsman, avid motorist and yachtsman. He revived the firm's interest in art-ware with a promotional appeal to 'Australian-made, Australian workmen, Australian artists and Australian clay'. With modern methods and high quality material, the new line of 'Regal Art' ware, including ornamental bowls, vases and jugs, was to provide articles equal to most that could be imported and at a price the average housewife could afford. Artists such as Loma Latour, wife of Raymond Lindsay [q.v.], were employed to make Art Deco pieces. Profit, however, depended on the production from 1932 of 'Bristol gloss' ware, especially sanitary and lavatory ware, and from 1935 of mass production methods.

In World War II the company received many government contracts for essential items, such as hospital wares, industrial chemical appliances and acid containers. After the war Mashman, as an elder statesman, fought to retain a tariff on sanitary ware, believing the industry required reasonable protection to permit expansion, and opposed government cuts on sewerage expenditure. In 1957 Mashman Bros Ltd was merged with Doulton & Co. Ltd, London, and the new plant officially opened in 1959. Mashman, who had become chairman of directors, retired in June 1960 and on 1 July the business became a fully owned subsidiary of Doultons: Doulton Sanitary Potteries (Australia) Pty Ltd.

Mashman died suddenly at his Newport home of a coronary occlusion on 29 November 1964 and was cremated with Anglican rites. His marriage had been dissolved in 1953; his only child Colleen survived him. His estate was sworn for probate at £94 159.

Clay Products J of Aust, 1 Aug 1934, p 15, 1 Nov 1934, p 11, 13, 1 Jan 1936, p 11, 1 Apr 1937, p 15, 1 Jan 1938, p 7, 14, 1 Aug 1940, p 16, Apr 1948, p 11, Apr 1950, p 11, 17; *Roy Doulton Review*, Mar 1961, p 35; *Clay Pipe News*, Nov 1961, p 11, Feb 1964, p 9, Jan 1965, p 13; E. Ungar, 'The Mashman Bros. pottery', in Aust Soc for Hist Archaeology, *Newsletter*, 6, no 1, Apr 1976; *SMH*, 12 May 1959.
                                        E. A. UNGAR

MASSIE, ROBERT JOHN ALLWRIGHT (1890-1966), sportsman, soldier and businessman, was born on 8 July 1890 at St Leonards, Sydney, son of Hugh Hamon Massie, banker and ex-international cricketer, and his wife Tryphena Agnes, daughter of (Sir) Thomas Dibbs [q.v.4]. Jack attended Sydney Church of England Grammar School (Shore) in 1900-10. He played for his school and later the University of Sydney as a left-arm bowler, and was selected for the New South Wales State side in 1911-12 against the Marylebone Cricket Club. He learned boxing from Larry Foley [q.v.4] and later represented the university as a heavyweight, gaining the State championship in 1914. When Massie left school he was senior prefect, with colours in cricket, football, rowing and athletics, and the Venour Nathan Shield for rifle-shooting. In his last term he was invited to row in the New

South Wales eight but this his father would not allow, thinking him too young. He rowed for the university instead, before enrolling.

In 1910 Massie commenced civil engineering at the University of Sydney and in 1914 graduated B.E. with first-class honours and the University medal. He won a half-blue in boxing and blues for cricket, Rugby, rowing and athletics and represented his State in cricket (1912-14), Rugby (1912-13) and athletics (Dunn Shield). In 1914 he was regarded by many as the best bowler in Australia and a certainty for the Australian team.

After graduation Massie joined the British-American Tobacco Co. He enlisted in the Australian Imperial Force on 17 August 1914, was commissioned second lieutenant, 4th Battalion, on 13 September and embarked for Egypt in October. Promoted lieutenant on 1 February 1915, he landed at Gallipoli on 25 April. Next day, acting on mistaken orders, his battalion advanced courageously but blindly towards Lone Pine and was decimated. When his commanding officer was killed, Massie carried the body towards their trenches but was turned back by Turkish fire. Wounded slightly on 25 June and 20 July and severely at Lone Pine on the night of 6-7 August, he was evacuated and in December declared unfit for active service for four months. For his service at Gallipoli he was mentioned in dispatches and awarded the French Croix de Guerre. On 1 December, while returning to Australia, he was promoted captain.

On 1 May 1916 Massie was promoted major and appointed second-in-command of the 33rd Battalion; he left Sydney for England. On 21 November his unit was sent with the rest of the 3rd Division to Armentières, France. Massie was attached to divisional headquarters in May-June 1917 and in October-December attended a senior officers' course in England. Again wounded in action on 3 February 1918, he recovered to undertake a course at the machine-gun training centre at Grantham, England, and in July he was passed 'technically qualified to command a Machine Gun Battalion'. He was attached to the Australian Corps School on 12 September and appointed commandant on 24 September; promotion to lieut-colonel was confirmed on 21 October. After the Armistice he was appointed organizer of sport for the Australian Corps. For his service in France and Belgium he was awarded the Distinguished Service Order and was twice mentioned in dispatches. His A.I.F. appointment ended on 16 August 1919.

Massie married Phyllis Wood Lang at Holy Trinity Anglican Church, Brompton, London, on 3 June 1919. He resumed his career with the tobacco company in December 1919, in the United States of America, then returned to Sydney where he worked for the company and was esquire bedell to the chancellor of the university until 1946. A war injury to his shoulder precluded further representative cricket: instead he wrote a book, *Bowling*, which he presented to the Cricket Association.

Massie was chairman of directors of the British Tobacco Co. (Aust) Ltd and W.D. and H.O. Wills (Aust) in 1937-46 and a director of the Commercial Banking Co. of Sydney Ltd. Appointed director-general of supply in June 1941, he resigned to join the Board of Area Management for New South Wales, Ministry of Munitions, from April 1942 and became its chairman in May 1943. In November 1941 he had resigned his directorship with the Commercial Banking Co. because of his commitment to war work. His wife died in 1943, the year their son John was killed in action. On 20 September 1947, in Washington, D.C., he married a widow, Elizabeth Emily Squire, née Crosse. In 1946-51 he was deputy chairman of the British American Tobacco Co. Ltd in London then retired to Australia. Survived by his wife and by two daughters of his first marriage, he died of cancer on 14 February 1966 at Mosman, Sydney, and was cremated.

C. E. W. Bean, *The story of Anzac* (Syd, 1921); G. E. Hall and A. Cousins (eds), *Book of remembrance of the University of Sydney in the war 1914-1918* (Syd, 1939); *London Gazette*, 28 Jan, 22 Feb 1916, 1 June 1917, 28 May, 3 June 1918; *Torchbearer*, 1964, 1966; War diary, 33rd Battalion AIF, *and* records (AWM).   ROSSLYN FINN

MASSON, SIR DAVID ORME (1858-1937), chemist, professor and man of science, was born on 13 January 1858 at Hampstead, near London, second child and only son of David Mather Masson, professor of English literature at University College, London, and his wife Emily Rosaline, née Orme. In 1865 his father took up the chair of rhetoric and English literature at the University of Edinburgh. Masson attended Oliphant's School in Edinburgh in 1865-68 before enrolling at Edinburgh Academy, a private establishment patronized by the professional élite. He matriculated at the University of Edinburgh, graduated M.A. in 1877 and then studied chemistry under Crum Brown, graduating B.Sc. in 1880. Undergraduate life was enriched by the presence of (Sir) James Barrie and Robert Louis Stevenson.

After the 'obligatory' excursion to Germany, including a short period in Wöhler's laboratory at Göttingen in 1879, Masson joined (Sir) William Ramsay, newly appointed professor of chemistry at Bristol University College, for a year as lecturer. The two young men teamed famously and established a lifelong friendship, one of the major influences in Masson's career. Returning to Edinburgh in 1881, he undertook research on the composition of nitroglycerine leading to his doctorate in 1884. The University of Edinburgh celebrated its tercentenary in 1884 and both Massons, father and son, were prominent in the festivities. The younger Masson had played a leading role in the establishment of the Students' Representative Council (the first of its kind in any university) and in the university union which followed.

The celebrations attracted a house guest, Mary Struthers, daughter of an old friend of the elder Masson. In a matter of weeks she became engaged to the tall and handsome Orme but their marriage awaited securing an appointment with an assured income. After various disappointments Masson was offered the chair of chemistry at the University of Melbourne, and the wedding took place on 5 August 1886 at Aberdeen according to the forms of the Church of Scotland. The Massons sailed a few weeks later.

Masson's initial responsibility in Melbourne was lecturing to first-year classes in which the preponderance of medical students was reminiscent of Edinburgh; regulations for the institution of a degree in science had only just been introduced. His inaugural lecture in 1887 made a striking impression as to content and elegance of style; from the outset his mastery of classroom discipline stemmed from the inherent charm and organization of his material. He was remembered by his former student (Sir) Kingsley Norris as 'the prince of demonstrators'. Masson was soon joined by two other gifted young professorial colleagues, (Sir) Baldwin Spencer and (Sir) Thomas Lyle [qq.v.], in biology and natural philosophy: they constituted a powerful trio for the establishment of teaching and research in the sciences. Outside the university Masson was appointed to the Victorian Board of Public Health in 1890—the first of many public commitments.

Despite the heavy burden of teaching and planning Masson always found time for personal research. His first paper from the Melbourne laboratory concerned relationships between the physical properties and chemical characteristics of liquids of the same chemical type. His presidential address for section B of the 1891 Christchurch meeting of the Australasian Association for the Advancement of Science dealt with the theory of solutions, from which emerged the term 'critical solution temperature'. Ramsay thought so highly of the paper that he arranged for its publication in *Nature* and the *Zeitschrift für physikalische Chemie*.

Though Masson was never interested in money as such, and had in fact earlier declined an opportunity to invest in the Broken Hill

Proprietary Co. Ltd, he was intent on preserving his savings in the financial crash of 1893 and hastened by cable tram to his city bank to withdraw his money only hours before it closed its doors. Thus he was able to take his family on leave of absence in 1895. Their arrival in Britain coincided with the discovery of helium and argon by Ramsay and his colleagues at University College, London. Masson, who for years had devoted much attention to the periodic classification of the elements, is credited with persuading Ramsay that these two newcomers were part of a hitherto undiscovered group, and that Ramsay should look for the others. Over the next few years Ramsay was to isolate the four missing members.

In 1899 Masson's abiding interest in ionic theory led to work on the velocity of migration of ions in solutions, and the ingenious equipment he devised was widely adopted. About this time he reported to the British government on the establishment of an Indian institute of science, but in 1901 he declined the post of foundation principal, remaining in Melbourne to become dean of the faculty of science in 1905. With increasing demands on his administrative abilities, he yet remained a steadfast teacher, continuing to produce brilliant scholars such as (Sir) David Rivett [q.v.] and his own son Irvine. His research work was mainly performed in collaboration with these and other gifted graduates. In 1905 he was joined as lecturer by his former student Bertram Steele [q.v.]. Working with the physicist (Sir) Kerr Grant [q.v.9], Steele devised a microbalance which brought a new dimension to the accurate weighing of minuscule amounts of matter. An improved version constructed in Ramsay's laboratories was the key to the determination in 1910 of the atomic weight of radon, the last member of the 'rare' gases to be isolated.

A long-held ambition had been realized by Masson in 1900 when the Society of Chemical Industry of Victoria was founded with him as president, bringing together over one hundred industrial and academic chemists covering a wide range of interests; in 1904 the growing scope and maturity of academic chemistry led him to form the Melbourne University Chemical Society. In 1911 Masson was president of the Sydney meeting of A.A.A.S., lending his considerable influence to the Australasian Antarctic Expedition then being planned by (Sir) Douglas Mawson [q.v.]. This was the beginning of Masson's twenty-five year involvement with Antarctic research. At the same meeting he announced that the British Association addressed by him a few months before had accepted the Commonwealth invitation to hold its 1914 meeting in Australia. As chairman of the executive committee, he largely fulfilled his hope that the meeting would be 'as brilliant, as memorable, as it should be', despite the outbreak of war.

Masson's administrative work materially increased with his chairmanship of the professorial board in 1912-16. But invited to succeed Ramsay at University College, London, he once again chose to remain in Australia. He was closely involved with the formation in 1916 of the Commonwealth Advisory Council set up to consider and initiate researches in connexion with primary and secondary industries, and became deputy chairman. He and his council colleagues were buffeted by the vehement opposition of State departments, the suspicion of many academics, and the vagaries and duplicity of some politicians. When after four years the long awaited draft bill was tabled to establish the permanent Institute of Science and Industry, it fell so far short of Masson's reasonable expectations that he resigned in protest, declaring that 'as a nett result of four-and-a-half years work I have no faith in politicians'. Fortunately there were politicians who retained faith in Masson, and when Prime Minister (Viscount) Bruce [q.v.7] convened a review conference in May 1925, Masson, though now in retirement, was selected as the speaker to follow him; he was unwavering in the promulgation of his original concepts for the institute. There were cries of dissent from some academics, including Steele, when he maintained that universities existed primarily for the education of students; but the Act of 1926 establishing the Council for Scientific and Industrial Research largely reflected his lofty ideals, and he was delighted when Rivett, his successor in the Melbourne chair, was appointed chief executive. Masson was a council-member until his death.

The decade 1916-26 undoubtedly saw the peak of Masson's accomplishments. Concurrent with his work towards the establishment of C.S.I.R. were activities connected with the formation in 1921 of the Australian National Research Council; Masson was president in 1922-26. A wartime concern was the professional organization of chemists. Determined to move towards proper professional standards in Australia, Masson had much to do with founding the (Royal) Australian Chemical Institute in 1917; he was first president of the Victorian branch (1917-20) and first general president (1923-24). During the war he was also a member of the Commonwealth Munitions Committee.

After Masson's retirement in 1923 and his appointment as emeritus professor he maintained a close association with C.S.I.R. and all the societies of which he was a founder. He acted as a consultant to the Electrolytic Zinc Co. of Australasia, was an elder statesman on the boards of the Union Trustee Co. and the National Mutual Life Association (1925-37), and served as a deputy commissioner of the State Electricity Commission (1925). Nor were the lifetime habits of research and study neglected, for he persisted with the development of theories connected with the conductivity of electrolytes.

Masson was elected a fellow of the Royal Society in 1903 and some years later a fellow of the (Royal) Institute of Chemistry of Great Britain and Ireland. He was appointed C.B.E. in 1918 and K.B.E. in 1923; the University of Edinburgh awarded him an honorary LL.D. in 1924. First and foremost he was a great teacher. Many of his students such as David Avery, (Sir) Herbert Gepp and (Sir) Russell Grimwade [qq.v.7,8,9] went on to occupy high positions in national affairs. Sir Macfarlane Burnet, describing an evening lecture delivered by Masson in 1920, wrote: 'I can remember sitting high up in the back row, entranced for the first time with the wonder and glory of discovery'. Masson used to good effect a single raised eyebrow as a quizzical mark of emphasis. From his early years he seems to have embraced a Huxley type of agnosticism. He possessed great stores of energy and endurance, was a strong walker, a skilled golfer and a foundation member of the (Royal) Melbourne Golf Club, and also played tennis and billiards. He cherished a great love for Edinburgh and the Highlands and, an accomplished correspondent, for many years wrote a weekly letter 'home' (unfortunately mostly destroyed). He was generous and supportive of his family.

Masson died of cancer at South Yarra on 10 August 1937, and was cremated. His wife, his daughter Flora Marjorie (Marnie), wife of (Sir) Walter Bassett and a gifted historian, and his son survived him. He was predeceased by his daughter Elsie Rosaline, wife of the anthropologist Bronislaw Malinowski; she published *An untamed territory: the Northern Territory of Australia* in 1915. A fine portrait of Masson by W. B. McInnes [q.v.] is in the foyer of the University of Melbourne chemistry department. The department fronts on to Masson Road and houses the Masson theatre. In 1931 a Masson lectureship was promoted by the A.N.R.C. and since 1939 the R.A.C.I. has offered the Masson memorial scholarship. A mountain range and an island in the Australian sector of Antarctica are named for him.

MARY MASSON (1862-1945) was born on 11 July 1862 in Edinburgh, fourth of seven children of (Sir) John Struthers, professor of anatomy at Aberdeen, and his wife Christina Margaret, née Alexander. In Melbourne she followed the rearing of her children with dedicated community work, although it was not until the war years that her true *métier* for community service developed and her nostalgia for Scotland faded. A founding member of the Victoria League (1908), she was president of the University branch of the Australian Red Cross Society (1914-19), executive member of the Australian Comforts Fund (1915-18) and foundation member of the New Settlers' League (1921) and the Country Women's Association in Victoria (1928). She belonged to the Lyceum and Alexandra clubs and the Victoria League, and was appointed C.B.E. in 1918.

Lady Masson adorned university society and drew the wives of sub-professorial staff 'who did not officially exist' into the social life of the campus. Although without scientific training she regularly attended meetings of the University Chemical Society, a custom maintained after her husband's death. Her valuable organizing ability was used with tact and imagination; she had a gift of creating harmony among men and women of diverging points of view and widening the lives of people lonely in an unfamiliar setting. Active in the Young Settlers' League, she was the mainspring of a Victoria League committee that arranged introductions for Australians going overseas.

In World War II she was still busy, especially in the formation of the Women of the University Fund which works for disadvantaged children. She was of diminutive stature, which combined well with a pleasant air of authority and purpose. On her death on 25 September 1945 at Armadale the university flag was flown at half mast. Her memory is honoured at the university by the Lady Masson memorial lecture.

SIR JAMES IRVINE ORME MASSON (1887-1962) was born on 3 September 1887 at Toorak. He was educated at Melbourne Church of England Grammar School and entered the University of Melbourne in 1904 (B.Sc., 1907). After taking the second year of the medical course he reverted to chemistry and was awarded an 1851 exhibition scholarship in 1910. He spent a year at Edinburgh, then moved to University College, London, to become Ramsay's last personal assistant— his father had been the first.

On 20 December 1913 Irvine Masson married his cousin Flora Lovell, daughter of George Lovell Gulland, professor of medicine at Edinburgh. During the war years he joined the research department at the Royal Arsenal, Woolwich. Back at University College in the post-war period he developed an interest in the history of chemistry and in bibliography; his *Three centuries of chemistry* (1925) was widely acclaimed. In 1924 he was appointed professor of chemistry at the University of Durham and head of the department of science. Though much involved in administration, for the next fourteen years he continued research, making significant con-

tributions in his study of nitration and of the organic compounds of iodine. In 1938 he became vice-chancellor of the University of Sheffield. During World War II he also directed a Ministry of Supply chemistry team.

Masson retired to Edinburgh in 1952 where he continued his study of *incunabula*, publishing in 1954 *The Mainz Psalters and Canon Missae, 1457-1459*. A man of extreme reticence, he was appointed M.B.E. in 1918, elected F.R.S. in 1939, and knighted in 1950. He died in Edinburgh on 22 October 1962, survived by his son.

DNB, 1931-40; G. Currie and J. Graham, *The origins of CSIRO* (Melb, 1966); F. K. Norris, *No memory for pain* (Melb, 1970); J. M. Gillison, *A history of the Lyceum Club* (Melb, 1975); *Science and Industry*, 1 (June 1919), no 2; *Obituary Notices* (1939) and *Biographical Memoirs* (1963) of the fellows of the Roy Soc; *Aust J of Science*, 3 (1940-41), p 139; Roy Aust Chemical Inst, *Procs*, Nov 1958, p 533; *Age*, 6 Oct 1945; Masson papers (Univ Melb Archives).　　　　　　　　L. W. WEICKHARDT

MASSY-GREENE, SIR WALTER (1874-1952), politician and entrepreneur, was born on 6 November 1874 at Camberwell, Surrey, England, second son of John Greene, brewer and hotel proprietor, and his wife Julia Eamer, née Sandeman. Walter spent his childhood at Wimbledon, and was educated at Lynton House College, Oxfordshire. When it was agreed that his delicate constitution needed the toughening of outdoor work his father gave him £10 and his passage to Australia, where he worked as a farm and sawmill labourer in northern Tasmania from 1891. His family joined him to farm near Kyneton, Victoria. In 1895 Greene joined the Bank of New South Wales and was posted to Kalgoorlie, Western Australia. Here, during the gold boom, he led a rather adventurous life for a young bank officer.

Greene was transferred to head office, Sydney, in 1901, then to Lismore as branch manager. From 1902 he farmed a property near Nimbin with his two brothers and became involved in local government, holding office as first president of Terania Shire Council. He joined the newly created Liberal League in 1909 and assisted in forming branches on the north coast and tablelands. He comfortably won the Federal seat of Richmond in 1910 with the support of small farmers. Likened to 'a schoolboy who had mistakenly strayed into a gathering of Presbyterian elders', Greene created an immediate impression in the parliament. His vivid mane of red hair and his aplomb singled him out. Early speeches were devoted to parochial questions of post offices, railways and rural markets but he soon widened his range, speaking with particular authority on banking and finance. He was extremely critical of the Labor government's legislation to take over the note issue and to establish a Commonwealth bank, being convinced that these matters should remain in the private sector. He remained extremely conservative on questions of banking, finance and currency. Re-elected in 1913, Greene was appointed whip to the Cook [q.v.8] government, which had a majority of one. He displayed considerable skill in organizing to maintain government numbers and showed a liking for parliamentary hurly-burly. Opposition whip after the government's defeat in 1914, during a turbulent debate on new banking legislation he was suspended, all the Liberals present walking out with him.

After the Labor Party split in 1916, Greene was appointed whip of the new Nationalist government led by W. M. Hughes [q.v.9]. He developed rapport with Hughes, with whom he shared a wide experience of working men and hard physical labour, and quickly emerged as his chief lieutenant. As a liberal in the mould of Alfred Deakin [q.v.8], Greene had little affinity with the conservative wing of the National Party. He strongly supported the conciliation and arbitration system, claiming that no one outside a lunatic asylum could deny that its principles were just, right and 'such as become civilised societies'. He also supported, and co-operated with, trade unions, believing that it was not possible for working men and women to better their conditions without unionism. Co-operative effort he described as 'sane socialism', attributing the success of north-coast farmers to its practice. He advocated profit-sharing and had practised it with his farmworkers. He also believed in high protection and taxes on wealth.

On 27 March 1918 Greene was appointed assistant minister and given responsibility for price-control (though he had once described price-fixing as 'the most fatuous futility that had ever addled the brain of man'). It brought him into close contact with every facet of Australian economic life. According to a critic; 'To Mr Greene fell the duty of fixing most of the things that Mr Hughes' fertile brain could suggest, from flax to the Army, and from knitting needles to HMAS Australia. No man ever fixed more things in shorter time'. He also administered wheat, wool and butter pools, and in April 1918 was appointed to the Board of Trade. On 17 January 1919 Hughes promoted him to the senior portfolio of trade and customs. Here he conducted delicate negotiations for resumption of post-war trade, particularly with the defeated powers. As customs minister he had important decisions to make on the development of the infant motor-body industry and on the social implications of imported films. He was involved with quarantine regulations and other domestic measures taken against the influenza epidemic. He participated in the planning of the repatriation scheme for ex-servicemen and the operation of the Transcontinental Railway. By mid-1919 he had the satisfaction of phasing out the price-controls which had made him especially unpopular with rural producers.

Greene's greatest achievement during the immediate post-war years was a major revision of the tariff schedule. He prepared for this huge task by an exhaustive programme of factory inspections and intensive analysis of the existing schedule with his departmental officers. The proposals were ready in March 1920 and approved in July 1921. During debate Greene displayed impressive command of the myriad detail of a labyrinthine tariff schedule. Subjected to a barrage of questions, pleas and threats, his control never faltered; his knowledge, imperturbability and readiness to compromise won him parliamentary commendation on a question where divisiveness and rancour traditionally prevailed. He was, however, disappointed that constitutional difficulties prevented him from producing a more scientific and comprehensive measure than 'the Greene tariff'. In 1921 he also carried legislation to establish the Australian Tariff Board.

He saw the tariff not as a narrow revenue-raising instrument but as a device for vigorous national development and population growth, and succeeded in infusing a visionary quality into debate on routine machinery aspects of the elaborate tariff structure. He saw high protection as essential for the stimulation of Australian industries to fill the many gaps in local production. Appalled by the economic waste he detected in excessive reliance on overseas supply, he urged the creation of factories at decentralized points along the coastline, supplied by raw materials from the interior and manned by a workforce boosted by immigration. His arguments for development and migration policies based on a high tariff structure foreshadowed the policies commonly associated with the Bruce [q.v.7]-Page [q.v.] government.

Greene was given the additional portfolio of health in March 1921 and was widely regarded within the government as Hughes's obvious successor. His appointment to succeed Cook as treasurer was regarded as a formality, but Hughes selected instead the relatively unknown S. M. (Viscount) Bruce. Greene's status as number two in the government was, however, confirmed and he was given the senior portfolio of defence in place of trade and customs, while retaining health. His relationship with Hughes remained as close as ever: he acted as prime minister and leader of the House in Hughes's absence. As health minister, he encouraged research and development in tropical medicine. As defence minister, he was responsible for unpopular economies, including modification of defence training schemes, retrenchment of personnel and curtailment of camps. As with the tariff, Greene acted through personal assessment in scrupulous consultation with those involved. A difficult and unpopular task was thus done with minimum bitterness and disruption. He was involved in plans to diversify the Lithgow small-arms factory and to establish an aircraft manufacturing industry at Mascot, Sydney. He directed the administrative measures necessary to reabsorb the wartime Navy Department into the Defence Department.

To general surprise, Greene was decisively beaten at the December 1922 election by the Country Party candidate Roland Green, who had lost a leg in the war. Green had used an ingenious punning campaign slogan: 'Vote for the Green without an E'. Lack of an E also gave him precedence on the ballot paper. Greene had neglected his electorate to some extent because of his ministerial and national campaign responsibilities. His price-fixing activities had made him unpopular in the country and his qualified support for the vigorous New State movement in northern New South Wales may have cost him votes. He made a tactical error by inviting the blunt Sir Granville Ryrie [q.v.], who was given to tactless indiscretions, to campaign for him. The Country Party polled well enough to secure the balance of power and Hughes was replaced by the Bruce-Page coalition. Had he held his seat, Greene might have become prime minister, although he would have had problems in reaching an accommodation with Page and the Country Party.

He felt the defeat keenly. A contemporary account describes him as a silent spectre walking round Parliament House: 'He never whines. But the grey face and subdued eyes tell their own tale'. He retained his links with public life, making a lecture tour advocating high protection and giving evidence to a royal commission on the sugar industry. Late in 1923 he was appointed to a Senate casual vacancy for New South Wales. He remained in the Senate for fifteen years but never regained prominence.

Greene became increasingly disenchanted with the National Party which he saw as so weighed down by conservatism that it had lost much of its democratic support, but he remained close to Hughes who he believed brought to the Nationalists a numerous and enthusiastic following who otherwise would vote Labor. He favoured creation of a 'genuine centre party', deriving perhaps from a further split in the Labor Party and incorporating elements of the Nationalists in a 'strongly Australian, anti-conservative and progressive' party. In the Senate he frequently criticized Page and the Country Party, and in 1924 led a major defection of government members to amend a roads bill sponsored by Page. He assisted Hughes with tactical advice in the crisis that led to the defeat of the Bruce-Page government in October 1929. But he did not join the rebel parliamentary group, nor did he become a member of Hughes's breakaway Australian Party although he gave advice on its organization and financing. His disenchantment with the Nationalists came to a head when (Sir) John Latham [q.v.] was elected leader. Greene told the party meeting that it had made a grave mistake and that he would no longer support the party or attend its meetings. A year later he relented and resumed attendance.

After some reluctance, Greene accepted a post as assistant minister in the United Australia Party government formed by J. A. Lyons [q.v.] in January 1932. He acted as assistant treasurer to Lyons, supervising arrangements for Premiers' conferences, chairing the Loan Council, negotiating a trade agreement with New Zealand and conducting general financial administration. He resigned in October 1933, remaining in the Senate until 1938, although his political involvement diminished and there was criticism of his irregular attendance.

Appointed K.C.M.G. in 1933, he soon incorporated the family name of 'Massy' into a hyphenated surname, to formalize the usage of Massy-Greene that had evolved during the preceding twenty years.

After his political defeat in 1922 Massy-Greene had been attracted to company directorships as an alternative source of income, his interest in industry having been stimulated by his experience with price-fixing and the tariff. Invited to join the boards of three pastoral companies connected with the Baillieu [q.v.7] family, he began an association with the Collins House group. So, approaching 50, he began the second career that made him an outstanding company director of his era, holding over forty directorships, some with the largest and most important Australian industrial enterprises.

In 1923 he became a director of the British-Australian Cotton Association Ltd which was extracted from its overwhelming problems as a result of his initiatives. He was equally successful in salvaging Austral Silk and Cotton Mills Ltd, of which he was a director, by persuading Bradford Cotton Mills Ltd into a takeover, after which he joined Bradford Cotton as a director and succeeded (Sir) Robert Webster as chairman. Also director of the Dunlop Rubber Co., he negotiated another successful and mutually profitable arrangement with Bradford. A long association with metals culminated after World War II in the chairmanship of Electrolytic Zinc Co. (Australasia) Ltd and in his recognition as a principal spokesman for gold producers. His major interest in textiles developed through Webster. Massy-Greene joined the board of Felt and Textiles of Australia before it became a public company, and through his advice and reorganization contributed much to its success. He was also associated with Yarra Falls Ltd.

His most distinguished involvement was with Associated Pulp and Paper Mills of Burnie, Tasmania, manufacturers of quality paper. As its first chairman (1936-52) he fathered this major industrial project from small beginnings. The company was the first to apply short-fibred eucalypt pulps from Australian hardwoods to the commercial manufacture of fine paper. It was also unusual in acquiring forestry rights and freehold forest lands. Throughout the difficulties of experimental techniques and the complications of wartime production, Massy-Greene's 'political grasp of the situation provided the example of inflexible purpose and unflagging energy; and restored his colleagues' faith in the venture'. His qualities as an outstanding industrial leader were matched by his flair for industrial relations. At Burnie his innovations in employee welfare, formulated by (Sir) Gerald Mussen [q.v.], were among the 'most original and advanced of their kind' in Australia.

After he left the Senate Massy-Greene maintained liaison with government departments on behalf of his companies, and appeared for them before the Tariff Board, once sharply reminding its chairman that he had established the board and was entirely familiar with its powers and precedents. During World War II he was a chairman of the Treasury Finance Committee, deputy chairman of the National Security Capital Issues Advisory Board, and member of the Defence Board of Business Administration. In October 1940 he led the Australian delegation to the Eastern Group Supply Council in New Delhi, co-ordinating the British Commonwealth war effort. He was a member of the Council of the University of Melbourne in 1939-49, and a foundation member of the council of the Institute of Public Affairs from 1944.

Massy-Greene had married Lula May Lomax of a Tenterfield pastoral family at St James' Church, Sydney, on 6 February 1915. The family moved from Nimbin in 1923 and lived at Manly and Mosman, then in Toorak, Melbourne, from the early 1930s, Massy-Greene working with a small secretariat from Collins House. He had a hobby-farm near Berwick and was a keen saltwater fisherman. He died in Freemasons' Hospital, East Melbourne, on 16 November 1952 after a gallbladder operation, and was cremated. His wife, two sons and a daughter survived him. He left his estate of £81 672 to his family. His son (Sir) Brian became a very prominent company director.

Of medium height, slim and very erect with clean-cut features and quiet eyes, Massy-Greene retained a sandy colouring until late in life. Something of the aura of a lost leader surrounds him, based on widespread acceptance that he failed to become prime minister by a hair's breadth. Page, with little reason to like him, recognized him as 'an outstanding parliamentarian and a man of great capacity'. His dual ascendancy in politics and industry is unusual in the Australian experience.

E. C. G. Page, *Truant surgeon*, A. Mozley ed (Syd, 1963); C. D. Kemp, *Big businessmen* (Melb, 1964); D. Aitkin, *The colonel* (Canb, 1969); C. Edwards, *Bruce of Melbourne* (Lond, 1965); L. F. Fitzhardinge, *The little digger* (Syd, 1979); *Punch* (Melb), 17 Nov 1921; *Table Talk*, 16 Jan 1930; Papers of W. M. Hughes *and* J. Hume-Cook *and* C. D. Kemp *and* J. G. Latham (NL); *SMH*, 17 Nov 1952; information from Sir B. Massy-Greene, Syd.

C. J. LLOYD

MATHER, JOHN (1848?-1916), painter, etcher and teacher, was born at Hamilton, Scotland, son of John Mather, surveyor, and his wife Margaret, née Allan. Little is recorded of his early life but as a young man he studied art at the Royal Institute of Fine Arts, Glasgow, before migrating to Australia in 1878. He had hoped to practise professionally but when he settled in Melbourne realized he would be unable to make an immediate living from painting, and worked as a house decorator. He was engaged to paint the inside of the dome of the Exhibition Building for £2000 and this contract gave him slight financial independence, enabling him to give more time to art.

Mather was a skilful and prolific etcher although better known as a landscape painter who worked with equal facility in oils and water-colours. He built a studio at Lilydale and much of his painting was done in the surrounding countryside; his pastorales were painted in quiet colours with faithful representation of the natural scene. Although Mather practised the *plein air* method of painting introduced by Louis Buvelot [q.v.3], he kept aloof from the 'Australian Impressionism' of his contemporaries, Arthur Streeton, Tom Roberts [qq.v.], Charles Conder [q.v.3] and others. As his pictures became popular he was known in the Australian art world as a 'best seller'. He conducted art classes and frequently lectured at the artists' camps at Eaglemont; although he was never considered a major influence in the period he had a large following.

A foundation member of the Victorian Artists' Society, Mather was president in 1893-1900, 1906-08 and 1911. In 1912 he joined Fred McCubbin, Max Meldrum, Walter Withers [qq.v.] and others to form a breakaway group, the Australian Art Association. After constant campaigning for the inclusion of an artist on the board of trustees of the Public Library, Museums and National Gallery of Victoria, Mather was appointed in 1892. He was a member of the Felton [q.v.4] Bequest Committee in 1905-16 and in this capacity, and as trustee, he strongly supported Australian art. It is told that Mather offered Streeton £150 for 'Purple Noon's Transparent Might' while another trustee, unknowing, offered £126. Three of his own paintings, 'Autumn in the Fitzroy Gardens' (oil), and 'Morning, Lake Omeo' and 'Wintry Weather, Yarra Glen' (water-colours), were purchased by the gallery. In 1911 he visited an exhibition of British art at Wellington, New Zealand, and advised on purchases.

Sensible of the great benefaction from Alfred Felton, Mather persistently suggested that a suitable memorial to him be erected, one of his proposals being that the tympanum of the portico of the National Gallery be filled with a bronze relief, 'Felton protecting, encouraging and rewarding fine arts'.

Mather was dark and saturnine in appearance, genial in disposition but forthright and with a liking for lively argument, a man of integrity and possessed of immense energy. He had a well-informed mind and was particularly interested in science and the philosophy of Herbert Spencer. On 16 September 1882 he had married, at Williamstown, Jessie Pines Best; they had a daughter and three sons, one of whom died in 1919 after serving in France. Mather died of diabetes at his home, Cadzow, South Yarra, on 18 February 1916 and was buried in Cheltenham cemetery. At the time of his death, still industrious, he was working on a water-colour from a sketch of Launching Place.

His widow arranged for a comprehensive exhibition of her husband's work, held at the Athenaeum Gallery in August 1916. Mather's work has been acquired by Australian State and provincial galleries and the National Art Gallery and Museum, Wellington, New Zealand. A charcoal portrait by E. Phillips Fox [q.v.8] is in the National Gallery of Victoria.

E. La T. Armstrong, *The book of the . . . National Gallery of Victoria, 1856-1906* (Melb, 1906); *Smike to Bulldog—letters from Sir Arthur Streeton to Tom Roberts*, R. H. Croll ed (Syd, 1946); Bernard Smith, *Australian painting 1788-1960* (Melb, 1962); *Studio*, 7 (1896); *Argus*, 21 Feb 1916; *Age*, 5 Nov 1932.   JUDY BLYTH

MATHER, JOSEPH FRANCIS (1844-1925), Quaker, was born on 6 April 1844 in Hobart Town, son of Joseph Benson Mather, draper, and his wife Anna Maria, née Cotton. He was educated at Clifton House, New Norfolk, Somerset House, Hobart, Frederick Mackie's Friends' School, briefly at the Hobart High School in 1859 and finally at H. M. Pike's School. He worked on his grandfather Francis Cotton's [q.v.1] estates at Kelvedon and Earlham, had a brief period with an architect and was an agricultural apprentice at Ellinthorp Hall, Ross, in 1865-68. He joined the long-established family clothing business in Hobart, becoming a partner in 1870 and proprietor on his father's death in 1890, until he sold out in 1912. On 19 March 1874 he married Margaret Ann Lidbetter (d. 1876) at the Friends' Meeting House in Hobart.

Mather was a generous employer, who endeavoured to apply his religious principles to the conduct of his business affairs. His character and integrity won the respect of Hobart's business community. He was a committee-member of the Hobart Chamber of Commerce, the Savings Bank, the Tasmanian Tourist Association and the Sanitary Association, concerned to develop public reserves to conserve natural beauty around Hobart. His philanthropic interests included temperance, the British and Foreign Bible Society, the Hobart Ethical Society, the Ragged School Committee and the Hobart Benevolent Society. He represented the Society of Friends on the Hobart Council of Churches.

Mather was secretary of the original committee to found The Friends' School, Hobart, and chairman in 1890-1923. He believed that the future of the Society of Friends depended on education and he gave the school his total commitment, even to the prejudice of his business. His own standing brought strong support to the school as a non-secular, non-sectarian institution, which stressed not only acquisition of knowledge but character building. He welcomed the progressive ideas of the first headmaster, Samuel Clemes [q.v.8]. During periods of difficulty Mather provided continuity of direction and firm 'pilotage'. His code address was appropriately 'Hopeful, Hobart'. In 1912 he produced a history of the school.

Mather was a prolific correspondent with the English Quakers Edwin Ransome and Charles Holdsworth. For many years he was editor of the *Australian Friend* in which he wrote copiously on education, militarism in schools, the history of Quakers in Australia and contemporary issues. Yet in spite of his exposition of Quaker principles he was considered a 'private' man, averse to publicity or involvement in politics. Thus he based his testimony against war on a consistent attempt to maintain a line of conduct in harmony with the mind and spirit of Christ and was doubtful about activists who made conscription a political issue. Nor did his pacifism prevent him from respecting those of differing views: when Friends' old scholars wished to erect an honour-board in the school after World War I, and some Quakers opposed it, Mather acknowledged the genuine feeling behind both views. The board was erected with the inscription, 'They followed where their sense of duty led'.

On 18 January 1905 he had married Lucy Margaret Thompson in Sydney. There were no children of either marriage. Survived by his wife, Mather died on 11 August 1925 in Hobart and was buried in Cornelian Bay cemetery. In a leader the *Mercury* paid tribute to him as 'The Good Citizen' and to his 'nameless, unremembered acts of kindness and of love'.

W. N. Oats, *The rose and the waratah* (Hob, 1979); *Mercury*, 12 Aug 1925; J. F. Mather correspondence (F 4/1-6, Univ Tas Archives).

WILLIAM N. OATS

MATHESON, Sir ALEXANDER PERCEVAL (1861-1929), businessman and politician, was born on 6 February 1861 in Mayfair, London, second son of Sir Alexander Matheson, 1st baronet of Lochalsh and Liberal member of parliament, and his second wife Eleanor Irving, née Perceval, a descendant of Spencer Perceval, the prime minister who was assassinated in 1812. Educated at Harrow, Alexander spent two years travelling, during which he married Eleanor Money, an Englishwoman, at New Gisborne, Victoria, on 18 October 1884. He then entered a London commercial house. In 1894 he migrated to Western Australia and next year established a store and commercial agency in Bayley Street, Coolgardie. From this base he managed branches in Perth, Fremantle, Kalgoorlie, Cue, Menzies and Lawlers, providing finance, in association with Bewick Moreing Ltd, for the development of mines, and selling mining machinery.

Matheson had brown hair with a gingery tinge and violet-blue eyes; he wore a full moustache and clipped beard. Well-groomed, he was popular on the goldfields despite his upper-class accent and, in 1897, was elected to the Legislative Council for North-East Province on an advanced or 'experimental' democratic policy. Probably about this time, he brought his family to Western Australia and settled, in style, in Perth; he became a sought-after member of society with regular social entry to Government House. He had been active in the political reform movement on the goldfields and became president of the Eastern Goldfields Reform League which helped to force a reluctant Western Australian government into Federation. In 1897-1900 he was a member of the Federal Council of Australasia. He was also an urban investor in Perth and was responsible for the subdivision of Applecross.

Matheson won a Senate seat in 1901 with a policy which included absolute free trade, industrial arbitration, old-age pensions, uniform franchise and White Australia. He did not join the Australian Labor Party, although he supported much of its policy, but had many friends in its ranks and corresponded with King O'Malley [q.v.] for many years. His wife had spent very little time in Western Australia and at the end of his first parliamentary term he resigned, returned to England to rejoin his family, and resumed his business career.

Matheson's three sons were killed in action in World War I. Although four daughters survived, the loss, following a financial disaster due to unwise speculation, contributed to breaking the marriage which was probably legally dissolved. He succeeded his half-brother as 3rd baronet in 1920 but soon left for New Zealand where he was a correspondent for *The Times*. He lived in Wellington and planned to marry again, but the engagement was terminated. In 1927 he settled in a Monaco flat. He died at Queens Gate, Kensington, London, on 6 August 1929.

P. W. H. Thiel & Co., *Twentieth century impressions of Western Australia* (Perth, 1901); *Kalgoorlie Miner*, 24 May, 8 July 1897, 16 Mar 1901, 16 Aug 1929; *Morning Herald* (Perth), 2 Apr 1901; *The Times*, 8 Aug 1929; J. S. Bastin, The West Australian Federation movement (M.A. thesis, Melb, 1952); D. Mossenson, Gold and politics (M.A. thesis, Univ WA, 1952); O'Malley papers (NL); family information.

H. J. GIBBNEY

MATHEW, JOHN (1849-1929), Presbyterian minister and anthropologist, was born on 31 May 1849 at Aberdeen, Scotland, fourth child and eldest son of Alexander Mathew, factory overseer, and his wife Jean, née Mortimer. He was educated at Kidd's school, Aberdeen, and at the Insch Free Church School where he was a pupil-teacher in 1862-64.

In 1864 Mathew migrated with a brother and sister to Queensland to live with their uncle John Mortimer on his station, Manumbar, on the Burnett River. Stockrider, bookkeeper, and storeman for six years, he became familiar with the language and culture of the Kabi and Wakka peoples, towards whom his Calvinist uncle acted humanely. For two years Mathew was a gold-digger at Imbil and Ravenswood. Next, he served the Queensland Department of Public Instruction as a teacher at Dalby (1872-75) and the Brisbane Normal School (1875-76).

Feeling a call to the ministry, Mathew moved in 1876 to Victoria where he matriculated and graduated from the University of Melbourne (B.A., 1884; M.A., 1886). Although his studies were interrupted by stints as tutor and station-manager he qualified for both degrees with first-class honours, having been awarded a scholarship in mental and moral philosophy in 1885. He took the full course in theology at Ormond [q.v.5] College in 1884-86. Inducted to the parish of Ballan in 1887, on 6 July he married Edinburgh-born Wilhelmina (Minnie) Scott (1863-1940). In 1889 Mathew was called to the suburban charge of Coburg, where he was minister until his retirement in 1923. He was elected moderator by the 1911 Victorian assembly and moderator-general for Australia in 1922-24. He was a home chaplain during World War I.

Mathew was a council-member of Presbyterian Ladies', Scotch and Ormond (chairman, 1910-26) colleges. He was a founder and office-bearer of the Melbourne College of Divinity; an advisory council-member of Coburg High School, and a long-standing member of the Royal Society of Victoria and the Australian Literature Society (president, 1915-20). In 1926-29 he served on the anthropological committee of the Australian National Research Council. His scholarship won him further degrees, from the University of St Andrews, Scotland (B.D., 1892), and the Melbourne College of Divinity (B.D. *ad eund.*, 1913; D.D., 1924).

Maintaining a lifelong interest in Aboriginal ethnography, Mathew published two books and numerous papers and articles between 1879 and 1928. In 1889 he won the prize and medal of the Royal Society of New South Wales for an essay 'The Australian Aborigines' which was the basis for his best-known publication, *Eaglehawk and crow* (1899). It was, as Mathew had anticipated, criticized by the established ethnographers (Sir) Baldwin Spencer [q.v.], A. W. Howitt and Lorimer Fison [qq.v.4]. Spencer wrote a scholarly critique of the book but Fison's attack seems to have been provoked by Mathew's challenge to his own theories of group-marriage, and perhaps also by his amateur status. Mathew received more encouragement and support from other independent workers such as R. H. Mathews [q.v.5] and Daisy Bates [q.v.7], who appreciated his assistance and advice.

In 1906 Mathew returned to Queensland to visit the Kabi and Wakka people living on Barambah Government Aboriginal Station and in 1910 he published *Two representative tribes of Queensland.* While his linguistic studies and ethnographic reporting are still well regarded, his more speculative discussion of the tri-hybrid origin of the Australian Aborigines, controversial at the time, is unsupported by data now available.

From youth Mathew was a keen musician, poet, humorist and handyman. He invented a system of shorthand called 'Breviscript'. Genial in society and a total abstainer, he was a short, trim man who sported a full bushman's beard until his thirties, later going bald. An eloquent preacher, he was both liberal in theology and ardently evangelical. Beside his ethnographic works he also published three volumes of verse.

Mathew died on 11 March 1929 at his Coburg home and was buried in Melbourne general cemetery. He was survived by his wife, daughter, and four sons who all served in World War I.

J. Greenway, *Bibliography of the Australian Aborigines and the native peoples of Torres Strait* (Syd, 1963); *Presbyterian Messenger,* 22 Mar 1929; *Oceania,* 46, no 1, Sept 1975; *Artefact,* Dec 1980; *Argus,* 12 Mar 1929; R. Y. Mathew, John Mathew 1849-1929 (typescript, John Oxley Lib, copies LaTL and Aust Inst of Aboriginal Studies); J. Mathew papers (Aust Inst of Aboriginal Studies); *EDB*/02 and /V2 (QA).   M. D. PRENTIS

MATHEWS, GREGORY MACALISTER (1876-1949), ornithologist, was born on 10 September 1876 at Merrygoen, New South Wales, second son of native-born parents Robert Hamilton Mathews [q.v.5], surveyor and ethnologist, and his wife Mary Sylvester, née Bartlett. Educated at Singleton Grammar School and The King's School, Parramatta, he enthusiastically collected birds' eggs. He worked for six years on a cattle-station near Charters Towers, Queensland, observing birds on droving trips and indulging his love for horses. He returned to New South Wales and became an orchardist. On 6 May 1902 at Parramatta he married a wealthy 37-year-old widow with two children, Marion Cecil Wynne (d. 1938), daughter of H. C. White of Havilah, and niece of James White [q.v.6]; they sailed for England, with Mathews, a believer in the powers of prophecy, confident that there lay his destiny.

Life in England was a continuous round of hunting, races and horse-shows until he visited the British Museum and conceived the idea of producing an exhaustive work on Australian birds. He met R. Bowdler Sharpe, keeper of the bird collection, who encouraged him and 'taught him how to work'. Once started on the huge undertaking, Mathews became fanatical. Sixteen-hour days were spent in research, writing, skin and book-collecting: he bought, exchanged or obtained by hired collectors 30 000 skins and amassed some 5000 books covering every aspect of ornithology but, 'essentially a bibliophile', he 'was not really interested in the living bird'. Correspondence sped between Australia and experts all over the world. The first volume of *The birds of Australia* was published in London in 1910. Next year Tom Iredale [q.v.9] became his secretary; in close partnership they produced a staggering amount of work until Iredale left for Australia in 1923.

In 1914 Mathews undertook a world tour, meeting ornithologists and extensively examining skins. Returning just before World War I he settled in Hampshire at Foulis Court, Fisher's Pond. Too old for enlistment, he grew vegetables, performed the 'obligations of a Squire of the Village' and continued *The birds of Australia*. The twelfth and final volume appeared in 1927. His other publications covered lists of Australian, New Zealand, Lord Howe and Norfolk Island birds, numerous articles and, with Iredale, one volume of a *Manual of the birds of Australia* (London, 1921). In 1912 he established the *Austral avian record*, editing it throughout its fifteen years of existence.

Mathews' place in Australian ornithology is controversial. His main interest lay in taxonomy, and originally, influenced by Sharpe, he adopted a conservative approach. His 'Handlist of the birds of Australasia' (*Emu*, January 1908), reflected this attitude. However he soon joined the school favouring sub-species, gaining the reputation of an arch 'splitter'. His 'Reference list to the birds of Australia' (*Novitates Zoologicae*, 18 January 1912), raised the number of forms from 800 to 1500! He constantly revised his taxonomy, at times inconsistently, and Australia's established ornithologists mistrusted his extremist ideas. Heated arguments raged, although with the passage of time some of his pronouncements have been accepted. In the latter stages of his work he reverted to conservatism, but by then the rest of the world had moved on.

A fellow of the Royal Society of Edinburgh, Mathews was associated with world-wide scientific bodies, received many honours and was appointed C.B.E. in 1939; he represented Australia at five international ornithological congresses. In 1939 he presented his library to Australia, and in 1940-45 supervised its housing in the National Library, Canberra; he published an autobiography, *Birds and books* (Canberra, 1942). He returned to England in 1945 and died of cancer at Winchester on 27 March 1949, survived by a son. His collection of skins, sold to Lord Rothschild in the 1920s, is now in the American Museum of Natural History, New York.

Mathews was tall, bronzed, with silvery hair, blue eyes aided by a monocle, and a thin, prominent nose. He spoke rapidly in a high-pitched voice. He usually dressed as a country squire and is depicted thus in a portrait by Basil Gotto held by the National Library.

H. M. Whittell, *The literature of Australian birds* (Perth, 1954); D. L. Serventy, *Checklist to the Mathews ornithological collection* (Canb, 1966); J. White, *The White family of Belltrees* (Syd, 1981); *Auk*, 44, no 3, July 1927, p 435; *Emu* (Melb), 49, no 2, Oct 1949, p 145, 49, no 4, Apr 1950, p 257; *SMH*, 3 Sept 1966; D. L. Serventy, G. M. Mathews collection (Roy Aust Ornithologists Union Archives, LaTL).   TESS KLOOT

MATHEWS, HAMILTON BARTLETT (1873-1959), surveyor-general, was born on 23 March 1873 at Deepwater, New England, New South Wales, eldest son of Robert Hamilton Mathews [q.v.5] and his wife Mary Sylvester, née Bartlett, and elder brother of Gregory [q.v.], the ornithologist. As a child he travelled constantly with his father before attending The King's School, Parramatta. In May 1894 he qualified as a licensed surveyor and practised privately. He studied at night at the University of Sydney (B.A., 1899), graduating with first-class honours in mathematics. On 16 June 1900 at Parramatta he married Enid Chatfield Mackenzie (d.1934).

Mathews had been appointed assistant surveyor in the Department of Lands on 31 August 1897 and worked under Charles Scrivener [q.v.] in the Metropolitan Land District until transferred to Maitland in August 1901. After service at Moree (1911-14) and Goulburn (1914-15), he was district surveyor at Forbes (1916-21) and Wagga Wagga (1921-26). Mathews was appointed surveyor-general and metropolitan district surveyor on 16 June 1926, chief mining surveyor in 1927, and an electoral districts commissioner in 1928.

His western experience had brought Mathews into close contact with soldier settlement; the non-viability of many subdivisions caused him substantial anguish, which he attempted to convey as chairman of the Soldiers' Settlements Appraisement Board (1925-28). His initial task as surveyor-general was to implement a policy, bitterly contested, of introducing motor transport in lieu of horse-drawn vehicles for field surveys. He resumed the trigonometrical survey and oversaw completion of triangulation of the ranges from Newcastle to the Queensland border.

Mathews played a key role with the university and Sydney Observatory in establishing a new standard of invar bands for long metre tapes in suspension, required for preparing the harbour bridge site. He strongly influenced the Surveyors Act of 1929 which provided for the registration of surveyors, regulated the making of surveys by amending existing legislation, and supplemented the reciprocal arrangements previously agreed to by the Australian States and New Zealand.

Identifying strongly with the emergence of surveying as a profession, Mathews regularly attended conferences of the staff surveyors where 'this fine old gentleman, formal and erect, in his old alpaca frock coat and stiff collars' relayed vivid impressions of earlier days. He married a widow Rachel Naomi Margaret Kearney (d.1949), née Tasker, at Turramurra on 1 July 1936. He retired next year.

A trustee of the Australian Museum, Sydney, from 1926 and president in 1945-58, Mathews developed a lifelong interest in its work. He was a member of the Royal Society of New South Wales from 1926 and of the board of visitors, Sydney Observatory, in 1927-58. He became a member of the Institute of Land Valuers in 1930, served as chairman of the Port Kembla Environs Planning Committee in 1934-40 and was elected an honorary fellow of the Institution of Surveyors, New South Wales, in 1938 and of the Australian Planning Institute in 1954.

Mathews' abiding interests were the Presbyterian Church (session clerk at Wagga Wagga, and at St Stephen's, Macquarie Street, 1947-58) and Freemasonry. He was initiated at Lodge Orient, Maitland, on 26 January 1906, and eventually served as grand master of the Grand Lodge of Mark Master Masons of New South Wales in 1930-46 and as first grand principal of the Supreme Chapter of Royal Arch Masons of New South Wales in 1934-40. He wrote the comprehensive article on Freemasonry in the 1958 edition of *The Australian encyclopaedia.*

Mathews died at his home at Potts Point on 21 January 1959 and was cremated. His son and two daughters survived him.

Dept of Lands (NSW), *Annual Reports*, 1926-37; *NSW Valuer*, 1, no 2, Apr 1930, p 50; *Aust Surveyor*, 30 June 1916, p 75, Mar 1959, p 324; *SMH*, 23 Jan 1959; *Bulletin*, 18 Feb 1959; information from grand secretary, United Grand Lodge, NSW, from J. Darby, Syd, Janet Mathews, Bayview, and Dr F. D. McCarthy, Northbridge, Syd, E. Miller, Glen Innes and C. C. Bradley, Armidale, NSW.

JOHN ATCHISON

MATHEWS, ROBERT HENRY (1877-1970), missionary and sinologist, was born on 13 July 1877 at Flemington, Melbourne, son of London-born William Mathews and his Australian wife Mary, née Whitlaw. Many sinologists have mistakenly assumed that the great lexicographer, author of Mathews' *Chinese-English dictionary*, was English. William had been a tinsmith and later worked in the Victorian Railways. His son studied lithography as part of his apprenticeship in the printing trade at the Working Men's College (Royal Melbourne Institute of Technology). Mathews was an intensely religious Congregationalist. While 'waiting and praying for light' he became interested in the evangelical work of the Christian missionaries, and the activities of the China Inland Mission in particular.

Abandoning his printing business, Mathews joined the C.I.M. in August 1906, after spending eighteen months in Adelaide where he received Bible instruction and ministered to the city's outcast population. He sailed for China on 4 October. After spending a short period at C.I.M.'s Shanghai headquarters he was sent to two stations in Honan Province. In 1915 Mathews was transferred to Hueichow in Anhwei Province where, as in Honan, he was confronted by 'a peculiar lack of response to the Gospel's message'.

His experience in Anhwei, however, first aroused Mathews' passion for the Chinese language. Noting the variety of dialects, and believing that 'a preacher must not only be understood, but easily understood', he developed a consuming interest in questions of language. In 1921 he returned to Honan to conduct Bible classes among the troops of Feng Yu-hsiang, a prominent warlord and convert. Before the rise of Chiang Kai-shek the C.I.M. looked to Feng to institute a new moral order in China. Comforted by the fervour with which Feng's army embraced Christianity, Mathews for the next four years travelled across Szechwan, leading Bible classes and supervising the work of young Chinese seminarians. In 1926 he returned to Australia for a brief vacation but the deterioration of the political situation in China and the evacuation of thousands of British missionaries forced him to remain in Australia until February 1928.

On his return to Shanghai he was asked to revise Baller's Chinese-English dictionary. After three years of intense work Mathews produced a volume of 1200 pages that contained 7785 Chinese characters and over 104 000 phrases, including classical, modern and technical terms. A *Chinese-English dictionary* compiled for the C.I.M. by R. H. Mathews was published in Shanghai in 1931. In 1943 Harvard University Press issued an American edition entitled simply *Mathews' Chinese-English Dictionary* and the work is now universally known simply as *Mathews.* In that year the C.I.M. compound in Shanghai was taken over by the Japanese army for use as its headquarters. Unbound copies of Mathews' own revised edition of his dictionary, printing blocks and the mission's library were confiscated and destroyed. For the next two years he was held in Japanese internment.

In 1945 Mathews returned to Melbourne for only the third time in forty years and retired from active missionary work. However his talents and command of Chinese were recognized by the Department of Defence. In 1948 he was recruited to work part time on translation of archival material and compilation of glossaries, and he was employed full time for six years from 1951.

Mathews was a quietly spoken and humble man who achieved a high standard of scholarship through patience, dedication and an unusual degree of linguistic skill. His dictionary, described by C. P. Fitzgerald as a 'monument of learning', became the standard text for English scholars. Its circulation was enhanced by the fact that many printings were made in America and Asia without Mathews' authorization. His *Kuoyü primer* suffered a similar fate.

His great achievement was made without any formal educational background in languages and his contribution long went without any official acknowledgement. In 1962, however, the University of Melbourne awarded him an honorary doctorate of letters. He is described as being short, slender and 'round shouldered like a scholar'. In his mission work he presented the Gospel in a forceful and practical way, as befitted his evangelical calling. He was invariably courteous and kindly. His colleagues in the Department of Defence regularly addressed him, with affection and respect, as 'Mr Ma' as he had been known in his Chinese households for so many years.

Mathews died in Melbourne on 16 February 1970 and was cremated. His first wife, Annie Ethel Smith, a New South Wales C.I.M. missionary whom he married on 30 December 1908, died in 1920; they had three children. In 1922 Mathews married another missionary Violet Ward (d. 1954) who collaborated very closely with him on his linguistic work.

M. L. Loane, *The story of the China Inland Mission in Australia and New Zealand 1890-1964* (Melb, 1965); China Inland Mission, *China's Millions*, 1 Oct 1906, 1 July 1909, 1 Apr 1911, 1 Sept 1915, 1 May 1920, 1 Aug 1921, 1 July 1943, 1 Mar 1954, 1 Mar 1970; *Meanjin Q*, 15, no 4 (1956); *Univ Melb Gazette*, Feb 1963; *Age*, 17 Dec 1962; information from Mr J. Spierings and Mr R. D. Botterill, Melb.   ARTHUR HUCK

MATHIAS, LOUIS JOHN (1886-1965), labourer and soldier, was born on 10 February 1886 at Boorooma station, Walgett, New South Wales, fifth child of James Mathias, farmer and contractor, and his wife Susanah, née Denewal. He attended Gun-

nedah Public School, and worked as a farm labourer and blade shearer around Gunnedah and Coolah. On 1 January 1912, at Gungal, he married Harriet Fanning of Coolah with Anglican rites.

Tall and well-built, Jack Mathias had won local fame as a bare-fisted boxer. On 2 February 1916 he enlisted in the Australian Imperial Force at Narrabri and embarked from Sydney in May with the 33rd Battalion ('C' Company) for training in England. He was promoted corporal on 14 November before proceeding to France with his battalion.

A 'capable and courageous leader and a fearless fighter', Mathias was promoted lance sergeant on 26 January 1917, sergeant on 26 June, and temporary company sergeant major on 20 December. He was known for his strong personality and energy and was highly regarded by his comrades. Said to be the champion heavyweight boxer of the battalion, he instructed in physical training and bayonet fighting. He was awarded the Distinguished Conduct Medal for the 'exceptional courage, initiative, skill and able leadership' he displayed between 22 September 1917 and 24 February 1918.

On 17 April Mathias was gassed at Villers-Bretonneux and was out of the line until 24 July. On 8 August with four men he captured three enemy strong-points in the advance through Accroche Wood, killing three and taking eighteen prisoners. Although cut off from the company by dense fog, Mathias continued to Long Valley and captured a field-gun, killing two gunners and taking two more prisoners. After the company reached its objective he assisted in the reorganization. He was awarded a Bar to his D.C.M., the citation praising his leadership, initiative and inspiring influence on all ranks.

Mathias was awarded the Military Medal for his part in operations near Bouchavesnes on 31 August, in the struggle for Mont St Quentin. Organizing a small party of the 33rd's left assaulting company, he brought heavy reverse fire from a Lewis-gun to bear on the enemy, leading to mass surrenders, and enabling the advance to continue. With his company commander Walter Duncan [q.v.8] he was prominent in capturing a strongly defended quarry and in establishing defensive posts. His judgement and leadership were again apparent in his company's second advance.

On 20 September 1918 Mathias joined an officers' training battalion and before rejoining the 33rd was commissioned second lieutenant on 5 January 1919. He was promoted lieutenant on 5 April, shortly before returning to Australia. His A.I.F. appointment ended in July.

Mathias obtained a soldier-settler farm at Oban, Coolah. From the mid-1920s, however, he worked in Sydney as a wharf labourer, for some years returning to the country for seasonal work as a shearer. A modest man, he rarely spoke of his wartime experiences, and devoted himself to his family. In his final years, when suffering from arterial disease and hemiplegia, he received a pension. Survived by his daughter, he died at Kensington on 21 June 1965 and was cremated. His medals are held by the Australian War Memorial, Canberra.

C. E. W. Bean, *The A.I.F. in France*, 1918 (Syd, 1937, 1942); *London Gazette*, 31 May 1918, 3 June supp, 3, 5 Dec supp, 13 May 1919, 14 May supp; *SMH*, 22 June 1965; information from Mrs M. Evans, Burwood, and Mr V. Donoghue, Gunnedah, NSW; War Diary, 33rd Battalion, A.I.F. (AWM).

GILLIAN FULLOON

MATSON, PHILLIP HENRY (1884-1928), sportsman, was born on 22 October 1884 at Port Adelaide, son of George Matson, bootmaker, poet and later a Commonwealth literary pensioner, and his wife Emma, née Duffield. Educated at state school, Matson moved to Western Australia as a youth and worked as a navvies' water-boy. He swam competitively in Perth from 1902 and played Australian Rules football. Matson dominated Perth swimming and held State free-style titles from 100 yards to a mile using the trudgen stroke. At the 1905 Australasian championships in Melbourne he won the 220 yards breast-stroke event. Over the next three years he lowered his time to 3 minutes, 14 seconds, a world record time, and retained his title in 1907 and 1908. He turned professional for a £20 stake in 1909. On 16 March 1907 at Boulder he had married his cousin Gertrude Ethel Jean Pope; they later separated.

Financial rewards came from football, despite its rules for amateurs. Matson chased transfer fees and job offers: to South Bunbury 1904-05; Boulder City 1906-08; Sturt (Adelaide) 1909-10; North Fremantle 1911; Subiaco 1912-17; and East Perth 1918-23. He played his best football in Adelaide, being fast, vigorous, an outstanding high mark, despite his height of 5 ft. 10½ ins. (179 cm), and versatile at half-back, half-forward and following. He represented South Australia in 1909-10 and Western Australia in 1908, 1911 and 1914 (as captain) in interstate matches.

Matson worked intermittently as a miner, tramways motorman, farmer (at Nippering), trans-Australian railway navvy, lumper, storeman and 'Spot-Lager' retailer. Formerly abstemious, he later drank socially and 'scorned few delights'. Heavy gambling made him alternately flush and broke. This lifestyle caused tension in his family who lived in tents at Crawley or moved house frequently. When rejected for war service on medical grounds, Matson favoured the casual life of a licensed Swan River fisherman and running two-up schools at Subiaco and Pelican Point and starting-price books at city hotels. In 1918-24 he held a trotting bookmaker's licence and ran an illegal gaming-house in Central Perth.

He became coach of East Perth Football Club in 1918. A dominant personality, Matson inspired confidence and respect with his systematic approach and ability to outwit opponents and to exploit their weaknesses. Strengthened by his recruitment of champion players, East Perth won seven premierships between 1919 and 1927. Matson commanded high fees for his success: he had played in twelve premiership teams and, in the last ten years of his career, coached teams into nine finals. A selector for the successful 1921 Western Australian interstate carnival team, he coached the 1924 and 1927 teams that lost narrowly to Victoria. He bluntly attacked Victorian officials in 1924 for initiating bashing tactics. Officialdom won, for, after coaching Castlemaine, Victoria, in 1925, he was refused permission by the Victorian Football League to coach Richmond. Matson's answer was to inspire Western Australia to two 'spiteful, vicious, brutal' victories over Victoria in 1926.

A witty, eloquent, unconventional, uninhibited yet popular individual, Matson lived hedonistically, without pretension, and accumulated few possessions. He was important in the professionalization of working-class sport, insisting upon fees to become the highest-paid Westralian footballer-coach of his era, and forcing the abandonment of amateur transfer rules. Injured in a truck smash, he died in Perth on 13 June 1928 and was buried in the Anglican section of Karrakatta cemetery. He was survived by his wife, their two sons and his *de facto* wife Kate Thompson, née Owens.

M. Glossop (ed), *East Perth 1906-1976* (Perth, 1976); C. T. Stannage (ed), *A new history of Western Australia* (Perth, 1981); *Western Mail* (Perth), 14, 21 June 1928; *Football 150* (Perth, 1979); *Westralian Worker*, 28 May 1915; *Express and Telegraph* (Adel), 31 Aug 1922; *Mirror* (Perth), 28 April 1923, 16 June 1928; *West Australian*, 12, 13, 14 June 1928; Subiaco Football Club, WAFL, Football records; P. H. Matson correspondence, papers, newspaper cuttings (held by P. G. Matson, Sth Perth); information from P. G. Matson, J. Dolan, East Fremantle, and A. G. Owens, Mount Lawley, WA.   LYALL HUNT

MATTERS, MURIEL LILAH (1877-1969), suffragist, was born on 12 November 1877 at Bowden, Adelaide, third of ten children of John Leonard Matters, cabinetmaker and later stockbroker, and his wife Emma Alma, née Warburton. She studied music and elocution, reciting Whitman and Ibsen, then lived for a time in Sydney and Melbourne, acting with the Robert Brough [q.v.3] Comedy Company. In 1901 she settled again in Adelaide, where she performed at the Cowandilla Salon, Mrs R. Quesnel's music rooms and elsewhere. In 1902 she directed Pinero's play *Sweet lavender* for the Appendreena Dramatic Club. She later moved with her family to Perth.

Both in Adelaide and Perth Muriel Matters was influenced by European friends who imbued her with socialist ideals. In 1905 she left for London where Peter, Prince Kropotkin, Russian revolutionary anarchist, and the journalist W. T. Stead encouraged her to further radical activity. She soon abandoned acting and in 1907 joined the Women's Freedom League.

Miss Matters lectured in Hyde Park and in 1908 took the first 'Votes for Women' caravan on a tour of villages in the south of England where she met Henry James, a supporter, at Rye. On 28 October she gained notoriety by chaining herself to an iron grille in the ladies' gallery of the House of Commons and declaiming women's suffrage aims. She was removed, still attached to the grille, and sent to Holloway Prison for a month; she adopted the cause of prison reform. Matters spent a year in Wales advocating votes for women and held meetings in Dublin. In 1909 she flew over London in an airship inscribed 'Votes for Women', scattering handbills over parliament. But she objected when more violent militants took over the movement.

In Australia next year Matters lectured in several States on feminism and socialism: her manner was earnest but humorous and she excelled at repartee. She denounced sweating and advocated women's unions, equal divorce laws, equal pay for equal work, endowment of motherhood, and support for unmarried mothers. With Vida Goldstein [q.v.9] she secured a resolution from the Senate to the British prime minister detailing the good results from the enfranchisement of Australian women. In London in 1911 she helped to form a women's settlement to further educational opportunities in the Lambeth slums. In 1916 she attended a training course by educationalist Maria Montessori at Barcelona, Spain, and later addressed the British Montessori Society. Muriel was a Christian.

The book *Australasians who count . . .* (London, 1913), edited by her sister-in-law Mrs L. W. Matters, included a chapter, 'My impressions as an agitator for social reform', by Muriel. On 15 October 1914 in the London Registry Office she married Dr William Arnold Porter (d. 1949), a divorced Bostonian dentist; they had no children. She organized a national conference of women in London on 14 April to discuss peace and disarmament.

In 1922 she lectured in Australia and in 1924 stood, unsuccessfully, as Muriel Matters-Porter, as a Labour candidate for the House of Commons for Hastings. Her brother Leonard (1881-1951), a journalist, was Labour member of parliament for Lambeth, Kennington, in 1929-31.

Mrs Porter was a slight, attractive and vivacious woman with a mass of golden hair. She lived on at Hastings, enjoying sea bathing and remaining lucid to a great age. She died there on 17 November 1969.

Quiz and the Lantern (Adel), 4 Apr, 30 May, 7 Aug 1901, 12 Dec 1902, 12 Feb 1904; *Critic* (Adel), 9 Aug 1905; *Women's Freedom League*, 4, 11 June, 10, 30 July 1908; *Southern Sphere*, 1 July 1910; *Aust and NZ Weekly*, 9 Feb 1911, 22 June 1916; *The Times*, 6 Jan 1909; *Weekly Times* (Melb), 7 Nov 1908; *Table Talk*, 23 June 1910; *Socialist* (Melb), 22, 29 July, 5 Aug 1910; *Woman Voter*, 1 July 1915; *Australasian*, 17 Jan 1925.

FAYETTE GOSSE

MATTHEWS, CHARLES HENRY SELFE (1873-1961), Anglican clergyman, was born on 16 November 1873 at Sandhurst, Berkshire, England, son of Rev. John Henry Dudley Matthews and his wife Edith Annie, née Selfe. His father, a master at nearby Wellington College, later became headmaster of Leeds Grammar School. Matthews was educated there and at King's College, Cambridge (B.A., 1896; M.A., 1902). After teaching science at Crewkerne Grammar School, he entered Wells Theological College, was made deacon on 18 December 1898 and ordained priest by Bishop Randall Davidson (later archbishop of Canterbury) on 21 December 1899.

After serving as curate at St Mary-extra-Southampton, an important centre of industrial mission work, Matthews was recruited in 1901 to the new Brotherhood of the Good Shepherd for service in New South Wales. He laboured in the western section of the diocese of Bathurst, which stretched to the Queensland border. At first he lived at the Brotherhood house, which he helped to extend, at Dubbo, but in 1904 he moved to Gilgandra. This involved a more settled ministry but still included many long journeys. While remaining English in outlook and habit, Matthews appreciated and, to an unusual extent, understood the problems and habits of the outback. He brought to them a dry humour and a practical spirituality and was quite devoid of the patronizing attitude so often adopted by English clergymen in Australia.

The Bush Brothers had to overcome opposition centred in Evangelical Sydney from supporters of the traditional parochial structure and from those who thought the Brotherhood's monastic-like discipline to be inimical to episcopal authority. Some believed the Brothers to be too English and others too Anglo-Catholic. Aware of these difficulties, as first editor of the magazine *Bush Brother* from 1904 Matthews expounded the Brotherhood case with vigour and a fair degree of success. In 1908 he returned to England and became vicar of Catsfield in the diocese of Chichester. That year he published in London *A parson in the Australian bush* (reprinted 1909, new edition 1910). At one level it was a vivid description, serious but with many a wry twist, of the life of a Bush Brother. At another, it showed an understanding of the outback that few other churchmen had approached.

At Kensington, London, Matthews married Gertrude Ethelwyn Malkin on 15 June 1909. Apart from serving as chaplain of Marlborough College (1930-38), he remained in the parish ministry until his retirement in 1948, serving at St Peter-in-Thanet, diocese of Canterbury, and Kenilworth and Fenny Compton, diocese of Coventry; he was an honorary canon of Coventry from 1946. A persuasive writer and a zealous editor, Matthews kept abreast of current religious and social developments and produced a steady stream of books and pamphlets, notably on Modernism, his chief theological concern. But he did not forget Australia—he published *Bill: a bushman* in 1914 and continued to serve on Brotherhood committees. He died at Wilcot, Wiltshire, on 30 September 1961, survived by his wife and at least one son.

J. W. S. Tomlin, *The story of the Bush Brotherhoods* (Lond, 1949); R. A. F. Webb, *Brothers in the sun* (Adel, 1978); *Bush Brother*, Dec 1961; *Church Times* (Lond), 30 Oct 1961; R. M. Teale, By hook or by crook: the Anglican diocese of Bathurst, 1870-1911 (M.A. thesis, Univ Syd, 1968).

K. J. CABLE

MATTHEWS, HARLEY (1889-1968), writer, soldier and vigneron, was born on 27 April 1889 at St Leonards, Sydney, son of Henry Matthews, clerk, and his wife Edith, née Morgan, both born in New South Wales. Registered at birth as Harry Matthews, he grew up on his parents' vineyard at Fairfield and was educated at Sydney Boys' High School. After working as an articled clerk in 1906-14 he enlisted as a private in the 4th Battalion, Australian Imperial Force, on 13 September 1914. He took part in the landing at Gallipoli on 25 April 1915, was mentioned in dispatches and wounded early in August. After service in France, in August 1916 he was posted to the Australian Army Pay Corps

at A.I.F. Headquarters, London; repatriated towards the end of 1917, he was discharged on 29 December.

Matthews next pursued a career in journalism, at first on the Sydney *Sun*, and from 1920 freelance writing in the United States of America. On his return in 1922 he briefly rejoined the *Sun* but soon afterwards, disillusioned by both the law and journalism, decided to become a wine-grower. He had married on 3 March 1920 Barbara Sarah Filder Goode at the Registrar General's Office, Sydney, and they bought 57 acres (23 ha), on the Georges River at Moorebank, which Matthews proceeded to clear and plant with characteristic energy and determination. Once established, his vineyard quickly became a popular venue for a large group of mostly Bohemian 'writers, artists, eccentrics and spare-time philosophers' (to use Kenneth Slessor's description) who frequented it in search of good talk and good wine.

In 1912-38 Matthews published in Sydney three books of verse and a volume of short stories. In his first volume of verse, *Under the open sky* (1912), Matthews is the 'simple chorister' of the Australian bush and the teller of romantic tales. It was published in London in 1916 under the same title but with mainly new content; amid the poems of Nature and fantasy were a sprinkling of war poems, notably the love-lyric, 'The Mirror'. *Trio* (1931) displayed qualities of vigour, drama, realism, and technical freedom previously lacking. His contribution to this volume was the Gallipoli narrative 'Two Brothers' (one of the other two poems being Slessor's 'Five Visions of Captain Cook'). 'Two Brothers' reappeared in Matthews's next volume *Vintage* (1938), a collection of four Gallipoli narratives and four lyrics, republished as *Vintage of war* in 1940. His volume of twenty short stories, *Saints and soldiers* (1918), illustrating the typical traits and exploits of diggers during the war, is most successful when the tone is humorous.

His life changed radically during World War II. On 23 December 1940 he was granted a dissolution of marriage. Then, on 10 March 1942, by an ironic stroke of fate the patriotic Matthews was wrongfully arrested as a seditionist. The Gallipoli veteran, who in 1916 had served as model in London for Jacob Epstein's bronze head of the soldier epitomizing 'the spirit of Anzac' (now in the Imperial War Museum), found himself confined in an internment camp at the Anzac Rifle Range, Liverpool. He remained there without being charged or brought to trial, as a suspected member of the Australia First Movement, for six months. The 'grave blunder' made by military intelligence in detaining Matthews was not publicly acknowledged until 12 September 1945. The report of the Clyne royal commission into the Australia First Movement then found that Matthews 'was not a member' and was 'a loyal subject', and recommended that he be awarded £700 compensation.

From 1943 Matthews lived alone on a mixed farm at Ingleburn where he planted a small vineyard, entertained his many visitors, and continued to read and write poetry. His early poem, 'The Breaking of the Drought', was republished as a separate booklet in 1940, but no further volume appeared until *Patriot's progress* (Adelaide, 1965). This collection of mainly lyrical pieces, written over many years, expresses the author's independent spirit, love of the Australian countryside, and scorn for conformists, town-dwellers, materialists, and seekers after 'gain or power'. The style is frequently reminiscent, as Slessor observes, of 'that other farmer-poet Robert Frost'.

Matthews's other publications were a selection of short stories, *Wet canteen* (1939); *We are the people* (1940), a three-act play on the theme of snobbery and class-distinction in Australia; and *Pillar to post* (1944), a short-story anthology which he edited.

Matthews, described by Douglas Stewart as 'a small, dark, wiry man', died at the Repatriation Hospital, Concord, on 9 August 1968 and was cremated. He left no children.

B. Muirden, *The puzzled patriots* (Melb, 1968); P. Hasluck, *The government and the people, 1942-1945*, 2 (Canb, 1970); K. Slessor, *Bread and wine* (Syd, 1970); D. Stewart, *A man of Sydney* (Melb, 1977); *Smith's Weekly* (Syd), 22 Sept 1945; *Daily Telegraph* (Syd), 13 Aug 1968; M. Franklin papers (ML); K. Slessor papers (NL); copies of letters and other documents relating to internment (F940. 950901,ML); holograph and typed copies of poems (MSS 1953, 1214, ML).   J. T. LAIRD

MATTHEWS, SUSAN MAY (1877-1935), child welfare inspector, was born on 9 March 1877 at Glen Innes, New South Wales, daughter of Sydney-born parents John Joseph Matthews, saddler, and his wife Mary Frances, née Lynch. The family moved to Sydney about 1888. Known as May, she was employed as a lady's help when she first appeared on the electoral roll. She joined the public service as a temporary typist in the Registrar General's Office in 1911, became active in the Australian Clerical Association and was a delegate to the Labor Council of New South Wales and Labor Party conference.

From 1913 Matthews convened the standing committee on trades and professions for the National Council of Women of New South Wales. She was concerned about the low wages paid to women and the common practice of dismissing women on their becoming eligible for adult rates. As an executive member of the Women's Progressive Association she campaigned for the appointment of women to public office, to the police force, to juries, as magistrates, and for women to be eligible for election to parliament. She opposed conscription, helped to organize relief for strikers in 1917, and became president of the Labor Women's Central Organising Committee in 1918 but increasingly espoused independent political views.

May Matthews completed a five-year course in economics conducted for the Workers' Educational Association by Meredith Atkinson and R. F. Irvine [qq.v.7,9]. Appointed an inspector in the reorganized Child Welfare Department in 1916, she did the same work as male inspectors, covering truancy, probation, affiliation, placements and adoptions, until 1923 when women were debarred from country inspections. Among the first women gazetted justice of the peace in 1921, as an executive member of the Women's Justices' Association she renewed efforts to extend eligibility for jury service to women. When refused leave in 1924 for study overseas, she resigned. A temporary appointment as migration officer enabled her to study industrial conditions in England. She was reinstated on her return and in 1927, invited by the prime minister to be an observer with the Industrial Delegation to the United States of America, was granted leave of absence. She stressed in her report the range of employment opportunities opening for women in America and the recognition there of the importance of the health and welfare of workers.

Matthews had continued to convene the National Council of Women's standing committee while becoming an executive member of the New South Wales Housewives' Association. Recognition of the work of mothers by payment of child endowment, and improved conditions for housewives through labour-saving routines and electrical appliances were among the causes which she supported. She consistently argued for equal pay. Before the royal commission on the Child Welfare Department in 1934 she stated that women welfare-inspectors were disadvantaged professionally by exclusion from country tours of duty and that female wards were deprived of advice on sexual matters.

She was a foundation member of the local branch of the League of Nations Union, a member of the Sunshine Club and the Good Film League and a supporter of the Parks and Playground Movement. In 1932 she stood unsuccessfully as a Federal Labor candidate. She died of cancer on 26 June 1935 at Moore Park, and was buried in the Roman Catholic section of Botany cemetery. For most of her adult years she had lived with her parents and three siblings at Darlinghurst. The *Bulletin* said her work was her best monument but her fellow workers in child welfare contributed the headstone on her grave.

PP (Cwlth), 1926-28, 5, p 1110; National Council of Women (NSW), *Biennial Report*, 1913-14 - 1934; *Progressive J* (Syd), Aug 1935; *SMH*, 29 July 1920, 18 Jan, 26 Aug, 2 Sept 1927, 28 June 1935; *Aust Worker*, 3 July 1935; Evidence before roy com into child welfare dept (J. E. McCulloch, SM) (court reporting, 6/1780, NSWA).   LYN BRIGNELL
                                HEATHER RADI

MATTHIAS, ELIZABETH (1882-1963), socialist and charity-worker, was born on 30 December 1882 in Crown Street, Sydney, daughter of Richard Miles, van proprietor, and his wife Alice, née Eagar, both from Kerry, Ireland. When her mother died in 1895, Betsy went to school in New York, United States of America, where her father's seven siblings had settled. One of her uncles, John Miles, a silk merchant, gave $1 million for the investigation of Sing Sing Prison, and was made foreman of the board of investigation by President Woodrow Wilson. Two cousins, both radical attorneys, became senators.

Betsy returned to Sydney in 1900. By 1905 associating with members of the International Socialist Club, she later joined its offshoot, the Australian Socialist Party. She left the party in World War I, enraged by its reluctance to support the pregnant wife and four children of an imprisoned comrade. Donald Grant [q.v.9] introduced her to members of the Industrial Workers of the World, who immediately gave her £5 and started a systematic collection for the distressed family. Though never a member of the I.W.W., Betsy was the most energetic and successful collector of funds to sustain the families of the imprisoned 'Twelve', and of the 100-odd members serving short sentences under the War Precautions Act, including her husband Rudolph Hamilton Matthias, baker, whom she had married on 25 October 1915 at the Sydney Registry Office. Her only child was born in 1919. Betsy was prominent also in the defence and release campaigns around these imprisonments, and in the 'No' campaigns during the conscription referenda. She was assistant secretary-treasurer of the Industrial Labor Party of New South Wales, which was as hostile to parliamentary activity as the I.W.W., and in 1917-19 edited its fortnightly newspaper, *Solidarity*. Betsy travelled frequently to industrial centres through the State, and proved to be a militant and effective agitator. In her writing and speaking she always enjoined working-class women to fight alongside their menfolk, and working-class men to encourage the participation of women in the struggle to end the poverty and misery caused by capitalism.

In the 1920s, while retaining links with the I.W.W. remnants, Betsy turned her attentions to the Australian Labor Party, hoping 'to purify it', and the established trade union movement. By 1927 she was the Unemployed Workers' Union delegate to the Labor Council of New South Wales. Over the next few years, she was active in the One Big Union of Unemployed, the Labor Women's Central Organising Committee, and in strike support work, notably during the 1929 timber-workers' strike. In the 1930s she sheltered many refugees from Nazi Germany; managed a hostel for destitute women; and served on the Bankstown District Hospital's board. Every year from the mid-1920s she organized a children's Christmas tree and became 'one of Bankstown's best-known and controversial identities'.

In 1959 Betsy was appointed M.B.E. especially for her work as secretary of the Labor Women's welfare committee. Two months later she led a deputation of old-age pensioners to Canberra, to protest to the Menzies government at the level of pensions at the time of a salary increase for parliamentarians. She died on 26 August 1963 at her home at Peakhurst. Predeceased by her husband and daughter, she was survived by her ward Len Bradford. Her body was delivered to the University of Sydney's medical school, and was later cremated without clergy. Arthur Calwell wrote that her 'life was well-spent'; and former I.W.W. member Mick Sawtell recalled the Christmas dinner Betsy gave him in gaol in 1917. The Betsy Women's Refuge at Bankstown was named in her honour in 1975.

ALP women's diamond jubilee souvenir (Syd, 1964); *Labor Daily Year Book*, 1933, p 157; ALP, *J*, Sept 1963, p 18; *Solidarity* (Industrial Labour Party) (Syd), 5, 19 Jan, 15 June, 27 July 1918; *SMH*, 1 Jan 1959; *Bankstown Observer*, 14, 21, 28 Jan 1959, 18 Feb, 4 Mar 1959; *Torch* (Bankstown), 2 Aug 1963; N. Wheatley, The unemployed who kicked (M.A. thesis, Macquarie Univ, 1975); M. Dixson, Notes from an interview with Betsy Matthias in Mar 1963 (held by M. Dixson, UNE); Intelligence reports, Qld, Syd and Melb, CP 407/1 (AAO).   VERITY BURGMANN

MATTINGLEY, ARTHUR HERBERT EVELYN (1870-1950), photographer and ornithologist, was born on 11 July 1870 at North Melbourne, fourth child of English parents Albert Mattingley, headmaster, and his wife Mary Jane, née Hayman. His younger brother Harold Vernon (d. 1961) became a leading Melbourne dentist. Educated at his father's school in North Melbourne and at

Scotch College, Mattingley worked briefly as a tea-taster for Herbert Henty [q.v.4] in 1891 before joining the Customs Department. His interests in photography, ornithology and conservation began early and were maintained enthusiastically all his life.

A pioneer of Australian bird photography, Mattingley published his first photograph in 1903 and in 1909 won a gold medal at the International Photographic Exhibition at Dresden, Germany. Many of his photographs appeared in books by Robert Hall [q.v.9] and Charles Barrett [q.v.7], and in the *Emu* and the *Victorian School Paper*. He made his greatest impact as a photographer and conservationist with an illustrated article in the *Emu* (October 1907), 'Plundered for their plumes', exposing the cruelty of slaughtering egrets for the millinery trade. Sets of his photographs were exhibited in London shop windows, shown as lantern-slides and published in *Bird Notes and News* by the Royal Society for the Protection of Birds of which Mattingley was made an honorary life member in 1909.

A member of the Royal Australasian Ornithologists' Union from its inception, Mattingley held the offices of treasurer (1903-04), honorary secretary (1904-08), vice-president (1911-13) and president (1913-14). The camp-outs he organized included the first to Shearwater rookeries on Phillip Island in 1902; he suggested banding the birds there as early as 1912. In 1908 he led an expedition to the Bass Strait Islands and persuaded O. G. Perry [q.v.] to film seals and birds—'unlike anything yet seen in Melbourne'. He was elected a corresponding member of the Zoological Society of London in 1907 and a corresponding fellow of the American Ornithologists' Union in 1921.

Mattingley helped to form the Bird Observers' Club, Melbourne, in 1905; he was president in 1928 and was made a life member in 1935. He was a founder of the Gould [q.v.1] League of Bird Lovers of Victoria (president, 1933) and of the Victorian Advisory Council of Flora and Fauna. In 1947 he was made an honorary member of the Victorian Field Naturalists Club. He was a founder of the Wyperfeld National Park; Mount Mattingley, its highest point, is named after him. He was also a member of the committee of management of Wilson's Promontory National Park.

As well as publishing ornithological articles, Mattingley wrote on imaginative uses of water resources and on the education of children in conservation methods. He was on the council of Melbourne Boys' High School. After retiring from the Customs Department as officer-in-charge of overseas parcels post, in 1934 he led a two-month expedition through central and north-eastern Australia,

covering nearly 7000 miles (11 300 km). Photographs and articles testify to his great interest in the Aborigines for whom he advocated a system of segregation. His negatives and lantern-slides, donated to the Education Department of Victoria, are now held by the La Trobe Library, Melbourne.

A somewhat stern man, Mattingley was slight, 5 ft. 10 ins. (178 cm) tall, with dark hair and brown eyes. He died on 2 October 1950 at Prahran and was cremated. He was survived by his wife Zenobia Anne, née Fenton, whom he had married at St Mary's Church of England, North Melbourne, on 22 March 1910, and by three sons.

H. M. Whittell, *The literature of Australian birds* (Perth, 1954); P. Slater, *Masterpieces of Australian bird photography* (Adel, 1980); *Emu*, 7 (1907), pt 2, p 71, 9 (1909), pt 2, p 108, pt 3, p 179, 14 (1914), pt 3, p 121, 51 (1951), pt 1, p 85; *ANA Advocate*, May 1942; Bird Observers' Club, *Monthly Notes*, Sept 1945, Dec 1947, Dec 1950; *Herald* (Melb), 1 Sept 1934; *Townsville Daily Bulletin*, 29 Sept 1934; *Courier Mail*, 23 Oct 1934; *SMH*, 23 Oct 1934; *Age*, 20 Oct 1961; Mattingley family papers (held by Mr F. Mattingley, Glen Iris, Vic).

TESS KLOOT

MAUDSLEY, SIR HENRY CARR (1859-1944), physician, was born on 25 April 1859 at Stainforth, Settle, Yorkshire, England, son of Thomas Maudsley, farmer, and his wife Ann, née Annistead. Henry Maudsley (1835-1918), founder of the Maudsley Hospital for mental diseases at Denmark Hill, London, was his uncle.

Maudsley was educated at Giggleswick School, near Stainforth, and at University College, London, where he matriculated. In 1880 he obtained the diploma of M.R.C.S. and graduated M.B., B.S. in 1881 from the University of London with first-class honours in medicine and surgery and the gold medal in surgery. Appointed house physician and surgeon at University College Hospital in 1880, he was resident medical officer there in 1882-87. He obtained his M.D. in 1883 and his M.R.C.P. in 1884. In 1887, however, he was unsuccessful in an application to join the hospital staff and next year migrated to Melbourne where he was immediately appointed to the out-patient staff of the Alfred Hospital, becoming an in-patient physician in 1892. Keen to work in a teaching hospital, he stood next year for election as an out-patient physician at the (Royal) Melbourne Hospital but, unwilling to canvass, did not succeed. Friends helped him to win election as an indoor physician in 1903, the year after his election as fellow of the Royal College of Physicians of London.

In 1908-21 Maudsley was lecturer in theory and practice of medicine at the University of Melbourne. His eminence during this period was widely acknowledged. He was a vice-president of the section of medicine at the International Congress of Medicine held in London in 1912, acting *in absentia*, and in 1920 presided over the neurology and psychiatry section of the Australasian Medical Congress in Brisbane.

With the outbreak of war in 1914 Maudsley, an honorary major in the Australian Army Medical Corps Reserve from 1909, was appointed to the 1st Australian General Hospital, Australian Imperial Force, as senior physician with the rank of lieut-colonel. The hospital was established at Heliopolis early in 1915 and while based there Maudsley visited Gallipoli and Mudros to inspect the sick and wounded. In 1916 he was made consulting physician at A.I.F. Headquarters, London, and promoted colonel. With Colonel (Sir) Charles Ryan [q.v.] he served as a medical board to assess the fitness of officers and men for duty, refusing appointment with the British Expeditionary Force in France because he felt that his work was with the Australians. Mentioned in dispatches (1916) for valuable services, he was appointed C.M.G. in 1916 and C.B.E. and K.C.M.G. in 1919. That year he returned to Melbourne to resume private practice; he retired from the active staff of the Melbourne Hospital but remained consulting physician there and at St Vincent's Hospital, establishing a neurological and psychiatric clinic at the Melbourne Hospital in 1923.

Maudsley was frail looking with a quiet voice and a friendly, whimsical manner. He seemed to know everything and everybody in the Melbourne medical world, yet was extremely modest and self-effacing. He was not entirely successful as a teacher for his wide knowledge and extensive reading did not allow him to dogmatize; nevertheless his clinics were always popular and he established neurology as a clinical entity in Melbourne. He taught students to consider every fact and circumstance, including the patient's home life and social background, before making a diagnosis. He had a remarkable memory, never forgetting a student or patient, and was at his best on his daily rounds with his house physicians. As a private consultant he was clear and definite. Not a fluent orator, he spoke little at meetings and wrote less, but when necessary was fearless in expressing his strongly held opinions.

On 18 February 1890 at St Mary's Church of England, Caulfield, Maudsley had married Grace Elizabeth, sister of J. F. Stretch [q.v.]. Lady Maudsley was a foundation member of the Victoria League in Melbourne and an executive member of the National Council of Women. Her interest in education led to her membership of the committee of Janet Clarke

[q.v.3] Hall, University of Melbourne, where, after her death in January 1933, the Grace Maudsley prize was founded by friends.

In his student days Maudsley had been a skilled mountaineer and for years he enjoyed an occasional climb in the Healesville district. In 1934, when taking his evening walk along Alexandra Avenue, South Yarra, he was hit by a car and sustained a cerebral injury which made him a complete invalid. He died in Melbourne on 5 March 1944 and was cremated. His daughter and his son Henry Fitzgerald (1891-1962), awarded the Military Cross in World War I and a prominent Melbourne neurologist, survived him.

Who's who in the world of women, 1 (Melb, 1930); *Lives of the fellows of the Royal College of Physicians of London 1826-1925*, 4 (Lond, 1955); A. M. Mitchell, *The hospital south of the Yarra* (Melb, 1977); A. G. Butler (ed), *Official history of the Australian Army Medical Services . . . 1914-18*, 1 (Melb, 1930); *British Medical J*, 1944, 1, p 437, 575; *MJA*, 29 Apr 1944, p 402; Roy Melb Hospital, *Clinical Reports*, 15 (1944), p 1; *Argus*, 7 Mar 1944.
K. F. RUSSELL

MAUGER, SAMUEL (1857-1936), social reformer, was born on 12 November 1857 at Geelong, Victoria, son of Samuel Mauger, carpenter and his wife Caroline, née Liz, both from Guernsey, Channel Islands. Young Samuel was educated at the Geelong National school, but left to be a hatter's errand boy when his father was struck down by rheumatic fever. In 1874, carrying character references, a Bible and *A young man's guide to immortality through life*, he sought work in Melbourne and was apprenticed to a hatter in 1876.

Mauger (pronounced Major) developed as an organizer and public speaker as superintendent of a Rechabite tent and as a Bible-class teacher at St Mark's Church of England, Fitzroy. There he met Hannah Rice whom he married on 13 May 1880. He was later Sunday school superintendent at St Paul's Congregational Church, North Fitzroy.

Mauger organized and became superintendent of volunteer fire brigades, convening a conference in 1883 to form an association. As its president he helped to draft the basis of the 1891 Fire Brigades Act. A government representative on the Metropolitan Fire Brigades Board in 1891-1936 and four times president, he contributed much to securing for firemen weekly and annual leave, promotion by merit and a superannuation scheme. He was sometime president and Trades Hall Council delegate of the Hatters' Union, and took a close interest in the clothing trades, assisting in the organization of the Tailoresses' Union. These enthusiasms did not wane when he went into business as a hatter at Fitzroy in 1889.

In 1892 Mauger was an unsuccessful Progressive Political League candidate for Fitzroy, but Labor's pledge later proved an insuperable barrier to his joining the party. Successively, he became secretary of the Protection, Liberal and Federation League from 1893, of the Protectionist Association which the league created in 1894, and of the National Anti-Sweating League of Victoria from 1895. No one did more to create and sustain Victoria's anti-sweating movement. During 1893 he led the P.L.F.L. in demanding amendment of the Factories and Shops Act, urged the case in a deputation to Premier Patterson [q.v.5], was the principal speaker at the Wesley Church public conference, and became secretary to the Methodist Central Mission's investigative committee. Mauger accompanied Rev. Charles Strong [q.v.6] on his inspections of homes where sweating was rife, and gave evidence to the Factories Act Inquiry Board of 1893-94.

In 1895 he arranged the inaugural meeting of the Anti-Sweating League and became secretary. The league's committee met above Mauger's hat shop at 66 Bourke Street. With H. H. Champion [q.v.7] he drafted the Factories and Shops Act (1896) and campaigned for an extension of the wages-boards system beyond the original six sweated trades and for adoption of minimum wage principles by municipalities and statutory authorities. The term, New Protection, was coined at his shop in 1899, and popularized by Mauger at interstate protectionist conferences in 1900-01: 'unless protection went further than the Customs House, and protected the wages, the homes, and the lives of the people, it was not worth the name'.

In 1899 (at his fourth attempt) Mauger was elected as a Liberal at a by-election for Footscray and became secretary to Sir George Turner's [q.v.] Opposition. He was returned unopposed for Footscray in 1900, and for the Federal seat of Melbourne Ports in 1901. In parliament he advocated high protection and immigration restriction, for which he argued in A white man's world (Melbourne, 1901). He secured minimum wage rates and maximum hours clauses in Federal government contracts, and weekly leave for government employees. Victorian Legislative Council resistance to expansion of the wages-boards system confirmed Mauger as a radical and independent Protectionist. With J. Hume Cook [q.v.8] he led the citizens' committee of 1903-04 to aid railway engine drivers dismissed by Premier Irvine [q.v.9] and attempted to gain their reinstatement. Supporting Federal Labor's attempts to extend the conciliation and arbitration bill to State employees, he joined the radical Liberal alliance with Labor in 1904, but in 1905 declined Deakin's [q.v.8] offer of the position of Liberal whip.

He was a member of the committee of management of Strong's Social Improvement Society in 1897, chairman from 1905, and chairman of the Young People's Guild from 1899. Despite this close association with the Australian Church and an abiding loyalty to Strong, Mauger's evangelicalism remained firm. By the early 1900s he was emphasizing individual salvation and the strengthening of the family as much as state socialism as the keys to social regeneration. President of the Melbourne Total Abstinence Society and of the Victorian Alliance, and a leading Rechabite, Mauger argued in parliament for 'dry' military canteens, and for prohibition in Papua. He took a prominent part in W. H. Judkins's [q.v.9] 1905-06 crusade against liquor and gambling in Victoria, and despite John Wren's [q.v.] campaign against him won the new seat of Maribyrnong. As postmaster-general (1907-08) in the Deakin ministry, after being honorary minister in 1906-07, he closed the mail and telephone services to purveyors of indecent literature, 'quack' medicines and lottery tickets, and to tote operators.

Mauger backed the campaign by the implement-maker H. V. McKay [q.v.] for protection against cheap, American stripper-harvesters, but the excise tariff device to ensure fair and reasonable wages in the industry failed. Previously Mauger had argued for a constitutional amendment to provide for uniform Commonwealth industrial laws, but in 1909 he joined the Fusion which opposed such a course. The result, as Mauger put it, was a 'knockout' by his Labor opponent J. E. Fenton [q.v.8] in 1910. Living on a handsome testimonial from admirers, he lectured to enthusiastic temperance audiences in Britain in 1911 where appalling poverty, drinking and industrial violence confirmed his principles. He wrote to Deakin of Labor hostility to Liberals, 'The more you do for them "the hotter they go for you"', but upon his return he found that Labor distrust was weaker than conservative and freetrader loathing of him as a dangerous radical. Mauger unsuccessfully contested the Senate in 1913 and 1914.

He was involved in the Victorian six o'clock closing movement in 1911, and was secretary of the successful 1916 campaign. His interest in prisons and prisoner rehabilitation found expression in membership of the Howard League and the Criminology Society, and in chairmanship (1912-36) of the Victorian Indeterminate Sentences Board. In 1914-15 he was chairman of the Melbourne unemployment relief committee. As well, the Child Welfare Association, the Gordon Institute, the Workers' Educational Association of Victoria, the Young Men's Christian Association and the United Friendly Societies claimed his time. During the 1920s he chaired several wages boards and in 1931 was vice-president of a revived Anti-Sweating League.

Increasing deafness, family illness and business reverses did not hamper his public duties. Mauger died on 26 June 1936 at Elsternwick and was buried in Melbourne general cemetery, with a fireman guard of honour, after a service conducted by Strong. His wife and six children survived him.

The *Age* remarked that 'scarcely a movement of any importance in Victoria to improve the average human lot and to secure a greater measure of social justice did not gain in coherence and strength from his influence'. *Labor Call* said that Mauger represented 'the finest type that Liberalism could produce'. Memorials were raised at Eastern Hill and Footscray, and in the Australian Church.

C. R. Badger, *The Rev. Charles Strong and the Australian Church* (Melb, 1971); J. Rickard, *Class and politics* (Canb, 1976); *Rechabite and Temperance News*, 1 Aug 1936; *Punch* (Melb), 10 Mar 1910; *Age* and *Argus*, 27, 29, 30 June 1936; F. H. Cutler, A history of the anti-sweating movement in Victoria, 1873-1896 (M.A. thesis, Univ Melb, 1956); E. M. Wilson, The campaign for national righteousness. The Methodist Church and moral reform in Victoria 1900-1916 (B.A. Hons thesis, Univ Melb, 1957); M. R. Parnaby, The socially reforming churchman: a study of the social thought and activity of Charles Strong in Melbourne 1890-1900 (B.A. Hons thesis, Univ Melb, 1975); Deakin *and* Hume-Cook *and* Groom *and* Aust Industries Protection League *and* Mauger *and* Strong papers (NL); Merrifield collection (LaTL). JOHN LACK

MAUGHAN, SIR DAVID (1873-1955), barrister, was born on 5 February 1873 at Paddington, Sydney, elder son of John Maughan, Scottish-born bank clerk, and his Sydney-born wife Bertha Windeyer, née Thompson, granddaughter of Charles Windeyer [q.v.2]. Educated at The King's School, Parramatta, he was school captain and won the Broughton and Forrest exhibition. On 20 October 1891 he matriculated at Balliol College, Oxford (B.A., 1895; M.A., 1912; B.C.L., 1912). He gained first-class honours in the B.C.L. examination in 1896 ahead of F. E. Smith (Lord Birkenhead) and (Sir) William Holdsworth. (Viscount) Simon and L. S. Amery were also fellow students. That year he tutored in law at Balliol.

Called to the Bar of Lincoln's Inn on 17 June 1896, Maughan returned to Sydney, was admitted to the New South Wales Bar on 18 November and read with (Sir) Langer Owen [q.v.]. His income rose rapidly from £42 in his first year of practice to over £300 two years later. At St Mark's Church, Darling Point, he married Jean Alice, daughter of Sir Edmund Barton [q.v.7], on 30 March 1909. They lived at Woollahra.

Although at first practising almost entirely in Equity, Maughan became expert in constitutional law and in 1919 was appointed K.C. He was an acting justice of the Supreme Court in 1924 and 1936-37. On 27 January 1926 he wrote to Amery, secretary of state for the dominions, asking him to intervene in the 'extraordinary and revolutionary' attempt by Premier J. T. Lang [q.v.9] to abolish the Legislative Council. Amery refused; however, this effort by Lang failed. When in 1930 the council passed Lang's bills to abolish it, Maughan offered his services gratis to the anti-abolition councillors led by (Sir) Arthur Trethowan [q.v.]; he obtained a declaration by the Supreme Court that the bills could not lawfully be presented for assent until approved at a referendum. He was counsel for Trethowan in appeals to the High Court of Australia and Privy Council, successfully defending the Legislative Council, and in 1934, before the Privy Council, the insertion into the Constitution of a new procedure for settling deadlocks between the Houses.

Long opposed to proposals to fuse law and equity and to amalgamate the two branches of the legal profession, Maughan publicly attacked the administration of justice bill in 1931. He often wrote to and for the *Sydney Morning Herald*. A council-member of the State branch of the Australian Institute of International Affairs in 1933-41, he consistently opposed adoption of the Statute of Westminster. Owen had interested him in the corporate organization of the Bar: he served on the Council of the Bar of New South Wales in 1914-19 and in 1936, and was a foundation council-member of the Bar Association and several times a member of the Barristers' Admission Board.

As president of the Law Council of Australia from 1941, Maughan described the use of the regulation-making power under the National Security Act as 'Star Chamber laws'. Strongly committed to civil and States' rights, he consistently opposed big government, even during World War II. He appeared before the High Court in important constitutional cases, including the uniform tax case in 1942 and the airlines case in 1945, but, although holding a retainer from the Bank of New South Wales, he stood aside in 1947 for (Sir) Garfield Barwick to lead the fight against the nationalization of the trading banks. He was knighted in 1951.

Maughan was a keen cross-country walker, mountaineer, surfer and golfer. He was a vice-president of the New South Wales Rowing Association and of the Rugby Union, and a member of Royal Sydney Golf Club. He was also a governor of The King's School, chairman of the Free Library Council and the Big Brother Movement, a director of Royal Prince Alfred Hospital and a member of the Australian Club.

Survived by his wife, son and daughter, Maughan died in Royal Prince Alfred Hospital on 3 November 1955 and was cremated with Anglican rites. His estate was valued for probate at £31 365.

Cyclopedia of NSW (Syd, 1907); J. M. Bennett (ed), *A history of the New South Wales Bar* (Syd, 1969); D. Marr, *Barwick* (Syd, 1980); *Aust Law J*, vol 29, 17 Nov 1955; *SMH*, 14 May, 28, 29 July, 9 Aug 1931, 12 May 1941, 4 May 1943, 1, 19 May 1944, 30 Apr, 2 June 1945, 15 Mar, 29 Apr 1946, 1 Jan 1951, 8 Feb, 4 Nov 1955; Maughan fee-books and papers (ML).   ANTHONY FISHER

MAURICE, FURNLEY; *see* WILMOT, FRANK

MAWSON, SIR DOUGLAS (1882-1958), geologist and explorer, was born on 5 May 1882 at Shipley, Yorkshire, England, second son of Robert Ellis Mawson, a cloth merchant from a farming background, and his wife Margaret Ann, née Moore, from the Isle of Man. The family moved to Rooty Hill, near Sydney, in 1884. Douglas was educated at Rooty Hill and at Fort Street Model School in Sydney. At the University of Sydney in 1899-1901 he studied mining engineering and graduated B.E. in 1902 when he was appointed as a junior demonstrator in chemistry. Next year he took six months leave to make a geological survey of the New Hebrides (Vanuatu), under the auspices of Captain E. G. Rason, the British deputy commissioner there. This was Mawson's introduction to scientific exploration, carried out in rugged country with dense jungle and among hostile inhabitants. His report, 'The geology of the New Hebrides', was one of the first major works on the geology of Melanesia.

He returned to further studies in geology in 1904 (B.Sc., 1905), having already published a paper (1903) on the geology of Mittagong, New South Wales, with T. Griffith Taylor [q.v.] and one (1904) on radioactive minerals in Australia, with T. H. Laby [q.v.9], in addition to several on the New Hebrides.

Through the early influence of Professor A. Liversidge [q.v.5], Mawson became a pioneer in the chemical aspects of geology and geochemistry. But the dominant influence was that of Professor (Sir) Edgeworth David [q.v.8], foremost among workers in the geological sciences in Australia.

In 1905 Mawson was appointed lecturer in mineralogy and petrology in the University of Adelaide. He immediately became interested in the glacial geology of South Australia. Also, continuing his interest in radioactivity, he identified and first described the mineral davidite, containing titanium and uranium, in specimens from the region now known as Radium Hill. That deposit was the first major radioactive ore body discovered in Australia.

The major work of his early South Australian period was his investigation of the highly mineralized Precambrian rocks of the Barrier Range, extending from the northern Flinders Ranges through Broken Hill, New South Wales. The country is a complex of metamorphosed, igneous and sedimentary rocks with varying degrees of mineralization. Mawson identified two groups: an older Archaean (Willyama) Series, and a newer, Proterozoic (Torrowangee) Series. This investigation led to publication of his 'Geological investigations in the Broken Hill area'; he had previously submitted the substance of this work to the University of Adelaide (D.Sc., 1909).

In November 1907 (Sir) Ernest Shackleton, leader of the British Antarctic Expedition, visited Adelaide on his way south. Mawson approached him with a view to making the round trip to Antarctica on the *Nimrod*. His idea was to see an existing continental ice-cap and to become acquainted with glaciation and its geological consequences. This interested him because in his South Australian studies he was 'face-to-face with a great accumulation of glacial sediments of Precambrian age, the greatest thing of the kind recorded anywhere in the world'. After consulting with David, who had agreed to join the expedition, Shackleton telegraphed: 'You are appointed Physicist for the duration of the expedition'. Mawson accepted, and so began his long association with the Antarctic.

Although he recognized that Shackleton's prime aim of reaching the South Pole was considered essential to financing the expedition, he would have liked more opportunity offered to the scientists. Nevertheless, the scientists' achievements proved to be considerable and Mawson had good opportunities for glaciological and geological investigations; he published significant accounts of his observations on the aurora and geomagnetism.

In March 1908 Mawson was one of the first party, led by David, to climb Mount Erebus. Next summer David (leader), A. F. Mackay and Mawson were the first to reach the vicinity of the South Magnetic Pole, manhauling their sledges 1260 miles (2030 km); Mawson was responsible for the magnetic observations and the excellent cartographic work. The return was difficult because of exhaustion and shortage of food. David, aged 50, suffered badly and at his request Mawson assumed leadership. The journey almost ended in disaster: having reached their main depot two days late and hearing a rocket distress signal fired from the *Nimrod*, Mawson, while rushing towards the ship, fell into a crevasse. Help from the ship was required for his rescue.

Shackleton's confidence in Mawson may be gauged from his instructions: should his own expedition to the South Pole not return in time, Mawson was to lead a search party. David said in public tribute: 'Mawson was the real leader who was the soul of our expedition to the Magnetic Pole. We really have in him an Australian Nansen, of infinite resource, splendid physique, astonishing indifference to frost'.

Mawson returned to Adelaide and his university post in 1909 but was still making reports on the expedition when his plans for further Antarctic work began to mature. Captain R. F. Scott was planning his second (1910-13) expedition and Mawson asked him for transport on the *Terra Nova* for himself and three others, to form an additional party of the expedition to be landed on the coast west of Cape Adare. Mawson expounded the potential scientific value of the proposed work but Scott was not persuaded. Instead he invited Mawson to join his South Pole sledging party. This did not interest Mawson, who was dedicated to scientific exploration. Mawson then approached Shackleton for help; he took over Mawson's plan as his own but failed to get adequate financial backing. Mawson waited until Scott had raised all the funds he could in Australia and New Zealand, and had sailed for Antarctica in 1910, before launching his own appeal for support of what was to be the Australasian Antarctic Expedition.

With substantial private and government backing and a prodigious effort on Mawson's part in planning, organizing, recruiting personnel, and acquiring equipment and supplies the A.A.E., including C. T. Madigan [q.v.], sailed in December 1911. Three bases were established: one at Macquarie Island which, apart from its scientific work, was to serve as a radio relay station; Main Base under Mawson at Commonwealth Bay (Scott having landed his second party at Cape Adare); and Western Base on the Shackleton Ice Shelf under Frank Wild. At each base, and in expeditions from them, major scientific investigation was pursued in geology, cartography, meteorology, aurora, geomagnetism and biology. Also, an extensive programme of marine science was carried out from the *Aurora* under Captain J. K. Davis [q.v.8].

At Commonwealth Bay building was largely completed by February 1912 and the scientific programme well established before winter set in. This included preparations for the several land expeditions of the following summer. Mawson took charge of the Far

Eastern expedition, which included B. E. S. Ninnis and X. Mertz, but was to become the most extraordinary epic of lone survival. When 310 miles (500 km) out, Ninnis, with sledge and dog team, broke through the lid of a large crevasse and disappeared. With seriously depleted provisions Mawson and Mertz began their return, progressively using their dogs to supplement their food supply. It was not known then that the dogs' livers were very rich in Vitamin A and potentially toxic. After twenty-five days on the return journey, and the combined effects of hard physical exertion and starvation, this toxicity may have hastened Mertz's death. Mawson, himself seriously debilitated, discarded everything that was not essential for survival, except his geological specimens and records of the journey. Using a pocket saw, he cut his sledge in half and dragged it unaided the last 100 miles (160 km), taking another thirty days to reach Main Base. As he approached he saw the *Aurora* on the horizon; she had come and gone. A small party had waited to search for him; they remained for another year. The scientific work at Main Base and Macquarie Island continued through 1913.

While recuperating, Mawson began writing his account of the expedition. *The home of the blizzard* (London, 1915), profusely illustrated by the magnificent photographs of Frank Hurley [q.v.9], is a classic of polar literature and described the first major scientific exploring venture by Australians beyond their shores.

Mawson was helped by other eminent scientists to analyse and report on the data collected; but so great was the task that publication of the A.A.E. *Scientific Reports*, in twenty-two volumes edited by him, was not completed until 1947. A.A.E. land parties had explored some 4000 miles (6400 km) in Adelie Land, King George V Land and Queen Mary Land. They outlined the geology of the country traversed and described the nature of the land and the coast between longitudes 90 degrees E and 155 degrees E and at Macquarie Island. They identified the characteristic feature of the Antarctic continental shelf: the bottom at first deepens on passing out from the shore, then shoals again before plunging to deep water beyond the edge of the shelf. New biological species, on land and at sea, were described. They recorded meteorological data simultaneously at the three bases; they maintained continuous geomagnetic field records at Commonwealth Bay for eighteen months and made further field observations to define more precisely the location of the Magnetic Pole; they systematically observed the aurora australis. The first to use radio in the Antarctic, they transmitted meteorological data to the weather bureau in Melbourne every day for two years from Macquarie Island and, during part of that time, from Commonwealth Bay also. The use of radio facilitated the accurate determination of longitude at Commonwealth Bay. It also enabled the transmission to Australia of Mawson's account of his tragic Far Eastern journey.

J. Gordon Hayes's assessment in 1928 has stood the test of time:

> Sir Douglas Mawson's Expedition, judged by the magnitude both of its scale and of its achievements, was the greatest and most consummate expedition that ever sailed for Antarctica. The expeditions of Scott and Shackleton were great, and Amundsen's venture was the finest Polar reconnaissance ever made; but each of these must yield the premier position, when fairly compared with Mawson's magnificently conceived and executed scheme of exploration . . . Its excellence lay in its design, its scope and its executive success; and [in its origin and conduct] by scientists of administrative ability . . . Mawson's was the first British [sic] Expedition which had clearly passed beyond the novitiate stage in Antarctic exploration, previously so painfully evident.

But in discussing the loss of Ninnis and consequent death of Mertz, Hayes is critical that they did not use skis. In fact Mertz was scouting ahead on skis; for Mawson and Ninnis, who were manoeuvring heavy sledges, this would have been difficult much of the time. In the event they made an error of judgement.

Mawson was knighted in 1914. In 1915 he applied to serve in a scientific capacity in World War I, and in May 1916 he was attached to the British Ministry of Munitions. He became embarkation officer for shipments of high explosives and poison gas from Britain to Russia. Later, working for the Russian Military Commission, he investigated and reported on production in Britain in order to increase output of high explosives in Russia itself. After the revolution he was transferred to the British staff of the Commission Internationale de Ravitaillement, concerned with the maintenance of supplies of high explosives, chemicals, poison gas and petroleum oil products; he held the military rank of major. In 1920 he was appointed O.B.E. After the war, until 1923, he was a committee-member of the Australian War Museum (Australian War Memorial).

Mawson returned to the University of Adelaide in 1919 and was appointed professor of geology and mineralogy in 1921. He successfully developed an effective teaching and research department, insisting on student involvement in geological field-work. His own research covered a wide scope and continued vigorously until his retirement. He made major contributions to the knowledge of Australian geology. His main interest during the

next thirty years was the 'Adelaide System' of Precambrian rocks, especially in the Flinders Ranges. He concentrated on Proterozoic stratigraphy and Precambrian glaciation, showing that glacial beds extended for 930 miles (1500 km) and that glacial conditions existed intermittently over much of Proterozoic time. His interests also included the geochemistry of igneous and metamorphic rocks, the geological significance of algae, the origin of carbonaceous sediments and the identification of the rarer minerals. His stature enabled him to draw widely on the assistance of specialists around the world in describing rocks and fossils collected in Australia and Antarctica.

Mawson's extensive field-work was carried out on foot, by horse-and-cart, camel, and with motor vehicles. He was usually accompanied by students, who learned not only about geology but also about camping and survival in the bush, an activity which Mawson always enjoyed.

As a result of his initiatives, the support of the Australian National Research Council, and the backing of the Australian government which resulted from a decision of the Imperial Conference of 1926, Mawson was invited to organize and lead the British, Australian and New Zealand Antarctic Research Expedition of 1929-30 and 1930-31. This expedition used the ship *Discovery* and did not establish land bases. They made extensive geological and biological investigations at Iles Crozet, Iles Kerguelen, Heard Island and at many points along the 1550 miles (2500 km) of coastline of Antarctica between 43 degrees E and 179 degrees E longitude. They were greatly assisted by the use of a small aircraft. Much of the coast was mapped for the first time and it was shown to be continuous from the Ross Sea to Enderby Land and beyond. This work provided accurate geographic data that supported the Australian Antarctic Territory Acceptance Act of 1933. The Act came into force in 1936 and, by arrangement with the British government, established the Australian Antarctic Territory.

But the main occupation of the expedition was marine science, which included extensive oceanographic work and marine biological sampling. Over the next fifty years detailed examination of the various species collected was carried out by specialists all over the world and their results described in the thirteen volumes of the B.A.N.Z.A.R.E. *Scientific Reports.* (Sir) Grenfell Price gives a cautious evaluation:

> Although future generations may continue to afford a high place to the gallant men of several nations who reached the South Pole, or who died in the attempt or achievement, they will, I think, pay increasing honour to the man

who, of all southern explorers, gave the world the greatest contributions in south polar science and his own people the greatest territorial possessions in the Antarctic.

Mawson's interest in Antarctica continued after World War II when he promoted the Australian National Antarctic Research Expeditions; he was a member of the Australian Antarctic Executive Planning Committee until he died.

Apart from geology and Antarctica, Mawson cultivated a broad range of interests including conservation, farming and forestry. He was a persistent advocate of decimal measures, a supporter of strict regulation of the whaling industry, and was influential in having Macquarie Island declared a sanctuary. Mawson owned and worked a small farm, which he named Harewood, at Meadows, south of Adelaide, and he was a founder and, for over thirty years, a director of S.A. Hardwoods Pty Ltd.

He retired at 70. That year the university published a volume of contributions to geology titled *Sir Douglas Mawson anniversary volume* and named the new geology building after him. The Mawson Institute for Antarctic Research was established within the University of Adelaide in 1959. Its library incorporates Mawson's collection of polar literature, his Antarctic diaries, a substantial collection of papers, correspondence, photographic records and objects of historical importance. In 1983 the Douglas Mawson chair of geology was created.

Numerous biological species and geographical places have been named in his honour, among them Mawson Coast and Mawson, the first permanent Australian station, established in 1954, in Antarctica. His image has appeared on several Australian postage stamps and on the $100 note.

He was a fellow of the Royal Society from 1923, a foundation fellow of the Australian Academy of Science, and president of the Australian and New Zealand Association for the Advancement of Science in 1935-37. Numerous honours and awards included: two Italian decorations, the Royal Geographical Society's Antarctic (1908) and Founders' (1915) medals, Polar medals, gold medals of the geographical societies of America, Chicago, Paris and Berlin, the von Mueller [q.v.5] medal of A.N.Z.A.A.S., and the Verco [q.v.] and Clarke [q.v.3] medals of the Royal societies of South Australia and New South Wales. In 1979 the Australian Academy of Science established the Mawson lecture. As part of the celebrations of the centenary of Mawson's birth in 1982, the Fourth International Symposium on Antarctic Earth Science was held at the University of Adelaide and the proceedings were dedicated to his memory.

The A.A.E. and B.A.N.Z.A.R.E. were important events in Australian history, and Mawson was one of the most outstanding explorers of this century. But he was first and foremost a scientist, dedicated to the advancement of his subject and the encouragement of his students. He did not propound new, fundamental theories but he extended and developed geological thinking and knowledge over a wide range of topics and locations, and through his leadership created opportunities for the realization of major developments in many disciplines. His lectures about Antarctica were widely acclaimed around the world. As a lecturer to undergraduates his reputation varies, but his inspiration is universally acclaimed. His infectious enthusiasm and friendliness were appreciated by students and colleagues. He was physically impressive, tall and strong but, more significantly, he was courageous, kind and noble. He ranks high among our national heroes.

Mawson had married, on 31 March 1914 at Holy Trinity Church, Balaclava, Melbourne, Francisca Adriana (Paquita) (1891-1974), daughter of G. D. Delprat [q.v.8]; they had two daughters. Lady Mawson was tall and stately and they made a striking couple in the social life of Adelaide and of the university. She wrote biographies of her father (1958) and of her husband (1964).

Mawson died at his Brighton home on 14 October 1958 following cerebral haemorrhage. He was accorded a Commonwealth state funeral and was buried at St Jude's Anglican Church, Brighton. A memorial service, arranged by the university, was held at St Peter's Cathedral, Adelaide.

Portraits of Mawson by W. Seppelt (1922), H. J. Haley (1933), Jack Carington Smith (1955) and Ivor Hele (1956) are held in the University of Adelaide; and by Ivor Hele (1959) in the Royal Geographic Society, London. Bronze busts by John Dowie (1982) are in North Terrace, Adelaide, and at Mawson, Antarctica, and by Jean Perrier (1980) in Canterbury Museum, New Zealand.

J. G. Hayes, *Antarctica* (Lond, 1928); A. G. Price, *The winning of Australian Antarctica* (Syd, 1962); P. Mawson, *Mawson of the Antarctic* (Lond, 1964); Roy Soc SA, *Trans*, 82 (1959) for list of Mawson's publications; *SMH*, 31 Mar 1909.

F. J. JACKA

MAXTED, SYDNEY (1845-1907), journalist and public servant, and EDWARD (1855-1902), charity worker, were born on 15 December 1845 in Sydney and on 30 September 1855 at Newcastle, New South Wales, eldest and fourth sons of George Maxted, English-born printer, and his Australian-born wife Martha, née Spencer. Their father published two short-lived newspapers at Newcastle and Maitland before establishing the *Newcastle Pilot* of which Sydney was co-proprietor from 1868. His polemical journalism led to a damaging libel action and after his father's death in 1871 the family lost control of the *Pilot*. Sydney married a widow Sophia Ann Richardson, née Gibb, at Newcastle on 15 June 1874. He was appointed master at the Protestant Orphan School, Parramatta, in 1878. The inspector of charities commended the 'pleasantly confidential relations' between officers and children and in 1881 Maxted became chief inspector and boarding out officer to the new State Children Relief Board. Sophia, after acting as matron, became a salaried officer of the board in 1884.

Sydney Maxted was largely responsible for successfully implementing the board's policy of fostering out orphaned or destitute children in institutions. He campaigned for legislative reforms directed to saving infant life, especially of children born illegitimate: under the Children's Protection Act of 1892 the private arrangements for the care of these children were brought under state control and the board's officers secured improved procedures for establishing paternal responsibility. From 1888 Maxted was also director of government asylums for the infirm (later director of charitable institutions), but had little success in obtaining funds for a rebuilding programme.

Edward had experience as a printer and in journalism. He was appointed manager of the Benevolent Society of New South Wales in 1884, and on 11 November 1885 married Anne Elizabeth Cottle at Darlinghurst. In press articles and in a series of special reports to the Benevolent Society he publicized the hardships experienced by the destitute and especially the unwed mother. Though he consistently ignored the medical and nutritional factors behind the high death rate for illegitimate children, his use of Benevolent Society records helped to confer credibility on the campaign against 'baby-farming' and was important to the passage of the Children's Protection Act.

The brothers looked to more systematic administration of charity and firmer action where family members were in a position to help. They neither believed in separating old couples in asylums nor in removing children to a foster home if a widowed mother was destitute. The State Children Relief Board had no statutory powers to pay the fostering out allowance to a child's own mother. Edward used the Benevolent Society provision of rent allowances to help such women; when the practice was well entrenched amending legislation in 1896 empowered the board to pay widows in need a small weekly sum to keep their children.

That the state had direct responsibility where the family could not help was the principle which the brothers advocated. Hence they looked to the extension of the state's authority and the bringing under state control of the work of private charities. The invitation to Sydney to attend the first Australasian Conference on Charity in 1890 evidences the respect for their work. At the second conference Sydney presented a scheme for appointing charity commissioners with overriding authority. The influence of the Charity Organization Society is apparent but his scheme was distinguished by the proposal that the state should become the co-ordinating authority.

With increasing demands on the Benevolent Society during the depressed 1890s, Edward stepped up publicity. Several pamphlets were published and in 1895-97 the *Charities Gazette* was sold door to door by the society's collectors. Sydney's evidence before the select committee on old-age pensions, 1896, largely foreshadowed the scheme later adopted. He opposed a contributory scheme as those most in need of pensions would not be able to maintain contributions; if means-tested, pensions would not depress wages; many men at 60 found difficulty finding work.

Both brothers had been in ill health for some time. Edward retired in 1901 and died at his Paddington residence on 30 May 1902, following collapse of his liver and kidneys, and was buried in the Anglican section of Waverley cemetery. His wife and son survived him. From 1892 Sydney was in mounting financial difficulties, having lost in a mining investment, and resorted to borrowing at high rates of interest; the dishonouring of a bill precipitated early retirement in 1897. His wife Sophia lost her position when he went into bankruptcy next year. Both were well regarded among officers of the board, who lent money to Sydney and spoke regretfully of Sophia's dismissal. Sydney mortgaged his pension to pay off the debt, living in penury and suffering from angina until he died on 10 July 1907. His wife, son and two daughters survived him. By their moves to document carefully the condition of the poor, the brothers had made a small but important contribution to the intellectual foundations of the welfare state.

Select cttee on the infants' and children's protection bills, Report, procs and minutes of evidence, *J*(LC NSW), 1891-92, 49, p 1067; Director of charitable institutions, Report, 1892, *V&P* (LA NSW), 1893, 2; Select cttee on aged pensions, 1896, *V&P* (LA NSW), 1896, 5; State Children Relief Bd, *Annual Report*, 1881-97; Benevolent Soc of NSW, *Annual Report*, 1884-1901; A'sian conference on charities, *Procs*, 1891, 1892; *Charities Gazette*, 1895-97; *SMH*, 14 Oct 1890, 12 Feb 1891, 9 Mar, 22 July 1892, 1 Oct 1895; *T&CJ*, 7 June 1902; *Bulletin*, 18 July 1907; B. K. Dickey, Charity in N.S.W. 1850-1914: a study in public, private and state provisions for the poor (Ph. D. thesis, ANU, 1968); J. D. Moody, The development of the newspaper press in Newcastle 1855-1880, and its social and political attitudes (M. A. thesis, Univ Newcastle, 1971); Select cttee on children's protection bill, Report and minutes of evidence, 1892 *and* bankruptcy file, 13030 (NSWA). HEATHER RADI

MAXWELL, GEORGE ARNOT (1859-1935), barrister and politician, was born on 30 April 1859 at Montrose, Forfarshire, Scotland, second of five sons of David Skinner Maxwell, Presbyterian minister, and his wife Margaret, née Arnot. He attended school in Fifeshire until 14 before migrating with his parents in 1875 when his father was appointed to South Yarra, Melbourne. George was briefly a jackeroo near Broken Hill, New South Wales, but after a sickly childhood was unsuited to outback life. In 1876-79 he was a clerk in the Flinders Lane warehouse of Beath, Schiess & Co., at the same time completing matriculation. He spent one year as resident master at Toorak College and eighteen months in a similar position at Caulfield Grammar School.

While teaching, Maxwell studied at the University of Melbourne (B.A., LL.B., 1890), succeeding only by perseverance, but demonstrating oratorical gifts as prelector of the Dialectical Society, Trinity College, as a Presbyterian lay preacher and as a National Association lecturer. After pupillage under J. B. Box he was admitted to the Bar in 1891 and within four years had a considerable practice in criminal cases.

Maxwell eventually, certainly by the 1920s, became the foremost advocate of the criminal Bar in Victoria, judged by Sir Arthur Dean as 'beyond all question the greatest [Victorian] criminal advocate of modern times' and by Sir Robert Menzies as 'the greatest criminal advocate I ever heard'. His appearance was impressive; tall, dark, sallow and aquiline, he possessed a resonant voice with an attractive Scottish burr. More important were the sincerity and earnestness derived from his religious convictions. He believed in the innocence of his clients; contemporaries claimed he had a remarkable faculty for self-conviction. He was a poor cross-examiner and lacking in order but his defects were outweighed by his persuasive powers.

Maxwell stood unsuccessfully for the Legislative Assembly on several occasions: Collingwood, 1891; Prahran, 1897; Warrnambool, 1900; Carlton, 1902; Evelyn, 1914. He also nominated unsuccessfully for the Aus-

tralasian Federal Convention. In 1917 he won for the National Party the Labor-held Federal seat of Fawkner.

Possessed of a strong social conscience, Maxwell was proud to have been chairman from 1897 of the board which set wages for workers manufacturing underclothing following the passing of the Victorian Factories Act. His conscience and his belief in his duties to his constituents made him an unreliable party man. He disliked what he saw as the sectionalism of the Country and Labor parties and was unhappy with the 1923 Bruce [q.v.7]-Page [q.v.] electoral pact. Following his conscience he voted against the Bruce-Page government on many issues in 1929, including the crucial maritime industries bill which led to the government's fall. Unopposed by Labor he was re-elected in 1929. He briefly joined W. M. Hughes's [q.v.9] Australian Party, but resigned in May 1930 and sat as an Independent until he joined the United Australia Party in 1931. Throughout these vicissitudes he was respected by political opponents for his integrity.

Maxwell had lost the sight of one eye suddenly in 1920, the result of a break in the retinal nerve. Most of his remaining sight was lost in 1921 and he became totally blind in 1929. He faced his affliction with fortitude, even using it to advantage in court appearances and in his electorate. He was appointed K.C. in 1926 and remained an active Presbyterian layman.

On 19 December 1896 Maxwell had married, at Yarra Glen, Jean Russell Ross; they had four daughters and one son. He died at his home at Canterbury on 25 June 1935 and was cremated.

A. Wildavsky and D. Carboch, *Studies in Australian politics* (Melb, 1958); A. Dean, *A multitude of counsellors* (Melb, 1968); R. G. Menzies, *The measure of the years* (Melb, 1970); *PD* (Cwlth), 1929, p 552; *Table Talk*, 7 Feb 1896, 15 Nov 1928; *Punch* (Melb), 11 July 1907, 5 Apr 1917; *Age* and *Argus*, 26, 27 June 1935; D. J. E. Potts, A study of three Nationalists in the Bruce-Page government of 1923-1929 (M.A. thesis, Univ Melb, 1972). NORMA MARSHALL

MAXWELL, JOSEPH (1896-1967), often claimed as the second most decorated Australian soldier in World War I, was born on 10 February 1896 at Annandale, Sydney, son of John Maxwell, labourer, and his wife Elizabeth, née Stokes.

Employed as an apprentice boilermaker in Newcastle, he enlisted in the Australian Imperial Force on 8 February 1915. He was posted to the 18th Battalion and served at Gallipoli before proceeding with his battalion to France in March 1916. Promoted sergeant in October, he went to a training battalion in

England, briefly returning to France in May 1917 before being sent back to attend an officer training school. Involved in a brawl with civil and military police in London, he was fined and returned to his unit. He was promoted warrant officer in August and appointed company sergeant major.

In September, during the 3rd battle of Ypres, Maxwell took command of a platoon after its officer had been killed and led it in the attack. Later he safely extricated men from a newly captured position under intense enemy fire. For this action he was awarded the Distinguished Conduct Medal and a few days later was commissioned in the field as second lieutenant; he was promoted lieutenant in January 1918. In March he led a scouting patrol east of Ploegsteert and after obtaining the required information ordered his men to withdraw. He was covering them when he saw a large party of Germans nearby. Recalling the patrol, he organized and led a successful attack, an action for which he was awarded the Military Cross.

In August, during the offensive near Rainecourt, Maxwell, the only officer in his company who was not a casualty, took command and, preceded by a tank, led his men into the attack on time. The tank received a direct hit and Maxwell, although shaken by the explosion, rescued the crew before the tank burst into flames. He continued the attack and the company reached its objective. He was awarded a Bar to his Military Cross.

Maxwell was awarded the Victoria Cross after an attack on the Beaurevoir-Fonsomme line near Estrées on 3 October. After his company commander was wounded he took charge. Reaching the strong enemy wire under intense fire, he pushed forward alone through a narrow passageway in the wire and captured the most dangerous machine-gun, disposing of the crew. His company was thus able to penetrate the wire and take the objective. Shortly afterwards, again single-handed, he silenced a machine-gun holding up a flank company. Later, with two men and an English-speaking prisoner, he encouraged about twenty Germans in a nearby post to surrender, and in doing so was briefly captured himself. Awaiting his opportunity, he drew a pistol concealed in his respirator haversack, killed two of the enemy and escaped with his men under heavy rifle-fire. He then organized a party and captured the post.

In just over twelve months Maxwell was awarded the D.C.M., the M.C. and Bar and the V.C., and he was only 22 when the war ended. After returning to Australia in 1919 he worked in a variety of occupations in Sydney, Canberra and New South Wales country towns. On 14 February 1921, describing himself as a reporter, he married a 19-year-old tailoress, Mabel Maxwell (not a relative) at Bellevue Hill, Sydney, with Catholic rites. There was a daughter of the marriage which was dissolved in 1926 with his wife as petitioner.

In 1932, helped by Hugh Buggy [q.v.7], Maxwell published the very successful *Hell's bells and mademoiselles*, an account of the war as he saw it; at the time he was working as a gardener with the Department of the Interior in Canberra. His health was often very unstable. He attempted, unsuccessfully because of his age, to enlist in the 2nd A.I.F., but eventually succeeded in enlisting in Queensland under a false name; his identity was discovered and he was discharged. On 6 March 1956, stating that he was a journalist of Bondi, he married a widow Anne Martin, née Burton, in Sydney. In 1964, with his wife, he attended the opening of V.C. Corner in the Australian War Memorial, Canberra. He was adamant that his V.C. would not end up there, as he took the view that 'lumping' all the V.C.s together cheapened the award.

On 6 July 1967 Maxwell collapsed and died of a heart attack in a street in his home suburb of Matraville; he had for some time been an invalid pensioner. After a service with military honours at St Matthias Anglican Church, Paddington, he was cremated. His widow donated his medals to the Army Museum, Victoria Barracks, Paddington.

L. Wigmore (ed) *They dared mightily* (Canb, 1963); *Reveille* (Syd), Sept, Nov 1932, July 1967; *SMH*, 15 Feb 1921, 7, 11, 31 July 1967; *Wentworth Courier*, 26 Sept 1979.   E. J. H. HOWARD

MAXWELL, WALTER (1854-1931), agricultural scientist, was born on 14 June 1854 at Paradise, Sedgefield, Durham, England, son of Walter Maxwell, farmer, and his wife Ann, née Walker. He reputedly studied at the Royal College of Science, London, and undertook research in physiological chemistry under Professor E. Schulze at Zurich, Switzerland and at Harvard University in 1888. Maxwell began sugar research in the United States Department of Agriculture under Dr H. W. Wiley and took charge of the Sugar Beet Experiment Station, Schuyler, Nebraska.

In 1893 Dr Maxwell resigned to investigate sugar-cane juice under Dr Stubbs at Audubon Park Sugar Experiment Station, Louisiana. His essay on reviving the cotton industry won a $500 newspaper prize. He became first director of the Hawaiian Sugar Planters' Association's Experiment Station in 1895. An aggressive, energetic worker with broad vision, he studied the lavas and soils of Hawaii and irrigation; sugar yields increased dramatically.

Confronted with declining prices, land

exhaustion and the termination of Melanesian labour, Queensland growers, supported by J. C. Brunnich [q.v.7] and H. Tryon [q.v.], were demanding full-scale sugar experiment stations. The Bundaberg Planters' and Farmers' Association funded a visit by Maxwell through J. V. Chataway [q.v.7], minister for agriculture.

Maxwell's *Report on investigation into the conditions in the sugar industry in Queensland* (Brisbane, 1900) recommended the establishment of experiment stations for research and educational services. He was appointed director of the sugar experiment stations on 27 October 1900, and negotiated an annual salary of £3000, the highest paid to a Queensland public servant.

Funded equally by government and industry, Maxwell acquired the existing station at Mackay, but established his headquarters and laboratory at Bundaberg. He initiated a complete system of soil analysis and experimented with irrigation, fertilizing methods, cultivation and cane-breeding. As comptroller, Bureau of Central Sugar Mills, from 27 October 1904, Maxwell eliminated preferential treatment for shareholder cane, reduced the price to meet debt repayments, modernized mills and threatened to enter possession of farms mortgaged to the goverment as collateral—six defaulting central mills were taken over initially. He was also honorary technical adviser to the Australian Sugar Producers' Association, formed in 1907 along lines he had recommended in 1900-01. Devoting increasingly less time to sugar experiment stations work, Maxwell antagonized many former supporters and was savagely criticized in parliament for his failure to educate independent farmers or to establish further stations, for meddling in the Pacific islander labour dispute and for not investigating insect pests and diseases in cane.

As Commonwealth government adviser Maxwell had reported on the cane sugar industry (1901) and on the sugar bonus (1905), which resulted in legislation that extended the controversial white-labour bounty till 1913. He left Australia in 1910, the year he again reported to the Commonwealth government on the condition of the industry. He then reported on the Philippines sugar industry for the United States Department of Agriculture, and advised the British government during World War I. He lost a son during the war. In retirement at Washington and New Hampshire, Maxwell published two volumes of verse. He died on 9 July 1931 at Conway, New Hampshire, and was cremated.

H. T. Easterby, *The Queensland sugar industry* (Brisb, 1933); Queensland Bureau of Sugar Experiment Stations, *Fifty years of scientific progress* (Brisb, 1950); *PD* (LA Qld), 1900, p 1828, 1903, p 936, 1906, p 687, 2119, 2130, 2140, 1907, p 680, 738; *V&P* (LA Qld), 1901, 4, p 271, 275, 291; *PP* (LA Qld), 1905, 2, p 597, 1911-12, 2, p 1048; *Sugar J and Tropical Cultivator*, Dec 1899, Feb, Mar 1900; *International Sugar J*, 2 (1900), p 170, 282, 4 (1902), p 38, 11 (1909), p 213; *Facts about sugar*, 27 (1932), p 24; *Hawaiian Planters' Record*, 36 (1932), p 3; *Bundaberg Mail*, 12 June 1899.

J. D. KERR

MAXWELL-MAHON, WILLIAM ION (1881-1956), actor, soldier and writer, was born on 19 February 1881 at Kingston-upon-Thames, Surrey, England, eldest son of John William Sims Mahon, secretary to the Junior Naval and Military Club, Portsmouth, and his wife Catherine Adeline Maxwell, née Gill. He was educated at Bowden House, Harrow, and King's College School, London. On 1 January 1900 he enlisted as a private in the Imperial Yeomanry, fought briefly in the South African War, deserted, and returned to England. As William Maxwell he enlisted as a trooper in the Royal Household Cavalry, 2nd Life Guards, but bought himself out on 7 July 1902.

Using Ion Maxwell as a stage name he joined Frank Benson's Shakespearean company in 1903 and toured the English provinces until 1905. He married Maud Marian Jay, a Gaiety girl, in London on 1 August 1906.

Separated from his wife, he migrated to Australia in 1907 with his brother Arthur Mahon to farm near Beaudesert, Queensland. He then taught music at the Southport School before joining J. C. Williamson's [q.v.6] Royal Comic Opera Company, Sydney. Maxwell-Mahon was in the first Australian performance at Her Majesty's, Sydney, in 1910 of *Our Miss Gibbs* and of *The Quaker girl* in 1912. After touring New Zealand for the second time with six of Williamson's musical comedies he took part in the first all-Australian revue at Her Majesty's in 1913. He appeared with Muriel Starr and Maggie Moore [q.v.5] in various productions during 1914. He married Gertrude Amy Phillips, a young Australian actress, on 5 September 1914 at Prahran, Melbourne.

On 15 August Maxwell-Mahon had enlisted in the 2nd Field Artillery Brigade, Australian Imperial Force, again using the name William Maxwell; he was wounded at Gallipoli on 21 June 1915. After promotion to sergeant in January 1916 and transfer to the 4th Division Artillery, he was wounded at Ypres and discharged medically unfit in Melbourne on 20 June 1918. Towards the end of 1918 he organized and toured Australian capital cities in the first 'Diggers' theatrical company.

Maxwell-Mahon was engaged by the

Maurice E. Bandman Operatic Company to tour India in 1919 with musical comedies and he went on with Bandman to Egypt. During 1920-21 he played revues as Ion Maxwell in the English provinces and pantomime in South Africa. He married Edythe Augusta Cowley, a South African singer and actress, in Sydney on 20 July 1922.

In 1922-25 he was a master at Toowoomba Grammar School, produced for the Toowoomba Operatic Society, and was co-editor of the *Countrywoman and Social*, contributing regularly as 'Neil Street'. Returning to the stage in 1925 he took his own small companies through northern Queensland and inland to Broken Hill, New South Wales. Bankrupted by this barnstorming he accepted engagements to perform with (Dame) Judith Anderson, Nellie Stewart [q.v.] and other contemporary actresses. He and his wife toured Tasmania in comedies for the Brandon-Cremer Players during 1927. With Gaston Mervale he produced and performed in the first Australian stage dramatization of Grand Guignol plays in Sydney during January 1928.

After casual broadcasting for 2BL and 2FC in 1926, he began a new career with the Australian Broadcasting Commission in the 1930s. As Ion Maxwell he was solely responsible for drama production of A.B.C. programmes in Queensland from 1942 and until his retirement in 1946 wrote and acted in scores of radio plays, sketches and revues for 4QG. He and his wife June Carter, an Australian actress born Mavis Jeannette Brayne, whom he married in Brisbane on 15 June 1933, helped to pioneer radio transmission of Shakespearean plays for schools in Queensland. He died at Nambour Hospital on 8 June 1956 and with Anglican rites was buried in Nambour cemetery. He had one daughter by each of his first, second and fourth wives and a son by his third wife.

C. G. Pearce, *Horace Henry Dixon and the genesis of the Southport School* (Brisb, 1976); *Footlights*, 14 Dec 1910, 13 Mar 1914; *Theatre* (Syd, Melb), 1 May 1911, 1 Jan 1913; *Teleradio*, 18 Dec 1927, 28 Aug 1937; *Old Southportian Review*, July 1976; W. Maxwell-Mahon, 'Ion Maxwell: forty years in Australian theatre and radio', *A'asian Drama Studies*, vol 2, no 2, Apr 1984, p 91; *Bulletin*, 10 Feb 1910; *Times of India*, 22 Apr 1919; *Sth African Pictorial*, 10 Dec 1921; *Mercury*, 11 July 1927; *SMH*, 2 Jan 1928; Maxwell-Mahon newspaper cuttings and programmes (LaTL) and Victorian Arts Centre Trust Archives); ABC Archives, Syd; personal information; family papers held by author (Univ Qld).

W. D. MAXWELL-MAHON

MAY, SYDNEY LIONEL (1882-1968), organist and music lecturer, was born on 30 May 1882 at Tent Hill, Rothschild, New South Wales, son of native-born parents Walter James May, teacher, and his wife Margaret, née Dodds. From Dunolly Public School he won a bursary to East Maitland High School (1896-98), but transferred to Sydney Boys' High School (1898-99). He gained a certificate in geology and metallurgy after two years at the Sydney Technical College School of Mines, and in 1902 became assistant metallurgist with the Sulphide Corporation at Cockle Creek, Newcastle. Eye trouble prevented him from continuing as a metallurgist.

Having studied the piano as a child he was now drawn to a career in music. May became organist and choirmaster at St John's Church of England, Newcastle, until late 1904, then took up duties as organist and choirmaster (1905-20) at the Central Congregational Church, Ipswich, Queensland. He taught the piano and music theory privately, conducted the Esk Musical Union (1907-10) and organized many concerts and musical evenings in Ipswich, Esk and Boonah. On 25 April 1910 he married Mary Ellen Williams in the church in which he performed. He lived in Ipswich till his death, although his work and interests were to take him away increasingly. May followed Percy Brier [q.v.7] as organist at the Brisbane City Tabernacle Baptist Church in 1920-35.

By 1924 he was a member of the University of Queensland Music Advisory Board, and in 1928 the university appointed him part-time organizer of Queensland examinations for the Australian Music Examinations Board. May became full-time organizer and lecturer from 1 January 1934, not without some controversy as he lacked any formal tertiary training. He maintained this position by one-year appointments until his retirement in 1952.

May was proud of his achievement in establishing the examination system in music and speech on a firm footing in Queensland. When he took over the university position it ran at a financial loss with about 700 entries in 1927. He worked hard over many years, travelling extensively even to small centres in outback regions to persuade teachers to submit candidates for examination. The scheme was soon financially self-sufficient and by 1952 over 11 000 candidates were entering annually. May organized summer schools in music and speech from 1946 to 1953 in Brisbane and Toowoomba, attracting hundreds of teachers and students. In 1955 he was on the Conservatorium Advisory Council, having been prominent in campaigns to establish a conservatorium of music in Queensland.

The university evidently lacked confidence in May's ability to offer worthwhile studies in music towards a B.A. degree, as only about one-tenth of the units for that degree could be taken in music during his time as lecturer. In his retirement he was somewhat embittered by the university's lukewarm acknowledgement of his contribution to the development of music over twenty-five years of service, and joined forces with Mrs Grace MacGibbon to found in 1963 a rival examinations body, the Council of Music and Drama in Queensland.

Particularly from about 1936 May developed enthusiasm for collecting the origins of place names and was, for a time, honorary secretary of the Queensland Place Names Committee. In *Local Government* (1957-64) he discussed at least 1900 place names, Aboriginal names and Melba's [q.v.] Queensland years. His theory on the origins of 'Waltzing Matilda' in *The story of Waltzing Matilda* (Brisbane, 1944) suffers from insubstantial evidence and irrelevancies.

Of sturdy build, with fair hair and somewhat rugged features, May often seemed forbidding on first acquaintance; he was gregarious, nevertheless, and loved travelling round Queensland, renewing friendships and discussing music and place names. He died at Ipswich on 21 November 1968, and was cremated. Two sons and two daughters survived him.

P. Brier, *One hundred years and more of music in Queensland* (Brisb, 1971); *Local Government*, June 1957, p 31; *RHSQJ*, 2, no 3, 1981-82, p 15; *Courier Mail*, 24 Dec 1949; *Telegraph* (Brisb), 27 Nov 1968; P. J. Fleming, History of C.M.D. (typescript, nd, Council of Music and Drama, Brisb) Univ Qld Archives; family papers held by Mrs H. Stannard, Wishart, Brisb.   G. D. SPEARRITT

MAY, WILLIAM LEWIS (1861-1925), conchologist, was born on 18 April 1861 at Wanstead near Mount Barker, South Australia, one of six children of William May, farmer, and his wife Mary, née Cotton. His Quaker parents were capable artists and naturalists and trained their children in these fields. In 1874 the May family settled in Tasmania, establishing a farm at Sandford. William and his brother Alfred, trading as May Bros, were pioneers in the shipment of apples to England. On 2 November 1887 William married Margaret Elizabeth Greer (d. 1901) at the Friends' Meeting House, Hobart. On 8 November 1904 he married Edith Ellen Lester at Ballarat, Victoria.

By the 1890s May had accumulated valuable collections of shells and knowledge which led to joint research with Professor Ralph Tate [q.v.6] of the University of Adelaide. Their second paper, carefully illustrated by May, was the important 'Revised census of the marine mollusca of Tasmania' (1901).

Mary Lodder generously made her conchological work available to Tate and May and in 1902 worked with May on the identity of J. E. Tenison-Woods's [q.v.6] type material in Hobart. From 1900 May published twenty-nine papers, almost doubling the known Tasmanian molluscan fauna; about 160 new species were described. A significant joint dredging expedition with Charles Hedley [q.v.9], east of Cape Pillar, enabled eighty species to be presented to the Royal Society of Tasmania. May continued dredging in eastern and southern waters. A joint paper with Tom Iredale [q.v.9] on 'The misnamed Tasmanian chitons' joined publications dealing with freshwater mollusca, Table Cape fossils and Bass Strait Island collections.

A check-list of the mollusca of Tasmania (Hobart, 1921) and *The illustrated index of Tasmanian shells* (Hobart, 1923), consolidated his research. The *Index*, with over 1000 drawings by May, realized his wish to illustrate the known species. This unique work of great value to malacologists is the monument to his careful research and artistic ability. A genus and many species honour his name.

May was also a keen bird observer and collector of eggs. His shell collection was purchased by Sir Joseph Verco [q.v.] for the South Australian Museum. His paintings of native birds and plants and a fine collection of butterflies and beetles are held by his family. May was elected to the Royal Society of Tasmania in 1895 and the Linnean Society of New South Wales in 1902. He was a member of the Clarence Road Board, held office with the Sandford Hall Committee and was an active sportsman. Following his father, May was interested in local and family history and edited *Two letters describing the voyage of the May family to South Australia in 1839* (Hobart, 1911). He was a devoted and active member of the Society of Friends and a governor of The Friends' School of which his father was one of the founders.

May died on 30 August 1925 in Sydney, while returning from a voyage in the Pacific, and was buried at the Friends' cemetery, Rookwood. His wife and three children by each marriage survived him.

Dept of Hist, Univ Tas, *Report on the historical manuscripts of Tasmania*, no 5 (Hob, 1960); *Aust Zoologist*, 4 (1927), p 351; *Nautilus*, 39 (1925), p 40; Linnean Soc NSW, *Procs*, 51 (1926), no 1, p v; *Tas Naturalist*, 50 (1977), p 1, 52 (1978), p 2; May family papers (access through Dept of Hist, Univ Tas); information from Mrs B. May and Mrs M. B. May, Sandford, Tas.   RON KERSHAW

MAYGAR, LESLIE CECIL (1872?-1917), soldier and grazier, was born on 26 May 1871 or 1872 at Dean station, Kilmore, Victoria, son of Edwin Willis Maygar, grazier, and his wife Helen, née Grimshaw, both from Bristol, England. His father's family were originally political refugees from Hungary. Leslie was educated at Alexandra and Kilmore State schools and privately. He was nearly 6 ft. (183 cm), and had brown hair and later a Kitchener moustache. He, his father and three brothers owned Strathearn station, Euroa. A very fine horseman, Maygar enlisted in the Victorian Mounted Rifles in March 1891.

At the start of the South African War he was not accepted among the first volunteers, owing to a decayed tooth, but went with the 5th (Mounted Rifles) Contingent, arriving in Cape Town in March 1901. For twelve months the contingent was constantly in action, north of Middelburg, East Transvaal, then at Rhenoster Kop, Klippan, Kornfontein and Drivelfontein. It was transferred to Natal in August. At Geelhoutboom, on 23 November, Lieutenant Maygar was awarded the Victoria Cross for rescuing a fellow Victorian whose horse had been shot. With the enemy only 200 yards (180 m) away Maygar dismounted, put the man on his own horse, told him to gallop for the British lines, and ran back under heavy fire. His V.C. was presented by Lord Kitchener. Before returning home in March 1902 he was also mentioned in dispatches.

Resuming work as a grazier at Euroa, Maygar also served as a lieutenant in the 8th (later 16th) Light Horse, V.M.R., and was promoted captain in 1905. He enlisted in the Australian Imperial Force soon after World War I broke out, on 20 August 1914 was appointed a captain in the 4th Light Horse Regiment and sailed for Egypt in October. On Gallipoli, with the dismounted light horse, he was promoted major. On 17 October 1915 he was given temporary command of the 8th L.H.R., both rank of lieut-colonel and command being confirmed in December. During the evacuation of Gallipoli Maygar, left in command of forty men, was instructed to hold the trenches, at all costs, till 2.30 a.m. He wrote: 'I had my usual good luck to be given command of the last party to pull out of the trenches, the post of honour for the 3rd L.H. Brigade'.

Maygar led his regiment throughout its service in Sinai and Palestine until his death and was a much-admired leader. During the 2nd battle of Gaza, on 19 April 1917, the 8th was in a most exposed sector and suffering heavy casualties. Maygar rode about the battlefield all day on his grey charger and 'in every crisis stirred the spirit of his regiment by his example in the firing line'. Sir Henry Gullett [q.v.9] records that Maygar was 'always very bold in his personal leadership' and writes of 19 April: 'It was a day when true

leaders recognised that their men needed inspiration, and Maygar gave it in the finest manner'. He was awarded the Distinguished Service Order in June 1917, and was thrice mentioned in dispatches in 1916-18. When Brigadier General J. R. Royston [q.v.] was invalided home, Colonel Maygar acted as brigadier general in command of the 3rd Light Horse Brigade.

Late on the day of the battle of Beersheba, 31 October 1917, a German aeroplane, using bombs and machine-guns, hit Maygar whose arm was shattered. The grey bolted into the darkness and was found later by 8th Regiment troopers but Maygar was not with him. 'He was picked up during the night by other troops . . . and, having lost too much blood, died the next day at Karm'. L. C. Maygar, 'Elsie' as he was affectionately known, was 'a true fighting commander'.

Aust Defence Dept, *Official records of the Australian military contingents to the war in South Africa*, P. L. Murray ed (Melb, 1911); H. S. Gullett, *The A.I.F. in Sinai and Palestine* (Syd, 1923); L. Wigmore (ed), *They dared mightily* (Canb, 1963); *Reveille* (Syd), Feb 1968; War diaries, 4th *and* 8th Light Horse Regiment, AIF (AWM); information from Mr I. Ferguson, Euroa, Vic.

ELYNE MITCHELL

MAYNE, JAMES O'NEIL (1861-1939) and **MARY EMELIA** (1858-1940), philanthropists, were born on 21 January 1861 and 31 December 1858 in Brisbane, youngest of five children of Irish parents Patrick Mayne, butcher and grazier, and his wife Mary, née McIntosh. Inherited real estate gave them independent means: neither they nor their siblings married. Mary was a pupil of All Hallows' Convent School until 1877 and thereafter hostessed many functions at Moorlands, the family home at Auchenflower. James attended Brisbane Grammar School, graduated B.A. (Syd.) in 1884, and studied medicine at University College, London (L.R.C.P., Lond, M.R.C.S., Eng, 1890).

Resident medical officer at Brisbane General Hospital in 1891-98, then medical superintendent, Mayne worked with 'unremitting personal effort and self-denial', paid for the hospital's first X-ray plant, and donated his salary to the building and grounds committee. He resigned in 1904 after his brother Isaac was committed to an asylum where he later suicided.

After this tragedy, and worried by his own health, Mayne lived very quietly at Moorlands. He relinquished vice-presidencies of the National Cricket Union and Brisbane Bicycle Club; however he later accepted office in the Amateur Fisherman's Association and Toowong Rowing Club. He eschewed telephone and motor car, but travelled widely abroad with his sister. In memory of their brothers they commissioned, from Harry Clarke of Dublin, a stained-glass triptych for St Stephen's Cathedral, where they were regular worshippers. Exceedingly patriotic, they helped to alleviate sectarian bitterness by making Moorlands available to Red Cross working parties during World War I, and gave liberally to the Anglican St Martin's War Memorial Hospital.

Courteous, gentle and shy, Mayne shunned publicity but became renowned for philanthropy. The principal benefactors of the University of Queensland, he and Miss Mayne gave it 693 acres (279 ha) of Moggill land for agricultural education in 1923, and after negotiations beginning in 1926 paid £63 000 to resume over 200 acres (81 ha) at St Lucia. Mayne was attracted to this extensive river site by memories of Sydney University's small ground space and lack of water frontage.

Mayne died at Moorlands on 31 January 1939. Miss Mayne, softly spoken, gracious, slender and taller than her brother, died in the Mater Misericordiae Private Hospital on 12 August 1940. They were buried in Toowong cemetery in the family tomb which the university was requested to maintain. Mayne's estate was valued for probate at £113 334, Miss Mayne's at £83 375. Chief assets were the Brisbane Arcade, Regent building and Moorlands. Identical wills provided that the estates be applied in perpetuity for the university's medical school.

They are commemorated by the Mayne chairs of medicine and surgery, the Mayne String Trio and Mayne Hall where there is a bronze plaque of them by Kathleen Shillam. A portrait of Mayne by Melville Haysom hangs in the University Art Museum. Moorlands, listed by the National Trust, now houses the Blue Nursing Service State Council and in its grounds is the Wesley Hospital.

Courier Mail, 1, 2 Feb 1939; *Brisb Grammar School Mag*, June 1939, p 123; *Univ Qld Gazette*, Dec 1954, p 4; *Alumni News*, 8 (1976), no 1, p 15; *Queenslander*, 30 Oct 1926; HOS 1/D14 (QA); Mayne material (Univ Qld Archives).

BETTY CROUCHLEY

MAYO, GEORGE ELTON (1880-1949), social theorist and industrial psychologist, was born on 26 December 1880 in Adelaide, eldest son of George Gibbes Mayo, draftsman and later civil engineer, and his wife Henrietta Mary, née Donaldson. Educated at Queen's School and the Collegiate School of St Peter, he lost interest in medicine at the University of Adelaide and, after 1901, at medical schools in Edinburgh and London. In 1903 he went to West Africa, and returned to London, writing articles for magazines and teaching English at the Working Men's College. He returned to Adelaide in 1905 to a partnership in the printing firm of J. H. Sherring & Co., but in 1907 he went back to the university to study philosophy and psychology under (Sir) William Mitchell [q.v.]. He won the Roby Fletcher [q.v.4] prize in psychology and graduated with honours (B.A.,1910; M.A.,1926) and was named the David Murray research scholar. In 1911 he became foundation lecturer in mental and moral philosophy at the new University of Queensland and in 1919-23 held the first chair of philosophy there. On 18 April 1913 in Brisbane he had married Dorothea McConnel.

In Brisbane Elton Mayo was a public figure, lecturing for the Workers' Educational Association and serving on the university's war committee. Influenced by Freud, Jung and Pierre Janet, he studied the nature of nervous breakdown and with a Brisbane physician, Dr T. H. Mathewson, pioneered the psycho-analytic treatment of shell-shock. His first book, *Democracy and freedom* (Melbourne, 1919), stated the basis of his social thought later developed in numerous articles and in his major works, *The human problems of an industrial civilisation* (New York, 1933) and *The social problems of an industrial civilisation* (London, 1945). Observing the disturbing level of industrial strife and political conflict in Australia, Mayo formulated an analogy between war neurosis and the psychological causes of industrial unrest. Drawing on social anthropology, he argued that the worker's morale, or mental health, depended on his perception of the social function of his work. He saw the solution to industrial unrest in sociological research and industrial management rather than in radical politics.

Mayo left Australia for the United States of America in 1922. A Rockefeller grant enabled him, as a research associate at the University of Pennsylvania's Wharton School, to investigate the high labour turnover at a textile mill. This work attracted the attention of the Harvard School of Business Administration where he was appointed associate professor in 1926 and professor of industrial research in 1929. There he joined and designed investigations into personal and social factors determining work output at the Western Electric Co.'s Chicago plant; these famous Hawthorne experiments were pathbreaking studies in modern social research. Mayo was one of the most influential, if controversial, social scientists of his day.

In 1947 he retired from Harvard to England where he died at Guildford, Surrey, on 1 September 1949; a short man, who smoked excessively, he had suffered from chronic hypertension. His wife and two daughters survived him. The Elton Mayo School of Management in Adelaide was developed as a tribute to him.

Dr Helen Mayo [q.v.] was his sister. His brother Sir Herbert (1885-1972) became a justice of the Supreme Court of South Australia and president of the Law Council of Australia. Another brother, John Christian (1891-1955), was a prominent Adelaide radiotherapist and surgeon and another sister Mary Penelope Mayo, M.A., (1889-1969) was a historian of early Adelaide.

L. F. Urwick, *Elton Mayo—his life and work* (Syd, 1960); R. C. S. Trahair, *The humanist temper: the life and work of Elton Mayo* (New Brunswick, USA, 1984); G. E. Mayo, *The mad mosaic: a life story* (Lond, 1984); H. Bourke, 'Industrial unrest as social pathology: the Australian writings of Elton Mayo', *Hist Studies*, no 79, Oct 1982; *Univ Qld Gazette*, no 15, Dec 1949, p 2; *The Times*, 7, 8 Sept 1949; Mayo papers (Baker Lib, Harvard Univ); Mayo family papers (SAA).

HELEN BOURKE

MAYO, HELEN MARY, (1878-1967), medical practitioner, was born on 1 October 1878 in Adelaide, eldest of seven children of George Gibbes Mayo, draughtsman and later civil engineer, and his wife Henrietta Mary, née Donaldson. Educated by a tutor at home—her studies included physics—and for two years at the Advanced School for Girls, she matriculated in 1895 and entered the University of Adelaide next year. Helen enrolled in arts because her father considered her too young to study medicine. She began medical studies in 1898, winning the Davies Thomas scholarship in 1901 and the Everard scholarship in 1902; she was the university's second woman graduate in medicine (1902). After a year as house surgeon at the (Royal) Adelaide Hospital, she left for London where she was a clinical clerk at the Hospital for Sick Children in Great Ormond Street. Following a course in tropical medicine, she gained experience in midwifery in Dublin and at St Stephen's Hospital for women and children in Delhi.

Returning to Adelaide in 1906 Mayo entered private practice, combining midwifery and the management of the medical problems of women and children; she was honorary anaesthetist at the Adelaide Children's Hospital. In 1911 she became clinical bacteriologist at the Adelaide Hospital and later established its vaccine department. She gathered material there for her thesis on biological therapy by the administration of vaccines, proceeding in 1926 to the first M.D. degree awarded to a woman by the university.

During World War I Mayo had been demonstrator in pathology at the university and in 1926-34 she was clinical lecturer in medical diseases of children. From 1919 she was physician to out-patients at the Children's Hospital and, from 1926, physician to in-patients. On retiring in 1938 she became honorary consulting physician, but in 1940 returned to the hospital as senior paediatric adviser for the duration of World War II, simultaneously organizing the Red Cross donor transfusion service and instructing in infant feeding.

In 1909 Mayo's paper on infant mortality had called for the early registration of births and advocated educating women for motherhood rather than relying on instinct. She envisaged a close social and psychological relationship between mothers, nurses, doctors and voluntary workers providing specialized attention for all mothers, regardless of economic circumstances. That year she and social worker Harriet Stirling set up a small clinic in the Franklin Street Kindergarten, to attend and advise mothers in and near the city. This grew into the School for Mothers' Institute and Baby Health Centre and in 1927 became the very effective Mothers' and Babies' Health Association; it eventually served the whole State. Mayo was honorary chief medical officer until 1967 and president in 1949-53. In 1921 her emphasis on the wellbeing of mother and baby led her to initiate ante-natal, and later post-natal, consultations for impoverished women in West Adelaide. She also supported the kindergarten movement. In 1935 her 'zeal for efficiency' was rewarded by appointment as O.B.E.

In 1913 Mayo and Stirling had called a meeting which, despite opposition from some doctors, resulted in their opening a small hospital for babies at St Peters. Financial problems led to the government taking over the hospital which moved to Woodville in 1917 as Mareeba Babies' Hospital. Dr Mayo dominated its policy formation: she was honorary physician and honorary responsible medical officer in 1921-47. She and her colleagues assessed and implemented overseas developments in new methods of infant feeding and the prevention of cross-infection. She travelled to England and Canada in 1920 and in 1933, after a paediatric congress in London, visited colleagues in Amsterdam and Germany. In hospitals, birth control and gynaecological clinics and children's welfare services she observed new techniques and ideas, some of which were later incorporated into M.B.H.A. nurses' training.

In 1914 Mayo had become the first woman university councillor in Australia; she continued to serve on Adelaide's council until 1960. She helped to establish St Ann's University College for Women and was chairman of its council in 1939-59. In 1909 she had been a founder of the Women's Non-Party Political

Association, a group of articulate, well-educated and mainly Protestant women. She was first president of the Lyceum Club for professional and artistic women in Adelaide in 1922. In 1939-45 she presided over the Australian Federation of University Women. Mayo was also a member of the South Australian branch of the British Medical Association and a foundation fellow of the (Royal) Australasian College of Physicians; she also joined the Australian Paediatric Association. For twenty years from 1943 she sat on the State Advisory Committee (later Advisory Council) on Health and Medical Services.

Dr Mayo was a progressive woman of forceful views. She was almost certainly a political conservative but she was never attracted by the nastier elements of the Progressive-Fabian emphasis on national efficiency through community health which was espoused by some Australian doctors between the two world wars. She was short and plump with curly hair, a round face and alert expression with a deep rich voice and infectious laugh. She preferred 'sensible English clothes' and had a brisk and bustling manner; her hobbies of sketching and embroidery evidence her concentration and patience. Unmarried, she shared a North Adelaide house with her partner Dr Constance Finlayson and Miss Gertrude Young, sister of financier Sir Walter Young [q.v.]. Helen Mayo served maternal and child welfare during four decades when South Australia's infant mortality rate fell by 60 per cent. She emphasized the social responsibility owed to the community by the medical profession and her foresight, tenacity and energy enabled her to complete many valuable projects.

She died on 13 November 1967 and was cremated. Her portrait by William Dargie hangs at St Ann's; and rooms there, and at the university, and an annual M.B.H.A. lecture are named for her.

Mothers' and Babies' Health Assn of SA, *Annual Report*, 1911-12 to 1967-68; *MJA*, 2 Mar 1968, 20 Feb 1971; *Advertiser* (Adel), 4 June 1935, 16 Nov 1947; PRG 127, and D444 6 (SAA).

NEVILLE HICKS
ELISABETH LEOPOLD

MEAD, ELWOOD (1858-1936), irrigation engineer and advocate of planned rural settlement, was born on 16 January 1858 at Patriot, Indiana, United States of America, elder son of Daniel Mead, farmer, and his wife Lucinda, née Davis. He graduated in agriculture and science from Purdue University (B.S., 1882; M.S., 1884; D.Eng., 1904) and from Iowa State College of Agriculture (C.E., 1883). He married Florence Chase, of La-

fayette, Indiana, on 20 December 1882, before taking up an appointment at Colorado State Agricultural College where he received rapid promotion to a professorship in irrigation engineering, the first of its type in the United States.

In Colorado and later as state engineer in Wyoming, Mead established a lasting national reputation for his unusual grasp of the social impact and political context of modern water-management technologies, repeatedly emphasizing the priority of overarching community rights and the necessity for a state-controlled technocratic establishment. These views reflected a deep-rooted agrarian idealism which had been nurtured in his boyhood experience of the disintegration of cherished rural communities.

In 1899 Mead moved into the federal sphere as director of irrigation investigations for the Department of Agriculture while working part time for the University of California at Berkeley. His lecture courses and official duties provided the basis for *Irrigation institutions* (1903) and other major publications. In 1901 his right arm was surgically amputated following a traffic accident. Supporting three children after the death of his first wife and an unsuccessful second marriage, he married Mary Lewis on 28 September 1905. Isolated in Washington after his opposition to the Federal Reclamation Act (1902), he accepted for six months an invitation from the Victorian government to become, at double his American salary, chairman of its newly formed State Rivers and Water Supply Commission. Mead and his family arrived in Melbourne in November 1907.

The high hopes for government-controlled irrigation in Victoria owed a great deal to the early efforts of Prime Minister Alfred Deakin [q.v.8], who expected Mead to advise at both national and State levels. The novelty and openness of the Australian situation revived his idealism and, abandoning all plans for a quick departure, he embraced the opportunity to demonstrate the social utility of an enlightened irrigation programme. Not content with proposing higher water-rates to attempt to recover maintenance, management and construction costs, he also insisted on the logical extension which demanded higher-yielding uses of water and land. The Water Act was passed in 1909 despite the fierce opposition of large landowners, and Mead's influence on rural development was massively increased by his assumption of overriding control in the planning of closer settlement in Victoria's irrigation districts. He claimed much of the credit for the hierarchical arrangement of allotment sizes which characterized these designs, but the novelty was rather in Mead's salesmanship, in the very scale and complexity of the commission's operations, and in the bureaucratic web in which the new settlers became enmeshed.

The Australian interlude consolidated Mead's international reputation. Some of his prodigious energy continued to be directed away from Australia: American contacts were carefully cultivated and he obtained generous overseas leave. In Victoria his contributions were generally well recognized in the irrigation settlements, but his American background and involvements were less popular. A serious drought was threatening the entire irrigation programme across south-eastern Australia and Mead's own insecurity intensified in proportion to the mounting hostility towards America's continuing neutrality in World War I. His resignation became effective in May 1915.

Appointed professor of rural institutions at the University of California, Mead became prominent in the abortive campaign for a national settlement scheme for returned soldiers. *Summary of soldier settlements in English-speaking countries* was published in 1918, to be followed by his best-known book, *Helping men own farms* (New York, 1920). As chairman of California's Land Settlement Board in 1917-23 he instituted 'agricultural colonies' but the plan was ill timed and abandonments and bankruptcies were common during the agricultural depression of the 1920s.

A four-month advisory tour of Australia in 1923 was punctuated by disputes with Sir Joseph Carruthers [q.v.7] and leading irrigation authorities in New South Wales over the selection and use of land in the Murrumbidgee Irrigation Area. Mead rejected plans for further fruit planting, advocating larger dairy farms and an improved co-ordination of grazing and irrigation enterprises which would favour stock fattening and the intensive production of lucerne. On his return he resigned from the University of California and in April 1924 took up his last major appointment, as federal commissioner for reclamation.

Survived by his wife, three sons and two daughters, Mead died in Washington on 26 January 1936 only four months after the official dedication of the giant Boulder Dam. In February 1936 the reservoir behind the dam was named Lake Mead. They were fitting memorials to a distinguished public service career devoted to the establishment and consolidation of modern irrigation administration in the western world.

J. M. Powell, *Environmental management in Australia, 1788-1914* (Melb, 1976); American Soc of Civil Engineers, *Trans* 102 (1937), p 1611; *Aqua*, Feb 1951; *JRAHS*, 67 (1982), p 328; *Punch*

(Melb), 9 Feb 1911; *Herald* (Melb), 28, 29 Jan 1936; *Argus*, 29 Jan 1936; J. R. Kluger, Elwood Mead: irrigation engineer and social planner (Ph.D. thesis, Arizona State Univ, 1970).

J. M. POWELL

MEAD, GERTRUDE ELLA (1867-1919), medical practitioner, was born on 31 December 1867 in Adelaide, daughter of Silas Mead [q.v.5], Baptist minister, and his first wife Ann, née Staple. She trained as a nurse at the Adelaide Children's Hospital in 1890-91 and then studied medicine at the University of Adelaide; she graduated (M.B., B.S., 1897) from Melbourne. On her way to Britain in 1898 for postgraduate work Mead stayed briefly at Perth where her colleague Dr Roberta Stewart [q.v.9 Jull] thought her 'a nice girl, a sufferer from mitral disease who is very philosophical about it'. Gertrude Mead spent two years abroad, as resident physician at an English children's hospital, at a Dublin women's hospital and as a house surgeon at Leith, Scotland.

In 1901 she returned to Perth to join her father, now a co-pastor there. Unmarried, she was the third woman doctor to register in Western Australia and practised from her home at Harvest Terrace, Perth. Her paramount interest was in women's and children's welfare. She was the delegate of the Western Australian branch of the Australasian Trained Nurses' Association to the Women's Maternity Hospital Committee formed in 1909, and its obstetric representative when the institution opened as the King Edward Memorial Hospital in 1916. She was also A.T.N.A. nominee on the Western Australian Council for Venereal Disease; her forthright report of 1918 stated that nurses were inadequately informed and needed education on that subject. Dr Mead was honorary physician to the Perth Children's Hospital, which had opened in 1909, and honorary medical officer for the House of Mercy for unmarried mothers in 1904-07. She was an active member of the Karrakatta Women's Club (vice-president, 1912-14), and successively chairwoman of the legal, educational, scientific and current affairs programmes, giving talks on China, Florence Nightingale, women's work and, during World War I, on Red Cross work. Dr Mead was a founder of the Children's Protection Society of Western Australia, where she proposed a day-care centre.

She was appointed to the inaugural Senate of the University of Western Australia in 1912 as a medical representative; a fellow senator recalled her as 'a small thin woman with a mild voice and manner but a keen brain'. She remained on the senate and as a member of its education committee until her death. During the war Dr Mead, an honorary life member of the St John Ambulance Brigade and a Perth divisional surgeon in 1915-19, lectured to Red Cross nurses and was an honorary medical officer at the Fremantle Base Hospital in 1918. Mrs Muriel Chase [q.v.7], who founded the Silver Chain Association, credited Dr Mead with the suggestion to use surplus donations for the salary of a district nurse in Perth; Mead joined the committee of the Silver Chain Nursing League in 1912. She proposed a scheme to build cottage homes for old people and promoted the idea through the Karrakatta Club. The first cottage, rented in Wright Street, North Perth, in 1916, was designed and furnished by Dr Mead and Mrs Chase.

Gertrude, although unwell, left Perth in 1919 to visit her medical missionary brother Dr Cecil Mead, on leave in Adelaide from India. She began to investigate the running of old people's homes in Adelaide, but died of cerebral embolism on 6 November. She was buried in West Terrace cemetery. It was said of her that 'She did not know her own energy and worked far too hard'. A deeply religious but practical woman, her philosophy had been expressed in a paper on 'Medical missions' (*W.A. Baptist*, 15 April 1907) in which she emphasized the need for doctors to embrace spiritual work as well as regular medical care—to win souls while healing bodies. She concluded with a plea for the women of India and the need for women doctors there. The Silver Chain Cottage Homes were opened in 1920; the only surviving one was named in 1981 the 'Dr Gertrude Mead Cottage Home'. A plaque at Silver Chain headquarters praised her as 'the beloved friend, inspirer and helper of the Silver Chain Nursing League . . . the solace and strengthening of many to whom she was both physician and friend'.

C. W. M. Cameron, *Karrakatta Club Incorporated 1894-1953* (Perth, 1954); N. Stewart, *Little but great* (Perth, 1965); V. Hobbs, *But westward look* (Perth, 1980); *West Australian*, 15 Dec 1916, 10 Nov 1919; R. Jull, Diaries, 10 Jan 1898, 6, 7 Nov 1919 (Battye Lib).   Prue Joske

MEAGHER, JOHN (1836-1920), storekeeper and politician, was born on 8 December 1836 at Kilrush, Clare, Ireland, son of Roger Meagher, fisherman and coastguard, and his wife Catherine, née Mahoney. He arrived in Sydney about 1863 and at St Mary's Cathedral married Mary Ann Byrne (d. 1895), housekeeper, on 19 September 1864. That year he moved to Bathurst where he was employed by Edmund Webb [q.v.6] who later became a commercial and political rival.

Meagher opened his own store at Bathurst in 1867, followed by branches at Hill End, Trunkey, Locksley and Dirty Swamp. Large stores were later established at Temora, West Wyalong, Barmedman, Forbes, Cootamundra, Parkes and Yass. He imported drapery, grocery, ironmongery, wines and spirits and furniture. By extending customer credit on the advice of their store-managers John Meagher & Co. assisted the development of the central and south-western districts of New South Wales.

A justice of the peace from 1878, Meagher was active in local politics as a Protectionist and in 1885 was defeated by (Sir) Francis Suttor [q.v.6] for the Legislative Assembly seat of Bathurst. In 1888 he sponsored the local celebrations for the centenary of the foundation of the colony and invited William Astley [q.v.3] to Bathurst as organizer. In 1896 he was a vice-president of the committee that sponsored the People's Federal Convention at Bathurst and entertained in his home (Sir) Edmund Barton [q.v.7], Cardinal Moran [q.v.] and many leading Federationists.

Nominated to the Legislative Council in 1900, Meagher proposed the building of the Temora-Wyalong railway line and was a vocal advocate of state aid for Catholic schools. He identified himself closely with the Irish Home Rule movement and frequently visited Ireland, making his last visit in 1919-20. He was prominent in greeting Irish delegates to Australia such as John and William Redmond [qq.v.6], John Dillon and Michael Davitt. Close personal friendships developed between Meagher, his family and William Redmond. In 1916 Meagher deplored 'the ruthless execution of the leaders' of the Easter rebellion in Dublin and strongly opposed conscription. In a letter to the *Daily Telegraph* on 23 November 1917 he defended Archbishop Mannix [q.v.] from allegations of sedition made by Judge Heydon [q.v.9].

Meagher was a devout Catholic, a daily communicant throughout his life, a generous donor to Catholic Orders and organizations, notably to the Sisters of Mercy when they were building their novitiate and establishing an orphanage at Bathurst, and to St Stanislaus' College. In December 1903 he was appointed knight commander in the papal Order of St Gregory the Great. A 'sterling, big-hearted Irishman', he continued to champion Irish-Catholic causes through years when sectarianism was a familiar tension.

Meagher died on 26 August 1920 in St Vincent's Hospital, Sydney, and was buried in the family vault in Bathurst cemetery. Predeceased by his only daughter who had become a religious of the Sacré Coeur order, he was survived by five of his seven sons. His estate was valued for probate at £44 737.

M. G. Meagher, *John Meagher 1836-1920* (Cootamundra, NSW, priv print, 1981); *PD* (LC NSW),

1920, p 550; *Freeman's J* (Syd), 12 Sept 1896, 9 June 1907; *SMH*, 25 July 1898, 22 June 1918, 27 Aug 1920; *Catholic Press*, 9 June 1900, 13 Nov 1902, 24 Aug 1905, 2 May 1907, 2 Sept 1920; *Daily Telegraph* (Syd), 3 Mar 1911, 13 Dec 1912, 12 Apr, 6, 16 May, 10 Aug, 26 Sept 1916, 17, 23 Nov 1917, 9, 15 Mar 1920; B. J. Pennay, Political concerns of Bathurst 1885-1910 (M.A. thesis, Macquarie Univ, 1974); information from Z. Denholm, San Isidore, NSW.   BRUCE PENNAY

MEAGHER, RICHARD DENIS (1866-1931), solicitor and politician, was born on 11 January 1866 at Bathurst, New South Wales, son of Denis Meagher, policeman, of Ireland, and his wife Jane, née Keleher, of Bathurst. His mother died when he was 2, and he was brought up by relations. Educated at St Stanislaus College, Bathurst, and St Aloysius College, Sydney, he was articled to J. A. B. Cahill in 1883, transferring to W. P. Crick [q.v.8] in 1887; he was admitted as a solicitor on 30 November 1889. At St Francis Church, Paddington, he married Alice Maude Osmond on 26 January 1891; they were childless.

Dick Meagher had been a lonely child. But he was a bright schoolboy and talented youth, with a flair for law and a taste for radical protectionist politics that placed him firmly in the unsubmissive Irish Catholic environment. In 1885 he helped E. W. O'Sullivan [q.v.] to campaign, and in the 1880s and early 1890s made a name as a speaker welcoming dissident Irish visitors John and William Redmond [qq.v.6], Michael Davitt and Joseph Devlin. Yet there was an ambivalence about Meagher for, since the days of J. H. Plunkett, E. Butler and D. H. Deniehy [qq.v.2,3,4], 'his people' had seen the law as an avenue for tribal recognition and social fulfilment.

He grew into a fleshy, tall, young man, with a long, oval face, flared nostrils and a wide gap between his upper lip and the base of his nose. His sulky looks complemented his hauteur, masking an emotional insecurity and gullibility that made him a bad judge of people. He could tell a joke, but could seldom see one. He acquired a fruity eloquence which under pressure could expand into protean oratory that gratified audiences with luscious imagery and sonorities, occasionally arousing them with searing vituperation. By 25 he was a Sydney identity. In 1892 he became Crick's partner, practising mainly in the Police Court; but he also appeared in higher courts, following an 1890 law amendment that allowed the 'solicitor on the record' to do so. Astute, cantankerous and earthy, Crick found Meagher's self-conceit hard to take, even as they prospered.

Helped by the publicity of the case of George Dean [q.v.8], Meagher won the seat of Sydney-Phillip on 24 July 1895. He had defended Dean in the Police Court in March against a charge of attempted murder of his wife by poisoning, and next month at his trial when he was sentenced to death. The judge, Sir William Windeyer [q.v.6], had shown antipathy to Dean, raising doubts about the verdict. But on 9 April, under pressure from Crick, Meagher tricked Dean into confessing. Meagher rationalized his duty to his client, kept the secret and stirred public and political opinion to have the case reviewed, thus provoking suspicion that the prisoner's stricken wife and her mother had bizarrely plotted to have him hanged. A royal commission's majority report resulted in a pardon for Dean on 28 June.

Meagher's vainglory intensified. When the *Daily Telegraph* reflected on his defence of Dean in July he sought advice from the leader of the Bar, Sir Julian Salomons [q.v.6], about a libel action. To impress him he disclosed Dean's guilt, but Salomons was appalled and in August divulged Meagher's confidences to J. H. Want [q.v.], attorney-general. Meagher, with Crick's unwitting help, brazened it out throughout September. But he was forced to confess on 8 October. His grandiloquence helped to sustain him: 'I am determined to endure mental torture no longer, nor to stifle the voice of truth . . . This awful lesson of my life I will endeavour to atone for in another clime'. He resigned from parliament. His father died on 28 October.

With Crick and Dean he was charged in December with conspiracy to defeat the ends of justice. Crick was acquitted, and Meagher and Dean's convictions were quashed in May 1896 on the grounds of the inadmissibility of certain evidence. Meagher was struck from the roll of solicitors by the Supreme Court on 1 June. He decided to stay in Sydney and to try to rehabilitate himself.

The Dean case had decimated Meagher's savings and he now had no income. He realized on oratory in lecture tours and became a land agent. In the 1898 general election he won the seat of the Tweed, where the Irish protectionists were strong. He regained his position as a Sydney celebrity in September when in Pitt Street he horse-whipped John Norton [q.v.], who had called him 'Mendax Meagher' in *Truth*; Norton pulled his revolver, but missed; Meagher was fined £5 for assault. That year he was responsible for the important Medical Practitioners' and Accused Persons' Evidence Acts. In a parliament confused by the advent of Federation, he helped (Sir) George Reid [q.v.] to bring New South Wales into the national fold. He became an effective and well-liked parliamentarian and by 1904, when his seat was abolished, he had retrieved much of his State-wide popularity. He was an alderman for Phillip Ward on the Sydney Municipal Council in

1901-20, a member of the Metropolitan Board of Water Supply and Sewerage in 1906-10, and on the committee to welcome the American fleet in 1908. He was a trustee of the Public Library of New South Wales in 1916-31, and a director of Royal Prince Alfred Hospital in 1916-18.

Meagher's consuming goal was to be restored to the roll of solicitors. Applications failed in 1900 and 1902, but in 1904 the chief justice, Sir Frederick Darley [q.v.4], intimated that a future request might succeed. In 1902-03 he had an apparently dubious association with W. N. Willis [q.v.], a fellow parliamentarian and land agent. The royal commissioner, Justice (Sir) William Owen [q.v.], who examined the administration of the Lands Department in 1905-06, reported adversely on Willis and Crick but not on Meagher. Willis was a plausible manipulator and Meagher was quite unable to comprehend his personality or methods. The Incorporated Law Institute of New South Wales opposed Meagher's application for readmission in 1909, when Sir George Simpson [q.v.6], acting chief justice, who knew Meagher well, found his relations with Willis in one instance 'reprehensible, but . . . [not] so reprehensible that it should prevent' his reinstatement; and in a second case Simpson stated that suspicion was raised, 'but unless those circumstances lead almost conclusively to a conviction of guilt, I am bound by every principle of law and justice to acquit'. He and Judge Cohen granted the application in July, with Judge R. D. Pring [q.v.] dissenting. Meagher resumed practice. But the Law Institute appealed against his readmission and the High Court of Australia reversed the decision in November. Thereafter he gave up his land work but continued before the Railway Appeal Board and the Public Service Appeals Tribunal.

In 1907 he had been re-elected to parliament for Phillip. In 1909 he joined the Labor Party and contributed much to its strength and achievements while it held government in 1910-16; on the executive in 1910-16, he was vice-president in 1913 and 1915-16 and president in 1914-15. He was parliamentary chairman of committees in 1910-13. In 1912 the governor Lord Chelmsford [q.v.7] put pressure on J. S. T. McGowen [q.v.] and W. A. Holman [q.v.9] to prevent Meagher from obtaining a cabinet vacancy, saying that he would not receive him socially. The same year a private member's bill to readmit him to the roll of solicitors passed the Legislative Assembly, but failed in the Legislative Council. He became Speaker in 1913 after caucus had supported him against McGowen, the choice of the premier, Holman.

Meagher's appointment by the government as the first Labor lord mayor of Sydney in January 1916 ended a deadlock on the council, but he was elected to the position for 1917. Pressed by the Churches, he set up a censor of street posters and said, 'While I occupy this chair the standard of decency will be maintained'; he introduced rating on unimproved land values and planned to increase the construction of workers' houses. He mediated unsuccessfully to end the 1917 transport strike, and collected money to help families in need because of the dispute. He was very active in raising men and money for World War I.

Like many other Australian-Irish 'Home Rulers', Meagher deplored the Dublin 1916 Easter rising, and he was troubled by those who favoured an Irish republic, some of whom were activists in the Labor Party. The problem crystallized as a large party majority rejected compulsion for overseas service in the war. Surprising many conservatives, Meagher supported Prime Minister W. M. Hughes's [q.v.9] conscription policy and was expelled from the party in November. He ran as Independent Labor at the 1917 election but was defeated after a bitter campaign, described by Meagher as a 'saturnalia of sectarianism and a veritable hurricane of hate'; during the campaign he and Holman had been hooted at the St Patrick's Day sports. Holman had him appointed to the Legislative Council in May.

That month Meagher made his fifth application to be restored to the roll. The court was headed by Chief Justice Sir William Cullen [q.v.8], who at one stage provoked Meagher's counsel, J. C. Gannon, K.C., to remark: 'I am beginning to think that for most people there is to be no possibility of reclamation'. The application was refused. A representative testimonial committee, including (Sir) S. Hordern [q.v.9] and (Sir) A. Meeks [q.v.], was established to help him financially. He tried again in November 1919 and clashed openly with Cullen, accusing him of having insulted and humiliated him in his position as lord mayor. Cullen denied it. Meagher said he had 'come here in no craven spirit seeking mercy', and in his reply savaged R. Broomfield, K.C., counsel for the Law Institute. Reinstatement was refused.

In December he failed in an appeal to the High Court, but Justice (Sir) Isaac Isaacs [q.v.9] said that he should go again to the Supreme Court and satisfy them 'that your attitude has really changed'. Meagher took the advice and by affidavit in March 1920 expressed his 'contrition for everything that has happened'. Broomfield argued that the sorrow was not genuine, and the court agreed. The High Court refused leave to appeal. Meagher now saw that his ordeal had involved a hopeless struggle against the hard conservative core of the legal profession, and sought justice from parliament.

He had resigned from the Legislative Council in February 1920 to contest Sydney at the March elections. Meagher lost but polled well, and there were signs of wide-ranging political support and public sympathy in his long fight to resume his career in law. With the support of J. Storey's [q.v.] Labor government and some members of the Opposition, in October W. Bennett of the Progressive Party brought down a bill to restore Meagher to the roll. Despite petitions from the Law Institute, presented by T. J. Ley [q.v.], and from the Council of the Bar of New South Wales, the Legal Practitioners Amendment Act of 1920 passed both Houses in December. The debate in the Legislative Council was highlighted by a compassionate speech by Sir Joseph Carruthers [q.v.7]. The *Sydney Morning Herald* said that the unique Act was 'a moral shock to the community'.

Meagher quickly re-established himself and was later joined by R. Sproule [q.v.] in a successful legal firm. Meagher's wife died in April 1924 and he visited the United States of America. As a memorial to her, in 1928 he donated land for the erection of the Church of Our Lady of the Nativity at Lawson. Next year he was appointed a papal knight of the Order of St Gregory. He suffered from chronic nephritis, died in Lewisham Hospital on 17 September 1931 and was buried in Waverley cemetery. His estate was sworn for probate at £32 580 of which £20 000 was left to Archbishop M. Kelly [q.v.9] for the education of priests; included in a long list of minor beneficiaries were D. C. Green, D. R. Haugh [qq.v.9], H. V. Evatt and W. Bennett.

In 1920 Meagher published *Twenty-five years' battle*, and in 1925 *American impressions*.

Report of the royal commission on . . . Lands Department (Syd, 1906); C. Pearl, *Wild men of Sydney* (Lond, 1958); L. Blackwell, *Death cell at Darlinghurst* (Lond, 1970); D. J. Murphy (ed), *Labor in politics* (Brisb, 1975); F. A. Larcombe, *The advancement of local government in New South Wales, 1906 to the present* (Syd, 1978); *NSW State Reports*, 9 (1909); *Cwlth Law Reports*, 9 (1909); *Daily Telegraph* (Syd), 24 Dec 1913; *T&CJ*, 31 Dec 1913; *Punch* (Melb), 14 May 1914, 24 May 1917; *SMH*, 12 Jan, 24 Aug 1916, 29 May, 29 Dec 1917, 8 Nov, 19 Dec 1919, 9 Mar, 22 Dec 1920, 18 Sept 1931; *Freeman's J* (Syd), 17 Aug 1916, 15 Mar 1917, 8 Jan, 14 May 1925; Carruthers papers (ML); CO 418/101.   BEDE NAIRN

MEAGHER, RICHARD JAMES (1871-1947), public service commissioner, was born on 21 July 1871 at Ballarat East, Victoria, son of James Meagher, tollgate keeper, and his wife Eliza, née Tracey, both Irish born. Richard was educated at the Christian Brothers' College, Ballarat. He joined the Post and Telegraph Office, Victoria, as a telegraphist and transferred to the Hobart Telegraph Office on 25 July 1891. On 9 September 1894 he married Adeline Mary Ann Nettlefold in Hobart. Almost immediately he was retrenched but was appointed a telegraphist at Kalgoorlie and Perth, Western Australia. He returned to Hobart in 1895 and was re-employed in the Hobart Telegraph Office in January 1896. He resigned in October 1902 to enter commercial life and later became secretary of St Joseph's Hibernian Australasian Catholic Benefit Society, and Tasmanian district secretary in 1907. An alderman on the Hobart City Council in 1910-18, he was mayor in 1914.

On 22 December 1905 Meagher was appointed government nominee on the first Tasmanian Public Service Board and became acting chairman in 1914 after his reappointment in 1911. When the board was abolished in 1918 and replaced by a single commissioner, Sir John Gellibrand [q.v.8], Meagher was appointed assistant commissioner. He became commissioner in 1922 on condition, as an economy measure, that he remain chairman of the wages and railway classification boards. Meagher supported this 'need for the exercise of every effort, even to the last ounce, in order to meet the exigencies of the State' and claimed that over fifteen months he saved 'about £750 . . . in my own office'. He was reappointed commissioner, though never permanently, and altogether served under seven premiers.

The wages board was a major initiative in Tasmanian industrial relations and Meagher had been the main architect of the Wages Board Act (1910). He was chairman until he resigned on 25 October 1935, when he pointed out that his duties as commissioner included the chairmanship of fifty-nine wages boards, as well as boards relating to awards of the Commonwealth Court of Conciliation and Arbitration, public service appeals, relief of workers suffering from occupational diseases and returned soldiers' employment. He was also a member of the government office accommodation board, visiting gaol magistrate and a trustee of the Hobart public cemetery.

Even after his retirement, in August 1941 Meagher remained chairman of two boards and was also government nominee on the public service classification and chairman of the Transport Commission appeal boards. On reappointment as public service commissioner in 1938 he had said: 'I shall return . . . to my aforementioned place in the field as full forward, ready and fit to play my part in the teamwork required to achieve success in the game'. He was chairman of the Tasmanian Football League.

A fellow of the Federal Institute of Accountants and of the Institute of Incorporated Secretaries, he was appointed O.B.E. in 1941. He had been first president of the Australian Natives' Association's Tasmanian board of directors in 1905-07. He was a member of the Athenaeum Club and found time to play golf and bowls.

Meagher died on 11 March 1947 and was buried at Cornelian Bay cemetery, Hobart. His wife and son survived him. His elder son had been killed in France in 1917.

Mercury, 12 Mar 1947.   R. J. K. CHAPMAN

MEARES, CHARLES EDWARD DEVENISH (1861-1940), dairy industry organizer, was born on 17 November 1861 near Kiama, New South Wales, son of Alfred Devenish Meares, dairy-farmer, and his Tasmanian wife Maria Louisa Antoinette, daughter of John Tooth [q.v.6 R. Tooth], brewer. In 1875 he became a junior clerk in the New South Wales Fresh Food & Ice Co. Book-keeping experience with a Sussex Street commission agent crystallized his ideas on producer co-operatives. Joining the South Coast and West Camden Co-operative Co. Ltd in 1881, Meares became accountant, then commerce manager. On 14 October 1899 at Enfield he married Annie Ellen Pechey who bore him two sons and died in 1906.

The banks foreclosed on the company in 1899 and next year Meares formed the Dairy Farmers' Co-operative Milk Co. Ltd and lobbied for a co-operative distributive company, Coastal Farmers' Co-operative Society Ltd, of which he became manager. He travelled incessantly, propounding the advantages of co-operation. Assisted by L. T. McInnes, director of dairying, he initiated major reforms: separation on the farm, co-operative distribution within Sydney and bulk carriage by rail; he initially opposed pasteurization of cream for butter-making and compulsory grading of butter. In 1909 he persuaded the North Coast Co-operative Co. Ltd (NORCO) and other co-operatives to use a joint selling floor and started a common export system.

Emphasizing primary industries, Meares helped to reorganize the Sydney Chamber of Commerce in 1912 and as vice-president (1916) and president (1918) energetically pursued its aims. With the formation of the Primary Producers' Union by C. J. McRae [q.v.] in 1916 to secure maximum production with a safe exportable surplus, Meares, as leader of its delegation, attempted to remove dairying from Necessary Commodities Control Commission jurisdiction. He vigorously opposed establishment of price-fixing boards and at the conference (Melbourne, 1916) of dairying and manufacturing interests advocated greater emphasis on section 92 of the Constitution.

A government nominee on the Commonwealth Dairy Produce Pool Committee, in 1919 Meares was hesitant about (Sir) Walter Massy-Greene's [q.v.] scheme for co-operative control of the dairy industry. But, as a provisional director, he energetically supported the subsequent Australian Producers' Wholesale Co-operative Federation Ltd. In London in 1920, with West Australian Basil Murray, Meares secured the coping-stone of his career: the federal co-operatives of Australia, New Zealand and South Africa united in the Overseas Farmers' Co-operative Federations. In 1922-23 with W. B. Chaffey [q.v.7] and F. L. McDougall [q.v.], he was a member of the Commonwealth delegation sent to Britain to seek larger markets for dried fruits. In 1929 Empire Dairies Ltd was formed in London to handle butter sales.

After achieving reconstitution of the 1922 Australian Dairy Council as a purely advisory body, Meares was appointed chairman. He spearheaded lobbying for the Dairy Produce Export Control Board which successfully reduced freight and insurance costs. In 1926 he was elected to the State Advisory Dairy Board. In 1925 NORCO's withdrawal from the co-operative selling floor threatened disintegration, but pressure from Casino achieved an amalgamation of Coastal Farmers with Berrima District Farm and Dairy Co. Ltd to form the Producers' Distributing Society Ltd. Meares was joint manager until 1931 and remained a director until 1938. He was cautious about William Paterson's [q.v.] All-Australian scheme in 1925 but, after its acceptance by the dairying industry, he resolved its financial impasse. In 1932 he published *50 years of co-operation 1881-1931*.

Meares was a foundation member of Rotary International, Australia, and a keen sportsman: he was honorary secretary of the New South Wales Lawn Tennis Association. He died at his Lindfield home on 14 November 1940 and was cremated with Anglican rites. His second wife Mary Anna, née Brown, whom he had married at Ashfield on 18 March 1908, and five sons survived him. For nearly forty years Meares was the master-mind in developing co-operative marketing for primary producers; he stressed efficiency, self-reliance and independence of government assistance.

R. S. Maynard, *His was the vision* (Syd, 1940); *Commerce* (Syd), 1 Aug 1918; *SMH*, 6 June 1919, 10 Nov 1920, 11 Oct, 14 Nov 1922, 16, 20 Nov 1940; D. H. McKay, History of co-operation in south-eastern Australia, 1860-1940 (M.A. thesis, Univ Melb, 1946); information from Dr S. D. Meares, Avoca Beach, NSW.   JOHN ATCHISON

MEEKS, SIR ALFRED WILLIAM (1849-1932), merchant and politician, was born on 15 April 1849 at Cheltenham, Gloucestershire, England, son of William Meeks, shoemaker, and his wife Maria, née Healing. The family migrated to Melbourne in 1854 and Alfred was educated mainly at St James' schools. He entered a business house and was an accountant when he married with Baptist forms his cousin Alice Freeman, English-born daughter of a bootmaker from Cheltenham, on 14 October 1873 at Richmond.

In 1878 Meeks became manager of a department of Bright [q.v.3] Bros & Co., merchants and shipping agents. He went to Adelaide in 1882 to establish a branch of Gibbs, Bright & Co. and considerably expanded the firm's business. He served on the commission on government stores (1886-87), chaired the finance committee for the Adelaide Jubilee International Exhibition in 1887, was a local director of the National Bank of Australasia and chairman of the Adelaide Chamber of Commerce.

Moving to Sydney in 1888 as senior resident partner of Gibbs, Bright & Co., Meeks became a director of the Australian Mutual Provident Society next year and was chairman in 1906-32. He also became chairman of Lysaght Bros & Co. Ltd and of the Sydney and Suburban Hydraulic Power Co. Ltd, and a local director of the Ocean Accident and Guarantee Corporation of London. He served on the royal commission into military affairs in 1892 and in 1895 was a founder of the Chamber of Manufactures of New South Wales. President in 1897-98 of the Sydney Chamber of Commerce, he chaired a congress of Australian chambers of commerce in 1897.

A staunch Protectionist and ardent Federationist, Meeks was a member of the executive of the Australasian Federation League of New South Wales from 1894. As joint treasurer of the United Federal Executive in 1899 he campaigned vigorously for the acceptance of the Constitution bill. In 1900 Meeks was nominated to the Legislative Council: liberal-minded, he supported female suffrage. He was an executive-member of the committee which initiated a testimonial fund for R. D. Meagher [q.v.] in 1917.

Meeks worshipped regularly at St Mark's Anglican Church after he had moved to Darling Point about 1907. He was sometime president and honorary treasurer for the Young Men's Christian Association, president of the Sydney City Mission and of the Sydney Industrial Blind Institution, and a committee-member of the New South Wales Bush Nursing Association and Toc H. During World War I he was honorary treasurer of the Y.M.C.A.'s war service funds, an executive-member of the Lord Mayor's Patriotic and War Fund and in 1919 senior vice-president of the Returned Sailors' and Soldiers' Imperial League of Australia. Next year he was appointed K.B.E. His wife worked for the Boys' Brigade, the Fresh Air League and the Surgical Appliance Aid Society. In 1930 they gave a small hospital to the Boy Scouts' Association in memory of their only son Victor who had served with the light horse on Gallipoli and died in 1926.

A dark, dapper man with a neat vandyke beard and waxed moustache, Meeks belonged to the Union Club and the Royal Australian Historical Society. He loved music, especially singing, and was a vice-president of the Sydney Liedertafel (Royal Sydney Apollo Club from 1916) in 1900-08 and president in 1908-32; he was presented with its gold lyre in 1920. He was also a vice-president of the Royal Philharmonic Society of Sydney. Retiring from Gibbs, Bright & Co. in 1929, Sir Alfred died at his Darling Point home on 6 March 1932 and was buried in the Anglican section of South Head cemetery; his wife died on 21 July. They were survived by a daughter, who inherited most of his estate, valued for probate at £84 573 in two States. In the Legislative Council Sir Joseph Carruthers [q.v.7] said that he had 'never heard Sir Alfred Meeks say an angry word, or a word that would cause pain to another man'.

Cyclopedia of N.S.W. (Syd, 1907); *PD* (NSW), 1932, p 8215; *Millions Mag*, 1 Dec 1919; *A'sian Insurance and Banking Record*, 21 Mar 1932; *SMH*, 4 June 1917, 28 Mar 1919, 27 Feb 1920, 2 Feb 1925, 10 May 1926, 20 Oct 1930, 7, 8 Mar, 22 July 1932; *Bulletin*, 9 Mar 1932; Deakin papers (NL).
                                    MARTHA RUTLEDGE

MEESON, DORA; *see* COATES, GEORGE

MEHAFFEY, MAURICE WILLIAM (1884-1970), engineer and public servant, was born on 17 December 1884 at Invercargill, New Zealand, son of William Graham Mehaffey, teacher, and his wife Violet Ann, née Mitchell. He was educated at Southland Boys' High School and Canterbury College, University of New Zealand (B.E. (Mech), 1910). He combined his studies with tennis and football and executive positions in student associations. In 1909-10 he lectured in engineering at Canterbury College, then joined the Auckland Harbour Board as assistant engineer.

In 1911 Mehaffey was appointed to the Queensland Railways, and was involved in the design of bridges. In 1912 he took up a position with the Queensland Harbour and Rivers Department and in 1914 was resident engineer at Bowen where he designed and constructed harbour and wharf extensions. In March 1916 he enlisted in the Australian Imperial Force, but after 300 days service he was discharged on the application of the Commonwealth government to permit his appointment to the Commonwealth Lighthouse Service as district lighthouse engineer, Queensland. On 3 July 1917 he married Alma Frances Le Neven in Cairns Presbyterian church. Between 1917 and 1923 Mehaffey supervised the construction of more than twenty lighthouses along the Queensland coast.

In 1923 he became assistant lighthouse engineer at the Melbourne headquarters. As an authority on harbour engineering and the Australian coastline, Mehaffey was twice seconded in 1924 and 1925 to the Prime Minister's Department to advise on national harbour projects. In 1927 he was appointed lighthouse engineer and in 1931-36 was director of lighthouses. His attendance at an international conference on signalling in Paris in 1933 resulted in the programme he initiated for the electrification of Australia's major lighthouses.

In 1936 Mehaffey was appointed Commonwealth director-general of works, and in January-April 1939 was acting director-general of civil aviation. In 1938 he had been responsible for the £400 000 extension of the General Post Office, Sydney. Political agitation led in 1939 to a royal commission into the 'almost fantastically complicated' circumstances relating to the largest Federal public works contract since the Depression. The commission found Mehaffey guilty of serious errors of administration, but not of improper motives. A departmental inquiry reprimanded him and he was transferred to Sydney as assistant director-general of works. From 1940 he was responsible for the construction of the Captain Cook [q.v.1] graving dock which was so important in the maintenance of naval shipping during the Pacific War. He retired in December 1949.

Mehaffey was an associate member of the Institution of Civil Engineers, London. He died on 25 July 1970 in a private hospital at Turramurra, Sydney, and was cremated. Two sons and a daughter survived him.

B. B. Schaffer and D. C. Corbett (eds), *Decisions* (Melb, 1965); M. Komesaroff, 'The Commonwealth Lighthouse Service: its formation and early development', *VHJ*, vol 48, no 2, May 1977; *Smith's Weekly* (Syd), 24 Mar 1945; MT267/1, file 43/1759 (AAO).   MICHAEL KOMESAROFF

MELBA, DAME NELLIE (1861-1931), prima donna, was born Helen Porter Mitchell on 19 May 1861 at Richmond, Melbourne, eldest surviving of ten children of David Mit-

chell [q.v.5], building contractor, and his wife Isabella Ann, née Dow. Her father's business acumen and strict code of behaviour strongly influenced Melba, who later declared that of all the men she had known he had meant most to her. Her mother shared her husband's taste for music and proficiently played a number of instruments including the family harmonium; she was the girl's first music teacher. Nellie was not, however, an infant prodigy. Although she first sang in public when 6, forming a lifelong attachment to 'Comin' thro' the Rye', it was her humming that visitors noticed. Unwittingly she had hit upon what she would later describe as an effective vocal exercise. She also whistled, and generally behaved like a tomboy.

Educated first by her aunts, Melba was sent to a boarding school at Richmond before entering as a day-girl at the new Presbyterian Ladies' College. There, in the context of the most advanced education then available to women in Victoria, she pursued her interests in singing and the piano: her teacher Mme Ellen Christian had been a student of the famous Manuel Garcia. Melba showed herself to be adept in elocution, accomplished at painting and in acquiring the social graces; in mathematics and English she was undistinguished.

Melba's leaving school in 1880 was overshadowed by her mother's death, followed by that of a sister. Deciding on a change of scene, David Mitchell contracted to buy a sugar mill near Mackay in Queensland. There the 21-year-old Nellie encountered Charles Nisbett Frederick Armstrong, tall, blue-eyed and three years her senior, a man who agreeably combined exceptional skills as a rough-rider with the recommendation of gentle birth: his father was a baronet. They were married in Brisbane on 22 December 1882. Sequestered in a tin-roofed house, Melba became bored with the incessant rain and frustrated by a foundering marriage. The birth of a son, George, did little to allay her growing ambition to sing professionally, and on 19 January 1884 she left Mackay for Melbourne.

Although Melba later repudiated her indebtedness to Pietro Cecchi, her then singing teacher, it was he who responded to her inquiring letter with an emboldening telegram, since he believed hers to be a voice which would enthral the world. Melba now applied herself totally, and on 17 May 1884 made her début at a Liedertafel concert at the Melbourne Town Hall. 'She sings like one out of ten thousand', wrote the *Australasian's* critic. It was here she met John Lemmone [q.v.], a flautist later to act as her accompanist, manager and opera company impresario, and who would be present at her deathbed.

After some success as a professional singer

(she earned £750 in the first year) Melba accompanied her father, appointed Victoria's commissioner to the Indian and Colonial Exhibition, to London in March 1886. At first she was captivated; but encouragement was not forthcoming. Sir Arthur Sullivan told her to keep on with her studies and in a years time he might offer her a small part in *The Mikado*; her one concert was smothered in fog and polite applause. However Melba had already arranged to have an audition in Paris with Mathilde Marchesi; a letter from Mme (Wiedermann-) Pinschof [q.v.], wife of the Austro-Hungarian consul in Melbourne and herself a former pupil of Marchesi, introduced her. Marchesi immediately recognized her potential. Nevertheless it was necessary to refine Mrs Armstrong's technique; the pupil's voice may have been indebted to the teacher for its extraordinary durability, though not for a great deal else.

In the seven years he had taught her, Cecchi had placed the voice, coached her in the leading Italian operatic roles, and won her confidence to the point where she asked him to form a touring company. Mme Marchesi's contribution was to send Melba forth to selected salons as much for her social education as for singing experience, and to introduce her to the various composers who visited the Ecole Marchesi. These included Delibes, Thomas, Massenet and in particular Gounod, who coached her in his operatic roles. The sense of indebtedness of 'Melba'—Marchesi had pressed on her the necessity of taking a suitable name, so she chose a contraction of that of her native city—was enormous. Habitually she addressed her in correspondence as 'Mother', and repeatedly stated that Marchesi had been her only teacher. Certainly Marchesi had transformed the girl.

Melba made her début as an opera singer at the Théâtre Royal de la Monnaie in Brussels, on 13 October 1887. She was an immediate hit as Gilda in *Rigoletto*, a daughterly role for a 26-year-old; she went against custom and appeared in plaits. Subsequently she appeared in *La Traviata* and in *Lucia di Lammermoor*; then, on 24 May 1888, sang Lucia at Covent Garden. It was not a conspicuous success; although she later sang her favourite role of Gilda, she seemed to make little headway, and on being offered a secondary part by the management in another opera, packed her bags and returned to Brussels. However she had found an ally at Covent Garden in the influential Lady de Grey, who wrote begging her to return. Melba consented, but meanwhile made her Paris début as Ophélie in *Hamlet* on 8 May 1889. Acclaimed by press and public alike, she moved on to Covent Garden, where she appeared with Jean and Edouard de Reszke in *Roméo et Juliette*. 'I date my success in London', she later recalled,

'quite distinctly from the great night of 15 June 1889'.

Melba was fortunate in that the greater part of her career coincided with Covent Garden's golden age, even though its architect, the impresario (Sir) Augustus Harris, had initially engaged her reluctantly. Harris mounted spectacular productions involving hundreds, broadened the repertoire and widened the audience while still drawing the aristocracy; the Royal Opera's extraordinary social status Melba found exhilarating. Even though some of her greatest triumphs occurred elsewhere, most notably at La Scala in 1893 and repeatedly in New York, it was to Covent Garden that Melba returned season after season, maintaining a permanent dressing room to which she alone held the key. There she reigned supreme: her eclipse by the ageing Patti in 1895 was temporary.. A powerful figure behind the scenes, Melba effectively blocked a number of rivals. In 1913 Covent Garden commemorated the twenty-fifth anniversary of her first appearance there with a gala performance: Melba appeared as Mimi in *La Bohème*, a role she had studied with the composer and made famous.

Assisted materially by her friend Lady de Grey, Melba moved freely in high society. It was remarked that she carried herself as if to the manner born. On first-name terms with the great, she would sing at their houses only when it pleased her: a not unreasonable attitude when, in addition to her tours to Continental opera houses, she had been invited to sing in St Petersburg before Tsar Alexander III, had sung in Stockholm before King Oscar II, in Vienna before Emperor Franz Joseph, and in Berlin before Kaiser Wilhelm II; she had also been commanded by Queen Victoria to Windsor. 'Years of almost monotonous brilliance' was the summation on her Covent Garden farewell programme. When she appeared in distant places, she was mobbed (much as pop-singers are today). Meanwhile friendly advice from Alfred de Rothschild strengthened her financial position. Shortly after the turn of the century she bought a house in Great Cumberland Place, London, to be her home for more than twenty years, employing French workmen to remodel it in the style of Versailles.

Although Charles Armstrong had sailed with Melba to Europe, he joined the army to keep himself occupied and occasionally visited his wife and baby in Paris. He was reluctant to shed the marriage; a spectacular row on the occasion of Melba's début in Brussels effectively ended it. In 1890 Melba met Philippe, duke of Orléans, the dashing heir of the Bourbon pretender to the French throne, then living in England. The pair were glimpsed together in London¦ Paris, Brussels,

St Petersburg, and Vienna where they indiscreetly shared a box at the Opera. The papers got hold of the story, and almost immediately Charles Armstrong filed a petition for divorce on the grounds of adultery. The case was eventually quietly dropped; diplomatic pressure may have been brought to bear. The scandal was enough to send the duke off on a two-year safari in Africa, and to impress upon a bereft Melba both the importance of discretion and an increased sense of solitariness. Armstrong, having spirited their son away to America, divorced her in Texas in 1900.

Melba's circle increasingly included Australians and she kept effective contact with her family. In 1902 her long-awaited return home took place, for a concert tour to all States and New Zealand: from the concerts in Sydney and Melbourne alone she netted £21 000, the takings of one Sydney concert setting a new world record. Melba's train journey was a royal progress southwards to Melbourne, where thousands turned out to greet her. A contingent from P.L.C. shrilled a 'coo-ee' as she alighted, while the Stock Exchange brokers waved their hats in the air as her carriage passed. For newly federated Australia, Melba represented glamour, success, and international acceptance: Melbourne in particular felt that she had made the place famous. Unfortunately, a week after she sailed for Europe in March 1903, John Ezra Norton [q.v.] penned an open letter in *Truth* which accused her of wilfulness, miserliness, parasitism and drunkenness. Norton made it plain that he would welcome a legal challenge and kept up the attack, but Melba, safely ensconced once more in London society, chose to ignore him. Unfounded stories of her fondness for the bottle continued to circulate for years afterwards.

Although she was entering her forties, Melba was at the peak of her career. She was commanded to sing for the president of France at Buckingham Palace; in 1904 she created the title role in Saint-Saëns' opera, *Hélène*, at Monte Carlo; and in 1906-07, since she was displeased with the Metropolitan, she deserted it for the recently founded, rival Manhattan Opera House, which she revived financially with a triumphant season. It was probably her finest hour. Shortly after that American tour she contracted pneumonia and, although she fulfilled her engagement at Covent Garden, found it necessary to go to Australia for a holiday. While she was away Luisa Tetrazzini, ten years younger, gave a season at Covent Garden and quickly became a sensation; however, once Melba returned she held her ground, even though on occasion she irksomely had to alternate roles. Tetrazzini's success was even greater in America, where she settled; although no longer challenged, Melba had been made

aware of the precarious nature of her primacy, and henceforth became increasingly concerned to develop her links with her homeland.

In 1909 she embarked on a 'sentimental tour' of Australia: she covered 10 000 miles (16 100 km), appearing in many remote towns. The further she toured, the deeper seemed the adulation: there were banquets, speeches, even small crowds at wayside stations as Melba progressed with an entourage consisting of her manager, a maid and a valet, together with two baby grand pianos. She would arrive a full twenty-four hours before a performance, and to sustain the excitement give her concert without an interval. On this visit she also began to promote what she regarded as the correct way of singing, essentially the Marchesi method as modified by herself. She bought a property at Coldstream near Lilydale, Victoria, and called in the architect and engineer John Grainger, father of Percy [q.v.9], to build Coombe Cottage. Increasingly it became the centre of her operations; nearly half of her remaining years would be spent in Australia. She returned in 1911 to head the celebrated Melba-Williamson [q.v.6] Opera Company; Williamson's arranged the venues, Lemmone and she engaged the artists. In England once more, she continued to command an extraordinary following: no fewer than seven kings and queens attended one gala performance at Covent Garden in 1914.

When World War I broke out, Melba had recently arrived at Coombe Cottage. To go back to Europe was difficult, but she did make three wartime concert tours of North America where she excited pro-allied sentiment, and also applied herself to raising funds for war charities at home, most notably by her spirited auctioneering of flags at the conclusion of her concerts. She probably raised as much as £100 000 for the war effort, and on one memorable occasion stated that she would be prepared, if necessary, to work on the wharves. When in 1915 two Austrian teachers (one of them Mme (Wiedermann-) Pinschof) resigned from the Albert Street Conservatorium to follow Marshall-Hall [q.v.] back to the University of Melbourne, Melba's response to what she saw as enemy action was to offer F. B. Hart [q.v.9] her full support. Her connexion with the university, where she had laid the foundation stone of Melba Hall in 1913, was snapped; that with Albert Street thereafter grew to the point where today it is known as the Melba Memorial Conservatorium. Her interpretation classes there became famous, and drew students from all over the country; a martinet, she would pace up and down in her high leather boots, ably drawing out general points from students' mistakes as they sang before her. To be taken up by Melba held terrors of its own. Stella Power, winner of a scholarship to Albert Street, was badgered beyond her temperamental capabilities since the diva was intent on establishing her as the 'Little Melba'. Eager to create a school of bel canto in Australia, Melba provided her services gratis to Albert Street and made the conservatorium responsible for publishing her singing tutor, the *Melba method* (1926).

The war over, Melba went to London to reopen Covent Garden; the city's weariness and shabbiness depressed her deeply. But the brown tweed coats she noted disapprovingly in the stalls, in place of the formal attire and tiaras of pre-war 'Melba nights', were but an indication of changed social conditions and the declining status of Covent Garden. She did not appear there again until 1923; in Australia she sang, offering cheap tickets, at the immensely successful Concerts for the People in Melbourne and Sydney in 1922, which drew some 70 000 people. A further Melba-Williamson opera tour took place in 1924; here she did her best to upstage the young Toti dal Monte. Beverley Nichols, who travelled with her while ghost-writing her *Melodies and memories* (1925), later writing the novel *Evensong* (1932) about her, observed the 'unutterable weariness of the perpetual struggle to keep her supremacy when her voice and her body were growing old'. Melba returned to England and on 8 June 1926 gave her farewell performance at Covent Garden. Three Australians sang with her in three of her best-known roles: one of them (at her insistence) was John Brownlee [q.v.7], making his Covent Garden début.

Melba now began a series of farewell appearances that, in 'doing a Melba', was to enrich the language as well as bolster her self-esteem. As early as October 1924 she had announced her Australian farewell to grand opera, but her last operatic performances, again in a portmanteau programme, occurred at the end of the third Williamson-Melba season (as the order had now become) in Sydney on 7 August and in Melbourne on 27 September 1928. Two months later in Geelong she gave her last Australian concert. Feeling that she had been away too long, Melba left for Europe for two years, and sang in Brighton before moving on to Paris and Egypt, where she developed a fever. She never quite shook it off; however she managed to sing one last time at a charity entertainment at the Hyde Park Hotel, London. Dreading another northern winter, Melba decided to return to Melbourne, but her health grew worse on board ship. Partly in the hope of getting better medical care, she later went to Sydney where, in St Vincent's Hospital, Darlinghurst, she died on 23 February 1931 of septicaemia, which had developed from facial surgery in Europe some weeks before.

Though tempered with some astonishment that so great a personage should have been a singer, the obituaries read as though for the passing of a monarch. 'Is it too much to say', asked the *Argus*, 'that she was the greatest Australian?'; in Canberra parliamentarians stood with heads bowed to honour her memory. As a visiting English musician had earlier written, it was difficult for anyone outside the country to realize the extraordinarily powerful position Melba occupied in Australia. She may indeed have told Dame Clara Butt to 'Sing 'em muck!'; certainly Melba felt obliged to pronounce on everything from the state of the Empire to the condition of the road to Portsea. In England she would trade on her Australianness to be brash and forthright, but in Australia, Beverley Nichols recalled, travelling with Melba 'was like travelling through France with Marie-Antoinette'. She would bestow graded, lavish tiepins as if they were decorations, certificates of approval to shopkeepers, and for her students at Albert Street designed a uniform complete with a blue letter 'M'. There were many acts of public charity and private generosity. Convinced of her own importance, she believed that the accidents which occurred during an American tour during World War I were German-inspired attempts to eliminate her, so effective had she been in the war effort. Her autobiography shows that Melba's social successes were quite as important to her as her singing ones. Yet, as she once remarked to an inquiring aristocrat, 'there are lots of duchesses but only one Melba'.

A splendid constitution and tenacity of purpose, allied with exceptional powers of concentration and attention to detail, were elements of a charismatic personality which enabled Melba to remain for so long in the forefront of the musical world. Her sense of theatre comprehended the audience as well as the piece in hand; on one occasion her direct intervention from the stage prevented a panic when fire broke out, and in a production of *The barber of Seville* in San Francisco in 1898, the year of the Spanish-American war, she won the hearts of a restless audience by singing 'The Star-Spangled Banner' in the music-lesson scene. Ruthless to rivals, she was quite capable of singing the same part from the wings in order to undermine a singer she did not like. A practical woman, she knew how to drive a hard bargain, while her feeling for show-biz gave her sureness of touch in dealing with the press.

Melba believed that her voice and personality were of a kind that came together only once a century. Certainly she drew the admiration of other singers, and even had the capacity to make them sing better. But not everyone rated her so highly. Whatever the case in London and New York, and to a lesser degree the Francophone countries, her standing was not quite so high beyond: Sir Thomas Beecham believed this to be because she was 'wanting in genuine spiritual refinement', while others spoke of her coldness. George Bernard Shaw, then a music critic, initially found Melba 'hard, shallow, self-sufficient and altogether unsympathetic', but by 1892—after the break with the duke of Orléans—he acknowledged her as not merely a brilliant singer but a dramatic soprano. Shortly afterwards Melba's limitations were made painfully apparent: her Brünnhilde in *Siegfried* at the Metropolitan in 1896 was a disaster, and her singing of the title role in *Aida* a few years later was scarcely more successful. Similarly, although Melba claimed that Puccini wrote the part of *Madame Butterfly* for her, and she studied it with him, something in the role eluded her and she never sang it.

She was at her best either in those parts which required a light voice, such as Gilda, Lucia, or Marguerite, or which did not require too great an exploration of psychological complexities, such as the lusty Nedda or the pathetic Mimi. In these parts she was so popular that her repertoire shrank to a dozen roles: she learned no new parts after 1904. She only twice created roles, both in undistinguished works; only after World War I did she put her aptitude for languages to use by singing *chansons*. The fact remains, however, that she sang with seeming effortlessness, producing a voice which Sarah Bernhardt described as being 'pure crystal', and which the soprano Mary Garden admired for the way it left the stage and seemed to hover in the auditorium like a beam of light. For Percy Grainger, 'Her voice always made me mindsee Australia's landscapes'.

It was as 'the Voice' that Melba sometimes chose to describe herself. 'Good singing', she stated, 'is easy singing'; nature had given her an almost perfect larynx and vocal cords. Her range was fully three octaves, while her registers were so well blended that even an eminent throat specialist thought they were one. A scientific measurement of her trill produced twenty feet of undulations between perfectly parallel lines. Instrumentalists admired her, not least for the way that, despite her imperious temperament, she scrupulously sought to realize the composer's intentions. From 1904 Melba began recording; she issued over one hundred records and helped to establish the gramophone. In 1920 she also became the first artist of international standing to participate in direct radio broadcasts.

Melba was appointed D.B.E. in 1918, and G.B.E. in 1927. She was survived by her son, and left an estate valued at £67 511: in 1914 she had been worth much more. Among her bequests was £8000 to the Albert Street Conservatorium for a singing scholarship, 'in the hope that another Melba may arise'. Of the portraits painted, those by Rupert Bunny [q.v.7] and John Longstaff [q.v.] are the best known; both are in the National Gallery of Victoria. Neither depicts the young Melba, with the electricity of her auburn hair and lively eyes, her majestic profile and frank mouth; nor do they show the Melba of later years, the one familiar to millions of Australians reading their newspapers, a cultural icon swaddled in furs and splendid isolation.

M. de Castrone Marchesi, *Marchesi and music,* (Lond, 1897); A. Murphy, *Melba* (Lond, 1909); P. Colson, *Melba* (Lond, 1932); B. Nichols, *All I could never be* (Syd, 1949), and *The unforgiving minute* (Lond, 1978); T. Waters, *Much besides music* (Melb, 1951); J. J. M. Thompson, *On lips of living men* (Melb, 1962); J. Wechsberg, *Red plush and black velvet* (Lond, 1962); J. Hetherington, *Melba* (Melb, 1967); B. and F. Mackenzie, *Singers of Australia* (Melb, 1967); H. Rosenthal, *Opera at Covent Garden* (Lond, 1967); J. Bird, *Percy Grainger* (Melb, 1977); *Musical Times,* 72 (1931), p 305; Melba Conservatorium (Melb), *Con Amore,* 1934, 1938, 1942; *Quadrant,* 2, no 3 (1958); *Argus,* *SMH* and *The Times,* 24 Feb 1931; Melba-Grainger correspondence (Grainger Museum, Univ Melb); Lemmone collection *and* Cochran collection *and* Van Straten collection *and* programmes, press cuttings and tapes (Performing Arts Museum, Melb); Melba-Marchesi correspondence (Podraghy collection) *and* Melba-Hart correspondence (NL); Melba biog file *and* McEwan collection *and* Beaumont scrap-book (LaTL).   JIM DAVIDSON

MELBOURNE, ALEXANDER CLIFFORD VERNON (1888-1943), historian, was born on 10 June 1888 at Hackney, Adelaide, son of William Clifford Melbourne, printer and trade union official, and his wife Elizabeth Agnes, née Braidwood. Alexander was educated at Norwood Public School and the Adelaide Pupil Teachers' School. For three years he taught at Unley Public School; then in 1908 he attended the University of Adelaide, winning the Tinline [q.v.6] scholarship in 1908 and first-class honours in history in 1910. He accepted a temporary assistant lectureship in the department of history and economics at the University of Queensland in 1913. Melbourne soon became honorary secretary of the newly formed Historical Society of Queensland and delivered its inaugural address.

With ten years experience in the citizen forces, on 20 August 1914 he enlisted as captain in the 9th Battalion, Australian Imperial Force, left with the first contingent, shared in the horrors of Gallipoli and was wounded on 25 April and 4 June 1915. Invalided out of active service in October, Melbourne returned to his previous position at the University of Queensland in 1916, but for much of 1916-18 worked in censorship and on troop-ships. On 20 November 1916 he married Ellen Mary Lowenthal in the Church of St Mary the Virgin, Kangaroo Point, Brisbane.

Melbourne returned to the university as lecturer in history and industrial history from 1919. He gained his M.A. in 1921 from the University of Adelaide for a thesis on the constitutional development of Queensland. He failed in 1922 to secure the foundation McCaughey [q.v.5] chair in history and economics for which Henry Alcock, an Oxford graduate, was preferred.

Regarded as a man of 'brilliance, bonhomie and restless initiative', 'always on the best of terms with his colleagues', Melbourne in 1920 was the first secretary of the University of Queensland academic staff association and the first non-professorial academic to be elected to the university senate in 1926-28 and 1932-43. He was a strong advocate of the St Lucia site and became heavily involved in the planning and construction of the new buildings. Vice-Chancellor J. D. Story [q.v.] was to remember Melbourne as 'one of the most virile and progressive members of the Senate' with 'a flair for organisation'.

In 1928 he was awarded a Laura Spelman Rockefeller fellowship, enabling him to study at the University of London for a Ph.D. (1930) under A. P. Newton, Rhodes professor in Imperial history. This was an unusual and imposing achievement for a Queensland scholar in humanities. His work in London led to his writing two chapters in volume 7, part 1, of the *Cambridge history of the British Empire* (1933), his John Murtagh Macrossan [q.v.5] lecture in 1932 on William Charles Wentworth [q.v.2] (Brisbane, 1934) and his classic study, *Early constitutional development in Australia* (Oxford, 1934). Returning to Queensland by early 1931 and without a party political affiliation, Melbourne was invited by Premier A. E. Moore [q.v.] to submit a scheme which would ensure reintroduction of a second chamber into the parliament. Melbourne's proposal was placed before Moore's party but nothing came of it.

At the suggestion of the public service commissioner and with financial support from the Moore government, the university senate sent him to Japan and China in 1931-32. Melbourne published his *Report on Australian intercourse with Japan and China* (Brisbane, 1932). He was Queensland government representative on the Queensland and Federal advisory committees on Eastern trade (chairman of both in 1933-35).

Having failed in attempts to secure chairs in Sydney (1929) and Adelaide (1934), Melbourne was appointed part-time foundation

librarian and promoted associate professor. He was a frequent and fine public lecturer and broadcaster.

In 1935 his application for the Australian trade commissionership in Tokyo was unsuccessful; the Japanese minister of foreign affairs, K. Hirota, supported him. Backed by the government and the university, Melbourne returned to East Asia in 1936 and compiled a *Report on a visit to the universities of China and Japan* (Brisbane, 1936). He also wrote several pamphlets on foreign policy for the Australian Institute of International Affairs. In 1937 he failed to secure the chair of history at the University of Melbourne. He was largely responsible for the engagement of a Japanese national, Ryonosuke Seita, to lecture in Oriental civilization in the University of Queensland's history department; Seita was interned soon after his arrival.

World War II brought Melbourne back into national service as a deputy district censor. He died, childless, of cerebral haemorrhage at Glenrowan Private Hospital, Brisbane, on 7 January 1943 and was cremated with Congregational forms. His wife survived him.

Introduction, A. C. V. Melbourne, *Early constitutional development in Australia*, R. B. Joyce ed (Brisb, 1963); M. I. Thomis, *The University of Queensland academic staff association—a historical outline* (Brisb, 1985); *Aust Lib J*, Jan 1961, p 73; *Chronicle* (Adel), 28 Jan 1932; *Queenslander*, 24 May 1934; *Courier Mail*, 8 Jan 1943; H. Bryan, The University of Queensland 1910-1960 (Syd, 1966, roneoed typescript, Fryer Lib); Melbourne papers (Fryer Lib); staff file for A. C. V. Melbourne, *and* Univ Qld Senate minutes (Univ Qld Archives).   MALCOLM I. THOMIS

MELDRUM, DUNCAN MAX (1875-1955), artist, was born on 3 December 1875 in Edinburgh, son of Edward David Meldrum, chemist, and his wife Christine, née Macglashan. He was educated at George Heriot's Hospital, Edinburgh, and arrived in Melbourne in 1889 with his father (who had taken a post with Felton, Grimwade [qq.v.4] & Co., wholesale druggists), his mother, two brothers and one sister.

After working briefly as a clerk in a wool store Meldrum enrolled in 1892 at the National Gallery School under Bernard Hall [q.v.9]. In 1895-96 he sometimes assisted George Coates [q.v.8] at his painting and life classes, was one of the artists in the Prehistoric Order of Cannibals club, and contributed cartoons to the socialist weekly the *Champion*. In 1899 he won the National Gallery travelling scholarship. To augment his travel funds he unsuccessfully requested the patronage of the trustees of the gallery for an art union which he proposed to conduct with his scholarship picture as the prize.

Proceeding to Paris in 1900 Meldrum began to work under L. J. R. Collin and Gustave Courtois at the Académie Colarossi. In March 1901 he was studying under Jean Paul Laurens at the Académie Julian as well as at Colarossi's, but he soon withdrew from both ateliers. In June he was living with a maternal uncle in Edinburgh and thence in December he shipped a nude study, painted in Scotland, to the Melbourne gallery trustees. He had already begun that year to copy works in the Louvre and on his return to Paris in 1902 copied a portrait by Tintoretto and Paolo Veronese's *Flight from Sodom*. Later that year he began to work on the original painting required by the terms of his scholarship. In Paris Meldrum met Charles Nitsch, a painter from Pacé near Rennes, who introduced Meldrum to his family; about 1907 he married Nitsch's sister Jeanne Eugenie, a singer of the Opéra Comique, Paris. From Rennes Meldrum exhibited 'La Leçon' at the Salon de la Société des Artistes Français in 1904, and from Paris 'Le contre-fa' in 1905. In 1907-08 he painted murals on commission, in the Chateau de Pacé. He exhibited 'Au Chateau de Pacé' and 'Un Paysan de Pacé' in 1908 at the Société des Artistes Français, and in 1911 'L'homme qui rit'. He was elected an associate of the Société Nationale des Beaux-Arts.

Returning to Melbourne with his family in 1912, Meldrum lived with his parents in East Melbourne, then at St Kilda. In 1915 he took a studio at 527 Collins Street, for a time sharing it with Harley Griffiths, senior, and opened an art school there. Among his students were Clarice Beckett [q.v.7], Colin Colahan, Auguste Cornels, John Farmer, Polly Hurry, Justus Jorgensen, Percy Leason [q.v.] and Arnold Shore [q.v.], and he influenced considerably the work of his friend Alexander Colquhoun [q.v.8], whose son Archibald Douglas was also a Meldrum student at that time. In 1916-17 he was elected president of the Victorian Artists' Society.

In 1919 *Max Meldrum his art and views*, edited by Colahan, was published, including a long essay by Meldrum entitled 'The invariable truths of depictive art' developed from a lecture in 1917. In it he argued that painting was a pure science, the science of optical analysis or photometry by means of which the artist, in carefully perceiving and analysing tone and tonal relationships, could produce an exact appearance of the thing seen. Tone was the most important component of the art of painting, next came proportion, 'the superficial area occupied by one tone', and then colour, the least important component. The decadence of civilization was revealed through art by the declining interest in tonal analysis and the increased contemporary interest in colour. The theory, despite its several constraints on proportion and colour, proved highly influential among his students and a Meldrum school of painting, impressed by the theory and methods of its master, developed in Melbourne. From the late 1930s his ideas were promulgated in Sydney by Hayward Veal, and in the United States of America by Leason at the Staten Island Institute of Art and Science.

Meldrum's school became the principal alternative in Victoria to the National Gallery's. Between 1916 and 1923 he held his classes in the city, then moved them to a large room in his home in Kooyong Road, Elsternwick. In April 1926 he sailed for France where he lived for some years, making a six-month tour of the U.S.A. in 1928 to lecture on his theory and methods of painting. Returning to Melbourne in 1931 he took a house at Armadale for six months, then moved to Olinda until 1933. In 1936 he bought a house in Belmont Avenue, Kew, and next year opened a new school in Collins Street. During the 1930s his students included John Farmer, Ron Crawford, Peter Glass, Hayward Veal and Ida Meldrum. He was a trustee of the National Gallery of Victoria in 1937-50, his strong opposition to the acquisition of modernist work bringing him into confrontation with Sir Keith Murdoch [q.v.]. Meldrum won the Archibald [q.v.3] prize for portrait painting in 1939 and again in 1940. In 1950 *The science of appearances as formulated and taught by Max Meldrum*, a substantial account of his theory and methods edited by Russell Foreman, one of his students, was published in Sydney. He died at Kew on 6 June 1955 and was cremated. His wife (d. 1966) and two daughters survived him.

Meldrum was probably the only Australian artist to develop a fully formulated theory of painting and to practise and teach it. Small in stature, generous to a degree, he was also argumentative and occasionally waspish. Lionel Lindsay [q.v.], intolerant of his fanatical dedication to his theory, dubbed Meldrum 'the mad Mullah' and Norman Lindsay [q.v.] depicted him as the dogmatic McQuibble in his novel *A curate in Bohemia*. A pacifist during World War I, he gave influential support to Egon Kisch on his arrival in Australia in 1934 and actively defended civil liberties over the years.

Meldrum became a foundation member of the Australian Art Association, in 1912. He held exhibitions of his work in Melbourne at the Athenaeum Hall (1913 and 1922) and Gallery (1931), at Georges Gallery (1945), and in Sydney at David Jones [q.v.2] gallery (1937) and Farmer's [q.v.4] Blaxland Gallery (1941). He also exhibited with the Royal Society of Portrait Painters, London. A retrospective exhibition of his work was held in the National Gallery of Victoria, the National Art Gallery of New South Wales and the Queensland National Art Gallery in 1954. The National Gallery of Victoria also held an exhibition of his work in 1961. He was awarded the medal of the Society of Artists, Sydney, for services to Australian art. There is a self-portrait in the Art Gallery of South Australia.

J. J. M. Thompson, *On lips of living men* (Melb, 1962); D. Meeson Coates, *George Coates, his art and his life* (Lond, 1937); C. B. Christesen (ed), *The gallery on Eastern Hill* (Melb, 1970); E. Hanks (comp), *Australian art and artists to 1950* (Melb, 1982); *Triad* (Syd), 10, no 6 (Apr 1925); *Meanjin Q*, 26, no 2 (June 1967); *Argus*, 2 Sept 1912, 23 July 1913; *Punch* (Melb), 18 June 1925; *SMH*, 1, 3 Nov 1937, 20 Jan 1940, 22 Jan, 14 Nov 1941, 11 Mar 1950, 10 July 1954; *Age*, 7 June 1955, 22 Aug 1959; *Sunday Mirror* (Syd), 23 Sept 1962; J. McGrath, The Australian Art Association, 1912-1933 (B. Soc. Sci. special study, Roy Melb Inst of Technology, 1974); Aust art and artists files (SLV) *and* unpublished letter, Meldrum to Leason, 23 July 1928 (Leason papers, SLV); biog cuttings and artists files (NL); Salon exhibition catalogues, Paris, 1903-06, 1908, 1911 (held by Société des Artistes Français, Paris); information from Mrs E. Thomson and Miss I. Meldrum, Kew, Melb.

JOYCE MCGRATH
BERNARD SMITH

MELROSE, CHARLES JAMES (1913-1936), aviator, was born on 13 September 1913 at Burnside, Adelaide, only child of James Melrose (d. 1922), pastoralist, and his second wife Hilda Westley, née Billing. While still at the Collegiate School of St Peter he joined the South Australian Yacht Squadron and took lessons with the (Royal) Aero Club of South Australia at Parafield, gaining his pilot's licence at 19. His widowed mother was his first passenger; he was influenced by her enthusiasm and by her English aviator uncle, Pemberton Billing. Sir John Melrose [q.v.] was another uncle.

Jimmy purchased a DH Puss Moth fitted with a powerful 120 horsepower (89 kw) Gipsy Major engine. He named the plane 'My Hildergarde' and in August 1934 flew 8000 miles (12 875 km) solo around Australia, reducing the previous record by almost two days, to 5 days, 10 hours, 57 minutes. A skilful and courageous natural flyer, Melrose was tall, flaxen haired and blue eyed; while conforming to the popular ideal of a hero, he avoided lionization. He exercised seriously, swimming at Glenelg where he and his mother lived; he kept early hours, neither smoked nor drank alcohol and ate 'Oslo' lunches.

On his twenty-first birthday he left Parafield in the Puss Moth for England, reaching Croydon in a record 8 days, 9 hours. At Mildenhall he joined the Melbourne Centenary Air Race as the youngest entrant and, in spite

of an emergency landing at Darwin, came third in the handicap and was the only solo flyer to finish. Awarded second prize of £500, he established a monoplane fund for the Aero Club of South Australia. In October 1934 he set a South Australian altitude record over Gulf St Vincent; two months later he made the first non-stop Adelaide-Tasmania flight, followed by a record time from Launceston to Sydney.

In January 1935 Melrose studied navigation and blind flying in England at the Air Service Training Centre, Hambling; returning to Australia in a new Percival Gull, he joined in the unsuccessful search for Sir Charles Kingsford Smith [q.v.9]. His first accident involved a forced landing at Penrose, New South Wales. On recovering from injuries he went to England, bought a five-seater Heston Phoenix monoplane, and in April 1936 used it on a goodwill flight home to publicize South Australia's centenary; a crowd of 8000 greeted him at Parafield. Later he started air taxi work, once flying the premier to a country meeting.

On 5 July 1936 Jimmy began a charter flight from Melbourne to Darwin. Over South Melton, Victoria, in turbulent conditions with low visibility his Heston Phoenix broke up, killing both pilot and passenger, A. G. Campbell, D.S.O. The cause of the accident was established as structural failure. Australians joined Prime Minister Joseph Lyons [q.v.], in mourning their 'chivalrous young knight of the air'. Funeral services were held simultaneously in Melbourne's and Adelaide's Anglican cathedrals. Schoolchildren lined the route from St Paul's to Springvale necropolis, as planes circled overhead. In Adelaide both Houses of parliament suspended their sittings and St Peter's Cathedral was packed, mainly with women, who had idolized Jimmy. Three Royal Aero Club Moths flew over as the service ended.

It was not until 1968 when his mother died that Melrose's ashes were buried, with her, at the North Road Anglican cemetery, Adelaide. His name is commemorated by a look-out tower at the Glenelg Surf Life-Saving Club and by James Melrose Road bordering Adelaide airport.

Roy Aero Club of SA, *Wing Tips*, Aug 1934-Nov 1936, no 68, 70, 71, 81, 95; *Chronicle* (Adel), 9 July 1936; *Advertiser* (Adel), 6, 8, July 1936, 7 June 1968; H. Jones interviews for ABC radio, Personalities remembered (typescript, SRG 196/18 SAA); information from Mrs C. E. Wigg, Gilberton, Adel.

HELEN JONES

MELROSE, SIR JOHN (1860-1938), pastoralist, was born on 12 January 1860 at Rosebank, near Mount Pleasant, South Australia, third son of George Melrose and his wife Euphemia Medina, née Thompson. After attending Prince Alfred College he worked in a mercantile office for a year before becoming assistant manager of his father's property, Wangaraleedini, at Franklin Harbour. From 1884 he was his father's manager at Ulooloo station in the mid-north of the colony, where he lived for the rest of his life. He was a member, and sometime chairman, of Hallett District Council for the next forty-nine years. On 17 April 1886 at the Congregational Church, Glenelg, he married Emily Eliza Edhouse.

In 1892 Melrose's father died. He bought Ulooloo from the estate and began a series of pioneering stock imports: in 1895 he brought the first Dorset sheep to Australia; in 1913 the first French Percheron draughthorses; in 1928 the first Wensleydale sheep, from New Zealand. With Henry Dutton he bought the 32 000-acre (12 900 ha) station, North Booborowie, for £96 320 in 1897. He also became a director of a station in Western Australia and of Oakbank Ltd, on the South Australian border with New South Wales.

About 1898 he began to go blind. He taught himself braille and made a frame to enable him to write his own cheques. He wore small, round, metal-rimmed spectacles and developed heightened hearing and touch. The latter he used to assess his stud sheep and their wool. By 1901 he had lost all sight but still managed his property, with his daughter Margaret Lily as constant companion. He was known affectionately as 'The Blind Squatter' and occasionally contributed articles to livestock journals under a pseudonym.

In 1910 the government, following a 'land for the people' policy, bought North Booborowie and opened it for closer settlement. Melrose was a big shareholder in the Broken Hill Proprietary Co. Ltd and became a philanthropist, giving over £20 000 to causes including Burra Burra Hospital, the Royal Institution for the Blind, and, notably, in 1927 £10 000 to the Waite [q.v.6] Agricultural Research Institute to build its first proper chemical laboratory. He desired 'to help research . . . with problems of any and every nature associated with the land'. In 1929 the building was named after him. The previous year he had been knighted.

In 1934 he financed his nephew, the aviator C. J. 'Jimmy' Melrose [q.v.], to enter the Melbourne Centenary Air Race. Despite his disability Sir John was admired as 'an heroic figure'; somewhat crusty when young, he mellowed to a kindly, gentle, optimistic old man. Predeceased by his wife, he died on 16 September 1938 at Calvary Hospital, Adelaide, and was buried in the Anglican cemetery, Mount Pleasant. His estate was sworn for probate at £142 749. He was survived by his daughter, who married Arthur Gaynor

Owen-Smythe—they managed Ulooloo till their deaths in 1970—and his son Alexander John (1889-1962) who was a member of the House of Assembly in 1933-41 and of the Legislative Council in 1941-62.

Marlene Richards, *Hallett—a history of town and district* (Adel, 1977); V. A. Edgeloe, *The Waite Agricultural Research Institute* (Adel, 1984); *Observer* (Adel), 24 Dec 1904; *Register* (Adel), 20 July 1927; *Advertiser* (Adel), 17 Sept 1938.

SUZANNE EDGAR

MELVIN, JOSEPH DALGARNO (1852-1909), journalist, was born on 15 August 1852 at Banff, Banffshire, Scotland, son of John Melvin, shore master, and his wife Isabella, née Gossip. Both sides of the family had connexions with trade and the sea. Joe was educated at Banff Academy where he showed aptitude as both a scholar and sportsman. Aged 12, he rescued a schoolfellow from the Moray Firth and became a local hero. On leaving school he worked in the local post and telegraph office, studied shorthand and aimed at a career in journalism. He joined the staff of the *Moray Advertiser* and later the Perth *Advertiser*. In 1875 Melvin's father returned from a long spell in Australia to arrange for his family to follow him to Melbourne where he later became a partner in Parsons Bros & Co., food and grain merchants. Active in the Congregational Church, Melvin senior also achieved some reputation as a lecturer on religion and science and as a magic lanternist.

Joseph Melvin worked on the *Argus* in the late 1870s, gaining a name for initiative. At the siege of the hotel at Glenrowan in 1880 he was in the thick of things: he helped to move the wounded Ned Kelly [q.v.5] indoors, was one of the first to interview him and 'scooped' other papers with his quickly wired reports on the Kellys' last stand. In 1885 Melvin secured a passage (by bribery or by posing as a crewman) aboard the *Iberia* which was transporting colonial troops to the Sudan. He was accredited as a war correspondent and sent back lively reports to the Sydney *Daily Telegraph* and the *Bulletin*. Subsequently he seems to have engaged chiefly in political reporting. His pamphlet *The Victorian electors' guide to questions and candidates* was published in 1892.

In mid-1892 Melvin set off on the assignment for which he is best known—a report on the Pacific Islands labour trade. He joined the *Helena* as supercargo and witnessed a typical recruiting voyage to the Solomon Islands. His vivid account, serialized in the *Argus*, provides one of the best first-hand descriptions of the trade. Melvin acquitted the recruiters of kidnapping, convinced that the islanders engaged in the business willingly and cannily. He wrote: 'No kidnapping, force, fraud, misrepresentation or cajoling was resorted to', a judgement broadly endorsed by recent historians.

In the 1890s Melvin worked as a parliamentary and political reporter for various newspapers and was appointed to the Victorian Hansard staff in 1905. Poor health, however, curtailed his activities. He had married Margaret Ann Booth on 30 November 1885 at St John's Church of England, Brisbane; they were childless and after her death in 1908 Melvin's own health deteriorated rapidly. A chronic sufferer from rheumatism, which his adventures perhaps aggravated, and other complaints, he died on 26 June 1909 at Surrey Hills, Melbourne. He left an estate valued for probate at £49, and was buried in Boroondara cemetery. His funeral was attended by many pressmen including the *Age*'s proprietor and the editor of the *Herald*. Obituaries in metropolitan and provincial newspapers testified to his high personal and professional standing.

H. Gordon, *An eyewitness history of Australia* (Adel, 1976); J. D. Melvin, *The cruise of the Helena*, P. R. Corris ed (Melb, 1977); *Bulletin*, 21 Mar 1885; *Argus*, 26, 28 June 1909; *Age*, 28 June 1909; *Ballarat Courier*, 29 June 1909.

PETER CORRIS

MENNELL, PHILIP DEARMAN (1851-1905), journalist and biographer, was born on 10 March 1851 at Newcastle-upon-Tyne, England, fourth son of George Mennell, cokemaker, and his wife Hannah, née Tuke. He was a grandson of the Yorkshire Quaker philanthropist Samuel Tuke. Educated privately, Philip showed early proficiency in writing when in 1872 he published *Lord John Manners, a political biography*. He studied for the law and was admitted as a solicitor in 1875. However, he soon abandoned his profession and migrated to Victoria. Mennell later wrote of the experiences of middle-class migrants who landed in Melbourne with meagre capital; the description by 'New Chum', published in A. Patchett Martin's [q.v.5] *Oak-bough and wattle-blossom* (London, 1888), may partly reflect Mennell's own experience.

From Melbourne he 'went bush' to Bairnsdale where he printed and published the *Advertiser* newspaper from May 1877 (and became part-owner in 1879) and where on 7 March 1879 with Anglican rites he married Ellen Elizabeth O'Meara; they had two sons and two daughters. He described Bairnsdale in general terms and with mixed feelings in 'Traits of the township', a sketch contributed to a book he edited in 1889, *In Australian wilds*. Mennell ran the *Bairnsdale Advertiser* successfully until April 1882 when, appar-

ently, the increased work-load of his job-printing business compelled him to admit J. W. Baker as his partner. Some doubt is cast on Mennell's success by the rival *Bairnsdale and Bruthen News* which implied that by April Mennell had already left for Melbourne to 'accept a subordinate billet on a paper of adverse politics'. Whatever reasons did prompt Mennell to leave Bairnsdale, he was for some months in 1882 acting sub-editor and leader-writer for the Melbourne *Age*. On 20 July he sold his share in the *Advertiser* to H. M. West and early next year returned to London to represent the cable syndicate controlled by the *Age*.

Mennell revisited Australia as special correspondent for the *Daily Chronicle* in 1891, penning enthusiastic articles (republished in 1892 as *The coming Colony*) on the latent resources of Western Australia. In August 1892, after eighteen months assiduous work, he also published his *Dictionary of Australasian biography*: with 542 pages containing nearly 2000 entries it was a substantial volume of collective biography relating to Australia as a whole, though it did not cover the pre-1855 period. Mennell had consulted journalists and publishers as well as government office-holders and historians and had achieved a fine balance between a particularity for local circulation and a condensed treatment for English readers.

From December 1892 until shortly before his death Mennell was editor-proprietor of the *British Australasian and New Zealand Mail*. He championed the cause of Federation and publicized Australian visitors to Britain. He returned to Australia briefly in 1895 for *The Times*, and again in 1900 for the *Morning Post*, each time visiting Western Australia where he appears to have had business interests; he was a member of the Coolgardie Club.

A Roman Catholic and a fellow of the Royal Geographical Society, Mennell died of cancer on 19 October 1905 at Bayswater, London, and was buried at Kensal Green. Philip spelt his name Mennell, as did his brother Henry Tuke and sister Edith. Two brothers, including the author Wilfred, used the name, Meynell.

G. Meudell, *The pleasant career of a spendthrift* (Lond, 1929); *Bairnsdale and Bruthen News*, 19 Apr 1882; *Bairnsdale Advertiser*, 2 May, 5 Sept 1882; *British A'sian*, 6 Oct 1904, 26 Oct 1905; *Argus*, 23 Oct 1905; *Leader* (Melb), 28 Oct 1905; *Bulletin*, 2 Nov 1905.   BILL TREVENA

MERCER, JOHN EDWARD (1857-1922), Anglican churchman and bishop, was born on 13 February 1857 at Eccleshill, Bradford, Yorkshire, England, son of Rev. Edward

Mercer and his wife Mary. Young Edward obtained a scholarship in 1871 to Rossall School, Lancashire, where he was a voracious reader and revelled in sport. In 1876 he went up to Lincoln College, University of Oxford (B.A., 1879; M.A., 1886; D.D., 1902). He was ordained in 1880 and began his ministry with short curacies in the Durham diocesan parishes of Tanfield (1880-82) and Penshaw (1882-83) where he won the approbation of working-class parishioners. On 18 April 1882 he married Josephine Antonia (d. 1907), daughter of Rev. William Archdall.

In 1883 Mercer was appointed Rossall School missioner (or school-financed curate) at another working-class parish, Newton Heath, Manchester, where the Mercers had full scope for work among the poor. Open-air services, youth clubs and temperance associations helped to raise local morale. In 1889 he was appointed rector of St Michael's, Angel Meadow, an inner Manchester parish described by Engels in 1844 as a grim victim of the industrial revolution. Mercer himself wrote vividly of the 'grinding poverty', 'besotted drinking' and prostitution which he strove to alleviate. He became a leading member of the Christian Social Union. In 1897 Mercer transferred to the nearby parish of Gorton, another industrialized area where his dash and enthusiasm rapidly developed the religious and social amenities of the parish.

Mercer was appointed fifth Anglican bishop of Tasmania in 1902 and arrived on 1 September. To the mounting fury of upper-class Tasmanians, the robust new bishop was an outspoken social reformer. He provided a cathedral service for the infant Labor Party's first conference in 1903, spoke frequently to Labor gatherings, and conducted missions to remote Bass Strait islands and mining camps. He participated vigorously in the exposure of 'sweating' among Hobart seamstresses, a campaign that helped to obtain Tasmania's first wages boards in 1910. His support of the Workers' Political League and trade unions earned him the title of 'the Socialist Bishop', and led to bitter attacks in the local press. Mercer was a good administrator, encouraging the building of new churches and schools. He was a compelling speaker and published prolifically while in Tasmania. An amateur poet and painter, he supported intellectual and cultural activities and was a keen bushwalker.

Mercer resigned and sailed home from Tasmania on 15 March 1914. After a period at Brighton he was appointed assistant to the bishop of Chester, accepting a residential canonry in September 1916. At Southampton he married on 27 April 1916 Harriet Ethel Bennion, twenty years his junior and a keen church-worker. He retained his enthusiasm for social reform. In 1919 he added the arch-deaconry of Macclesfield to his duties and participated vigorously in the Church of England convocation. His death from erysipelas on 28 April 1922 came as a shock. Mercer left no children by either marriage but an adopted daughter Sarah was mentioned in his will of 1916.

Of Mercer's numerous books and pamphlets, the most notable are *Social equality* (Sydney, 1905), *The soul of progress* (Melbourne, 1907, Moorhouse [q.v.5] lectures), *The science of life and the larger hope* (London, 1910), *Nature mysticism* (London, 1913), *The mystery of life* (London, 1915) and *Why do we die? An essay on thanatology* (London, 1919).

E. Hudson, *The Rossall mission* (priv print, 1911); R. P. Davis, *Bishop John Edward Mercer*, Univ Tas Occasional Paper, 34 (Hob, 1982); *Rossallian*, 8 Apr, 16 Oct 1889, 16 June 1922; *PTHRA*, 30 (June 1983), no 2.   R. P. DAVIS

MEREDITH, JOHN BALDWIN HOYSTEAD (1864-1942), soldier and doctor, was born on 11 November 1864 at Derrylough, Rosenallis, Queen's County, Ireland, seventh child of William Meredith, landowner, and his wife Annie, née Hoystead. The Merediths were a Welsh family. John was orphaned when he was 9 and was educated at Arlington College, Port Arlington. Unable to afford either an army commission or to play football for Ireland, in 1882-87 he studied medicine. In the leading hospitals in Dublin under the auspices of the Royal College of Surgeons in Ireland, in 1888 he qualified as a licentiate of the Royal colleges of Surgeons and Physicians, Edinburgh, and of the Faculty of Physicians and Surgeons, Glasgow.

He hoped to marry and practise in Ireland but decided, after asking his fiancée if she would go to one of the colonies, to try for a passage as ship's doctor. Only after signing on did he realize he was going to Australia. He arrived in 1888 and bought a practice at Raymond Terrace, New South Wales. His fiancée, Harriett Eveline Waters of Kildare, arrived two years later, after her father, who had prevented her leaving, had died. They were married on the day she landed, 20 May 1890, in St Phillip's Anglican Church, Sydney. Of their three children, Marjorie married (Lieut-General Sir) Iven Mackay.

Meredith became government medical officer for a large area. He had joined the Hunter River Light Horse and volunteered for the South African War, going as medical officer in the Citizen's Bushmen's Contingent in 1900. He served in Rhodesia, the Transvaal, Orange River Colony, Cape Colony and at the relief of Mafeking and was awarded the Queen's Medal with four clasps. In 1905, as second lieutenant, he formed a troop of light horse at Raymond Terrace, part of the 4th Light Horse Regiment; he was promoted captain in 1906 and major in 1908.

Meredith took his family to England and Ireland in 1908-09 and was attached to the 18th Hussars for training in Ireland. While overseas, he bought a bull calf and a cow in calf for his Leigh Jersey stud and also a motor car. In 1910 he commanded the 4th Light Horse Regiment; promoted lieut-colonel in 1911, he commanded the 6th L.H.R. (Hunter River Lancers) in 1912.

On the outbreak of World War I Meredith joined the Australian Imperial Force on 28 August 1914 in command of the 1st L.H.R. which fought dismounted on Gallipoli from May 1915 until the evacuation. In November he was temporary commander of the 1st Light Horse Brigade. In mid-January 1916, back in Egypt, the brigade was up the Nile from Cairo. In May Meredith commanded in the Sinai desert while 'Fighting Charlie' Cox [q.v.8] had sick leave. He was in command during the battle of Romani when his three regiments held back the Turks throughout the night of 3-4 August. (Sir) Henry Gullett [q.v.9], in his official history, wrote: 'by their calm and dogged work in the night Romani had virtually been won'. Later, 'in February [1917] the 4th Australian Light Horse Brigade was created in Egypt under Meredith, who had handled the 1st Light Horse Brigade so admirably at Romani'. Meredith was awarded the Distinguished Service Order in December 1916 and in February 1917 the Order of the White Eagle (Serbia). He was promoted colonel and temporary brigadier general in May 1917 and in November, just before the battle of Beersheba, he embarked for Australia for 'family reasons'. His A.I.F. appointment ended on 3 January 1918. In 1921 he commanded the 2nd Cavalry Brigade, Australian Military Forces, and he retired in 1923 as honorary brigadier general.

Meredith was a well-built, athletic man, with a great zest for life. He was successful and popular in medical practice. His Jersey stud was of great interest to him and he became vice-president of the Jersey Herd Society of New South Wales. He loved animals and had many pets, usually about nine dogs, retrievers, setters and pointers. After his wife's death, he married 20-year-old Alice Christina Mowbray Windeyer on 19 October 1921, at St John's Anglican Church, Raymond Terrace. Meredith died at Maitland on 1 January 1942 and was cremated. He was survived by a son and two daughters of his first marriage, and by his wife and four young sons.

Aust Defence Dept, *Official records of the Australian military contingents to the war in South* *Africa*, P. L. Murray ed (Melb, 1911); H. S. Gullett, *Sinai and Palestine* (Syd, 1939); G. W. Nutting, *History of the Fourth Light Horse Brigade*, AIF (Brisb, 1953); records (AWM); family information from Lady Mackay, Roseville, Syd.

ELYNE MITCHELL

MERRETT, SIR CHARLES EDWARD (1863-1948), merchant and agriculturalist, was born on 8 January 1863 at South Yarra, Melbourne, son of English parents Samuel Headen Merrett, civil servant, and his wife Sarah Ashton, née Baxter. His father, who had migrated to Victoria in 1853, built railways in suburban Melbourne and designed its first Exhibition Building. A victim of the 'Black Wednesday' 1878 retrenchments, he died soon after. Charles, at Melbourne Church of England Grammar School, was forced to forgo a university education, and in 1880 joined the firm of Welch, Perrin & Co., machinery merchants and manufacturers' representatives, as an office-boy. He worked his way up to become a partner in 1890 and managing director in 1916.

Merrett's career in the armed forces began in 1880 when he joined the St Kilda Rifles. He rose through the ranks, transferring to the Victorian Mounted Rifles in 1883, becoming lieutenant and quartermaster (1889) and captain (1892). Transferring to the Australian Light Horse, he served as captain (1903) and major (1905) with the 10th, 11th and 29th brigades before becoming, in 1915, lieut-colonel of the 5th Light Horse Brigade and the oldest serving light horse officer. To his disappointment he was not to go overseas in World War I, but served instead on the selection committee for officers of the Expeditionary Forces. He retired in 1920 with the rank of colonel.

Related to his military career was Merrett's long association with the sport of rifle-shooting, beginning in 1878. In 1907 he became chairman of the Victorian Rifle Association and later also chaired the Commonwealth Council of Rifle Associations. In 1914, 1928 and 1937 he took the Bisley team to England and in 1941 was elected a vice-president of the National Rifle Association in England. A council-member of the Victorian Rifle Association for over thirty-three years, he is commemorated by the Merrett Rifle Range at Williamstown.

From the time he began work at Welch, Perrin & Co., Merrett showed a developing interest in agriculture and the land. Long-standing service to the Royal Agricultural Society of Victoria culminated in his record term as president in 1915-47. Melbourne *Punch* believed that the R.A.S. had 'never had a more energetic or able president'. Large land purchases extended the showgrounds, and a building programme added pavilions, halls and grandstands, most of which are still in use. Merrett's aim was to produce a better educated farmer, and he built up the Melbourne Show accordingly. He was also associated with the founding of Young Farmers and of the Country Women's Association.

Politics attracted Merrett and he joined the People's Liberal Party (Victoria), founded in 1910 to muster support for the Fusion. In his only parliamentary attempt he stood unsuccessfully for the Federal seat of Melbourne Ports in 1913. Thenceforth he concentrated on party organization, becoming an executive-member of the National Federation after it merged with the People's Liberal Party. By the 1920s he was disenchanted with the Nationalists. He called for a return to liberalism and with T. R. Ashworth [q.v.7] of the Employers' Federation formed the Liberal Union, as a breakaway from the National Union, protesting against its continued support of W. M. Hughes [q.v.9]. They rallied financial support and in 1922 supported the successful Federal election campaign of (Sir) John Latham [q.v.], as an Independent Liberal. The Liberal Union's policy manifesto supported private enterprise, efficiency and economy in government. S. M. (Viscount) Bruce [q.v.7] saw it as conservative but it gained enough support to operate through the 1920s, still supporting candidates in the 1929 elections.

In State politics Merrett emerged in the mid-1920s as one of the key figures protesting at the government's neglect of the metropolitan area. He was one of the five founders in 1926 of the Australian Liberal Party which, although short-lived, brought down the Allan [q.v.7]-Peacock [q.v.] government.

Merrett collected a large number of public commitments. He was a South Melbourne councillor in 1915-37 and mayor in 1922-23. He chaired the Canned Fruits Export Control Board, the Big Brother Movement, the Empire Day Movement, the New Settlers League, the State Employment Council and the Society for the Protection of Animals. A justice of the peace from 1919, he was appointed C.B.E. in 1929 and knighted in 1934.

Merrett had married Annie Florence Slocombe at St Peter's Church, Melbourne, on 21 April 1891. He died at his Brighton home on 11 November 1948, survived by a son and a daughter. His other son Charles, a flight lieutenant, was killed at Dover, England, in 1916.

F. H. Noble and R. Morgan, *Speed the plough* (Melb, 1981); *Punch* (Melb), 3 Feb 1916, 29 Sept 1921; *Table Talk*, 22 Sept 1927; *Age* and *Argus*, 12 Nov 1948; M. Vines, The instability of govern-

ments and parties in Victoria in the 1920s (M.A. thesis, Univ Melb, 1975).   MARGARET VINES

MERRIMAN, SIR WALTER THOMAS (1882-1972), sheepbreeder, was born on 18 May 1882 at Ravensworth, Yass, New South Wales, second son of GEORGE MERRIMAN (1847-1915), sheepbreeder, and his wife Mary Ann (d. 1927), née Dowling. A grandnephew of James Merriman [q.v.5], George was born at Berrima on 13 May 1847. He began to build his fine-wool merino stud, Ravensworth, in 1865 on Mudgee and Tasmanian blood lines. After being bred within itself, the stud was augmented in the 1880s and 1890s by some notable sires from Cullenbone stud, Mudgee, and the Glasslough and Esk Vale studs in Tasmania. A keen exhibitor, he won many show prizes in the farmers' class. A justice of the peace and a member of the Yass Pastures and Stock Protection Board, he died at Ravensworth on 28 August 1915, survived by his wife, whom he had married at Yass on 29 October 1866, and by two daughters and three sons. His estate, valued for probate at £51 359, was divided between his sons.

Walter was educated at Murrumbateman Public School under C. G. Dyce. In 1903 he acquired a small draft of fine-woolled Ravensworth ewes and the sire, Mountain King, from his father and began his own small stud, Merryville, on part of Ravensworth. He campaigned against the American Vermont sheep introduced by (Sir) Samuel McCaughey [q.v.5], which he described as 'wrinkled horrors'. He shore his ram at the Yass Show in 1904 and its wool won first prize in the open class; it subsequently won eleven more firsts. At the Anglican church, Mundoonan, he married Kate Sleeman, daughter of a local grazier, on 18 November 1908.

In 1911 Merriman introduced Peppin [q.v.5] blood into part of his flock to produce plain-bodied sheep with medium to fine-medium wool and augmented this by purchasing the medium-wool sire, Sir Francis, from the Wanganella Estate of F. S. Falkiner [q.v.4] for 1000 guineas in 1917 when Merryville became a closed flock. However, it was as a breeder of fine-woolled sheep that he became renowned. In 1915 he had received a quarter of the ewes and rams from his father's estate and in 1921 bought 680 stud ewes at the Murgha dispersal sale. Kept separate, this flock was registered as the Merryville-Murgha stud. Unlike most sheepbreeders, he was an expert woolclasser and for many years prepared his own clip for sale.

In 1937 Merriman formed a family company, becoming managing director of Merry-

Merriman

A.D.B.

ville Pty Ltd which embraced sundry properties around Yass and Boorowa on the south-
western slopes. Merryville Poll Shorthorn
stud at Hillview, Murrumbateman, was
founded in 1943 and the Merryville Poll
Hereford stud in 1960 with stock from Milton
Park, Bowral, and the Brewarrina stud,
Narrandera.

Merryville sheep and wool won many
prizes including grand championships, and the
Stonehaven [q.v.] Cup for pens of five at the
Sydney Sheep Show a record twelve times,
the Weatherly [q.v.] Trophy (Melbourne), a
record six times in succession, and the Albury
Sheep Show's Mungadal Cup a record
twenty-one times. In 1953 Merryville won
every major award at the Sydney Sheep
Show; in the 1950s the stud's rams and super-
fine wool brought record prices. In over fifty
years as a sheepbreeder Merriman maintained the fine quality of his wool while
increasing the average yield of his flock to
fourteen lb. (6 kg) a head and at the same time
more than doubling the yield of his top breeds.
In 1954 he was knighted. He was a council-
member of the New South Wales Sheepbreeders' Association for many years and of
the Graziers' Association of New South
Wales.

Sir Walter was very prominent in local
affairs. He was a member of the Goodra-
digbee Shire Council (1906-10), president of
the Yass Pastoral and Agricultural Association (1923-25), captain and president of the
local bush fire brigade, director of the Yass
District Hospital, Pastures Protection Board
and District Soldiers' Memorial and Literary
Institute, a leading Freemason and a vice-
president of the Yass Picnic Race Club.

Hard-working, modest and hospitable with
a dry humour, Merriman was also a keen
sportsman. An enthusiastic cricketer and
amateur boxer in his youth, he played tennis,
golf and billiards well into old age, despite a
serious stockyard accident in the 1940s which
permanently damaged vital nerves controlling head movement and speech. Roses and
his collection of pre-1956 Holden cars were
other interests.

Merriman died at Yass on 25 January 1972,
survived by his two sons and four daughters
and was buried in the Anglican section of
Murrumbateman cemetery. His estate was
valued for probate at $169 099.

Register of stud merino flocks of the Commonwealth of Australia, 8 (Syd, 1929); NSW Sheepbreeders' Assn, The Australian merino (Syd,
1955); Pastoral Review, 16 Sept 1915, 16 July
1927, 16 Feb 1928, 10 June 1941, 16 Mar 1949, 19
Jan 1954, 25 Feb 1972; Aust Country Mag, July
1972; Australasian, 5 June 1937; SMH, 1 Nov
1937, 13 May 1953, 26 Jan 1972.
G. P. Walsh

MESSENGER, HERBERT HENRY
(1883-1959), footballer, was born on 12 April
1883 at Balmain, Sydney, third son of Charles
Amos Messenger, boatbuilder, from Middlesex, England, and his Melbourne-born wife
Anne Frances, née Atkinson. Nicknamed
'Dally' after W. B. Dalley [q.v.4], he was educated at Double Bay Public School, where he
played football. He then worked in the family
boatshed, in the down-at-heel fishing and
ferrying enclave within the otherwise upper-
class harbour-side eastern suburbs.

Messenger's father and grandfather had
been champion scullers and Dally was a good
cricketer and sailor of 18-footers and a champion canoeist in 1899-1905. From about 1900
he played Rugby Union football with the
Warrigal club in the city and suburban competition. In 1905 he joined the Eastern
Suburbs district team and captained its winning second-grade side. At this time his tactical theory was rudimentary: 'Just bung the
ball out to me, boys, as quickly as you can'.
Next year he made first grade and played for
New South Wales against Queensland and
New Zealand's All Blacks. He quickly won a
large following, drawn by his great ball-skills,
cheeky tricks (such as diving over defenders
or carrying the ball behind his back) and his
accurate, long-range kicking with either foot.
A centre three-quarter, whose 'feints, dodges
and swerves completely baffle a tackler', he
weighed 12 stone (76 kg) and was 5 ft. 7½ ins.
(172 cm) tall. He was sturdy and good looking, with brown hair and a determined mouth
and chin.

In 1907 Messenger was a key member of
the State and Australian sides against the
touring New Zealanders. In August he played
three games against a New Zealand professional team, receiving £180. Expelled from
the Rugby Union code, he joined the New
Zealand team for their visit to Britain, playing
Northern Union football. The outstanding
player of the tour, he returned to Sydney in
April 1908 with £200 in his pocket and well
fitted out with new clothes. He captained
Eastern Suburbs, runners-up in the inaugural
Sydney Rugby League competition. In
August he left to tour Britain with the first
Kangaroos, whom he led in two Tests.

In 1908-13, as Rugby League became the
dominant winter sport in Sydney, Messenger
was its star player. He captained all three
Tests against the 1910 English tourists, and
the New South Wales tour of Queensland. He
played five Rugby League matches for Australia, fifteen for his State against Queensland
and New Zealand, and other famous encounters such as the three 1909 Kangaroos versus
Wallabies matches. Within the Rugby League
code his unorthodox exploits became legendary. In a 1910 club game, tackled by C.
McKivatt [q.v.] and held by one foot, he repu-

488

tedly kicked a field-goal. Against South Sydney he once scored three tries which led to rule changes: kicking ahead, he ran off the field around the defence, then back on to gather and score; later he punched the ball ahead, caught it and scored; the third try resulted from a collapsed scrum, when he stepped on and over the grounded forwards. He brought place-kicking to a new level of skill. An unpredictable individualist on the field, off it he was a gentle man of few words. His 1911 season tally of 270 points was a record until passed by Dave Brown [q.v.7] in 1935.

On 14 October 1911 in Sydney, with Congregational forms, Messenger married a divorcee, Annie Maud Macaulay, née Carroll, owner of the Albion Hotel which they managed together in 1911-17. Because of family and business commitments, he declined to tour Britain with the second Kangaroos in 1911-12. Having led Eastern Suburbs to premiership victories in 1911-13, he retired. His brother Wally played Rugby League for Australia in 1914.

About February 1917 Messenger took up a banana plantation at Mount Buderim, Queensland, then in July became proprietor of the Royal Hotel, Manilla, New South Wales. After his wife's death from influenza in 1919 he returned to Sydney, where he worked as a carpenter with the Department of Public Works. He married Annie Elizabeth Thurecht on 1 September 1922. A non-smoker, he did not drink alcohol until well after his football days. In his last years he lived at the Leagues' Club, Phillip Street. Survived by his only son, he died on 24 November 1959 on a visit to Gunnedah, and was buried in the Anglican cemetery, Botany, Sydney. A typical working-class Australian, who became famous through sporting prowess and saw the world, but kept little of the money which he made, Dally Messenger was Rugby League's first and greatest hero.

Dally R. Messenger, *The master* (Syd, 1982).
                                              CHRIS CUNNEEN

MESTON, ARCHIBALD LAWRENCE (1890-1951), educationist, historian and anthropologist, was born on 5 June 1890 at Launceston, Tasmania, elder son of Andrew Meston, carpenter, and his wife Louisa, née Lawrence. He was a remote cousin of Archibald Meston [q.v.5]. Educated at Glen Dhu Primary School, Launceston, 'Arch' Meston trained as a teacher under J. A. Johnson [q.v.9] at the Teachers' College, Hobart, in 1906-08; he also undertook part-time and extra-mural studies in arts and law at the University of Tasmania (B.A., 1914; M.A. with first-class honours in English, 1922).

After holding positions in primary schools at Battery Point and at Queenstown and Gormanston on the west coast, Meston was promoted in 1914 to secondary teaching. He became headmaster of Devonport High School in 1929 and of Launceston High in 1932. In 1938, after he had represented the Commonwealth at the Seventh International Conference on Public Education in Geneva, he was appointed government education officer in Hobart; at his death he was education officer for high schools. For many years Meston was an examiner in matriculation English as well as a member of the Tasmanian Schools Board (from 1944) and of the university's faculty of arts.

Meston interpreted the purpose of education as fitting people to live as reasonable beings with due regard for others, while yet adopting the way of life best suited to their temper. A leader of the liberal view in the Education Department, he fought for and to some extent implemented far-reaching reforms in teaching: he replaced the examination system in his schools by accrediting and assessment methods, urged university status for all teachers and supported the introduction of school libraries and innovative teaching aids.

In 1934 Meston published *A junior history of Australia*, commissioned by Oxford University Press. He also published articles on Tasmanian history and anthropology in the *Papers and Proceedings* of the Royal Society of Tasmania (of which he was a member from 1921, several times vice-president, and chairman of the northern branch in 1936-37) and in the *Records of the Queen Victoria Museum*, Launceston. His history of the Van Diemen's Land Co. was published posthumously in the *Records* in 1958. He wrote a number of anthropological papers. An experienced, intrepid bushman, Meston explored the areas about which he wrote, attempting to better the understanding of his subject and to reconstruct the customs of the Aboriginal people; he also made an extensive collection of Aboriginal stone implements. He was a trustee of the Launceston Library Board and of the Tasmanian Museum, a founding member of the editorial board of *Historical Studies—Australia and New Zealand*, and in 1949 vice-president of the anthropological section at the Hobart meeting of the Australian and New Zealand Association for the Advancement of Science.

Meston's many friends delighted in him. He was an outgoing, unconventional person, giving generously to those who wanted advice and helping the young especially to make reasonable research choices. He loved English literature and readily shared his fine library of literary texts and historical and anthropological works. He was at his best on the walking trips which gave him so much pleasure, and those privileged to accompany him experienced not only the joys of bushwalking but those of good conversation. Such explorations led to probably his most important anthropological work, the discovery and description of the rock carvings at Mount Cameron West in 1933. Another major addition to the study of Tasmanian prehistory was his initiation of large-scale excavation in the shell midden at the South Cave, Rocky Cape. One practical outcome of Meston's love for the Tasmanian bush was the proclamation of the Cradle Mountain Reserve for which he had been the driving force. Fittingly, he was the first chairman of the board set up to administer the reserve.

About 1949, an old head injury brought about Meston's declining health. He died of cerebro-vascular disease at his Glenorchy home on 21 December 1951. He was survived by his wife Winifred, née Rockwell, whom he had married in Sydney on 5 January 1916, and by three daughters; he was buried in Cornelian Bay cemetery. Meston's collection of implements and other Aboriginal relics is now housed in the Museum of Victoria; his library is the property of the City of Launceston.

Tas Education, June 1952, p 213; Roy Soc Tas, *Procs*, 86, 1952, p 159; *Mercury*, 22 Dec 1951; R. Jones, Rocky Cape and the problem of the Tasmanians (Ph.D. thesis, Univ Sydney, 1971).

N. J. B. PLOMLEY

MEUDELL, GEORGE DICK (1860-1936), stockbroker, company promoter and accountant, was born on 29 January 1860 at Sandhurst (Bendigo), Victoria, son of William Meudell and his wife Elizabeth Strachan, née Taylor. Educated at Warrnambool Grammar School and Sandhurst High School, he matriculated aged 14. A childhood accident which left him blind in one eye frustrated his intention of reading for the Bar so he joined the Sandhurst branch of the Bank of Victoria, where his father, a university-educated Scot, was manager.

William Meudell (1831-1911) had migrated to Victoria in 1852 and joined the bank in 1854. He was manager at Heathcote, Echuca, Beaufort and Warrnambool before returning to Sandhurst. In 1881 he was appointed by Henry ('Money') Miller [q.v.5] general manager in Melbourne and in 1889-91 was manager in London.

George moved with the family to Collins Street, Melbourne, in 1881 and joined the Melbourne Savings Bank, becoming manager at Carlton and Emerald Hill and then personal assistant to its actuary John Alsop. In 1884 he investigated banking practices in Europe and the United States of America.

A passionate nationalist, inventor in 1882 of the slogan, 'Australia for the Australians', Meudell was active in the Australian Natives' Association, where he enjoyed making 'inflammatory speeches' about 'the decadent British Empire, the glorious destiny of Australia and the superiority of the native Australian', and was prominent in urging the annexation of New Guinea and the New Hebrides. He was a regular contributor to the press, especially to the *Bulletin*, whose editor J. F. Archibald [q.v.3] he had known from his Warrnambool days.

Resigning from the bank in 1886 Meudell became a public accountant. In 1888 Benjamin Fink [q.v.4] 'lured' him from his comfortable practice to become assistant-manager of the 'ill-fated' Mercantile Finance and Guarantee Co. Ltd for which Meudell prepared land boom prospectuses—'a rare farrago of high-priced rubbish'. He claimed to have lost £20 000 buying company shares before resigning to become secretary of the Australian Property Co., whose affairs he organized in London in 1889.

In January 1890 Meudell became a member of the Stock Exchange of Melbourne, with the help of a £2000 loan from William Knox [q.v.9], who wanted his assistance with the share business of the Broken Hill Proprietary Co. Ltd. During the depression and bank crashes of the 1890s Meudell prudently rented a safe-deposit box and accumulated one thousand gold sovereigns. He organized a 'Legion of Relief' which collected £1500 for food and clothing for the unemployed. In 1893 he joined Knox in his money-raising visit to England on behalf of the Mount Lyell Mining & Railway Co. Ltd and in 1895 helped the recovery of the company's fortunes by advising the issue of debentures convertible into ordinary shares. On 27 June 1898 he married Lillie Elizabeth Dougharty in London.

Contracting tuberculosis in 1907, Meudell defied doctors' predictions of imminent death to travel the world looking at oilfields and return to an unsuccessful nineteen-year attempt to launch an Australian oil industry. This was one of many abortive schemes: it was preceded by enthusiasm for brown coal and hydro-electricity, and followed by an interest in oil-shale.

A 'short, rotund figure' in frock-coat and top-hat, a *bon vivant*, Meudell believed that to be well dressed afforded greater solace than religion. Bustling, energetic and forceful in his opinions, he 'had a mania for establishing leagues and associations', many of them short lived. He was a founder of the Young Victorian Patriotic League (1892), the Bimetallic League (1893), the Kyabram reform movement (1901), the National Citizens' Reform

League (1902) and the People's Liberal Party (1910). He stood for the Legislative Assembly seat of Grenville in by-elections of 1899 and 1900 but, despite the use of a gramophone and comic songs in his campaign, was unsuccessful. In 1927 he published *The romance of Australian banking*. An indefatigable traveller, he claimed to have covered 50 000 miles in forty-eight countries.

'My way of joking', Meudell wrote, 'is to tell the truth'. When he chose to tell the truth about the Victorian land boom in a rambling, idiosyncratic and uninhibited autobiography, *The pleasant career of a spendthrift*, its publication in 1929 caused a sensation. On the instruction of its chairman J. M. Gillespie, a land-boomer, Robertson [q.v.6] & Mullen's withdrew it, and other booksellers were warned of possible legal consequences of stocking it. For a time Meudell sold his book privately but in 1935 published an expurgated version, *The pleasant career of a spendthrift and his later reflections*.

Meudell was a member of numerous clubs including the Athenaeum and the Australian. He was a fellow of the Statistical Society of London (Royal Statistical Society), and the Incorporated Institute of Accountants. Predeceased by his wife he died childless on 26 or 27 May 1936 at St Kilda, and was cremated, leaving almost no assets.

J. Smith (ed), *Cyclopedia of Victoria*, 1 (Melb, 1903); A. D. Mickle, *Many a mickle* (Melb, 1953); M. Cannon, *The land boomers* (Melb, 1967); K. Dunstan, *Ratbags* (Melb, 1980); *VHM*, 13, (1928-29), p 87; *Table Talk*, 14 Apr 1893; *Punch* (Melb), 8 Sept 1898; *Australasian*, 22 Apr 1911; *Argus*, 28 May 1936.   DIANE LANGMORE

MEYER, FELIX HENRY (1858-1937), medical practitioner, was born on 19 June 1858 in Melbourne, son of Menk Meyer, businessman, and his wife Rebecca, née Fink. His Prussian-born father had come to Victoria in 1853. Felix received his first schooling from James Bonwick [q.v.3], then attended the St Kilda Collegiate Academy, the Flinders National Grammar School at Geelong, and finally Wesley College where he was dux in 1875. Retaining a lifelong affection for Wesley, Meyer was president of the Old Collegians in 1897-98 and in 1932 published a biography of its famed headmaster, L. A. Adamson [q.v.7].

Meyer entered the University of Melbourne medical school in 1876 and in 1880, with T. R. H. Willis, convened a meeting which led to the founding of the Medical Students' Society. He graduated M.B., B.S., 1880-81, and M.D. in 1902. In 1881-85 he was sole resident medical officer at the Lying-in Hospital (Royal Women's Hospital); during this time he initiated both systematic clinical teaching of students and formal training of midwives, and founded the Victorian Nurses' Association and the nursing journal *Una*, which he edited for five years. In 1887 he was appointed to the honorary staff of this hospital and in 1891-1918 was senior gynaecological surgeon. His private practice in obstetrics and gynaecology was conducted first at Carlton, and then in Collins Street until he retired in 1935. He lectured in these subjects at the University of Melbourne in 1914-18 and published many articles on them in medical journals. In 1932 he delivered at Brisbane the Jackson [q.v.9] oration, 'The makings of obstetrics'.

Meyer's commitment to his profession is reflected in his appointments: president of the Victorian branch, British Medical Association, 1894; creator of the board of examiners for the Victorian state certificate of midwifery and its first chairman, 1916; and member of the obstetrical research committee set up by the faculty of medicine in 1925, which led to the establishment in 1929 of the chair of obstetrics in the University of Melbourne. He was a foundation fellow, 1927, of the College of Surgeons of Australasia (Royal Australasian College of Surgeons).

Proud of his Jewish origin, Meyer was a man of wide culture. A master of languages, a lover of books and learning, art and music, he was a member of the faculty of music of the University of Melbourne and of the board of the Lady Northcote Permanent Orchestra Trust, and a regular attender at concerts and exhibitions. He wrote elegant verse and prose and was a brilliant speaker and conversationalist. He was a keen spectator-sportsman, enjoyed the camaraderie of clubs such as the Beefsteak, Wallaby and Yorick and attracted the friendship of men as diverse as Samuel Alexander [q.v.7], Sir John Monash and Sir John Longstaff [qq.v.]. He died at Armadale on 31 August 1937 and was cremated.

On 20 January 1904 Felix Meyer had married Mary Fisher (1878-1975), second daughter of Professor E. J. Nanson [q.v.], a talented artist who had studied under E. Phillips Fox [q.v.8]. In 1965 she held a retrospective exhibition at the Lyceum Club, of which she was an original member. There were no children and on her death on 7 March 1975, she left an estate of about $874 000. She bequeathed to the University of Melbourne $130 000 to endow postgraduate scholarships in literature and in obstetrics and gynaecology, both in her husband's name, and $20 000 to the Brownless [q.v.3] medical library.

J. Barrett, *In memoriam Felix Henry Meyer* (Melb, 1937); F. M. C. Forster, *Progress in obstetrics and gynaecology in Australia* (Syd, 1967); J. M.

Gillison, *A history of the Lyceum Club Melbourne* (Melb, 1975); K. F. Russell, *The Melbourne Medical School 1862-1962* (Melb, 1977); *MJA*, 9 Oct 1937, p 626, 12 Jan 1957, p 28; *Age*, 27 May 1975; F. Meyer papers (Univ Melb Archives).

FRANK M. C. FORSTER

MICHELIDES, PETER SPERO (1878-1966), tobacco grower and manufacturer, was born on 3 June 1878 at Castellorizo, an Aegean island near Turkey, son of Spero Peter Michelides, retired captain and store-keeper, and his wife Jasmine, née Hatzipetro. At 17 he went with his family to Cairo where, without formal study, he mastered six languages as well as Greek. He was apprenticed for a year to a tobacco-manufacturer. In 1901 Michelides migrated to Western Australia intending to establish tobacco production. He was a waiter in the Perth restaurant of compatriot John Doscas who, in 1904, lent him money to buy a few bales of Turkish tobacco and a hand-operated tobacco-cutting machine. Until 1924 Michelides was also part-time customs interpreter and administered the dictation tests in European languages devised to exclude non-white immigrants.

Operating from one room in Murray Street, Michelides worked twelve hours daily, hand-making cigarettes and canvassing hotels for orders. His younger brother Michael joined him in 1905 and the rest of their family next year; the venture flourished and orders from Government House raised its prestige. On 8 August 1911, in the district registrar's office, Fremantle, Peter Michelides married an Englishwoman, Ethel Pearl Freeman Dodd; they had three daughters and three sons. In 1913 Peter visited Greece.

In World War I his acceptance of honorary consulates for France, Spain and Russia indicated strong pro-allied sympathies. Wartime orders helped his business to a prosperity that accelerated after the peace. In 1921 a public company was formed, a factory was opened in Roe Street and city retail outlets were bought. Michelides Ltd's President cigarettes, Luxor tobacco and RizLa cigarette papers (made under licence from a French firm) became household names. Early attempts to grow tobacco at Waroona had been unsuccessful but, following a study trip by Peter to America in 1931, growing began on an increasing scale at Manjimup and Pemberton. By World War II the company had about 1000 acres (405 ha) under crop, more than two-thirds of Western Australia's production. In 1939 they built a new factory.

In the mid-1950s Michelides Ltd experienced a set-back, although it was claimed to be Australia's third-biggest tobacco manufacturer, employing 400 men and girls making a million cigarettes a day. Overseas companies promoted 'king-size' cigarettes with special packaging and filter tips, which required a leaf darker than the local product. The company lost money until sold for $156 000 in 1960 to an Adelaide firm. Plantations were disposed of and diverted to other crops.

Michelides's consular services—he also became Greek consul—earned him French, Russian and Greek decorations notably, in 1940, the silver cross of the Royal Order of George I of Greece. Small-framed and courteous, he remained active and alert in old age. His scholarly mind, independence, and charisma as a speaker had made him a leader in Perth's Greek community; in 1924 his mother was invited to lay the foundation of the Greek Orthodox Cathedral for which he had raised considerable funds. Michelides's multilingual library, evidencing his interest in history and philosophy, was a retreat·in his charming home at the foot of Mount Eliza, overlooking Perth Water. Survived by five children, he died there on 17 November 1966 and was buried in the Greek Orthodox section of Karrakatta cemetery. His estate was sworn for probate at $80 156.

G. Wilson and J. Graham (eds), *Western Australia's centenary, 1829-1929* (Perth, 1929); *West Aust Mining and Commercial Review*, 2, no 9 (Nov 1937); *People* (Syd), 29 Aug 1951; *West Australian*, 18 Nov, 24 Dec 1966, 21 Feb 1967; A. O'Brien, The life and work of Peter Michelides (typescript, 1968, Battye Lib); information from Mr E. Michelides, Mosman Park, Perth.

E. R. JOLL

MICHELL, ANTHONY GEORGE MALDON (1870-1959), engineer and inventor, was born on 21 June 1870 at Islington, London, second son and youngest of five children of John Michell (pronounced Mitchell), miner, and his wife Grace, née Rowse. His parents, both from Devonshire, joined the gold rush to Victoria in 1854 and settled at Maldon. George, born during the family's visit to England in 1870-73, spent his childhood at Maldon and in Melbourne where, after tutoring by his sister and his brother John Henry [q.v.], he attended South Yarra State School. In 1884 the family once again returned to England: Michell gained distinctions in classics and mathematics at Perse Grammar School, Cambridge, and attended lectures in physics, chemistry, mechanics and classic Greek art at the University of Cambridge before returning to Victoria in 1890 to study civil and mining engineering at the University of Melbourne. He graduated with first-class honours (B.C.E., 1895; M.C.E., 1899).

Michell's principal teacher at the Melbourne engineering school, apart from Professor W. C. Kernot [q.v.5], was the civil and hydraulic engineer Bernhard A. Smith. Michell became his pupil-assistant and later his partner; they jointly developed and patented a design for a regenerative pump. In 1902-03 he was also an examiner of patents in the Victorian Patents Office. He established his own consultancy business in 1903, dealing with projects for irrigation, water-supply and sewerage. Next year he published in the *Philosophical Magazine* (London) 'The limits of economy of material in frame-structure'; the Michell theorem, derived from this, has been employed as a basis for computer programmes.

Michell's reputation was established internationally when he took out a patent in England and Australia on 16 January 1905 for the Michell thrust-bearing. Developed from his research on the mechanical properties of fluids and mathematical studies of fluid motion, viscosity and lubrication (published as 'Lubrication of plane surfaces' in *Zeitschrift für Mathematic und Physic*, 1905), his invention revolutionized thrust technology, especially in the field of marine propulsion, making possible, for example, the building of ships up to the size of the *Queen Mary*. The Michell thrust-bearing, having an allowable pressure more than ten times greater, replaced the massive plane-faced collars which made contact with fixed plane shoes. The unique feature of the bearing is the tilting slipper pad. The bearing has a ring of sector-shaped pads making contact with a fixed collar through a pivot or ball-joint. The collar attached to the shaft bears against the pads and as the shaft rotates oil is introduced between collar and pads. The load is taken by the oil film.

To market the invention, Michell and his friend in England, Henry Newbigin, issued licences to interested manufacturers at £1 per inch of shaft diameter. But it was not until 1913, after a report that Krupps was installing the thrust-bearing in German battleships, that British engineers adopted the design. In 1920 four companies (Vickers, Cammell Laird, John Brown & Co., and Fairfield) combined to take over and develop the plant; the total capital was £100 000 in £1 shares of which Michell was given 29 000; he later sold them back to the company for £38 000. The original 1920 company was taken over in 1969 by Vickers alone and continued as Vickers Michell Bearings. In the United States of America, however, as a result of a rival patent granted in 1911 (a blow which Michell found hard to accept), the bearing is known as the Kingsbury thrust-bearing.

Michell was a member of the Institute of Patent Attorneys of Australia and from 1931, when he became a registered patent attorney, he prosecuted all his own patent appli-

cations. In addition to his thrust-bearing his inventions included journal bearings, pumps and turbines of special types, the Michell viscometer, a telegraph cypher system, a cypher decoding machine and, finally, the Michell crankless engine.

The crankless engine invention application was made on 19 June 1917. The engine is in the form of an oblique slice of a solid cylinder mounted on a horizontal shaft. As the shaft rotates the oblique slice reciprocates back and forth. A group of pistons operate in cylinders arranged at equal intervals around the shaft. Contact between pistons and 'slant' is via Michell slippers. Thus, with an oil film intervening, no metal to metal occurs. Motion is purely harmonic and the weight of the 'slant' and the pistons is determined by a single formula which results in a complete balance at all speeds.

The Crankless Engine Co. was established to develop designs, manufacture prototypes and endeavour to secure licences from overseas manufacturers for large-scale production. Crankless Engines Ltd was formed in 1920 and from a Fitzroy workshop produced pumps, compressors, automobile engines and aero and gas engines. Construction numbers were assigned to fifty-four machines and of these at least forty-five were built. The company ceased active operations in Australia in 1928 but design and building proceeded in England and U.S.A. The principal overseas manufacturer, George Waller & Sons of Stroud, Hampshire, England, had by 1971 built 116, mainly gas, compressors, ranging in capacity up to 500 000 cubic feet (14 160 m³) per hour.

Michell's outstanding designer was Louis Sherman, a Queensland engineering graduate who became Crankless's representative in England and then worked in America. Two of the machines he designed, an 800-horsepower petrol engine (1929) and a 2000-horsepower opposed piston diesel engine (1943) are held by the Smithsonian Institute, Washington; an automobile engine built in Melbourne in 1923 is in the Museum of Victoria.

In his private practice Michell had been consultant to the Mount Lyell Mining & Railway Co. Ltd; designer of the pumping machinery for the Murray Valley irrigation works; and investigator (1919) for the Victorian government of the hydro-electric possibilities on the Kiewa River. He gave up his practice in 1925 to concentrate on the manufacture of the crankless engine and spent several years overseas, returning to Melbourne about 1933.

Michell became a fellow of the Royal Society in 1934; he received the University of Melbourne's Kernot medal in 1938, and in 1943 was awarded the James Watt International medal by the Institution of Mechanical Engineers, London. His own achievements indeed have been likened to those of James Watt.

Michell has been described as 'of medium height, of slight build, with sandy hair and moustache, keen intelligent eyes and . . . round wire-framed spectacles'. He was quiet and modest and well liked. T. H. Laby [q.v.9] was a valued friend. Unmarried, Michell lived at Camberwell with his brother and spinster sisters and also owned a country property, Ruramihi, at Bunyip which he considered 'a sanctuary . . . essential to his mental health and comfort'. His leisure interests rested in his rural retreat, his technical writing, his remarkable 'exotic' garden at Camberwell, music and continued reading. At 80 he published his massive book *Principles of lubrication*, a work which demonstrates his facility in expressing his orderly process of thought. On the title page is the working motto of his life, a quotation from Leonardo da Vinci: 'Theory is the Captain, practice the Soldiers'.

Sadly, his lifetime of great achievement closed with his complete loss of mental capacity. He died at Camberwell on 17 February 1959 and was buried in Boroondara cemetery with Anglican rites, leaving an estate valued for probate at £174 009. The library of the Michell brothers was presented to the University of Melbourne, but was not retained as an entity; A. G. M. Michell's personal records were destroyed. The A. G. M. Michell award was created in 1978 by the Institution of Engineers, Australia, to perpetuate the memory of one described by Professor John Crisp as 'arguably Australia's most versatile engineer', and a bronze plate in the civil engineering building, University of Melbourne, also commemorates his name.

DNB, 1951-60; F. W. Niedenfuhr and J. R. M. Radok, *The collected mathematical works of J.H. and A.G.M. Michell* (Groningen, 1964); *Engineering* (Lond), July-Dec 1915, 20 Feb 1920; *Biographical memoirs of fellows of the Roy Soc*, 8 (1962); *International J of Mechanical Sciences*, 11 (Feb 1969), no 2; *Aust Official J of Patents, Trade Marks and Designs*, 49 (1979), no 5, supp, p 13; *SMH*, 30 Dec 1972; S. E. A. Walker, 'Modest man of genius: a complete history of the Michell crankless engine' (MS held by the Inst of Engineers, Aust).

SYDNEY WALKER*

MICHELL, JOHN HENRY (1863-1940), mathematician, was born on 26 October 1863 at Maldon, Victoria, eldest child of John Michell (pronounced Mitchell), miner, and his wife Grace, née Rowse, who had migrated from Devonshire in 1854. His parents were energetic and adventurous but above all serious-minded people, very respectful to scholarship and quick to recognize the intellectual promise of their sons John and George [q.v.].

In 1877 the family moved from Maldon to Melbourne, mainly so that John might be placed at Wesley College under Henry Martyn Andrew [q.v.3], a severe but inspiring teacher who had been a Cambridge wrangler. Here, where he won the Draper and Walter Powell [q.v.5] scholarships, and at the University of Melbourne to which he proceeded in 1881, Michell was always at the top of the mathematical classes, and he stood high also in the classical and other courses which he attended. On his graduating B.A. with first-class honours in 1884, his teachers in mathematics (Professor Nanson [q.v.]) and natural philosophy (Andrew, who had moved to the university) urged him to pursue his mathematical studies at the University of Cambridge; and there, accordingly, his parents moved.

Michell proceeded to justify their faith in his powers by attaining the senior wranglership in 1887—one of four bracketed equal for this honour, an unprecedented happening—a Smith's prize in 1889, and a fellowship of Trinity College in 1890. Shortly after that award he returned, with his family circle, to Melbourne to take up a newly created lectureship in mathematics at the university. In this position, where he was responsible for the teaching of applied mathematics, he remained until he succeeded Nanson as professor in 1923 and turned his attention to the teaching of pure mathematics. He greatly enlarged the activities of the school, establishing practice-classes and tutorials, providing class-rooms with models and large-scale drawings and inaugurating special lectures and courses. Among his distinguished pupils were (Sir) Kerr Grant [q.v.9], H. S. W. Massey, E. J. G. Pitman, J. M. Baldwin [q.v.7] and S. B. McLaren [q.v.]. He retired at the end of 1928 with the title honorary research professor. He did not marry, and after his Cambridge days did not again travel beyond Australia.

Michell attained a reputation as one of the leading mathematicians in the world through his researches in the theories of hydrodynamics and elasticity, published in the period 1890-1902. In hydrodynamics his papers on the theory of free stream lines, the highest waves in water and the wave resistance of a ship were works of major importance whose conception and execution showed imagination and skill of the highest order. Most of his publications, however, were in elasticity, to which subject he was a major contributor in the period of systemization and consolidation which followed the pioneer researches of the nineteenth century. He was the first to formulate the complete system of fundamental equations in terms of stress-components only, he gave the first account of thin-plate theory which was free from questionable assumptions, he systematized and extended the theory of flexure and torsion of beams, and he gave ingenious solutions of a variety of special problems. These researches were recognized in his election to a fellowship of the Royal Society in 1902. However, Michell never showed concern for recognition of his work and for the most part did not exploit his theories by working out special cases.

His only publication after 1902 was a textbook, *The elements of mathematical analysis* (London, 1937), written with M. H. Belz, his colleague in the mathematics department of Melbourne University during the 1920s. This book embodied the pedagogical ideas which Michell had been pondering and developing during his later years as a teacher; in an interesting and original way it combines twentieth century rigour with nineteenth century clarity and spaciousness in exposition.

Michell's predominant interest lay in the applications of mathematics to the elucidation of natural phenomena, but he had also a wide and precise knowledge of pure mathematics; throughout this field he read continually, and he was constantly incorporating new works in his lectures. His concern for the applicability of his work was nourished by contact with his engineer friends, and by some experimenting by himself. In 1906 he helped to found the Mathematical Association of Victoria, to whose meetings he presented original papers almost to the end of his life, and for a time he occupied the chair of the Victorian Schools Board. He was a most skilful teacher; his pace appeared to be slow, but by judicious selection of material he covered an astonishing amount of ground. His skill in condensing what he wished to say to its essentials was shown also in his conversation and in his published work.

Michell was reckoned to be a shy man; but here the essence was that he had exceptionally high standards of intellectual and moral integrity, and was irked by the company of those who seemed at all insincere. When he gave his friendship he gave it without reserve. He was punctilious in attending to his teaching and examining responsibilities, to the extra-tutorial functions of his position, and (after the death of his father) to his duties as head of his family circle. He found relaxation in classical music—he was a capable performer on the organ—in wide reading and in gardening; he was a learned connoisseur and lover of plant life, especially Australian trees and shrubs.

Michell died, after a brief illness, at Camberwell, on 3 February 1940 and was buried in Boroondara cemetery.

F. W. Niedenfuhr and J. R. M. Radok, *Collected mathematical works of J. H. and A. G. M. Michell* (Groningen, 1964); *Obituary notices of fellows of the Royal Society*, 1940; J. H. Michell papers (Univ Melb Archives).   T. M. CHERRY*

MICHIE, JOHN LUNDIE (1882-1946), professor of classics, was born on 4 June 1882 at Lochnalair, Crathie, Aberdeenshire, Scotland, son of Charles Michie, blacksmith, and his wife Mary, née Lundie. He attended school at Robert Gordon's College, Aberdeen, graduated M.A. with first-class honours in classics in 1904 from the University of Aberdeen and then entered Trinity College, Cambridge, as an exhibitioner. Here he was awarded the Ferguson classical scholarship, regarded as the highest honour attainable by a Scottish student of classics. He obtained a double first in the classical Tripos (B.A., 1907; M.A., 1911) and returned to the University of Aberdeen, where he became assistant (1908-09) to the professor of humanity, Sir William Ramsay, and later lecturer in Roman history (1909-10). Besides distinguishing himself academically Michie also displayed great athletic prowess, as a hammer-thrower in Scotland and as a shot-putter at Cambridge, where he won a blue. His massive frame and mild disposition were to win him the reputation of a gentle giant and the nickname 'Michie Mouse'.

His appointment to the foundation chair of classics at the newly established University of Queensland, which he took up in February 1911, was controversial. Although the London committee had believed him a 'sound steady safe quite excellent man', they had placed him second and subsequently attempted to overturn the senate decision. It seems not unreasonable to suppose that Governor Sir William MacGregor [q.v.5], the first chancellor, also an Aberdonian, was not averse to offering a helping hand to this 28-year-old man of promise from home, who then became one of the four professors entrusted with the task of creating a university. Michie was undoubtedly a key figure in the great matriculation debate which led to the decision to make a classical language a prerequisite for arts students, acting in close collaboration with MacGregor against the utilitarians, who wanted a university that would meet Queensland's practical requirements rather than one embodying traditional academic attitudes from the old world. Michie married Isabella Harriet Crombie Sword on 9 February 1926 in the Presbyterian Church, Stanthorpe.

For thirty-five years he was one of the most

respected leaders of the university community as chairman (1911-22) and dean (1928-32, 1939-46) of the faculty of arts, senator (1916-23, 1926-32)—during which time he rarely made a speech—and president (1917-22) of the board of the faculties. He was well liked by his students for his kindness, courtesy and shyness (especially with female students), his infinite patience and great learning and wisdom in his lectures. He was no writer and justified his failure to publish by arguing that what he could do best, which was translate from Latin and Greek, was well enough done already. His energies, which were considerable, were consequently directed towards teaching and administration. His early distinguished students included Jack Lindsay and Eric Partridge [q.v.].

From February 1946 Michie needed to take leave on health grounds, and he died on 23 June at Hamilton, survived by his wife and two daughters. His estate was sworn for probate in three States at £33 753. He had made bequests to the universities of Queensland and Aberdeen. The J. L. Michie memorial scholarship fund was created by his former students and colleagues, who were quickly able to present the senate with £1000 to launch the scholarship for an honours undergraduate in classics. The best-known memorial to him in the modern university is the Michie Building, the humanities block built during the early 1970s, where classics continues to be taught in Queensland.

J. Lindsay, *Life rarely tells* (Lond, 1958); *Univ Qld Gazette*, Aug 1946; *Courier Mail*, 24 June 1946, 24 Jan 1947; Univ Qld, Senate Minutes (Univ Qld Archives); PRE/A360 (QA).

MALCOLM I. THOMIS

MICKLEM, PHILIP ARTHUR (1876-1965), clergyman, was born on 5 April 1876 at Waltham St Lawrence, Berkshire, England, son of Leonard Micklem, company secretary, and his wife Dora Emily, née Weguelim. He was educated at Harrow School, Hertford College, Oxford (B.A., with first-class honours in *litterae humaniores*, 1899; M.A. 1902; D.D. 1924), and Cuddesdon College. While assistant master at Harrow, Micklem was made deacon on 5 October 1902 and priested by the bishop of London on 4 October 1903. By this time, he had entered the parish ministry as curate of Shene, Surrey.

Micklem was first and foremost a scholar. His six years at Shene were given over to biblical studies. In 1909 he became a lecturer at St Augustine's College, Canterbury. A year later, responding to a call from Archbishop St Clair Donaldson [q.v.8], he migrated to Brisbane to become principal of the local theological college of St Francis. Here he proved an effective teacher and administrator, while completing his commentary on St Matthew's Gospel. As residentiary canon of the cathedral and incumbent of a small parish, Micklem participated in diocesan affairs, but his austere, fastidious temperament and his reserved manner made it difficult for him to be a part of Queensland life. The bitterness of the conscription issue deeply offended his strong Imperialism. In 1917 Micklem was glad to remove to the Church of St James, Sydney.

A city church with a widespread congregation, St James' had developed an 'advanced' ritual out of its Tractarian tradition. Under Micklem's direction, it became an Anglo-Catholic parish, with elaborate choral services. Such a stance separated him from the predominantly Evangelical diocese and gave him little opportunity to occupy important diocesan positions. In specialist areas, such as publicizing spiritual healing and advocating social services, Micklem was allowed some scope. Elsewhere his Incarnational theology—expressed in his 1931 published Moorhouse [q.v.5] lectures, *Values of the Incarnation*—cut him off from the mainstream of Sydney Anglicanism.

Interested in the debates about constitutional autonomy for the Church in Australia, Micklem published his Moorhouse lectures for 1920 as *Principles of Church organization*. While they failed to persuade his Sydney colleagues, his studies turned him into an historian of Australian religion; in 1936 he completed F. T. Whitington's [q.v.] biography of Bishop Broughton [q.v.1] and helped to arrange the Broughton centenary celebrations. As rector of a church built by Francis Greenway [q.v.1], he was a pioneer advocate of the preservation of early colonial architecture and strenuously opposed the removal of St Andrew's Cathedral to the Hyde Park Barracks site.

On 29 March 1932 Micklem married a 25-year-old teacher, Evelyn Muriel Auriac. No longer was the bachelor rector wedded to his parish. With the election of Archbishop Mowll in 1933 and the triumph of the conservative Evangelical party in the diocesan councils, Micklem realized that his ministry would become less creative. In 1937 he resigned and returned to England. Soon after his arrival he became provost of Derby cathedral, where he officiated for ten years. Wartime difficulties hampered his work but the influence of Archbishop William Temple aroused a new interest in the problems of post-war industrial society which he expressed, in a generalized historical context, in his Bampton lectures for 1946, *The secular and the sacred* (1948). In a series of pamphlets for the Industrial Christian Fellowship, he attempted to give practical application to his ideas. The septuagenarian classical scholar, with his remote, even icy, manner, was at the same time a compassionate and constructive social thinker.

In 1947 Micklem retired to Staplecross, Sussex. Survived by his wife, he died at Hastings on 5 December 1965. His ashes were placed in Derby cathedral and a memorial tablet was erected in St James' Church, Sydney.

K. J. Cable, *St James' Church, Sydney* (Syd, 1982); *Brisb Church Chronicle*, 1 Feb 1966; *Anglican*, 16 Dec 1965.   K. J. CABLE

MIETHKE, ADELAIDE LAETITIA (1881-1962), educationist, was born on 8 June 1881 at Manoora, South Australia, sixth daughter among the ten children of Carl Rudolph Alexander Miethke, Prussian schoolmaster, and his South Australian wife, Emma Caroline (Louisa), née Schultze. Addie suffered from asthma. She was educated at country schools and Woodville Public School before becoming a pupil-teacher in 1899 and in 1903-04 attending the University Training College. Her first appointment was to Le Fevre Peninsula School. In 1916 she became first female vice-president of the South Australian Public School Teachers' Union, and was a forceful advocate of salary rises. From 1915 she had taught at the Woodville High School, from 1920 being senior mistress of the girls' section. She studied part time to complete her degree (B.A., 1924).

In 1915 Adelaide Miethke had addressed the Women's Non Party Political Association, supporting the widely held view that 'technically gifted girls should have a chance of developing their bent'. That year she was founding president of the Women Teachers' League, which impressed W. T. McCoy [q.v.], director of education, with the need to recognize women teachers' contributions. He began to place women as headmistresses and appointed Miethke as an inspector of schools on 30 November 1924, at £525. Next year he established metropolitan central schools with a vocational bias.

She was to inspect high schools, including domestic arts classes, in high schools and to organize and supervise domestic and secretarial training in the home-making (later girls' central) schools; these were formed by adding several super-primary classes to primary schools. Initially they offered pre-vocational training to 748 girls, aged 13 to 16; 1358 were enrolled by 1930. However, some pupils felt themselves to be, and were often seen as, inferior to those attending the few high schools. General secondary subjects were studied in the mornings. The afternoons were devoted to 'manual classes': laundry work, cookery, household management, first aid, drawing and applied art, needlework and dressmaking; second-year girls received millinery and secretarial training. Goods produced in the schools were displayed annually at the spring show of the Royal Agricultural and Horticultural Society to which Miss Inspector Miethke belonged.

From 1934 central school students could sit for the new Intermediate technical certificate. The schools were said by the Education Department to be training young women to become housewives of 'skill and taste'. In the *Housewife* Miethke expounded her theories about 'The central schools and the housewife of the future' (June 1930) and 'Preparing girls for their ultimate career' (September 1938): while her home was a woman's place, it need not be her prison.

In 1939 four central schools were reorganized, to re-open next year as separate girls' junior technical schools. Their educational aim was broader and commercial subjects were dominant. Miethke applied rigorous teaching standards; schools under her administration were to be bright and attractive, adorned with flowers and pictures. She was now on the executive of the New Education Fellowship which explored progressive methods.

In 1936 Miethke had been president of the Women's Centenary Council of South Australia which, as a memorial to pioneer women, raised £5000 to establish the Alice Springs base of the Australian Aerial Medical Service (later Royal Flying Doctor Service), and built the Pioneer Women's Memorial garden in Adelaide. The council produced *A book of South Australia: women in the first hundred years*. She also designed and organized a grand Empire pageant, her stentorian voice being ideal for rallying the 14 000 schoolchildren involved. The pageant symbolized 'in rhythmic movement, colour and music the major expansions of our great Empire'. Next year she was appointed O.B.E.

In 1941 she retired as inspector, to general praise. Brisk and cheerful, this stout, buxom teacher who dressed in tailored suits had been an intimidating inspector whom teachers respected and feared. Some associates found her abrasive and excessively managerial. An ex-pupil recalled: 'You couldn't get away with much with Miss Miethke. They had *authority* in those days'. Although she was a stickler for formality, her outspoken methods helped to improve teachers' industrial conditions and to raise the status of women in the Education Department.

Miethke had spent years overseeing

schools for future wives and mothers, yet personally she was committed to a professional life. But in this paradox she was like many single women teachers of her time. She spent the little free time she allowed herself in motoring interstate with lifelong friend Phebe Watson [q.v.], reading, gardening and organizing charitable, professional and patriotic causes.

Notable among her causes was mobilization of schoolchildren for fund-raising and scrap-collecting in the two world wars. Of German ancestry, she possibly needed to demonstrate her loyalty. In 1915-17 Miethke organized the South Australian Children's Patriotic Fund. In 1940-46 she directed the Schools Patriotic Fund of South Australia; £402 133 was raised and she wrote pamphlets about both campaigns. From 1941 she served on the Women's War Service Council.

S.P.F. money remaining after World War II went to buy a hostel, Adelaide Miethke House (opened 1951), for country girls studying in Adelaide: it bore a plaque inscribed 'Children loved her'. The hostel was administered by the Young Women's Christian Association, to which Miethke belonged.

Further S.P.F. money went to the (Royal) Flying Doctor Service; Miethke, a friend of John Flynn [q.v.8], was the State branch's first woman president in 1941 and edited *Air Doctor*. In 1946 while travelling to Alice Springs, she noticed the shyness of outback children. The idea of ' "bridging the lonely distance" seized her mind' and suggested her 'most constructive work'. She devised, and single-mindedly set up as a branch of the F.D.S., the world's first School of the Air. It began operating from Alice Springs Higher Primary School on 20 September 1950, using individual, pedal-wireless sets on remote homesteads to link the children.

In 1941-46 Miethke had edited the monthly schoolchildren's magazine, *Children's Hour*. In 1942 she was founding president of the Woodville District Child Welfare Association which established four pre-schools; the Adelaide Miethke Kindergarten (opened 1953) still flourishes. 1949 saw her last organizing feat—the United Nations Appeal for Children. She once admitted, 'I fear work has become almost a disease with me!', and she was unwell at this time. But she maintained unabated her appetite for clubs and committee work: the Girl Guides' Association (commissioner and State council-member); the Royal Commonwealth Society; the National Council of Women, of which she was State and national president; the Adelaide Women's Club and the Catherine Helen Spence [q.v.6] Scholarship Committee.

Addie remained single. A relative recalls that her father had been wont to take a stock-whip to importunate suitors of his eight unmarried daughters. In 1962 she was ill but refused to go to hospital. She died at her Woodville home of seventy years on 4 February and was buried in Cheltenham cemetery.

S. Marsden, *A history of Woodville* (Adel, 1977); H. Jones, *Nothing seemed impossible* (Brisb, 1985); Annual Reports of director of education (SA), *PP* (SA), 1925-42; *Education Gazette* (SA), Jan 1900; *Guild Chronicle*, 20 June 1941; *Children's Hour*, May 1951; *Register* (Adel), 5 July 1916; *Advertiser* (Adel), 3 June 1930, 5 Feb 1962; *The Times*, 4 Dec 1952; *Chronicle* (Adel), 15 Feb 1962; J. F. Wormwell, Adelaide Miethke: a lifetime contribution to public education in South Australia 1905-1950 (B. Ed. thesis, Salisbury College of Advanced Education, SA, 1984); D5390 (Misc) 26, PRG 107, pkts 2, 4, 5, SRG 266, Dorothy Marshall cuttings (SAA); information from Mr G. R. Miethke, Lower Mitcham, Miss M. Douglas, North Adelaide, Mr L. Dodd, Fulham, Adel.   SUZANNE EDGAR
HELEN JONES

MILERUM (1869?-1941), shearer and Aboriginal ethnologist, also known as Clarence Long, was born about 1869 at Jung-gurumbar, Younghusband Peninsula, South Australia, son of Puningeri of the Karagarindjeri clan, Tanganekald tribe, Djeri-mangap moiety. His mother was Lakwunami, of the Potaruwutj tribe from the Keilira region. Wiantalan was his child name and korowale, the white-faced heron, his totem. He grew to be a man of classic Murrayian physical type.

His intensely conservative grandparents had avoided encroaching white settlers, especially after the murders of passengers on the ship *Maria* in 1839. They lived in the wilder swamp and mallee karst country east of the Coorong. Milerum's parents continued as hunters and gatherers till 1875, when his father became on ox-driver for William Barnett; Milerum accompanied Puningeri, transporting wool to Portland, Victoria, and learned to talk with the last of the Bunganditj people of the Beachport area. He was 6 before he saw white folk and was given his first clothes so that he could play with little Mary Jane Barnett, at a Rosetown house now preserved as a national treasure. Later he was picker-up during shearing at the McCourt family's Woakwine station.

Both before and after initiation at about 14, as a red-ochred youth, his parents taught him much of their history and tradition so that in effect he became the final repository of the details of their culture. Although unschooled, at Woakwine Milerum learned to speak English well, becoming favoured employee there. In 1914 he was champion blade shearer of the South-East; he visited the district annually for shearing well into the 1930s. About 1925

Milerum is said to have organized the last ceremonial gathering held by Aboriginal survivors at Point McLeay.

Milerum's first marriage was to Kuleinji, also known as Lydia Thomson. In 1931, recently widowed from his second wife Polly Beck of the Ngaralta tribe from the Murray Bridge area, he was living at Point McLeay mission on Lake Alexandrina with his four children. Here he met the present author, son of Mary Jane Barnett; the subsequent ten-year friendship was perhaps strengthened by Milerum's discovery of this association. Although reticent, when he realized that phonetic transcriptions made possible proper recording of his words and sayings, he began to communicate his parents' previously unrecorded languages.

Each year after shearing, Milerum went to Adelaide for the summer and camped in the sandhills at Fulham. He visited the South Australian Museum and, under a shady grapevine on the Old Military Barracks' porch, he made baskets and wooden weapons, which were sought as treasures by museums far and wide. Imparting his knowledge was his pleasure; and in conversation he recalled ever more detail of the songs he sang and the stories he told in his two principal languages. He also widened his remembrance of the speech of others. All was recorded by the museum officers. Many a passing university teacher and student stopped to learn from him.

Milerum's infant name Wiantalan provided a first lead in pronouncing one aspect of Australian and Tasmanian speech; for the 't' sound was only understood when an amused Jarildekald tribesman told museum staff, 'Stick your tongue out man!'. Thus the interdental series of sounds was discovered by white Australians, enabling tribal languages to be better transcribed.

Milerum planned and enacted for films a record of his people; many of his songs, recorded on wax cylinders and flat discs, have been studied by musicians, including Harold Davies [q.v.8]. He guided H. K. Fry and the author over parts of his country, giving names, places, and the limits of the clans, and recollecting events and traditions. He became an anthropologist in his own right, seeking verification of data from old Aborigines.

In 1941 Milerum entered Royal Adelaide Hospital fearing that his illness was due to long-dead men of the Ngaralta, who had resented his marriage, exerting magic to 'bruise' him and cause his death. He died of coronary vascular disease on 21 February. A non-smoker and non-drinker, he was a model for any Australian. Leslie Wilkie's [q.v.] portrait is in the South Australian Museum.

N. B. Tindale, *Aboriginal tribes of Australia*

(Berkeley, California, USA, 1974); *Aboriginal Q*, 1, no 2, Apr-June 1968.   Norman B. Tindale

MILES, BEATRICE (1902-1973), Bohemian rebel, was born on 17 September 1902 at Ashfield, Sydney, third surviving of the five children of William John Miles [q.v.], Sydney-born public accountant, and his wife Maria Louisa, née Binnington, a Queenslander. Residing at St Ives, she was educated at Abbotsleigh. An inheritance from her paternal grandmother allowed her to escape the violent scenes that characterized her relationship with her father. She enrolled in arts at the University of Sydney, but discontinued her studies after a year 'because they did not teach enough Australian stuff'. Soon after, she contracted encephalitis. Conflicts with her father continued, over her lifestyle and sexual 'freedom'. In 1923 he had her committed to the Hospital for the Insane, Gladesville, where she remained until publicity in *Smith's Weekly* led to her release in 1925.

Thereafter, Miles became notable for her outrageous, disruptive conduct in public places, and her outspoken criticism of political and social authorities. Irresolvable differences over her behaviour and life-style occasioned the end of her long relationship with Brian Harper when she was 38. He wanted to marry, while she despised men who got married.

Henceforth Miles had 'no fixed address'. Well-known in Sydney, she could be seen about city and suburban public transport wearing a green tennis shade, tennis shoes and a scruffy greatcoat over a somewhat ample body. She had a number of ingenious methods of obtaining goods, services and daily support. One method was to give recitations from Shakespeare, with a sixpence to three-shilling price range. She became notorious for refusing to pay fares, especially in taxis: cabbies often refused to pick her up. Sometimes in retaliation she would leap on their running-boards, bumper-bars or bonnet, or hurl herself against their sides, detaching doors from hinges; however, in 1955 she paid a female taxi-driver £600 to drive her to Perth and back, taking nineteen days. From the 1940s her closest friend was a taxi-driver John Beynon, but this could not prevent the ire of unpaid drivers; she was assaulted several times in the 1950s.

Bee Miles was constantly harassed by police and she claimed to have been falsely convicted 195 times, fairly 100 times, though obituaries give lower estimates. She haunted the Public Library of New South Wales, reading many books each week, until she was banned from the building in the late 1950s. The final years of her life were dogged by ill health, and in 1964 she entered the Little Sisters of the Poor Home for the Aged at Randwick. In old age she reputedly claimed: 'I have no allergies that I know of, one complex, no delusions, two inhibitions, no neuroses, three phobias, no superstitions and no frustrations'. After renouncing her lifelong atheism and receiving Roman Catholic rites, she died of cancer on 3 December 1973 and was cremated.

As well as advocating free love Miles was a fervent nationalist: at her request Australian wildflowers were placed on her coffin, and a jazz band played 'Waltzing Matilda', 'Tie me Kangaroo down Sport' and 'Advance Australia Fair'. In 1984 *Better known as Bee*, a musical comedy based on her life, was performed by the Q Theatre Company, Penrith. Her portrait by Alex Robertson was entered for the 1961 Archibald [q.v.3] prize.

D. Hewett, *Bobbin up* (Syd, 1959); *SMH*, 24 May 1958; *Sun-Herald* and *Sunday Telegraph* (Syd), 9 Dec 1973; Frank Johnson papers *and* P. R. Stephensen papers (ML); Case papers, Gladesville Hospital, 1923-25 (held by NSW Health Commission, Syd).   JUDITH ALLEN

MILES, EDWARD THOMAS (1849-1944), merchant seaman, politician and entrepreneur, was born on 24 June 1849 at Hobart Town, son of Alfred Miles, shoemaker, and his wife Elizabeth. In 1863 he went to sea as ship's boy, subsequently serving in many parts of the world and gaining his master's certificate in 1873. On 11 February 1874 in Hobart he married Charlotte Eliza Reynolds; they had seven sons and four daughters.

After operating out of New Zealand for a time, Miles returned to Tasmania in 1879. He briefly partnered his brother in a manufacturing business, then purchased the first of many small coastal vessels which he resold or used for short-term shipping leases and charters. The profits enabled him to enter the Tasmanian coastal trade in 1889, and after succeeding on the east coast, Miles and his father-in-law, as T. A. Reynolds & Co., moved to the Hobart-Strahan run; that year they also won the contract to build the Strahan-Zeehan railway.

A dapper man with a neat spade beard, Teddy Miles was quick and decisive in his business methods and not unprepared to bend the law to suit himself. His company soon absorbed its main rival, the Launceston & North-West Coast Steam Navigation Co., and in 1896 sold out at a profit to the Union Steamship Co. of New Zealand. In 1898 Miles moved to Strahan to manage his considerable property investments and that year became first master warden of the Strahan Marine Board.

Miles had entered public life in 1888 as a member of the Glebe Town Road Trust and the Hobart Marine Board (master warden 1897-98), and in December 1893 he was elected to the House of Assembly for Glamorgan, becoming minister for lands and works in May 1899. His political career was brief, ending spectacularly after an 1899 select committee investigated allegations of dishonesty involving the Strahan Marine Board and the proposed construction of the Macquarie Harbour breakwater. Evidence revealed 'a deliberate purpose on [Miles's] part to obtain and use the position of Master Warden for his own ends', and indicated that, 'improperly and secretly interested in two of the tenders for the West Breakwater', he employed 'unworthy means to secure the acceptance by the Board of the higher of these'. After discussions with Premier Braddon [q.v.7], Miles resigned from the ministry on 2 October 1899; the committee's report was accepted by the assembly on 4 October and a motion of no confidence in the government moved next day; the Braddon government lost the vote on 6 October and resigned six days later.

Miles nominated for the seat of Hobart in 1900, and surprised by gaining election under the proportional representation voting system. The outcry was immediate and, ostracized by fellow members, he resigned his seat within six weeks. In 1901 he unsuccessfully contested South Hobart and in 1903 both Lyell and the Senate.

By 1900 Miles had purchased enough west coast property to have a yearly rent roll of £2000, but falling land values saw this reduced to £500 by 1902 and he was forced to seek restoration of his fortunes. In 1903 he travelled to East Asia where on behalf of New Zealand and Australian interests he negotiated the sale of several ships in China and Japan. He also contracted for the supply of wooden paving blocks for Manila streets, established a timber plant in the Philippines and made sleeper sales to Indian railways.

More importantly, in Siam (Thailand) Miles gained the Tongkah Harbour Concession Agreement for working tin deposits on Phuket Island, in return for which he constructed a deep-water dock and shipping channel. In 1906 he helped to float the Tongkah Harbour Tin Dredging Co. Ltd in Hobart and was appointed general manager. (Sir) Henry Jones [q.v.9] and his associates were major shareholders but Miles, loath to advertise the 'damn jam', abandoned the IXL name given to the initial prospecting company. A bucket dredge, constructed in Scotland to Miles's design, was assembled at Penang, Malay Peninsula, in December 1907; then Miles took his last command, the steamer *Padang*, to tow the uninsured dredge 200 nerve-wracking miles (320 km) across open sea to the work site. The enterprise, continued by Miles's sons, laid the foundation of the modern Thai tin-mining industry.

In 1909 Miles settled at Ringwood, Victoria, where he owned orchards and other property. He retired from the Tongkah Harbour Co. board in 1911 but was for many years managing director of companies operating at Ranong, Siam.

Miles died at his home, Glamorgan, on 6 July 1944, survived by ten of his children. His estate was valued for probate at £27 976. An imposing monument to his tin-mining work was unveiled on Phuket Island in 1969.

V&P (HA Tas), 1899, 41 (61); *Mercury,* 8 July 1944; T. A. Miles (comp), The life story of Captain Edward Thomas Miles master mariner and pioneer of tin dredging (1969, typescript, based on the memoirs of E. T. Miles, held NL).

SCOTT BENNETT

MILES, JOHN CAMPBELL (1883-1965), prospector, was born on 5 May 1883 at Richmond, Melbourne, eighth of nine children of Thomas Miles, compositor and sometime goldminer, and his wife Fanny Louisa, née Chancellor. Little is known of his childhood or education. According to folklore he panned his first pennyweight of gold at the age of 7 on the family's Melton farm, and at 12 ran away to work with a Melbourne bootmaker. By 18 he was a farm-hand at Stawell.

In 1907, lured by the promise of higher wages, he moved to Broken Hill, New South Wales, and worked underground for several months. When news of a rush to the Oaks alluvial goldfield reached Broken Hill, Miles and a companion bicycled the 1550 miles (2500 km) to the North Queensland strike only to find the ground fully pegged. Subsequently, he prospected on the Etheridge field, but was again disappointed. In 1908 Miles was navvying on the Einasleigh railway. Over the next decade he was itinerant in every sense, working on stations, cutting sugarcane and fossicking.

Back in Melbourne in 1921, he decided to try his luck in the Northern Territory. His journey was unhurried: by the following Christmas he had progressed only as far as the deserted Cloncurry, Queensland, copperfield. In early February 1923 Miles camped at the Leichhardt River, six miles (10 km) below Lagoon Creek. Observing mineralized outcrops, he took up a shoeing hammer and casually collected samples, ten of which he subsequently dispatched to the government assayer at Cloncurry. As Miles later admitted, 'I was not prospecting . . . I knew the piece of stone must contain mineral from its weight, but what it was I did not know'. The samples were lead carbonate assaying from

49 to 73 per cent lead, with rich silver contents.

Miles invited Bill Simpson of nearby Mica Camp to join him. They pegged three areas, forty-two acres (18 ha) around the original outcrops, soon known as the Black Star and Racecourse leases. Six months later the name, Mount Isa, was conferred on Miles's find, by which time several consignments had been sent to Cloncurry, and much of the new field taken up. Already, however, the field's future had passed into the hands of William Corbould [q.v.8] who, with Douglas MacGilvray, had options over most of the leases, including those of Miles and Simpson.

Mount Isa Mines Ltd was floated in January 1924; 12 250 shares of £20 each were allotted to the promoters to secure the optioned leases. Miles received 500 shares, nominally worth £10 000, some of which he sold over the following twenty months to sustain his prospecting at Lawn Hills. In December 1925 Miles still held 8680 £1 shares; that dwindled to 2900 by 1929. In 1933 he sold his last 400 shares.

Miles's whereabouts was unknown to Mount Isa for almost three decades, years which he dismissed as 'wanderings'. In 1957 he was invited to inspect the company's huge mining and metallurgical undertaking. It was probably characteristic of the wiry, weather-hardened prospector, whose only admitted vice was pipe-smoking, that he should return to the north-west overland by car, camping under the stars, and then accept accommodation only in the workers' barracks. Miles died unmarried on 4 December 1965 at Ringwood, Melbourne, and was cremated. In 1968 his ashes were interred beneath the memorial clock-tower in Miles Street, Mount Isa.

G. Blainey, *Mines in the spinifex* (Syd, 1960); K. H. Kennedy (ed), *Readings in North Queensland Mining History,* 1 (Townsville, 1980); I. Hore-Lacy (ed), *Broken Hill to Mount Isa* (Melb, 1981); *Qld Government Mining J,* Oct, Nov 1923; Dept of Mines (Qld), *Annual Report,* 1923; *Mimag,* Oct 1957, Aug, Nov 1962; *North-West Star,* 29 May 1973; *North Qld Register,* 22 Oct, 12 Nov 1923, 9 June 1924, 5 Jan 1925; information from M. I. M. Holdings' share registry and public affairs division (Mount Isa Mines Ltd).   K. H. KENNEDY

MILES, WILLIAM JOHN (1871-1942), rationalist and businessman, was born on 27 August 1871 at Woolloomooloo, Sydney, only child of John Balfour Clement Miles (d. 1908), wealthy Tahitian-born public accountant, and his English-born wife Ellen, née Munton, widow of W. J. Cordner [q.v.3]. Entering his father's firm, Miles, Vane & Miles (from 1908 Yarwood, Vane & Miles), he became a fellow of the Australasian Corporation of Public Accountants; from 1912 he practised as an independent consulting accountant. He was a director of Sydney Meat Preserving Co. Ltd (in 1909), British General Electric Co. Ltd and the fashionable mercers, Peapes & Co. Ltd (in 1912-42), of which he had a 70 per cent shareholding. At St Philip's Anglican Church on 23 April 1897 he had married Maria Louisa Binnington, a Queensland fishmonger's daughter.

About 1912 Miles helped to found and became first secretary of the local branch of the Rationalist Press Association, London (later Rationalist Association of New South Wales), publishing in 1914 its *Sydney Rationalist Annual*. He regarded war as 'biologically inevitable', but opposed conscription for overseas service and was active in the referenda campaigns of 1916 and 1917. In October 1917 he established the Advance Australia League, which, under his slogan 'Australia first', opposed Imperial Federation. Now associating with R. S. Ross [q.v.] and contributing to *Ross's Monthly of Protest, Personality and Progress* and the *Socialist*, he left the rationalist association in 1920. From about 1923 he concentrated on business. He made five visits overseas, the last about 1929.

Miles retired in 1935 and, with an annual income of about £6000, devoted himself to secularist and chauvinist propaganda. In July he began a monthly magazine, the *Independent Sydney Secularist*. Impressed by P. R. Stephensen [q.v.], whom he now employed as 'literary adviser' at £5 per week, from July 1936 Miles funded and edited the *Publicist*, a pro-monarchical, pro-fascist, pro-Aboriginal, anti-British, anti-communist and anti-Semitic monthly. He published Stephensen's *The foundations of culture in Australia* (1936) and Xavier Herbert's *Capricornia* (1938). In 1937-38 he financed the Aborigines' Progressive Association, formed by William Ferguson [q.v.8] and Jack Patten [q.v.]. The outbreak of World War II curtailed Miles's pro-Axis editorials and the *Independent Sydney Secularist* ceased in April 1940.

From his late twenties Miles had suffered angina pectoris. Late in life one foot became gangrenous, but he hobbled daily to the *Publicist* bookshop-cum-office in Elizabeth Street. Eventually confined to bed, he ran a sweep on when he would die. He took no part in Stephensen's Australia First Movement, founded in October 1941, but from 1 January 1942 transferred the *Publicist* to Stephensen and two others. Miles died at his home at Gordon on 10 January, survived by his two sons and three of his four daughters, including Beatrice [q.v.]. He was cremated after a rationalist service. In March the *Publicist* ceased when Stephensen and others were interned.

'A peppery, authoritative little man with a strong nose, heavy moustache and booming voice', Miles was an athlete, cricketer and Rugby footballer in his youth, had a good bass voice and played the piano. He represented New South Wales at chess, was honorary treasurer of the Shakespeare Society of New South Wales, and a systematic but unsuccessful punter who rarely missed a Randwick race meeting. With dangerous obsessions and money to spend, Miles represented an unstable element in Australian society.

B. Muirden, *The puzzled patriots* (Melb, 1968); C. Munro, *Wild man of letters* (Melb, 1984); *Ross's Monthly*, 14 Feb 1920; *Publicist*, 1 Feb 1942; *Nation*, 14 Feb 1959.   CHRIS CUNNEEN

MILLEN, EDWARD DAVIS (1860-1923), journalist and politician, was born on 7 November 1860 at Deal, Kent, England, son of John Bullock Millen, Cinque Ports pilot, and his wife Charlotte, née Davis. Educated in England, he worked in a marine insurance office before migrating to New South Wales about 1880. He was a journalist living in Walgett when he married Constance Evelyn Flanagan on 19 February 1883 in a civil ceremony at Bourke. They soon moved to Brewarrina, where Millen took up nearby grazing leases, and about 1887 to Bourke. He joined the staff of the *Central Australian and Bourke Telegraph* and reputedly became part-owner of the paper. By 1889 he was editing the *Western Herald and Darling River Advocate*, which he owned in partnership with Philip Chapman until 1901. In the late 1890s Millen set up as a land, mining and financial agent; by 1902 he had an office in O'Connell Street, Sydney, and a house at Burwood.

Standing unsuccessfully in 1891, Millen had been elected to the Legislative Assembly for Bourke in 1894 as a free trader and follower of (Sir) George Reid [q.v.]. He 'fought strenuously' for improved conditions for the man on the land. He believed in Federation but mistrusted the leadership of (Sir) Edmund Barton [q.v.7] and was rejected for the Australasian Federal Convention in 1897. Fiercely critical of provisions in the draft constitution that he considered either undemocratic, notably the powers and composition of the Senate, or unfair to New South Wales, next year he campaigned vigorously for 'No' at the referendum, and in consequence narrowly lost Bourke. However, on 8 April 1899 he was nominated to the Legislative Council, pledged to support Federation.

Resigning from the council in 1901, Millen represented New South Wales in the Senate in 1901-23. A skilled debater and forceful speaker, he brought to the Senate a reputation for political astuteness, a profound knowledge of parliamentary tactics and a fund of funny stories. Only 5 ft. 4 ins. (163 cm) tall, he had wavy, dark hair and a luxuriant moustache. Still supporting Reid, he became Opposition leader in the Senate in 1907. He was vice-president of the Executive Council in Deakin's [q.v.8] Fusion ministry in 1909-10. As government leader of a minority in the Upper House he managed to carry legislation with consummate skill and tact, then led the Opposition again in 1910-13.

Minister for defence under (Sir) Joseph Cook [q.v.8] from 24 June 1913 to 17 September 1914, in August Millen was closely involved in the government's response to the outbreak of war. He supervised recruiting and equipping 20 000 men for the Australian Imperial Force and by 19 August the Australian Naval and Military Expeditionary Force was dispatched against German New Guinea. However, after the government lost the election in September he again became Opposition leader in the Senate. From late 1915 he was a member of a parliamentary sub-committee on repatriation.

In 1916 the Labor Party split over conscription: when W. M. Hughes [q.v.9] formed his Nationalist ministry on 17 February 1917 Millen was again appointed vice-president of the Executive Council, with charge of repatriation; from 28 September he was formally minister for repatriation. He appreciated what he was undertaking: it 'will kill me, either politically or physically'. With the help of Major (Sir) Nicholas Lockyer [q.v.] he had to create an entirely new government department: since it was staffed almost exclusively by returned soldiers lacking administrative experience, blunders occurred. According to C. E. W. Bean [q.v.7] in 1918 all soldiers had 'a dread of Millen as a politician first, last and all the time'. As well as sustaining the 160 000 men returning after the Armistice until they were absorbed into the workforce, vocational training and housing schemes were devised, medical services provided and widows and children supported. Millen was the target for bitter attacks in the press, especially for administrative failures and scandals in the war service homes branch, and accepted 'responsibility for errors made by certain officials, without his knowledge or sanction'.

Meanwhile, during the absence of Hughes and illness of W. A. Watt [q.v.], Millen was acting prime minister in July 1919 and, with his 'nimble, suave and tactful methods', successfully mediated in the seamen's strike. However the strain of office was affecting his health and he contemplated retiring: on 30 July the governor-general Sir Ronald Munro Ferguson [q.v.] wrote to him that 'it has seemed to me all along that the practical working of the Commonwealth administration renders it a kind of Suicide Club for leading Ministers'. One of Hughes's closest

colleagues, Millen retained his portfolio until 9 February 1923. In November-December 1920 he represented Australia at the first meeting of the General Assembly of the League of Nations at Geneva and secured all the promised mandates despite Japanese displeasure. He visited war graves then went on to London where he reorganized Australia House, promoted government-assisted immigration and arranged for the funding of the Commonwealth's debts before returning to Australia in March 1921.

Millen died of chronic nephritis on 14 September 1923 at Caulfield, Melbourne. Granted a state funeral, he was buried in Rookwood cemetery, Sydney, after Presbyterian services in Parliament House, Melbourne, and St Stephen's Church, Sydney. His wife and two daughters survived him and inherited most of his estate, valued for probate at £18 309.

E. Scott, *Australia during the war* (Syd, 1936); L. F. Fitzhardinge, *The little digger* (Syd, 1979); *Western Herald*, 26 Apr 1890, 4 May 1898, 19 Sept 1923; *Punch* (Melb), 18 Apr 1912, 30 Apr, 20 Aug 1914, 7 Apr 1921, 20 Sept 1923; *Fighting Line*, 19 Mar, 19 Apr 1913, 18, 20 June 1914, 20 Apr 1917, 27 Sept 1920; *SMH*, 12, 28 Aug, 19 Sept 1914, 6 Jan, 19 Oct 1915, 27 Jan, 17 May, 7, 19 July 1916, 21 Feb, 17 May, 19 July 1917, 5 Apr 1918, 12, 17 June, 25 July, 16 Sept 1919, 3 Apr, 23 Sept, 10, 16 Dec 1920, 6, 13 Jan, 4 Feb, 14, 24, 25 Mar, 14 Apr, 21 Dec 1921, 11 Nov 1922, 15, 17 Sept 1923; *Aust National Review*, 20 Sept 1923; *PD* (Cwlth), 1924, 16, p 1; Parkes papers (ML); Novar papers (NL); Bean diaries (AWM).   MARTHA RUTLEDGE

MILLEN, JOHN DUNLOP (1877-1941), mining engineer and politician, was born on 3 May 1877 at Londonderry, Ireland, son of John Millen, draper, and his wife Kate, née Dickson. The family migrated to Queensland in 1884, settling at Toowoomba where his father established a drapery. Millen was educated at Toowoomba Grammar School, completed a diploma course with honours at Sydney Technical College and acquired other qualifications in engineering, metallurgy and analytical chemistry.

He moved, probably in 1904, to Tasmania, worked for several years in the Mount Bischoff Tin Mining Co. smelting works at Launceston, and undertook consultancies such as his work on the Renison Bell tin-mine at North-East Dundas. On 6 February 1906 he married Janet May Scott at St Andrew's Kirk, Launceston. In 1906-19 he was general manager of the Mount Bischoff mine at Waratah, overseeing an improvement in the company's prosperity, aided by his own detailed petrological investigations.

Millen returned to Launceston in 1919 and, 'a fluent and brilliant speaker', successfully contested the Senate for the National Party. Over six feet (183 cm) tall and heavily built but with cherubic features, Millen was a popular and hard-working member. Like all Tasmanian senators of the post-Federation years, he was a firm believer in the right of his State to special compensation for the impact of Federation on its finances. He had a particular interest in technological subjects, including the development of the Commonwealth Council for Scientific and Industrial Research. He was a member of the Joint Committee on Public Accounts in 1920-25 and of the wireless agreement committee of 1921-22. In 1923-27 he chaired the royal commission on 'national insurance as a means of making provision for casual sickness, permanent invalidity, old age and unemployment'. Their extensive recommendations were seriously considered and partly adopted in a government bill late in 1928 which, however, lapsed. Always well-prepared, he delivered his memorized speeches at a rate that was the despair of reporters, for whom he was always prepared to repeat anything that had been missed. In his later years declining health made his parliamentary duties onerous.

A director of Amalgamated Wireless (Australasia) Ltd and of the Australian Provincial Assurance Association, Millen acted as advisory engineer to the Vacuum Oil Co. and just before his death became managing director of Hadfields Steel Works at Alexandria, Sydney. He was a foundation member and president (1924) of the Institution of Engineers, Australia.

He held his Senate seat in 1925 and 1931, on the latter occasion as a United Australia Party candidate. Defeated in 1937, he was again unsuccessful in the 1940 election. Millen suffered from diabetes mellitus and died on 1 August 1941 at Launceston. Survived by his wife and three sons, he was buried in Carr Villa cemetery.

Millen seems to have made friends easily. At his death many parliamentarians, including Prime Minister (Sir) Robert Menzies, claimed him as a friend. According to a fellow senator this was because 'what he had to say was said with a quiet reserve and a gentility of manner which disarmed even his keenest opponents'.

PD (Cwlth), 1941, 168, p 5; *Examiner* (Launc) and *Mercury* (Hob), 2 Aug 1941; information from Mr L. D. Millen, Launceston, Tas.

SCOTT BENNETT

MILLER, ALEXANDER (1842-1914), retailer and philanthropist, was born in 1842 at Aberdeen, Scotland, son of William Miller, cooper, and his wife Annie, née McKenzie.

Several years later Alexander arrived with his mother at Geelong, Port Phillip District, where William Miller, who had migrated earlier, had tried unsuccessfully to establish himself in the fishing industry. Eldest of three sons and three daughters, Alexander was forced to work after only minimal formal education and became an apprentice with Hall Bros, drapers.

When the family inherited £100 from Alexander's maternal uncle, he started a drapery business in Pakington Street, Geelong West. By 1868 he had set up as a draper at Ballarat but in 1873 returned to Geelong, opening a store at Victoria House, Moorabool Street. In 1890 he opened new premises in Moorabool Street which were the centre of his rapidly expanding activities.

From the 1880s Miller extended his business interests to other country towns, becoming an initiator of chain-store organization in Victoria. By 1884 he had opened a shop at Horsham and in 1893 he established a business at Geelong House, Benalla. By 1895 there were other branch stores of A. Miller & Co. at Euroa, Hamilton, Maryborough and Shepparton and, by the time of his death, also at Numurkah, Rushworth and Echuca. As his business prospered, he diversified his activities to include farming, real estate and general stores.

Although dour and self-effacing and an exacting employer, Miller gained during his life a reputation as a philanthropist and benefactor. Influenced by Rev. A. R. Edgar [q.v.8], he sought to use his wealth in a Christian way. He established almshouses in East and West Geelong, Chilwell and Benalla, donated statuary to public gardens in Geelong, Shepparton and Benalla, and gave financial aid to needy cases who came to the attention of Geelong police magistrate George Read Murphy [q.v.]. He opened the gardens of his substantial Geelong home, Rannoch House, for use by charitable organizations.

Miller died, unmarried, at Armadale, Melbourne, on 27 April 1914. After a service at Yarra Street Methodist Church, Geelong, of which he had been steward and trustee, he was buried in Geelong cemetery. His estate, valued for probate at about £172 000, after providing bequests to various religious and charitable organizations, was committed to the building and endowing of homes for the poor, to be known as the Alexander Miller Memorial Homes, in Geelong, Euroa, Numurkah, Benalla, Rushworth and other country towns. The homes were to be administered by local advisory committees comprised of clergymen and businessmen. By 1944, 168 homes had been erected at the cost of £95 000 and the estate, valued at £275 000, included £180 000 to provide annuities for charitable organizations. By 1984 there were 195 Alexander Miller Memorial Homes.

W. A. Brownhill, *The history of Geelong and Corio Bay* (Melb, 1955); A. J. Dunlop, *Benalla cavalcade* (Melb, 1973); G. Seaton, *The Ashby story* (Geelong, 1978); *Investigator*, 20, no 4, Dec 1985; *Argus* and *Shepparton Advertiser*, 30 Apr 1914; *Age*, 30 Apr 1914, 5 Apr 1944; *Benalla Independent* and *Euroa Advertiser*, 1 May 1914; *Herald* (Melb), 4 Apr 1944.   DIANE LANGMORE

MILLER, DAVID (1857-1934), public servant and soldier, was born on 27 March 1857 at Glebe, Sydney, son of Irish-born Frederick Thomas Miller, timber merchant, and his English wife Martha, née Croxford. After a public school education he joined the New South Wales survey branch of the Department of Lands in February 1875, becoming clerk to the surveyor-general in 1882. He was assistant accountant in the department in 1887. On 2 April 1878 in Sydney he had married Emily Eliza Langdon (d. 1883); they had one son. On 23 April 1890 he married Jane Mary Elizabeth Thompson at Harris Park. After a period as chief clerk in the Government Printing Office, he was appointed a treasury inspector in August 1898.

A citizen soldier since 1885, Miller was major commanding the New South Wales Army Service Corps when he embarked with the Imperial Bushmen's Contingent in April 1900 for the South African War, returning after fourteen months service with the Queen's South Africa medal and four clasps. Appointed lieut-colonel in 1902 and I.S.O. in 1903, he became honorary colonel in 1912.

On his return from the war Miller had entered the Federal service in November 1901 as the first secretary of the Commonwealth Department of Home Affairs. In Melbourne 'the Colonel' efficiently ordered his rapidly expanding department. C. S. Daley [q.v.8] described him as alert and vigorous with an impressive military manner, decisive in his dealings but considered by some to be an over-strict disciplinarian. He dealt diplomatically with a succession of ministers, but had his troubles with King O'Malley [q.v.], who, making no secret of his contempt for the public service and its procedures, spoke of Miller as the 'gilt-spurred rooster'.

Not the least of Miller's departmental responsibilities was the search for a Federal territory, the conduct of an international competition for the design of the capital and the formidable task of establishing the new city. He was the chairman of a departmental board appointed in 1912 by O'Malley to report on the competition designs. The board did not recommend Walter Burley Griffin's [q.v.9] winning design but produced its own plan, which was adopted by the government in January 1913 but widely condemned. Deeply committed to the creation of the Federal capital and the board's plan, Miller arranged to be seconded as administrator of the capital territory, transferring to Canberra in October 1912. His 'residency' was its first permanent building. He was appointed C.M.G. in the following year.

When Griffin was appointed Federal capital director of design and construction in October 1913, and the departmental board and its plan was abandoned by O'Malley's successor W. H. Kelly [q.v.9], Miller was humiliated. In the not entirely baseless belief that Griffin's ideas were too extravagant to be realized and that his three-year appointment would not be extended, Miller did his best to ignore Griffin's contract and his design. He was encouraged by the next minister, W. O. Archibald [q.v.7], who detested Griffin and his ideas.

O'Malley's return as minister in October 1915, now as enthusiastic ally of Griffin, made things impossible for Miller who arranged a further secondment to the Department of Defence in January 1916. With the title of commandant of A.I.F. camps in New South Wales and the rank of temporary colonel, he reviewed and submitted a report on camp administration in September. He retained his official residence in Canberra.

A royal commission was set up in June 1916 to inquire into the administration of the Federal capital. In the course of the seven-month inquiry, on 14 November, O'Malley resigned from his portfolio before the formation of the second Hughes [q.v.9] National Labor ministry. The new government made the works branch of home affairs a separate Department of Works and Railways, with W. D. Bingle acting for Miller as its permanent head. The following month Miller resumed his post of administrator of the Federal territory.

Miller's credibility had suffered under six days examination before the royal commission in September and October 1916 and Wilfred Blacket's [q.v.7] finding, delivered in March 1917, that there was 'a combination, including the Honorable W. O. Archibald and certain officers hostile to Mr Griffin and to his design for the city' was, unlike many of his other findings, irrefutable.

Miller had already sought early retirement and took leave from Canberra in June 1917, retiring officially on 31 August. He retired from the army, as honorary brigadier general, in 1920. Until his death he lived with his wife and son Selwyn on a grazing property at Wellingrove near Glen Innes, New South Wales. He died on 27 November 1934 at Glen

Innes and was buried in the local cemetery with Anglican rites.

Aust Defence Dept, *Official records of the Australian military contingents to the war in South Africa*, P. L. Murray ed (Melb, 1911); A. R. Hoyle, *King O'Malley 'The American bounder'* (Melb, 1981); Roy com on Federal capital administration, Report, *PP*(Cwlth), 1914-17, 2, p 1067, 1917, 2, p 1; *Punch* (Melb), 24 Jan 1907, 23 July 1908, 27 Jan 1910, 30 Apr 1914, 28 Oct 1915, 27 Jan 1916; *SMH*, 1 Dec 1934; *Canb Times*, 1 Aug 1964; staff cards, A151/1, Dept Home Affairs *and* A199, FC 17/125, Miller to Bamford, 2 Feb 1917 (AAO).

PETER HARRISON

MILLER, SIR DENISON SAMUEL KING (1860-1923), banker, was born on 8 March 1860 at Fairy Meadow, near Wollongong, New South Wales, son of Samuel King Miller, schoolteacher, and his wife Sarah Isabella, née Jones. Most of his boyhood was spent at Deniliquin, where his father was headmaster of the public school. At 16 he was employed as a junior in the Deniliquin branch of the Bank of New South Wales and after six years was transferred to head office in Sydney, where he rose steadily in the bank hierarchy. On 17 February 1885 he married Maud Eveline Dean at St John's Church of England, Darlinghurst. After seventeen years service he was appointed assistant accountant, and two years later accountant. On 13 June 1895 at Young, the widowed Miller married Laura Constance Heeley. In 1899 he became assistant to the general manager, in 1907 general manager's inspector, and two years later metropolitan inspector, the second most-senior position in the bank. In 1911 he went on a world tour.

Miller, however, was relatively unknown when Prime Minister Andrew Fisher [q.v.8] appointed him governor of the Commonwealth Bank from 1 June 1912. The terms were generous: £4000 a year, the second-highest salary paid to a banker in Australia and substantially more than the salary of the prime minister or the chief justice of the High Court of Australia. He was also entitled to travelling expenses equal to those of High Court justices.

In the long political campaign leading to the establishment of the Commonwealth Bank some sections of the labour movement had seen the bank as an instrument of radical reform: an institution which would control what were considered to be the rapacious activities of the private banks. King O'Malley [q.v.] saw it also as a central bank which would exercise a good deal of control over all the trading banks. In fact the bank, legislated into existence by Fisher and developed by Denison Miller, differed little from the existing banks: where there was a difference it was in the greater conservatism of the Commonwealth Bank. With a nice mixture of caution and initiative Miller proved to be unusually well suited to preside over such an institution.

In order to avoid any appearance of political control, the Commonwealth Bank Act (1911) provided for an autocrat: 'the bank shall be managed by the Governor of the Bank'. Even the deputy governor, James Kell, who was required to exercise the powers of the governor if by reason of illness or other cause he was unable to carry out his responsibilities, was granted only minimal authority.

Miller exercised his authority to the full. In the first six months after his appointment the spare and wiry governor travelled Australia from Cairns to Perth, setting up branches of the Commonwealth Savings Bank, beginning at Melbourne in July 1912. At the same time he was finding premises and appointing staff to carry on the general banking business. Seven and a half months after his appointment the trading bank opened, with the head office in Sydney and branches in all State capitals, Canberra, Townsville and London. Miller maintained his close and detailed supervision. He not only made decisions on sites and plans for new buildings, but also decided on fittings and furniture. Only in 1921, when the bank was quite a large institution, was there any significant delegation of authority, and then only to permit the inspector and secretary, third and fourth in the hierarchy, to approve branch purchases of furniture. Even then the governor instructed that he should be kept informed of what was being bought. All staff, from managers to cleaners, were his personal concern.

The details of banking policy were also determined by Miller, set out in a letter to the Commonwealth treasurer about a year after taking up his position. His aim, he wrote, was to build a bank that would not interfere with the existing banks, that would do the business of the Commonwealth and such of the State governments as might elect to do business with it, and when it could be done safely, meet those needs of the public which could not be accommodated by their own bankers. In regard to private business Miller was at pains to emphasize that he was not competing aggressively with the private banks; the interest rate for overdrafts was a uniform 6 per cent with 5 per cent for charities and churches; the fixed deposit rate was ½ per cent less than the other banks; and business was declined if it was discovered that it was offered to secure a lower rate than was being charged by the applicant's own bank. In the face of gibes about 'sovereigns for all' and 'Fisher's flimsies', Miller took care not to convert vague distrust into hostility. An expanding banking frontier eased this task.

At the outbreak of war in 1914 the bank was a very modest concern, but the demands of war financing soon gave it a key position in the banking structure. The two problems with which the war confronted the banks were how to raise the necessary funds to pay for war expenses, and how to finance Australia's international trade under war conditions. The Commonwealth Bank took the lead in solving the banking side of both problems.

Australia entered the war expecting to pay for it from revenue and loans raised in London, but revenue proved insufficient and the London money market was soon restricted. So Australia was thrown back on its own resources. The Commonwealth had never raised a loan in Australia and nobody had any clear idea of what could be expected from that source. In the event, internal loans raised and managed by the bank provided more than half the total spent on the war. The ten war loans raised £250 million.

The bank also played a big part in financing the export trade. Before the war the export of wool, wheat, meat, and other primary products was handled by wool-broking firms, grain merchants, and others. But the war limited the available shipping, upset the established means of payment, and varied the demand for Australian products in Britain. The answer was to pool commodities, arrange finance for producers, and control exports. Wheat and wool made up two large pools, but there were others for meat, rabbits, cheese and butter. Though all banks played a part in financing these operations, the Commonwealth Bank had the central role.

By the end of the war the bank was firmly established as the Australian government's banker and its agent in most financial matters. The physical evidence of its maturity was the imposing head office, opened in 1916 in the heart of Sydney, in whose building and furnishing Miller had taken a close and detailed interest. An undercurrent of objection to the governor's exceptional personal power was kept in check by Miller's impressive record. But after the war he was accused of nepotism with regard to architectural and other services to the bank. In June 1919 he was appointed to a second term of office. The K.C.M.G. with which he was invested by the visiting prince of Wales on 17 June 1920 was a recognition of personal achievement as well as of the stature of the bank.

Displaying a 'faculty for combining conventionality in thought with enterprise in action', Miller in 1920 released sufficient currency to cushion Australia from the post-war slump, and in 1921 he confirmed to a deputation of the unemployed that he was prepared to finance the country for productive purposes in the same way as in wartime.

Vance Palmer [q.v.] observed that though Miller's personality was 'neither dramatic nor colourful it made a deep impression on the public mind'. It was appreciated that the new bank might have been as outstanding a failure in the hands of the wrong man, as it had been a success in Miller's. His ability to secure co-operation and loyalty was not the least of his strengths.

Miller was a man of wide interests. He was closely associated with the Barnardo scheme, the Millions Club, the Million Farms Campaign Association and the New Settlers' League. A founder and honorary treasurer of the Institute of Bankers of New South Wales, he was a life governor of Sydney Hospital and the Royal Alexandra Hospital for Children whose executive he chaired. He was for many years president of the Australian Golf Club, and a member of the Australian Club and the Royal Sydney Yacht Squadron.

Miller died suddenly of heart disease at his home, Cliffbrook, Coogee, on 6 June 1923. He was buried in the Church of England section of Waverley cemetery. His wife, four sons and two daughters survived him. His son Clive of his first marriage was killed in France in 1917. Miller's estate was sworn for probate at £29 791. A public meeting inaugurated the Denison Miller Memorial Fund that established a post-graduate scholarship in economics at the University of Sydney in 1924.

C. C. Faulkner, *The Commonwealth Bank of Australia* (Syd, 1923); R. Gollan, *The Commonwealth Bank of Australia* (Canb, 1968); *PD*(Cwlth), 1924, 106, p 985; Reserve Bank of Aust Archives, Head office, Syd.   ROBIN GOLLAN

MILLER, EDMUND MORRIS (1881-1964), scholar, was born on 14 August 1881 at Pietermaritzburg, Natal, son of Scottish parents David Miller, tailor, and his wife Georgina Agnes, née Morris. The family moved to Melbourne in January 1883 and settled at Flemington. Ed's mother was ardent in her devotion to the Church of Christ, his father to liberal politicians such as W. E. Gladstone and Alfred Deakin [q.v.8].

After an early education at the local state school and a spell in his maternal grandfather's boot workshop Miller attended University High School and Wesley College. In 1900 he began a professional career at the Public Library of Victoria and also enrolled at the University of Melbourne, graduating B.A. in 1905 and M.A. with first-class honours in philosophy in 1907. The achievement of Federation deepened his political interests and nationalist enthusiasm, while, under the influence of Professor Henry Laurie [q.v.], he developed an abiding passion for Kant and idealism. His life at the library was less happy as he asserted himself against bureaucratic and hierarchic norms.

In 1906 Miller worked for the short-lived Australian National Party, writing his first articles on Australian culture and history. Next year, as secretary to the Imperial Federation League in Melbourne, he made contact with Deakin and the two developed something of a father-son tie. In 1908 Miller travelled, notably in Scotland and Germany. He visited Rudolph Eucken, whose ethical idealism came close to his own world-view, and on Deakin's introduction met L. S. Amery and other notables of Imperial federation. On his return to Melbourne he published several pamphlets in this cause as well as his first Kantian essay—an attempt to develop a synthesis of Kant and modern relativists (particularly William James) and so provide an ethical basis for active citizenship.

A central figure in the formation of the Library Association of Victoria in 1912, Miller that year published the first Australian monograph in librarianship, *Libraries and education*. It reflected his absorption of functional ideas: 'where the need is socially urgent, there the library should be most ready to press its service'. But Miller was by now hoping for an academic career. Further research in Melbourne's philosophy department resulted in *Kant's doctrine of freedom* (1912) and in April 1913 he became lecturer in philosophy and economics at the University of Tasmania. From the outset he gave skilled leadership to the university's modest library and promptly helped to found the Workers' Education Association of Tasmania.

Miller soon forsook his work in economics but became increasingly absorbed in applied psychology. He drafted the Mental Deficiency Act (1920) and in 1922 was appointed first director of the State Psychological Clinic whose chief task was to test children's intelligence and advise on special education. Miller became an enthusiast for 'mental hygiene' while avoiding the harsher elements of racial and social eugenics. Both before and after being appointed full professor of psychology and philosophy in 1928 he drew part of his salary directly from the state. From 1924 Miller was also president of the (Royal) Tasmanian Institution for the Blind and Deaf, and from 1925 chairman of the Mental Deficiency Board. A trustee of the Tasmanian Public Library, he became chairman in 1923 and was a founder of the Library Association of Australia in 1928.

These community endeavours resulted in part from Miller's feeling that within the university he was slighted and undervalued. Tension persisted between himself and such traditional purists as R. L. Dunbabin [q.v.8], notwithstanding Miller's Litt.D. awarded by the University of Melbourne in 1919, his publication of further monographs on Kant (in 1924 and 1928) and his presidency of the Australasian Association for Psychology and Philosophy in 1929-30. In 1926 he offered for the chair of philosophy at the University of Sydney which in the event went to John Anderson [q.v.7]. He also stood, in vain, that year for the University of Tasmania's council, seeking support primarily from interested laymen rather than fellow academics; he gained a place in 1928. In 1933 lay backing won him election as vice-chancellor (part-time).

Miraculously, Miller not only sustained these various roles throughout the 1930s but established his major right to fame—as author of the bibliographic *Australian literature from its beginnings* (two volumes, 1940). Although F. J. Broomfield [q.v.7], Sir John Quick [q.v.] and others contributed to this work, Miller's effort was prodigious. The bibliography is comprehensive; it gives much biographical and publishing detail; and Miller's commentaries, if sometimes amateurish, are much more often shrewd and enlightening. His nationalistic faith suffuses the whole.

The 1940s saw a lessening of Miller's responsibilities. In 1940 he ceased being head of the Blind and Deaf Institution which had struggled worthily through financially straitened times. Soon afterwards the State Library of Tasmania was restructured in a way which Miller did not wholly support and he resigned his chairmanship: the theme of his tenure had been survival rather than vigour, although he had encouraged work for children and an Australian collection. In 1939-40 Miller took pride in organizing the transfer from the Commonwealth of a new site for the university at Sandy Bay. Yet remaining tensions conduced to his abandoning the vice-chancellorship in 1945. He still taught, without enthusiasm, until 1951. His leadership of the Mental Deficiency Board and the Psychological Clinic ended in 1946, albeit briefly resumed in 1951-52.

In retirement Miller remained a thinker and scholar. The chief fruit of his increasingly engrossing enthusiasm for Australian literature was the solid and informative *Pressmen and governors: Australian editors and writers in early Tasmania* (1952). Retaining an interest in the university, he upheld his successor in the chair of philosophy, S. S. Orr, after his dismissal in 1956 for alleged sexual misconduct.

Long a believer in the right of scholars and *literati* to enjoy public honours, Miller accepted appointment as C.B.E. in 1962. He had earlier been awarded the gold medal of the Australian Literature Society and elected a fellow of the British Psychological Society

(1943) and of the International Institute of Arts and Letters. He died on 21 October 1964, survived by his wife Catherine Mackinnon, née Carson, a Scottish-born milliner whom he had married in Melbourne on 1 June 1914, and by their daughter. He was cremated.

Miller did not possess an intellect of the highest order. At times he could be 'political' in the pejorative sense, and his own tendency, as well as Tasmanian circumstance, was to spread his interests too widely. Yet such reservations mean little against his extraordinary record of public service and scholarly achievement. The central library of the University of Tasmania bears his name; within hangs a portrait by J. Carington Smith which conveys the subject's genial and tenacious qualities.

L. Rodda (comp), *E.M.M.* (Hob, 1970); J. Reynolds and M. Giordano, *Countries of the mind* (Hob, 1985); M. Roe, *Nine Australian progressives* (Brisb, 1984); D. Drinkwater, Librarian errant: E. Morris Miller and Australian librarianship (M.A. thesis, Monash Univ, 1984); *Mercury* (Hob), 22 Oct 1964.

MICHAEL ROE
JOHN REYNOLDS*

MILLER, SIR EDWARD (1848-1932), financier, pastoralist and politician, was born on 3 August 1848 at Richmond, Melbourne, second of five sons of Henry 'Money' Miller [q.v.5] and his wife Eliza, née Mattinson. He was educated privately and at Melbourne Church of England Grammar School after it opened in 1858 until 1862.

Edward was introduced to the financial world under his father's guidance, gaining experience with the Victoria Insurance Co. and eventually becoming chairman of directors. He replaced his father as director (and later was chairman) of the Bank of Victoria, remaining on the board when it amalgamated with the Commercial Banking Co. of Sydney in 1927. On his father's death in 1888, he inherited his mantle as Melbourne's leading figure in banking, insurance and real estate. Unlike Henry Miller, who regarded mining investments as a dangerous gamble, Edward was chairman of directors of the Pioneer Tin Mining Co. of Tasmania and of the Goldmining Association of Charters Towers, Queensland, whose capital of £4500 returned £550 000 in gold. Interested in Broken Hill from its inception, he held the first scrip issued by the Broken Hill Proprietary Co. Ltd. Edward was a careful conservator of his inheritance, constantly developing and modernizing his valuable city properties and managing the family's Victorian pastoral interests and further property acquired at Windoora and in the Rocklands estate near Camooweal, Queensland.

Miller shared the family interest in horse-racing, although breeding and training were managed by his brothers Albert and Septimus. After their steeplechaser Redleap, trained on the family's private track at Alphington, won the Victorian Grand National Hurdle in 1889, the Millers built elaborate stables at Mill Park, Bundoora, where the Findon Harriers were housed. This beagle pack had been started by Edward Woods in 1870, and previously accommodated by Miller at Findon, in Kew. Miller was master of the hunt for twenty years after 1871. In 1896 the pack was opened to public subscription as the Findon Harriers Hunt Club.

Miller was a member of the Legislative Council of Victoria, representing South Yarra (1892-1904), then East Yarra Province until he retired in June 1913. Noted for a meticulousness in all his concerns, he spoke frequently in financial, pastoral and land policy debates.

When the Australian branch of the British Red Cross Society was founded in 1914 (from 1916 Australian Red Cross Society), Miller became its honorary treasurer until 1928. He was also treasurer of the Talbot [q.v.] Colony for Epileptics, and a committeeman of the (Royal) Children's Hospital, the Eye and Ear Hospital and the Royal Victorian Institute for the Blind. Knighted in 1917, he was president of the Melbourne Club in 1923.

Miller died on 26 September 1932 at his home Glyn in Kooyong Road, Toorak, and was cremated. He was survived by his wife Mary Elizabeth, née Darlot, whom he had married on 5 September 1877, and two sons, Edward Eustace, and Everard Studley [q.v.]. His estate was sworn for probate at £104 669. Lady Miller had in 1918 been appointed O.B.E. in recognition of her war work.

A. Sutherland et al, *Victoria and its metropolis*, 2 (Melb, 1888); E. Scott, *Australia during the war* (Syd, 1936); H. B. Ronald, *Hounds are running* (Kilmore, Vic, 1970); *PD* (Vic), 1893, 2nd S, p 4, 1932, 2nd S, p 1196; *A'sian Insurance and Banking Record*, 21 Oct 1932; *Table Talk*, 31 Mar 1893; *Australasian*, 9 June 1917; *Argus*, 27, 28 Sept 1932; *Age*, 27 Sept 1932, 1 July 1933; *Bulletin*, 5 Oct 1932; *Herald* (Melb), 1 July 1966.

E. M. FINLAY

MILLER, EMMA (1839-1917), seamstress and women's rights and labour activist, was born on 26 June 1839 at Chesterfield, Derbyshire, England, daughter of Daniel Holmes, a Unitarian cordwainer, and his wife Martha, née Hollingworth. Eldest of four children, she walked with her Chartist father to political meetings up to ten miles (16 km) away; he influenced her to rebel against the existing social order. On 15 September 1857 at Chesterfield Register Office she married Jabez Mycroft Silcock, a book-keeper with whom she had eloped. They had four children whom she eventually supported in Manchester by sewing twelve hours a day for six days a week. Emma, now widowed, married on 30 August 1874 at Salford, Lancashire, William Calderwood (d. 1880), a stonemason. With her children, the couple migrated to Brisbane, arriving in March 1879. Her third husband was Andrew Miller (d. 1897), a widower whom she married at Brisbane Registry Office on 21 October 1886.

As a shirtmaker, in 1890 Emma helped to form a female workers' union, mainly of tailoresses. In 1891 she gave evidence to the royal commission into shops, factories and workshops and marched with shearers' strike prisoners when released. She was the first woman to travel west organizing for the Australian Workers' Union and was the first woman member and a life member of the Brisbane Workers Political Organization.

Emma Miller championed equal pay and equal opportunity for women and was foundation president of the Woman's Equal Franchise Association (1894-1905), urging legislation to grant women the franchise on the principle of one adult one vote; although its policy was similar to Labor's she denied the association was allied to any political party. She admired William Lane [q.v.9], a champion of women's rights. She became president of the Women Workers Political Organisation (Qld) after 1903. In 1908 she was one of two women to attend a Commonwealth Labor conference, only the second time a woman was a delegate.

On 'Black Friday' of the 1912 strike Mrs Miller led a large contingent of women to Parliament House, braving the batons of foot and mounted police. She reputedly stuck a hatpin into the horse of Police Commissioner Cahill [q.v.7] who was thrown and injured. A staunch secularist, she campaigned for free speech in 1914-16. Her hatred of militarism led her to take an energetic part in the anti-conscription campaigns: as president of the Queensland branch of the Women's Peace Army, she was a delegate to the Australian Peace Alliance Conference in Melbourne in 1916.

Her steadfast position as a Labor agitator earned her the proud title of 'Mother Miller' and 'the grand old labor woman of Queensland'. Though very frail when old, in 1915 she campaigned in the Murilla State electorate for J. S. Collings [q.v.8]. She believed that the basis of the labour movement was industrial and stressed that it was of equal importance to women and men. She had no time for those who wavered from bedrock labour principles.

When she died at Toowoomba on 22 Janu-

ary 1917, survived by one son, the flag on the Brisbane Trades Hall flew at half mast and the Australian Meat Employees' Union conference was adjourned. Emma was buried at Toowong cemetery. On 22 October 1922 a publicly funded marble bust of her was unveiled in the Trades Hall.

J. Harris, *The bitter fight* (Brisb, 1970); Roy Com on shops, factories and workshops, *V&P* (Qld), 1891, 2, p 1177; *Official Bulletin* [1912 strike], no 4, 3 Feb 1912; *Ross's Mthly*, 23 Sept 1916, 17 Feb 1917; *Brisbane Courier*, 28 Apr, 1, 26 May 1894; *Worker* (Brisb), 6 May 1899, 2, 18 July, 31 Oct 1908, 27 Jan, 1, 3 Feb, 11 May 1912, 25 Jan, 1, 8, 15 Feb, 8 Mar 1917, 26 Oct 1922; *Daily Standard*, 11 July, 1, 5 Sept 1914, 27 Feb, 6, 29 Mar 1915, 23, 25, 27 Jan, 10, 12, 16 Feb 1917; *Woman Voter*, 27 Apr, 1 June 1916, 1 Feb 1917; S. G. Svenson, William Lane—the Brisbane years, 1885-1892 (B.A. Hons thesis, Univ Qld, 1982); IMM/116, p 232, 233, 321, 368 *and* PRE/A415, Chief Sec, 04252, p 30 (QA).   PAM YOUNG

MILLER, EVERARD STUDLEY (1886-1956), philanthropist, was born on 24 October 1886 at Studley Park, Kew, Melbourne, younger of two sons of (Sir) Edward Miller [q.v.], banker, and his wife Mary Elizabeth, née Darlot, and grandson of Henry ('Money') Miller [q.v.5]. He was educated at Melbourne Church of England Grammar School and at Sherborne School, Dorsetshire, England. Though he would have liked to have gone to the University of Cambridge and become a don, he followed the wishes of his father and returned to take up his position in the family business of the Bank of Victoria, probably until 1927 when the bank amalgamated. He had continued studies under (Sir) Archibald Strong [q.v.], classical scholar and writer. In 1914 he joined the (Royal) Historical Society of Victoria and attended meetings of the Classical Association.

Miller collected small *objets d'art* and prints, particularly Arundel chromolithographs reproducing Italian Primitives. His chief interests were engineering and photography. He practised the latter from 1903, increasingly for the purpose of historical study, as an aid to preserving 'the monumental memories of early Australia'; he assembled his work in a series of albums, the first of which was called *Historical monuments in Victoria I*. In the pursuit of family history and the history of pioneers he travelled extensively, first in Tasmania and later in Great Britain and Europe. Between 1914 and 1919 he joined Isaac Selby [q.v.] in protesting against the resumption of the old Melbourne cemetery which contained monuments to distinguished pioneers of the Port Phillip settlement.

Daryl Lindsay [q.v.], from 1941 director of

the National Gallery of Victoria, on whom Miller called frequently, remembered that he showed considerable interest in the administration of the Felton [q.v.4] Bequest.

In increasingly poor health after World War II, Miller lived quietly at the family house Glyn, designed by the architect Rodney Howard Alsop [q.v.7], in Kooyong Road, Toorak, until his death on 5 July 1956. He was cremated with Anglican rites. A bachelor, tall and distinguished-looking, he was shy and retiring in manner, inclined to contemplation rather than business or society. His most cherished ambition took form in a will which, from an estate sworn for probate at £262 950, bequeathed property and money to the value of £170 000 to the National Gallery of Victoria, as a purchasing fund to be used for the acquisition of 'portraits of individuals of merit in history, painted, engraved or sculptured before 1800'. Purchases were made from about 1960 until 1977 when the fund was exhausted. His collection of photographic material was left to the Royal Historical Society of Victoria; the classics department of the University of Melbourne obtained a selection of his library.

U. Hoff, 'The Everard Studley Miller bequest', in A. Bradley and T. Smith (eds), *Australian art and architecture* (Melb, 1980); *SMH*, 19 Sept 1956.   URSULA HOFF

MILLER, GUSTAVE THOMAS CARLISLE (1851-1918), newspaper proprietor and politician, was born on 26 November 1851 at Prospect, New South Wales, son of William Richardson Miller, farmer of Smithfield, Parramatta, and his German-born wife Catherine, née Engel. He was educated at St Philip's and Fort Street Model schools and was apprenticed to his uncle John Engel, a printer. In 1876 he went to Cooma to work on G. W. Spring's *Manaro Mercury and Cooma and Bombala Advertiser*. After a disagreement with Spring over its political reports, Miller left the *Mercury* in 1879 and with the help of John Gale [q.v.4] founded the *Cooma Express*. At Cooma on 5 May 1881 he married Emmeline Annie Hewison. As a journalist Miller was described as a 'Jack Blunt' and was several times successfully sued for libel. He retained the *Express* until 1918, sometimes leasing it; when editing it himself in the 1880s it was noted for ardent republicanism.

In December 1889 Miller won a Legislative Assembly by-election for Monaro and held the seat until 1918. The mainspring of his policies was support for the worker and the selector. A Protectionist, he favoured breaking up big estates, electoral reform, land and income tax and female suffrage, and criticized the high salaries and pensions given to ministers, judges and senior public servants. He long advocated Federation and, although he knew he had no chance of election, stood for the Australasian Federal Convention as a republican in 1897. Believing that the libel laws discouraged newspaper proprietors from exposing crime and corruption, he somewhat ambiguously supported John Norton [q.v.] as 'a necessary evil . . . a political scavenger', who could be of some service to the people, in the privilege debate of 1901.

Priding himself on his political independence, Miller once described himself as belonging to a party of one, but joined the Labor Party in 1901 when he felt that protection was dead as a State issue. He had opposed sending troops to South Africa and China in 1899 and 1900, and in 1916 vigorously campaigned against conscription. An assiduous local member, he chaired the Parliamentary Standing Committee on Public Works in 1914-16 and in 1916 was joint chairman of the royal commission on border railways.

Gus Miller was a good footballer and active in local social, sporting and cultural affairs; he was chairman of the Cooma Co-operative Mill & Flour Co. Ltd and an executive-member of the Cooma Pastoral and Agricultural Association. Especially interested in music and drama, he was capable of 'obliging with a song'. He was affectionately known as 'the Monaro Foghorn' and was rather brusque in manner, but moved by personal hardships and injustice. Romantic-looking, with classical features, wavy, dark hair and a carefully tended moustache, he was described by W. A. Holman [q.v.9] as a picturesque and attractive figure with 'a heart of gold under an exterior of granite'.

Impoverished, Miller died of heart disease at his Marrickville home on 20 October 1918 and was buried in the Anglican section of Rookwood cemetery. His wife, four of their five sons and two daughters survived him.

PD(NSW), 1891-92, p 305, 1894, p 2940, 1899, p 1575, 1900, p 1332, 1901, p 723, 2852, 1918, p 2241; *Bulletin*, 21 Aug 1880, 27 Aug 1887; *Daily Telegraph* (Syd), 31 July 1894, 24 Oct 1916, 7 Mar 1917; *Cooma Express*, 25 Oct 1918; *SMH*, 25 Oct 1918.   D. B. WEBSTER

MILLER, HORATIO CLIVE (1893-1980), pioneer aviator, was born on 30 April 1893 at Ballarat, Victoria, only son of John Pettigrew Miller, clerk, and his Irish wife Mary Ann, née Hurley. Mary Ann Miller died of typhoid at Mildura in 1893, leaving Horrie and his sister Annie in their father's care. Miller left school while young and worked in Melbourne as a baker's errand boy, a cleaner and rouseabout to a car firm. He was apprenticed at Sunshine Harvester Works for two years, became interested in aviation and built his first model aircraft. After finishing his apprenticeship Miller worked for the Tarrant [q.v.] Motor Co. where he met Hawker, Kauper [qq.v.9] and Busteed, 'the three Harrys', all destined to make their names.

In 1911 the three went to England, hoping to break into aviation; Miller, with a friend Bob Cousins, followed in 1913. Hawker and Kauper were working at Sopwith Aviation Co.'s works. Miller and Cousins joined them there: as a mechanic Miller learned to fly and won repute for his knowledge of aerodynamics.

On the outbreak of World War I he returned to Australia. While waiting to join the Australian Flying Corps he built his first aircraft, which he flew himself. After training Miller became a member of the first flying unit to go to England in 1916. He was trained as a fighter pilot, posted to No 2 Australian (68) Squadron where he obtained his commission and was transferred to No 3 (69) Squadron. Late in 1917 he saw action in France. Early next year, in poor health, he returned to Australia and spent the rest of the war at Point Cook, Victoria, as a test pilot. In 1919 Miller became a mechanic with a small South Australian aviation company. He then worked for the Department of Defence and flew an Avro 504 in a job that called for aerobatics over towns, encouraging people to invest in the Second Peace Loan. In 1920 he left the department to take delivery of an Armstrong Whitworth war disposal aircraft and, with Arthur Kennedy, formed the Commercial Aviation Co.

In 1922 the partnership was dissolved and Miller sold the Armstrong Whitworth to Queensland and Northern Territory Aerial Services Ltd; it was one of the first two planes QANTAS owned. Miller spent 1923-24 on charter work and joy flights in Queensland and won the speed and handicap sections of the 1924 Aerial Derby in Sydney. He returned to work at Point Cook in the engine-repair section but, feeling that he had become caught again in military discipline, soon left.

In 1927 Miller reopened the Commercial Aviation Co. Next year his friend David Robertson introduced him to his brother (Sir) Macpherson Robertson [q.v.], the confectionery magnate, who agreed to pay for a new aircraft. In 1928 the MacRobertson-Miller Aviation Co. was registered; three new planes were bought and two pilots employed. Miller was managing director, chief pilot and chief engineer. He also opened a flying school at Mount Gambier, South Australia. Next year he made headlines when in a De Havilland 9 aircraft he won the Sydney-to-Perth centenary air race, carrying a prize of £1000. In 1934 MacRobertson-Miller Aviation suc-

cessfully tendered for an air service from Perth to Daly Waters, Western Australia, to connect with the QANTAS airmail service to Singapore, thus starting M.M.A.'s operations in the West.

By 1939 the company's main coastal route had been extended to Darwin. M.M.A. supported the Flying Doctor Service and the Air Beef Scheme in 1949-53; the latter flew beef out of the remote Kimberleys abattoirs. In 1955 M.M.A. amalgamated with Airlines of Western Australia and Miller became regional director at Broome. He had ended his commercial flying days in the late 1940s though he continued to fly privately. In 1963 Ansett Transport Ltd gained control of M.M.A. but Miller remained a director till the late 1960s. He retired to live in Perth in 1972 and in 1978 received the highest aviation award, the Oswald Watt [q.v.] medal, and was appointed O.B.E. His name is given to a Broome museum containing his old Wackett aircraft.

Miller had married Jean Auburn Knox on 31 May 1934 at the Registry Office, Adelaide; they had one daughter. The marriage was dissolved in 1938. On 2 December in Melbourne he married the writer, (Dame) Mary, daughter of M. P. Durack [q.v.8]; they had two sons and four daughters including Robin Miller (d.1975), the flying nurse. Miller's book *Early birds* (Adelaide, 1976) covered his pioneering aviation experiences. A tall, bronzed man, he had sharp, hawk-like features, but his eyes were gentle. After a stroke in 1977 his health gradually declined. He died at Dalkeith on 27 September 1980; he was cremated and his ashes were interred in Broome cemetery.

F. M. Cutlack, *The Australian Flying Corps* (Syd, 1923); *People* (Syd), 22 Apr 1953; Miller papers (held by Dame Mary Durack, Nedlands, Perth).   GERALDINE BYRNE

MILLER, MONTAGUE DAVID (1839-1920), radical and labour organizer, known as Monty, was born on 7 July 1839 at Clarendon, Van Diemen's Land, son of Thomas Miller, carpenter, and his wife Elisabeth, née Passey. In childhood or youth he went to Victoria where he worked as a gold digger and claimed to have fought at the Eureka stockade. On 3 July 1862 he married Sarah Elizabeth Scott at Ballarat, where they lived for some years before moving to Melbourne. A carpenter, Miller was an active trade unionist and participant in the debates on democracy, protection, land and education which gripped the colony. He became a rationalist and thoroughgoing radical propagandist, a member of the Melbourne anarchist group.

Miller moved to Perth about 1897 and was

soon prominent in labour circles as a militant unionist, and a founder of the Labor Church and the Social Democratic Federation. His motion, which was carried, at the 1902 Trades and Labor Congress of Western Australia urging 'establishment of an Industrial Commonwealth founded on collective ownership of land and capital and upon direct popular control of legislation and administration', marks him as a socialist. Disillusioned with the Labor Party, for which he had earlier worked, he embraced the principles of the Industrial Workers of the World—industrial unionism and direct action in the class struggle—when they became known in Australia from 1907. As a member of the I.W.W. he was tried in Perth in December 1916, found guilty of conspiracy, but released. He continued his court-room defiance outside, touring Australia condemning the war, and next year in Sydney was again sentenced to gaol for his membership of an illegal organization, and again released because of his age. The bitter divisions of World War I had brought him into greatest prominence at the end of his life. He died, as he wanted it known, with 'atheistic fortitude', in Perth on 17 November 1920 and was buried in the interdenominational section of Karrakatta cemetery, the mourners singing 'The Red Flag'. His wife, three daughters and one of his two sons survived him.

Miller was an outstanding example of a self-educated artisan of great intellectual powers. Supporting himself at his trade, he studied social sciences, humanities and natural sciences. His book, *Labor's road to freedom* (1920), acknowledges Plato and Shakespeare as well as Carlyle, Emerson and Ingersoll. In his last twenty years he became a Marxist, more mechanical than dialectical, stressing the economics of surplus value and exploitation, and the inevitable progression of stages of society succeeding each other as their modes of production evolved, to culminate in socialism. But he remained also a humanitarian and a rationalist. He is remarkable too as a lifelong revolutionary throughout Australia's most bourgeois age. His resolute search to find ways to transform society was the mainspring of his extraordinary vitality. His talents received little recognition but his life personified sixty years of radicalism and socialism in Australia.

Miller was tall and erect, in later years his hair and moustache white, his face grave and lined, his compassion and natural dignity evoking respect even from opponents. He was best remembered as a speaker, proclaiming with the eloquence of a prophet the vision of a better world and calling for action to bring it into being.

E. Fry, 'Australian worker Monty Miller', in E.

Fry (ed), *Rebels and radicals* (Syd, 1983), and for bibliog.   ERIC FRY

MILLER, ROBERT WILLIAM (1879-1958), mine and ship-owner, was born on 27 January 1879 at Queensferry, West Lothian, Scotland, son of Robert Miller, clerk, and his wife Christina, née Fraser. Apprenticed at 14 as a cabin boy in sailing ships he made many trips round Cape Horn and qualified as master mariner. About 1901 Captain Miller migrated to Australia and served with Huddart [q.v.4], Parker & Co. Pty Ltd, ship-owners, on the Australia-New Zealand and the Melbourne-Geelong runs. On 8 February 1910 he married Annie May Kieran at St Mary's Roman Catholic Cathedral, Sydney.

In 1907 Miller had left the sea and begun business on Sydney Harbour in stevedoring and lighterage, mainly coal transport. In 1919 he founded a private company, R. W. Miller & Co. Pty Ltd, and was governing director until 1958. His first ship, the 180-ton *Audrey D.*, was put on the Newcastle-Sydney run. He soon purchased the *Meeinderry* and *Herga* and in 1923 ordered in England the *William McArthur*, the first collier with engines aft and equipped with grabs to unload, resulting in faster turn-around in port. After surviving the loss of the *Annie M. Miller* off Macquarie lighthouse (1929), cargo-handling techniques were systematically developed by his son Roderick (1912-1971) who, in 1931, became sales manager and director. The firm later developed road transport of coal in New South Wales and Victoria, but in 1952 Miller strongly opposed the proposal by the Menzies government that various private owners be offered a chance to buy the Commonwealth shipping fleet.

In 1920, on the recommendation of Professor Sir Edgeworth David [q.v.8], Miller had purchased Ayrfield Colliery near Branxton. With the later acquisition of Wallsend Borehole, Belmont and Preston Extended (Curlewis) mines the company became a major producer of coal in New South Wales, notably for the Sydney market through the 'Sixty Milers' fleet, and later throughout Australia.

In the 1930s Miller faced frequent confrontations with the Australasian Coal and Shale Employees' Federation, the Seamen's Union of Australasia and the Department of Mines over techniques of extraction and working conditions. The 'breast' system of mining pillars of coal designed for Ayrfield was cheaper and enabled coal to be run off, during strikes, with unskilled labour, but was opposed by inspectors on the grounds of safety, supervision, the frequent detection of 'fire-stink' and surface subsidence. The Court of Mines ruled in favour of the company in 1934, albeit with criticism of management diligence, but mining and transport unions lobbied a sympathetic government for an inquiry led by a technical expert. A raging underground fire in Ayrfield No. 1 and the reopening in 1935 of Ayrfield No. 2, closed since 1930, helped to resolve the difficulties.

Purchase of Britton's brewery in 1935 signalled capital diversification to inaugurate a major expansion of company interests in a chain of hotels. Although the development of the company into a major conglomerate was engineered principally by Roderick, R. W. Miller was actively involved until his death.

Miller belonged to the Highland Society of New South Wales, the League of Ancient Mariners, Royal Automobile Club of Australia, Australian Jockey Club, Sydney Turf Club and several golf clubs. He died on 10 February 1958 in Lewisham Hospital and was cremated after a service at St Stephen's Presbyterian Church. He was survived by his wife and three sons, all directors of R. W. Miller & Co. His estate was valued for probate at £148 794. A colourful businessman with great capacity and resourcefulness, Miller built a very efficient organization in a competitive industry and developed into one of the great executives of the Australian Coal Association.

R. W. Miller (Holdings) Ltd, *Prospectus*, 1962; N. L. McKellar, *From Derby round to Burketown* (Brisb, 1977); *Aust Brewing and Wine J*, 76, no 5, 20 Feb 1958; *Ports of NSW*, Mar 1979; *SMH*, 9 Feb 1929, 10 Apr 1933, 21 July 1934, 21 Nov, 13, 21 Dec 1934, 19 Apr, 8, 11 July 1935, 27, 28, 29 Aug 1935, 28 Jan 1945, 8, 9 Mar 1949, 12 Feb 1958; *Maitland Mercury*, 12 Feb 1958; *Newcastle Morning Herald*, 12 Feb 1958, 25, 28 Apr 1971; *Newcastle Sun*, 27 Apr 1971; *Australian*, 11 May 1984; information from the secretary, R.W. Miller (Holdings) Ltd.
                                          JOHN ATCHISON

MILLER KNOWLES, MARION; *see* KNOWLES, MARION

MILLIGAN, STANLEY LYNDALL (1887-1968), soldier and surveyor, was born on 27 April 1887 at Aberdeen, Scotland, son of Robert Angus Milligan, solicitor, and his English wife Margaret Katherine, née Lyndall. The family migrated to South Africa when Milligan was 9. He was educated at the South African College, Cape Town, and passed the Surveyor's Board (public service) registration examination. Milligan, his mother and brother then migrated to New South Wales where he joined the public service in Sydney. He enlisted in the New South Wales Scottish Rifles in 1908, was discharged with the rank of sergeant on the inauguration of compulsory military training and was com-

missioned as a lieutenant in the Australian Military Forces in 1911.

Milligan was working in Sydney as a survey draughtsman when he joined the Australian Imperial Force on 27 August 1914 as a second lieutenant in the 4th Battalion. He embarked for Egypt in October, was promoted lieutenant on 1 February 1915 and landed at Gallipoli on 25 April. He performed valuable service from late April to early May and was mentioned in corps routine orders. Wounded on 14 June, he rejoined the battalion on 9 August as a captain and was appointed acting adjutant next day. The 4th Battalion served on the left sector of Lone Pine until the end of August. Milligan was appointed staff captain, 1st Brigade, on 30 November and left Gallipoli on 19 December; his service in the evacuation brought another mention in corps routine orders. On 1 March 1916, in Egypt, he was appointed temporary deputy assistant adjutant and quartermaster general, 1st Australian Division. Promoted major and appointed brigade major, 1st Brigade, on 12 March, he sailed for France that month. In July-August he served in the battle of the Somme at Pozières and Mouquet Farm and was awarded the Distinguished Service Order and mentioned in dispatches.

On 17 March 1917 Milligan was appointed to command the 2nd Battalion as lieutcolonel. In March-April the battalion fought during the German retreat at Bapaume and on 9-10 April in the capture of Hermies. It served at Bullecourt in May and in the 3rd battle of Ypres in September-November. For excellent service as commanding officer during September-October Milligan was appointed C.M.G. On 19 December he was promoted general staff officer, grade II, on 1st Divisional Headquarters and held this post until 26 October 1918. He was G.S.O. II, Australian Corps Headquarters, from then until February 1919 and G.S.O. I, 5th Division, from February 1919. His A.I.F. appointment ended on 12 January 1920. Apart from his C.M.G. and D.S.O. he was mentioned in dispatches five times during the war.

Milligan was granted a commission as captain in the Highland Light Infantry, British Army, in 1921, with seniority from November 1917 and was seconded to the Egyptian Army. He served in the Sudan in 1921 and in the Darfur campaign and was awarded the Sudan General Service Medal. He was a member of the Anglo-French Sudan Boundary Commission delineating the boundary between the Sudan and the Wadi area of French Equatoria in 1922-23 and was assistant quartermaster general, Sudan Defence Force in 1924-27. He resigned from the army in January 1927 when he was appointed director of surveys in Anglo-Egyptian Sudan. When he retired in 1937 he was awarded the

Order of the Nile. In World War II he commanded military training centres in England and Wales in 1940-44.

Milligan had married Sylvia Nora Evelyn Turnbull on 30 June 1934 at Torquay, Devonshire, England. Survived by his wife, a son and a daughter, he died on 15 April 1968 at Weymouth, Dorset.

H. W. Cavill, *Imperishable Anzacs* (Syd, 1916); F. W. Taylor and T. A. Cusack (eds), *Nulli secundus: history of the 2nd Battalion, A.I.F., 1914-19* (Syd, 1942); *Reveille* (Syd), Jan 1933; *Roy Highland Fusiliers J*, June 1968; Milligan file, war records section (AWM).　　　　　　　　J. K. HAKEN

MILLS, ARTHUR EDWARD (1865-1940), physician and professor of medicine, was born on 13 February 1865 at Mudgee, New South Wales, youngest of three sons of native-born parents Thomas Edward Mills, publican, and his wife Mary, née Tuckerman and late L'Estrange. Educated at Mudgee, Dubbo and Gulgong, he was influenced by the Gulgong schoolmaster Robert John Hinder, who married his sister Sarah and became headmaster of Sydney Boys' High School. Mills became a pupil-teacher but, having difficulty in controlling older boys, boarded in Sydney with Hinder and matriculated at the University of Sydney (M.B., Ch.M., 1889).

A resident at Royal Prince Alfred Hospital in 1889, he demonstrated in anatomy at the university in 1890 and entered general practice in 1892 at Picton. On 10 August at Palmer's Island, Clarence River, he married Ida Cecilia Archibald, and moved to Strathfield, Sydney, in 1894. Mills was appointed assistant physician at Prince Alfred in 1898, physician in 1910 and consultant in 1930; he set up as a consultant physician in Macquarie Street in 1910.

From 1901 Mills had lectured at the university in the diseases of children. He visited the Infants' Home, Ashfield, as honorary medical officer for thirty-five years and introduced a modified Truby King feeding schedule which greatly reduced infant mortality from gastro-enteritis. In 1906 he visited medical schools in Berlin and was impressed with the importance given to teaching the physiological and biochemical principles underlying clinical medicine. He was one of the earliest to teach in this modern way in Sydney.

In his early years Mills was a controversial figure. He presented papers at meetings of the State branch of the British Medical Association and was a forthright critic of whoever or whatever appeared illogical or inaccurate. His appointment as lecturer in the principles and practice of medicine in 1910 was unpopular with the profession because other senior physicians were passed over. While his lectures were not profound they were not understood at first and the students complained to the dean. Later 'Artie' became a popular lecturer and bedside teacher, noted for his lively manner and the blackboard and chalk he took with him on the wards. In 1915 he joined the Australian Imperial Force as major, served overseas at No.1 Australian Auxiliary Hospital, Harefield, and at administrative headquarters, London, and was recalled to the university next year.

First professor from 1920 to 1930 of the principles and practice of medicine, Mills was dean in 1920-25. Less autocratic and domineering, Mills was more popular as dean than Professor Sir Thomas Anderson Stuart [q.v.], his intimate friend for thirty years, and exercised considerable power in the faculty less blatantly. He was a fellow of the senate in 1920-25 and 1929-39 and deputy chancellor in 1936-38. He was known as a fighter for what he believed in and for his candour and bluntness, in response to pomposity, insincerity and self-satisfaction, thereby earning some enmity. He was a foundation fellow of the Royal Australasian College of Physicians (1938).

In 1926 Mills had accepted Sir John Garvan's [q.v.8] offer of the post of chief medical officer for the Mutual Life & Citizens Assurance Co. Ltd. His wife died in 1929, and he married Garvan's sister Helena Mary at St Mary's Cathedral on 11 June 1932. He died suddenly in Martin Place of coronary occlusion on 10 April 1940 and was cremated with Anglican rites. His wife and two sons and one of two daughters of his first marriage survived him.

His portrait by William Rowell [q.v.] and a cartoon by Norman Lindsay [q.v.] are held by the University of Sydney.

A. G. Butler (ed), *Official history of the Australian Army Medical Services in the war 1914-19*, 3 (Canb, 1943); J. A. Young et al (eds), *Centenary book of the University of Sydney faculty of medicine* (Syd, 1984); *MJA*, 22 June 1940; *SMH*, 13 Apr 1940; Roy A'sian College of Physicians Archives (Syd); Univ Syd Archives; Biog card index and notes (Basser Lib, Canb); information from Mr A. Gray, Mutual Life & Citizens Assurance Co. Ltd, Syd.　　　　　　　　C. R. B. BLACKBURN

MILLS, ARTHUR JAMES (1883-1964), soldier and dentist, was born on 10 July 1883 at Glebe, Sydney, son of Arthur William Mills, importer from Birmingham, England, later a jeweller, and his wife Margaret Elizabeth, née Phelps, of Sydney. Educated at St Patrick's Catholic School, Parramatta, he became a dentist. He enlisted in the New South Wales

Lancers in 1901, was commissioned second lieutenant in the 1st Light Horse Regiment (Parramatta Squadron) in December 1904 and was promoted lieutenant in June 1908.

Mills married Betsy Florence Raphael at St John's Anglican Church, Parramatta, on 10 September 1910. They had two sons, one of whom, George Millard Mills, was killed in action in World War II. At the outbreak of World War I Mills was adjutant of the New South Wales Lancers (7th Light Horse) and spent two weeks guarding Sydney's water-supply. He joined the Australian Imperial Force at Liverpool on 9 February 1915 as a captain, was promoted major on 1 March and embarked for Egypt in May with the 5th Reinforcements to the 1st Light Horse Regiment. He joined his unit on 1 January 1916 and served for six months in the Western Frontier Force. He was appointed to command 1 Double Squadron and a squadron of the 1st L.H.R. on 1 July.

In November Mills joined the Australian Training Camel Regiment and in February 1917 became second-in-command of the 1st Camel Battalion, Imperial Camel Brigade, which fought in the long and successful battle for Rafa. In the 2nd battle of Gaza the Cameliers suffered heavy casualties. On 29 December Mills was promoted lieut-colonel and given command of the 4th (Anzac) Battalion, Imperial Camel Corps. Brigadier G. F. Langley wrote: 'The 4th hailed him with delight and had implicit confidence in his leadership. He too reciprocated his men's feelings'.

The Australian War Memorial has two diaries kept by him in 1918; it is obvious that he took close care of his men and had great pride in them. He was deeply impressed by the stamina of the camels, the distance they could travel, and the length of time they could go without water. 'To my mind the most interesting period for me was while I was with the Camel Corps . . . (I once did 75 hours without a rest)'. He and his 4th Brigade were in the raid to Amman, when they had to push, pull and coax the camels up steep, rocky hillsides during torrential rain. He describes the return from Amman when light horsemen and cameliers helped the Armenian Christians who were fleeing from the Turks. He carried a 4-year-old girl, sleeping in his arms, on his camel. In April 1918 Mills led the 4th Battalion in operations at Es Salt.

The fighting ended, then, for the Imperial Camel Corps. Mills wrote to his mother: 'We have been turned into Light Horse. I have command of the 15th Light Horse Regiment . . . I have two nice horses, nothing very "flash" about them, but there, I was never very "flash" was I, Mum'. He was transferred to the 15th L.H.R. on 1 July and he was in command during the great race for Dam-

ascus, at the time of the Armistice. His A.I.F. appointment ended on 19 January 1920. For his war service he was awarded the Distinguished Service Order and was twice mentioned in dispatches.

After the war Mills resumed dental practice in Sydney and continued in the Light Horse, Australian Military Forces, commanding 4th Cavalry Brigade in 1927 and again in 1931, with the temporary rank of brigadier. In 1936 he was made honorary colonel of the 7th Light Horse. He was appointed C.B.E. in 1935.

During World War II Mills was temporary brigadier commanding permanent ship's staff (military) in the troopship, *Queen Mary*. He was placed on the retired list, A.M.F., in 1943. He had a lifelong interest in sailing: in 1946 he took part as a deckhand in the Sydney-Hobart yacht race. He died at Mosman, Sydney, on 5 August 1964 and was cremated. His wife and son survived him.

H. S. Gullett, *Sinai and Palestine* (Syd, 1941); G. F. and E. M. Langley, *Sand, sweat and camels* (Kilmore, Vic, 1976); *SMH*, 8 Aug 1964; A. J. Mills file, War records section, and diaries, 1918 (AWM).

ELYNE MITCHELL

MILLS, CHARLES (1877-1963), soldier, businessman and pastoralist, was born on 3 December 1877 at Charters Towers, Queensland, second son of Thomas Mills, English-born pioneer of the Charters Towers and Gympie goldfields, and his Scottish wife Elizabeth, née Buchanan. After education in England at Alleyn's College of God's Gift (Dulwich College) and Hollesly Bay Agricultural College, Mills worked as a jackeroo at Michael Studholme's property Waimate, near Canterbury, New Zealand, and for Robert Gray at Hughenden, North Queensland. In 1907 he married Maud Elsie Jane, daughter of Albert Duckett White of Bluff Downs, and later that year moved to Panshanger, the historic Tasmanian property near Longford built by Joseph Archer [q.v.1], acquired for him by his father.

On the outbreak of World War I, already a lieutenant in the 26th Light Horse, Mills enlisted in the Australian Imperial Force and was posted second-in-command of C Squadron, 3rd Light Horse. He was promoted major in February 1916 and served through the Sinai and Palestine campaigns, acquitting himself with distinction in reconnaissance and supply operations as well as in combat. Wounded in the battle of Romani in August and mentioned in dispatches in December, he was again wounded on 9 January 1917 in the battle of Rafa when he led his squadron in a hazardous advance against a high-positioned, well-entrenched enemy; cover could only be contrived by digging the hard ground with bayonets. He was also later stricken with malaria. After his return home in November 1918 and his discharge from the A.I.F. next January, Mills remained in the Citizen Forces, retiring in 1937 as honorary colonel.

Mills became less engaged in the family pastoral business, which increasingly was managed by his sons Maurice and Ernest, and turned to industrial management. In 1923 he helped to form the Tasmanian Cement Co. whose works were constructed, under the supervision of E. G. Stone, on the shale deposit near Railton. After Dorman, Long & Co., the firm building the Sydney Harbour Bridge, took over the company's general management and a substantial shareholding, Mills became a founding director of the resulting Goliath Portland Cement Co. (incorporated in July 1928) with H. J. Brock [q.v.7], (Sir) John Ramsay, (Sir) Thomas Nettlefold [qq.v.] and L. Ennis. Like his Tasmanian co-directors Mills was commended for private investment in the new company 'not entirely for personal gain, but rather in pursuit of a great ideal of Tasmanian development'.

Goliath Portland Cement expanded rapidly. From marketing 17 416 tons in 1927 it raised its production capacity to 65 000 tons in 1930 and 100 000 tons in 1939, an important boost to the Depression economy. Mills was chairman of directors in 1944-54 and remained an influential, 'keen and active' director until he retired in 1961.

There was an active innovatory turn of character which placed a stamp on Mills's life whether as a serving officer, an industrial businessman or, notably as an observer of change: he encouraged his son Ernest to obtain the world's first autogiro licence in England in 1934. Mills was a member of the Launceston Club and an active golfer. He died on 26 March 1963 at Launceston, survived by his daughter and two sons, and was cremated. His estate was valued for probate at £109 846. His sons continued to manage the extensive and expanding family pastoral interests; Maurice also became a director of the Goliath Portland Cement Co.

L. Broinowski (ed), *Tasmania's war record 1914-1918* (Hob, 1921); H. S. Gullett, *The A.I.F. in Sinai and Palestine* (Syd, 1923); *Cyclopedia of Tasmania* (Hob, 1931); Goliath Portland Cement Co. Ltd, *Fiftieth anniversary, 1923-1973* (Railton, Tas, 1973); *Tas Year Book*, 5, 1971; *Mercury*, 6, 12, 27 July, 1-4 Aug 1928, 28 Mar 1963; *Weekly Courier*, 17 Aug 1933; information supplied by Mr E. D. Mills, Longford, Tas.   PETER CHAPMAN

MILLS, RICHARD CHARLES (1886-1952), economist and educationist, was born on 8 March 1886 at Mooroopna, Victoria,

third child of Victorian-born parents Samuel Mills, schoolteacher, and his wife Sarah, née Bray. Educated at University High School and Wesley College, he resided in Queen's College while studying law, history and political economy at the University of Melbourne (LL.B., 1909; LL.M., 1910). At the university he won sundry scholarships, was treasurer and secretary of his college sports and social club, prize orator of the William Quick [q.v.5] Club, and first president of the Students' Representative Council in 1907. A good footballer, he played tennis and cricket well into middle age. He tutored at Queen's College in 1909-11 and in 1911 was university lecturer in constitutional history, law, Roman law and jurisprudence.

In 1912-15 Mills studied at the London School of Economics and Political Science, winning the Hutchinson medal and graduating D.Sc. in economics. His thesis, published as *The colonization of Australia 1829-42* (1915), gave a careful account of E. G. Wakefield's [q.v.2] plan for scientific colonization and its Australian application, and examined Wakefield's views within a perspective of leading contemporary views on the political economy of colonies. He later wrote the introduction to the Everyman edition of Wakefield's *A letter from Sydney* (London, 1929) and the entry on W. E. Hearn [q.v.4] for the *Encyclopedia of Social Sciences* (New York, 1932).

Mills had enlisted in the British Expeditionary Force on 10 December 1915, and after attending the Inns of Court Officers' Training Corps and various cadet schools, was commissioned in October 1916. Before embarkation for France he married Helen Elizabeth Crawford at Ballymena, Antrim, Ireland, on 14 October. He served with the 61st Siege Battery in France and Belgium from 22 October until 17 February 1919 and was acting captain from 15 May 1917, gassed at Armentières on 9 April 1918 and mentioned in dispatches. Returning to Melbourne, he tutored in history at Queen's College in 1919 and served on the Victorian royal commission on high prices.

In 1921 Mills lectured in economics and commerce at the University of Sydney and from 1922 until 1945 was professor of economics and dean of the faculty. During the 1920s and 1930s he built up the school by appointing F. C. Benham [q.v.7] as lecturer and later employed Sydney graduates but, recalling his own valuable postgraduate experience in London, appointed them as temporary lecturers only until they had completed advanced studies overseas. As dean, Mills laid the foundations for curriculum and staffing developments until the early 1950s. The university senate claimed that his faculty 'became the leading economics school in Australia'.

In 1924 Mills helped to establish the Economic Society of Australia and New Zealand, acting as chief adviser to the editor of its journal, the *Economic Record*, to which he contributed many articles. With Benham, in 1925 he published a textbook, *The principles of money, banking, and foreign exchange, and their application to Australia*, and acknowledged J. M. Keynes and Edwin Cannan as major influences. In the thirteenth Joseph Fisher [q.v.4] lecture, *Public finance in relation to commerce* (Adelaide, 1929), Mills put forward the then unusual view that taxes might have purposes other than raising revenue. He opposed income tax duplication by the Commonwealth and States and defended in general the appropriateness of individual and business income taxation. His second text, *Money*, published in 1935 with (Sir) Ronald Walker, went through thirteen editions and was used until the mid-1950s. Among the reasons for its success was its claim to be the first Australian text presenting Keynes's new theories. It remains historically and biographically interesting as later editions record Mills's views on the recommendations of the 1935 royal commission on monetary and banking systems.

A talented administrator, Mills was elected chairman of the university professorial board for four successive terms (1933-41) and was a member of the university senate in 1934-46, where he became 'a powerful figure, prominent in a number of battles'. His success arose partly from skills in 'drafting rapidly and clearly the general sense of a meeting with which he was not necessarily in accord', a talent of even greater importance in drafting government reports which occupied him from 1941 onwards.

Mills had served on the economic commission on the Queensland basic wage in 1925. However, with his wife and children, he was in the United States of America as a Carnegie visiting professor in 1930 and temporarily escaped being drawn into Depression tasks. In 1932 he was appointed to a committee to prepare a preliminary survey of Australia's Depression-induced economic problems, and in 1932-36 acted as consultant to the New South Wales Treasury and adviser to Premier (Sir) Bertram Stevens [q.v.].

With J. B. Chifley and others Mills was a member of the royal commission appointed in November 1935 to inquire into the monetary and banking systems. He greatly influenced the structure and large parts of the initial draft of its report, and was appointed O.B.E. in 1936. Since the commission's recommendations were largely implemented in 1945, S. J. Butlin did not exaggerate when he described the effects of Mills's membership as 'deep and long lasting'. Moreover, Mills gained Chifley's friendship which from 1941 involved him increasingly in public service.

Even more enduring was his work as chairman of the Commonwealth Committee on Uniform Taxation in 1942 in replacing the existing 'eleven [State] taxes on income at widely differing rates' with a uniform Federal income tax, generating significant ideas for income tax legislation and laying the foundations for financial compensation for the States. The last connected with his work as chairman in 1941-45 of the Commonwealth Grants Commission, which considered applications from the States for financial assistance.

However Mills's most important contribution was his administration of Commonwealth education policy in its initial phase of substantial financial involvement with the universities. This grew out of Commonwealth war activities in research, technical training and education schemes for servicemen. Mills resigned from the university in 1945 to become full-time chairman of the Universities Commission and director of the new Commonwealth Office of Education. In 1947 he chaired the interim council which established the Australian National University and in 1949 persuaded Chifley of the importance of continuing financial assistance for university students beyond repatriation requirements, thereby fathering the Commonwealth scholarships scheme.

In 1950 Mills chaired a special committee on the financing of universities which recommended a grants system allowing them not only to meet their existing commitments, but also to expand their teaching and research and to lift academic standards. (Sir) Robert Menzies saw this as a most significant development in his term as prime minister. As director of the Commonwealth Office of Education Mills was responsible for activities ranging from the administration of Aboriginal schools in the Northern Territory to Australia's involvement with the United Nations Educational, Scientific and Cultural Organization and other forms of overseas educational aid.

Mills was 'tall and dignified in person' and 'commanded the respect of strangers by his appearance and bearing'. He had 'great personal charm and wit', a love of literature, poetry and the theatre, and expertise at bridge. In the 1930s he revealed his humour in a weekly column, 'Diary of a Doctor who was Told', a parody of another column also in the *Sunday Sun*, and anonymously published short stories. For most of his married life he lived at Mosman.

Having suffered for years from chronic nephritis and arteriosclerosis, Mills died in hospital at Mosman on 6 August 1952 and was cremated with Anglican rites. His wife, two daughters and two sons survived him. He left his estate, valued for probate at £12 669, to his wife. The tribute passed by Sydney's faculty of economics on his death records that Mills 'spent himself to the limits of his capacity in the service of his university and country'. The University of Sydney inaugurated the R. C. Mills memorial lecture in his honour in 1957.

G. E. Hall and A. Cousins (eds), *Book of remembrance of the University of Sydney in the war 1914-1918* (Syd, 1939); S. J. Butlin, *War economy, 1939-1942* (Canb, 1955); L. F. Crisp, *Ben Chifley* (Melb, 1961); R. G. Menzies, *The measure of the years* (Melb, 1970); W. Prest and R. L. Mathews (eds), *The development of Australian fiscal federalism* (Canb, 1979); *Economic Record*, 1, no 3, Nov 1925, 23, no 2, June 1947, 28, no 3, Nov 1952, S. J. Butlin, 'Richard Charles Mills', 29, no 3, Nov 1953, and for publications, 60, no 171, Dec 1984; Faculty of Economics, Univ Syd, *Economic Review '70 Jubilee Issue*, Aug 1970; *Aust Economic Hist Review*, 22, no 2, Sept 1983; Univ Syd, Faculty of Economics minutes, 1933-52 *and* Professorial Bd minutes, 11 Aug 1952 *and* Senate minutes, 8 Sept 1952 (Univ Syd Archives).   P. D. GROENEWEGEN

MILLS, STEPHEN (1857-1948), public servant, was born on 23 September 1857 in Sydney, second son of John Mills, grocer's assistant, and his wife Emily, née Stidolth, both English born. Educated privately, he joined the New South Wales Department of Public Works as a surveyor in December 1877. On 3 September 1890 he married Alice Maud Hudson at Homebush. In January 1901 he was appointed assistant engineer and in April became engineer and secretary to the City Improvement Advisory Board. In 1902 he appeared before the interstate royal commission on the River Murray and in 1903 he was secretary to royal commissions on government docks and workshops (New South Wales) and on a Federal capital site (Commonwealth), impressing by his zeal and 'professional and literary ability'. He was admitted to the New South Wales Bar in 1903, and became assistant engineer and an executive member of the Metropolitan Board of Water Supply and Sewerage the same year.

On 1 December 1903 Mills was appointed secretary to the Commonwealth Department of Trade and Customs, Melbourne. Dismissing objections to Mills's membership of a board of enquiry into Port Adelaide customs staff in May 1907, his minister Sir William Lyne [q.v.] commended his 'impartiality and freedom from bias'. Mills was appointed collector of customs in New South Wales in 1909, then succeeded (Sir) Nicholas Lockyer [q.v.] as comptroller general of the Department of Trade and Customs in September 1913. His temporary appointment to the Inter-State Commission in 1917 was converted to membership in June 1918, but he continued nominally as comptroller general until his retirement from the public service in September 1922. He was appointed C.M.G. in 1920.

Mills was a member of several other Commonwealth royal commissions: the sugar industry (1919), taxation (1920), and the effect of tariffs on Western Australia (1924) when he objected to proposals for independent State customs duties as contrary to the principles of Federation. In the majority report of the royal commission on child endowment (1927) Mills recommended against a Commonwealth scheme on constitutional and economic grounds. He entered the contemporary tariff debate with *Taxation in Australia* (London, 1925), examining Australia's position as a high-tariff country and criticizing industries 'wholly dependent upon high prices made possible by high import-duty upon competing goods'.

In 1925 Mills was chairman and one of two external members of an economic wage commission appointed by the government of South Africa. Its majority report (1926) recommended integration of black and white labour interests, encouragement of the economic status of black labour and the arrest of migration to the towns. Mills, as was natural to someone who had worked so long with the practical consequences, took a keen interest in the problems of Federation, contributing articles to the *Sydney Morning Herald* in the 1930s on such subjects as the financial agreement of 1927 and the Supreme Court of the United States.

Mills died at home at Glen Iris, Melbourne, on 1 November 1948 and was cremated. Two sons survived him.

SMH, 22 Sept 1890, 23 Sept 1922; *Advertiser* (Adel), 25 May 1907; *West Australian*, 24, 26 Sept 1925; Higgins papers (NL).
D. I. MCDONALD

MILLS, WILLIAM GEORGE JAMES (1859-1933), stud sheep-breeder, was born on 7 September 1859 at Native Valley near Adelaide, second son of Richard Mills, farmer, and his wife Margaret, née Henry. He was a grandson of Kentish migrants Richard and Sarah Mills, who arrived in South Australia in 1840. William attended Nairne Public School and the Presbyterian Grammar School of Rev. A. Laws at Mount Barker. He lived on his father's property, Millbrae, where he was to achieve an Australia-wide reputation as a merino sheep-breeder. In 1881 his father retired and sold all of Millbrae except 500 acres (200 ha) around the homestead, which was leased to the two eldest sons, Richard and William, with a gift of 400 sheep and some horses; Richard relinquished his share to William. Next year, on 19 July, William married Englishwoman Lizzie Martha Champion.

By 1900 the property had grown to 5000 acres (2000 ha) including neighbouring Bondleigh. In 1923 Mills left Millbrae to his eldest son Alec and moved to Sturtbrae, south of Adelaide, where he bred sheep until his death in 1933. His real success in sheep-breeding had come after 1900 as a result of buying three rams which brought to his stud the qualities of three of Australia's most famous flocks.

On 14 December 1915 Mills was among thirty-six South Australian farmers who met in Adelaide and established a Farmers and Settlers' Association. Mills, who was president from 1916 to 1921 except briefly in 1918, emphasized uniting the farming community. He knew that tensions existed in the organization because of disparate farming interests, wealth and family origin. Mills favoured operating as a pressure group without parliamentary representation, but others preferred to transform the association into a political party.

The decision to form the Country Party was taken by the association in September 1917; alterations to the constitution were agreed upon in December. The F.S.A. endorsed Mills and six other candidates for parliament at the 1918 State election; he won the Legislative Council seat for the Northern district. He was now president of the Country Party but there was some ambiguity, since the party's two members of parliament were variously identified as F.S.A. representatives, members of the Independent Country Party and members who 'sit in the House as independent farmers' representatives'. The Country Party name was formally adopted after the 1921 election.

Mills's farming experience had made him sympathetic to the radical wheatgrowers of the Mallee country who attacked the interests of city capital, represented by the Liberal Union. But he opposed any move suggestive of support for the Labor Party. Because of his pioneering background Mills celebrated personal initiative, thrift and hard work; but he also sympathized with unfortunate people who lacked his advantages. He was most at home as a respected, successful farmer in the rural areas where community spirit still existed; and he distrusted urban politicians whose class divisions defined their political behaviour. He tried to carry his allegiance into politics by representing himself as the spokesman for all rural people.

Although his parliamentary career began with the foundation of the Country Party, he had not founded it, as has been claimed. In 1921 he supported moves to create the Pro-gressive Country Party, which he believed would widen the party's base of support. The rejection of these moves by the F.S.A. membership led to his resignation as president. He remained a committed spokesman for rural interests in the Legislative Council until his retirement in 1933. The formation of the Liberal and Country League in 1932, which he had refused to join, reflected the weakness of the Country Party as an independent force; its formation had highlighted deep divisions among farmers.

Survived by his wife, four daughters and three sons, Mills died on 20 September 1933 and was buried at Blakiston. His will provided for the building on his land near Blackwood of homes for aged or infirm farmers no longer able to earn a living.

Pastoral Review, *Millbrae, Native Valley and Sturtbrae, Sturt, South Australia* (Adel, nd); Garden and Field Pty, *Our pastoral industry* (Adel, 1910); U. R. Ellis, *A history of the Australian Country Party* (Melb, 1963); R. Cockburn, *Pastoral pioneers of South Australia*, 2 (Adel, 1927); B. D. Graham, *The formation of the Australian Country parties* (Canb, 1966); M. Mills, *Millbrae and its founding family* (Adel, 1973); P. Hetherington, *The making of a Labor politician* (Perth, 1982); *Advertiser* (Adel), 21 Sept 1933; PRG 35 (SAA).

PENELOPE HETHERINGTON

MILNE, EDMUND OSBORN (1886-1963), railway official and soldier, was born on 8 November 1886, at Bundanoon, New South Wales, son of Edmund Milne, railway stationmaster (later deputy chief commissioner), and his wife Emily, née Cork. Educated at Goulburn, he joined the New South Wales Government Railways in 1901 as a probationer in his father's office. He shared a number of his father's interests and was active in ambulance work and rifle-shooting, becoming a lieutenant in the rifle club reserves of the military forces. After joining the railways head office staff in Sydney he became active in the Railway Institute, editing its monthly journal, *Budget*. He and his father wrote in 1906 *The Australian transcontinental railway problem*.

In December 1910 Milne was commissioned lieutenant in the Australian Intelligence Corps as railway representative. On 22 September 1914 he enlisted as a lieutenant in the Australian Imperial Force from Harden, where he was traffic inspector, and raised the 1st Railway Supply Detachment which embarked for Egypt in December. He was promoted captain in March 1915 and appointed railway transport officer in Cairo in May. His detachment was sent to Gallipoli to operate a light railway intended to connect inland positions with the beach but the short length of track laid along the foreshore never operated.

His unit was employed in off-loading and distributing water, rations and medical comforts. In November he was temporarily appointed major and principal supply officer at Anzac in charge of the Army Corps Reserve Supply Depot and next month took command of the 11th Company, Australian Army Service Corps.

After the A.I.F. withdrew to Egypt, Milne became involved in light railway operations at Tel-el-Kebir, Ferry Post, Serapeum and Ismailia. In March 1916 he was appointed senior supply officer with the 4th Divisional Train and promoted major substantively. Awarded the Distinguished Service Order in June, he was mentioned in dispatches in July and in January 1917. Next July he was made deputy assistant quartermaster general of the 4th Division, transferring in September to the same appointment on 1st Australian Corps Headquarters. He was again mentioned in dispatches in December 1917 and December 1918. On 11 August 1918 Milne's sword was used by King George V to invest the corps commander, Lieut-General Sir John Monash [q.v.], with his knighthood.

In 1918 Milne married, in England, Sister Myra Septima Hutchinson Wyse of the Australian Army Nursing Service; they had no children. While in England he made a comprehensive tour of railway networks. In January 1919 he was awarded the French Croix de Guerre and returned to Sydney where his A.I.F. appointment ended in July. Reverting to his pre-war rank, he was promoted captain and brevet major in the Australian Military Forces.

Promoted substantive major, A.A.S.C., in September 1920, Milne remained active in the militia. He filled staff appointments on the headquarters of the 2nd Division and with the Engineer and Railway Staff Corps before being given command of army service corps troops of 2nd Division in July 1928; he was promoted lieut-colonel in April 1929. In civil employment he was outdoor superintendent in the chief traffic manager's branch, general manager of the Metropolitan and Newcastle Transport Trusts in 1930-32, then superintendent of passenger transportation with the government railways. In June 1937 he was appointed commanding officer of the 34th Battalion (Illawarra Regiment).

Seconded to the 2nd A.I.F. in November 1939, Milne proceeded on active service as assistant adjutant and quartermaster general and was appointed O.B.E. in 1940. In August he was placed in command of the Australian Port Detachment on the Suez Canal and in December was promoted colonel and appointed to the staff of the 7th Division until May 1941. Returning to Australia, he became assistant quartermaster general at Headquarters, Home Forces. In 1942-44 he was controller of docks on the staff of land headquarters and helped to reduce serious delays at the port of Melbourne. In November 1944 he was transferred to part-time duty with the Volunteer Defence Corps and was placed on the retired list in 1946. He retired from the New South Wales railways in 1951.

A foundation member of the Legacy Club in Sydney, Milne was president in 1950-51 and was also involved in managing Legacy's war veterans home from 1938. He was active in the Returned Services League for forty-four years, especially as councillor and metropolitan vice-president; he was also marshal of the Sydney Anzac Day march until his death. A member and sometime chairman of the State executive committee of the Institute of Transport, he belonged to twelve Masonic lodges, was director of the anti-tuberculosis association, chairman of the Burwood branch of the Liberal Party, and honorary secretary of the Forestry Advisory Council of New South Wales.

Survived by his wife, he died at the Repatriation General Hospital, Concord, on 11 April 1963 and was cremated.

C. E. W. Bean, *The story of Anzac*, 2 (Syd, 1924); R. McNicoll, *The Royal Australian Engineers, 1919 to 1945* (Canb, 1982); *London Gazette*, 2 June, 11 July 1916, 2 Jan, 25 Dec 1917, 31 Dec 1918, 7 Jan 1919; *Reveille* (Syd), Sept 1935, Oct 1937, Jan 1940; *SMH*, 9 Aug 1915, 24, 25 Aug 1917, 5 June, 10 Dec 1928, 27 July 1929, 12 Dec 1939, 11 July 1940, 16 Feb 1946, 19 Nov 1952, 24 Nov 1954, 8 Oct 1962, 13 Apr 1963; valedictory address by Colonel W. Wood, 17 Apr 1963 (NL); records (AWM).

C. D. COULTHARD-CLARK

MILNE, JOHN ALEXANDER (1872-1918), farmer, agent and soldier, was born on 23 March 1872 at Woodside, Cromar, Aberdeenshire, Scotland, son of Alexander Milne, labourer, and Jane McCombie, and was educated at Torphins School. He arrived in Brisbane as a free immigrant on the *Dorunda* in August 1890. Initially a farm-labourer in the Wide Bay district, he was a miner in 1897 and then engine-driver on the Gympie goldfield, and in 1903-06 a farmer at Kilkivan Junction. He became a commercial traveller for hardware firms, based at Maryborough and from 1908 at Bundaberg, where he established a commission agency in 1913 and was a dealer for the International Harvester Co. of Australia Pty Ltd.

An excellent rifle-shot, Milne was from 1908 an officer in the Wide Bay Regiment's 1st Battalion (later the 4th Infantry Battalion). He enlisted in the 9th Battalion, Australian Imperial Force, as a captain on 20 August 1914 and sailed on the first troopship to leave Queensland.

On 25 April 1915 Milne took 'E' Company

ashore at Gallipoli; although wounded five times he continued encouraging his men until he collapsed and was dragged down to the beach where it was realized he was still alive. After treatment in hospital he returned to Gallipoli but on 11 November, two days after his promotion to major, he was evacuated because of fever and in January 1916 was invalided to Australia.

After enthusiastic civic welcomes in Maryborough and Bundaberg, Milne told in recruiting speeches, 'cheered to the echo', of his pleasure in leading such men as the Australians, unveiled the honour board of St Andrew's Presbyterian Church, Bundaberg, and enjoyed a short fishing holiday at Urangan. On 1 May 1916 he resumed duty with the A.I.F. and was appointed second-in-command of the 41st Battalion. Reaching France in November, he was promoted lieut-colonel and given command of the 36th Battalion on 24 February 1917. Gassed at Messines, and injured by a shell at Passchendaele, he was awarded the Distinguished Service Order in August for 'great capacity and initiative' and was mentioned in dispatches in December.

In March 1918 Milne successfully organized and executed two important raids on German defences near Warneton, and at Villers-Bretonneux on 4 April led a spectacular bayonet charge. Generals Birdwood, Goddard [qq.v.7,9], Monash and Rosenthal [qq.v.] appreciated Milne's achievements but before receiving official recognition he was killed on 12 April 1918 by a shell and was buried in Heath cemetery, Harbonnières.

Strong, broad-shouldered, seemingly fearless, with a powerful voice and marked Scots accent, the sandy-haired Milne was well liked and respected by his troops. A rugged individualist, with little respect for formality though a rigid disciplinarian, he was an eminently practical and competent soldier with a strong sense of duty.

On 6 October 1898 at Kilkivan Junction, Queensland, in a Primitive Methodist ceremony performed by Rev. John Adamson [q.v.7], Milne had married Mary Elise May Bull who, with their three sons, survived him.

C. E. W. Bean, *The A.I.F. in France*, 1918 (Syd, 1937); N. K. Harvey, *From Anzac to the Hindenburg line* (Brisb, 1941); *London Gazette*, 24 Aug, 28 Dec 1917; *Maryborough Chronicle*, 16, 22 Feb 1916; *Brisbane Courier*, 27 Apr 1918; *Sydney Mail*, 22 May 1918; information from and family papers held by Mrs D. Hope, Mackay, Qld, and Mrs B. Curry, Riverwood, NSW.   BETTY CROUCHLEY

MINAHAN, PATRICK JOSEPH (1866-1933), boot manufacturer and politician, was born on 27 March 1866 at Killaloe, Clare, Ire-

land, son of Patrick Minahan, bootmaker, and his wife Mary, née Murphy. He arrived in Sydney about 1870 and by 1890 had opened a boot factory at Newtown. On 5 September 1900 at St Patrick's Catholic Church he married Catherine Kinsela (d. 1914).

Minahan joined the Labor Party and was an executive-member in 1907-13, vice-president in 1909 and president in 1910 when he contributed much to the organizing and financing of the State and Federal electoral victories. He held the State seat of Belmore in 1910-17. On 1 July 1909 he chaired the meeting that established the Catholic Club (president, 1909-24).

At Rathgar Catholic Church, Dublin, on 3 June 1915 Minahan married Elizabeth Mary Ward. Back in Sydney next year he was stirred by the Dublin Easter rising. With D. M. Grant [q.v.9] he was joint treasurer of the No-Conscription Campaign Committee and was a generous and effective chairman of the 1917 transport strike relief committee. Defeated for pre-selection for Belmore in 1917, he ran against ex-Labor premier W. A. Holman [q.v.9] at Cootamundra, and lost.

Minahan had become wealthy, with retail properties in Sydney, and was known as the 'Boot King'. He combined Irish and Australian nationalism with romantic gusto. Impulsive and quick-tempered, in his presidential address to the Catholic Club in 1918 he asserted that 'we . . . will enforce our rights when necessary [as] we are a fourth of the community, and generally are of the intellectual and wealthy portion of the population'. Standing in 1920 for Sydney, he claimed that secret groups had planned that if conscription had been carried in 1916, 'there would probably have been a republic in Australia'. The Labor leader J. Storey [q.v.] said Minahan's 'little joke' was part of his platform oratory. He had signed the petition of the Labor Council of New South Wales for the release of the twelve Industrial Workers of the World prisoners and as a result had his endorsement withdrawn; but he won a seat as Independent Labor and was admitted to caucus when Storey formed a government.

In parliament with P. F. Loughlin, C. C. Lazzarini [qq.v.] and others Minahan defended Catholic institutions against criticism from Sir Thomas Henley [q.v.9] and T. J. Ley [q.v.] and praised Archbishop Mannix [q.v.]. Active in the St Vincent de Paul Society, he had helped to found St Vincent's Boys' Home (Westmead) in 1891-96, and contributed to other Catholic charities. He became foundation chairman of the Knights of the Southern Cross on 22 March 1919, and was national president in 1922-23. In 1920 he received the papal knighthood of St Sylvester.

In 1922 Minahan provided finance for the

Daily Mail; it lost money, and next year was taken over by the *Labor Daily*. He was unpredictably active in party factionalism at that time and supported the executive's action in making J. J. G. McGirr [q.v.] leader in place of James Dooley [q.v.8]. In 1923 he was recommended for two years expulsion over the 'sliding panel' ballot-box scandals, but the 1924 conference did not approve it. The Labor Sydney Electorate Council refused his endorsement at the 1925 election, but the executive reinstated him and he gained a seat when J. E. Birt died before being sworn in. He was bemused by renewed pressure of industrialists (trade unionists) under A. C. Willis [q.v.] for control of the party in 1926-27, and was suspicious of Premier J. T. Lang's [q.v.9] links with them. But he welcomed the reforms of the government.

Minahan joined T. D. Mutch's [q.v.] group opposed to Lang when he reconstructed his ministry in May, and claimed that the new 'red rules' opened the door to 'Sovietism'. Commenting that the Labor Party was no longer the one he had known 'for over thirty years', he added that members of branches, who were 'representatives of science, literature and commerce, small manufacturers and employers', were now subordinate to trade unionists. He ran against Lang at Auburn as an Independent in the October elections, but lost.

Minahan died of coronary occlusion at his home at Lewisham on 3 October 1933, survived by his wife, five children of his first marriage and two of his second. He was buried in Rookwood cemetery. His wealth and restless individuality had made him an unusual member of the Labor Party; nevertheless he belonged there as a radical Irish-Australian, distrustful of authority and responsive to demands for social reforms, though antagonistic to what he saw as communist extremism.

James Mark Minahan (1872-1941) was his brother and associate in business. He was a member of the Legislative Council in 1925-34. The brothers belonged to a large, but diffuse and disunited group of Catholics in the Labor Party which increased from eight parliamentarians out of thirty in 1901 to forty-three out of 100 in 1925. Religiously, Paddy Minahan seems to have been the most politically active of them, but his party influence was negligible, and they never dominated events or policy, though at opportune moments of complex factionalism certain individuals may have gained from the connexion and the numbers.

Freeman's J (Syd), 10 Feb 1910, 9 Dec 1920, 4 Sept 1924; *Sydney Mail*, 19 Apr 1922; *SMH*, 2, 8 Mar, 13 Dec 1920, 23 Apr 1924, 25 June 1925, 24 Jan, 26 July, 23 Sept 1927, 4 Oct 1933.

BEDE NAIRN

MINCHIN, ALFRED CORKER (1857-1934), zoo director, was born on 24 September 1857 in Victoria, son of Richard Ernest Minchin [q.v.5] and his wife Ellen Rebecca, née Ocock. Educated at North Adelaide Grammar School, he worked for land agents G. W. Cotton [q.v.3] and Green & Co. before running his own agency in 1883-93. He gained zoological knowledge at the Melbourne zoo and was twice honorary director of the South Australian Zoological and Acclimatization Society. He became honorary assistant director in 1891 and, succeeding his father, director of the Adelaide Zoological Gardens from 1893 until his death. The society's council was a powerful body whose members collected during their overseas trips; but it depended on an annual government grant and benefactions. Minchin added new buildings and stock to the zoo; but by its silver jubilee in 1903 the annual report reflected hard times: the replacement of the hippopotamus, the purchase of giraffes and polar bears 'and other ideals of the energetic director, Mr Minchin, must remain unrealized unless the Society is more liberally supported'.

There was progress in 1908-14; grants facilitated reconstructive work, new animals drew crowds. The council found Minchin 'a most competent authority' who 'has made a paradise of the gardens'. In 1911 he was elected to the Zoological Society of London. The 1915 drought and further slashing of grants meant that the zoo deteriorated, not recovering fully until 1925.

He had married Florence Euphemia Scammell on 9 October 1888. They lived happily with their daughter and two sons in the stately director's residence. A tall, imposing man, Minchin 'held court' on Sunday mornings at the zoo where the lemurs were his favourites. He was a member of the Adelaide Club. He died on 20 September 1934 and was buried in North Road cemetery.

His second son RONALD RICHARD LUTHER (1904-1940) was born on 26 February 1904 at the zoo and was educated at the Collegiate School of St Peter. In 1923 he joined the zoo's staff. In 1929, as assistant director, he bought new species from Java and Singapore, and from New Zealand in 1933. He was director from 1935. Ron, whose hobby was bird watching, was an aviculturist, specializing in Australian parrots and breeding rare types, particularly seven members of the genus *Neophema*. New aviaries were built, attendances increased, and in 1938 the society became the Royal Zoological Society of South Australia.

Ron had married Elizabeth Margaret Ashwin on 21 October 1936; they had one son. Quiet and unobtrusively efficient, he had a distinctive sense of humour. He died of cancer on 4 February 1940. His wife scattered his ashes before the parrots' cages.

ALFRED KEITH (1899-1963), Alfred Minchin's elder son, was born on 24 May 1899 at the zoo and was also educated at the Collegiate School of St Peter. In South Africa and Britain in 1924-25 he collected animals for the Adelaide zoo. He opened a snake park in the north parklands in 1929 with about 200 species. Two years later he was crippled by poliomyelitis, having to use crutches and, later, a wheel-chair. But in 1936 he expanded, and introduced koala bears; his notes, 'Weaning of young koalas', were published in 1937. He released surplus koalas onto his land on Kangaroo Island. His Koala Farm closed in 1960; council inspections had criticized the stables and enclosures. He also ran an aquarium off the Glenelg jetty, 'the best bob's worth on or off the beach'. By 1942, however, the Glenelg Council deplored the aquarium's disgraceful state; it was destroyed in 1948.

Keith was controversial: some found him dominating, argumentative and over-fond of publicity; to others he was jovial, one of Adelaide's characters. Despite his disability he was an adventurous photographer. Although vice-president of the zoological society from 1935, he rarely attended meetings. Unmarried, he died on 1 August 1963 and was buried near his father.

C. E. Rix, *Royal Zoological Society of South Australia, 1878-1978* (Adel, 1978); Sth Aust Zoological and Acclimatization Soc, *Annual Report*, 1883-1936; Roy Zoological Soc of Sth Aust, *Annual Report*, 1936-63; *Advertiser* (Adel), 21 Sept 1934, 3 Aug 1963; *Chronicle* (Adel), 15 Feb 1940; Adel City Council Archives; Sth Aust Harbours Bd Archives; information from Mrs E. M. Brummitt, Norwood, and Mrs A. M. Madden, Toorak Gardens, Adel.   JOYCE GIBBERD

MINIFIE, RICHARD PEARMAN (1898-1969), airman and company director, was born on 2 February 1898 at Alphington, Melbourne, son of James Minifie, a flour miller from Shropshire, England, and his Geelong-born wife Beatrice Kate, née Earle. He was educated at Melbourne Church of England Grammar School where, in 1915, he became a prefect and a cadet-lieutenant.

On 11 June 1916 Minifie joined the Royal Naval Air Service in London as a temporary probationary flight sub-lieutenant and during the next six months was posted to R.N.A.S. establishments at Eastbourne, Cranwell, East Fortune and Dover for pilot training. He was confirmed as a flight sub-lieutenant in October, was posted to No. 1 Squadron, R.N.A.S., and arrived in France in December. The squadron was equipped with Sopwith Triplane fighting scouts and in February-March 1917 was continually in action on the Somme. The Triplanes also became engrossed in large aerial engagements, or dogfights, and the squadron was highly effective in ground-strafing, particularly during the battles of Bullecourt and Messines in May and June.

Between July 1917 and March 1918 Minifie was promoted acting flight lieutenant, flight lieutenant and acting flight commander and took part in the battles of Ypres and Passchendaele. He was an excellent fighter pilot and his score of victories against enemy aircraft rose rapidly. Like his Australian contemporaries in the R.N.A.S.—B. C. Bell, R. S. Dallas, S. J. Goble [qq.v.7,8,9] and R. A. Little [q.v.]—he found the Triplane very manoeuvrable and efficient.

In October 1917 No. 1 Squadron returned to England to re-equip with Sopwith Camel scouts, and was back in France in February 1918. On 17 March, fifteen days before he was promoted captain, Minifie crash-landed his Camel, owing to engine failure, in the German lines. He was taken as a prisoner of war at Roulers, and spent the rest of the war in P.O.W. camps at Karlsruhe and Clausthal. Major Dallas, who had been Minifie's commanding officer from June 1917 to March 1918, wrote to Mrs Minifie to let her know that her son had been taken as a P.O.W. and 'that he is all right'. Referring to Minifie as 'a brilliant pilot and air fighter', Dallas added that 'his aerial victories were gained by clean, clever fighting and he was always so modest about his great achievements'.

Minifie was officially credited with destroying twenty-one enemy aircraft, mostly when aged 19, and was the seventh highest scoring Australian pilot of World War I. His prowess as a fighter pilot was exemplified in the outstanding and rapid sequence of awards of the Distinguished Service Cross on 2 November 1917, Bar to the D.S.C. on 30 November, and second Bar on 17 April 1918.

In May 1919 Minifie returned to Australia and was demobilized as a flight lieutenant, Royal Air Force, on 1 September. He decided to study mathematics and science and took up the scholarship at Trinity College, University of Melbourne, which he had won in 1915; however, he soon withdrew, feeling that his first allegiance was to the family business. He joined his father and his partner, James Gatehouse, in the flour company of James Minifie & Co. Pty Ltd.

On 19 October 1921 Minifie married Nellie Frances, daughter of W. J. Roberts [q.v.] at Holy Trinity Church, Kew. Next year James Minifie died and his sons Richard and James, together with Gatehouse, successfully expanded the business over three decades. During World War II Minifie was a squadron leader with the Prahran Wing of the Air Training Corps. He was appointed president of the Victorian Flour Millers' Association in 1948 and from 1949 was managing director of James Minifie & Co. Pty Ltd and associated companies. That year he became president of the Federal Council of Flour Millowners of Australia, a position he retained until his retirement in 1966. He was also the flour millowners' representative on the Australian Wheat Board in 1949-66.

Survived by his wife, son, and three daughters, he died on 31 March 1969 at Malvern and was cremated. Dick Minifie was a tall, slim, good-looking man with an engaging smile, and a courteous and patient manner. He was also modest and very few people, including his family, knew of his important wartime exploits. He enjoyed home life, had a wide circle of friends, and was highly regarded by his employees.

F. M. Cutlack, *The Australian Flying Corps* (Syd, 1934); B. Robertson (ed), *Air aces of the 1914-18 war* (Letchworth, Eng, 1959); C. Cole (ed), *Royal Air Force 1918* (Lond, 1968); E. Hadingham, *The fighting triplanes* (Lond, 1968); J. Rawlings, *Fighter squadrons of the R.A.F. and their aircraft* (Lond, 1969); K. Isaacs, *Military aircraft of Australia, 1909-1918* (Canb, 1971); information from R. L. Minifie, Milawa, Vic.   KEITH ISAACS

MINNS, BENJAMIN EDWIN (1863-1937), water-colourist and black-and-white artist, was born on 17 November 1863 near Dungog, New South Wales, son of Irish-born Bridget Murray, aged 17, who in 1869 married George Minns, farmer. He spent his early years at Inverell, where he had lessons in painting and drawing. At 17, intended for a career in law, Minns went to Sydney and entered the offices of (Sir J. P.) Abbott [q.v.3] & Allen. However, he met Charles Conder [q.v.3] with whom for a time he shared a studio. He studied at Sydney Technical College under Lucien Henry, joined A. J. Daplyn's [qq.v.4] life class of the Art Society of New South Wales, and had lessons from Julian Ashton [q.v.7], an accomplished *plein air* painter. He joined the society's Sketch Club with Ashton, Phil May [q.v.5] and Nerli [q.v.].

Conder, employed by the *Illustrated Sydney News*, got Minns his first job there. Minns also drew for the *Sydney Mail* and in 1887-1937 regularly contributed to the *Bulletin*, becoming particularly well known for his humorous drawings of Aborigines. On 9 June 1888 at St John's Church, Darlinghurst, he married Harriet Ford. The National Art Gallery of New South Wales purchased his 'Season of Mists' from the annual Art Society exhibition in 1891 and in 1894 acquired some of his first paintings of Aborigines, including portrait

heads that combine a somewhat sentimental charm with a genuine respect.

In 1895 Minns and his wife went to England. He sent back drawings to the *Bulletin* and contributed to *St Paul's Magazine*, *Punch*, the *Strand Magazine*, the *Bystander* and other journals. He steadily developed his water-colour painting, sketching in England and France, and exhibited successfully at the Royal Academy of Arts, the Royal Institute of Painters in Water Colours in London, and the Société Nationale des Beaux-Arts (New Salon) in Paris. He was also commissioned by Colonel Frank Rhodes to paint a series of water-colours of the family seat at Dalham, Suffolk.

Minns returned to Australia in 1915; unfortunately the paintings he had with him were destroyed by a shipboard fire. It was not until the early 1920s that exhibitions of Minns's water-colours in Sydney and Melbourne won him recognition as one of Australia's foremost water-colourists. His usual signature was B. E. Minns. He was a founder in 1924 and first president (until 1937) of the Australian Water-Colour Institute. He was also a member of the Society of Artists, Sydney, and with Lambert [q.v.9] and Longstaff [q.v.] was among the artists commissioned by the Art Gallery in 1928 to paint a self-portrait.

A tall, well-built man, Minns was popular with fellow artists and generous in appreciation of their work. He established his home and studio at Gordon, a bush setting on Sydney's north shore; he was an enthusiastic gardener and keenly interested in photography. A good horseman, he often included animals and birds in his landscapes. Survived by his wife and childless, Minns died suddenly at Taronga Zoological Park on 21 February 1937 and was cremated with Anglican rites. He was posthumously awarded the Sydney sesquicentenary prize for a historical oil painting in 1938.

His water-colours, somewhat neglected after his death, are noted for a lucid and sympathetic handling of wash and show some influence of the fine decorative sense of Conder and of the blue and gold vision of the early Streeton [q.v.]. Most highly regarded are his lyrical views of Sydney, its harbour, streets and beaches, and his paintings of the Aborigines and their way of life, based on memories of his early years in the Hunter valley.

J. Campbell, *Australian watercolour painters, 1780-1980* (Adel, 1983); *Lone Hand*, 2 Mar 1914; *B.P. Mag*, June-Aug 1930; *Art in Aust*, no 2, 1917, Dec 1932; *SMH*, 22 Feb 1937; *Bulletin* and *Worker* (Syd), 24 Feb 1937.   JEAN CAMPBELL

MINOGUE, MICHAEL ANDREW (1862-1923), public servant, and HENRY (1897-

1947), barrister, were father and son. Michael Andrew was born on 20 November 1862 near Kyneton, Victoria, son of James Minogue, farmer, and his wife Catherine, née McGrath, both Irish born. After education at the local Catholic school and the Kyneton Collegiate School, Minogue joined the Victorian Public Service aged 14. Except for three years as an accountant with the Department of Mines and Water Supply, he spent his whole career with the Department of Treasury, working his way through its ranks to the position of under-treasurer in August 1908. He remained head of the department until his retirement in 1922, serving the State with distinction.

A prominent Catholic layman and 'indisputably an Irishman', Minogue had an unconventionally 'breezy' and independent style, yet he exerted great influence. Roy Bridges [q.v.7] described him as a 'genius for finance' and referred to the 'Ministry's implicit reliance on his guidance'. He had advanced views on government spending, believing that in times of stress more money should be spent than in times of plenty. He drafted the Melbourne tramways bill, passed in 1918, which resulted in the state takeover of the metropolitan tramway system.

Minogue was a keen bushwalker who trekked through much of Victoria. His colleagues considered that the greatest monument to his work was his plan for financing the construction of roads in outback districts. In 1912 he was granted leave of absence from the Treasury for ill health. He travelled to Europe and while in London began negotiations for the conversion of a major Victorian loan due in the following year. When he retired early, suffering from angina, he was appointed to the newly formed State Tourism Committee but at its first meeting on 16 February 1923 he collapsed and died. He was survived by his wife Amelia, née Bouchier, whom he had married on 28 October 1891, five sons and two daughters. After a requiem Mass in the Church of the Immaculate Conception at Hawthorn, attended by politicians of all parties, he was buried in Burwood cemetery.

Henry, his second son, was born on 4 January 1897 at Hawthorn, Melbourne. He was educated at Xavier College where he was dux in 1914. On leaving school he volunteered for war service but was rejected on medical grounds. Assisted by an Ormond [q.v.5] College exhibition he studied at the University of Melbourne (LL.B., 1921), becoming in 1916 co-winner of the Mollison [q.v.2] scholarship for French.

During his student days Minogue was active in both literary and political affairs. He contributed to and was an assistant editor of *Melbourne University Magazine* and was for a time literary editor of the Catholic *Advocate*. He was involved in the wave of Catholic social militancy when, from 1911, movements aimed at promoting distinctively Catholic social thought and action emerged. Minogue became active in the Catholic Workers' Association, the Catholic Democrat Club and the Leo Guild. In 1917 a number of young men associated with the Leo Guild and the Democrat Club launched *Australia: a Review of the Month*, a Catholic journal of social and literary comment. As founding editor Minogue attacked capitalist individualism and promoted the corporate ideal—'the right of every man in industry to a share in the profits'. An ardent anti-conscriptionist and staunch supporter of Archbishop Mannix [q.v.], he resigned after being tried and fined for publication in May 1918 of an article 'Peace: the unwooed goddess', which was judged to be disloyal. The magazine ceased publication in 1920.

Admitted to the Bar in 1922, Minogue pursued a successful legal career. He married Thelma Constance Townsend Bucknill on 24 October 1939 at St Patrick's Cathedral. In World War II he was commissioned captain in the Army Service Corps, but did not see overseas service. He died of malignant hypertension at Yackandandah on 8 January 1947 and was buried in Burwood cemetery. His wife and two sons survived him.

Henry Minogue was a solidly built, dark-haired man with a booming voice and a jovial, kind and exuberant personality. He was a wit and raconteur, a linguist who spoke French, Italian and Spanish fluently and a member of the Vintage and Oakland Hunt clubs. After 1920 he took no further part in radical or political activities, nor was he prominent in any Catholic organization, although he remained a devout Catholic all his life. His professional integrity was praised by colleagues who remembered his common sense, fairness, sincerity and frankness.

R. H. Croll, *I recall* (Melb, 1939); R. Bridges, *That yesterday was home* (Syd, 1948); U. M. L. Bygott, *With pen and tongue* (Melb, 1980); Xavier College, *Xaverian*, 10, no 4, Dec 1947; C. E. Close, The organisation of the Catholic laity in Victoria 1911-1930 (M.A. thesis, Univ Melb, 1972); C. H. Jory, The Campion era: the development of Catholic social idealism in Australia 1929-1939 (M.A. thesis, ANU, 1974); *Punch* (Melb), 29 April 1915; *Argus*, 17 Feb 1923, 10 Jan 1947; *Advocate*, 22 Feb 1923; *Age*, 10 Jan 1947; Minogue biog file (LaTL).

JOHN ARNOLD
COLIN H. JORY

MITCHELL, SIR EDWARD FANCOURT (1855-1941), barrister, was born on 21 July 1855 at Richmond, Surrey, England, son of (Sir) William Henry Fancourt Mitchell [q.v.5] and his wife Christina, née Templeton. He was educated at Geelong and Melbourne Church of England Grammar schools, winning the matriculation exhibition in mathematics in 1874. In 1876 he entered Trinity Hall, Cambridge (B.A., LL.B., 1880; M.A., 1883).

Called to the Bar at the Inner Temple, London, in 1881, Mitchell returned to Australia and was admitted to the Victorian Bar in the same year. He began his career as junior to J. L. Purves [q.v.5] and soon built up a considerable practice, appearing almost exclusively before the Supreme Court. Contemporaries remembered him not only for his legal expertise but also for his height, gentlemanly bearing and courteous manner.

On 16 December 1886 he married ELIZA FRASER MORRISON (1864-1948), daughter of Alexander Morrison [q.v.5], headmaster of Scotch College, Melbourne, and his wife Christina, née Fraser. Born at Scotch College on 30 March 1864, Eliza had been educated at home and at Presbyterian Ladies' College, and had travelled extensively through Europe in 1882-83. They had four daughters, including Mary and Janet [qq.v.].

In 1893, as a result of the bank crisis in Victoria, Edward Mitchell was asked by the directors of Goldsbrough, Mort [qq.v.4,5] & Co. Ltd to represent the company in London. Successful in persuading the debenture holders not to force the company into liquidation by claiming their money, he was appointed chairman of directors on his return. On a similar mission two years later, he succeeded in negotiating major modifications on behalf of the shareholders. After serving as chairman in 1893-96 Mitchell was the company's adviser, only giving up the position in order to win back a leading place at the Bar. Following a further business trip to London in 1897, he devoted much of his time to working for a favourable vote in the 1898 Federation referendum.

After Federation Mitchell became one of the leading barristers in the fields of constitutional and equity law, appearing in most of the important constitutional cases to come before the High Court of Australia and the Privy Council. In 1902 he and his wife again travelled to London when he was briefed to appear in three cases before the Privy Council. Appointed K.C. in 1904, by 1913 he was generally acknowledged as pre-eminent at the Victorian Bar.

In 1910 Mitchell became chancellor of the diocese of Melbourne and as such, despite misgivings of Church members, advised Archbishop Clarke [q.v.8] to bring his successful libel action against *Truth* newspaper. A devout layman, Mitchell continued to work for the Church as chancellor until his death.

From his youth, when he placed a bet on Adam Lindsay Gordon's [q.v.4] steeplechase winner, Mitchell had wide sporting interests. He was a founding member of the (Royal) Melbourne Golf Club, but his main interests lay in tennis and cricket. Having represented Victoria against New South Wales in 1886 and 1887, he became vice-president of the Lawn Tennis Association of Victoria in 1893 and later induced the association to obtain its Kooyong property. He became its patron in 1906 and a life member in 1908. A member of the Melbourne Cricket Club from 1873, he was president in 1933-41, a trustee of the ground and in 1907-08 Victorian representative on the Australian Board of Control for international cricket matches.

As chairman of the Edward Wilson [q.v.6] Trust, Mitchell was responsible for the distribution of funds to charitable organizations. In 1918 he attempted to enter the House of Representatives, standing unsuccessfully for National Party preselection for the seat of Flinders against S. M. (Viscount) Bruce [q.v.7] who attributed Mitchell's failure to his dreariness as a public speaker. Anecdotes also bear witness to his ponderousness and lack of 'verbal felicity'.

At the start of World War I Eliza Mitchell was appointed a foundation member of the Red Cross council and became chairman of the Victorian Red Cross home hospitals committee in 1914-15. Late in 1915 the family travelled to England for Mitchell to appear again before the Privy Council. As chairman of the committee for hospital visiting, Eliza continued to work for the Red Cross until she was appointed assistant commissioner of the Australian Red Cross Society in England in January 1918. That year she was appointed C.B.E. and Edward K.C.M.G., a rare honour for members of the legal profession other than judges.

On her return to Australia in 1919 Lady Mitchell became widely involved in voluntary work. She was re-elected to the councils of the Australian Red Cross and of its Victorian division, remaining a member for many years. In 1920 she led an appeal for £20 000 for the Queen Victoria Hospital for Women, and the new wing of the hospital built with the funds raised was named after her. A founding member of the Victoria League in 1908, she became president of its immigration committee. She chaired the women's standing committee of the New Settlers' League, as well as devoting much of her time to promotion of the Bush Nursing Association (president, 1927). She enlisted the support of her husband to arrange funding by the Wilson Trust and the Victorian government for the training of nurses. In addition she helped to found the Victorian Country Women's Association and was its president in 1928-30. Much of her work for these organizations is described in her autobiography, *Three-quarters of a century* (London, 1940).

Meanwhile Sir Edward Mitchell continued his distinguished career, opposing Premier Lang's [q.v.9] financial policies in New South Wales through articles published in the *Argus* in 1930-31 and his book, *What every Australian ought to know* (1931), a work dealing with the legality of financial agreements between the Commonwealth and States. He was also prominent in the conversion of the internal public debts of Australia by ensuring the immunity of new bonds from Federal tax increases.

Mitchell died in Melbourne on 7 May 1941 and his wife at Brighton on 1 October 1948. Both were buried in the family grave in St Kilda cemetery. Their four daughters survived them.

J. Mitchell, *Spoils of opportunity* (Lond, 1938); C. Edwards, *Bruce of Melbourne* (Lond, 1965); N. Adams, *Family fresco* (Melb, 1966); A. Dean, *A multitude of counsellors* (Melb, 1968); *Argus*, 4 June 1918, 31 Oct, 8 Nov 1930, 28 Mar 1931, 8 May 1941; *Age*, 8 May 1941; information from R. J. McArthur, East Malvern, Melb.

ELISE B. HISTED

MITCHELL, ERNEST MEYER (1875-1943), barrister and politician, was born on 12 February 1875 at Wynyard Square, Sydney, eldest child of Philip Mitchell, jeweller from Germany, and his Sydney-born wife Rosalie, née Brodziak. He was educated at Sydney Grammar School where he was school captain and winner of the Knox [q.v.5] prize twice. At the University of Sydney he won several prizes, gained his rowing blue and was treasurer of *Hermes* before graduating B.A. with first-class honours in classics in 1896 and LL.B. in 1900 with the University medal. He was admitted to the Bar on 26 October and elected president of the Sydney University Law Society in 1905.

In 1907 Mitchell was appointed Challis [q.v.3] lecturer in common law subjects at the university. An unorthodox lecturer, he walked around the room as he spoke. Meanwhile he practised at the Bar in a wide variety of cases.

On 14 April 1915 Mitchell married Mabel Daisy Black, a masseuse, at the Unitarian Church, Liverpool Street. In November next year he enlisted in the Australian Imperial Force and served in France with the 4th Battalion from October 1917. Commissioned in June 1918 he was transferred to the 1st Machine Gun Battalion. After the Armistice he was attached to the A.I.F. education scheme under Bishop Long [q.v.]. Returning to Sydney in July 1919 he retained a military connexion with the Australian Army Legal Division until transferred to the reserve of officers in 1926, having been promoted lieut-colonel in 1924. He briefly continued university lecturing and was a member of the senate in 1925-34 and of the joint committee for tutorial classes.

Resuming practice at the Bar, Mitchell took silk in 1925 and appeared in important constitutional cases in the High Court of Australia; his special contribution was to the interpretation of section 92 of the Australian Constitution, guaranteeing the freedom of trade and commerce. In 1930-31, with (Sir) David Maughan [q.v.], he appeared gratis for (Sir) Arthur Trethowan [q.v.] and others opposing the abolition of the New South Wales Legislative Council. He also appeared for the Commonwealth in the three garnishee cases in 1932 when Premier J. T. Lang [q.v.9] challenged the validity of the Financial Agreements Enforcement Act. He also acted for the aviator Goya Henry [q.v.9] in his two appeals to the High Court in the 1930s. He was frequently consulted by State and Commonwealth governments, trade unions and employer associations.

In December 1933 Mitchell was elected to the reconstituted Legislative Council for three years and in 1936 for twelve years. He was an influential adviser of both sides of the House on legal issues, carefully considering every bill as a critic of particular provisions rather than as an initiator of legislation. Although conservative himself and a member of the United Australia Party, he often proclaimed that he was not opposed to Labor.

Mitchell's parliamentary activity declined during World War II. A diabetic, he died suddenly of atherosclerotic heart disease on 21 April 1943 at his Phillip Street chambers and was buried in the Anglican section of Northern Suburbs cemetery. His wife survived him; the marriage was without issue. Essentially a private and humble man, Mitchell declined offers of judicial positions. He was a learned and incisive advocate, well known for his lack of pretension, courtesy and willingness to help others.

G. E. Hall and A. Cousins (ed), *Book of remembrance of the University of Sydney in the war 1914-1918* (Syd, 1939); T. R. Bavin (ed), *The jubilee book of the law school of the University of Sydney* (Syd, 1940); *PD* (NSW), 1943, p 2611; *Cwlth Law Reports*, 44, p 394, 46, p 155; *SMH*, 22 Apr 1943; Incorporated Law Inst (NSW), *Report* 1933 (ML).

ANTHONY FISHER

MITCHELL, ISABEL MARY (1893-1973), author, and JANET CHARLOTTE (1896-1957), journalist and author, were born in Melbourne on 25 August 1893 and

3 November 1896, third and fourth daughters of (Sir) Edward Mitchell [q.v.] and his wife Eliza Fraser, daughter of Dr Alexander Morrison [q.v.5], principal of Scotch College, Melbourne.

The four Mitchell daughters grew up at Scotch College and in family homes in East Melbourne and at Mount Martha and Mount Macedon, where they were educated by governesses. The academic and literary tastes of Dr Morrison influenced his granddaughters, as did their parents' interest in welfare organizations such as the Red Cross. Extended European tours 'finished' their education, some visits being made in conjunction with Edward Mitchell's appearances before the Privy Council in London.

Mary Mitchell visited England in 1906, 1911 and 1916, returning in 1921 for secretarial training at the Women's Institute, London. She then worked for the Australian Red Cross Society as assistant secretary and until 1932 was secretary of the Victorian Junior Red Cross. Writing was a hobby until, after two unsuccessful attempts, her novel, *A warning to wantons* (London, 1934) was published. Described as 'a combination of ultra-sophisticated worldliness and romantic melodrama in a Ruritanian setting', it was a popular success, occasioning surprise that a gently bred woman from the colonies should produce a work so daring and cosmopolitan. The Gothic fantasy of the plot and the charm of the gamine heroine's innocence and amorality, in contrast to the ironic astringency of the social observation, appealed widely; it became a Book Society's book of the month and was translated into Swedish, Hungarian, French and German. In 1949 it was filmed. Mary Mitchell travelled extensively in Europe in 1935, visiting the settings of many of her later novels.

Pendulum swing, a novel set in Melbourne depicting the relationship between two girl cousins from differing social backgrounds, appeared in 1935, then *Maidens beware* (London, 1936), and thereafter more than twenty novels until 1956. In the 1930s Mary Mitchell also published three detective stories under the name of Josephine Plain. No other work achieved the popularity of *A warning to wantons* although Miss Mitchell herself preferred *One more flame* (London, 1942), a study of an Australian farming family and its relationship with the land.

In 1947 Mary Mitchell became aware that she was going blind and adapted her methods of writing to her failing vision. Determined to prove that a blind person need not become dependent, she mastered the technique of touch-typing and use of a dictaphone and produced eight novels after losing her sight. Living independently at Kalorama in the Dandenongs, she published in 1963 *Uncharted country*, an attempt to present in lay language the everyday problems of the blind. A tall, fair, reserved, dignified and elegant figure, Mary Mitchell became the first woman president of the P.E.N. Club and vice-president of the Braille Library of Victoria; in 1970 she was appointed M.B.E. She died at Box Hill on 24 July 1973, and was cremated.

Janet Mitchell became a licentiate of the Royal Academy of Music in 1917 and graduated B.A., University of London, in 1922. She was education secretary of the Young Women's Christian Association, Melbourne, in 1924-26 and directed the thrift service of the Government Savings Bank of New South Wales in 1926-31. Active in the League of Nations Union, in 1925 and 1931 she was an Australian delegate to conferences of the Institute of Pacific Relations in Honolulu and Hangchow, China. She went on to Harbin at some risk to report the Japanese occupation of Manchuria, an experience which formed the basis of her only novel, *Tempest in paradise* (London, 1935), which was dedicated to her cousin 'Chinese' Morrison [q.v.]. An autobiography, *Spoils of opportunity*, followed in 1938.

In 1933 Janet Mitchell was acting-principal of the Women's College, University of Sydney, and in 1936, after journalism in London and semi-official work with the League of Nations in Geneva, she became warden of Ashburne College in the University of Manchester, resigning in 1940 for health reasons. She was assistant in youth education, Victoria, for the Australian Broadcasting Commission in 1941-55. Delicate from childhood, she lived at Armadale, Melbourne, until her death on 6 September 1957. A convert to Catholicism, she was buried in St Kilda cemetery.

AGNES ELIZA FRASER (NANCY) (1890-1968), Mary and Janet's elder sister, was born on 15 July 1890. She worked at American Naval Headquarters, London, during World War I and married George Hill Adams, wine merchant, at St Paul's Cathedral, Melbourne, in 1921. During World War II she managed G. H. Adams & Co. Pty Ltd and later wrote a novel, *Saxon sheep* (1961), based on the experiences of her forbears who imported Saxon merino sheep into Van Diemen's Land. In 1966 Nancy Adams published *Family fresco*, memoirs of the Mitchell and Morrison families. She died in Melbourne on 22 August 1968.

Lady Mitchell, *Three-quarters of a century* (Lond, 1940); M. Harding (ed), *This city of peace, being the conversion stories of 25 Australian converts to the Catholic Church* (Melb, 1956); J. Hetherington, *42 faces* (Melb, 1962); *Bohemia*, 13, no 2, Oct 1957; *Argus*, 6 Oct, 13 Dec 1933, 9 Jan 1934, 16 Apr, 10 Dec 1935; *Herald* (Melb), 16 May 1935, 19 Oct 1963; *Age*, 20 Nov 1962, 26, 27 July

1973; *Sun-News Pictorial*, 1 Jan 1970; Age biog file
for Mary Mitchell (LaTL).   E. M. FINLAY

MITCHELL, SIR JAMES (1866-1951),
premier and governor, was born on 27 April
1866 at Paradise Farm, Dardanup, near Bunbury, Western Australia, eldest of thirteen
children of William Bedford Mitchell, estate
manager and grazier, and his wife Caroline,
née Morgan. Educated at Bunbury, he joined
the Western Australian Bank in 1885 and was
posted to Geraldton. On 17 September 1888
at Bunbury he married Clara Robinson
Spencer; they had three sons and a
daughter.

From 1890 Mitchell managed the bank's
branch at Northam, soon the railhead for the
Yilgarn and eastern goldfields. The Avon Valley district, centred on Northam, throve as
the ideal source of produce for the developing
goldfields, and Mitchell throve too. He was
ready to back enterprising farmers, sometimes too hopefully. From 1892 he himself
engaged in farming, soon making a sound
local reputation. A keen horseman, he was
thought to have the best collection of hacks in
Western Australia. He was twice captain of
the local volunteer movement, and was made
justice of the peace in 1897.

Mitchell's farming experience was
gathered in the well-watered, long-established Avon valley at a time of unpreced-
entedly buoyant markets. This led him habitually to underestimate the hazards of pioneer farming, and confirmed his enthusiasm
for agricultural expansion. He shared Sir John
Forrest's [q.v.8] faith in the potential of the
150 miles (240 km) east of Northam, though
it was only with the development of William
Farrer's [q.v.8] Federation wheat that agriculture became feasible in this drier area; this
development coincided felicitously with Mitchell's entry into State politics. In October
1905 he won the Northam seat in the Legislative Assembly. Handsome in the heavy-
moustached style of his day, though already
somewhat portly, Mitchell was a presentable
and popular figure, soon marked out for
advancement. No great public speaker, he
earnestly advocated agricultural settlement
and deplored Western Australia's dependence on imported produce, seeking to place
families on the land, particularly as the goldfields declined and miners looked elsewhere.

In May 1906 Premier (Sir) Newton Moore
[q.v.] appointed Mitchell honorary minister
with oversight of agricultural expansion. In
June 1909 he was promoted to minister for
lands and agriculture, next year adding industries to his portfolio. He was responsible for
recruiting William Lowrie [q.v.] as director of
agriculture. The Agricultural Bank Acts had

been consolidated in 1906, increasing the
bank's scope for advancing loans, and providing inspectors as rural advisers at most major
country centres. In 1906-11 the frontier of
agricultural settlement was pushed to the
Yilgarn. Stimulated by the introduction of
superphosphate, the acreage under wheat
trebled.

Following the ministry's landslide defeat by
Labor in October 1911, opinion swung
against Mitchell. The winters of 1911, 1912
and 1914 saw unusually low rainfall, so that
many farmers in the new wheat-belt had difficulties. Mitchell was blamed for his bland
optimism in allegedly throwing new settlers
into the bush with just an axe, claiming that
new railways and 'a little muscular activity'
only were required for success. He was a
prime target for the Farmers and Settlers'
Association, founded in 1912. When, two
years later, the association returned the first
eight Country Party members to parliament,
Mitchell became a hindrance to an anti-Labor
alliance. He was dropped as deputy leader of
the Liberals in 1915 in favour of (Sir) Henry
Lefroy [q.v.]. Next July, when the Labor ministry was ousted, the Country Party insisted
that Mitchell should not be minister for lands
or agriculture.

Premier Frank Wilson [q.v.] made him minister for railways and industries and he
became responsible for the Industries Assistance Board set up by the previous government to pump government subsidies into primary industry. He intervened actively in rural
policy, creating a royal commission to inquire
into the wheat-growers' plight. He also
revived negotiations with the Federal and
British governments to settle returned servicemen on the land, envisaging that up to
25 000 British migrants might be attracted
annually. Mitchell now saw the South-West as
the focus for development, with dairy-farm-
ing as its potential staple industry. Thus he
became 'Moo-cow Mitchell'. In November
1916 he dominated the cabinet sub-committee which put forward a plan for intensive
cultivation on holdings of 100-160 acres (40-
65 ha), part of which would be cleared and
fenced by migrants guided by experienced
supervisors. This was the genesis of the
group settlement scheme which was to dominate Mitchell's career.

A setback followed. After the Labor Party's
split over conscription in 1917 Wilson and
Mitchell were ousted from office in June to
make way for a broadened coalition under
Lefroy. By following Wilson into the wilderness Mitchell consolidated his reputation for
integrity and avoided association with the
drift and indecision of Lefroy's ill-assorted
ministry. The *West Australian* backed Mitchell, even when he sometimes voted with the
Labor Opposition. In September 1918 he

even launched what was taken as a motion of no confidence in the Lefroy government, attacking its failure to promote soldier settlement and the improvement of virgin land in the South-West. He was successfully opposed by Lefroy's attorney-general, R. T. Robinson [q.v.], who advocated forest conservation.

But next April a party revolt overthrew Lefroy. Mitchell's old Northam ally (Sir) Hal Colebatch [q.v.8] became premier, restoring Mitchell to the Lands Department. On 17 May Colebatch, unable to find an acceptable seat, resigned the premiership in Mitchell's favour: 'Mitchell may last a month', forecast a commentator. 'If he lasts longer he will be a miracle worker'. But the miracle was worked. The Country Party consented to serve under him. His only significant rival, Robinson, resigned from cabinet in June and soon left politics. Mitchell won the election in March 1921 and remained premier until April 1924.

His early years saw several achievements. Women were admitted to parliament in 1920. Motor traffic control was placed under a centralized authority. A ministry for the North-West was created; the Wyndham meatworks had opened in 1919, and a resident commissioner for the North-West was appointed in 1921 to encourage cotton-growing and other tropical agriculture. But none of these initiatives prospered.

Overshadowing all else came the group settlement scheme. In 1921 pilot projects placed unemployed men on the land, and Mitchell concluded an agreement with the British government providing for 15 000 migrants. The scheme gained considerable publicity in Britain after Mitchell's one and only visit in 1922. But the migrants and their Australian foremen were often poorly chosen and lacked the skills and resources to clear hardwood timber and succeed as dairy farmers. When Mitchell left office in 1924, 42 per cent of the British settlers had already walked off the groups; but the scheme continued under his successors so that, at much human cost, a dairying industry was established in the South-West.

Mitchell was a poor political manager. Impatient with party politics, he did little to court the financial and extra-parliamentary bodies supporting the coalition. Strong-tempered and imperious, he overruled his colleagues although usually leaving them much responsibility for the detail of policies. He and his senior ministers, Colebatch, Scaddan [q.v.] and W. J. George [q.v.8], antagonized conservative businessmen by their pragmatic willingness to maintain state-owned industries and state intervention in price-fixing and other industrial activities. The Legislative Council was ill disciplined and rejected several measures, including the reform of government hospitals. Mitchell also avoided redistributing parliamentary seats, thus giving Labor an advantage through its command of the decaying goldfields constituencies. Several government back-benchers transferred to the Country Party so that by the end of 1920 its numbers exceeded Mitchell's followers; but its leaders continued to back him and in 1923 a split occurred between the official Country Party, keen to leave the coalition, and a ministerialist Country Party which remained. A policy of multiple endorsements also weakened the Mitchell ministry's hold on some assembly seats. Not surprisingly, Mitchell lost the 1924 elections to the Labor Party, led by Phillip Collier [q.v.8].

This did not produce any marked shifts in policy. According to one journalist, Mitchell and Collier 'went in and out of office like cricket teams going to bat and bowl, and their controversies were always conducted on a high level'. The anti-Labor factions composed their differences, forming a United Party under Mitchell from 1926 to 1928; but it was as a Nationalist-Country Party coalition that they regained office in April 1930.

As premier and treasurer, Mitchell confronted the Depression with promises of 'work for all', an impossible goal. Unemployment was nearly 30 per cent by 1932; wheat prices fell disastrously; the government concentrated on coping with the havoc. In 1931 the State Savings Bank of Western Australia was transferred to the Commonwealth Bank, and the Farmers' Debts Adjustment Act was passed, allowing farmers to stay on their properties while working off their liabilities. Experiments were made in the bulk handling of wheat, but failed to satisfy the militant Wheatgrowers' Union who, in the harvest of 1932, attempted a 'strike', withholding the delivery of crops. Mitchell was dismayed at demonstrations in Perth by the unemployed; Western Australia had the least niggardly unemployment relief rates in Australia. His only remedy was to provide sustenance work on irrigation schemes and other public works. To arrest falling revenue, the government introduced an entertainments tax and, in 1932, established a lotteries commission to support charities.

In 1930-33 the Dominion League channelled many Depression tensions into a populist movement for secession from Australia. Uneasily sympathetic, Mitchell authorized a referendum to coincide with the State election of 8 April 1933. Secession gained a 'Yes' vote of 68 per cent, but Mitchell was swept from office, and like every Nationalist member of cabinet, lost his seat. He remained bitter towards the Commonwealth.

In July Collier, again Labor premier, offered the lieutenant-governorship to his friend and rival. In the absence of a British-appointed governor, Mitchell performed with conspicuous success. Fortunately he encountered no constitutional crises, and the role gave him scope for his unaffected geniality and sociable avuncular temperament. Daily he strolled along St George's Terrace with the slightly old-fashioned formality of a successful country banker—striped trousers, bowler hat, pince-nez and a silver-mounted stick—greeting acquaintances and tipping children with threepences for ice-cream. He enjoyed urging young men to go on the land and women to become farmers' wives and mothers. He was perhaps happiest in the country districts, though the punctilious deplored his reputed habit of keeping fish-hooks and bait in the pockets of his formal clothes. Courteous, florid, ample in paunch and jowl, he said: 'I have lived in the world's best climate and done justice to the world's best food'. During World War II he was a stalwart figurehead. In 1948 he was formally appointed governor.

Mitchell's last years in Government House were saddened by the deaths of his wife (1949) and all but one of their children; in June 1951 he was persuaded to retire. After spending the day shooting with his son, early on 26 July Sir James died in his sleep in the vice-regal railway carriage, at Glen Mervyn in the South-West. After a state funeral he was buried in the Anglican section of Karrakatta cemetery. His affable and unpretentious occupancy of Government House almost erased criticisms of his political performance. With his drive and optimism he had sustained the burgeoning wheat-growing and dairying industries, but insufficient realism in detailed planning, and tunnel vision about the virtues of agriculture, led him to support unbalanced economic growth which bred hardship for many. Nevertheless this benign autocrat remains among the best loved of the State's father figures.

Mitchell had been nominated C.M.G. in 1911 but the award was only granted in 1917. He was promoted K.C.M.G. in 1921 and G.C.M.G. in 1947. The northern section of Perth's metropolitan freeway is named after him. His estate was valued at £12 167.

G. L. Sutton, *Comes the harvest* (Perth, 1952); F. K. Crowley, *Australia's western third* (Lond, 1960); J. P. Gabbedy, *Yours is the earth* (Perth, 1972); G. C. Bolton, *A fine country to starve in* (Perth, 1972); *The Times*, 27 June 1915; B. K. Hyams, The political organisation of farmers in Western Australia from 1914 to 1944 (M.A. thesis, Univ WA, 1964); D. W. Black, The National Party in Western Australia, 1917-1930: its origins and development with an introductory survey of 'Liberal' Party organisation, 1910-1916 (M.A. thesis, Univ WA, 1974).   G. C. BOLTON

MITCHELL, JOHN (1848-1928), schoolteacher and palaeontologist, was born on 9 March 1848 at Ballieston, near Glasgow, Scotland, son of James Mitchell, contractor and mine-manager, and his wife Margaret, née McNab. He arrived in New South Wales with his parents in 1849 and lived and was educated at Newcastle. On 21 March 1870, with Baptist forms, he married Sarah Ashton at Wallsend.

In 1873 Mitchell joined the Department of Public Instruction and trained as a teacher at the Fort Street Training School. After teaching briefly in the Newcastle district he was transferred to Balranald where, in his spare time, he collected beetles and butterflies. In 1883 he was moved to Bowning near Yass where he amassed a fine collection of fossils and began to study palaeontology seriously. Next year he joined the Linnean Society of New South Wales and in 1886 published the first of a number of papers in its *Proceedings*.

Moved to Narellan in 1888, Mitchell collected fossil insects and plants from the Wianamatta Series and in 1890 discovered the first Australian specimens of *Leaia*, described by Robert Etheridge [q.v.8] under the name of *Leaia mitchelli*. In January 1898 he was appointed science master at Newcastle Technical College with a salary of £275. Next year he gave evidence to the Victorian government's royal commission on technical education. As well as his administrative duties he lectured on a wide range of subjects including geology, botany, chemistry and assaying, and continued his palaeontological research and publications. In 1909 he recorded the discovery of *Estheriae* (first collected by him near Glenlee in 1890) in the Newcastle coalmeasures.

Mitchell's published work was largely confined to the groups Trilobita and Brachiopoda on which he was highly regarded as an authority. Between 1890 and 1917 he collaborated with Etheridge and produced six important papers on the Silurian trilobites of New South Wales; in 1918 he published a summary paper on Australian Carboniferous Trilobita. In 1920 he collaborated with W. S. Dun [q.v.8] on the Palaeozoic *Atrypidae* of New South Wales.

Mitchell visited technical colleges in Europe in 1910 and accompanied Sir George Reid [q.v.] to an educational conference in Belgium. A short, portly man with a full white beard, he retired in 1913, but remained very active in the field and discovered the first fossil insects in the Newcastle coal-measures. These insects, including the notable *Belmontia mitchelli*, were described by R. J. Tillyard [q.v.]. Mitchell's last paper, on Australian *Estheriae*, was read to the Linnean Society in 1927.

He died on 14 January 1928 in the War Memorial Hospital, Waverley, Sydney, survived by his wife, three sons and three daughters, and was buried in the Anglican section of Sandgate cemetery, Newcastle.

C. F. Laseron, *Ancient Australia* (Syd, 1954); Linnean Soc NSW, *Procs*, 42 (1917), p 480, 721, 44 (1919), p 231, 50 (1925), p 438, 52 (1927), p 106, 53 (1928); *Newcastle Morning Herald*, 17 Jan 1928; Teachers' records (Dept of Education, Archives, Syd).   G. P. WALSH

MITCHELL, ROBERT (1851-1929), clergyman, was born on 12 January 1851 at Meigle, Perth, Scotland, son of Robert Mitchell and his wife Agnes, née Stewart, and younger brother of Thomas Mitchell [q.v.]. His parents arrived in Adelaide with four children in 1855. Robert was educated at Salt Creek School and John Whinham's [q.v.6] North Adelaide Grammar School. He began studying for the ministry under Rev. James Roddich in 1868, while working on his father's rented farm near Mount Pleasant. He was sent to Clare in February 1872 and on 20 August became the first Presbyterian to be ordained in South Australia. On 22 August in the Flinders Street Presbyterian Church, Adelaide, Mitchell married Mary Fraser.

His pastoral work at Clare included setting up outlying preaching stations and conducting missions to shearers. In 1882 he established a congregation at Port Augusta. With money given by the Clare people he bought a printing press which he used for Church purposes. When the northern railway was built, he extended his ministry up the line, sending advance notices which he printed. Seeing the need to regularize this work, he and Rev. W. F. Main organized the Smith of Dunesk Mission, named after Mrs Henrietta Smith of Dunesk, Scotland, who had given the Free Church of Scotland an endowment for its South Australian work.

Mitchell became the mission's first agent in October 1894. From his base at Beltana he travelled by buggy and train through an area of about 2900 square miles (7500 km²) administering the usual religious services and medicines and first aid, even setting broken limbs and extracting teeth; he repaired his own house and occasionally helped others with theirs. During this period he was accompanied by one of his daughters, while his wife and other children lived at Gawler. Mitchell had been moderator of the Presbyterian Church of South Australia in 1889-90. In 1899 he moved to Goodwood in Adelaide where he was convener of the Smith of Dunesk Mission committee and formed a new church at Hawthorn. A tall, gaunt man with a ragged white moustache, he rode his bicycle on pastoral calls, even when they extended to Morphett Vale. The Mitchell Memorial Church at Goodwood was named after him. After retirement from Goodwood in 1922 he ministered for three years to the Morphett Vale congregation and, at 78, served another ten months as Smith of Dunesk missioner. He died at Goodwood on 28 February 1929, survived by his wife, son and three daughters and was buried in Payneham cemetery.

Although his term as Smith of Dunesk missioner had been his shortest pastorate, it was his most influential. He was not the first clergyman to travel north of Port Augusta, nor was he the only one in his time. But he conceived and carried out a full-time, permanent, itinerant ministry. From this mission, following Mitchell's example of combining ecclesiastical duties with medical and dental treatment, Rev. John Flynn [q.v.8] developed the Australian Inland Mission and the (Royal) Flying Doctor Service of Australia.

Goodwood Presbyterian Church. Souvenir of jubilee of Rev. Robert Mitchell (Adel, 1922); J. R. Fiddian, *Robert Mitchell of the inland* (Melb, 1931); *Farm, Stock, Station J*, 10 Feb 1905; Uniting Church in SA Hist Soc, *Newsletter*, no 7, Feb 1980; *Chronicle* (Adel), and *Observer* (Adel), 9 Mar 1929; Mitchell papers and other records, SRG 123 (SLSA).   J. H. LOVE

MITCHELL, SAMUEL JAMES (1852-1926), politician and judge, was born on 11 May 1852 near Mount Barker, South Australia, son of John Mitchell, tailor, and his wife Lydia, née Phillip. He was educated at R. C. Mitton's Grammar School, Adelaide, and other private schools before working at Mount Gambier and later at Melrose. In 1871 he moved to Port Augusta where he became a successful auctioneer. He was a district councillor and mayor for two years, as well as master of the Masonic lodge.

Mitchell returned to Adelaide and worked as a draper. On 15 September 1875 he married Eliza Ann Gardener at Trinity Church, North Terrace. In 1885 he was articled to H. E. Downer who entrusted him with management of his office. After graduating LL.B. from the University of Adelaide in 1890 he was admitted to the Bar that year and practised in association first with Paris Nesbit, Q.C. [q.v.], and, later, with Rupert Ingleby, Q.C.; he became one of Adelaide's most able and astute barristers. He was also a committee-member of the Glenelg Institute and the first president of the South Australian Electric Telegraph Association.

In 1900 Mitchell stood unsuccessfully for

parliament, but next year won the House of Assembly seat for the Northern Territory at a by-election. He was re-elected in 1902 and 1906 and worked hard for the territory, advocating the construction of a transcontinental railway connecting Adelaide and Port Darwin. From June 1909 he was attorney-general in A. H. Peake's [q.v.] ministry for six months before being replaced in a cabinet reshuffle.

With the transfer of the territory to control by the Federal government imminent, Mitchell resigned from parliament in January 1910 to become government resident and judge in the Northern Territory; he travelled in India and South-East Asia first. In Palmerston (Darwin) he tried to revive the economy by introducing a public works programme and by encouraging mineral prospecting and investment. In 1911 he helped to effect the transfer of control of the territory to the Commonwealth. Although he remained the territory's acting administrator and judge of the new Supreme Court, he resigned in 1912 after the Federal authorities refused to guarantee the independence of his judicial office by making his appointment tenable for life.

Returning to South Australia, Mitchell became a stipendiary magistrate at Port Pirie. In 1916 he was transferred to the Adelaide Police Court. With the death of Commissioner J. G. Russell [q.v.] early in 1918, he was promoted to commissioner of insolvency, a title altered to judge in 1926; he was also stipendiary magistrate of the Adelaide Local Court and the Taxation Appeal Court. He was the royal commissioner investigating the State Bank's thousand homes contract (1925), and police bribery (1926). During the sitting of the latter Mitchell became ill. He died of pneumonia on 3 October 1926 and was buried in North Road cemetery after a service at Holy Trinity Anglican church. His wife, son and two daughters survived him; Dame Roma Mitchell, Australia's first woman Q.C. and judge, is a granddaughter.

A small, dignified man, noted for his courtesy, Mitchell was a shrewd judge of character, energetic and fair. He was a staunch low church Anglican. He played the flute and was a Dickens [q.v.4] enthusiast. As commissioner, and in 1926 judge of the Insolvency Court, he delivered judgment on many complex cases that drew on his wide judicial and business experience; his decisions were seldom upset by appeal.

J. J. Pascoe (ed), *History of Adelaide and vicinity* (Adel, 1901); H. T. Burgess (ed), *Cyclopedia of South Australia*, 1 (Adel, 1907); *Public Service Review* (SA), Aug 1898, Feb 1918; *Quiz and the Lantern*, 29 Aug 1902; *Honorary Magistrate*, Mar 1918; *Advertiser* (Adel), and *Register* (Adel), 4 Oct 1926; Letter from Mitchell to Gill, Palmerston, 10 June 1910, SAA Gen Cat 1313/3 C4, *and* Government Resident's Office records *and* Insolvency Court records (SAA).   ROBERT THORNTON

MITCHELL, THOMAS (1844?-1908), farmer, was born in Forfarshire, Scotland, eldest son of Robert Mitchell, farmer, and his wife Agnes, née Stewart, who migrated to South Australia with their younger children, including Robert [q.v.], in 1855, leaving Thomas behind. In 1862 Thomas joined his family, farming at South Rhine near Adelaide and subsequently at Mount Crawford. Later he selected 400 acres (162 ha) at Canowie Plains, grew wheat, and did well. On 21 March 1873 he married Susan Maitland in the Presbyterian manse, Clare; they had two sons and two daughters. In 1879 Thomas moved to Eldena, a larger property near Jamestown, producing principally wheat.

Northern wheat-farmers felt that they were being exploited by collusive buyers underpaying for output and overcharging for wheat-sacks. Working on ideas derived from New Zealand, and encouraged by A. Molineux, secretary of the government's Agricultural Bureau, Mitchell proposed a producers' union to combat the effects of depressed agricultural prices and the power of dealers. He aired his ideas at a private meeting that he chaired at Jamestown on 28 February 1888, when a committee was formed. As earlier attempts at farmers' co-operation had failed, there was considerable scepticism. Nevertheless the scheme matured: in October the South Australian Farmers' (later Co-operative) Union Ltd was floated, with a paid-up capital of under £300, ninety-four shareholders, John Pearce [q.v.] as managing director and Mitchell a director. Following heavy losses in the first year, directors personally guaranteed the co-operative's overdraft, and appointed Pearce paid manager. Mitchell became managing director (until his death) and travelled the countryside in pursuit of new members and agencies, in order to expand capital and increase the volume of business.

After a few precarious years the union was 'able to give farmers more for their grain than they would get elsewhere, and that is as good as a dividend', as Mitchell reminisced. In 1893 the union declared its first profit and paid a dividend of 8 per cent on paid-up capital of £3000. It thereafter expanded beyond its mid-north base and penetrated the west coast, Yorke Peninsula and the South-East. In 1895 the head office was transferred to Adelaide; a merchandise store was established at Port Adelaide. Business was diversified to include dealing in wheat-sacks, machinery and superphosphate, whose use the union promoted.

Mitchell served a term on the Belalie District Council, was a justice of the peace, and was narrowly defeated in a bid for the Burra seat in the House of Assembly in 1899, possibly because of his temperance views. He supported moderate protection, the existing land tax, Federation and religious instruction in government schools. Deeply religious, he was an elder of the Presbyterian Church for over thirty years, taught Sunday school and was secretary to the board of management. Mitchell was also a kindly and conscientious benefactor to every worthy movement at Jamestown.

When he died on 2 August 1908, after a period of illness and an operation in a local hospital, Mitchell was recognized as 'the man who founded the Union, and fought for it ever since'. His twenty years leadership had been important in establishing a vigorous co-operative with a substantial and continuing role in South Australia's rural economy. A son Robert later became a director of the union.

W. F. Morrison, *The Aldine history of South Australia*, 2 (Adel, 1890); C. Hill, *Fifty years of progress* (Adel, 1938); *PP* (SA), 1908 (20); *Farm, Stock and Station J* (Adel), June 1904, Aug-Oct 1908, June-Aug 1909, Jan 1916; *J of Agr and Industry* (SA), Oct 1899; *Agriculturist and Review* (Jamestown), 4 July, 10 Oct 1888, 7 Aug 1908; *Advertiser* (Adel), 4 Aug 1908; *Chronicle* (Adel), 17 Mar 1938; G. M. Messner, The formation and early history of the S.A. Farmers Co-operative Union Ltd (B.A. Hons thesis, Adel, 1964).   ERIC RICHARDS
JOAN HANCOCK

MITCHELL, SIR WILLIAM (1861-1962), scholar, educationist and administrator, was born on 22 or 27 March 1861 at Inveravon, Banffshire, Scotland, son of Peter Mitchell, a hill-farmer who died when William was 5, and his wife Margaret, née Ledingham. He attended school at Elgin, where Ramsay MacDonald was a fellow pupil-teacher, for twelve years before entering the University of Edinburgh in 1880; following a very distinguished undergraduate record he graduated M.A. with first-class honours in philosophy (1886) and D.Sc. by thesis (1891) in the department of mental science.

Mitchell became a lecturer in moral philosophy (1887-90) and examiner in philosophy and English (1891-94) at the university. He lectured in education at University College, London, from 1891 to 1894 and was twice guest lecturer, and in 1894 examiner in education, for the University of Cambridge. He was also a lecturer and examiner in English for the Royal University of Breslau, Germany. In 1892 he declined an invitation to the chair of philosophy and economics at the University of New Brunswick, Canada.

Threatened tuberculosis led Mitchell to seek in 1894 the Hughes [q.v.4] professorship of English language and literature and mental and moral philosophy in the University of Adelaide, and on taking up duty in March 1895 he rapidly established himself as an intellectual and educational leader among his colleagues and the wider community. In his first public address in 1895 he emphasized the importance of analysis and criticism; the contribution to appreciation and mastery of English that study of foreign languages could make; and the development, through philosophy, of understanding and interest in one's daily work. Next year he was elected to the university council on which he sat for fifty-two years. By 1900 he had achieved a fundamental restructuring of the curriculum for the arts degree which remained operative for over twenty years; and, in collaboration with (Sir) William Bragg [q.v.7], had laid the foundation for significant development in the education of teachers, in accordance with principles that he had first expounded in 1895.

He had pleaded then for schools to provide 'general education in opposition to the widely-accepted view that education was simply a means for "getting on"'. He defined general education as 'the formation of an intellectual, an aesthetic, and a moral character, together with various kinds of skill'; and he saw the 'thorough professional education of teachers' as the governing factor in providing it. Professional education should embrace instruction in the principles, practice and history of education, practical demonstrations by accomplished teachers in a wide range of school classes, and seminar discussions on both.

The Mitchell-Bragg plan involved the university in forgoing fees for two years undergraduate study by all trainee teachers, even infant-teacher trainees, and the Department of Education in granting the university a part in the education and training of teachers; the trainees were housed within the university. Twenty years later the training programme for prospective secondary teachers had become a bachelor's degree in the subjects to be taught, followed by a year studying the theory of education and the craft of teaching. Mitchell also advocated the organization of schools on a regional basis. In the 1940s he proposed that the Adelaide Teachers College should become independent, with its own governing body, a transformation that took some thirty years.

Mitchell was vice-chancellor (unpaid) of the university from 1916 until 1942 when he became chancellor. For nearly half a century he had been so immersed in university life that he continued to discharge many of the functions of a vice-chancellor. He retired as chancellor in 1948 to remove any impediment that he might constitute, or be thought to constitute, to the ideas and policies to be expected of the new full-time vice-chancellor A. P. Rowe.

As vice-chancellor Mitchell had believed that the quality of the university lay in its human rather than its material resources. In the appointment of professors he supported young men of proven intellectual capacity whose greatest achievements lay ahead of them: historian (Sir) Keith Hancock, econo-mist (Sir) Leslie Melville, and English scholar Innes Stewart.

In a submission to a 1917 government com-mittee of inquiry he defined the two functions of a university as, at undergraduate level, the giving of knowledge (and thereby power); and at postgraduate level, the creating of know-ledge (and power) and the acquisition of expertise. He argued, without immediate suc-cess, for the development of the postgraduate function, believing that postgraduate students would contribute to the creation of knowledge and, by teaching, exert a beneficial influence on undergraduates. Another future development that he foresaw was the impor-tance of interrelations between academic dis-ciplines. In seeking a substantially increased government grant he desired growth and expansion, not explosion. The government responded by increasing the limit of subsidy on endowments to a figure well beyond what the university could qualify for at once; and later (1927) by providing, under the Agricul-tural Education Act, support for the Waite [q.v.6] Agricultural Research Institute, to increase steadily from £5000 to £15 000 a year over a decade. In the introductory address to the conference of Australasian uni-versities in 1937 Mitchell expanded his views on the functions of a university to include the giving of a view of the universe, the fostering of a sense of values through the pursuit of knowledge, and the promotion of the exercise of reason.

During his administration Mitchell saw the establishment of a dental school (1920), the Waite Institute (1924) and the school of econ-omics; there was great development in the engineering and medical schools, and a trebling of the university's physical re-sources. His administration has been criti-cized for apparent failure to nurture corres-ponding growth in the humanities and the social sciences. But nearly half the state grant came as subsidies on endowments; some ben-efactors expected the government subsidy to be applied to the same or a cognate purpose. Twentieth-century endowments had been predominantly for buildings, the medical school and science; the university council hesitated to use the government subsidy for other purposes. In establishing the chair of economics in 1928 it anticipated an endow-ment promised for the indefinite future

(received thirty years later), and kept vacant a chair in science.

An interesting instance of Mitchell's in-dependence from the current emotional atmosphere was his public address, 'The national spirit', in December 1918. In it he rejected the jingoistic doctrine of 'my country, right or wrong' and propounded the conception of true patriotism as identifying oneself with 'the country's task, welfare, hon-our, and shame'.

Throughout his term as professor (1895-1922) he taught psychology, logic, ethics and general philosophy. He taught also a little English language and literature (until 1900), education (until 1909) and economics (until 1917) and so, as he said, his chair was more like a sofa; but he considered himself pri-marily a philosopher. His listeners valued some of his occasional lectures sufficiently to publish them; and his forward thinking in the realm of education exerted a profound long-term influence in South Australia. But it was his scholarship and original thinking in psych-ology and philosophy that brought him over-seas acclaim.

Mitchell's first major contribution to inter-national thought was *Structure and growth of the mind* (London, 1907), regarded by Nor-man Kemp Smith of Princeton University as 'undoubtedly one of the most important philo-sophical publications of recent years'; for more than a quarter of a century it was a text-book over which university students, in Adel-aide at least, sweated. In 1924 and 1926 he gave two ten-lecture series of Gifford lec-tures in the University of Aberdeen. The first was published in 1933 as *The place of minds in the world*, but the second, 'The power of the mind', did not reach the printer. The main theme of *The place* was the nature of know-ledge and the impact on knowledge of recent advances in physics. J. W. Harvey regarded it as 'a book of the first importance', despite its being 'as difficult . . . as profound'; H. B. Acton complained of its 'great obscurity' and of the absence of treatment of the latest rel-evant philosophical thought—defects which he expected to be remedied in the second volume. Mitchell also published reviews in the *Philosophical Review, Mind* and *Philos-ophy*. In 1929 he gave the John Murtagh Macrossan [q.v.5] lectures in the University of Queensland, and in 1934 the Henrietta Herz lecture of the British Academy.

On 18 January 1898 he had married Mar-jorie Erlistoun (d. 1913), daughter of Robert Barr Smith [q.v.6]; they had a son and daughter. The son was (Sir) Mark, professor of biochemistry and physiology (1938-62) and deputy vice-chancellor (1951-65) at Adelaide, and chancellor of the Flinders University of South Australia (1966-71). In 1934 Mitchell provided a set of iron gates for the main entrance to the university grounds; in 1937 he paid for the hosting of a conference of Australian and New Zealand universities; that year he also gave £20 000 to endow the chair of biochemistry to which Mark had already been appointed. To the sum of £55 000 provided by his wife's family for the university's Barr Smith Library, Mitchell added £5000 in 1940. The university in 1961 named its original building, now devoted to administration but during his time used also for teaching, the Mitchell Building. It had previously commissioned a portrait by W. B. McInnes [q.v.] which hangs in its great hall.

Mitchell, who had been appointed K.C.M.G. in 1927, had the capacity to deal with people as man to man, irrespective of any disparity in age or status. 'There was absolutely no pretentiousness or pomposity about him'.

Physically incapacitated during the closing years of his life, Mitchell died, aged 101, on 24 June 1962 and was privately cremated; his ashes were placed near his wife's grave in Mitcham cemetery.

Mind, 43, no 170, Apr 1934, p 243; *Philosophy*, 9, no 33, Jan 1934, p 103; *A'sian J of Philosophy*, 40, no 3, Dec 1962; *Advertiser* (Adel), 19 Dec 1895, 12 Dec 1918; records (Univs Adel, Aberdeen, Edinburgh).   V. A. EDGELOE

MOFFAT, JOHN (1841-1918), mineowner and entrepreneur, was born on 26 May 1841 at Newmilns, Ayrshire, Scotland, son of James Moffat, starcher, and his wife Elizabeth, née Loudoun. Trained as a commercial clerk in Glasgow, he migrated to Queensland in 1862, became a shepherd on an outstation of Mount Abundance, and in 1864 began work in J. & G. Harris's [qq.v.4] Brisbane store. Ambitious for material success and independence, Moffat opened stores with Robert Love in Queen Street, Brisbane, South Brisbane (1866) and Stanthorpe (1872). He bought tin for the Brisbane smelters and gained some prominence on the Stanthorpe and New England tinfields, erecting the Tent Hill smelter. The result was a financial débâcle which culminated in the liquidation of Love & Moffat in 1876.

The discovery of the Great Northern tin-lode at Herberton in 1880 by Moffat's former employees John Newell [q.v.5] and William Jack transformed his career. With the backing of Sydney merchants Caird [q.v.3], Maxwell & Co. and the skilled negotiations of James Forsyth [q.v.8], Moffat's Glen Smelting Co. secured a monopoly over mining and reduction works. Within five years John Moffat & Co., the North Queensland branch, had developed tin-lodes and reduction works at Herberton, Watsonville and Irvinebank. The

Loudoun mill, with battery and smelter, began work at Irvinebank on 10 December 1884. Over the next twenty years it acquired forty head of stamps working three shifts a day within earshot of Moffat's modest timber house. During the boom on the British and southern capital markets Moffat sold the company's prime leases to repay the mortgages. The prospect of high returns after a relatively short wait and small initial outlays on prospecting drew him into the Montalbion silver and Glen Linedale (Oberlin Tin Co.) ventures from 1886. His substantial share in floating these companies on the British capital market enabled him to phase out the Glen Smelting Co. and in 1890 to form the Irvinebank Mining Co. That year on 1 March in Brisbane he married Margaret Linedale with New Jerusalem Church forms.

Moffat floated Montalbion and Muldiva silver-mining companies and Oberlin Tin Mining Co., eliminating his mortgages, but none paid dividends. The Vulcan tin-mine, opened in 1889 at Irvinebank, turned out a spectacular success. His initial control of almost 40 per cent of the capital of the Vulcan Tin Mining Co. rose to 75 per cent in 1906. The mine became the deepest in Australia and the mainstay of Irvinebank district tin-production for twenty years, and the company was the first on the North Queensland tin-fields to pay a dividend. By 1919, when it closed, it had paid £117 000.

The Irvinebank Mining Co. survived the 1890s depression. A steady output from the Vulcan, Great Southern and Tornado mines at Irvinebank was augmented by supplies from Tate River, California Creek and Koorboora. From 1888 Moffat was quietly developing the rich surface copper deposits in the Chillagoe district. The Chillagoe Pty Co., promoted in 1897 to construct a railway, stimulated the North Queensland copper boom. However, fierce opposition by Labor politicians against the company's (unlawful) leases of 'public lands' and its proposed hydro-electrically powered smelters above the Barron Falls forced Chillagoe Railway & Mines Ltd (formed June 1898) to construct expensive, coal-fuelled smelters inland. When estimates of ore reserves decreased, Moffat withdrew from the board of directors in mid-1901 and forced a reconstruction of the financially crippled company with more reasonable provisions for small investors.

Entrusting several ventures to new partners, he invested heavily on the outskirts of his empire at Arbouin and O.K., north-west of Chillagoe, in Mount Mulligan coal mines (1907), wolfram at Wolfram Camp, Koorboora on Mount Carbine, as well as oil shale at Baffle Creek and coal leases near Lowmead in central Queensland. His interests also extended to the patenting and marketing of the Moffat-Virtue shearing machine, part-ownership of the *Walsh and Tinaroo Miner* at Mareeba, establishment of a sawmill at Ravenshoe and maize-growing at Atherton. Other, unrewarding, involvements and misjudgements, insufficient ore reserves and conflict with unionists contributed to his empire's decline.

A deeply religious man, a member of the New (Swedenborgian) Church, Moffat was quietly spoken, hospitable and a keen supporter of the Good Templar movement. Believing that his religion obliged him to serve his neighbours, he perceived as crucial his development of their material resources. His honesty was rare among mining entrepreneurs. When the Montalbion project was deemed unprofitable, he refunded £20 000 of the purchase price to the British company. In 1910 he offered to sell his Bailey's Creek land at the original price if a sugar mill was erected. Surrounded by relatives and tradesmen from Tent Hill days, many from the west of Scotland, his manner with workmen blended equality with authority. He neglected, however, to train a successor to the empire and was forced by the Queensland National Bank to retire to his Cremorne home in Sydney in 1912.

Moffat died from influenza at Toowoomba on 28 June 1918 and was buried with Presbyterian forms in Toowoomba cemetery. He was survived by his wife and two daughters. His estate was valued for probate at only £29 431. In 1919 the Queensland government took over the Loudoun mill as a State treatment works.

G. C. Bolton, *A thousand miles away* (Brisb, 1963); R. Kerr, *John Moffat's empire* (Brisb, 1979); John Moffat's letter-books, 1882-92 (held by Cairns Hist Soc and Roy Hist Soc of Qld).

RUTH S. KERR

MOFFITT, ERNEST EDWARD (1871-1899), artist, was born on 15 September 1871 at Sandhurst (Bendigo), Victoria, son of John Thomas Lowry Moffitt, draper, and his wife Mary Emily, née Rogers. Little is known of his early life, but from 1890 he was active in Melbourne's art and music circles. That year he enrolled at the National Gallery of Victoria's art schools and left after a term of drawing from plaster casts.

In 1891 Moffitt became Professor G. W. L. Marshall-Hall's [q.v.] first student in the faculty of music, University of Melbourne. Although failing the theoretical course, he became a skilled practical musician playing bassoon, banjo and church organ. In 1893-95 he was employed by the music firm of Allan [q.v.3] & Co. and from 1896 until his death was secretary of the Melbourne Conservatorium of Music. Here he worked closely with his mentor Marshall-Hall, organizing, producing posters for and playing in his orchestral concerts.

Marshall-Hall encouraged Moffitt to renew his practice of the visual arts and he returned to the gallery schools in 1893; but as Lionel Lindsay [q.v.] noted, 'any suggestion of regulated study was ill suited to his original temperament'. Despite Moffitt's casual attendance he was an immediate stimulus, starting a sketching club and according to Lindsay 'in all things leading the thought and life of that curious heterodox society'. From this time he associated with the young Bohemian artists centred around Lindsay. He was a member of the Cannibal Club and was often to be found at Fasoli's Café which it is claimed he 'discovered'. From 1898 his weekends were spent at Charterisville near Heidelberg, painting, sketching and enjoying the pagan pleasures of Nature with Lindsay and other artist friends. Moffitt regularly exhibited water-colours and drawings with the Victorian Artists' Society from 1893 and in 1897 he designed the title-page of Marshall-Hall's *Hymn to Sydney*.

As an artist Moffitt is principally remembered for his pen-drawings, woodcuts and etchings. His early landscape drawings show the influence of James McNeill Whistler, but by 1895 his work became more decorative, inspired by the English illustrators of the 1860s. His last works show his response to the Aesthetic movement, probably through his study of such magazines as *Studio* and *Harper's Bazaar*.

Moffitt's house in Yarra Street, Alphington, was a meeting-place for artists. He was well known for the artistic furniture he made, and for his collection of old English pottery, beautifully bound books, Japanese furniture and carved pipes.

He died, unmarried, of acute enteritis at Alphington on 23 March 1899 and was buried in St Kilda cemetery. The pallbearers at his funeral—Marshall-Hall, John Longstaff and Frederick McCubbin [qq.v.] from the Victorian Artists' Society, Mr Dierich and Carl Pinschoff [q.v.] from the Austrian consulate, and Charles Tait [q.v.]—attest to his popularity in the Melbourne cultural community.

A book on Moffitt by Lionel Lindsay, financed by Marshall-Hall, was published in 1899; the first monograph devoted to an Australian artist, it commemorated 'a fine artist and what is saddest, the promise of a great one'.

L. A. Lindsay, *A consideration of the art of Ernest Moffitt* (Melb, 1899), and *Comedy of life* (Syd, 1967); *Alma Mater* (Univ Melb), 4, no 1 (1899), p 62; *Weekly Times* (Melb), 1 Apr 1899.

ROGER BUTLER

MOLESWORTH, HICKMAN (1842-1907), judge, was born on 23 February 1842 in Dublin, son of Sir Robert Molesworth [q.v.5] and his wife Henrietta, née Johnston. The family migrated to Victoria in 1852 and Hickman studied law at the University of Melbourne, being called to the Bar in April 1864. On 9 July 1868 he married Eliza Emily (d. 1881), daughter of William Rutledge [q.v.2], at Warrnambool; on 15 June 1882 he married Alice Henrietta Peck at Sale. Molesworth built up a reputation defending criminal cases, and his personal popularity with juries was such that some brought in verdicts 'for Mr Molesworth'. He was appointed to the County Court bench in December 1883, becoming permanent judge of the Insolvency Court soon after.

There he fought the abuse of the insolvency system by land speculators that aggravated the depression of the 1890s. Whenever he could legitimately do so Molesworth would refuse approval of secret compositions arranged with their creditors by insolvents applying for release from sequestration. In 1895, when he refused an application from J. M. Davies [q.v.4] for his brother's discharge, he pointed out that, as County Court judges were dependent on parliament for their salary, the application would better be made before independent judges of the Supreme Court. In the storm that followed Molesworth was reprimanded by the attorney-general but in his public reply revealed that the Crown Law Department was attempting to remove him and that a request from County Court judges in 1894 for a guarantee of freedom from political interference had received no reply. Supported by public and judiciary, Molesworth remained in his position and in 1896 was appointed special commissioner to investigate the collapse of the City of Melbourne Bank. He was chairman of the Metropolitan Licensing Court, of General Sessions and the Court of Mines, and, during 1891, an acting justice of the Supreme Court.

Known for his lively personality and optimistic and cheerful nature, he was of a mediating and tolerant disposition. Picturesque and unconventional, especially in his dress, he refused to robe for court. Even as a judge he enjoyed socializing with the Bar and showed 'palpable relief' upon being 'freed of the judicial harness' when court rose. A member of the Melbourne Club from 1872, Molesworth was a keen rider to hounds and enjoyed shooting. In 1893 he became a committee-member of the Charity Organisation Society.

In 1907 on medical advice Molesworth took leave and sailed for Queensland. He died of cirrhosis of the liver on board R.M.S. *Omrah* on 18 July 1907, and after a service at St Columb's Church, Hawthorn, was buried in Boroondara cemetery. His wife and their three children, and four of his first marriage, survived him.

P. A. Jacobs, *Judges of yesterday* (Melb, 1924); A. Henderson (ed), *Australian families* (Melb, 1941); M. Cannon, *The land boomers* (Melb, 1976); *Australasian*, 3 Sept 1898; *Punch* (Melb), 17 Mar 1904; *Age*, 19, 20 July 1907; *Argus*, 19, 24 July 1907.
                                              ELISE B. HISTED

MOLESWORTH, VOLTAIRE (1889-1934), journalist and politician, was born on 29 December 1889 at Balmain, Sydney, second surviving son of Hobart-born James Molesworth, wharflabourer, and his Sydney-born wife Elizabeth Ellen, née Vibert. Aged 3, he went with his parents to William Lane's [q.v.9] New Australia settlement in Paraguay for about a year. After primary education in Sydney, he became a warehouse clerk and in 1912 joined the staff of the *Cumberland Times*, moving to a metropolitan daily, the *Evening News*, in 1914. He specialized in industrial affairs.

In October 1913 Molesworth became a delegate to the Nepean Federal Labor Council, over which J. T. Lang [q.v.9] presided, and next September was defeated for the Federal seat of Nepean. Several times rejected for the Australian Imperial Force because of a heart defect, he became a leading opponent of conscription. Nonetheless, he opposed the anti-recruiting group in the Labor Party, regarding them as 'extreme internationalists'. He was finally accepted by the A.I.F. in 1918 but after three months his health failed and he returned to the *Evening News*.

Throughout the war Molesworth pursued two careers simultaneously, serving as secretary of the Nepean Labor Council (1914-18) and making a name for himself in journalism. As honorary auditor of the Australian Journalists' Association, he revealed that many members were not paying their subscriptions and was soon elected treasurer; after two years he was elected State president in 1919. That year he became chief of staff of the new newspaper *Smith's Weekly*.

Molesworth relished Labor politicking, playing a leading role in the Industrial Vigilance Council. A moderate, he opposed socialists like J. S. Garden [q.v.8] and the One Big Union movement. In August 1919, while president of the Randwick Labor Council, he was attacked for using his talents on a capitalist paper and as an enemy of the working class, but managed to retain his recently secured position on the central executive of the State branch of the Labor Party and was a delegate to the Commonwealth Political

Labor Conference that year. In March 1920 he was elected to the Legislative Assembly for Cumberland. Entering parliament at a time of leadership struggles within the party, Molesworth had leadership aspirations himself; in 1921 he was defeated for whip and in 1923 for secretary. Next year Lang tried to have Molesworth expelled for supporting a leadership challenge by T. D. Mutch [q.v.]. Molesworth explained his decision to retire from politics in *Smith's Weekly* on 6 December 1924: 'Labour in N.S.W. is torn with strife, intrigue and political corruption . . . One cannot be loyal to the Labour movement and be loyal to Mr Lang'.

Editor of the *Daily Guardian* since its foundation in July 1923, Molesworth delighted in exposing scandals, especially any involving Lang, but he lost his position in a management reshuffle in 1929. Next January he signed an agreement with R. C. Packer [q.v.], whose Associated Newspapers Ltd had taken over Smith's Newspapers Ltd, to continue as managing editor on a salary of £50 a week, but in 1931 the contract was broken and he received substantial recompense. In 1932 he became managing editor of Sporting Life Publications Ltd, a Packer organization, and next year acquired Packer's shares to become a major shareholder; the company owned *Turf Life* which Molesworth ran in 1933.

He had turned to the Nationalists, serving them and their successors, the United Australia Party, as a voluntary publicity director. He also served as president of Motion Picture Distributors Association of Australia. Nominated to the Legislative Council by the Stevens [q.v.] government in 1932, he did not stand for the reconstituted council in 1933.

Molesworth had married Ivy Vick at All Saints Church, Woollahra, on 6 November 1915; they had two daughters and a son, but Molesworth had little time for family life. In 1920 they had set up house at Burwood, in 1925 moved to Randwick and in 1932 to Vaucluse. He was an omnivorous reader, his books were his companions; he also collected coins and stamps. His career was cut short when he died as a consequence of mitral stenosis on 5 November 1934; he was cremated with Anglican rites. Lang later described him as a 'larrikin journalist', a master of political invective and innuendo.

E. Baume, *I lived these years* (Lond, 1941); J. T. Lang, *I remember* (Syd, 1956); G. Souter, *A peculiar people* (Syd, 1968); R. B. Walker, *Yesterday's news* (Syd, 1980); *PD* (NSW), 1922, p 2767, 1924, p 129; *A'sian Journalist*, 15 Sept 1919; *Newspaper News*, 1 Dec 1934; *Journalist*, 31 Dec 1934; *SMH*, 23 Mar 1920, 6 Nov 1934; *Daily Guardian* (Syd), 17 Oct 1924; *Smith's Weekly* (Syd), 6 Dec 1924; *United Aust Review*, 21 Sept 1932; V. Molesworth papers (ML and NL).   PETER SPEARRITT

MOLLISON, CRAWFORD HENRY (1863-1949), medical and forensic pathologist, was born on 1 August 1863 at Sandhurst (Bendigo), Victoria, son of Crawford Mollison, goldfields warden, and his wife Elizabeth, née Hobson. At 7 he was sent to school at Tunbridge Wells in England and later to Geelong and Melbourne Church of England Grammar schools. He then studied medicine at the University of Melbourne (M.B., 1884; B.S., 1885). Resident medical officer at the Melbourne Hospital for two years, he subsequently travelled overseas gaining membership of the Royal College of Surgeons in England in 1887. After studying ophthalmology and dermatology in Vienna for seven months, he returned to Melbourne to set up in general practice and become demonstrator in anatomy at the university.

Mollison married Emily Beatrice Smith at Hawthorn on 23 October 1889. After her death in childbirth in April 1891 Mollison, feeling that he could no longer practise medicine, turned to pathology and became honorary pathologist at the Children's Hospital (1891-1904). He was appointed assistant pathologist at the Melbourne Hospital in 1892 and senior assistant pathologist in 1911, holding that post until 1938 when he was appointed consulting pathologist. In 1893 he became coroner's surgeon and pathologist to the Women's Hospital, a position he occupied until the appointment of a full-time pathologist in 1939. He was lecturer in forensic medicine at the University of Melbourne in 1904-43.

As coroner's surgeon for over fifty years Mollison was involved in most of the famous criminal cases of that period, including the Deeming [q.v.8] trial (1892), the Gun Alley murder (1922), the Leonski murders (1942) and the 'pyjama girl' case (1934-44). A short, stocky man of 'almost cherubic countenance, with rosy cheeks, pleasant smile and soft voice', Mollison was quiet and unassuming, with a dry sense of humour. He was the ideal scientific witness who presented his findings in simple, unambiguous English, and insisted on giving only factual evidence. His composure impressed hearers and carried conviction. He remained even tempered although, as a disinterested expert witness, he sometimes felt that remarks made by legal counsel were unfair.

A fine histo-pathologist and a keen observer, Mollison attracted only one pupil, Dr Redford Wright-Smith, who died three years after succeeding Mollison at the morgue. In 1946, aged 83, Mollison returned to work until a replacement could be found. He published one book, *Forensic medicine lectures* (1921), and some contributions to the Medico-Legal Society of Victoria, of which he was elected first medical president in 1932.

Active in many professional organizations Mollison was a member of the board of the Walter and Eliza Hall [qq.v.9] Institute of Research in Pathology and Medicine, chairman of the British Medical Insurance Co. and of the British Medical Agency of Victoria Pty Ltd, and a member of the Victorian Medical Board. Treasurer of the Victorian Medical Society from 1895, he was one of the movers for amalgamation of the society with the Victorian branch of the British Medical Association. In 1943 he was awarded the B.M.A.'s gold medal.

Mollison was surgeon to the Victoria Racing Club for many years and was a champion royal tennis player. He loved bridge and was a keen rosarian. On 18 December 1900 at St John's Church, Toorak, he had married Corientia Elizabeth (d. 1920), daughter of Thomas Browne ('Rolf Boldrewood') [q.v.3]; they had three sons. Mollison died in Melbourne on 6 April 1949 and was cremated. He was survived by his third wife Grace Elizabeth, née Thomas, whom he had married on 16 October 1929, a daughter from each of his first and third marriages and two sons from his second. His eldest son was lost on service in World War II. Mollison's portrait by W. B. McInnes [q.v.] is in the council-room of the Australian Medical Association (Victorian branch).

K. F. Russell, *The Melbourne medical school 1862-1962* (Melb, 1977); Medico-Legal Soc of Vic, *Procs 2*, 1933; Roy Melb Hospital, *Clinical Reports*, Dec 1949; *MJA*, 28 July 1951, 12 Jan 1957; *Punch* (Melb), 1 Oct 1908, 25 Sept 1924; *Age*, 7 Apr 1949.   J. BIRRELL

MOLLISON, ETHEL KNIGHT; *see* KELLY, ETHEL

MOLLOY, THOMAS GEORGE ANSTRUTHER (1852-1938), builder, speculator and local government politician, was born on 4 October 1852 at Toronto, Canada, son of John Molloy, a soldier who served in the Crimean War and the Indian Mutiny, and his wife Jane, née Curtis. They migrated to the penal colony of Western Australia, John as a pensioner guard, in 1862. Thomas attended the Christian Brothers' College, Perth. After leaving school at 13, he worked in a printing office and with J. T. Reilly [q.v.], a notable figure in the Perth co-operative movement and Mechanics' Institute. As manager of the city branch of the Co-operative Stores, Molloy substantially increased the Co-operative Society's assets, especially with the purchase of a central city block of land. On 18 February 1873 in Perth, he married Amelia Littlejohn Molloy; they had two daughters and a son. He worked in South Australia for two years, but from 1875 his career in Perth stabilized and prospered.

He owned and ran a baker's shop, with cottages for his employees. From 1881 he worked on the *Daily News*; in 1884 he became commercial manager for the *West Australian*. His real estate speculations in the central and western parts of the city were most profitable, especially when he bought land and hotels from James Grave's estate. His wife had died, and on 23 January 1889 he married Mary Reaney; they had two daughters.

By the mid-1890s the city's rate clerk described Molloy as being of independent means and in 1895 he was appointed justice of the peace. Next year he built the Theatre Royal, Perth's first substantial theatre and one of the city's largest buildings; it was completed by Gustave Liebe [q.v.] and opened on 19 April 1897. By 1904 Molloy had also built the Metropole Hotel in central Hay Street, and His Majesty's Theatre—for many years it had the largest stage in Australia—and His Majesty's Hotel further to the west of the city. By judicious selling of real estate as West Perth developed, Molloy's fortunes further increased. In 1912 the Theatre Royal was remodelled for £9000 to fulfil lease conditions made with Cozens Spencer [q.v.], a Sydney movie mogul. Molloy spent most of 1913 in Britain and returned home via North America.

His class and religious background and his early contact with the co-operative movement ensured that his politics would be populist in character. He represented the West and Central wards on Perth City Council from 1884, more or less continuously, through World War I. He was mayor in 1908-09 and 1911-12. On the council Molloy was seen as radical, largely because he espoused municipal socialism, particularly in matters of gas and water supply, transport, drainage and sewerage. He sought to provide people with no-charge recreation and bathing facilities and in 1912, subtly supported by Town Clerk W. E. Bold [q.v.7], he ended the Perth Gas Co.'s monopoly of the provision of the city's power and lighting. A typical contention in Molloy's annual report reads: 'The lighting of the City is a service which is created by the people, and the people should have the profits which accrue therefrom'. His term ended before he could accomplish municipal council control of Perth's transport. Despite his many attempts to be mayor again, he was thought to be too stubborn and disputatious to work with, and he failed.

In 1892 he won the seat of Perth in the Legislative Assembly. He advocated abolition of the property qualification and backed attempts to introduce manhood suffrage.

Indeed, Molloy supported universal suffrage, to the annoyance of more conventional colleagues; it is believed that he introduced barmaids to Perth's hotels! At the 1894 elections his parliamentary career ended abruptly. As a Catholic he had argued for the dual system of education and against the abolition of state aid to church schools. He and the other sitting members for Perth were routed by abolitionists, and state aid to church schools ceased. Molloy was chagrined, blaming 'religious bitterness'. He stood again unsuccessfully many times between 1901 and 1932. He became a staunch member of the National Party.

Molloy was litigious and occasionally would resort to violence. In 1937 he appealed unsuccessfully to the High Court of Australia against assessments for land taxation. He became a rather mean and negligent landlord; buildings of his in St George's Terrace degenerated into slums. His second wife had died in 1925. He was anxious for a knighthood, and in 1931 was created a papal knight commander of the Order of St Gregory, after which he used the title 'Sir'. It was engraved on his tombstone in Karrakatta cemetery where he was buried after his death at Subiaco on 16 February 1938 and a requiem Mass at St Mary's Cathedral. A daughter of his second marriage survived him and inherited most of his estate, which was sworn for probate at £150 873. His will, however, led to protracted litigation.

J. T. Reilly, *Reminiscences of fifty years residence in Western Australia* (Perth, 1903); J. S. Battye (ed), *Cyclopedia of Western Australia*, 1 (Adel, 1912); L. W. Matters, *Australasians who count in London* (Lond, 1913); V. Courtney, *All I may tell* (Syd, 1956), and *Perth and all this* (Syd, 1962); C. T. Stannage, *The people of Perth* (Perth, 1979); *Morning Herald* (Perth), 29 Jan 1897; *West Australian*, 6 Oct 1926, 17 Feb 1938.

TOM STANNAGE

MOLONEY, PARKER JOHN (1879-1961), teacher, politician and public servant, was born on 12 August 1879 at Port Fairy, Victoria, son of Maurice Moloney and his wife Mary, née Bowe. He worked on the family farm at Boot Pool and attended school at Port Fairy and later at the Hamilton Academy. A childhood friend was Thomas Joseph Ryan [q.v.]. Solidly grounded in mathematics and classics, Moloney became a teacher at J. B. O'Hara's [q.v.] South Melbourne College in 1902 and then at University High School. His lodgings were close to the Trades Hall, and he began to mix with industrial and Labor leaders. Like his political peers, James Scullin [q.v.] and Frank Brennan [q.v.7], Moloney developed his debating skills through the Catholic Young Men's Association.

From 1906 he was principal of Beechworth College but in 1910 he won the Federal seat of Indi for Labor. He lost in 1913, but regained the seat in the Labor landslide of 1914. Moloney's strong opposition to conscription lost him rural Indi in 1917. He crossed the border to win Hume in New South Wales in 1919, as its first Labor representative. Moloney moved his residence to Melbourne, but built up strong personal support in Hume, touring regularly by bicycle and open car. On 15 April 1914 he had married Margaret Mary Mills of Bendigo.

Under Scullin, Moloney was minister for markets and transport in 1929-31. He attended the 1930 Imperial Conference in London, then went to the United States of America for trade consultations. He negotiated the first Australian trade treaty with Canada at Ottawa, an achievement that won him a parliamentary ovation. Moloney attended the crucial conferences which framed the Premiers' Plan in mid-1931, and prepared for the 1932 Imperial Economic Conference at Ottawa, but lost his seat when the Scullin government was swept from office in December 1931.

In the era before parliamentary pensions, he was left virtually destitute. He sold his house at Moonee Ponds, Melbourne, and moved his family into an aunt's home. In partnership with R. V. Keane, another defeated Labor parliamentarian, Moloney scraped together enough to buy two old mining dumps near Bendigo. When the Collins House group bought the dumps for £3000, he invested his share of £1500 in property. For some years he worked as a mining consultant from an office in Collins House. Extremely conscious of his reputation for probity, Moloney did not sell shares in the Fiji Mining Lease of Blue Mounts Alluvial purchased on the advice of an old political colleague Edward Theodore [q.v.], when they fluctuated advantageously and mysteriously on the Stock Exchange.

He was Victorian State president of the Australian Labor Party in 1939. He twice stood unsuccessfully for the Senate, but withdrew from Labor's winning team in 1943. In later years Moloney lost touch with the A.L.P. and joined the Democratic Labor Party. He was chairman of the Victorian Dried Fruits Board in 1936-57, retiring only after his family surreptitiously lobbied Prime Minister (Sir) Robert Menzies for a pension, and was chairman of the Commonwealth Wheat Industry Stabilisation Board in 1947-49. Moloney was closely associated with Archbishop Daniel Mannix [q.v.], who was his confessor. His principal interest outside public life was horse-racing.

Moloney died on 8 May 1961 and was buried in Melbourne general cemetery after a state funeral. His two sons and a daughter survived him. A calm, dignified man of medium height, 'bearing the stamp of the pedagogue', with a piercing, reedy voice well suited to parliamentary debate, Moloney was a distinctive representative of a generation of Catholic Labor politicians of Irish descent. Archbishop (Sir) Guilford Young described him as 'outstanding among a great generation of Catholic men who had a special Catholic ethos'.

Table Talk, 7 Aug 1930; *Aust Worker*, 4 Dec 1929; *Punch* (Melb), 9 June 1910, 9 May 1912; Moloney papers, (NL); information from Fr Parker Moloney, Canb.   C. J. LLOYD

MONASH, SIR JOHN (1865-1931), soldier, engineer and administrator, was born on 27 June 1865 in West Melbourne, eldest of three children and only son of Louis Monash (1831-94) and his wife Bertha, née Manasse. Several generations of John's paternal ancestors had lived at Krotoschin (Krotoszyn), Posen province (Poznán, Poland), Prussia, near Breslau (Wroclaw). Almost one-third of the town's population was Jewish. John's grandfather Baer-Loebel Monasch was a learned publisher and printer. His uncle by marriage Heinrich Graetz was the eminent historian of the Jewish people. His father Louis migrated to Melbourne in 1854, prospered as a merchant, was naturalized in 1856 and was secretary of the Deutscher Verein. He returned to Europe in 1863, married Bertha (of Dramburg, near Stettin (Szczecin)), and next year took her back to Melbourne.

John was brought up bilingually (but never acquired any Yiddish); his parents spoke good English. For three years he attended St Stephen's Church of England School, Richmond. His father had suffered 'terrible losses' and was never again to be well off. He opened a store at Jerilderie, New South Wales, where John attended the public school in 1875-77 under William Elliott who delighted in the boy's intelligence and taught him all the mathematics he knew. In some anguish Bertha returned with the children to Melbourne late in 1877, to further their education; Louis followed five years later with enough savings to build a modest villa at Hawthorn. John enrolled at Scotch College under Alexander Morrison [q.v.5]. His parents had largely abandoned religious practice, but John sang in the choir at the East Melbourne synagogue and celebrated his bar mitzvah there. His mother attracted a wide circle of friends to her Richmond home; they were musical, German or Jewish but included the Deakin and Hodgson [qq.v.8, 4] families. Bertha was a

proficient pianist; John had begun to play by 5.

Classically Jewish in their expectations for their first-born son, John's parents drove him hard. In her husband's absence, Bertha talked much with the boy who developed a precocious articulateness and ease in adult company. At school he was studious and quiet, without games skills; later he was a good runner, a mediocre horseman and a fair shot. He retained a lifelong affection for Scotch College. He matriculated at 14 and in 1880, in the sixth form under Moses Moses, was second in mathematics and logic to (Sir) James McCay [q.v.], his lifelong friend and rival. Morrison persuaded him to return for another year; after a highly ingenious prize essay on *Macbeth*, he was equal dux in 1881 and at the public examinations won the mathematics exhibition and came fourth in the class list in French and German.

John had firmly decided to take arts and engineering at the University of Melbourne. (Nearly fifty years later, distributing the prizes at Scotch, he instructed the dux in mathematics, (Sir) Archibald Glenn: 'You'll do engineering, of course'.) His first-year lecturers did not excite him and he began his own course of concentrated reading at the Public Library of Victoria, mainly in English literature and history; he was also stagestruck, attending the theatre twice a week (deceiving his mother), spoke and debated at the Wesley Church Mutual Improvement Society of which he became secretary, began to keep diaries and experimented with journalism and writing stories. He attended lectures by Thomas Walker [q.v.6] the secularist, but his reading had already led him to a freethinking or pantheist attitude to religion. He failed his first-year examinations.

He knuckled down, however, and in 1883 passed with third- and in 1884 with second-class honours, becoming passionately interested in mathematics. He tutored a few students and managed almost to keep himself. He played much chess and kept up the piano, sometimes performing in public; a Chopin 'Polonaise' was his star piece. Monash furthermore became deeply involved in student politics, being a co-founder of the Melbourne University Union, active in arranging debates, socials and concerts, and editor of the first twelve issues of *Melbourne University Review* in 1884-85. He was also in 1884 one of the first to join the university company of the 4th Battalion, Victorian Rifles: 5 ft. 8¾ ins. (175 cm) tall, well-built but slim and agile, the raw recruit rose to colour sergeant within fourteen months.

His ambition to contest for the glittering prizes had been naked. His awareness of his talents—of being predestined or chosen—the high expectations of his parents, his relative poverty and the consciousness of being an outsider—doubly so as a Jew of Prussian parentage—all made for an unusually determined assertiveness. Yet as a student he had a rare ideal of what a university and what a university student ought to be. His ingratiating and yet combative manner, his craving to be the centre of attention, his sensitivity to slights, his vanity were all obvious, but his intellect and achievements won respect and friendships.

During his mother's long fatal illness in 1885, Monash abandoned his course. Highly distressed, he trod an erratic path for the next few years. His father was stricken and his business as a financial agent was yielding little. John had to contribute to the family finances. His sister Mathilde, dux of Presbyterian Ladies' College in 1886 and later a language-teacher, was running the household and looking after her sister Louise. Through his friend J. B. Lewis, Monash found a post on construction of Princes Bridge over the Yarra which gave him valuable experience for more than two years. After a bungled attempt in 1886, he passed his university third-year in 1887 as a part-time student, but abandoned his intention of sitting for honours in mathematics. Early in 1888 he was fortunate to be given charge of construction of the Outer Circle eastern suburban railway-line which he capably concluded after three years 'enormous and extensive experience', having in August 1890 lucidly and unpretentiously addressed the university's Engineering Students' Society on 'The Superintendence of Contracts'. In November 1891, after the collapse of the boom, he was grateful to find a post with the Melbourne Harbor Trust.

During the peak years of the boom, when Monash pursued a giddy social career, his chief centre was the German Club; but by 1889 he largely abandoned it because his sympathies were 'too English'. In 1886-87 his performance as a pianist reached its highest point. Balls and dances, the opera and theatre, annual walking trips (especially to Mount Buffalo and the Alps) and—particularly—girls filled his leisure time. Habitual flirtation led to several embarrassing close associations and eventually, in 1888-89 to a tempestuous *affaire* with Annie Gabriel, a non-Jewish married woman. In September 1889, in a markedly unstable condition, Monash reached the point of attempting to abscond with her to another colony and thus, in disgrace, to abandon his cultural heritage—but just in time her husband carried her off to Sydney. A month later, impulsively, he became engaged to 20-year-old Hannah Victoria Moss whom he married on 8 April 1891. Their only child Bertha was born on 22 January 1893. Before and after marriage, seemingly incompatible but bonded by deep attrac-

tion, they fought and made up constantly. Indeed they separated for ten months in 1894-95.

In 1890 Monash resolved to complete his degrees. On 4 April 1891 he took out his B.C.E., having won the *Argus* scholarship with a high second-class honour. In 1891-92 he crammed himself through the exams for municipal surveyors' and water-supply engineers' qualifications. Identifying a possible lucrative monopoly in legal engineering, again in 1891-92 he forced himself through a law degree, by last-minute cramming, probably without having attended a single lecture. In December 1892 he completed arts by conquering his bugbear Latin. He formally graduated (M.Eng., 1893; B.A., LL.B., 1895) when he could afford the fees. It had been an astonishing spare-time programme. Given opportunity and concentration, he might have won first-class honours in any of engineering, mathematics, modern languages, philosophy or English literature.

The university company had been disbanded in July 1886. Monash had applied unsuccessfully for a commission in the Engineers; but joined the North Melbourne Battery of the Metropolitan Brigade of the Garrison Artillery, whose fixed guns defended the Victorian ports, being appointed probationary lieutenant on 5 April 1887. By then he had almost settled on a combination of engineering and soldiering as his life's work. Military theory had begun to excite him and he enjoyed the control of men in a hierarchical disciplined structure. Moreover a military commission carried much more status than the professions of engineering and teaching.

Monash made many blunders in his early relations with fellow officers, especially at the annual Easter camps at Queenscliff; he got on better with other ranks. He joined the Naval and Military Club. He was chiefly responsible for construction of a dummy practice-gun which served for several years as a useful training device. He lectured frequently on artillery, weapons, explosives, practical mechanics and many other subjects, within the militia and in public, and his expository ability won recognition. By 1893 he was senior subaltern in the Garrison Artillery. He was active in and became secretary of the United Service Institution of Victoria. Under the patronage now of Lieut-Colonel W. H. Hall, he was promoted captain at last on 18 October 1895. Next year he sat the examinations for major (which, he calculated, made 94 written exams in 17 years) and was promoted on 2 April 1897 with command of the North Melbourne Battery, which he was to retain for another eleven years. Although work in coastal artillery was highly specialized and something of a backwater, it was there that Monash developed his gift for administration and learned to command men with fatherly authority. He did not volunteer for and was not invited to take part in the South African War. Coastal artillerymen were irrelevant, men of his age with family and business responsibilities were hardly expected to go; moreover his support for the war was less than whole-hearted.

Retrenched by the Harbor Trust in the depth of the depression in April 1894, Monash boldly launched into private practice with his friend J. T. Noble Anderson as civil, mining and mechanical engineers and patent agents. For three years they struggled on, carrying out a wide variety of minor tasks; a contract to design and install an 'aerial tramway' for transporting quartz at Walhalla gave hard-won experience but little profit. Their situation, however, improved from mid-1897 when Monash came suddenly into demand as an advocate and expert witness in legal-engineering work. Over the next two years he spent three-quarters of his time in other colonies, visiting Queensland four times and New South Wales six, and passing twelve months in Western Australia successfully conducting claims against the government arising from a railway-construction project.

Meanwhile Anderson had gained from the Sydney contractor-engineer F. M. Gummow the patent rights in Victoria for Monier reinforced concrete construction. Monash & Anderson now concentrated on contracting for bridge-building and planned to manufacture concrete pipes with David Mitchell [q.v.5] and his employee John Gibson. Their bridge-building was highly successful until one of their Bendigo bridges collapsed under testing and they had to rebuild at their own cost. Then the shires of Corio and Bannockburn refused to make the large final payment for their Fyansford bridge and, in an eccentric judgment, were upheld by the Supreme Court of Victoria early in 1902. All their capital was gone and they were deeply in debt. Anderson, with a large family to support, left for a job in New Zealand.

Humiliated, and justifiably complaining of his 'cursed bad luck', Monash endured three more years of poverty. Toughened by hard experience and backed by business associates who recognized his capacity, he began to switch to constructing buildings and in 1905, with Gibson as managing director, formed the Reinforced Concrete & Monier Pipe Construction Co. Ltd. He had paid off his debts at the rate of £1000 a year. Protected still by the Monier patents and largely monopolizing concrete construction, the company undertook a dozen jobs at a time and formed a South Australian subsidiary. By 1913 Monash was worth over £30 000. In 1910 he had made his first overseas trip: to Britain, the Continent

and, briefly, the United States of America whose technological achievements deeply impressed him. In England he formed an intimate friendship with the scientist Walter Rosenhain [q.v.] who had married his sister Lou.

Meanwhile his military career had taken a marked turn for the better. In 1907 he had seemed to be in a dead end. But Colonel McCay, commanding the Australian Intelligence Corps (militia), offered him charge of the Victorian section and Monash was promoted lieut-colonel on 7 March 1908. Military mapping—disgracefully backward—was the prime task, general intelligence gathering was also important but, in alliance with his new friend Major (Sir) Julius Bruche [q.v.7], Monash involved himself in general staff work. He attended Colonel Hubert Foster's [q.v.8] schools in military science at the University of Sydney; helped to prepare for Lord Kitchener's inspections; suggested, umpired and reported on tactical exercises. Above all he studied military history and in 1911 won the first army gold-medal essay competition on 'The Lessons of the Wilderness Campaign, 1864' (*Commonwealth Military Journal*, April 1912). From 1 June 1913 he was appointed to command the 13th Infantry Brigade, as colonel. His conduct of manoeuvres in February 1914 won the warm approval of the visiting General Sir Ian Hamilton. Monash's pamphlet, *100 hints for company commanders*, became a basic training document.

Monash was now a pillar of Melbourne society, in the inner swim of business affairs. He had bought a Toorak mansion and a luxurious motor car, with a chauffeur and other servants to match, and was the calm centre of his extended family. He lectured and examined in engineering at the university, became chairman of the graduates' association and president of the University Club, then from 1912 was elected to the university council and its more important committees. As president of the Victorian Institute of Engineers, in 1913 he gave a constructive radical critique of his profession and worked towards foundation of a national body. He was prominent in the Boy Scout movement. He was at peace with himself, recognized enough now with a fair measure of fame and a wide circle of friends; he could relax and be more altruistic. But his career showed signs of a dying fall. Yet he had superb qualities for any large job which might crop up: absolute self-confidence, skill in the manipulation of men to his forceful will, a magnificently developed administrative competence and an intellect never yet subjected to adequate challenge.

On the outbreak of war Monash acted as chief censor for four weeks before he was appointed to command the 4th Infantry Brigade, Australian Imperial Force. It was an Australia-wide brigade which had to be organized and gathered at Broadmeadows, Victoria, and given elementary training before sailing with the second contingent on 22 December 1914. Monash chose as his brigade major Lieut-Colonel J. P. McGlinn [q.v.]; they were soon intimate friends. Monash commanded the convoy of seventeen ships which reached Egypt at the end of January 1915. The 4th Brigade went into camp near Heliopolis as part of Major General Sir Alexander Godley's New Zealand and Australian Division. Godley and the corps commander Lieut-General Sir William Birdwood [q.v.7] were well satisfied with Monash's training of the brigade. At the Gallipoli landing it was in reserve: Monash did not land until the morning of 26 April, and was given the left-centre sector including Pope's Hill and Quinn's Post to organize while the Turks counter-attacked. His brigade was still not fully gathered by the 30th but Monash had an orderly conference of his battalion commanders that day. The night offensive on Baby 700 of 2 May, which Monash had opposed, was disastrous; according to C. E. W. Bean [q.v.7] it left him 'unstrung, as well it might'. The brigade played its part in withstanding the Turkish offensive of 19 May and the break-in to Quinn's on the 29th, and was relieved from the line at the end of the month.

In July Monash learned of his tardy promotion to brigadier general at a time when wild rumours were circulating in Cairo, London and Melbourne that he had been shot as a German spy and traitor; there had been a similar vicious whispering campaign in Melbourne the previous October. The brigade now prepared for the battle of Sari Bair and its part in the left hook on Hill 971. Their night-march of 6 August was delayed and a vital wrong turning made. Monash forced himself to the front, punched his battalions into position and made good progress against moderate resistance. But the maps were faulty, the men were lost and exhausted, and next morning could only dig in. On the 8th, after attacking, they had to withdraw. Most of the men were sick, many had paratyphoid. The remnants then took part in the unsuccessful attacks on Hill 60, before being withdrawn to Lemnos. Monash had three weeks leave in Egypt where he learned of his appointment as C.B. The brigade returned to a quiet sector on Gallipoli. On the final night of the evacuation Monash was not one of the last to leave, but rashly sent home an illegal diary-letter implying that he had been. Gallipoli had given him a devastating education. Bean, Birdwood and others left an impression that his performance had been mediocre; but his brigade had performed at least as well as any of the other three and he had little or no part in the battle-

plans he had to attempt to carry out. His performance on 7-8 August is open to criticism, but it came to be recognized that the attack on Hill 971 was totally impossible of achievement. Bean reported the saying that Monash 'would command a division better than a brigade and a corps better than a division'.

In Egypt in January 1916 he wearily began retraining his reconstituted brigade, distressed by the news of his wife's operation for cancer. The brigade, after dismemberment to form daughter units, joined 4th Division and spent two months in the local defences east of Suez Canal. In June they moved to France, to the Armentières sector, and were immediately tagged for a substantial diversionary and unsuccessful night-raid on 2 July. That month Monash was promoted major general in command of the new 3rd Division arriving on Salisbury Plain, England. He was given two first-rate British professionals to watch over him, Lieut-Colonels G. H. N. Jackson and H. M. Farmar, who soon became his admiring devotees. Training proceeded vigorously. Monash had a flattering triumph when King George V himself inspected the division. In November they moved into the Armentières sector as part of Godley's II Anzac Corps and General Sir Herbert Plumer's Second British Army. Field Marshal Sir Douglas Haig inspected on 22 December. Monash had established and retained a remarkably low crime-rate in the division. By an extraordinary feat of will-power he had reduced his weight drastically to 12½ stone (79 kg), which considerably added to his authority. His good fortune was, unlike the other Australian divisions, to serve under Plumer and Major General Harington, and that his first major battle, Messines in June 1917, was Plumer's masterpiece. According to Bean, Monash 'concentrated upon the plans an amount of thought and care far beyond that ever devoted to any other [A.I.F. operation]'. 'Wonderful detail but not his job', Harington commented. In the autumn, during 3rd Ypres, at Broodseinde Monash brought off the greatest A.I.F. victory yet. But the weather had broken and in the following week Monash and his 3rd Division suffered the misery of Passchendaele.

3rd Division, which Monash was sure was 'one of the Crack Divisions of the British Army', spent most of the winter quietly in the Ploegsteert sector. In November it had at last joined the other divisions in I Anzac Corps. Monash dined privately with Haig who let it be known that he wanted him as a corps commander; at the New Year he was appointed K.C.B., not a mere knighthood. In March 1918, in the face of the great German offensive, he brilliantly deployed his division to plug the gap in front of Amiens. They were, however, in the eye of the storm, and saw little serious action. But in late April and May they were heavily involved in aggressive 'peaceful penetration'. Then, to the general satisfaction of the A.I.F., Monash was appointed corps commander from 1 June and promoted lieut-general; Birdwood remained general officer commanding the A.I.F. Bean and the journalist (Sir) Keith Murdoch [q.v.], however, carried on a relentless campaign for more than two months to replace Monash with Major General (Sir) Brudenell White [q.v.] and Birdwood with Monash. He stood to win both ways, but was determined to test himself in the field at corps level.

The battle of Hamel of 4 July—'all over in ninety-three minutes . . . the perfection of teamwork', Monash wrote—proved his point. The Americans participated, and Monash had to withstand, by extraordinary force of personality, a last-minute attempt by General Pershing to withdraw them. Military historians have acclaimed it as 'the first modern battle', 'the perfect battle'. 'A war-winning combination had been found: a corps commander of genius, the Australian infantry, the Tank Corps, the Royal Artillery and the RAF'.

Returned soldiers including many senior officers, and Australian patriots in general, broadly assumed that Monash inspired the great offensive of 8 August and thus 'won the war'. He himself was never quite sure. He and his army commander, General Rawlinson, were thinking along similar lines, but it is almost certain that Rawlinson anticipated Monash and allowed him to believe he was the instigator. At all events, in conjunction with the Canadians, the break-out on 8 August, 'the black day of the German army', was a classic set-piece. On 11 August an extraordinary chance gathering at Villers-Bretonneux of senior allied generals and politicians made Monash and Lieut-General Sir Arthur Currie, the Canadian, the centre of congratulations. Next day the king invested Monash with his knighthood.

The sixty days from 8 August, with the A.I.F. as virtual spearhead of the British army, were glorious. There was a minor botch on 10 August near Proyart, but thereafter, until about the end of September, a series of conclusive victories followed—at Chuignes, Mont St Quentin and Péronne especially (where Monash's ability in a fluid battle was finally proved), and Hargicourt. The breaking of the Hindenburg line, during which Monash commanded some 200 000 including Americans, was a much more uncertain matter; and the very last A.I.F. infantry action at Montbrehain, with heavy casualties, was probably unnecessary. But it was a series of victories unsurpassed in the annals of the British army and, according to military historians, the 5000 A.I.F. dead were a remarkably light cost. During the battles Monash had

had to deal with Prime Minister Hughes's [q.v.9] decision to send 6000 veterans home on leave, the British army's enforcement of disbandment of some battalions, and the tragic 'fatigue mutiny' of some of the 1st Battalion. Exhausted, Monash sought seclusion in England. Blessedly, the A.I.F. was moving back into action only on the day of the Armistice.

Monash perhaps won more than his fair share of fame, as against other Australian generals, for he had the great luck to take command of a magnificent fighting body just when the tide was about to turn conclusively in the allies' favour. But the task could hardly have been better done. None of the A.I.F. generals compare with him in intellect, articulateness or personal magnetism, though White does in administrative capacity. He won the undying respect of nearly all his peers, including the greatest fighting generals. Remarkably, no serious charge was ever held against Monash of 'butchery'. His reputation remains undiminished. Bean, as historian, remained rather ambivalent, combining effusive praise with trivial criticism and some personal distaste. Monash's international reputation, largely British, derives from Sir Basil Liddell Hart's admiration, which has uncritically been accepted by a succession of historians. Monash was sometimes admired as 'the best man in France' but, although he might have been offered an army if the war had continued into 1919, the conjecture that a Jewish colonial militiaman of German origin could ever have become British commander-in-chief is absurd. He never had the opportunity to succeed, or fail, at the level of high strategy.

As a general, Monash had the first essential qualities, the capacity to bear great strain and to make quick and clear decisions. His sheer intellect, breadth of grasp, his articulateness especially, together with his forceful personality, induced respect and confidence among his juniors. He worked closely with his staff, extracting the best from them: the partnership with his devoted admirer at corps, Brigadier General (Field Marshal Sir Thomas) Blamey was famous. He developed the practice of conferences of senior officers, not merely to cover a mass of detail, but to facilitate knowledge of what was expected right down the line. He held the view that warfare was essentially a problem in engineering, of mobilizing resources, like the conduct of a large industrial undertaking; in 1918 the men in the line knew that all was right behind them. He eagerly made use of the most recent innovations. He took the view that an energetic offensive policy, 'feeding the troops on victory', was the short way to end the slaughter and misery. He was of the new scientific breed of generals, did not attempt to hob-nob with the troops and seek their popularity, and so was often criticized by the traditional 'inspirational' school of thought. His chief weaknesses were his status-hunger, craving for publicity and honours, and his own habit of exaggerating his men's and his own achievements.

The efficient and harmonious repatriation of 160 000 Australian soldiers, almost entirely within eight months, is among the most remarkable of Monash's achievements. He compelled the government to alter its initial policy of slow repatriation for fear of employment difficulties, and aggressively fought for and found ships, despite the shortage. He delighted in presiding over the superb A.I.F. Education Scheme. Commonwealth governments, in 1919 and later, entirely neglected to honour him or treat him with any generosity or ordinary courtesy, until the Scullin [q.v.] government eventually promoted him general. Meanwhile in London Monash enjoyed his considerable fame. From early August in about a month—another amazing feat—he wrote *The Australian victories in France in 1918*; it was propaganda, but not far off the truth. Monash left for home on 15 November and had a tumultuous welcome in Melbourne on Boxing Day. But his happy homecoming was ruined by his wife Vic's illness; she died on 27 February 1920.

Monash had been uncertain about his future. He seriously considered standing for the Senate in 1919, but the Nationalist politicians blocked his path. He was looking for a national job, but negotiations for him to head the Institute of Science and Industry fell through. The salaries attached to the most senior military posts were meagre. He picked up the threads of his enterprises which Gibson had carried on, but could not resist a takeover offer for the Concrete Constructions Co. by W. R. Hume [q.v.9]; Monash became a director of the Hume Pipe Co. (Aust) Ltd and picked up other directorships. Then in late June 1920 came the offer of the general managership of the State Electricity Commission of Victoria, which he was happy to accept, withdrawing from the Reinforced Concrete Co.

His new task was of great public importance, difficulty and attractiveness to an engineer. Making abundant cheap power available by harnessing the huge deposits of Gippsland brown coal would remove a crippling handicap to development of industry. He had strong fellow commissioners—Sir Robert Gibson [q.v.8], (Sir) Thomas Lyle and George Swinburne [qq.v.]—and Hyman Herman [q.v.9] as chief technical expert; Monash himself was soon appointed chairman. Unexpected high moisture content of the coal produced a grave early crisis, but power from Yallourn, the model garden-town, was turned on in 1924. German technology was used to solve many problems. Monash faced great political difficulties and distrust of the project which required all his forceful pugnacity to overcome; he could not tolerate (Sir) Frederic Eggleston [q.v.8], his minister in 1924-27, who distrusted Monash's 'ruthless egotism'. He survived a major inquiry in 1926, and next year the commission showed a profit. By 1930 the initial task was completed, the S.E.C. grid covered the State and the commission was established as a highly successful state enterprise. Monash himself had inspired a degree of creativity, loyalty and affection, probably unparalleled in any other large Australian corporation then or since. As in the A.I.F. he displayed his gift both of exciting their best from his colleagues and making them his personal friends. 'He was a great leader', Herman wrote, 'and a genius in getting to the heart of any problem and finding its solution . . . the ablest, biggest-minded and biggest-hearted man I have ever known'.

Innumerable demands were made on him. His advice on military matters was occasionally sought and he sometimes publicly condemned starvation of the forces. He was the natural spokesman for returned soldiers. He took command of the Special Constabulary Force during the police strike of November 1923 and chaired the subsequent royal commission. From 1925 he led Melbourne's Anzac Day march and from 1927 was its chief organizer. The cause closest to his heart in his last years was the Shrine of Remembrance of which he was in practice chairman of the constructing body. Premiers constantly pestered him for advice. From 1923 he was vice-chancellor of the university (acting chancellor for a year in 1925-26), which involved heavy burdens. He was president of the Australasian Association for the Advancement of Science in 1924-26. He advised and lobbied governments on engineering appointments and other matters relating to the profession. The clubs he most enjoyed, other than the Naval and Military, were the Wallaby and Beefsteak, and he was president of Melbourne Rotary in 1922. His haven was the family home, Iona, where he lived with his daughter and delighted in his grandchildren; he had a great gift with children. His constant companion was Lizette Bentwitch, a miniature-painter; he also remained in touch with Annie Gabriel.

The great Anglo-Jewish families had rushed Monash in London in 1919. His quiescent communal feeling revived. He had habitually ignored anti-Semitism and denied that he had ever been subject to discrimination. But he was well aware of his own unusual position as a Jew leading the army of one of the world's most democratic peoples. On return home, he could not have escaped, even if he wished to, the degree of leadership of the Jewish people thrust upon him. He accepted some formal duties, including inactive membership of the board of management of the St Kilda congregation, sympathized with the liberal Jewish position, sometimes acted as communal spokesman, and eventually occasionally attended services. He also adopted moderate Zionism—an unusual stance among prominent contemporary Jews—and in 1927 became national president of the Australian Zionist Federation on the understanding that he could be little more than a figure-head. In the 1920s he never had to speak in protest about any major local incident of anti-Semitism. His own presence and prestige, Colin McInnes claimed, 'made anti-Semitism, as a "respectable" attitude, impossible in Australia'.

In the 1920s Monash was broadly accepted, not just in Victoria, as the greatest living Australian. The soldiers had to have a representative hero who was a volunteer; he was acceptable to the community as a seemingly unpretentious outsider, not really part of the Establishment. His commanding intellect was sensed as well as his basic honesty and decency. He was one tall poppy who was never cut down. His knowledge ranged extraordinarily widely, but was neither very profound nor original. He achieved greatness essentially as an administrator, by cultivating to a super-pitch of excellence the ordinary qualities such as memory, concentration, stability and common sense, allied with temperamental capacity to work harmoniously with colleagues. He had the gift of being able instantaneously to turn from one task to the next. He was a great teacher, supremely articulate, 'the greatest advocate I ever listened to' said Sir Robert Menzies. No one in Australia's history, perhaps, crammed more effective work into a life; but, he said, work was the best thing in life. In later years at least, his charm, courtesy and impression of simplicity were striking, though traces of deviousness, sensitivity to slights and constant need for approval remained.

From 1927 Monash was troubled with high blood-pressure. With his eyes open he continued to work. Early in 1930 the Scullin government briefly considered him as a possible governor-general. In 1930-31 he rebuffed sporadic attempts to persuade him to lead a right-wing political movement. Early in 1931 he enjoyed representing the Australian government at the durbar for the opening of New Delhi. By August his health had markedly deteriorated and he died of coronary vascular disease at Iona on 8 October. His state funeral, with crowds of at least 250 000, was probably the largest in Australia to that time; he was buried in Brighton cemetery with Jewish rites. Numerous memorials were raised, including an equestrian statue near the Shrine of Remembrance. The Australian War Memorial holds portraits by John Longstaff and James Quinn [qq.v.] and shares with the National Library of Australia his huge collection of private papers and memorabilia.

G. Serle, *John Monash: a biography* (Melb, 1982) and for bibliog; P. Pedersen, *Monash as military commander* (Melb, 1985).   GEOFFREY SERLE

MONCKTON, CHARLES ARTHUR WHITMORE (1873-1936), magistrate, was born on 30 May 1873 at Invercargill, New Zealand, son of Francis Alexander Monckton, surgeon, and his wife Sarah Ann, née Newton. Educated at Wanganui College, in 1895 he went to British New Guinea seeking employment in the magisterial service. Unsuccessful in this attempt, he went prospecting for gold at Woodlark Island, then pearling and trading in the Louisiades. In 1896 and 1897 he published two short articles on native customs in the *Journal of the Polynesian Society.* He returned to New Zealand to study navigation, and then in 1897 sailed a small boat from Sydney to Port Moresby.

This time, Lieutenant-Governor Sir William MacGregor [q.v.5] was able to offer Monckton relief posts as resident magistrate in the Eastern Division, the Mekeo district and the South-Eastern Division during 1897-99. His first permanent appointment was to the newly created North-Eastern Division; he arrived at Cape Nelson with the new lieutenant-governor, (Sir) George Le Hunte [q.v.], on 4 April 1900. This station was established to gain better control over numerous belligerent indigenous clans as well as to provide law and order for miners on the Yodda goldfields.

Accompanied by his native police whom he had trained to a high degree of efficiency, Monckton mounted a series of expeditions, some punitive, some exploratory. Tough, efficient, quick-witted and ruthless, he conducted each expedition as if it were a military campaign. In bringing under control combative people such as the Doriri, Dobodura and Paiwa, his policy was to 'shoot and loot'. With more peaceful people, such as the Agaiambu who, living in the swamps of the Musa River, were marked by a physique that made it difficult for them to walk on land, he showed some anthropological awareness. While some contemporaries admired him as a 'fearless . . . fighting man', others deplored his readiness with a gun, his callous punishments and his sexual exploitation of local women. His handling of the 'Paiwa affair', when his police went berserk with bayonets, provoked widespread criticism. Relations with miners in the area, generally mutually helpful, sometimes became explosive, particularly with those who thought an even tougher line should be taken against the Papuans. In 1903 Monckton was given the additional responsibility of the Northern Division. He was also appointed to both the Legislative and Executive councils.

Two major exploratory expeditions were initiated from his headquarters. His was the first party (1906) to climb Mount Albert Edward (13 100 ft., 3993 m). When miners began to intrude into German New Guinea north of the Waria River, Monckton used a necessary border survey as an excuse to cross the island by taking his party down the Lakekamu River into the Gulf of Papua. He had exceeded his instructions and was reprimanded. The report of the royal commission on Papua, published in 1907, criticized Monckton's friends in government. Although the commission commended him personally, he resigned from the service on 4 June 1907 and went to London.

On 24 July 1907 at Holy Trinity Church, Brompton, Monckton married Margaret Louisa Arkwright. Returning to New Zealand, he managed a farm near Otago in 1910-14; here he began writing the first of his three books. War interrupted, however, and he went to England to enlist, became a captain in the Sherwood Foresters and served in India. After the war he and his wife settled at Walmer, Kent, where he continued writing. He was elected a member of the Royal Central Asian Society in 1923 and was later made a fellow of the Royal Anthropological Institute, the Zoological Society and the Royal Geographical Society. Survived by his wife, he died of blackwater fever and influenza in London on 1 March 1936.

Monckton's writing style was readable and racy; every page was packed with adventure. To British armchair travellers he became the epitome of the colonial white man bearing the burden of civilizing native races. His supreme egoism was tempered by astute observations on the customs of the Papuans and peppered by strong opinions on the virtues and faults of his colleagues, missionaries, miners and traders. His official reports, well written and detailed, were used as a basis, and often quoted in full, in *Some experiences of a resident magistrate* (London, 1920) and *Last days in New Guinea* (London, 1922). These two books, though biased in judgements, are factually accurate except where he comments on events outside his province, such as the Goaribari affray. His last book, *New Guinea recollections* (London, 1934), sullied his reputation. It is an inaccurate series of unconnected anecdotes in which he attempted to exonerate himself.

N. Lutton, 'C. A. W. Monckton' in J. Griffin (ed),

Papua New Guinea portraits (Canb, 1978), *and* C. A. W. Monckton's trilogy of his adventures in New Guinea (B.A. Hons thesis, UPNG, 1972), and for bibliog; *The Times*, 2 Mar 1936.

NANCY LUTTON

MONCRIEFF, ALEXANDER BAIN (1845-1928), engineer, was born on 22 May 1845 in Dublin, eldest son of Alexander Rutherford Moncrieff, corn merchant, and his wife Anne, née Bain. After attending Belfast Academy he was articled at 15 to the Great Southern and Western Railway of Ireland; this included manual work in the blacksmith's shop which gave him a lifelong understanding of fellow workers. He then had jobs in engineering works in Drogheda, Glasgow, Scotland, and Hertfordshire, England. In November 1874, dissatisfied with his prospects, with his brother Joseph Cowan Bain he went to South Australia as an engineering draughtsman in the civil service. On 23 August 1877, at Kent Town, he married Mary Bonson Sunter; they had a daughter and two sons.

Next year Moncrieff helped (Sir) Peter Scratchley [q.v.6] to design and construct fortifications at Largs Bay and Glanville; upon their completion he became resident engineer for the Great Northern Railway at Quorn. In 1888 Moncrieff returned to Adelaide as engineer-in-chief, succeeding H. C. Mais [q.v.5]. The position had been stripped of much of its former authority in railway management, but the Department of Harbours and Jetties and the Hydraulic Department (waterworks and sewers) were brought under his control. He now held 'one of the most senior positions in the Civil Service', although the radical press suggested that he was 'drawing a nice fat salary with minimal responsibilities'.

This was unfair. Moncrieff was largely responsible for the design of several lighthouses, ably supervised difficult and controversial work on Adelaide's Outer Harbour, and designed and implemented far-sighted drainage schemes in the South-East (1911). His Barossa dam was hailed by an American engineering journal as fit 'to rank with the most famous dams in the world' for 'the boldness of its design'. He also accumulated other responsibilities: chairmanship of the Supply and Tender Board (1895-99); presidency of the Institution of Surveyors in 1901; chairmanship of the Municipal Tramways Trust in 1907-22; and, from 1909, railways commissioner. He was appointed C.M.G. that year. He had been elected to the British Institution of Civil Engineers, London, in 1888 and the American Society of Civil Engineers in 1894.

Moncrieff retired as railways commissioner in 1916; he had been unable to concentrate fully on railway matters because of his chairmanship of the tramways and was unfortunate to be commissioner at a time when parliament wanted developmental railways. He fought against these lines, and his 1912-13 report warned that railway finances must suffer. But he was perhaps a qualified success. He was not very conversant with the work of traffic branch and in the 1916-18 reports of the North Terrace reserves and railway centres royal commission he was criticized, mainly for the antiquated design of the new Mile End goods yards and signalling devices installed at Adelaide station. He relished the fact that during his seven-year chairmanship no serious accident occurred for which a railway employee could be blamed; his motto was 'safety first'. Moncrieff's approach to transport was democratic: he deplored the two-class system of travel on the railways and prevented it on trams, where he kept fares cheap; he supported unionism and encouraged employees to 'feel that they and we are running the concern'; and he was proud of the trams' 'psychological effect'—they 'put more life into Adelaide than ever it had before'.

He was a Freemason and a pledged teetotaller from schooldays: 'Drunkenness and dishonesty', he said, 'are the two unpardonable crimes of a railwayman'. He expected high moral standards in public life and worked hard, holidaying only when compelled by illness. Moncrieff was a member of the Prisoners' Aid Society, and enjoyed gardening and mechanics. He was an Anglican lay preacher and an insatiable reader. He died at his Rose Park home on 11 April 1928 and was buried in Main North Road cemetery.

R. I. Jennings, *W.A. Webb, South Australian railways commissioner, 1922-1930* (Adel, 1973); M. Williams, *The making of the South Australian landscape* (Lond, 1974); *PP*(LA Vic), 1912, 3 (16); *Quiz* (Adel), 26 Jan 1894, 15 June 1899; *Public Service Review* (SA), 9, no 6, 1903; *Observer* (Adel), 5 May 1888; *Mail* (Adel), 18 Jan 1913; *Register* (Adel), 13 Apr 1928; family papers held by A. H. Moncrieff, Blackwood, Adel.
A. J. STIMSON
ALEX H. MONCRIEFF

MONCRIEFF, GLADYS LILLIAN (1892-1976), soprano, was born on 13 April 1892 at Bundaberg, Queensland, youngest child of Melbourne-born parents Reginald Edward Moncrieff, piano-tuner, and his wife Amy Lambell, née Wall, a professional singer. Gladys attended school at Maryborough, Bundaberg, and Townsville. At her stage début when 6 in the Queen's Theatre, Bundaberg, where she sang 'The merriest girl that's out', her accompanist father rewarded her encore

with one shilling. At West End State School, Townsville, she sang roles in Gilbert and Sullivan works, which 'toured' to Charters Towers. She was successful in the junior soprano section of the Charters Towers annual eisteddfod.

After leaving school Gladys toured remote North Queensland with her family, using Cobb & Co. coaches, coastal boats and trains to entertain isolated audiences with moving pictures, music and lantern slides. She was billed as 'Little Gladys—The Australian Wonder Child'. In 1908 at Townsville she sang the soprano lead in *The Messiah*. A testimonial concert there in April 1909 raised funds for her to pursue a singing career in Brisbane, where she worked in picture theatres and on vaudeville stages (including Toowoomba) before accompanying her mother to Sydney for further experience.

In late 1911 she was auditioned in the presence of (Dame) Nellie Melba [q.v.] by Hugh Ward [q.v.], managing director of J. C. Williamson [q.v.6] Theatres, who gave her a three-year contract with an initial salary of £3 per week, increasing to £6. It was a kind of apprenticeship and included eighteen months of singing lessons from Madame Grace Miller, Ward's wife, a noted concert singer and teacher. After extensive chorus and understudy work Moncrieff sang in 1914 for Williamson's Australasian Gilbert and Sullivan season in a local chorus with English principals, graduating to Josephine in *H.M.S. Pinafore* and other leading roles. The company performed in Sydney, New Zealand and Melbourne. Roles followed in *The geisha*, *The Quaker girl*, *Forty thieves* and *Florodora*.

During 1915-16 Moncrieff was well received during a seven-month, Williamson-sponsored engagement in South Africa with an English company. She sang in *The merry widow*, *The pink lady*, *Katinka* and *Maytime* in Australia and New Zealand in 1918-19. Her first great theatrical success was as Teresa in *The maid of the mountains* at the Theatre Royal, Melbourne, on 2 January 1921. The *Herald* critic wrote: 'It was good to hear a crowded Australian audience acclaim the success of a slim, straight young Australian girl . . . It was a personal triumph in which hard work, talent and youth bore fine fruit'. The *Argus* commented on the 'richness and purity' of her voice, and said her acting 'had a quiet force in defiance, passion and tragedy'. *Theatre* magazine spoke of the 'snowy purity and velvet lusciousness of her voice'. Many critics noted her dark, attractive, gypsy-like beauty. Management doubled her salary to £50 a week. The show ran for twenty-seven weeks and Gladys attracted up to eighteen curtain-calls a time. The Australian season extended to more than two years. *The maid* was to become the most frequently revived musical of the Australian stage and Moncrieff appeared in it some 2800 times.

On 20 May 1924 at St James' Church, Sydney, Gladys married Thomas Henry Moore, a member of the chorus in a revival of *The merry widow*, and subsequently her manager. Honeymooning in France and England, she made her first ten gramophone recordings for the Vocalion Company. By the mid-1920s Gladys had established herself as the leading performer of the musical comedy stage and, at £150 a week, as one of the highest-paid performers in the history of Australian theatre. At the peak of her success she sailed for London in January 1926 and took lessons from Anne Williams, a well-known Australian teacher who had coached protégées of Melba. Her English career was launched at the Gaiety Theatre in a new musical, *Riki-Tiki*. The show, however, was disliked for its poor libretto and closed within two weeks.

Failing to obtain a worthwhile role in another major musical comedy, Gladys eventually accepted the role of Blanka in Franz Lehár's *The blue mazurka*, which opened on 19 February 1927. 'Before the night concluded', wrote a reviewer, 'even the dullest critic must have realized that a new star of amazing brilliance had climbed above London's theatrical horizon'. The show ran for twenty-six weeks. In 1926-27 Moncrieff recorded thirty-seven titles with the Vocalion Co. Twelve performances used the acoustic (open horn) method, the others the new electrical process with a microphone. Exported to her homeland, these recordings sold extremely well.

Her marriage a failure, she began to live apart from her husband. Gladys was very homesick and returned to Australia to play the name-role in *Rio Rita*, a new musical staged by John Fuller [q.v.8]. The show was an artistic triumph and commercial success for 'Australia's Queen of Song'. She continued to sing in revivals of musicals and undertook appearances in cinemas. Her first broadcast had been a test transmission in 1918. During the 1930s she extended her radio activities and undertook tours for the New Zealand Broadcasting Service.

In 1933-35 Moncrieff starred in two moderately successful Australian stage musicals, *Collitt's Inn* and *The cedar tree*. An ill-fated 1934 film version of *Collitt's Inn* with Gladys as the heroine was not completed by Efftee Productions; only stills and some soundtrack recording survive. In 1936 comedian Arthur Stigant dubbed her 'Our Glad', a term of endearment which identified her to the Australian community for the rest of her life. Involved in a road accident in March 1938 she was absent from the stage until 10 June 1940 when she sang for the Australian Broadcasting Commission in Sydney.

Williamson's signed Moncrieff to a four-year contract in 1942 to revive noted musical comedies. She also entertained the armed forces at home, and in December 1943 took a concert party to Papua New Guinea. The final concert at Port Moresby showground was attended mainly by 17 000 troops and nurses. On her return home she worked constantly to raise funds for charities.

In 1948-49 in Perth Moncrieff sang in her final season of operetta revivals for Williamson's. In August 1951 she toured for the Department of the Army to entertain British Commonwealth occupation forces in Japan and troops in Korea. On the eve of her appointment as O.B.E. in June 1952, she commenced an Australasian season in a Harry Wren production, *Gay fiesta*. A series of radio programmes for the Macquarie broadcasting network were produced in the mid-1950s, including 'The Gladys Moncrieff Show'. Then followed a farewell stage tour of Australia and New Zealand in 1958-59 for Wren under the title 'Many Happy Returns'. Her final stage appearance was at Hamilton, New Zealand. Her last public performance as a singer was in 1962 on television in Brisbane.

Moncrieff made highly successful gramophone recordings in Australia for the Columbia Gramophone Co. between 12 October 1928 and 4 June 1935. She was a regular visitor to the company studios at Homebush, Sydney, making eighty-four titles which were released on either Regal, Regal-Zonophone or Columbia labels as ten-inch discs. These well-known musical comedy favourites sold far better than similar material by many famous overseas artists. Most of these recordings were reissued by EMI Records Australia and enjoyed healthy sales.

Gladys Moncrieff had a powerful, wide-ranging, rich soprano voice, and excellent diction. Undemonstrative in behaviour, she approached her singing like a craft, meticulously and unostentatiously. She dressed simply and did not shun menial tasks. Her large, informal parties were memorable for her superb cooking, especially for her pie with seventy dozen oysters. Perhaps it was also her sense of fun and tender-heartedness that attracted her large following of 'gallery girls', women who queued for standing room and followed her movements with flowers and mail. She became a legend in Australia in her lifetime, respected by her professional colleagues and loved by her devoted public. Her autobiography, *My life of song* (Adelaide, 1971), was ghosted by Lillian Palmer.

Moncrieff retired to the Gold Coast, Queensland, in January 1968, where she died, childless, in Pindara Private Hospital, Benowa, on 8 February 1976.

G. Moncrieff, biog file (NL).   PETER BURGIS

MONDALMI (c.1910-1969) was an Aboriginal woman of the Maung people, ngalangila subsection, born at Wighu, South Goulburn Island, Western Arnhem Land, Northern Territory. Her father Mayjburn (English name Charlie), who helped to collect trepang for 'Macassan' (Indonesian) traders, belonged to the small Manganowal group, whose country was between the Maung and the Yiwadja to the west. Her mother Ngalmiyjalwarn was from the Junction Bay area on the mainland. Mondalmi's second name was Milimili; her nickname was Ngalwububul, abbreviated to Bubu, meaning a short person. She was proud of being one of the saltwater people of the islands and adjacent mainland: 'I'm not a bush woman . . . My country is on the beach'. They suffered more severely from outside intrusion, over a longer period, than did the people of eastern Arnhem Land; but they retained their language and something of their traditional ways, despite increasing contact also with other Aborigines from adjoining areas. Besides Maung, Mondalmi spoke Yiwadja, Gunbalang and English, and understood Gunwinggu.

As a child, following her first fearful contact with 'white-skinned' strangers, Mondalmi was taken to the Methodist mission station on South Goulburn Island, established in 1916. There she learned to read and write English, sew and make baskets. Although she had been betrothed early to an older man, he agreed to her marriage at Goulburn Island Methodist Church on 27 June 1927 with a Gunwinggu-speaking man from the mainland, Gadawar also known as Ganaraidj (c.1906-1971), English name John, a lay preacher at the mission. In keeping with Maung custom, she kept her own names on marriage. Her seven sons and two daughters were born between 1928 and 1953. She brought up her children carefully in traditional ways to become independent within a co-operative context. But the 'balanda' (European) presence had interrupted the passing on by older people of much traditional knowledge. Mondalmi regretted this: 'They should have taught us these things, so we would know what to do. We can't find out now—they all gone without telling us'. One of her sons 'little Bunug' later went to Kormilda College, near Darwin, and he and a group of other Aboriginal students compiled *Djugurba: tales from the spirit time* (Canberra, 1974).

On the mission, Mondalmi was a capable and conscientious domestic helper, kindly and patient. She and her husband were of the dependable core-population who must have made the missionaries feel that their efforts were worth-while. Her brother Lazarus Lamilami became an ordained Methodist minister, but he saw this as essentially compatible with Maung religion. The mission was not only a refuge and a buffer: its policy was 'to keep what is best in the Aboriginal culture'. Nevertheless, it was part of the invading society.

Mondalmi was a keen observer and social commentator. From 1947 she tried thoughtfully and critically to teach the author about Maung life and culture, traditional and changing. The wide range that she covered included kinship-terms, relationships and behaviour, family life, myths and stories, relations between people and land, children's songs, hand-sign as well as verbal vocabularies, plant foods and medicines, and more complicated topics such as explanations of religious beliefs and ritual events, especially from women's perspective.

Basically resilient, cheerful and active, by 1964 Mondalmi, unwell, was disillusioned about relations between Aborigines and Europeans. But she kept her confident authority and assurance about her place in the world as a Maung woman. She died of cancer on 23 October 1969 at Goulburn Island and was buried there.

L. Lamilami, *Lamilami speaks, the cry went up* (Syd, 1974); C. Berndt, 'Mondalmi: One of the saltwater people' in I. White et al (eds), *Fighters and singers* (Syd, 1985).   CATHERINE BERNDT

MONDS, ALBERT WILLIAM (1864-1945), businessman and civic leader, was born on 22 November 1864 at Launceston, Tasmania, second son of eight children of Thomas Wilkes Monds [q.v.2] and his wife Angelina, née Hall. He was educated at Mr Baxter's school at Hagley, Horton College, Ross, and Mr Leech's school at Launceston. After brief commercial experience Albert joined the family milling business at Carrick. As a result of the illness of his elder brother he became the effective manager of the mill when his father retired to Launceston in 1888. Later, his younger brother Charles was admitted to partnership, the two surviving sons each holding equal shares with their father. On 23 February 1898 Albert married Fanny Robertson at Westbury.

Of Wesleyan and later Congregational conviction, the Monds family was always pious, reflecting their Huguenot origins. Albert took a leading part in Church affairs. Conservative, diligent and considerate, he was scrupulously honest, enjoying an honourable reputation with employees, customers, farmers who supplied grain and with all public bodies.

For most of his life Monds was active in civic affairs. A chairman and treasurer of the Carrick Road Trust and councillor of the Westbury municipality, he was an alderman of Launceston City Council in 1919-37, and exercised his financial acumen as mayor in 1920, 1921 and 1932. In the footsteps of his father, from 1925 he was a board-member (chairman, 1933-45) of the Launceston Bank for Savings, chairman of the Equitable Building Society, and after 1918 head of the merged competing family companies reconstituted as Monds & Affleck Pty Ltd. A skilled engineer, he supervised the installation of roller milling equipment at Carrick and later directed the construction of a new flour-mill at Launceston.

Monds was a member of the Tasmanian Turf and Longford Racing clubs and president of the National Agricultural and Pastoral Society. A committeeman of the Northern Fisheries Association, he was also president of the Launceston City Band and a member of the Launceston Public Library Board. His interest in young people never flagged: he was a board-member of Broadland House Church of England Girls' Grammar School, the Launceston Girls' Home and the Ministering Children's League. He enjoyed travel and visited England in 1898 and again in 1925 when he went to America as well. He was a keen fisherman and noted in his youth as an excellent shot.

Monds died on 10 February 1945 and was cremated. A son and a daughter survived him; his wife had died in 1939.

Cyclopedia of Tasmania, 2 (Hob, 1900); T. W. Monds, *Autobiography* (Launceston, 1907); *Examiner* (Launceston), 12 Feb 1945.

ALAN WARDEN

MONGER, FREDERICK CHARLES (1863-1919), speculator and politician, and ALEXANDER JOSEPH (1869-1947), pastoralist and businessman, were born on 25 January 1863 and 26 January 1869 at York, Western Australia, sons of John Henry Monger junior, merchant and grazier, and his wife Henrietta Joaquina, née Manning. Both were educated at Wesley College, Melbourne.

Frederick returned in 1879 to join his father's business. With Neil McNeil [q.v.5] and seven others, he launched the Wealth of Nations gold-prospecting syndicate in 1892. Relinquishing his partnership in J. H. Monger & Co. in 1895, with a loan of £3000 he speculated as an investor and agent. Associated with many mining ventures, he was joint owner of Wooramel station, Carnarvon, and the Excelsior Hotel at Cue. On 18 April 1895, in St George's Anglican Cathedral, Perth, he married Ethel Margaret Sherard; they had four daughters. Monger gambled on the turf (in 1897 his horse Snapshot won the Perth Cup), but he suffered substantial losses. He appeared in the Supreme Court in 1899 and, after protracted proceedings, was declared

bankrupt on 20 March 1903 with an indebtedness of £40 000.

A member of the York Municipal Council in 1892, Monger withdrew in October and took his father's former seat of York in the Legislative Assembly. Financially embarrassed, he resigned in 1899 but was immediately re-elected. He again resigned in 1903, to be returned after his successor R. G. Burges's death in October 1905. He was defeated in 1914. A Forrest [q.v.8] ministerialist, Monger later followed the Liberal League. He did not join his brother Alexander in the Country Party from 1913 because of its caucus-like pledge, but after the pledge requirement was relaxed he unsuccessfully contested York for the party in 1917.

He had gained valuable amenities for York. He boasted that he secured the State's first agricultural railway, from York to Green Hills, but it ran at a loss and thereafter Monger opposed state-funded railways. He supported the Kalgoorlie water scheme, opposed interests bringing tick-infested cattle from the Kimberleys to Fremantle, and fought the female franchise. On 26 September 1906, in response to Western Australia's losing the remainder of its tariff autonomy, the Legislative Assembly passed a resolution submitted by Monger that favoured secession. His bill to provide for a referendum on the subject was defeated in November.

Frederick Monger had been a member of the Perth Stock Exchange. A generous, gentlemanly person, he died of cancer on 15 November 1919 and was buried in Karrakatta cemetery.

Alexander also joined his father's business in York. As both father and son were volatile and 'impassionate', they fell out. Alexander took a camel team to Coolgardie. There, with £2000 borrowed from Dalgety [q.v.4] & Co. Ltd, he established a store and built two others at Southern Cross and Kalgoorlie. He floated Monger's West Australian Stores Ltd in London in 1897 with its head office at Fremantle; it was overcapitalized and went into voluntary liquidation in 1904. In partnership with (Sir) Ernest Lee Steere [q.v.], in 1900 he had bought the 30 000 acre (12 100 ha) Woongondy estate which, much improved, they resold to the State government. With Lee Steere and A. Watson, Monger owned Hamelin Pool station. From his father's estate he bought Daliak near York and, advised by G. L. Sutton [q.v.], developed it into a show property. Monger was a founder of the Fremantle Freezing & Meat Works and chairman of the Western Australian Meat Exports Co. On 29 August 1906 in Perth he married Florence McCracken with Methodist rites; they had a daughter and two sons. They lived from 1909 at Faversham House, the Monger home at York which he restored.

Conservative and a leader (known as 'the Czar'), Alexander supported primary producers' co-operation. As chairman of the York Association in 1912, he scathingly rebutted the Rural Workers' Union log, which aimed to bring them within the Commonwealth arbitration system. This led to the formation of the Farmers and Settlers' Association (Primary Producers' Association, 1920) of which Monger was president in 1912-24. A March 1913 resolution that a political party should be formed was based on his motion to the F.S.A.; through the association Monger powerfully influenced the emergent Country Party. Never a parliamentary aspirant, however, he rejected an association request to contest the York seat in 1917. He clashed with Sir John Forrest [q.v.8] about the implications of a third political party; he opposed Premier Scaddan's [q.v.] land distribution policy; and he disagreed with (Sir) James Mitchell [q.v.] over his government's agricultural settlement programme in uncertain rainfall areas. In 1915 Monger's conservative executive undermined the party's radical parliamentarian, James Gardiner [q.v.8]. Complaining in 1924 that the Country Party was keeping the Nationalists in office, Monger resigned as president of the Primary Producers' Association over a rift between its executive and parliamentary wings.

Typical of Perth's 'St George's Terrace farmers', Alexander Monger was a familiar figure, daily waving his handkerchief at the William Street intersection to ascertain the wind's direction. He was State chairman of the Mutual Life Association of Australasia, chairman of the Perpetual Executors Trustees & Agency, Sydney Atkinson Motors Ltd, Australian Outturns Ltd, Berry Barclay and Foy & Gibson [qq.v.8] Pty Ltd. From its inception in 1933 to 1944, he was chairman of Co-operative Bulk Handling, and as a founding trustee of the Wheat Pool of Western Australia, he understood international wheat marketing.

Monger was a foundation member of the Western Australian Bush Nursing Trust in 1920, a member of the Fairbridge [q.v.8] Farm School Committee, and on the Council of the Church of England Schools. He was appointed O.B.E. in 1941. Tall, dark and personable, the 'Beau Tibbs of Perth', he moved in exclusive circles. In 1941 he gave Faversham House to the Australian Red Cross Society for use as a convalescent hospital in World War II. Monger died in Perth on 3 November 1947 and was cremated. His estate was sworn for probate at £22 702.

Truthful Thomas, *Through the spy-glass* (Perth, 1905); F. R. Mercer, *On farmers' service* (Perth, 1955); R. Pervan and C. Sharman, *Essays on Western Australian politics* (Perth, 1979); C. T.

Stannage (ed), *A new history of Western Australia* (Perth, 1981); *PD* (WA), 1906, p 1871, 2271, 2829; *Univ Studies in History*, 3, no 2, Oct 1958; *Kalgoorlie Miner*, 9 Nov 1904; *West Australian*, 24 Feb, 6 May 1914, 4 Nov 1947; oral history transcript from Mrs A. J. Monger, 1975 (Battye Lib).

WENDY BIRMAN

MONK, CYRIL FARNSWORTH (1882-1970), violinist, was born on 9 March 1882 at Surry Hills, Sydney, son of James Monk, grocer from England, and his native-born wife Rosa Agnes, née Bullen. His mother began teaching him the piano when he was 4 and he was later sent to Samuel Chudleigh for the violin. He made frequent public appearances until he became a pupil of Josef Kretschmann and of Alfred Hill [q.v.9] who taught him theory and composition. In 1894 he won a gold medal at the Sydney Eisteddfod. He was a member of the orchestra conducted by Roberto Hazon [q.v.9] for J. C. Williamson's [q.v.6] Italian opera season in 1901-02 and was first violin with the Sydney Philharmonic Society in 1901-03.

Financially assisted by a benefit concert, in September 1904 Monk went to London to study with Guido Papini at the College of Violinists, London, and also visited France and Germany. In 1906 he was awarded the college's diploma and gold medal. After his return from London in 1906 he was engaged as a soloist by Hill for the New Zealand International Exhibition's orchestral concerts at Christchurch and next year he toured New Zealand with the orchestra.

Settling in Sydney, Monk began teaching and in 1908 presented his first students' recital. He formed the Austral String Quartet (which included Hill) in 1910 and introduced many new works by such composers as Ravel, Debussy, Milhaud, Englishmen Herbert Howells and York Bowen and the Australian Arthur Benjamin [q.v.7]. On 22 December 1913 at St Philip's Church, Sydney, he married ISABEL VARNEY DESMOND PETERSON (1892-1967), composer and pianist; they lived at Mosman, where he enjoyed gardening and chess and she collected Australian first editions and antique furniture.

When the New South Wales State Conservatorium of Music was founded in 1916, Monk was appointed to its staff. He was leader of its orchestra under three directors, Verbrugghen, Arundel Orchard [qq.v.] and Edgar Bainton [q.v.7], and conservatorium examiner for the Australian Music Examinations Board; he composed various educational pieces. In addition, in 1919-23 he was principal violinist in the New South Wales State Orchestra. Although the Austral String Quartet had been disbanded when Verbrugghen formed the Conservatorium Quartet, Monk continued to give annual recitals and to play new works including Eugene Goossens's *Violin sonata* in 1923. At his last public recital on 5 April 1927 he was accompanied by Frank Hutchens [q.v.9] and displayed 'an admirable technique'.

Thereafter Monk concentrated on teaching and occasionally gave lecturette recitals when he would play part of a work as illustration. In 1932 he stressed the need for a professional orchestra. He was a member of the first Federal Council of Music Teachers and president of the Musical Association of New South Wales. He retired from the conservatorium in 1955. Survived by his son and daughter, he died in Royal North Shore Hospital on 7 March 1970 and was cremated.

His wife, known professionally as Varney Desmond, was born on 18 January 1892 at Bacchus Marsh, Victoria, daughter of Ernest John Peterson and his wife Miriam Jane, née Roberts. She wrote many songs and in 1923 won the *Sunday Times* song competition; she set to music lyrics by A. L. Gordon, H. Kendall [qq.v.4,5] and H. Lawson [q.v.]. Her elaborate musical romance, *Collitt's Inn*, involving redcoats, bushrangers and Aborigines, was staged by Frank Thring [q.v.] and ran for seven months in Melbourne in 1933; the cast included George Wallace and Gladys Moncrieff [qq.v.]. A Sydney season followed. Another operetta, *The cedar tree* (1934), was staged in Sydney and Melbourne. In 1966 she won the Henry Lawson Festival award at Grenfell for song-writing. She died on 7 February 1967.

SMH, 2, 6 Apr 1927, 6 Nov 1947, 9 Feb 1967, 11 Mar 1970; C. Monk, newspaper cuttings (held by Mrs P. Evans, Mosman, Syd).

HELEN BAINTON

MONTEFIORE, DOROTHY FRANCES (1851-1933), women's suffragist and socialist, was born on 20 December 1851 and baptised on 18 January 1852 at St Nicholas' Church, Tooting Graveney, London, eighth of thirteen children of Francis Fuller, surveyor and railway entrepreneur, and his wife Mary Ann, née Drew. Brought up at Kenley Manor in Surrey, Dora was educated by governesses and tutors and at Mrs Creswell's school at Brighton. She later described herself as a dark-haired tomboy, devoted to her father. In 1874 she came to Sydney to assist the delicate wife of her eldest brother. After returning temporarily to England, she married a Jewish merchant George Barrow, son of Joseph Barrow Montefiore [q.v.2], on 1 February 1881 at St Mark's Anglican Church,

Darling Point. They lived at Paddington where her daughter was born in 1883 and son in 1887. Her husband died at sea on 17 July 1889. Upon learning that as the widow she had no automatic right to guardianship of her children, she became an advocate of women's rights. The first meeting of the Womanhood Suffrage League of New South Wales was held at her home on 29 March 1891.

Dora Montefiore left Australia in 1892 and lived in Paris for some years, before returning to England. In 1898 she published a volume of verse, *Singings through the dark*. An executive-member of the London-based National Union of Women's Suffrage Societies led by (Dame) Millicent Fawcett, she soon joined the Women's Social and Political Union recently formed by Emmeline and Christabel Pankhurst. Of medium height with grey eyes and aquiline nose, she spoke 'up and down the country' and gave of her means. In May 1906 she received much publicity when she refused to pay taxes without representation and barricaded her Hammersmith home; after a six weeks siege her furniture was sold by distraint. In October, with Adela Pankhurst [q.v.] and other suffragettes, she was arrested and imprisoned for rowdily demanding votes for women in the lobby of the House of Commons. She successively joined Charlotte Despard and other socialists in the Women's Freedom League, the executive of the Social Democratic Federation and the British Socialist Party, and was a delegate to many international women's and socialist conferences.

In 1910 Mrs Montefiore visited her son Gilbert, an engineer who had settled in Sydney. Owing to the illness of Henry Holland [q.v.9], in 1911 she edited his newspaper, the *International Socialist Review of Australasia*. In her editorials she castigated the introduction of compulsory military training for school-age boys, thereby causing great public controversy. Her principles, however, did not prevent social contact with the Holmans [qq.v.9].

Mrs Montefiore returned to England in 1912. Next year she devised a scheme to send some 300 starving children to England pending the settlement of strikes in Dublin. At the instigation of the Catholic clergy in Dublin, she was arrested and charged with kidnapping; although the charges were dropped, considerable press discussion culminated in an anti-Semitic attack upon her by G. K. Chesterton.

World War I was a time of great disillusionment for Montefiore: her international socialist friends were harried and Gilbert, while serving with the Australian Imperial Force, was severely gassed. Somewhat doleful, she presided over the dinner at the Lyceum Club to celebrate the enfranchisement of women over thirty. In 1920 she was elected to the provisional council of the United Communist Party of Great Britain.

Gilbert died in 1921, but the Australian government refused to allow Mrs Montefiore to visit Australia to see his grave and her grandchildren until Holman intervened, pleading her age and poor health; she had agreed in writing not to carry on communist propaganda. Police spying disclosed that she defied the restrictions and befriended Christian Jollie Smith [q.v.]. She represented the Communist Party of Australia in Moscow in 1924.

Back in England, Dora Montefiore published her autobiography, *From a Victorian to a modern*, in 1927. She died at Hastings on 21 December 1933 and was cremated. Her daughter survived her.

R. Fulford, *Votes for women* (Lond, 1957); J. Marcus (ed), *The young Rebecca* (Lond, 1982); *The Times*, 25 May, 24 Oct 1906, 22-24 Oct 1913, 1 Jan 1934; *Daily Herald* (Lond), 16, 20, 22-24 Oct 1913; Womanhood Suffrage League of NSW, Minutes, Rose Scott papers *and* correspondence (ML); Prime Minister's Dept, Suspended and undesirable persons 1916-25, CRS A 3932/SC 292/pt 2 (AAO).   JUDITH ALLEN

MONTFORD, PAUL RAPHAEL (1868-1938), sculptor, was born on 1 November 1868 at Kentish Town, London, son of Horace Montford, sculptor, and his wife Sarah Elizabeth, née Lewis. Horace Montford was curator of schools at the Royal Academy of Art; Paul learned modelling in his father's studio and drawing at the Lambeth School of Art. He entered the Royal Academy of Arts' schools in 1887 on scholarships and after an outstanding studentship travelled to Italy, Spain and France on another scholarship won in 1891, along with the academy's gold medal.

Montford regularly exhibited portrait-busts at the Royal Academy but specialized in the sculpture of architectural decoration. He completed the façades of Battersea Town Hall (1892) and Polytechnic, reliefs for the Charles Street bridge, Westminster, and for the Cardiff City Hall and Law Courts, bronze groups for Kelvin bridge, Glasgow (1914), and a war memorial at Croydon. His memorial of Sir Henry Campbell-Bannerman is in Westminster Abbey. Montford taught sculpture at the School of Art, Chelsea, in 1898-1903, and was modelling master at the London Polytechnic for five years. On 11 September 1912 he married Marian Alice Dibdin, portrait painter.

Commissions became scarce, however, after World War I and at 53 the energetic and enthusiastic Montford came to Australia, motivated by his belief that its light was conducive to great monumental sculpture. But he found little prospect of earning a living as a sculptor. He taught at the Gordon Institute of Technology, Geelong, Victoria, and in July 1924 exhibited at the Geelong Art Gallery. The critic J. S. MacDonald [q.v.] suggested the establishment of a sculpture school at the National Gallery of Victoria under Montford's direction. It failed to eventuate but he became influential through his lectures at the Victorian Artists' Society of which he was president in 1930-31. Montford's *avant-garde* opinions concerning the social and environmental role of sculpture in the modern city were regularly aired, with his usual zeal. His unconventional, flamboyant and theatrical personality, his sculptural practices, Bohemian life-style and his Toorak studio were continuously featured in the Melbourne press.

In 1927 Montford won the commission for the exterior sculptural groups at Melbourne's Shrine of Remembrance. His work for the project was disparaged in *Stead's Review* and *Smith's Weekly* but he was restricted from the outset by the architectural and thematic requirements. Accusations that he habitually looked to the classical world for inspiration are refuted by his exhaustive efforts to present other Australian subjects with precise contemporary detail and historical authenticity. His seated statue of Adam Lindsay Gordon [q.v.4] in Spring Street Gardens, Melbourne, condemned in the Australian press, won the gold medal of the Royal Society of British Sculptors (1934). His nearly seventy Australian works include statues of John Wesley (Wesley Church, Melbourne), George Higinbotham [q.v.4] near the Treasury, and the memorials to Carlo Catani [q.v.7] (St Kilda), Benjamin Chaffey [q.v.7] (Mildura), Sir Ross Smith [q.v.] (Adelaide), and 'Pioneer Women' (Sydney).

Montford died on 15 January 1938 of leukaemia, at Richmond. His ashes were scattered in the woods at Leatherhead, Surrey, England. His wife, two daughters and son returned to England and were granted a civil list pension in 1939 for Montford's services to sculpture.

M. Spielmann, *British sculpture and sculptors of today* (Lond, 1901); A. Pratt, *The national war memorial of Victoria* (Melb, 1934); G. Sturgeon, *The development of Australian sculpture 1788-1975* (Lond, 1978); K. W. Scarlett, *Australian sculptors* (Melb, 1980); S. Beattie, *The new sculpture* (New Haven, Connecticut, 1983); *Architects' J*, 56, 1922; *Art in Aust*, no 7, Mar 1924; *Stead's Review*, 2, Dec 1929; *Argus*, 21 Apr 1923; *Herald* (Melb), 29 July 1924, 22 May 1928, 15 Aug 1931, 6 Aug 1936; *Evening Sun*, 25 Apr 1925; *Table Talk*, 25 Sept 1930; *Smith's Weekly* (Syd), 27 Dec 1930; *Age*, 1 Aug 1931; *Sun-News Pictorial*, 17 Jan 1938.   JENNY ZIMMER

MONTGOMERY, CHRISTINA SMITH (1870-1965), headmistress, was born on 21 March 1870 at Kelso, Scotland, eldest child of William Montgomery, draper's assistant, and his wife Janet, née Smith. She attended Kelso Grammar School where she acquired a lifelong love of classical studies. After the family arrived in Melbourne in 1884, she and her younger sister Margaret (d. 1917) attended Cambridge Street State School, Collingwood, and in September 1886 were appointed pupilteachers there. In 1891 they both enrolled and became prizewinners at the new Melbourne Teachers' College. Matriculating in 1892, Christina attended the University of Melbourne (B.A., 1897; M.A., 1900), becoming one of the first women graduates employed in the State Department of Education.

Throughout, she taught full time at Ballarat and Drouin but her studies did not diminish her glowing inspectors' reports, which referred to her 'care and energy'. The first director of education, Frank Tate [q.v.], noted that as a very young, 'undersized' junior teacher, by her mere presence she quelled classes that defeated men over six feet (183 cm) tall. Christina waited for promotion until she was 29, her progress impeded by her studies and the further handicaps imposed on women in the depression. In 1898 she took leave to become head of evening classes at Perth Central Girls' School, which confirmed her preference for teaching older students. She was promoted on returning in 1899.

When Melbourne Continuation School opened in 1905, Christina Montgomery was appointed Latin teacher. In 1923 she became headmistress, under the principal, Joseph Hocking; but in 1927, after the school had been condemned on health grounds, the boys moved to the new Melbourne High School at Forest Hill, while the girls remained in the renamed Melbourne Girls' High School. From this inauspicious beginning Miss Montgomery established the first girls' academic high school, eventually renamed MacRobertson Girls' High School.

Unashamedly flaunting her classical prowess, she named the houses after Greek nymphs, adopted 'Potens Sui' as the motto, and launched a students' paper, Pallas. Monty's raison d'être was to rival both the brother school and independent schools academically. Her girls were not to suffer the disabilities she had overcome. Moreover, World War I had convinced her that any hope for a sane future lay in women's hands. Her speech nights resounded with the glories of her girls' achievements. She established the school's enduring scholarly reputation, successfully resisting attempts to make its curriculum more 'domestic' and even to close it down. Her greatest triumph came when in 1931 it was moved from a 'penitentiary'-like slum to Government House. Determined that her girls would be at home with high culture and social graces, Monty continued an established weekly 'social hour'.

She had won parents' militant loyalty in the political battle to save the school in 1930. Between 1927 and 1932, the year of her retirement, enrolments rose from 340 to 805, despite the Depression and the £6 per term fees, but the demands imposed by the school's vulnerability drained her considerable energies. She felt she dare not err. Her feminism was characterized by a touchily nervous jealousy of the girls' reputation. Being embattled made her seemingly aloof, formidable and humourless to some pupils and teachers, yet she had a dry wit. Her imperious dignity counterbalanced her minuteness and possibly a fieriness that matched her flaming auburn hair. By her dowdiness and undemonstrative reserve this female dominie concealed a warmth and a suppressed sentimentality that escaped occasionally when she talked of travel or her mother, 'to whom I owe all'. Monty approved of the 'new education'; and while her teaching style was thorough and didactic, she admired good teachers who could unbend. But in battling for women's equality she was uncompromisingly meritocratic.

Like a shrewd champion sportswoman, Christina Montgomery gave up at her peak. School had been her whole world; but more than a third of her life was to be spent in retirement, during which she wrote a travel book, Recaptured in tranquillity, and a detailed textual study, Shakespearean afterglow (1942). The Montgomery family had prospered as Fitzroy retailers; Christina died, at Brighton on 27 August 1965, considerably more prosperous than she was born. She was buried in Melbourne general cemetery.

G. Dow and L. Scholes, 'Christina Montgomery', in R. J. W. Selleck and M. Sullivan (eds), Not so eminent Victorians (Melb, 1984); Board of inquiry regarding the administration of the Education Department 1931: transcript of evidence (typescript, faculty of education, Univ Melb); Pallas, 1927-32; MacRobertson Girls' High School Archives; file 10249 (PRO, Vic); information from Miss R. Gainfort, Camberwell, Melb.

GWYNETH DOW

MONTGOMERY, SIR HENRY HUTCHINSON (1847-1932), bishop, was born on 3 September or 3 October 1847 at Cawnpore, India, eldest son of (Sir) Robert Montgomery, magistrate and collector and later lieut-governor of the Punjab, and his wife Ellen Jane, née Lambert. Montgomery was educated at Harrow, where he excelled at sport, and at Cambridge (B.A., 1870; M.A., 1873; D.D.,

1889) where, as an athletic Trinity College undergraduate, he was reputed to have achieved the formidable leap up the hall steps. Trained for the ministry by Charles Vaughan, his first headmaster at Harrow, he was made deacon at Chichester in 1871 and ordained priest in 1872.

Montgomery's clerical advancement was rapid. Appointed curate of Hurstpierpoint, Sussex, in 1871, he moved to Christ Church, Southwark, in 1874, St Margaret's, Westminster, in 1876 and, as vicar, to St Mark's, Kennington, in 1879. In 1889 he was chosen as fourth bishop of Tasmania.

On 28 July 1881 at Westminster Abbey, Montgomery had married Maud, the 16-year-old daughter of Frederic William Farrar, canon of Westminster and formerly Montgomery's housemaster at Harrow. Farrar was a noted 'Broad Churchman' and Montgomery's own theological position was described as 'much the same . . . only less so'. From Vaughan he had imbibed a deep regard for Scripture and Church, and from A. P. Stanley, dean of Westminster, to whom he had been private secretary, he derived a belief in the importance of a national Church. The practicalities of domestic life he left to his determined young wife who organized their nine children (according to the most famous of them, Bernard Law, later Viscount Montgomery of Alamein) along military lines.

'A man must be a leader in the Colonies', Montgomery later wrote of the role of bishop. 'The quiet, harmless man will fail. It is all push . . . all *pioneer work*, even in the cities'. Immediately on arrival in Tasmania he proceeded with the completion of the cathedral as a diocesan focus, notwithstanding objections from country parishes. But he also journeyed to remote west-coast mining settlements and showed deep concern for Bass Strait Aborigines. In Hobart and Launceston he encouraged pastoral work among the disadvantaged: he attempted to develop the ministry to the Chinese—somewhat hampered by the missioner Yung Choy's lack of English—and created a home and hospital for prostitutes and unmarried mothers.

Montgomery believed that the Church had to witness to a high moral standard in a particularly corrupt society. He thus opposed George Adams [q.v.3], gambling and drinking, although not himself a total abstainer. He argued for Church instruction in schools, the revival of the Sunday School movement and the strengthening of church schools.

Above all he saw himself as a missionary bishop. He wrote to the archbishop of Canterbury in 1901: 'It is because the work is all Missionary here that I love it so. Great questions such as Education, Temperance, Social problems between classes, come to me as *duties*. Missionary questions come to me as

joys'. His vision outdistanced Tasmania. He dreamt of an Anglican Church in Australia with an effective general synod, a national primate and an indigenous clergy. Such a Church, he believed, could lead to the conversion of the Pacific. In 1892 he lobbied for the creation of the diocese of New Guinea and after visiting the diocese of Melanesia wrote a significant report on missionary strategy, *The light of Melanesia* (1896). He was also locally bedevilled by narrow-minded Evangelical criticism concerning ritualism, confession and prayers for the dead.

During Montgomery's Tasmanian episcopate Church membership grew from nearly 81 000 to nearly 88 000 and the number of buildings from 75 to 125. Montgomery organized the first Tasmanian Church Congress (1894) and celebrations for the jubilee of the Australian Board of Missions (1900). But clearly he found the challenge of Tasmania too small. In June 1901 he accepted the episcopal secretaryship of the Society for the Propagation of the Gospel and took up the post next January.

A prebendary of St Paul's, London, from 1902, Montgomery was Ramsden preacher that year and in 1918. In 1905 he was appointed a prelate of the Order of St Michael and St George and in 1908 received honorary degrees from the universities of Oxford and Durham. He retired in 1919 and from 1921 lived on the family estate, New Park, Moville, Northern Ireland. He was appointed K.C.M.G. in 1928.

Montgomery published many papers and books ranging from impassioned pleas for the protection of mutton-birds to biographies of eminent ecclesiastics, reflections on mission work, visions of the Church, old age and personal joy. He died at New Park on 25 November 1932, survived by his wife, five sons and two daughters.

Viscount Montgomery of Alamein, *Memoirs* (Lond, 1958); *The Times*, 28 Nov 1932; P. R. Hart, The Church of England in Tasmania under Bishop Montgomery, 1889-1901 (M.A. thesis, Univ Tas, 1965); Letter-books (Diocesan Registry, Hob).

GEOFFREY STEPHENS

MONTGOMERY, SYDNEY HAMILTON ROWAN (1869-1916), psychiatrist, was born on 25 October 1869 in Belfast, Ireland, second son of Rev. Robert Montgomery and his wife Margaret, née Wylie. He attended the Royal Belfast Academical Institution in 1879-88 and graduated M.B., Ch.B. from the Royal University of Ireland in 1894. After two years as ship's surgeon in the *City of*

Agra, sailing to Indian and South American ports, he entered general practice at Liscard, Cheshire, England.

Montgomery was interested in mental disorders and in 1897 became an assistant at the Nottingham City Asylum for the Insane; there he met a Mr Hine, who had designed several asylums and from whom he learned the principles of asylum construction. On 18 July 1900 Montgomery married Mabel Callaghan at New Brighton, Cheshire; they had six children. Next year he went as superintending medical officer of asylums to Western Australia, arriving at Fremantle on 20 June. He was responsible for the care and treatment of 231 patients in the Fremantle Hospital for the Insane and 45 at Whitby Falls (Mundijong); the latter was a farm used as overflow accommodation for the crowded Fremantle asylum.

Shortly after Montgomery's arrival he visited the eastern States with the principal architect of the Public Works Department J. H. Grainger (father of Percy [q.v.9]) to inspect New South Wales and Victorian asylums before designing a new institution to replace the outdated Fremantle asylum. He also reviewed the lunacy Acts in the other States and in New Zealand. In 1901 he chaired a committee formed to select a site for the new asylum, and in early 1903 chose 394 acres (159 ha) at Claremont, near Perth. Temporary buildings were set up and on 18 August twenty 'quiet and chronic' patients were moved there from Whitby Falls. Transfer of patients from Fremantle soon began, but it was 1909 before all patients had been moved and the old asylum closed. At this time Montgomery was drafting a new Lunacy Act, which became law on 1 January 1904 and regulated the treatment of the insane in Western Australia for the next sixty years. He also drafted the Inebriates Act of 1912, which enabled alcoholics to be treated as patients in mental hospitals and which operated until 1963. In 1914 Whitby Falls was converted into a home for inebriates where farm work and other forms of rehabilitation were carried out.

In 1905, with Dr W. P. Birmingham, Montgomery had established a three-year training course for mental nurses, with the award of a certificate of competency. A 'mental ward', the first of its kind in Australia, was set up at the Perth Public Hospital in 1908 so that the 'suspected insane' could enter the general hospital and be treated without the stigma of being incarcerated in an asylum. Montgomery presented a paper on the functioning of this ward to the local branch of the British Medical Association in 1909. That year he became president of the branch, and later read a paper on 'The evolution of the treatment and care of the insane'; he also published an article, 'Syphilis as a cause of insanity', in the *Australasian Medical Gazette*.

In 1915 Montgomery influenced amendments to the Lunacy Act that increased the number of the statutory board of visitors to the mental institutions from two to three, and provided for the appointment of a woman to the board. In addition to his work as inspector general and medical officer for the insane (his title since 1903) and his participation in the British Medical Association, Montgomery played golf, tennis, Rugby, lacrosse and billiards; he was also a Freemason and a member of the Weld Club. He helped to organize and control the State's pure milk supply, and was part-owner of a wheat-farm in the south-west.

Montgomery died from heart disease on 1 March 1916, and was buried in the Anglican section of Karrakatta cemetery. His wife and five young children survived him. A tenacious, driving, far-sighted man, he was possibly one of the State's greatest public servants. He fought apathy and prejudice to help those who had no voice of their own; many of his ideas are as relevant now as they were eighty years ago.

J. S. Battye (ed), *Cyclopedia of Western Australia*, 1 (Adel, 1912); A. S. Ellis, *Eloquent testimony* (Nedlands, 1984); *Daily News* (Perth), 25 Aug 1916; *West Australian*, 2 Mar 1916; *A'sian Medical Gazette*, 28 (1909), p 422; *RWAHSJ*, 7 (1975), pt 7, p 39.   A. S. ELLIS

MOORE, ANNIE MAY (1881-1931) and MINNIE LOUISE (1882-1957), photographers, were born on 4 January 1881 and on 6 October 1882 at Wainui, New Zealand, eldest and second daughters of English-born Robert Walter Moore, sawyer and farmer, and his wife Sarah Jane, née Hellyer, a New Zealander. May studied at the Elam School of Art and Design, Auckland, and in 1906-07 sold pencil and ink sketches at the New Zealand International Exhibition at Christchurch. Moving to Wellington, she painted oil portraits in a rented studio in Willis Street.

Mina, as Minnie was known, was a schoolteacher and had no artistic training. She became interested in photography while developing pictures she took with a borrowed camera on a visit to Australia in 1907. On her return to Wellington the sisters bought the Willis Street studio, and before the old staff left May learned camera work, and Mina printing. They quickly developed a distinctive style of close-up-head studio portraiture, the only light coming from an open window to shine on one side of the face. They pioneered sepia tonings, bromide paper and limp mounting-boards. Avoiding the prevalent 'stodgy backgrounds and stiff accessories', they chose a simple hessian or cloth back-drop. Avid theatre-goers, they specialized in costume studies of visiting companies. Both believed that in good portrait photography it was essential to put the sitter at ease and to gain 'some insight into his character'. In 1909 the Sydney-based *Australasian Photo Review* reproduced the first of many May Moore portraits.

In 1910, when May was visiting Sydney, friends arranged a temporary studio for her in the *Bulletin* building, and Livingston Hopkins [q.v.4], David Low and the Lindsays [qq.v.] were among her first sitters. In 1911 she opened a studio in George Street, and later moved to King Street.

Mina managed the Wellington studio and began operating camera until she joined May in Sydney in 1911. In 1913 the sisters opened a studio in J. and N. Tait's [qq.v.] auditorium in Collins Street, Melbourne, for Mina to manage. She concentrated on theatrical studies, including the entire Quinlan Grand Opera Company, and she soon had a large clientele. She worked with a freelance woman journalist for a time, combining interview and portrait sessions.

The sisters' photographs of actors, musicians, writers and artists were published in such magazines as the *Home, Lone Hand* and *Triad*; they were often co-signed, although for all but two years they ran separate studios in different cities. In World War I they turned their attention to taking portraits of uniformed servicemen; they prospered and became household names. At St Philip's Church, Sydney, May married a dentist Henry Hammon Wilkes on 13 July 1915. He gave up his practice to help in her studio. Mina married William Alexander Tainsh, company secretary and poet, on 20 December 1916 in Melbourne.

May was a handsome, assured woman, humorous and direct. Six feet (183 cm) tall, she had a strong stride and wore loose, flowing dresses. She was 'determined, sink or swim', to put her ideas into practice. She employed only women, except in the darkroom, and encouraged others to enter the profession. Illness forced her to retire about 1928, but she continued to paint landscapes. She was a member of the Society of Women Painters, Sydney, the Professional Photographers' Association of Australia, the Musical Association of New South Wales and the Lyceum Club, and reputedly became a Christian Scientist. She was survived by her husband—they had no children—when she died of cancer at her Pittwater home on 10 June 1931; she was buried in the Anglican section of Manly cemetery. Six months later the Lyceum Club held a memorial exhibition of her portraits.

Mina retired from business after the birth of her first child in 1918, although she was tempted to return after photographing for, and directing, a presentation book for the Shell Co. of Australia Ltd in 1927. She found, however, that 'family calls' were too strong. Except for 1918-22 in Sydney, they lived in or near Melbourne. Mina's friends included the artists Clara Southern, Jessie Traill [qq.v.] and Jo Sweatman. She died at Croydon on 30 January 1957 and was cremated. Her husband, son and two daughters survived her.

J. Cato, *The story of the camera in Australia* (Melb, 1955); B. Hall et al, *Aust women photographers, 1890-1950* exhibition cat (Melb, 1981); *Harrington's Photographic J*, 22 Oct 1910, 22 Feb 1911; *A'sian Photo-Review*, 22 June 1911; *Austral Briton*, 5, 12 Feb 1916; *SMH*, 17 Dec 1930, 17 June 1931; *Aust Worker*, 24 June 1931.

BARBARA HALL

MOORE, ARTHUR EDWARD (1876-1963), farmer and premier, was born on 9 February 1876 at Napier, New Zealand, son of Edward Moore, English banker, and his New Zealand-born wife Emma Bayley, née Newman. Eldest of three children, he attended Akaroa State School and, in 1887-92, Melbourne Church of England Grammar School when his father was general manager of the Union Bank of Australia Ltd, Melbourne. Failing to matriculate, he sought farming experience and worked in a vineyard while his family settled in London. His father visited Melbourne in 1897 and assisted him to purchase Waipawa, a 1000-acre (405 ha) wheat and dairy property at Brymaroo near Jondaryan on Queensland's Darling Downs. On 12 April 1899, in St James' Church, Toowoomba, Arthur married Mary Eva ('Nellie') Warner, daughter of a local Anglican clergyman.

Moore's farming was not initially prosperous, but his financial position gradually improved as hard work transformed the property. He also made a commercial success of two cheese factories. At first the demands of the farm left little time for other activities, but in 1905 he was elected to the Rosalie Shire Council and was its chairman in 1911-29. In 1913 he was elected to the executive of the Local Authorities' Association of Queensland and served several terms as vice-president and president in the 1920s.

Moore entered State parliament in 1915 when, as a Farmers' Union candidate, he defeated the incumbent Liberal in the assembly seat of Aubigny, which he was to hold until his retirement. His election coincided with the defeat of the Denham [q.v.8] Liberal government and the commencement of fourteen years of Labor rule. Labor's dominance was facilitated by the chronic divisions within and among the conservative parties. Leaders changed with alarming regularity, explaining Moore's rise to the position of deputy Opposition leader in 1920. He welcomed the formation in 1925 of the Country and Progressive National Party, an amalgam of National and Country Party groups. Because of personal and factional rivalries, the C.P.N.P.'s birth was traumatic and its future unassured; which is perhaps why the able, consensual, but somewhat retiring Moore gained preferment as leader that year.

Some power-brokers within the C.P.N.P. saw Moore as a conciliatory, stop-gap leader to be replaced later by someone more dynamic. His retention of the leadership can be explained by the new party's good showing at the 1926 State election and by his handling of the divisive A.C. Elphinstone [q.v.8]. Aided by economic stagnation, the disturbed industrial situation and by internal strife within the Labor Party, Moore campaigned skilfully and debated forcefully during the 1929 campaign and in May led his party to victory over William McCormack's [q.v.] Labor government—Moore's greatest political achievement.

He assumed the premiership with the enthusiasm and good will of primary industry and commercial groups throughout the State. Yet, because of the great Depression, his government lay in ruins only three years later. Many of the policies he adopted, in a vain attempt to ameliorate the economic collapse, both inflamed his traditional opponents and alienated his supporters. He managed to unite the labour movement against him by alterations to the conciliation and arbitration system, by his enthusiastic support for the deflationary Premiers' Plan and by his pursuit of E. G. Theodore [q.v.] over the Mungana scandal. On the other hand, increases in personal income tax to fund Queensland unemployment relief measures and his inability to re-establish the Legislative Council lost him support among business and commercial interests. Moore also had a cabinet which was inexperienced and, with one or two exceptions, inept. Despite a favourable electoral redistribution in 1931, his government was defeated in June 1932 by a revived Labor Party led by William Forgan Smith [q.v.].

Moore again became Opposition leader, but at the 1935 election the Labor Party won such an overwhelming victory that the C.P.N.P. disintegrated. The Country Party, which emerged as a separate entity in March 1936, agreed to embrace the country C.P.N.P. parliamentarians provided Moore was replaced as leader. Rather than provoke division Moore stood aside and was replaced in 1937 by E. B. Maher. He remained on the

Opposition front-bench until he retired from parliament on 28 March 1941.

Moore was active in a wide range of business and community organizations. He served on the boards of the Australian Mutual Provident Society (1938-51) and Queensland Trustees Ltd (1937-49). He maintained long associations with the Red Cross Society, the Queensland Country Women's Association (as returning officer) and the Queensland Bush Nursing Assocation. In 1958 he was appointed C.M.G. Moore was a devout Anglican benefactor, who prayed daily and who was actively involved in Church affairs from 1913 until his death. He was a tall, handsome man possessed of a gentle sense of humour which he often directed against himself. He was well liked by colleagues on both sides of politics and all attest to his scrupulous honesty.

After his period as premier he did not return to the farm but in 1935 purchased Brisbane's second-oldest residence, Bulimba House (built 1849). He lived there and at his Caloundra seaside cottage until his death. Moore became a wealthy man through inheritance and wise investments. He and his wife nevertheless continued to lead quiet, unpretentious lives. His hobbies were the simple ones of gardening, fishing and reading.

Arthur Moore died in St Martin's Hospital, Brisbane, on 7 January 1963. His wife and two of their three sons survived him. He was cremated after a State funeral at St John's Anglican Cathedral. He left an estate valued for probate at £154 778.

C. A. Bernays, *Queensland—our seventh political decade, 1920-1930* (Syd, 1931); A. J. Campbell, *Memoirs of the Country Party in Queensland 1920-1974* (Brisb, 1975); B. J. Costar, 'Arthur Edward Moore: odd man in', in D. J. Murphy and R. B. Joyce (eds), *Queensland political portraits—1859-1952* (Brisb, 1978); *PD*(Qld), 1963, p 26; *Elector*, 7, no 2, 15 Apr 1933; *Aust Country Party Mthly J*, 3, no 29, June 1936; *Courier Mail*, 8 Jan 1963; B. J. Costar, Labor, politics and unemployment: Queensland during the great Depression (Ph. D. thesis, Univ Qld, 1981); family information.   B. J. COSTAR

MOORE, CAROLINE ELLEN (1882-1956), actress, was born on 31 July 1882 at Geelong, Victoria, third of nine children of Robert William Moore, Newfoundland-born labourer, and his Victorian wife Mary, née Wyatt. Educated locally, she regularly attended Sunday school and occasionally appeared in amateur theatricals. At 14 Carrie was taken by an uncle to sing for J. C. Williamson [q.v.6]; she made her first professional appearance in December 1896 in Williamson's pantomime, *Djin-Djin*.

After returning briefly to school Carrie played in several pantomimes. While understudying the role of Suzette in *The French maid,* she stood in for Ada Willoughby in Sydney in October 1897 and for Ada Reeve in Melbourne in March next year, when she 'sang and danced with vivacity and high spirits'. In November 1899 in Sydney she sang Maid Marian in Koven's opera *Robin Hood*—and was 'a prima donna at seventeen'. She found *Iolanthe* 'one of the loveliest of Gilbert and Sullivan operas and [Phyllis] one of the loveliest parts'. She remained four years with Williamson's Royal Comic Opera Company, playing many leading roles: her favourite was Maid Marian.

In 1901 Carrie Moore became engaged to Ernest Tyson, great-nephew of James Tyson [q.v.6], and wore his presents of diamond star and swallow on stage in *Florodora*. When he failed to attend the wedding she sued him for breach of promise and £5000 damages, thereby creating a sensation. The case was settled out of court.

In July 1903 Carrie Moore sailed for England to a definite engagement with the comedian George Edwardes and immediately went on tour in *San Toy*. She soon made her London début as Ellen in *The girl from Kay's* at the Apollo Theatre. Next year she joined Robert Courtneidge to play the principal boy in *Aladdin* at Liverpool. Carrie became 'a much-paragraphed and much-photographed actress of the best London theatres' and played the principal boy in Christmas pantomimes at Liverpool or Birmingham, between appearances in London in *The dairy-maids* (1906) and as Honour in *Tom Jones* (1907); she thoroughly enjoyed touring with *Tom Jones* as she motored through England.

In May 1908 Carrie Moore was lured back to Australia by Williamson to create the role of Sonia in *The merry widow* and once again captivated audiences and critics. Called by some 'the Vital Spark', she was small in stature, with large sparkling, deep brown eyes. 'Sartor' described 'her keen eager face, framed in its dark hair, with those eyes catching the light, responding to every emotion her part bespeaks, her light, sinuous form bending and swaying to the music'. On 30 September at the Whitefield Congregational Church, Sydney, Carrie Moore married Percy Plantagenet Bigwood, an English racehorse-owner and businessman, and announced that she would leave the stage. An Englishwoman then issued Bigwood with a writ for breach of promise. Late in the year they returned to England.

William Proctor, to whom Carrie had been engaged, attributed his bankruptcy to betting and the jewels that he had bestowed on her. She continued to play in pantomimes and starred as Zingarie in *The Persian princess* (1909) and in 1910 toured in the title role in *Our Miss Gibbs*; she also earned £200 a week in vaudeville. She visited Australia in 1912-13

and appeared in variety, and in 1917, looking 'plump and matronly', toured Australia in *A little bit of fluff* and *Mr. Manhattan.* Bigwood was killed in action in World War I; on 14 May 1918 at Coogee, Sydney, she married the divorced Horace Vernon Bartlett, better known as John Wyatt, a bookmaker. This time she did leave the stage and lived lavishly in Macquarie Street until she secured a judicial separation in 1933 and an annuity of £500.

Carrie Moore continued to live in Sydney, refreshed by long visits to her sisters in Britain and the United States of America. In 1933 in Australia she appeared in *Music in the air*, in 1938 in a command performance in London. Unable to get an American work permit in 1939-44, she perforce refused several film offers from Hollywood. In 1945 she was the midwife in Charles Chauvel's [q.v.7] film, *The sons of Matthew.* Reduced to living in a room at Kings Cross, in 1953 she successfully applied for increased maintenance from her husband's estate. She died childless in Sydney on 5 September 1956 and was cremated with Congregational forms. Reputedly owning diamonds worth £23 000 in her twenties, she had sold her jewellery: her estate was valued for probate at £504. Four of her sisters, Lily, Eva, Olive and Ivy, made successful stage careers.

British A'sian, 2, 16 Jan 1902, 5 Nov 1908; *Red Funnel,* 18 May, 1 Aug 1908; *People* (Syd), 10 Oct 1951; *Argus,* 18 May 1897; *SMH,* 2 Oct 1897, 27 Dec 1939, 10 May 1946, 6 Oct 1950, 21, 28 Nov 1953, 6 Sept 1956; *Australasian,* 12 Mar 1898, 9 June, 15 Sept 1900, 12 Jan 1901, 3 Oct 1908, 3 July 1909; *Bulletin,* 2 Dec 1899, 26 July, 20 Sept 1917; *Punch* (Melb), 4 July, 22 Aug, 8 Oct 1901; *T&CJ,* 20 May 1908; *Sun-News Pictorial,* 16 Dec 1932, 2 Mar 1933; *Herald* (Melb), 5 Sept 1956, 6 Nov 1957.   MARTHA RUTLEDGE

MOORE, DONALD TICEHURST, (1892-1972), soldier and accountant, was born on 28 March 1892 at Flowerbank, Singleton, New South Wales, son of Thomas Henry Moore and his wife Jane, née Anderson, both born at Singleton. His father was the manager of James Moore & Co., a major local trading business. Educated at Singleton Superior Public School and St Leonards Public School in Sydney, Donald later attended the Smith Premier Business College, Sydney, where he studied accountancy. His military career began with service in the senior cadets and he was then appointed second lieutenant in the 18th (North Sydney) Infantry and promoted lieutenant in February 1914.

On the outbreak of World War I Moore was appointed a lieutenant in the 3rd Battalion, Australian Imperial Force, on 28 August and embarked for Egypt in October. On 25 April 1915, then a platoon commander in 'C' Company, he landed at Anzac Cove, in the second wave of the assault. The battalion was in continual action until 9 August when it was relieved and moved back to Lemnos. On 2 May Moore was promoted captain and company commander and was leading an attack on Lone Pine on 6 August when, jumping into a trench, he fell on the bayonet of a dying Turk and was severely wounded. Convalescing in England, he was promoted major in December; he returned to the 3rd Battalion in Egypt on 24 February 1916 and sailed for France in March.

After a short period of training Moore's battalion entered the front line at Fleurbaix on 5 May and was in action until 4 July when it was moved to Amiens to prepare for a new offensive which culminated in the capture of Pozières. Moore was awarded the Distinguished Service Order for leading his men through heavy shell-fire and an intense barrage to an advanced position at Pozières. The next major action for his battalion was the capture of Mouquet Farm where on 18 August the unit came under a heavy artillery bombardment; Moore was again wounded and evacuated to England.

On 1 December Moore was appointed commanding officer of the 3rd Battalion, vice Lieut-Colonel O. G. Howell-Price [q.v.9] who had died of wounds. On 9 December Moore returned to his unit, was promoted lieut-colonel and remained as C.O. until the battalion was disbanded on 20 January 1920.

During 1917 the 3rd Battalion was engaged in severe actions including Bullecourt and the 3rd battle of Ypres. It served continuously until September 1918 and fought in the battle of the Lys and finally in the battle of the Hindenburg outpost line. Moore returned to Australia in January 1920 and his A.I.F. appointment ended in May. For his war service, apart from his D.S.O., he was appointed C.M.G., mentioned in dispatches three times and awarded the Belgian Croix de Guerre and the Ordre de la Couronne. He was highly regarded by his battalion and was one of only eight A.I.F. battalion commanders who were aged 24 or less when given command.

Following his return to civilian life Moore was president of his battalion association for many years. He practised accountancy in Sydney and also retained his military interests, being appointed to command the 18th Battalion (militia) in 1921; he was placed on the reserve of officers in 1929. In World War II he served in various home appointments in 1939-44 and was retired in 1951 with the honorary rank of colonel.

Moore married Eileen Mary Blattman at Concord on 23 April 1952 and died on 25 December 1972 at Mona Vale, being survived by his wife.

C. E. W. Bean, *The story of Anzac* (Syd, 1921, 1924), and *The A.I.F. in France*, 1917-18 (Syd, 1933, 1937, 1942); E. Wren, *Randwick to Hargicourt, 3rd Battalion, A.I.F.* (Syd, 1935); D. T. Moore file, War records section *and* nominal roll of 3rd Battalion AIF at embarkation 20 Oct 1914 *and* war diary, 3rd Battalion, AIF (AWM).

K. R. WHITE

MOORE, ELEANOR MAY (1875-1949), pacifist, was born on 10 March 1875 at Lancefield, Victoria, daughter of William Ainsworth Moore, builder, and his wife Sarah Martha, née Prout. From a solidly middle-class background, Eleanor was educated in Melbourne at Hawksburn State School, Presbyterian Ladies' College, and Stott's Business College. She became a skilled stenographer and in 1897 was the second woman in Victoria to qualify as a court reporter, an occupation she could not pursue because of her sex. Her main employment on leaving school was as a Hansard reporter and as a secretary for eight years at Dalgety [q.v.4] & Co. Ltd. She had some writing talent and later supplemented her inherited income with freelance reporting. Remaining single, she lived with her parents, and in 1905 travelled to Europe with her sister Alice.

Sceptical about religion, she joined Dr Charles Strong's [q.v.6] Australian Church, mainly for its social welfare concerns. She was also active in the Try and City Newsboys' societies. Moore became involved in the peace movement in March 1915 when Dr Strong founded the Sisterhood of International Peace, of which she became international secretary. She was also an executive-member of the Australian Peace Alliance, which advocated a negotiated peace, and campaigned on the platform and in pamphlets against conscription in 1916 and 1917; for this she was expelled from the National Council of Women of Victoria. In May 1919 she was S.I.P. representative at the International Women's Congress in Zurich, Switzerland, where she met and was inspired by the veteran American peaceworker Jane Addams.

In 1920 the S.I.P. became the Australian section of the Women's International League for Peace and Freedom, the most enduring group in the Australian peace movement. Its objective was to educate the public about the causes and effects of war; it favoured persuasion over provocation and its activities were characterized by decorum, restraint and persistence. Moore was to be its secretary from 1928 and its motive force until her death. Much in demand as a speaker, she travelled around Australia for groups such as the Australian Union of Democratic Control for the Avoidance of War, the Peace Society in Sydney and the Melbourne section of the World Disarmament Movement. In 1928 and 1930 she represented the W.I.L.P.F. at the Pan Pacific Union Women's conferences in Honolulu, lecturing in New Zealand before returning home. In 1936-38 she toured Victoria and New South Wales speaking on 'Peoples of the Pacific' for the Country Women's Association. Meanwhile the relatively conservative W.I.L.P.F. had dissociated itself from the International Peace Campaign and the left-wing Movement Against War and Fascism.

Japan's aggression in China and the outbreak of World War II created new problems for Moore. Contrary to the policy of the head office of the W.I.L.P.F she vehemently opposed, mainly on humanitarian grounds, the idea of a general boycott of Japan. Moore and the Australian section remained 'absolute pacifists', and she was 'violently anti-communist' at a time when other pacifists tended to be pro-Russian.

Eleanor Moore was much admired as a calm, gentle, self-effacing woman who was an uncompromising pacifist. Old age and ill health did not lessen her activism; she spoke against the manufacture and use of atomic bombs shortly after Hiroshima, and over the next three years attended interstate conferences of the Federal Pacifist Council of Australia. Her semi-autobiographical *The quest for peace* was completed only a few months before her death at Toorak, Melbourne, on 1 October 1949.

R. Gibson, *The people stand up* (Melb, 1983); H. Josephson (ed), *Biographical dictionary of modern peace leaders* (Connecticut, USA, 1985); *Peacemaker*, Nov 1949; M. Colligan, Brothers and sisters in peace: the peace movement in Melbourne 1900-18 (B.A. Hons thesis, Monash Univ, 1973); E. M. Moore papers (ML); MS 9377, box 1723/4, no ii/89 (LaTL); information from Miss J. and Miss A. O'Neil, Cowra, NSW.   MIMI COLLIGAN
                                          MALCOLM SAUNDERS

MOORE, JAMES LORENZO (1887-1951), sheepdog expert, was born on 4 November 1887 at Kew, Melbourne, son of native-born parents George Watton Moore, commission agent, and his wife Octavia Frances Gordon, née McCrae. He spent some of his early years in the Hillston-Hay districts of New South Wales and was for a time overseer on a station at Wyalong before moving to Tasmania, where he imported and bred working sheepdogs.

Describing himself as a 'sheep grazier' and claiming experience as a school cadet, he enlisted in the Australian Imperial Force at Pontville on 27 August 1914. His war service was brief. He joined 'C' Squadron of the 3rd Australian Light Horse at Gallipoli on 29 September 1915 and ten days later fell ill with tuberculosis. In January 1916 he returned to Australia and was discharged medically unfit in Tasmania in July.

By February 1917, 'late 3rd L.H.', Moore had re-formed his kennel at St Leonard's and, claiming that his dogs had won more than sixty trials overseas and in Australia, was advertising Scotch border collies, kelpies and barbs for sale. His first sire was The Gaffer (Boss) sired by Moss of Ancrum, bred by Tom White of Victoria and for which he paid Arthur Collins £100. Moore imported many notable champions from England and Scotland, including Macpherson's Moss, Brown's Shep, Brown's Nell and Cayley of Thornhill.

In 1920 Moore demonstrated his dogs at work for the prince of Wales and Field Marshal Sir William Birdwood [q.v.7] and in 1921 became a life member of the International Sheep Dog Trial Society. On 12 April 1922 at Launceston he married Charlotte Lucia Cargill; they were divorced in December 1947. In 1923 he moved to Melbourne where he worked as a manager and in conjunction with his friend H. J. Smith relocated his 'Tasmanian Kennels' at the Nook, Kyneton. By 1929 he had kennels in Victoria, Tasmania, Western Australia, New South Wales and New Zealand.

Moore wrote (probably with assistance) many authoritative articles on the breeding and training of sheepdogs, chiefly for the *Pastoral Review* and the *New Zealand Loan Quarterly Magazine*. In 1929 he published *The canine king: the working sheep dog* with a preface by Birdwood. Moore was no A. P. Terhune and though the book failed to live up to the extravagant claims of its editor, Frank Russell, it contained a wealth of knowledge and rare entertainment according to C. J. Dennis [q.v.8]. In 1931 Moore made *The master of the flock*, a talkie film demonstrating the capabilities of his dogs. He gained wide repute as breeder, dog and trial judge and publicist, especially for the border collie sheepdog. He was a keen supporter of field trials and from 1920 urged the establishment of a working sheepdog stud book. He always bred from broken stock.

In 1932 he went to South Africa and H. J. Smith carried on the kennel in Moore's name. On his return in 1939 he was general manager of the South African Fruit Canners' Council. An active worker for incapacitated ex-servicemen, Moore was president in 1945-51 of the Gallipoli Legion of Anzacs of Victoria. He died childless on 3 March 1951 in Melbourne and was cremated. His second wife Edna May, née Pearce, whom he had married at Cairns Memorial Church, Melbourne, on 19 March 1948, survived him.

Pastoral Review, 16 Mar 1921, 16 Jan 1926, 16 Nov 1931, 15 Apr 1939, 16 Oct, 16 Nov 1940, 16 Apr 1941, 16 Mar 1951; *NZ Loan Q Mag*, Mar, June 1924, Mar 1925; *New Nation Mag*, 1 Dec 1931; *Argus*, 5 Mar 1951; *Australasian*, 10 Feb 1917, 4, 31 Aug 1918, 18 Jan, 1 Feb, 25 Oct 1919, 10 Jan, 21 Aug 1920, 9 Apr 1921, 15 Sept, 6 Oct 1923, 24 May 1924, 22 June 1929, 10 May 1930, 2 July 1932.

G. P. WALSH

MOORE, JOHN CHARLES (1887-1918), soldier and mechanic, was born on 2 June 1887 at Waterloo, Victoria, third son of Thomas Macedon Moore, miner, and his wife Mary Jane, née Robinson, both Victorian born. He was schooled at either Waterloo or Beaufort near Ballarat, then worked in Melbourne for Massey Harris & Co. as a mechanic.

Having served in the Australian Military Forces in the 64th Battalion, Moore enlisted in the Australian Imperial Force on 6 June 1916 and joined the 5th Reinforcements for the 60th Battalion. He was made acting corporal in July after attending an instructional school at Geelong and embarked for overseas service on 25 September. He arrived in England on 11 November and was sent to the 15th Training Battalion. In France by late December, he joined the 5th Division Base Depot, reverting to the rank of private.

After short periods acting at higher rank Moore joined the 60th Battalion as a private near Delville Wood on 8 February 1917. He was promoted corporal that month and sergeant on 5 May and in mid-May saw action in the battle of Bullecourt where he won the Military Medal for bravery under fire. Sent to an officers' training school at Cambridge, England, in September, he was commissioned as a second lieutenant in the 60th Battalion on 23 January 1918. He was awarded the Military Cross for conspicuous gallantry as the officer in charge of one of two raiding parties at Wytschaete on 13-14 March; single-handed, Moore took an enemy post, capturing four prisoners. When the raiding party withdrew he remained behind with two of his men to bring in the wounded under very heavy machine-gun fire.

Soon after his promotion to lieutenant on 1 April Moore fought in the 2nd battle of Villers-Bretonneux and was awarded a Bar to his M.C. For four days he organized resistance to German attacks, arranging for the removal of wounded, the continuance of supplies, the collection of intelligence and the accurate directing of artillery fire.

On 8 May Moore was detached by Brig-adier General H. E. Elliott [q.v.8] to the 15th Australian Light Trench Mortar Battery to help counter difficulties caused by the issue of inferior 'blue ring' mortar ammunition. He was serving with the 15th Battery when he was killed on 4 July 1918 in the battle of Hamel during a heavy German bombardment. He was buried in the British cemetery at Méricourt, France.

Moore had married Ada Jane Hendy Cooper on 31 May 1916 at Bendigo, Victoria; there were no children of the marriage.

C. E. W. Bean, *The A.I.F. in France*, 1918 (Syd, 1942); *London Gazette*, 17 July 1917, 10 May 1918, 13 Sept 1918; *Bendigo Advertiser*, 14 May 1918; *Ballarat Courier*, 16 July 1918; *Bendigo Independent*, 20 July 1918; records (AWM).

MATTHEW DICKER

MOORE, JOHN DRUMMOND MAC-PHERSON (1888-1958), artist and architect, was born on 6 September 1888 at Waverley, Sydney, son of Frederic Moore, draughtsman, and his wife Emily Mary, née Macpherson. He was educated at Sydney Grammar School and later studied painting at Julian Ashton's [q.v.7] Sydney Art School. Articled in 1908 to McCredie & Anderson, architects, about 1913 he visited San Francisco, United States of America, and worked in the New York office of the architect B. G. Goodhue in 1914-15. Moving to London he enlisted in the Royal Engineers in 1915, was commissioned and served in France. After the war he studied in London at the Polytechnic School of Art and the Architectural Association school.

Returning to Sydney in 1919 after some months in New York, Moore set up practice as an architect and was known professionally as John D. Moore. In 1919-35 he was instructor in architectural design and draughtsmanship at the University of Sydney. At Wahroonga on 2 October 1924 he married Casiphia Dorothy Morton; she died in 1931, leaving two sons. On 23 June 1932 he married GLADYS MARY OWEN (1889-1960) at St Michael's Anglican Church, Vaucluse.

Of medium height and sturdy build, Moore was a man of even temper with many friends. A partner in Wardell, Moore & Dowling from 1927, he managed a satisfying balance between painting and architecture in his professional life. Most of his architecture was domestic, but he also designed projects for hospitals and schools and a Roman Catholic cathedral (as yet unbuilt) for Canberra. A friend of Winifred West [q.v.], he designed many buildings for her school, Frensham, winning the Sulman [q.v.] prize for its West wing in 1937; he later served on the school council and encouraged her to develop the craft centre, Sturt. In the 1930s Moore campaigned for the preservation of the Hyde Park Barracks and in 1937 was appointed to the Board of Architects of New South Wales. In World War II he was deputy director of camouflage for New South Wales in 1942-45.

A fellow of the Royal Australian Institute of Architects and an associate of the Royal Institute of British Architects, from 1943 he practised in several short-lived partnerships and sometimes alone. In magazine articles, radio broadcasts and his book, *Home again* (1944), Moore deplored reliance on 'styles' and 'isms', advocating a rational approach to planning and design in keeping with Australian conditions. Philosophically his ideas had much in common with those of the architects Hardy Wilson and Leslie Wilkinson [qq.v.].

As a painter in water-colours and oils, Moore was noted for his freshness of approach to the Australian landscape. In the 1930s he was a member of the Contemporary Group of Sydney and was classed among such 'moderns' as Rah Fizelle [q.v.8] and Margaret Preston [q.v.], more because of his skill at composition and distinctive palette of pinks and indigos than for any urge to adopt forms of expressionism or abstraction. Between 1925 and 1951 he held eight exhibitions at the Macquarie Galleries, Sydney. He was a vice-president of the Society of Artists and in 1954 was awarded its medal. His best-known painting is probably a sparkling oil of Sydney Harbour, bought by the National Art Gallery of New South Wales in 1936; it was painted from the family home he designed at Vaucluse.

Survived by his wife and sons of his first marriage, Moore died at Vaucluse on 9 December 1958 and was cremated with Anglican rites.

His second wife Gladys was born on 1 July 1889 at Hunters Hill, daughter of (Sir) Langer Meade Loftus Owen [q.v.] and his wife Mary Louisa Dames, née Longworth. Educated privately, she studied painting with Gerald Fitzgerald and Dattilo Rubbo [q.v.] and at the Grosvenor School of Modern Art, London, and in Europe.

During World War I Miss Owen was foundation joint honorary secretary (1914-27) of the local branch of the British Red Cross Society under Mrs Eleanor MacKinnon [q.v.]. An executive member of the local Victoria League and vice-president of the Women's Loyalty League of New South Wales, she addressed recruiting meetings and campaigned early for conscription. In 1918 she was appointed O.B.E.

Gladys Owen visited Britain and Europe in 1924: her paintings were accepted by the Spring Salon in Paris and by the Royal Insti-

tute of Painters in Water Colours, London. She was a member of the Australian Water-Colour Institute and held several exhibitions. Nancy Phelan described her as 'a lively painter with dangling earrings and plaits round her ears like Chelsea buns'. In the 1930s she wrote many articles and book reviews for the *Sydney Morning Herald*. Employed full time by the Australian Broadcasting Commission, she was in charge of the State 'Women's Session' in 1933-36 and talks editor in 1936-38, Federal supervisor of the 'Children's Session' and adviser on women's interests in 1938-40, and part-time talks officer in 1946-49. In 1937 she was appointed a trustee of the Public Library of New South Wales.

Gladys Moore had continued her work for the Red Cross. She was director of the civil section of the Women's Australian National Service in 1940, a council-member of the State division of the Red Cross in 1940-49 and of national headquarters in 1943-49, and honorary secretary of the State Red Cross Field Service in 1941-43. From 1950 she was president of the Council of Social Service of New South Wales. She died, childless, of heart disease at Edgecliff on 18 July 1960.

An early portrait of John Moore by David Barker is held by his son David, a distinguished photographer, and one by Norman Carter [q.v.7] is in the Art Gallery of New South Wales.

P. Kennedy, *Portrait of Winifred West* (Syd, 1976); *Art in Aust*, no 8, 1921; *Art and Aust*, 2, no 4, 1974; *SMH*, 3 Oct 1924; W. H. Gill and Winifred West papers (ML).   CEDRIC FLOWER

MOORE, SIR NEWTON JAMES (1870-1936), premier, soldier and businessman, was born on 17 May 1870 at Fremantle, Western Australia, son of James Moore, auctioneer and later mayor of Bunbury, and Elizabeth Dawson, schoolteacher. He attended the Bunbury primary school and, later, Prince Alfred College, Adelaide. At 14 he began work as a sales assistant at Geraldton and was later articled to the surveyor Alexander Forrest [q.v.8] in Perth. His years as a surveyor (1886-1904) coincided with the granting of responsible government to the colony and increased prosperity following the discovery of gold. Moore travelled widely throughout Western Australia gaining knowledge of its potential, its difficulties and notable developments. His map was for many years the official guide to the position and extent of the State's forests and commercial timber resources; in 1903 he was a member of the royal commission on forestry. He was associated with the flotation of some of the largest jarrah companies on the London market. On 6

April 1898 at Bunbury Congregational Church he had married Isabel, sister of William Lowrie [q.v.]; they had three daughters and one son.

Next year Moore became a member of the Bunbury Municipal Council and was mayor in 1901-04. He supervised much construction work on roads, drains, footpaths and windmills, and in later life often gave his occupation as 'surveyor and civil engineer'. Moore was president of the Western Australian Municipal Association in 1904 and he was a keen Freemason. In 1893 he had also joined the Bunbury Rifles in which he rose to the rank of lieutenant. When Western Australia's first mounted infantry were raised in 1900, Moore was given command and promoted captain; he commanded the 18th Regiment, Australian Light Horse, from 1901 to 1908. He then, as lieut-colonel, led the State branch of the Australian Intelligence Corps.

Moore admired Sir John Forrest [q.v.8], premier in 1890-1901 and also a Bunbury man. In the 1901 elections Moore narrowly failed to enter State parliament, but he won the Bunbury Legislative Assembly seat in 1904 and held it until his retirement from State politics in 1911. In his maiden speech Moore, essentially a conservative, emphasized his Western Australian birth and advocated immigration, land settlement, taxation on unimproved estates and better harbour facilities for Bunbury. It was a period of political instability: between the departure of Sir John Forrest for Federal politics in 1901 and Moore's accession to the premiership in May 1906, six ministries 'shuffled across the political stage'. When the Daglish [q.v.8] Labor government fell in August 1905, Moore became minister for lands and agriculture under (Sir) Hector Rason [q.v.].

Although the *West Australian* had predicted his appointment, Moore was not Rason's first choice. But it was a crucial appointment for Moore, enabling him to establish himself among his parliamentary colleagues. When Rason retired in April 1906, Moore became premier on 7 May after Frank Wilson failed to form a ministry. Moore was selected partly because his position was somewhere between the liberal and conservative wings of the large, amorphous, non-Labor group known as the Ministerial Party. After a difficult first year during which he was lampooned in the press and nicknamed 'Buglepumpkin' for his mistakes and inexperience, Moore grew increasingly popular. Winning the 1908 election conclusively, he retained the premiership for four years. He kept the lands portfolio until 30 June 1909 when he became colonial treasurer.

A personable, genial man of burly figure, a 'hustling politician', Moore helped to hold the government together after a period of in-

decision had interrupted development. Successive governments had recognized the need for developmental programmes to consolidate the prosperity of the gold rushes of the 1890s; but because of the brevity of their tenure of office they had been unable to act. Although so inexperienced, Moore soon emerged as an astute leader who became a cohesive element in his heterogeneous party.

Like his minister for agriculture (Sir) James Mitchell [q.v.], Moore believed in the State's 'unlimited' farming potential. He was the driving force behind programmes which helped to establish Western Australia's wheat-growing industry. By liberalizing the terms of credit of the Agricultural Bank, so that finance was more freely available to farmers, and by heavy government loan expenditure, particularly on light railways, by 1910 Western Australia was a strong wheat-exporter. Yet Moore was proud that gold-mining was not neglected. Of 950 miles (1530 km) of railways authorized during 1906-10, about 550 miles (885 km) served agricultural districts, while the remainder ran to and from gold-mining areas.

An important policy initiative was the attraction of new settlers. In 1906 the net gain from migration was only 319; next year 7500 more people left the State than came to it. By 1910 and in the years until World War I however, urged on by Moore, Western Australia experienced an immigration boom. His expansionist policies helped to lift the State out of the economic recession into which it had slumped. Other important legislation included the Municipal Corporations Act (1906); the Electoral Act (1907); Western Australia's first land and income tax Acts (1907) after conflict with the hostile Legislative Council which resulted in compromise low rates; and the State Children Act (1907) which established the Child Welfare Department and the Children's Court. Moore attended several vital premiers' conferences and fought for more favourable financial consideration for his State. The financial agreement of 1909, with its special terms and new sliding scale for Western Australia, was the climax of his negotiations with the Federal government and gave new confidence to business in the West.

Under Moore the Ministerialists embraced a tighter party organization, although he was reluctant because it was contrary to his Burkeian view that members should speak and vote as their conscience dictated. But the nature of the Labor Party's organization forced him to tighten his party's performance in the assembly. Policy was thrashed out in cabinet and controversial decisions were usually referred to the party caucus.

Moore was appointed C.M.G. in 1908 and

K.C.M.G. in 1910. He resigned the premiership on 16 September 1910 and went as agent-general for Western Australia to London in 1911. During his first term until 1914, he exuberantly promoted and fostered a spectacular amount of migration to Western Australia. He approved the first twelve boys who were selected for the Fairbridge [q.v.8] Farm School near Pinjarra in 1912 and those sent out to learn farming under Rev. Henry Freeman's scheme. Moore reorganized the agent-general's London office, recommended the purchase of Savoy House as its new premises in 1913, and promoted the State's primary produce in Britain and Europe. He was invited and agreed to continue for another three years, but this period was interrupted by World War I.

In May 1915 Moore took command, as lieut-colonel, of the depot for Australian and New Zealand troops at Weymouth, Dorset; in December he was promoted temporary brigadier general commanding the relatively few Australian Imperial Force troops then in Britain. From July 1916 he took charge of A.I.F. camps and depots, which involved supervision of the training of reinforcements. C. E. W. Bean [q.v.7] noted his success: 'under a bluff exterior he had, though slow of speech and heavy of movement, a wide experience of men and the ability to handle them . . . with the politician's sense of what men were feeling, a kindly humour, marked determination, and loyal . . . nature'. On 14 February 1917 Moore was promoted temporary major general and in April was replaced by Major General (Sir) James McCay [q.v.].

In September 1918 Moore was returned unopposed as an Imperialist to the House of Commons seat of St George's, Hanover Square, previously held by Sir George Reid [q.v.]. In his maiden speech he supported women's eligibility to be members of parliament. He represented North Islington in 1918-23 and Richmond in 1924-32 as a Conservative. He was chairman of the Standing Orders Committee during two parliaments and in 1919-32 of the Overseas Parliamentary Committee.

His British parliamentary career took second place to his growing business interests. In 1917 he had become a director of one of Western Australia's oldest mining ventures, the Great Boulder Pty Gold Mines Ltd, later controlled by C. A. de Bernales [q.v.8]. Moore was chairman of this company when he died in 1936 and also of Hampton Gold Mining Areas; he was a director of the British General Electric Co., Consolidated Tin Mines of Burma, Carmen Valley Gold Mines, Southern Cross Gold Development, Great Boulder No. 1 and Odhams Press. He was also president of four major Canadian companies: the Dominion Coal Co., the Nova Scotia Steel & Coal Co., the Halifax Shipyards, and the Dominion Steel & Coal Corporation of Canada, one of the Dominion's largest industrial concerns; Moore had assumed its presidency when in 1932 he had moved to live in Montreal. Mainly because of his vigorous sales promotion, at the time of his resignation in 1936 the company's huge steel plants had not only recovered their pre-Depression output but had reached their highest peak since World War I.

Moore's recreations were shooting, hunting and bowls, and he belonged to leading social clubs in three continents. Survived by his wife and children, he died after surgery in a London nursing home on 28 October 1936. He was buried in Warnham parish church, Sussex, and left an estate of nearly £100 000 in Australia and England.

J. S. Battye (ed), *Cyclopedia of Western Australia*, 2 (Adel, 1913); C. E. W. Bean, *The A.I.F. in France*, 1916 (Syd, 1929); *West Australian*, 24 Sept 1910, 29 Oct 1936; *Sunday Times* (Perth), 6, 22 July, 12 Aug 1906; *Western Mail* (Perth), 24 Sept 1910; *Punch* (Melb), 13 Apr 1916; *The Times*, 29 Oct, 2 Nov 1936; *Countryman* (Perth), 13 Oct 1960; F. D. Adams, A biography of Sir Newton James Moore with special reference to his role in Western Australian politics (M.A. thesis, Univ WA, 1973); James papers (outward correspondence 1905-06, Battye Lib, Perth).   DAVID ADAMS

MOORE, NICHOLAS (1862-1941), detective, was born on 27 February 1862 at Waterford, Ireland, son of Nicholas Moore, brewery manager, and his wife Mary, née Barron. After serving with the Liverpool police in England, he migrated about 1890 to Sydney where he joined the New South Wales Police Force on 4 August 1891. He served mainly at the Redfern Police Station rising to sergeant 2nd class; in January 1913 he was promoted detective 1st class, Sydney Metropolitan District. His duties included political surveillance and attending the Domain on Sundays to report upon public speakers.

On the outbreak of World War I Moore was seconded at the army's request to the local branch of Military Intelligence to assist in the detection and prosecution of opponents of the war, including the Industrial Workers of the World. After the Labor Party had split in 1916 over conscription, Prime Minister W. M. Hughes [q.v.9] had the I.W.W. banned. Moore had been watching the I.W.W. from 1914 and, with the army, raided its premises several times and arrested and prosecuted its members.

Late in 1916 twelve I.W.W. members including Donald Grant [q.v.9] were arrested on charges of conspiring to commit arson, allegedly as a protest against the gaoling of Tom Barker [q.v.7], editor of their paper,

Direct Action. Moore drew on his local knowledge and contacts with radical groups to prepare comprehensive reports to aid the Crown's case which led to the gaoling of the twelve for a total of 150 years. All the detectives involved were congratulated by the judge and later given awards; Moore received £25.

He later reported on moves to have the case reopened by E. E. Judd, who had obtained statements from some Crown witnesses that they had been pressured by the police to give false evidence. An inquiry was conducted by Justice (Sir) Philip Street [q.v.] into the actions of the police under a specially introduced Police Inquiry Act. Apparently under renewed pressure, the informants revoked the confessions they had given to Judd and returned to their original statements. Accordingly, Street declared in December 1918 that the police had not acted improperly, but a second inquiry in June 1920 by Justice N. K. Ewing [q.v.8] led to the immediate release of ten of the twelve. Moore was well rewarded for his efforts: in 1919 he was given £50 by the Commonwealth government for services rendered and in 1921 was awarded the King's Police medal.

Despite having worked for many years in the slum area of Redfern, Moore had little sympathy for the working class. His suspicion of their leaders and reformist programmes appeared in all the highly literate and thorough reports he prepared about them. His main contribution to the area of political surveillance lay in this judgemental and reporting pattern which came to be perpetuated by his successors.

On 7 May 1921 Moore married a widow Ellen Secret Kelly, née Daniel, with Presbyterian forms at Westmead, and in October retired from the police force. He died at his Westmead home on 24 September 1941 and was cremated with Presbyterian forms.

I. Turner, *Sydney's burning* (Melb, 1967); F. M. Cain, *The origins of political surveillance in Australia* (Syd, 1983); NSW Police Dept, IWW special bundle (NSWA).   FRANK CAIN

MOORE, SAMUEL WILKINSON (1854-1935), mine-manager and politician, was born on 7 February 1854 at Bua, Vanua Levu, Fiji, son of Rev. William Moore, Wesleyan minister, and his wife Mary Ann, née Ducker. The family arrived in Sydney in 1864. Sammy was educated at Newington College and was a student teacher (assistant master) at G. Metcalfe's private Goulburn High School in 1870-72.

Moving to the Tingha-Inverell district in 1873, Moore established a strong following among miners. With his father, Jasper Tyson and Rev. Francis Tate, he formed the Britannia Tin Mining Co. Building a verandahed, weatherboard house which survives, Moore was manager, leading assayer of minerals and chief tin-buyer for Britannia. Appointed a justice of the peace in 1879, he carried the burden of magisterial work for the local court for several years. On 18 June 1876 he married Isabella Leah Sawkins, at Tingha. A strong batsman, Moore scored highly for both Inverell club and for New England against A. Shaw's and the Hon. Ivo Bligh's English elevens in the early 1880s.

A free trader and supporter of Sir Henry Parkes [q.v.5], Moore was elected to the Legislative Assembly for Inverell in 1885 and held the seat in 1887. Although criticized for being motivated by 'personal aggrandisement' he was widely regarded as a very capable member and an 'upright and faithful steward' to his constituents. His advocacy of the Inverell-Glen Innes railway occasioned comment about his land and mining speculations along the proposed route. He served on the Board of Technical Education in 1886-87.

Moore did not seek re-election in 1889, but represented Bingara in 1894-1910, first as a supporter of (Sir) George Reid [q.v.], then as a Liberal from 1901. Although ideology made him unpopular with most small landholders, he found strong support from the influential Forster [q.v.8] family at Abington, Bundarra. A member of the Parliamentary Standing Committee on Public Works in 1901-04, Moore joined the Carruthers [q.v.7] ministry as secretary for mines and agriculture in August 1904. Hard-working, he carried into effect 'much needed relief and improvement' in the mining industry. When (Sir) Charles Gregory Wade [q.v.] took over as premier in October 1907, Moore became secretary for lands. He implemented the first compulsory Crown acquisition in 1908 under the Closer Settlement (Amendment) Act (1907) of 99 618 acres (40 314 ha) of the Peel estate from the Peel River Land and Mineral Co. and then, under the same Act, the acquisition of 45 006 acres (18 214 ha) at Warrah from the Australian Agricultural Co. F. L. Livingstone-Learmonth [q.v.] found Moore firm but fair in his determination to administer legislation opposed by large landholders.

Defeated at the 1910 general election, Moore was appointed a commissioner of the Western Land Board. After retirement in 1922 he lived at Roseville where he died on 15 February 1935; he was cremated with Methodist forms. His wife, son and four daughters survived him.

Our present parliament (Syd, nd, 1886?); W. F. Morrison, *The Aldine centennial history of New South Wales* (Syd, 1888); G. N. Hawker, *The par-*

liament of New South Wales, 1856-1965 (Syd, 1971); E. Wiedemann, *World of its own* (Inverell, NSW, 1981); H. Brown, *Tin at Tingha* (Armidale, 1982); A. Harris, *Abington, a history of a station and its people* (Armidale, 1982); Dept of Mines (NSW), *Annual Report*, 1876, 1877, 1881; *Sydney Mail*, 9 Feb 1889; *Armidale Express*, 19 May 1891; *Daily Telegraph* (Syd), 28 July 1894; *T&CJ*, 7 Sept 1904, 21 Aug 1907; *SMH*, 2 Dec 1922, 18 Feb 1935.   JOHN ATCHISON

MOORE, THOMAS BATHER (1850-1919), prospector and explorer, was born on 26 November 1850 at New Norfolk, Van Diemen's Land, fourth child of John Anthony Moore, surgeon from Northumberland, England, and his wife Martha Anne, née Read, of New Norfolk. After elementary schooling in the colony, Moore completed his education at Windermere College in the English Lake District under the guardianship of an uncle. He returned to Tasmania in 1868.

In 1873 Moore participated in a tin-mining venture in Victoria and next year commenced his exploration of Tasmania's west coast by examining the area south of Mount Bischoff for tin and gold. He followed this with eighteen months in New South Wales and some time in north-east Tasmania. On 1 January 1877 with his brother James and James Andrew he left New Norfolk to investigate recent mineral discoveries around Mount Heemskirk. His route, cutting across the Tyndall Plateau, became a supply line for the west coast, but his prospecting claims proved disappointing, as did those he worked at Heemskirk next summer for the Corinna Co.

Moore spent February to May 1879 on a solitary, unbacked prospecting venture covering the area from Macquarie Harbour to Port Davey and the region south of the Arthur Range. One of the first white men to have seen the range from the south, he reported his journey to the Lands and Survey Department, noting mapping corrections, particularly in the river system. He found no worthwhile mineral traces, but the trip presaged many journeys over the next forty years, often undertaken on behalf of the government.

On 9 January 1889 at the Church of All Saints, Hobart, Moore married Jane Mary Solly. They settled at Strahan where Moore became inspector of roads and works for the west coast. Unable to conform to the constraints of bureaucracy, however, he resigned in 1891 to resume prospecting and track-cutting. From 1904 he was head of the outside prospecting party of the Mount Lyell Mining & Railway Co. He came to know the west better than any other man and the map is sprinkled with his nomenclature. His most notable achievement was blazing a track (now the Lyell Highway) from Lake St Clair through to the West Coast Range.

Moore was a competent botanist and geologist, and a founder and life member of the Queensland branch of the Royal Geographical Society. His expeditions were always undertaken with the anticipation of adding to the scientific corpus. He was the first to write on the glacial formation of the Tyndall Range (in a paper to the Royal Society of Tasmania, 1893); he collected plant varieties for Sir Ferdinand Mueller [q.v.5] and is credited with the discovery of *Coprosma moorei* and three liverworts; and his fossil specimens were acknowledged by R. M. Johnston [q.v.9] in his *Geology of Tasmania*. Handicapped by lack of formal education, he magnified his achievements in an endeavour to establish his reputation. Nevertheless his work amply justified his use of the signature 'T. B. Moore F.R.G.S., explorer'.

Dark-complexioned, of medium height and sturdy build, Moore was admired for his bushman's skill and endurance: he frequently walked twenty miles (32 km) through virgin bush in a day, packing a heavy load. But he was an authoritarian employer and quarrels in his camp were frequent. Sadly, his acceptance of the solitary life led to estrangement from his family. When knee trouble and chronic bronchitis obliged him to accept a desk job with Mount Lyell he sought refuge in hard drinking and the company of other bushmen.

Moore died on 14 August 1919 at Queenstown, survived by his wife, one son and three daughters. An active church member for much of his life, he was buried with Anglican rites at Strahan.

C. J. Binks, *Explorers of western Tasmania* (Launc, 1982); *V&P* (HA Tas), 1878-79, 35 (85), p 8, 1886, 9 (138), p 3; *Examiner* (Launc), 15 Aug 1919; Moore papers (held by Mrs M. G. Elliston, Latrobe, Tas).   IAN McSHANE

MOORE, WILLIAM (1859-1927), surgeon, was born on 30 July 1859 at Western Suburbs (Milton), Brisbane, third son of William Moore, gardener and later Baptist minister from Somerset, England, and his Welsh wife Margaret, née Hitchings. Entering the University of Melbourne in 1878 from Brisbane Grammar School with the nickname 'Jerry' and a high scholastic record, he graduated M.B. in 1882 and B.S. in 1883, dux of his year. He was house surgeon at the (Royal) Melbourne Hospital in 1883-84 and afterwards demonstrator in anatomy at the university. Following his marriage on 29 April 1884 at Hotham Hill to Grace Emily Poole, governess and Baptist clergyman's daughter, he resumed his studies to become the first recipient of the University of Melbourne's M.S. degree, conferred in 1885 at the same ceremony as his M.D.

'Jerry' Moore was appointed surgeon for skin diseases at the Melbourne Hospital in 1885 and in 1887 out-patient surgeon. Commencing private practice in Spring Street, in 1890 he took over the Collins Street practice of E. M. James, a senior hospital colleague and a timely and benevolent patron. He continued at the Melbourne Hospital, as surgeon on the full staff from 1902, until 1910 when he became consulting surgeon; he was also honorary surgeon to St Vincent's Hospital in 1899-1906, a member of the committee of the Austin Hospital in 1895-1907 and one of the few surgeons to run his own private hospital, Milton House, in Flinders Lane.

The amount and variety of surgery which Moore undertook was prodigious and his results, published in pamphlets and in numerous contributions to the *Intercolonial Medical Journal of Australia*, outstanding. By 1908 his reputation was such that Melbourne *Punch* termed him 'the perfect surgeon'. He was pre-eminent in two directions: he led in the application of Listerism to abdominal surgery, demonstrating new standards of lower mortality rates; and he had a special interest and skill in reconstructive surgery on which he published one of the earliest books, *Plastic surgery*, in 1899. His work in this field at the 11th Australian General Hospital during and after World War I was far advanced for his time.

Moore's greatest contribution to the Melbourne Hospital was his abolition of the system of hospital appointment by public canvass and vote. Successively promoting the appointment of allies to the hospital board—he was a member himself in 1904-25—he achieved his objective in 1910 with the establishment of the independent electoral college system of appointments. In 1886 he had been a strong advocate for moving the Melbourne Hospital from Lonsdale Street to its present Parkville site, but was outvoted. He was also critical of the charge levied on patients, believing the hospital should remain a charitable institution for the underprivileged.

As a student Moore helped to found the Medical Students' Society and later served on the councils of the Medical Society of Victoria and the Victorian branch of the British Medical Association. In 1889-93 he co-edited the *Australian Medical Journal* with (Sir) George Syme [q.v.]. He was, nevertheless, a loner in professional circles, always self-reliant, outspoken on matters of principle and intolerant of other viewpoints. His isolation was exacerbated when in 1906 he was charged with unprofessional conduct by a col-

league whose patient Moore had visited for a 'friendly chat'. An investigation involving the parent B.M.A. continued until 1911, making the case a *cause célèbre*. Though ultimately exonerated, Moore withdrew from the centre of medical affairs; he did not rejoin the B.M.A. until 1926.

Apart from surgery, sport (cricket, tennis and cycling) and the Church were said to be Moore's only interests. Captain of the university cricket team in the 1880s and later club president, he subsequently had his own team, The Medicos. As a dedicated Baptist, he initiated the founding of Carey Baptist Grammar School where his name remains on a foundation stone and in Moore House. A non-drinker and non-smoker, completely humourless and with an unattractive voice, he was the object of some ridicule by the medical student body. He had, however, the lifelong respect of many of Melbourne's leading physicians and surgeons, (Sir) Richard Stawell [q.v.] in particular recording that Moore 'imbued a new spirit into hospital work . . . in Melbourne'.

Moore died suddenly at Fitzroy on 8 September 1927 before he could take his seat on the first credentials committee of the College of Surgeons of Australasia to which he had been elected a foundation fellow earlier in the year. Buried in Box Hill cemetery, he was survived by his wife, four daughters and a son.

J. Smith (ed), *Cyclopedia of Victoria*, 1 (Melb, 1903); K. S. Inglis, *Hospital and community* (Melb, 1958); B. K. Rank, *Jerry Moore and some of his contemporaries* (Melb, 1975); *MJA*, Dec 1927; *Punch* (Melb), 18 June 1908.   B. K. RANK

MOORE, WILLIAM GEORGE (1868-1937), journalist and art critic, was born on 11 June 1868 at Sandhurst (Bendigo), Victoria, son of Thompson Moore (1832-1912), businessman and politician, and his wife Emily, née Capper. After education at Scotch College, Sandhurst, he was employed in a merchant's office. Thereafter, for more than a decade, he pursued an itinerant life-style, locally and overseas, as a member of various theatrical companies.

Returning to Melbourne in 1904 he became art and drama critic for the *Herald*. His anecdotal writings on art were collected in *City sketches* (1905) and *Studio sketches* (1906), and his dramatic interests culminated in what was perhaps the first sustained promotion of locally written plays, a series of annual Australian drama nights in 1909-12. Plays written by Moore, including *The tearoom girl* (1910) and *The mysterious moonlight* (1912), were among those produced.

After the last drama night Moore left for London where he continued promoting Australian art and drama, and his own playwriting and acting, as a member of Granville Barker's theatrical company. During World War I he served in the British Army Service Corps in France. While in London he met the New Zealand poet Dora Wilcox and after the death of her husband married her on 1 October 1923 in Sydney.

In 1919 Moore had settled in Sydney which, owing to the work of S. Ure Smith [q.v.] and the launching of *Art in Australia*, he judged to be the centre of art publishing in Australia. He wrote for many periodicals and newspapers including the *Daily Telegraph*, the *Brisbane Courier*, and the *Home* and in 1926 contributed the concise and balanced article on art to the *Australian Encyclopaedia*. On the eve of publication of his life's work, *The story of Australian art* (1934), he was awarded the Society of Artists', Sydney, medal for distinguished services to his country's art.

Moore's two-volume *magnum opus* was the first monographic survey of Australian art. Much of its information was obtained directly from the artists themselves or from close contemporaries, and thus it remains a basic reference work which was reprinted in 1980. However, its lack of critical judgement and sustaining methodology, attributable to Moore's journalistic background, greatly limits its value. Although the work was very favourably received, one lone hostile review condemned it as an 'encyclopaedic stream of facts', many of them trivial or irrelevant. Moore's sometimes trite evaluations damn with faint praise and his constant efforts to find something encouraging to say belie any real critical strength or stand. It was to be another decade before a more 'academic' approach to Australian art historiography appeared in Bernard Smith's *Place, taste and tradition* (1945), which acknowledged a debt to Moore's pioneering work. William Moore thus holds an important place among Australia's leading art critics and publicists and, with Blamire Young [q.v.], stands in a direct line of descent from James Smith [q.v.6], James Green (J. G. De Libra) and Sidney Dickinson [q.v.8].

In 1937 Moore edited with T. Inglis Moore *Best Australian one-act plays*, and contributed an introductory essay on the development of Australian drama. He died in Sydney on 6 November 1937 and was cremated. Contemporaries remembered him as a man with 'a genius for friendship'. A portrait by G. J. Coates [q.v.8] is in the National Library of Australia.

His wife MARY THEODORA JOYCE WILCOX (1873-1953), poet and playwright, was born on 24 November 1873 at Christchurch, New Zealand, daughter of William Henry Wilcox, saddler, and his wife Mary Elizabeth, née Washbourne. Educated privately and at Can-

terbury College, she contributed to the *Bulletin* and taught for several years at Armidale, New South Wales, before travelling to England where she published *Verses from Maoriland* (1905) and *Rata and Mistletoe* (1911). Dora Wilcox married Jean Paul Hamélius, professor of English at Liège University, Belgium, in London on 14 October 1909 and served with the Voluntary Aid Detachment in London in 1915-18. After her marriage to Moore she devoted much time to helping him to research *The story of Australian art*. She published *Seven poems* (1924) and in 1927 won the *Sydney Morning Herald's* prize for an ode commemorating the opening of the Commonwealth parliament. In 1931 she won a prize for a one-act play, *The raid*, while another, *The fourposter*, was included in *Best Australian one-act plays*. A contributor to Australian, English and European periodicals, Dora Wilcox also published *Samuel Butler in Canterbury, New Zealand* (1934), a lecture given to the Sydney branch of the English Association of which she was a patron. She died, childless, in Sydney on 14 December 1953.

L. Rees, *The making of Australian drama* (Syd, 1973); *Spinner*, 2, no 25, May 1926, p 79; *Pandemonium*, 1, no 11, Dec 1934, p 11; *B.P. Mag*, 10, no 2, Mar 1938, p 70, 73; *Southerly*, 15, no 1, 1954, p 63; *Art and Aust*, 19, no 2, Winter 1982, p 451; *Argus*, 8 Nov 1937; R. H. Croll *and* P. Serle papers *and* J. K. Moir collection (LaTL); William Moore scrapbook (NL) and papers (James Hardie Lib of Aust Fine Arts, Syd).   ROBERT HOLDEN

MOORE, SIR WILLIAM HARRISON (1867-1935), academic and constitutional lawyer, was born on 30 April 1867 in London, son of John Moore, printer and later journalist, and his wife Jane Dorothy, née Smith. After leaving school at 17 Moore worked as a journalist in the gallery of the House of Commons before entering the Middle Temple in 1887. Aided by scholarships, in 1891 he graduated B.A. from King's College, Cambridge, where he headed the first class in both parts of the law tripos, and LL.B. from the University of London and was called to the Bar. In 1892 he succeeded Professor Edward Jenks [q.v.9] in the chair of law at the University of Melbourne; he held it until 1927 and was appointed professor emeritus in 1928.

Harrison Moore was a small, fine-boned man and upon his arrival members of the university council were taken aback by his bright, boyish appearance. As dean of the faculty he immediately proposed reforms, including elimination of procedure as an undergraduate course and abolition of Roman law. Neither suggestion was adopted although later, under his leadership, the Melbourne law school pioneered the teaching of administrative law as an independent subject. He saw an important role for the school in the young colony, a conviction he maintained at his retirement. 'It is inevitable', he wrote in 1927, 'that Dominion Courts should owe less to British Courts in the future than they have done in the past . . . our courts are now accumulating a mass of case law . . . we shall become more dependent on schools of law and on the literature of the law to keep the systems in harmony'.

Moore's aims within the university reflected late nineteenth-century utilitarian ideals: the school should turn out 'really competent professional men . . . a Law School should not become too academic'. Similarly, in a university report published in 1899, he advocated a university system which would not only provide a scientific training in the structure and organization of modern industry and commerce but bring the university into touch with the commercial sector of the community. Although his report was shelved, the proposed curriculum provided the basis for the commerce degree introduced in 1925.

Moore also stressed the moral and social value of legal education. He favoured linking the study of law with history and politics and accordingly shaped his jurisprudence course to include political philosophy, and introduced broad historical themes in constitutional and legal history. He thus addressed both law and history students and, innovatively, the general public. Sir Keith Hancock described these lectures as 'the best course that I have ever known at any of my many universities'. The themes were broad, the methods exact and the whole delivered with Moore's sardonic wit and customary precision in speech. When speaking, he would twist between his fingers a pellet of wool, pulling it to pieces as if separating the strands of an argument and rewinding it into a ball.

In his monthly addresses to the Law Students' Society (recorded in the student magazine *Summons*), Moore used his wide-ranging knowledge to trace the development of legal institutions and provide a rationale for their existence. He also advocated reform of the existing law. In a speech on arbitration in 1896 he urged establishment of a permanent international court or college of arbitrators; in 1898 he questioned the validity and utility of the jury, and on another occasion criticized the statutory method by which lawyers were obliged to set out their fees, claiming that this procedure often resulted in lawyers being overpaid.

Undoubtedly, Moore's major contribution to the thought of his generation lay in constitutional law. He took an immediate interest in the work of the Federalists at the 1893

Corowa conference and in the drafting of the proposed constitution. By the time the Australasian Federal Convention's first meeting in Adelaide in 1897 ended, Moore was an acknowledged authority on the drafts and was 'used as a human reference library' by convention members. In 1902 he published *The Constitution of the Commonwealth of Australia*. It was his major work and the first scholarly study of the subject. It included a history of the Federation movement and a detailed examination of the Constitution. He maintained that national sentiment in favour of Federal power would, in time, recede and be reflected in constitutional amendments. 'The great facility', he wrote, 'with which the Australian Constitution may be altered, makes it probable, that its development will be guided, less by judicial interpretation, and more by formal amendment, than the development of the Constitution of the United States'. But, as J. A. La Nauze has commented, 'his famous pupils would have had less to do if he had proved to be a true prophet'. Moore published his second book, *Acts of State in English law*, in 1906.

Moore's Cambridge background, his correct English manner and outlook, and a pronounced puritanical streak enabled him to fit easily into the Melbourne Establishment; he was a member of the Melbourne Club. His social position was ensured by his marriage on 10 November 1898 to Edith Eliza, daughter of (Sir) Thomas à'Beckett [q.v.3]. Edith was an intelligent and strong-minded woman who omitted the conventional vow of obedience during their wedding ceremony at the Toorak Wesleyan Church. She was active in social movements, helping to secure the establishment of the Queen Victoria Hospital for Women and vigorous in her work for female suffrage. The Moores had no children and their domestic life at Arolla, a gracious house set in a rambling garden, was quiet.

Moore was a conservative, although his friends (Sir) Ernest Scott and (Sir) John Latham [qq.v.] remarked on his political neutrality and detachment, claiming that 'he was a liberal supporter of . . . societies . . . [concerned with] political issues', but 'careful never to ally himself with any political section'. During World War I he warmly supported conscription. In 1920 he criticized the concept of the caucus in 'Political systems of Australia', a chapter in M. Atkinson [q.v.7] (ed), *Australia: economic and political studies*; but his partisanship was more evident after his retirement. Four months after Labor's election in 1929 Moore actively advocated the need for a restriction of the activities of the Federal government, and in 1930 he censured Labor when it nominated only one person for the position of governor-general, although he did not question Sir Isaac

Isaacs's [q.v.9] fitness for the office. By May next year his political leanings were quite open: in a letter to the *Argus* on the conversion loan, an authoritative statement on the economic situation culminated in a ringing denunciation of the Labor leaders, Scullin, Theodore [qq.v.] and Lang [q.v.9].

Harrison Moore was closely involved with the Victorian government as its official adviser on constitutional matters (1907-10), and with conservative Federal governments; Sir Ronald Munro Ferguson [q.v.] also consulted him on constitutional questions. He was appointed C.M.G. in 1917 and K.B.E. in 1925. Much of his research in the early 1920s was directed to assisting Sir Leo Cussen [q.v.8] to prepare the Victorian Imperial Acts Application Act (1922). In October 1927 he attended the Rome conference revising the Bonn convention on artistic and literary copyright and afterwards travelled through Europe, visiting universities and assessing attitudes to the League of Nations; he also participated in the league's attempted codification of international law. In May 1928 he was appointed an Australian delegate to the league. Reappointed in 1929 and 1930, he played a significant role in the league commission in Geneva which revised the rules of the Permanent International Court of Justice.

Moore was also keenly interested in Imperial relations. As early as 1908 he had advocated a regular conference of lawyers of the Empire and called for the creation of a legal administrative union to collect and disseminate information. In 1927 he addressed the University of Chicago on the British Empire and its problems, as well as on the White Australia policy, and in 1929 he represented Australia at the Operation of Dominion Legislation Conference in London which led to the Statute of Westminster (1931). Moore subsequently wrote an article in support of the suggestion of an Empire tribunal.

After 1930 Moore was chairman of the Victorian division of the Royal Institute of International Affairs and a member of the executive committee of the Institute of Pacific Relations, leading a delegation to a conference in Shanghai, China, in November 1931. The last two years of his life were devoted to the completion of an article on the law to be applied in suits between governments in Canada and Australia. Characteristically, it was a lucid, meticulously researched piece which led him, like much else in his studies, into the borderland between constitutional and international law.

Moore died at Toorak on 1 July 1935 after a life remarkable for its dedication and hard work, and was cremated; his wife survived him. One of his most enduring contributions to Australia was his emphasis on Federal constitutional law and international law within the University of Melbourne; it has been claimed that the esteem enjoyed by the High Court of Australia reflects Moore's influence as a teacher on several of its members.

E. Scott, *A history of the University of Melbourne* (Melb, 1936); W. K. Hancock, *Country and calling* (Lond, 1954); G. Blainey, *A centenary history of the University of Melbourne* (Melb, 1957); Joan Lindsay, *Time without clocks* (Melb, 1962); J. A. La Nauze, *The making of the Australian Constitution* (Melb, 1972); L. Re and P. Alston, 'William Harrison Moore. Third dean of the faculty of law', in R. Campbell, *A history of the Melbourne law school, 1857 to 1973* (Melb, 1977); *Herald* (Melb), 1 July 1935; *Age*, 2 July 1935; *Argus*, 6 July 1935; Law Faculty, Univ Melb, Minutes (Univ Melb Archives); W. H. Moore papers (Univ Melb Archives).

LORETTA RE

MORAN, CHARLES JOHN (1868-1936), politician and farmer, was born on 20 November 1868 near Toowoomba, Queensland, son of Irish parents John Hacket Moran, labourer, and his wife Anne, née Armstrong. After education at local state schools and St Killen's College, Brisbane, he became a qualified pupil-teacher and matriculated to the University of Sydney in 1890, but did not proceed to higher study.

Late in 1890 he migrated to Western Australia and was articled to the architect A. Stombuco; he superintended part of the construction of the General Post Office (later Treasury) building. Following the discovery of gold at Coolgardie and Kalgoorlie Moran worked briefly for a contractor supplying water to the goldfields. He participated in the abortive Siberia rush of late 1893, and gained such repute that next year he won the Legislative Assembly seat for the new mining constituency of Yilgarn, defeating former Opposition leader L. V. De Hamel [q.v.8]. A handsome man with thick wavy hair and a luxuriant moustache, Moran was a fluent but unpolished speaker. He walked and cycled hundreds of miles, carrying swag and billy, while electioneering. In parliament as an Independent he staunchly supported the developmental policies of the Forrest [q.v.8] ministry, especially the goldfields water-supply scheme. Despite prevalent anti-Forrest goldfields sentiment, he was re-elected in 1897 for the East Coolgardie seat based on Kalgoorlie. He was now a director of several mining companies.

Against most of his constituents, Moran opposed Federation in 1900 as premature, broke with the Forrest ministry over the issue and supported a motion of no confidence; and after Forrest's retirement to enter Federal politics in 1901, he accepted office as commissioner of crown lands under

George Throssell [q.v.]. He lasted only long enough to authorize F. S. Drake-Brockman's [q.v.8] expedition to the Kimberleys. At the April 1901 elections he was ousted after a turbulent campaign. He contested West Kimberley unsuccessfully at a by-election in July but a year later won West Perth as an opponent of (Sir) Walter James's [q.v.9] Liberal government.

After the 1904 elections, seven survivors of the old Forrest party joined with Labor to carry a vote of no confidence in the James ministry. Moran then formed with three others an Independent group whose support gave Henry Daglish [q.v.8] the majority that enabled him to form Western Australia's first Labor government. Ambition and pique partly motivated Moran, but he was also spurred by a strong, if uncritical, belief in economic development, especially in agriculture. The 'mark time' policy of the Daglish ministry in its first year dissatisfied Moran and his followers and, in July 1905 after a cabinet reshuffle, the Independents negotiated an agreement under which the government pledged itself to a more energetic developmental policy. In August however the Independents voted against the terms on which the government intended to purchase the privately owned Midland Railway Co., and the ministry fell. Conjecture that Moran would form a ministry proved groundless; instead the Liberals came to power and at the October elections won a large majority. Moran was among the casualties and never again sat in parliament.

In 1907 he began farming at Wagin. He was prominent in the Farmers and Settlers' Association formed in 1912 and its offshoot, the Country Party. In 1921 he became a trustee of the Agricultural Bank. As such he was associated with its expansive credit policies in the 1920s and shared the censure when a 1934 royal commission accused the trustees of laxity; they were replaced next year. Moran wrote many articles on land settlement and was also a trustee of the Rural Relief Board. The government consulted him on rural policy until his death at West Perth on 18 December 1936.

On 28 August 1895 at Fremantle Moran had married Elizabeth Frances Healy, who survived him with three sons and three daughters. Moran died intestate; he was buried in the Roman Catholic section of Karrakatta cemetery.

W. B. Kimberly (comp), *History of West Australia* (Melb, 1897); *Morning Herald* (Perth), 25 June 1904; *West Australian*, 19 Dec 1936; D. Mossenson, Gold and politics: the influence of the eastern goldfields in the political development of Western Australia, 1890-1904 (M.A. thesis, Univ WA, 1952).   G. C. BOLTON

MORAN, HERBERT MICHAEL (1885-1945), surgeon, was born on 26 April 1885 at Darlington, Sydney, second son of Michael Moran (d. 1951), Irish-born baker, and his Australian wife Annie, née Quain (d. 1890). He was educated at Darlington Public School, St Aloysius' College, Surry Hills, and briefly at St Joseph's College, Hunters Hill, before proceeding to the University of Sydney (M.B., 1907; Ch.M., 1929).

Moran played Rugby Union for the Rose Bay club and then for the university; in 1906 he represented New South Wales against Queensland. Next year he was resident medical officer at (Royal) Newcastle Hospital. He captained the first Wallaby tour of Britain in 1908. Dogged by injury, he played in the Test against Wales which Australia lost. The series over, he took his F.R.C.S., Edinburgh, in 1909, then worked in hospitals in London and Dublin.

Back in Sydney next year, Moran practised at Balmain and later in Macquarie Street. At St Mary's Cathedral on 21 April 1914 he married Eva Mann. Already a captain in the Australian Army Medical Corps, in 1915 he went to Britain to join the Royal Army Medical Corps and served as a lieutenant at No. 23 Stationary Hospital, Indian Expeditionary Force, in Mesopotamia. Returning to Sydney in July 1916, he was honorary surgeon at St Vincent's Hospital.

Moran had a notable surgical career; his great interest lay in cancer research and the then new use of gamma irradiation through the medium of metallic radium. In this he was far ahead of his time and he travelled widely, published in journals and studied and lectured in many parts of the world. In 1927 he spent ten months at the cancer research centre in Paris. He was honorary consultant for radium treatment at Royal Prince Alfred, Lewisham and Royal North Shore hospitals and honorary radium therapist at Prince Henry Hospital in the 1930s. Editor of the *Journal* of the University Cancer Research Committee, he was a fellow of the Royal Society of Medicine, London, the Royal Australasian College of Surgeons, and St John's College, University of Sydney.

All his life Moran was haunted 'by the art, letters and antiquities of Italy and the majestic history of Rome and the Renaissance'. He spoke Italian, as well as French and German, and was a life member and president of the Dante Alighieri Art and Literary Society (Sydney) and deputy president of the Modern Language Association. In 1930 he gave £1000 for a lectureship in Italian at the university. He interviewed Signor Mussolini in 1932 and the next year was appointed cavaliere of the Order of St Maurice and St Lazarus. Leaving his wife and son in 1935, he revisited Italy and went to Britain to try and mend the deterioration in Anglo-Italian relations by lobbying political leaders. He visited the Italian army in Abyssinia and later was appointed commendatore of the Order of the Crown of Italy. In 1936 he published *Letters from Rome: an Australian's view of the Italo-Abyssinian question*. Initially impressed by Mussolini he later changed his opinion.

In World War II he served with the R.A.M.C. in 1940-45; promoted lieut-colonel, he was appointed an additional president of medical boards of Eastern Command in Britain based on Colchester, Essex. In 1945, stricken by his great enemy, he died of malignant melanoma in a Cambridge nursing home on 20 November, survived by his wife and son, with whom he was reconciled.

Moran's three largely autobiographical books show considerable literary talent and a very individual style. He was essentially a destructive critic of medical, social and religious mores—though he remained throughout a devout Catholic; his work exhibits a strong sense of sardonic humour and sympathy with the underdog. *Viewless winds* (London, 1939) had unusual success and caused much indignation in certain circles. *Beyond the hill lies China* (Sydney, 1945) vividly depicts social conditions and medical practice in Sydney before World War I and *In my fashion* (London, 1946) dealt with his work for the British Army and the symptoms and course of the disease that killed him.

G. E. Hall and A. Cousins (eds), *Book of remembrance of the University of Sydney in the war 1914-1918* (Syd, 1939); J. Pollard, *Australian Rugby Union* (Syd, 1984); *British A'sian*, 12 Nov 1908, 1 Sept 1910, 2 Dec 1915, 16 Mar 1916; *MJA*, 23 Mar 1946, p 415, 23 Apr 1946, p 535; *Aust and NZ J of Surgery*, 45, no 2, May 1975, p 119; *SMH*, 11 Nov 1927, 20 June 1930, 12, 29 Sept 1932, 21 Sept 1933, 26 May 1934, 23 Nov 1945; *Bulletin*, 16 Oct 1946; information from Prof P. A. P. Moran, ANU, Canb.　　　　　　　　　　　G. P. WALSH

MORAN, PATRICK FRANCIS (1830-1911), cardinal, was born on 16 September 1830 at Leighlinbridge, Carlow, Ireland, youngest of five children of Patrick Moran, businessman, and his wife Alicia, née Cullen and formerly Murphy. For both his parents, who had complex family relationships through the Mahers, it was a second marriage.

Born into material comfort, Moran was deprived of emotional security. His mother died when he was fourteen months old, his father when he was 11, and three siblings died young. The Cullens of Craan, Carlow, provided a home for him until, in 1842, he was placed in the care of his mother's half-brother (Cardinal) Paul Cullen [q.v.3], rector of the Irish College, Rome, who was to be the formative influence in his nephew's life.

In Rome Moran was a model student, diligent and industrious. At 15 he spoke Italian and Latin 'as well as any man in Rome', according to Cullen. Over the next ten years he added French, German, Spanish and Irish, as well as Hebrew and biblical Greek. He studied theology at the Roman Seminary under the Jesuits Perrone and Passaglia, and at the Urban College of Propaganda Fide where in 1852 he was awarded a doctorate with Cardinal Pecci (later Pope Leo XIII) as one of his examiners. His studies had been only slightly disturbed by the Roman revolution of 1848-49 and he was ordained priest on 19 March 1853.

At the Irish College Moran was at the centre of a missionary enterprise with worldwide interests. In 1856 he was appointed vice-rector, but he preferred missionary work to an episcopal career in Ireland; his strong sense of missionary vocation was to underlie his willingness to go to Australia in 1884. He developed good working relations with Roman officials and in the 1850s and 1860s regularly wrote memoranda to officials, drafted reports on Irish affairs, and even wrote some of Cullen's pastoral letters. He acted as translator, interpreter and guide for both metropolitan and overseas Irish: in 1859 he helped Archdeacon McEncroe [q.v.2] to prepare the colonial Irish clergy's case against Archbishop Polding [q.v.2] of Sydney.

In 1857 Moran was appointed professor of Hebrew in the Propaganda College, where he also taught Scripture. He had studied palaeography and, urged by Cullen, began the first systematic study of the sources for the history of the Irish Church. On 2 May 1859 Cullen secured special papal authorization for Moran to make copies of relevant codices in Roman archives. For the rest of his life Moran maintained his interest in the search for relevant manuscripts and built up a collection of books and maps dealing with Australasia and the Pacific. He regularly recorded archaeological details and visited the sites of former Celtic monasteries.

Moran wrote five substantial books on Irish Church history including *Historical sketch of the persecutions suffered by the Catholics of Ireland under the rule of Cromwell and the Puritans* (1862), *Essays on the origin, doctrines, and discipline of the early Irish Church* (1864) and a *History of the Catholic archbishops of Dublin, since the Reformation* (1864). He wrote many scholarly articles, pamphlets and formal lectures, some of which were collected in *Occasional papers* (1890). He also edited *The pastoral letters and other writings of Cardinal Cullen, archbishop of Dublin* (1882), and *Spicilegium Ossoriense* (1874, 1878, 1884), a three-volume collection of documents illustrating Irish ecclesiastical history from the Reformation until 1800, and made other compilations of source material.

Well versed in hagiology, Moran published *Irish saints in Great Britain* (1879). Although some of his work was antiquarian and his purpose often apologetic or polemical, he saw himself as rescuing the Irish past from the dominance of the Protestant ascendancy represented by J. H. Todd and Trinity College, Dublin. However, he was a pioneer in the use of archives, and some of his work belongs to the wider context of the creation of a modern Irish cultural identity. He was an early advocate of compulsory Irish for university matriculants, and remained a strong supporter of the language revival. By the 1870s he had acquired some of the analytical skills and understanding of a historian, but his development was increasingly restricted by pressure of work, and his intended biography of Cullen was never written. His massive *History of the Catholic Church in Australasia* (1895) was essentially a compilation of source material, but organized with specific apologetic and polemic aims. He made other, much shorter, contributions to Australian historiography, most notably *Discovery of Australia by De Quiros in the year 1606* (1906), in which scholarly caution was overridden by his eagerness to claim first arrival for his Church. Historical research gave him a strong sense of change over time and of the need to respond to that change.

In 1866, newly promoted monsignor, Moran returned to Ireland to become Cullen's private secretary. From 1864 he had been joint founding editor of the *Irish Ecclesiastical Record*, which he later made the model for the *Australasian Catholic Record* he launched in Sydney in 1895. He was appointed professor of Hebrew and Scripture at Holy Cross College, Clonliffe, the Dublin diocesan seminary, and was also appointed to the staff of the troubled Catholic University of Ireland as professor of Scripture and scriptural languages and of Irish history. In 1869 he was elected a fellow of the Royal Irish Academy.

In 1871 Cullen arranged for Moran to be appointed coadjutor-bishop in Ossory and on 5 March 1872 consecrated him bishop of Olba *in partibus*. In August Moran succeeded automatically when the octogenarian bishop died. After moving to Kilkenny, he visited each of the forty-one parishes at least twice in his first three years. He concentrated on raising the educational standards of the clergy, strengthening their discipline and reorganizing the local seminary, St Kieran's College, reviving liturgy, increasing the number of nuns, and establishing industrial schools. He strongly advocated total abstinence, a policy he pursued vigorously in his early years in Sydney but later moderated. He inherited a serious situation in the town of Callan where the learned but eccentric parish priest Robert O'Keeffe had defied suspension measures, launched civil actions against the old bishop, and added further libel actions against Moran and Cullen. The legal saga ended in 1875 with O'Keeffe's defeat, setting precedents for church-state relations in Irish law.

Moran was 6 ft. 3 ins. (191 cm) tall, an impressive figure but reserved, shy and seemingly aloof. He kept his emotions under tight control, but was subject to bouts of weeping which he overcame only in his forties. One of his priests said later that he was 'very much respected, a good deal feared, but little loved'. He was a man of simple piety and well-regulated habits. He meditated daily on life as a 'pilgrimage', regularly using Bishop Challoner's *The garden of the soul*. He was probably the only nineteenth-century bishop actually to publish a devotional book, *The Catholic prayer book and manual of meditations* (Dublin, 1883) which, characteristically, included translations of early Irish prayers. His health was never robust: he suffered from bronchitis and congestion of one lung.

Many of the Irish bishops and clergy regarded Moran with suspicion because of his close relationship with Cullen, but most bishops, and especially Roman officials, recognized his competence. He was secretary for one of the commissions of the 1875 Maynooth Plenary Council; the task of getting the council's decrees approved by Rome facilitated the smooth functioning of his own three plenary councils in Australia. He was several times authorized by the Vatican to mediate in disputes between Irish bishops and clergy and over land agitation, and to negotiate with the British government on education reform.

Some clergy and laity mistakenly regarded both Cullen and Moran as favourably disposed towards British rule: both had a strong sense of Irish nationality but condemned Fenianism on the practical grounds that it would only result in increased British repression. Publicly cautious on national issues, Moran, asked by Leo XIII in 1888 secretly to investigate Irish conditions, upset the Vatican with the forcefulness of his condemnation of British policy.

From the 1850s Moran had been an interested observer of Australasian events. In 1866 he was appointed non-resident vicar-general of the diocese of Maitland, New South Wales, and as Bishop James Murray's [q.v.5] proctor attended sessions of the first Vatican Council. He thought of New Zealand as an integral part of a common region, and later strongly opposed a Roman decision to separate New Zealand from the Australian colonies for Church purposes. In 1878 the New South Wales Irish suffragan bishops appointed him their agent to argue their case in Rome against the English Archbishop Vaughan [q.v.6], especially in defence of Bishop O'Mahony [q.v.5], which Moran quickly realized was a lost cause. Despite anti-Irish lobbying by English Catholic bishops and a British government agent, Moran had the strong support of Propaganda officials and the endorsement of Pope Leo XIII himself. He was appointed archbishop of Sydney on 25 January 1884 and arrived on 8 September.

His settling in was disrupted on 1 May 1885 by a summons to Rome. He believed he would be offered the see of Dublin, but determined to urge Leo XIII to allow him to return to Sydney. On arrival he was informed that he was to be made a cardinal. Far from a consolation prize, this was both a confirmation of Moran's high personal standing in Rome and an affirmation of Leo's belief in the importance of the new worlds. On 27 July he was raised to the rank of cardinal-priest, with a titular link to the Roman church of St Susanna, and became a member of three Roman congregations, Propaganda, Consistory and Religious; but he had few opportunities to join in curial government. When Leo died in 1903, Moran failed to reach Rome in time for the conclave that elected Pius X.

Before his return to Sydney in 1885 he was appointed apostolic delegate to preside over the Plenary Council of Australasia, held in November to reorganize Church structure and discipline. He was given similar authority for the second and third councils of 1895 and 1905 and, since this covered intervening years in which council decrees were being processed, Moran, for most of his Australian years, occupied a most unusual position as both the senior member of the local hierarchy and the Pope's representative in dealing with that hierarchy. This dual role confirmed the Pope's high opinion of Moran. Rome had wanted a plenary council to be held in Australia since the 1870s to consolidate the widespread Church structure. Moran acted skilfully and decisively and the three councils in a period of economic development and vital political change laid the foundations of the national Church in the twentieth century.

Before Moran's arrival, the Australasian colonies had been heavily dependent on migrant priests. He soon commissioned Sherwin & (J. F.) Hennessy [q.v.9] to design a seminary and his official residence (completed 1886) at Manly. St Patrick's College, initially intended to provide priests for all the colonies, was opened in 1889; Moran contributed a library of several hundred books, a collection of medieval manuscripts, and items for a museum.

Within two years Moran, with typical thoroughness, had not only visited every one of the forty-six parochial districts of his diocese (which then extended to the Victorian border), but also the suffragan dioceses of Maitland and Armidale, and New Zealand. In 1887 he sailed to both Brisbane and Adelaide to confer palliums on new archbishops, and to Perth to consecrate a bishop. Before his death he had visited almost every diocese in Australasia including Western Australia in 1887 and 1911 and New Zealand in 1885, 1905 and 1908. He dedicated cathedrals at Armidale, Bathurst, Goulburn, Lismore; Melbourne and Bendigo, Victoria; Hobart; Rockhampton, Queensland; and Auckland and Dunedin, New Zealand. He made five journeys to Rome on Church business in 1885, 1888, 1893, 1902 and 1903.

Moran was determined to have all Catholic children in schools staffed by religious Orders. By 1911 more than three-quarters of the Catholic children in Sydney of primary-school age were in his system, and he had laid the basis for a similar secondary system. He almost trebled the number of teaching brothers and more than trebled the number of nuns. He had authorized the expenditure of more than £1 250 000 on building churches, schools and institutions. On the twentieth anniversary of his arrival he noted that he had personally blessed eighty-eight foundation stones for churches or schools in the diocese. The largest single building project was the near-completion of St Mary's Cathedral. He had first finished the northern end, then built the central section including 'the Cardinal's Tower' by 1900, and was able to consecrate it all, debt free, in 1905. In his last years he decided to begin work on the southern part of the original plan, set a foundation stone in 1909, and in the second half of 1910 was speaking almost weekly in a tour of parishes to raise money.

The colonies had a long history of sectarian conflict before Moran's arrival, exacerbated by disputes over education in the 1870s and 1880s. His Irish experience made him deeply distrustful of other denominations. In the 1880s he rejected offers from the Anglican Bishop Barry [q.v.3] to co-operate for common Christian objectives, and resisted pressure from the governor Lord Carrington [q.v.3], with similar aims. In the 1890s he increasingly believed that Catholics' political and civil rights were threatened and, in 1896, saw deliberate discrimination in a situation where 'no office of first, or even second, rate importance is held by a Catholic'.

In 1901 he refused to attend the official inauguration of the Commonwealth because precedence was given to the Church of England. As his public role developed, he made numerous enemies for himself and his Church by his attacks on other denominations. When his secretary D. F. O'Haran [q.v.] was cited as co-respondent in the

Coningham [q.v.8] divorce cases in 1899-1901, he regarded this as a Protestant conspiracy aimed at himself, but rejoiced that 'the Catholic spirit has been wonderfully aroused'.

In deliberately developing an active public role, Moran acted on the assumption that in colonial society leadership was needed. While his sermons remained, as in Ireland, 'so learned that he was hard to follow', he delivered brief, impromptu speeches at Church functions which, by the 1890s, had become the delight of Sydney journalists. In this role he became one of the best known public figures in Australasia. Increasingly in the 1890s he advocated Federation and in 1896 was invited to address the People's Federal Convention at Bathurst. Next year he agreed to stand for election to the Australasian Federal Convention and, when sectarian feeling erupted, he persisted in his candidacy, believing that the civil rights of Catholics were at issue, but failed to win a position in the New South Wales delegation of ten. In the 1900s he continued to strongly advocate an independent defence and foreign policy, repeating earlier calls for a separate Australian navy and supporting schemes for military training programmes.

In the 1880s and 1890s Moran denounced anti-Chinese legislation as unchristian and specifically defended Chinese migrants, though pilloried in front-page caricature by the *Bulletin* as 'The Chows' Patron'. His vision of Australia as the base for the Christianization of Asia and the Pacific was threatened. He had originally intended to establish a Chinese College in Sydney. His junior seminary, St Columba's College, Springwood, was planned as a missionary college. He gave the French Sacred Heart missionaries a Sydney base and seminary at Kensington for their work in Melanesia. Through the 1880s and 1890s he urged the Propaganda Congregation to provide missionaries for both Melanesia and Polynesia, sending detailed advice on ethnology, geography, social conditions and means of travel. At the 1885 Plenary Council of Australasia he introduced a scheme for annual collections throughout the colonies to support missionaries working among Australian Aborigines, especially in Queensland and Western Australia; but he received little support from most of the other bishops, despite his constant reminders.

There was an unconventional side to Moran which marked him out among his contemporaries in the Irish episcopate and in the College of Cardinals. Although in no real sense a liberal Catholic, he had no sympathy with the integralist trends of European Catholicism. He criticized French Catholic anti-Semitism during the Dreyfus case, and paid a sympathy call on the chief rabbi of Syd-

ney after pogroms in Russia. In Ireland he had opposed political activity by women; in Australia he became a strong advocate of female suffrage and authorized use of his name for female suffrage campaigns in Europe. In 1907, in response to Pius X's directive to all Catholic bishops, he dutifully set up a vigilance committee to search for evidence of 'modernism' but decided there was nothing to be worried about in Australia. The radicalization of his political and social attitudes in his last fifteen years involved no questioning of theological implications. He remained within the conventional theology of his early years, and enjoyed making disparaging remarks about Cardinal Newman as a theologian.

His increasing public support for the trade union movement, for the new Labor Party, and for what he called 'Australian socialism' alarmed conservative Catholics in Australia and overseas. In 1890 he had supported the trade union cause in the maritime strike, a year before the appearance of the papal encyclical *Rerum novarum*, for which he tried to provide Australian relevance in his 1891 public lecture, 'The rights and duties of labour'. At first cautious, by 1900 he had criticized many aspects of the industrial system, and on one occasion even quoted Karl Marx on the social consequences of capitalism. To some extent, his support for the Labor Party was influenced by his belief, expressed publicly in 1901, that Labor was 'the only party above religious prejudice'. By 1902 he was being criticized by other bishops for putting social reform ahead of their demands for 'educational justice'. In 1905 he upset both Prime Minister (Sir) George Reid and the leading Catholic editor J. Tighe Ryan [qq.v.] by denying that the Labor Party's platform made it unacceptable to Catholics. The great enemy of Australia, he said, was 'not socialism . . . but imperial jingoism'. In his last year, he both intervened in State politics to persuade a Catholic not to abandon support for the tottering McGowen [q.v.] Labor government and provoked worried letters from American Catholic bishops, including Cardinal Gibbons, because of his strong public support for the 1911 'socialist' referenda proposals.

In 1889-99 Joseph Higgins [q.v.9] served Moran faithfully as auxiliary bishop. When Higgins was given his own diocese in 1899, an ageing Moran was in even greater need of help. Since arriving in Sydney he had depended heavily in administrative matters on his secretary O'Haran, 'a treasure to me'. Seemingly oblivious to growing criticism of O'Haran from clergy and laity, well before the Coningham case, Moran nominated him as his auxiliary, and was upset by Rome's reply that the nomination was opposed by several Australian bishops. Angered to find that his old friend Bishop Murray was among O'Haran's critics, Moran contemplated resignation and retirement to Rome. He refused to make any other nomination and hastily decided to have, instead, a coadjutor with the right of succession. Uncritically, he endorsed the first choice of the clergy and bishops, Michael Kelly [q.v.9], a man quite unsuited for Australian conditions and probably too simpleminded to be a successful bishop anywhere. From Kelly's arrival in 1901 the relationship was one of constant friction. Annoyed by Kelly's repeated public-relations blunders and, above all, by his failure to give priority to episcopal visitations, Moran tried unsuccessfully to minimize the consequences of his own misjudgement.

In August 1911, after a visit to Perth, Moran retired to Manly for a few days rest. He was found dead in his room on the morning of 16 August. He was buried in the crypt of St Mary's Cathedral.

Portraits of Moran are in St Patrick's College and the Archbishop's House at Manly, and at St John's College, University of Sydney. A bronze statue by Bertram Mackennal [q.v.] is outside the south entrance of St Mary's Cathedral.

J. T. Donovan, 'His Eminence' (Syd, 1902); P. MacSuibhne, Paul Cullen and his contemporaries, 1-5 (Naas, Kildare, Ireland, 1961-77); P. Ford, Cardinal Moran and the A.L.P. (Melb, 1966); R. G. Ely, Unto God and Caesar (Melb, 1976); P. O'Farrell, The Catholic Church and community in Australia (Melb, 1977); E. M. O'Brien, 'Cardinal Moran's part in public affairs', JRAHS, 28, no 1 (1942); A. E. Cahill, 'Catholicism and socialism: the 1905 controversy in Australia', J of Religious Hist, 1, no 2 (1960), and 'Cardinal Moran and the Chinese', Manna, 6 (1963); also J. M. Mahon, same issue of Manna; Moran papers (Catholic Diocesan Archives, St Mary's Cathedral, Syd); Irish College Archives and Sacred Congregation of Propaganda Fide Archives and Vatican Secret Archives (Rome); Catholic diocesan archives (Maitland in NSW, Melb, Perth, and Dublin and Kilkenny in Ireland).   A. E. CAHILL

MORANT, HARRY HARBORD (1864?-1902), horseman, balladist and soldier, was born probably on 9 December 1864 at Bridgwater, Somerset, England. He arrived at Townsville, Queensland, on 1 April 1883. He later claimed to be the son of Admiral Sir George Digby Morant of Bideford, Devon, and to have entered the Royal Naval College.

On 13 March 1884, at Charters Towers, Edwin Henry Murrant, son of Edwin Murrant, and his wife Catherine, née O'Reilly, married Daisy May O'Dwyer. It is almost certain that he was Morant, then a groom at Fanning Downs station, and that she was Daisy Bates [q.v.7]. After being acquitted of a charge of stealing pigs and a saddle, he separated from her and went to Winton, later overlanding cattle south.

Acquiring a reputation as horse-breaker, drover, steeplechaser, polo player, drinker and womanizer, from 1891 he contributed bush ballads to the Sydney Bulletin as 'the Breaker'. He was in Adelaide when the South African War broke out in 1899 and enlisted in the 2nd Contingent, South Australian Mounted Rifles, as Harry Harbord Morant.

In South Africa Morant's skill as a horseman was soon well known, and having qualities of education and manners he was engaged as a dispatch rider by General French, and later worked with Bennett Burleigh, a British war correspondent. At the end of his one-year enlistment he received good reports and accepted but did not take up a commission in Baden Powell's South African Constabulary. He went to England, and is supposed to have been welcomed into society and to have become engaged. Becoming close friends with Captain Percy Hunt, who had also served in the war, he followed him back to South Africa in March 1901. In changed conditions, irregular units were formed to counter Boer guerillas. One such, the Bush Veldt Carbineers, formed at Pietersburg, north of Pretoria, was composed largely of time-served colonials, but was not an Australian formation. Its commander, Major R. W. Lenehan [q.v.], commissioned Morant and sent him into the Strydpoort area south-east of Pietersburg where he served with distinction.

To the north, known as the Spelonken, the British commander, Captain Robertson, was weak, and Captain Taylor, an intelligence officer from Rhodesia, a man of sadistic brutality. When six Boers came into Fort Edward wishing to surrender, they were shot by the B.V.C. Not long afterwards a B.V.C. patrol led by Lieutenant P. J. Handcock [q.v.9] returned with one of its number, Van Buuren, a turncoat Boer, mysteriously shot. There was also insubordination and looting by some troopers and Robertson was recalled. Hunt was posted to Fort Edward, to be joined by Morant and Lieutenants Picton and Witton. On patrol on 4 August 1901 Hunt was mortally wounded. Some mutilation was done to the body, and clothing taken. There is evidence that Africans, not Boers, may have been responsible for the atrocities, but Morant, now in command, morose and incensed, encouraged by Taylor, became bent on vengeance. He led a patrol after the Boers, and caught up with them late in the evening.

Because of his premature order to attack, all but one, Visser, wounded in the ankle, got away. Morant wanted to shoot Visser immediately, but was dissuaded. The patrol next morning returned some distance towards Fort Edward, and on 11 August Visser was shot. Morant had alleged that Visser was wearing some of Hunt's clothing, but the evidence is to the contrary. Then eight Boers approaching Fort Edward to surrender were met by a patrol led by Morant and including Handcock. The Boers were spoken to by a passing missionary, Rev. C. A. D. Heese, a British subject of German extraction who attempted to reassure them, but on 23 August Morant had them shot. Heese left, rejecting Morant's advice not to go on to Pietersburg alone. Morant then spoke to Taylor, and Handcock rode out.

Later, Heese was rumoured killed, and Handcock reported finding his body. On 7 September Morant, Handcock and two others shot three Boers coming in to surrender. Morant then led a successful patrol to capture alive an Irish-Boer leader, Kelly. After leave in Pretoria he returned to the Spelonken but on 22 October was, with Lenehan, Taylor, Picton, Witton and others, arrested.

A court of inquiry dragged on until on 15 January 1902 charges were laid. Morant was charged with inciting various persons to kill Visser, the eight Boers, the three Boers, and Heese. Major J. F. Thomas, a solicitor from Tenterfield, New South Wales, was ordered at short notice to represent the accused and on 17 January the trial in relation to Visser began. On 23 January Boers attacked the blockhouses at Pietersburg where the court martial was taking place. Morant, Handcock and others were recalled to service and helped to beat off the attack. The hearing then continued. The existence of orders to take no prisoners, and the difficulties of guerilla warfare, were pleaded.

On 1 February the case of the eight Boers commenced. As in the first case, no finding was pronounced, nor was it after the next hearing, in relation to the three Boers. At the trial in relation to the missionary, Handcock, who was charged with and had originally confessed to the murder, gave an alibi. He claimed to have visited two Boer ladies at their farms on the day in question, and they corroborated his story. But other evidence leaves an irresistible inference that Heese was murdered at Morant's instigation. In 1929 Witton informed Thomas that Handcock had confessed the murder of Heese to Witton, and had implicated Morant as the instigator of 'a most premeditated and cold blooded affair'. The alibi was, however, accepted and acquittals pronounced on this charge.

Morant was convicted on each other charge, and sentenced to death, although the court recommended mercy on the grounds of provocation, good service and want of military experience. On 26 February Morant and Handcock were informed that they would be shot in the morning. Thomas in desperation sought to see Lord Kitchener, but he had gone out on trek. The sentences were duly carried out, and bravely endured, Handcock and Morant being shot by firing squad on 27 February in Pretoria. After Morant's execution Admiral Morant denied he was his father. The Defence Act (1903), limiting the offences for which sentence of death could be imposed by court-martial, and requiring such sentence to be confirmed by the governor-general, perhaps reflected public concern over the executions.

Probably the charge of which Morant was acquitted was the impetus for his execution. The acquittal, while certainly open on the evidence, is with hindsight and in the light of additional evidence best supported by the defence of condonation, based on the call to service during the attack on Pietersburg. That defence would not have had to deny what is now virtually undoubted, namely Morant's reprehensible incitement of the homicide of an innocent civilian. The defences put in the other cases were rightly rejected. Even if an order to take no prisoners had been lawfully given, the deaths of the Boers, who had ceased to resist and been taken prisoner, did not occur in pursuance of such an order. As folk hero he should be rejected, but he may be accepted as a man of many talents who, under the influence of weak or sadistic peers, was corrupted by the brutality of war.

The film *Breaker Morant* was released in 1980.

F. Renar [Fox], *Bushman and buccaneer* (Syd, 1902); G. Witton, *Scapegoats of the Empire* (Melb, 1907, 1982); R. Kruger, *Goodbye Dolly Gray* (Lond, 1959); G. Jenkin, *Songs of the Breaker* (Adel, 1960); F. M. Cutlack, *Breaker Morant* (Syd, 1962); R. L. Wallace, *The Australians at the Boer War* (Canb, 1976); M. Carnegie and F. Shields, *In search of Breaker Morant* (Melb, 1979); K. Denton, *Closed file* (Syd, 1983); *Northern Miner*, 14 Apr 1902; personal records, 83/120 (AWM).   R. K. TODD

MORDAUNT, EVELYN MAY (1872-1942), author, was born on 7 May 1872 at Cotgrave, Nottinghamshire, England, fifth child of St John Legh Clowes, gentleman farmer, and his wife Elizabeth Caroline, née Bingham, daughter of the 3rd Baron Clanmorris. She spent her childhood at Charlton House near Cheltenham, Gloucestershire, and her teens near Heythrop, in the Cotswolds. Tall like her brothers, and 'stoutly made', Evie grew up with a love of horses, hunting and open-air life. She learned little from a series of governesses but later took up landscape painting and fabric and wallpaper design, and studied German, Latin, Greek and shorthand.

In 1897 Evelyn went to Mauritius as companion to her cousin Caroline, wife of (Sir) George Le Hunte [q.v.]. On 18 August 1898 in the Plaines Wilhems district, she married Maurice Wilhemn Wiehe, a sugar-planter. Her two children of this unhappy marriage were stillborn. Wasted by malaria, she returned alone to England; in convalescence she completed *The garden of contentment.* But before the first edition appeared in 1902, under her pen-name 'Elenor Mordaunt', she had left in the sailing-ship *Loch Katrine* for Melbourne, arriving on 10 June. On 9 March 1903 she gave birth to a son, Godfrey Weston Wiehe.

In Australia Evelyn made some lifelong friends, initially through Dr Edith Barrett [q.v.7]. Except when incapacitated by illness or injury she refused all offers of help, living in cheap lodgings and earning her keep by sewing blouses and muslin cushions, painting parasols, posters and friezes and decorating white furniture. She tried her hand at stained-glass window design and for some months ran a small metal workshop. She briefly edited a woman's monthly magazine. Friendship with C. Bogue Luffman [q.v.] led to work designing and building a garden; she lived at his house at the School of Horticulture, Burnley, for some two years from late 1903. While there she wrote *Rosemary: that's for remembrance* (Melbourne and London, 1909). On 14 July 1909 she and her son left for England.

To support herself Evelyn turned to writing, using several pseudonyms but from 1913 principally 'Elinor Mordaunt'; she changed her name by deed poll to Evelyn May Mordaunt on 1 July 1915. Altogether she published over forty volumes, mainly novels and short stories. Her reputation as a travel writer resulted from her round-the-world trip by sail and cargo steamer for the London *Daily Mail* in 1923.

In her autobiography, *Sinabada* (1937), Evelyn Mordaunt recalls her antipodean years with affection, but few of her books have Australian settings. *A ship of solace* (1911) describes a voyage by sailing-ship to Melbourne; *Lu of the ranges* (1913) is set in Victoria; the hero in *The pendulum* (1918) becomes involved in trade union and labour politics while in Australia. Short stories published in *The island* (1914) first appeared in the *Lone Hand* in 1910 and 1912; 'The Ginger Jar' in *Old wine in new bottles* (1919) is about the Chinese of Melbourne's Little Bourke Street. A more practical appraisal of Australian society is contained in her handbook, *On the wallaby through Victoria*, by E. M. Clowes (1911). The product of both reminiscence and research (some of it unreliable), this book is interesting as the memoir of a woman who had learned to adapt to unfamiliar class values.

During World War I, Mrs Mordaunt lived at Greenwich, London. In the 1920s she bought a house in the south of France but sold it when her travels took her far afield to Central and North America, the Pacific and Africa. On 27 January 1933 at Tenerife, Canary Islands, she married Robert Rawnsley Bowles, 66, a retired barrister from Gloucestershire; in her own words, the marriage 'ended in tragedy'. She died on 25 June 1942 at the Radcliffe Infirmary, Oxford.

R. B. Johnson, *Some contemporary novelists— (women)* (Lond, 1920); S. J. Kunitz and H. Haycraft, *Twentieth century authors* (NY, 1942); National American Woman Suffrage Assn, *Woman's J* (NY), Mar 1929; *Wilson Bulletin*, vol 3, no 18, Feb 1929, p 470; *Aust Book Buyer*, June 1912; *The Times Literary Supp*, 14 Sept 1911; *The Times*, 18 Sept 1931, 23 Oct 1937, 27 June 1942.

SALLY O'NEILL

MORELL, SIR STEPHEN JOSEPH (1869-1944), businessman and lord mayor, was born on 15 August 1869 at Carlton, Melbourne, son of Esteban (Stephen) Murell, Spanish restaurateur, and his Victorian-born wife Ada, née Scott. By the time Stephen was 3 he and his family were living in Spain where he received his early education, but in 1883 they returned to Melbourne. Murell had a hotel on the corner of Bourke and Russell streets from 1884 to 1893 when he expanded his interests to set up his children; the Orient Hotel on the corner of Swanston and Collins streets was transferred to Stephen in 1894.

In 1885-87 Stephen had attended Scotch College. He excelled at rowing, which remained a lifelong interest: he helped to coach the college crew in 1891-92, joined the Mercantile Rowing Club in 1891 (president, 1907-33), and was a member of the Victorian champion four in 1896 and of the champion eight in 1896 and 1897; at his death he was president of the Victorian Rowing Association. In the 1890s he was also actively involved in the Metropolitan Amateur Football Association and was later a vice-president of the Melbourne Cricket Club.

Consolidating the start his father had given him in the hotel trade, Morell, who worked briefly for a firm of indenters, invested in Queensland pastoral runs and more city property. In 1914 he took over the Princes Bridge Hotel (Young and Jackson's). When the Melbourne breweries combined in August 1903 to raise the price of beer he helped to establish the successful Melbourne Co-operative Brewery at Abbotsford; he became its chairman and joined the expanded board when Carlton and United Breweries absorbed the co-operative in 1925. From 1911 Morell was a director of Windsor Pictures and from 1928 of the Victoria Insurance Co. and of Equity Trustees, Executors & Agency Co. Ltd.

He was popular and affable, yet shrewd. From 1901 until 1939, when he retired, he represented Gipps Ward on the Melbourne City Council. He served on seven council committees and was chairman of the licensed vehicles and electric supply committees. He was a member of the Melbourne Tramway Trust in 1901-05 and joined the Melbourne and Metropolitan Tramways Board in 1929. In 1925 Morell was made an alderman and in 1926 succeeded Sir William Brunton [q.v.7] as lord mayor. In this capacity he entertained the duke (later King George VI) and duchess of York in 1927 and was knighted. He was unanimously elected to a second term and, in 1928, declined a third. Bridges over the Yarra were an issue of his mayoral years, as was the work of the Metropolitan Town Planning Commission, but initiatives were frustrated by the division of metropolitan authority. Morell was a supporter of a unified Greater Melbourne Council, but was ideologically unable to support the adult suffrage necessary for reform.

A cosmopolitan, Morell visited Japan in 1933; he was honorary consul for Spain prior to the Civil War and but for the outbreak of hostilities would have been motoring there in 1936. He died at his South Yarra home on 6 July 1944, survived by his wife Elizabeth Rutherford, née Telford, whom he had married on 27 November 1901 at Richmond with Presbyterian forms, and by three sons and a daughter. He was cremated after Masonic rites and left an estate sworn for probate at £65 219. Morell Bridge over the Yarra was renamed after him in 1936 in tribute to his municipal service and his enthusiasm for rowing.

J. Smith (ed), *Cyclopedia of Victoria*, 1 (Melb, 1903); *VHM*, 23 (1950), p 74; *Table Talk*, 14 Nov 1901, 9 Dec 1926; *Herald* (Melb), 9 Oct 1926, 17 Jan, 12 Nov 1927, 9 Feb 1948; *Argus*, 13 Jan, 9 May, 11 Oct 1927, 7 July 1944; *Age*, 19 Oct 1936, 7 July 1944.   DAVID DUNSTAN

MORGAN, SIR ARTHUR (1856-1916), newspaper proprietor and premier, was born on 19 September 1856 at Rosenthal station, Warwick, Queensland, son of James Morgan [q.v.5] and his wife Kate, née Barton, both Irish born. Arthur's schooling in the Warwick district was cut short when his father bought the *Warwick Argus* newspaper and printing business on 1 June 1868. Arthur learned the trade from back room to front office. By 18 he was manager, as his father's responsibilities in the Legislative Assembly took him away increasingly from 1873. A justice of the peace before he was 20, Arthur became editor and,

with his brother, proprietor of the *Argus* a few months before his father died in 1878. The paper became a bi-weekly publication from 26 August 1879, and a month later moved into new commodious premises. On 26 July 1880 Arthur married Alice Augusta Clinton at Warwick with Church of England rites. By August 1888 the *Argus* was asserting that its circulation bordered on one thousand each issue, double that of its competitor, the *Examiner and Times*.

Arthur Morgan entered politics at the local level in 1885 when elected to the Warwick Municipal Council; he served as mayor in 1886-90 and 1898. On 18 July 1887 he was elected to the Legislative Assembly for Warwick and represented this electorate until 4 April 1896 when he stood aside to allow T. J. Byrnes [q.v.7] to pursue the premiership via the seat. He was chairman of the royal commission on local government that year. Morgan regained Warwick on 2 October 1898 at the by-election after Byrnes's death and, enjoying 'the confidence of all parties', served the assembly as Queensland's first native-born Speaker from May 1899 until September 1903. He resigned after a series of dramatic political events surrounding the defeat of the Philp [q.v.] government. Labor leader W. H. Browne [q.v.7], unable to form a government, recommended that the governor send for Morgan. Drawing on support from the 'Darling Downs bunch' (seceders from (Sir) Robert Philp), he formed a composite group from farming representatives, liberal progressives and the Labor Party.

When the Morgan-Browne coalition ministry was sworn in on 17 September 1903, one commentator noted that the member for Warwick had before him a particular opportunity for performing 'a master stroke of statesmanship'. Morgan became premier, chief secretary and secretary for railways. The coalition was returned overwhelmingly in 1904. It was responsible for the mildly progressive Income Tax Amendment Act of 1904 and introduced the franchise for women in State elections. According to T. O'Sullivan [q.v.], Morgan was a dignified, courteous and sensitive man who became 'thoroughly disillusioned' by the hurly-burly, factionalism and strife of parliamentary politics. He relinquished the premiership, accepting the presidency of the Legislative Council from 19 January 1906 after the death of Sir Hugh Nelson [q.v.]. William Kidston [q.v.9] became premier.

In 1907, about the time he was knighted, Morgan effectively stepped aside as editor of the *Warwick Argus*. For nearly thirty years he had followed a moderately liberal political line. Never a member of the Queensland Club, actively identified with agricultural and acclimatization bodies, he compared city people to drones who were simply useful machines for paying taxes. It was the miner, pastoralist and farmer who produced the wealth on which the city people lived and grew fat.

Morgan released his reins on the *Argus* overtly in 1910 when he ceased to be sole proprietor and became chairman of directors of Warwick Argus Ltd, which was incorporated on 4 June with a capital of £8000. Andrew Dunn [q.v.] and sons bought the paper on 31 March 1914.

On Kidston's recommendation, in 1907 the governor Lord Chelmsford [q.v.7] reluctantly appointed Morgan—'the lesser evil of the two', who was still close to politics—lieutenant-governor, by-passing (Sir) Pope Cooper [q.v.8]. Morgan deputized in 1907 and 1908 during Chelmsford's absences and, in 1909 and 1914, was lieutenant-governor on the retirement of governors Chelmsford and Sir William MacGregor [q.v.5]. He was still president of the Legislative Council when he died at his Brisbane residence, Clinton, Upper Paddington, on 20 December 1916 after a long illness; he was buried in Toowong cemetery after a state funeral and service at St John's Anglican Cathedral. His estate was valued for probate at £8790. Morgan was survived by his wife, five sons and three daughters. His eldest son Arthur Clinton served with the 11th Light Horse at Gallipoli and briefly became a member of parliament.

C. A. Bernays, *Queensland politics during sixty (1859-1919) years* (Brisb, 1919?); Commercial Publishing Co. of Syd. Ltd, *Annual Review of Qld*, 1902; Qld Trustees Ltd, *Trustees Quarterly Review*, Jan 1917; *RHSQJ*, 10 (1978-79), no 4; *Warwick Argus*, 4 July, 5 Dec 1878, 26 Aug, 27 Sept 1879, 25 Aug, 25 Sept 1888; *Brisbane Courier*, 18 Sept 1903, 21 Dec 1916; *Warwick Examiner*, 11 Jan, 1 Feb 1908; *Toowong Chronicle*, 21 Dec 1916; B. A. Knox, The Honourable Sir Arthur Morgan, Kt: his public life and work (B.A. Hons thesis, Univ Qld, 1956); T. O'Sullivan, Reminiscences of the Queensland parliament, 1903-15 (nd, Oxley Lib, Brisb); GOV/68, 3 Feb 1906, 4 May 1907 *and* A/18942 (QA).   ROD KIRKPATRICK

MORGAN, GODFREY (1875-1957), journalist, grazier and politician, was born on 29 July 1875 at Landsborough, Victoria, second surviving son of English parents Godfrey Morgan, printer and later newspaper proprietor at Donald, and his wife May Elizabeth, née Williamson. Young Godfrey was educated at Coodie's and Hawthorn colleges, Melbourne. When his father died in 1891, he became a reporter and manager of the *Donald Times* and three years later its editor and proprietor. He organized and founded the

Victorian Provincial Newspapers' Association and twice held office as its president. On 8 December 1896 Morgan married Annie Jane Pace at Donald.

Responding to a Queensland government call for settlers to take up prickly-pear-infested selections, he took up 7000 acres (2830 ha) on the Condamine River near the town of Condamine. The selection, called Arubial, was occupied by his family in 1908. Inexperienced in pastoral pursuits, Morgan battled to turn his selection from virgin scrub into prime grazing land, introducing irrigation to offset drought. He extended his land holdings, bred and judged Shorthorn cattle and Corriedale sheep and became an authority on the grazing industry and related matters. Keenly interested in bloodstock horses, he gained an insight into horse-racing and its administration; his horses won many races in Brisbane. In 1933-39 he was president of the Queensland Breeders', Owners' and Trainers' Association.

In 1909 Morgan was elected to the Murilla Shire Council at Miles and on 2 October he won Murilla as a ministerial supporter in the State elections. His political career was exemplified by faithful service to his rural electorate, by his indefatigable work on solving problems of prickly-pear-infestation, of lack of roads and water. His attendance on horseback at waterhole meetings and annual picnics led to the view that 'the Murilla electorate was to Godfrey Morgan the whole world'.

After fourteen years of parliamentary opposition, Morgan expected to be given the lands portfolio when A. E. Moore [q.v.] led the Country and Progressive National Party to power in 1929. However Moore wanted a tough man for a tough portfolio, so Morgan became secretary for railways (1929-32) and minister for transport (1932).

Although the Moore government lost power in June 1932, Morgan retained his seat and unmercifully badgered the Forgan Smith [q.v.] Labor government; he was one of the party's more able debaters. In 1935 he won the new electorate of Dalby, but broke away from the C.P.N.P. Following redoubled efforts by Labor he lost the 1938 election as a Country and United Australia Party candidate. Although he then retired from politics the Country Party drive he started in 1935 continued to gain impetus.

Resident in Brisbane now, Morgan visited Arubial periodically and maintained his interest in horse-racing. He died in St Martin's private hospital, Brisbane, on 29 August 1957, survived by his wife, two daughters and four sons, and was cremated with Church of England rites after a state funeral.

A contemporary regarded Morgan as a politician with strong convictions and uncompromising views, a genial companion with a keen appreciation of a joke.

C. A. Bernays, *Queensland—our seventh political decade, 1920-1930* (Syd, 1931); H. M. Ferguson, *A history of Tara and district 1840-1960* (Brisb, 1961); C. Lack (ed), *Three decades of Queensland political history, 1929-1960* (Brisb, 1962); G. Morgan, *We are borne on as a river (my first seventy years)* (Brisb, 1971); *Qld Country Life*, 5 Sept 1957; *Courier Mail*, 30 Aug 1957; Morgan family papers (held by author, Indooroopilly, Brisb).

J. C. H. GILL

MORGANS, ALFRED EDWARD (1850-1933), mining investor and politician, was born on 17 February 1850 at Ochr Churith Machen Lower in Monmouthshire (now Gwent, Wales), son of Morgan Morgan, mine engineer, and his wife Mary Ann, née Tucker. After education at private schools and schools of mines, he was apprenticed at Ebbw Vale and worked in various regions of Britain as a mechanical engineer specializing in iron and coal-mining. In 1878-95 he spent much time in Central America representing British investment in mining and railways, especially in Guatemala and Nicaragua. From this period he retained many picturesque anecdotes, claiming acquaintance with the Mexican dictator Porfirio Diaz and other notable people. Morgans also developed an interest in Aztec and Mayan archaeology and sent artefacts to British museums.

Early in 1896 he came to Western Australia to inspect mining properties for London capitalists and stayed as local managing director and attorney. He was responsible for the development of the Mount Morgans field, the establishment of a short-lived copper-smelting plant at Murrin Murrin, and for several more gold and asbestos enterprises. In May 1897 he entered the Legislative Assembly as member for Coolgardie and, despite his capitalist beliefs and background, easily retained the seat against all opponents until his retirement in June 1904. A prosperous-looking figure with waxed moustache and pince-nez, Morgans was a good-humoured and diplomatic personality who largely confined his public utterances to the advocacy of goldfields railways and public works. He was a powerful supporter of the Coolgardie goldfields water scheme and promoted civic amenities which would encourage families to settle permanently on the goldfields.

In politics he described himself as an independent cross-bencher but usually voted with the Forrest [q.v.8] ministry. After Forrest entered Federal politics early in 1901 a period of political instability followed which brought Morgans to the fore. In November George Leake's [q.v.] first ministry lost a vote of confidence in the Legislative Assembly, largely over railway policy. The leader of the Opposition F. H. Piesse [q.v.], a former railways minister, was unable to form a cabinet and the task was entrusted to Morgans, as a practical man of experience. He became premier on 21 November. Of his five ministers three were recruited from among Leake's following; but at the ensuing ministerial elections in December all three were defeated. Morgans sought a parliamentary dissolution from the governor Sir Arthur Lawley [q.v.], who refused. Several backbenchers then defected to Leake from Morgans, who resigned on 23 December. He never sought parliamentary office again and retired at the next election. Among the consolations of an opulent private life he numbered a grazing property in the Porongorups on which he tried to acclimatize fallow deer.

From 1910 the goldfields were in decline and Morgans' fortunes with them; he occupied himself with a variety of honorary offices. He was consul for Austria-Hungary in 1910-17, vice-consul for Spain in 1915, and consular agent for the United States of America in 1921-30, having acted in that post since 1918. Between 1918 and 1920 he served on the North Fremantle Municipal Council and he was president of the acclimatization committee administering the Perth Zoological Gardens in 1921-29. He died at South Perth on 10 August 1933 and was buried in the Anglican section of Karrakatta cemetery. His estate was sworn for probate at £3658. Morgans had married Fanny Ridler at Westbury on Severn, Gloucestershire, England, on 19 March 1872. She and their son Morgan Morgans, also a mining investor, predeceased him.

W. B. Kimberly (comp), *History of Western Australia* (Melb, 1897); P.W.H.Thiel & Co., *Twentieth century impressions of Western Australia* (Perth, 1901); J. Raeside, *Golden days* (Perth, 1929); C. F. H. Jenkins, *The Noah's ark syndrome* (Perth, 1977); G. S. Reid and M. R. Oliver, *The premiers of Western Australia 1890-1982* (Perth, 1982).

G. C. BOLTON

MORIARTY, DANIEL (1895-1982), sportsman, was born on 21 August 1895 in Adelaide, tenth of fourteen children of Irish migrants Daniel Moriarty, carter, and his wife Jane, née Condon. His father worked for the Adelaide City Council and the family lived near the Victoria Park racecourse. The boys attended Christian Brothers' College, Wakefield Street, a well-known nursery of sportsmen. Following the death of his mother when he was 13, Dan at 14 joined the accounts branch of the Postmaster-General's Department, where he spent most of his working life.

Moriarty was almost 24 when he played his first South Australian National Football League match for South Adelaide in 1919; he soon established a brilliant record. At 5ft. 10in. (178cm) he had a fine physique, was broad shouldered and well muscled through a lifelong habit of systematic exercise and vigorous sport; he did not smoke. Quick and agile, Moriarty showed superb judgement of pace. He proved to be an exceptional footballer. However, other factors in his short career contributed to the legend which grew up. He came to the league fully formed and at the top of his powers and won the Magarey medal, as the fairest and most brilliant player, in his first three seasons (1919-21)—a feat which has never been repeated. He played for South Australia at centre-half-back in his first year, and was an automatic selection thereafter.

On 5 November 1924 in St Francis Xavier's Cathedral he married Clarice Mary Corona Teresa Thornton, a photographer's assistant; they had a daughter and a son. When Moriarty retired in 1926, still at the top of his powers, he made a clean break with the game, though suited by character, prestige and discipline to be a football administrator or coach. Just as he left no memories of a young footballer gradually acquiring skill, so there were none of an ageing champion's decline.

As a boy Moriarty had fallen under the spell of the thoroughbred horses exercising and training at Victoria Park, and racing had remained in his thoughts. He now embraced what was to be in turn a pastime, a passion and almost a profession. He was special racing writer for the Catholic weekly *Southern Cross*, and then regular track reporter for the Adelaide *News*. In 1935 he resigned from the public service to freelance, specializing in racing journalism. He became an owner and had many successes with shrewdly chosen horses such as Torlea, Trellios, Welloch, First Scout, Serene Princess and St Pierre. After giving up journalism in 1955 he devoted his long retirement to his family, business, farming, golf and racing.

Moriarty was popular on South Australian race-tracks; the aura of success from his football youth stayed with him, while his expertise was widely acknowledged and admired. But other qualities won him the affection of his fellow-sportsmen—a delight in the game itself, a most genial temperament and a moral earnestness that seemed to make him an elder statesman in any group.

Moriarty died in Calvary Hospital on 12 November 1982 and, after requiem Mass at St Ignatius Church, Norwood, was buried in Centennial Park cemetery. He was survived by his wife and children and the South Adelaide Football Club struck a perpetual trophy to commemorate him.

C. K. Knuckey, *South Australian football, the past and present* (Adel, 1965); B. Whimpress, *The South Australian football story* (Adel, 1983); *Sth Aust Football Budget*, 9 May 1981; *News* (Adel), 7 Sept 1976; *Advertiser* (Adel), 13 Nov 1982.

J. H. PASH

MORICE, LOUISE (LUCY) (1859-1951), kindergarten worker and social reformer, was born on 1 March 1859 in Adelaide, daughter of John Brodie Spence, official assignee, and his wife Jessie, née Cumming. She was educated at private schools and was much influenced by her family's Unitarianism and political interests. Her aunt Catherine Helen Spence [q.v.6] became her greatest friend. She married JAMES PERCY MORICE (1858-1943) on 20 March 1886 in a Unitarian service at her father's home, Fenton, Glenelg; they had one son. Pretty, poised and sociable, Lucy read avidly and developed an idealistic vision of a just society; she frequently despaired of its realization.

She and 'Auntie Kate' founded the Woman's League in 1895, after female enfranchisement, 'to educate women politically and to work for the interests of women and children'. Its early failure, Lucy believed, was because of the absorption of women into party politics and men's conservatism and fear of their wives being exposed to 'disturbing ideas and suggestions'. In 1902 the all-female South Australian Co-operative Clothing Co. opened Adelaide's first electrically powered clothing factory, designed to protect women workers from 'sweating'. Lucy Morice was a foundation shareholder and Catherine Spence chaired it until she died in 1910, her hand in Lucy's. Although they had agreed that she would complete her aunt's unfinished autobiography, another niece forestalled these plans. Lucy chaired the co-operative until its liquidation in 1913, caused by economic competition and, she thought, the individualism and lack of co-operation of Australians. She and her husband helped to found an Adelaide Fabian group; in 1903 they had met the Shaws and other Fabians in England. She turned to the Anglican Church and theosophy, claimed to be a socialist and in 1905 she joined a United Trades and Labor Council committee to form a new trade union, the Women's Employment Mutual Association, of which she was an active honorary member.

Freed by domestic help, Lucy enjoyed music and in 1911-12 was on the board of the Adelaide Literary Theatre. She attended Government House balls and held 'salon' afternoons on Sundays for interesting and intellectual persons of varied persuasions. In 1905 she had helped to found the Kindergarten Union of South Australia which became her most passionate commitment. With Lillian de Lissa [q.v.8] she battled to maintain the union's early independence and sought widely for funds. Initially minute secretary, in 1913-32 she was honorary organizing secretary, in 1912-31 on the executive, in 1922-51 on the education committee and vice-president from 1932 to 1951. She lectured in history of education to Kindergarten Training College students in 1908-25 and stimulated them to read widely. Her belief in kindergarten as a hope for society's future was allied with distaste for what she saw as the regimentation of the state school system. Her compassion for children caused her, with Dr Helen Mayo [q.v.], to found the School for Mothers Institute in 1909; as its president she campaigned against high infant mortality rates.

That year, on Vida Goldstein's [q.v.9] advice, she initiated the Women's (later Non-Party) Political Association, which took practical and successful steps to stimulate reform in numerous areas affecting women and children; political lobbying was continually employed. She succeeded her aunt as president. In 1916-17 she was a vice-president of the League of Loyal Women and was later a committee-member.

In 1935 the Lucy Morice Kindergarten, to which she had donated £500, was opened at lower North Adelaide. In 1936 she was appointed M.B.E. Her correspondence with Miles Franklin [q.v.8] from the 1930s describes experiments with Christian Science and the trials of her husband's physical and mental decline. Lucy Morice died in a nursing home on 10 June 1951. She was cremated, having requested that 'no-one shall wear mourning for me . . . nor send any flowers'.

Her husband James Percy, parliamentary librarian and clerk, was born on 18 November 1858 at Brixton, London, son of James Morice, general merchant's clerk, and his wife Cecilia Margaret, née Swan. He was educated at Bedford Grammar school and migrated in 1877, becoming a clerk in the South Australian Survey and Crown Lands Department in 1878. In 1886 he was appointed librarian to the South Australian parliament. Though genial, he battled with members who were irresponsible with books, magazines and newspapers. He banned smoking from the reading-room from 1892 until 1915, when a members' vote reversed the decision. Morice supervised the library's move to the old Legislative Council chamber in 1909 and organized a card catalogue in 1916.

He was clerk assistant and sergeant-at-arms of the Legislative Council 1901-18 and of the House of Assembly in 1918-20. In 1918 he resigned as librarian and became clerk of the council in 1920, and clerk of parliaments in 1925-36, when he developed an unrivalled knowledge of parliamentary procedure. A member of the Adelaide Club, he was at the heart of political affairs through his work; these advantages helped his wife. He supported her as treasurer in 1913-20, general secretary in 1914-20 and trustee in 1922-37 of the Kindergarten Union. He retired in 1936, died at his North Adelaide home on 26 March 1943 and was cremated.

H. Jones, 'Lucy Spence Morice and Catherine Helen Spence: partners in South Australian social reform', *JHSSA*, no 11 (1983); *Advertiser*, 25 Feb 1902, 29 Mar 1943; *Herald* (Adel), 1 Mar 1902, 12 May 1906, 28 Apr 1908; *Daily Herald* (Adel), 28 June 1913; L. S. Morice, Auntie Kate (nd, typescript), *and* South Australian Co-operative Clothing Co. records, *and* League of Women Voters, executive and committee minutes, *and* Kindergarten Union of SA, Annual Report, 1906-07 to 1952 and executive and organizing cttees papers and minute-books, 1905-52, *and* Woman's League records (SAA); A. Wainwright, A tribute to Lucy Spence Morice (1962, typescript, Thiele Lib, SA College of Advanced Education); SA Parliament, Joint Lib cttee, Minute-book, 1881-1917 (Parliamentary Lib, Adel); Lucy Morice to Rose Scott, 12 Apr 1910 (R. Scott correspondence, ML); S. M. Franklin letters (ML).   HELEN JONES

MORLEY, WILLIAM (1854?-1939), Congregational minister, was born at Cransley, Northamptonshire, England, son of George Morley, postal official, and his wife Anne, née Moore. From 1875 he studied for the Congregational ministry at New College, London. He married Alice Micklem at Littlewick, Berkshire, on 19 July 1881. Morley began his ministry at Thame, Oxfordshire (1880-89), was a director of the London Missionary Society and served at Littlehampton, Sussex (1889-92).

Soon after migrating to Melbourne in 1892 Morley was invited to fill a vacancy at Prahran. Later he served congregations at Rockhampton, Queensland (1897-1900), and Dulwich Hill, Sydney (1901-08). In 1906-27 he was New South Wales auxiliary secretary of the London Missionary Society, devoting his whole time to the society from 1908.

A foundation executive-member of the Association for the Protection of Native Races in Australasia and Polynesia, formed in Sydney in 1911, Morley became co-secretary in December 1915 and soon assumed sole responsibility, proving himself adept at organization. Although Aborigines were an early priority, over the next ten years attention was largely confined to Papua, New Guinea and Melanesia. In 1923 Morley could rejoice at the absence of serious complaints or injuries to Aborigines in recent years. The association ceased to function in 1925 but was reactivated in November 1927, after the Onmalmeri massacre in Western Australia.

Over the last twelve years of his life Morley worked tirelessly to improve conditions of Aborigines. In August 1928, on his motion, the A.P.N.R. adopted a policy of 'physical, mental and moral improvement'. By 1929 he was calling for Federal control, increased spending, extension of reserves, improved conditions on pastoral stations, and reforms in the administration of justice. In 1928-30 he launched a campaign to arouse public opinion, raised money to assist starving Aborigines in Central Australia and demanded a royal commission to investigate the Coniston killings. In 1929 he recruited Professor A. P. Elkin to the A.P.N.R.'s executive and persuaded him to assume its presidency in 1933.

Throughout the 1930s Morley was in almost constant contact with Federal authorities and to a much lesser extent their State counterparts, although he failed to establish relations with Aboriginal leaders or to support actively their campaign for citizenship. He was prominent in the agitation over the Tuckiar (1933-34), Borroloola (1933-36) and McKinnon (1934-35) cases and was responsible for establishing the A.P.N.R.'s journal, the *Aborigines' Protector*, in 1935.

Morley was an uncompromising crusader for justice, in the process alienating senior officials. He met ministers and politicians when possible, but more often doggedly argued the case in closely reasoned correspondence; where all else failed he tried to publicize issues through the press. Bitterly disappointed by the unresponsiveness of governments, the disregard of the record of 'ill-treatment, outrage, and massacre', he was forced by illness to resign in November 1938. He urged that his successor should not be a moderate, for 'moderatism will never help the cause of our natives'. As no replacement was found, he resumed the position in April 1939, but died on 19 August at his Killara home and was cremated. His wife, two daughters, and son Norman (1883-1940) who also worked for Aborigines, survived him.

Assn for the Protection of Native Races, *Annual Report*, 1912, 1930-39; *Vic Independent*, Oct 1939; *Aborigines' Protector*, no 7, Nov 1941, p 4; Association for the Protection of Native Races, Aboriginal matters, Dept of the Interior (AAO), *and* Minute-books, correspondence (Univ Syd Archives); information from Mr J. Creasey, Dr Williams's Library, Lond.   ANDREW MARKUS

MORONEY, TIMOTHY (1890-1944), railwayman and union official, was born on 15 November 1890 at Nundah, Queensland, son of Irish immigrants Thomas Moroney (d. 1900), labourer, and his wife Bridget, née O'Dea. Tim was educated at Nundah State School and Brisbane Normal School and in 1906 was employed by the Queensland Railway Department as a lad porter. He lost his job because of his activities with the railway strike committee in 1912 but was reinstated as a clerk in 1913.

He married Norah Violet Ruane in St Stephen's Cathedral, Brisbane, on 11 August 1915; they had two sons and a daughter. Norah died in 1936 and on 26 January 1938 in Holy Spirit Church, New Farm, Tim married his secretary Kathleen Annie Scully, who also bore him two sons.

His activities in the labour movement began in 1910 when he became a founding member of the Queensland United Railway Employees' Association; in 1917-20 he was general secretary of the Queensland Railway Union. When the Q.R.U. combined with 'all grades' organizations in other States to form the successful, militant Australian Railways Union in 1920, he became State secretary until his death. Moroney was Q.R.U. delegate in 1916-20 and 1923-26 to the State central executive of the Australian Labor Party and to the 1918, 1923 and 1926 Labor-in-Politics conventions.

He resigned temporarily from the central executive in January 1920 in protest against its acceptance of a delegate from the Returned Soldiers' and Sailors' Labor League. Having been on the State Railway Strike Council in 1925, Moroney and the other A.R.U. delegates were expelled—largely due to Labor premier McCormack's [q.v.] influence—from the 1926 convention, and subsequently the party, on the grounds that only under protest had they signed pledges declaring that they were not members of the Communist Party. George Rymer and Moroney in 1927 led the A.R.U. in bitter clashes with the Labor government during the protracted South Johnstone strike and railway lockout. In 1929 Moroney joined the Militant Minority Movement of disillusioned Labor supporters before the elections in which McCormack was defeated.

A big, able man with a sense of humour, Moroney was the adored centre of his extended family. He was a fearless and forceful advocate, a convincing, logical speaker and a gifted writer, admired by fellow workers for the strength and humanity of his personality. He lectured for the Workers' Educational Association and was a driving force behind the education and propaganda classes initiated by the A.R.U. Many of his books, which formed part of the A.R.U. library, were from the George C. Kerr group of socialist publications and were influential in the development of his syndicalist philosophy. A critic of compromising Labor politicians, Moroney saw socialism and direct intervention by unions as the only answer to poverty and injustice. His interests included international affairs, the peace movement and the fight against fascism.

Moroney had been active in the anti-conscription campaign during World War I and had supported the Industrial Workers of the World against unjust persecution. With the A.R.U. isolated politically and industrially from the A.L.P., Moroney helped to found the Railway Transport Council, was general president of the A.R.U. in 1935-44 and inaugural president of the Combined Railway and Transport Unions Federal Council in 1936. During World War II he joined the Volunteer Defence Corps as an anti-aircraft gunner. In 1942-44 he was vice-president of the Australasian Council of Trade Unions.

Moroney edited the A.R.U. *Advocate* in 1930-44 and wrote several pamphlets on trade union and political subjects. He learned to pilot small planes for union business, had an interest in ciné photography and was a member of the Queensland League of Wheelmen. In his later years he became a strict teetotaller. He died on 10 September 1944 in Genazzano Private Hospital, Brisbane, from coronary occlusion and was buried in Nudgee cemetery with Catholic rites.

F. Nolan, *You pass this way only once* (Brisb, 1974); V. Daddow, *The puffing pioneers and Queensland's railway builders* (Brisb, 1975); D. J. Murphy (ed), *Labor in politics* (Brisb, 1975); D. J. Murphy et al (eds), *Labor in power* (Brisb, 1979); *Labour Hist*, 31 Nov 1976, p 1; *Telegraph* (Brisb), 11 Sept 1944; *Advocate* (Brisb), 15 Sept 1944; *Courier Mail*, 11 Oct 1944; information from Mr T. Moroney, Sheldon, Brisb.   JOY GUYATT

MORRES, ELSIE FRANCES (1874-1958), teacher, was born on 6 September 1874 at Sandhurst (Bendigo), Victoria, daughter of Henry Morres, surveyor, and his wife Emily Augusta, née Moore. Starting school when only 4, she matriculated from Tintern Ladies' College, Melbourne, in 1888 aged 13. In 1890 she enrolled at the University of Melbourne and as a non-resident student of Ormond [q.v.5] College. Her course was made more difficult by the absence of both Greek and Latin in her secondary education, but she was determined and hard working; she was awarded the exhibition in Natural Philosophy I and graduated B.A. in 1901, having been president of the Committee of University Women. She received her M.A. in 1903 and later maintained her interest in university affairs, being for some years on the committee of the Victorian Women Graduates' Association.

Since childhood, when she had 'taught' her brother's toy soldiers, Elsie Morres had wished to become a teacher. She served a seven-year apprenticeship at Melbourne Church of England Girls' Grammar School, and became, in 1906, founding headmistress of The Hermitage, a new Anglican grammar school for girls at Highton, Geelong. She remained headmistress for over twenty-seven years, retiring at the end of first term 1933.

During her years as headmistress, The Hermitage's enrolments grew from 45 to 200. It grew physically as more properties were bought, new buildings erected and old ones modified; it grew academically and in sporting prowess, but remained essentially a family school. The emphasis was always on boarders, particularly girls from Western District families, to whom the headmistress regarded herself as a mother. She later commented that though she had borne no children she had daughters unnumbered.

The Hermitage under Miss Morres maintained close ties with the Church of England. Herself a sincere Christian, she had qualified as associate of theology, and she strove to impart to the girls her deep personal faith and the principles and precepts of the Church. In 1926 she had the joy of seeing Archbishop Lees [q.v.] dedicate 'the Sanctuary' at the school.

Many of her 'daughters' went on to the university, often as residents of Janet Clarke [q.v.3] Hall, and embarked on professional careers, but Miss Morres was not a feminist in the post-World War II sense of the term; she regarded women as equal but different. To her mind a girl 'should be a woman and a home-maker first and let her business or her profession come after'. This belief and the realization that non-academic girls had other talents to be developed, led her to pioneer at The Hermitage a course in domestic economy which included dressmaking, cookery and laundry.

After her retirement Elsie Morres lived in a cottage in the Dandenongs, but maintained close contact with the school and with her former pupils. She died at Footscray on 17 November 1958 and was cremated. A portrait by William Dargie is at The Hermitage.

I. Southall, *The story of The Hermitage* (Melb, 1956); The Hermitage, *Coo-ee*, 1932, 1933, 1958; *Geelong Advertiser*, 15 Feb, 18 Dec 1906, 18 Dec 1907, 16 Dec 1908; *Age*, 21 Apr 1933, 18 Nov 1958; M. Y. Blight, Attitudes towards women in Victoria gaining a university education and subsequent graduate employment 1900-1920 (B.A.Hons thesis, Monash Univ, 1970).   LYNDSAY GARDINER

MORRIS, ALBERT (1886-1939), botanist and assayer, was born on 13 August 1886 at Bridgewater, South Australia, second son of Albert Joseph Morris, stonecutter from England, and his wife Emma Jane, née Smith. The family moved to the new silver-field of Thackaringa, New South Wales, and in 1890 to Broken Hill. From an early age Albert developed a strong interest in the plant life of the arid interior. His lifelong passion for botany may have resulted from an injury to his foot in infancy that left him crippled for life and debarred him from sport. He was educated at Burke Ward Public School and at Broken Hill Technical College, where he obtained a diploma in metallurgy; he grew and sold pepper trees to pay his fees. He was employed by the Central Mine from 1902 and became its chief assayer.

At Broken Hill on 13 April 1909 he married Ellen Margaret Sayce, dressmaker. She was a forceful personality and a staunch member of the Society of Friends; in 1918 Morris also became a Quaker after an Anglican upbringing. They built a tiny cottage in Cornish Street, Railway Town, an area most exposed to soil erosion and drifting sand: trees had been cut for fuel and years of overstocking and the rabbit plague had denuded the land.

Morris cultivated a desert garden and, assisted by Edwin Ashby [q.v.7], experimented with a wide range of plants from dry areas, including Arizona and South Africa. He found that species grown from seed collected locally withstood drought conditions better than others. In 1920 with W. D. K. MacGillivray he helped to found the Barrier Field Naturalists' Club and served as its secretary until his death. Numerous field expeditions in his spare time greatly increased his knowledge and his collection to over 5000 pressed specimens, which his wife later gave to the Waite [q.v.] Institute of South Australia. Strongly practical, he gave away hundreds of trees and shrubs to schools and public bodies and worked to preserve the Aboriginal paintings and rock carvings at Mootwingee from vandalism.

Until 1936 no mining company was willing to control sand drift by implementing Morris's idea of a green belt, which he asserted would 'not only help, but will wholly remove the problem . . . providing you fence a fairly large area with stock and rabbit-proof fencing, and give some help for the first few years'. W. S. Robinson [q.v.], managing director of the Zinc Corporation Ltd, decided to support Morris, who showed a remarkable understanding of the three basic principles of natural regeneration: the exclusion of grazing animals and rabbits; careful positioning of fences to protect trees from prevailing winds; and choice of local plants well adapted to the hot, dry conditions.

In May 1936 the company established a twenty-two-acre plantation, later named the Albert Morris Park. Morris provided seedlings and advised the planting of native grasses, gum trees and old man salt bush, a species that had almost disappeared. Within eighteen months the results were so impressive that the North Broken Hill and Broken Hill South companies joined the scheme.

Morris did not live to see the greening of Broken Hill by the regeneration area, parks, bowling greens and recreation areas. Survived by his wife, but childless, he died of a cerebral tumour on 9 January 1939 at Broken Hill and was buried with Anglican rites. A drinking fountain in front of the Technical College commemorates his work. Gentle and a tireless amateur botanist, Morris also enjoyed music and reading. Known simply as 'Uncle Bert', he was a kind host to many nurses sent to Broken Hill to train at the hospital.

A. Morris, *Plantlife of the West Darling*, Barrier Field Naturalists Club comp (Broken Hill, NSW, 1966); W. S. Robinson, *If I remember rightly*, G. Blainey ed (Melb, 1967); R. H. B. Kearns, *Broken Hill 1915-39*, 3, and *1940-73*, 4 (Broken Hill, NSW, 1975 and 1976); *Walkabout*, 1 Nov 1938, p 33; *Vic Naturalist*, 55 (1938-39), p 180; *Barrier Daily Truth*, 10 Jan 1939.   B. E. KENNEDY

MORRIS, SIR JOHN NEWMAN; *see* NEWMAN-MORRIS

MORRIS, MYRA EVELYN (1893-1966), author, was born on 15 May 1893 at Boort, Victoria, daughter of English-born Charles William Morris and his Victorian-born wife Bessie Lily, née Sydenham. Her father owned a series of grocery and produce stores at Allansford, Warrnambool, Rochester, Maldon, St James and Camperdown. Growing up in bush towns, the five Morris children shared their mother's delight in the natural world; she, rather than her husband, nurtured Myra's literary abilities. Myra was educated at Rochester Brigidine Convent where, lively and vibrant, she was encouraged by her English teacher and published verse in the *Bulletin*.

Without further formal training Myra embarked on a career as a freelance writer, publishing her first selection of poetry, *England, and other verses*, in 1918. In 1922 *Us five*, a children's novel, was published after being serialized, and Myra with her youngest sister moved to a flat in Melbourne. In 1927, with her parents and elder sister, she moved to Frankston, where she lived for the remainder of her life. It was an easy-going, sociable household and the family was relatively well-off but Myra, staunchly independent, paid board and did her share of housework and entertaining. She described herself as a 'lazy, vagabond sort of person who has no aesthetic fancies, no neurotic leanings and no secret sorrows'. She published her steady output of short stories and verse in major Australian journals, newspapers and popular magazines. Many were included in the main anthologies. She did some book-reviewing and editing and wrote essays, but her preference was for short stories.

In 1930 Myra travelled to England, where she had an affair with the ship's captain. On her return to Frankston she became increasingly involved in literary, journalistic and artistic circles. A person of 'boundless energy, swift enthusiasms and great vivacity', she had diverse interests: she studied art for two years under Alexander Colquhoun [q.v.8], was a talented woodcarver, a dedicated gardener, and a bushwalker and swimmer. In 1938 her novel, *The wind on the water*, was published and she was active in founding and organizing the Melbourne branch of P.E.N. International. In 1939 she completed her novel, *Dark tumult*.

Myra Morris has been acclaimed as one of Australia's best short-story writers. Her clear pictures of life in country and town contain a wide range of characters and reveal her tolerance and understanding of humanity in its struggles. Like her novels, her stories combine earthy realism, poetic imagery and a broad humour. Sometimes her plots are marred by the demands of the popular market, but her often beaten-down and defeated people always contrast with her lyrical evocation of landscapes. In her poetry (a second volume, *White magic*, was published in 1929), there is an occasional haunting melancholy, but more often she celebrates the individual's spiritual connexion with the land, equating it with the search for God.

Myra's later years were difficult. Katharine Prichard [q.v.] recalled her unassuming and undemanding ways with friends and family, but sensed her frustration; in the mid-1940s she had a nervous breakdown, but was awarded a Commonwealth literary fellowship. In 1947 *The township*, a selection from her innumerable short stories, was published, and her work was broadcast on Australian and British radio and on Australian television. Translations were published in Germany, Austria and Switzerland.

Crippled with Paget's disease, Myra Morris died at Frankston on 18 August 1966 and was cremated with Anglican rites.

C. Roderick, *20 Australian novelists* (Syd,

1947); *Aust Woman's Mirror*, 19 July 1927; *Book News*, Oct 1947; *Bohemia*, 1 Dec 1966; *Age*, 2 Aug 1961, 19 Aug 1966; International P.E.N. Club papers *and* Lavater papers (SLV); information from N. Morris, Frankston, Melb.

D. J. JORDAN

MORRISON, CHARLES NORMAN (1866-1909), educationist, was born on 4 December 1866 at Geelong College, Skene Street, Newtown, Victoria, third son of George Morrison [q.v.5], proprietor and principal of the college, and his wife Rebecca, née Greenwood. G. E. 'Chinese' Morrison [q.v.] was his brother. Norman spent his whole life as part of the school: even during his few years of study and teaching in Melbourne it was his family home. His education there flowed from cradle to junior classes to matriculation and first-year arts. He was a good student; handsome, tall, straight, slender, he was also a strong athlete and footballer.

In 1885 he entered Ormond [q.v.5] College, University of Melbourne, majoring in classics and philology (B.A., 1886; M.A., 1889). He won a university blue for football and stroked Ormond eights. In 1889-90 he was an assistant master at Brighton Grammar School under Dr G. H. Crowther [q.v.8]. He joined the colonial military forces, gaining a commission in 1890.

Morrison returned to Geelong College in 1891 to be vice-principal, gradually taking over responsibility from his father who died in 1898. He toured Britain and Europe in 1894-95. He remained unmarried, a benevolent despot, exercising strict discipline and making or unmaking rules at will. Friendly and sincere, he became known affectionately as 'The Skipper'. His initiatives brought enlarged grounds and buildings and the teaching of 'modern' sciences and languages. He led the cadet corps to great efficiency, especially in rifle-shooting; he had transferred to the Geelong Battery, Militia Garrison Artillery, in 1892, becoming captain in 1894.

But he was not satisfied with the standing of his college in the community. Leading church schools had formed an influential group, the Associated Public Schools of Victoria, from which Geelong College, as a private concern, was excluded. So Morrison, with Crowther, formed a Victorian Schools' Association, hoping to raise the standard of other private schools and rival the A.P.S. When the experiment failed Morrison conceded that the desired status could be attained only by joining the A.P.S. This consummation was realized in 1908, the college being purchased by the Presbyterian Church and governed by a council, with Morrison as salaried principal. Although involving financial loss and a painful renunciation by the

Morrison family, it was a smooth transition. The future looked bright.

On 12 November 1909 Morrison was killed, attempting to get through a fence, when out shooting at Mount Moriac. He who taught so sternly the use of firearms had himself for a moment tragically relaxed. He was buried in Geelong western cemetery.

It seemed that Morrison's life's work had been perfected in 1908: as 'skipper', he had accurately set the little colonial private school on a new course into the twentieth century. Only his own highly personal style could not be handed on, and for a time his successors floundered, suffering odious comparison, while friends and ex-pupils remained Morrison's lifelong admirers. In the Norman Morrison Memorial Hall at Geelong College are a bronze bust by Paul Montford [q.v.] and a portrait by G. R. Mainwaring, both posthumous.

G. McL. Redmond, *Geelong College, history, register and records* (Melb, 1911); B. R. Keith (ed), *The Geelong College 1861-1961* (Geelong, 1961); Geelong College, *Pegasus*, Dec 1909; *Geelong Advertiser*, 15, 17 Nov 1909; Geelong College archives.   B. R. KEITH

MORRISON, EDWARD CHARLES (1888-1955), soldier, policeman and court official, was born on 5 December 1888 at Blessington, Tasmania, son of James Morrison, labourer, and his wife Elizabeth, née Shepherd. After farming for some years at Blessington, he became a labourer for Hinman, Wright & Manser Ltd of Launceston.

On 8 July 1915 Morrison enlisted in the Australian Imperial Force as a private and embarked from Hobart in August. On 4 December he joined the 12th Battalion on Lemnos and on 1 March 1916 transferred to the new 52nd Battalion, forming at Tel-el-Kebir, Egypt. The battalion embarked for the Western Front in June; Morrison saw action at Sailly, France, and suffered from shell-shock on 12 July.

On 14 March 1917 Morrison was promoted sergeant and awarded the Distinguished Conduct Medal for 'leading his men in a bombing attack upon the enemy who were forming up for a counter-attack'. He afterwards 'showed great courage in an attack upon a strong point where he remained in an isolated position with a small party until all his bombs were exhausted'.

In July-August Morrison attended the 2nd Anzac Infantry School and achieved good results. On 9 September, however, he was found guilty and reduced to corporal by a court martial for 'improper interference after an order had been given by his superior officer'. He was detached on 2 October from the battalion and sent to the 13th Training Battalion in England; the timing suggests an attempt to save an otherwise first-class non-commissioned officer from some of the embarrassment of his reduction in rank.

Morrison rejoined the 52nd Battalion on 9 February 1918 and on 5 April was wounded twice at Dernancourt. He nevertheless 'continued to take up exposed positions and fire rifle-grenades and throw bombs on the enemy inflicting heavy casualties on them. His fine courage and skill greatly inspired the men of his platoon and caused the enemy attack to be stemmed'. For this he received a Bar to his D.C.M. He did not see any further active service and was invalided to Australia in October.

Following demobilization on 3 March 1919 Morrison joined the Tasmania Police Force and served in numerous towns until 1935 when he resigned for health reasons. He resumed farming at Blessington before joining the Court of Requests in 1937; he later became a court crier at the Supreme Court of Tasmania and between 1943 and retirement in 1953 was judge's attendant to Sir John Morris.

At White Hills Anglican Church on 3 June 1919, Morrison had married Gladys Gertrude Whittle. Survived by his wife, son and daughter, he died from hypertensive cerebrovascular disease in the Repatriation General Hospital, Hobart, on 22 September 1955 and was buried in Cornelian Bay cemetery.

C. E. W. Bean, *The A.I.F. in France*, 1918 (Syd, 1937); *London Gazette*, 24 Aug 1917, 3 Sept 1918; information from Mr A. C. Morrison.
     RODNEY K. QUINN

MORRISON, GEORGE ERNEST (1862-1920), journalist, traveller and political adviser to the Chinese government, was born on 4 February 1862 at Newtown, Geelong, Victoria, eldest son of George Morrison [q.v.5] and his wife Rebecca, née Greenwood. C. N. Morrison [q.v.] was his brother. He was educated at his father's school, Geelong College, where he recalled that 'we lived healthy, happy lives, giving more time to outdoor play than to study' and where he acquired his lifelong habits of keeping a diary, collecting—at first stamps and shells, later books on China—and walking long distances. At the end of his school life he also became interested in journalism. He grew into a moderately tall, fair-haired, blue-eyed youth who retained his solid good looks into middle age. His biographer Cyril Pearl suggests that, although his father took great pride in his achievements, Morrison always had much closer ties with his mother.

Early in 1880, before beginning medical

studies at the University of Melbourne, Morrison walked about 750 miles (1200 km) around the coast to Adelaide through much still unsettled country. He sold his diary of this 'walking tour' to the *Leader*. The following summer, he canoed down the Murray from Wodonga to the sea, walking back to Geelong. More *Leader* articles resulted. His medical studies were less successful and in March 1882 he failed a crucial examination.

This setback left him free to travel to North Queensland in April to investigate the Kanaka 'blackbirding' trade for the *Age*. He joined the *Lavinia* as an ordinary seaman for a three-month recruiting cruise and six mildly critical articles appeared in the *Leader* between October and December. Morrison meanwhile had gone on to visit Port Moresby and Thursday Island and then Normanton, on the Gulf of Carpentaria, from where he set out on 19 December to walk to Melbourne, roughly back-tracking the route followed by Burke and Wills [qq.v.3,6]. After two months he was at Cooper's Creek and by 21 April 1883 in Melbourne, having covered over 2000 miles (3220 km) in 123 days. He wrote to his mother that it was 'no feat of endurance—only a pleasant excursion'. The *Argus*, hostile to him as an *Age* cub, decried this as the curious and purposeless feat of a swagman; his future employer *The Times*, however, praised it as 'one of the most remarkable of pedestrian achievements', which it surely was.

Soon after his return Morrison denounced 'the Queensland slave trade' in a letter to the *Age*, prompting questions to the Queensland government from the Colonial Office. After a perfunctory enquiry in June (Sir) Samuel Griffith [q.v.9] reported a lack of supporting evidence. Governor Sir Anthony Musgrave [q.v. 5], however, writing to the earl of Derby, was 'unable quite to agree' with his premier, and Morrison's articles and letter remain significant accounts of the trade.

In June Morrison, financed by the *Age* and the *Sydney Morning Herald*, had left Melbourne to explore New Guinea. He proceeded inland from Port Moresby at the end of July, accompanied by two white men and several indigenes. How far the party penetrated is unclear; early in October Morrison received severe spear wounds, one below his right eye, the other in the abdomen, and the explorers struggled back to Port Moresby. After convalescence there and at Cooktown, Queensland, Morrison returned 'defeated and wounded' to Melbourne. Only his strong constitution and indomitable will enabled him to survive. In March 1884 he sailed for Edinburgh where, after a tapering spearhead 'the size of your second finger' was removed from his side, he resumed his medical studies.

After graduating M.B., Ch.M. in August 1887 Morrison travelled, on very limited finance, to North America and the West Indies. From May 1888 he worked in Spain for eighteen months as medical officer at a British-owned mine and then resumed his rather aimless wanderings, drifting back to Australia at the end of 1890. Next April he was appointed resident surgeon at the Ballarat base hospital but two years work there ended in a dispute with the hospital committee and Morrison's ready return to his 'nomad' life. He travelled through the Philippines then up the coast of China, for economy's sake as a missionary in Chinese dress. In Japan he decided to walk across China into Burma, again reversing the path of his rare predecessors. His journey of 3000 miles (4830 km), begun from Shanghai in February 1894, took over three months and cost, he calculated, less than £30. In Calcutta he recovered from a near-fatal attack of fever and was back in Australia by the end of the year.

But he chose not to stay. In February 1895 he returned to London with a written account of his journey. While seeking a publisher he completed a thesis on the hereditary transmission of malformations and abnormalities and graduated M.D. in Edinburgh in August. By then his book, *An Australian in China, being the narrative of a quiet journey across China to Burma*, was published. It was very favourably received. In it Morrison confessed that his 'lively sympathy and gratitude' had begun as the 'strong racial antipathy to the Chinese common to my countrymen'. He wrote ironically of the missionaries and with concern about the opium problem. The book retains some value as a clear-eyed though culture-bound account of provincial China in the 1890s.

His enterprise won Morrison appointment, on a secret and trial basis, as a special *Times* correspondent in Asia. Late in 1895 he travelled via Saigon into Indo-China as far as Bangkok, reporting trenchantly on the French presence in the region. His reports were highly praised, both by (Sir) Valentine Chirol, foreign editor of *The Times*, and by the Foreign Office, and his position was soon confirmed as the first permanent correspondent of *The Times* in Peking. He took up his post there in March 1897; it was to be his base for over twenty years. Without ceasing to be something of a wanderer he became, for Westerners at least, 'Chinese Morrison', the foreign expert on the politics of China, though he never acquired a thorough command of Chinese.

Morrison was fortunate to arrive in Peking at a time when mounting tensions ensured the noteworthiness of his dispatches. As a representative of *The Times* he also enjoyed unusual authority and entrée. Nevertheless, his resourcefulness and the high level of detail and accuracy of his reports denote not just a lucky but a great newspaper correspondent.

His first major scoop came in 1898 when he reported a Russian ultimatum to China demanding a lease on Port Arthur; at first little regarded by the British government, the report was soon shown to be wholly accurate. In 1900 Morrison wrote the last terse and reliable reports before the Boxer siege of the foreign legations and the first full account after it. He also proved his physical courage, being severely wounded while rescuing another defender. His own newspaper, accepting a *Daily Mail* report of the massacre of all Europeans in Peking, published on 17 July three lengthy obituaries, bracketing Morrison with the British minister, Sir Claude MacDonald, and the head of the Imperial Customs Service, Sir Robert Hart. All three in fact survived. Morrison was praised as 'in every way a striking personality, essentially modest and unassuming, yet at the same time resolute and virile' who had sent reports which 'savoured of genius'.

Although he was to revise his ideas radically, in the years immediately following the Boxer crisis Morrison became a vigorous protagonist for Japan as a counter to the growing Russian pressures on China. He welcomed war between Russia and Japan in 1904 and accompanied the Japanese forces on their triumphal entry into Port Arthur in January 1905. A few months later he was sent to report on the peace conference presided over by President Roosevelt at Portsmouth, United States of America. In spite of Morrison's pro-Japanese stand, the chief Russian negotiator, Count de Witte, sought him out for a lengthy discussion. Returning to China via England and Europe, Morrison exercised some influence on the choice of a new British minister to Peking and in the development of British policy ending the opium trade from India. He had reached the apogee of his political and diplomatic influence.

He was, however, entering another period of uncertainty. He clearly felt the lack of any sustained, close personal relationship; his health, no doubt affected by the rigours he had experienced, was worsening, while he was increasingly dissatisfied with the editing of his reports. In 1907 he rejected an invitation to become foreign editor of *The Times* in London, and he speculated about returning to Australia, which he had revisited in 1900 and 1902-03, in order to enter political life. He corresponded occasionally with prominent Australians including Alfred Deakin [q.v.8] and H. B. Higgins [q.v.9], his brother-in-law. Another idea he entertained was to become British minister in Peking. But in fact he

remained as *The Times* representative there, albeit often absent. He was present in 1911, however, to report, once again more sharply and accurately than other correspondents, on the revolutionary events culminating in the end of Manchu rule.

In August 1912 Morrison quickly accepted President Yuan Shi-kai's offer of a well-paid place as government adviser. On 26 August at Croydon, Surrey, England, he married his New Zealand-born secretary, Jennie Wark Robin, twenty-seven years his junior. He found in his marriage a new happiness and emotional security. But his change of professional status was far less rewarding and he was soon complaining of being more in the dark than when he was a correspondent. Nevertheless, he had some limited successes. He must take some of the credit, for example, for the tempering of Japan's notorious Twenty-One Demands on China in 1915; although he did not participate in negotiations, he obtained publication of the demands in foreign papers which had initially doubted their authenticity.

Convinced that the new republic must enter actively into world diplomacy, Morrison worked to bring China into the war against Germany. He also wanted to maintain China's integrity in the face of what he now saw as the major threat of an aggressive, exclusivist Japanese imperialism; he considered the best way to do this was to preserve the old links with Britain. China's entry into World War I gave it a place at the 1919 Versailles conference and Morrison helped to prepare its submissions. These were quite unsuccessful in preventing China's 'allies' from subordinating her interests to Japan's and the great surge of Chinese nationalism known as the May Fourth movement erupted. Morrison, however, was to see nothing of this. By then very ill, he left Paris in May for England. After a year of suffering and desperate searches for a cure, he died of inanition associated with chronic pancreatitis at Sidmouth, Devon, on 30 May 1920; survived by his wife (d. 1923) and three sons, he was buried in Sidmouth cemetery.

Morrison had visited Australia once more in late 1917. Although deeply attached to the country of his birth he was very critical, especially of the defeat of the second conscription referendum which he interpreted as a triumph for Catholic and women voters. He spoke publicly for conscription, but even more of trade prospects with China and to warn that an easy-going Australia could not for long ignore hard-working Japan. Earlier, he had sold his remarkable library of Western language works on China—over 20 000 volumes, maps and pamphlets. The collection is now held by the Tokyo Toyo Bunka Kenkyusho. Morrison's eldest son Ian (1913-

1953) was killed reporting the Korean War for *The Times*. In 1932 an annual series of lectures on China was founded in honour of Morrison by Chinese residents in Australia; the series continues under the auspices of the Australian National University.

F. Clune, *Sky high to Shanghai* (Syd, 1939), and *Chinese Morrison* (Melb, 1941); W. A. Morrison, *Ernest Morrison* (Melb, 1962); C. Pearl, *Morrison of Peking* (Syd, 1967); R. Hatton and M. S. Anderson, *Studies in diplomatic history* (Lond, 1970); H. Trevor-Roper, *Hermit of Peking* (NY, 1977); H. M. Lo (ed), *The correspondence of G. E.Morrison*, 1-2 (Cambridge, 1976, 1978); *JRAHS*, 20 (1934), p 401, 48 (1963), p 426; *J of Oriental Soc of Aust*, June 1963, p 42; A. G. Moller, G.E.Morrison: political adviser to Yuan Shih-k'ai 1912-16 (M.A. thesis, Univ Melb, 1975); Morrison papers (ML).

J. S. GREGORY

MORRISON, SIBYL ENID VERA MUNRO (1895-1961), barrister, was born on 18 August 1895 at Petersham, Sydney, daughter of Charles Henry Victor Emanuel Gibbs, Victorian-born pastoralist, and his second wife Alexandrina Caroline Elizabeth, née Munro, from Parramatta. Educated at Shirley, Edgecliff, and Presbyterian Ladies' College, Croydon, she was resident in Women's College while at the University of Sydney (LL.B., 1924). She interrupted her legal studies to visit Britain in 1923 and in London on 1 October married a 'ranch owner' Charles Carlisle Morrison. Returning to Sydney she completed her law course and on 2 June 1924 was admitted to the New South Wales Bar, where she was the first woman to practise. An uncle and her half-brother were lawyers.

In her first appearance as a barrister Sibyl Morrison was briefed by D. R. Hall [q.v.9] to act for a plaintiff widow claiming under the Testator's Family Maintenance and Guardianship of Infants Act. She established herself at the Bar and was on occasions briefed by her 'sisters-in-law' Christian Jollie Smith [q.v.] and Marie Byles, both of whom had been admitted as solicitors in 1924.

Active in the Sydney University Women Graduates' Association, Mrs Morrison, in an address on vocations at the university, asserted that 'if you have ability the law is one of the best professions you can take up and one for which women are specially suited'. With her legal knowledge she was welcomed as a member of the National Council of Women of New South Wales and was convener of their laws committee. She presented a paper on divorce in Australia in November 1926 when the National Council of Women was advocating uniform Federal marriage and divorce laws. She divorced her husband in 1928.

Again in London in 1930, Sibyl Morrison was called to the Bar of the Middle Temple in May. Back in Sydney, she married an architect Carlyle Greenwell on 16 March 1937 at St Stephen's Presbyterian Church. After her marriage she was no longer listed as a practising barrister. In 1940-42 she was first president of the Law School Comforts Fund, becoming a life vice-president in 1942. She was also involved with what became the Business and Professional Women's Club of Sydney.

Although Sibyl Morrison had been in competition with male colleagues, she did not lose her femininity and a magazine noted that she was 'an exceedingly smart up-to-date frocker'. Predeceased by her husband and childless, she died of cancer at Collaroy on 29 December 1961 and was cremated with Anglican rites. From an estate valued for probate at £72 011, she made two bequests of £1000 for annual prizes or scholarships in the faculty of law to be named after her mother and herself. After several other bequests, she left the residue to the University of Sydney, to be known as the Sibyl Greenwell Bequest and used to support the small animal section of the Rural Veterinary Centre at Camden.

She was painted in wig and gown by Norman Carter [q.v.7].

Cwlth Home, 16 Oct 1925; *Sun* (Syd), 19 Dec 1924, 24 Jan, 23 May 1926; *SMH*, 20 Dec 1924; *Christian Science Monitor* (Boston), 13 July 1925; *Evening News* (Syd), 24 Apr 1926; *Daily Guardian* (Syd), 5 Dec 1925, 25 Feb 1926; *Daily Telegraph* (Syd), 5, 8 Nov 1926.

JOAN M. O'BRIEN

MORT, EIRENE (1879-1977), artist, was born on 17 November 1879 at Woollahra, Sydney, third child of Canon Henry Wallace Mort, Queensland-born Anglican clergyman, and his wife Kate Macintosh, daughter of R. M. Isaacs [q.v.4]; her father was a nephew of T. S. Mort [q.v.5]. Eirene attended St Catherine's Clergy Daughters' School, Waverley, and studied painting with Dattilo Rubbo [q.v.] and A. H. Fullwood [q.v.8]. In 1897 she travelled alone to London where she completed courses at the Grosvenor Life School, the Royal School of Art Needlework and the Royal College of Art, South Kensington, gaining its art-teacher's certificate.

Returning to Sydney in 1906 Eirene Mort set up a studio with her lifelong friend Nora Kate Weston. Pre-Raphaelite philosophy appealed to her and the activities of the studio, which became one of Sydney's earliest centres for professional design and applied art, were influenced by William Morris. That year she was a founder of the Society of Arts and Crafts of New South Wales and was a vice-president until 1935. She helped to organize and publicize the Australian Exhibition of Women's Work in 1907: her many exhibits included 'fine embroideries and bold decorative designs' for every branch of applied art. She also wrote and illustrated articles for the *Sydney Mail* and *Art and Architecture* and designed the cover of A. G. Stephens's [q.v.] *Bookfellow*.

Visiting England again in 1909, Eirene Mort studied mediaeval art, illustration and illumination, and etching with Luke Taylor. On her return she made many etchings using historical and rural subjects. She illustrated Florence Sulman's [q.v.] *A popular guide to the wild flowers of New South Wales* (1913, 1914). The well-designed and botanically accurate drawings were later used by A. B. Blombery in *A guide to native Australian plants* (1967, revised 1977). In 1914 Eirene Mort taught Sydney Ure Smith [q.v.] the etching process and in 1927 exhibited a series of etchings of the Canberra district.

In the 1920s her many bookplates revealed her knowledge of heraldry, her skills in etching, woodcuts and pen-drawing, her love of Australian subjects and her individual sense of humour. Eirene Mort was a founder in 1921 and council-member of the Australian Painter-Etchers' Society, honorary treasurer of the Australian Ex Libris Society and a member of the Australian Bookplate Club. She was also a founder of the Australian Guild of Handicrafts. A respected teacher of art, she served as principal of the Women Painters' Art School and taught at such schools as Abbotsleigh, Kambala, and Sydney Church of England Girls' Grammar School, Darlinghurst, and later at Frensham, Mittagong. She wrote and illustrated several books about Australian fauna and flora for children, and, at the request of the Department of Education, *The story of architecture* (1942). She lived at Greenhayes, Mittagong, from 1937 and continued to teach until she moved to Bowral in 1960.

Unmarried, Eirene Mort found time in her busy life to maintain contact with her large extended family, becoming its focal point and historian until she died at Bowral on 1 December 1977; she was cremated. The scope of work and the variety of media that she mastered are impressive. Contemporary reviews praised her skilled craftsmanship, her attention to detail, and her witty and inventive use of Australian motifs. She constantly sought to improve the quality of Australian design.

Bookfellow, 1, no 1, Jan 1907; *Art and Architecture*, 4, no 5, Sept-Oct 1907; *Art in Aust*, no 9, 1921, s 3, no 5, Aug 1923; *Sydney Mail*, 11 Sept 1907; P. A. Starr, Wielding the waratah—Eirene Mort. A study of an artist/craftswoman's training and working experiences from the period 1879 to 1910 (B.A. Hons thesis, Univ Syd, 1980); information from and family papers held by M. Mort, Newcastle.   MARGARET HENRY

MORTON, ALEXANDER (1854-1907), museum director and naturalist, was born on 11 September 1854 near New Orleans, United States of America, son of Thomas William Morton, who migrated to Queensland as general manager of the Manchester Queensland Cotton Co. Alexander was a seaman for about two years, at first on a vessel bringing Melanesian labour to Queensland cotton and sugar plantations. He visited England and Europe briefly but returned to Australia and studied the natural sciences. In 1877 he was appointed curator's assistant at the Australian Museum, Sydney. That year Morton accompanied the explorer Andrew Goldie [q.v.4] on his expedition to New Guinea; his collections, mainly of birds from forests near Port Moresby and from Yule Island, proved his ability and he was sent to Palmerston (Darwin). In 1881 he visited the Solomon Islands and in 1882 explored the Burdekin and Mary rivers in Queensland and Lord Howe Island. When he left the museum it retained him as a field collector.

On 25 January 1884 Morton was appointed curator of the Royal Society of Tasmania's museum in Hobart. He was also given charge of its library, which he ordered and catalogued, including a register of all papers published in the society's journal. In 1885 the Royal Society's museum and gardens were renamed the Tasmanian Museum and Botanical Gardens and incorporated with a board of trustees. Morton was reappointed curator and became secretary as well. From January 1904 he was director of both the museum and gardens. He was also honorary secretary of the Royal Society from 1887 to 1907. He helped to establish the Queen Victoria Museum and Art Gallery at Launceston and acted as honorary curator in 1891-96.

Under Morton 'one of the finest and largest museums in the Commonwealth' was developed. Two new galleries were opened in 1889. He was keenly interested in acquiring an art collection in Hobart, and a floor of the new wing temporarily became an art gallery; extensions opened in 1902 provided a permanent gallery and more than trebled the museum's display space. He concentrated on display until, by 1891, he had reorganized the museum, using the latest British Museum labelling methods, and evolved a highly regarded system of classification and arrangement.

Morton was an executive commissioner for Tasmania at the Melbourne International Centennial Exhibition (1888-89), honorary secretary of the Tasmanian section of the

Paris Exposition Universelle (1889) and director of the executive management committee of the Tasmanian International Exhibition (Hobart, 1894-95). As general secretary of the Australasian Association for the Advancement of Science (Hobart, 1892), he edited its report and papers. A member of the Technical Board of Hobart and a commissioner of fisheries for Tasmania, he was also a member of the permanent committee of the Tasmanian Improvement and Tourist Association, a committee-member and secretary of the Hobart Horticultural Society and honorary secretary of the Domain Committee. He was a fellow of the Linnean Society, London (1889).

Persevering and valued for his warmth and loyalty, Morton was described as 'a steady, intelligent, hard-working man, whose soul is wrapped up in natural history'. He was a Freemason and an adherent of the Free Church of Scotland. On 8 July 1884 he had married Caroline Eliza Mills in Hobart. He died of heart disease on 27 May 1907 at Sandy Bay and was buried in Cornelian Bay cemetery. His wife, three daughters and a son survived him.

Cyclopedia of Tasmania, 1 (Hob, 1900); S. L. Clemens, *Following the equator* (facsimile, Melb, 1973); R. Strahan et al (eds), *Rare and curious specimens* (Syd, 1979); Roy Soc of Tas, *Papers and Procs*, 1906; *PTHRA*, 28, no 1 (Mar 1981); *Bulletin*, 25 May 1905; *Mercury*, 28 May 1907; Scrapbooks prepared by A. Morton, 1887-1900 (held by Tas Museum and Art Gallery, Hob); Council, Roy Soc of Tas, Minute-books, 1882-1907 (Univ Tas Archives); Tas Museum and Botanical Gardens, correspondence, 1874-1907, *and* Trustees, Minute-books, 1886-1907 (Tas Museum and Art Gallery); information from Mr E. C. Thompson, Newport, NSW.   PETER MERCER

MORTON, FRANK (1869-1923), journalist and author, was born on 12 May 1869 at Bromley, Kent, England, son of James Morton, plumber, and his wife Rhoda, née Hookham. He was educated at a private school at Stoke-on-Trent, Staffordshire, and aged 16 migrated to Sydney with his family. He began work as an engineering apprentice, but in 1889 shipped before the mast in the *Conqueror*, leaving the vessel at Hong Kong.

Making his way to Singapore, Morton taught at a Methodist mission school and later that year joined the staff of the *Straits Times*, discovering his aptitude as a journalist 'in a flash'. On 5 August 1891 he married Louise Susan Chicherley Holloway, born in Calcutta; they moved to India where he worked on several Calcutta newspapers and became sub-editor of the *Englishman*. As special correspondent he accompanied the theosophist Annie Besant on her Indian tour, the wanderings of the opium commission and Sir Mortimer Durand's mission to Afghanistan.

In 1894 Morton returned to Australia and was in Sydney in 1895-96, when he began contributing to the *Bulletin*, before moving to Queensland to work on the *Brisbane Courier*. About 1898 he went to Hobart where he freelanced and worked for the *Mercury*. In 1905 he joined the *Otago Daily Times*, Dunedin, New Zealand, but left abruptly about 1908 and moved to Wellington. He became editor of a sixty-page monthly magazine, the *Triad*, and wrote most of it, under such pseudonyms as 'M', 'F. T. Monk-Orran', 'Epistemon', 'Selwyn Rider', and 'Booklander'. In Wellington Morton published *Laughter and tears: verses of a journalist* (1908) and wrote two novels, *The angel of the earthquake* (Melbourne, 1909) and *The yacht of dreams* (London, 1911).

Returning to Sydney about 1914, Morton settled at Manly. He contributed to the *Bulletin, Lone Hand, Native Companion, Bookfellow, Steele Rudd's Magazine* and other journals. From 1915 he became the mainstay of the new Australian edition of the *Triad* and later was associated with the *Sunday Times*. He published four more volumes of mainly light love poetry and children's verse; they included *Verses for Marjorie and some others* (1916), written for his daughter, *The secret spring* (1919), an erotic poem, and *Man and the devil: a book of shame and pity* (1922). Bald, bespectacled, with a full, sensuous mouth, Morton was intensely proud of his 'happy Bohemian home . . . where every meal was a movable feast', despite appearing in his writings as 'the Great Lover—a disillusioned, yet still dangerous *roué*'. He was 'tolerant, broad-minded, generous and genial' and had a great knowledge of books, especially French literature, and of the East.

Morton died of acute nephritis at Stanmore on 15 December 1923 and was buried in the Baptist section of Rookwood cemetery. His wife, three sons and two daughters survived him. A prolific writer, he knew all the tricks and his idiosyncrasies were easily and frequently imitated. To J. F. Archibald [q.v.3] he was one of three journalists who lifted journalism to the plane of literature; to A. G. Stephens [q.v.] he wrote 'clever, light, sparkling verse & prose—good craftsman . . . Personally—nice little fellow'; to Adam McCay [q.v.] he had 'more words than any other writer among us'.

Triad, 11 Feb, 10 Nov, 1 Dec 1924; *Pacific*, 29 Feb 1924, p 10; *Aust Worker*, 17 Dec 1908; *SMH* and *Mercury* (Hob), 17 Dec 1923; *Bulletin*, 20 Dec 1923; *Queenslander*, 22 Dec 1923; A. G. Stephens, Notes on Australian authors for A. W. Jose 1899 (ML).
                              B. G. ANDREWS
                              MARTHA RUTLEDGE

MOSS, ALICE FRANCES MABEL (MAY) (1869-1948), campaigner for women's rights, was born on 27 April 1869 at Ballarat, Victoria, daughter of English-born John Alfred Wilson, sharebroker and later licensed victualler, and his Scottish wife Martha Brown, née Lamb. She was educated at Presbyterian Ladies' College, East Melbourne, and on 10 March 1887 married in Melbourne in a civil ceremony, Isidore Henry Moss, grazier (d. 1938), son of Mark Moss, financier. They lived in New South Wales for some thirteen years.

While her two daughters were young, Mrs Moss began working for the rights of women. As vice-president of the Australian Women's National League in 1906-14 she campaigned in Victoria for female suffrage. An early member of the National Council of Women of Victoria, formed in 1904, she was appointed in 1927 an alternate Australian delegate to the League of Nations Assembly at Geneva, where she was the first woman member of the finance committee and served on other committees. She was also Australian delegate to the first World Population Conference at Geneva and the first Women's Peace Study Conference at Amsterdam, Holland. After attending an executive meeting in Paris of the League of Nations Union, she returned to become vice-president of its Victorian branch in 1928.

While in Europe Mrs Moss was Australian representative at the executive meeting at Geneva in 1927 of the International Council of Women. Next year she was elected a vice-president, a position she held until her death. In 1930, as an Australian delegate, she attended the I.C.W. Meeting in Vienna and the Codification of International Law Conference in The Hague, on the nationality of married women, then of particular concern to women's national organizations.

Mrs Moss served as first president of the National Council of Women of Australia in 1931-36. After repeated requests from its Victorian council, of which she was president in 1928-38, for the inclusion of women, she was appointed to the executive of the Victorian and Melbourne Centenary Celebrations Council (1933-34). At the same time she chaired the Women's Centenary Council, which established the Pioneer Women's Memorial Garden and prepared a Book of Remembrance containing records of some 1200 early women settlers. In 1934 she was appointed C.B.E. and awarded the gold badge of the N.C.W. for distinguished service.

Actively interested in other community organizations such as the (Royal) Women's Hospital, the Collingwood Crèche and the Free Kindergarten movement, Mrs Moss also served on the board of management of the City Newsboys' Society in 1906-48 and

was the first woman lay-member of the National Health and Medical Research Council in 1936-45. She was recognized for her outstanding ability and her distinguished contribution to the community, as for her dignity, charm and grace. She was always quick to praise the work of other people: 'I like to give a rose to someone who can smell it'. A member of the International and Lyceum clubs, she was interested in the theatre, painting and woodcarving. She died in East Melbourne on 18 July 1948 and was cremated with Presbyterian forms.

H. Gillan, *A brief history of the National Council of Women of Victoria 1902-1945* (Melb, 1945); M. O. Reid, *The ladies came to stay* (Melb, 1960); A. M. Norris, *Champions of the impossible* (Melb, 1978); *Herald* (Melb), 4 June 1934, 19 July 1948; National Council of Women (Vic), records (Melb); personal information.   ADA M. NORRIS

MOTT, HAMILTON CHARNOCK (1871-1963), newspaper proprietor, was born on 1 June 1871 at Hamilton, Victoria, eighth son of GEORGE HENRY MOTT (1831-1906), London-born newspaper proprietor, and his wife Allegra Haidée (d. 1905), née Charnock; they had married in London on 18 December 1852 and migrated to Victoria. George, after newspaper experience in Melbourne and on the goldfields, moved to Albury, New South Wales, and established the *Border Post* in 1856. George campaigned for separation of the Riverina, organized an anti-customs league and was mayor of Albury in 1868. His greatest work was the formation of the North-Eastern Railway League, which resulted in the completion of the Melbourne-Wodonga line and the eventual link with Albury. In early 1869 he returned to Victoria and bought a partnership in the *Hamilton Spectator*. Moving to Melbourne in 1885, he was managing director of Gordon & Gotch [q.v.4] Ltd for nine years before buying the *Kew Mercury* which his son Walter had founded in 1888. George served on the Kew Borough Council for four years and died at Kew on 7 January 1906.

Hamilton was educated at Hamilton Academy and Kew High School. He absorbed the atmosphere of the newspaper world as a boy and later helped his father to run the *Mercury*. In the wake of gold discoveries, with three brothers, he went to Western Australia where Decimus and Sydney started Kalgoorlie's first paper, the *Western Argus*. Hamilton soon replaced Sydney; the partnership founded the *Tothersider* at Coolgardie and engaged in job-printing. After 1900 the brothers returned to Victoria. On 27 May

1902 Hamilton married Evelyn May Grave (d. 1961) at the Australian Church, Melbourne.

After the demise of the *Border Post*, Hamilton and Decimus moved to Albury and established the daily *Border Morning Mail* on 24 October 1903. They were skilled, confident, and assertive newspapermen—their paper flourished. The partnership ended in 1923 and Decimus went to Melbourne where he and his family built up extensive newspaper interests in the Leader Publishing Co., Northcote. In 1925 Hamilton bought and closed his opposition, the *Albury Daily News*.

While overseas for the coronation in 1937, Mott bought a photo-engraving plant and the *Mail* became the first country newspaper in New South Wales and Victoria to install a full photo-engraving section: the paper later won the Sommerlad [q.v.] and other awards for news photography. Four of his five sons, Milton, Tennyson, Clifton and Melbourne, joined him in the newspaper business, while his daughters Haidée, Thalia and Aglaia worked for the *Mail* at various times. In 1948, the year that ownership passed to a family company, a rotary press was installed and the paper converted to tabloid. In 1962 Mott saw a Hoe rotary press installed in larger premises, but never saw it in action.

Handicapped by severe deafness for most of his life, Mott concentrated on the indoor work of editing and sub-editing. Daily he checked every word in the *Mail*. His strong sense of a newspaper's duty led him into several libel actions—he won some, lost some.

Impeccably dressed, courtly and erect, a disciplinarian yet tolerant and understanding, Mott earned the respect of the community and the devotion of his employees. His hobby was gardening. After studying Mendelism, he evolved a new winter-flowering variety of sweet pea, without the usual hooded formation, which is known by the name 'Mott'. He crossed and perfected varieties, and changed the colour of the flowers at his home, Murray Bluffs, and through commercial growers in Queensland and South Australia sent seed throughout the world.

At 91 Mott was still working. He died on 2 February 1963 and was cremated after a service in St Matthew's Church of England, Albury.

C. A. Mott, *The runaway family* (Wodonga, Vic, 1980); *Argus*, 9 Jan 1906; *Border Morning Mail*, 24 Oct 1953, 4 Feb 1963; information from H. L. Davidson and G. R. Dowling, Albury, and C. A. Mott, Yackandandah, Vic.   PAT STRACHAN

MOULDEN, BEAUMONT ARNOLD (1849-1926), lawyer and politician, and SIR FRANK BEAUMONT (1876-1932), solicitor

and mayor, were father and son. Beaumont was born on 19 October 1849 at Southwark, London, son of Joseph Eldin Moulden, solicitor, and his wife Margaret Perkins, née Hinton. Migrating to South Australia with his parents next year, Moulden was educated at J. L. Young's [q.v.6] Adelaide Educational Institution. He was articled and admitted to the Bar in 1870, following his father's interests rather than his own, which were in chemistry. He joined his father in what became the well-known firm of Moulden & Sons.

Beaumont was a tall, large man of powerful voice—'a dominant figure in any room where people . . . gathered'— who showed 'almost fanatical insistence' on his point of view, good manners and punctuality, even on fishing trips. In politics he 'placed principle before popularity'; perhaps this explains his mixed success. Despite many attempts, he was a member of the House of Assembly only in 1887-90 and of the Legislative Council in 1903-12. Yet during that time he was a founder, and president for nine years, of the Australasian National League, the major opponent of the recently formed United Labor Party.

While a member for Albert in the South-East, he saw through the Intercolonial Debts Act (1887), which other colonies copied, to deal with debtors absconding across borders. In 1889 he was attorney-general in Cockburn's [q.v.8] ministry but resigned next year in protest against the proposed progressive land tax. Later, as council-member for Central District, Moulden opposed the proliferation of wages boards, further land taxation and forced closer settlement—'class legislation of a vicious and dishonourable character'. But he supported the 1911 Act allowing women to practise as lawyers.

Moulden embraced commerce and mining, being chairman of Broken Hill South Silver Mining Co., director of Electrolytic Zinc Co. of Australia Ltd and other mining interests, managing director of Haussen and Co., and local chairman of the Commercial Union Assurance Co. For years he travelled to Melbourne for fortnightly company meetings. He was a member of the Adelaide Club from 1902 and had been a volunteer soldier. Like his father, Moulden pursued municipal affairs, and in 1891 was mayor of St Peters. His five visits to England and Europe extended these interests: in 1886 he was admitted to the Livery Company of Farriers and to freedom of the City of London; in 1900 he was awarded the grand star of the Primrose League of England, a leading conservative organization.

Moulden had married Anna Mary Cramond on 25 September 1872; they had four children. He died on 20 December 1926 and was buried in North Road Anglican cemetery.

His second child Frank Beaumont was born on 25 June 1876 at Norwood, Adelaide. Educated at the Collegiate School of Saint Peter and the University of Adelaide, he was articled to his father, admitted to the Bar in 1897 and joined the family firm in 1900.

Moulden gave twenty-eight years to Adelaide's government. He was a popular councillor in 1904-13, an alderman in 1913-19 and 1922-32, and mayor in 1919-21. Chairman of the council's parliamentary and by-laws committee in 1905-24, he modernized regulations for traffic control.

Although interested in sport and motoring, Moulden was not strong physically. Rejected for active service in World War I, he worked for soldiers, their dependants and the allies. On 10 April 1918 he married a widow, Deborah, Lady Hackett [q.v.9], whom he had met while skiing at Mount Kosciusko. Next year he became consular agent for France in South Australia and was honoured by the French government for his war work. As mayor, encouraged by his wife, particularly during the prince of Wales's visit, he began a period of 'unique hospitality which had never been . . . imagined in South Australia'. Young, pretty and charming, Deborah Moulden welcomed her new social opportunities; 'Bay' was quiet and retiring. He was knighted in 1922. In 1929 he became an officer brother of the Order of St John of Jerusalem. He also belonged to the Adelaide Club.

Moulden continued legal work, though with increasing ill health, and was a company director. After a cerebral haemorrhage he died on 8 April 1932. His colleagues praised his courteous friendliness, logical mind and hard work. Having no children, he helped to raise his wife's five and the three of his late brother. Moulden was buried in North Road Anglican cemetery.

H. T. Burgess (ed), *Cyclopedia of South Australia*, 1 (Adel, 1907); Associated Publishing Service, *The civic record of South Australia, 1921-1923* (Adel, 1924); *Register* (Adel), 30 May 1912, 21 Dec 1926; *Chronicle* (Adel), 25 Oct 1919; *Advertiser* (Adel), 9 Apr 1932; Aust National League (Liberal Party) Records (SAA); family papers (held by Mrs B. Brummitt, Stirling, SA).   ELIZABETH KWAN

MOULDEN, DEBORAH VERNON; *see* HACKETT, DEBORAH

MOULDS, CONSTANCE (1897-1972), trotting trainer, was born on 14 February 1897 at Rylstone, New South Wales, daughter of London-born Dudley Joseph Stephens, mounted-police constable, and his Victorian wife Mary Eleanor, née Calvert. In 1908 the family moved to Rouse Hill and on leaving school Connie worked as a clerk. On 17 May 1919 she married George Francis Moulds, butcher, at Christ Church, Rouse Hill. Her only child Lawrence was born in 1923.

By 1922 George was a smallgoods man at Riverstone and from 1925 a fruiterer. Although he suffered from spinal arthritis, they began to train trotters after the purchase of Tiny Loche for £30; the mare won her first three starts (which carried total prize money of six guineas) and later established a family of winners. Constance trained the horses full time, sometimes for other owners.

After winning open events against all-comers at shows, in 1924 Mrs Moulds was granted by the New South Wales Trotting Club a trainer-driver licence to compete at registered meetings outside the metropolitan area. She was the only woman granted such a licence in New South Wales although there were women drivers in other States. At Richmond on 10 June she rode Chester in a rough race and finished second. A fortnight later at Menangle, she had weighed in when she was notified that she could not compete. The stewards later said that men might be inhibited by chivalry from protesting against interference by women drivers. Thereafter her racing was confined to events restricted to women. This action set back the cause for women's participation in registered trotting in New South Wales for many years.

By the early 1930s the Moulds had about twelve horses in constant work. After George was killed on the Windsor Road while driving Charming Ribbons in 1932, Mrs Moulds was 'granted permission' to continue training but kept only one pacer, Robert Loche, a winner on provincial tracks and at Victoria Park, and used him to pass on her knowledge and training expertise to her son Lawrie, who became a leading reinsman.

In the 1940s she twice rescued a nondescript gelding, Machine Wood, from the knackery. Her kindness and gentle training were rewarded when the gelding gave Lawrie his first win at Harold Park in 1944. At the inaugural night-trotting meeting at Harold Park on 1 October 1949 Machine Wood won the New Zealand Handicap. She was soon frustrated when ordered to transfer her horses to a man before they could compete at Harold Park; so, many of her entries appeared under Lawrie's name. Nonetheless Constance Moulds was largely responsible for training Van's Dream and Miss Josephine, winner of the Tom Austin Cup at Richmond.

At trotting meetings, her dumpy little figure was conspicuous in wide-brimmed hat and jodhpurs—she was rarely seen in a dress. She was affectionately known as 'the little mother' for her sympathy and practical help. Survived by her son, Constance Moulds died at Blackheath on 27 September 1972 and was buried in the Anglican cemetery at Rouse Hill.

M. J. Agnew, *Australia's trotting heritage* (Melb, 1977); *Aust Trotting Record*, 14 Jan 1925; *Racetrack Mag*, Sept 1968; *Sydney Sportsman*, 17 June, 1 July 1924; *Labor Daily*, 17 Dec 1924; *Trotguide*, 26 Nov 1969; *Sun-Herald*, 26 Dec 1982.

GREG BROWN

MOUTON, JEAN BAPTISTE OCTAVE (1866-1946), New Guinea trader and plantation owner, was born on 9 October 1866 at Velaine, Belgium, son of Maximilien Mouton, impoverished commercial traveller, and his wife Rose, née Josse. He left school at 11, became an apprentice barber and in 1881 migrated with his father to the ill-fated Free Colony of Port-Breton. The venture—brainchild of a half-demented French aristocrat, the Marquis de Rays [q.v.6]—ended in utter failure. About one-half of the 700 colonists perished and only about a dozen, the Moutons among them, remained in New Guinea.

In 1882 the Moutons settled on the Gazelle Peninsula as copra traders under contract to Thomas Farrell, the common law husband of E. E. Forsayth, known as Queen Emma. Next year they moved to Kinigunan (Vunanami), east of Kokopo, signed a contract with one of Farrell's competitors, Hernsheim, and were still working for him when Mouton senior died in 1888. Octave soon started to trade for the Deutsche Handels- und Plantagen-gesellschaft der Südsee-Inseln zu Hamburg and in 1891 planted his first coconut trees on land acquired by his father at Kinigunan. With the financial backing of the Sacred Heart Mission, Mouton became in 1894 the first independent trader in New Guinea, and by getting his trade goods directly from Sydney and selling his copra to Burns [q.v.7], Philp [q.v.] & Co. Ltd, gradually managed to break the virtual foreign trade monopoly of the big companies. In 1897, together with Captain Rondahl, a Swede, and Captain Monrad, a Dane previously employed by Queen Emma, he founded the trading firm, Mouton & Co., and gradually expanded his trading activities to northern New Ireland, Kapingamarangi and Ontong Java while continuing to plant coconuts. He was the envy of all struggling traders and planters, but one observer attributed his prosperity to his 'industry' and 'clear-headedness'.

In 1902 Mouton made the first of several business and pleasure trips to Australia. On his next visit he met a Sydney girl, Monantha Davis, and married her on 1 September 1903; they had one son. He bought a property near Port Hacking but was forced to spend much of his time in New Guinea, since he could not rely on his managers. In 1911 Mouton became a naturalized Australian. The same year he divorced his wife and married on 8 June 1914 Helen Collier (d. 1930); they had one son. After the war he divided his time between Sydney and Kinigunan. In 1929 he sold his plantation to the Sacred Heart Mission, and retired to Bellevue Hill, Sydney, marrying a widow, Jessie Jamieson Vallerie, née Barnsley, on 27 September 1930. But he retained a connexion with New Guinea: in 1930 he bought the *Rabaul Times*, and later formed Rabaul Recreations Ltd which ran Rabaul's only cinema. He died of cirrhosis of the liver at Bellevue Hill on 7 September 1946 and was buried in South Head cemetery with Anglican rites.

Mouton's *Memoirs*, written in the early 1930s, are an important record of colonial New Guinea, for unlike the pioneer missionaries and government officials, the early traders left few documents for posterity. They are written in a somewhat clumsy style since Mouton, while a fluent speaker of pidgin, never quite mastered the intricacies of the English language. He emerges as down-to-earth and pragmatic, with an appreciation of 'kanaka ways'. Moderately wealthy, he lived with some style and travelled widely, spending almost two years in Europe in 1908-09 and 1919-20. In New Guinea, his household included a much commented on rarity, a governess from Sydney; in Sydney his second wife had Tolai servants. He sold his plantation at a most opportune time, only a few months before the crash in 1929. His estate was valued for probate at £143 571.

J. B. O. Mouton, *The New Guinea memoirs of Jean Baptiste Octave Mouton*, P. Biskup (ed), (Canb, 1974); H. Blum, *Neu-Guinea und der Bismarck-archipel* (Berlin, 1900); J. H. Niau, *The phantom paradise* (Syd, 1936).

P. BISKUP

MOYES, MORTON HENRY (1886-1981), Antarctic explorer and naval officer, was born on 29 June 1886 at Koolunga, South Australia, second son of John Moyes, headmaster, and his wife Ellen Jane, née Stoward. Two brothers were John Stoward (1884-1972), Anglican bishop, and Alban George (Johnnie) (1892-1963), journalist and cricket commentator.

Moyes was educated at the Collegiate School of St Peter, Adelaide, and the University of Adelaide, graduating B.Sc. in physics and mathematics in 1910, and representing the university at football and athletics. He was South Australian high and broad-jump champion in 1906-08 and in 1909, while teaching at Townsville Grammar School, represented Queensland in the Australasian amateur athletic championships.

At university Moyes had been greatly impressed by his geology lecturer (Sir) Douglas Mawson [q.v.] and from Rockhampton Grammar School he successfully applied to join Mawson's Australasian Antarctic Expedition of 1911-14. He was meteorologist for the western base party under Frank Wild which was to winter on the Shackleton Ice Shelf; he had received a few days of instruction in meteorology in Hobart in November 1911. In November 1912 Moyes was left alone in the winter-quarters hut while a group, led by Wild, went on a sledging trip. The loss of a sled delayed the group's return and Moyes endured nine weeks of anxious solitude, sustained by his strong religious faith.

After returning to Australia in March 1913 Moyes became headmaster of the University Coaching College in Sydney. He was recruited as a naval instructor at the newly established Royal Australian Naval College in February 1914. Initially he specialized in mathematics but soon began to teach navigation and in 1915 spent some months in the cruiser H.M.A.S. *Encounter*, gaining practical navigating experience. He was promoted senior naval instructor in January 1916 and his polar experience was recognized when he was made navigating officer of the *Aurora* which, commanded by Captain J. K. Davis [q.v.8], sailed from New Zealand to the Ross Sea in December to rescue marooned members of (Sir) Ernest Shackleton's Trans-Antarctic Expedition.

Moyes found it galling to be 'chained to an office' at the naval college while others went to war. The naval board twice refused him leave to enlist in the Australian Imperial Force and rebuffed his plea for 'active service in the Navy' as his duties were considered of national importance. Finally, in October 1918 his resignation was approved for 31 January 1919, too late to achieve its purpose. On 11 January 1919 Moyes married Miriam Esther King at St James' Church, Sydney. He applied to rejoin the navy and was accepted as an instructor lieutenant in December with seniority for previous service. For nearly a decade his postings alternated between time at sea in cruisers instructing junior officers and sailors and shore service at H.M.A.S. *Penguin* and H.M.A.S. *Cerberus* where he supervised schoolmaster and instructor officers; he was promoted instructor lieut-commander in 1920 and commander in 1924.

In September 1929, at Mawson's request, Moyes was seconded to the British, Australian and New Zealand Antarctic Research Expedition, which was to assert British territorial claims in Antarctica by means of two voyages in the auxiliary barque, *Discovery*.

Moyes hoped to sail as a ship's officer but Davis, again in command, believed he lacked appropriate training. He joined the scientific staff as survey officer, spending long hours operating a defective echo-sounder, taking sights and drawing charts, helping with townets, and assisting Mawson in executive matters. The first B.A.N.Z.A.R.E. voyage, from October 1929 to April 1930, was not happy. Everyone became 'heartily tired of the bickering' between Mawson and Davis; Davis considered the crew and scientists formed 'two distinct parties' and was sceptical of the value of Moyes's work. However, the New Zealand meteorologist R. G. Simmers recalled Moyes as being 'very serious, precise and conscientious about his work' and 'a good steadying influence' on the younger expedition members. For private reasons Moyes did not undertake the second voyage in November 1930.

Resuming his naval career, Moyes spent nearly six years in H.M.A.S. *Australia* as fleet instructor officer and became the navy's first (acting) instructor captain in June 1941. Debarred from sea service by age and seniority, in November 1943 Moyes was appointed the first director of educational and vocational training at Navy Office, Melbourne, where he set up correspondence courses for those at sea and began a psychology section for vocational guidance. When his naval career ended in 1946 he became the chief rehabilitation officer for the Commonwealth until 1951 and supervised the postwar training of some 11 000 ex-servicemen and women. In his long retirement he was an active president of the Naval Association of Australia and with rising public interest in Antarctic affairs became a minor celebrity as one of the last veterans of the 'heroic age' of Antarctic exploration.

In recognition of his three Antarctic expeditions Moyes was awarded Polar medals in silver and bronze and a bronze clasp; he was appointed O.B.E. in 1935. He was a fellow of the Royal Geographical Society and president of the Geographical Society of New South Wales in 1933-35. He contributed substantially to an A.A.E. meteorology volume and the B.A.N.Z.A.R.E. report, 'Soundings'; later he published several reminiscences of his Antarctic experiences.

Moyes was sturdily built, erect in bearing and with a direct gaze; his sanguine temperament stood him in good stead during his Antarctic expeditions. A widower without children, he died in Sydney on 20 September 1981 and was cremated after a service at St Andrew's Church, Roseville. He is commemorated by several Antarctic place-names.

D. Mawson, *The home of the blizzard* (Lond, 1915); C. F. Laseron, *South with Mawson* (Syd,

1947); A. G. Price, *Geographical Report*, BANZARE 1929-31 (Adel, 1963); *Walkabout*, Oct 1964; *Hemisphere*, June, July, Aug 1975; *Navy News*, 9 Oct 1981; *Weekend Australian*, 14-15 Jan 1978; H. M. Moyes papers (Mawson Inst, Univ Adel, *and* ML *and* Mr A. G. Moyes, Syd); J. K. Davis papers (LaTL); Dept of Defence (Navy), MP 124/6, 150, 151, 692, 856, 1214 (AAO, Melb); information from Instr Capt R. G. Fennessy, Canb, and Dr R. G. Simmers, Wellington, NZ.   DENIS FAIRFAX

MUECKE, HUGO CARL EMIL (1842-1929), customs and shipping agent, was born on 8 July 1842 at Rathenow, near Berlin, eldest son of Dr Carl Wilhelm Ludwig Muecke [q.v.5] and his first wife Emilie. The family arrived in Adelaide in 1849. Educated at Tanunda High School, at 16 Hugo joined John Newman's commercial and shipping agency, which required a German-speaking clerk. In 1866 he became a partner, and also a naturalized British subject. On 2 April 1863 at Tanunda he had married Margaret Elisabeth Julia Le Page from Guernsey, Channel Islands; they had four daughters and four sons.

After Newman's death in 1873, Muecke took over the business, renamed H. Muecke & Co. It owned large bond stores at Port Adelaide, handled consignment and customs business, acted as agent for Norddeutscher-Lloyd and other steamship lines, and owned and operated small coastal vessels. In 1877 Muecke became vice-consul for Germany, and was consul in 1882-1914, an honorary position (apart from occasional fees). He was also a justice of the peace. First elected to the Adelaide Chamber of Commerce committee in 1880, he served almost continuously until 1915, including terms as deputy chairman (1884) and president (1885-86). A successful and highly respected member of the business community, Muecke became a director of the Broken Hill Proprietary Co. Ltd in 1892. He joined the boards of the Bank of Adelaide, Adelaide Steamship Co. Ltd and Executor Trustee & Agency Co. of South Australia Ltd and the local boards of South British Fire & Marine Insurance Co. and National Mutual Life Association of Australasia (1878-1915). He served as warden of the Marine Board and on the Port Adelaide, Rosewater and Walkerville municipal councils. In 1900 he became a member of the Adelaide Club; he was active in the German Club and a prominent Freemason. In 1903 he entered the Legislative Council for the Central District as a conservative; he was defeated in 1910.

In April 1914 Muecke became chairman of B.H.P. When war came, this key role in the steel industry nourished suspicion generated by his German birth and trade activities, despite his long residence in South Australia, his naturalization, and his assurance to the governor of 'good and loyal citizenship in this State'. In November B.H.P. offices were raided by 'defence authorities'; no evidence of any offence was found. After asking the board in January 1915 to release him from the chairmanship and to grant six months leave of absence as director, Muecke resigned his directorship in October. Already in May he had relinquished involvement in the Chamber of Commerce.

In November he nevertheless sought re-election as director of the Executor Trustee & Agency Co. He published advertisements repudiating Germany's war conduct and countering 'disparaging remarks' about his loyalty. He protested that his family was 'enthusiastically British' and did not speak German; his youngest son, a surgeon wounded at Gallipoli, was then serving with the British in France. Muecke's re-election campaign succeeded, but Defence authorities were not persuaded. He was interned in April 1916 at Fort Largs and, following appeals on his behalf by local businessmen, from May at his own home in Medindie, 'in charge of one man stationed in the house'. This military custody ended in October. Two sons carried on the business, which is still conducted by descendants.

Muecke died at Thorngate on 6 June 1929, and was buried privately with Anglican rites. His estate was valued at about £100 000.

A. Trengove, *'What's good for Australia ...'* (Syd, 1975); *PP* (SA), 1900 (135); *Quiz and the Lantern* (Adel), 29 Apr 1904; *Register* (Adel), 21 Sept 1903, 6, 7 Aug 1914, 19, 30 Nov 1915; *Observer* (Adel), 10 July 1915; *Advertiser* (Adel), 8 June 1929; *Daily Commercial News*, supp, 2 May 1980; Records of Adel Chamber of Commerce (SRG 78, SAA); information from Ms D. Wheeler, Corporate Archivist, BHP, and from Mrs M. Maitland, Prospect, Adel.   JOAN HANCOCK
ERIC RICHARDS

MUIRDEN, WILLIAM (1872-1940), school proprietor, was born on 9 May 1872 at Golspie, Sutherland, Scotland, son of Alexander Muirden, sheriff-officer and auctioneer, and his wife Catherine, née Mackay. The family fell upon hard times and William's elder brother Alexander migrated to South Australia. In 1887 he formed Adelaide's first business college, the Adelaide Shorthand Institute. In 1892 William joined him in the business, but Alexander left Adelaide next year. William combined with William Hogg to operate the Shorthand and Business Training Academy which provided the earliest correspondence education in the colony, from 1895 teaching country students by letter. In 1900 William Muirden established, as sole proprietor, the consistently successful Muirden

College Ltd. On 14 December 1897, at Mile End, he had married Mabel Florence Lambell; they had a daughter and three sons.

Mostly begun as institutions to teach shorthand, by the 1890s nearly all business colleges had established typing as a core subject, supplemented by disciplines like bookkeeping. By the late 1890s Muirden could boast that his graduates worked in over ninety per cent of Adelaide's business houses. The colleges prepared students for a wide range of public and private organizations, including State and Commonwealth public services.

From 1913 to 1934 Muirden published his Commonwealth Series—widely used and republished booklets on grammar, spelling, commercial practice, etc., for use by students preparing for public examinations all over Australia. A deacon at Stow Memorial Congregational Church, he was influenced by Rev. W. R. Fletcher [q.v.4], who possibly urged him to study for his arts degree at the University of Adelaide (B.A., 1910). He formed the William Muirden Book Club, and belonged to the Wayville Literary Society and the Caledonian Society.

His professional reputation assured by his conduct of the business colleges, he became a public advocate for commercial education and helped to prepare the path—long and tortuous—for its acceptance as a subject suitable for academic study at the highest levels. Perhaps it was his 'love of the best in art, music, and literature' that made him unusual in supporting the inclusion of general education (as distinct from technical, skill-training aspects); Muirden College's curriculum reflected this. In February 1914 Muirden was appointed by the State government as an honorary commissioner to inquire into and report on commercial and technical education in Britain and Europe; he was away eight months. In 1924 he helped to establish, and was a director on the first board of King's College, a private Congregational and Baptist school (now Pembroke School).

Muirden bought Hassett's Business College in Prahran, Melbourne, in 1923, and moved there in 1925 to direct it, as Muirden's Business College (in 1936 the name reverted to Hassett's Commercial College). He was assisted by two of his sons; the other remained in Adelaide to run the college, which is still directed by a grandson of William Muirden.

A robust, tall and handsome man, but modest, Muirden was a perfectionist. He conducted his Melbourne school successfully, enjoyed bowls and became an active Methodist. He impressed associates with 'the balanced symmetry' and 'harmony' of his nature. Survived by his wife and family, Muirden died of coronary vascular disease at his East Mal-

vern home on 25 November 1940. He was cremated and his estate was sworn for probate in Melbourne and Adelaide at £9792.

H. T. Burgess (ed), *Cyclopedia of South Australia*, 2 (Adel, 1909); M. Figg (comp), *A brief history of Muirden College, 1900-1980* (Adel, 1982); *Herald* (Melb), 26 Nov 1940; *Age*, 27 Nov 1940; H. Jones, The history of commercial education in South Australia with special reference to women (M.A. thesis, Univ Adel, 1957); newspaper clippings books held by Muirden College, Adel; information from I. B. Muirden, Malvern, SA.

BRIAN CONDON

MULLALY, JOHN CHARLES (1895-1973), planter, was born on 3 September 1895 at Richmond, Melbourne, second of fourteen children of John Henry Mullaly, clerk, and his wife Cecelia Eleanor, née Needham. Educated at Christian Brothers' College, East Melbourne, in 1902-12, he entered the Department of External Affairs in May 1913. In October 1914 he enlisted in the 3rd Light Horse Brigade, Australian Imperial Force, and sailed with the 1st reinforcement on 2 February 1915. He served in Egypt, London, France and Belgium, where he was transferred to the 43rd Infantry Battalion in September 1917; wounded next month, he was promoted sergeant in May 1918 and commissioned lieutenant in April 1919. He returned in October to Australia where his A.I.F. appointment was terminated in February 1920.

Appointed Commonwealth audit inspector to the Expropriation Board in the Mandated Territory of New Guinea in 1921, Mullaly became an inspector in the Department of Native Affairs in 1924 and district officer and magistrate in New Ireland in 1925. He soon resigned when he acquired Natava plantation, New Britain, one of the German properties expropriated by the Australian government after the war. In 1926 he became a foundation member of the New Guinea Planters' Association, formed to look after the planters' interests as they had no political representation. Mullaly served as vice-president of the association in 1929-32 and 1938-40 and as president in 1932-38 and 1940-41. He played a major role in the planters' efforts to break the oligopoly in the copra industry of the big trading companies, Burns [q.v.7], Philp [q.v.] & Co. Ltd. and W. R. Carpenter [q.v.7]. & Co. Ltd. Because of low world market prices for copra, many of the Australian ex-servicemen on expropriated properties were in financial difficulties. After the association's appeal to the Federal government, they were granted a moratorium and payments were suspended from July 1930 to June 1936.

When the New Guinea Legislative Council was established Mullaly was appointed one of the non-official members (1933-45) and the non-official member of the Executive Council (1933-39). In the Legislative Council in 1940 he pressed for government control and marketing of copra through a statutory authority. He was appointed O.B.E. in 1937.

On the outbreak of war in 1939 Mullaly served as lieutenant and adjutant (1940) of the New Guinea Volunteer Rifles. Transferred to the Australian Intelligence Corps in 1941, he was seconded to Allied General Headquarters, South-West Pacific Area, in 1942 and directed its Combined Operations Intelligence Centre in 1943-44. Promoted lieut-colonel in 1945, he commanded the Training Battalion, Pacific Islands Regiment, until his retirement in July 1946. He settled in Sydney about 1949.

Slightly built, 5 ft. 8 ins. (173 cm) tall, with brown hair and eyes, Mullaly married a nurse, Ruth Saunders, of Singleton, New South Wales, on 9 February 1926 at Kavieng, New Guinea. He was always a keen sportsman: his recreations included cricket, golf, tennis and riding. He belonged to the Papua, Rabaul, Imperial Service, Australasian Pioneers' and Melbourne Cricket clubs. He died at Mosman, Sydney, on 25 March 1973 and was cremated. His wife (d. 1977) and daughter survived him.

PD (LC NG), 12th S, meeting 1, April 1940; *PIM*, June 1973; *SMH*, 2 Dec 1935, 2, 4, 27 Mar 1936, 2 May, 15 Dec 1937; P. W. Hopper, Kicking out the Hun (M.A. thesis, UPNG, 1981); information from Miss D. Mullaly, Mont Albert, and Mrs B. A. Cole, Toorak, Melb.

PATRICIA W. HOPPER

MULLAN, JOHN (1871-1941), public servant, union organizer and politician, was born on 8 September 1871 at Loughlinstown, Dublin, son of John Ponsonby Mullan and his wife Mary, née Stanley. His parents died during his childhood and he was cared for by relatives. He was educated at National and private schools in Dublin.

Arriving in Melbourne in 1888, Mullan worked for two years as a clerk before going to Queensland. There he briefly became a railway maintenance worker, then a letter carrier and postal assistant in the Post and Telegraph Department, Charters Towers, before joining the Government Savings Bank there. He married Mary Ellen Farrelly, a miner's daughter, in St Columba's Catholic Church, Charters Towers, on 11 September 1895.

Mullan was a miners' union organizer in 1905-06, secretary of the Amalgamated Workers' Association (later Amalgamated Workers' Union) in 1912-13, and general organizer for the Queensland central execu-

tive of the Australian Labor Party in 1917. He attended Labor-in-Politics conventions in 1910 and 1920-38 and was a convention delegate to the central executive in 1920-23 and 1926-41.

After failing to win a by-election for the seat of Charters Towers in 1905 and Townsville in 1907, he won Charters Towers in 1908. His defeat in 1912 was attributed to an electoral redistribution and the general strike. Elected to the Senate for Queensland in 1913 and 1914, Mullan was on the executive of the Parliamentary Labor Party in 1916-17. An anti-conscriptionist, he lost his seat largely because of the way the 1917 Senate vote was counted. In 1918 he won the State seat of Flinders, merged after 1932 in the new Carpentaria electorate, which he held until his retirement from politics in 1940.

Mullan was in turn parliamentary whip (1909-12), minister without portfolio (1919-20) and attorney-general (from 12 November 1920 to 21 May 1929 and 17 June 1932 to 14 November 1940). His long term as attorney-general was interrupted when the Moore [q.v.] government won office. A close friend and valued counsellor of Premier Forgan Smith [q.v.] and acting premier on many occasions, Mullan was a capable, fair-minded minister who gave no quarter in debate but who had few enemies. It was said that his many successful reforms to the State legal system were possible because he did not belong to the legal profession. He had a personal library on legal subjects and was well respected by lawyers and officials of the Justice Department for his common-sense analysis of the advice he received. His speeches in parliament were based on a sound understanding of the matters being debated. His belief that major and lasting reforms could be achieved by Labor in power never flagged.

A small man with a shock of black hair, a high forehead and bright eyes, he was known as Johnny Mullan and, affectionately by public servants in the Justice Department, as 'the little man in the brown suit'. Speaking of himself as the only attorney-general who was neither an attorney nor a general, he was the first of a line of attorneys-general in Queensland without legal qualifications. After his health began to decline, Mullan spent much time at his house at Surfers' Paradise where he refused to install a telephone, saying that if the premier really wanted him the police would let him know. He died in the Mater Misericordiae Private Hospital, Brisbane, on 1 October 1941, survived by his wife, three sons and six daughters. A requiem Mass at St Stephen's Cathedral was followed by a state funeral to Toowong cemetery.

C. A. Bernays, *Queensland—our seventh politi-*

cal decade, 1920-1930 (Syd, 1931); J. Larcombe, *Notes on the political history of the labour movement in Queensland* (Brisb, 1934); *PD* (Qld), 1941, p 569; *Aust Law J*, 15, 1941, p 196; *Daily Mail* (Brisb), 30 Sept 1924; *Worker* (Brisb), 14 Jan 1941; *Truth* (Brisb), 19 Jan 1941; *Telegraph* (Brisb), 2 Oct 1941; Mullan papers (QA); information about Mullan family from J. Fahy, Booval, and F. J. Waters, Ashgrove, Brisb.   JOY GUYATT

MULLEN, LESLIE MILTIADES (1882-1943), soldier, accountant and prison administrator, was born on 15 August 1882 at Williamstown, Victoria, son of William Rowland Mullen, stationmaster, from Liverpool, England, and his second wife Caroline, née Loughhead. Educated to Intermediate certificate level at Queen's College, Maryborough, he joined the 5th Victorian (Mounted Rifles) Contingent as a private in February 1901 and served in the South African War until April 1902. He then settled in Tasmania and worked for the Emu Bay Railway Co. and later the Tasmanian Farmers' Co-operative Association as an accountant. At St Mary's Anglican Church, Caulfield, Melbourne, on 16 August 1910, he married Alma Hoper Langeveldt.

In 1906 Mullen had been commissioned as a second lieutenant in the Tasmanian Rangers (militia); by 1914 he was area officer at Burnie. On 28 August he enlisted in the Australian Imperial Force as a lieutenant and was appointed the 12th Battalion's transport officer. Promoted captain on 22 May 1915, he went ashore at Gallipoli and led 'A' Company, 12th Battalion, in operations there in May-August; his unit left Gallipoli in November. On 20 February 1916, in Egypt, Mullen was promoted major and second-in-command and embarked for France in March. On 4-16 October he commanded the 11th Battalion and on 1 December was promoted lieut-colonel in command of the 9th Battalion.

Mullen led the battalion in operations on the Somme in February 1917 and on 25 April-12 May temporarily commanded the 3rd Brigade at Bullecourt. Awarded the Distinguished Service Order in June, he saw further action in September at Polygon Wood and then at Broodseinde where on 9 October he was severely wounded in the chest and shoulder. In 1917 he was twice mentioned in dispatches.

Mullen rejoined the 9th Battalion on 9 January 1918 and at Hollebeke, on 6 March, he was gassed. He led the battalion at Meteren, Lihons, Cappy, Villeret and against the Hindenburg outpost line in May-September. He commanded the 1st Training Brigade at Sutton Veny, England, from October to January 1919 and then became commandant of the 3rd A.I.F. Depot. Awarded the Belgian

Croix de Guerre, he embarked for Australia on 4 June and was discharged from the A.I.F. on 6 September.

On 1 July 1920 Mullen joined the Tasmanian Public Service as an inspector with the Audit Department. In May 1928 he became superintendent of the New Town Infirmary and on 1 September was appointed controller of prisons and governor of Hobart gaol. He had continued serving in the militia, commanding the 2/12th Infantry Regiment, Australian Military Forces, from 1920 and the 12th Battalion from 1921. He was placed on the reserve of officers in 1929.

In 1919 Mullen joined the Hobart sub-branch of the Returned Sailors' and Soldiers' Imperial League of Australia. Elected State president in June 1922, he represented Tasmania at many national league conferences and was an Australian delegate to the British Empire Service League conferences in Melbourne in 1924 and Canada in 1931. In 'recognition of his distinguished work in the returned soldier movement', he was appointed C.M.G. in June 1934.

An active sports administrator, Mullen held various executive appointments with the Tasmanian Cricket Association (chairman, 1926-33). He was also a committee-member of the Tasmanian National Football League. In World War II he commanded the Volunteer Defence Corps, Tasmania, in 1942.

Survived by his wife and daughter, Mullen died of coronary vascular disease on March 1943 in Hobart and was cremated. A 'sturdy, competent commander', he was remembered as a 'strict but never a harsh disciplinarian [whose] friendliness and commonsense methods made the [9th Battalion] a well-knit and supremely contented unit'.

L. M. Newton, *The story of the twelfth* (Hob, 1925); *Cyclopedia of Tasmania* (Hob, 1931); N. K. Harvey, *From Anzac to the Hindenburg Line* (Brisb, 1941); C. E. W. Bean, *The A.I.F. in France*, 1917-18 (Syd, 1933, 1937, 1942); *Reveille* (Syd), 1 July, 1 Aug 1934; *Weekly Courier* (Launc), 22 Aug 1928, 9 Oct 1929, 7 June 1934; *Examiner* (Launc), 1, 22 July, 23 Oct, 1, 30 Nov 1939; records, Returned Services' League, Hob; information from Mr B. C. Williams, New Town, Hob.

RODNEY K. QUINN

MULLER, FREDERICK (1881-1962), manufacturer, was born on 21 July 1881 at Neustadt, Prussia, Germany, son of Wilhelm Müller, tourist guide, and his wife Elizabeth, née Hock. The family reached Sydney in the *Bombay* on 9 June 1885. Known as Fritz he attended several schools and after his father's death helped his mother to run their Viennese-style café. At 13 he started work for the sheet-metal-working firm, Wunderlich [q.v.] Patent Ceiling and Roofing Co. Ltd. A devout

Lutheran, he married Gertrude Amelia Katherine Jope at the Lutheran Church in Goulburn Street on 11 April 1903. He was naturalized in 1904.

Next year Muller opened his own sheet metal workshop in a small loft in George Street, equipped with a blowlamp, a primus stove and a soldering-iron. After successfully repairing a car radiator for Mark Foy [q.v.8] and a mudguard for John Norton [q.v.], he specialized in radiator and mudguard repair and manufacture. He invented an all-metal mudguard and, as motoring became more popular, his business grew rapidly. By 1911 he had moved to larger premises in Crown Street. Expansion continued during World War I and in 1919 he bought a large block on Parramatta Road, Camperdown, where he later built a three-storey factory.

In the early 1930s Muller began to manufacture refrigerator components, which previously had been imported. He imported specially designed plant as the equipment was unavailable in Australia. Developing a hard-solder technique, Muller made submerged and flooded coils, condensers, evaporators and other sheet metal and tubular parts for commercial and domestic refrigerators, as well as air-conditioning equipment.

In 1937 he set up the private company, F. Muller Pty Ltd. The business flourished during World War II with the acceptance of government contracts; production included radiators for cruiser tanks, power-generating plants for Australian-produced vehicles, and self-sealing fuel and oil tanks for Mosquito aircraft. The firm also helped to establish the operational value of new inventions for the Army Inventions Directorate.

Known as the 'Chief', Muller was a strong, thick-set man with an 'air of quiet purpose'. Cautious and meticulous, he always thought modestly of himself as 'a sheet metal worker'. With his ingenuity and mechanical expertise he made a considerable contribution to the development of Australian secondary industry and was one of the most successful of Australia's German immigrants. In 1955, the fiftieth anniversary of his firm, he retired in favour of his sons, but continued to take a keen interest in the business. In 1959 the firm merged with National Radiators Ltd (now National Consolidated Ltd).

Survived by his wife, three sons and two daughters, Muller died at his Caringbah home on 23 March 1962, and was buried with Lutheran rites in Woronora cemetery. His estate was sworn for probate at £95 144.

People (Syd), 12 Jan 1955; *Refrigeration, Cold Storage and Air Conditioning*, 30 Apr 1955, 31 May 1962; *Refrigeration J*, 2 Aug 1955; *SMH*, 11 May 1962; naturalization files A1/04/3368 (AAO).

J. TAMPKE

MULLINS, JOHN LANE (1857-1939), solicitor, was born on 4 June 1857 in Sydney, second son of Irish parents James Mullins, clerk, and his wife Eliza, née Lane. He was educated at Richard Creagh's and Mrs Saclier's schools, then by the Benedictines as a boarder at St Mary's College, Lyndhurst, and at St John's College, University of Sydney (B.A., 1876; M.A., 1879). In May 1876 he was articled to R. B. Smith [q.v.6], solicitor. After touring Europe in 1882-83 he was admitted as a solicitor on 28 February 1885. At St Mary's Cathedral he married Jane Mary Frances, sister of John and (Sir) Thomas Hughes [qq.v.9], on 14 April.

Income from his father's investments, mainly in city real estate, freed John from the necessity of earning all his income and enabled him to pursue cultivated and gentlemanly ideals. Like his father he was a prominent Catholic layman: he was treasurer (or secretary) of St Mary's Cathedral Building Fund from 1879, a director of St Joseph's Building and Investment Society, active in the Society of St Vincent de Paul in Australia, a fellow of St John's College (1885-1939), and secretary then treasurer of St Vincent's Hospital. A founder of, and solicitor for, the *Catholic Press* in 1895, he was a trusted confidant of and adviser (especially on financial matters) to Cardinal Moran [q.v.] and Archbishop Kelly [q.v.9]. He was appointed papal chamberlain in 1903 and a knight commander of the papal Order of St Gregory the Great in 1920.

Mullins mixed an affection for England and English Catholicism with a pride in his Irish origins and Australian birth. In 1896 he helped to form the New South Wales Irish Rifle Regiment, and was a captain from 1898. He planned to accompany the 3rd New South Wales contingent to the South African War as adjutant, but was elected to the Sydney Municipal Council for Bligh Ward. Elected chairman of the finance committee in 1902, he contributed to reorganization of the city's finances. In 1909 as chairman of the library committee he helped to arrange the transfer of the lending branch of the Public Library of New South Wales, to form the basis of the Sydney Municipal Library. He lost interest in municipal affairs after being defeated for mayor in 1910 and with his family visited Europe for almost two years.

Nominated to the Legislative Council in 1917, Mullins generally voted with the Nationalists and was especially interested in legislation affecting Catholics, hospitals and charities, local government and certain businesses. In 1931 he joined the All for Australia League and supported the United Australia Party from 1932. He did not stand for election to the reconstituted council in 1933. In 1918 he was appointed to the State Children Relief

Board and was an executive-member of the Royal Society for the Welfare of Mothers and Babies, the National Association for the Prevention and Cure of Consumption, president of the Citizens' Rights and Liquor Reform Association and a vice-chairman of the Metropolitan Hospitals Contribution Fund from 1932. He became a director of the City Mutual Fire Insurance Co. in 1923 and of Tooheys [q.v.6] Ltd in 1927.

Mullins was a notable patron of the arts. He had studied music and was adept at repoussé metal work. As a youth he had assisted the sculptor Achille Simonetti [q.v.6]; later he arranged the publication of Hugh McCrae's [q.v.] first work and supported him financially. Mullins collected finely bound and printed books and book plates, and also paintings; and he encouraged these activities by founding and presiding over the Australian Ex Libris Society and the Australian Limited Editions Society and using his influence to obtain commissions for artists. He was secretary and treasurer of the Society of Artists, Sydney, in 1907-39, and from 1916 a trustee of the National Art Gallery of New South Wales (president, 1938-39). Mullins provided an important link between artists and Sydney's business and political élite. He was also active in the local Numismatic and Philatelic societies, a member of the (Royal) Australian Historical Society and a vice-president of the Wattle Day committee.

Mullins was admitted to the Bar on 1 August 1930, to encourage a grandson to do the same. Survived by four daughters, he died on 24 February 1939 at Elizabeth Bay and was buried in South Head cemetery. His wife had died in 1926 and his only son Brendan was killed in action in 1917. A terracotta bust of Mullins by Simonetti is held by the Mitchell [q.v.5] Library, Sydney.

Cyclopedia of N.S.W. (Syd, 1907); *SMH*, 25 Feb 1939; *Catholic Press*, 2 Mar 1939; J. L. Mullins papers (ML). MARK LYONS

MULQUIN, KATHERINE (1842?-1930), educationist, was born at Adare, Limerick, Ireland, daughter of John Mulquin, landowner, and his wife Catherine, née Sheehy. Her family was well known and comfortably situated. Educated at the Faithful Companions of Jesus Convent, Laurel Hill, Limerick, she joined the Congregation of the Presentation of the Blessed Virgin Mary and was professed in 1863, taking the religious name Mary Paul.

On 22 October 1873, as Superior of a projected foundation in Melbourne, she left Limerick in response to a plea for teaching assistance from Fr J. F. Corbett [q.v.8], parish priest of St Mary's Catholic Church, St Kilda. She and six other Sisters arrived in the *Great Britain* on 21 December to make the first Presentation foundation in Victoria. To give them temporary accommodation the priests vacated St Mary's presbytery. Within a month the Sisters took over the girls' section of the parochial school. On the presbytery verandah they also conducted a fee-paying 'select school'. This adaptation of the original aim of the Presentation Order to educate the poor was necessary in Australia to answer the need for secondary classes; moreover fee-paying students at both primary and secondary levels helped towards general expenses. A short time later, when they had purchased a house in Dandenong Road, Windsor, opposite the presbytery, the nucleus of Presentation Convent and College, the Sisters enrolled isolated students as boarders.

Mother Paul was an assiduous correspondent and many of her letters to and from her family and friends in Ireland are extant. These and the detailed diary she kept on the voyage out demonstrate perception, humour, strength of character and strong spirituality, qualities which enabled her to deal capably with the vicissitudes of life in the colony. She spoke French and Italian fluently, was very fond of music and gently insisted on the social graces: 'the noiseless opening and closing of doors, the proper way to fold a letter, the courteous inclination of pupils when passing their teachers, the keeping of appointments or a timely excuse for failure, the immediate expression of gratitude for favours'. Her teaching was integrated and time-tables foreign to her. However, when the University of Melbourne opened to women in 1881, stimulating the academic element in the education of girls, examinations began to take precedence over accomplishments. Although Mother Paul had reservations about this new trend, she appreciated the value of examinations as a key to a girl's independence. Here, too, was an application of the Presentation principle that girls be trained to earn their own living.

By the mid-1880s Windsor was sending candidates for the matriculation examination, and the school soon achieved a considerable reputation for combining personal spiritual development with genuine intellectual enquiry. Several country and city convents and many parish primary schools were founded on Windsor personnel and resources.

In 1890 Mother Paul retired as Superior. However she was again Superior in 1891-94 after her successor's death, and also from 1899 until succeeded by Mother Ita Cagney in 1906. The amalgamation of the various Victorian Presentation convents in 1908 met with her approval.

Mother Paul became a semi-invalid in her last years but always retained her keen alertness. She died at Windsor Convent on 10 February 1930.

K. D. Kane, *Adventure in faith* (Melb, 1974); *Aust Women's Weekly*, 28 Nov 1973; *Advocate* (Melb), 27 Dec 1873, 3, 10, 17, 31 Jan 1874, 13, 20 Feb 1930; M. Kavanagh, The educational work of the Presentation Sisters in Victoria 1873-1960 (M.Ed. thesis, Univ Melb, 1965); Presentation convents' archives (Limerick, Eire, *and* Windsor, Melb). KATHLEEN DUNLOP KANE

MULVANY, EDWARD JOSEPH (1871-1951), public servant, was born on 17 February 1871 at St Kilda, Melbourne, son of Michael Mulvany, carpenter, and his wife Johanna, née Ryan, both Irish born. Educated at the Christian Brothers' College, East St Kilda, after his matriculation he entered the Victorian Department of Customs in May 1888. He was a member of the Australian Natives' Association, and for a time president of its Brunswick branch, and in 1894 was president of the Catholic Young Men's Society. On 25 October 1899 he married Annie Hegarty, a schoolteacher, at St Francis' Church, Melbourne.

Mulvany transferred to the Commonwealth Public Service after Federation, and served a period in the office of the minister C. C. Kingston [q.v.9]. In 1912 he took charge of the customs branch at the high commissioner's office, London, travelling throughout Europe, Canada and the United States of America to assess dutiable values. At the beginning of World War I he was involved in gathering information about firms suspected of trading with the enemy. When he returned to Australia in 1916 he was seconded to the Treasury to work on the issue of war gratuity bonds.

In 1921 he was in charge of the commerce branch of the Department of Trade and Customs, responsible for the control of fruit pools and Commonwealth assistance schemes for primary producers. When, in 1925, these functions were combined with the immigration office of the Prime Minister's Department to create the Department of Markets and Migration, Mulvany was appointed secretary. In January 1927 he was appointed to the Commonwealth Board of Trade. For his 'valuable work' as a recognized specialist on the fruit industry and particularly for his effectiveness in extending overseas markets for Australian produce he was appointed I.S.O. in 1927. W. M. Hughes [q.v.9] is reputed to have said of him: 'Mulvany is never in the way, and never out of the way'. In 1928 he became a member of the Development and Migration Commission, and when it was abolished in 1930 he returned as secretary and permanent head to the Department of Markets (renamed Department of Commerce in 1932). During this period he was also the Commonwealth representative on the Australian Overseas Trade Publicity Committee and the Australian National Travel Association. In 1934 he took leave and retired officially in 1935.

In 1935-51 Mulvany acted as economic adviser to the Commonwealth Dried Fruits Control Board, and was a member in 1940-46. He was also active as a vice-president and president of the Victorian regional group of the Institute of Public Administration. He had a lifelong interest in horse-racing and was a member of the Williamstown, Moonee Valley and Victoria racing clubs. Predeceased by his wife, Mulvany died suddenly on 7 June 1951 at his St Kilda home and, following a requiem Mass at St Columba's, Elwood, was buried in Melbourne general cemetery. Of his nine children, five sons survived him.

Argus, 6 Apr 1912; *SMH*, 3 June 1927; *Herald* (Melb), 6 Dec 1934, 7 June 1951; *Smith's Weekly* (Syd), 28 Mar 1925, 6 Jan 1940; *Age*, 8 June 1951; information from Mr T. J. Mulvany, Melb. I. G. CARNELL

MUMMERY, JOSEPH BROWNING (1888-1974), tenor, was born on 12 July 1888 at Carlton, Melbourne, only son of Joseph Ernest Mummery, jeweller, and his wife Matilda, née Henry. He was educated at the local state school where he excelled at cricket and singing. His family circle was musical but, a trade being basic, he was successfully apprenticed to an engineering firm tolerant of warbling at the lathe. Known as Joe Mummery, he was, like his friend John Curtin, a member of the Victorian Socialist Party. Italian-trained A. C. Bartleman eliminated any vocal faults before, without rehearsal, Mummery displaced an erratic Latin in Gounod's *Faust* with the Rigo Opera Company. In 1919-20 he toured Australasia with Amy Castles [q.v.7] in the Williamson [q.v.6] Opera Company.

Henceforth known as Browning Mummery, he married a pianist, Alice Martha Jane Craven, at Albert Park on 22 April 1919 and in 1921 went to England without introductions. Next year Percy Pitt engaged him for the British National Opera Company and later included him in the first-ever broadcast of opera (*Faust*) from Savoy Hill. In 1923 at Birmingham he sang Rodolfo in *La Bohème*, (Sir) Malcolm Sargent's first conducted opera. His soaring upper register broadcast sympathetically, and his studious and expressive self-presentation coupled with an amenable cheerful practicality gained him a seven-year contract with a subsidiary of His Master's Voice. By 1926 he had made nineteen double discs with Zonophone.

Mummery studied in Italy before being recalled to sing in *Der Rosenkavalier* at Covent Garden with Lotte Lehmann and Elizabeth Schumann. In 1926 Melba [q.v.] engaged him and John Brownlee [q.v.7] for her Covent Garden farewell. Under Vincenzo Bellezza, their two acts of *La Bohème* provided the first on-stage land-line broadcast and earned Mummery three further valedictory co-performances plus an engraved diamond-tipped pin (which he lost) from the diva. The autographed photo of the three Australians shows Mummery smiling discreetly, stocky, barrel-chested, with sparse slicked hair parted in the centre, and hands deferentially gripped. But when, at Melba's absolutely last farewell in Melbourne's His Majesty's Theatre on 27 September 1928, she insisted that only the handsomer, taller, younger Brownlee take curtain-calls with her, he joined them from upstage to collect applause and a playful slap. He had been in Australia for Williamson's season with Toti dal Monte and a La Scala cast.

From 1929 to 1932 Mummery sang in New York and Chicago with the National Broadcasting Company, becoming a radio favourite and singing in the historic Christmas broadcast to Admiral Byrd in the Antarctic in 1931. Returning to England in 1932 he sang in films for Gaumont British, notably with Evelyn Laye in *Evensong* (1933), based on Beverley Nichols' notorious satire of Melba. After touring his homeland again in 1934 with, among others, Florence Austral [q.v.7] for Sir Benjamin Fuller's [q.v.8] Victorian centenary season, he remained in Melbourne where he turned to teaching, making occasional broadcasts and appearances in New Zealand and throughout Australia.

Mummery was Australia's most celebrated tenor between the wars. Lyrical but robust, glowing and vibrant, his voice had neither the mellifluous languor of the great *tenori di grazia* nor the clarion effrontery of a *lyrico spinto* like Martinelli. He was a precise, supportive lead rather than a florid virtuoso. He had a well-memorized repertoire of thirty roles, negotiated all Puccini sonorously, but amiably recorded hogwash such as 'Josephine' and (with chorus) 'The Bells of St Mary's'. His most historic disc, duets from Verdi's *Il Trovatore* with Austral, owes its celebrity to her assumption of a contralto role on one side when another performer failed to appear.

A sanguine, decent, rather Edwardian man, Mummery died in Canberra on 16 March 1974 and was cremated. His wife and son survived him.

Complete catalogue of Zonophone records (Brisb, 1927); His Master's Voice, *Catalogue of records 1936*(Lismore, NSW); I. Moresby, *Australia makes music* (Melb, 1948); J. Hetherington, *Melba* (Melb, 1967); B. and F. Mackenzie, *Singers of Australia* (Melb, 1967); N. Melba, *Melodies and memories*, J. Cargher introd and notes (Melb, 1980); *Punch* (Melb), 24 Apr 1924; *Herald* (Melb), 11 May 1928, 5 Dec 1930, 25 Sept 1935; *Table Talk*, 7 June 1928; *Australian*, 23 Feb 1967; recorded interview, 11 Aug 1972 (tape 625, NL Sound Archive); personal information.   JAMES GRIFFIN

MUNRO, ANDREW WATSON (1858-1944), obstetrician, was born on 1 March 1858 at Tain, Ross-shire, Scotland, son of Hugh Munro, master plasterer, and his wife Barbara, née Watson. After studying medicine at the University of Edinburgh (M.B., C.M., 1883; M.D., 1892), he migrated to Sydney about 1884 and set up in practice in York Street. In 1888-91 he was honorary physician at Sydney Hospital. He visited Edinburgh in 1892, gained his doctorate and was elected a fellow of the Royal College of Surgeons, Edinburgh.

Back in Sydney, with (Sir) James Graham, David Fell [qq.v.4,8] and Dr L. E. F. Neill, in 1893 Munro helped to found and to finance the Women's Hospital in Hay Street to train obstetric nurses. On 24 December 1894 at Woollahra he married Sophia Gunning, who had arrived from Ireland in 1888 and trained as a nurse at (Royal) Prince Alfred Hospital. She too became involved in the Women's Hospital, furnishing and decorating its first indoor department when it moved to Crown Street in 1897. In 1900 it became a teaching hospital of the University of Sydney. Munro was honorary obstetrician and gynaecologist from 1893 until 1909, when he became a consultant, and was a director until 1908 and in 1911-12. He also examined in materia medica and pharmacology at the university in 1894-1902.

In London, Munro was an honorary assistant bacteriologist at Guy's Hospital in 1915-17. On his return to Sydney, he worked throughout 1918-19 as a pathology demonstrator at the university. He maintained private consulting rooms until 1924, but became increasingly involved in public health causes. In the 1920s he wrote many letters to the *Sydney Morning Herald* urging the establishment of a chair of obstetrics at the university and deploring the lack of agitation on the issue by women's groups. His campaign succeeded in 1925 with the appointment of J. C. Windeyer [q.v.] as professor. Munro's letters were intensely rhetorical and often vitriolic: in 1925 he crossed swords with S. R. Innes-

Noad [q.v.9] over lower infant mortality rates in New Zealand. That year he was president of the State branch of the Health Association of Australasia.

In the late 1920s and 1930s Munro devoted his attention to reducing the maternal mortality rate and in 1935 sent a sketch of a department of maternity hygiene to W. M. Hughes [q.v.9], who as Commonwealth minister for health was launching the George V and Queen Mary Maternal and Infant Welfare Memorial Jubilee Fund. Like Hughes, Munro was obsessed with the idea that Australia must 'populate or perish'. His letters to the press increasingly dealt explicitly with population issues and the declining birth-rate, warning darkly of the dangers to Australia of contraception and abortion ('*homicide*, of course') and the perils of an empty continent so close to the teeming millions of Asia.

Dark-haired and clean-shaven, Munro had a profound knowledge of the works of Shakespeare, Burns and Carlyle. His wife died in 1929 and at Dulwich Hill on 27 May 1930 he married Helen Maria (d. 1937), née Gibson, widow of Sir William McMillan [q.v.]. Watson Munro died childless at his Woollahra home on 7 September 1944 and was cremated with Presbyterian forms. He left the residue of his estate, valued for probate at £30 838, to the University of Sydney for research into the causes of death and disease of women in pregnancy, parturition and the puerperium and of children in the first two years of life.

Syd Hospital, *Annual Report*, 1888-91; Health Assn of A'sia, *Bulletin*, 1925-26; *SMH*, 24, 28 Aug, 3, 9 Sept 1925, 6 Feb 1929, 2 Nov 1937, 9 Sept 1944; Health Soc of NSW, *and* Public Health Assn of A'sia, *and* Crown St Hospital, Annual Reports 1922 (ML); Faculty of Medicine, *and* Senate, Univ Syd, minutes, *and* book of newspaper clippings relevant to Univ Syd (Univ Syd Archives); W. M. Hughes papers (NL).   T. FITZSIMONS

MUNRO, EDWARD JOY (1882-1950), soldier and political party administrator, was born on 1 March 1882 at Scone, New South Wales, second surviving son of Arthur William Munro, sexton, and his wife Marianne, née Easterbrook, both Sydney born. Educated at Glen Innes Superior Public School and privately, he joined the New South Wales Railways where he remained until the outbreak of World War I, thereby obtaining 'an intimate knowledge of most of the country districts of the State'. On 16 September 1911 he married Irene Frances Johnson at St Matthew's Anglican Church, Manly.

Munro had begun his military career in 1899 as a driver in the militia. He was commissioned in 1908 and later commanded the 6th Army Service Corps. On 17 August 1914

he enlisted in the Australian Imperial Force and was appointed as a lieutenant in the 1st Australian Divisional Train. Promoted captain in September, he sailed for Egypt in December. He served briefly at Gallipoli before returning to transport duties in Egypt. From December 1915 until March 1916 he was engaged in the Senussi campaign. Promoted major before embarking for France, from April 1916 to July 1918 Munro was engaged in transport work on all fronts in France and Belgium occupied by the 1st Division. In August 1918 he took command of the Australian Army Service Corps Training Depot in England. He had been awarded the Distinguished Service Order in 1917 and was also mentioned in dispatches. After the Armistice Munro was attached to the staff of Lieut-General Sir John Monash [q.v.] in London for a year as staff officer of rail transport.

Returning to Australia late in 1919, Munro retired from the railways in 1922 and established a general agency business. In 1925 he led the Ormildah Oil Development Co. Ltd expedition some 400 miles (650 km) up the Sepik River, Mandated Territory of New Guinea. Promoted lieut-colonel in the Australian Military Forces in 1920, Munro held various commands in the A.A.S.C. until 1934. He was returned to the active list in 1940 and commanded the A.A.S.C., 1st Division. He retired with the rank of colonel in 1941.

Munro was appointed general secretary of the Australian Country Party, and New South Wales secretary, in February 1927 and retired from those positions in June 1948. Described as a rather flamboyant personality whose plans were inclined to be grandiose and incapable of realization, Munro was 'something of a jack-of-all-trades. He was a superb organizer, an efficient campaign director, and a trained accountant, who accustomed himself to travelling long distances each year to keep in touch with party stalwarts all over the state'. Early in his appointment Munro rapidly built up branches of the Country Party. In 1933-34 he gave extensive evidence in favour of possible new States to the Commonwealth royal commissioner H. S. Nicholas [q.v.].

Although never seeking to displace politicians from the public spotlight, Munro spoke for the Country Party on a variety of issues. He successfully built up its head office 'as the linch-pin of the party's organisation, with himself as the essential link between the Central Council and the local organisation'.

Munro became an associate of the Chartered Institute of Secretaries (England) in 1934. Active in Legacy (president of the Legacy Club of Sydney in 1944-45) and with the War Veterans' homes, he also took an interest in scouting and was commissioner for the City of Sydney district Boy Scouts' Association in 1940. A member of the Imperial Service Club, he enjoyed rifle-shooting, surfing and gardening.

Survived by his wife and son, Munro died of coronary occlusion on 27 August 1950 at Manly and was cremated after an Anglican service. In making public tributes (Sir) Arthur Fadden and (Sir) Michael Bruxner [q.v.7] described him as 'one of our most distinguished and loyal citizens'.

D. Aitkin, *The Country Party in New South Wales* (Canb, 1972); *London Gazette*, 1 June 1917; *SMH*, 5 June 1917, 11 Feb 1927, 28 Aug 1950; records (AWM). MATTHEW DICKER

MUNRO, GRACE EMILY (1879-1964), a founder of the Country Women's Association, was born on 25 March 1879 at Gragin, Warialda, New South Wales, second of seven daughters of George Hollinworth Gordon, grazier, and his Victorian wife Eliza Frances, née Macdonald. She was educated by governesses and at Kambala school, Sydney. An accomplished horsewoman, she could drive a buggy at a gallop as well as any man. She was also a good shot, an expert needlewoman and a knowledgeable gardener.

At Gragin on 14 July 1898 she married 36-year-old Hugh Robert Munro [q.v.] of Keera. They had four children, the youngest dying in 1911 while Grace was absent in Sydney with another child having an emergency appendectomy. This experience made her determined to improve the conditions of and the availability of medical help for all women and children in the country. Recuperating from her loss, she travelled restlessly between 1911 and 1914. She stayed with (Sir) Hubert Murray [q.v.] in Papua and sailed with him in his yacht to the Trobriand Islands and up the Fly River. She later visited Tonga, Samoa and Fiji, and in 1914 Egypt, Europe and Britain.

During World War I Grace Munro lived mainly in Sydney at Bellevue Hill. In 1915 she was honorary organizing secretary of the Australian Army Medical Corps' comforts fund and also worked for the Australian Red Cross Society under Eleanor MacKinnon [q.v.], particularly at Holsworthy army camp. Using her Clement-Talbot car, she and her driver transported supplies to the camps round Liverpool each week. She helped to provide facilities at the Sydney showground for country volunteers during the 1917 strike and ran the post office there. She qualified in first aid, home nursing and hygiene with the St John Ambulance Association and had advanced instruction from Sister A. B. Parry [q.v.]. After the war she gave first aid classes at Keera and in recognition of her work was appointed a serving sister of the Order of St John of Jerusalem. She was a member of the Bingara Hospital Board.

In 1922 Mrs Munro helped to organize and publicize the conference in Sydney which formally established the Country Women's Association of New South Wales. Elected president, she insisted that the association was to be non-political. She travelled throughout New South Wales and Queensland speaking to country-women and helping to form branches. By 1923 there were sixty-eight branches, seventeen rest-rooms for mothers and children, two seaside homes and maternity centres in many towns. She met cabinet ministers to urge the establishment of maternity wards in country hospitals and improved conditions in trains and at railway refreshment rooms for women and children. Ill health forced her to retire in 1926 after 100 branches had been formed and a membership of 4500 attained. She continued to raise large sums of money for such causes as rest-centres and holiday homes, the Australian Inland Mission's Aerial Medical Service, the Red Cross and St John. Appointed M.B.E. in 1935, she was a member of the advisory council of New England University College at Armidale from 1938.

Over the years Grace Munro visited Kashmir, India, Burma, China, Japan, The Philippines, Indonesia, North America, Europe and South Africa. In 1928 she accompanied the administrator, Brigadier General E. A. Wisdom [q.v.], on his annual tour of the ports of the Mandated Territory of New Guinea, and 400 miles up the Sepik River. From 1952 she annually visited the Great Barrier Reef, gathering a remarkable shell collection. She did not live at Keera after her eldest son's marriage in 1936, but developed a series of properties at Scone and Bundarra and houses in Sydney's eastern suburbs.

Survived by two sons and a daughter, Grace Munro died in Sydney on 23 July 1964 after suffering from severe curvature of the spine; she was cremated with Presbyterian forms and her ashes were scattered over Keera. Her estate was valued for probate at £64 525. With her independent wealth she lived a largely separate life from her husband although he remained amusedly tolerant and proud of her activities. She was thin and 5 ft. 7 ins. (170 cm) tall, and had a forceful, even dominating and self-centred personality, although devoted to her family.

Country Women's Assn of NSW, *The silver years* (Syd, 1947), and *The golden years* (Syd, 1972), and *Report*, 1922-26; *Stock and Station J*, 2, 5, 12, 26 May 1922; *Land Annual*, 19 Oct 1960, p 38, 39, 56; *Pastoral Review*, 17 Aug 1964; family papers (held by author). JILLIAN OPPENHEIMER

MUNRO, HUGH ROBERT (1862-1958), pastoralist, was born on 14 February 1862 at Keera, Bingara, New South Wales, youngest of ten children of Donald Munro (d. 1866), and his wife Margaret, née McPherson. His parents and four children had migrated from Dingwall, Scotland, in 1848 and had bought Keera in 1858. After being tutored at home, Hugh was educated at Newington College, Sydney. At 19 he was managing Keera while his elder brothers developed their own pastoral partnership.

In 1885 Munro joined Thomas Cook of Turanville, Scone, as junior partner and general manager of T. Cook & Co. To Cook's 380 000 acres (154 000 ha) he added the 250 000 acres (101 000 ha) of Keera. For more efficient breeding and fattening of cattle on a large scale, they sold five stations and bought Oakhurst near Boggabilla, Gundibri near Merriwa, and Moogoon and Wyaga near Goondiwindi, in Queensland. Munro actively encouraged the export of chilled beef to Britain: he was chairman of the Australian Chilling & Freezing Co. Ltd at Aberdeen and a director of Pitt [q.v.5], Son & Badgery [q.v.3] Ltd in Sydney. When Cook died in 1912 Munro bought Oakhurst, Wyaga and Gundibri from his estate. He had married Grace Emily Gordon [q.v. Munro] on 14 July 1898 at Warialda. With his sons he later formed the Gundibri Estate Co. Pty Ltd, the Dingwall Pastoral Co. and the Keera Pastoral Co.

An authority on breeding beef-cattle and horses, Munro imported Shorthorn and Aberdeen Angus cattle from the United States of America, Scotland and New Zealand and used the Angus-Shorthorn cross to produce high-quality steers for market, winning numerous prizes at livestock shows. He founded the Wyaga merino sheep and Oakhurst poll merino studs; he also bred Canadian Berkshire pigs. He was for many years chairman of the Warialda Pastures Protection Board and a council-member of the Graziers' Association of New South Wales.

Chairman of the Northern and North Western Racing Association and a member of the Australian Jockey Club, Munro imported the stallion, Thespian, from New Zealand and successfully bred and raced horses throughout New South Wales and Queensland for seventy-six years. His biggest wins were the A.J.C. Metropolitan in 1921 with Laddie Blue and the Doncaster in 1931 with Sir Chrystopher. As a young man he rode his own horses at picnic race meetings: later such famous jockeys as Myles Connell [q.v.8] and Jim Munro [q.v.] rode for him. He was patron of many country and picnic race-clubs as well as the Inverell Polo Club.

Munro was a staunch Presbyterian: he financially supported churches at Bingara and Canberra, St Andrew's War Memorial Hospital in Brisbane, and Rev. John Flynn's [q.v.8] Aerial Medical Service. After World War I he made part of Keera available for soldier settlement and after World War II part of Gundibri and all of Cubbaroo.

Munro was tall, with twinkling blue eyes and waxed moustache and often wore a topee and leggings. He loved Scottish literature, especially the works of Scott and Burns and their Australian counterparts A. L. Gordon [q.v.4] and A. B. Paterson [q.v.]. Rarely at home at Keera for more than a few days, he travelled constantly—and, although a member of the Australian and Royal Sydney Golf clubs, used the Australia Hotel as his Sydney base.

Survived by his wife, daughter and two sons, Munro died on 14 February 1958, his ninety-sixth birthday, at his daughter's home at Walcha, where he had flown to attend a race meeting at which his horse won. He was buried in the Presbyterian section of Bingara cemetery. His estate was valued for probate at £194 616. A portrait of Munro by Gundars Eglentals is held by his family.

H. G. Lamond, *From Tariaro to Ross Roy* (Brisb, nd); G. N. Griffiths, *Some northern homes of NSW* (Syd, 1954); H. G. Munro (comp), *The monument at Keera* (Bingara, NSW, 1960); N. Gray, *Thomas Cook of Turanville* (Scone, NSW, 1977); *Pastoral Review*, 17 Mar 1958; *Northern Daily Leader*, 20 Feb 1958; family papers (held by author).

JILLIAN OPPENHEIMER

MUNRO, JAMES LESLIE (1906-1974) and DAVID HUGH (1913-1966), jockeys, were born on 7 September 1906 and 5 March 1913 at Caulfield, Melbourne, sons of Hugh Munro (d. 1925), horse-trainer, and his wife Susannah Catherine, née Dunn. The Munros were steeped in thoroughbred lore and racing: Hugh trained Revenue, the winner of the 1901 Melbourne Cup; he also had Wakeful, a champion mare which ran second in the 1903 Cup. The Munros moved to Randwick, Sydney, about 1916.

Jimmie Munro was absorbed in horses and stables. His precocious riding skills were recognized by astute horsemen Richard Wootton and William Kelso, but his father refused their offers and indentured him to himself; he completed his apprenticeship with E. F. Walker. At 15 Munro had his first ride, at 6 st. 9 lb. (42 kg), in the Melbourne Cup; in 1923 he was second on Rivoli, but won on Windbag in 1925 and on Statesman in 1928. His first big win had been on Prince Charles, owned by J. Brown [q.v.7], in the 1922 Sydney Cup. In the 1920s he won many major races in Sydney and Melbourne on several other outstanding horses, including Phar Lap, Amounis and Valicare. In 1927 he was disqualified for a year for his ride on Songift at Canterbury.

Munro was a strong rider, proficient with the whip and with hands and heels. He had an instinctive perception of pace and tactics. Most races until his day were run at a leisurely speed with jockeys holding their mounts up for a final sprint. But Munro would often daringly clap the pace on in the early or middle stages, breaking the field up and often emerging an easy winner. In 1930 he went to Germany to ride for Baron Oppenheim; he won the German Derby on Alba, which he said was the best horse he ever rode. In 1933-34 he rode in India for A. Higgins. Back in Sydney with a high international reputation he maintained his form, but increasing weight limited his rides and in November 1938 he retired. He became a trainer next year, but was content with a small team with which, however, he had much success; in the early 1940s he won nineteen races with Tel Asur. In 1945 he was granted a No.1 licence, but he retired in the early 1950s to spend time in England with his daughter who had married a leading English jockey, G. Lewis.

Munro died at Randwick on 24 July 1974, survived by his wife Florence Ita Mary, née Duncombe, whom he had married on 14 May 1932 at St Michael's Church, Daceyville, and by a daughter. He was buried in the Catholic section of Waverley cemetery.

David, 'Darby', Munro went to the Marist Brothers' College, Randwick, and was apprenticed to his brother John. He won his first race at 14 on Release, defeating Jimmie's mount by a head. He won the 1930 Australian Jockey Club Challenge Stakes and Doncaster Handicap on Venetian Lady, and soon established himself as a daring and vigorous rider, constantly engaged by leading trainers, including M. (Jack) Holt [q.v.9], Bailey Payten [q.v.] and Peter Riddell. In 1933 he won the A.J.C. Derby and Victoria Racing Club Derby on Hall Mark, and next year his first Melbourne Cup on Peter Pan; in 1944 he won on Sirius and on Russia in 1946. He also rode three Sydney Cup and one Brisbane Cup winners.

By 1939 Munro was hailed as Australia's best jockey. Swarthy and poker-faced, he was known, among other names, as 'The Demon Darb'. His relations with punters were ambiguous: they occasionally hooted when he lost, especially on a favourite, but cheered when he won. No one doubted his skill or courage. He was a very strong rider with a punishing whip style, but he could nurse a tiring mount with consummate artistry. He always looked good on a horse. Like Jimmie he was a great judge of pace, and dominated many weight-for-age races in Sydney and Melbourne in the 1930s and 1940s with his clever tactics. He rode nine winners at the 1940 A.J.C. Easter carnival, including the Doncaster-Sydney Cup double. Perhaps his best ride was on Shannon, carrying 9 st. 9 lb. (61 kg), in the 1946 Epsom at Randwick when he was accidentally left at the post but pursued the field, manoeuvring his mount through needle-eye openings, coming second by a half head.

In 1940 Munro's riding weight rose to 8 st. 5 lb. (53 kg) and he had a constant struggle to keep it down. He had trouble with the racing stewards and in 1941 his licence was revoked for six months. He enlisted in the army on 25 June 1942 and served in the salvage section but was discharged medically unfit on 11 February 1944. He was disqualified for two years in October 1948 because of his ride on Vagabond at Caulfield: in retrospect it seems the stewards misread his expert handling in the straight of a horse that could do no more and lost by a head. As a result of this case he failed to obtain a licence to ride in England in 1953, but he rode in California, United States of America, and France that year. He retired in 1955 and was granted a No.1 trainer's licence, but he had only moderate success.

In 1964 Munro's left leg was amputated because of diabetes. He died on 3 April 1966 in Sydney Hospital from cerebral haemorrhage, survived by his wife Kathleen Waverley, formerly Frauenfelder, née Trautwein, whom he had married on 24 June 1958 at North Sydney Registry Office, and by two daughters of his second marriage. He was buried in the Catholic section of Randwick cemetery. He had married Iris Veronica Fisher in St Aloysius Church, Cronulla, on 14 May 1934, and Elsie Joyce Dixon (Shirley Allen) at Paddington Registry Office on 28 August 1941—both marriages ended in divorce.

In 1981 Munro was featured on a 22-cent stamp.

People (Syd), 11 Oct 1950; *Daily Telegraph* (Syd), 3 June 1925; *SMH*, 23 June 1927, 3 Dec 1930, 24 Nov 1938, 1 Apr 1940, 8 Apr 1941, 19 May 1953, 22 June 1955, 4 Apr 1966, 28 July 1974.
BEDE NAIRN

MUNRO FERGUSON, SIR RONALD CRAUFURD, VISCOUNT NOVAR OF RAITH (1860-1934), governor-general, was born on 6 March 1860, at Raith House, Fife, Scotland, eldest child of Lieut-Colonel Robert Ferguson, M.P., and his wife Emma Eliza Ferguson, née Mandeville. In 1864, inheriting from a cousin the estates of Novar in Rossshire and Muirton, Morayshire, his father took the additional surname Munro. Ronald was educated at home and at the Royal Military College, Sandhurst, and served in the Grenadier Guards in 1879-84.

He entered parliament in 1884 as a Liberal, winning and losing Ross and Cromarty before taking Leith Burghs, the seat he held until 1914. He had the patronage and friendship of Lord Rosebery [q.v.5 Primrose], whom he served as parliamentary private secretary and as a junior lord of the treasury. Other political associates were the 'Liberal Imperialists' Grey, Asquith and Haldane; his closest friend was the diplomat and poet (Sir) Cecil Spring Rice, who persuaded him to support Home Rule and to admire Theodore Roosevelt's America. On 31 August 1889 after a visit to India, Munro Ferguson married Lady HELEN HERMIONE BLACKWOOD (1865-1941), daughter of the viceroy, the marquess of Dufferin and Ava, an able and imperious woman on whose judgement of politics and of protocol he relied absolutely.

Disappointed by his exclusion from the Liberal government of 1905 Munro Ferguson vainly 'asked for Bombay'. He remained active in parliament but, disliking Asquith and his 'vulgar pushing mob', showed increasing indifference to party discipline. Made a privy councillor in 1910, he refused Asquith's offered peerage, preferring to continue as the first country gentleman of Scotland rather than wear the badge of political failure. Anxious to find a billet suitable for his talents, he refused the governorship of Victoria (as he had that of South Australia in 1895), but accepted the governor-generalship and a G.C.M.G. in February 1914. Despite Australian complaints that the British government was ridding itself of a failed colleague, Munro Ferguson was soon to prove himself the ablest of the early governors-general. He arrived in Melbourne on 18 May.

Munro Ferguson was determined to maintain British parliamentary principles, to represent Imperial policies as the sole official channel of communication between the governments, and to maintain the prestige of the infant Commonwealth against the pretensions of the States, and especially their governors. He was soon in bitter conflict with Sir Gerald Strickland [q.v.], the pugnacious governor of New South Wales. Aware that the governor-general had specific constitutional powers as well as the monarch's prerogative to advise and warn, he intended to be politically impartial. He believed Labor to be the party of federalism, though he distrusted the power of its caucus and found some Liberals more congenial company. His private observations on Australia were sharp and candid. A handsome, energetic man, he was kind if frequently choleric, with much of his wife's disdain for the socially inappropriate. Tree-felling was his favourite recreation, even in Melbourne. He came to admire some aspects of Australian life while deploring many others, and seemed most at home with country folk, whom he compared with his Scottish tenantry.

Munro Ferguson's political acumen was tested when Prime Minister (Sir) Joseph Cook [q.v.8] on 2 June 1914 requested a double dissolution, hoping to strengthen his precarious majority. Munro Ferguson had excellent precedents for claiming a discretion to refuse the request, and he rejected the arguments of Attorney-General Sir William Irvine [q.v.9] that the governor-general was obliged to follow the advice of the prime minister; but after consulting the chief justice Sir Samuel Griffith [q.v.9], convinced that it was in the best interests of both parties, he granted the dissolution. Munro Ferguson was increasingly annoyed that his action was interpreted as acceptance of Irvine's narrow interpretation of his powers. He believed he could seek advice from any source, even the Opposition, and acted on his assumption that he could discuss confidential government business with any privy councillor.

Before the political storm was stilled by the Opposition's decisive victory in the September elections, war intervened. Cabinet was dispersed electioneering, and Munro Ferguson was perforce involved with the minister for defence and the attorney-general in major policy decisions. War transformed his daily role. He continued to travel widely, but social commitments were reduced (and the ballroom of Melbourne's Government House given over to Lady Helen's work for the British Red Cross Society, which earned her appointment as G.B.E. in 1918). Promotion of the war effort became his chief concern: as commander-in-chief he inspected camps, corresponded with British and Australian generals as one soldier to another, complained of the presumptions of the navy (which had its own direct communication with the Admiralty), saw almost as much of the minister of defence as of the prime minister, and judged politics and society in terms of the Empire's struggle for survival, increasingly regarding Australia as a 'Fools' Paradise' ignorant of external realities. Privately he chafed at his distance from Europe, mused that a different fate might have made him minister for war, and considered (perhaps rightly) that Lady Helen had more of the qualities needed to lead the Empire in war than Asquith.

Munro Ferguson did not hesitate to advise and warn Prime Minister Fisher [q.v.8] and the Colonial Office on all sorts of issues, and complained vigorously when not consulted. In August 1914 he had forced Sir John Forrest [q.v.8] to consult Fisher concerning emergency fiscal measures. In September he cabled directly to the governor-general of New Zealand warning against the dispatch of troop-ships without assurance of safety from

German cruisers. In March 1915 he refused to appoint a royal commission on the New Hebrides until London had been informed. In May he mediated between British generals and the Australian government on the disputed appointment of a successor to Major General Sir William Bridges [q.v.7] on Gallipoli. He deplored Australia's attitude to non-European allies and willingly responded to a secret request from the British government in January 1915 that he prepare 'his Ministers' for post-war occupation of German colonies north of the Equator by the Japanese. He shared British concern over the inefficiency of Australian security measures, and consented in January 1916 to Lieut-Colonel (Sir) George Steward [q.v.], his official secretary, becoming head of a new Counter-Espionage Bureau, active in surveillance of dissidents as well as enemy agents. He was annoyed, however, when seedy associates of 'Pickle the Spy' intruded into Government House.

In October 1915 W. M. Hughes [q.v.9] succeeded Fisher, beginning five years of an increasingly complex personal and political relationship between prime minister and governor-general. Aware that Hughes was never fully frank with him, he came to believe 'my little Welshman' indispensable to the war effort, and acquiesced in manipulation of his goodwill to Hughes's political benefit, risking the appearance, if less often the substance, of the impartiality required of his office.

Munro Ferguson welcomed Hughes's conversion to the cause of conscription in 1916, though critical of his tactics, and when the cabinet crumbled on the eve of the first plebiscite he crossed Sydney Harbour at midnight to console 'the poor little man' in a taxi on the quay. Nevertheless he refused to promise Hughes a dissolution in advance. He was also unhappy with his involvement in the manoeuvres by which the new National government tried vainly to avoid an election. As the war news worsened he supported a second attempt to win conscription, but advised a dissolution rather than another plebiscite. He deplored Hughes's pledge to resign if the vote was lost, and when the prime minister reacted to hostility in Queensland by creating a Federal police force he argued successfully for a more rational plan. The bitterness of the campaign, and especially Archbishop Mannix's [q.v.] part in it, shocked him.

Munro Ferguson refused Hughes's request to keep secret their meeting in Melbourne to discuss the defeat of conscription, complaining that he was no Charles II to hide in an oak tree 'and besides, a gum don't give much cover'. On 29 December 1917 he urged him to resign and recommend another Nationalist; Hughes delayed until 8 January and left it

to the governor-general to conclude, after diligent interviews with leading figures in government and opposition, that the Labor leader could not guarantee supply and that only Hughes was acceptable to all Nationalists. Opposition criticism of the renewed commission was not allayed by his explanatory memorandum. He attempted to bring all parties together at his special recruiting conference held at Government House in April 1918, but critics continued to identify him with Hughes's political interests. In so far as the charge was justified, it arose from his belief that the cause of the Empire at war overrode domestic considerations.

Munro Ferguson attempted to use Hughes's apparent dependence on him to renew his request that the Executive Council should consider measures as well as approve them. Hughes rebuffed him, then undermined his authority by winning at the 1918 Imperial War Conference the right of direct communication with the British prime minister. Munro Ferguson was shocked, predicting greater Australian independence and eventual alignment with the United States of America, and foreseeing a need for British political representation separate from the governor-general. The dilemmas of Imperial defence uncovered by Lord Jellicoe's visit of 1919 also alarmed him, and although he shared Hughes's contempt for President Wilson and his League of Nations, he watched 'the little man pull the noses of the Mikado and Wilson at the Peace Conference' with trepidation.

Despite some disillusionment Munro Ferguson agreed to extend his term from May 1919 until 6 October 1920, in part to organize the visit of the prince of Wales. During the tour his insistence on Federal precedence so offended some of the State governors that they asked that the Colonial Office never again appoint so overbearing a governor-general. Nevertheless the public farewells to the Munro Fergusons were warm, and the press rightly praised his contribution to such causes as forestry, encouragement of science and the beautification of Melbourne. Munro Ferguson was surprised to find himself sorry to leave, though pleased to return to his estates and consoled with elevation to the peerage.

His public career was not over. In October 1922 he took office as secretary for Scotland under Bonar Law. Baldwin dropped him in 1924, losing patience with the Ferguson brand of political independence. He chaired the committee reviewing political honours in 1925, was appointed a knight of the Thistle in 1926 and received various other honours. His meticulously ordered papers of his period in Australia were used by (Sir) Ernest Scott [q.v.] for his volume of the official history of the war. A portrait by W. B. McInnes [q.v.] hangs in Parliament House, Canberra.

Lord Novar died at Raith on 30 March 1934. Childless, he had selected a sister's grandson as his heir. Lady Helen died on 9 April 1941.

E. Scott, *Australia during the war* (Syd, 1936); G. Sawer, *Australian Federal politics and law, 1901-29* (Melb, 1956); L. F. Fitzhardinge, *William Morris Hughes*, 1-2 (Syd, 1964, 1979); C. Cunneen, *Kings' men* (Syd, 1983); Novar papers (NL *and* Scottish Record Office).   J. R. POYNTER

MURAMATS, JIRO (1878-1943), pearler and storekeeper, was born on 6 September 1878 at Kobe, Japan, second son of Sakutarō Muramatsu and his wife Sada of Fujieda, Shizuoka prefecture.

Sakutarō set up in business at Cossack, Western Australia, in 1891 as an importer and storekeeper for the Japanese community. He died there in 1898 and his tombstone is one of the few surviving relics in that ghost-town. Jirō arrived in 1893. He attended Cossack State School and in 1895-97 boarded at Xavier College, Melbourne. On his father's death he, with his elder brother Tsunetarō, reconstituted the family firm as J. & T. Muramats, which operated in Australia until World War II. Jirō managed operations in Australia; Tsunetarō, until his death in 1925, those in Japan. On 17 January 1905 Jirō married Hatsu Noguchi (born in Nagasaki) who had arrived in Australia in 1896; they had one daughter.

In Western Australia coloured aliens had since 1892 been denied pearling-boat licences. Muramats was in 1899 granted naturalization in Victoria which became effective throughout Australia in 1904. He received his first boat licence in 1906 and acquired another nine before Western Australia in 1912 banned the grant of new licences to all persons of Asiatic or African race. But, like others who combined pearling, storekeeping and the provision of credit, his influence extended beyond his own luggers. In 1915 the local Customs officer reported that most of the freehold properties at Cossack belonged to him and that seven more luggers (whose owners were required to purchase their provisions and dispose of their shell through him) were under mortgage to him, giving him control of more than half the Cossack pearling fleet. In the years that followed, using a floating station, he operated his luggers up to 250 miles (400 km) south and 100 miles (160 km) north of that port.

Following the revival of pearling in Darwin in 1928, Muramats moved five of his luggers there during 1929 and 1930. Thereafter Darwin was his domicile, although he continued to make regular visits to his Cossack establishment. In 1931 he and two other Darwin pearlers alone stood out against a national scheme to curtail production voluntarily and, as a result, the minister imposed drastic restrictions under the Northern Territory Pearling Ordinance. This act of independence was held against Muramats next year when he sought Federal permission to purchase seven luggers at Port Hedland. The minister vetoed the transaction, informing Muramats that Federal policy on master-pearlers of non-European race conformed with that of Western Australia and that he would not be permitted to increase his eight current licences in Darwin and Western Australia beyond the ten allotted to him in Western Australia in 1912.

The political rights conferred by naturalization had also proved hollow. Amendments to the Western Australian Electoral Act in 1907 disfranchised British subjects who were 'aboriginal natives of Australia, Asia, Africa or the islands of the Pacific'. As the Federal franchise was linked to the State franchise, this deprived Muramats of the vote in Federal elections also. In 1923 he appealed to the High Court of Australia maintaining that, since the Ainu were the aboriginal natives of Japan, he was entitled to the vote. Justice Higgins [q.v.9] dismissed the appeal, arguing that by such reasoning the Australian Aborigines would be entitled to the franchise as they had arrived after the Tasmanian Aborigines and that this was patently contrary to the intention of the legislature.

In December 1941 Muramats was interned along with the Japanese community. He died at Tatura Internment Camp, Victoria, on 7 January 1943 of cancer. In 1946 his widow returned from Tatura to Cossack, where in the late 1950s she was virtually the last inhabitant. She died at Yokohama, Japan, on 12 August 1959 leaving an estate in Western Australia of £7670.

W. A. Thompson, *Cossack: 1863-1887* (mimeograph, Roebourne, WA, 1959); photograph of Jirō and Hatsu Muramats in M. A. Bain, *Full fathom five* (Perth, 1982), p 131; *Cwlth Law Reports*, 32 (1923), p 500; Japanese Foreign Ministry Archives, MT 3.8.2.275 (mfm G16163, NL); A1 24/24078 31/1339, A433 41/2/2244, A659 43/1/7347 (AAO); J. & T. Muramats business papers (Battye Lib); Fisheries 24/33 (WA State Archives).

D. C. S. SISSONS

MURDOCH, JAMES (1856-1921), Orientalist, was born on 27 September 1856 at Fetteresso, Kincardineshire, Scotland, son of William Murdoch, labourer, and his wife Helen, née McDonald. After attending the local parochial school and the Grammar School, Old Aberdeen, he topped the entrance examination at the University of Aberdeen in

1875 and graduated M.A. with first-class honours in classics in 1879. The Fullarton travelling scholarship then took him to Worcester College, Oxford; but on 26 June 1880, three months after passing Responsions, he married Lucy Parkes (daughter of a Congregational minister at Lyme Regis) and soon afterwards returned to Aberdeen as assistant to the professor of Greek.

Murdoch arrived in Queensland in July 1881 as headmaster of the new Maryborough Grammar School. He became unpopular with the trustees (possibly because of his atheism and the deterioration of his marriage) and in March 1885 they summarily dismissed him for resisting their instructions that his staff give lessons at the Girls' Grammar School. For the next two years he was second master at Brisbane Grammar School. In 1886 he also sat the Bar examinations, but failed in two of the eight papers because he, mistakenly, attempted to answer every question. He left Brisbane Grammar at his own wish and, after some months working with William Lane, Francis Adams [qq.v.9,3] and other kindred spirits on the radical nationalist journal, the *Boomerang*, embarked in April 1888 for a visit to East and South-East Asia. In a series of articles for that paper, key elements of his radicalism emerge: he disparaged in highly racist terms the Chinese communities in the ports he visited; he predicted that within a generation the Australian colonies would form a republic, and that Australians would be driven to nationalize land (a process in which he thought blood might be shed).

After briefly returning to Brisbane to wind up his affairs, Murdoch in September 1889 took up a lectureship in European history at the First Higher School, a highly selective institution which young men attended before entering Tokyo Imperial University. In addition to his teaching duties, the next four years saw him vigorously engaged in literary activities. In June 1890 he published a long piece of satirical verse, *Don Juan's grandson in Japan*. In November he launched a weekly magazine, the *Japan Echo*, which lasted for six issues. In 1892 he published *From Australia and Japan* (a volume of short stories which went through three editions) and a novel, *Ayame-san*. These were romances in which the heroes tended to be socialists of high competitive achievement in the academic and sporting fields, and the women either mercenary and cruel or paragons of erudition, beauty and good breeding. He also wrote several descriptive texts for pictorial works addressed to the historically minded tourist and edited the memoirs of Hikozō Hamada, the castaway who became the first Japanese to acquire American citizenship.

In September 1893 Murdoch left Japan to join Lane's 'New Australia' commune in Para-guay. By the time of his arrival, however, about one-third of the colonists had seceded. He remained only a few days and, leaving his 12-year-old son in South America, proceeded to London. After five months at the British Museum translating the letters of sixteenth-century European *religieux* in Japan he returned to that country. From 1894 to 1897 he taught English at the Fourth Higher School at Kanazawa. On 23 November 1899, while teaching economic history at the Higher Commercial College (today's Hitotsubashi University) in Tokyo, he married Takeko Okada.

In 1901 Murdoch moved to the Seventh Higher School at Kagoshima. A severe illness in South America (diagnosed as sunstroke) had weakened him and he hoped to benefit from the milder Kyushu winters. The first volume of his *A History of Japan*, dealing with the century of early foreign intercourse, 1542-1651, appeared in 1903. The sources in European languages—Latin, Spanish, French and Dutch—he sought out and translated himself. The Japanese sources were selected for him by a young history graduate, Kenko Murakawa, and translated into English by Murdoch's former pupil, Isoo Yamagata.

In 1908 his teaching contract was not renewed. Murdoch, nevertheless, remained at Kagoshima. He contributed regularly to the *Kobe Chronicle* and, to supplement this income, planted a citron orchard. Although he was never to achieve fluency with the spoken language, he had now become proficient in classical Japanese and had no longer to rely on Japanese assistants. The next volume, *From the origins to the arrival of the Portuguese in 1542 A.D.*, appeared in 1910.

In 1915, following the completion of the manuscript of the third volume, *The Tokugawa epoch 1652-1868*, straitened circumstances forced Murdoch to teach at junior high-school level, at Shibushi. In February 1917, however, he was able to return to Australia to teach Japanese at the Royal Military College, Duntroon, and at the University of Sydney, concurrent appointments instituted on the initiative of the Defence Department. The following year, in response to an attractive bid by Waseda University, the Sydney position was raised to a chair. In return for £600 a year from the Defence Department, the university permitted Murdoch to supervise a deputy at Duntroon and to visit Japan annually to brief the department on shifts in Japanese public opinion and foreign policy. The first such visit resulted in a memorandum by Murdoch's friend, the director of military intelligence (E. L. Piesse [q.v.]), highly critical of Australia's intransigence on the racial equality issue at the Paris Peace Conference. Similarly, two years later Murdoch was called to Melbourne to give the prime minister his views on the renewal of the Anglo-Japanese alliance.

Murdoch died of cancer at his home at Baulkham Hills on 30 October 1921. He had just completed the research for the fourth volume of the *History* but had not begun writing. He was survived by his son (in South America) and by his wife (who returned to Japan).

As testimony to Murdoch's vigour and influence, within eighteen months of his arrival Japanese was being taught at two Sydney high schools by native speakers recruited by him in Japan and the first matriculation examination was held in 1921. The subject had not, however, become firmly established and in the years that followed failed to make progress—either at the university or at Duntroon. Murdoch's lasting contribution was the *History* (whose third volume was published posthumously in 1926). It was a pioneer work and remained the standard work until the late 1950s.

K. Maki, *Kindai ni okeru seiyōjin no nihon reki-shi kan* (Tokyo, 1950); S. Hirakawa, *Sōseki no shi mādokku sensei* (Tokyo, 1984); *American Hist Review*, 17 (1911), p 630; *Aberdeen Univ Review*, 9 (1922), p 109, 226; P. H. T. Dowding, *Okayama Shōdai Ronsō*, 18, no 2-3; T. Sugiyama, *Okayama Shōdai Ronsō*, 18, no 3, 19, no 2, 20, no 1-2; *SMH*, 5, 26 Nov 1921; *Japan Weekly Chronicle*, 17 Nov 1921; D. C. S. Sissons, Australia's First Professor of Japanese: James Murdoch, 1856-1921 (unpubl., 1982, NL MS 3092).   D. C. S. SISSONS

MURDOCH, SIR JAMES ANDERSON (1867-1939), retail trader, politician and philanthropist, was born on 10 March 1867 in Edinburgh, son of Thomas Murdoch, master cabinetmaker, and his wife Margaret, née Anderson. Educated at Adair's and Herriot's schools, at 13 he joined George Barclay & Sons, wholesale woollen merchants. In 1884 he migrated to Melbourne and, after working as a salesman and in a hosiery shop, moved to Sydney in 1887. While employed by Edward Hordern, he became active in the Early Closing Association of New South Wales and in 1889 was founding secretary of the Shop Employees' Union. Late that year he joined Finney, Isles & Co., Brisbane, but returned to Sydney next year to manage the menswear firm F. J. Palmer. At St Stephen's Presbyterian Church, Sydney, he married Isabella Binning on 26 August 1891. From 1896 they lived at Midhope, Wahroonga, with a renowned garden.

In 1893, seeking independence, he opened a men's mercery, Murdoch's, in Park Street. His business slowly prospered in the 1890s and by 1914 he had 400 employees. He attributed his early success to dealing directly with manufacturers, avoiding wholesale firms. Priding himself on their welfare, he gave his employees annual bonuses, distributed according to efficiency. In 1909 he formed a limited liability company and instituted a co-partnership scheme which attracted great public interest. Hard-working employees were offered either a cash bonus or four-shilling shares in the company, which paid the same dividend as ordinary £1 shares and were retainable only while in Murdoch's employ. As a result he claimed that he had fewer labour problems and greater efficiency and retention of workers.

In October 1915 Murdoch volunteered for service (at his own expense) with the Australian branch of the British Red Cross Society. In Egypt next February he was appointed third commissioner. Transferred to France in April, he was appointed honorary lieut-colonel in September. He administered depots at Boulogne and Rouen until he moved to England in 1917 as chief commissioner; he was closely involved in work for prisoners of war. His 'valuable services' were twice brought to the attention of the secretary of state for war and he was appointed C.M.G. in 1918, returning to Sydney in December.

Murdoch's Ltd in Park Street expanded rapidly after the war. In 1922 seven-storey factories were built at Surry Hills, in 1928 Murdoch's Ltd was registered as a public company and next year it acquired additional premises in George Street. Remaining chairman of the company, Murdoch was also a director of the Commonwealth General Assurance Corporation Ltd (1920-30), Melbourne Hotels Ltd (1922-38), Standard Portland Cement Co. Ltd (1924-38), Arthur Rickard [q.v.] & Co. (Extended) Ltd (1925-30), Linoleum Holdings Ltd (1937-38) and National Studios Ltd (1937-38).

Murdoch was a council-member (president, 1920-22) of the Master Retailers' Association (from 1921 Retail Traders' Association of New South Wales). Under his leadership it presented an organized front against the solidarity of labour; advocating co-operation, he criticized trade unions and the arbitration system. He also served on the Employers' Federation of New South Wales and the Sydney Chamber of Commerce and was a foundation executive-member of the State branch of the National Roads Association of Australia in 1920-29. In 1919, as an assessor, he had assisted Justice R. D. Pring [q.v.], royal commissioner enquiring into wheat contracts and the State Wheat Office.

In 1920 Murdoch joined the National Consultative Council and that year was a founding vice-president of the Citizens' Reform Association (president, 1922-30). He believed in applying business principles to politics (later expressing admiration for Mussolini) and was determined to 'clean up the city' by organizing against Labor politicians on the Sydney Municipal Council. In 1927 his demands for a royal commission influenced the Bavin [q.v.7] government to appoint three civic commissioners, replacing the elected council, to fight corruption. A powerful behind-the-scenes organizer, Murdoch had been nominated to the Legislative Council in 1923. He spoke seldom there and then mainly on business, arbitration and local government. He did not seek election to the reconstituted council in December 1933 but was chairman of the United Australia Party Consultative Council in 1934-35. In 1930 contracts granted to Standard Portland Cement Co. Ltd had been questioned in parliament; in 1938 J. T. Lang [q.v.9] resurrected claims of collusion over these contracts and accused Murdoch and others of secret dealings in the sale of the State Monier Pipe Works. A royal commission exculpated Murdoch of all charges.

He loved Scottish causes. In 1919 he had joined the board of Burnside Presbyterian Orphan Homes under its founder Sir James Burns [q.v.7] and was chairman in 1923-37. In 1922 he donated a school (leased to the Department of Public Instruction) for the orphans. In all he contributed some £18 000. He spoke with a Scots accent and was a vice-president of the Highland Society of New South Wales in 1927-30. He was also a director of Sydney Hospital (vice-president, 1925-30), a trustee of Kuring-gai Chase and vice-president of the Australian Federal Capital League. From 1927 chairman of the Canberra Burns Memorial Fund, he contributed £500 towards the statue of Burns (unveiled 1935), and gave £5000 for the organ in St Andrew's Presbyterian Church, Canberra. He was appointed K.B.E. in 1928.

Enjoying racing, fishing and golf, Murdoch was a committee-member of the Australian Jockey Club in 1928-39. He was fairly successful as an owner in the 1920s, although success in the big races eluded him. He established a stud, Bendooley, at Bowral, better known for its Aberdeen Angus cattle and private golf-course than horses. A Freemason, he belonged to the New South Wales Club. The press and his peers viewed the small, jovial and public-spirited figure with affection and regard for his honesty and integrity. Survived by his wife and three daughters, Murdoch died of cardiovascular disease at Manly on 30 January 1939 and was cremated with Presbyterian forms. He left the bulk of his estate, valued for probate at about £370 000, to his family. His portrait by Jerrold Nathan is held by the Burnside Homes; another is owned by his grandchildren.

F. A. Larcombe, *The advancement of local government in New South Wales, 1906 to the present* (Syd, 1978); *Scottish A'sian*, 10, no 109, 6 Jan 1919, p 6655, 12, no 138, 14 Feb 1921, p 7870, 25, no 8, 21 Feb 1935, p 83; *Sydney Tatler*, 28 Dec 1922; Retail Traders' Assn of NSW, *J*, 5, no 3, Sept 1923, p 61; *Daily Telegraph* (Syd), 3 Aug 1923; *SMH*, 31 Jan 1939; letters and correspondence of J. A. Murdoch, 1915-18 (Red Cross Archives, Melb); family papers held by Mr M. M. Johnson, Warrawee, NSW.   HOWARD WOLFERS

MURDOCH, JOHN SMITH (1862-1945), architect and public servant, was born on 29 September 1862 at Cassieford, Elgin County, Scotland, son of John Murdoch, farmer, and his wife Bathia, née Smith. Educated at Rafford School and Forres Academy he trained as an architect in Edinburgh and worked at Inverness, Glasgow, and with the Scottish railways before migrating to Victoria about 1884. He was a draughtsman in Queensland's Department of Mines and Works in 1885-87 then worked privately. Rejoining the public service, in March 1894 he became a draughtsman in the Department of Public Works, rising to district architect in 1902.

In July 1904 he transferred to the Commonwealth as senior clerk, public works branch, Department of Home Affairs. Senior assistant to the director-general Percy T. Owen [q.v.] from 1909, Murdoch was a member of the reviewing board for the national capital design competition, won by Walter Burley Griffin [q.v.9] in May 1912. While overseas that year in connexion with plans for Australia House, London, he negotiated with the Royal Institute of British Architects on a proposed international competition for a parliament house and in Chicago, United States of America, called on Griffin. The two later fell out, partly over Griffin's belief that Murdoch was one of the departmental officers who was hostile to his capital design and partly over differences about conditions for the parliament house competition, which in any case was finally abandoned.

Promoted architect in 1914, and chief architect, Department of Works and Railways, in 1919-29, Murdoch was responsible for the design and construction of many early Canberra buildings, such as the provisional parliament house, the power-house and the Hotel Canberra. With (Sir) John Sulman [q.v.] and K. A. Henderson [q.v.9] he assessed residential-area plans for Canberra in 1923. In 1926 he was an adjudicator of competitions for design of the Australian war memorials in Canberra and Villers-Bretonneux, France. As Commonwealth architect he was responsible for the design of the General Post Office, Perth (1923), Spencer Street Post Office and the High Court of Australia (1925, now Federal Court), Melbourne. He laid out Forrest Place, Perth, and Anzac Square, Brisbane.

Director-general of works from 1927, Murdoch transferred with the department to Canberra in 1929. He retired in September and was appointed to the Federal Capital Commission, serving until its abolition in April 1930. C. S. Daley [q.v.8], a close colleague greatly influenced by Murdoch, remembered him as a man of 'wide cultural and human studies', generous in his 'quiet and constant benefactions to charity, and assistance to public servants in misfortune'. He had been interested in Scouting and the Canberra Relief Society. A fellow (1914) and councillor (1925-30) of the Royal Victorian Institute of Architects, he was a fellow (1926) of the Royal Institute of British Architects and foundation member of the Royal Australian Institute of Architects. In 1927 he was appointed C.M.G.

Murdoch, a bachelor, died on 21 May 1945 at Brighton, Melbourne, and was cremated. A dour Scot, Murdoch had been mindful of the need to conserve public funds. Although in 1916 he had 'no particular enthusiasm' for the Canberra project, describing it as 'a sort of mythical thing' on which expenditure could not at the time be justified, during the period of inter-war development he made a positive contribution to its architecture and was responsible for significant Commonwealth buildings throughout Australia.

D. I. McDonald, 'Architect J. S. Murdoch and the provisional parliament house', in *Canberra Hist J*, Mar 1985, p 18, and for bibliog.

D. I. McDonald

MURDOCH, Sir KEITH ARTHUR (1885-1952), journalist and newspaper proprietor, was born on 12 August 1885 at West Melbourne, second son and third of seven children of Rev. Patrick John Murdoch [q.v.] and his wife Annie, née Brown, children both of Presbyterian ministers, who had migrated from Scotland the year before. Keith grew up in semi-rural Camberwell in the stringent economy of a clergyman's large family. He was afflicted with a humiliating stammer which made school a torture; his speech would collapse under stress, he sometimes could not even buy a railway ticket without scribbling a note. Extreme shyness, difficulty in making friends and possibly unusually determined ambition were the consequences. He attended in turn Camberwell State School, a small local one and his uncle (Sir) Walter Murdoch's [q.v.] school and, in 1901-03, Camberwell Grammar of which he was dux. He taught Bible class and Sunday school at his father's church. Golf, a family recreation, was his only sporting skill.

His parents were ambitious for him and when Keith determined to take up journalism his father was disappointed that he had no interest in going to university. However, he introduced him to his friend David Syme [q.v.6] who, impressed by the boy's shorthand skill, employed him at 1½d a line as district correspondent for Malvern, a middle-class suburb unsympathetic to the *Age*. For four years, working very long hours, Murdoch was highly successful in working up local news and increasing circulation in the area, and graduated to staff reporting assignments. He had saved £500 when in April 1908 he sailed steerage for London, primarily to seek advice for his ailment.

London for eighteen months was a miserably lonely experience. His sheaf of introductions from Alfred Deakin [q.v.8] and others led to little journalistic work. He attended lectures at the London School of Economics, read widely and was interested by the radical sociological theories of L. T. Hobhouse. He was wondering whether he might feel a call to the ministry, but became worried by his lack of faith. Treatment for his stammer improved it a little. 'The survival of the fittest principle is good because the fittest become very fit indeed', he wrote home. 'I'll be able to learn much here . . . and with health I should become a power in Australia'. In mid-1909 he almost won a post on the *Pall Mall Gazette*, but at the final interview 'my speaking collapsed'.

He left for home via the United States of America. (Sir) Geoffrey Syme [q.v.] kept his half-promise of an *Age* job and by the end of 1911 had raised Murdoch's salary from £4 to £7 a week. His stammer was now under reasonable control. Becoming Commonwealth parliamentary reporter, he was soon on close terms with Prime Minister Andrew Fisher [q.v.8] a friend of his father, W. M. Hughes [q.v.9], (Sir) George Pearce [q.v.] and other Labor ministers and members, entertaining some of them at his aunt's guesthouse in the Dandenongs. He was a founding member of the Australian Journalists' Association in 1910. Then in 1912 he became Melbourne political correspondent for (Sir) Hugh Denison's [q.v.8] lively Sydney evening *Sun*. In July 1914 he provisionally accepted the offer, at £800 a year, of news editor on Labor Papers Ltd's projected Sydney *World*, with the promise of future editorship of a new Melbourne daily, but the scheme was deferred after war broke out.

When in September the A.J.A. appointed an official Australian war correspondent, Murdoch lost narrowly to C. E. W. Bean [q.v.7]. In 1915, however, Denison transferred him to London as managing editor of the United Cable Service (of the *Sun* and Melbourne *Herald*). Fisher and Pearce had both advised him not to enlist but to continue his important work. Possibly concerned primarily to gain a first-hand report on the progress of the Gallipoli campaign, they commissioned Murdoch to investigate Australian Imperial Force mail services and associated matters. Late in August he won permission from General Sir Ian Hamilton to visit Anzac and signed the standard official declaration to observe the rules of censorship. Murdoch had only four days on Gallipoli, sending home some emotional dispatches, but he met the chief war correspondent. The British journalist Ashmead-Bartlett, appalled by the conduct of the campaign, persuaded him to carry a letter addressed to Prime Minister Asquith which, betrayed by another correspondent, Murdoch had to surrender to a British army officer at Marseille, France. However, before his ship reached England he had composed an 8000-word letter to Fisher which he sent on 23 September. It was a remarkable document which lavishly and sentimentally praised the Australians and attacked the performance of the British army at all levels, including many errors and exaggerations.

In the next few days Murdoch made contact with Geoffrey Dawson and Lord Northcliffe, editor and proprietor of *The Times*, who arranged for him to meet Lloyd George, Bonar Law, Carson and other cabinet ministers; his letter was printed as a secret state paper. It provided ammunition for the 'anti-Dardanelles' faction and contributed to Hamilton's recall and the eventual evacuation. Australian and British senior officers held Murdoch in contempt over this episode. He later defended himself vigorously before the Dardanelles royal commission. Many years later Bean concluded that Murdoch was 'glowing with patriotism' and 'dearly loved the exercise of power', but that he was wrong to break his pledge and could have made his case without such 'gross overstatements'. Writing to Bean in 1933, Murdoch admitted he had made mistakes, which he greatly regretted.

In England he made the most of his notoriety and began to hob-nob with the men of great power—at the age of 30. On Prime Minister Hughes's visits to England in 1916 and 1918 he acted as his publicist, fixer and runner, helping him with speeches and editing a volume of them (1916), giving private dinner-parties for him with such guests as Lloyd George, Bonar Law, Milner and General Sir Henry Wilson. He largely organized the campaigns to persuade the troops at the front and in England to support the National government and the two conscription plebiscites, but warned Hughes that their votes could not be relied on and advised suppression of the figures. He acted as intermediary between Hughes and Lloyd George and

relayed confidential information to Hughes in Australia. The embattled prime minister once replied: 'My dear old chap . . . I miss you dreadfully'.

Murdoch visited the front irregularly as an unofficial war correspondent; some of his dispatches, in 1918 especially, were vivid, though opinionated, and in some respects superior to Bean's. Late in 1917, pursuing governmental policy to bring the A.I.F. divisions together into an Australian corps officered entirely by Australians, he attempted to negotiate with Field Marshal Haig, and with Bean urged the replacement as Australian commander of General Sir William Birdwood [q.v.7] by Major General (Sir) Brudenell White [q.v.], while belittling Major General (Sir) John Monash [q.v.]. The corps was formed, but in May 1918 Monash was given its command while Birdwood remained general officer commanding. Bean, Murdoch and others attempted to persuade Hughes to give White the corps and make Monash G.O.C., distracting the Australian higher commanders during the most vital period of the war. On 6 June Murdoch explicitly put the 'offer' to Monash, flattering him, suggesting promotion to general as G.O.C., reminding him that his cables went to 250 newspapers. Birdwood and Monash, however, were not to be bullied or bribed and launched a counter-offensive which demonstrated that Bean and Murdoch almost totally lacked support from the A.I.F. Murdoch continued to nag Hughes through July, but the prime minister told him he had found no one who agreed with him. The successful battle of Hamel and the August offensive closed the question. Late in the year Murdoch, again unsuccessfully, tried to persuade Hughes that White, not Monash, should control repatriation.

About this time Murdoch and Hughes fell out seriously. Early in 1919 Murdoch wrote powerfully in support of Monash's determination to repatriate the troops as quickly as possible, against the government's wishes. At the Paris Peace Conference, where he was the only Australian journalist to witness the signing of the treaty, Murdoch privately described Hughes as 'pursuing an utterly reckless mischievous line of policy'.

In 1918 Denison had raised Murdoch's salary to £1200 and a further term of three years was agreed. He extended the United Cable Service to India and South Africa. In 1920 he covered for *The Times* the prince of Wales's visit to Australasia. He had developed an almost filial relationship with Northcliffe; working from *The Times* office, he saw much of him and was soon barging in unannounced. Northcliffe introduced him to clubs and played golf with him. As early as 1916 Murdoch called him 'as good a friend as I have ever had', but he recognized that if he became an employee their relationship would inevitably be destroyed. Murdoch once wrote to him as 'My dear Chief . . . the Chief of All Journalists (of all ages)'. Modelling himself closely on him, especially in his ruthless use of power, Murdoch may never have realized how manic Northcliffe was in his last years. At Murdoch's farewell banquet from London, he was photographed at Northcliffe's right hand; the photograph was to have pride of place in his office.

In 1920 Murdoch had reached an understanding with Theodore Fink [q.v.8], chairman of the Herald & Weekly Times Ltd, and in January 1921 was appointed chief editor of the Melbourne evening Herald at £2000 a year. Denison, whom Murdoch had played off against Fink, was angered. The Herald was a stodgy journal, without competition, ripe for reform; but at least a new building was being constructed in Flinders Street. Murdoch quickly had the general manager demoted by the board and himself retitled managing editor. He soon found Fink 'almost insufferable' but got on well with director W. L. Baillieu and his son (Lord) Clive [qq.v.7] who possibly financed him personally.

Northcliffe sent critical commentaries on the Herald to Murdoch, who modelled it on Northcliffe's Daily Mail and Evening News, including many more pictures and 'human interest' stories and thoroughly overhauling the paper. He was not to be allowed to forget an early experiment in sensationalism when the Herald 'tried and convicted' the 'Gun Alley' murderer. He did not move far in that direction, however, but rather went in for whipping up political issues. Murdoch employed young journalists on good salaries, engaged the popular poet C. J. Dennis [q.v.8], invited celebrities to contribute and published serious criticism of the arts. Copying Northcliffe, in 1924 he began 'Managing Editor's Notes', critical comments on the previous day's issue for his top executives, and House News in 1929. The Sporting Globe was established in 1922 and 3DB radio was bought in 1929.

The Herald thrived on a major challenge from Denison. Knowing that he intended to move on Melbourne, Murdoch gained a promise of £5000 from Northcliffe and from December 1921 unsuccessfully attempted to win control of the Sydney Evening News, rival to Denison's Sun. Denison established the tabloid Sun-News Pictorial in Melbourne in September 1922 and followed with the pink-papered Evening Sun next April, both launched by Monty Grover [q.v.9]. After a bitter contest Denison threw in the towel in April 1925; the Evening Sun closed down and the Herald bought the Sun-News Pictorial. The Herald's circulation had increased by half in Murdoch's four years. The Victorian Farm-

ers' Union's Morning Post (1925-27) was merged with the Sun. The later battle with the Argus & Australasian Ltd's evening Star (1933-36) was never in doubt. Murdoch's touch with journals was not so sure. In 1924 he acquired Melbourne Punch and had great hopes for a national weekly, recruiting J. B. Dalley, Will Dyson [qq.v.8], Percy Leason [q.v.] (at £1750 a year), C. R. Bradish, Kenneth Slessor and others, but amalgamated it in 1926 with Table Talk which petered out in 1939.

'Lord Southcliffe' (or KM as he was generally known in the office) had greatly increased profits and was appointed a director in 1926; in November 1928 he became managing director. Henceforth he had to leave much more to his editors. The Herald remained his true love, his 'personal journal'; he was less interested in the Sun, even though he saw it as 'the best tabloid in Australia' and it was rising to the highest circulation of any Australian daily.

Tall, dark and handsome and an expensive dresser, the 'burly man with the quizzical eyebrows' had been an eligible young man about town. He had lived in a service-flat at Cliveden Mansions, East Melbourne, for two years, then in South Yarra with a butler and other servants, and bought a property at Langwarrin (later named Cruden Farm); Desbrowe Annear [q.v.7] remodelled both houses. Murdoch early began collecting furniture, paintings and objets d'art; (Sir) Daryl Lindsay and Dame Nellie Melba [qq.v.] helped him to acquire taste. Australian Home Beautiful, a Herald publication, devoted an article to the South Yarra house in April 1928. On 6 June that year at Scots Church Murdoch married 19-year-old Elisabeth Joy, daughter of Rupert Greene, a Melbourne merchant; they moved to Toorak and had four children. Parents and children out riding near Cruden Farm were an impressive spectacle. He was a good family man.

Murdoch's interstate empire had begun in 1926 with the purchase from the Hackett [q.v.9] estate of the West Australian by a syndicate including W. L. Baillieu and W. S. Robinson [q.v.] and the Herald board, which formed West Australian Newspapers Ltd. Partly because of resentment at Melbourne ownership, Murdoch abandoned direct control by the early 1930s and disposed of the syndicate's interest. In 1929 he had attacked the Adelaide Advertiser, owned by the aged Sir Langdon Bonython [q.v.7], by purchasing on behalf of the Herald the morning Register, reducing its price and so boosting its circulation that Bonython was frightened into selling for £1 million. Murdoch became chairman of Advertiser Newspapers Ltd, put in (Sir) Lloyd Dumas as managing editor, closed the Register in 1931, and that year also negotiated a controlling interest by the *Herald* in the evening *News*—thus Adelaide's newspapers came under monopoly control. In the late 1920s Murdoch had personally bought a share in John Wren's [q.v.] Brisbane *Daily Mail*; in 1933 they bought the *Courier*, amalgamated it as the *Courier-Mail* and formed Queensland Newspapers Ltd with Murdoch in personal control provided a certain level of profit was maintained. But for intervention by John Fairfax [q.v.4] & Sons Pty Ltd, the *Herald* might have bought Consolidated Press from (Sir) Frank Packer in 1939. By 1935 Murdoch and the *Herald* had interests in 11 of the 65 commercial radio stations, and campaigned to limit the development of the Australian Broadcasting Commission and to prevent it establishing an independent news service. Whatever the prime motive—profit, power or pulpiteering—Murdoch had forged the first national media chain.

In the 1920s the *Herald* had been politically independent. Indeed in 1929 Murdoch instructed: 'It MUST be realised that we are not a Nationalist organ'. He emphasized that it was an Australian paper and Imperial interests should not be played up. And that year the *Herald* was reasonably objective concerning the striking timberworkers and the mineowners' lockout. But from then Murdoch came down heavily on the ultra-conservative side, supporting S. M. (Viscount) Bruce's [q.v.7] arbitration bill and throwing all his weight against the Scullin [q.v.] government in a massive campaign. J. A. Lyons [q.v.] was lunching at the *Herald* even before he left the Labor Party to become United Australia Party prime minister. But Murdoch was not among the prime plotters, though he threw all his resources behind Lyons, once his course was known. In 1931 Victorian trade unions imposed a boycott on purchase of the *Herald* and *Sun* with little effect. In office, Lyons was no puppet and Murdoch's 'kingmaker' role remains largely a myth. Lyons rejected his offer to act as a go-between to bring about a coalition with the Country Party. Murdoch's pressure on Lyons to give Hughes a ministry may have been important, but, according to Pearce, 'Murdoch gave the impression of greater influence than he in fact had'. Stating his worries in frequent letters to Clive Baillieu and Robinson, from about 1936 Murdoch became increasingly impatient with Lyons's leadership—'I put him there and I'll put him out', he was overheard saying—but he was never sure that (Sir) Robert Menzies was a suitable successor and turned against him in 1940-41.

From the 1930s the 'Murdoch press' was widely criticized, especially in Labor quarters. *Smith's Weekly* condemned 'the would-be press and radio dictator' and the dangers of a chain of newspapers with identical policies.

One enemy, Sir Frederic Eggleston [q.v.8], named Murdoch with R. A. G. Henderson and Frank Packer as 'vindictive populists', 'the major cause of the deterioration of Australian politics' in his lifetime. Murdoch had kept the 'loathsome Dunstan' [q.v.8] in power in Victoria and had driven Eggleston and other 'intelligent liberals' out of State parliament.

In 1933-34 Murdoch had been laid up for some twelve months with a heart condition. On his return he narrowly withstood an attempt by the Fink interests to overturn him on the *Herald* board. He was knighted in 1933; he had reputedly refused such an honour about 1919 from Lloyd George and Hughes.

Murdoch dominated the Australian Newspaper Conference. In 1935 he took the lead in amalgamating the existing cable services into Australian Associated Press Ltd, of which he was chairman until 1940. It was his idea to form a partnership between A.A.P. and Reuters in 1946. Similarly, Murdoch was interested in L. R. S. Benjamin's [q.v.7] early experiments in making newsprint from eucalypts and in 1938, with the *Sydney Morning Herald* as the other dominant partner, established Australian Newsprint Mills Pty Ltd (from 1947 a public company) at Boyer, Tasmania, and was its chairman until 1949. The mill began production in 1941.

On 8 June 1940 the wartime prime minister Menzies appointed Murdoch director-general of information. He immediately blundered, tactlessly issuing without adequate consultation a regulation requiring correction of newspaper reports in extreme cases. As he put it, the government might say: 'That statement has been harmful. Here is the truth. Print it and print it where we tell you'. Inevitably, his fellow proprietors reacted vehemently, the regulation was amended and Murdoch resigned in December. Meanwhile, however, with (Sir) Richard Boyer he had set up an American division of his department, aiming to entice the U.S.A. into the war, and was the leading founder of the Australian-American Association, of which he remained president until 1946.

On Fink's death in 1942 Murdoch became *Herald* chairman. His policy for his papers was an all-party national government and 'one army' (conscription for overseas service and amalgamation of A.I.F. and militia). He once recommended that, after formation of a national government, the Imperial parliament should extend the life of the Commonwealth parliament until victory was won. Bitterly disappointed with the war effort, he expressed his fervent patriotism in writing extensively and ponderously for his chain under his own name, exhorting, calling on the 'spiritual sources' of the nation, pontificating on military strategy, in his most Messianic mood almost incoherent. He incessantly attacked Prime Minister John Curtin, whose popularity and stature he could not recognize, and General Sir Thomas Blamey (who heartily reciprocated hostility, remembering 1915 and Murdoch's successful campaign against him as Victorian chief commissioner of police). General MacArthur described him as a quisling and recommended vigorous application of the censorship against him (which occurred at least once).

Labor's sweeping victory in 1943 muted Murdoch. He continued to travel extensively overseas. In his later years his campaigns were as extreme as ever—attacking bank nationalization, immigration policy ('You bloody old scoundrel', Arthur Calwell called out one day), and the communists whose outlawing he vehemently favoured.

In art politics, which became his major private interest, Murdoch was a cultural liberal. In 1931 he had sponsored an exhibition lent from private collections including works by Matisse and Modigliani. He was appointed a trustee of the Public Library, museums and National Gallery of Victoria in 1933. With Daryl Lindsay and Basil Burdett [q.v.7], *Herald* critic in 1936-41, he confronted the highly conservative Melbourne art establishment of which the director of the gallery J. S. MacDonald [q.v.] was a leading spokesman. Murdoch himself admired George Bell [q.v.7] and allied himself in art politics with S. Ure Smith [q.v.] in Sydney; while he could not appreciate Picasso and Braque or abstractionism, his taste was moderately advanced and broadly tolerant. Late in 1939 the *Herald* arranged an exhibition of French and British modern art, organized by Burdett, which was a famous turning-point in Australian art appreciation. That year Murdoch also became president of the library, museums and gallery trustees and soon forced replacement of MacDonald by Lindsay, with whom he reinvigorated the gallery; meetings of trustees were enlivened, however, by the hostility of Fink's son-in-law R. D. Elliott [q.v.8] and Max Meldrum [q.v.]. Murdoch did much to force the long overdue creation of separate authorities for the library, museums and gallery and from 1945 was chairman of gallery trustees. He also founded the *Herald* chair of fine arts at the University of Melbourne, helped to arrange reservation of the St Kilda Road site for a new gallery, and encouraged formation of a society of gallery friends. He had become the leading figure in a new art establishment.

Murdoch retired in 1949 from almost all his posts except the *Herald* chairmanship. In his last years he underwent major operations for prostate and cancer. He died in his sleep at Cruden Farm on the night of 4-5 October 1952, survived by (Dame) Elisabeth, charity worker and philanthropist, his son Keith Rupert and three daughters, and was cremated.

His estate was sworn for probate at some £400 000. Murdoch had invested in 1938 in the pastoral property Wantabadgery, near Wagga Wagga, New South Wales, and, when it was largely taken for soldier settlement, in Booroomba, near Canberra; they were poor investments and Booroomba was heavily mortgaged. Murdoch had been obsessed with providing for his family's security and for a newspaper base for his son. About 1948 he persuaded the *Herald* board to sell him its holdings in the Adelaide *News*, then invested heavily in it and in Queensland Newspapers Ltd, building his holding in the latter to about 40 per cent and retaining few *Herald* shares. His trustees were forced to sell out of the *Courier-Mail*. Rupert Murdoch built his empire from the Adelaide *News*. Remarkably, Sir Keith had planned to leave the *Herald* and, in conjunction with the London *Daily Mirror* group which owned the *Argus*, to form a chain in which he would have a majority interest; he was to take over the *Argus* himself. However, the proposed deal fell through. About 1950 he had been interested in the *Canberra Times* and tried to save *Smith's Weekly* as a national institution.

The luck of being in the right place at the right time together with powerful friends and family contacts gave Murdoch a great start to his career. His enormous capacity for work, limitless driving ambition, a phenomenal memory and belief in himself carried him on. His Presbyterian upbringing remained basic —he was strait laced and easily shocked— and he sought a high moral purpose for his newspapers. He was a 'big thinker', with close contacts with many international leaders, and strove to further Australia's long-term interests. But his judgement was faulty and, as Eggleston asserted, he had no 'real social philosophy'.

Murdoch hired young reporters personally, would chat informally with them, had a capacity to inspire them with enthusiasm for their craft, and invited them home to awesome dinners. Many of his 'young men', like Angus McLachlan, liked and admired him; Bradish considered him 'the most generous and kindliest employer for whom I had ever worked'; Douglas Brass found 'not the slightest tinge of personal spite in his make-up'. But Cecil Edwards regarded him with some cynicism and others, like Clive Turnbull and John Hetherington, detested him. In a scathing biographical essay Hetherington concluded that Murdoch was essentially 'a calculating, undeviating, insatiable seeker after worldly riches and temporal power'. But his detractors would usually admit, 'At least he's a newspaperman'.

Like most newspaper tycoons, Murdoch backed conventional conservative stances of his day and lacked the originality to make many useful contributions to public policy; but he was an able journalist, a brilliant editor in his youth and a remarkable entrepreneur and organizer of his industry.

Herald & Weekly Times, *Keith Murdoch, journalist* (Melb, 1956); J. Hetherington, *Australians* (Melb, 1960); D. Lindsay, *The leafy tree, my family* (Melb, 1965); L. B. Cox, *The National Gallery of Victoria, 1861 to 1968* (Melb, 1970?); C. Edwards, *The editor regrets* (Melb, 1972); C. Hazlehurst (ed), *Australian conservatism* (Canb, 1979); D. Zwar, *In search of Keith Murdoch* (Melb, 1980); R. Haese, *Rebels and precursors*, (Melb, 1981); G. Souter, *Company of heralds* (Melb, 1981); G. Serle, *John Monash. A biography* (Melb, 1982); G. Munster, *A paper prince* (Melb, 1985); *Newspaper News*, 1 Dec 1928; *Nation* (Syd), 4 July 1959, 29 June 1963; Murdoch papers (NL); F. Eggleston, Confidential notes: journalists and press barons (Menzies Lib, ANU); C. E. Sayers, unpublished biography, C. E. Sayers papers (LaTL); Bean papers (AWM).

GEOFFREY SERLE

MURDOCH, MADOLINE (NINA) (1890-1976), writer, was born on 19 October 1890 at North Carlton, Melbourne, third daughter of Victorian-born parents John Andrew Murdoch, law clerk, and his wife Rebecca, née Murphy. The family moved to Woodburn, New South Wales, where Nina grew up. She conveyed her love for the bush in lyric poetry which she began writing while at Sydney Girls' High School in 1904-07. After leaving school she herself taught at Sydney Boys' Preparatory School. In 1913 she won the *Bulletin* prize for a sonnet about Canberra. She met journalist Adam McCay [q.v.], who encouraged her to work on the Sydney *Sun* where she was trained by Monty Grover [q.v.9] and became one of the first women general reporters. In 1915 she published a book of verse, *Songs of the open air.*

On 19 December 1917 at St Philip's Anglican Church, Church Hill, Nina married James Duncan Mackay Brown, an ex-teacher and journalist who had lost an arm. She was part of the literary and journalistic coterie clustering round the *Bulletin*. Some of them, including her friend Rose Scott [q.v.], farewelled the Browns at a luncheon before they moved to Melbourne: Nina was dark, attractive and vivacious 'in her powder-blue costume, edged with lamb's wool, her marmot furs and little pointed velvet toque'.

They worked on the *Sun News-Pictorial*, Nina often using the pen-name 'Manin'. An independent woman, in 1927 she travelled alone in England and Europe, developing a lifelong obsession that she expressed in travel books, beginning with *Seventh heaven, a joyous discovery of Europe* (1930). A novel, *Miss Emily in black lace* (1930), was the first in a series of three pot-boilers. By 1934 *Seventh heaven* reached its fifth edition; it abounded in ecstatic enthusiasm for European art, antiquity and graciousness.

In Melbourne in 1930 Nina and other married women were retrenched from the *Herald* because of the Depression. She gave travel talks on the wireless and, from the inception of the Australian Broadcasting Commission in 1932, managed Children's Corner at 3LO. She formulated the idea for, and as 'Pat' began running, the Argonauts' Club. Its pledge epitomized her style: 'I vow to stand faithfully by all that is brave and beautiful; to seek adventure, and having discovered aught of wonder or delight, of merriment or loveliness, to share it freely with my comrades'. Members were known by the name of a Greek ship and their number in its crew; their original contributions were read over the air. It was novel children's programming that introduced cultural content to an area previously dominated by bunnies, kookaburras and birthday calls; but some thought it too highbrow. Brown moved to Adelaide to work for News Ltd in 1933 and Nina followed next year, so having to leave the A.B.C. The club ceased, but was revived along similar lines in 1941 and ran very successfully till 1972.

Nina was in Europe in 1934-35 and wrote *She travelled alone in Spain* (1935). On her way home she journeyed down the Amazon. She was abroad again in 1937. She loved the Austrian Tyrol, but wrote for the Australian press warning against Nazism. Murdoch published two more travel books and undertook war work and some broadcasting in Adelaide before returning to Victoria about 1942. She was a member of the Lyceum Club, the Incorporated Society of Authors (London) and the Fellowship of Australian Writers.

In 1948 her last book appeared, *Portrait in youth*, the only biography of John Longstaff [q.v.]. She enjoyed walking, boating, Russian ballet and good films; but looking after her mother, who was blind and lived to 105, and her asthmatic husband who died in 1957, left her little time: 'You can't hold a pen in one hand and an egg-beater in another', she commented. Nina Murdoch died childless on 16 April 1976, and was cremated, after spending her last years in an Anglican nursing home at Camberwell.

A. W. Thomas, *Broadcast and be damned* (Melb, 1980); K. S. Inglis, *This is the ABC* (Melb, 1983); *A'sian Journalist*, Apr 1927; *SMH*, 13 Feb 1936, 5 Apr 1938; *Bulletin*, 8 May 1976; Angus & Robertson papers (ML); Mackaness papers (NL); SP 1572 (AAO, Syd); information from Miss G. Machin, Syd, and Mrs F. Bell, Woodhurst Park, Oxted, Surrey, Eng.

SUZANNE EDGAR

MURDOCH, PATRICK JOHN (1850-1940), Presbyterian minister, was born on 10 June 1850 at Pitsligo, Aberdeenshire, Scotland, son of Rev. James Murdoch, Free Church of Scotland minister, and his wife Helen, née Garden. Patrick was raised in the highly erudite atmosphere of a Free Church manse at Rosehearty, the herring-fishing port of Pitsligo on Moray Firth. He graduated M.A. after four years at the University of Aberdeen and completed his training for the Free Church ministry as Cunningham scholar at New College, Edinburgh, and assistant minister at Regent Square Presbyterian Church, London, and South Free Church, Aberdeen. His contemporaries and co-religionists included (Sir) William Robertson Nicoll, founding editor of the *British Weekly* and the *Bookman*, whose career in religious journalism was later upheld as an ideal in the Murdoch family, and his friend the popular writer John Watson, alias 'Ian Maclaren'. Licensed to preach in 1878, Murdoch was ordained as minister at Cruden, Aberdeenshire, where he married Annie Brown on 5 January 1882. In 1884, when a crisis was disrupting the Free Church of Scotland, he accepted a call to the West Melbourne Presbyterian Church.

Murdoch and a large family party including his parents and his 10-year-old brother (Sir) Walter [q.v.], arrived in Melbourne on 2 October 1884 only to find that the Victorian Church had its own crisis regarding Charles Strong [q.v.6]. After three years at West Melbourne Murdoch was called to Trinity Church, Camberwell, in August 1887 and remained there until his retirement in 1928. He held prominent positions in the Presbyterian Church, being convener of the Victorian General Assembly's business committee in 1892-1918, joint convener of the 20th Century Fund, clerk of the presbytery of Melbourne South in 1896-1920, moderator of the Victorian General Assembly in 1898-99 and moderator-general of the Presbyterian Church of Australia in 1905-06. A churchman of strict principle, he demonstrated that the covenanting spirit was not dead during the *Ronald* v. *Harper* [q.v.9] slander and libel case in March 1909 when he spent a night in 'the sheriff's quarters' at Melbourne gaol for contempt rather than obey Justice Hodges's [q.v.9] demand to produce a letter in the possession of the presbytery of Melbourne South without its authority. Murdoch upheld the legal nature of the presbytery as an ecclesiastical court, whereas the judge took the view that he could 'no more allow members of the Presbyterian Church, through oaths administered to one another, not to produce documents . . . than [he] could allow two thugs, by virtue of similar oaths, to do the same thing'.

A cleric who valued social connexions, exemplified in his love of golf and bowls, Murdoch was tall, 'broad-shouldered, straight-backed and full of Christian fun'. He established friendly relations with persons of consequence: prime ministers as diverse as Andrew Fisher, Alfred Deakin [qq.v.8] and (Sir) Robert Menzies were his friends or admirers, and he had many contacts in the newspaper world. A theologian of the liberal Free Church tradition, he published *Sidelights on the shorter catechism* (1908), *The central doctrines of the Christian faith* (1915) and *Laughter and tears of God and other war sermons* (1915). Despite his orthodoxy he was better known for his reforming zeal, humanitarian and ecumenical interests, and his sympathy for the underdog. Rev. (Sir) Irving Benson saw him as one of the architects of the Presbyterian Church in his day as well as 'a prince of preachers'.

Patrick Murdoch died at Auburn on 1 July 1940. A portrait of his wife (d. 1945), painted by George Lambert [q.v.9] in 1927, won the Archibald [q.v.3] prize. They were survived by one daughter and three sons, including (Sir) Keith Arthur [q.v.].

A. MacKay, *Cruden and its ministers* (Adel, 1912); A. Macdonald, *One hundred years of Presbyterianism in Victoria* (Melb, 1937); C. McKay, *This is the life* (Syd, 1961); A. Dean, *A multitude of counsellors* (Melb, 1968); J. La Nauze, *Walter Murdoch* (Melb, 1977); D. Zwar, *In search of Keith Murdoch* (Melb, 1980); *Table Talk*, 17 Nov 1899; *Argus*, 16, 17 Mar 1909; *Herald* (Melb), 9 Nov 1928, 1, 2, 6 July 1940.   NIEL GUNSON

MURDOCH, THOMAS (1868-1946), politician and businessman, was born on 15 March 1868 in Hobart Town, fourth son of John Murdoch, merchant, and his wife Margaret, née Anderson, both from Scotland, and grandson of Dr James Murdoch [q.v.2]. He was educated at The Hutchins School. In 1884 he joined the audit department of the Tasmanian Main Line Railway Co. as a junior clerk and in 1890-97 worked in the Bank of Van Diemen's Land and the Commercial Bank of Australia. With his brother Harry he established Murdoch Bros, merchants and auctioneers, with butter and cheese factories in Hobart and country districts.

Murdoch represented Hobart in the Legislative Council in 1914-26 and Buckingham in 1927-44; he was deputy president in 1927, chairman of committees in 1932-37 and president in 1937-44. In 1932 he had been one of the four members whose seats were briefly forfeited when the solicitor-general found unconstitutional the holding by members of loans from the Agricultural Bank. One of the most forceful debaters in the council,

Murdoch was a militant Tasmanian, introducing a motion for secession in December 1924.

As a crusader for Tasmanian industries and agent for Cadbury-Fry-Pascall Pty Ltd, he selected a site for their Australasian factory at Claremont. He was a successful promoter of the Australian Newsprint Mills, the Electrolytic Zinc Co. and a Sydney-Hobart shipping service, and was an active member of the committee for the apple and pear scheme. He served as a member of the Hobart Marine Board in 1909-38 (four times master warden) and was four times president of the Hobart Chamber of Commerce. As consul for Belgium from 1917 Murdoch was twice decorated by the Belgian government. He was honorary agent for the British Emigration Society of London, for over thirty years chieftain of the Caledonian Society of Tasmania, a life member of the Hobart Regatta Association and Tasmanian representative of the Australasian Pioneers' Club. In 1943 he was appointed C.M.G.

Murdoch died on 29 June 1946 in Hobart and was cremated. On 15 September 1898 in Hobart he had married Mabel Mary Pearce who died in 1903, leaving a daughter. On 14 December 1907 in Melbourne he married LESLEY ELIZABETH (1881-1961), daughter of Boston-born Hubert Tope and his Scottish wife Jessie, née Taylor; she had been born in Melbourne on 18 October 1881. Lesley Murdoch was an outstanding hostess and organizer, with many legal, political and artistic friends. In 1920, with the help of a committee, she organized a citizens' ball and reception in honour of the prince of Wales at the City Hall, Hobart, connected by a walkway to the supper-room in Murdoch Bros' Building.

Mrs Murdoch was the third woman to stand for election to parliament in Tasmania, but was unsuccessful in 1934 as an Independent. She was the first woman to be elected to the Council of the University of Tasmania (1932-35, 1937-44). Petite and blue-eyed but of forceful personality, she worked to improve the status of women; she found employment for girls and frequently spoke for women in court. She was a member of the National Council of Women of Tasmania, the Child Welfare Association, the Women's International League for Peace and Freedom, and was a founding member of the Women's Non-Party League.

Lesley Murdoch died on 13 October 1961 at Wagga Wagga, New South Wales, and was cremated; a son and daughter survived her.

Univ Tas, *Calendar*, 1941; *SMH*, 17 May 1930, 12 July, 11 Oct 1932, 20 Mar 1940; *Mercury*(Hob), 1 July 1946, 14 Oct 1961; Diary with entries by T. and L. Murdoch and family papers (held by T. B. and H. M. G. Murdoch, Sandy Bay, Tas); personal information.
ELIZABETH B. JONES

MURDOCH, THOMAS (1876-1961), military engineer, was born on 16 April 1876 at Milawa, Victoria, son of James Murdoch, farmer and former stonemason, and his wife Elizabeth, née Doig, both Scottish born. He was educated at South Melbourne College and at the University of Melbourne (B.C.E., 1898). He also became a licensed surveyor. In 1897 he joined the civil engineering staff of the Victorian Railways.

In 1901 Murdoch was commissioned in the Victorian Railways Infantry, a militia regiment. In 1904 he transferred as a lieutenant to the Corps of Australian Engineers and by mid-1906 was a captain commanding No. 2 Electric Company. In 1910 he passed an examination for appointment to the Permanent Military Forces. He was commissioned as a lieutenant in the Royal Australian Engineers and appointed staff officer (Works) for Victoria. Before long he was director of engineers at Army Headquarters, Melbourne, as well as director of works. In 1913 he was promoted captain.

On the outbreak of war in 1914 Murdoch was 38, too old for most postings in the Australian Imperial Force. He remained in Australia, consoled at the end of 1915 with a brevet majority for meritorious service. It was not until June 1917 that a place was found for him in the A.I.F., as a major. By September he was at the Engineer Training Depot at Brightlingsea, Essex, England, and in November he took command of the 1st Field Company, then in the quiet Messines sector after months of fighting in the 3rd Ypres battles. In April 1918 Murdoch was promoted lieutcolonel and appointed to command the 1st Pioneer Battalion. He held this command throughout the final six months of the war, for much of which the battalion worked under the chief engineer of the Corps. He was awarded the Distinguished Service Order in the 1919 New Year honours.

Murdoch returned to Australia in April 1919 and took up duty as director of works at Army Headquarters. His duties remained unchanged when he was transferred to the Department of Defence in 1928. In 1930 he resigned from the Permanent Military Forces, staying on as director of works in a civilian capacity. In 1936 he was made a life member of the Victorian Institute of Engineers which he had joined in 1910. He retired from Defence in January 1937 with an honorary colonelcy, his stated intention being to play a lot of golf.

The outbreak of World War II called for an enlarged army works service and in November 1939 Murdoch was called back to the active list and appointed deputy director general of engineer services with the rank of colonel. A year later he was made director general, and a brigadier. By the time he retired from the directorate in November 1941 the severe staff shortages had been overcome and a substantial volume of work done, though there were still shortcomings in the handling of engineer stores.

After a year of inactivity Brigadier Murdoch joined the Department of Munitions, where he was concerned with the allocation of power generation resources and took part in the early planning for the post-war hydro-electric development of the upper Snowy River. He remained with Munitions until the end of the war.

On 25 April 1905 at Elsternwick, Melbourne, he had married Kathleen Tiernan; they had two daughters and three sons, who included Major General Ian Murdoch and Air Marshal Sir Alister Murdoch. Predeceased by his wife and a daughter, Murdoch died at Geelong on 13 July 1961 and was buried in Geelong western cemetery with Presbyterian forms.

G. Drake Brockman, *The turning wheel* (Perth, 1960); R. McNicoll, *The Royal Australian Engineers, 1919 to 1945* (Canb, 1982); family information.   RONALD MCNICOLL

MURDOCH, SIR WALTER LOGIE FORBES (1874-1970), popular essayist and university professor and chancellor, was born on 17 September 1874 at Rosehearty, a fishing village north-west of Aberdeen, Scotland, fourteenth and last child of Rev. James Murdoch, minister of the Free Church of Scotland, and his wife Helen, née Garden. Rev. P. J. Murdoch [q.v.] was his eldest brother. After a childhood at Rosehearty and in England and France, Walter arrived with his family in Melbourne, aged 10. He attended Camberwell Grammar School and Scotch College. At the University of Melbourne (B.A.,1895; M.A.,1897), as a member of Ormond [q.v.5] College, he won first-class honours in logic and philosophy.

After teaching experience, country and suburban, to the end of 1903, Murdoch's academic career began with appointment as a Melbourne University assistant lecturer in English. This was in what had virtually become a combined department under the classics professor T. G. Tucker [q.v.]. Murdoch published his first essay, 'The new school of Australian poets', in 1899, and he continued writing for the Melbourne *Argus*, under the pen-name of 'Elzevir', in a column which appeared weekly from 1905 titled 'Books and Men'. On 22 December 1897 at

Hawthorn, Melbourne, Murdoch had married Violet Catherine Hughston, a teacher.

1911 marked a turning-point in Murdoch's life. Passed over in favour of an overseas applicant, (Sir) Robert Wallace [q.v.], for the re-created independent chair of English at Melbourne University, he spent the next year as a full-time member of the *Argus*'s literary staff. He was then selected as a founding professor of the University of Western Australia, where in 1913 lectures began, and continued for many years, in tin sheds in the heart of Perth.

The literary and other friendships formed in Melbourne still exerted a strong nostalgic influence upon the middle-aged Murdoch. This has been established by his warmly sympathetic, but not uncritical, biographer John La Nauze; but the fact that he felt deeply his geographical and intellectual isolation in Perth was not evident to even his close associates there. Through the inter-war years, Murdoch broadened his influence upon Australian life—most noticeably within the western State but extending throughout the Commonwealth.

On the young campus he had a considerable following outside his own department and his immediate academic colleagues. In addition to the appeal of his wide-ranging and often informal literary lectures, of his sardonic wit and his ready debunking of the pompous and ultra-respectable, Murdoch was known for his help to students and junior colleagues in difficulties.

Sympathy for underdogs and a willingness to champion lost causes extended beyond Murdoch's academic environment. It coloured his second major contribution to Western Australian life: his association with several other members of the foundation professoriate in building closer links between the university and the community. His most effective medium was the column he contributed to the 'Life and Letters' page of the *West Australian* on alternate Saturday mornings. Combined from 1933 with occasional day and evening talks on radio—he was to prove a very effective broadcaster—and appearances on public platforms, frequently in the chair, it brought Murdoch a wide and varied local following. Simple language, challenging titles, erudite literary allusions, subtle or open criticisms of popularly accepted practices or beliefs, served to attract, in his biographer's words, varying types of people 'who read him, all with interest, most with pleasure, some with disapproval, over many years'. 'No other writer in the history of Australian letters has built so wide a reputation on the basis of the essay as a form of communication.'

These essays should be judged in the first instance as part of the community activities of the University of Western Australia. They were directed at the widespread literate, but by no means academic, population of the still very isolated State. But Murdoch's audience did not stop there. Indeed, the 'Elzevir' articles had begun to reappear in the *Argus* in 1919, and the essays in varying forms found an all-Australian market when Murdoch succumbed to the persuasion of his flamboyant nephew (Sir) Keith Murdoch, and his writings were syndicated on the Melbourne *Herald* network. Walter Murdoch's essays came to be read by others, then and much later, through collection and book form, from *Speaking personally* (1930) onward. Moreover, in old age, for nearly twenty years from 1945, he conducted a weekly 'Answers' column, 'little essays' on any and every question, syndicated throughout most States and New Zealand and read by a huge public.

It is perhaps fortunate that Murdoch did not in his best creative years allow himself the leisure to write more ambitious works than his essays and some early textbooks. What he described as his one 'real book', *Alfred Deakin: a sketch* (1923), was the result of work done in a year's leave in and around Melbourne. It was not successful financially, nor as an introduction either to a larger joint biography (later abandoned) or to La Nauze's definitive two-volume *Alfred Deakin: a biography* (1965).

Murdoch's limited interest, in his middle and later years, in Australian writing has often been criticized. However, in 1918 he published the *Oxford book of Australasian verse* (revised, 1923, 1945) and in 1951, after many years delay, with Henrietta Drake-Brockman, *Australian short stories* which was much better received than the verse anthology.

In addition to his academic teaching and the benefits which the young university obtained from his extramural activities, Murdoch was to remain a member of its governing body after he resigned from his chair in 1939. Chancellor in 1943-48, he was appointed C.M.G. in 1939 and K.C.M.G. in 1964; the university awarded him an honorary D.Litt. in 1948. He had been president of the local League of Nations Union from its foundation in the early 1920s until 1936, was president of the Kindergarten Union in 1933-36, and supported movements for women's rights.

Murdoch did not escape contemporary campus criticism, either for his teaching or his administrative policy. Literary purists deplored his lack of linguistic studies and specialist courses for advanced students. Some members of the university senate declared that, as chancellor, he made a poor chairman. On the first charge most observers would have accepted his biographer's assessment: 'He was a good academic man for the

time, the place and the circumstances'. This judgement is consistent with admission that, as his tenure of the chair of English lengthened, Murdoch became bored with teaching, was less accessible on the campus and no doubt less prompt in returning student assignments. His study at South Perth was a retreat where he might concentrate on keeping his own literary deadlines.

In matters of academic policy and administration, his limitations as chairman were more than offset by his grasp of basic principles and his readiness to work for a cause—before World War II in intimate collaboration with the university's first full-time vice-chancellor, Hubert Whitfeld [q.v.]. Murdoch sometimes engaged in vigorous public controversy; more often, as he aged, in subtle and skilful manoeuvring. As chancellor he brought great dignity to the office and the university profited thereby.

The friendliest of critics should note one phase of Murdoch's life and one aspect of his writings: his passionate advocacy during the 1930s of Douglas Credit. For a time this limited the credibility of his essays; it also affected his judgement on some aspects of university policy, such as the filling of a vacant chair of economics. The phase symbolized his sympathy for the underdog—in this case, the many affected by the Depression, and his search for an escape from its cause. It did not prevent him from actively opposing the idea of secession from the Commonwealth as a solution to Western Australia's economic ills. Much later, in 1950-51, he vehemently and stalwartly fought the attempt to outlaw the Communist Party.

Though the last years of Murdoch's long life were spent more or less as a recluse, with increasing deafness and declining eyesight, he remained mentally alert to the end. In 1964 he paid the last of several visits to his beloved Italy. When in the month of his death he was given a bedside message from the premier that the State government was to name its second university after him, he was able to send an appreciative acceptance. He added, *sotto voce*, 'It had better be a good one!'

The Murdoch family at South Perth was a closely knit household with Violet Murdoch keeping open house for a large circle of friends, academic and otherwise, until her prolonged post-war decline, and death in 1952. The only surviving son Will had begun a journalistic career but died in 1950. There was a close intellectual and personal relationship between father and elder daughter Catherine King, who gained distinction from running for many years an Australian Broadcasting Commission women's session which had a wide range of listeners, rural and metropolitan, of both sexes. Murdoch was frequently cajoled into taking part.

On 8 March 1962 at Perth Registry Office, Murdoch married his secretary-companion and nurse, Barbara Marshall Cameron. Survived by her and by the two daughters of his first marriage, he died on 30 July 1970 at South Perth and was buried in the Anglican section of Karrakatta cemetery.

An oil portrait of Murdoch by Louis Kahan is in the senate room of the University of Western Australia; Kahan's pen and wash drawing is in the foyer of the senate room at Murdoch University, which also holds a bust by Hetty Finley. Murdoch's gold-rimmed spectacles had always seemed poised halfway down his nose. His audiences were often beguiled by his genial if mischievous smile, the pipe which he smoked incessantly, and by his simple, sometimes satirical, introductory comments—all of which tended to disguise the often unconventional and unpopular opinions which he proceeded to present forcefully.

F. Alexander, *Campus at Crawley* (Melb, 1963); J. La Nauze, *Walter Murdoch: a centenary tribute* (Perth, 1974), and *Walter Murdoch: a biographical memoir* (Melb, 1977) and for bibliog; F. Alexander, 'John La Nauze on Walter Murdoch', *Westerly*, Dec 1977; Murdoch papers (NL). FRED ALEXANDER

MURDOCH, WILLIAM DAVID (1888-1942), musician and author, was born on 10 February 1888 at Sandhurst (Bendigo), Victoria, son of Andrew Murdoch, engineer, and his wife Annie, née Esler. Although his parents were 'a little musical' he showed no interest until, aged 11, he began piano lessons. He was soon competing successfully in solo competitions at Bendigo, Ballarat, Geelong and Melbourne and in 1903 was awarded the first Bendigo Austral scholarship. Murdoch also won an Ormond [q.v.5] exhibition and began piano studies with W. A. Laver [q.v.] at the University of Melbourne's Conservatorium of Music. In 1906 he won the [W. J.] Clarke [q.v.3] scholarship which, together with funds raised by public subscription, enabled him to study at the Royal College of Music, London.

Under the guidance of Frits Hartvigson, the eminent Danish pianist and teacher, Murdoch won two gold medals, a Bechstein grand piano and personal acclamation from Sir Hubert Parry, who described him as one of the most 'gifted' and 'charming' personalities to study at the R.C.M. Murdoch gave his first public recital in 1910 and next year, with (Dame) Clara Butt, played in South Africa, the first of many tours which included the Butt-Rumford visit to Australia and New Zealand in 1913. On 5 August 1915 he married, in London, Ellen Josephine Tuckfield. From 1916 he served in France as a bandsman in the Grenadier Guards and in 1918-19 was sent to Scandinavia as a cultural ambassador.

After meeting Albert Sammons, the leading violinist of his time, Murdoch's celebrated career in chamber music began. He was associated in 1919 with Sammons, W. H. Reed, Raymond Jeremy and Felix Salmond in the première performance of Elgar's Quintet in A minor, formed the highly successful Chamber Music Players with Sammons, Lionel Tertis and Lauri Kennedy, and made many recordings of piano trios with Arthur Catterall and W. H. Squire for Columbia.

Besides frequent solo recordings, recitals and concerto appearances with all the major orchestras in England, Murdoch performed in Europe and the United States of America during the 1920s and in 1929 undertook another concert tour of Australia in association with Harold Williams [q.v.]. During this tour he urged the formation of permanent professional orchestras in Sydney and Melbourne. On his return to England he was appointed professor at the Royal Academy of Music, and became a director of the Royal Philharmonic Society and a council-member of the Incorporated Society of Musicians.

In 1933 Murdoch published *Brahms*, a biography and analytical study of all the piano works and pianoforte chamber music. This was followed by *Chopin: his life* (1934), which revealed considerable literary flair as well as detailed scholarship. Several of his own songs and piano compositions were also published. He made piano arrangements of several Bach choral preludes and wrote a concerto in D minor for piano and orchestra from the Bach-Vivaldi transcription.

After the death of his first wife Murdoch married a divorcee Dorothy Violet Lang, née Mascall, on 21 March 1921 in London: four years later she divorced him and he married the co-respondent, Antonia Dorothea Meek, née Simon, on 25 November 1925. He died on 9 September 1942 at Holmbury St Mary, Surrey. His wife, two sons and two daughters survived him.

Audiences and critics around the world acclaimed the originality, musicality and technical security of Murdoch's performances. The exacting critic W. J. Turner [q.v.] wrote in 1916: 'Even when we get to the best pianists it is rarely, if ever, that we find a combination of exceptional technical mastery with tone-power, delicacy of touch, brilliance, command of colour, sensitiveness of phrasing, variety of feeling, imagination and vital passion. Mr. Murdoch possesses all these qualities to a high degree'.

Columbia records purple label series catalogue (Lond, 1924); R. Foster, *Come listen to my song* (Syd, 1949); *Musical Standard*, 10 Apr 1909, 20 Mar 1926; *Aust Musical News and Musical Digest*,

1 June 1913, 1 Aug 1928; *Musical Opinion*, 15 Oct 1942; *New Statesman* (Lond), 15 Apr 1916; *Argus*, 14, 16 May 1929; *Table Talk*, 23 May 1929; *SMH*, 12, 17 June 1929, 26 Sept 1942; *The Times*, 12 Sept 1942; *Bendigo Advertiser*, 14 Sept 1942.

J. A. PROVAN

MURPHY, ARTHUR WILLIAM (1891-1963), engineer and airman, was born on 17 November 1891 at Kew, Melbourne, son of Adelaide-born Charles Hubert Murphy, joiner and later engineer, and his English wife Mary, née Fisher. He was educated at Melbourne High and Footscray Technical schools, served a five-year apprenticeship with Austral Otis Engineering Co. and worked in several engineering establishments. He was one of the first five Australians to enlist in 1914 in the Aviation Instructional Staff of the Permanent Military Forces for training as air mechanics at the Central Flying School, Point Cook.

With the Australian Flying Corps preparing to send its first full squadron into active service overseas, in early 1916 Sergeant Murphy volunteered for the Australian Imperial Force, entering as a private but being immediately promoted to technical warrant officer. He embarked on 16 March 1916. His work in the maintenance of the squadron's aeroplanes and equipment under trying conditions in Egypt, the Sinai desert and Palestine was recognized by a mention in dispatches in 1917.

Selected to undergo a pilot's course, Murphy trained in Egypt with the Royal Flying Corps and was granted a temporary commission as second lieutenant in the A.I.F. on 24 October. After service with the R.F.C. and further training he returned to the Australian squadron in Palestine. He and his observer accounted for several enemy aeroplanes and carried out valuable bombing and reconnaissance missions, many in support of Colonel T. E. Lawrence and his irregular forces in the Hejaz. For this work Murphy was awarded the Distinguished Flying Cross and the Hejaz Order of Nahda.

On return to Australia and termination of his A.I.F. appointment, Murphy reverted to non-commissioned rank in the regular forces, combining technical with flying duties. Late in 1919, to secure information for competitors in the first flight from England to Australia, he and Captain H. N. Wrigley, flying from Melbourne to Darwin, were the first to cross the continent by air. In an old BE2e, the airmen made about twenty landings, many of them forced, in which Murphy's practical engineering experience proved invaluable. In Darwin they met (Sir) Ross and (Sir) Keith Smith [qq.v.] who had just arrived from England, winning the £10 000 prize. Wrigley and Murphy were both awarded the Air Force Cross. On 17 October 1922 Murphy married Alicia Logan Shoebridge at Erskine Presbyterian Church, South Carlton, Melbourne.

Joining the Royal Australian Air Force with the rank of flying officer shortly after its formation in 1921, Murphy continued in technical and flying roles, making several pioneering flights including a formation flight around Australia with the then chief of the air staff, Wing Commander (Air Marshal Sir) Richard Williams [q.v.] in 1927. In 1936 he was on the overseas mission which selected an American-designed aircraft, rather than a British type, for manufacture in Australia. He also participated in 1939 in negotiations to manufacture Beaufort aircraft and the establishment of the Government Aircraft Factory.

With the onset of World War II and the expansion of the R.A.A.F., Murphy played an important role in the co-ordination of aircraft production and in equipment maintenance. He reached the rank of air commodore in 1943—a striking achievement for a man who had enlisted as a trainee air mechanic. His contribution to aviation was recognized by his election as a fellow of the Royal Aeronautical Society. He left the R.A.A.F. in January 1946.

Contemporaries spoke highly of his integrity and described him as a kindly but somewhat shy man with a dry sense of humour. 'Spud' Murphy died of heart disease at Essendon, Melbourne, on 21 April 1963 and was cremated at Fawkner. He was survived by two sons and a daughter.

F. M. Cutlack, *The Australian Flying Corps* (Syd, 1923); L. W. Sutherland and N. Ellison, *Aces and kings* (Syd, 1935); R. Williams, *These are facts* (Canb, 1977); *London Gazette*, 6 July 1917, 3 June 1919, 1 Apr, 9 July 1920; information from Air Vice-Marshals H. N. Wrigley, Balwyn, Melb, and E. Hey, Campbell, ACT, and Mr L. A. Murphy, Essendon, Melb.

ALAN FRASER

MURPHY, BENNETT (BERNARD) FRANCIS (1888-1964), teamster, farmer and soldier, was born on 19 June 1888 at Geraldton, Western Australia, son of Andrew Murphy, farmer, and his wife Emma, née Snowdon. He was educated at Chapman Valley, near Geraldton, to about fourth grade and after leaving school worked as a teamster and farmer in the Murchison and Gascoyne areas. He trained teams of camels, horses and donkeys but is particularly remembered for a team of large camels (said to be the best in the Murchison district) which he trained for carting copper from the mines around Meekatharra.

Murphy left his team at Peak Hill to be sold and joined the Australian Imperial Force as a private at Blackboy Hill on 2 June 1915. He was tall, active, a keen athlete, a horse-breaker and champion roughrider. He enlisted as Bernard Francis Murphy and used this first name for the rest of his life, though he was usually called Barney. He embarked from Fremantle on 22 July for Gallipoli with the 2nd Reinforcements for the 28th Battalion. After the evacuation of Gallipoli and training in Egypt the battalion was transferred in March 1916 to France. During the next twenty months Murphy fought with the 28th in France and Flanders through the battles of Pozières, Bullecourt, Messines and Passchendaele and was promoted corporal and sergeant in October 1916. In March 1917 he was awarded the Distinguished Conduct Medal for gallantry, especially for volunteering to lead dangerous patrols. His coolness and daring were again recognized in December when he gained valuable information during scouting patrols and was awarded the Belgian Croix de Guerre.

In January 1918 Murphy volunteered for a special mission with Dunsterforce (British Army) which was to serve in Persia, Russia and Armenia. Selection for the contingent was confined to outstanding soldiers and Murphy was one of the twenty Australian non-commissioned officers sent to England for training. He served with Dunsterforce until March 1919 and fought in actions at Kermanshah, Hamadan, Kazvin, Zenjan, Takan Tepe, Sain Kala and Miandoab. On 6 May 1918 he was in a small party covering a withdrawal at Samkaleh and because of his courage and determination the enemy attacks were beaten back. For his part in this action and for aiding a wounded officer when practically surrounded by enemy troops he received a Bar to his D.C.M.

Murphy was discharged from the A.I.F. in June 1919 in Perth. With little money and without a team of horses or camels he worked as a horse-breaker and station-hand near Carnarvon. In 1922 he acquired land under the soldier-settlement scheme and established Erong station. That year he trained a number of prize racehorses including the first official winner of the Landor Cup. On 30 January 1924 he married Ethel Maud Trenaman at Christ Church, Nannine; they had three sons and a daughter. In 1944 Murphy leased Madoonga station, purchased it a few years later and lived there until retirement in 1952. He sold Erong in 1948 and bought the adjoining property, Kalli; both properties were managed separately by his sons Bernard and Stanley until 1974 when Madoonga was sold.

Barney Murphy retired to a small property at Armadale which he worked as a hobby farm. He also pursued his interest in horse-racing and joined the Western Australian Turf Club; he had been a member of the Murchison Race Club while living at Madoonga. In 1959

he moved with his wife to St James, a suburb of Perth. He died on 3 December 1964 in Hollywood Repatriation Hospital and was cremated.

H. B. Collett, *The 28th* (Perth, 1922); C. E. W. Bean, *The A.I.F. in France*, 1918 (Syd, 1937); *West Australian*, 9 Dec 1964; War diary, 28th Battalion, AIF (AWM); information from Mr and Mrs S. R. Murphy, Bentley, Perth.   R. C. H. COURTNEY

MURPHY, EDWIN GREENSLADE (1866-1939), journalist, was born on 12 December 1866 at Castlemaine, Victoria, tenth child of Irish-born Edward Murphy, plasterer and clay modeller, and his English wife Ellen, née Greenslade. He had five years schooling at South Melbourne—his handwriting remained almost illegible—before going to work for his father in City Road. He spent some time in Gippsland and then used his pleasant tenor voice to join the chorus of the Gilbert and Sullivan operas being presented by J. C. Williamson [q.v.6]. Murphy was attracted to the gold discoveries in Western Australia; he carried a swag 350 miles (560 km) from Perth to Coolgardie, arriving in 1894. He did a little dryblowing at Fly Flat, and enjoyed the nightly sing-songs around pub pianos.

Murphy helped Billy Clare to launch his *Coolgardie Miner*, contributing a weekly gossip column, including jingles, using the penname 'Dryblower'. This originated when a friend sent one of his rhymes to the Sydney *Bulletin*, saying that it had been written by a local dryblower; Murphy used the name for the rest of his life.

He went north-east to the new find at I.O.U. (Bulong) where, with two mates, he struck a rich patch at the end of 1894, dollying gold worth about £2000 (a tidy sum for penniless prospectors). With one of the mates he set off in March and floated the mine, the Esmeralda, in London. It slumped and he came home, but soon returned to England where he wrote for financial and social papers and helped to expose the hoaxer Louis de Rougemont [q.v.8] before conducting him on a lecture tour.

In London Murphy enjoyed the theatre, especially Gilbert and Sullivan operas, in which he sometimes sang; he sent articles home about 'Fogopolis', as he called the city. On 25 September 1895 at Hackney Register Office he married Emma Eleanor Lowndes, daughter of a retired builder, and returned to Australia at the time of the South African War. Inspired by English patriotic fervour, he wrote a song, 'Hands Across the Sea', which was set to music by George Snazelle, a popular operatic figure. Returning to parched red soil from lush England, 'Dryblower' wrote 'The sun is flooding this gasping globe with myriad miles of flame'.

His crisp, humorous writing won him a job on Kalgoorlie's weekly *Sun*, where his chief regular feature was 'The Mingled Yarn'. After a few years he moved to Perth's *Sunday Times*, his 'Verse and Worse' column containing gems of satire. As co-proprietor with J. E. T. Woods, in April 1905 he founded the penny *Sporting Life*, to print racing news; it only ran for a year and Murphy returned to the *Sunday Times* where he had to write so as 'to make profits for MacCallum Smith' [q.v.], the owner. He also produced a column on theatre. Murphy continued this work for over thirty-five years, occasionally missing a column when, as he said, celebrating unduly.

'Dryblower' wrote local content of songs for visiting musical comedy companies; when in 1908 the American fleet arrived, one of his lines, 'We've Got a Big Brother in America', was repeated widely. In World War I Murphy worked indefatigably for patriotic causes and his poem, 'My Son', inspired by his son Harry's enlistment, was greatly admired. Like many Australian humorists of the period Murphy responded to and encouraged popular sentiments of racism and jingoism.

He published a novel about Coolgardie, *Sweet boronia*, in 1904. Four years later his *Jarrahland jingles* appeared; it was one of the first books of substantial verse published in Western Australia and contained a preface by C. W. A. Hayward [q.v.9] that applauded Murphy's 'playful banter' and 'stinging satire', but Hayward noted that much of it was 'quick pressure work' and gave only two poems real praise. Murphy's verses became better known than those of any other Western Australian writer and in 1926 he published *Dryblower's verses*.

Public men feared his lampooning pen, which did not deter him from running in 1934, unsuccessfully, as an Independent candidate for the Senate.

This exuberant raconteur was thickset and ginger haired with an aggressive turned-up nose; he was drawn by a cartoonist in 1907 with full drooping moustache, thumbs stuck boastfully in his waistcoat, straw boater and tight stove-pipe trousers. He died of cancer at East Perth on 9 March 1939, survived by his wife and three sons of his five children; 'Dryblower' was buried in the Anglican section of Karrakatta cemetery, having left an estate of £288.

V. Courtney, *All I may tell* (Syd, 1956); B. Bennett (ed), *The literature of Western Australia* (Perth, 1979); A. L. Bennett, *Dryblower Murphy—his life and times* (Perth, 1982); *Bookfellow*, 30 May 1907; *Daily News* (Perth), 9 Mar 1939.

ARTHUR L. BENNETT

MURPHY, GEORGE FRANCIS (1883-1962), soldier, teacher and administrator, was born on 24 September 1883 at Pyrmont, Sydney, son of Michael Murphy, plumber, and his wife Catherine Ann, née Clarke, both Australian born. Educated at Pyrmont, Darlinghurst and Goulburn Public schools, he qualified as a teacher in the New South Wales Department of Public Instruction and later attended the University of Sydney as an evening student. He was teaching at Young when, on 30 December 1907, he married Marian Eliza Swain, also a teacher, at St Barnabas Anglican Church, Sydney.

Murphy's military career began in 1910 with his appointment as a lieutenant in the New South Wales cadets; in 1913 he passed the examination for entrance into the Administrative and Instructional Staff, Australian Military Forces, and was posted in December 1914 to Liverpool camp. Before that he had been first assistant teacher at Bathurst High School. On 5 May 1915 he joined the Australian Imperial Force as a captain and officer commanding 'A' Company, 20th Battalion; next month he was promoted major and embarked for Egypt in June. He reached Gallipoli on 22 August. After the 18th Battalion's attack on Hill 60 in August he was transferred to it and in November-December temporarily commanded it at Courtney's and Steele's Posts, building up a reputation as 'an alert and aggressive commander, with thorough grip of detail'. During the evacuation of Anzac he commanded rear parties.

Murphy embarked from Eygpt for France in March 1916 as second-in-command of the 18th Battalion; in April he served at Bois Grenier. At Pozières Heights on 27 July he was reconnoitring at night when he was severely wounded by heavy German artillery fire; he resumed duty in late October at Flers. On 7 November he took command of the battalion as a temporary lieut-colonel (his rank was confirmed on 1 December) and from then on led his battalion in all its major actions. At Bullecourt in 1917 Murphy personally led 200 of his men in the attack, moving during the advance to both flanks to steady first the right and then the left; for outstanding leadership he was awarded the Distinguished Service Order. In September-October he commanded the 18th in the costly battles of Menin Road and Broodseinde.

In April 1918 Murphy's battalion was sent south to help counter the German breakthrough near Amiens. A few miles to the east at Villers-Bretonneux he led an attack at Hangard Wood and next month at Morlancourt. C. E. W. Bean [q.v.7] later described him as 'a most competent commander and an able tactician'. Later in May, at Ville-sur-Ancre, with the aid of his scout sergeant, he captured seven German machine-gunners, rushing their post 'across 100 yards of open country', and for this action received a Bar to his D.S.O. In 1918 he was appointed C.M.G. for outstanding work at Broodseinde. He led the 18th in operations at Villers-Bretonneux in June-July before temporarily commanding the 7th Brigade from mid-July to 24 August, except for four days when he rejoined the 18th Battalion for the decisive battle of 8 August. He was evacuated to England with illness and then commanded the 18th from October 1918 to February 1919. In 1917-18 he was mentioned in dispatches five times.

Murphy's A.I.F. appointment ended in January 1920 but he continued to serve part-time in the A.M.F. In 1921-22 and 1924-31 he commanded the Sydney-based 17th Battalion. In 1920 he was appointed under-sheriff of New South Wales and was sheriff in 1925-35; he was deputy marshal of the High Court in 1935-39. Appointed assistant comptroller of New South Wales prisons in 1939, he became comptroller in 1940 and after World War II service resumed the post in 1947; he retired in September that year. In 1932-39 he was also custodian of the Sydney Cenotaph. During World War II Murphy served as a temporary colonel and director of the Volunteer Defence Corps in 1941-42; in 1941-43 he was also provost marshal at Army Headquarters. From April 1943 he was director of the military prisons and detention barracks at land headquarters and from May 1943 was also director of the military prisons and detention barracks service. He retired as an honorary colonel in November 1946.

Murphy was an outspoken member of the Returned Sailors' and Soldiers' Imperial League of Australia and was State president in 1941. He was also an active Freemason and a foundation member of Sydney Legacy.

Murphy's wife had died in 1934 and on 13 October 1936 he married Bessie Irene Hodge at Wesley Chapel, Castlereagh Street, Sydney. Survived by her, their son and three daughters, and by two sons and a daughter of his first marriage, he died on 13 September 1962 at Concord, and was cremated with Methodist forms.

C. E. W. Bean, *The A.I.F. in France*, 1916-18 (Syd, 1929, 1933, 1937, 1942); *T&CJ*, 2 June 1919; *Reveille* (Syd), Apr 1937; *SMH*, 20 July 1920, 16 Oct 1925, 20 Aug 1932, 18 Nov 1938, 29 June 1939, 1 Feb, 20 June 1940, 23 Jan 1941, 18 Jan 1947, 14 Sept 1962; G. F. Murphy file, War records section, *and* War diary, 18th Battalion AIF (AWM).   L. B. SWIFTE

MURPHY, GEORGE READ (1856-1925), public servant, inventor and writer, was born on 17 May 1856 at Prahran, Melbourne, eldest son of Henry Morgan Murphy, mer-

chant, and his wife Edith, née Read. His Dublin-born father was a member of the Victorian Legislative Council in 1864-73. After attending Melbourne Church of England Grammar School, Murphy was appointed to the Victorian Public Service as a clerk of courts on 5 January 1874, the youngest officer ever given charge of a court. His public service career extended over forty years and embraced a variety of duties in seventeen country and suburban localities. He was at times clerk of courts, coroner and police magistrate.

But Murphy's public service career, distinguished as it was, seemed to be merely a source of financial security which allowed him to pursue a busy intellectual life. From his youth he wrote verse and prose and letters to editors on a wide range of social issues. When a serious coach accident in 1886 necessitated his taking extended sick leave from the public service, he went to London and immersed himself in the issues of the day. He studied torpedo, invented some twenty years earlier, and patented the 'Victoria' torpedo, which was commended in *The Times*. A company purchased the rights to manufacture for £500 a year but failed to sell them to the Royal Navy because of the expense involved in changing from the existing systems. He lectured to the British Association for the Advancement of Science in 1890 on torpedoes.

While in London Murphy wrote his first novel, *The Blakely tragedy* (1891), which was in reality a plea for legislation to banish prostitutes from the streets. Returning to Victoria to resume his legal duties at Geelong, he published *Beyond the ice* (London, 1894). The subtitle suggests an adventure story about a trip to a newly discovered region near the North Pole; it is in fact a Utopian novel, showing how Australia (Zara), America (Ura), England (Gurla) and the civilized dependencies (Roda) might attain a state of universal happiness in a socialist society guided by the philosophy of Christ. In 1894 he also published at Geelong his *History of Federation*, a fictitious presentation in dialogue form. He also lectured and wrote on prison and racing reform, socialism and reform of the petty sessions, and he was largely responsible for bringing about the royal commission on law reform in 1897.

Murphy retired as police magistrate at Ballarat in 1916. He had married Ellen Stock at Sandford, Victoria, on 3 November 1904; they had no children. He lived in retirement in Melbourne and published his last book, *Peace*, in 1920. He died of pneumonia in Sydney on 11 September 1925 and was buried with Anglican rites in Northern Suburbs cemetery. His wife survived him.

M. M. McCallum, *Ballarat and district citizens*

and sports at home and abroad (Ballarat, 1916); *Table Talk*, 25 July 1901; *Argus*, 16 Sept 1925.

ANNE BEGGS SUNTER

MURPHY, HERBERT DYCE (1879-1971), sometimes known as Dyce-Murphy, gentleman adventurer and raconteur, was born on 18 October 1879 at Como, South Yarra, Melbourne, son of Alexander Dyce Murphy and his wife Ada Maud Florence, daughter of John Rout Hopkins [q.v.4]. Herbert's other grandfather was Sir Francis Murphy [q.v.5].

In his childhood Lord Lucan told him the story of the charge of the Light Brigade, which inspired lifelong study of the Crimean War. Herbert attended Cumloden school, Melbourne Church of England Grammar School (1889-90), visited Russia with his mother and went to Tonbridge School, Kent (1894-95). His uncle Sir William Waller, lord lieutenant of Suffolk, took him as a schoolboy on three Arctic voyages on the yacht *Gladiator*. Herbert then made two trips to Australia on the barque *Loch Broom*, apparently as third mate under the notorious 'Bully' Martin. When he informed his parents that he would not dedicate himself to the family's massive Queensland and New South Wales pastoral interest ('I had seen people on stations becoming vegetables'), his financial support was withdrawn.

Murphy matriculated from Brasenose College, Oxford, in May 1900 and passed Responsions. No further examination record survives, but he claimed to have held scholarships, studying history and engineering, and styled himself M.A. (Oxon). He was acquainted with Hilaire Belloc, John Buchan and Herbert Asquith among others, and some years later enjoyed escorting the Empress Eugénie with whom he shared Kirkpatrick forbears. During vacations he enlisted as navigator on the Dundee whaler *Balaena*, returning from Franz Josef Land and northwards with accounts of extraordinary adventure; shipped in the *Hope*, transporting reindeer from Norway to Russia; and visited the United States of America.

After seeing Murphy perform a female role in a Greek play at Oxford, the director-general of military intelligence recruited him for secret work. Murphy already held a territorial commission. Trained by a family friend Lady Broughton—entering and leaving hansom cabs was the most difficult trick—he lived for several years as a woman. In a period of poor diplomatic relations with France and Belgium, 'Edith' Murphy closely studied their railways. 'There were 100 000 wagons on the French northern railways and I must have examined each one twice'. He wrote technical papers on engineering matters. For a period

he shared a house at Kew with a retired ship's master 'who could never work out how I knew so much about a ship'; a painting shows Murphy in elegant dress and hat with the mariner, who eventually bequeathed him considerable property.

He greatly enjoyed his feminine life. A French lieutenant proposed to him in the Bois de Boulogne. Photographs survive of him at Henley, and he always firmly claimed that he was the delightful, auburn-haired woman, with white parasol, in Phillips Fox's [q.v.8] 'The Arbour', originally sketched at Bath about 1902, the artist being unaware of his identity. Murphy asserted that he worked for the War Office for some five years and was awarded two service medals—that no records survive means little—but the period was probably shorter. His voice was becoming more masculine, his hands were growing and he found it difficult to keep up the impersonation.

Murphy's story goes that he next shipped out from the Canary Islands on a two-year voyage on a New Bedford whaler under ruthless Quaker officers; he was navigator, and tutor to the skipper's daughter. His stories of adventure and near-disaster on this voyage, including visits to sub-Antarctic islands, are convincing in their verisimilitude and there are external corroborations. After he deserted in New Zealand, by his own account he was received coolly in Melbourne by his family, now aware of his transvestite activities. He returned to Europe and worked and invested in Norwegian whaling, about 1906 buying for £2500 the fine brigantine-rigged yacht *Francesca*. He adopted two Norwegian orphan girls whom he educated and launched successfully into the world. They accompanied him on many voyages, including one to Tierra del Fuego and another to Novaya Zemblya where the yacht was frozen in for nine months; they were reduced to eating seals, Arctic owls, and lemmings which Murphy said tasted 'beastly'.

Murphy volunteered for Ernest Shackleton's 1908 Antarctic expedition as a surveyor, but was turned down for supposed effeminacy—a charge he always vigorously denied. (Sir) Douglas Mawson [q.v.], however, accepted him for his 1911-14 expedition. Murphy was dog-handler, in charge of stores, during 1912 in command of the southern supporting party, and of winter quarters during Mawson's absence. Mawson wrote of him as 'Our stand-by in small talk, travel, history, literature and what not' and elsewhere referred to his 'services cheerfully rendered'. C. F. Laseron [q.v.9] commented: 'He tells of social life in Melbourne, of one of his friends who proposed to two girls in one evening, and of how both accepted him, and of complications which followed. From this he wanders to . . . hair-raising scandals with lurid details of complicated domestic situations with ludicrous climaxes . . . He holds himself up to ridicule as well as his other characters. Yet he never loses his air of diffidence; his whole method is apologetic. His stories have a curious suggestion of truth; they are convincing and at the same time too impossible to be true'.

During World War I, after a year in army intelligence, Murphy returned to Australia, joined the Australian Imperial Force in 1916, but was discharged for inferior vision. He was then described as 5 ft. 8¼ ins. (173 cm) in height, and his occupation as orchardist. He bought a property at Whittlesea, Victoria, and ran sheep. He later moved to Mount Martha where his rambling, weatherboard house became a holiday centre for many Melbourne boys and girls—Murphy preferred the girls—often from underprivileged backgrounds. Many of them recall the 'golden' days with excitements ranging from motor excursions and the trolley-railway in the garden to Murphy's library, log-fires at night and his anecdotes of the Arctic and Antarctic. Murphy silently assisted the education of several needy children.

A High-Churchman, Murphy was for at least thirty-five years a member of synod and was a Mornington shire councillor in 1926-36 (president, 1932-33). He was a skilful photographer, a life member of the Royal Automobile Club of Victoria and of the Ship Lovers' Society to whose *Dog Watch* he contributed spirited articles (1948-53) on his experiences, and was in wide demand as a speaker and singer of shanties. Although a member of the Melbourne Club for some thirty years, he claimed to have entered it only once. On 13 February 1934 at St John's Church, Toorak, Murphy married Muriel Idrene Nevile Webster.

His interest in Antarctica had continued: from 1920, for three months annually, he became ice-master to the Norwegian whaling fleet there, his task the handling of the mother-ship in the ice. He claimed to have continued this work until 1965; the Norwegian underwriters 'nearly had a fit' when they discovered he was 85.

Few Australian lives can compare in variety and adventure with Murphy's. The drive and confidence of his personality stemmed from the social status of the 'Port Phillip gentlemen'. Though he stepped outside this tradition, he remained bound to it in many ways, not least in the determined self-confidence, comparable with Percy Grainger's [q.v.9], with which he maintained, and sometimes flaunted, his aberrant psycho-sexuality. He was right to deny effeminacy, though the extent to which his physical exploits were a deliberate offset to his admiration of girls and

women, and his desire to enter into their roles, may be considered.

Behind Murphy's infectious charm and unaffected manners lay an organized mind with magnificent powers of recall and reminiscence. Something of a Munchhausen perhaps—some of his claims appear to be fantasies. However, much of even his most outrageous stories 'check out', and in his embellishments he was striving for the symmetry of art. It was therefore fitting that Patrick White used Herbert Murphy as a model, in part, for the character of Eddie Twyborn in *The Twyborn affair*.

Survived by his wife, Murphy died childless on 20 July 1971 at Mornington and was buried in the cemetery there.

C. F. Laseron, *South with Mawson* (Syd, 1947); *Bohemia*, 1 May 1947, 1 July 1950, 1 Dec 1951; *People* (Syd), 1 Dec 1954; Shiplovers' Soc of Vic, *Newsletter*, Oct-Dec 1971; *A'sian Post*, 11 Mar 1965; *Mornington Leader*, 12 Dec 1963, 4 Aug 1971; tape-recorded interview with S. Murray-Smith, (LaTL); interview notes by J. W. Gliddon (held by A. Woodley, Crib Point, Vic).

S. MURRAY-SMITH

MURPHY, JEREMIAH MATTHIAS (1883-1955), priest and university educationist, was born on 13 July 1883 at Kilkenny, Ireland, son of James Murphy, headmaster, and his wife Mary Kate, née McGrath. His parents died while he was young and he boarded at St Kieran's College, Kilkenny, where, although a moderate scholar, he excelled in classics. He entered the Society of Jesus in 1901, studying at St Stanislaus' College, Tullamore. In 1904-07 he attended University College, Dublin, graduating M.A. with first-class honours in classics. In 1908 he undertook non-degree postgraduate studies at Oxford under Gilbert Murray [q.v.] and A. E. Zimmern, whose liberal influence is evident in his rather florid essay, 'Athenian Imperialism', in *Studies* (1912).

In 1910 and 1913 Murphy taught classics at Clongowes Wood and Belvedere colleges, interspersed with theological studies at Milltown Park, Dublin. After his ordination in 1916 his health failed, although he taught for some time and spent 1919 studying theology at Canterbury, England. Next year he sailed for Melbourne where he was senior classics master at Xavier College in 1920-22, and rector of Newman College in 1923-53. With another Kilkenny Jesuit, W. P. Hackett [q.v.9], he became confidant and adviser to Archbishop Mannix [q.v.]; this influence may explain what was, for his Order, an unusually long rectorship.

Murphy's Newman years were significant for his contribution to better understanding between Catholics and the rest of the community. He was outward looking, insisting that college students participate fully in university life and not adopt utilitarian attitudes to study. He set a personal example, serving long terms on numerous university bodies, including the council, the boards of management of the union and the university press; for years he was a member of the Schools Board and the Council of Public Education. He encouraged graduates to further research, including overseas study, believing that they should become community leaders. Mannix's opposition to the foundation of a Catholic university, a Sydney proposal of the 1940s, must have owed much to Murphy's Melbourne success. He certainly played a major role, in 1950, in establishing the Archbishop Mannix travelling scholarship.

Always prominent in diocesan intellectual life, Murphy was a frequent public preacher and speaker. He served as chaplain to various bodies, including the Newman Society and the National Catholic Girls' Movement; he assisted the establishment of the Catholic Teachers' Association. Although he never adopted an aggressive or ostentatious Catholicism, he was a successful exponent of ideas to the general public. He proved his abilities as a Catholic Evidence lecturer and, from 1932, in Catholic broadcasting. He gave evidence on behalf of the archbishop to the 1941 parliamentary committee on broadcasting.

Murphy raised the academic quality of Newman by developing a tutorial system across many disciplines, tutoring in classics himself and employing others who later became prominent in professional and academic life. Out of this intellectual ferment grew, in the early 1930s, the Campion Society.

Murphy possessed an irrepressible sense of fun, and, despite a misleading manner of appearing impatient and superficial, was a good listener. When needed, his tolerance and wisdom prevailed. His genial smile and his old-world sense of courtesy were surely taxed, however, by the pressures of increased student numbers and changed post-war expectations. Unfortunately he failed to grasp the architectural importance of Burley Griffin's [q.v.9] college design, and under his custodianship the fabric deteriorated and disastrous alterations were made to the dome.

Senior university administrators sought his advice, appreciating his shrewd, penetrating and moderate judgements. He also could be consulted regularly in the front row of the Carlton Football Club members' stand. His educational contribution was recognized in 1954, when the university conferred upon him a doctorate of laws and he was appointed C.M.G.

Transferred rather abruptly from the rectorship to semi-retirement at Xavier at the end of 1953, Murphy died on 17 May 1955 and was buried in Kew cemetery. His portrait by William Dargie hangs in Newman College.

U. M. L. Bygott, *With pen and tongue* (Melb, 1980); H. Dow (ed), *Memories of Melbourne University* (Melb, 1983); *Univ Melb Gazette*, Mar 1954, June 1955; Xavier College, *Xaverian*, Dec 1955; Murphy papers (Soc of Jesus Provincial Archives, Hawthorn, Melb); Irish Provincial Archives, Dublin; personal information.   D. J. MULVANEY

MURPHY, PETER (1853-1925), businessman, was born on 29 June 1853 at Mohill, Leitrim, Ireland, son of James Murphy, storekeeper, and his wife Ann, née King. Educated at National schools, he worked in an uncle's wine and spirit store at Mohill before reaching Brisbane in the *Indus* in July 1871 as a nominated immigrant. Labourer, bullockdriver, police constable in North Queensland, and grocer at Red Hill, Brisbane, he obtained a spirit dealer's licence in 1879. Later he conducted the Railway Co-operative Store and a wholesale spirit agency in partnership with William Healion whose niece, Ellen Imelda Bulcock, he married on 16 February 1885 in St Stephen's Cathedral.

Murphy became licensee of the Burgundy Hotel, Roma Street, in 1883 and in 1884 opened the Transcontinental, which soon had the largest bar trade in Brisbane. President of the Queensland United Licensed Victuallers' Association for several terms and a successful hotel broker, from 1893 he was a director (later chairman) of the reconstituted brewery firm, Perkins & Co. Ltd. With his usual business acumen he became a shareholder in its rivals, Queensland Brewery Ltd, and Castlemaine Brewery and Quinlan Gray & Co. Brisbane Ltd.

Diversifying his interests, Murphy invested mainly in businesses of Catholic friends, in particular in Cummins [q.v.8] & Campbell Pty Ltd, Townsville, and McDonnell [q.v.] & East [q.v.8], of which he was the initial financial backer and alternate managing director. He held directorships in the City Electric Light Co. Ltd and the Union Trustee Co. of Australia Ltd and from 1907 to 1914 partnered P. J. Leahy [q.v.John Leahy] in a stock and station agency. His property holdings were extensive: tenants included hotels, the Theatre Royal and the State Butchery Department.

Appointed to the Legislative Council on 4 May 1904, Murphy for a time was the only member sympathetic to Labor, although he never joined the party. His most significant role was as spokesman of the liquor trade. Overseas travel had instructed him in prohibition and 'local option', and he surprised the Denham [q.v.8] government by the vigour and efficacy of his opposition to the 1911 liquor bill. When the Ryan [q.v.] government took office the pragmatic Murphy, father-in-law of J. A. Fihelly [q.v.8] and with influential Labor friends, was untroubled by fears of the ascendancy of the temperance faction. His confidence was not misplaced; Queensland was the only State in which hotels remained open until 11 p.m. throughout World War I.

The archetypal Irish-Australian, genial, generous, honorary life member of the Philanthropic Institute, Murphy believed drinking and gambling were inherent in human nature. An advocate of State lotteries, a racehorse owner, committee-member of the Queensland Turf and Brisbane Tattersall's clubs, and a Toombul Racecourse trustee, he financed the sporting paper, *The Pink 'Un*, with M. J. Barry, later Brisbane's first Labor mayor.

Murphy died at his home Glostermin, Hamilton, on 24 February 1925 and was buried in Nudgee Roman Catholic cemetery. His wife, four sons and four daughters survived him and inherited most of his estate, valued for probate at £295 839.

Brisbane Courier, 4 May 1904, 25 Feb 1925; *V&P* (Qld), 1901, 3, p 939, 969; information from Mr P. F. Murphy, Kenmore, Brisb, and Mrs A. Toakley, Tweed Heads West, NSW.

BETTY CROUCHLEY

MURRAY, SIR GEORGE JOHN ROBERT (1863-1942), judge, was born on 27 September 1863 at Murray Park, Magill, Adelaide, second surviving son of Alexander Borthwick Murray, a Scots pastoralist and politician, and his second wife Margaret, née Tinline. He largely took charge of the family's business concerns on his father's death. His family was wealthy by colonial standards and in 1874-75 he attended the High School, Edinburgh, after early tuition at J. L. Young's [q.v.6] Adelaide Educational Institution. On his return from Scotland, at the Collegiate School of St Peter he demonstrated outstanding academic attainments and prowess in sport. He matriculated to the University of Adelaide in 1880, winning an entrance scholarship and taking an arts degree in 1883, after annually obtaining first-class honours. That year he was awarded the South Australian scholarship, which enabled him to read law at Trinity College, Cambridge, with financial support from the colonial government.

At Cambridge Murray represented his college in cricket and rowing, and was equal first in the law tripos examinations for the bachelor of laws degree in 1887. His ability was noted by F. W. Maitland, the most distin-

guished English legal historian of the period, who suggested that he consider taking up the study of legal history as a vocation. However, with financial assistance from his family and an Inns of Court scholarship, Murray completed the requirements for admission to the Bar and was called to the Inner Temple in 1888. Returning to Adelaide next year, while recovering from an accident which permanently curtailed his sporting activities, he was admitted to legal practice in South Australia at a bedside ceremony conducted by Chief Justice (Sir) Samuel Way [q.v.].

By 1900 Murray had established a firm position for himself in legal and academic life. He began his long-standing professional relationship with Way when he served as his associate on the Supreme Court in 1889-91. Later, in private practice, he specialized in civil matters. The amalgamated nature of the legal profession enabled him to build up an extensive clientele as a solicitor in the commercial area. In appearances in court as a barrister he was not a forceful advocate, but developed a solid reputation for logic and clarity of argument. He was appointed K.C. in 1906 and in mid-career surprised some contemporaries when he visited England and completed the requirements for the Cambridge master of laws degree in 1909. By then he was also involved deeply in the affairs of the University of Adelaide. He had undertaken a heavy lecturing commitment in the law school during the absence of F. W. Pennefather in 1891. He was elected to the university council that year, beginning a direct, active association which was to continue for fifty years. His correspondence reveals his deep interest in the quality of legal education, the attributes of appointees at professorial level and the nature of the curriculum.

Murray was reticent about taking up a judicial appointment and refused an acting judgeship of the Supreme Court in 1911. Next year, however, pressed strongly by Way who suggested that it was his patriotic duty to join the court, he accepted appointment as a puisne judge. Murray was concerned at the small judicial salary, as he viewed it; but as much as anything he was reluctant 'to change my present mode of life'. After Way's death, the senior puisne judge Sir John Gordon [q.v.9] was offered the chief justiceship, but declined because of ill health; Murray was then promoted to be Way's successor. His appointment by the Vaughan [q.v.] Labor government was acknowledged as marking a non-political approach to appointments to the court, in contrast to what had often been the situation. Murray's preference had been for the conservative side of politics and, meticulously, he had resigned from membership of the Liberal Union before his initial appointment to the bench. He had, however, steadfastly refused over the years to accept nomination as a parliamentary candidate.

A 'long lean man', who often seemed reserved, even austere, Murray was a dominant influence on the Supreme Court for the remainder of his life. He held strongly to a traditional view of the role of law in society. This was marked early in his chief justiceship when he successfully helped to resist efforts to have the president of the State Industrial Court, Dr Jethro Brown [q.v.7], appointed also to the Supreme Court. As under Way, the court had little influence through its decisions outside South Australia, particularly as Murray as much as any of his colleagues tended in appellate and other decisions to eschew detailed reasoning in his judgments. Nevertheless, there was a strongly held tradition in the local legal profession, often justifiably, that Murray had an admirable capacity to reflect accurately the condition of the law and apply it dispassionately to the cases in hand. In this mould, the Supreme Court showed little innovatory zeal, but served in its own way to preserve the character of community values as Murray conceived them.

Appointed K.C.M.G. in 1917, Murray on elevation to the chief justiceship also became lieut-governor. This proved to be no sinecure: he administered the State on 103 occasions in 1916-42, for a period totalling over six years. As a frequent resident of Government House during vacancies in the office of governor, or absences of a governor, he undertook ceremonial and other vice-regal duties. The university also claimed his continuing attention; six times elected chancellor from 1916 to 1942, he presided regularly over council meetings, concerning himself quite strongly at times in the conduct of the university's affairs. His close knowledge of the university, dating back to his student days, his membership of many of its committees down the years and his standing as one of its most noted graduates, made him a powerful force in regulating its activities.

Murray had followed his mentor Way as chief justice, chancellor of the university and lieut-governor. After Way's death in 1916, Murray often seemed to remain in the shadow of his formidable predecessor. But this was not entirely so. The similarities between them were based on shared beliefs in conservative values relating to the law and the conduct of public affairs. At least in Way's final years, Murray had been almost certainly often dominant in their relationship, with the aged chief justice deferring more and more to the younger man's views. Like Way, Murray mostly sought and obtained his personal fulfilment within his home State and through his contributions to its way of life. Endowed with a keen intellect, he had the capacity to make significant contributions to the law and other

fields. However, he increasingly preferred to be seen as an embodiment of traditional, conservative and often localized values and as a focal point for helping to preserve those from untoward influences, as he viewed them. Even Way had 'never known a judge who was such a partisan'.

Murray was not an aggressive nationalist but he had a deep pride in his success as a South Australian, pointing out not long before his death that he was the first person of colonial birth to serve on the State's Supreme Court and the first native-born chief justice and chancellor. His views and outlook were Australian, tempered but never displaced by his contacts with Britain down the years, in the manner of the era in which he lived.

Murray did not marry and lived at Murray Park with his unmarried sister Margaret; he remained, personally, something of an enigma. He was a trustee of the Adelaide Club. An avid stamp collector from his youth, he had a fine collection of the stamps of the Australian colonies which, with his Australian paintings, he bequeathed to the Public Library, Museum and Art Gallery of South Australia. He endowed the Tinline [q.v.6] scholarship in history to commemorate his mother's family from 1907, and he gave generously to the university: £10 000 for a union building in 1936, surrender of a life interest in £53 000 in 1937, and other gifts.

In accord with his wishes, eschewing the pomp and circumstance which he had shunned during his lifetime, on his death on 18 February 1942 Murray was buried privately beside his sister in St George's Church of England cemetery, Magill. The university council minuted that he had been revered 'for the austerity of his life as for his manifest uprightness'. His estate was sworn for probate in Victoria, New South Wales and South Australia at £225 700. The residue of above £83 000 was bequeathed to the university. His extensive library was shared between it and the Law Society of South Australia, which named its library in his memory.

Public Service Review (SA), May 1915; *Honorary Magistrate*, 15 Apr 1942; *SA Homes and Gardens*, 1 Apr 1948; Roy Inst of Public Administration, *Bulletin*, Nov 1978; *Observer* (Adel), 28 July 1906, 4 Oct 1924; *Mail* (Adel), 17 Aug 1912; *Chronicle* (Adel), 29 Sept 1932; *Advertiser* (Adel), 19 Feb, 14 May 1942; Murray papers, PRG 259 and GRG 36/49/,1889-1892 *and* S. J. Way letter-books, 1912, p 221, May-Dec 1903 (SAA); Minute-books, Council of Univ Adel (Univ Adel Archives).

ALEX C. CASTLES

MURRAY, HENRY WILLIAM (1880-1966), soldier and grazier, was born on 1 December 1880 at Evandale, Tasmania, son of Edward Kennedy Murray, farmer, and his wife Clarissa, née Littler. His father died when he was young and after leaving Evandale State School Harry helped to run the family farm. His military career began with six years service in the Australian Field Artillery (militia) at Launceston. At 19 or 20 he moved to Western Australia, working as a mail courier on the goldfields, travelling by bicycle or on horseback. When he enlisted as a private in the Australian Imperial Force on 13 October 1914, describing himself as a 'bushman', he was employing men cutting timber for the railways in the south-west of the State. He was handsome, tall, solidly built with dark hair, modest but strong-willed in character, resourceful and a natural leader.

Murray was posted to the 16th Battalion and belonged to one of the unit's two machine-gun crews when he landed at Gallipoli on 25 April 1915 with his mate and Number 1 gunner, Lance Corporal Percy Black [q.v.7]. Next day both gun-crews on the rear slope of Pope's Hill sniped at the Turks creeping onto Russell's Top. C. E. W. Bean [q.v.7] recorded that 'The 16th Battalion machine-guns were in charge of men of no ordinary determination'. Both men, though wounded, refused to leave their guns on that day or through any of the heavy fighting of the next week. Murray, from wounds received on 30 May, was evacuated and rejoined his unit on 3 July. Promoted lance corporal on 13 May, he won the Distinguished Conduct Medal for 'exceptional courage, energy and skill' between 9-31 May. He was wounded again on 8 August when the machine-gun section of the 4th Brigade, later described by Bean as 'possibly the finest unit in the A.I.F.', covered the withdrawal after the attack on Hill 971. On 13 August he was promoted sergeant, commissioned second lieutenant and transferred to the 13th Battalion. 'Cool, determined and confident', Murray remained 'a compelling, ubiquitous figure' on Gallipoli.

On 20 January 1916, in Egypt, he was promoted lieutenant and captain on 1 March. Late that month the 13th Battalion went to France where Murray took part in every major fight in which the unit was engaged. At Mouquet Farm in August, with fewer than 100 men, he stormed the remains of the farm, capturing his objective, but after beating off four German counter-attacks ordered his men to withdraw. The farm was eventually recaptured by 3000 men. Murray received the Distinguished Service Order, for, although twice wounded, he had commanded his company 'with the greatest courage and initiative'. Later when an enemy bullet 'started a man's equipment exploding he tore the equipment off at great personal risk'. Evacuated with wounds, he rejoined his battalion on 19 October.

On 4-5 February 1917 Murray led his com-

pany in an attack on Stormy Trench, near Gueudecourt. The night attack was launched across frozen snow and Murray's men reached the objective trench and set up a barricade. The Germans counter-attacked, shattering the barricade, and Murray fired an S.O.S. signal, which brought artillery support. The enemy continued attacking and were bombing heavily when Murray called on twenty bombers and led a brilliant charge which drove them off. From midnight to 3 a.m. fierce enemy bombing continued. Murray observed movement in an adjacent trench and called again for artillery support. By daylight his party had occupied the trench and held it until relieved at 8 p.m. For this work Murray was awarded the Victoria Cross.

In April, in the 1st battle of Bullecourt, Murray's unit, following the 16th Battalion, saw them caught against the wire in a torrent of machine-gun fire. 'Come on men', he shouted, 'the 16th are getting hell'. The gallant Percy Black was killed trying to find a gap in the wire. Murray got through to the German trenches and sent a message that the position could be held with artillery support and more ammunition. However, the artillery was not permitted to fire and under a heavy German barrage Murray withdrew his men; for his part in the battle he received a Bar to his D.S.O. On 11 April, the day of the battle, he was promoted temporary major (confirmed on 12 July) and towards the end of the year he temporarily commanded his battalion.

Promoted lieut-colonel on 8 May 1918, Murray was appointed to command the 4th Machine-Gun Battalion, a post he held until the end of the war. In January 1919 he was awarded the French Croix de Guerre and next May was appointed C.M.G. In 1917-19 he was mentioned in dispatches four times.

After the Armistice he toured Britain studying agricultural methods and on return to Australia began looking for a sheep-farming property. His A.I.F. appointment ended on 9 March 1920. After discharge in Tasmania he moved to Queensland and became a grazier at Blairmack, Muckadilla. On 13 October 1921, at Bollon, he married an estate agent, Constance Sophia Cameron. They lived at Muckadilla until 1925 when they separated and Murray went to New Zealand. Their marriage was dissolved on 11 November 1927 and on 20 November, at the Registrar's Office, Auckland, Murray married Ellen Purdon Cameron. They returned to Queensland and in April 1928 Murray bought Glenlyon station, Richmond, a 74 000-acre (29 900 ha) grazing property where he lived for the rest of his life.

In World War II he commanded the 26th Battalion in North Queensland until April 1942; in August he became lieut-colonel commanding his local battalion of the Volunteer Defence Corps; he retired from military service on 8 February 1944. Although a shy man who shunned publicity he attended the V.C. centenary celebrations in London in 1956. Survived by his wife and their son and daughter, he died on 7 January 1966 in Miles District Hospital, Queensland, after a car accident. He was cremated with Presbyterian forms.

The historian of the 16th Battalion wrote of him: 'To Murray belongs the honour of rising from a machine-gun private to the command of a machine-gun battalion of 64 guns, and of receiving more fighting decorations than any other infantry soldier in the British Army in the Great War'. The 13th Battalion historian noted: 'Not only was the 13th proud of him but the whole brigade was, from general to Digger. His unconscious modesty won him still greater admiration . . . Murray's courage was not a reckless exposure to danger like that of Jacka [q.v.9] or Sexton [q.v.7 M. V. Buckley] who didn't know fear'. He was a sensitive man who believed in discipline and wrote that it transformed thousands of men '—nervy and highly-strung like myself— enabling them to do the work which without discipline, they would have been quite incapable of performing'. Bean called him 'the most distinguished fighting officer in the A.I.F.' His portrait, by George Bell [q.v.7] is in the Australian War Memorial, Canberra.

C. E. W. Bean, *The story of Anzac* (Syd, 1921, 1924), and *The A.I.F. in France, 1916-18* (Syd, 1929, 1933, 1937, 1942); T. A. White, *The fighting Thirteenth* (Syd, 1924); C. Longmore, *The old Sixteenth* (Perth, 1929); L. Wigmore (ed), *They dared mightily* (Canb, 1963); *London Gazette*, 3 Aug 1915, 14 Nov 1916, 2 Jan, 9 Mar, 15 June, 25 Dec 1917, 31 Dec 1918, 7 Jan, 3 June, 11 July 1919; *Reveille* (Syd), Aug 1930, July 1956, Feb 1966; *Brisbane Courier*, 12 Nov 1927; *Courier Mail*, 24 Feb 1940, 8, 14 Jan 1966; *Age*, 8 Jan 1966; *Canb Times*, 8 Jan 1966; *Queensland Country Life*, 13 Jan 1966; War diaries, 13th and 16th Battalions, A.I.F. (AWM); information from Mr Douglas Murray and Mr Donald Murray, Richmond, Qld, *and* Mrs N. Waugh, Buderim, Qld. MERRILYN LINCOLN

MURRAY, JOHN (1837-1917), pastoralist and politician, was born on 15 August 1837 at Mauchline, Ayrshire, Scotland, son of Peter Murray, coachman, and his wife Jean, née Witherspoon. He was formally educated at Mauchline, and throughout his life read widely. About 1852 he arrived on the Victorian goldfields with his parents and siblings. Ten years later John Murray and his brothers Thomas and Campbell began business in New South Wales, shipping live cattle from Twofold Bay and Newcastle to New Zealand. This terminated two years later when New Zealand banned cattle imports, because of pleuro-pneumonia in Australia.

Riding overland from Brisbane, John reached Rockhampton about December 1864. His eldest brother Peter had settled there. In 1869-71 John selected almost 2000 acres (810 ha) of good land on what was then the Rockhampton agricultural reserve and named his property Fitzroy Park. He successfully grew sugar-cane as early as 1872 and was largely responsible for the establishment of the Pandora Sugar Co. Ltd in 1880 (liquidated 1884). In these years he demonstrated the resourcefulness and determination which distinguished him to the end.

At Rockhampton on 1 September 1873 with Primitive Methodist forms, Murray had married Jane Elizabeth Hartley (d. 1877) by whom he had two sons and one daughter. On 3 January 1882 he married Margaret McGavin also at Rockhampton; they had three sons and one daughter.

Murray was a foundation member of the Gogango Divisional Board, becoming chairman for three terms. Having shown his ability to think analytically and speak forcefully, he was elected to the Queensland Legislative Assembly in May 1888 for Normanby as supporter of McIlwraith's [q.v.5] National Party. On 16 November 1903 he resigned from parliament to contest the Senate election, but was defeated. A true conservative, he believed the then Labor balance of power in the Commonwealth parliament meant 'government from the gutter'. This was typical of his Scottish forthrightness.

For most of Murray's political career, he endeavoured to steer a middle course between the supporters and opponents of Central Queensland separation. Declaring his support for separation in 1890, he later declined a cabinet seat in the Griffith [q.v.9]-McIlwraith coalition. The ultimate success of the separationists seemed in no doubt. It was a different matter in 1898 when he accepted the portfolio of secretary for railways and public works (April 1898-February 1901) under the premiership of T. J. Byrnes [q.v.7] and (Sir) James Dickson [q.v.8]. In the south he was seen as a politician capable of rising above the 'narrow endeavour' to play off the smaller question of separation against Federation. According to the separationists, however, Murray had aligned himself with their declared enemies. On 12 March 1901 he was appointed to the Legislative Council. From February 1901 to August 1902 he was secretary for public instruction, then minister without portfolio in the Philp [q.v.] ministry until his retirement in September 1903.

At 66, feeling that 'time was running short', he returned to the pastoral industry, eventually acquiring eight pastoral leases. In 1911 when he purchased Beaconsfield East and West stations, Ilfracombe, his wife Margaret told their sons they must endeavour 'to make the name of Murray a power in the land ... there is no doubt [your] father has a master mind and is no ordinary man'.

In his later years Murray lived chiefly at Tullibardine, Brisbane. He took ill while on a visit to Beaconsfield and died at Longreach on 18 November 1917. Buried at Longreach, his remains were later reinterred in Toowong cemetery, Brisbane, with Presbyterian forms. His estate was sworn for probate at £48 775.

M. J. Fox, *The history of Queensland*, 3 (Brisb, 1923); *V&P* (Qld), 1889, 4, p 301; *Capricornian*, 24 Nov, 8 Dec 1917; *Morning Bulletin*, 10 Sept 1873, 3 Dec 1877, 22 Apr 1879, 9, 27 Aug, 27 Nov 1880, 13 Aug 1881, 7 Jan 1882, 15 Apr 1893, 17 Jan, 18, 23 Feb 1889, 24 Jan, 7 Mar 1899; *Brisbane Courier*, 24 Mar 1919; A. E. Hermann, Development of Rockhampton and district (ms, nd) and minute-book, Rockhampton Land Court (both held by Rockhampton and District Hist Soc); information from P. Murray, Ilfracombe, Qld, and Mrs E. Taylor, Paddington, Syd.

LORNA L. MCDONALD

MURRAY, JOHN (1851-1916), grazier and premier, was born on 8 July 1851 at Koroit, Victoria, son of James Murray (d. 1885) and his wife Isabella, née Gordon. His strict Presbyterian parents had migrated from Scotland in 1839. James farmed at Koroit, then took up Glenample station at Port Campbell. Jack, as he was always known, attended Allansford National School and, eventually from 1868, Henry Kemmis's Warrnambool Grammar School on the Hopkins River. His education was thorough. He remained very widely read with an unusual capacity for extended quotation; Burns and Sir Walter Scott were his prime loves and he knew the Bible thoroughly. His younger friend J. F. Archibald [q.v.3] recalled: 'Jack came of a physically ponderous family, but mentally he was most alert. Even in his youthful days he was a Doctor Samuel Johnson in figure and in wit'.

Murray visited Britain when about 20 and reportedly was horrified by the poverty he saw. He returned to the family property near Allansford and became a well-to-do grazier. As the local favourite son, enormously popular for his good fellowship but condemned by the *Warrnambool Standard* as the leader of the 'wayward' and 'troublesome' native-born faction, he stood unsuccessfully in 1883 for Warrnambool in the Legislative Assembly against J. G. Francis [q.v.4]. On the latter's death next year Murray won the by-election and remained undefeated for thirty-two years, becoming 'Father of the House'. He had cobbled together support from radicals,

trade unionists, Catholics and the native-born, and soon proved himself as an efficient local member by his part in gaining the railway extension from Camperdown to his town. On 4 April 1888 he married Alice Jane Bateman at Warrnambool.

He was quite uncommonly radical for a provincial member. He had imbibed the doctrines of 'red-hot liberalism' from Sir Graham Berry [q.v.3], supported Henry George's [q.v.4] land tax, Irish Home Rule, one man one vote and the female franchise, hated militarism especially as displayed in the 1890 strike, and was a mocking republican. He detested the plutocracy: 'the desire for the accumulation of wealth destroyed everything that was noble and admirable in the human character'. W. G. Spence [q.v.6] listed him as in 1892-97 a parliamentary member of the Progressive Political League. However, Murray never signed the Labor pledge and always regarded himself as a Liberal.

Alcohol was his problem; as often as not, by most accounts, he was under the influence in the House. 'Never was man more tantalising. He seemed capable of anything, yet achieved nothing ... He could not lead, and he would not follow ... He was caustic, cynical and unequalled in epigrammatic wit ... but perversity possessed him'. In the late 1890s, however, he was cured by J. T. P. Caulfield, became a total abstainer and henceforth frequently lectured frankly on the evils of drink.

Murray outraged Imperial loyalists by vehemently and persistently opposing Australian participation in the 'capitalist' South African War, though he condemned Boer treatment of black Africans. He was often reviled as a traitor but he held his seat narrowly in 1900 against George Maxwell [q.v.]. Thereafter he was unopposed in four elections and in 1908 and 1911 doubled the opposing vote.

Surprisingly the conservative (Sir) William Irvine [q.v.9] selected him in June 1902 as chief secretary and minister of labour after he had seconded the no confidence motion against Peacock [q.v.]. When (Sir) Thomas Bent [q.v.3] took over from Irvine in February 1904 Murray became president of the Board of Land and Works and commissioner of crown lands and survey and carried legislation for closer settlement which had become a widely agreed policy. On 15 August 1906, however, he resigned dramatically on the floor of the House over the issue of compulsory land purchase which Bent opposed; Murray had had enough of Bent's domineering leadership. For two years now, in alliance with W. A. Watt [q.v.] he waged guerilla warfare, satirizing Bent's ebullient style. (Sir) Frederic Eggleston [q.v.8] compared the struggle to 'a bull fight, with Bent the bull,

Murray the toreador, and Watt the chief matador'. 'There never was a more delightful and exasperating stone-waller than Murray. His lambent sarcasm never failed.' Late in 1908 Murray and Watt moved for the kill: Bent's authority was crumbling, several ministers resigned, and on 3 December Murray carried a no confidence motion. After the election Murray was commissioned to form a ministry and Watt backed him as treasurer; Murray took the Chief Secretary's and Labour departments.

Murray's government (8 January 1909-18 May 1912) was essentially a Liberal-country coalition but also covered the period when Liberal factions were formally consolidating in the face of growing Labor strength. At the November 1911 election he won a large majority with two-thirds of the assembly more or less in support. His government continued developmental policies but the Legislative Council blocked its measures of land reform. However, a basic development in state secondary education was carried through, the Country Roads Board was initiated, and public utilities reorganized. Murray spent much of his trip to the Coronation in 1911 examining schemes of electrified public transport. Watt had been generally recognized as the driving-force of the ministry and in mid-May 1912, under some pressure in cabinet, Murray passed the premiership to him while retaining his portfolios.

Murray's health was deteriorating. Roy Bridges [q.v.7] noticed that 'his natural good humour was lost in periods of mental and physical depression'. His heart was giving trouble and he resigned his ministries on 19 February 1913. On 22 December, however, he rejoined Watt as chief secretary, continued under Peacock from June 1914 and in August 1915 even resumed the ministry of labour. Murray withdrew entirely, however, when Peacock reconstructed his ministry in November.

His advanced views on a range of questions before 1900 had taken some living down: that he became a largely disillusioned radical, and 'mellowed', helped him to win the political following which his intellect and parliamentary qualities inspired. He had great natural tact and subtlety in judging the temper of members, together with honesty and generosity. Those who knew him best were certain that his apparent indolence was an affectation of lethargy and that he was a speedy, efficient administrator. His ultimate political achievement, however, was a puny reflection of his hopes and capacity.

One unorthodox cause Murray continued to maintain was his defence of Aborigines, especially those at Framlingham near Warrnambool, many of whom he knew personally. In 1890 he saved part of Framlingham

Reserve in the face of governmental attempts to disperse the Aborigines. As chief secretary in 1902-04 and from 1909 he was formal chairman of the Board for the Protection of the Aborigines and, like none of his predecessors, took his duties seriously. He repeatedly intervened, legislated in 1910 to require the unwilling board to aid half-castes, and eventually in 1913-14 attended all board meetings, then did not convene it but administered directly. Murray was allied with his two sisters, especially Mary who nurtured the Framlingham folk for decades as well as generally working for the local poor.

Jack Murray had hundreds of friends and by all accounts stuck to them. He had keen interests in racing, especially trotting, and cricket and was a trustee of the Melbourne Cricket Ground.

On 4 May 1916 Murray's pony bolted in a Warrnambool street; he pulled him up but when he stepped down from the trap fell dead. He was buried with Presbyterian forms after a state funeral attended by close on 2000 people including Aborigines from Framlingham; the procession was nearly two miles (3 km) long. A portrait is held by the Warrnambool Public Library. His wife and three daughters survived him.

R. Osburne, *The history of Warrnambool from 1847 to 1886* (Melb, 1887); A. Sutherland et al, *Victoria and its metropolis*, 2 (Melb, 1888); E. H. Sugden and F. W. Eggleston, *George Swinburne* (Syd, 1931); C. E. Sayers, *By these we flourish* (Melb, 1969); L. M. Field, *The forgotten war* (Melb, 1979); S. Lawson, *The Archibald paradox* (Melb, 1983); D. Barwick, 'Equity for Aborigines? The Framlingham case' in P. Troy (ed), *A just society?* (Syd, 1981); *Warrnambool Standard*, 15, 18 Feb 1884, 5 May 1916; *Bulletin*, 2 Jan 1892; *Punch* (Melb), 2 Feb 1905, 30 Sept 1909; *T & CJ*, 13 Jan 1909; *Age* and *Argus*, 5 May 1916; *Freeman's J*, 11 May 1916; K. Rollison, Groups and attitudes in the Victorian Legislative Assembly, 1900-1909 (Ph. D. thesis, La Trobe Univ, 1972).

GEOFFREY SERLE

MURRAY, SIR JOHN HUBERT PLUNKETT (1861-1940), colonial administrator, and GEORGE GILBERT AIME (1866-1957), scholar, were born on 29 December 1861 and 2 January 1866 in Sydney, children of (Sir) Terence Aubrey Murray [q.v.2], pastoralist and politician, and his second wife Agnes Ann, née Edwards. Born into a family that had position and property in New South Wales, the boys grew up without advantages of wealth. Having lost his Yarralumla and Winderradeen stations, Terence Murray lived from 1865 on his salary as president of the Legislative Council. The boys absorbed family pioneering stories, but only Hubert had even slight experience of bush life.

Although Sir Terence bequeathed no capital on his death in 1873, he influenced the value that his sons placed on physical and moral courage, public service, learning and tolerance. The boys were imbued with an Irish suspicion of those who presumed privilege and righteousness. The Murrays, Gilbert recalled, were Home Rulers, members of the Aborigines' Protection Society and 'keen on the protection of animals, children, foreigners, heretics, unpopular minorities and the like'. Agnes Murray was an Anglican while Sir Terence respected, and 'but very partially accepted', the Catholicism of his youth. Hubert, named after his father's friend J. H. Plunkett [q.v.2], was baptized as an Anglican, and in 1869 both boys were baptized Catholics. From a family which was 'greatly interested but sceptical', Gilbert became strongly opposed to organized religion. His stance was a central part of his English liberalism. Hubert's later adoption of Catholicism and his interest in his Irish forebears confirmed his view of himself as an outsider among the Australian ascendancy.

For a time a pupil at a non-denominational school, Hubert shifted with the family south of Sydney Harbour through homes of decreasing size to a leased house at Darlinghurst. Aged 9 he sailed to Melbourne to attend a preparatory school. In 1872 he returned to Sydney to go to Sydney Grammar School. By his final year in 1877 he was school-captain and his scholarly and sporting prowess was recognized by numerous prizes.

When Sir Terence died, Lady Murray purchased Springfield, a girls' school close to her Darlinghurst home. Gilbert, after local education, went to Southey's school at Moss Vale and later at Mittagong. Lady Murray and Gilbert sailed in 1877 for England which to Gilbert was 'home'. Hubert followed a year later to attend Brighton College, from which he was expelled for punching a master who called him a 'wild Irishman'. Mature, aloof, accustomed to taking alcohol and confident of his abilities, Hubert seemed to taunt his teachers. He spent part of 1880-81 learning German at a Rhineland academy.

At Oxford Hubert excelled in sport and graduated (B.A., 1886) with first-class honours in Greats. Gilbert, who went from Merchant Taylors' School to be a year behind Hubert at Oxford, recalled his brother sitting 'silent and perhaps bored' among sporting companions who were not his intellectual equal. Hubert went down to London to read for the Bar at Inner Temple and again demonstrated his capacity for mental and physical contest. Without any intellectual or reformist passion for law, Murray passed his examinations, played Rugby for the Harlequins, and won the English amateur heavyweight boxing title. He was called to the Bar in May 1886.

When he sailed for Australia that year he was 14 stone (89 kg), 6ft. 3ins. (191 cm) in height, broad shouldered and agile. Few men had arrived in Sydney with such physical and mental endowment.

At St John's College, Oxford, Gilbert (B.A., 1888) won a succession of scholarships and prizes to establish a reputation as a brilliant classical scholar. Without Hubert's commanding physique he was handsome, and where Hubert was reserved and critical, he was generous and charming. In 1888 Gilbert was offered a fellowship at New College, Oxford, and aged 23 was appointed professor of Greek at the University of Glasgow. It was an exceptional elevation for an inexperienced teacher. On 30 November 1889 he married Lady Mary Henrietta Howard at Castle Howard, Yorkshire.

In Sydney Hubert was given few briefs at his shared Phillip Street chambers and he drank more heavily. His mother, in Sydney to attend his wedding to Sybil Maud Jenkins on 17 July 1889, wrote to Gilbert that it was his 'saunter that annoys the Attorneys'. The apparent arrogance that may have masked some vulnerability, the refusal to engage in small talk and the despondency which sometimes descended on him, all kept clients away. To increase his earnings, Murray went on circuit as a judge's associate and acted for absent crown prosecutors. In 1892 he took a position as a New South Wales parliamentary draftsman, finding some escape from that 'living death in Macquarie St' by continuing to act as a prosecutor. In 1896 he was himself appointed a crown prosecutor, and 'although he had not entirely lived down the infamy of having been at Oxford' he picked up private briefs in country towns.

At first 'bitterly opposed' to the war in South Africa, Hubert sailed for Cape Town as a special service officer in command of a troop-ship in January 1900. He explained that his commitment to military training as officer commanding the volunteer New South Wales Irish Rifles overcame his political and moral doubts. Gilbert maintained his opposition. At first posted to rear areas Hubert eventually fulfilled his ambition for battle near Pretoria in June with the 1st Mounted Infantry Brigade, and later he pursued mobile Boers. Supervising the burning of Boer farms, Murray hated 'the whole business'. He left South Africa after ten months. Commended as an administrator and in action, Murray held the rank of lieut-colonel in the Australian forces and of major in the Imperial service.

Returning to a 'tedious way of earning a living' in the courts of western New South Wales, Murray was now sober and a practising Catholic. His abstemiousness and Catholicism gave him stability but further distanced him from his fellows.

In 1904 he was appointed chief judicial officer of British New Guinea. He had been acting as a district court judge and his application was strongly supported by legal and political leaders, including Sir Edmund Barton [q.v.7]. Murray was 42, physically fit, father of three young children, his marriage under strain, and conscious that he had under-used his intellectual talents. British New Guinea was an escape and an opportunity.

Accompanied by his wife, Murray arrived in Port Moresby in September 1904. Sybil returned to Sydney after a week, and over the next thirty-five years Murray was rarely to have both wife and children in his official residence.

The only trained lawyer in British New Guinea, normally sitting without defence, prosecution or jury, Murray heard all cases coming before the Central Court. He drafted legislation, tendered legal advice to the administration, and was a member of the legislative and executive councils. Within a fortnight he had heard his first cases and he was soon travelling on the government boat to take cases in outer administrative divisions, constantly resisting the special pleading of white settlers. Although aware that in some British colonies attempts were being made to rule through customary laws and to use influential villagers on local courts, Murray maintained the English-Australian legal system. His court procedure was simple, in English and therefore often dependent on interpreters, and at sentencing he took customs into account. From the late 1920s a few Papuans were invited to assist at minor trials, but in 1938 Murray still thought that it would be a long time before even 'trivial offences' could be handed to Papuan magistrates.

Murray had arrived in Port Moresby at a critical time. The colony's population of just over 500 whites generated little income and the few government officers in 'disreputable old tin shanties' were feuding among themselves as they waited for the transformation of the area from British New Guinea to the Australian Territory of Papua. Immediately after the proclamation of the Papua Act in 1906 a Commonwealth royal commission arrived in Port Moresby. In evidence given over two days Murray accused the administrator F. R. Barton, of having a 'nervous dread of Australia and Australian ideas', and of being weak and spiteful; he gave details of the treasurer's drunkenness; and he charged two senior officers with shooting Papuans. The commissioners' report opened the way for the Australian government to remove many of the senior officials and to appoint Murray as acting administrator, then as lieutgovernor in 1908. At what point Murray saw that his evidence would result in his own advancement is unclear, but he was obliged to say in public what he had already written privately in a letter to Prime Minister Alfred Deakin [q.v.8]. Some of those whose careers were damaged by the royal commission stayed in Papua as settlers; their hatred of Murray was intense.

He came to power in an administration committed to providing cheap land for white settlers. After a brief boom the white population stabilized at just over 1000. Murray's protective policies were not tested by strong settler demands for Papuan lands and elected representation. Faced with declining prospects some settlers in 1920 launched a virulent attack on Murray's administration for its 'hostility to progress' and 'its contempt of the white race'. Murray countered with well-argued letters to the minister and in published writings.

Claiming that Papuans would have no reason to be grateful to Australians if they were just 'hewers of wood and drawers of water for European settlers', Murray introduced the Native Taxation and Native Plantations Ordinances. By the time the trees which villagers were required to plant had matured, the 1929 Depression had reduced prices, and the Papuans had to be compelled to keep the plantations in production. The tax money paid a subsidy to mission schools and placed reading books and some sports equipment in a few villages.

Murray travelled frequently by boat and foot, and insisted that his outside officers patrol regularly. His strongly worded instructions of 1909, telling officers that they were never justified in 'firing on natives by way of punishment' and warning them that self-defence would not always protect them from charges of manslaughter, were issued when punitive expeditions were common in German New Guinea and still took place in north Australia. Partly as a result of the poverty of his administration and partly conforming to his ideals, most exploring expeditions were small and dependent on bushmanship, endurance and a calm confidence to advance peacefully. By the late 1930s Murray was justly proud of the way his 'outside men' had opened vast areas to government influence.

Murray read current anthropology and created the post of government anthropologist. He was influenced by the functionalists' view of culture and depopulation, but he took issue with those who wanted to stand in the way of all change. Most of Murray's opinions derived from wider humane studies and his own shrewd observations. The rejection of 'the unity of mankind' was, he thought, the basis for the worst outrages on black people and he denounced those who argued that the native was a child. Murray believed that some Papuans could be trained to be lawyers and doctors, but that the average Papuan was less intelligent than the average European. His views were more liberal than those of nearly all white residents in Papua. He published two books, *Papua or British New Guinea* (1914) and *Papua of today* (1925), and his annual reports were widely read.

In 1919 Murray served as chairman of the royal commission into late German New Guinea. Angry at the flogging and shooting that continued under Australian rule, Murray wanted to combine the two territories and head the new administration. The government accepted the report of his fellow commissioners Atlee Hunt [q.v.9] and Walter Lucas [q.v.] to keep the territories separate and impose harsh expropriation penalties on the Germans. Murray admitted that he had 'great difficulty in not killing' Hunt and Lucas. By the late 1930s Murray opposed amalgamation, fearing that the combined territories would then pass to less humane control. Papua, he argued, was ultimately to be an Australian State, and New Guinea, under the terms of the mandate, was to be independent.

Murray was reluctant to impose the death penalty. Only two Papuans were hanged in the last twenty years of his rule while some sixty-five men were hanged in the Mandated Territory of New Guinea. But he administered similar petty discriminatory laws about dress and behaviour, and he legislated for savage penalties for attacks on white women.

Sybil Murray died in 1929. Companionship escaped Murray a second time. He married an Irish widow, Mildred Vernon, née Trench, at St Mary's Cathedral, Sydney, on 20 February 1930. In the 'affair Mildred' Murray suffered 'a torrent of abuse' and financial loss before a separation was arranged. In spite of long absences, he maintained affectionate relationships with his three children. Leonard Murray, his nephew, served as official secretary in Papua for twenty-five years and succeeded Hubert in office.

By the 1930s Murray's worst enemies had died, his writings had gained him a reputation beyond Papua, and many white residents had come to take pride in what they believed was an advanced and benign 'native policy'. Murray was appointed C.M.G. in 1914 and K.C.M.G. in 1925. Throughout his long career he often complained of boredom, feared that anti-Catholics or conservatives would have him replaced, and privately greeted all honours with self-mocking cynicism. He had the friendship and respect of many Papuans who confidently approached him for aid and advice.

After his death from lymphatic leukemia in office at Samarai on 27 February 1940, Murray was mourned by all peoples in Papua. On his modest grave in the old Port Moresby cemetery the epitaph in Latin proclaims: 'If you seek a monument look about you'. It is inappropriate. Murray's administration never had the funds to build and Murray sought no physical monuments. His achievements lay in his probity, his capacity to instil loyalty and pride in a poorly paid staff, and his determination to reduce the blatant injustices of colonialism. Without Murray more Papuans would have been shot, bashed and become landless labourers. Ahead of much educated opinion at his appointment, Murray in his last decade in office could have done more to educate Papuans and give them greater responsibility in government. But after three decades in Government House he was probably still better informed about recent developments in colonial administration and more enlightened in practice than any likely replacement.

Gilbert and Hubert rarely met in later life, but their correspondence was frank and they took pride in each other's achievements. Appointed Regius professor of Greek at Oxford in 1908, Gilbert was a brilliant lecturer and a distinguished and productive scholar. His many translations opened classical Greek literature to a generation of English readers, and his historical and critical writings influenced the perception of Greek culture. Active in the English theatre, he had a wide interest in contemporary literary and intellectual movements.

Near the end of his life Gilbert said that not a day had passed when he had not thought about working 'for peace and for Hellenism'. From the start of World War I he began campaigning for an international movement to ensure a sustained peace. He was foundation chairman of the League of Nations Union in 1923-38 and president of its successor, the United Nations Association. After he retired from his Oxford chair in 1936 he remained active as a writer and as a speaker and organizer for liberal causes. In 1941 he was awarded the Order of Merit.

Married into the English aristocracy and a lifelong Liberal, Gilbert was more interested in bringing benefits to the under-privileged than in encouraging them to act for their own advantage. By the 1950s he was out of sympathy with the aspirations of the new nations outside western Europe. Survived by two of his five children, he died on 20 May 1957 at his Berkshire home; his ashes were buried in Westminster Abbey. His *Unfinished autobiography* was published in 1960.

L. Lett, *Sir Hubert Murray of Papua* (Syd, 1949); F. West, *Hubert Murray* (Melb, 1968), and (ed), *Selected letters of Hubert Murray* (Melb, 1970) and *Gilbert Murray, a life* (Lond, 1984); Murray family papers (NL); Murray papers (ML); Dept of Territories files (AAO, Canb).   H. N. NELSON

MURRAY, PEMBROKE LATHROP (1846-1929), journalist and soldier, was born on 26 July 1846 at Kangaroo Point, near Hobart, son of Robert William Felton Lathrop Murray [q.v.2] and his wife Eleanor, née Dixon. In 1849 he went to England with his mother to join his father who had returned to claim his estate in Shropshire. Following his father's death in 1850 his mother sold the property and returned to Melbourne in 1853.

Initially Murray intended to train for the law and in March 1863 was articled to a Melbourne solicitor. On 30 September 1865 he sailed for England 'to study for the Bar for three years', but returned in November 1866. He moved to Sydney and on 21 May 1870, describing himself as a reporter, married Margaret Mary Therese McDermott at St Patrick's Catholic Church. That year his *The three bears and little Silverhair the charming*, a burlesque pantomime, was produced at the Royal Victoria Theatre on Christmas eve, his dialogue being described as 'smart, witty and fresh, being full of new-made puns and social and political hits'.

In 1871 Murray enlisted in the New South Wales volunteer artillery; he was appointed second lieutenant in 1874 and promoted lieutenant next year. On 5 September 1876 he was commissioned in the colony's permanent artillery. Promoted captain in October 1878, he went to Newcastle in September 1879 with troops sent to settle a colliery strike.

During these years Murray continued writing, contributing articles and stories to the *Australasian* as 'L' for over fifty years; these were chiefly on early Melbourne and Sydney, and the last appeared two days after his death. He also wrote on military subjects. The first of two articles published in the *Sydney University Magazine* in 1878-79 was an account of the development of artillery. Despite his journalistic activities he suffered recurring indebtedness which threatened the loss of his commission, a situation averted by financial assistance from his brother Kynaston. He was granted brevet rank of major in 1888, confirmed in rank in 1891, and for several years commanded a company of artillery in Sydney.

Following his wife's death he married Dublin-born Constance Nora Frances Connors on 2 May 1900 at St Patrick's Church. During the arrival of the governor-general Lord Hopetoun [q.v.9] in Sydney on 15 December Murray commanded a 100-man guard of honour. In March 1901 he went to South Africa in charge of troops on the *Ranee*, and saw active service until July with the column under Lieut-Colonel W. H. Williams. He returned to Sydney in February 1902 but almost immediately was appointed paymaster to the 3rd and 4th Battalions, Australian Com-

monwealth Horse, as a captain. He sailed again in April, returning in August, and was retired on 1 September with honorary rank of lieut-colonel.

Murray was probably the compiler of an unpublished 1903 manuscript entitled 'Historical record of the New South Wales regiment of Royal Australian Artillery'. He was employed after retirement in the Department of Defence, Melbourne, where he compiled and edited *The official records of the Australian military contingents to the war in South Africa* (1912). He described his work— still a standard source—as 'not a history of the war' but 'a statistical register and reference'.

He returned to Sydney about 1926 and lived at Woollahra. Survived by two sons and two daughters of his first marriage, he died in the Sacred Heart Hospice on 26 September 1929 and was buried in South Head cemetery.

J (LC NSW), 1875-76, 2, p 797, 1876-77, 2, p 593; *London Gazette*, 2 Apr 1902; *Town Courier* (Hob), 28 Feb 1849; *Argus*, 2 Oct 1865, 24 Nov 1866, 11 Oct 1929; *SMH*, 26 Dec 1870, 28 Sept, 1 Oct 1929; information from, and records in possession of, Mr G. G. L. Murray, Port Macquarie, NSW, and Mr C. L. Murray, Bairnsdale, Vic.

C. D. COULTHARD-CLARK

MURRAY, RUSSELL MERVYN (1877-1945), mining engineer, was born on 12 July 1877 at Elliminyt, Victoria, son of Victorian-born parents Andrew Strachan Murray, grazier, and his wife Florence Eleanor, née Blunden. His grandfather Hugh Murray, son of Hugh Murray [q.v.2], had settled in the Colac district during the Tasmanian pastoral exodus in the 1830s. Russell was to re-cross Bass Strait as a pioneer of modern mining.

Educated at Colac Grammar School and the University of Melbourne (B.C.E., 1900), Murray applied several times for employment with the Mount Lyell Mining & Railway Co., Tasmania, before being appointed draftsman and assistant surveyor at Gormanston in 1900. He became acting manager of the Mount Lyell mines on the death of W. T. Batchelor in 1906 and formally engineer-in-charge next year. He succeeded Robert Sticht [q.v.] as general manager in 1922.

Murray had the sort of careful, analytical mind which avoided misplaced optimism and promoted efficiency. He looked, and was, kind and dependable. His courageous and calm direction of rescue operations during the fire at North Lyell in 1912, when forty-two died, earned him the Royal Humane Society's silver medal and the respect of the miners. His subsequent initiation of a scheme for improved living conditions, resembling the welfare programmes evolving at Port Pirie and Wallaroo, South Australia, earned him, in addition, the miners' gratitude. He deprecated the term 'welfare', preferring 'self-preservation': he saw that the renovation of houses at Gormanston, the provision of social clubs, of cheap firewood, food, electricity and railway fares, the subsidizing of bands, school of mines and soldiers' clubs would prevent the development of that acrimony which the 1912 disaster might have wrought between men and management. Later, Murray's policy proved of great importance in enabling the company to survive the post-war slump in copper prices.

During his period of management Murray introduced large-scale changes in mining operations. In 1906-22 he oversaw the development of the Mount Lyell complex as the biggest group of underground mines in Australia. From 1922 until he retired in 1944, crippled by arthritis, he supervised the swing back to open-cut mining as appropriate for the large-scale exploitation of the remaining low-grade copper deposits. He recommended the installation of an electrolytic copper refinery after his visit to the United States of America in 1926.

A leading exponent of industrial legislation, Murray was president of the Australian Institute of Mining and Metallurgy in 1927; he was also a member of the American Institute of Mining and Metallurgical Engineers. In a peripatetic profession he was unusual in spending his entire working life on one field. Locally he remained popular: he was elected warden of Gormanston every year from 1920 until his death from coronary disease at Queenstown on 22 January 1945.

Murray had married Vivienne Douglas with Anglican rites in Hobart on 15 November 1905. She survived him with their two daughters and three sons, the eldest of whom, Hugh Mervyn, became general manager of Mount Lyell in 1948. Murray's estate, consisting mainly of government bonds, was valued for probate at £27 737.

G. Blainey, *The peaks of Lyell* (Melb, 1967); *Weekly Courier* (Launc), 18 May 1922; *Mercury*, 23 Jan 1945.   ANN G. SMITH

MUSCIO, BERNARD (1887-1926), philosopher and pioneer industrial psychologist, was born on 7 April 1887 at Purfleet, Manning River district, New South Wales, son of Bernard Muscio, Swiss farmer, and his native-born second wife Eliza Anne, née Isaacs, formerly White. He suffered from organic heart disease and was educated privately by L. F. Meagher. Entering the University of Sydney in 1907, he won the Lithgow scholarship for philosophy in 1909 and graduated B.A. in 1910 and M.A. in 1912, both times with first-class honours and the University medal in logic and mental philosophy; his thesis was 'Pragmatism—the present position of psychological theory'.

Awarded the Woolley [q.v.6] travelling scholarship he studied philosophy with James Ward and others and psychology with C. S. Myers, while at Gonville and Caius College, Cambridge, (B.A., 1913; M.A., 1919). In 1913 he won the Burney prize for his essay, 'Determinism and freewill' and next year a Burney studentship; he wrote a thesis on 'Idealism and the neo-realism'. Rejected for military service, he was demonstrator in experimental psychology (1914-16). On 31 March 1915 at West Derby, near Liverpool, he married Florence Mildred Fry [q.v. Muscio]. In 1913-16 he published three papers in leading philosophical journals and a long experimental report in the *British Journal of Psychology*.

Back in Sydney in 1916 Muscio was acting lecturer in logic and mental philosophy at the university for three years. His series of public lectures on industrial psychology embodying recent empirical work in the United States of America, Britain and Europe, and dealing with such topics as fatigue, vocational selection and methods of work, were published in Sydney in 1917 and reprinted in London in 1919. This publication was the earliest British statement of the aims, scope and value of industrial psychology.

Muscio returned to Cambridge in 1919 to become organizing secretary and lecturer for the Industrial Fatigue Research Board. He wrote some nine reports for the board based on surveys of current thought, experimental investigations and studies in factories, which were published as monographs or as journal articles. Two of these were of considerable significance, one dealing critically with current conceptions of fatigue and the other with an experimental demonstration that motor ability was not a unitary trait.

In 1922 Muscio was appointed to the Challis [q.v.3] chair of philosophy at the University of Sydney, after strong support from Ward who praised his philosophical talents but regarded his activities in experimental and industrial psychology as an unfortunate diversion from his main field. In the event Muscio made a greater mark in industrial psychology than in philosophy. He wrote some papers but they were comments on philosophy rather than analyses of particular problems and concepts; he had not worked out his basic position but he seems to have been shaking off the remnants of earlier idealism. He was a founder and first president of the Australasian Association of Psychology and Philosophy.

Muscio was still adjusting to his professorial tasks when he died, childless, of heart disease at his Potts Point home on 27 May 1926; he was cremated. His wife survived him.

A'sian J of Psychology and Philosophy, 4, no 3, 1926, p 157; *Aust J of Psychology*, 23, no 3, 1971, p 235; *SMH*, 28, 29 May 1926.   W. M. O'NEIL

MUSCIO, FLORENCE MILDRED (1882-1964), feminist, was born on 28 April 1882 at Copeland, New South Wales, eldest daughter of English-born Charles Fry, telegraph master, and his native-born wife Jane, née McLennan. Known as Mildred, she was educated at the Sydney Girls' High School and the University of Sydney, graduating B.A. in 1901 with first-class honours in logic and mental philosophy and M.A. in 1905. Next year, with her sister Edith, she published *Poems*. She worked as a teacher while completing her studies, and was principal of the Brighton College for Girls, Manly, in 1906-12.

In England she taught at Crosby, Lancashire, before marrying Bernard Muscio [q.v.] on 31 March 1915. She shared her husband's interests, and his university posts allowed her to continue studying and enjoy the company of students and graduates. Back in Sydney permanently from 1922, she was president of the Sydney University Women Graduates' Association (1923-26) and the Sydney University Women's Union (1927-28), and later an executive-member of the Sydney University Settlement. After her husband's death in 1926 she helped to form the Institute of Industrial Psychology in Sydney, and lectured in psychology for the University Extension Board.

Mildred Muscio's association with the National Council of Women of New South Wales began in 1922 when she was invited to organize the Good Film League. She joined the council's executive and was president in 1927-38. She was also federal president in 1927-31 and led the Australian delegation to the Vienna conference of the International Council of Women in 1930. During the Depression she defended the right of women to employment and maintained that a separate women's movement was necessary. In 1931 she considered standing for the Federal Senate.

Mrs Muscio served on the Commonwealth royal commission on child endowment in 1927; the minority report she submitted with John Curtin called for the immediate introduction of a Federal child endowment scheme. In 1929 she was a founding member of the Board of Social Study and Training, which issued a certificate for professional training in social work, and when the two-year diploma course was taken over by the university in 1940 she continued on the supervisory board. She served on the government committee inquiring into the system of examinations and secondary education in 1933. Before the 1934 inquiry into the Child Welfare Department, she stressed the need for welfare officers trained in psychology and advocated the establishment of counselling clinics.

Among her many other activities, including writing and broadcasting, Mrs Muscio was president of the Lyceum Club and vice-president of the New South Wales Society for Crippled Children, and worked for the Racial Hygiene Association, the Australian Red Cross Society, the New South Wales Bush Nursing Association, the Australian Aerial Medical Services, the Council of Social Services, Travellers' Aid Society, theatrical groups and the sesquicentenary celebrations. Active in the local branch of the League of Nations Union, she was an alternate delegate at the league's general assembly at Geneva in 1937. A friend of Margaret Bailey [q.v.7], for many years she served on the council of Ascham School where her sister Eva was senior mathematics mistress in 1917-45.

Mildred Muscio was appointed O.B.E. in 1938. A gifted speaker, fluent and logical, she was admired for her organizing ability, generosity, impartiality and 'sympathetic spirit'. She died, childless, in hospital at Ryde on 17 August 1964 and was cremated with Anglican rites.

National Council of Women (NSW), *Biennial Report*, 1933-34, 1936-38; *Housewife* (Syd) Dec 1933; *National Council of Women News*, Oct 1964; *Australasian*, 22 Oct 1927; *Queenslander*, 3 Nov 1927; *SMH*, 18 Apr 1931, 3 July 1934, 11 June 1937, 9 June, 3 Dec 1938.   MEREDITH FOLEY
GILLIAN FULLOON

MUSGRAVE, ANTHONY (1895-1959), entomologist, was born on 9 July 1895 at Cooktown, Queensland, son of Anthony Musgrave, Antigua-born deputy commissioner and government secretary of British New Guinea, and his Queensland-born wife Elizabeth Anne, née Colles; he was a great-nephew of Sir Anthony Musgrave [q.v.5]. Educated at Hayfield Preparatory School, Homebush, and at Sydney Church of England Grammar School (Shore), he joined the Australian Museum, Sydney, as a cadet in February 1910. After a year in the library he was appointed assistant to the entomologist W. J. Rainbow and began his life's work with an insect survey of Sydney's (Royal) Botanic Gardens and an expedition in 1916 to the Barrington Tops, New South Wales.

He studied art with Julian Ashton [q.v.7], passed examinations in zoology at the Sydney

Technical College and the University of Sydney (though he did not take a degree), and on Rainbow's death was appointed entomologist at the museum on 1 June 1920. The appointment was later altered to curator of entomology.

Musgrave developed a profound knowledge of insects and arachnida but chose to specialize in *Hemiptera* and *Diptera* (notably *Nycteribiidae*), venomous spiders and ticks. He carried out extensive field-work in every State (except Western Australia), New Guinea, the Great Barrier Reef and Lord Howe Island. He contributed almost two hundred notes and papers (many early ones illustrated by his own drawings) to scientific journals including the *Australian Museum Magazine*, but is perhaps best remembered for his monumental and meticulous *Bibliography of Australian entomology, 1775-1930; with biographical notes on authors and collectors*, published by the Royal Zoological Society of New South Wales in 1932 and subsequently kept up to date on cards. For about twenty years he compiled all the zoological entries for *Australian Science Abstracts* until they ceased publication in 1957.

In 1920 he joined the Linnean Society of New South Wales and became a member of its subcommittee on phenological observations. He was a council-member of the Zoological Society, 1920-35, president 1929-30, and fellow (1933). He was also a fellow of the Entomological Society, London. In July 1934 he represented the museum at the Museums' Association conference at Bristol, England, and visited Ireland and the Continent.

Musgrave also contributed material to the first two editions of the *Australian encyclopaedia*. He joined the Royal Australian Historical Society in 1950 (councillor 1956-57); in 1954 he published a history of his native Cooktown in its *Journal and Proceedings* of which he and others in 1958 published a comprehensive index. Unmarried, he died suddenly of heart disease in Royal North Shore Hospital, Sydney, on 4 June 1959 and was cremated with Anglican rites.

An excellent lecturer and photographer, illustrating many of his talks with slides of great technical excellence and beauty, Musgrave was of a retiring nature and disliked publicity. He always found time to identify thousands of specimens brought by a continuous stream of museum visitors. A 'natural gentleman', he enjoyed music, theatre and literature, especially of travel and philosophy, and golf was his favourite weekend relaxation. *Punch* and the lyrics of Gilbert and Sullivan appealed to his rich sense of humour; he told his friend and colleague G. P. Whitley that Talbot Mundy's *Om* (Indianapolis, 1924) was the novel that most influenced him.

In his presidential address to the Zoological Society in 1930 Musgrave had divided the history of Australian entomological research from 1770-1929 into three periods: the Fabrician to 1830, the Westwoodian to 1861 and the Macleayan [q.v.2 W. S. Macleay] to 1929. According to Whitley, posterity might well regard Musgrave's great systematic work on the subject from 1930 to 1959 as the Musgravian period.

R. Strahan (ed), *Rare and curious specimens* (Syd, 1979); Roy Zoological Soc NSW, *Procs*, 1958-59; *Aust Museum Mag*, 13, no 3, Sept 1959; *J of Soc for Bibliog of Natural Hist*, 3, no 7, 1960, p 380; *RAHSJ*, 45, Jan 1960, p 281; Linnean Soc NSW, *Procs*, 86, pt 1, 1961, p 11.   G. P. WALSH

MUSKETT, ALICE JANE (1869-1936), artist and author, was born on 28 April 1869 at Fitzroy, Melbourne, only daughter of English parents Charles Muskett, bookseller, and his wife Phoebe, daughter of Arthur Charlwood, printer and bookseller. After Charles died in 1873 Phoebe carried on the business. In 1885, with Alice, she followed her son Philip, medical practitioner, to Sydney. Next year she died.

From this time Alice was the second pupil of Julian Ashton [q.v.7], who was persuaded to provide Sydney's first life-class for women. He recognized her ability, 'refined and sensitive nature' and beauty: his 1893 study in oils shows her in class with light auburn hair, high-necked white dress and pince-nez. She exhibited annually from 1890 with the Art Society of New South Wales (council-member, 1894) and with the professional breakaway Society of Artists, Sydney, from its first exhibition in 1895.

In 1895-98 Alice Muskett studied at the Académie Colarossi in Paris and wrote a lively description for the Sydney *Daily Telegraph*. In 1896 she exhibited at the Salon de la Société des Artistes Français and her work was included in the 1898 Exhibition of Australian Art in London. Her 1898 'Study of Roses' and 'In Cumberland Street' (Sydney, 1902) were bought by the National Art Gallery of New South Wales.

In Sydney Alice also published verse and short stories. She was a committee-member of the revived Society of Artists in 1907. In 1909 D. H. Souter [q.v.] called her 'probably the most talented of our women painters', noting her preference for a decorative, imaginative approach in which design dominated subject. She lived with her brother Philip, also unmarried, in Elizabeth Street. He wrote widely-sold books on infant health and diet and medical guides that featured women's diseases and their reproductive functions. He died following a nervous breakdown on 9 August 1909. Next year Alice Muskett went abroad, visited the exhibition of the Royal Academy of Arts and wrote a tart account for *Art and Architecture*—British art did not impress her.

Back in Sydney by 1912, she was active in the Society of Women Painters and shared a studio with Florence Rodway [q.v.]. During World War I she worked at a soldiers' canteen in London, returning to Sydney in 1921. In 1928 she endowed the annual Philip Muskett prize at Ashton's Sydney Art School to encourage landscape painting.

As 'Jane Laker' (her maternal grandmother's name) Alice published a novel, *Among the reeds*, in 1933. It had been written and set in Sydney in 1913 and, like her short stories, seems partly autobiographical. Her fiction suggests a love affair which came to nothing: there is a recurring renunciatory theme, or perhaps she lost a lover in the war. *Among the reeds* is remarkable for its feminist point of view; it depicts conflict between Bohemian, artistic values and middle-class conventions and the dilemma faced by women of 'Jane's' class in choosing between marriage and a career. The narrator advocates her version of rights for women: to learn a trade, craft or profession; to enjoy everyday happiness or one big ecstasy; to have a room of her own; at least once to be made love to; and to know the joy of payment for work. The style is anecdotal and discursive but shows flashes of psychological insight, and reveals the author's 'engaging and vigorous' personality. The book evokes a lively sense of the city and of the 'North Shore line'.

The Depression eroded Miss Muskett's finances. From the late 1920s she rented rooms at Neutral Bay. In 1933 she suffered a cerebral haemorrhage and died on 17 July 1936 at Cremorne; she was cremated and her ashes buried in Philip's grave in the Anglican section of Waverley cemetery. Her many small bequests included books to neighbourhood children and £50 to Ashton 'for use during illness'. Ashton made three portraits of Alice: his 1893 study and 'The Coral Necklet' are in the Art Gallery of New South Wales and Will Dyson's [q.v.8] wash drawing of a diminutive, dainty Alice is in the Australian National Gallery, Canberra.

J. R. Ashton, *Now came still evening on* (Syd, 1941); C. Ambrus, *The ladies' picture show* (Syd, 1984); *Art and Architecture*, 6, no 2, 1909, 7, no 4, 1910; *VHM*, May 1935; *Australasian*, 7 June 1873, 28 Aug 1909; *Table Talk*, 17 Apr 1896; *Daily Telegraph* (Syd), 24 Feb, 2 Mar, 22 Aug, 12 Sept 1896, 27 Aug 1898; *T&CJ*, 1 Sept 1909; *SMH*, 13 Sept 1928; Lambert family papers (ML); H. M. Green papers, held by D. Green, Campbell, ACT; information from D. Dysart, S. H. Ervine Gallery, Syd, Dr L. Marun, Registrar, Art Gallery of NSW, Syd, C. Bruce, Power Inst of Fine Arts, Univ Syd, R. Ashton, Dee Why, Syd.   SUZANNE EDGAR
DOROTHY GREEN

MUSSEN, SIR GERALD (1872-1960), entrepreneur, journalist and industrial relations consultant, was born on 17 October 1872 at Dunedin, New Zealand, son of Henry Garrett Mussen, surveyor, and his wife Harriett Alice, née Drew. He was educated at Southland High School, Invercargill. In 1897 he joined the gold rush to Coolgardie where he survived typhoid fever, then became a freelance journalist in Sydney. On 21 November 1900 he married Florence Elizabeth Gordon at Roseville and next year moved to Melbourne to report Federal politics for the Sydney *Daily Telegraph*. He became a close friend of W. S. Robinson [q.v.] and an associate of W. L. Baillieu [q.v.7], superintending his investments in 1908-10 and investigating plans in London and Germany to develop Victoria's brown coal. Through his friendship with the Labor leaders J. C. Watson [q.v.] and W. M. Hughes [q.v.9] Mussen helped to reconcile the Labor government and the mining companies after Hughes's military raid on Collins House in November 1914.

W. S. Robinson, as managing director of Broken Hill Associated Smelters Pty Ltd at Port Pirie, South Australia, in 1915 turned to Mussen, who 'understood and sympathised with the Australian worker' and agreed about worker welfare schemes for assisting with labour and community problems. In 1917 Mussen was the company's full-time industrial adviser, heading its welfare and publicity department with journalistic flair, imagination and drive. He found Port Pirie a raw, industrial town where workers' families 'walk the dusty streets, look in the shop windows and as there is nowhere to sit down and nothing to see they go home again'.

There were no amenities at the plant and no sickness and accident insurance, despite the serious risk of lead poisoning from dust and fumes. Mussen, supported by Robinson and (Sir) Colin Fraser [q.v.8], introduced housing, industrial safety and health measures: smelter workers had lunch and changing rooms, accident and sickness insurance, first-aid care and a provident fund. To reduce living costs B.H.A.S. established boarding-houses, a co-operative store and a firewood scheme, and to discourage absenteeism in a vital war industry Mussen developed a seaside holiday-camp. He collaborated with town planner Charles Reade [q.v.] to improve conditions: B.H.A.S. donated £1000 to a soldiers' memorial park, contributed to charities, and commissioned Reade to design a housing estate. Hundreds of men in what Mussen publicized as 'the world's largest working bee' built a twelve-acre (5 ha) children's playground in one day. During the conscription and industrial turmoil of 1916-17 Mussen used his influence with the local press and unions to isolate militants from Broken Hill, New South Wales, and consolidate support behind the war effort.

While he preached the 'gospel of happiness', delivering the Joseph Fisher [q.v.4] lecture at the University of Adelaide in 1919 on 'The humanizing of commerce and industry', Mussen promoted himself as the 'single and lone specialist in Australia on this particular type of work'. After his success at Port Pirie he was appointed 'consulting industrialist' to the troubled field at Broken Hill in March 1919, reluctantly accepting £1000 a year instead of the £5000 he had nominated. Delays and disagreements notwithstanding, his proposals for a welfare trust won support from Baillieu, Fraser, Robinson, W. E. Wainwright [q.v.], James Hebbard and (Sir) Herbert Gepp [q.v.8], and the companies subscribed £42 900 to the Barrier Industrial Association formed for this purpose.

Mussen found his efforts to improve industrial relations nullified by mounting conflict over the miners' union's 'revolutionary' log of claims and by demarcation disputes, but he worked with the hospital board and union leaders to fund a children's ward and, during the influenza epidemic, organized treatment facilities. Militants, however, denounced his policies as 'palliatives, sops, and doles to chloroform the worker' and the union paper attacked him as 'the greatest menace Broken Hill unionists have ever had to fight'. Mussen was a negotiator during the strike of 1919-20, suggesting a lead bonus to soften the hard line of Cyril Emery, the irascible president of the mine managers' association. With his assistant Baxter Cook [q.v.8] he supervised the purchase and refitting of the Palace Hotel as a club for the Returned Soldiers' Association, the funding of the Barrier Distress Association and municipal relief works, and assisted the medical commission of Professor H. G. Chapman [q.v.7].

Mussen's close association with the owner-editor of the *Barrier Miner*, J. E. Davidson [q.v.8], led to the founding of the Adelaide *News* in 1922-23. It was as a newspaper proprietor that Mussen followed experiments to make paper pulp from short-fibred eucalyptus hardwood. In 1924 he was a negotiator between the Van Diemen's Land Co. and Amalgamated Zinc (de Bavay's [q.v.8] Ltd (controlled by Collins House) for tracts of Tasmanian forest and an intended mill site at Burnie. When Collins House lost interest, Mussen bought 125 000 acres (51 000 ha) and the mill site from the V.D.L. Co. and further options, all of which he transferred to Canberra Activities Pty Ltd. He lobbied the

Tasmanian and Federal governments and urged his case before two parliamentary committees. The Lyons [q.v.] Tasmanian government legislated to encourage a wood pulp and paper industry. Canberra Activities sold out in 1930 to Paper Makers Pty Ltd, which Mussen helped to form with the essential support of (Sir) Colin Fraser [q.v.8]. The project continued to languish through the Depression. In 1936, however, Associated Pulp & Paper Mills Ltd was formed. Throughout tortuous manoeuvres, Mussen had remained supremely confident. The company's first chairman Sir Walter Massy-Greene [q.v.] considered him 'an optimist—perhaps dangerously so', but recognized his pluck and courage. Mussen remained a major shareholder. In 1939 he was knighted.

Mussen formulated a comprehensive social welfare policy for the 750 employees at Burnie. Family medical and hospital cover was provided for a nominal contribution and in 1941, a dental clinic, financed by a production bonus. Such further innovations as a life assurance scheme and a scholarship fund, administered by a council of employees and management, were among the most original and advanced in Australia.

Mussen was active also as chairman of the Victorian Central Citrus Association (1924-30) and of the Federal Citrus Association (1927-30). He developed the fish-canning industry at Port Lincoln, South Australia, from 1937. During World War II he was a vigorous publicist for the war effort and national planning, advocating in many speeches the goals of full employment, improved health and education services, better housing and town planning. In 1944 he published *Australia's tomorrow*. Ever an optimist, Mussen believed most causes of human suffering and misery were 'remediable'. His confidence was infectious and his broad sympathies and liberal views lifted the spirit of his staff and employees, who knew him simply as 'Muss'. He was personally reticent and preferred to avoid the limelight. His strength lay in negotiation and public relations rather than in original thought.

After a lingering illness Mussen died on 21 March 1960 in a Melbourne private hospital and was cremated with Anglican rites. Two sons and a daughter survived him.

W. S. Robinson, *If I remember rightly*, G. Blainey ed (Melb, 1967); B. Kennedy, *Silver, sin and sixpenny ale* (Melb, 1978), and *A tale of two mining cities* (Melb, 1984); *Bulletin*, 9, 16 Dec 1959; C. B. Johnstone, A history of the origins, formation and development of B.H.A.S. Pty. Ltd. at Port Pirie, South Australia (Ph.D. thesis, Univ Melb, 1982); A. G. L. Shaw, MS on Australian Pulp & Paper Mills Ltd.   B. E. KENNEDY

MUSTAR (MUSTARD), ERNEST ANDREW (1893-1971), soldier and aviator, was born on 21 September 1893 at Oakleigh, Victoria, son of William Edward Mustard, labourer, and his wife Alice, née Usher, both Victorian born. He was educated at state schools and in 1911 was appointed clerk in the engineering branch of Victorian Railways. That year he became an early possessor of an amateur wireless licence.

After a year in the Corps of Australian Signallers and two years in the 21st Signal Troop, Australian Engineers (both militia), Mustard enlisted as a private in August 1914 in the 1st Signal Troop, Australian Imperial Force, and embarked two months later. He served at Gallipoli from the landing (with the 29th British Division at Cape Helles) to the evacuation, and was promoted corporal in November 1915. From July 1916 to January 1917 he served with the signals in the Sinai campaign. Wounded at Bir el Abd on 9 August 1916, he was promoted sergeant in September. After the battle of Rafa he transferred to the Imperial Camel Corps as second lieutenant and signal officer attached to headquarters of the 4th Anzac Battalion.

In June 1917 Mustard joined No. 1 Squadron, Australian Flying Corps, in which, after instruction in aerial gunnery, he became an observer. Short, 'sturdy, snappy and wiry', 'Pard', as he was invariably called, earned respect for his 'bag' of enemy planes and for the accuracy and comprehensiveness of his reconnaissance reports. His exploits with Captain (Sir) Ross Smith [q.v.], such as interrupting their breakfast to shoot down German aircraft at Deraa, won them a reputation as one of the outstanding pilot-observer partnerships of the war. Mustard was awarded the Order of the Nile and the Distinguished Flying Cross. After flying instruction with the Royal Air Force in England in 1918 he returned to Australia in April 1919.

Demobilized, Mustard spent a short period flying commercially, offering joy-rides to residents of country towns, then in 1922 joined the Royal Australian Air Force as captain. He conducted aerial surveys of Lake Eyre in 1922 and, with the Royal Australian Navy, of the Great Barrier Reef in 1925. Turning to civil aviation, Mustard next year became chief pilot and instructor of the Aero Club of Victoria. While working at Essendon he was approached by representatives of Guinea Gold, No Liability, on behalf of its founder C. J. Levien [q.v.], who sought to introduce air transport to the Mandated Territory of New Guinea, to service its new Edie Creek goldfield, perched at 7500 ft. (2290 m) on a mountainside near Wau.

In March 1927 Mustard arrived with his DH37 by sea at Rabaul and flew it to Lae. In April he lifted it across the densely wooded,

precipitous mountains behind Lae and, after three fruitless attempts to locate Wau, landed on 17 April on its newly constructed airstrip. On this pioneer flight of 1½ hours his payload of 600 lbs (272 kg) represented the work of fifteen carriers for three weeks. Later that year as chief pilot of Guinea Airways, a subsidiary of G.G.N.L., he visited Dessau, Germany, and purchased a Junkers W34, an all-metal monoplane, which he assembled at Rabaul and flew to Lae and Wau in April 1928. On his return he was appointed a director of Guinea Airways. In December he flew a second Junkers, as a seaplane, from Point Cook in Victoria to New Guinea. The progress of the first seaplane flight along the entire eastern Australian coast until its completion on schedule was closely monitored by the Australian press.

Exhausted by continual flying and debilitated by malaria, Mustard left New Guinea in March 1929 to become an aviation representative for the Vacuum Oil Co. in Melbourne. On 19 April at Scots Church he married Margot Sara Munro, who had persuaded him to change his name to Mustar. While in Melbourne he encouraged Placer Development Ltd, a Canadian company with an option over the Bulolo valley, to initiate the transportation by air of dredging machinery, and negotiated with Junkers the purchase of a three-engined G31, modified to his specifications. Returning to New Guinea in January 1931 to establish a fuel depot for Vacuum Oil at Lae, he supervised the preparations for the flying-in of the dredges, which in March began operation in the Bulolo valley.

In 1934 Mustar returned to Australia and next year was appointed managing director of Australian Transcontinental Airways. In World War II he served on R.A.A.F. headquarters staff at Laverton and in 1941 was appointed squadron leader. After the war he became officer in charge of records, Department of Air, retiring with the rank of group captain. He died suddenly on holiday at Coolangatta, Queensland, on 10 October 1971 and was cremated. His wife, son and daughter survived him.

F. M. Cutlack, *The Australian Flying Corps* (Syd, 1923); I. Idriess, *Gold-dust and ashes* (Syd, 1933); L. W. Sutherland and N. Ellison, *Aces and kings* (Syd, 1935); F. Clune, *D'air devil* (Syd, 1941); *Pacific Islands Mthly*, Sept 1932, Aug 1940, Nov 1941; *Argus*, 21 Feb 1940; C. V. T. Wells papers (NL).

DIANE LANGMORE

MUTCH, THOMAS DAVIES (1885-1958), journalist, politician and historian, was born on 17 October 1885 at Lambeth, London, eldest child of William Mutch, Scottish omnibus driver, and his second wife Sarah, née Davies. He arrived in Sydney on 24 March 1887 with his parents and four half-brothers. Educated at Double Bay Public School, he left home and school after his mother died in 1899 and worked for four years in outback shearing-sheds. An enthusiastic reader, he absorbed socialist literature and the bush tradition. He was an executive-member of the Australian Workers' Union in 1903-17.

Returning to Sydney in 1903, Mutch joined the staff of the *Australian Worker* and met Henry Lawson [q.v.]. He tried to wean Lawson from drink, in 1910 camped with him at Mallacoota, Victoria, and Cape Howe, and in 1914 accompanied him on a pilgrimage to his boyhood home at Eurunderee. At Neutral Bay, Sydney, on 23 September 1912 Mutch had married a divorcée Edith Marjorie Hasenkam, née Coskerie.

In 1909 he had organized the Australian Writers' and Artists' Union, which in 1913 merged with the Australian Journalists' Association; he was president of the State branch and vice-president of the federal council in 1915-16.

A member of the State Labor central executive in 1913-17, Mutch was a delegate to federal Labor conferences in 1916 and 1918. A socialist visionary, stubborn with a burning sense of justice, he was regarded as a radical within the party. At its Easter conference in 1916 he was a founder of the 'Industrial Section' and was among the first to vigorously campaign against conscription.

In March 1917 Mutch was elected to the Legislative Assembly for Botany; Lawson told the electors that Mutch 'is the straightest mate I ever had'—even if he did take 'pyjamas in his swag'. He worked tenaciously for the release of Donald Grant [q.v.9] and the other eleven imprisoned members of the Industrial Workers of the World. A member of the Unions' Defence Committee during the 1917 strike, he was put on a good behaviour bond for calling the police 'paid mental prostitutes' at a Domain meeting. In parliament Mutch soon made his mark as a vibrant speaker: his 'lithe form pulsating with nervous energy; the handsome features lit up by the dark eyes gleaming with merriment or with enthusiasm, or with anger'.

After visiting the United States of America with James Dooley [q.v.8] in 1919, Mutch served as minister of public instruction and for local government from April 1920 to October 1921 under John Storey [q.v.] and continued until April 1922 in his education portfolio under Dooley. An able administrator, he contended with increased classes and chronic shortages of teachers, classroom accommodation and funds. He tried to get more Australian content into school curricula, abolished high school fees, caused a stir when he banned war trophies in schools, gave priority to technical education, and strove to improve educational opportunities in the country. He also reorganized the State Children Relief Department, creating the Child Welfare Department.

An alderman on Mascot Municipal Council in 1921-27, Mutch introduced Acts which established county councils and compulsory registration of architects. He also tried to establish a main roads board.

However, Mutch's ministerial achievements were obscured by the bitter faction fighting that convulsed the State Labor Party in the 1920s. In 1920 he and Dooley were exonerated by a royal commission into charges of bribery, made by Jack Bailey [q.v.7]. Matured by the realities of office and leader of the Freemasons in caucus, Mutch gradually drifted to the right. In April 1922 he was defeated for the deputy leadership. In 1923 he remained stubbornly loyal to Dooley and castigated Bailey and the communists. On 27 June 1924 Mutch challenged J. T. Lang [q.v.9] for the leadership and lost by one vote, thereby incurring Lang's enmity.

However, Mutch served in Lang's first ministry in 1925-27 as minister for education. He endured pinpricks from the premier and such severe cuts in loan funding that he was goaded into publicly criticizing Lang for starving his department. Lang ordered a secret inquiry by the auditor-general into the Child Welfare Department. In parliament Mutch vigorously defended his departmental officers and denounced the report. Lang blandly ordered a royal commission (which eventually exonerated Mutch and his department). The dissension in cabinet was intensified by the party's new 'Red Rules'; Mutch accused Lang of assuming dictatorial powers. On 27 May 1927 he was excluded from Lang's reconstructed ministry.

Losing pre-selection, he was expelled from the party and fought two vituperative election campaigns against R. J. Heffron during which he became involved in several libel suits. He held Botany as an Independent in 1927 but lost in 1930. Bitter at his treatment by Lang, Mutch was a foundation council-member of the All for Australia League in 1931 and, next year, found himself, somewhat uncomfortably, a member of the United Australia Party. Defeated for the Federal seat of Werriwa in 1934 and the State seat of Bathurst in March 1938, he won a by-election for Coogee in June. In the assembly he was caught up in E. S. Spooner's [q.v.] and other discontented back-benchers' plots against Premier (Sir) Bertram Stevens [q.v.]. Utterly disillusioned with politics he was defeated in 1941.

Unemployed after his defeat in 1930, Mutch led a hand-to-mouth existence there-

after as a freelance journalist, writing historical articles for the *Sydney Morning Herald*
and the *Bulletin*. From 1936 he also broadcast regularly for schoolchildren and from
1940 provided the Rural Bank of New South
Wales with research for broadcasts. He was
also an alderman on Randwick Municipal
Council in 1931-37, a member of the Board of
Fire Commissioners in 1936-54, and editor of
the *Bulletin*'s 'Red Page' in 1936-37. Imprac-
tical with money, he was a director of several
small companies and unsuccessfully speculated in mining and real estate.

Mutch had been a foundation member of
the Henry Lawson Memorial Committee in
1922 and in 1933 published *The early life of
Henry Lawson*. He became deeply interested
in the voyages of the early Dutch navigators
and secured the help of the Netherlands consul-general to procure and translate documents. In 1942 he presented a paper to the
Royal Australian Historical Society on *The
first discovery of Australia with an account of
... the career of Captain Willem Jansz*
(privately printed). He was elected fellow of
the society in 1943 and was a council-member
in 1943-47.

A professional genealogist, Mutch was a
council-member of the Society of Australian
Genealogists in 1945-46 and was elected fellow in 1946. He compiled a comprehensive
index to the early settlers of New South
Wales and Van Diemen's Land from parish
registers, convict indents, musters and land
records; the 'Mutch Index' is now in the Mitchell [q.v.5] Library. A trustee of the Public
Library of New South Wales (1916-58) and a
member of the Mitchell Library committee
(1924-58), he secured Jansz's [q.v.2 Janssen]
original charts for the library, successfully
lobbied for establishment of the State
Archives in 1942, and in 1945 persuaded the
National Library of Australia to co-operate in
a joint copying project of documents relating
to Australia in the Public Records Office, London.

Tall and impeccably dressed in tailor-made
suits, Mutch was attractive to women, but his
addiction to work, desire for perfection and
later crankiness placed great strains on his
domestic life. He was divorced in 1927 and in
Melbourne married a schoolteacher Dorothy
Annette Joyce on 26 March 1928; they parted
about 1955. Survived by his wife and their son
and daughter, he died of cancer at his Clovelly
home on 4 June 1958 and was buried in the
Anglican section of Waverley cemetery after
a service in St James' Church. The Society of
Australian Genealogists established the T. D.
Mutch memorial lecture in his honour.

J. T. Lang, *I remember* (Syd, 1956); *PP* (NSW),
1920, 2, 2nd S, p 1373, 1927, 2, p 773; *PD* (NSW),
1958, p 37; *RAHSJ*, 44 (1958), p 375; *Aust
Genealogist*, 9, Autumn 1959, p 37; *Descent*, 1
(1961-62), pt 1, p 5; *SMH*, 24 Aug, 8 Sept, 31 Oct
1917, 3 Dec 1920, 5 Jan 1921, 21 Feb, 8 June, 11
Sept 1922, 8 June 1923, 22 Nov 1926, 14, 15 Feb,
30, 31 May, 2 June, 25 July, 8, 31 Aug, 29 Nov
1927, 4 May 1931, 2, 9 Dec 1933, 11 Feb 1936, 1
Nov 1943, 6 June 1958, 25 June 1960; *Labor Daily*,
17 June 1925, 14 Feb, 8 Sept 1927, 4, 5, 8 Sept
1928; *Daily Telegraph* (Syd), 25 May 1931; G. E.
Lewis, A biography of the Honourable Thomas
Davies Mutch, M.L.A., F.R.A.H.S., F.R.A.G.S.
(M.A. thesis, UNE, 1977); Miles Franklin papers
(ML); H. E. Boote papers *and* G. Mackaness papers
(NL).   MARTHA RUTLEDGE

MYER, SIMCHA (SIDNEY) BAEVSKI
(1878-1934), merchant and philanthropist,
was born on 8 February 1878 at Kritchev in
the Russian province of Moghilev, within the
Pale of Settlement, youngest of eleven children of Ezekiel Baevski, Hebrew scholar, and
his wife Koona Dubrusha, née Shur.

His elder brother ELCON BAEVSKI (1875-
1938) was born on 4 December 1875 at
Mogilso, attended the Jewish Elementary
School in Kritchev, then a higher school, and
later managed his mother's drapery business.
In 1894 he migrated to Australia, finding
employment in Melbourne in the clothing
trade with a relation, Lazer Slutzkin. Simcha
attended the same schools as his brother, distinguished himself as a student, and in turn
managed his mother's store. He too migrated
and in March 1898, almost penniless, joined
Elcon for a time in Slutzkin's underclothing
business in Flinders Lane, teaching himself
English. Several months later, adopting the
family name of Myer (the second name of
their eldest brother Jacob), the brothers
moved to Bendigo and opened a small drapery
shop. Sidney plied a rapidly growing trade in
fabrics and garments in country districts, first
on foot, later with a horse and cart.

In 1902 the brothers formally became
partners in new premises in Pall Mall, and on
12 March Elcon married Rose Marks (d.
1927) of Melbourne. But the partnership soon
foundered on Elcon's strictly orthodox opposition to Saturday trading, and he returned to
Melbourne, establishing himself as a clothing
manufacturer in Flinders Lane. Sidney
bought him out for £320 and remained in Bendigo, but they continued in close association,
with Sidney as Elcon's biggest customer. On
8 March 1905 Sidney married Hannah
(Nance) Flegeltaub at Ballarat; they had no
children, but from 1911 Sidney acted as
guardian to his nephew (Sir) Norman Myer
(1898-1956).

The Bendigo drapery, decked out in exotic
style, drew crowds of customers with irresistible bargains and novelties temptingly displayed; Sidney Myer had a flair for discerning
new fashion trends and presenting stock at-

tractively. He also advertised boldly, in a style both sensational and persuasive, appealing to women's shopping habits and predilections with a sure touch. By 1907 'Bendigo's Busiest Drapers' had over sixty staff and had expanded its premises. In 1908 Sidney Myer bought Craig Williamson Pty Ltd, a leading drapery firm, for £22 000, and a 'hurricane sale' of its stock repaid his creditors. Now Bendigo's foremost merchant, he increased his turnover in three years from £38 000 to £160 000, with a net annual profit of £15 000.

Late in 1909 Sidney travelled overseas to study British and European merchandising methods and to establish contact with manufacturers and exporters. In April 1911 he seized the opportunity to purchase Wright & Neil, a drapery store in Bourke Street, Melbourne, for which he paid £91 450. He raised staff wages, then closed the store for a fortnight's stock-taking and ordering; and in May, after a spate of full-page newspaper advertisements, Melbourne experienced its first Myer sale. Old stock sold for a song, new stock was priced almost at cost, goods once kept behind counters were strewn upon tables, and the rush lasted for a week.

The newly acquired store continued under its former manager Edwin Lee Neil [q.v.], but Elcon Myer now rejoined his brother and, with another deputy, managed the two Bendigo shops until their sale in 1914 for £50 000. Sidney purchased the freehold of the Bourke Street site; and in 1912 he also bought land in Post Office Place. In 1913 he purchased the Civil Service Stores, Flinders Street, to accommodate business while the outgrown Bourke Street store was rebuilt. The move was made in a single night; custom was retained by a free bus service and by an almost continuous series of bargain sales. Modelled upon San Francisco's 'Emporium' and bearing the same name, the new £70 000, eight-storey building opened in July 1914 with a hugely successful gala sale.

When World War I began, Elcon was on his way to London, to establish a buying and export office and organize shipments of cloth. In 1915 he joined the Army Service Corps, serving first in England, then from May 1917 at the front. He returned to Australia early in 1919, to become merchandizing manager for the Myer Emporium, a post which involved frequent journeys overseas.

During the war the London office greatly assisted Sidney's determination to maintain his imports, despite an initial slump in the retail trade. Convinced that the struggle would be long, and fearing lest Australia would be cut off from overseas supplies, he also increased purchases of locally made softgoods and began manufacturing on his own account. Already, in 1913, Myer had opened a fitting factory in Barkly Place; in 1915 he built a clothing factory in Condell's Lane and bought the Doveton Woollen Mills at Ballarat in 1918. He bought more land off Post Office Place for a men's wear store; and at the end of 1917 he formed Myer's (Melbourne) Pty Ltd, with a capital of £500 000 and himself and Neil as directors.

The two men were opposites: Sidney 'open, informal, and genial though moody', Neil 'reserved, formal'; yet they complemented one another admirably. While Neil was the expert manager, Myer provided creative energy, commercial intuition and sheer merchandising genius. His influence was almost charismatic. He could speak harshly when he saw fit, or at moments of sudden wrath, but generally treated staff with consideration, criticizing constructively, consulting freely, rewarding initiative and encouraging effort. Department managers might well dread his frequent forays through the store, as with an unerring eye he detected their errors of judgement, or on an inspiration upset their domains. But in return for his generosity and the responsibility he bestowed, they gave loyalty and a capacity to excel that made Myer the envy of other employers. He was a remarkable judge of character; and his own infectious enthusiasm, natural dignity and persuasive charm won an eager response.

At once frank and courteous, Sidney had a lively sense of humour, offset by an underlying wistfulness. He was tall and elegant, with dark crinkly hair and light blue eyes, high cheek-bones, neat moustache and an expressive mouth. In his quiet voice there lingered a Russian accent that became stronger when he spoke, reluctantly, in public. The accent was more noticeable in Elcon, who tended to 'splutter' under pressure and whose capacity for mispronunciation 'sometimes verged on genius'. Short and stocky, with a walrus moustache and a fatherly manner, Elcon was 'impossible to dislike'.

In mid-1919 Sidney left Neil in command and visited the United States of America, to investigate department stores. He also obtained a divorce in Nevada and was converted to Christianity. On 8 January 1920, at San Francisco, he married 19-year-old (Dame) Marjorie Merlyn, daughter of George Baillieu, of Melbourne. They subsequently spent several months each year in California where their four children were born.

By 1920 the Myer Emporium was a vast affair of 200 departments, famous for its 'Friday specials' and Monday 'star bargains', and equipped with a fleet of motorized delivery vans. In that year a new holding company, Myer's (Australia) Ltd, brought together all firms solely owned by Sidney Myer, with a capital of £2 million; and a London subsidiary was incorporated. In 1921 warnings of a post-war slump overseas prompted Sidney to anticipate the collapse of import prices and cut his losses with a Million Pound Master Sale. It cost Myer over £500 000, half his fortune; but, by restocking with the cheaper imports, he traded out of crisis by the year's end, while other firms languished.

Sidney now offered on easy terms 73 000 'staff partnership' shares of £1 each. He also began distributing shares (more than 200 000, all told) among his executives and managers, according to his estimation of their merit. Increasingly, Myer looked upon his staff as a community; by 1926 they numbered over 2000. Weary managers received paid vacations, a sick fund was instituted, holiday homes were established, and an elaborate free hospital provided in the store. Social activities included annual staff balls and picnics, football and cricket matches, a Christian Fellowship, and choral society concerts in aid of charity.

The Myer Emporium grew steadily, its business expanding threefold between 1922 and 1925. The Bourke Street frontage increased as the neighbouring drapery stores of Robertson & Moffatt and Stephens & Sons were purchased. The first section of an eleven-storey Lonsdale Street store opened in 1926. To finance this growth, a new company, the Myer Emporium Ltd, was formed in 1925, with a capital of £3 million. Sidney Myer and Lee Neil continued as governing and as managing director, but a large assisting directorate was appointed also. In 1927 this company's net profit was £328 000, and shareholders received a dividend of 17½ per cent. In 1928 Myer took over the department store of James Marshall [q.v.5] & Co. of Adelaide, establishing The Myer Emporium (S.A.) Ltd under the joint direction of his nephew Norman and James Martin.

While the Lonsdale Street store was being extended, Myer bought out Thos. Webb & Sons, tableware merchants, in 1930 and in 1931 W. H. Rocke & Co. Ltd, quality furniture dealers. Myer's now catered for all needs, pockets and tastes. In 1926 it had opened Melbourne's first 'Cash and Carry' grocery; then came one of the world's largest self-service cafeterias and in 1933 the handsome 'Mural Hall'.

With the Depression at its worst, in 1931 Sidney Myer launched a £250 000 reconstruction of his Bourke Street store, deliberately aimed at creating employment and restoring confidence. In 1930, anticipating the Scullin [q.v.] government's tariff embargoes and import restrictions, he had reduced his overseas buying and inaugurated a 'Made in Australia Week', displaying locally made goods and urging customers to 'lessen unemployment by helping to open up new avenues of industry'. To meet the decline in purchasing power he limited profit margins to 5 per cent. All staff, himself included (except for those affected by a wages board), endured a 20 per cent pay-cut for eighteen months, so that no employee need be retrenched. The staff shareholder dividend was reduced by 6 per cent in August 1931.

Stressing the connexion between spending power and recovery, Myer declared: 'It is a responsibility of capital to provide work. If it fails to do this it fails to justify itself'. Late in 1931 he urged the wealthy to donate funds for government projects, so that people might have work and a happier Christmas. He himself gave £10 000 for immediate continuation of the Yarra Boulevard scheme, which employed many hundreds of men; and over the next two years he contributed a further £12 000. On Christmas Day 1930 he had endeavoured to cheer the unemployed by holding a vast Christmas dinner for over 10 000 people at the Exhibition Building; free tram travel was provided, a band played, and every child received a present.

Much of Myer's liberality was privately bestowed, but on occasion gifts were made publicly, to draw attention to the cause. The objects of his philanthropy were sometimes cultural, rather than charitable. In 1926, learning of the University of Melbourne's financial plight, he gave it 25 000 Myer shares, worth £50 000, with the sole request that the shares not be sold until they doubled their value. This 'princely munificence' was honoured by the naming of the Sidney Myer chair of commerce.

In 1928 Myer backed the trans-Pacific flight of aviator (Sir) Charles Kingsford Smith [q.v.9]; and, when 'financial stringency' was forcing the Children's Hospital to close its wards in 1929, he donated £8000. His love of classical music inspired him to provide £1000 annually for free open-air concerts by the Melbourne Symphony Orchestra. Then he engineered its amalgamation with the University Symphony Orchestra, to form a new M.S.O. in 1932, and established a trust fund for its support with a gift of 10 000 Myer shares. He also endowed an annual series of free orchestral concerts at the university conservatorium. In 1932 also he gave £5000 to Melbourne's Shrine of Remembrance.

From May 1931 Sidney Myer served with energy and generosity on the committee of management of the (Royal) Melbourne Hospital, largely contributing to a reform of its business system, purchasing methods and patient records. Early in 1933 he was appointed to the executive committee of Victoria's Centenary Council, and raised over £20 000. He organized the musical arrangements for the celebrations, and donated many prizes for centenary competitions. One of his last gifts was an ambulance for the Victorian

Civil Ambulance Service. At the time of his death he was planning to endow the Anglican Church with £100 000 for a training farm for indigent boys.

Sidney Myer died suddenly of cardiac failure on 5 September 1934, near his home in Toorak, and was buried in Box Hill cemetery. Survived by his wife, two sons (Kenneth Baillieu and Sidney Baillieu, both of whom became managing directors of Myer's) and two daughters, he left an estate worth well over £1 million. By his will one-tenth of his wealth was placed in trust for the charitable, philanthropic and educational needs of 'the community in which I made my fortune'. His portrait by John Longstaff [q.v.] is held by the family.

Neil replaced him briefly at the head of the firm, which by now had an issued capital of £2 479 950 and 5300 employees. He was succeeded by Elcon, with Norman Myer as managing director. As chairman, Elcon presided over the completion of the modern Bourke Street store and the celebration, in 1937, of its silver anniversary.

A retiring yet sociable man, Elcon was active in many charitable causes, and served on the board of the Alfred Hospital. He was also a leading member of St Kilda Synagogue.

He died on 18 February 1938 in the Mercy Hospital, of cancer after a long illness, and was buried with strict Jewish rites in Brighton cemetery. His estate in Victoria was sworn for probate at £114 353. Elcon was survived by the two sons of his first marriage and by his second wife Myrtle Audrey Fisher, née Levy, whom he had married in 1929.

When Sidney Myer first established himself in Melbourne, Lee Neil had judged him to be 'inordinately ambitious', but withal 'a man of vision and high enthusiasm and warm human sympathies'. The combination made Myer 'one of the most magnetic personalities' Neil had ever met. Myer's bold optimism and fine philanthropy, his commercial foresight and innovative courage, and above all the brilliance with which he wrought a retailing revolution and changed the heart of Melbourne, have established him as one of the great men of his time.

J. W. Barrett, *Eighty eventful years* (Melb, 1945); A. Marshall, *The gay provider* (Melb, 1961); A. Pratt, *Sidney Myer* (Melb, 1978); *Age*, 1 Jan 1931, 6 Sept 1934, 19 Feb 1938; *Argus*, 6 Sept 1934, 19 Feb 1938; A. H. Tolley, Notes on the biography of Mr Sidney Myer (typescript, nd, 1935?, Myer Museum, Melb); Myer records (Univ Melb Archives).   ANTHEA HYSLOP

N

NANGLE, JAMES (1868-1941), architect and educationist, was born on 28 December 1868, at Newtown, Sydney, eldest of five children of Irish Catholic parents Thomas Nangle, coachman, and his wife Maria, née Carney. He began working part time at 9, and on leaving school at 11 obtained unskilled work in an engineering firm. At 15 he was apprenticed as a carpenter and joiner to a Newtown builder, then worked as a journeyman, clerk of works and draughtsman. He attended classes at Sydney Technical College and at the University of Sydney in the 1880s.

Nangle was a quietly ambitious man with wide interests and contacts. Small, neat, fair and compact in appearance, he was always to enjoy an enviable reputation for courtesy, tact and integrity, while his cheerfulness, good manners and adaptability attracted the goodwill of professional colleagues.

In 1891 Nangle began practice as an architect and on 7 December next year married Helen Van Heythuysen at Newtown Registry Office. Active in the Sydney Architectural Association from the early 1890s, he became an associate of the Institute of Architects of New South Wales in 1896 and as honorary treasurer from 1897 helped to stave off the institute's financial collapse. He later became its secretary.

Most of Nangle's architectural work was residential, institutional and commercial. Two of his best-known buildings were the stores erected for Marcus Clark [q.v.8] at Newtown and on the Pitt and George Street corner. He also carried out commissions for the Roman Catholic Church, including the Sacred Heart Church, Darlinghurst, St Columba's Seminary, Springwood, and St Mary's Cathedral Girls' School. Later he designed the portable classrooms used for many years by the Department of Public Instruction, the Turner hall extension and the new architectural and building block at Sydney Technical College, Ultimo, and the Balmain Trades School.

In 1890 Nangle had begun teaching mechanical drawing part time for the technical education branch of the Department of Public Instruction. He offered to publicize new classes and to canvass for students. By 1894 he was conducting two weekly classes and delivering public lectures. In 1897 he was responsible for all drawing instruction at Newtown. Next year he was transferred to Sydney Technical College where in 1905, at the urging of (Sir) George Knibbs [q.v.9], Nangle became lecturer-in-charge of the department of architecture. He restructured the existing courses, improving relationships between the architectural and building trades classes. The Institute of Architects later recognized his redefined courses as part of the qualifications necessary for membership. In 1911 conflict of interests led him to quit practice although he maintained a small consultancy until 1913.

As a student in the university's engineering laboratories Nangle had developed a lifelong interest in materials testing. His *Australian building practice* (1900) was widely used as a text-book. He delivered papers and published articles in journals such as the *Australian Technical Journal* and the *Technical Gazette of New South Wales* on the properties of materials and the strength of structures, especially Australian timber and stone. He was an early supporter of the use of concrete and steel in buildings, and for many years the official testing architect for the Institute of Architects.

Nangle was appointed superintendent of technical education in 1913. His predecessor J. W. Turner [q.v.] had recommended him as 'most suitable . . . very capable, efficient and held in great respect by the entire staff of the college'. Nangle immediately became involved in the reforms instituted by the director of education Peter Board [q.v.7]. Reform in technical education was directed mainly at upgrading the status and content of training and redefining it more strictly within vocational limits. New trade courses were designed and the diploma courses, which eventually set the high standards required for award of associate of Sydney Technical College, introduced. To achieve the necessary co-operation of educators, employers and employee organizations, Nangle suggested the establishment of course advisory committees containing union and industry representatives as well as college staff, which formed the basis of the committee system of course review still operating in New South Wales.

The 1913 reforms were not an unqualified success. The relationship between preliminary trade work in school and trade courses was unsatisfactory, and insufficient funding led to persistent accommodation crises despite the extra land acquired at Ultimo in 1910 and the development of East Sydney Technical College in the 1920s. In addition, the limited meaning given the term 'vocation' reduced the scope of technical education, forcing Nangle into stratagems to defend some courses and to enable others to be extended. By 1920 he had managed to so redefine and extend the applied art courses that their number and prestige increased. Their relocation in the early 1920s at East Sydney marked the establishment of the college's 'National Art School' with its subsequently highly regarded courses.

Nangle also increased the range of the branch's activities when he persuaded the department to take over the aircraft mechanics' section of the pilots' training scheme set up by the Holman [q.v.9] government at Richmond in 1916. Transferred to East Sydney in the 1920s, the section formed the basis of the department's present aircraft engineering courses.

The worst effects of the reorganization were those caused by the continuing problems of increased numbers of students and insufficient space, funds and equipment. Nangle was denied direct access to his minister and forced to work through the director of education whose interests were mainly school based. Nangle found this unfair, frustrating and a brake on the development of technical education. Nevertheless his ability to operate within restrictive limits highlighted his exceptional ability to assess needs and make very inadequate ends meet. These qualities, rather than educational innovation, contributed to Nangle's long-standing success as superintendent between 1913 and 1933.

In 1919 he accepted the position of director of vocational training under the Commonwealth Department of Repatriation. His administrative talents and skill with course advisory committees were considered indispensable to the acceptance of large numbers of partly trained men into the workforce. He oversaw the training of some 20 000 ex-servicemen in trade and other courses operated by State Education departments and a smaller number in universities and other institutions. Nangle was appointed O.B.E. in 1920. As the training agreements signed by each State allowed them to keep considerable quantities of equipment and sometimes buildings at reduced costs, he was able to influence the choice of the facilities retained for New South Wales technical colleges. He also persuaded the department to retain courses such as automotive engineering and commerce provided under the scheme and some staff as well.

This post-war windfall became all the more important in the 1920s when Nangle struggled against a constantly increasing student backlog, lack of space and staff unrest. As late as 1927 technical education was allocated less than 4 per cent of the total education vote.

In 1927 Nangle advised on the establishment of a technical education system for Western Australia, as he had for Tasmania in 1916; and in 1930 he chaired an unemploy-

ment research committee set up by the Bavin [q.v.7] government. Courses he had already introduced at Sydney Technical College for unemployed boys and girls formed the basis of the committee's emergency day training scheme. Some 4500 students attended these courses between 1932 and 1937. This experience, and his war-time experiences, confirmed Nangle's view of the inadequacy of statistical data on employment and of the need for juvenile employment bureaux. In 1933 he served as consultant to the technical education commission set up by D. H. Drummond [q.v.8], minister for education, submitting a lengthy report. He retired the same year.

An amateur astronomer of merit, Nangle had designed a small observatory at his Marrickville home, built and operated telescopes, written several papers on his observations and joined official expeditions to view eclipses of the sun in 1910 and 1923. A member from 1905 and many times president of the local branch of the British Astronomical Association, he was elected a fellow of the Royal Astronomical Society of London in 1908. He was also a member of the 1912 committee advising on the reorganization of the work of Sydney Observatory, and in the 1920s helped to replan the observatory building and residence, where he moved his family when he was appointed honorary government astronomer in 1926. Nangle strongly supported the educational role of observatories and published *Stars of the southern heavens* (1929) and *The Sydney Observatory: its history and work* (1930). Under his direction the six-pip time-signal was introduced.

Nangle was also an office-bearer of the Engineering and Town Planning associations of New South Wales and of the State committee of the Council for Scientific and Industrial Research. A member of the Royal Society of New South Wales from 1893 and president in 1920-21, he published several articles in its *Journal and Proceedings* on timbers and building stone. He was also an additional member of the first Board of Architects of New South Wales appointed in 1921, and president of the Royal Australian Institute of Architects in 1936-37. In 1937 he was elected a fellow of the Royal Institute of British Architects. A fellow of the Senate of the University of Sydney in 1913-34 Nangle supported the establishment of chairs of architecture and mechanical engineering and the introduction of courses in domestic science.

His last years as superintendent of technical education were marred by ill health. After his retirement he continued to work as government astronomer while running a small private correspondence school, the Nangle Institute of Technology, which was operated by his family until the 1960s. Survived by three sons and a daughter, Nangle died of heart disease on 22 February 1941 at the observatory and was buried with Congregational forms in Rookwood cemetery.

Cyclopedia of N.S.W. (Syd, 1907); *Quarter century of technical education in New South Wales* (Syd, 1909); J. M. Freeland, *The making of a profession* (Syd, 1917); Repatriation Dept, Interim report upon the organisation and activities of the Repatriation Com, *PP* (Cwlth), 1917-19, 162, p 117; Repatriation Com, Annual Report, *PP* (Cwlth), 1921-26; Roy Astronomical Soc, *Monthly Notices*, 69, pt 1, 1908; Roy Soc, NSW, *J*, 75, pt 4, 1941, p xxxi; *Building* (Syd), 24 Mar 1941; L. J. Dockrill, James Nangle: architect, astronomer, educator (B. Arch thesis, Univ NSW, 1975); Dept of Technical Education files including box 10/14346, 10/12/1912 (NSWA); Repatriation Dept files (AAO, Canb).   JOAN COBB

NANSON, EDWARD JOHN (1850-1936), university professor and electoral reformer, was born on 13 December 1850 at Penrith, Cumberland, England, son of John Nanson, hatter, and his wife Isabella, née Bowman. From Penrith Grammar School he went to Ripon Grammar School where he was a favourite pupil of the headmaster, Canon J. F. McMichael, whose eldest daughter Elizabeth he married at Ripon Cathedral on 21 April 1875. In 1870 he had entered Trinity College, Cambridge (B.A., 1873); as second wrangler and second Smith's prizeman, he became a fellow of Trinity College in 1874 and was appointed that year professor of applied mathematics at the Royal Indian Engineering College, Cooper's Hill, Surrey. After W. P. Wilson [q.v.6] died, Nanson was appointed professor of mathematics, pure and mixed, in the University of Melbourne, arriving in June 1875.

Nanson did not profess a popular discipline. He was frustrated by low first-year standards and the perfunctory attitude of arts and engineering students undertaking a compulsory study. Unlike his predecessor he did not develop natural philosophy interests or associate himself directly with the pragmatic concerns of the growing engineering school. Kind but reserved in manner, mild in temperament, a field naturalist given to solitary rambles, Nanson received unsympathetic treatment from the reforming royal commission on the University of Melbourne (1902-04) which criticized student absenteeism and lack of tutorial teaching, but affirmed his industry and stature as a mathematician. A disciple of Cayley, Sylvester and Salmon, Nanson was of the dominant English 'aesthetic' school of pure mathematics whose great achievements were in formal algebra and its applications in geometry. He kept abreast of the most advanced theoretical studies in this field, notably matrix theory, and contributed regularly to the *Messenger of Mathematics* (Cambridge) and to the *Proceedings* of the Royal societies of London, Edinburgh and Victoria. Intellectually lonely in his theoretical interests he found some companionship in the Mathematics Association of Victoria of which he became first president in 1906.

Widely known as an electoral reformer, of the school of Thomas Hare and J. S. Mill, Nanson advocated proportional representation, using the preferential vote and the principle of the quota in multi-member electorates as 'the only way the true will of the people can be ascertained'. From the early 1880s at public meetings, in the daily press and in numerous journal articles and pamphlets, such as *Electoral reform* (1899) and *The real value of a vote* (1900), he analysed contemporary elections and assessed electoral reform proposals. His ideas were embodied in an electoral reform bill introduced in the Legislative Assembly of Victoria in August 1900 by Sir George Turner [q.v.] and Alfred Deakin [q.v.8] and in the first Commonwealth electoral bill drafted by (Sir) Robert Garran [q.v.8] in 1901. The bills were amended and did not implement his theories but Nanson continued his critique of Australian elections in *How to secure majority rule* (1904). The Council of the University of Melbourne was elected on a scheme proposed by him.

Nanson had a life-appointment but negotiated a pension settlement with the university and retired as emeritus professor in December 1922. His wife had died in 1904 and he married Mavourneen Bertha, née Wettenhall, in Melbourne on 10 March 1913. He was a trustee of the Public Library, museums and National Gallery of Victoria in 1879-1913 and was an active Anglican layman. He died on 1 July 1936 at Glen Iris and was buried in St Kilda cemetery. His wife, a son and five daughters of his first marriage, and four daughters of his second, survived him. A portrait by Bernard Hall [q.v.9] is held by the University of Melbourne.

Alma Mater (Univ Melb), May 1896, Jan 1902; *Age*, 2 July 1936; *The Times*, 28 July 1936; Univ Melb Archives.   G. C. FENDLEY

NANSON, JOHN LEIGHTON (1863-1916), journalist and politician, was born on 22 September 1863 at Carlisle, Cumberland, England, son of John Nanson, solicitor and town clerk, and his wife Caroline Fletcher, née James. He was educated at the local grammar school and King William's College, Isle of Man. He left school at 16, worked for a solicitor for a year, and migrated to Australia, hoping to better his fortune and his health. His cousin Edward John Nanson [q.v.] was professor of mathematics at the University of Melbourne.

John Nanson first worked on a station near Broken Hill, New South Wales, but in 1881 he joined the Commercial Bank of South Australia. In 1891 he moved to Perth as accountant in its new Western Australian branch but two years later lost his job when the bank went into liquidation. On 8 October 1887 he had married Janet Drummond Durlacher in the Fremantle Anglican church; they had one daughter and a son who died young.

Nanson joined the *West Australian*, Perth's morning daily, and became the Fremantle representative; he alone managed both reporting and commercial affairs. He was soon promoted to Perth as a sub-editor. After visiting England in 1897, he became associate editor and chief leader-writer. Both the owner-partners, Charles Harper and (Sir) Winthrop Hackett [qq.v.9], were in parliament; Nanson was in a position to be politically interested and useful.

In 1901, after obtaining Hackett's permission to stand, he won the Legislative Assembly seat of Murchison by one vote. At first he supported Premier Leake [q.v.], but in October crossed the floor to vote with the Opposition, having criticized Leake's stand on duties on certain imports, large-scale government borrowing, recognition of unions in the conciliation and arbitration bill, and alleged tacit support for criticisms of British royalty published in the *Sunday Times*. In November the month-long Morgans [q.v.] cabinet included Nanson as minister for lands. He was a prolix, easily nettled, leader of the Opposition in 1902-03 and, now a Liberal, held office briefly again as works minister under (Sir) Walter James [q.v.9] in 1904. His anxious look and gangling appearance made him a gift to cartoonists. In 1904-05 he represented Greenough, which was adjacent to his previous electorate.

In 1902 Nanson had left the *West Australian* and bought a controlling interest in the *Morning Herald*, launched by the owners of the *Daily News* to compete with his old paper. He became chairman of directors on 15 September, but after two and a half years the effects of his tuberculosis forced him to sell to J. Dreyer, nominee of Bishop Gibney [q.v.8].

Nanson went to Switzerland, and later to England where he studied law. He was called to the English Bar in July 1908, practised briefly with a leading common law barrister, and returned to Perth just in time to win back Greenough. When (Sir) Norbert Keenan [q.v.9] resigned the following May, Nanson became attorney-general and minister for education for the last fifteen months of the

(Sir) Newton Moore [q.v.] government. He held similar portfolios in the first Wilson [q.v] ministry of 1910-11. He joined A. Despeissis [q.v.8] in 1912 in Santa Rosa Wine & Distilleries Ltd.

Nanson's illness again became serious: he left Western Australia in 1913 and went again to Switzerland and to Italy and England where he lived in Dorset. He retired from parliament in 1914 and on 29 February 1916 died at Vaynor, Broadstone. His estate was sworn for probate at about £20 000.

JANET NANSON (1868-1943) had also been a journalist, from the time when her husband was associate editor of the *West Australian*. As 'Sigma' she was Perth's first social writer and the original 'Aunt Mary' of the *Western Mail*, Harper and Hackett's weekly for country people. After her husband bought the *Morning Herald* she wrote political journalism, but left work when he sold the paper. After his death she lived alternately in Perth and London, where her daughter was an actress. She died in Perth on 14 December 1943 and was buried in the Anglican section of Karrakatta cemetery.

Truthful Thomas, *Through the spy-glass* (Perth, 1905); N. Stewart, *Little but great* (Perth, 1965); *Aust and NZ Weekly*, 27 Aug 1908; *WA Newspapers Q Bulletin*, 2, no 1, Feb 1963; *West Australian*, 22 Oct 1901, 2 Mar 1916, 5 Jan 1933, 8 Dec 1938, 15 Dec 1943; *Punch* (Melb), 16 Mar 1916; Memoirs of A. R. Grant (NL).

O. K. BATTYE

NANYA (c.1835-1895), founder of one of the last New South Wales Aboriginal families to live by traditional hunting techniques, was a Maraura of the lower Darling. His childhood coincided with incursions in 1839-46 of European explorers, aggressive overlanders and punitive expeditions which killed most of his people, notably in the 1841 Rufus River massacre by South Australian police led by Thomas O'Halloran [q.v.2].

About 1860 Nanya left his camp at Popiltah station, forty miles (64 km) north of Pooncarie. With two women and a steel axe, he went into the waterless mallee country between the Great Anabranch and the South Australian border, known as the 'Scotia blocks', where he lived for over thirty years. Records compiled in 1897-1908 by amateur ethnographers suggest causes for Nanya's self-imposed exile; possibly he had eloped with a woman of his own Makwarra moiety, an offence considered incestuous and meriting death.

Nanya's people kept themselves closely concealed: there were some reports of tracks and piles of freshly cut mallee roots, but very few sightings, although Aboriginal stockmen were well aware of their movements. By the early 1890s the press reported more frequent sightings of the 'wild tribe'. Station-workers found that Nanya's people were obtaining water by operating tank machinery on Cuthero station, and noticed from tracks that Nanya's family was steadily increasing. White settlers, previously indifferent, became anxious for the family's, and their own, welfare.

In 1893 Aboriginal stockmen Harry Mitchell, Don McGregor and Fred Williams tracked down the family and persuaded them to return to the river. This 'capture' was perhaps encouraged by a false rumour of a £50 government reward, but the rescuers' descendants recall that the family was brought in lest they be shot by settlers. The twelve men, eight women and ten children, all in good physical condition, reached Popiltah station on 11 August. Nanya still had his steel axe, now worn wafer-thin.

The station-owner described the dwellings, tools and food-gathering skills of Nanya's group, noting that they initially refused to eat bread, tea or sugar. Yet a photograph taken at the Adelaide exhibition of 1895 of Nanya with two daughters shows that the graceful women of 1893 had become stout on a flour and sugar diet. The Aborigines Protection Board selected a site at Travellers Lake, near Wentworth, but Nanya's people preferred hunting-camps in the vicinity of Poon-carie.

Nanya's case is of interest to demographers as an example of population growth in arid regions. He died in 1895 and was buried near the Great Anabranch. Many of his children, with no acquired resistance to intro-duced disease, died soon after their isolation ended. In 1905 his son Billy, educated for a time in Adelaide, was being transferred by the paddle-steamer *Gem* to Point McLeay mission, on Lake Alexandrina. Tormented to desperation by crew-members, Billy jumped into the steamer's engine and was cut to pieces.

B. Hardy, *West of the Darling* (Brisb, 1969), and *Lament for the Barkindji* (Adel, 1976); N. B. Tindale, *Aboriginal tribes of Australia* (Berkeley, California, 1974); *Report of the Aborigines Protection Bd* (NSW), 1893; *Report of the fifth meeting of A.A.A.S.* (Adel), 1894, p 524; *Science of Man*, 6, no 8, Sept 1903, p 119; *Aust Museum Mag*, 10, no 6, 15 June 1951, p 172; *Barrier Miner*, Christmas 1898, supp; material in the possession of Dr D. Barwick, Canb; information from Mrs M. Smith, Dareton, Mr R. J. Whyte, Wentworth, and Mr J. Whyman, Wilcannia, NSW, and Miss G. D. Parker, Leabrook, Adel; N. (Warrakoo) Smith typescript (nd, copy held by R. J. Whyte, Wentworth, NSW).   ROBERT LINDSAY

NASH, CLIFFORD HARRIS (1866-1958), Anglican clergyman, was born on 16 December 1866 at Brixton, London, son of Frederick John Nash, merchant, and his wife Ellen, née Holden. He was educated at Oundle School, where he became school captain and won a classical scholarship to Corpus Christi College, Cambridge, in 1885. A tall, handsome young man, he was, as at school, successful academically (B.A., 1888), in debating and in sport. The Cambridge Inter-Collegiate Christian Union fostered his evangelical faith and introduced him to students from Ridley Hall, where he studied theology (1888-89).

Too young to be ordained, Nash taught for eighteen months at Loretto School, Mussel-burgh, Scotland, under its progressive head-master Dr Hely-Hutchinson Almond. He was made deacon in 1890 and moved to the busy industrial parish of St Peter's, Huddersfield, Yorkshire. After a short tour of overseas missions, he was ordained priest in Wakefield Cathedral on 26 February 1893.

Two years later Nash's promising career was curtailed because it was alleged that while engaged to his vicar's daughter he had made advances to her younger sister. In February 1895 he sailed for Tasmania, where he worked on a sheep-station, then became superintendent of a new settlement for un-employed people at Southport.

In February 1897 Bishop Saumarez Smith [q.v.] of Sydney invited Nash to resume his ministry and appointed him assistant at St Philip's, Sydney. He became superintendent of the Mission Church at Ultimo and an hon-orary secretary of the Church Missionary Association. On 31 January 1899 he married Louise Mary Maude Pearse, at St Philip's.

After a short term as acting rector of St Paul's, Redfern, Nash became in January 1900 incumbent of St Columb's, Hawthorn, Melbourne, a thriving parish. He also became involved in home mission work in the Dandenongs and planned the building of St Hilda's, a training house for deaconesses established in 1901. Canon of St Paul's Cathedral in 1903-07 and a Melbourne diocesan theological lecturer at Trinity College (University of Melbourne), Nash was in great demand as a preacher and teacher at Church functions and student meetings. A founder of the Parker Union formed in 1902 as a brotherhood of evangelical clergy, he was elected in 1905 as a clerical member of the provincial synod of Victoria.

At Archbishop Lowther Clarke's [q.v.8] request, Nash moved in 1906 to Christ Church, Geelong, where he was also chaplain to Geelong Church of England Grammar School. But in October 1907 the archbishop called a special meeting of the cathedral chapter and confronted it with reports of Nash's affection for a young, female Hawthorn parishioner, at the same time alluding to alleged past indiscretions. Nash was required to resign, despite opposition from fellow clergy and laymen, many of whom felt that he should have been properly tried by the Court of Ecclesiastical Offences. After Nash's renomination to the incumbency of Christ Church was vetoed by the archbishop, a Geelong committee paid for him to travel to England to vindicate himself. Attempts by the archbishop, in England for the Lambeth Conference, to investigate further Nash's past behaviour were terminated when they aroused strong criticism. Nash was relicensed in August 1908 and invited by Dr Pain, bishop of Gippsland, to become rector of St Paul's, Sale, and archdeacon of Gippsland.

On 16 October 1909 a slanderous article was published by John Norton [q.v.] in Melbourne *Truth*, attacking the 'condemnable, contemptible, cowardly conduct' of Clarke in 'crucifying his clerical confrere, Canon Nash'. The archbishop took successful legal action but the incident damaged the Church and in particular Nash, whose alleged improprieties became public knowledge. For the third time he resigned from the Anglican Church.

Nash's turbulent middle life preceded another forty years of active ministry during which he continued to exert a profound influence through his teaching, preaching and pastoral work. In 1913-15 he ran a boys' school at Kew, and in 1915-21 was pastor of the Prahran Independent Church and principal classics master at Caulfield Grammar School.

In 1920 Nash began the most significant work of his life by starting the Melbourne Bible Institute (Bible College of Victoria) at Prahran. He trained over one thousand students before retiring in 1942. On his sixtieth birthday in 1926 Archbishop Harrington Lees [q.v.] relicensed him. In 1927-41 he served as curate at St James' Old Cathedral, Melbourne, and from 1941 until his death assisted at various parishes.

Unfailingly active in the wider concerns of evangelical Christianity, Nash was a council-member of the China Inland Mission in 1916-43 and a member and first president of the Bible Union of Victoria. A popular convention speaker, he also organized and led city Bible classes from 1925. In 1927 he joined the committee of the Church Missionary Society and helped to form its League of Youth. In 1936 he was a founder of Campaigners for Christ. In his later life he led various ordination retreats in Sydney.

Nash died at Royal Park on 27 September 1958. After a service at St Paul's Cathedral he was buried in Dromana cemetery. His wife, three daughters and three sons survived him. His writings included two books, *Christ*

interpreted (1940) and *The fourfold interpretation of Jesus Christ* (1946).

D. H. Chambers, '*Tempest-tost*' (Melb, 1959); *Argus*, 9 Nov, 5, 6, 7, 21 Dec 1907, 18 June 1910, 10, 14 Feb 1911, 18, 19, 20, 21 June, 1 Aug 1912; *Bulletin*, 30 Jan 1908; *Punch* (Melb), 3 Sept 1908; *Truth* (Melb), 9, 16 Oct 1909; *Herald* (Melb), 1 Dec 1926; *Age* and *Sun-News Pictorial*, 29 Sept 1958; bibliographical file (LaTL); newspaper clippings, *Clarke* v. *Norton* (1912) (held at Mollison Lib, Trinity College, Melb).   B. B. DARLING

NATHAN, SIR CHARLES SAMUEL (1870-1936), businessman and government adviser, was born on 23 July 1870 in South Melbourne, second of six sons of Solomon (Sathiel) David Nathan, auctioneer, and his wife Flora, née Levy, both English born. He attended the Normal School at Christchurch, New Zealand, and was articled to solicitors before becoming a commercial traveller in Dunedin. He moved to Sydney in 1890 and Perth in 1894. On 15 June 1898 at the Fremantle synagogue Nathan married Bessie Lichtenstein; they had a daughter, who died at 16, and two sons.

In 1901 Nathan joined the South Australian firm, Charles Atkins & Co. W.A. Ltd, at Fremantle; it dealt in abrasives, pulleys and other commodities for gold-mining. Later he bought the branch and, about 1911, transferred it to Perth. Atkins Pty Ltd (W.A.) became a leading mercantile and engineering enterprise that handled a diverse range of tools, machinery, electrical household goods, radios, and automotive supplies and parts.

Nathan devoted himself to a broad range of public activities, including membership of the East Fremantle Municipal Council (1902-05) and the Fremantle Tramways and Electric Light Board. In 1914 he was mayor of Perth. During World War I he was a co-founder of the State branch of the Australian Red Cross Society, and also belonged to the Trench Comforts Fund, the War Loan Campaign and the Young Men's Christian Association.

Nathan possessed generosity, organizing ability, and a capacity to deal with people. His long relationship with the Returned Sailors' and Soldiers' Imperial League of Australia culminated in his wardenship of the State War Memorial in 1932. In 1920-23 he had chaired the Western Australian Council of Industrial Development and in 1921 led a State trade delegation to Malaya and Java. In 1918 he was appointed to the executive committee of the Advisory Council of Science and Industry and in 1927-28 was an executive-member of the Council for Scientific and Industrial Research; he was also a committee-member of the Commonwealth Forest Products Laboratory. As an Australian commissioner for the British

Empire Exhibition at Wembley, London, he spent two years in England in the mid-1920s. In 1926-27 he was a 'meticulous and methodical' vice-chairman and financial adviser of the Commonwealth Development and Migration Commission; he waived a salary. Appointed C.B.E. in 1926, he was knighted in 1928. He had retired the previous year.

In London in 1928 Nathan was negotiating improvement schemes for Australia's beef cattle industry with the British firms, Vestey Bros and Bovril Ltd. He acted as unofficial adviser to the Bruce [q.v.7]-Page [q.v.] government on northern development.

In the post-war period Nathan had organized fund-raising for the National Party; he chaired the Westralian Consultative Council in 1925. In 1930-34 he held the Metropolitan Suburban seat in the Legislative Council. An individualist, he attracted animosity because of his stand against secession, which partly reflected his merchandising interests; in 1931 he was president of the Federal League and in 1933 led the referendum fight against separation from the Commonwealth. He was a member of the Perth Club.

Nathan played a major part in reducing the indebtedness of the Perth synagogue. Integrity, modesty and acumen had characterized his career, and his contribution to Western Australian and Australian economic planning in the decades between the wars was notable.

From 1933 Nathan was unwell. Survived by his wife (d. 1948) and sons, he died of cerebro-vascular disease on 5 June 1936. He was buried in the Jewish section of Karrakatta cemetery and his estate was sworn for probate at £14 698. His son Lawrence became managing director of Atkins Pty Ltd.

Westralian Judean, 1 July 1936; Aust Jewish Hist Soc, *J*, 6 (1964-69), no 7; *West Australian*, 6 June 1936; Nathan papers (Battye Lib); Sir G. F. Pearce papers (NL).   D. MOSSENSON

NATHAN, SIR MATTHEW (1862-1939), governor, was born on 3 January 1862 at Paddington, London, second son of Jewish parents Jonah Nathan, businessman, and his second wife Miriam, née Jacobs. After private tuition, in 1878-80 he studied with distinction at the Royal Military Academy, Woolwich, and in 1882 left the School of Military Engineering, Chatham, as lieutenant, Royal Engineers. He served in Sierra Leone and Egypt (1883-87) and India and Burma (1887-90). From 1895 he was secretary of the Colonial Defence Committee and was promoted major in 1898.

Acting governor of Sierra Leone in 1899, Nathan was governor of the Gold Coast (1900-04), Hong Kong (1904-07) and Natal (1907-09). He was appointed C.M.G. (1899), K.C.M.G. (1902) and G.C.M.G. (1908), and promoted lieut-colonel (1908). Having fallen out of favour with the Colonial Office, he became secretary of the British Post Office in 1909, secretary of the Board of Inland Revenue in 1911, then under-secretary for Ireland in 1914. Blamed for failing to detect the signs of impending revolution in 1916, reassuring his chief as late as 14 April that 'all was well in Ireland', he resigned two days after the Easter rising. First secretary of the pensions ministry in 1917, he was removed by Lloyd George to the secretaryship of a commission into higher wages for women. Nathan never married, but conducted discreet *affaires* with, among others, Constance Spry, author of books on cooking and flower arranging.

Nathan accepted the offer of the governorship of Queensland in June 1920, in succession to Goold-Adams [q.v.9], and assumed office on 3 December. After some early difficulties he established a reasonable working relationship with Premier E. G. Theodore [q.v.], who had failed to persuade the Colonial Office to appoint an Australian governor. Nathan's term was relatively free of political crises, although he was petitioned to recommend refusal of royal assent to the bill to abolish the Legislative Council. Convinced of the absence of 'any very strong or widespread feeling in the country against this assent', he recommended it on 1 December 1921. In November, a similar example of Theodore's determination to implement Labor policy had placed Nathan in a position of sympathy with the senior judiciary affected by the judges retirement bill, but also in the constitutional position of refusing to refer the bill for royal assent. Relations were also somewhat strained by Theodore's legislation for proxy voting in the Legislative Assembly. Disapproving of Theodore's manipulation of the constitution, in December 1921 Nathan suspected that his next move would be an attempt to abolish governorships, but this Theodore denied at the time.

Despite a slight decline in health, Nathan travelled extensively within Queensland, visited the southern States in 1922 and spoke willingly and at length on public occasions. He appears to have gained general public approval, despite the earlier reservations of those Irish Catholics who retained painful memories of 1916. He actively supported the boy scout and girl guide movements, sought to promote British immigration to Queensland and interested himself in study of the Great Barrier Reef, as well as local history and the origin of place names in Queensland. He was chancellor of the University of Queensland in 1922-26 and was awarded an honorary LL.D. in 1925.

Nathan left Queensland in September 1925. Involved from 1922 in the planning, organization and financing of the British Great Barrier Reef expedition (1928-29), he was chairman of sub-committees of the Civil Research Committee and the Economic Advisory Council. In 1927-28 he advised on the Ceylon Constitution. He retired to his house at West Coker, Somerset, and was high sheriff of the county to 1934. Nathan died at West Coker on 18 April 1939 and was buried in the Jewish cemetery at Willesden, London. Portion of his library was donated to the John Oxley [q.v.2] Library, Brisbane, after World War II.

DNB, 1931-40; A. P. Haydon, *Sir Matthew Nathan* (Brisb, 1976), and for bibliog; *Queenslander*, 26 Sept 1925; *The Times*, 19, 22 Apr, 8 June 1939; Governor's despatches and correspondence, Gov/58-59, 69 (QA).   PAUL D. WILSON

NAYLOR, HENRY DARNLEY (1872-1945), classical scholar and advocate of collective security in international relations, was born on 21 February 1872 at Scarborough, Yorkshire, England, son of John Naylor, composer and organist of York Minster, and his wife Mary Ann, née Chatwin. He was educated at St Peter's School, York, and at Trinity College, Cambridge, where he gained a first class in the classical Tripos in 1894 and the Walker prize. He also distinguished himself as a footballer and a mountaineer.

In 1895, for health reasons, he took up the post of lecturer at Ormond [q.v.5] College in the University of Melbourne; from 1903 he was vice-master. In 1906 he was appointed professor of classics in the University of Adelaide. He had married on 21 July 1898 Jessie Cairns Lloyd (d. 1913) of Melbourne, by whom he had a daughter; on 4 January 1916 he married Ethel Richman Wilson, a nurse and leading member of several women's organizations, by whom he had a son.

Powerfully built and athletic, Naylor was a singularly handsome man: with clean-cut features, massive forehead, thick white hair and candid blue eyes. His natural charm was heightened by his voice and diction, by his humour, cheerfulness and friendliness, and by his wide interests, including music and the literature and history of England, France and Italy, as well as of the classical world (he knew five modern languages). An uncommonly stimulating teacher, he left a lifelong mark on his students, morally and socially as well as intellectually. He advocated the reform of classical teaching and rejoiced in what he saw as the 'marked disappearance of class distinction' in Australia. Although of Anglican background, he was now a Presbyterian and opposed gambling. Among his hobbies was bridge, which he played well. He was a founder and president of the South Australian Amateur Football League.

Like his mentor Gilbert Murray [q.v.], he was a serious scholar and a serious citizen of the world. His specialist interests were Euripides, Horace, and Latin word order. He contributed frequently to the *Classical Review* and the *Classical Quarterly* as well as to the *Encyclopaedia Britannica* (1929). Among his published works were *Latin and English idiom* (Cambridge, 1909), which is also a study of Livy; *Short parallel syntax of Latin and Greek* (Adelaide, 1910); *More Latin and English idiom* (Cambridge, 1915); and *Horace, odes and epodes* (Cambridge, 1922). He was vice-president of the British Classical Association in 1913. He gave much effort to conserving and improving the quality of English in Australia, spoken and written, but became pessimistic about it.

On the creation of the League of Nations Naylor perhaps did more than anyone to make Australians aware of its existence, purpose and activities. At the time he was active as a member of the council of the University of Adelaide, as the founding chairman of Scotch College, Adelaide, as chairman of the Workers' Educational Association, and, soon, as a member of the council of St Mark's College, but the League of Nations Union, which he founded and guided in South Australia, took up a part of every day.

In 1927 Naylor retired to Cumberland in England to give his time mainly to public affairs, particularly the League of Nations Union. His campaigning, devoted and tireless, increased in proportion to the worsening of the international situation. In 1929 he stood, unsuccessfully, as a Liberal Party candidate for Whitehaven. The outbreak of World War II gave him a desolatory sense of failure, a little heightened by his son's record as a gallant soldier. Naylor died on 8 December 1945 at Cockermouth, Cumberland.

Mail (Adel), 15 Mar 1913; *The Times*, 11 Dec 1945; *Advertiser* (Adel), 12 Dec 1945; D5390, miscellaneous (SAA); personal knowledge and information from Dr V. A. Edgeloe, Kensington Gardens, Adel.   W. R. CROCKER

NAYLOR, RUPERT (RUFUS) THEODORE (1882-1939), sporting entrepreneur and gambler, was born on 14 August 1882 at Chippendale, Sydney, third son of Henry John Naylor, native-born labourer, and his South Australian wife Susannah, née Phillips. After basic education at West Wyalong, from 12 he worked as a miner and at 17 was a licensed bookmaker. He promoted sporting contests in Queensland, and on the Western Australian goldfields in 1906.

In 1908 Naylor took a stable of athletes to South Africa and next year staged match races in Johannesburg between Jack Donaldson [q.v.8], Arthur Postle [q.v.] and the American Charles Holway. He quickly established business interests including a sports stadium and a chain of picture theatres. He spent 1913-17 based in London as overseas manager of African Theatres Trust Ltd. Returning to Johannesburg he founded a weekly newspaper, *L.S.D., Life, Sport and Drama* and extended his gambling interests with casinos and a lottery in Lourenço Marques, Portuguese East Africa (Mozambique), running a special Friday night train, 'the Rufe Naylor Express' for his Johannesburg patrons. He also kept a string of racehorses, and opened several proprietary racecourses after a bitter fight with the Jockey Club of South Africa. In 1919 he was elected to the Johannesburg Municipal Council and that year was acquitted of charges of bribery.

After some years in India, Naylor had returned to Sydney by 1925 and set up as a bookmaker on Associated Racing Clubs' courses and was then licensed by the Australian Jockey Club. His activities over the next decade were colourful. He was managing director of Empire Theatres Ltd which built the vast Empire Theatre in Sydney, and promoted mechanical-hare greyhound racing, boxing and cycling. Giving up bookmaking in 1930 after being questioned by A.J.C. stewards about his alleged ownership of racehorses with Fred Angles, a big punter, he devised a profitable scheme for selling 'shares' in lottery tickets, but was prosecuted next year. He was separately charged with keeping 'a common gaming house'. Turned punter, he founded the weekly *Racing Reflections* and became known for the radio programme, 'Racing Revelations', which he broadcast over 2KY; he was warned not to transmit betting information in codes in 1931. He befriended Cyril Angles and arranged for him to call races for 2KY. In 1933 he managed the racehorse Winooka on an expedition to the United States of America. Next year he was defeated as an Independent for the Federal seat of Lang.

That year Naylor was warned off registered racecourses by the A.J.C. for allegedly giving misleading false information to the committee. His injunction against disqualification was upheld by the Supreme Court, but in 1937 he lost when the A.J.C. chairman Sir Colin Stephen [q.v.] appealed to the Privy Council, and was formally disqualified at 'the committee's pleasure'. In his long legal battle Naylor symbolized the 'little man's' fight against bureaucratic authority and class legislation, which was seen as protecting the gambling interests of the wealthy while attempting to destroy those of the working classes, and so he became a minor folk-hero in the 1930s.

Naylor died of heart disease at his Centennial Park home on 25 September 1939. He was survived by his wives Catherine, née Hammersley, and Phyllis, née Penberthy, and by a son of his first marriage. He bequeathed his body to Sydney Hospital for research and the ashes to Catherine in London.

E. Rosenthal (comp), *Southern African dictionary of national biography* (Lond, 1966); *Worker* (Syd), 23 Jan 1909; *Smith's Weekly* (Syd), 30 May 1925; *SMH*, 22 Oct, 6 Nov 1931, 4 Dec 1933, 30 Mar, 14, 18 Apr, 8 May 1934, 8 Apr 1935, 21 Jan 1936, 4, 7 May 1937, 26 Sept 1939; State Broadcasting Advisory Cttee papers MP544/1 (AAO, Melb); information from editor-in-chief, *Dictionary of South African Biography*.   JOHN O'HARA

NEALE, WILLIAM LEWIS (1853-1913), educationist, was born on 12 May 1853 in London, son of Hilary Williams Neale, shoemaker, and his wife Anne, née Lewis. The family arrived in Adelaide on 1 January 1856.

It was natural for Neale to regard himself as a South Australian. He attended Pulteney Street school and at 15 became a pupil-teacher there, beginning a distinguished career in primary education in South Australia as teacher, headmaster and inspector. He had firm Methodist beliefs. As a protégé of J. A. Hartley [q.v.4] he was headmaster at Kapunda (1878-83) and Sturt Street, Adelaide (1884-90). While at Kapunda he gave important evidence on behalf of the masters of model schools to the 1882-83 royal commission on the working of the education Acts; and at Sturt Street he established the sixth or exhibition class which was arguably the beginning of state secondary education for boys in South Australia. In his inspectorial years (1891-1904) he was, as a New Educationist, almost as scathing about education in South Australia as he was to be about schooling in Tasmania. He was also active in both States in instituting superannuation schemes for teachers and the public service.

In February 1904 Neale was invited by Premier W. B. Propsting [q.v.] to inquire into the educational administration and system of primary education in Tasmania. On the strength of Neale's reputation and his terse, yet comprehensive and forthright report, (Sir) John Evans [q.v.8], who had succeeded Propsting in July, appointed Neale director of education from 1 January 1905 and charged him with the task of implementing his recommended reforms.

Neale made the training of teachers his priority. Appointed to instil 'firmer discipline' into a service notoriously lax and steeped with political influence, he nevertheless offended public opinion when the tone of his correspondence in censuring his teachers became known. As an administrator he was accused of rigidity, harshness and, above all, lack of tact. His alleged discourtesy to some of his women teachers especially lost him public sympathy. His system of education—his curriculum and teaching methods as distinct from his administration—also attracted criticism but far less antagonism. A fundamental cause of discontent was that certain Tasmanian teachers considered that South Australian teachers imported by Neale were receiving preferential treatment.

Agitation from some teachers, boards of advice and politicians led to three royal commissions to inquire into Neale's administration: two in 1907 and one early in 1909. By mid-1908 the disaffected teachers had gained control of the executive of the Teachers' Union and the committee of classifiers and were supported by politicians hoping to embarrass the Evans government. The Hobart *Mercury*, mouthpiece of the Legislative Council, was particularly hostile towards him. This combination proved too strong for both Neale and the ministry that had appointed him. The five politicians of the 1909 commission, but not P. Goyen, an educationist from New Zealand, recommended that Neale be dismissed. He resigned in June and refused the offer of the principalship of the Teachers' College, Hobart. Despite opposition to his schemes and methods, Neale achieved much-needed reform of the antiquated educational system.

Though the government finally agreed to pay him compensation for loss of office, the Tasmanian episode was a personal disaster for Neale; he ran the 'gauntlet of troubles'. He left Tasmania, however, with the knowledge that he had been able to lay the foundations of what promised to become an efficient, modern and progressive system.

Neale returned to Adelaide in 1910 where he died from cerebral haemorrhage on 16 December 1913. His wife Nancy, née Leaver, whom he had married on 15 February 1874, two sons and two daughters survived him. Denied reinstatement in the South Australian Education Department, he had spent the last two years of his life as senior clerk in the local land tax branch of the Commonwealth Treasury.

Roy Soc of Tas, *Papers and Procs*, 104, 1970, p 51; *Mercury* (Hob), and *Register* (Adel), 17 Dec 1913; PL 56/1 and GRG 18 Series 2 2390/1909 (SAA); letter from W. L. Neale to A. Williams, 24 Oct 1909 (SAA); information from Mr B. Pirkis, Launc, Tas.   P. H. NORTHCOTT

NEIGHBOUR, GEORGE HENRY (1848-1915), teacher, lawyer and acting judge, was born on 4 June 1848 in London, son of Henry Thomas Neighbour, engineer, and his wife Mary, née Black. He received his early education in Sheffield, Yorkshire, passing the Cambridge local examinations with first-class honours at the age of 15, and came to Melbourne with his family in 1864 because of his father's indifferent health. Next year he entered the University of Melbourne (B.A., 1868; M.A., 1870; LL.B. 1871). He was admitted to the Bar in 1872. On 7 February 1877, at St Paul's Church, Neighbour married Mary James, eldest daughter of the university registrar.

Neighbour at first turned to coaching, then in January 1872 founded Carlton College (later Essendon Grammar School) in Nicholson Street, Fitzroy. He remained its headmaster until he commenced practice as a barrister in 1877, reading with Edward de Verdon, Q.C., and G. H. F. (later Mr Justice) Webb [q.v.6]. He continued at the Bar for the next thirteen years, some of that time as an amalgam barrister and solicitor. While in practice he also lectured on the law of obligations, equity and insolvency at the University of Melbourne until he was appointed chief clerk (equivalent to master) of the Supreme Court (1900-15). In 1901 he was appointed K.C.

As chief clerk Neighbour also acted as commissioner of patents and trade marks and as master in Equity and lunacy. In 1901 he presided over the first interstate conference of commissioners of patents. His most important additional duties were those of an acting county court judge. He sat in the Insolvency Court and in General Sessions for periods totalling nearly four years in 1901-11. The appointment was popular, but the discharge of judicial duties concurrently with tenure as a permanent public servant attracted repeated protests from the legal profession and complaints by the Law Institute. The practice was discontinued in 1911.

In July 1906 Neighbour became involved in a minor scandal concerning John Wren [q.v.] and his Collingwood tote. An extensive anti-gambling campaign, led by W. H. Judkins [q.v.9], a zealous Methodist lay preacher, forced the Bent [q.v.3] government to introduce an anti-gaming bill. Judkins alleged extensive corruption against Wren, including bribery of the police, and implicating the chief secretary, Sir Samuel Gillott [q.v.9]. When Neighbour quashed on appeal the convictions against Wren and his associates, because of the unsatisfactory police evidence, Judkins suggested that he had been corruptly influenced by Wren. The allegations led Neighbour to make a public statement to the press, unprecedented in a member of the judiciary, justifying his decision and denying the charges.

Neighbour died of tuberculosis at his home on 19 December 1915 and was buried with Anglican rites in Boroondara cemetery; his wife, two sons and four daughters survived him. Described as a 'scholarly gentleman' he had wide interests and great dedication to his work. Neighbour held a commission as captain in the Victorian Militia and assisted with the design of military fortifications at Queenscliff and Point Nepean. He was a member of the Institute of Actuaries, London. He left no estate. His widow unsuccessfully petitioned the government for an *ex gratia* payment equivalent to two years salary, in recognition of his additional official duties. An illuminated address to him is in the principal's office at Penleigh and Essendon Grammar School.

J. Smith (ed), *Cyclopedia of Victoria*, 1 (Melb, 1903); A. Dean, *A multitude of counsellors* (Melb, 1968); N. Brennan, *John Wren* (Melb, 1971); R. Campbell, *A history of the Melbourne Law School, 1857 to 1973* (Melb, 1977); E. H. Buggy, *The real John Wren* (Melb, 1977); *J of Religious Hist*, 10 (1977-78), no 1; *Argus*, 16 Feb 1877, 18, 19 Sept 1906, 20 Dec 1915; *Table Talk*, 17 May 1900, 13 Jan 1916; *Bulletin*, 2 June 1900; *Age*, 22, 24, 25 Sept 1906, 20 Dec 1915; Neighbour papers (LaTL).   H. A. FINLAY

NEIL, EDWIN LEE (1872-1934), businessman, was born on 13 October 1872 at Charlton upon Medlock, Lancashire, England, son of a Scot, James Neil, salesman, and his wife Margaret, née McCallum. He left school at 12 and with his family migrated to Sydney in 1884. After working in warehouses, Neil joined the English, Scottish & Australian Bank. Posted south to head office, he observed the collapse of 'Marvellous Melbourne'. In 1895 he joined his father's drapery firm, Wright & Neil, as its accountant and when it was taken over by Sidney Myer [q.v.] in 1911, stayed on. On 11 September 1900 he had married Lucy Harriet Hunt at Christ Church, South Yarra.

A tall, careful, religious, conservative man, who wore pince-nez, Neil became responsible for the financial planning and delicate negotiations underpinning Myer's ambitious schemes. Neil's caution, business connexions and experience complemented Myer's intuitive flair and energy. In running the Myer Emporium, Neil especially concerned himself with the control and training of the staff. In the manner of a Christian patriarch, at times severe, at times lenient, he cultivated loyalty and enthusiasm by inspections, lectures and exhortations, stressing the desirability of good health and manners, and the avoidance of strong drink (Myer's did not sell liquor during his lifetime). He installed a doctor and nurses who daily attended staff and customers. With incorporation in 1917, Neil became manager and co-director with Sidney Myer, and in 1925 when the Myer Emporium Ltd was formed, managing director. He groomed A. H. Tolley as his successor. In the 1920s when Myer was often absent for up to six months in a year, Neil was in charge, an arrangement that encouraged speculation about growing misunderstanding. In the few months between Myer's death and his own, Neil was chairman of directors, addressing shareholders from his sickbed.

Apart from his work Neil's chief interests were music and the Church. He played the organ at St Hilary's, East Kew, and although his mother had been a fervent Congregationalist, Neil was a committed Anglican: member of synod, the Church Missionary Society, the Melbourne Bible Institute, a leader in the Days of Prayer movement, and a lay canon of St Paul's Cathedral.

Appointed to the board of the Melbourne Homeopathic (Prince Henry's) Hospital, Neil found the institution's sturdy loyalty to homeopathic principles incompatible with the need for reorganization, and after some years of frustration resigned. In 1925 Prime Minister S. M. (Viscount) Bruce [q.v.7] appointed him commissioner in charge of the Australian section at the British Empire Exhibition, Wembley, London. Using the opportunity to press for an Imperial preference scheme, he criticized the government's failure to foster Australian products by advertising. He was appointed C.B.E. in 1926.

During the Depression Neil took a public stand on national policy, opposing E. G. Theodore's [q.v.] scheme of expenditure (Neil belonged to the 'balance the books' school), and J. T. Lang's [q.v.] plan of repudiation. In February 1931 Neil helped to found the Citizens' League, was joint vice-president with G. J. Coles, and wrote a pamphlet, *Why we need a citizens' league*. The league amalgamated with the All for Australia League which late in the year was absorbed into the United Australia Party.

Neil, who had not been well since he fell off a ladder while cleaning a gutter, died on 17 December 1934 at home at Kew and was buried in Box Hill cemetery. At his funeral the Salvation Army, the Myer Emporium choir and metropolitan choral societies sang his favourite hymns. He was survived by his wife, a missionary son and three daughters. His estate was sworn for probate at £28 506. In death as in life, Neil epitomized that successful marriage of commerce with Protestantism, which was once the hallmark of Melbourne.

A. Marshall, *The gay provider* (Melb, 1961); J. Templeton, *Prince Henry's* (Melb, 1969); R. Cooksey (ed), 'The great Depression in Australia', *Labour Hist*, 1970, no 17; *C of E Messenger* (Vic), 21 Dec 1934; *Table Talk*, 11 Mar 1926; *Argus*, 20 Apr 1927, 16-26 Feb 1931, 18, 19 Dec 1934; P. Nicholls, The rise of the United Australia Party (M.A. thesis, Univ Melb, 1971); A. H. Tolley, Untitled memoir on E. Lee Neil (nd, 1935?, Univ Melb Archives).   P. H. DE SERVILLE

NEILD, JOHN CASH (1846-1911), insurance agent and politician, was born on 4 January 1846 at Bristol, Somerset, England, second son of John Cash Neild, surgeon, and his wife Maria, née Greenwood. In 1853 the family migrated to New Zealand but, caught up in the Taranaki wars, moved to Sydney in 1860. John junior was educated privately before entering the office of (J. L.) Montefiore, Joseph [qq.v.5,4] & Co. In 1865 he set up as a commission agent, but soon switched to insurance. He became manager of several companies and later worked as an arbitrator and adjuster.

As a young man Neild was active in the Free Church of England; on 29 October 1868 at Paddington he married (with Congregational forms) Clara Matilda Gertrude, daughter of Rev. Philip Agnew. Their only child died in 1876 and Clara in 1879. At St Paul's Anglican Church, Redfern, he married Georgine Marie Louise Uhr on 19 February 1880.

Politically ambitious, Neild served on the Woollahra Municipal Council in 1876-90 and was mayor in 1888-89. After standing unsuccessfully in 1882, he represented Paddington as a free trader in the Legislative Assembly in 1885-89, 1891-94 and 1895-1901. On 23 June 1886 he spoke for nine hours against the Jennings [q.v.4] government's introduction of mild *ad valorem* duties, thereby earning the sobriquet 'Jawbone'. In parliament he was indefatigable, serving on the public works, elections and qualifications and joint library committees and on numerous select committees. He introduced some twenty-one different bills (some repeatedly) but few became law. From 1887 he had charge in the assembly of Sir Alfred Stephen's [q.v.6] divorce extension bill, which was eventually enacted in 1892, and that year carried the Children's Protection Act. In 1895 he served on the Public Service Board.

Neild had a genius for getting into trouble —and for wriggling out of it. His expenses (amounting to £4950) as New South Wales executive commissioner for the Adelaide Jubilee International Exhibition in 1887 were questioned in parliament for several years, but he was cleared of accepting an office of profit under the crown in 1887 and of extravagance in 1890. While grand master of the Loyal Orange Lodge of New South Wales in 1891-93 he outraged extreme Protestants by publicly praying for the recovery of the Pope.

In 1895 Neild began agitating for old-age pensions: he was a member of the 1896 select committee and in 1896-98 was honorary royal commissioner in Europe on old-age pensions, state insurance and charitable relief. In 1898 he published his report, which the *Sydney Morning Herald* conceded was 'admittedly of great value, and involving a great deal of work'. In pecuniary difficulties, he received £350 to cover personal expenses. Although Neild was again cleared of accepting an office of profit, the Reid [q.v.] government was defeated on a related no confidence motion in September 1899—Neild had helped to precipitate the downfall of the strongest government in New South Wales since 1856.

Meanwhile in 1896 he had raised a volunteer regiment and on 11 June was gazetted captain commanding the St George's English Rifle Regiment. Although lacking previous military experience and 'tact and judgement', he was promoted major in July and lieutcolonel on 27 April 1898. By 1899 governor Lord Beauchamp [q.v.7] recorded that the regiment was 'in a state of ridiculous insubordination. Officers abused officers, the men never attended. Signs of incapacity were noticed at the Easter manoeuvres'. Claiming parliamentary privilege, Neild attacked his critics and superior officers in the press, but in April was placed under 'open arrest'. A military court of inquiry in 1900, although censorious, left him in command.

In 1901-10 Neild represented New South Wales in the Senate; he was a member of the Committee of Disputed Returns and Qualifications for some years. Impervious to rebuffs, he continued to harangue the House in 'virile and robust' tones on 'every conceivable subject'. He used the Senate to attack the military administration and Major General Sir Edward Hutton [q.v.9], who tried to have him retired because of near mutiny in his regiment. Neild complained of intimidation. A Senate select committee on privilege in 1904 cleared Brigadier H. Finn [q.v.8] but found that Hutton had tried to interfere with Neild in the discharge of his duties as a senator. Neild retired from the militia next year, but was appointed honorary colonel in 1906.

A big man physically, he had a Garibaldi beard, wore loud check suits, and curled 'his moustache fiercely like the "Dashing Militaire"'. His recreations were cricket and literature—in the 1870s he was music and drama critic for the Catholic *Evening Post* and in 1896 published a volume of verse, *Songs of the Southern Cross*.

Neild suffered from hepatic cirrhosis and, survived by his wife, son and daughter, died on 8 March 1911 at his Woollahra home; he was buried with military honours in the Anglican section of Waverley cemetery. His estate was valued for probate at £595.

Cyclopedia of N.S.W. (Syd, 1907); B. Nairn, *Civilising capitalism* (Canb, 1973); *PD* (NSW), 1885-86, 20, p 2881, 2909; *PP* (NSW), 1890, 8, p 73, 1899, 1, p 433; *PD* (Cwlth), 1901-02, 10, p 13701, 1903, 17, p 5383, 1904, 18, p 46; *PP* (Cwlth), Senate, 1904, 1, p 541; *ISN*, 15 June 1887; *Daily Telegraph* (Syd), 18 June, 28 July 1894, 15 Feb 1896; *Table Talk*, 10 Apr 1896; *Punch* (Melb), 30 Aug 1906; *SMH*, 9 Mar 1911; *T&CJ*, 15 Mar 1911; *Freeman's J* (Syd), 16 Mar 1911; M. Rutledge, Sir Alfred Stephen and divorce law reform in New South Wales, 1886-1892 (M.A. thesis, ANU, 1966); M. Lyons, Aspects of sectarianism in New South Wales circa 1865 to 1880 (Ph.D. thesis, ANU, 1972); Deakin papers (NL); Beauchamp diary (ML).
MARTHA RUTLEDGE

NEILSON, JOHN SHAW (1872-1942), poet, was born on 22 February 1872 at Penola, South Australia, eldest son of Scottish-born JOHN NEILSON (1844-1922), bushworker and selector, and his wife Margaret, née McKinnon. Known as Jock, he attended the local school for less than two years and as a small child worked as a farm-labourer for his father. In 1881 John Neilson senior and his half-brother Dave Shaw joined the South Australian farmers making the long trek by wagon over the border to take up selections under the Victorian Land Act (1869), and were each allotted 320 acres (130 ha) north of Lake Minimay.

In the first year on their selection, the Neilsons cleared six acres (2.4 ha) and ploughed, sowed and harvested by hand, but after deducting the money owed to the storekeeper found they had made £7 from the crop. Impoverished and bankrupt, they were forced to seek station work to exist, and only devoted their spare time to the selection where the family lived in a crude mud-plastered house for eight years. Neilson senior asked for extensions in which to pay the annual rent year after year, until in 1888 the storekeeper foreclosed. By June 1889 they had shifted to Dow Well, a few miles west of Nhill. Although he did his share of clearing and working the land, Shaw Neilson found time to wander the swamps and woodlands as a keen observer of Nature, gathering eggs and listening to birdsongs, foraging for mushrooms, and tracking wild bees, and for some months went to school in 1885-86, leaving when he turned 14.

Neilson and his father generally worked as farm-hands, timber-cutters, or road-workers for the shire council, but were also staunch unionists when shearing. Both belonged to the local literary society, and both won prizes for verse in the Australian Natives' Association competitions in 1893. The father was a published bush poet, who appears to have started writing verse when he was about 30, and contributed to local newspapers and Adelaide *Punch*. He won another prize for verse in 1897, but achieved his widest popularity in outback shearing sheds with a song, 'Waiting for the Rain'. Although he obviously lacked 'the outstanding poetical genius of his son', he was a writer of some achievement in the face of a lifelong bitter struggle for existence and little schooling; his verse was issued in book form, *The men of the fifties*, in 1938.

Frank Shann, editor of the *Nhill Mail*, printed verse by Shaw Neilson for some years. Most was conventional and undistinguished. The family moved into Nhill in mid-1893, still deep in poverty and existing on municipal contracts and farm work, but by May 1895 they were on the road again travelling north to take up a scrub-covered Mallee selection near Lake Tyrrell, which had to be rolled and burned and grubbed before ploughing and sowing. Battling drought and bushfire to survive, there was little time or energy for writing poetry. One of Shaw's few poems appeared in the Sydney *Bulletin* in December 1896 and nothing more until the end of 1901.

The Neilsons continued share-farming combined with scrub-clearing for wages and contract work, but moved to a house at Kaneira to be closer to the shire work for a while, before shifting once more to an area totalling 2400 acres (970 ha), about 26 miles (42 km) north of Sea Lake, in the parish of Eureka. Despite the general drought, the Eureka district had heavy rains in 1902 which enabled the Neilsons to harvest some hay and provide agistment for horses. While their finances improved, personal grief struck hard: Neilson's sister Maggie, who had been ill for some years, died in 1903, followed by another sister Jessie in 1907. He himself was in very poor health, and did little writing for nearly four years, but contributed to the *Bulletin* several times between 1901 and 1906, with some lighter verse and limericks appearing in Randolph Bedford's [q.v.7] *Clarion* a little later. About then his sight began to fail, and for the rest of his life he was unable to read and write legibly and depended on the assistance of family members or fellow workmen.

John Shaw Neilson is often called 'the green singer', because of his fondness for that colour, and sometimes 'the roadmender' because most of his adult life was spent making roads, quarrying stone, or on bush work, and always in poverty. [Dame] Mary Gilmore [q.v.9] spoke of her first meeting with him: 'and when I saw his work-swollen hands, with the finger-nails worn to the quick by the abrading stone, I felt a stone in my heart'. Yet he was so much more than an unschooled navvy; he was, as Percival Serle [q.v.] describes him, 'a slender man of medium height with a face that suggested his kindliness, refinement and innate beauty of character'.

The unique gifts of Shaw Neilson may never have survived without the encouragement and practical assistance of A. G. Stephens [q.v.], who placed all his work, although much of it was never paid for, and edited, punctuated and arranged the rough manuscripts sent to him. Neilson was largely self taught in the techniques of poetry, and shows immense change and development in both theme and technique over the years that led Tom Inglis Moore to claim: 'as a pure singer Neilson at his best stands unsurpassed in modern English-speaking poetry, and he can take his rightful place in company with the finest lyrists of all English literature'. When Stephens's *Bookfellow* magazine was revived in 1911, Neilson became a regular contributor, and the editor began collecting his poems which were revised and included in *Heart of spring* (1919).

In 1923 Louise Dyer [q.v.8] paid £100 for the printing of *Ballad and lyrical poems*, which consisted of the first book and twenty additional poems. A volume of *New poems* (23 poems) was published in 1927, followed by his *Collected poems* in 1934, which included the previously published poems and only twelve new ones. When *Beauty imposes* (14 poems) was issued in 1938, the young R. D. Fitz-Gerald said 'no other Australian poet has Neilson's skill with words and rhythms', although he pointed to what he considered limitations in vocabulary and weaknesses in construction. Lesser claims have been made on behalf of Neilson's subtle craftsmanship; H. J. Oliver, for example, has seen him as 'a fascinating minor poet, who in his best lyrics wrote with an unusual delicacy of expression'. Other critics have looked beyond his lyricism. A. R. Chisholm recognized Neilson's instinctive affinity with the French Symbolist poets and H. M. Green wrote of him as 'perhaps the most notable of all Australia's mystic poets', whose images from Nature hint at a beauty beyond the objects portrayed: 'at his best Neilson's vision is so intense that it seems to carry him beyond himself'. A recent assessment by Vivian Smith rates him with Christopher Brennan [q.v.7] as 'the foremost poet of his generation'.

Shaw Neilson spent much of his life in tents, in navvy camps and in cheap boarding-houses while working at casual jobs all over Victoria (and in parts of New South Wales) to an estimated total of 200 jobs in thirty years. By the time he was in his mid-fifties the strain of hard physical labour had taken its toll on a man who had never been robust. A group of Melbourne literary people worked to obtain Neilson a tiny Commonwealth Literary Fund pension, and eventually in 1928 he was employed as a messenger and attendant in the office of the Victorian Country Roads Board, which was set in the gardens surrounding the Exhibition Building. Neilson stuck at this permanent work for thirteen years although he hated the 'dreadful noise of the city', living all that time with relations at Footscray, but not writing many poems. Early in 1941 he took extended sick leave and went to Queensland to visit James Devaney, who left a picture of this ailing, frail, but cheerful man stepping from the train in Brisbane wearing a dressing gown.

He returned to Melbourne in ill health in spite of patient care and died, unmarried, of heart disease on 12 May 1942. Neilson was buried in the Footscray cemetery where Sir John Latham [q.v.], a fervent admirer, addressed the mourners, and fellow poet Bernard O'Dowd [q.v.] made an oration. Vance Palmer [q.v.] recorded that Shaw Neilson 'in his coffin . . . looked like a small wax image of some saint of the Middle Ages', but the poet's death passed with little notice, partly because poetic fashions had changed, but mainly because of the intensity of the war. After his death several collections of his poetry were made, including *Unpublished poems of Shaw Neilson* (1947), *Witnesses of spring* (1970), and *The poems of Shaw Neilson* (1965, revised and enlarged 1973). His partial autobiography was published in 1978, and his earliest printed verse, *Green days and cherries* in 1981. A number of Neilson's poems have been set to music by composers from 1925 to the present, including W. G. Whittaker, Frank Francis, Alfred Hill [q.v.9], and especially Margaret Sutherland. 'Shaw Neilson', Devaney so accurately said, was 'the poor working-man who has left us a legacy of endless wealth'.

John Shaw Neilson: A memorial (Melb, 1942); J. Devaney, *Shaw Neilson* (Syd, 1944); L. J. Blake, *Shaw Neilson in the Wimmera* (Horsham, Vic, 1961); H. Anderson, *Shaw Neilson* (Syd, 1964); H. F. Chaplin, *A Neilson collection* (Syd, 1964); H. J. Oliver, *Shaw Neilson* (Melb, 1969); H. Anderson and L. J. Blake, *John Shaw Neilson* (Adel, 1972); H. Anderson and L. Blake (eds), *Green days and cherries* (Melb, 1981); L. Kramer (ed), *The Oxford history of Australian literature* (Melb, 1981); *Southerly*, 17, no 1, 1956.   HUGH ANDERSON

NEITENSTEIN, FREDERICK WILLIAM (1850-1921), prison reformer, was born on 8

January 1850 at Shoreditch, London, son of Frederick Henry John Neitenstein, sugar refiner, and his wife Mary, née Nutkins. Educated at Sherman College, Kent, he entered the mercantile marine and served with the Devitt & Moore Line. In 1872 he arrived in Sydney and, liking the colony, stayed. On 6 October 1873 he was appointed mate and clerk in the Nautical School Ship, *Vernon*, and on 1 April 1878 commander and superintendent. In St Thomas' Church, Balmain, he married Marion Walker on 26 July 1879.

His new position allowed Captain Neitenstein, as he was always known, to introduce reform of the treatment of juvenile offenders. Unlike other reformers who favoured the boarding-out system, he believed that institutional treatment could be effective. The essence of his system was discipline, surveillance, physical drill and a system of grading and marks. He aimed at creating a 'moral earthquake' in each new boy. Every new admission was placed in the lowest grade and, through hard work and obedience, gradually won a restricted number of privileges. He gained considerable pleasure from this process and preferred the challenge of tackling boys who showed a 'little sturdy hot-headedness at first'. In 1892 the *Vernon* was closed and he became superintendent of the new N.S.S. *Sobraon*.

In 1896, his reputation as a reformer already established, Neitenstein was appointed comptroller-general of New South Wales prisons. Adapting many of his schemes for juvenile reform, he introduced the grading, mark and physical drill programmes, and developed the policy of 'restricted association' and other schemes to reduce contact between inmates as a means of separating different classes of prisoner.

Hoping to turn the prison into a 'moral hospital', Neitenstein sought to remove first offenders, inebriates, juveniles, lunatics and summary offenders from the inmate population. Only 'real criminals' were to be subjected to the new 'reformative regime'. The apparent success of many of these policies in the 1900s was achieved partly through skilful manoeuvring—in 1906 he was able to transfer the cost of maintaining lunatics in prison to the Lunacy Department, thereby effecting on paper a substantial cut in both prison expenditure and the number of recorded prisoners.

Neitenstein was an occasional member of the Public Service Board and served on the Public Service Tender Board, the Central Board for Old-Age Pensions and the 1906 royal commission on weights and measures. He had been a prominent Freemason, was a founder of the Discharged Prisoners' Aid Society and belonged to the Howard Prison Reform League. In 1906 he was appointed I.S.O.

In 1909 Neitenstein retired as comptroller-general and next year from the public service. Parliament granted him a gratuity of £500. Thick-set and round faced, with heavy brows and a luxuriant Edwardian moustache, he was considered an aloof, prudish man, who revelled in the trappings of office and demanded absolute obedience from his subordinates. An earnest bureaucrat, he listed his recreations as reform and philanthropy.

After returning from a two-year visit to England, Neitenstein became a virtual recluse in his Burwood home. Ill health marked his declining years. On 23 April 1921, survived by his daughter, Neitenstein died at home of cerebro-vascular disease and was buried in the Congregational section of Rookwood cemetery.

School Ships *Vernon* and *Sobraon*, Annual Report, 1878-91, 1892-95, *PP* (LC & LA NSW); Prisons Dept, Annual Report, 1896-1909, *PP* (NSW); *Magistrate* (Syd), 1 Sept, 1 Oct 1909; *SMH*, 25 Apr 1921; M. L. Sernack-Cruise, Penal reform in NSW: Frederick William Neitenstein, 1896-1909 (Ph.D. thesis, Univ Syd, 1980); Neitenstein papers (ML).   S. GARTON

NELIGAN, MAURICE WILDER; *see* WILDER-NELIGAN

NELSON, CHARLES (1896?-1948), coalminer and trade unionist, was born at Broxburn, West Lothian, Scotland, son of John Nelson, engineer, and his wife Annie, née Watson. Orphaned at 2, he was reared by his grandparents who indelibly impressed him with their anti-militarism. Forced to leave school at 13 and work in the mines to supplement family income, he joined the Independent Labour Party in 1911 and the Scottish Shale Miners' Association in 1913, but migrated to New South Wales next year.

Active in the 1916 anti-conscription campaign, Nelson joined the Industrial Workers of the World while working on railway construction near Mittagong. He had left the I.W.W. by 1917 and went to the coal-shale mines at Newnes, where he organized for the One Big Union. He married a widow Pauline Feltis, née Radecki, daughter of an artist, on 29 December 1919 at the Central Methodist Mission in Sydney. After campaigning with J. S. Garden [q.v.8] and A. C. Willis [q.v.] for the O.B.U. in Sydney, he returned to Newnes, but suffered the first of several physical breakdowns from over-work.

After his recovery, in 1925 Nelson went to work in the State Mine at Lithgow where he became a leader of the local Militant Minority Movement, a communist front. There he ran classes on Marxism which attracted William

Orr [q.v.]. In 1929 Nelson became president of the State Mine lodge and in 1931 was elected vice-president of the western district of the Australasian Coal and Shale Employees' (Miners') Federation. He also became prominent in the Communist Party of Australia, from which he was expelled briefly in 1932 for placing his union obligations before party loyalties. Nelson attacked the lack of initiative shown by the Miners' Federation's 'oldguard' leadership and the labour movement in general over the 1929-30 northern lock-out and stood unsuccessfully as a M.M.M. candidate for the federation's executive. However, he was resoundingly elected general president in 1934. In mid-1937 the Miners' Federation, under Nelson's guidance, served a substantial log of claims on employers with great success. A supplementary log in 1938 was rejected and in September resulted in the first general coal strike since 1916, which forced concessions.

In February 1938, after a long and involved wrangle between the Labor Council of New South Wales, J. T. Lang [q.v.9] and several trade unions over the *Labor Daily*, Lang lost control of it. Nelson became a director of the newspaper and managing director in August. Next year he continued as managing director of its successor, the *Daily News*.

In December 1940 Nelson was appointed to the Central Reference Board, one of many instrumentalities created in wartime by successive Federal governments to quell coalfield disputes. In February 1941 he was also appointed to the Commonwealth Coal Board and from August was consultant to the Commonwealth coal commissioner, a position he resigned at the direction of the Miners' Federation. That year he was opposed by rank and file over industrial policy and was denigrated for allegedly accepting a £300 bribe to prevent industrial action. A royal commission on secret funds did not clear Nelson, but neither did it satisfactorily vindicate Attorney-General Hughes [q.v.9] nor Prime Minister Fadden, who had ordered the payment. In December 1941 Nelson was narrowly defeated as general president by Harold Wells, another communist.

Suffering from chronic emphysema, Nelson retired to a small orchard near Gosford. Survived by his wife and two daughters, he died there on 26 May 1948 of coronary occlusion and was cremated without religious rites.

E. Ross, *A history of the Miners' Federation of Australia* (Syd, 1970); *Communist Review*, Oct 1937; *Common Cause*, 20 May 1939; *SMH*, 25, 26, 27, 30 Sept, 11, 15, 16, 21, 22 Oct, 12, 13, 25, 26, 27, 29 Nov 1941, 27 May 1948; D. P. Dingsdag, Technological change in N.S.W. underground coalmines, 1904-71 (uncompleted Ph.D. thesis, Univ Wollongong); Militant Minority Movement and Plebs League, Brisb, 1927-29 (bound volume of misc publications, hand-bills and typescripts, ML); interview by author with Mr W. Parkinson, general president, Miners' Federation, 1955-67.

DON DINGSDAG

NELSON, HAROLD GEORGE (1881-1947), engine driver, trade union official and politician, was born on 21 December 1881 at Botany, Sydney, son of Scottish-born John Nelson, shopkeeper, and his wife Elizabeth Ann, née Tighe. Little is known of his early years and nothing of his education. As a young man he was an engine driver in Queensland, where he mainly lived at Gympie and Mount Perry. He married Maud Alice Lawrence with Presbyterian forms at Mount Perry on 17 March 1904.

With his wife and five children Nelson moved to Pine Creek, Northern Territory, in 1913. There he was an engine driver and organizer for the Australian Workers' Union. In July 1914 he became the A.W.U. organizer in Darwin and in 1917 first secretary of the union's Darwin branch. An able administrator and a fiery orator, he was largely responsible for a substantial increase in the A.W.U.'s Territory membership. In 1917 he was also elected to the Darwin Town Council.

Nelson was a dominant figure in the campaign of boycotts and strikes which forced Vestey Brothers to raise wages for their meatworks employees in Darwin. He campaigned for Northern Territory representation in the Commonwealth Parliament and called for removal of the administrator, J. A. Gilruth [q.v.9], who had often clashed with the trade union movement. On 17 December 1918, in an incident later described as the 'Darwin Rebellion', Nelson marched with a few hundred supporters to Government House and demanded that Gilruth leave. Continuing agitation resulted in the government recalling the administrator in February 1919. The subsequent royal commission which investigated Gilruth's administration generally supported Nelson, but the commissioner, Justice N. K. Ewing [q.v.8], was criticized for using Nelson's paid assistance at its hearings.

In April 1921 Nelson stood down as A.W.U. secretary. He was gaoled briefly in June after refusing to pay taxes in a campaign for 'no taxation without representation' that resulted in the Territory being allowed a nonvoting member with limited rights, in the House of Representatives. Nelson was elected narrowly as the Territory's first Federal parliamentarian in December 1922. He stood as an Independent but had trade union support and shortly after his election joined the Australian Labor Party. He spoke ably and frequently in parliament, yet had little success in his attempts to obtain greater expenditure on the Territory or some form of self-government. Defeated by a conservative opponent in September 1934, he later worked as an agent at Alice Springs. He died there of cardiac failure on 26 April 1947, survived by his wife and five children. A son John Norman was to become a member of the House of Representatives and administrator of the Northern Territory.

Nelson's appearance was unimpressive—of medium build, he was quick to put on weight. His spirited speeches, however, nearly always aroused great passions. Trade unionists often saw him as a hero in their struggle for economic and political rights while many others viewed him as a dangerous revolutionary. He was certainly prepared to threaten violence but for the most part believed in a steady accumulation of gains for working people rather than great leaps forward. He closely identified his personal ambitions with those of the movements he supported.

A. Powell, *Far country* (Melb, 1982); F. X. Alcorta, *Darwin rebellion 1911-1919* (Darwin, 1984); P. F. Donovan, *At the other end of Australia* (Brisb, 1984); *Northern Perspective*, 4, no 1, 1981; *Northern Standard* (Darwin), 2 May 1947; Blain papers (Darwin Institute of Technology Lib); information from Mr J. N. Nelson, Alice Springs, NT.

DAVID CARMENT

NELSON, SIR HUGH MUIR (1833-1906), premier and pastoralist, was born on 31 December 1833 at Kilmarnock, Ayrshire, Scotland, son of William Lambie Nelson (d. 1887), stationer, later Presbyterian clergyman and squatter, and his wife Agnes, née Muir. Educated at Edinburgh High School and at the University of Edinburgh for two years, Hugh migrated with his family to Queensland in 1853, became a storekeeper's clerk at Ipswich and then a station-hand at Nelson's Ridges. He managed his father's stations, Tartha, Binbian and Myra, and, subsequently, Burenda Station near Charleville before superintending Eton Vale for Hodgson [q.v.4] and Watts (his brother-in-law) in 1862-72. With Watts he acquired the 40 000-acre (16 200 ha) freehold property Loudon near Dalby, and developed a prize-winning and lucrative stud and wool-producing flock, selling out for £60 000 in 1892 just before the crash.

Unsuccessfully contesting Northern Downs in 1879, Nelson was elected chairman of the Wambo Divisional Board in 1880 and was member of the Legislative Assembly for Northern Downs (7 September 1883-18 May 1888) and Murilla (19 May 1888-22 April 1898).

A strong McIlwraithian [q.v.5], he was secretary for railways from 13 June 1888, and railways and public works from 4 January 1890, in B. D. Morehead's [q.v.5] administration. In the 'Griffilwraith' coalition Nelson was briefly vice-president of the executive council and acting colonial treasurer, then treasurer in McIlwraith's government (27 March to 27 October 1893). Succeeding as premier (27 October 1893 to 13 April 1898) on McIlwraith's prudent resignation, Nelson was vice-president of the executive council, colonial treasurer (until 6 August 1896), chief secretary (from 29 March 1895) and treasurer (6 August 1896 to 2 March 1898). During years of crisis he was the linchpin in Queensland politics.

Upon Nelson fell much of the burden of preserving pastoral and mercantile capitalism against the attacks of newly organized labour. Behind the Scots commonsense and probity of a Presbyterian elder was a shrewd, ruthless, political manipulator and worthy head of the remaining Pure Merino pastoral elite—most having departed for England, the civil service, or bankruptcy. 'Old Never Mind' did mind and was effective when confronted with public crises.

Inheriting McIlwraith's political largesse and dynamic entrepreneurial flair, Griffith's [q.v.9] propertied liberal legalisms and the wealthy's fear of Labor and the lower orders, Nelson framed a series of bleak budgets and unadventurous policies. During the failed shearers' strike in 1894 he fathered the Peace Preservation Act which, while not then enforced, later proved a cheaper, more effective way for the state to use its power than armed force, and set useful precedents for the future. His handling of the Queensland National Bank crisis was his greatest and shrewdest service to colonial capital and bourgeois society. When the Q.N.B. suspended payment on 15 May 1893, Nelson and his friend A. H. Barlow [q.v.7] investigated its affairs and declared it 'basically sound' although aware of its true state. The government then rescued the bank, largely at its own and the depositors' expense. The death of the general manager E. R. Drury [q.v.4] in February 1896 precipitated a deeper political crisis. Nelson used brilliant tactics to preserve the bank, his government and all their friends except the absent McIlwraith, who was ultimately sacrificed by those who '[committed] many illegal things [subsequently] legalized' in these 'necessarily' lawless days. A wedge was driven into Labor and the *status quo* conserved.

Nelson had been appointed K.C.M.G. in 1896 and, while representing Queensland with T. J. Byrnes [q.v.7] at the Queen Victoria Diamond Jubilee celebrations in London in 1897, was made a privy councillor, Hon.

D.C.L. Oxford, Hon. LL.D. Edinburgh and a freeman of Kilmarnock. On 26 July 1898 he became president of the Legislative Council. He was lieut-governor of Queensland in 1904-05.

In private life this dignified, 'splendid physical specimen' with snow-white beard and 'courtly grace of manner' was a 'warm pairson' with a keen sense of humour. He believed that finally 'our minds and souls are ourselves, the rest is only ephemeral', but reasoned that if everyone now devoted himself to these high speculative studies 'where would we get our food and raiment?'. Practising the politics of 'practicalities and the provision of bread and butter', Nelson was more at home with herds and flocks than with rising social democracy.

He was president of the Royal Geographical Society of Australasia (Queensland), the Colonial Political Association and the Queensland Club. He visited British New Guinea in 1898 and acquired 'unrivalled knowledge' of policy there. A chief originator of the Royal Agricultural Society of Toowoomba, he was also chairman of the Brisbane and the Toowoomba Grammar schools trustees, and trustee of the Public Library of Queensland.

Nelson died of cancer at Gabbinbar, Middle Ridge, Toowoomba, on 1 January 1906, and was buried in Toowoomba cemetery after Presbyterian rites and a state funeral. He was survived by his wife Janet, née McIntyre, whom he had married at Toowoomba on 11 August 1870, and by two sons and three daughters. His estate was valued at £26 292.

C. A. Bernays, *Queensland politics during sixty (1859-1919) years* (Brisb, nd, 1919?); J. Kershaw (comp), *Repose with achievement* (Orange, NSW, nd, 1973?); *PD* (Qld), 1893, p 96, 1894, p 472, 1897, p 1058, 1906, p 14; *Echo* (Brisb), 26 Nov 1896; *HSQJ*, 5, no 1, 1953, p 771; *Qld Heritage*, 3 no 9, 1978, p 3; *Brisbane Courier*, 20 Sept, 24 Nov 1897, 5 Mar 1898, 16 Mar 1905, 2 Jan 1906; *Queenslander*, 23 Apr 1898, 6, 13, 27 Jan 1906; *Darling Downs Gazette*, 2 Jan 1906; J. McCormack, The politics of expediency. Queensland government in the eighteen nineties (M.A. thesis, Univ Qld, 1975); Palmer-McIlwraith papers (Oxley Lib); Premiers' correspondence 1893-98 (QA).

D. B. WATERSON

NELSON, WALLACE ALEXANDER (1856-1943), journalist, rationalist and politician, was born on 29 April 1856 at Aberdeen, Scotland, son of John Nelson, comb-factory manager, and his wife Jean, née Dow. Self-education rather than schooling seems to have shaped his lively mind. He ran away to London and at 15 contributed republican verse to *Reynold's Weekly Newspaper*. Revelling in the writings of Darwin, Huxley,

[qq.v.1] Spencer and Bain, he delivered his first lecture, on utilitarianism, in his teens. On 28 December 1877, a journeyman comb-maker, he married Ann Middleton at Aberdeen. In 1880 they went to Sheffield, where the diminutive Nelson (4 ft. 8 ins. (142 cm) tall) was an energetic freethought lecturer from 1883. A member of the Radical Party he associated with socialist luminaries, including William Morris and Edward Carpenter.

Fearing himself 'a dying man', Nelson arrived at Brisbane early in 1888. He was an instant success on Australasian freethought platforms alongside Joseph Symes, Thomas Walker [qq.v.6] and W. W. Collins, lecturing regularly at Brisbane's Gaiety Theatre and debating with all-comers. Restored to health, he became editor of the *Stockwhip* in 1890, encouraged perhaps by William Lane [q.v.9] whom he admired but opposed.

After bungled attempts at parliamentary candidature for Gregory (1893) and Musgrave (1896), Nelson succeeded James Charles Stewart in 1896 as editor of the Rockhampton crusading weekly, the *People's Newspaper*, of which William Kidston [q.v.9] was a proprietor. Having opposed Federation, Nelson became its ardent advocate, contesting the Federal seat of Capricornia for Labor in 1901. Zeal and wit brought the pro-Boer 'fearless Freedom fighter', campaigning against Kanaka labour, to within 160 votes of return.

In July 1901 he arrived at Kalgoorlie to succeed Thomas Henry Bath [q.v.7] as editor of the *Westralian Worker*. Finding employment by trade unionists less than 'unsullied joy', he resigned in December 1902, editing thereafter the Kalgoorlie *Sun* and the unsuccessful Labor-backed *Figaro*. In June 1904-October 1905 Nelson represented the new goldfields constituency of Hannans while the first Western Australian Labor government was in office. His gifts were appreciated in parliament, but political life proved uncongenial and he did not seek re-election. In association with Bath he edited the short-lived Perth *Democrat* (1905), then was leader-writer for the Perth *Daily News*. On 19 May 1908 he was declared bankrupt. Undaunted, he vigorously defended his adopted land, 'the freest democracy in the world', in *Foster Fraser's fallacies and other Australian essays* (Sydney, 1910), and contributed to the Perth literary journal, *Leeuwin*. Appointed official immigration lecturer by the Western Australian government, Nelson while in England in 1914-16 represented several Australian newspapers.

He returned to Sydney, an anti-conscriptionist, as founding editor of the *Australasian Manufacturer* until 1943, ably assisted by his journalist second wife Nora Claire, née Cleary, a 29-year-old Catholic from Beechworth, Victoria, whom he married in Sydney on 21 January 1918. The paper, later sub-titled 'A Weekly Newspaper devoted to Industrial Science and Efficiency', urged organization and modernization. The themes of protection and harmony between capital and labour were elaborated in *Letters to John Workman* (Sydney, 1919), and in his favour-ite column, 'After Business Hours', Nelson added literary whimsy to trade information. By the 1920s he felt Labor had lost its way, and his late-Victorian evolutionary optimism focused on ability. This progression was far from atypical, and it seems to have earned him few enemies.

Supporting economic nationalism as vigor-ously as he had once supported political nationalism, Nelson co-founded the Australia-Made Preference League (1924) and was of-ficial lecturer on the 'Great White Train' which toured New South Wales between Nov-ember 1925 and May 1926. He contributed frequent articles to the *Sydney Morning Her-ald* after 1926.

Survived by his wife and two children of his first marriage, Nelson died on 5 May 1943 at Wollstonecraft, and was cremated. His estate was sworn for probate at £862. 'Known and admired throughout the whole of Australia', Nelson was saluted by the *Rationalist* as the last of a band of stalwarts who 'never wavered in opposition to superstition'.

H. J. Gibbney (comp), *Labor in print* (Canb, 1975); E. Royle, *Radicals, secularists and repub-licans* (Manchester, Eng, 1980); *Aust Manufac-turer*, 15, 22 May, 10 July 1943; *Rationalist*, 19, no 10, June 1943; *Aust Worker*, 6 Apr 1901; *Morning Bulletin* (Rockhampton), 6 Sept 1957.

J. I. ROE

NERLI, GIROLAMO PIERI BALLATI (1860-1926), properly Girolamo Ballati Nerli Pieri Pecci, artist, was born on 21 February 1860 in the Palazzo Pieri Pecci at Siena, son of Italian nobleman Ferdinando Ballati Nerli Pieri Pecci and his wife Henrietta, daughter of Thomas Medwin, biographer of the poet Shelley and author of *Journal of the conver-sations of Lord Byron*, and Ann, Baroness Hamilton of Sweden. Nerli was sometimes called 'Marchese' although his correct title (honorific) was 'Patrizio di Siena'. He was often known in Australia as Signor Nerli.

He studied at the Accademia di Belle Arti in Florence under Antonio Ciseri, whose acad-emic style had been tempered by the in-fluence of the Macchiaioli, a loosely as-sociated group of painters who rebelled against the illusionism of the official art of the academies and advocated painting in the open air. Like the French Impressionists they were concerned to portray light, but were less con-cerned with momentary effects than with conveying a metaphysical intensity of light aimed at permanence. They often painted on small wooden panels, as Whistler and the Aus-tralian Impressionists were later to do. It was the influence of the Macchiaioli rather than the literary and romantic aspects of nine-teenth-century Italian painting (which Nerli also absorbed and brought with him) that en-abled him to contribute fresh ideas to Austral-asian painting.

With Italian fellow-artist Ugo Catani, Nerli travelled from Italy, visiting Madagascar, Mauritius and Bourbon before arriving in Melbourne in November 1885. He shared a studio in Collins Street with Catani and Artur Loureiro [q.v.5] for almost a year before moving to Sydney. He joined the sketch club attached to the Art Society of New South Wales where, in 1887-88, he probably met Charles Conder [q.v.3]. Conder's friend and colleague Arthur Streeton [q.v.] considered that Conder was much influenced by 'the bril-liant Nerli' whose example thus assumes a special significance for Australian art at this time, though the gifted Conder soon sur-passed Nerli.

James Green writing in the *Australasian Art Review* (June 1899) under the pseudonym 'De Libra' states that Nerli 'with a thorough European training, was the first to introduce to New South Wales the daring independence of Southern neo-Continentalism . . . in its dis-regard of generally accepted trammels and its frequent substitution of the mere sketch for finished work, which has since influenced a number of Australian painters'.

Late in 1889 Nerli went to Dunedin, New Zealand, to assist in setting up the New South Wales loan collection for an international exhibition, in which he exhibited nine works. He returned to Sydney in 1890. Some time was spent in Melbourne painting bayside beaches, and Nerli may also have visited Hobart. In 1892 he was painting at Mosman Bay, Sydney, with Tom Roberts [q.v.]. In August he visited Apia in Samoa where he met and painted Robert Louis Stevenson, making portraits in oil, pastel and charcoal. Stevenson wrote some verse about Nerli in the painter's autograph album.

By June 1893 Nerli was conducting art classes at Dunedin. In February 1894 with L. W. Wilson and J. D. Perrett he started a school, the Otago Art Academy, which held life classes and was very successful. Threat-ened by its popularity, the Dunedin School of Art appointed Nerli 'teacher of painting' from early 1895. Frances Hodgkins was one of his pupils. A contemporary described Nerli as 'a memorable figure . . . rather tall, with black, pointed beard'. He was considered flamboy-ant, light-hearted and Bohemian.

Moving north to Auckland in October 1896, Nerli exhibited with the Auckland Society of Arts. On 5 March 1898 he married Marie Cecilia Josephine Barron at Christchurch. By December Nerli and his bride were in Western Australia where they attended the opening of the third exhibition of the West Australian Society of Arts and Crafts in which he exhibited seven works. In 1899 he exhibited with the Society of Artists, Sydney, and in 1902-03 with the Victorian Artists' Society, Melbourne.

Little is known of Nerli's life after he left Australia. William Moore [q.v.], believed that he was attached to the Italian Embassy in London during World War I. In 1915 his work 'Kensington Palace' was exhibited at Auckland. His last years were spent at Nervi, near Genoa, Italy, where he died on 24 June 1926.

His wife died at Siena in 1947. No children are known to have been born of the marriage. A portrait by Grace Joel is in the Art Gallery of New South Wales. He is represented in the Australian National Gallery, Canberra, and other major Australian galleries including those in Melbourne, Sydney, Perth and Brisbane.

E. H. McCormick, *The expatriate* (Wellington, NZ, 1954); P. Entwhistle, *William Mathew Hodgkins and his circle* (Dunedin, NZ, 1984); *A'sian Art Review*, 1 June 1899; National Gallery of SA, *Bulletin*, 3, no 1, July 1941; *Auckland Art Gallery Q*, no 45, 1969; B. Chapman, 'Girolamo Nerli', *WA Art Gallery Feature*, no 2, 1976; *Art and Aust*, 16, no 1, Sept 1978, letter B. Chapman to editor, 16, no 3, Mar 1979; *Table Talk*, 12 Oct 1888; *Bulletin*, 1 Dec 1900.   BARBARA CHAPMAN